PERSONALITY: DYNAMICS, DEVELOPMENT, AND ASSESSMENT

Irving L. Janis

Yale University

George F. Mahl

Yale University

Jerome Kagan

Harvard University

Robert R. Holt

New York University

Irving L. Janis, *Editor*

 HARCOURT, BRACE & WORLD, INC.

New York   Chicago   San Francisco   Atlanta

PERSONALITY

DYNAMICS, DEVELOPMENT, AND ASSESSMENT

ISBN 0-15-569585-1

Library of Congress Catalog Card Number: 69-17520

Printed in the United States of America

ACKNOWLEDGMENTS AND COPYRIGHTS

The authors wish to thank the companies and persons listed below
for permission to use material in this book.

Textual Material

Chapter 1   Opening quote: From William Golding, *Pincher Martin*, Faber
and Faber Ltd., 1956; Harcourt, Brace & World, 1957 (under the
title *The Two Deaths of Christopher Martin*). © 1956 by William
Golding. By permission of the publishers.

Case study from Charles Thurmond, "Last Thoughts Before Drowning," in *Journal of Abnormal and Social Psychology*, 1943, 38, 165–
84, by permission of the American Psychological Association.

2   Opening quote: From *The Inferno* in *The Divine Comedy* by
Dante Alighieri, translated by Lawrence Grant White. Copyright
1948 by Pantheon Books, Inc., a division of Random House, Inc.
Reprinted by permission of the publisher.

3   Opening quote: From Edgar Allan Poe, "The Bells," in *The Best
Known Works of Edgar Allan Poe*, Blue Ribbon Books, copyright,
1927, 1943 by Walter J. Black, Inc.

Experiment from D. Campbell, R. E. Sanderson, and S. G. Laverty,
"Characteristics of a Conditioned Response in Human Subjects
During Extinction Trials Following a Single Traumatic Condition-
ing Trial," in *Journal of Abnormal and Social Psychology*, 1964, 68,
No. 6, 627–39. Copyright 1964 by the American Psychological As-
sociation, and used by permission of the American Psychological
Association and Dugal Campbell.

*Acknowledgments and copyrights for further textual material and for illustrative
material continue on page 830.*

PREFACE

The psychology of personality is coming of age. Although not all basic issues are settled, personality research and theory have reached the stage at which textbooks can concentrate on substantive knowledge—on descriptive *generalizations* and explanatory *principles* that are supported by empirical *evidence*. Our concern with substantive content and supporting evidence has guided the choice of topics and the presentation of them throughout this book.

The major goal of the book is to give students a sound introduction to the scientific study of personality. While our basic orientation is substantive and empirical, we do not neglect *theories* of personality. In every chapter we attempt to convey the relation between outstanding theoretical contributions and empirical investigations, which often requires exploring the intricacies of current research problems. We try to show the contemporary relevance of learning theories, psychoanalysis, and other theoretical approaches that have strongly influenced personality research during the past half-century, as well as the recent developments in cognitive theories that are helping to fill in some gaps in our knowledge of the human personality.

We believe that an in-depth approach will prove to be more enlightening and intellectually stimulating for students than a rapid encyclopedic tour that does not stop at any place long enough to let them find out what is really there. In a field like the psychology of personality, which has hundreds of research subtopics and dozens of points of view, students will probably benefit more from gaining a genuine comprehension of significant topics than from being exposed to a multitude of theories and experimental detail.

We have organized the subject matter to enable students to grasp most easily the central problems, concepts, methods of investigation, and established findings that constitute the core of the psychology of personality. The four parts of the book deal with (1) stress and frustration, (2) conflict and defense, (3) personality development, and (4) personality assessment. Each of these areas involves a somewhat different type of methodology and expertise, and each author specializes and currently does research in the area he is writing about. Part I is by Irving L. Janis; Part II is by George F. Mahl; Part III is by Jerome Kagan; and Part IV is by Robert R. Holt.

We start the book with the dynamics of stress and frustration because this area ties in most closely with what the students will have learned in their introductory psychology courses about such topics as Pavlovian and operant conditioning, the nature of emotions, and the formation of cognitions and attitudes. After studying Part I, students may be better prepared to comprehend the less familiar theoretical concepts, clinical observations, and experimental results on conflict and defense, discussed in Part II. Next comes personality development, which takes up the origins of major patterns of behavior covered in the first two parts. Then, having learned about the concepts and variables dealt with in the first three parts, students may be able to understand more readily the intricate issues of personality assessment in the final part. We have tried to select the best sequence for the typical student, but we realize that some instructors will want to assign the parts in a different order. They will probably find that this can be done successfully because, by and large, each part can be read independently. Rearrangement is also facilitated by the cross-references to important concepts, hypotheses, or variables that are more extensively discussed elsewhere in the book.

In our experience, all four areas can be well covered in a one-semester or one-quarter personality course. We have also found that it is relatively easy to coordinate the four parts of this book with supplementary readings, whether these are on theories of personality or on current research. The separate references listed for each part of the book may be helpful to the instructor who wishes to make up his own set of supplementary readings.

In addition to its in-depth treatment of basic problems of personality, the book has several other features that should be noted here:

1. We decided that the most important aspects of personality to present are those pertaining to normal people. Consequently we have made no attempt to cover all the chronic problems of maladjustment that constitute the subject matter of abnormal psychology—severe neurosis, psychosis, chronic drug addiction, and the like. But throughout the book, examples of common forms

of maladjustment—such as exaggerated fears, misplaced aggression, sexual inhibitions—are presented. These examples, which are often used as focal points of the discussion, are likely to interest all types of students. Of course, we also look at the other side of the coin, presenting examples of the successful patterns of adjustment that enable people to cope effectively with external and internal obstacles.

In this connection a word is in order about the case-study method, since this book presents a number of case studies (distinguished from the rest of the text by a different typeface). Case studies have a bad reputation among some psychologists, primarily because clinical investigators sometimes err in leaping to general conclusions from their single case. All too often they overlook the fact that the wider applicability of their observations cannot be ascertained without well-controlled observations from research studies that use adequate sampling techniques. Nevertheless, case studies remain an extraordinarily rich source of suggestive hypotheses concerning mediating psychological processes. We regard them as one of the best pedagogical tools for helping students to grasp the significance of many key explanatory concepts and hypotheses concerning patterns of adjustment in normal people.

2. We devote considerable discussion, especially in the first half of the book, to the influence of situational events, such as warnings and actual disasters that arouse strong emotions (Part I) and temptation situations that arouse conflict (Part II). This emphasis reflects a growing trend among research psychologists to regard the emotional and motivational changes induced by environmental variables as central problems in the study of personality. This point of view is vigorously expressed by Walter Mischel in his book *Personality and Assessment* (1968). Mischel calls into question the commonly held assumption that personality attributes—such as aggressiveness, anxiety, dependency, need for achievement, self-control, and sociability—are stable predispositions or traits. Mischel urges psychologists to concentrate on studying the environmental conditions that give rise to a person's *changes* in aggression, anxiety, dependency, and so on. One need not fully agree with Mischel's position on the specificity of human behavior to accept his view that "a viable approach to personality must bridge the gap between the principles and methods of general experimental psychology and the problems confronting the personality psychologist concerned with the assessment and modification of complex human behavior [Mischel, 1968, p. 148]." Throughout this book we try to show how the relevant findings from experimental studies on the effects of external events can be related to personality phenomena.

3. We do not include separate chapters on such topics as biological and social determinants of personality. Instead we discuss the most relevant material from the biological and social sciences in the context of specific personality problems. For example, recent findings from physiological studies of sleep and dream deprivation that bear on psychological stress are presented in Part I; studies of sensory deprivation that are related to fears of self-disintegration are discussed in Part II; the genetic bases for individual dif-

ferences in temperament are described in Part III; the complex ways in which hormones and other biochemical factors influence personality characteristics are given attention in Part IV. Similarly, the student will encounter throughout the book concepts and observations bearing on cultural factors, social attitudes, norms, and the influence of the family, peer groups, and other components of the social milieu.

4. Because incontrovertible evidence is hard to come by in the field of personality research, heated controversy is very easy to come by. We do not hesitate to touch on a number of disputes, such as the current debate between behavior therapists and psychoanalysts on the causes and cures of phobias. We think that the student can better grasp the relation between hypotheses and evidence if he occasionally grapples with an unsettled controversial issue. But for proper perspective, we try to present these controversies in the context of other, well-tested hypotheses for which there is solid supporting evidence.

No guides to the study of personality, of course, are noncombatants, free from bias, no matter how objective they are trying to be. Our team has at least one built-in safeguard: We do not see eye to eye on all issues and we do not share any single point of view or theoretical approach to personality. In the course of repeatedly exchanging manuscripts, each of us has been required to work out a way to present fairly all sides of each controversial issue. Moreover, one of the authors, as editor of the book, kept a constant lookout in every draft for ambiguous or incomplete formulations that might mislead the student and for gaps in our coverage that needed to be filled in.

As a group, we feel that the clinical approach has been unduly neglected during the past decade. Three of us take the position that psychoanalysis, despite the overly dogmatic certainty and quasi-religious loyalty it receives from some of its staunch adherents, should be presented in sufficient detail so that students can see that at least it is a valuable source of hypotheses concerning the causes and consequences of motivational conflicts. But the three relatively pro-psychoanalysis authors share with the fourth a critical view of the inadequate evidence offered in most psychoanalytic reports.

We also believe that it is necessary to be skeptical when learning theorists, cognitive theorists, or eclectic experimentalists extract broad generalizations from a few seemingly rigorous investigations, which sometimes have unintentional methodological flaws or deal with quite trivial aspects of behavior that are labeled as though they were analogues of important personality variables. Nevertheless, we give precedence to objective evidence from psychological experiments and systematic correlational studies *whenever they are relevant* for testing hypotheses about personality dynamics, development, or assessment.

Many people helped in the preparation of this book. Our list of acknowledgments (beginning on page iv) mentions a number of individuals, publishers, and organizations that kindly granted us permission to use textual and illustrative material. Here we would like to add our thanks to those who assisted each of us as we worked on our manuscripts in their several drafts. Geoffrey

Nowlis provided expert advice concerning the presentation of the psycho-physiological data in Part I, and Charlotte Janis aided in preparing the references on stress and frustration. Genoveva Palmieri was a devoted helper in preparing the manuscript of Part II. Respect and gratitude are also expressed to those persons who, by sharing their inner life with him in psychoanalysis, made it possible for the author of Part II to gain for himself and to attempt to convey some sense of the psychoanalytic conceptions of conflict and defense. Grateful acknowledgment is made to Mrs. Doris Simpson and Mrs. Henriette Salek, who helped in preparing the manuscript of Part III. Special mention should be made of "William Morris Brown," the subject of the extended study in Part IV, who permitted the account of the intensive interviews and personality tests administered to him in 1940 and 1966 to be published in this book. His extraordinary generosity, trust, and candor won him the author's gratitude and admiration. A considerable debt of gratitude is owed also to Robert Freed Bales of Harvard University, who was the collaborator on the original case study of "Morris Brown" in 1940 and who permitted the joint report to be drawn on freely here.

Irving L. Janis
George F. Mahl
Jerome Kagan
Robert R. Holt

CONTENTS

2

Psychological Trauma, 20

3

Basic Learning-Theory Concepts, 38

4

Psychodynamic Theories of Trauma, 63

5

Sensitization to Threat Cues, 74

6

Adaptive Personality Changes, 86

7

Fear, Shame, and Guilt, 106

8

When Warnings Fail, 123

9

Frustration and Aggression, 145

10

Grief, 170

PART TWO

CONFLICT AND DEFENSE

11

Origins of Psychoanalytic Ideas, 201

12

Types and Examples of Conflict, 217

17

Projection, Over-Reactions, and Unconscious Homosexual Conflicts, 313

18

Over-Reactions and Unconscious Conflicts About Aggression, 325

19

Interference with Defenses and Reality Contact, 335

20

Defense Against Unpleasant External Situations, 349

21

Defense Against Drives and Affects, 369

22

Organization of Defenses and Individual Differences, 392

PART THREE

PERSONALITY DEVELOPMENT

23

What Is Personality Development? 405

24

The First Critical Period:
Birth to 18 Months, 414

25

Initial Socialization:
18 Months to 3 Years, 441

26

The Period of Identification:
3 to 6 Years, 457

27

Sex Typing During the Preschool and Early School Years, 474

28

Major Motive-Behavioral Systems in the Young Child, 492

29

Personality and Intellectual Development in the School-Age Child, 517

30

Peer and Sibling Influences, 541

31

The Influence of Parents, 556

PART FOUR

ASSESSING PERSONALITY

32

The What and Why of Personality Assessment, 575

33

Major Processes of Informal Assessment, 590

INTRODUCTION

*What a chimera, then, is man! What a novelty! What a mon-
ster, what a chaos, what a contradiction, what a prodigy! Judge
of all things, feeble worm of the earth, depositary of truth, a sink
of uncertainty and error, the glory and the shame of the universe.*
PASCAL. Pensées VIII

All of us are lifelong students of personality. We soon
discover the unique fascination of learning about
ourselves and the people around us—the motives,
feelings, aspirations, and ideals that help to explain
our thoughts and actions. By the time we have
reached college age, most of us have acquired a deep curiosity about chimerical
man—his contradictions, his glories, and his shames.

College students seek to satisfy that curiosity in various ways. Some
choose the road of literature, philosophy, and other humanistic disciplines.
These students are sure to encounter many profound insights into the nature
of man. But anyone interested in the inner life of men and women, the quality
of their character, their adjustment to their social milieu, and their potentialities for self-fulfillment may well find the psychology of personality the most
relevant study of all.

What Is Personality?

"Personality" designates the *patterns of behavior and predispositions that determine how a person will think, feel, and act.* The major
components of personality, according to most psychologists, are those charac-

teristics that most directly affect a person's adjustment to his environment—including his motives, emotions, abilities, and skills in getting along with others. Beyond such a very general definition, however, one encounters disagreement. For as Nevitt Sanford has noted, the leading psychologists in this field do not agree about "what the elements of personality are, how they are organized, what the boundaries of personality are, and how personality interacts with other [psychological] phenomena [Sanford, 1968, p. 587]."

Despite all the disagreements about how to define and study personality, psychologists show fairly good agreement about what types of problems are central. We discuss in this textbook the major problems that have been extensively investigated and the answers that have emerged so far.

As a field of study, personality includes two interrelated types of investigations: (1) research on variables that account for *differences between individuals* exposed to similar environmental circumstances, and (2) research on variables that account for *changes within a person* in different situations and during different periods of his life. Research on these two aspects of personality has not yet developed as fully as research in such older areas of experimental psychology as sensation, perception, and learning. No single theoretical approach, method of inquiry, or broad set of principles unifies the study of personality. Some of its subject matter overlaps with other areas, including social and experimental psychology, psychiatry, and neurophysiology. Nevertheless, a number of topics, including the causes and consequences of difficulties in adjustment among *normal* people, are unique to this area. The scope and organization of the subject matter can best be conveyed by considering the distinctive problems on which each of the four parts of the book are focused.

Stress and Frustration

The first part of the book deals with some fundamental principles and observations concerning the dynamics of personality. As the word "dynamics" implies, the focus is on *changes* within the individual and the motivational forces that influence variations in behavior.

The dynamics of stress and frustration pertains to a variety of changes that are provoked by disruptive environmental events. Under this heading we study the powerful impact of external crises, accidents, and personal disasters, which directly affect a person's adjustment. Sometimes the outcome is a marked change in the basic features of a man's personality, which lasts for years and may even be permanent. Much more frequent, however, are instances of mild stress or frustration, which induce changes in a person's emotional state that last from a few hours to a few days.

The question of whether a change in behavior is attributable to stress or frustration arises whenever we see someone in a state of emotional turmoil, particularly if he has become so upset that he can no longer function adequately in ordinary situations. A typical example is the man who, after having performed well on his job for many years, unexpectedly becomes apprehensive, distracted, and inefficient. Usually the man's state of anxiety is manifested in his private life as well. He may no longer be pursuing his normal social activities; his relationship with his wife may also have become impaired. When we ask "What is causing all these changes?" the first possibility to be considered is that something new and different has occurred in his environment. If we can identify the external provocation—for instance, a medical report revealing a small growth in his body that poses a threat of cancer or an impending reorganization of his business firm that threatens the security of his job—we can predict that this man's adjustment will probably return to normal if the external stressful stimuli are removed (for instance, if his physician assures him that the growth is not malignant or if his boss assures him that his job status is guaranteed despite the reorganization).

Part I examines the main reactions that are typically evoked by many different types of stressful and frustrating events. Also considered are the factors that promote rapid recovery after the distressing stimuli are no longer present.

Conflict and Defense

After considering in Part I the problems of individual adjustment entailed by stress and frustration, we continue the discussion of personality dynamics in Part II by focusing on more subtle changes arising from motivational conflicts that are sometimes referred to as *internal* sources of frustration. Also of concern will be various modes of reducing conflict, particularly those that become habitual defense mechanisms.

Suppose that a careful appraisal of a person's life circumstances fails to turn up any evidence of stress or frustration that could account for his change in affect and action. We then begin to think in terms of internal difficulties. If a physiological dysfunction has been ruled out, a psychological analysis may enable us to understand why the person has changed. Part of the problem is to determine whether the strong emotional reactions are evoked by some seemingly neutral external events or cues that are particularly significant to the individual. These cues are much more difficult to detect than the gross environmental onslaughts identified as causes of stress or frustration.

For instance, a man who has become anxiety-ridden and inefficient might be able to tell us about a special provoking circumstance that he himself has identified but cannot understand. Perhaps the mere presence of a particular person—a slightly handicapped co-worker, let us say—regularly brings on his worst spells of distressing feelings and distraught behavior. The clinical investigator who listens patiently to what the man says about his troubles may notice that certain seemingly unimportant words in their conversation are regularly followed by anxiety. He may also learn a great deal about the dire images and fantasies that accompany the man's over-reactions to relatively neutral stimuli. The explanation for many such over-reactions, as will be seen in the series of case studies and experiments described in Part II, involves a conception of motivational conflict and defense. These are regarded as dynamic concepts because they refer to motivational forces and are used to explain puzzling changes in a person's behavior, including the appearance and disappearance of psychological symptoms as well as ups and downs in mood that affect the adjustment of any normal person.

Personality Development

Although certain developmental issues are discussed in the first two parts, Part III concentrates on the *long-term* development of personality characteristics. Here the aim is not to explain why adults suddenly change but to describe how their patterns of behavior evolved. Let us consider again the man whose anxiety led to an impairment in his work. If his symptoms are over-reactions based on an inner conflict, the developmental problem is that of describing and explaining how such a conflict arose. Did behavioral signs of the conflict appear at earlier ages? When did the first signs appear? What biological factors in the man's make-up contributed to the strength of the opposing motives that enter into the conflict? If the conflict arose during childhood, how was it later reinforced or modified by experiences during adolescence and adulthood?

A similar set of developmental questions can be posed about emotional reactions and adjustment difficulties attributable to stress or frustration. Here again, we need to look into the life history to find out how the person got that way. Anyone who worries about the possibility of suffering from cancer or from loss of job status must first have learned about the nature of such threats. Such learning involves the acquisition of some basic concepts about the self and the outside world, the capacity to visualize future events, and a variety of reassuring or nonreassuring concepts about what is required to reduce such threats. Organic constitutional factors in the person might also play a crucial role, since they determine the intensity and duration of physiological arousal evoked by emotional stimuli. The developmental aspects of stress and frustration are especially pertinent to the uncovering of individual differences in the capacity to tolerate stress, to cope with disruptive environmental events, and to plan constructive solutions rather than succumb to ineffectual hostility or apathy when progress toward a goal is blocked.

The problems of personality development are by no means limited to explaining the history of symptoms, maladjustments, and low tolerance for stress. Similar inquiry is needed into the origins of personality *strengths*—including the development of social skills and a satisfying sexual relationship, the capacity to maintain high self-esteem, adherence to basic ethical standards, and the pursuit of a variety of interests that enable a person to live a rich, productive, and enjoyable life.

The main task of the final section, Part IV, is to give a comprehensive picture of how personality is assessed by present-day psychologists, both those primarily concerned with research on normal adult personalities and those concerned with practical tasks, such as evaluating clients who come to a clinic seeking help for adjustment difficulties, screening out unsuitable candidates for professional training, or selecting mature men for leadership roles. All these assessors draw on a large body of research dealing with personality attributes in relation to behavior in life situations.

The problems of assessment cut across all the aspects of personality mentioned under the preceding three headings. A psychologist working with the man who has become anxiety-ridden and inefficient in his job would inquire into the context of his symptoms to find out how well he is functioning in other important areas of his life. He would take account of the genetic, neurological, hormonal, biochemical, and other organic features of the man's biological make-up to determine the extent to which they might account for the ways his behavior differs from that of other people. The psychologist would also assess the subject's self-awareness and self-control. To what extent can this man control his anger and other emotional impulses? Is he aware of the obstacles in his environment and within himself that frustrate achievement of his goals? Can he make decisions for himself and live up to them? What are his main strengths and weaknesses?

The personality assessor tries to provide specific answers to such questions. If he becomes careless or cuts too many corners, he may end up settling for an over-inclusive diagnostic label or formulating a set of vague or ambiguous generalizations. To be useful, a personality report must contain precise formulations that capture specific features of an individual's personality, whether these features are unique or are shared with many other persons.

There are two quite different traditions in present-day assessment work. One tradition is oriented toward making precise predictions based on tests that can be administered rapidly to a large number of persons and that provide quantitative scores on a few personality variables. These scores may then be correlated with objective records such as course grades, job efficiency ratings, and marital status. The other tradition is oriented toward obtaining as full a picture as possible of each person who is being studied, usually for such clinical purposes as selecting the most effective psychological treatment.

As yet very few research projects have tried to combine the precise statistical methods of analysis used by quantitatively oriented psychologists with the techniques for assessing qualitative variables used by clinical psychologists. As might be expected, therefore, research on personality assessment is marked by lively, heated controversies. Part IV attempts to familiarize the reader with the issues that are subject to constructive debate, to describe the values and limitations of both the objective and the clinical approaches to personality assessment, and to indicate how data from both approaches can be synthesized.

Theoretical Orientations

Each of the four areas described in this book employs somewhat different theoretical concepts and uses somewhat different methods in its investigations. A personality psychologist who is a specialist in one area usually is not an expert in any of the other three. This is one reason for the collaborative nature of this book.

The contributions of the great pioneers of modern psychology and the more recent theorists who have left their stamp on the field of personality research also fall into different areas. For example, Pavlov's work helps to explain the development of positive emotions toward persons who are present when such unconditioned stimuli as food and sexual stimulation occur. But Pavlov's main influence in the field of personality has been on our conceptions of human reactions to stress. As shown in Part I, his ideas have gained further support from subsequent experiments that show how noxious stimuli give rise to new forms of anxiety and other negative emotional habits. Freud, too, had important things to say about psychological trauma and the emotional development of the child, but his most outstanding contributions pertain to the dynamics of conflict and defense. The major contributions of Jean Piaget deal with cognitive development and have most strongly influenced systematic investigations of the way children change as they go through the successive stages of childhood.

In this book much more space is devoted to Freud than to Pavlov, Piaget, or any other theorist, for several reasons. Pavlov's experiments and Piaget's systematic approach have been influential in psychological research, but for the most part their work has been peripheral to the psychology of personality. Freud's writings, in contrast, are focused directly on the problems of personality as he encountered them in his clinical efforts to understand and cure those he treated for neurotic disorders. Although Freudian psychoanalysis is often criticized, sometimes justifiably and sometimes not, most of what is now known about the dynamics of motivational conflict and the mechanisms of defense comes directly from the clinical observations of Freud and his followers. This point has been forcefully stated by Richard Lazarus (1961), a leading experimental psychologist who does systematic research on human emotions and personality variables:

> It would be inconceivable for anyone to write a textbook on personality without devoting a substantial portion to psychoanalysis. The impact of Freud's work upon modern psychological thought, and indeed upon our entire culture, has been enormous. Many of the now commonplace notions about personality (such as unconscious motivation, internal conflict, and defense mechanism) . . . were either introduced by Freud or influenced by

his work. Thus the importance and influence of Freud is such as to require special and extensive treatment [Lazarus, 1961, p. 137].

Accordingly, we shall deal with Freud's contributions in several parts of this book, but especially in Part II, which presents many of his outstanding discoveries.

Even though Freud is generally recognized as one of the great geniuses of this century, his important discoveries are either not known or misunderstood by the vast majority of well-educated people. Most writings of psychoanalysts are flawed by obscure formulations of hypotheses and inadequate accounts of the relevant evidence, mixed in with untestable theoretical speculations. Most books about Freud by nonpsychoanalysts grossly distort his hypotheses and convey little or nothing about the clinical evidence in which they were grounded. Part II of this book is designed to provide a systematic account, unexpurgated and undistorted, of the major psychoanalytic hypotheses bearing on personality dynamics. Freud's own case studies, supplemented by studies reported by other psychoanalytic observers, are repeatedly drawn upon to enable the reader to see for himself the nature of the evidence that led Freud and his followers to account for failures in personal adjustment in terms of motivational conflicts. These conflicts, of which the person is not fully aware, can give rise to intense anxiety and motivate a person to engage in such defensive activities as repression, reaction formation, denial, and rationalization.

The clashes between the objective and clinical approaches mentioned in regard to personality assessment have their counterparts in each of the three other areas of personality research. Some of the relevant research studies on psychological stress, on human conflict, and on personality development come from two distinct and somewhat incompatible traditions. All four authors of this book value highly the recent trend toward developing new research strategies that combine the positive features of both the experimental and the clinical traditions. We think that as this new combined tradition takes hold, sufficient evidence will eventually become available to settle many long-standing controversies. We also feel that it is worthwhile to try to extract the best of both worlds, both in substance and in method.

The Empirical Basis for Generalizations

The field of personality suffers from an embarrassment of riches— too many rich ideas that are embarrassingly unsupported by substantial evidence. Suggestive ideas about personality permeate our lives, from the great works of literature to hack prose, from ageless bits of folk wisdom to the sudden insights of our daily encounters. How can we ascertain which of these are valid?

As psychologists, we do not pursue our inquiries into the nature of the human personality in the same way as literary writers or speculative philosophers do, even though we value and sometimes make use of their suggestive insights. Like them, we try to make sense out of what we hear people say about their intentions, aspirations, and shortcomings and what we see them actually doing, with due attention to discrepancies between saying and doing. But we regard any insight that may come from our own impressionistic observations or from the fascinating anecdotes related to us by others as a *tentative hypothesis that requires verification*. Thus, we regard the formulation of a hypothesis—whether it comes from a humanist, a psychologist, or anyone else—as only one of the early stages of the inquiry, to be followed by careful investigations guided by the scientific method. The later stages, of course, require objective observations of a representative sample of the people whose behavior the hypothesis purports to describe or explain, using all available safeguards to keep error and bias to a minimum. Such investigations enable us to decide whether the hypothesis is: (a) sufficiently confirmed, so that we can continue to accept it; (b) partially but unequivocally confirmed, so that it can be accepted if appropriately modified; (c) not consistently confirmed, but not consistently disconfirmed either, suggesting that in order to avoid persistent confusion it must be reformulated or tested in a more effective way; or (d) so completely unsupported by the findings that it should be discarded. We feel convinced that only those descriptive generalizations and explanations that are subjected to the rigorous tests of empirical verification furnish us with dependable knowledge about the psychology of personality.

The main implication of this objective orientation is that any generalization about personality is regarded as warranted only when confirmed by evidence that can be reproduced by a trained observer who carries out the same steps as the original investigator. The task of meeting this requirement is, however, a difficult one. First the empirically oriented psychologist must translate any challenging new idea into the mundane language of a testable proposition. Then, if he still thinks it embodies a new truth worth pursuing, he must arduously collect the evidence necessary for confirming or disconfirming it. All too often the empirical results show that the new idea is not worth much. Even if the results are positive, the report usually gets a mixed reception. The best the researcher can hope for is that his critical peers will accept his contribution with only minor reservations.

But the bitterest pill for him to swallow is the frequent response, "Didn't we already know that? It sounds obvious." Psychologists and other social scientists are frequently accused of coming up with findings that everyone already knew. But almost any plausible generalization about human nature is doomed to sound obvious. What systematic psychological investigation tries to do is to establish which of the apparently obvious generalizations are in fact *true*.

Perhaps the best refutation of the "obvious" label is one offered by Paul Lazarsfeld, an eminent sociologist. Lazarsfeld was appalled by the unfavorable response to *The American Soldier*, a two-volume work published in 1949, in which a group of social scientists presented a series of studies of military morale carried out during World War II. It featured many psychological hypotheses that were systematically tested by large-scale surveys. Several well-known historians and literary critics who reviewed the work dismissed it as a dull account of the "statistical soldier," containing little more than the obvious facts that were already well known from the popular writings of journalists who had been in the Army.

Lazarsfeld responded by pointing out that whenever a research study reports a prevailing regularity, many readers conclude that the study has only expressed in technical jargon elementary truths that were already obvious to everyone. Lazarsfeld went on to suggest that the reader might be helped to recognize this reaction in himself if he were to look over a few significant differences typical of those reported in *The American Soldier*. Among the conclusions he offers as examples are the following, which are here paraphrased from Lazarsfeld's article:

1. White privates were more eager than Negroes to become noncommissioned officers. (Wouldn't we expect black draftees to withdraw and be suspicious in a white authoritarian institution like the Army?)

2. As long as the fighting in Europe continued, combat infantrymen were more eager to return to the United States than they were after the German surrender. (Isn't it obvious that the dangers of being killed would motivate men to want to be sent home? And how would men be expected to react after the surrender, when there was the opportunity to be in a victorious army in a country full of *frauleins?*)

3. Soldiers from rural backgrounds usually expressed greater satisfaction and higher morale during their Army training than men from city backgrounds. (After all, which men would we expect to be accustomed to outdoor hardships?)

4. Better-educated men were more likely than those with less education to complain about having psychosomatic and anxiety symptoms. (Wouldn't we expect greater sensitivity to frustration and to the anticipated dangers of combat from the well-educated man than from the more impassive man in the street?)

Here are Lazarsfeld's comments about these obvious findings:

> We have in these examples a sample list of the simplest type of interrelationships which provide the "bricks" from which our empirical social science is being built. But why, since they are so obvious, is so much money and energy given to establish such findings? Would it not be wiser to take them for granted and proceed directly to a more sophisticated type of analysis? This might be so except for one interesting point about the list. *Every one of these statements is the direct opposite of what actually was found.* . . . [For example,] Negroes were more eager for promotion than whites . . . .
>
> If we had mentioned the actual results of the investigation first, the reader would have labeled these "obvious" also. Obviously something is wrong with the entire argument of "obviousness." It should really be turned on its head.

Since every kind of human reaction is conceivable, it is of great importance to know which reactions actually occur most frequently and under what conditions.

Fortunately, the field of personality research provides us with a number of discoveries that certainly were not expected by knowledgeable people, with the exception, perhaps, of a few remarkable geniuses whose insightful writings could not be fully appreciated until these very discoveries had been made. In fact, some of the findings we shall discuss border on the incredible and will perhaps require another generation before they begin to sound obvious to most readers. But such discoveries are rare. In pursuing the available evidence wherever it takes us, we most often end up with conclusions that sound as plausible as the ones cited by Lazarsfeld. As we discuss the evidence bearing on each of the fundamental issues, however, we shall try to convey to the reader that special form of excitement that comes from finding out which of several possibilities, whether obvious or incredible, is the one that embodies the truth.

Irving L. Janis

PART ONE
STRESS
AND FRUSTRATION

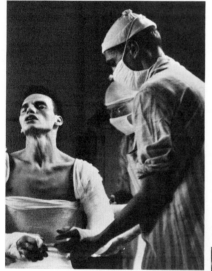

He began to swim again. His breathing laboured. He stared out of his arches intently and painfully at the back of each swell as it slunk away from him. His legs slowed and stopped; his arms fell. His mind inside the dark skull made swimming movements long after the body lay motionless in the water.

· · ·

The slow fire of his belly, banked up to endure, was invaded. It lay defenseless in the middle of the clothing and sodden body.
"I won't die! I won't!"

· · ·

He began to curse and beat the water with the flat of his white hands. He struggled up the swells. But even the sounds of his working mouth and body were merged unnoticed in the innumerable sounds of travelling water. He hung still in his belt, feeling the cold search his belly with its fingers. His head fell on his chest and the stuff slopped weakly, persistently over his face. Think. My last chance. Think what can be done.

WILLIAM GOLDING. Pincher Martin

CHAPTER 1
MAN'S STRUGGLE TO COPE WITH STRESS: AN OVERVIEW

Certain conditions of stress call forth intense emotional reactions and give rise to marked changes in the attitudes and actions of normal personalities. What those conditions are and how people react to them is the theme of the next ten chapters. In the first six chapters we shall examine the consequences of stresses that profoundly threaten man's physical survival. Then we shall see how people react to other stresses that can disrupt their everyday lives, including those "names," more painful than sticks and stones, which we might wish to believe can never hurt us. We shall consider the psychological effects of verbal warnings —warnings that we might fail in our work, be rejected by friends, or be unable to gratify our sexual and affectionate needs. Such purely verbal threats may lead to temporary changes as drastic as if the danger or frustration had actually materialized. For example, a young man who is characteristically calm, relaxed, and thoughtful reads a letter from his draft board and becomes so tense, restless, and impulsive that he appears to act like an altogether different person. In the following chapters we shall analyze the causes and consequences of these temporary stress reactions as well as the longer-lasting changes in personality generated by stressful life experiences.

Laboratory experiments, field investigations, and case studies will be drawn upon extensively in our discussion. Most of the experimental evidence comes from studies of minor types of stress. Many college students have first-hand knowledge of such experiments, having allowed themselves to be harassed by the threat of electric shocks, startled by films showing gory surgical procedures, or thwarted by attempts to solve insoluble puzzles. These experiments provide the most dependable evidence concerning cause-and-effect relationships, but we must rely mainly upon field investigations as the principal source of data about human reactions to the most severe forms of stress. Thus, we shall make use of findings from large-scale surveys based on interviews and direct observations of survivors who have been exposed to wartime and peacetime disasters. Case studies of persons in extreme situations also yield important clues to why a person reacts as he does when confronted by signs of threat or by actual deprivation.

We shall also consider some important theories that attempt to explain why one type of stressful or frustrating situation arouses intense emotions and has drastically disruptive effects on the average person's behavior whereas other, similar circumstances do not. These theories help us to understand the influence of *situational factors* that affect everyone, regardless of personality strengths or weaknesses, whenever a stressful or frustrating event occurs. We shall also examine some *individual differences* in personality attributes that help us to predict how well a particular person will be able to cope with life stresses.

"Last Thoughts" of a Drowning Man:
A Case Study

A remarkable but little-known case study will introduce our analysis of stress behavior. The subject was a young man who underwent a harrowing personal disaster and whose subsequent "reliving" of that experience was recorded in full (Thurmond, 1943). The resulting document in ways resembles the stream-of-consciousness technique used in such novels as James Joyce's *Ulysses*. Of course, an authentic record cannot be expected to convey the fullness of characterization and social context of a literary masterpiece; we should not feel at all dissatisfied if it enables us merely to catch a few glimpses into a private world of apperceptions, moods, memories, and fantasies ordinarily closed to direct psychological observation. Like all case material, this account has the limitation of dealing with only one person; furthermore, it covers only a very narrow span of time. Still, it offers a rare opportunity to examine microscopically important psychological phenomena that ordinarily can be studied only macroscopically.

The ordeal began at Wakonda Beach, Oregon, on the Pacific Ocean. It was 4:30 p.m. on an unusually stormy Saturday afternoon in late fall. Don O'Daniel, a 19-year-old student at Oregon State College, was jumping the breakers, when suddenly he was swept out to sea by the powerful undertow of the outgoing tide. His anguished companions gave him up for lost, never dreaming that anyone could possibly survive for many hours far out from shore in those huge, battering ocean waves.

At 8:30 p.m. Don was found unconscious on the beach. He was put to bed in a friend's cottage, where he lay inert except for sporadic groaning accompanied by convulsive contractions of his bruised body. After 3 hours, Don began writhing as though he were in great mental agony. With his eyes still closed, he began verbalizing in his delirium a detailed account of the disaster, as though he were reliving it in a dream and talking aloud in his sleep. Every word Don said was written down by Charles Thurmond, who later checked those details that could be objectively confirmed. Thurmond, a college teacher and a friend of Don's, had given him emergency treatment when he was rescued and remained with him throughout the period of delirium.

Verbalized reliving of a stressful experience occurs infrequently on such a purely spontaneous basis, but it is often encountered among surgical patients waking up from an anesthetic. Moreover, during World War II, psychiatrists in evacuation hospitals deliberately gave injections of hypnotic drugs, such as sodium pentothal, to large numbers of traumatized infantrymen and fliers in order to induce precisely this type of subjective reliving of distressing danger episodes, because it seemed to help them recover more rapidly.

Naturally, some of the statements made in the delirium state must remain inexplicable, but in this case most of the obscure material was promptly clarified by subsequent interviews. While Don was recovering in the college infirmary, Thurmond discussed the transcript of Don's entire delirious account with him in detail. Together they were able to trace out the meaning of many cryptic references to past events in Don's life history and to identify his relationship to all the persons whose names he mentioned. The interviews also supplied additional information that helps us to reconstruct the sequence of events.

In his delirium Don began in the middle of the story, reliving his experience of battling the waves far out in the ocean; then he went back to the beginning and talked about being caught up by the undertow; next he skipped to the end, when he was lying on the beach. As his delirium continued, he frequently jumped back and forth in time. As Thurmond noted, it was as though Don were playing a phonograph record of his subjective thoughts but allowing the needle to skip here and there, sometimes returning to the same spot a number of times.

We shall now consider, in sequence, six phases that can be reconstructed from Don's account, the entire transcript of which is included here. In order to extract suggestive hypotheses from the case material, we shall adopt the working assumption that the things Don said during his delirium were fairly accurate repetitions of the thoughts and feelings he had while struggling to keep alive in the ocean.

Phase 1:
Preliminary Warning or Threat

Since Don was preoccupied during his delirious recital with the most intense moments of anxiety and suffering, the information about the precrisis period comes mainly from the subsequent interviews. At the moment Don entered the ocean, he must have been aware of the potential danger, for on that afternoon the area was being hit by one of the worst storms of the year. He also must have noticed the unusually strong undertow as soon as he waded out into the water and began jumping the huge waves churned up by the storm. Yet he ignored all the obvious signs of danger, probably because he was in a very elated mood. Before going into the water, he had been intently following a radio broadcast of a football game. His own team was not playing, but the outcome of this game would determine what team would go to the Rose Bowl on New Year's Day. An enthusiastic member of the Oregon State football team, Don was elated when he heard that their main rivals had been defeated, making his team the conference champion. In unusually high spirits, he impulsively decided to plunge into the ocean and jump the breakers.

Denial of danger at a time like this is by no means unusual. Certainly Don's elation contributed to his lack of reflection about the consequences of his action. But even without this factor, people often ignore signs of ominous threats, especially if they have seen the same signs several times before and feel confident about their ability to cope with an emergency should it arise. As in this case, a person is most likely to ignore danger if he has not been warned by trusted authorities. Whenever the danger is regarded as remote, improbable, or easily manageable, the average person tends to be unresponsive to warning signs and feels, "Nothing will happen to me. I don't need to worry about it."

Don's sense of knowing just what to do in an emergency also contributed to his readiness to ignore the danger. In one of the interviews Don said, "I had lived on the ocean all my life. I had seen lots of people get drowned. I had made up my mind what I'd do if I ever got caught myself." He would swim out past the breakers until the tide changed, save his energy by merely keeping his head above water as he floated on the waves, and then swim in with the incoming tide. This was the plan he actually followed, and this was why he remained far out in the ocean for such a long time that his friends thought he must have drowned.

Phase 2:
The Impact of Disaster

Time and again during his delirium Don suddenly became frantic; his body became tense and rigid, as if he were preparing for superhuman exertion. After regaining consciousness, Don explained that he had suddenly found himself knocked off his feet by a wave and had fought hard to regain his upright position, but was knocked down over and over again: "Like when you roll down a hill—you regain your feet, but you keep on rolling."

In his delirious state Don's recapitulation of his response to the sudden onset of disaster seems to have been expressed more in body language than in words. Many signs of physiological mobilization were apparent: the tensing up of his body and the characteristic symptoms of autonomic nervous system activation—pounding heart, rapid breathing, hairs erect all over the body, skin quivering with goose pimples. Such a state of arousal, when evoked by a real emergency, can greatly facilitate the performance of protective actions. But unexpected danger may instead produce overwhelming panic. The person might wildly thrash about or freeze up in stunned terror, losing whatever momentary opportunity there may have been to save himself. Like most people suddenly confronted with disaster, Don was in a state of acute emotional excitement, but he oriented his behavior toward protective emergency action in a way that helped him to survive. In this respect his prior training and experience probably played a crucial role in preventing disorganized reactions: Don automatically knew what to do. It is noteworthy that in this phase, as he relived it during his delirium, he kept giving terse commands to himself, in much the way the captain of a sinking ship might talk to his crew:

> dive under it—dive under the breaker to get back—don't drink any salt water—don't swallow any salt water—take off your pants and shirts—they will help you float—don't take them off it will help you float—keep them on—take it easy—you will be all right—try to hold your own until the tide turns—you will be O.K., but you're getting tired—you were crazy to come out in the first place—you have gone out too far—you know better than that—don't swallow any water—it'll choke you . . .

> you must have stepped in a hole—the tide took you out—it's a good thing you know how to swim—but don't swim too hard—get out past the breakers before you get caught—you thought you had it figured out—how you'd make it—now's your chance

Here we see some *appraisal responses* that characteristically accompany or immediately follow emergency actions when disaster strikes. Don takes stock of the situation, trying to understand the catastrophe that has just hit him, and he quickly assesses what needs to be done. Like the man in Golding's novel, quoted at the beginning of this chapter, Don quickly tells himself to think what can be done. It is during the onset of a disaster that advance training and planning may have their biggest payoff.

Don instituted his prearranged emergency plan almost immediately. Once he could start breathing normally, he deliberately swam away from the shore with the outgoing tide, and he resisted the temptation to try to swim back through the region of powerful breakers until he thought the tide had started back. In an interview on the day after the accident he said, "I knew if I thrashed around trying to swim against the outgoing tide I'd wear myself out."

During the initial impact of danger, well-practiced motor responses may be needed for survival. Don's automatic actions to prevent the undertow from submerging his head were based on practice. They may have been equivalent to an infantryman's hitting the dirt at the sound of an explosion, an action that is drilled into soldiers during basic training. But such motor responses alone would not enable a person to survive a prolonged danger situation like the one Don was facing; he would also need a plan for coping with the danger. We note that Don recalled his emergency plan at the crucial moment it was needed. Later, during the hours he was executing it, Don repeated the plan to himself as a reminder and an incentive to stick with his exhausting course of action. In fact, Don's very first words when he began to moan out loud at the beginning of his delirium were, "Stay out past breakers until tide changes!" He repeated this formula over and over, as though his life depended on it.

Don's awareness of how well prepared he was for just such an emergency probably helped him to maintain a high level of confidence in his ability to survive and helped to prevent him from being overwhelmed with terror. His *attempt to reassure himself* is clearly manifested by his remark, "It's a good thing you know how to swim." This is not a very logical thought, since if he had not known how to swim, he would not have gone swimming in the rough ocean in the first place. He does, in fact, blame himself for foolishly going out too far, as if he were a strict parent reprimanding a child ("you know better than that!"). But this is one of the few times in the entire record that he criticizes himself for getting into such a predicament. Most of his thoughts, plans, and memories seem to be *mobilized toward carrying out the emergency tasks at hand*. While fighting off incipient feelings of hopelessness, he may have dimly realized that he could not allow himself to become further depressed or demoralized by pursuing ideas that would make him feel ashamed about having made such a bad mistake. Like most survivors of dire emergencies, Don does not dwell on his own shortcomings when energetic action is required.

Phase 3:
Prolonged Exposure
to Danger and Deprivation

In large-scale disasters the stock-taking and planning that immediately follow impact are usually self-centered, with each individual feeling that he is the only one stricken. As the typical disaster victim struggles to comprehend what has happened, he begins to realize that others are equally affected, and, at the same time, he begins to worry about his family, his friends, and other people whose survival is important to him. He then makes a strong effort to reestablish contact with loved ones. This evidently fulfills a number of important psychological needs, which will be discussed in detail later.

Don's thoughts soon turn to *concern about his family and friends*, even though he knows perfectly well that he is the only one in serious trouble. Time and again during the long hours of suffering in the raging ocean he conjures up images and memories of his mother and others in his family. During the first hour or so, however, he seems to focus on current friends, especially a girl he has just met. Serving partly as a distraction, this may also have helped bolster his morale. The following information, from interviews and comments by Thurmond, may clarify the full context of Don's thoughts about this girl. She was regarded as one of the most beautiful coeds on the Oregon State College campus. She was also considered "very sophisticated" and had spent much of her time at "swank" places such as Hollywood, California, and Seaside, Oregon. Recently, Don had felt embarrassed walking home with her from class. He felt so inferior to her that he did not have the nerve to ask her for a date, but he privately wished she would become his girl friend.

> you've learned lots of things—that phoney girl—talking about Hollywood—crazy people—Seaside—she's stringing you along—she thinks she's big time—Chuck's [Charles Thurmond's] on to her—think about something—keep your mind busy—don't worry—you're an Irishman—as good as any of them—they don't let down—you're Irish and you don't quit—that girl is just trying to pull the wool over somebody's eyes—peculiar people—sort of cute—but she thinks she's good—don't be a dink—it's a good thing you didn't ask her for a date—you're better than she is—she talks too much—you won't get to go to Puget Sound next year—you're a fool—they always told you you were dumb—you're trying to bluff your way through—you can't bluff now—you gotta produce the goods—you'll make it—just take it easy—God, you have been out here a long time . . .

> that girl—that's a laugh—think of something else—Seaside—Hell! that's a laugh—she probably stopped there to get a drink of water

We may wonder why Don's thoughts about the girl are so aggressively antagonistic. Perhaps he is trying to bolster his self-esteem ("you're better than she is") at a time when he needs to maintain high confidence for survival. In any case, he soon finds that thinking about her is not a satisfying distraction ("think about something—keep your mind busy"), and he immediately attempts to reassure himself in a different way by *reminding himself of his national group identity* ("you're Irish and you don't quit"). Here we see a typical tendency to rely on affiliation with a large group as a source of self-confidence. Perhaps this is also an added source of encouragement to put up a good fight, as good Irishmen should, with the implication that otherwise he would be letting them down.

During the long waiting period, Don shows continual awareness of the omnipresent danger and the corrosive effects of prolonged deprivation, which he tries to counteract by fresh efforts at reassurance:

> gee, that makes lots of noise—beautiful ocean—still a lot for you—dive under the big ones—you can't ride 'em all—it's getting so dark—if it wasn't for that light you might be going the wrong way—I hope they don't turn it out . . .

> you'll make it—just take it easy—God, you have been out here a long time . . . you can't play shuffleboard out here—you can't dance—you haven't got a boat—you're making it the hard way . . .

> God, I never knew there could be so much water on the bumpy, bumpy road to hell—you're doing fine—you'll be a success—why couldn't a boat come?—break it to them gently—that my heart belongs to you—kiss them good-bye—I got one over on them—eleven men go to the Rose Bowl—one kid gets the whole Pacific Ocean—what are you going to do with it?—it is not half as crowded as it will be in the Rose Bowl—Father Dailey—Sister Mary—laughed when you got me out of the other wreck—I'll never laugh again if you'll get me out of this one—any time that you would spend two hours on knees for me, why should I laugh?—I'll never laugh again

Giving himself some "bucking-up" formulas about being a success, reminding himself about the Rose Bowl prize, joking about possessing the entire ocean— all these can be regarded as *attempts to ward off disturbing thoughts* about what might be in store for him. But Don's efforts to make light of his predicament are not entirely successful, and he finally reverts to his memory of a quasi-religious experience.

Don later explained that when addressing Father Dailey and Sister Mary, he was recalling a serious auto accident in which he had been injured. Although he was a Catholic, he had been quite skeptical about the religious ideas he encountered in the Catholic hospital to which he had been taken. Now that he is again in a situation of mortal danger, he is temporarily willing to *renounce his former skepticism about the power of the deity.* At this point Don speaks as though he were a child making a confession to a parent, asking for help, comfort, and forgiveness. Perhaps we have here an example of reversion to a childhood attitude under extreme stress, a return to a primitive conception that personifies God as a powerful father figure who might be persuaded through prayer to save one from being badly stricken.

Don's situation at this time was comparable in many ways to that of a combat infantryman on the battlefield. The ocean was bitter cold (47° F. was registered on that late fall afternoon), and Don's shivering body was being relentlessly buffeted by huge waves as the storm mounted in fury—his face lashed by stinging rain, his muscles aching, his stamina being eroded. Don's plea for divine intervention reminds one of the old adage, "There are no atheists in foxholes." Obviously, this is a desperate effort to gain reassurance at a moment when all hope seems lost.

Akin to "foxhole" conversions are "deathbed" conversions, when a mature man returns to the religious faith of his childhood, after having been an agnostic or an atheist throughout his adulthood. Similar conversions sometimes occur after a serious accident or during recovery from a painful illness. The effects of these religious experiences of "fear and trembling" may persist for the rest of a person's life. But most often—and this is what apparently happened in Don's case—the return to a religious form of reassurance during an episode of extreme distress is soon forgotten and leads to no apparent change in the person's subsequent religious beliefs and practices.

Phase 4:
Exhaustion and Demoralization

As Don's suffering continued, a new and insidious source of danger gradually began to overpower him—the danger of developing a *sense of utter hopelessness and resignation.* We can see many traces of his sustained *struggle against apathy* in his attempt to avoid giving in to a seemingly peaceful surrender that would inevitably mean drowning.

> your 19 years are going to be over quick—you are not even going to know what life is about . . . kiss them goodbye—only thing smacks you is a wave . . .

the wind is pushing you past—you won't make it—you can't make it—float for a while—maybe I can make it—cramps—take it easy or you are going to cramp—do you think you can make it?—it's getting dark—water logged—keep moving to keep warm—what will my folks think—Mother will go crazy—I have been out here two hours already—I'm crazy—Rose Bowl—you won't get to see it—I won't be able to collect it—you are all through in school—you have wasted your folk's money—what will Rose think of this—you won't pass your exam—you are going to make it . . .

Mother—she'll go crazy—what will she do when she finds out?—she is not well enough to stand it—you got out of your wreck all right—they said you wouldn't—you'll be all right

During this phase, Don shows a dim awareness of the necessity to ward off feelings of hopelessness and demoralization. He again summons up the recollection of his earlier survival of a disaster in an effort to reassure himself by analogy ("you got out of your wreck all right—they said you wouldn't"). This type of *recollection of past disasters* is often observed during a prolonged crisis situation, for example during recovery from serious surgical operations. But Don's most powerful incentive to continue the struggle seems to be the *fantasy image of his grieving mother,* to which he resorts as a last-ditch effort to mobilize his dwindling resources, to maintain his vigilance, and to execute his plan for survival.

As the crisis continues unabated and Don's physical and psychological resources diminish, a new automatic type of defense emerges: a *confused mental state* with a *momentary loss of personal identity* that allows him to forget about the painful reality situation. But still the inner struggle goes on. He is unable to sustain any gratifying denial fantasies; the presence of danger reasserts itself time and again into his consciousness, in the form of phantasmagoric images similar to those that appear in nightmares. These horrifying reminders of danger seem to alternate with more pleasant images of safety and release from the painful struggle:

I can't remember back any more—what's happening to your mind?—what's your name? how'll they know your folks?—why worry about that when you are out in the ocean?—I always said I would be buried at sea—you always wanted to be buried at sea—here's your chance—I hope you never wash up on the beach—if your mother should find you—the birds'll pick your eyes out—that's fine . . . you'll go a long ways—I hope I don't wash up on the beach—I saw a guy that did once—you know what he looked like—one leg was gone—crabs ate the eyes out of his head—he fell off the jetty—you might as well shake hands with yourself—this is the last time you'll have both of them—why don't people sit by the fire like this and talk more often?—I hope a fish doesn't grab you—I wonder if there are fish on the bottom that are saying, "paddle your own canoe"—you can't hand the paddle to the guy in the back—you've got to paddle your own canoe—get a grand-daughter and lose a son—what will my folks think?—she looks like you, Mother says—you've been awfully damned ornery—this'll finish it sure

We see here that in addition to struggling against apathetic resignation, Don appears to displace the source of his intense concern. Instead of worrying about his mounting exhaustion and lack of physical strength to return through the breakers to the shore, he thinks about a comparatively unimportant threat of being unable to remember anything after he is saved. This is a realistic source of worry, but obviously it is much less distressing than the realization that he might have no mind or body left to worry about.

Later he resorts to a second, more desperate attempt to divert his attention from the immediate danger of drowning. This time he *displaces his fear* by imagining how horrified his mother would be to see his mutilated body washed up on the shore. Embedded in this displaced image, however, is an implicit acceptance of the horrible realization that he can no longer expect to survive.

There are numerous indications in the passage just quoted that Don now thinks his life is coming to an end—for example, "This'll finish it, sure"; "I hope I don't wash up on the beach"; "I saw a [drowned] guy that did once." And he adds to this a bit of gallows humor: "You might as well shake hands with yourself—this is the last time you'll have both of them." Most impressive is Don's fantasy image of himself as a corpse whose eyes are being picked out by birds, which seems to be his way of symbolizing his own death. Yet his vivid memories of just such mutilations seem to function as a strong goad to keep him from becoming inert and fully accepting death.

From the subsequent interviews we learn that throughout his early years, as a frequent visitor to Pacific Ocean resorts, Don had been deeply shocked several times by seeing dismembered bodies that had washed up on the beach. It is these memories that come to his consciousness during this phase. This phenomenon of *recalling horrifying sights and personal disasters* (such as Don's recollection of his auto accident) poses important questions for our understanding of human stress reactions. A series of case studies suggests that some traumatic past events suddenly recollected during a stressful experience are memories that up to that moment had been repressed (Janis, 1958, pp. 179–94).

The recovery of repressed memories as a reaction to severe stress is paradoxical, since it is well known that traumatic experiences produce amnesia for the traumatic events and for some associated past events. Yet men under stress sometimes recall seemingly forgotten events from the past. This might be a rudimentary basis for the popular belief that at the moment a person is about to die, his entire life will flash before his eyes. In case studies of disaster survivors who thought they were going to be killed, we find no indications that at the "moment of truth" they had been flooded with memories recapitulating their entire life histories. Nor did this occur in Don's case. But, like many disaster victims, Don vividly recaptured certain bits and pieces of his past life, which evidently did "flash before his eyes." Many of Don's recollections were disturbing memory images of past catastrophes that he would have been unlikely to dwell on voluntarily. Hence, the material from Don's delirium appears to be in line with the suggestive generalization that exposure to severe stress induces people involuntarily to revive disturbing memories from their past that up to that time they had seldom or never recalled. This generalization has not yet been confirmed by systematic research and so we must regard it as a tentative hypothesis, but it could have some important implications for the relationship between fear and memory functioning. For example, it may turn out that there is a tendency for disaster victims to recollect analogous threats of annihilation in the past, which they had managed to survive, in order to gain reassurance about surviving the present one. However painful the memories may be, they may still provide a psychological gain by enabling the person to obtain the type of consolation expressed by Don: "You got out of your wreck all right—they said you wouldn't—you'll be all right."

Not all Don's memories during the crisis were unpleasant. His positive feelings toward his family and his friends, as well as his intense longing for all varieties of warmth, are condensed into the memory image of sitting in a heated room next to a friend; he asks himself, "Why don't people sit by the fire like this and talk more often?" The later interviews reveal that this image was based partly on the events of the night before, when Don had sat listening to his literary friend Chuck Thurmond read poetry while he gazed into a log fire, comfortably protected from the raging storm outside. Don further explained that his mother always enjoyed sitting before a log fire and that in recent years he rarely joined her because he usually preferred to go out with his friends. If we allow ourselves to take Don's explanation as a "free association," we can surmise that when he contemplated this image of peaceful warmth while struggling for his life in the frigid waters, he was allowing his thoughts to go back to a time in childhood when he was physically and emotionally close to his mother.

This is one of several instances in the record of his delirious reenactment where we have an indication that Don experienced one of the most basic psychological needs activated by stressful events—the *longing for contact and psychological warmth from protective parents or parent substitutes*. This longing is tacitly acknowledged in a popular phrase used when talking about an acquaintance who has recently been hurt: "What he needs right now is some t.l.c." Alone and miserable, with dim prospects of surviving, a man can satisfy this need only in fantasy, perhaps without quite admitting to himself that what he wants is some tender loving care.

Don's recollection of the warmth of the fireside is soon followed by thoughts about a little baby who had just been greeted lovingly by all his family (his married brother had a newborn daughter). In a way, Don equates himself with the baby; he thinks of her as filling the gap in his parents' lives that will be left by his own death ("get a grand-daughter and lose a son . . . she looks like you, Mother says").

Don's intense longing for family warmth becomes explicit as he focuses on the traditional symbol of the affectionate family circle, the Christmas reunion at home. While verbalizing this part of his account, he began to sob bitterly.

> you'll have a nice Christmas—you can come home—you can come home and be with us—you are going to have your Christmas all by yourself—it's a good thing Chuck didn't come along—with those big boots—it's a good thing he didn't come along—he couldn't have made it—he has gone a long way—he has a long way to go—but you, you are losing nothing—come home for Christmas with us—you'll be like this for all time—I remember when you lost your little boat—I never knew then you were going to be next—we'll have Christmas together—isn't that ocean pretty?—it looks like hell! you can have Christmas—just the three of us—we'll all be together—it's a good thing you wrote just before you left—I hope they call and tell them—break it to them gently—you played football to get out of high school—you are going to have to swim to get out of the ocean—I'm getting so tired—being out here for hours—give up—just give up—give one more try—what difference does it make if you do drown?—sailors are drown-

ing in Europe every day—you're no better than they are—the mighty Pacific —it's gonna defeat you—aye, an' sure enough you're from Ireland—you can make it—everything is beginning to spin—if I can just make it—either make it all the way or not make it at all—if your mother found you on the beach she'd go crazy—you know how that other fellow was—his hand gone—his eyes gone—his bones showing through his skin

During this period of extreme crisis, with his outlook becoming blacker and blacker, Don tolerates sentiments that in almost any other circumstance he would not allow himself to take seriously. Like most college students, Don would dismiss feeling lonesome and tearful about not being home for Christmas as sentimental drivel.

It is noteworthy that Don never mentions his father during his delirious account. We can only speculate that this omission might reflect current unfriendly feelings toward his father, like those of many other young men struggling to gain independence during their late teens or early twenties. Perhaps Don's father is present in his thoughts, after all, in a somewhat disguised fashion, when he gives terse commands to himself, like a ship's captain or a football coach. These commands might represent the voice of his father, as an internalized part of Don's own personality. At any rate, when Don tells himself to "just give up," he immediately counters, as though speaking from another part of his own personality, with "give one more try." Don's intense conflict between giving up and struggling on seems to be directly expressed, as the internal debate continues, in a series of arguments and counterarguments. He assures himself that there is nothing wrong with giving up the struggle and that people drown every day. He defies the ocean, avows that it will not defeat him, and then reminds himself again of his Irish origins, to encourage himself not to give up the fight. And then once more he resorts to the ultimate goad—a vivid image of his mother agonizing over his mangled corpse.

We can see in the themes Don expresses that he is now trying to cope with an inner threat quite different from the one he had to counteract at the beginning of the episode. Then, the main internal danger involved feelings of terror and utter helplessness generated by the sudden confrontation with catastrophic danger, which might become so overwhelming as to interfere with effective emergency action. Now, as the crisis continues hour after hour, it is *feelings of hopelessness* that must be counteracted. Many of the memories and fantasies we have just been discussing can best be understood as defenses that Don is using to ward off demoralization, apathy, and resignation. As his stamina wears down, he begins to think more and more about the desirability of death, almost the same way a suicidal, depressed patient would.

One is reminded here of the well-known assertion, "Every man has his breaking point." Although this may be too broad a generalization, it points up the high frequency of breakdowns in normal soldiers and disaster victims who temporarily become incapacitated by anxiety symptoms after undergoing a terrifying catastrophe. Less well known are the less dramatic breakdowns that take the form of depressive symptoms, including suicidal ideas, that develop gradually when normal people are exposed to prolonged suffering with no apparent signs of letup. In some cases the ensuing depression is so profound that there is little emotional relief when the letup finally does come; the person remains depressed long after the episode is over. But there are marked individual differences in this respect, as will be seen in the next chapter. In Don's case the most obvious suicidal thoughts seem to have subsided rapidly after he was saved, but we do not know to what extent a persistent depressive mood entered into the emotional disturbances from which he suffered for many months afterward.

Phase 5:
Escape and Rescue

It was mentioned earlier that a decisive element in Don's struggle against apathy was the recollection of his plan. At a certain point, while in a somewhat dazed state after the long hours of struggle, he had the impression that the time had come to execute the final action. And so he made a desperate effort to swim to shore. But in his confused state he misinterpreted the signs of the turning of the tide. While he was fighting his way back to shore, the tide actually was still going out. His belief that the tide had begun to turn was an *error of judgment* that in fact led to a final, successful mobilization of all his energies. Such errors seem to be quite frequent in times of stress. They resemble the life-saving errors sometimes made during fires: Believing himself unscathed, many a desperately wounded person has thereby managed to run full speed from the flames. Don might not have been able to accomplish his great feat if he had not made the mistake of assuming that he was moving in the same direction as the tide. Otherwise, like any other knowledgeable swimmer, he would have had to admit to himself that his chances of making it to shore at that time were too poor to risk the attempt.

it's getting dark—the tide's turning—see the light—it's getting plainer —take it easier—you'll be all right—the water stings my face just like needles—you are going to make it to the breakers—swim with the breakers— you are going to make it . . .

that sand stings my face—it's cold—drag yourself—why doesn't somebody come?—take it easy—you're out of the water—I can't yell—why doesn't my flashlight work?—I can't yell—my voice doesn't work—my throat is all stopped up—crawl out of the water before it takes you back out

Don has now returned to action, after the long period of contemplative fantasying, and his style of thinking changes. He again addresses himself like the captain of a ship, announces the dangers to be warded off, and gives himself crisp advice about how to cope with the difficulties. His realistic anticipations and his successful performance are all the more impressive when we consider that while carrying out this final action, his *state of mental confusion* has by no means cleared up. For instance, he thinks he has a flashlight. (We learn from subsequent interviews that he used to take a flashlight along whenever he jumped breakers at night.)

After safely arriving on the edge of the beach, Don is so weakened by exhaustion that he can no longer execute simple body movements—he cannot yell for help, and he can barely drag his body away from the waves breaking on the shore; thus there is still the danger of being dragged out into the ocean again.

But despite his exhaustion and confusion, he mobilizes himself to assess the situation, to find out where he is, and to figure out what he should do.

> you are starting all over again—what are you gonna do here?—get to the light—this doesn't seem familiar—crawl through the bank—crawl through the canyon—where are you?—this is the end of the line—you can't make it any farther—you can't go on—you're just a weakling—you can't make it—this is as far as you can go—you're just a weakling—you still got your rabbit foot?—your mother bought that for you—it's a good thing you took that along—your 165 pounds is too heavy—you can't pull it—it's too heavy—there's a log—lean over it and throw up—stick your finger down your throat—throw up and then you can breathe—you can't get up the bank —you'll have to go up the canyon

In his confused state Don shows some typical symptoms of unrealistic thinking. This is most obvious in his *reliance on a primitive form of magic*, the rabbit's foot, which he normally would have dismissed as a mere keepsake. When asked a few days later about the rabbit's foot and the phrase "keep your fingers crossed" (which he repeated four times at the very end of his delirium), he laughed and treated these superstitious ideas as a joke.

It is not unusual, of course, for people to revert to childhood forms of re-assurance when in a state of extreme stress and to feel slightly embarrassed when reminded of them later. Often the superstitious ideas are expressed jokingly, but even so they are likely to be taken half-seriously at the time. They can be re-garded as indicating a mild regressive tendency that, unlike the severe regressions manifested by the mentally ill, may have a benign function. Such half-believed superstitions can help a person injured in a disaster to sustain his hopes of being rescued and to exert himself to the utmost to avoid entrapment.

Another, more subtle sign of a *temporary impairment of higher mental processes* is Don's apparent inability to discriminate between safety and danger. Having already crawled well up on the beach, he has fully escaped from the danger of drowning. But instead of feeling relieved, he thinks that he must keep on moving in order to survive, as though he were still out in the ocean ("you can't go on . . . you can't make it"). In fact, he dragged his bruised, exhausted body a phenomenally long way along the shore, though he could have obtained aid much sooner from the nearby houses (whose lights he saw) if he merely had rested long enough to regain his voice sufficiently to call out for help.

Incidentally, the details Don gave in his delirious account about what he did on shore were fully authenticated. On the basis of what Don said, one of his friends was able to trace his entire path, leading up to a small gorge, which Don perceived as an almost insurmountable canyon. There were also clear-cut marks in the sand where his wrists and the rabbit's foot remained imprinted.

Although Don was in a profoundly disorganized state and was momentarily regressing to childlike modes of thinking, he still retained some crucial remnants of his higher mental functions. For example, if his strenuous movements along the beach were somewhat unnecessary, they nevertheless did take him away from the ocean and close enough to the houses so that he was soon rescued and given first aid. Moreover, he effectively administered some first aid to himself by lying across a log and forcing himself to vomit in order to rid his body of the sea water he had swallowed. Here again he was relying on well-ingrained knowledge about what to do in just such an emergency, and it is quite remarkable that he could still retain sufficient psychological stamina to be able to carry out this essential bit of self-help.

The Aftermath:
Emotional Shock and Gradual Recovery

In a small portion of the record of Don's delirium we find some references to his here-and-now situation, as he lay in bed in the cottage to which he had been carried right after he was found on the beach. At one point he looked around dazedly, uncomprehendingly, and said:

> where are you?—I don't remember this—this is all new to me—where is this?—where were you before you came here?—where was I before I came here?—where are your folks?—where do they live?—wait till you come to—you don't know anyone—they are all strangers—can't I remember where I am?—better go back and see where you lost your senses

In the last statement of this passage Don suggests that going back over what happened to him might help him regain his senses. Later we shall see that this might well be a correct insight that helps explain why someone who has been traumatized in a disaster has such a powerful need to repeat the distressing experience in his dreams and in his waking thoughts. For the present it will suffice to note that the dazed, confused state in which Don was found at the time of rescue is typical of disaster survivors after undergoing a narrow escape from death. Often they are completely disoriented and have no recollection of what has happened to them. Don showed precisely this type of amnesia when he woke up after the delirium. The delirium state had gone on for about 3 hours, with many of the above-quoted statements being repeated over and over, some of them dozens of times. Then, when he finally awakened 6 hours after having been rescued on the beach, Don had a glassy, unnatural look in his eyes, and his face was expressionless. Nevertheless, he immediately answered questions put to him by his friends. His responses clearly indicated that he not only had total amnesia for the preceding events but also was unable to identify who he was and could recall only disconnected fragments of his past life. Among the statements indicating his *loss of personal identity* during the post-delirium interview were the following:

> I can't remember where I've been or where I'm going—where is this?—Wakonda Beach?—where is that?—where am I going?—home?—where is home?—I go to school?—No. I finished school!—who are you?—Chuck?—how did I get here?—is this the Navy?—this is like the time in football when I was knocked out for 5 hours—Corvallis?—I remember when I used to go to Corvallis [the town in which his college was located] when my brother was down there—but have I ever gone to school there?—ocean?—swimming?—have I been to the ocean?—how could I get here and not know a thing?—all I can remember is my folks trying to talk me out of going into the Navy—we're going to Corvallis tomorrow?—I am going to school there?

The loss of memory and of his sense of personal identity, which evidently had begun while he was out in the ocean, continued and became even more pronounced when he woke up from the delirium state. This is characteristic of the *gross impairment of mental functions* that is likely to occur in any disaster victim when he emerges from a situation of seemingly inescapable danger.

Even after being told during the interview that he was a student at Corvallis, that he had had an accident while swimming in the ocean, and that he had been picked up on the beach, Don was not able to regain his orientation. Nor could he identify his close friend, Chuck Thurmond, who was interviewing him. Don was able to produce only a few fragmentary memories, such as "This is like the time in football when I was knocked out for 5 hours" and "All I can remember is my folks trying to talk me out of going into the Navy."

After almost 8 hours of sleep, however, Don awakened and was able to recognize his friend and even to recall what they had talked about earlier. He said, "It's beginning to get clear, I remember you now, Chuck. I am beginning to remember Oregon State. Gosh, my shoulders hurt me, and my arms and legs."

As usually happens in cases of post-traumatic amnesia, Don slowly recovered his memories of recent events, as well as his orientation. Among other things, he recalled that during the hours he was out in the ocean he had felt convinced at times that he was going to drown and was concerned that the news be broken to his parents gently. These disturbing memories of the traumatic episode were not confined to recollections during the waking state. Don's sleep was markedly interrupted, night after night, by *terrifying dreams* during which he would call out, "I can't make it!—I won't make it." These dreams, which imply a basic change in attitude concerning his personal vulnerability, continued for several months and then gradually disappeared.

In the next chapter we shall examine evidence about personality changes produced in normal adults by traumatic disaster experiences comparable to Don's. In succeeding chapters we shall consider the main psychological themes that help us comprehend how and why various types of adaptive and maladaptive stress reactions—like some of those displayed by Don—are likely to be evoked in men and women at times when they are emotionally aroused by actual danger stimuli or by signs that remind them of past dangers and deprivations.

Like one who having battled with the waves,
In safety on the shore, with panting breath
Looks back upon the perils of the deep:
So did my soul, which still in terror fled,
Turn back to contemplate with awe and fear
That pass which man had never left alive.

DANTE. Inferno

CHAPTER 2
PSYCHOLOGICAL TRAUMA

D on O'Daniel provides a dramatic example of emotional shock produced by a narrow escape from death. His feelings of apprehensiveness, temporary confusion, amnesia, loss of cognitive abilities, and repetitive nightmares are all symptoms of the emotional state referred to as anxiety. They are typical of the temporary personality changes that follow an episode of harrowing personal danger. In this case these symptoms—together with the tremors, pounding heart, and other manifestations of extreme physiological arousal—are clearly the result of *psychological trauma*, which denotes a state of emotional shock induced by severe stress or frustration. Often the anxiety symptoms clear up within a few days, but they may last for months or even years, and some of them may remain unobservable until the person is again exposed to severe stress.

When the anxiety symptoms are so incapacitating as to prevent the person from resuming his work or his usual social activities, the condition is called *traumatic neurosis*. Don's acute symptoms gradually subsided during the first few months following the episode; his condition during this recovery phase would be called an *acute* traumatic neurosis. If we had subsequent follow-up information on Don indicating that his symptoms had not entirely cleared up after many years, we would label his condition a *chronic* traumatic neurosis. In the latter condition the patient usually develops additional neurotic symptoms that contribute to his inability to engage in normal activities, such as phobic reactions, excessive fatigue, and psychosomatic disorders, stemming directly or indirectly from the increased level of anxiety induced by the traumatic events.

In this chapter we shall examine the evidence concerning personality changes produced by exposure to severe environmental stress. We shall be particularly concerned with obvious disruptive changes; the more subtle effects of severe stress will be discussed in later chapters. At the end of this chapter we shall consider some recent discoveries concerning detrimental effects of psychological trauma that persist for years, perhaps permanently, even though the person may seem to be free of symptoms. After a person shows recovery from an acute traumatic neurosis, as Don presumably did, he might be left with a *latent* traumatic neurosis, which may go undetected for years, until a new crisis reactivates the acute symptoms.

Acute Traumatic Neurosis

THE SYMPTOMS

The term *traumatic neurosis* applies to both temporary and persistent forms of incapacitating personality changes that follow traumatic events. Such changes may occur after narrow escapes or after actual injury, even though the person had previously functioned well and had never before shown any neurotic symptoms. Sometimes merely an accumulation of mildly stressful events may produce traumatic neurosis.

Many cases of traumatic neurosis have been observed among soldiers after harrowing combat. Some of the soldiers wander aimlessly for hours in a disoriented state similar to the state Don was in when he reached the shore. Others suddenly become overexcited and recklessly attack enemy positions; some, stricken with panic, flee from the combat area. Following the acute phase of breakdown on the battlefield, the men show a fairly consistent pattern of aftereffects. In particular, three types of symptoms have been observed in most cases of traumatic neurosis:

1. spells of uncontrollable emotion, usually anxiety, but sometimes rage and depression;
2. sleep disturbances, including insomnia and terrifying dreams in which the traumatic event is relived;
3. blocking or partial loss of various personal skills, inability to concentrate, and loss of other "ego functions."

Military psychiatrists point out that the symptoms of war neurosis are not fundamentally different from those seen in the civilians who develop traumatic neuroses following automobile accidents or peacetime disasters. Survivors of a peacetime disaster typically show an initial state of terror, as Don did, followed by a period of disorientation and stunned immobility. Then, after the obvious signs of danger have disappeared, they show the characteristic symptoms of emotional shock—lethargy, depressive feelings, and irritability, together with sleep disturbances, jitteriness, and other anxiety symptoms, all of which are the same as in war neuroses. In some traumatized persons it is anxiety that predominates, while in others it is depression or sullen withdrawal.

Studies of men and women in cities destroyed by air attacks in wartime or by natural disasters indicate that only a small percentage develop *chronic* traumatic neurosis following a catastrophe, but a very high percentage develop *acute* traumatic neurosis (Janis, 1951; Tyhurst, 1957). Fritz and Marks (1954) found that approximately 90 percent of the survivors of a tornado disaster in Arkansas reported that they suffered from acute anxiety symptoms or psychosomatic reactions the day after the disaster, and 75 percent reported that these symptoms lasted for several days. The most frequent anxiety symptoms were general excitability and insomnia and related sleep disturbances; many also reported headaches, loss of appetite, and inability to concentrate. These temporary symptoms and the accompanying impairments in everyday behavior are essentially the same as in the infrequent cases of chronic traumatic neurosis, some of which involve permanent personality changes. As long as the symptoms persist, the person is unable to work effectively, lacks interest in normal social activities, and does little or nothing about rehabilitating himself or his community.

Maslow and Mittleman (1951) suggest that everyone at some time in his life probably experiences at least a mild, temporary form of traumatic neurosis, such as emotional shock following an automobile accident or some other disaster that brings the person close to the possibility of injury or death. They point out that relatively little is known about why one person can shake off the experience quickly, whereas others succumb to it and have persistent, perhaps permanent, distressing symptoms. Part of the answer may lie in the type of danger stimuli to which the person is exposed; later, we shall examine some of the main situational factors that increase the chances of psychological trauma (pages 24–29). In addition, the individual's personality make-up undoubtedly contributes to his predisposition to a traumatic neurosis. Some clinical follow-up studies suggest that the incapacitating symptoms of traumatic neurosis are most likely to become chronic in predisposed personalities who have a history of neurotic disturbance prior to the catastrophic event (Grinker & Spiegel, 1945a; Kardiner & Spiegel, 1947; Janis, 1951, 1958); but the evidence is still quite incomplete. The important point is that even in the most stable personalities, the acute symptoms of traumatic neurosis will usually occur at least temporarily following direct involvement in a disaster.

Studies of wartime and peacetime disasters indicate that the most severe and prolonged forms of emotional disturbance occur among people who are injured or undergo *near-miss* experiences. In addition to narrow escapes, the near-miss category includes all types of *victimization* resulting from a disaster; for example, when the person suffers physical injury or personal loss (such as destruction of his home), which clearly demonstrates to him that he could have been killed. In such instances the survivor, after recovering from the most incapacitating symptoms of emotional shock, remains keenly aware of how close he came to being badly mutilated, incapacitated for life, or killed. Similar reactions occur following exposure to nonphysical forms of danger, such as being humiliated in front of one's friends, being fired from one's job, or being unable to control one's violent rage against a rival.

A World War II study provides some impressive evidence about the power of near-miss experiences. Fraser, Leslie, and Phelps (1943) examined the medical records from all the first-aid posts in a large English city that had just been through a period of heavy bombing. The investigators tracked down every case they could find of civilians who had been rated by physicians at first-aid posts as uninjured after having been knocked down or personally affected by a bomb explosion. They were able to interview almost 100 such cases.

Forty percent of the civilians had suffered from emotional disturbances severe enough to keep them away from work for at least 3 weeks following the near-miss experience. Absenteeism among civilians in the same community who were remote-misses was less than 10 percent. (The term *remote-miss* was applied to people who were in the general neighborhood of a bomb explosion but were not directly affected.)

The investigators subdivided the uninjured survivors of bombing attacks who had undergone near-miss experiences into two groups, those who subsequently developed symptoms of traumatic neurosis and those who did not. The people afflicted with traumatic neurosis had undergone much more severe forms of victimization than the others: 50 percent of the afflicted group had been pulled out of the ruins of their destroyed homes, had had a friend or relative killed in the raid, or had suffered some other personal loss; only 4 percent of the nonafflicted group experienced any such victimization. The near-miss cases with the most persistent symptoms of traumatic neurosis were those who had been buried beneath debris of a building that was directly hit by a bomb.

Other studies in the bombed cities of England and Germany and in American cities damaged by tornadoes or other natural disasters also suggest that *the greater the degree of victimization produced by exposure to severe stress, the higher the probability of emotional disturbance afterward* (Janis, 1951; Fritz & Marks, 1954).

Military studies tend to confirm this generalization. The findings from one such study, presented in Figure 2-1, show that ratings of high anxiety—based on such symptoms as insomnia, tremors, stomach disturbances, and distressing feelings of nervousness—were more likely to occur among men on front-line duty in an active combat area than among those behind the lines who were subjected only to sporadic artillery fire or air raids. The latter men, in turn, had more symptoms than the soldiers in safe rear areas who had not yet been under enemy fire. Thus the incidence of anxiety symptoms appears to depend on the degree of exposure to actual danger. The most severe anxiety was produced in those men who were "fugitives" of the kind portrayed by Mauldin in Figure 2-2.

Similar results have been reported from World War II studies of combat fliers who lived in comfortable English towns and were exposed to enemy fire only about three times a week for a few hours at a time. A much higher incidence of anxiety symptoms was found in air crew members who had completed their tour of combat duty (20 missions over enemy territory) than among those who had flown fewer missions; practically no symptoms were observed in the men before their first mission (Janis, 1949a). Most of the fliers who had flown a dozen or more combat missions experienced startle reactions at any sudden noise in the barracks, uncontrollable spells of panic-like dread, and involuntary recollections of harrowing combat missions (Hastings, Wright, & Glueck, 1944; Shaffer, 1947). Many of these men doubled or tripled their usual alcohol consumption, thereby seeking a

Figure 2-1   Relation between anxiety symptoms and proximity to combat dangers, based on a cross-section survey of 4222 American soldiers in the European Theater of Operations, April 1945. (Adapted from Star, 1949)

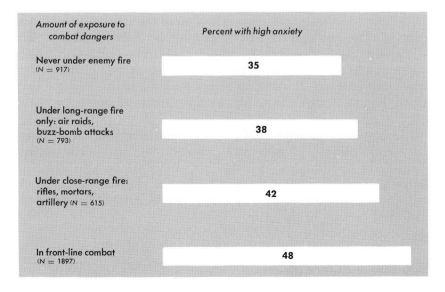

"I feel like a fugitive from th' law of averages."

Figure 2-2 A soldier's image of combat. (Drawing copyrighted 1944 by United Features Syndicate, Inc.)

refuge typical of men who are unable to cope adequately with unbearable stress in their daily lives. Perhaps the most disruptive anxiety symptoms were the sleep disturbances that ubiquitously plague men under stress.

SLEEP DEPRIVATION
AND DISORGANIZED BEHAVIOR

Insomnia and related sleep disturbances, which characteristically follow every traumatic experience, pose a special problem for the mental health of the victim, because sleep deprivation in itself can lead to disorganized behavior. Sleep disturbances also occur during any stressful period of a person's life, whenever he is confronted by the threat of personal failure or a loss affecting his love life, friendships, or career. Involuntary wakefulness appears to be extraordinarily persistent during periods of mourning. In an unselected group of 72 clinically normal widows, insomnia was found in about 80 percent of the cases during the first months of bereavement (Marris, 1958).

People who go without sleep for long periods of time show a marked loss in mental efficiency, display poor judgment, and sometimes become so disorganized in their thinking that they are temporarily in a psychotic state, no longer able to differentiate between reality and their own fantasies. This appears to be a reversible form of organic psychosis, attributable to transient physiological changes in the brain.

Many apparent senile psychoses in elderly persons may be essentially the symptoms resulting from sleep deprivation that would develop in any person suffering from chronic insomnia. Many older persons are constantly kept awake by physical aches and pains or by emotional stress created by awareness of approaching death, separation from their families, or signs of being rejected. In these cases, when sleep is restored through psychological treatment or sedative drugs, the person is no longer so forgetful and confused. Even in adolescents and young adults undergoing the stresses of college examinations, a temporary breakdown that appears to be schizophrenic might sometimes be attributable to the fact that they were getting very little sleep night after night for many weeks (Cameron, 1963). It has also been observed that the most disorganized behavior of men and women who have recently undergone traumatic disaster experiences begins to clear up quite rapidly once they are able to return to their normal sleeping habits.

The relation between sleep deprivation and emotional disorder is not fully understood. Some fascinating clues have recently emerged, however. The main breakthrough was the discovery in 1953 by Aserinsky and Kleitman that rapid eye movements (REMs), together with distinctive brain-wave patterns, regularly occur at periodic intervals during normal sleep. When normal subjects were awakened while they were having these rapid eye movements, it was discovered that this was the time they were having dreams. Dement (1960) and Fisher and Dement (1963) conducted a series of experiments designed to determine whether the nightly amount of dreaming shown by the normal person was essential for normal psychological functioning. They used the method of forced awakening with subjects who slept in their laboratory for as many as 16 nights. This method, although quite straightforward, turned out to require a tremendous amount of experimental effort (and resulted in the experimenters losing a considerable amount of sleep themselves, since they had to stay awake all night collecting their data). Using an apparatus like that shown in Figure 2-3, the experimenters carefully monitored the eye-movement records, watching for signs that the subject was beginning to have a dream. Each time the REMs appeared, they awoke the subject, kept him up for a few minutes, and then allowed him to go back to sleep. This procedure was continued throughout the subject's entire sleeping period for several nights. During a subsequent recovery night, when the subject's sleep was not at all disturbed, each one showed a marked increase in the amount of dreaming, which seemed to compensate for the lack of dreams during the preceding period of forced awakenings. In other words, the amount of dreaming lost during the period of the experiment was being made up for at the first opportunity. No such increase in dreaming time was found in the control group of subjects who were awakened just as often, but only at times when they were not showing rapid eye movements.

Two dream-deprived subjects, when given a special form of visual stimulation, showed evidence of hallucinating while awake. All subjects who were put through the dream-deprivation procedure for 5 consecutive nights showed a gradual deterioration in a variety of psychological functions; they had great difficulty in concentrating and became noticeably anxious and irritable. The investigators concluded that dreaming is necessary for the well-being of the human organism: A person deprived of the opportunity to dream for a long enough period can enter a psychotic-like state in which he performs dreamlike activity while awake—resulting in hallucinations, confused thinking, and disorganized action.

It seems probable that whenever a person has insufficient opportunity to dream because of lack of sleep over a long period of time, the same type of disorganized mental state will be produced. One experiment (Snyder, 1963) showed that after 5 days of complete sleep deprivation normal subjects began to have hallucinations and delusions, which became more marked at night and occurred with a periodicity of from 90 to 120 minutes,

Figure 2-3 Experimental setup for the study of eye movements and brain waves during dreams and dream deprivation. (From Research Center for Mental Health, New York University)

An eye-movement electrode has been placed at the side of each eye, and brain-wave electrodes have been placed on the scalp. The apparatus on the lower part of the ear is a ground. The wires are thin and are arranged so as to interfere as little as possible with the subject's movement. They run to a wall mount and then through the ceiling to the recording apparatus outside the room. This machine, at which the experimenter is stationed, amplifies and records the electrical activity.

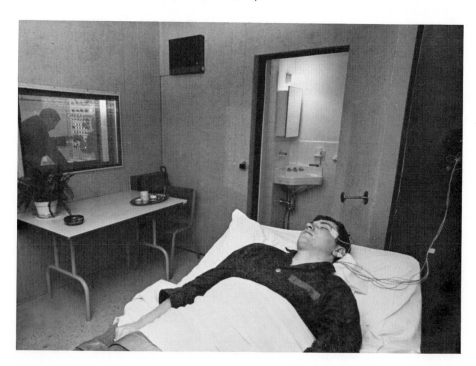

which happens to correspond closely to the periodicity with which spontaneous dreams usually occur during a normal night's sleep.

Clearly, it is important to restore sleep as rapidly as possible in any case of acute traumatic neurosis and in any person who is suffering from insomnia following an emotionally disturbing crisis in his life. A number of experiments involving forced awakening of normal subjects indicate that when people obtain only half their usual night's sleep, they develop symptoms of tension and anxiety, irritability, and difficulty in concentrating. Perhaps many of the most severe symptoms and disorganized forms of behavior could be prevented—especially those giving rise to gross errors of judgment that can lead to serious accidents or to impulsive suicidal acts—if disaster victims were regularly given sufficient sedation to induce sleep artificially or some special form of psychological treatment that would help them to recover their normal sleeping habits. Unless emergency treatment is given to counteract insomnia, a traumatized person may be unable to benefit from psychotherapy sessions in which he is encouraged to verbalize and unlearn his extreme emotional responses to cues that remind him of the traumatic events.

Chronic Traumatic Neurosis

Not all persons who suffer from acute traumatic neurosis show the expected pattern of recovery during the weeks and months after the traumatic event. Some develop lasting personality defects—recurrent anxiety symptoms, loss of interest in normal daily activities, and such marked disruption of ego functions that they are unable to keep working at even the most routine jobs (Kardiner & Spiegel, 1947). In these cases of chronic traumatic neurosis the patient shows great dependence on others to take care of his elementary needs, and in some cases he withdraws into the highly restricted world of the invalid.

Often the patient gets "secondary gains" for retaining his symptoms—such as pensions, insurance payments, and free room and board at a hospital. A more subtle form of secondary gain is the continuing fulfillment of the patient's strong dependency needs by members of the family or by nurses who are no longer objectively needed. Sometimes the patient shows irritability and overt hostility toward those who minister to him, thereby disguising his underlying passivity or reacting to the frustration of his insatiable longing for attention. Unlike the deliberate malingerer, the chronic patient is seldom fully aware of being influenced by the secondary gains he is receiving.

In general, the chronic condition is likely to be avoided if the individual is not given financial or other inducements for remaining incapacitated and instead is exposed to a social and work environment that allows him to resume his normal activities gradually. Even when there is no apparent secondary gain, however, some symptoms of anxiety may persist. One symptom is especially likely to become permanent—hypersensitivity to loud noises or to other threat cues (that is, stimuli similar to those that were present at the time of the traumatic event).

SYMPTOMS UNIQUE TO THE CHRONIC STATE

The relatively constant features of chronic traumatic neurosis include the same symptoms that characterize the acute form of traumatic neurosis. But they are usually accompanied by some new, more pervasive symptoms—a generalized form of apprehensiveness and timidity that seems to extend to the whole social and physical environment, indicating that the traumatized person now regards his entire world as an unsafe place. He shows a marked loss of confidence in himself, especially in his ability to face up to any future stresses. He may also feel disappointed in authority figures or in the friends and relatives on whom he normally relies for protection in times of crisis.

Kardiner and Spiegel (1947) suggest that the patient's distrust of himself and others to ward off traumatic dangers might account for the characteristic withdrawal behavior, overt expressions of resentment, and uncooperativeness shown by combat soldiers after undergoing harrowing battle experiences. They refer to "the increasing selfishness, the rudeness, explosiveness, and profanity which accompany the irritability and the gradual loss of confident orientation [p. 74]."

Year after year the demoralized patient suffers from preoccupation with the traumatic events and from nightmares in which he relives them. At the same time he withdraws more and more, gradually developing a deeply pessimistic outlook concerning his chances of recovery. His wife and other relatives may come to share his pessimism, as they see him surrendering to passivity. Yet many clinical reports suggest that even the most persistent anxiety symptoms may be reversible. Kardiner and Spiegel (1947, pp. 381–89) discuss cases of men who, after years of incapacitation, recovered from traumatic neurosis with psychiatric help. One of their highly instructive case studies, which is summarized below, illustrates the dramatic improvement that can be produced by a relatively small amount of therapeutic treatment.

RECOVERY FROM CHRONIC TRAUMATIC NEUROSIS:
A CASE STUDY

The patient, whom we shall call Tom, was 31 years old when he first came to the clinic with complaints of a variety of anxiety symptoms that prevented him from doing any work at all. Tom told the psychiatrist who interviewed him about his constant apprehensiveness, his fainting attacks, his fear of high places, his insomnia, and his distressing dreams—all of which are typical symptoms of a traumatic neurosis. Like many other incapacitated war veterans, he was wholly dependent on the government for financial support. Over the years he had refused any opportunity for work or for further vocational training, on the grounds that his symptoms were much too distressing. For almost 7 years he had confined himself to his home and remained completely dependent on his wife to take care of him.

What disturbed Tom most were the fainting spells, which occurred about three times a week. Precipitated by sudden noises or by other mild but unexpected stimuli, these spells usually lasted about a half-hour. Each time one of them began, he felt a queer sensation at the pit of his stomach and sometimes a slight pain in his forehead as well; then he lost consciousness and could not be aroused. While unconscious, he muttered to himself and sometimes moved convulsively. Upon regaining consciousness, he found himself very weak and sweating with agonized tension. This same agitated state followed upon his awakening from his terrifying nightmares, which happened so often that he preferred to lie awake exhausted rather than fall asleep. The queer stomach sensations generally accompanied his anxiety dreams, the manifest content of which always concerned falling from a great height. During his waking life, Tom sometimes became preoccupied with apprehensive thoughts about falling from high places.

All Tom's symptoms could be directly traced to an accident he suffered while serving as an airplane mechanic in the U.S. Air Force. He was injured when a routine flight ended in a serious crash; a friend of his was the pilot. Tom remembered little about the accident preceding the point when he was being carried to the hospital. Soon after the crash he had begun to experience the incapacitating anxiety symptoms, and he had never been able to work again. Thus the onset of this man's symptoms, like those of many people who develop a traumatic neurosis after a serious auto or airplane accident, could be precisely attributed to the traumatic event. Moreover, the specific content of his anxiety symptoms (fear of falling and distressing sensations in the pit of his stomach) could be directly related to the horrifying events of the accident.

When Tom was first brought to the psychiatric clinic by his wife, he was quite uncooperative. Only after much evasion in his first interview did he admit to the psychiatrist that he disliked being asked about the accident. "I don't like to be thinking about those things you make me think about; I'm trying to forget them." This avoidance reaction is typical of a patient suffering from a traumatic neurosis; many such patients try to avoid coming into contact with any friend, relative, or therapist who insists on making them talk about the distressing events. In this case the therapist used the patient's complaints about the disturbing questions to help him learn something about his symptoms.

The therapist was struck by Tom's remark that he had wanted to stop answering the questions because he had "queer sensations in the pit of the stomach—the way I often get before I go off" (into a fainting attack). The therapist pointed out that Tom's reaction to the questions was similar to his fainting spells: In both instances he had a sinking sensation in his abdomen, which he must have originally experienced when he was in the falling plane during the accident. After accepting this elementary insight, Tom began to speak much more freely about his troubles and fears. But it took many weeks of psychiatric interviews before this defensive patient regarded the therapist as a helper rather than a tormentor. He was then able to produce a few more recollections about what had happened during the traumatic airplane crash, and his symptoms began to improve noticeably. His fainting attacks occurred less frequently, he had fewer disturbing dreams, and he was able to get much more sleep.

By the sixth month of treatment Tom showed remarkable improvement in all his other symptoms as well. For the first time he could go back to work as a mechanic. Once again he could tolerate the sound of sudden noises and was no longer thrown into a spasm by the backfire of an automobile. Tom even recovered his self-confidence to the point where he felt a desire to try going up in an airplane again. Then came the great day when he actually did go on a flight and found that he could do so without any mishaps. Because of this considerable improvement the therapist decided to terminate the treatment, but he arranged for a series of follow-up interviews, to take place approximately every 6 months.

From the first of three follow-up interviews the therapist learned that all was going well. But when Tom returned for his second follow-up interview, about 15 months after the treatment had begun, he reported that although he had been able to work continually and was entirely self-supporting, he had recently had a setback. He had had a recurrence of his fainting spells, "the worst attack I ever had in my whole life." At first the therapist felt quite disappointed about this setback, but then as he listened to Tom describe the vivid dream images that accompanied this particular attack, he noticed that for the first time Tom was giving many of the missing details concerning the airplane crash—details he had never before consciously recollected. In the dreamlike fantasy that accompanied the fainting attack Tom took the controls of the airplane from his friend, and then just as he was about to land, he suddenly noticed a black object coming out of the clouds. Next he heard a crash as the right wing collapsed, and this was followed by a horrifyingly rapid descent, ending with the sensation of striking the ground. The fantasy ended with Tom futilely attempting to rescue his buddy, who was caught in the space between the motors, and then climbing out on the tail of the plane.

As Tom talked about this fantasy during the interview, his amnesia for the traumatic events began to lift. Now he could recall for the first time that he actually was in charge of the controls when the accident took place, that the accident had been caused by a collision with another plane, that the right wing of his plane had in fact broken off, that he had been deeply concerned about his friend's injuries and had tried to help him get out after the crash. Thus the last "spell" was a remarkable reproduction of the accident for which the patient had previously had almost complete amnesia. Moreover, it turned out that the night on which this extraordinary spell occurred was the eighth anniversary of the accident, to the day.

This type of recovery of amnesia for a traumatic disaster rarely occurs except under the influence of very deep hypnosis or hypnotic drugs, though, as we saw earlier in the case of Don, such episodes can be relived in a spontaneous delirium or dreamlike state. The only unusual thing about the present case was the patient's ability to recapture, from the content of his dream-spell, the seemingly lost memories of the traumatic episode so many years after it had happened.

A third follow-up interview 6 months later found Tom to be in an excellent state of mental health. He continued to work well, was relatively free from anxiety symptoms, and had no recurrences of the fainting spells.

The therapist noted that the positive results of the therapy could not be attributed to the lifting of the amnesia, since this occurred to only a small degree during the 6 months of actual treatment, while the patient was making his most rapid progress in recovering from the chronic traumatic neurosis. The lifting of the amnesia, which occurred almost a year after the treatment was over, should rather be regarded as the final step in recovery from the traumatic neurosis. Kardiner and Spiegel (1947) point out that an amnesia of this kind is likely to improve only when "the individual's picture of the outer world has been changed, when his courage and resources in handling this new external reality had been increased or restored, at least in part [p. 389]." The authors emphasize the social importance of the patient's recovery: For more than 6 years this man was a public charge and in need of constant care from his wife; 6 months of treatment enabled him to be completely rehabilitated. There is no reason to believe that this recovery could not have been produced by the same type of treatment shortly after the onset of the traumatic neurosis. Such early treatment might have saved the patient all those wasted, miserable years of his life. This case study illustrates an important point that has both practical and theoretical implications: At least in some cases, *the symptoms of chronic traumatic neurosis, like those of acute traumatic neurosis, are reversible.*

Latent Traumatic Neurosis

Successful treatment of a long-standing neurosis in a patient like Tom makes a psychotherapist feel optimistic about being able to cure other such cases. This outlook is reinforced by the results of numerous clinical surveys that support two important conclusions: (1) Most persons who develop the symptoms of acute traumatic neurosis following exposure to accidents or disasters spontaneously recover quite rapidly, usually within a few weeks; and (2) the persons who fail to recover spontaneously are more likely than the others to have a history of emotional disorder. It is quite understandable, therefore, that many specialists in this field believe that almost everyone who undergoes a traumatic experience can recover completely. The only exceptions would be those unusual individuals whose pathologic personality make-up predisposes them to chronic mental disorder in any case; in such cases *any* stress could trigger the long-lasting anxiety symptoms. According to this view, the people who permanently suffer adverse personality changes are those who would have had some sort of an emotional breakdown anyhow. The normal personality—so runs this argument—might be momentarily shaken by stressful events and develop a transient traumatic neurosis, but will soon return to the normal state of mental health.

This highly optimistic view concerning the *complete* reversibility of the symptoms is now being seriously challenged. Recent evidence suggests that we cannot assume that when disaster-stricken persons recover from the acute phase of traumatic neurosis, they recover permanently; rather, we must be alert to the possibility of *latent* changes that will show up on the surface later in their lives.

In a review of the recent evidence from follow-up studies, Archibald and Tuddenham (1965) conclude: When the average person has undergone traumatic stress, his anxiety symptoms may persist for many years and perhaps be permanent, although they are manifested in his behavior only when subsequent stress is encountered. Some of their evidence comes from long-term studies of American veterans of World War II, who were reexamined some 20 years after they had completed their military service. A group of veterans who were known to have developed war neurosis (traumatic neurosis induced during combat service) was compared with an equivalent group who had not. About 7 out of every 10 men who had recovered from war neurosis were again showing clear-cut symptoms of excessive jumpiness, irritability, restlessness, and depression. Furthermore, over 50 percent of the men in this group had additional neurotic symptoms, such as recurrent combat dreams, momentary blackouts, dizziness, and heart palpitations (see Figure 2-4). Thus, 20 years after their supposed "full recovery," the men were suffering from the same symptoms that had temporarily incapacitated them during the war. Such symptoms were rarely found in two control groups of war veterans who had not developed a war neurosis. (The first control group consisted of noncombat veterans who had to be treated for other psychiatric disorders while in military service, and the second consisted of "healthy" veterans who had never required treatment for any psychiatric disorder.) A follow-up study of Korean War veterans confirmed these findings. Surprisingly, about one-third of the veterans of both wars who had supposedly recovered from war neurosis were unemployed at the time of the study; a sizable additional percentage had unstable employment records, suggesting that their symptoms were severe enough to interfere with their work. On the basis of all their findings, Archibald and Tuddenham state that "the combat fatigue syndrome [acute traumatic neurosis], which was expected to vanish with the passage of time, has proved to be chronic [p. 481]." They bolster this conclusion with additional evidence indicating that latent personality changes may persist below the surface in traumatized men who had formerly been emotionally stable, even though they seem to have recovered and receive no secondary gains. Most of the veterans in these studies had received no special compensation. Nor did they receive any psychiatric treatment until long after leaving the service, when the stresses of later life precipitated a recurrence of the same type of anxiety symptoms that had temporarily incapacitated them during the war.

Methodological problems in any such follow-up study that relies on interview data prevent us from regarding the conclusions as definitive, but there is other supporting evidence. For example, an impressive experimental procedure was used by Dobbs and Wilson (1960) to investigate the stress

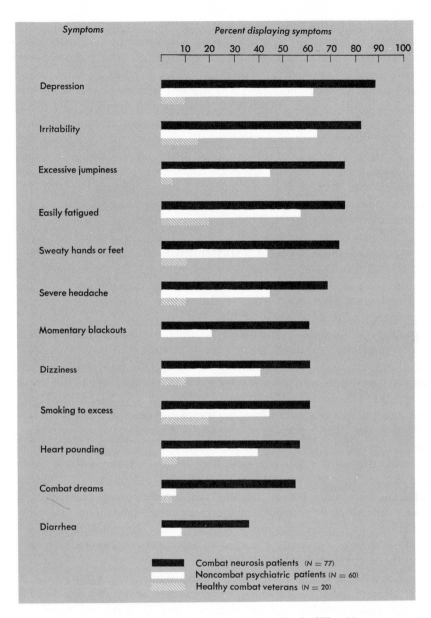

Figure 2-4 *Incidence of symptoms in World War II veterans, approximately 20 years after military duty. (Adapted from Archibald & Tuddenham, 1965)*

For every symptom, the war neurosis patients differ significantly from each of the other two groups. For a number of other symptoms (including difficulty in falling asleep and memory disturbances), there were differences in the same direction that were not statistically significant.

tolerance of equivalent groups of war veterans. They exposed the subjects to tape recordings of realistic battle noises. The men who had once developed traumatic neuroses and had seemingly recovered completely showed extreme behavioral and physiological disturbances when exposed to these sounds of battle. Some of them became panic-stricken and displayed acute anxiety symptoms like those seen in the acute phase of war neurosis. These extreme reactions were very seldom observed in a comparable group of combat veterans who had never developed traumatic neurosis; such reactions did not occur at all in a second control group of men who had never been in combat. These findings support the view that even when no symptoms are present on the surface, the personality changes induced by traumatic experiences may exist at a latent level and become manifest as acute anxiety symptoms only when the threat cues are reinstated.

Evidence of the recurrence of startle reactions, anxiety attacks, sleep disturbances, and other signs of hypersensitivity to threat stimuli has also been found in follow-up studies of victims of the Nazi concentration camps (Chodoff, 1963). The studies show a remarkably high frequency of anxiety symptoms years after the release of the victims from the camps. Research on peacetime disasters yields similar results. Leopold and Dillon (1963), for example, traced the subsequent histories of individuals who had survived a maritime explosion, giving special attention to those survivors who had shown the usual post-disaster anxiety symptoms followed by apparently complete recovery. Observations made 3 to 4 years after the explosion showed that the majority (71 percent) of the formerly traumatized survivors were again displaying symptoms of traumatic neurosis. The authors conclude that the high incidence of emotional disturbance detected years after the disaster may be attributed to the severity of the stresses and that it represents lasting personality changes. This evidence from civilians, like that from the war veterans, indicates that in about 7 out of every 10 persons the symptoms of anxiety evoked by terrifying experiences continued to create serious difficulties in life adjustment many years later. The "resistance to extinction" of anxiety symptoms acquired from exposure to traumatizing stimuli has been repeatedly observed in laboratory experiments, as we shall see in the next chapter.

The evidence cited above casts doubts upon older, optimistic views of total recovery from a traumatic experience. Taking the new and more cautious view, we must assume that in some yet-unknown percentage of cases, the disappearance of acute symptoms merely masks certain permanent personality changes—mainly a lowering of stress tolerance and an acquired predisposition to break down with incapacitating anxiety symptoms in response to life stresses that could have been tolerated if the individual had been free from the residue of the earlier traumatic experience. A "sustained" or "permanent" change in personality refers to instances where the individual lacks the opportunity for a corrective reversal, or unlearning, of the traumatic experience. The evidence indicates that traumatic neurosis is reversible when a person has such an opportunity—either in therapy or in corrective life experiences. If the incapacitating symptoms in a chronic patient like the aircraft mechanic can be eliminated, less severe cases may well be accessible to alleviation or cure. Each year more than 10 million people are injured in accidents or disasters in the United States, and there are millions of such victims in every other large country in the world (National Safety Council, 1967). The recent findings imply that even when these victims show a quick return to normal shortly after the traumatic event, many of them may still profit from a brief course of psychological treatment. Such treatment may prevent a latent traumatic neurosis and thereby reduce the chances that severe anxiety symptoms will recur at some later date.

Hear the loud alarum bells—
  Brazen bells!
What a tale of terror now their turbulency tells!
In the startled ear of night
How they scream out their affright!
Too much horrified to speak,
They can only shriek, shriek,
  Out of tune,
In a clamorous appealing to the mercy of the fire,
In a mad expostulation with the deaf and frantic fire
Leaping higher, higher, higher,
With a desperate desire. . . .

Oh, the bells, bells, bells!
What a tale their terror tells.

EDGAR ALLAN POE. The Bells

CHAPTER 3
BASIC
LEARNING-THEORY
CONCEPTS

H aving surveyed some of the main facts concerning the drastic psychological impact of traumatic events, we are ready to examine the key ideas by which theorists attempt to account for the observed phenomena. There are today three dominant types of theoretical approaches to human motivation, and all three have been used to a limited extent to explain the personality changes resulting from environmental stress or frustration.

One approach is favored especially by experimental psychologists whose research is focused on the laws of learning. It emphasizes the parallels between the anxiety symptoms acquired by men who undergo stress and the learned fear reactions acquired by laboratory animals who are exposed to painful or aversive stimuli. This *learning-theory* approach to man's emotional behavior will be examined in this chapter.

A second type of explanation is referred to as *psychodynamic* theory and comes largely from intensive case studies reported by clinical observers. This theoretical approach, which is associated most prominently with Freud, embraces a wide range of stressful events and human emotions. In the next chapter we shall examine the psychodynamic formulations that bear directly on psychological trauma.

The third type of theoretical orientation can be labeled the *cognitive* approach, because it stresses the role of perception and understanding; it emphasizes the importance of the person's appraisals of threat and his judgments about alternative means for coping with future dangers. This approach is based on recent attempts to take account of cognitive processes involved in personality functioning (Witkin, Lewis, Hertzmann, Machover, Meissner, & Wapner, 1954; Kelly, 1955; Schachter & Singer, 1962; Lazarus, 1966; Klein, Barr, & Wolitzky, 1967). Special emphasis is placed on the person's verbal concepts about what might happen to him in the future and the labels he uses to designate his current affective state. According to several cognitive theorists, these verbalizations have a "steering" function that exerts a marked influence on the direction of the person's subjective and overt behavior by influencing the types of information he will seek and the plans he will make for dealing with the threat. So far, the contributions of the cognitive approach apply primarily to the ways people react to warnings and threat cues that occur *before* any powerful danger stimuli are present; hence, we shall consider this theoretical approach when we take up the effects of preliminary warnings (pages 108–11).

For a theoretical understanding of the nature of psychological traumas such as those described in the preceding two chapters, we must rely mainly on learning theories and psychodynamic theories. These approaches illuminate different aspects of emotional behavior, and each has its own forte, explaining certain types of stress reactions about which the other has little or nothing to say. The learning-theory approach we are about to examine is somewhat limited in the range of stress phenomena to which it can be applied with precision, but many leading psychologists are confident that it can ultimately be extended to the more complex processes dealt with by the cognitive and psychodynamic theories. It is, however, an open question as to how much of these other two types of theories can be reduced to the simpler and more objective behavioral language of learning-theory formulations.

We shall begin with the classical conditioning model, which provides a simple explanation of the new anxiety reactions that people acquire as a result of being exposed to a painful accident or disaster. Then we shall see how the laws of operant conditioning can account for more complicated symptoms of traumatic neurosis, such as loss of ego functions, that may also be learned as a result of undergoing stressful experiences. Finally we shall see how the two types of conditioning principles, classical and operant, provide a rationale for some of the therapeutic procedures used in the treatment of persons suffering from phobias and other avoidance reactions that interfere with normal life activities. In the course of the discussion, however, we shall note the limitations and criticisms that have led many psychologists to feel that the learning-theory approach must be supplemented with other sources of observation and theory.

The main concepts of the psychology of learning that underlie this discussion are presented in introductory psychology textbooks. A summary is provided in Figures 3-1 (on classical conditioning) and 3-3 (on operant conditioning). Included there are the key concepts and definitions that are most relevant for explaining changes in behavior resulting from psychological stress.

Traumatic Conditioning
in Human Beings

PAVLOVIAN CONDITIONING: A BRIEF REVIEW

One of the central ideas emphasized by leading proponents of a learning-theory approach is that the laws of conditioning, as worked out through animal experiments by Pavlov (1927) and his followers, can be applied to the acquisition of human emotional reactions, including the common fears of normal persons and the morbid anxiety symptoms of neurotics. (See Figure 3-1.) As part of man's innate biological make-up, fear is assumed to be an unlearned response—an *unconditioned reflex* evoked by intense pain and other powerful noxious stimuli. But fear is "learnable," in the sense that essentially the same pattern of emotional response can be attached to neutral stimuli, stimuli that originally evoked no emotional response at all. This characteristic of fear has been repeatedly demonstrated in experiments on emotional learning in which animals are subjected to conditioning trials that pair neutral cues with powerful electric shock or other pain stimuli. Gantt (1965), for example, has reported that after a single pairing of a neutral tone with an electric shock, dogs develop a conditioned reflex of emotional excitement in response to the neutral signal that is extremely difficult to extinguish. Other animal experiments have also shown that a single exposure to a traumatic unconditioned stimulus that elicits severe pain can produce a lasting fear reaction that remains highly resistant to extinction over hundreds of trials.

AN EXPERIMENTAL PROCEDURE

Do the findings apply to human beings? Until quite recently, this question was answered by precarious extrapolations from lower animals to man, since there was no dependable evidence of traumatic conditioning in human subjects. For humanitarian and ethical reasons, experimental psychologists have understandably abstained from carrying out painful conditioning experiments that would expose human subjects to potentially damaging stimuli such as those used in the animal experiments. In 1964, however, Campbell, Sanderson, and Laverty performed an extraordinary conditioning experiment using 5 male patients in a hospital for chronic alcoholics. They made use of a newly discovered unconditioned stimulus that induces a

Figure 3-1   The classical conditioning model: key concepts and definitions. (Based on Hilgard & Atkinson, 1967)

Classical conditioning *involves the formation of a new association between a conditioned stimulus and a response, conforming to the pattern of Pavlov's experiments, as shown in the following diagram:*

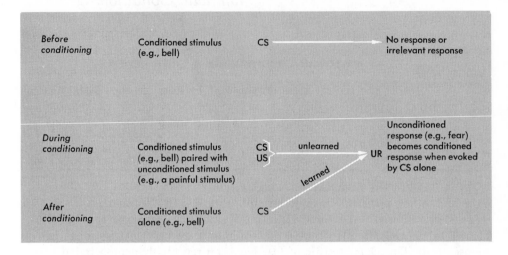

Conditioned stimulus: A stimulus that was originally neutral—that is, it did not evoke the response before being paired with the unconditioned stimulus; after the pairing it functions as a signal that elicits a response similar to the unconditioned response.

Unconditioned stimulus: A stimulus that dependably evokes a discernible response and that functions as the *reinforcement* for establishing a conditioned response when it is paired with a previously neutral stimulus.

Unconditioned response: The discernible response elicited by the unconditioned stimulus, the connection being based on either an innate reflex or prior conditioning.

Conditioned response: A response acquired by conditioning—that is, a response aroused by a conditioned stimulus that did not originally evoke it. A *conditioned emotion* is one type of conditioned response—an emotional response (such as fear) that is evoked by a conditioned stimulus.

Traumatic conditioning: One type of emotional conditioning resulting from the pairing of a neutral stimulus (such as the sight of a dentist's drill) with a powerful noxious stimulus (such as pain) that evokes intense emotional excitement. The excitement is usually manifested by behavioral signs of physiological arousal—palpitations, sweating, and other responses mediated by activity of the sympathetic nervous system.

Extinction: The reduction in strength or the total disappearance of a conditioned response, resulting from presenting the conditioned stimulus without the reinforcement or unconditioned stimulus.

Spontaneous recovery: The return in strength of a conditioned response after a lapse of time following extinction.

Generalization: The tendency for a conditioned response to be evoked by any new stimulus that is similar to the conditioned stimulus.

Gradient of generalization: The orderly decrease in strength of the generalized conditioned response with decreasing similarity of the new stimulus to the original conditioned stimulus, often plotted as a descending curve.

Discrimination: The differential in response to a positive (reinforced) conditioned stimulus as against a negative (nonreinforced) stimulus that previously had evoked a generalized conditioned response.

momentary state of utter horror without causing pain or any known physical damage. The authors justified the experiment on the grounds that the subjects were chronic patients who had volunteered to expose themselves to the unpleasant experimental experience because they hoped to gain help with their drinking problem.

Each patient was given only *one* conditioning trial, during which he heard a neutral tone (the conditioned stimulus) while being injected with a fast-acting drug known as Scoline (the unconditioned stimulus). Although this drug appears to be harmless physiologically, it promptly induces an unconditioned state of intense fear by producing a horrifying state of complete paralysis; the subject suddenly finds himself unable to move or breathe for almost two minutes. All 5 men reported that they thought they were dying during those excruciating moments of suffocation. One subject said that this drug experience was far more distressing than his most traumatic experience as a rear gunner in a combat bomber crew during World War II.

After being exposed to this single traumatic experience, each of the subjects was tested with the tone alone. Every one of them showed a remarkably powerful conditioned fear reaction to the tone, with all the characteristic autonomic changes noted in cases of acute traumatic neurosis. The sound of the tone itself now had the capacity to evoke horror, like the sound of the bells in Poe's poem.

Of special interest is the long-lasting character of the conditioned emotional reaction in 3 of the 5 human subjects. After 100 unreinforced trials—trials in which the conditioned stimulus (in this case, the tone) was presented without the horrifying unconditioned stimulus—these 3 subjects still showed absolutely no signs of extinction. They continued to show an intense emotional response to the bell, even though they had been given only *one* trial in which the bell was paired with the unconditioned fear stimulus. The experimenters were especially persistent in attempting to extinguish the conditioned fear reaction, partly out of a sense of responsibility to the subjects. They used sodium amytal and certain emotional deconditioning procedures, which had previously been reported as effective in eliminating various types of fears. But all these methods were completely ineffective. This high resistance to extinction of the emotional response seems analogous to the persistence of chronic anxiety symptoms in soldiers and civilians who for years after a single harrowing incident continue to have marked startle reactions and severe anxiety attacks in response to stimuli similar to those present during the traumatic experience.

The other 2 subjects showed extinction of their emotional response to the neutral tone during the first 10 trials; but when they were later given additional extinction trials, they showed spontaneous recovery of the conditioned response. This phenomenon is exactly parallel to that observed by Pavlov, who noted that immediate extinction was generally followed by spontaneous recovery of conditioned reflexes in his dogs. Surprisingly, however, the 2 men showed no further extinction despite being given 100 unreinforced trials; they continued to show exactly the same sort of conditioned emotional response as the 3 men who never showed any extinction at all. The return of the anxiety reaction is reminiscent of latent traumatic neurosis, as described earlier: In many war veterans and disaster survivors anxiety symptoms clear up rapidly following the traumatic events, but then months or years later the same anxiety symptoms recur spontaneously and are difficult to eliminate.

The main findings of this experiment are essentially the same as the findings from the earlier animal experiments. All 5 subjects showed clear-cut indications of emotional arousal in response to the formerly neutral tone stimulus, and this arousal reaction showed no diminution after 100 or more extinction trials were given over a period of 3 weeks.

HOW EMOTIONAL CONDITIONING IS MEASURED

Four different measures of emotional conditioning were used in the experiment by Campbell et al., and we shall examine them in some detail because they include basic measures used in current studies of psychophysiological aspects of human emotions. Figure 3-2 presents illustrative records from a typical subject.

Figure 3-2 Psychophysiological responses that reveal emotional conditioning. (Adapted from Campbell, Sanderson, & Laverty, 1964)

These charts show the responses of one of Campbell, Sanderson, and Laverty's subjects at three points in the experiment: before, immediately after, and 3 weeks after the single conditioning trial. Specifically, the charts show his responses during the fifth preconditioning trial, the second unreinforced postconditioning trial, and the eighty-ninth postconditioning trial.

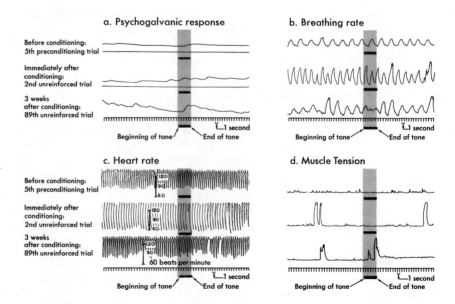

Psychogalvanic
Response   The upper left portion shows the psychogalvanic reactions (PGR), which were measured
by placing one electrode on the palm of the subject's hand and a second
electrode on his wrist and wiring both to a polygraph (like the device shown
in Figure 2-3, page 28), which records on a moving tape the fluctuations in
electrical resistance of the skin. These responses reveal activity of the sweat
glands, which indicates arousal of the autonomic nervous system. In Figure
3-2 we see the PGR record obtained at three stages:

1. The top row shows the response to the conditioned stimulus (the
tone) before any conditioning took place. The subject's reaction was relatively constant throughout this entire preconditioning (habituation) period.
When the tone was presented (shown by the short solid bar below the line),
there was only a very slight rise in the amount of skin resistance. This was
the fifth preconditioning trial, and the tone had become such a familiar and
expected signal that it evoked little arousal.

2. The next row shows the way the same subject reacted shortly after
the single conditioning trial during which the tone had been paired with the
horrifying unconditioned stimulation (injection of the drug Scoline). During
the 10 seconds preceding the onset of the tone signal, there was a slight rise
in the galvanic skin reaction, which probably reflects the increase in variability and excitement produced by the apparatus and the general situation
in which the paralyzing drug had been given. With the onset of the tone
there is a second slight rise in the amount of skin resistance, and immediately after the end of the tone there is a further slight increase. This
was the typical pattern for all subjects throughout all conditioning trials.

3. The third row shows an unreinforced trial given 3 weeks after conditioning. It is apparent that even though almost 90 unreinforced trials have
been given by this time, no extinction has occurred. With the onset of the
tone there is a very marked rise in skin resistance and other irregularities also
indicative of emotional arousal. All the subjects showed similar reactions to
the tone toward the end of the extinction series, which continued for more
than 100 trials before the experiment was brought to an end.

Breathing Rate   The upper right portion of Figure 3-2 shows
the simultaneous observations of breathing
reactions. The breathing records were obtained by a special apparatus known
as a Manning pneumograph, which is essentially a form of bellows that is
strapped around the chest. Each time the subject inhales and exhales, the
pneumograph makes a recording on the polygraph tape. A normal breathing
record was obtained on the fifth preconditioning trial, shown in the first row.

Shortly after the conditioning trial, breathing became much more
irregular, more rapid, and deeper than before, as shown by the record in the
second row. Especially noteworthy is the height of each respiration curve,

which varies considerably throughout this second unreinforced trial, in contrast to the uniform heights in the preconditioning record shown in the top row. The sample extinction trial obtained 3 weeks after conditioning shows even more irregularities. This was typical of all the subject's extinction trials up to that point and all the ones that followed, indicating that his breathing pattern continued to be disrupted by the tone in the same way it would be by any powerful stress stimulus.

Heart Rate   The lower left portion of Figure 3-2 presents the corresponding records for heart rate. This electrocardiogram (EKG) was obtained in the standard way used by a physician carrying out a routine medical checkup: One electrode is placed on the inner surface of each of the subject's forearms and on each of his shins in order to pick up his heart beats. Before conditioning, a normal heartbeat record was obtained. It is highly regular, with a relatively constant rate. In addition, there are smooth "scallops" along the bottom edge of this record, indicating a regular periodic increase and decrease in heart rate. This phenomenon, known as sinus arrhythmia, is characteristic of records from unaroused subjects. In the record obtained immediately after conditioning, shown in the next row, there is much more irregularity, especially toward the end of the tone signal, where we can see a very fast double beat. This is an indicator of extreme excitement, equivalent to the heart's "skipping a beat"; no such reaction ever occurred before conditioning. The record after 3 weeks again shows irregularities in heart rate while the subject is hearing the tone and for about 20 seconds after, which can be noted by observing the differences in the lengths of the lines.

Muscle Tension   The fourth measure is known as the electromyogram (EMG). This measure is obtained by placing a needle electrode just below the surface of the skin, immediately over the left and right frontalis muscles of the temple. Slight variations of the tension of this muscle have been found to be related to changes in muscular tension throughout the entire body and hence provide a record of the degree to which the person is tensing his muscles. A nearly straight horizontal line indicates calm relaxation or a constant state of tonus in the muscles of the body, whereas any spikes in the record indicate momentary muscular tension, which generally accompanies affective arousal. But since the same spikes often occur when a person is not emotionally aroused, the electromyogram is regarded as the least dependable of the four measures of emotional conditioning.

In the preconditioning record, shown in the lower right portion of Figure 3-2, we observe only a slight amount of muscular tension, with no discernible change when the tone is sounded. Immediately after conditioning, this record shows no change in response to the tone, but there are spikes immediately before the trial period and immediately after. Thus, after the conditioning trial the subject showed an increase in muscular tension, but the changes were not always related to the occurrence of the tone or to any other detectable external stimulus. In the bottom row we see a characteristic EMG reaction to the conditioned stimulus. Here we have some irregularities before the onset of the tone, but the irregularities become much more pronounced while the tone is sounding. Although this type of record was not obtained consistently on every extinction trial, it occurred frequently enough so that the EMG data can be regarded as crude evidence that supplements the consistent evidence of emotional conditioning obtained from the records of PGR, breathing, and heart rate.

CONTROLS FOR EMOTIONAL CONDITIONING

To varying degrees, all four measures show the sustained effect of the single conditioning trial. No single measure is highly dependable, but taken together they provide unambiguous evidence that each subject, like the one shown in the sample records in Figure 3-2, underwent a drastic alteration in his emotional response to the formerly neutral tone stimulus. The fact that sudden changes in skin resistance, breathing, heart rate, and muscle tension sometimes occurred when the tone was not sounding is by no means unusual, since the tone was certainly not the only neutral stimulus that accompanied the occurrence of the traumatic stimulus. The sight of the apparatus and the sensations of being strapped in it are also potential conditioned stimuli that could evoke the emotional response after the traumatic conditioning trial.

In order to conclude that genuine emotional conditioning has taken place, the changes occurring after the conditioning trial must be attributable to the pairing of the unconditioned with the conditioned stimuli. To make sure this pairing was responsible, two separate control conditions were included in the Campbell et al. experiment. In one control condition 3 hospitalized alcoholics were given only the unconditioned stimulus (the Scoline injection) for one trial, without the tone being sounded. Afterward these subjects showed a slight change in emotional arousal, as expected, in response to the general experimental situation. But they did not show any special response when they heard the tone, in contrast to the 5 subjects who received the tone paired with the unconditioned stimulus. The second group of controls consisted of 3 other hospitalized alcoholics, each of whom was given only the conditioned stimulus (the tone) for the same number of times it had been given to each of the experimental subjects. This control group, as expected, did not show any signs of an acquired emotional reaction. The results from the control subjects led the investigators to conclude that genuine emotional conditioning had occurred as a result of the single pairing of the unconditioned and conditioned stimulus.

A single experiment of this type, dramatic and convincing as the evidence may seem, cannot be regarded as conclusive until it has been verified by other, similar experiments in which other types of subjects are used. For example, chronic alcoholics may conceivably be especially susceptible to emotional conditioning. But although many questions remain to be investigated, it seems unlikely that this unique experiment will soon, if ever, be repeated, because there are so many objections to exposing human beings to an extremely distressing experience for purposes of scientific experimentation. Nevertheless, we can expect in the future to have more definitive evidence concerning emotional conditioning if, for instance, experimental psychologists can find some way of investigating systematically the emotional responses to painful medical treatments. Emotional conditioning might often be produced by the powerful unconditioned stimuli administered by physicians when they resort to unavoidably painful therapy in their efforts to cure patients who have not responded to milder forms of treatment, and some medical clinics might be willing to arrange for systematic studies of the patients' emotional responses.

Acquisition of Avoidance Habits

A CASE STUDY

An additional set of learning principles can be brought to bear on the new avoidance habits that often accompany the symptoms of acute anxiety generated by terrifying danger experiences. Let us consider a case study of a woman who developed a traumatic neurosis after a harrowing experience. The following account is based on the report of Cobb and Lindemann (1943):

The woman was at the Coconut Grove night club in Boston on the night the entire building was destroyed by fire. This fire was one of the worst disasters of the last 30 years, resulting in almost 500 people being burned to death and hundreds of others being seriously injured. Temporarily trapped by the roaring fire, the woman suffered severe burns of her face and hands. Like everyone else who was able to do so, she dashed for the exit, but it was already blocked by other panic-stricken people. The frantic crowd shoved her over the injured and dead bodies in front of the door, until finally she was outside.

In the hospital, she showed the typical symptoms of traumatic neurosis. She complained particularly about anxiety attacks, nightmares, and daytime reveries during which her thoughts involuntarily returned to the disaster. Months later, after recovering physically and being discharged from the hospital, she continued to show symptoms of traumatic neurosis, the most pronounced being phobic reactions (excessive fear and avoidance of situations or objects that are not dangerous). Specifically, she was unable to go to any large gathering place. A sociable person, she attempted repeatedly to overcome this phobia, but each time she suffered overwhelming anxiety attacks. For example, once when she was at a restaurant with her family she suddenly recollected fire breaking out and tables and chairs being tipped over, just as they had in the Coconut Grove disaster, and she had to flee the room, in a frantic state of terror. Another time she attempted to sit through a movie, but she had a similar anxiety attack as she looked at the people sitting around her; again she had to return home.

In this case the acute anxiety attacks were evoked by highly specific situations that resembled the one in which the victim had been exposed to the unconditioned terror-evoking stimuli—the painful sensation of being burned, the sight of the encroaching fire, and the visible mutilation of fellow human beings. For this woman the neutral cues of restaurants, theaters, and other large gathering places became potent conditioned stimuli, equivalent to the bell in the Campbell et al. experiment. These places now evoked intense anxiety that was manifested by signs of physiological arousal and subjective feelings of terror. In addition, the woman engaged in a new type of action, as typified by her refusal to go to gathering places. A mere verbal invitation from a friend to go to such a place could now induce at least a mild degree of anxiety, and this motivated her to decide to stay away. This staying-away reaction can be classified as a separate type of habit, an avoidance habit, based on the conditioned anxiety reaction.

Thus we can analyze this woman's phobic reactions into *two* recently acquired habits. The first habit, acquired at the time of the disaster, is the *anxiety reaction* evoked by formerly neutral cues (conditioned stimuli), such as the sight of large numbers of seated people. The second is the *avoidance habit*, which she acquired after she left the hospital; it resulted from the new anxiety reaction that continued to be aroused each time she tried to go to a gathering place.

THE OPERANT CONDITIONING MODEL

Most psychologists believe that the laws of Pavlovian conditioning do not explain the acquisition of new avoidance habits, because the conditioned avoidance response cannot be described as resembling an unconditioned response evoked by some known unconditioned stimulus with which the conditioned stimulus had been paired. A more appropriate theoretical model for such habits is provided by the laws of operant learning (also referred to as *instrumental* conditioning). According to this learning model, the main source of reinforcement is a reward that follows an action. (See Figure 3-3.) This type of reinforcement occurs after the response has been emitted, in contrast to the reinforcement in Pavlovian conditioning, which is provided by an unconditioned stimulus that evokes the response, as illustrated by the Campbell et al. experiment.

In terms of operant conditioning, whenever a new avoidance habit is learned, the main source of reinforcement is the *relief from fear or anxiety* that follows the performance of the avoidance act. Any conditioned anxiety reaction—whether newly acquired from a recent disaster experience or acquired years earlier in the course of childhood training and socialization—

Figure 3-3   The operant conditioning model: key concepts and definitions. (Based on Hilgard & Atkinson, 1967)

Operant conditioning *involves the strengthening of an emitted response by presenting a reward if and only if the response occurs, conforming to the pattern of Thorndike's and Skinner's experiments, as shown in the following diagram:*

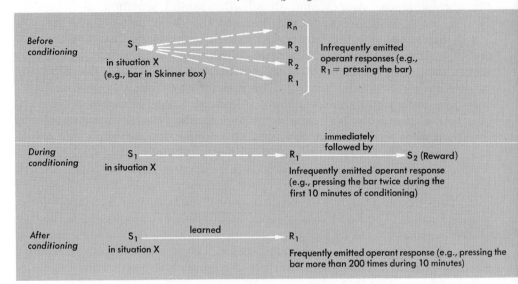

Operant response: Any observable act that is occasionally or frequently emitted in a given situation and that is not unequivocally tied to any given stimulus. The frequency of emission of the response depends on the stimulus to which it leads (reward), rather than the stimulus that happens to elicit it. Hence such responses are also referred to as *instrumental* acts. This category includes verbalizations and any other human acts that are voluntary or self-initiated.

Reward: A positive incentive that functions as a reinforcing stimulus for an operant response, including any stimulus-object or state of affairs capable of satisfying a drive. This category includes escape from pain or from social punishment as well as inherently positive objects that give rise to pleasure (e.g., food).

Avoidance learning: A form of operant conditioning in which the reward is evasion of pain or some other form of aversive stimulation. This category applies to any instance in which the learning of a perceptual, motor, or cognitive act is motivated by the fear or anxiety evoked by cues that signify the threat of punishment, when partial or complete removal of the threat cues functions as the reward.

Escape learning: A special case of avoidance learning, for which the reward is complete elimination of the aversive stimulation. The person either leaves the unpleasant situation or acts in a way that completely stops the unpleasant stimulation from continuing.

Partial reinforcement: A procedure that consists of presenting the reward on some fraction of the trials rather than on every occasion when the operant response is emitted. Partial reinforcement often results in greater resistance to extinction, that is, greater persistence of the operant response despite nonreinforcement. It corresponds to the procedure of *intermittent reinforcement* in classical conditioning, in which the unconditioned stimulus is omitted from a fraction of the conditioning trials.

Extinction
Spontaneous recovery ⎤
Generalization   ⎬ Same definitions as for classical conditioning (see Figure 3-1, page 42)
Gradient of generalization ⎥
Discrimination ⎦

is assumed to function as a source of drive, which can serve as a basis for learning new overt responses. Those actions or thoughts that result in escape from the cues that are evoking the distressing state of fear or anxiety will tend to be strongly reinforced and thus will become habitual, as in the case of the woman who stayed away from all gathering places after being traumatized by the Coconut Grove disaster.

The implications of instrumental-learning principles for the acquisition of avoidance habits in normal and neurotic personalities have been extensively discussed by Mowrer (1950) and Dollard and Miller (1950). Dollard and Miller refer to fear as a *response-produced stimulus*. By this they mean that the emotional state, once aroused, is a response that has the same cue properties and the same drive properties as pain stimuli. To put it another way: Whenever fear is aroused, regardless of the type of stimulus that is evoking it, the person's behavior will be influenced in essentially the same way as though he were suffering from a powerful aversive motivational state, such as physical pain from a powerful electric shock. This assumption has two important implications. First, fear is expected to function as a *cue* and thus to elicit habits that have previously been learned as responses to other fear-producing situations. Second, fear is expected to function as a *drive*, impelling the emotionally aroused person to attempt to escape from the fear-producing cues. Any new avoidance response that is followed by an immediate diminution in the intensity of the distressing emotional state would tend to be strengthened.

It should be mentioned that not all learning theorists agree that the rewards or reinforcements that lead to the acquisition of new instrumental habits always entail the reduction of a strong drive such as fear. An impressive accumulation of experimental evidence indicates that neither animals nor human beings uniformly seek a tension-free state of nirvana in which all internal and external stimulation is kept to a minimum (Holt, 1965). On the contrary, when relatively unstimulating conditions are set up in the laboratory, human subjects quickly become bored or restless and begin seeking more stimulation. Moreover, animal experiments show that some rewards entail an increase rather than a decrease in stimulation. For example, monkeys will work for the reward of being given an occasional opportunity to look through a window into an adjacent laboratory room (Harlow, 1953); male rats will exert effort and learn new responses when the only reward is contact with a receptive female followed immediately by removal from the goal box, so that the sexual drive is aroused without opportunity for discharge (Sheffield, Wulff, & Backer, 1951). Thus there appear to be positive types of motivation involving pleasure-seeking or increased stimulation as well as the negative types involving efforts to reduce pain or unpleasure. These considerations obviously argue against any learning-theory assumption that *all* rewards involve drive reduction. However, almost all psychologists who discuss human fear from a learning standpoint, despite their use of different vocabularies for talking about the learning of defenses and avoidance habits, accept a somewhat more limited assumption: that *reduction of fear or anxiety functions as a positive reinforcement.*

We noted a moment ago that fear is assumed to have the functional properties of a drive. This implies that it has the same energizing effects as other drives, such as hunger and pain. Many phenomena point to fear as a powerful goad to action (Selye, 1956). For example, a man who is in an excited emotional state will show exaggerated startle responses and may become capable of performing seemingly superhuman feats to escape from danger. Don's extraordinary endurance in his struggle against the outgoing ocean tide illustrates this. Some experiments in animal conditioning suggest that any action in progress will be carried out more vigorously and will be learned more rapidly when fear is aroused (Brown, Kalish, & Farber, 1951; Brown, 1961). A similar conclusion is supported by human studies that show that highly anxious persons acquire conditioned reflexes more rapidly than do relatively unanxious persons (Taylor, 1956; Spence, 1958). But the interpretation of these findings is still under debate, especially since there is also some evidence that fear arousal can have a markedly inhibitory effect on learning (Brown, 1961). Thus fear functions sometimes as an energizer and sometimes as an inhibitor, but we do not yet know exactly under what conditions one or the other effect will be obtained.

The disagreements about the energizing effects of fear call into question the notion that fear has *all* the expected properties of a drive, but they do not have any bearing on the central theoretical assumption that the reduction of fear reinforces new instrumental avoidance responses. Learning theorists repeatedly use this assumption to explain the acquisition of precautionary actions, such as cutting down on smoking after reading about lung cancer statistics, as well as maladaptive habits that may underlie neurotic symptoms.

Perhaps the most clear-cut examples of maladaptive habits that can be readily explained in learning-theory terms are the phobic-avoidance reactions that frequently occur after a traumatic accident. We have already discussed one such case—that of the woman who was in the Coconut Grove disaster. A second, parallel example is the phobic behavior displayed by Tom, the airplane mechanic whose traumatic neurosis was described in the preceding chapter. Here again, his phobic-avoidance symptoms can be analyzed into two habits: the acquired *anxiety reaction* evoked by formerly neutral cues (classical conditioning) and the subsequently acquired *avoidance reactions* (operant conditioning). We can readily explain Tom's newly acquired anxiety reaction in the presence of airplanes and in high places by using the principles of emotional conditioning if we assume that during and immediately after the harrowing episode of the midair collision he was exposed to intensely fear-provoking stimuli: The gut sensations accompanying the rapid descent and the impact of the crash were paired with neutral cues, such as the sight of the airplane and the ground far below. Thereafter, intense fear was evoked by all such cues whenever Tom was near an airplane or looked down from a high building. This fear formed the basis for the second type of habit, the avoidance of airplanes and of high places. Since the sight of airplanes, or even thoughts about flying, generated considerable fear, his avoidance responses would be reinforced by the reduction of fear. Staying away from airplanes and high places and avoiding thinking about the airplane crash—these avoidance responses would remove the cues that elicit intense fear and would thus become strong habits. Dollard and Miller (1950) point out that essentially the same learning-theory analysis can be applied to less dramatic avoidance habits, such as keeping one's hands off hot stoves and staying on the sidewalk when speeding cars are coming down the street.

A number of learning theorists agree with the point of view we have been adopting, namely that the acquisition of new avoidance reactions involves a combination of two habits, one resulting from the classical type of conditioning of fear reactions to formerly neutral cues and the other from the reinforcement of operant avoidance responses that were followed by reduction of fear. A *two-factor theory of learning*, specifying this dual process, was first suggested by Schlosberg (1937) and Skinner (1938). According to their theory, the first type of habit consists of conditioning *visceral* reactions—including all the physiological symptoms of fear—on the basis of the Pavlovian learning principle of *contiguity* (pairing of the conditioned stimulus with an unconditioned stimulus). The formation of the second type, however, involves the learning of new *verbal* responses or new movements of the *skeletal* muscles, and *reward* is the basis of reinforcement in accordance with the principles of *operant* conditioning.

Mowrer (1950) and others who favor the two-factor theory assume that the same two principles of learning apply to all types of negative emotional reactions, including anger, guilt, and grief as well as anxiety. In all instances the starting point is the pairing of neutral cues with unconditioned emotion-arousing stimuli during one or more stressful experiences, so that new visceral habits are formed; then new verbal or motor habits are acquired, since they are rewarded by alleviation of the unpleasant emotional state whenever they lead to avoidance of those previously neutral cues.

Fear Reactions as Habits:
Theoretical Implications

The human conditioning experiment by Campbell et al. (1964), described earlier, provides fairly strong support for the assumption that fear reactions in humans can be learned in essentially the same way as in animal conditioning experiments. The autonomic components of emotions evidently can be conditioned and extinguished just like any other habit. Hence we would expect that whenever a person undergoes a traumatic accident, the strength of the acquired fear reaction evoked by any neutral cue that was present at the time of the accident (for example, the sight of the vehicle) will depend upon certain variables that determine the strength of any conditioned reflex. They include:

1. The *intensity of the pain* (unconditioned stimulus) that occurs contiguously with the neutral stimulus during the traumatic episode;

2. The *length of the time interval* between the person's perception of the neutral stimulus and the onset of the unconditioned pain stimulus;

3. The *number of times the neutral stimulus and the unconditioned pain stimulus are paired* during the traumatic episode itself and afterward, while the person is still suffering from the injurious effects of the accident.

We would also expect the newly acquired fear reactions following a traumatic event to show other properties characteristic of all habits. One, to be discussed shortly, is the tendency for the new habit to *generalize* to other stimuli that are similar to, but not the same as, the neutral cues present during the conditioning trial or trials. Another, which has considerable relevance to the reversibility of phobias and other neurotic symptoms, is the capability of learned reactions to be *unlearned*. The ease of eliminating fear reactions depends upon the strength of the habit. This, in turn, depends upon the circumstances under which conditioning took place, including the three factors listed above. If it is not too strong, an emotional habit will be unlearned during a series of extinction trials, when the conditioned stimulus is presented alone, without the unconditioned stimulus.

Animal experiments have also shown that strong emotional habits, which are very resistant to extinction, can be effectively eliminated by *deconditioning* procedures. In contrast to extinction trials, which present only the conditioned stimulus, the deconditioning trials present the conditioned stimulus paired with a new unconditioned stimulus. The latter is selected to elicit relaxation or some other pleasant response that is incompatible with the unpleasant emotional response and prevents it from occurring in its full strength. Certain types of deconditioning procedures—examples of which will be given shortly—appear to be far more effective than mere extinction trials, as indicated by the fact that spontaneous recovery of the emotional habit is much less likely to occur after deconditioning than after extinction.

Can the same type of deconditioning procedures that eliminate acquired fear reactions in animals be applied also to man, as we would expect if the conditioning theory of human fear is valid? Can anxiety symptoms be cured by deconditioning procedures that enable the phobic person to acquire an incompatible response to the cues that had formerly evoked anxiety? In recent years strong affirmative answers have been put forth by a number of psychologists who are attempting to apply Pavlovian conditioning techniques to the treatment of persons suffering from phobias and related neurotic disorders.

Behavior Therapy

A number of proponents of behavior therapy have made some remarkable claims about successful cures produced by applying the principles of conditioning. Wolpe (1965), for example, states:

> It is implicit in conditioning theory that recovery from neurosis should be achieved by applying the learning process in a reverse direction: Whatever undesirable behavior has been learned may be unlearned. In experiments performed about fourteen years ago I demonstrated in cats that had been made neurotic experimentally how this unlearning can be brought about. . . . Anxiety reactions had been strongly conditioned to a small confining cage and to other stimuli, and could not be made to extinguish despite repeated exposure to the stimuli. The anxiety response habits could, however, be overcome in piecemeal fashion by counterposing feeding to weak anxiety responses. At first, stimuli distantly similar to the conditioned stimuli were used, until anxiety decreased to zero, and then, step by step, stimuli closer in resemblance to the original conditioned stimuli were introduced, until even the strongest eventually lost its power to evoke anxiety. These findings led to the framing of the reciprocal inhibition principle of psychotherapy, which is that *if a response inhibitory of anxiety can be made to occur in the presence of anxiety-evoking stimuli it will weaken the bond between these stimuli and the anxiety.*
>
> Experience with human neuroses indicates that the principle has quite general validity; in addition to feeding, a good many other kinds of responses, each of which, empirically, appears to inhibit anxiety, have been successfully used to weaken neurotic anxiety-response habits and related neurotic habits. The reciprocal inhibition principle also affords an explanation for the therapeutic effects of interviewing as such (which is seemingly the main basis of the successes of the traditional therapies) and for so-called spontaneous recoveries [Wolpe, 1965, pp. 10–11].

SYSTEMATIC DESENSITIZATION

Wolpe has developed a new technique of therapy called *systematic desensitization,* which is based directly on the reciprocal inhibition principle. His starting point is the earlier research of Jacobson (1938), which indicated that when a person is trained to be able to relax the muscles throughout his body, he will undergo a decrease in the autonomic responses that accompany anxiety. As a result, his mood will temporarily improve. Wolpe has a three-step method for deconditioning a person who is suffering from anxiety symptoms, which can often be completed within a few weeks:

1. In diagnostic interviews the therapist tries to identify the stimuli to which the patient is currently reacting with anxiety. He ranks the stimulus situations in order of intensity of evoked anxiety. For example, (a) riding in the same car in which the person had been injured during a highway accident, (b) riding in other cars, (c) riding in a bus, (d) seeing cars on a highway, (e) seeing a parked car.

2. The therapist next conducts a series of interview sessions during which he gives the patient training in relaxation. He asks the patient to relax as completely as he can (sometimes under hypnosis).

3. Then the therapist tells the patient to imagine the weakest of the anxiety-evoking stimuli for a few seconds (for example, the sight of a parked car). After brief rest periods he repeats the relaxation instruction over and over, until the patient is able to remain relaxed and unemotional each time he thinks about the stimulus. The same procedure is repeated for each of the other anxiety-arousing stimuli on the therapist's diagnostic list, always beginning with the *least* disturbing item left on the list.

Wolpe's claims for the effectiveness of this desensitization method in treating neurotic patients have not gone unchallenged by other therapists, particularly since he has repeatedly used his findings to launch highly provocative attacks against psychoanalysis and other forms of psychotherapy. Many therapists are convinced that anxiety symptoms in the majority of psychoneurotics cannot be cured without uncovering unconscious sources of anxiety, and they doubt that the apparently quick cures achieved by deconditioning procedures will stand the test of time. Nevertheless, the controversies engendered by Wolpe's method and related conditioning therapies have given a powerful impetus to research on emotional deconditioning.

During the early 1920's, when Pavlov's conditioning experiments first became widely known to psychologists, there was a flurry of interest in a behavioristic approach to problems of neurosis and mental health. Now, half a century later, new contingents of experimental and clinical psychologists are trying to apply conditioning principles to human emotional reactions. But this time, as we have just seen from Wolpe's procedures, they are making a concerted effort to develop new methods, rather than merely adopting a new vocabulary that translates the language of the clinic into the language of the experimental psychology laboratory. In their investigations they try to employ sophisticated research methods to test predictions derived from the principles of conditioning by collecting systematic data on the effects of various conditioning procedures on the anxiety symptoms of human subjects.

It may be easy to induce relaxation in the subjects being treated by the deconditioning method, but it is certainly not easy to induce relaxation in the large group of psychotherapists who vigorously oppose behavior therapy. Some regard it as unpromising and risky because it might give rise to new neurotic symptoms that could be much more harmful. On the sidelines are large numbers of more or less neutral psychologists who are waiting to see how successful this new therapeutic development will prove to be. The controversy will not be settled until we have the data from careful follow-up studies, carried out over periods of months and years, to determine whether the apparent cures persist and to make sure there is no outcropping of new neurotic symptoms that replace the old.

REPLACEMENT OF UNDESIRABLE
AVOIDANCE HABITS

Even if successful, Wolpe's methods may be applicable to phobias and related symptoms arising from specific traumatic events but not to many other neurotic symptoms that are based on other sources of anxiety. Another group of behavior therapists has begun to try out special techniques for building up desirable instrumental responses to replace a person's maladjustive forms of warding off anxiety. Drawing upon the principles of operant conditioning, Bandura and Walters (1963) have described three ways of modifying undesirable avoidance habits, in addition to simple extinction and deconditioning, that may be especially applicable for helping children overcome social withdrawal reactions and other asocial habits:

1. Positive reinforcement. For example, the adult provides special rewards on a number of occasions when the withdrawn child participates in social activities.

2. Negative reinforcements combined with positive reinforcements to produce discrimination learning. For example, the adult expresses mild disapproval each time the child withdraws and strong approval each time the child approaches his peers.

3. Social imitation. For example, the withdrawn child is allowed to observe a prestigeful older child who regularly engages in the desired types of social activity, and the withdrawn child is rewarded for imitating the model.

One of the main findings suggested by Bandura and Walters' research with children is that *occasional rewards* presented in a random sequence are more effective in modifying children's social behavior than is a fixed schedule of regular rewards. These observations support findings from animal learning experiments on *partial reinforcement*, which indicate that new instrumental habits are more strongly established when the subject is given a schedule of reinforcement that provides intermittent rather than continuous rewards (see Figure 3-3, page 50).

The learning-theory approach to replacement of neurotic and asocial habits gives added importance to a new trend in basic research on young children, which attempts to discover the innate and learned responses that alleviate or inhibit anxiety. Mandler (1962) has pointed out that some revisions of learning-theory explanations of stress behavior might emerge from this research development:

It has recently been suggested (Kessen and Mandler, 1961) that apart from the flight-from-trauma interpretation of anxiety and fear, we might entertain the additional hypothesis that some events such as sucking and rocking have inhibitory powers over states of distress. In other words, even in the presence of hunger and cold, the sucking response is followed rather rapidly and effectively by quieting and a cessation of all the signs of distress. Thus, sucking and some other events are classed as inhibitors—simply to indicate that their onset is followed by the cessation or inhibition of distress or anxiety. One such dramatic example of the effects of non-nutritive sucking is shown [by experimental data indicating that] the average activity of a group of newborns (four days old) drops drastically following the onset of the sucking response (Kessen and Leutzendorff, 1962). While we are only at the beginning of the exploration of these mechanisms and have little notion how far they apply to the adult, we can entertain the notion of mechanisms other than flight or removal of a noxious stimulus as reducing anxiety and distress. It has also been suggested that the absence of the mother (separation anxiety) can be viewed as the absence of a person who has been consistently paired with inhibition (sucking and rocking in particular) and that these manifestations of anxiety might be disinhibition phenomena. In other words, anxiety (and possibly some other emotions) occur not always because a traumatic event has taken place but sometimes because events that have served to inhibit and suppress distressful feelings and states have ceased to be present [Mandler, 1962, pp. 336–37].

Applying the Principle
of Generalization

Not all the implications of learning theory are as controversial as those pertaining to the therapeutic value of deconditioning procedures. Much more widely accepted—or at least tolerated—is the use of certain principles of conditioning to explain some of the characteristic features of traumatic neurosis. Few therapists who work with patients suffering from traumatic neurosis question the potential relevance of the principle of generalization. (See Figure 3-1, page 42.) For example, we have noted earlier that men who survive a plane crash may develop a generalized fear of all aircraft and of all activities associated with flying. This generalized fear can readily be explained by the similarity of these cues to those perceived by the person at the time he was exposed to the terrifying stimuli of the accident.

According to the related principle of *generalization decrement,* the intensity of emotional reactions evoked by similar cues should decrease as those cues become less and less similar to ones originally present in the emotional conditioning situation. This learning principle is consistent with the observation that a person suffering from a traumatic neurosis as a result of an airplane crash will show a smaller degree of emotional arousal in response to *words* that evoke visual images of the traumatic situation than in response to the actual *sight* of the vehicle in which the trauma occurred. The vehicle itself provides visual cues almost identical with those originally present at the time of the emotional conditioning experience, whereas the words provide cues only remotely similar to the original cues. The airplane mechanic who developed an incapacitating traumatic neurosis could not bear the intense anxiety produced by the sight of airplanes, but he could tolerate the low level of anxiety aroused by talking about the accident with his therapist and thus was able to verbalize enough details for the process of therapy to begin. The principle of generalization decrement, as suggested in the quotation from Wolpe (page 55), may be applicable to a number of standard therapeutic procedures used with patients suffering from acute anxiety. In psychotherapy, as well as in behavior therapy, the skilled therapist is likely to focus the patient's attention first on those topics that arouse relatively little anxiety, that is, those that are only somewhat similar to the original arousal stimuli. Then, as therapy continues, the patient will master increasingly larger doses of anxiety as he passes along the generalization continuum to more disturbing topics that are more closely related to the central sources of anxiety underlying his neurosis.

Applying the Principles of Avoidance Learning

Most of the avoidance habits cited so far involve actual physical avoidance of objects or places that arouse fear or other distressing emotional states. But, as we have noted, the laws of operant learning are assumed to be equally applicable to many other types of avoidance responses, including the evasion of anxiety-provoking words and images. Particularly important is the application of the principles of avoidance learning to well-known defense mechanisms, such as repression, reaction formation, and displacement. (See Part II, Chapter 21.) Other avoidance habits are those verbal responses that function as "reassurances," helping to reduce the intensity of fear evoked by conditioned fear stimuli. For example, combat soldiers and fliers not only become more fearful as they are exposed to successive dangerous missions but also develop new interests, diversions, and beliefs that can be seen as efforts to gain reassurance. When possible, they manage to forget about the war by indulging in distracting games, including those played with women and leading to sexual gratification. When confined to an isolated front-line military post, they become highly dependent on other men in their combat unit for companionship, and they avidly share in gallows humor, sometimes expressing ghoulish images similar to those that flashed through Don's mind when he was struggling physically and psychologically against being overwhelmed by the threat of drowning.

Men under stress, as pointed out earlier, also show a marked increase in consumption of alcohol. The acquisition of the drinking habit can be readily understood as an operant response that is reinforced by reduction of anxiety or other unpleasant emotional states. This explanation applies especially to those types of personalities who appear to be predisposed to obtain temporary relief from "superego" reactions of guilt and inferiority feelings by turning to alcohol. One wit has even suggested that the superego might be defined as the part of the human personality that is soluble in alcohol.

The new avoidance habits acquired by people under stress occasionally turn out to be more constructive modes of problem solving than the person had previously been using, and they can lead to favorable personality changes (see pages 87–99). More often, however, the drinking habits and distracting activities that are reinforced during long stressful periods of apprehensiveness about career failure, family discord, or illness are likely to interfere with adequate adjustment once the external sources of stress have subsided. Certain avoidance habits acquired following a brief exposure to a single traumatic episode can also be highly maladaptive—notably the extreme forms of social withdrawal and constriction of cognitive ego functions that characterize persons who have been traumatized. Consider, for example, the long-lasting memory losses following a traumatic experience. Don's symptoms of amnesia, it will be recalled, lasted for several months after his near-drowning episode; Tom's amnesia was still present 7 years after his plane crash and began to clear up only after he obtained psychotherapeutic treatment. In terms of learning theory, post-traumatic amnesia can be understood as a means of warding off thoughts and memories that evoke anxiety. By shutting off from awareness the symbolic cues that pertain to the accident, a person may be strongly rewarded by a reduction of anxiety, just as when someone resorts to alcohol to "forget his troubles." Nevertheless, the psychological gain is far from complete. The traumatized person's efforts to keep the disturbing memories from consciousness do not wholly succeed. The repressed memories frequently break through and appear in the nightmares that disturb the person's sleep and in the obsessional images that disturb his waking concentration.

Some Criticisms
of Learning Theories

The "leakage" of the repressed anxiety-provoking cues into other mental activities involves many complications that are difficult to explain by learning theory. This is one of the main reasons many psychologists and psychiatrists have severely criticized learning theorists and have accused them of oversimplifying complex personality functions. They also criticize learning theories as being too narrowly based on a simple model constructed from animal experiments on reactions to painful stimulation. Although few doubts are expressed about the applicability of these experiments as a model for human traumatic learning, many serious questions are raised about extending the model to include other types of human anguish that often arise in stressful life circumstances—grief over the loss of a loved one, shame about failing on an important task, guilt about violating one's ethical standards, and those vague feelings of self-discontent described so expressively by existentialist writers. These emotions have powerful motivating effects, which presumably can become even stronger than fear of external harm, since they can compel a person to commit suicide. But they seem to be based on cognitive processes that have a uniquely human quality, involving conceptions of the self and anticipations of future interaction with fellow human beings. Much of the strong opposition to learning-theory approaches centers upon doubts that these human cognitive processes can ever be translated validly into the simple laws of conditioning derived from animal research.

The more moderate critics simply say—with considerable justification, it would seem—that at present the learning-theory approach is valuable for understanding certain aspects of stress behavior but is inadequate for explaining all the personality changes observed in persons who have gone through a stressful crisis. These critics raise such issues as this one: A learning-theory explanation might readily account for many of the specific avoidance reactions produced by stressful experiences after the reactions have already been observed, but it provides little basis for predicting whether the reactions will be adaptive or maladaptive. In other words, the theory furnishes a great deal of plausible hindsight but little foresight that leads to testable predictions. Nor does it carry us very far in trying to understand individual differences—why some men break down immediately while others manage to keep going for long periods of time in the face of danger and deprivation.

Confronted by a number of such unanswered questions, many psychologists recommend a combination of skepticism of and receptiveness to new theoretical approaches that may furnish some of the missing answers.

For example, researchers are attempting to apply cognitive theories in order to learn how and why a person's conception of the threats he will face in the future and his capabilities for coping with them can be modified by social communications in a way that influences his emotional behavior. (See pages 93–95, 109–11.)

Many psychologists continue to draw upon the writings of Freud and other psychoanalysts for insights concerning the changes in children, adolescents, and adults exposed to typical life stresses. In the next chapter we shall extract from the clinical literature those psychodynamic concepts that appear to be especially illuminating as supplements to the concepts derived from learning theories.

Fear had shown itself suddenly to him, and had seized upon his person as an exclusive and sovereign mistress. . . . That evening, confined in his cell, he had been carried away and lashed by a wave of mad terror. As long as he had gone freely forward to meet danger and death, as long as he had held his fate in his own hands, however terrible it might be, he had appeared tranquil and even joyous. . . .

Suddenly a brutal, bewildering change had taken place. . . . He could no longer choose between life and death; they led him to death, certainly and inevitably. . . . He was nothing but an animal destined for the slaughter. Whatever he might say, they would not listen; if he started to cry out, they would stuff a rag in his mouth. . . . If he resisted, if he struggled, if he lay down on the ground, they would be stronger than he; they would pick him up, they would tie him, and thus they would carry him to the gallows. And his imagination gave to the men charged with this execution, men like himself, the new, extraordinary, and terrifying aspect of unthinking automata, whom nothing in the world could stop, and who seized a man, overpowered him, hanged him. . . .

. . . Almost mad with fear, he tried to fancy to himself that these people had tongues and spoke, but he did not succeed.

LEONID ANDREYEV. The Seven That Were Hanged

CHAPTER 4
PSYCHODYNAMIC THEORIES OF TRAUMA

The laws of learning carry us a certain distance in our quest for understanding of the consequences of exposure to stress, but they do not fully explain the puzzling emotional scars that remain unhealed long after the external danger is over. In this chapter we shall examine some illuminating leads from Freud's psychoanalytic contributions that bear on the causes and consequences of psychological trauma. We shall also consider the psychodynamic theories put forth by neo-Freudian psychoanalysts and other observers who use intensive interviews to study the problems of human anxiety.

Psychodynamic theories focus on the changes in a person's motivations, both conscious and unconscious, that underlie his feelings, aspirations, intentions, and actions. In studying human motivations clinical observers have been concerned not only with the ways people respond to realistic threats to personal safety but also with responses to many other stressful events, including career failures, family discord, loss of social status, identity crises, blocking of efforts to develop personal competence, and uncertainty about the future. Thus psychodynamic theories deal with many emotions in addition to fear of real dangers—such emotions as shame, guilt, grief, anger, resentment, and feelings of being unloved and rejected.

In this chapter we shall restrict ourselves to examining psychodynamic contributions to the understanding of extreme apprehensiveness, panic, and traumatic neurosis resulting from actual disaster experiences. We shall be particularly concerned with motivational concepts that link the person's conscious and repressed memories of past dangers with his current anticipations, fantasies, and attitudes about present dangers. (In later chapters we shall continue to draw upon psychodynamic theories concerning guilt and other emotions evoked by other types of stresses and frustrations.)

This chapter does not discuss "theories" in the sense of presenting well-integrated formulations of fundamental principles. Rather, we shall examine a number of suggestive explanatory hypotheses that can be extracted from the extensive clinical literature on the psychodynamics of stress. Unfortunately, however, the evidence is unsystematic and is often interpreted in terms of confusing metaphors. It should also be noted that no attempt is made here to review all the basic tenets of psychoanalysis that stand behind these hypotheses.

Freud's Hypotheses
About the Causes of Trauma

For Freud and other psychoanalysts, trauma is a relative concept, dependent on three sets of causal factors: (1) personality predispositions, (2) the person's physical condition, especially states of fatigue, exhaustion, or illness, and (3) the situational opportunities for action and defense that prevail just before and during the traumatic event (Freud, 1926; Fenichel, 1945). Freud recognized that some extreme danger stimuli could have a traumatic effect on all human beings, but he concentrated on the ways individuals differ in reacting to mild stresses. His case studies provide important clues that help to explain why neurotic personalities—people with lifelong histories of phobias, compulsions, or other anxiety symptoms—are especially likely to be overwhelmed by ordinary life stresses. For such persons a mild external danger may be associatively linked with inner dangers involving the loss of control over forbidden impulses. Because of this association, the mild external danger can precipitate attacks that resemble those observed in traumatic neurosis. (The personality predispositions that underlie such over-reactions to mild stress are discussed in detail in Part II.) This chapter deals mainly with the intense emotional reactions of normal persons who are not likely to break down unless they are exposed to extraordinarily severe stress. The hypotheses to be discussed deal mainly with the third factor; they help to explain why certain types of extreme situations are especially likely to provoke panic and to induce symptoms of traumatic neurosis in any human being, normal or abnormal.

Psychoanalysts point out that the same types of circumstances that lead to overwhelming fear and traumatic neurosis in an individual can provoke a collective panic in a group. They single out three conditions that are especially likely to induce panic: (1) signs of oncoming danger that cannot be readily averted, (2) lack of opportunity for acting when the danger is at hand, and (3) loss of emotional ties with loved persons, esteemed leaders, or members of a primary group, resulting from death, separation, or alienation (Freud, 1921; Anna Freud, 1937). A person exposed to these three conditions is likely to see himself as helplessly subjected to intolerable deprivations, bodily damage, or death. Subsequently he may over-react to the threat cues that were present during his terrifying confrontation with danger. Later in this chapter we shall return to the question of why these panic-provoking conditions give rise to a mild or severe form of traumatic neurosis. We shall see that there are strong reasons for expecting every panic-producing situation to produce a more or less sustained traumatic effect on the survivors, although exposure to such a situation is not the only cause of traumatic neurosis.

Observations Bearing on the Causes of Panic

Observational data from wartime and peacetime disasters support the psychoanalytic hypotheses about the circumstances that incite panic. There appears to be one main type of situation in which people become distraught and engage in wild flight, trampling of fellow human beings, and other excited actions that decrease everyone's chances of survival. The essential conditions are those of *potential entrapment*. (See Janis, Chapman, Gillen, & Spiegel, 1955.) Such situations have two components: (1) The individual is keenly aware of signs that serious danger is present, and (2) he realizes that any escape routes open to him are rapidly closing. These circumstances of panic are essentially the same as those described in Chapter 2 (pages 22–26), where we discussed narrow escapes and near-miss episodes that give rise to feelings of helplessness and produce traumatizing effects on disaster survivors. The existing evidence does not support a conception spread by imaginative journalists and fiction writers: that uncontrolled mob hysteria is nearly inevitable any time a population faces a serious threat of large-scale devastation from a natural disaster or war. Outbreaks of mass panic are not likely to occur unless bottlenecks in the escape route keep a large crowd confined at a time of danger, for example when a fire suddenly breaks out in a movie theater or a night club that has few exits. In the excitement everyone heads for the exit at the same time, shoving and pushing urgently forward with such force that the doorway becomes blocked. As a result, many people in front are crushed or trampled to death, while those in the rear are consumed by the encroaching flames.

Experimental social psychologists have recently undertaken laboratory investigations of collective panic. In one such experiment Kelley and his co-workers (1965) confronted male and female undergraduates with the threat of painful electric shocks. Their results indicate that the greater the perceived danger in a situation of perceived entrapment and the higher the level of fear, the smaller the percentage of subjects who end up escaping entrapment.

Obviously, panic does not occur every time the prime panic-producing conditions of potential entrapment are present. The chances of panic are increased when there is restriction of activity, which heightens the individual's sense of helplessness. Research studies of Army and Navy units in combat indicate that fear symptoms occur most frequently among those men who must sit passively and wait to see what the enemy will do (Janis, 1949b; Haggard, 1949). Recent laboratory experiments have highlighted the importance of an active role in dealing with danger stimuli. Faced with the threat of painful electric shocks, college students show the greatest degree of emotional disturbance when they are unable to predict the time of the shock and are given no opportunity to control its onset or termination (Champion, 1950; D'Amato & Gumenik, 1960; Pervin, 1963). These experimental findings, together with the field studies of combat and disaster, support the psychoanalytic hypothesis concerning the fear-intensifying effects of restrictions on motor and cognitive activities that augment feelings of helplessness in a threatening environment.

A number of additional experiments and field studies also contribute some support to Freud's views concerning the importance of maintaining contact with and positive emotional attachments to parents, leaders, and fellow members of primary groups. Separation from family and friends appears to be a prime factor in augmenting a frightened person's propensity to lose emotional control even when he knows that his chances of being entrapped or victimized are not very great. The evidence concerning the effects of separation and the reassuring effects of group affiliation under conditions of external danger will be reviewed in Chapter 6 (pages 92–93).

Freud's Hypotheses About "Working Through" the Trauma

One of Freud's major contributions to the theory of psychological trauma resulted from observations of traumatized soldiers during World War I. Freud was impressed by the frequency of dreams and daydreams in which the soldiers relived their terrifying experiences in the front-line trenches. He hypothesized that their mental repetitions of the distressing events were "belated attempts at mastery" motivated by painful feelings arising from their awareness of their helplessness in the face of danger. To put it another way: Preoccupation with painful reminiscences about a disaster helps a person to assimilate the experience, to work out a new conception of the danger and of his resources for coping with it; eventually this new conception results in a restoration of the person's emotional equilibrium. This process is sometimes referred to as "working through" the trauma (Fenichel, 1945).

Disasters and near-miss accidents in adult life are also likely to be followed by mental repetitions of the upsetting events, and these too would be expected to require adequate working through before the person could again face the same danger situation without becoming disorganized. In children even minor threats seem to require the same repetitive attempts at inner mastery. Freud's views have alerted specialists in child psychology to the potentially positive value of the child's repetitive play-acting, for example when he repeats a distressing visit to the doctor, reversing the doctor's role and his own.

The Basic Attitude Change:
A Lost Sense of Invulnerability

What is it that needs to be worked through? Why are new attempts at mastery necessary? Freud's theoretical statements pose these questions but do not give definite answers. From the case studies reported by a number of other psychoanalysts we can extract additional psychodynamic hypotheses concerning the damage to the human personality that gives rise to the extreme symptoms of traumatic neurosis and other personality transformations following exposure to severe stress.

During World War II, temporary emotional breakdowns occurred in large numbers of persons who had presumably been clinically normal before their war experiences. Many such cases were carefully studied by observers who were trained in psychoanalysis and who were accustomed to looking for subtle motivations underlying anxiety symptoms. Among the outstanding clinical investigators in the U.S. Army were Grinker and Spiegel. They carried out detailed analyses of psychiatric casualties, including combat infantrymen who broke down on the battlefield (1945b) and Air Force veterans who broke down during or immediately after completing their tour of combat flying duty (1945a). These investigators tried to understand how and why sustained anxiety symptoms arise following exposures to severe stress. At the same time Melitta Schmideberg (1942) and several other neo-Freudian analysts who were treating civilians in England during the war began making detailed case studies of men and women who broke down following direct personal involvement in the air raids. Both lines of investigation led to similar findings concerning the psychological changes that mediate the disruptive emotional effects of stressful events. Grinker and

Spiegel concluded that the fundamental change was a *loss of self-confidence concerning personal invulnerability*. Schmideberg arrived at the same conclusion: "A person's conviction that nothing can happen to him is sometimes painfully shattered if something actually *does* happen to him. In that case the shock of being hurt or losing his property will be intensified by the shock of realizing his vulnerability [Schmideberg, 1942, p. 166]."

Once a person has been utterly powerless to protect himself from danger, he can no longer maintain a basic sense of confidence about his future safety. After his house has crashed down around him or after he has been entrapped in a bombed-out shelter, the traumatized person cannot dispel from his fantasies and images of the future the memory of the harrowing experience in which he was helpless; he now anticipates, consciously or unconsciously, that the same thing can happen to him again at any time. He no longer regards himself as immune to extreme misfortune, injury, and death. He no longer feels the world to be a safe place where he can cope with whatever adversity may arise. He now perceives every new threat as similar to the traumatic danger situation during which he felt helpless.

That a loss of self-confidence has a markedly detrimental influence on performance under stress is one of Grinker and Spiegel's main themes (1945a). They found that the onset of this basic attitude change was the first step preceding marked decreases in efficiency of performance among combat fliers. Almost all of these men had begun their series of missions with high morale, as volunteers who were confident they could survive the hazards of combat flying. Most of them had originally felt that "others may die, but nothing will happen to *me*." They began to lose this sense of security after a few difficult missions, especially if they had a narrow escape or saw friends in other planes in their formation being shot down. Their fear of enemy attack markedly increased when they first encountered a convincing demonstration of damage from antiaircraft fire or enemy fighter planes. After a dramatic, unnerving experience of helplessness in the face of danger, some fliers became so apprehensive that they could no longer perform their flying tasks dependably and had to be grounded at least temporarily. A morbid change in basic attitude took place in these men: from "Nothing terrible will happen to me" to "Something terrible is *bound* to happen to me."

Other men were able to continue flying a while longer after a harrowing near-miss episode by developing a new type of defensive attitude that involved open admission of pessimism. The attitude was expressed this way: "I'll probably get it on my next mission, but I don't give a damn any more." In these men, the breakdown of invulnerability feelings was accompanied by depression or apathy, which was motivated by a strong need to ward off overwhelming fear. But this defensive attitude was likely to break down sooner or later, especially when the flier realized he was approaching the end of his tour of duty and began thinking about returning home to his loved ones. As soon as he began to hope for his survival, the defensive attitude of resigned indifference was no longer effective, and he would suddenly develop intense anxiety attacks, resulting in inefficient performances on his flying missions (Grinker & Spiegel, 1945a).

Grinker, in collaboration with several psychologists, obtained some systematic data on this relationship from a questionnaire study of 544 flying officers who had recently completed their tour of combat duty (Grinker, Willerman, Bradley, & Fastovsky, 1946). They investigated feelings of personal invulnerability by asking the officers whether they had felt that "while others might be hurt or killed, it couldn't happen to you." Affirmative answers were given by only a small percentage of the 284 flying officers who had developed acute neurotic symptoms during their combat duty or immediately after; affirmative answers were given by a relatively high percentage of the 260 flying officers who had undergone similar combat experiences without developing symptoms. Although the findings do not establish the causal sequence, the statistically significant difference between these two groups is consistent with the general hypothesis under discussion, which predicts that if a man develops the characteristic pattern of anxiety symptoms following exposure to danger, he will also show a change in attitude concerning his personal vulnerability.

The psychodynamic hypothesis concerning loss of self-confidence about coping with danger also helps to explain the findings cited earlier concerning the higher incidence of emotional breakdown among disaster victims who had near-miss experiences than among those who had remote-miss experiences. The critical disaster experiences that give rise to severe anxiety reactions appear to be those capable of evoking a feeling of being powerless to avert actual danger. Narrow escapes from danger, loss of persons with whom one feels identified, and witnessing maimed bodies appear to shatter the entire set of psychological defenses that maintain expectations of personal invulnerability.

The same type of basic attitude change has also been detected among survivors of peacetime disasters, automobile crashes, and other accidents (Wolfenstein, 1957). We caught glimpses of a loss of self-confidence in Don when he was recovering from the near-drowning accident. A woman who escaped uninjured from a devastating tornado in Texas said this about her change in outlook:

> I was terrified. I was like a trapped animal that didn't know what way to run. We had been planning a storm cellar and hadn't gotten one. And I don't know, I just—when those storms come up, I just—just feel like for sure this may be the end. That it could be a cloud that could swoop down before you could get to protection. They are murderous things. There's—there's a fear you can't conquer. A fear of storms. I used to enjoy a thunderstorm, a display of lightning. It just gave me a feeling of the importance of the Creator to watch it. But I don't now;

when I see a storm coming now you always imagine there is destruction in it, even if it is a rainstorm. Just don't get over that fear. I have noticed two or three times that we've just walked the floor wondering if we would have to leave. And this past week we did finally, we just couldn't constrain ourselves. We finally got in the car and ran from it. Just an instinct to try to run from it and get away [Moore, 1958, p. 257].

Changes in the individual's conception of his personal vulnerability have also been noted in persons exposed to danger during severe illness and surgical operations (Janis, 1958). Once he has lost his sense of personal invulnerability, an ill or injured person begins to think of himself as a condemned man, like the character in the passage from Andreyev quoted at the beginning of this chapter.

Attitude Changes Induced
by Prolonged Deprivation

We have so far been speaking about the basic attitude change produced by a single disaster or traumatic event. The same kind of attitude change may develop gradually if a highly stressful and frustrating life situation continues for a long time, for example in a person suffering from a prolonged illness or an infantryman kept in the front lines under highly deprivational circumstances for many months. The relentless accumulation of stresses day after day lowers the person's stress tolerance to the point where he begins to react to every minor stress as though it were a serious threat. Examples were cited earlier, when we examined the symptoms that precede severe emotional breakdown in combat soldiers. In these men, expectations of personal invulnerability gradually wore down until their basic attitude resembled that of men who had undergone a single traumatic accident. There is an important difference, however, because in the chronic stress situation the man's mood is much more likely to be colored by depression and apathy along with the anxiety symptoms.

As severe frustrations continue unabated, the person feels that he has been abandoned, that no one cares what happens to him (Rado, 1942). People who have undergone a long period of hospitalization and drastic surgery without being cured develop the same feelings. They may realize that everyone is trying to help them, but they cannot dispel the feeling that no one really cares and no one can be trusted. A chronically ill patient may react to painful treatment with intense feelings of aggrievement, like a child who feels he is being excessively punished or neglected by his mother just when he most needs help.

Bitter weeping and other depressive reactions are especially likely to be prominent if the person feels that "it serves me right, I have behaved badly." A combination of depression and anxiety is frequently encountered among combat soldiers who had felt envious of or angry at a buddy shortly before he was killed. The stressful events of combat have a much more powerful emotional impact once the man starts to feel that he deserves to be punished, since this self-deprecation contributes not only to his depression but also to his loss of self-confidence about surviving the ordeal. When a man's basic attitude of self-confidence about coping with danger has been severely shaken by an accumulation of prior stresses over a long period of time, a very minor source of stress may induce the onset of a traumatic neurosis. Thus it appears that the weaker the attitude of self-confidence, the less powerful the traumatic event required to induce emotional breakdown.

When we speak about an attitude of high or low self-confidence, we are referring to more than the person's conscious expectations about surviving environmental dangers. Such expectations are an important component of the attitude, but other components need to be assessed if we are to be sure that the person is not merely displaying irrational cockiness or denial of danger. We shall return to this point when we discuss the ways in which the person's verbalized expressions of his attitudes may give a distorted impression of his basic sense of confidence. The most dependable attitudes of high self-confidence, as we shall see, are likely to be those that take account of at least a limited degree of personal vulnerability to danger. "Blanket reassurances" of total invulnerability usually prove to be very flimsy defenses (see pages 95–105).

Therapy and Prevention
of Traumatic Neurosis

The psychodynamic theories discussed in this chapter have markedly influenced the treatment of persons suffering from traumatic neurosis. They have also strongly influenced practical policies for preventing damaging emotional scars in the inhabitants of disaster-stricken communities. Many psychotherapists who treat traumatized persons see their job as that of helping each person to do the amount of working through the trauma that is needed for him to regain his basic sense of self-confidence. They generally try to adopt a permissive, unthreatening manner of talking with the patient and sometimes introduce special techniques—such as eliciting free associations to details of the patient's repetitive nightmares or giving him a hypnotic drug that induces reliving of the traumatic events—in order to help him recall what happened and gain some insight into what it meant to him. This type of approach evidently can be successful many years after a disaster, as illustrated by the case of Tom, the airplane mechanic who responded well to treatment 7 years after the onset of his traumatic neurosis (see pages 30–33).

The concept of working through the trauma to regain mastery has also been applied in administering psychiatric first aid to children and adults following accidents or disasters. The assumption is that if they evade all reminders of their harrowing experience, they are more likely to be left with chronic traumatic neurosis. Thus disaster victims are encouraged to verbalize their recent distressing experiences. In addition, special efforts are made to give them reassurances and solicitous care so as to help reestablish their sense of confidence in the world about them. We do not yet know whether these preventive measures succeed in reducing substantially the incidence of sustained emotional disorders.

Although our understanding of psychological trauma remains incomplete, the observations and psychodynamic hypotheses introduced by clinical investigators enable us to give a tentative answer to a fundamental question raised earlier in this chapter: What needs to be restored in a person who has been severely traumatized? We have seen that the underlying personality changes produced by prolonged stress exposures as well as by sudden catastrophes involve a damaged sense of self-confidence about coping with environmental threats. Thus what has to be restored is the person's sense of basic security about his capacity to avert injury and annihilation in a world where man is vulnerable to sudden misfortunes, to uncontrollable dangers, and ultimately to death. The traumatized person, in short, must come to terms with the basic human condition.

Joseph made answer—far too quickly and far too low. . . . Joseph's heart—that heart which Jacob, far off, believed long stilled in death, whereas here it was in Egypt, ticking away and exposed to all the perils of life—that heart stood a moment still, then, as a heart does, throbbed the faster in order to overtake its lost beats.

THOMAS MANN. Joseph in Egypt

CHAPTER 5
SENSITIZATION TO THREAT CUES

In this chapter we shall continue our analysis of personality changes resulting from stressful life experiences by examining reactions that are much more subtle than the anxiety attacks and other disruptive symptoms considered so far. We shall concentrate on one important type of reaction: increased sensitization to threat cues.

On the basis of the learning principles discussed in Chapter 3, we would expect a person who had undergone a terrifying episode, such as Don's near-drowning experience, to show characteristic changes in his emotional reactions to cues that were present during the danger experience. For example, the mere sight of the seashore and of ocean waves might now arouse much more uneasiness than they ever had before. We would also expect symbolic cues, such as those present in movies or novels about the sea, to evoke a certain amount of unpleasant feeling that they had never evoked before. Despite every effort to appear calm, the survivor of a harrowing episode will betray his agitation when someone happens to broach the sensitive topic. Like Joseph in the passage quoted from Mann's novel, he will show his emotional arousal through a change in his manner of speaking or through involuntary movements, which can be regarded as the expressive language of the body.

The concept of *sensitization* applies to all instances of increased arousal evoked by formerly neutral cues. Sensitization is often manifested in a very subtle way. For example, only a quick inner signal of anxiety may be aroused by a threat cue, so fleeting that the person can easily keep it hidden from others, though he may feel a momentary pang.

Detecting Sensitization Effects

Special psychological techniques are needed to detect subtle sensitization effects. The Word Association Test, for example, is sometimes useful in uncovering acquired sensitization reactions in people who are motivated to maintain a calm exterior and to avoid admitting even to themselves that they are upset. With a person like Don, who had been traumatized by a near-miss accident, we would expect to find residual sensitization effects many months, perhaps years, after recovery from the more obvious symptoms of acute traumatic neurosis.

When used to detect such effects, the Word Association Test presents the subject with a number of "critical" words, stimulus words that refer to the danger episode. In testing a person who had undergone an experience like Don's, for example, such words as "swim," "waves," "water," and "drowning" might be embedded in a long list of neutral and irrelevant stimulus words, such as "fly," "jump," "air," and "parachute." The subject is asked to respond to each stimulus word with whatever word comes into his mind. The psychological examiner records the man's reaction time, expressive behavior (such as blushing, tremors, or speech disturbances), and verbal response to each stimulus word. In analyzing the record, he watches for disturbances in the responses to the critical words that do not appear for the neutral words. These differential indicators of emotional disturbance are sometimes supplemented by psychophysiological measures obtained during the Word Association Test—changes in heart rate, electrical potential of the surface of the skin, and other indicators of autonomic nervous system activity. Here again the investigator would look for signs of greater emotional disturbance in response to words pertaining to the stressful near-drowning episode than to words about irrelevant activities such as parachuting and flying in an airplane. If, instead, the stressful episode had involved a horrifying experience during a parachute jump, the words pertaining to jumping and flying would be the "critical" words.

Sensitization Effects
in Sports Parachutists

Parachute jumpers are, as a matter of fact, the subjects of the most complete and reliable studies now available on sensitization effects produced in human beings exposed to actual danger. An extensive investigation of sports parachutists, including the use of a Word Association Test and accompanying psychophysiological measures, has been carried out by Fenz (1964) and Epstein (1965). Their studies show that marked changes take place in the emotional reactions of college-age men who volunteer for what is probably the most exciting—and stressful—of all sports. Acute sensitization, followed by gradual desensitization, is the characteristic response of those who survive the physical and emotional rigors of the training program.

We shall examine the Epstein and Fenz experiments in some detail. They help us to understand the emotional changes induced in the men who develop obvious symptoms and who soon give up the threatening activity. The experiments also help to explain the changes in the men who continue their training and who seem unperturbed, as though they were immune to the unnerving emotional impact of an extremely rapid free fall that can be fatal if there is any malfunctioning in the man or his equipment. After reviewing the findings, we shall apply the theories discussed in the preceding two chapters to the observed phenomena.

The sport of parachute jumping in recent years has attracted thousands of young men, and fresh recruits continue to flock to jump-training centers throughout the United States. Although most of the volunteers are courageous men with a stomach for dangerous thrills, it is quite apparent from the descriptions given by participants and observers that a free fall from an airplane induces overwhelming feelings of terror in practically all the men when they make their first jump. The extreme fear reactions of novice parachutists seem comparable to the most extreme emotional symptoms observed among men in military combat or in peacetime disasters. For an hour or two after the first jump many parachutists are in a state of mild emotional shock, similar to Don's condition after his rescue from the ocean. They are likely to be confused, unresponsive to social stimulation, and either excessively agitated or excessively exhausted, out of all proportion to the amount of physical exertion of the jump activity itself. When the men start talking about how they feel after the first jump, they commonly say things like, "I never, never, ever want to go through it again" or "It was the most frightening experience of my life."

Objective evidence of the emotional impact of the first jump is provided by a study of 2800 men who volunteered for sport parachuting (Istel,

1961). All of them intended to become regular jumpers, but 85 percent of them showed a marked avoidance reaction by failing to return after the first jump. Of the 15 percent who did return, only a minority continued after the second or third jump. Thus, the vast majority of men reacted adversely either to the very first jump or to the next few jumps, developing such a powerful aversion to the activity that they decided to quit the training. This decision is not necessarily an unrealistic over-reaction to the objective threat; the average novice becomes so excited during the early jumps that he is likely to behave ineptly, and there is considerable risk of a serious accident (Moore, 1963).

Trainers and observers regularly report that after the first free fall, many of the sports parachutists who continue to receive training no longer look forward with keen anticipation to the joyful thrills of the sport. Most of them become quite apprehensive and jittery, although they may not readily admit it. They have to screw up their courage at each training session to force themselves to put on their gear and enter the plane.

Taking account of these observations, Epstein and Fenz decided to investigate the changes in parachutists' emotional reactions during the period following their first jump from the airplane. All the subjects were men who came back for more training after the first jump, since those who quit after their first jump were not available. Consequently, the emotional stamina of the men investigated was probably well above average.

Each novice parachutist was tested three times: two weeks before his next jump was scheduled, the day before it was scheduled, and a few hours before he went up to make the jump. In each session, the man was given a different (but equivalent) form of a Word Association Test, and his physiological reactions were assessed by measuring his psychogalvanic response (PGR) as he gave his verbal response to each word.

The main findings bearing on sensitization are shown in Figure 5-1. As we noted when discussing the Campbell, Sanderson, and Laverty experiment on emotional conditioning (Chapter 3), the PGR reflects activity of the sweat glands stimulated by the autonomic nervous system and is one of the most frequently studied human physiological responses. It is presumed to be at least a rough indicator of emotional arousal in certain circumstances (although it is sometimes an undependable measure and may fail to differentiate between fear and nonemotional reactions such as attentiveness to indistinct stimuli).

The words on the base line of the X-axis ("anxiety," "neutral," "low," "medium," and "high") represent the five categories of stimulus words that were presented, in random order, to the subjects. At the extreme right we have the average responses to the words most highly relevant to parachuting, including "parachute," "ripcord," and "fall." It will be noted that in all three sessions these most relevant words elicited stronger arousal than did the "medium," or moderately relevant, words, such as "opened," "aircraft," and

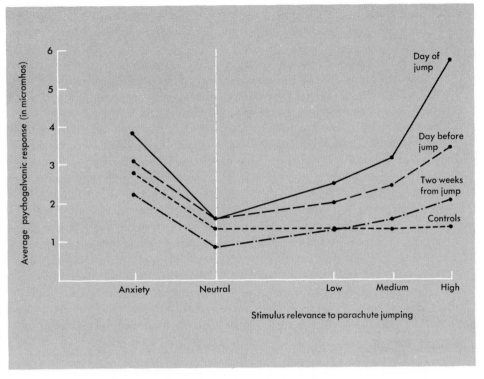

Figure 5-1   Psychogalvanic responses evoked in 27 parachutists and a control group of 27 nonparachutists by various types of stimulus words on the Word Association Test. (Adapted from Fenz, 1964)

"flying." The latter words, in turn, evoked more emotional arousal than did the "low," or least relevant, words, such as "sky," "swift," and "airport."

The base level of arousal was estimated by using neutral words that had nothing to do with parachute jumping, such as "music," "stove," and "paper." In addition, the experimenter introduced a standard set of "anxiety" words—disturbing words such as "killed," "hurt," and "fear," which generally induce some degree of anxiety arousal in the average person. These terms did, in fact, elicit almost as much arousal as the most relevant words (as can be seen from the results shown at the extreme left of the figure).

The curves in Figure 5-1 are especially revealing because each parachutist is used as his own control in determining his emotional responses at various times before the critical danger event. Emotionality is highest on the day of the jump, and it reaches a peak for those words that refer either to the jump scheduled for that day (the most relevant words) or to the risks of injury and death (the standard set of disturbing words). A similar curve was obtained on the day before the jump, but at a much lower level; this curve, in turn, was somewhat higher than the curve obtained two weeks before the jump.

There is further evidence of the men's worrisome preoccupation with the parachute jump on the day of the jump: They reacted more slowly to the most relevant words than they had during the two previous sessions, and there was a marked increase in the number of their word responses that referred explicitly to parachute jumping. On the day of a jump the parachutists are repeatedly confronted with clear-cut signs of the approaching threat. For example, they hear everyone around them talking about the day's jump schedule, they see the airplane warming up, and they are given the parachute gear to strap on. After their first jump the men probably become sensitized to all these threat cues. The differences in physiological response induced by words of varying degrees of relevance suggest the following generalization: *After a person has engaged in a hazardous activity, the more specifically any new threat cues denote the activity or its dangerous consequences, the more intense will be the person's emotional reaction.*

The investigators point out that a high degree of sensitization sometimes affects a man's performance unfavorably—he may pay so much attention to the threat cues that he neglects other important bits of information.

One parachutist who gave completely adequate responses to the Word Association Test on the day before the scheduled jump showed obsessional and somewhat bizarre reactions the next day. Shortly before the scheduled jump he gave words relevant to parachute jumping frequently and indiscriminately, even in response to stimulus words that had no relationship to jumping. For example, to the word "stove," his response was "jump master"; to "chair," his response was "sky diver." A few hours later, while the plane was taking off, he showed an extreme reaction of the opposite type. In contrast to being keyed up during the test, he now fell deeply asleep while being flown to the target area and had to be awakened as the plane approached the position for the jump. His falling asleep under these circumstances was most remarkable, given the blast of the wind and the noise of the airplane engine. Evidently he was resorting to an extreme form of inhibition for controlling his fear as the threat began to mount.

A number of cases of this type suggest that when hypersensitivity to threat cues is manifested shortly before the jump in the testing session, the man will later prove to have relatively low stress tolerance, which will be manifested by generalized inhibition or other extreme forms of defensive behavior when he is confronted with the actual danger.

Disavowal and Displacement of Fear

Psychological tests provide evidence concerning the defenses the men sometimes used for coping with their heightened sensitivity to threat cues after their first jump. On the day the second jump was scheduled, the men were given a projective personality test—a version of the Thematic Apperception Test, which involves showing each subject a series of somewhat ambiguous pictures and asking him to use his imagination to make up stories about what is happening. The recurrent themes in these fantasy-like stories reveal a great deal about the subject's motives and defenses; what he says about the anxieties of the hero is likely to apply directly to himself. (For a detailed description of this type of test, see Part IV, pp. 696–711.) The investigators used a special set of pictures designed to represent situations of varying relevance to parachute jumping (see Figure 5-2). They gave the same test to an equivalent control group of college students, none of whom had volunteered for parachute jumping or had ever jumped.

The parachutists showed a peculiar pattern of response in their stories that was not found at all among the nonparachutists. This pattern consisted of two seemingly contradictory types of verbal reactions: (1) When they told stories about pictures that depicted a parachutist inside an air-

Figure 5-2 Examples of the pictures in the Thematic Apperception Test used in a study of fear reactions of sports parachutists. (From Fenz, 1964)

plane (see part *d* of Figure 5-2), the novices disavowed feelings of fear by saying things like "He is not afraid at all" or "He will have a wonderful jump; it will be great, just great!" (2) But when they told stories in response to irrelevant pictures, such as the one depicting two young boys running (see part *a* of Figure 5-2), the parachutists expressed an exceptionally high degree of fear. They made such comments as "He looks worried . . . and he thinks: Am I gonna die?" Apparently, the storytellers displaced their fear away from the relevant pictures to the neutral or irrelevant pictures. This pattern suggests that on the day of the jump the parachutists are in a state of high emotional arousal, but they tend not to acknowledge their fear of parachuting and to displace it onto unrelated topics. This is a typical defense that many people use when they face a dangerous task; it helps them to ward off distressing feelings of apprehensiveness. Such defenses may enable parachutists to maintain a calm exterior, but the underlying fear may nevertheless show up in their involuntary physiological responses to relevant threat cues.

We cannot be certain that all the reactions revealed by Epstein and Fenz's research are a consequence of the stressful experience of the first jump, since the nonparachutist control group, which was used for certain comparative purposes, did not consist of volunteers for parachute jumping. Nevertheless, the changes observed following the stressful event—particularly the consistent increase in physiological reactions as the time for their next jump approached—appear to be genuine manifestations of sensitization to threat cues. The evidence points to the following general conclusion: *People exposed to actual danger generally acquire a marked increase in sensitivity to subsequent signs of threat.* This conclusion is also supported by several field studies of soldiers in combat and civilians exposed to peacetime disasters, which were cited in earlier chapters.

The emotional reactions of the novices, as revealed by the psychological tests, could have both adaptive and maladaptive consequences. On the one hand, the special sensitivity to parachuting cues implies a high degree of alertness to the oncoming danger situation. This alertness might make the men more vigilant and more cautious. On the other hand, the defensive reactions as well as the high emotional excitement might lead to inadvertent errors that could increase the danger and contribute to the high accident rate among novice parachutists. Disavowal and displacement of fear can reduce the person's capacity to appraise the danger accurately and to cope with it effectively. We shall discuss these adverse effects in a later chapter, where we shall examine the relationship between pre-stress denial and post-stress emotional disturbances. (See pages 96–99. See also Part II, pp. 377–78, for a discussion of counterphobic defense.)

Applying Learning-Theory Concepts

CONDITIONED EMOTIONAL RESPONSES

Most of the sensitization phenomena discussed so far can be readily accounted for in terms of the learning-theory concepts presented in Chapter 3. The increased emotional arousal shown by the parachutists after their first jump from an airplane can be regarded as *conditioned emotional responses* that were acquired during or shortly after the distressing free fall. We would expect these sensitization reactions to share the main functional properties of all conditioned responses, as specified by the laws of Pavlovian conditioning. The *unconditioned stimuli* include sensations of falling rapidly through space as well as fear-evoking stimuli based on prior conditioning. The powerful unconditioned stimuli during the free fall are accompanied by a variety of neutral stimuli (such as the sight of the airplane) and thoughts, images, and words that refer to the jumping activity, the equipment being used, and so on. After the initial frightening jump, all these formerly neutral cues become fear-producing cues, as a result of their contiguity with the unconditioned fear stimuli.

THE PRINCIPLE OF GENERALIZATION

We have also seen that the change in sensitivity displayed by the novice parachutists extends to a variety of cues relevant to jumping, as we would expect from the principle of *generalization*. The supplementary principle of *generalization decrement* accounts for an important feature of the curves presented in Figure 5-1. The curves show that the intensity of the emotional reaction tends to decrease as the cues become less and less similar to those present during the emotional conditioning situation. The same principles of conditioning could be used to account for the sensitization phenomena observed among combat soldiers and civilians after a terrifying disaster.

INSTRUMENTAL LEARNING

Principles of *operant* or *instrumental* conditioning help us to account for the newly acquired defenses that accompany changes in emotionality in the wake of a disaster. The survivors frequently show marked changes in their attitudes, plans, and actions, all of which are operant responses. Apparently these changes are reinforced by reduction of fear. After San Angelo, Texas, had been partially destroyed by a tornado, many inhabitants said they had "learned a lesson from the tornado" and explained that they were now making realistic plans to construct storm shelters before there were any more tornado warnings (Moore, 1958). They asserted that they had now become jittery, that they had never before realized how important it is to have shelters and to pay attention to warnings from the weather bureau. As one respondent said, "I'm not going to let them [storm clouds] slip up on me like that." Their thoughts about how to protect themselves in the future seemed to be oriented toward keeping down their present distressing fear, which had been much less intense before the disaster. Each of the operant responses involved in planning and constructing shelters would continue to be reinforced insofar as it continued to be promptly followed by a momentary or persistent lessening of fear.

The changes in behavior just described seem to fit in well with the two-factor theory of learning. The survivors showed signs of having acquired new conditioned fear reactions to threat cues that were formerly ignored. At the same time, they undertook new forms of instrumental activity that were rewarded by the alleviation of their fear. This activity included seeking the reassuring presence of friends and relatives as well as constructing shelters.

Psychodynamic Hypotheses
About Indiscriminate Sensitization

Let us now consider whether the psychodynamic concepts discussed in Chapter 4 can further our understanding of sensitization phenomena.

We noted in Chapter 4 that the emotional symptoms seen in near-miss cases appear to be consequences of a basic attitude change concerning personal vulnerability to danger. Indiscriminate sensitization to both remote and relevant threat cues can be viewed as one type of anxiety symptom resulting from a shattering of all those inner defenses that formerly enabled the disaster survivor to contemplate the possibility of danger with sufficient equanimity to make full use of his coping resources. When a person shows indiscriminate fear during the days following an extreme near-miss experience, we surmise that he has lost his former basic attitude of personal invulnerability and has not yet built up any defenses to restore his self-confidence. In this defenseless state, he responds to any reminder of the threat with an image of himself as utterly helpless in the face of overwhelming danger. He over-reacts to even the mildest of warnings, responding as though annihilation were imminent.

In contrast, people who have undergone a remote-miss experience are much less likely to display indiscriminate sensitivity to nonrelevant threat cues. This is because after the disaster they are able once again to rely upon a set of inner reassurances; they can envision themselves as surviving anticipated dangers without being seriously injured or annihilated. Their self-confidence may have been shaken at the time of the disaster, but it was not destroyed.

The distinction between near-miss and remote-miss experiences is purely descriptive. It simply helps us to predict which persons in a disaster-stricken area are likely to develop extreme emotional symptoms, including indiscriminate sensitization to threat cues. But such predictions can be improved if we take account of qualitative differences among remote-miss experiences. For example, several studies of large-scale disasters indicate that people who witness casualties will show various anxiety symptoms, including a marked increase in sensitivity to threat cues, even though they were not personally involved in the danger (Fritz & Marks, 1954; Wolfenstein, 1957). These findings suggest that any remote-miss case who perceives one or more mutilated persons during a disaster can come away with an "object lesson" about what could happen to him when disaster strikes. After such a lesson the person can no longer maintain his complacent outlook. In short, expectations of total personal invulnerability can be modified by a certain type of remote-miss experience, just as they can be modified by a near-miss experience. Here again the crucial type of information seems to be the vivid demonstration that a person can be unprotected in a disaster.

There is no hard and fast line between the effects of near-miss and remote-miss experiences; the near-miss experiences are merely *more likely* to provide a demonstration of helplessness in the face of danger. Such a demonstration, whether produced by a near-miss or a remote-miss episode, is usually accompanied by a loss of faith in the reassuring protectiveness offered by one's own primary group, by authority figures, and by other persons who are normally counted on to shield one against misfortune.

Once we encounter a vivid demonstration of our vulnerability to a potential source of danger, we cannot maintain a relaxed attitude. We can no longer assume that the danger applies only to other people, that we shall never be touched by it. But the outcome need not necessarily be that we become indiscriminately sensitized to reminders of the danger or that we over-react to all warnings. Provided we are not traumatized by the demonstration, our anticipations of *total invulnerability* will tend to be transformed into anticipations of *partial vulnerability*, which make us somewhat more fearful but do not result in severe anxiety symptoms. This sense of partial vulnerability makes us selectively sensitized to the most serious warnings we encounter and more receptive to information about protective actions to ward off the threat. These adaptive changes will be discussed further in the next chapter, when we examine the conditions under which sensitization to threat is diminished.

I have lain in prison for nearly two years. . . . I have passed through every possible mood of suffering. . . . I could not bear [my sufferings] to be without meaning. Now I find hidden somewhere away in my nature something that tells me that nothing in the whole world is meaningless, and suffering least of all. That something hidden away in my nature, like a treasure in a field, is humility.

It is the last thing left in me, and the best: the ultimate discovery at which I have arrived, the starting-point for a fresh development.

OSCAR WILDE. De Profundis

CHAPTER 6
ADAPTIVE PERSONALITY CHANGES

We have been concentrating on the disruptive effects of danger, examining the temporary and persistent changes in personality functioning that prevent the individual from coping adequately with life stresses. But sometimes a stressful episode brings about a *positive* change, making the individual more responsive to relevant warnings, causing him to plan realistically for future emergencies, and even helping him to develop greater emotional control in dealing with similar dangers. And, as Oscar Wilde suggests in his autobiographical essay, written when he was in prison, a man is inclined to find in his suffering some meaning that enables him to feel he can correct the weaknesses that led to his misery. In this chapter we shall examine the conditions under which experiences of threat and danger lead to adaptive changes that enable a person to cope more effectively with stress.

Emotional Adaptation
in Sports Parachutists

Suggestive evidence concerning adaptive changes comes from certain observations made by Epstein and Fenz (1965) in their research on sports parachutists. These investigators compared a group of highly experienced sports parachutists, all of whom had made more than 100 jumps, with relatively inexperienced men who had made from one to five jumps. They found marked differences in emotional reactions, which suggest that with increased experience the men became *desensitized*; that is, after making a large number of jumps the men showed only a mild emotional reaction, in contrast to the intense emotional reaction they may have had earlier in the series. This type of change with increased exposure to a threat situation is referred to as *emotional adaptation*.

A special questionnaire was given to both the experienced and the inexperienced men immediately after they completed a jump. Each man was asked to rate the strength of his fear at 14 different time points leading up to the completion of his jump; he was told to give a rating of 10 to the point of strongest feelings of fear and a rating of 1 to the point of weakest feelings. As shown in Figure 6-1, the inexperienced jumpers reported becoming more and more fearful as the time for their next jump approached. Fear apparently reaches its maximum when the novice jumper, aloft in the airplane, receives the "ready" signal. He then goes out the open door onto the step above the wheel to wait for the final signal to jump. Once outside the plane, the man has reached the point of no return; at this crucial moment, fear begins to decrease. It continues to decrease during the free fall, which is actually the time of greatest danger. The investigators interpret these findings as indicating that maximum fear usually occurs when the novice realizes he is about to commit himself irrevocably to the dangerous action: As soon as the final decision is made, fear declines.

A quite different type of curve was obtained from experienced parachutists; this curve is also shown in Figure 6-1. The curve for the experienced jumpers shows the highest level of fear on the morning of the jump. Afterward the amount of fear decreases steadily up to the point where the final hazardous action occurs (the free fall before the parachute opens). It is only after this point of greatest danger has passed that the experienced jumpers show an increase in fear.

As descriptive terms, "desensitization" and "emotional adaptation" can be applied to the lessening of fear at the airport and in the airplane, when the men are exposed to the series of threat cues that regularly precede the onset of actual danger. But the fact that they show a rise in fear after the danger is over suggests that this change in their fear reaction involves a process of active emotional control or defense, over and beyond any simple extinction or deconditioning that might result from repeated exposures to the conditioned stimuli.

The data shown in Figure 6-1 cannot be regarded as unequivocal evidence of the effects of increased exposure to the danger situation, since the two groups being compared were self-selected. Only a small proportion of novices decided to continue training to the point where they became experienced parachutists; thus this self-selected group might differ in important personality characteristics from the inexperienced men. Nevertheless, the findings are consistent with other evidence that also points to a striking diminution of fear evoked by threat cues as the men progress through the later stages of training. For example, trainers and other observers at sports parachuting centers report that experienced jumpers gen-

Figure 6-1 Parachutists' self-ratings of fear experienced before, during, and after a jump. (Adapted from Epstein & Fenz, 1965)

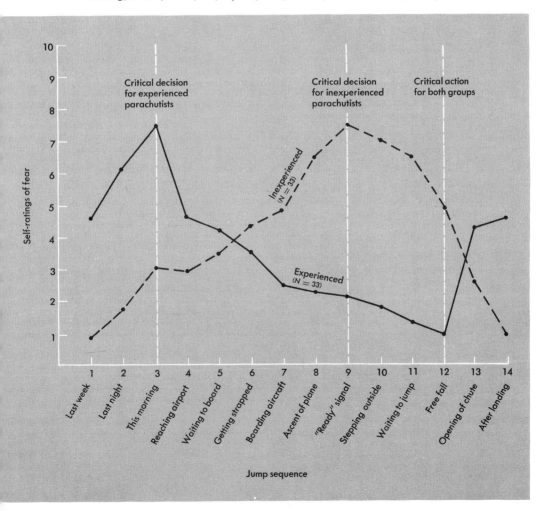

erally look forward to the jump each day and feel exhilarated, confident, and keyed up for action as the time for each jump approaches. At the beginning of their training these same men had shown the characteristic pattern of increasing fear before their next jump, as well as considerable conflict about wanting to avoid the danger but not wanting to be cowardly.

It seems most probable, therefore, that desensitization and highly discriminatory fear reactions occur among parachutists as a result of repeated exposure to the frightening situation of jumping from a moving airplane—provided, of course, that they continue to survive each jump unscathed. The beginners react strongly to the suspense and uncertainties of the approaching dangerous event. But evidently they gain confidence after a series of successful jumps and become much less emotionally aroused during the waiting period before each scheduled jump. The same type of emotional adaptation or habituation occurs among airplane pilots, scuba divers, professional skiers, mountain guides, and others who face repeated risks while undergoing training for highly dangerous occupations.

Emotional Adaptation
in Combat Soldiers

Research during World War II showed that when infantrymen first entered the front lines they usually failed to discriminate between dangerous and nondangerous explosions; they took cover whenever they heard any projectile. They gradually learned to discriminate, eventually taking cover only in response to sounds emitted by projectiles approaching close by (Janis, 1949b). Similarly, combat troops learned to discriminate among enemy weapons. For example, they gradually became less afraid of air attacks and more afraid of weapons that had greater potential for inflicting casualties, such as the German 88-millimeter artillery gun.

These wartime observations, like those made of the sports parachutists, indicate that an adaptive process of learning to make discriminations can go on during a period of repeated exposures to a hazardous environment. This process seems to have a dual effect: It decreases the person's fear reactions to exaggerated sources of apparent threat, and it increases his reactions to sources of real danger that he had formerly underestimated. "Green" troops often entered battle with considerable bravado and cockiness, carelessly disregarding the safety precautions they had been taught; their complacency disappeared when they had their "baptism by fire." After becoming seasoned combat men, they made far fewer errors of certain types (Smith, 1949). For example, they were less likely to huddle in groups when the enemy opened fire.

As the men in combat became increasingly responsive to real threats and less fearful of startling sights or sounds that could safely be disregarded, their judgments and actions became more appropriate in the face of danger. Insofar as these acquired discriminations increased the men's chances of survival, they are regarded as adaptive changes in behavior.

Paradoxical Effects of False Alarms

The foregoing observations concerning the acquisition of new discriminations in a recurrent danger situation seem to be in line with popular expectations that real danger will sensitize people to threat, while false alarms will tend to desensitize them so that they ignore future warnings. This view of false alarms is part of the folklore of our culture, as exemplified by the story of the shepherd boy who mischievously cried "Wolf! Wolf!" so often that no one reacted at all when he tried to give a real warning that his flock was actually being attacked. The "Wolf! Wolf!" myth does sometimes hold true, not only for community dangers but also for more intimate personal dangers, such as those that incline some women to make similar outcries at weekend drinking parties. But the available evidence indicates that false alarms can have either sensitizing or desensitizing effects, depending upon whether they increase or decrease the person's awareness of his personal vulnerability.

Killian (1954) reports a study that indicates the power of a false alarm. He interviewed a sample of the population of Panama City, Florida, a few days after that city had accidentally been given a false hurricane warning. The majority of the people interviewed reported that they were now more inclined than ever to take emergency action in the event of new hurricane warnings. Increased sensitivity to the hurricane threat was shown not only by those residents who had evacuated in response to the false alarm but also by a sizable percentage of those who had decided not to do so. All of these people had received the impressive warning that led them to believe that their city would be hit and that their lives would be endangered. Although this warning proved to be a false alarm, they learned from news reports that the windstorm caused enormous damage in areas less than 100 miles away. Thus, although their own city was unharmed, many of the people came to realize what the full force of the hurricane could have done to them if it had not changed its course.

The false alarm evidently produced a marked increase in vigilance because the new information interfered with previously established expectations of blanket immunity. Most residents now felt that "it *can* happen to me—it almost did." Any alarm, whether true or false, can probably produce the same type of emotional change. But we would not expect the outcome to be adaptive every time information is conveyed that makes the person aware of his vulnerability to a threat, particularly if it shatters his defenses against overwhelming fear. (The conditions under which warnings about realistic threats are likely to have adverse effects will be discussed in detail in Chapter 8.)

The Need
for Social Reassurance

Observations of both wartime and peacetime crises suggest that in times of danger most people have a heightened need for social reassurance. This is shown most frequently by overt efforts to avoid being separated from companions and authority figures who are capable of giving reassurance. The mere presence of a person's family, friends, and trusted leaders in the immediate neighborhood appears to dampen emotional excitement (Glover, 1942; Janis, 1951, 1958). Men in combat have frequently been observed trying to maintain contact with members of their unit. Time and again combat soldiers appeared to be acting against their own self-interest in their attempts to ward off separation fears and guilt about "letting the other guys down." Men who had performed well in battle sometimes refused a promotion if it meant they would be shifted to another group. Injured men sometimes went absent without leave from a safely located hospital or replacement depot and tried to rejoin their comrades at the front (Smith, 1949). Combat fliers who were physically ill and suffering from acute anxiety symptoms avoided going on sick call because they did not want to be separated from their air crews (Janis, 1949a). From all these observations, social psychologists and psychiatrists have inferred that sustained contact with the primary group is a crucial factor in the soldier's morale (Spiegel, 1944; Grinker & Spiegel, 1945a, 1945b; Shils & Janowitz, 1948; Stouffer, Lumsdaine, Williams, Smith, Janis, Star, & Cottrell, 1949; Glass, 1953).

In a series of social psychological experiments, Schachter (1959) has shown that there was at least a momentary increase in the need for affiliation when fear was aroused in female college students by telling them that they were about to receive an electric shock. For example, when the shock was described as being severe and painful (high threat), 20 out of 31 (65 percent) chose to wait together; but when it was described as mild and painless (low threat), only 10 out of 30 girls ($33\frac{1}{3}$ percent) chose to do so. These findings indicate that the preference to be with others increases with increased threat.

Taking account of additional findings from similar laboratory experiments, Schachter concludes that two different motives might give rise to the increased need for affiliation: (1) the need to evaluate one's own feelings and emotional symptoms by comparing them with those displayed by others and

(2) the need to obtain reassurance from being in the presence of others who will be supportive because they are in a similar predicament.

Of course, not all companions will be equally desirable. Rabbie (1963) found that subjects in a high state of fear preferred companions who would provide fear-reduction to those who were themselves in a high state of fear and would stimulate more fear.

This preference for being in the presence of others who are thought to be potentially helpful can be regarded as a form of reassurance-seeking that is a potentially adaptive mode of response to external stress. Affiliative behavior often involves "sharing of fear" in informal group discussions and in interchanges of gallows humor (Janis, 1968a, b). These interchanges may provide temporary relief from apprehensiveness and may also help each person to become better prepared psychologically for facing subsequent stress. (Later in this chapter we shall see how a person prepares himself psychologically when he is worried about future danger.) Moreover, the opportunity to talk about his fear in a friendly group setting can sometimes enable a person to correct his exaggerated views of the oncoming danger. Perhaps even more important is the increase in motivation to conform to the norms of the group in order to satisfy the heightened need for affiliation. If the group's norms concerning appropriate ways of dealing with the danger are based on sound information and realistic judgments, each individual who joins in the group discussions will become more ready to adopt some new reassuring beliefs and to adhere to the recommended precautionary measures, which can reduce his chances of becoming overwhelmed by feelings of helplessness.

Experiments
on Preparatory Communications

We have noted that exposure to actual danger can have favorable effects by building up adaptive discriminations and increasing the need for social reassurance. Exposure to warning communications can also initiate an adaptive learning process that enables the person to respond more effectively to subsequent stressful events. Studies of this process are important to understanding the psychology of stress and may lead to valuable practical applications in preventing emotional disturbances. Government agencies and national health organizations, including those in the mental health field, issue a constant stream of warning messages and recommendations to the public via news releases, magazine articles, pamphlets, movies, radio talks, and television programs. These messages in the mass media are "preparatory communications" in that they are intended to prepare people in advance to resist the adverse effects of a variety of stressful

events, including illness, accidents, bereavement, economic loss, job disloca-
tion, and divorce. The object of such preparation is to reduce the incidence
of preventable emotional disturbance. Similar preparatory messages are often
given in a more personal way by men and women in professional roles—at-
torneys, clergymen, physicians, social workers, teachers, employee counselors,
and others—when they help their clients prepare for future adversity.

What makes preparatory communications successful? Studies indicate
that a preparatory message can dampen the emotional impact of a subsequent threatening event if it correctly predicts the event, provided that it
does not make the potential danger appear to be so overwhelming that
nothing can be done to avert or minimize it. In one such study, Janis,
Lumsdaine, and Gladstone (1951) investigated the way the impact of a
major "bad news" event was modified by preparatory communications given
several months in advance. The experiment was started in June 1949, at a
time when the United States had a monopoly on atomic weapons. High
school students were presented with tape recordings of radio talks that discussed the Soviet Union's ability to produce an atomic bomb in the near
future. Three months later, when President Truman unexpectedly announced that Russia had succeeded in producing its first atomic bomb, the
same students were given a follow-up questionnaire to assess their emotional
reactions and attitude changes.

The findings indicated that the preparatory communication reduced
the psychological impact of the bad news event. The students in the control
group had not received the advance warning. Following President Truman's
announcement, they were much more likely than the forewarned students
to believe that Russia would soon have a large supply of A-bombs and that
within a few years Russia would launch a nuclear war against the United
States. The unwarned students also reported feeling more worried about the
possibility that their own city might be destroyed by an atomic bomb than
did those who were warned. Thus, the advance warnings tended to prevent
pessimism and apprehensiveness in response to the dramatic piece of bad
news. These findings indicate that an advance warning of an unfavorable
event can have a significant dampening effect even for a relatively non-
personal type of threatening news involving national security.

The findings from this experiment support the general hypothesis
that the intensity of fear evoked by a stressful event can be reduced by
prior exposure to a preparatory communication that predicts the event.
Further support for this hypothesis comes from a number of laboratory investigations of human reactions to experimentally induced stress. For example, an outstanding series of experiments by Lazarus and his co-workers
(1962, 1964, 1966) shows that advance information can significantly reduce
the emotional impact of distressing perceptions of bodily damage. In these
experiments male college students were shown an anthropological film of a
primitive society's puberty rite, during which young boys had to undergo

a crude type of circumcision. The stress reactions of the audience as they saw the color film sequence depicting the mutilation of the boys' genital organs were measured by self-ratings of their mood as well as by psychophysiological measures of heart rate and galvanic skin reactions. In one of the experiments Lazarus and Alfert (1964) found that much less fear was aroused when a commentary was given to the students before they saw the distressing scenes. This preparatory communication informed them that the procedure would appear to be very painful but that it was not actually disturbing to the young boys who experienced it in this particular cultural setting.

In such experiments the effectiveness of the forewarnings might involve more than merely changing the subjects' psychological set. The very warning that one will soon be confronted by horrifying sights functions as a mild source of stress, touching off a low or moderate level of fear and motivating the person to seek new forms of reassurance that might reduce fear.

Stress Tolerance
in Surgical Patients

A series of studies on surgical patients (Janis, 1958) highlights the crucial importance of developing relevant reassurances for coping with stress. Since major surgery involves pain, a profound threat to bodily integrity, and a variety of frustrations, a great deal can be learned on the surgical wards of a general hospital about the processes of normal adjustment to severe stress.

The investigations were designed to help answer some basic questions pertinent to a general theory of stress tolerance: What is the relationship between the intensity of the patient's fear before surgery and the way he reacts to the pains and discomforts of the postoperative period? Is the popular belief true that the more anxious a person becomes when confronted with the threat of impending danger, the poorer he will adjust to the stress when he encounters it? Is a patient better able to cope with postoperative stress if he has been given realistic information beforehand on what is likely to happen?

With these questions in mind, the author carried out a study on the surgical ward of a large community hospital. As a first step, interviews were given to 23 typical patients before and after they underwent major surgery. Each of the patients was facing a highly dangerous and painful operation, such as removal of a lung or part of the stomach. Hospital records, including the physicians' and nurses' daily notes on each patient's behavior, were used to supplement the intensive interviews.

THREE DEGREES OF ANTICIPATORY FEAR

Three general patterns of emotional response were observed:

1. *High anticipatory fear.* These patients were constantly worried and jittery about suffering acute pain, being mutilated by the surgeon, or dying on the operating table. Openly admitting their *extreme feelings of vulnerability*, they tried to postpone the operation, were unable to sleep without sedation, and continually sought reassurances, even though these gave only momentary relief. After the operation they were *much more likely than others to be anxiety-ridden.* They had stormy emotional outbursts and shrank back in fright when the time came for routine postoperative treatments. Their excessive fears of bodily damage appeared to be based on a chronic sense of personal vulnerability.

2. *Moderate anticipatory fear.* These patients were occasionally worried and tense about specific features of the impending operation, such as the anesthesia. They asked for and received realistic information about what was going to happen to them from the hospital staff. They were able to be reassured, to engage in distracting activities, and to remain outwardly calm during most, though not every minute, of the day before the operation. They felt *somewhat vulnerable*, but their concerns were focused on realistic threats. After the operation they were *much less likely than others to display any emotional disturbance.* They consistently showed high morale and good cooperation with the hospital staff, even when asked to submit to uncomfortable drainage tubes, injections, and other disagreeable postoperative treatments.

3. *Low anticipatory fear.* These patients were constantly cheerful and optimistic about the impending operation. They denied feeling worried, slept well, and were able to read, listen to the radio, and socialize without any observable signs of emotional tension. They appeared to have unrealistic expectations of *almost complete invulnerability*. After the operation, however, they became acutely preoccupied with their vulnerability and were *more likely than others to display anger and resentment toward the staff.* Most of them complained bitterly about being mistreated and sometimes became so negativistic that they tried to refuse even routine postoperative treatments.

ANTICIPATORY FEAR AND POSTOPERATIVE ADJUSTMENT

The main hypotheses suggested by this series of intensive case studies were supported by a second study, a questionnaire survey conducted among more than 150 male college students who had recently undergone surgical operations. Several measures were used as indicators of each patient's postoperative adjustment. The measures included feelings of anger, complaints against the hospital staff, and current emotional disturbance when recalling the operation. Each of these indicators was examined in relation to what the patient had reported about his fear level before surgery. In each instance a curvilinear relation was found, as shown in Figure 6-2. The essential feature of this relation is the location of the peak of the curve somewhere in the middle of the fear continuum, rather than at one end or the other.

This outcome clearly contradicts the popular assumption that placid people—those who are least fearful about an impending ordeal—will prove to be less disturbed than others by subsequent stress. One of the main implications of these findings from the surgical studies is this: Whenever people are exposed to severe stress, those who had been most calm and most confident about their invulnerability at the outset will tend to become much more upset than those who had been part-time worriers beforehand.

Apparently, a moderate amount of anticipatory fear about realistic threats is necessary for the development of effective inner defenses for coping with subsequent danger and deprivation. The patients who were somewhat fearful before the operation mentally rehearsed various unpleasant occurrences they thought were in store for them. They were motivated to seek and take account of realistic information about the experiences they would be likely to undergo from the time they would awaken from the anesthesia to the end of the period of convalescence. Seldom caught by surprise, these patients felt relatively secure as events proceeded just about as they had expected. Not only were they highly responsive to authoritative reassurances from the hospital staff, but also they could reassure themselves at moments when their fears were strongly aroused. In their postoperative interviews

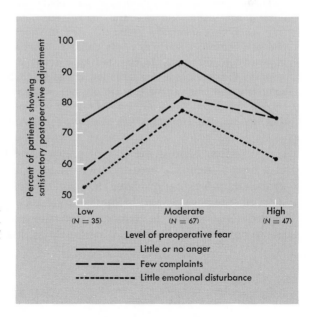

Figure 6-2   Relation between preoperative fear and postoperative adjustment. (Adapted from Janis, 1958, 1968b)

such patients frequently reported instances of self-reassurance; for example, "I knew there might be some bad pains, so when my side started to ache I told myself that this didn't mean anything had gone wrong."

Those who displayed excessively high anxiety before the operation appeared to benefit relatively little from preliminary mental rehearsals of the dangers. In the intensive interviews conducted both before and after the operation they revealed that they felt highly vulnerable to bodily damage and were unable to develop effective inner defenses for coping with the threat. Most of these patients were found to have a history of neurotic disorder, including past episodes of anxiety attacks. Their postoperative emotional reactions can be regarded as a continuation of their long-standing neuroses and not just a response to the external dangers of surgery.

The patients who were relatively free from anticipatory fears before the operation seem to have remained emotionally calm only by denying or minimizing the possibility of danger and suffering. As soon as the inescapable pains and harassments of normal recovery from a major surgical operation began to plague them, they could no longer maintain their expectations of personal invulnerability and became upset.

As an illustrative example, let us consider the reactions of a 21-year-old woman who had earlier undergone an appendectomy. At that time she had been given realistic information by her physician. Before the operation she had been moderately worried and occasionally asked the nurses for something to calm her nerves, but she showed excellent emotional adjustment throughout her convalescence. About two years later she came to the same hospital for another abdominal operation, the removal of her gall bladder. In the preoperative interview with the investigator she reported that her physician had assured her that "there's really nothing to it; it's a less serious operation than the previous one." This time she remained wholly unconcerned about the operation beforehand, apparently anticipating very little or no suffering. Afterward, experiencing the usual pains and deprivations following a gall bladder operation, she became markedly upset, negativistic, and resentful toward the nursing staff.

Chronic personality predispositions do not seem to account fully for this patient's reactions, since she was capable of showing an entirely different pattern of emotional response, as she had on a previous occasion. The patient's adjustment to the fear-producing situation appeared to be influenced mainly by the insufficient and misleading preparatory communications she was given before the second operation. Since nothing distressing was supposed to happen, she assumed that the hospital staff must be to blame for her postoperative suffering.

In some persons the lack of preoperative fear may be a manifestation of a type of neurotic predisposition that involves using extreme defenses of denial and projection of blame in order to ward off anxiety; probably nothing short of intensive psychotherapy could change this characteristic personality tendency. Most of the patients who showed little or no fear, however, seemed to be clinically normal personalities. Like the patient just described, they never received the type of realistic information that would induce them to face up to the distressing implications of the impending surgery. If they are given clear-cut information by a trustworthy authority, such persons are capable of modifying their defensive attitude and becoming appropriately worried about what they now realize is in store for them. But if they are not given adequate preparatory warnings about postoperative pain and suffering, they will cling to their expectations of personal invulnerability as long as possible, until suffering itself teaches them that they are not invulnerable after all.

The Role of Information

As we have just seen, the patients who did not worry beforehand appeared to be much less able to cope with the stresses of surgery than those who had been moderately worried. When the two types of patients were compared on a variety of background factors, the only significant difference turned out to be in the amount of advance information they had obtained. A careful check showed no significant differences as to type of operation, amount of pain, degree of incapacitation, type of anesthesia, or prognosis; nor were there differences between the groups as to age, education, sex, ethnic origin, or the number of prior hospitalizations.

But the two groups did differ on one important factor: the amount of prior information. Patients in the low-fear group had little idea of what to expect, whereas those in the moderate-fear group had been far better informed.

The survey of male surgery cases provided systematic evidence on this point. Illustrative results are shown in Figure 6-3, which compares preoperative fear and postoperative adjustment in the two groups of men who had undergone major surgical operations: 51 men who reported having been informed beforehand about the specific unpleasant experiences in store for them and 26 men who reported having been completely uninformed. The two groups differed in two ways: (1) the well-informed men were more likely to report that they had felt worried or fearful before the operation; and (2) the well-informed men were less likely to report that they had become angry or emotionally upset during the postoperative period of convalescence.

Since these correlational data are based on retrospective reports, they cannot be accepted as conclusive evidence. Nevertheless, they point in the same direction as the observations made in the intensive case studies, suggesting the following hypothesis: If no authoritative warning communications are given and if other circumstances are such that fear is not aroused beforehand, the normal person will lack the motivation to build up effective inner preparation before the onset of the danger, and he will thus have relatively low tolerance for stress when the crisis is actually at hand.

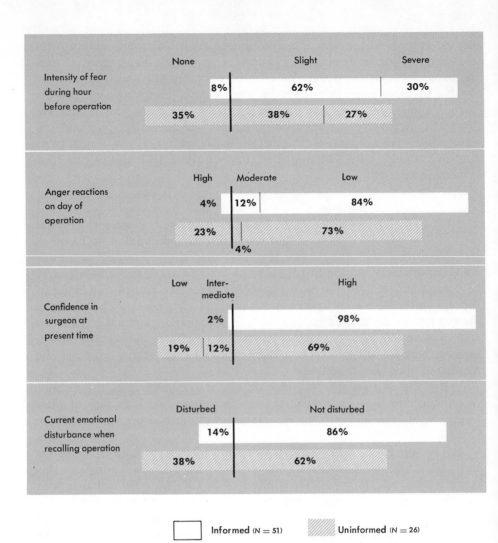

Figure 6-3 Preoperative fear and postoperative adjustment in informed and uninformed surgical patients. (Adapted from Janis, 1958, 1968b)

THE "WORK OF WORRYING"

The observations and findings from the surgery research suggested a concept of the "work of worrying," a theoretical construct that emphasizes the potentially positive value of anticipatory fear (Janis, 1958). The "work of worrying" might involve psychological processes similar to the "work of mourning" (discussed in Chapter 10), but there are likely to be some important differences. Freud postulated that the work of mourning begins *after* a blow, such as the death of a loved one, has struck; the work of worrying is assumed to begin *beforehand,* as soon as the individual becomes aware of signs of *impending danger* that might affect him personally.

**When the Work
of Worrying Is Incomplete**   Sometimes an endangered person remains quite unworried and then finds himself unexpectedly confronted with actual danger stimuli. This is evidently what happens to many surgical patients who are given no explicit warning information that induces them to face up to what is in store for them. They anticipate little or no pain or suffering until the severe stresses of the postoperative period are encountered. Then they are unable to reassure themselves and no longer trust the authorities whose protection they had expected. The patient's failure to worry about the operation in advance seems to set the stage for intense feelings of helplessness as well as resentment toward the members of the staff who, until the moment of crisis, had been counted on to take good care of them, just as good parents would do.

At moments of grave crisis most people are likely to blame the doctors or other authorities for unexpected stress. Many observations of surgical patients and of people exposed to comparable stress situations suggest the following sequence:

Absence of anticipatory fear
↓
Absence of mental rehearsal of the impending danger
↓
Feelings of helplessness when the danger materializes
↓
Increased expectations of vulnerability and disappointment in protective authorities
↓
Intense fear and anger

This sequence can be regarded as the major consequence of *failing to carry out the work of worrying.* Such failures are to be expected whenever a stressful event occurs under any of the following three conditions: (1) if the person is accustomed to suppressing anticipatory fear by means of denial defenses, by overoptimism, and by avoiding warnings that would stimulate the work of worrying; (2) if the stressful event is so sudden that it cannot be prepared for; and (3) if an adequate prior warning is not given, or if strong but false reassurances encourage the person to believe that he is invulnerable.

In order for the work of worrying to be complete, it seems that each source of stress must be anticipated and "worked through" in advance. This necessity is suggested by some outstanding instances of fright and rage observed in surgical patients who had displayed a moderate degree of anticipatory fear.

A young housewife, for example, had been somewhat worried before a lung operation and then, like most others in the moderately fearful group, showed excellent cooperation and little emotional disturbance throughout the postoperative period—except for one brief crisis she had not expected. She knew in advance about the acute incision pains and other unpleasant aspects of the postoperative recovery treatments, since she had undergone a similar operation once before and had asked her physician many pertinent questions about the impending second operation. But on the first postoperative day a physician entered her room and told her she would have to swallow a drainage tube, which she had never heard about before. She became extremely upset, could not relax sufficiently to cooperate, and finally begged the physician to take the tube away and let her alone. During an interview the following day she reported that she began to have extremely unfavorable thoughts about the physician at the time he made the unexpected demand; she suspected that he was withholding information about the seriousness of her condition, that he was unnecessarily imposing a hideous form of treatment on her, and that he was carrying out the treatment "so badly it was practically killing me." At no other time during the long and painful convalescence following the removal of her lung did she have any such doubts about this physician or any other member of the hospital staff; nor did she at any other time display any form of overt resistance. Evidently this was the one stressful event she had not anticipated and for which she had not, therefore, carried out the work of worrying.

This episode might help to explain why other patients who are caught by surprise display so much fright, anger, and uncooperative behavior. Those calm, seemingly stoic patients who do practically none of the work of worrying beforehand would be likely to encounter the same type of disruptive episode many times over during each day of their convalescence.

Preparatory Communications as a Prerequisite for Constructive Worrying: Some Further Evidence

Other studies on the psychological effects of surgical operations, severe illness, community disasters, and combat dangers provide many bits of evidence that are consistent with the foregoing hypotheses derived from the study of surgical patients (Grinker et al., 1946; Cobb, Clark, McGuire, & Howe, 1954; Cramond & Aberd, 1954; Titchner, Zweling, Gottschalk, Levine, Silver, Cowett, Cohen, & Colbertson, 1957; Janis & Leventhal, 1965). Like the surgery research, these studies suggest that if a normal person is given accurate prior warning of impending pain and discomfort, together with sufficient reassurances so that fear does not mount to a very high level, he will be less likely to develop acute emotional disturbances than a person who is not warned.

We know that there are exceptions, of course, such as neurotic personalities who are hypersensitive to any threat cues. But this does not preclude the possibility that moderately fear-arousing information about impending dangers and deprivations will function as a kind of emotional inoculation, enabling normal persons to increase their tolerance for stress by developing coping mechanisms and effective defenses. This process is called emotional inoculation because it may be analogous to what happens when antibodies are induced by injections of mildly virulent viruses.

If these inferences are correct, we should find that a group of surgical patients given appropriate preparatory communications before their operations will show better adjustment to the stresses of the postoperative period than an equivalent group of patients given no special preparatory communications other than the information ordinarily available to any hospitalized patient.

This prediction was tested and confirmed in a carefully controlled field experiment with 97 adult surgical patients at the Massachusetts General Hospital (Egbert, Battit, Welch, & Bartlett, 1964). The patients, hospitalized for elective abdominal operations, were assigned at random to the experimental and control groups. The two groups were equated on the basis of age, sex, type of operation, and so forth. On the night before his operation each patient was visited by the anesthetist, who gave him routine information about the operation—its time and duration, the nature of the anesthesia, and the fact that he would awaken in the recovery room. The patients in the control group were told nothing more. Those in the experimental group were given four additional types of information intended to help them carry out the work of worrying and to provide some useful coping devices: (1) a description of postoperative pain—where they would feel it, how intense it would be, how long it was likely to last; (2) explicit reassurance that postoperative pain is a normal consequence of an abdominal operation; (3) advice to relax their abdominal muscles in order to reduce the pain, along with special instructions about how to shift from one side to the other without tensing muscles in the sensitive area; and (4) assurance that they would be given pain-killing medication if they could not otherwise achieve a tolerable level of comfort. The information contained in the preparatory communication was repeated to the patients in the experimental group by the anesthetist when he visited them following the operation. Neither the surgeons nor the ward nurses were told about this experiment, to make sure that the experimental (informed) and the control (uninformed) patients would receive equivalent treatment in all other respects.

What difference did the special information make? During the 5 days just after surgery, patients in the experimental group required only half as much sedation as did patients in the control group. Comparisons of the total amounts of morphine administered to the two groups of patients during the postoperative period are shown by the curves in Figure 6-4. On the day of the operation (day zero in the figure) both groups required about the same amount of narcotics, but on each of the next 5 postoperative days the experimental group required significantly less than the control group.

The investigators tried to rule out the possibility that the well-informed patients might be suffering in silence in order to "please the doctor." They arranged to have the interviews conducted on the first and second postoperative days by an anesthetist whom the patients had never seen before. This independent observer was completely unaware of the type of treatment any of the patients had received, and his "blind" ratings indicated that the patients in the experimental group were in better emotional and physical condition than the controls. Further evidence of the more rapid improvement of the well-informed patients is provided by data on the duration of hospitalization. Completely unaware of the experiment, the surgeons sent the well-informed patients home an average of 2.7 days earlier than the patients who had not been given the special preparatory communication. In line with the earlier correlational findings shown in Figure 6-3, the investigators also noted that the uninformed controls made many complaints to the staff, such as "Why didn't you tell me it was going to be like this?" Such complaints were rare in the experimental group.

Thus, the experiment provides some systematic evidence concerning the positive value of advance information about postoperative stress. In this experiment the preoperative information was reiterated during the first few postoperative days, and this repetition may have contributed to the effectiveness of the preparatory communication. Conceivably, the postoperative reassurances alone might have been responsible for the outcome. There are other possible interpretations that will have to be checked in subsequent studies. It should be noted, however, that the results of this study show essentially the same positive outcome as two similar controlled ex-

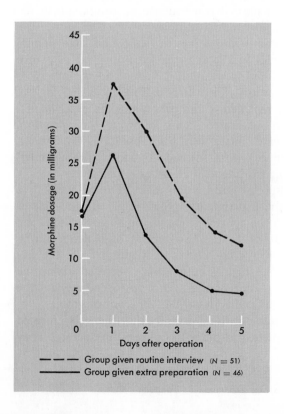

Figure 6-4 Postoperative narcotic treatment for two groups of surgical patients—those given a special preparatory communication and those given a routine interview. (Adapted from Egbert, Battit, Welch, & Bartlett, 1964)

periments on the effects of preparatory communications, one conducted by Moran (1963) with children on pediatric wards and the other by Miller and Treiger (1969) with dental patients before and after they had oral surgery. The studies reviewed in the last part of this chapter point to one general conclusion: A person will be better able to tolerate suffering and deprivation if he worries about it beforehand rather than remaining free from anticipatory fear by maintaining expectations of personal invulnerability. This generalization, if confirmed by research in other stress situations, might turn out to hold true for many nonphysical setbacks and losses such as career failures, marital discord, and bereavement. We shall return to this concept of the work of worrying when we discuss further the ways people can be helped to deal constructively with the major crisis in their lives (pages 196–98).

I'll not meddle with it [conscience]. . . . it makes a man a coward. A man cannot steal but it accuseth him; he cannot swear but it checks him; he cannot lie with his neighbor's wife but it detects him. It is a blushing shamefast spirit that mutinies in a man's bosom; it fills one full of obstacles. It made me once restore a purse of gold that I found; it beggars any man that keeps it. It is turned out of all towns and cities for a dangerous thing.

WILLIAM SHAKESPEARE. Richard III

CHAPTER 7
FEAR, SHAME, AND GUILT

Thus far we have been concerned mainly with the effects of powerful sources of stress, such as those a person encounters in a disaster or before and after surgery. In the next four chapters we shall examine the effects of other types of stressors, including warning signals and social communications that arouse distressing emotional states. This chapter discusses theoretical concepts, derived from recent research on human emotions, that help us to understand the causes and consequences of fear, shame, and guilt. In Chapter 8 we shall examine experimental evidence that shows how communications that arouse these emotions influence a person's mental efficiency, attitudes, decisions, and actions. Chapters 9 and 10 deal with the causes and consequences of two other distressing emotions that also arise under conditions of stress: anger and grief.

Three Types of Threat

The most frequent source of stress in everyday life is not danger itself but words that refer to threats or potential dangers. A news bulletin about an airplane crash can give you a jolt of anticipatory *fear* as you think of the flight you have just booked. A friend's comment about a social error you have made can convey an image of yourself as losing the high regard of your friends and can generate acute feelings of *shame*. A relative's report that a hospitalized member of the family is looking forward to seeing you can evoke a temporary sense of *guilt* as you realize that you have been planning to leave town without going to visit him at the hospital.

The same communication may evoke all three types of reaction simultaneously. For example, a young man who is informed by a physician that he has contracted a venereal infection becomes *fearful* about the threat of future damage to his body as he contemplates the possibility that the infection may prove to be resistant to medical treatment. He may also feel considerable social anxiety or *shame* as he anticipates the criticism and disapproval of certain friends and relatives who might find out about his disease. In addition, he is likely to feel some *guilt*—with keen awareness of the "blushing shamefast spirit that mutinies in a man's bosom," that "fills one full of obstacles"—as he tells himself that from now on he is going to live up to his own standards of personal hygiene. The three emotional reactions combine to create much more emotional disturbance than would one reaction alone.

The news bulletin, the friend's comment, the relative's report, the doctor's diagnosis—all these communications are the kind of stress stimuli that arouse distressing thoughts or anticipations of threats to our physical well-being, to our social acceptability, and to our self-esteem. Every day, dozens of communications stimulate in us states of fear, shame, or guilt. Some of these emotional reactions are only momentary twinges, while others persist as long as we continue to think that the threat cannot be disregarded. The normal person is able to tolerate these stresses: He is emotionally responsive to clear-cut signs of threat, but he can usually recover his emotional equanimity rapidly by making plans to avoid a recurrence of the source of fear, shame, or guilt.

When we analyze the behavioral consequences of these three types of emotion, we find that in some fundamental ways they are similar, although in a number of specific ways they are different. In the sections that follow we shall first concentrate on the similarities and then turn to the differences.

Anticipatory Emotions:
Key Concepts

Not surprisingly, we call an emotion "anticipatory" when it is a response to *anticipated* danger or loss. The strength of an anticipatory emotion—and its rise and fall—depends not on actual suffering at the present moment but on the course of the individual's *thinking* about the suffering that might be in store for him. Thus, the strength of an anticipatory emotion—whether it be fear, shame, or guilt—depends on the person's *cognitive appraisals* of threats to his future well-being. The strength of these emotions, in turn, determines the strength of the person's *motivation* to counteract the threat or to ward off distressing thoughts about it.

Anticipatory emotions have been getting a great deal of attention in recent studies of human emotion, particularly in the work of two outstanding research psychologists, Stanley Schachter and Richard Lazarus. We shall briefly review the key concepts introduced by these two investigators and their predecessors. Then we shall turn to some new theoretical formulations (Janis, in preparation) that may help to integrate the cognitive and motivational aspects of anticipatory emotions.

Schachter (1964) has formulated what he calls a "cognitive-physiological" theory of emotion. As its name indicates, it explains emotions by relating them to thought processes and bodily responses. A rough outline of Schachter's theory may be a useful preliminary to our discussion:

1. When a cue arouses emotional excitement in a person, his body undergoes marked physiological changes.

2. In an attempt to understand and label his bodily responses, the person is motivated to get information about what is happening to him.

3. Cognitions—thoughts and perceptions based on the person's past experience and on whatever new information he receives—"steer" the person into labeling the emotion as joy, fear, or whatever.

4. The label he gives to his state of emotional arousal determines how the person behaves.

Now let us examine the theory in more detail. Schachter has taken as his point of departure the well-known formulation by William James, who offered the first comprehensive psychological theory of emotion. Two assertions make up the core of James's conception (James, 1890, II, p. 449):

1. "Bodily changes follow directly the perception of the exciting fact."

2. "Our feeling of the same [bodily] changes as they occur *is* the emotion."

Schachter accepts the first proposition and postulates a general pattern of visceral reactions, resulting from the arousal of the autonomic nervous system, as a characteristic of all states of emotional arousal. But he substitutes for James's second proposition the assumption that the person's cognitions about his situation will have a "steering function," which determines how the person will label and respond to his stirred-up state. Schachter takes an extreme position on the question of how much influence these cognitions have on the person's feelings and emotional behavior. He assumes that the cognitions determine whether the person will label his state of physiological arousal as a positive emotion (such as euphoria) or a negative one (such as fear) and that the person will act accordingly.

Another of Schachter's key assumptions is more widely accepted: that whenever any environmental cue arouses emotional excitement (whether as an unconditioned or a conditioned stimulus), the person will become motivated to obtain information about what is happening to him, in an attempt to understand and label his bodily feelings. He postulates that

> a drive exists to evaluate, understand, and label ambiguous body states. . . . Given a new, strange, or ambiguous bodily state, pressures will act on the individual to decide exactly what it is that he feels and to decide how he will label these feelings [Schachter, 1964, pp. 76–77].

Schachter supports these assumptions with a number of his experiments. These show that the subjects' way of labeling their emotions is markedly influenced by the information they are given; the labels, in turn, determine whether they will act in an elated, aggressive, or frightened manner (Schachter & Singer, 1962; Schachter, 1964). In each of these experiments the subjects are given injections of a drug, such as epinephrine, that induces a bodily state of emotional arousal by activating the sympathetic nervous system. The experimenter then manipulates the subject's cognitions about what is happening—for example, by giving him information (or misinformation) about the expected effects of the injected drug or by allowing him to see the reactions of a fellow subject who supposedly has received the same injection but is actually a "stooge." Through these cognitive manipulations the experimenters have induced widely disparate forms of emotional behavior, ranging from euphoria to fear, as reactions to the same state of physiological arousal.

The steering function Schachter assigns to cognitive factors seems to be especially relevant to the psychology of fear and fits in well with some observations of how people react to ambiguous stressful events, when their emotions are highly aroused and they do not know the precise nature of the external threat. For example, during the initial phases of a flood disaster, when no one knows how to react, a single informative announcement to the residents of a threatened city can make the difference between a mass flight in terror and a relatively calm, stoical effort to maintain business as usual (Janis, 1962). Furthermore, Schachter's theory can readily account for research findings showing that when a person is confronted with a danger signal, his mood and actions depend upon the cognitions he has acquired from prior experience about the danger situation, such as whether the anticipated pains from an impending operation are likely to be mild or severe. It still remains an open question, however, whether Schachter's notions are valid concerning the extent to which the quality of an emotional state can be altered by informational inputs. Particularly questionable is his assumption that fear can be readily transformed into joy merely by inducing emotionally aroused people to change their verbal labels. Although some of his research suggests the possibility of just such a transformation, the evidence comes from experiments in which physiological arousal is artificially produced by a powerful drug. We simply do not yet know whether such arousal is comparable to emotional arousal in everyday life.

Lazarus's (1966) theoretical views, which resemble Schachter's in limited respects, are based on field studies as well as laboratory experiments. He agrees that emotional responses can be influenced to some extent by verbal information. We have already noted his experiment showing that prior communications dampened the emotional arousal evoked in young men exposed to a film depicting the mutilation of male genitals (see pages 94–95). Lazarus also agrees with Schachter that one of the consequences of emotional arousal is a heightened motivation to obtain relevant information, which makes the person more alert to internal and external cues. But Lazarus emphasizes some aspects of cognitive changes induced by emotional arousal that Schachter's theory does not deal with at all. Lazarus points out that when a person becomes apprehensive he will start thinking about the resources available for coping with the threat. As he does so, he will try to gain reassurance by planning a strategy that will effectively use those resources. Lazarus also assumes that when confronted with a threat, a person is likely to resort to defensive avoidances that ward off full awareness of the threat if he fails to gain emotional relief from his vigilant search for an effective means for coping with it. These important behavioral consequences of emotional arousal in response to external threats will be examined more fully in a later part of this chapter.

Motivating Effects of Anxiety

Long before these theoretical developments occurred, anticipatory emotional states had acquired an important place in the major psychological theories of human personality, including the classical psychoanalytical theory of Freud and his followers; the neo-Freudian theories of Erich Fromm, Karen Horney, and Harry Stack Sullivan; the phenomenological theories of Kurt Lewin and Carl Rogers; and the learning theories of John Dollard, Neal Miller, Hobart Mowrer, and B. F. Skinner. These theories differ in important details, but a few common themes run through their accounts of the behavioral consequences of "anxiety," which most theorists use as a generic term that includes fear, shame, and guilt.

There appears to be general agreement that whenever any form of anxiety is aroused, whether by a verbal communication or by a direct encounter with signs of danger, the person becomes motivated to get rid of the unpleasant emotional state. If the threat cues that arouse the distressing state do not promptly disappear as a result of environmental changes, the emotionally aroused person will exert his own efforts toward coping with them or will try to escape, either physically (for example, by turning off a distressing newscast) or psychologically (for example, by distracting himself by pleasant daydreams). Thus, when a person's attention is directed to a worrisome external danger or personal weakness, his mounting emotion will be followed by characteristic shifts in his fantasies, plans, and actions. These shifts may lead to constructive planning or to marshaling of defenses. In either case, the aim is to ward off external signs and internal anticipations that give rise to the distressing state.

As we saw in Chapter 3, the learning theorists attempt to specify the conditions under which habitual modes of avoidance will be acquired and maintained. They hold that any response will gain in habit-strength if it is immediately followed by escape from cues that arouse an unpleasant emotional state. This applies not only to physical avoidance actions but also to purely verbal responses, such as the reassuring beliefs and plans that a person thinks about when fear, shame, or guilt has been aroused by a verbal communication.

This learning-theory view was influenced to some extent by Freud's (1926) theory, which emphasized the powerful motivating effects of anxiety as a source of inhibitions and defenses. Freud recognized that fear, shame, and guilt share some important motivating effects, and he suggested that we should regard them as different forms of anxiety. He used the term "objective anxiety" to refer to fear produced by external dangers, "social anxiety" to refer to shame induced by anticipated ridicule or social criticism, and "conscience anxiety" to refer to guilt.

We had previously been talking about unpleasant emotions in general. But there are important differences between them that must be taken into account when we try to understand or predict human reactions to stress. As we just saw, Freud distinguished between fear, shame, and guilt on the basis of the different conditions that *cause* them; in fact, he assumed further that each of the three emotions could be traced to quite different formative experiences in childhood. But while concentrating on causes, Freud also recognized that fear, shame, and guilt give rise to somewhat *different motivating effects*. These behavioral consequences have been elaborated in more recent psychological analyses, which are concerned with the predictive value of distinguishing among unpleasant emotions. For example, in the case of a young man who has just been informed by his doctor that he has contracted a venereal disease, we would predict that the patient will seek different kinds of reassurances depending on whether the emotion that predominates is fear, shame, or guilt. When his fear of painful, destructive illness predominates, the patient is likely to seek reassurance from a medical authority, whose prescriptions and recommendations increase his hopes for a prompt and complete cure. When shame is predominant, the patient will seek reassurance that he still has the basic social acceptance of his friends and family. When guilt predominates, he will be preoccupied with the violation of his own standards of proper conduct and may reassure himself by acts of expiation that will restore his sense of self-esteem and moral worth. Accused by his own conscience, as Shakespeare observed, he may end up resolving never again to "lie with his neighbor's wife."

FREUD'S DISTINCTION
BETWEEN NORMAL AND NEUROTIC ANXIETY

Continuing our discussion of the differences among various unpleasant emotions, we turn next to one of Freud's most fundamental distinctions, which he regarded as vital for making sound diagnoses and prognoses in clinical work: *normal* versus *neurotic* anxiety. Normal, or objective, anxiety, according to Freud (1926), is always evoked by "real danger . . . which threatens from some external object [p. 151]." Neurotic anxiety involves intense emotional reactions and defensive efforts that are out of all proportion to the relatively mild or nonexistent threat to which the person attributes his distress. For example, if someone has just been warned by several friends that henceforth they will not put up with his disgusting antics, his intense emotional reaction of social anxiety, or shame, would be regarded as normal. But if a man knows that his friends have no cause to give him any such warning and yet cannot avoid intense feelings of shame from the train of thought engendered each time he hears someone else being criticized, his emotional reaction would be regarded as neurotic. Similarly, overreactions of guilt in response to very mild threats to self-esteem and excessive fear of bodily damage in response to mild threats of possible illness are classified as neurotic emotional reactions. The latter reactions are called *morbid fears* or *phobias* when a person greatly exaggerates relatively mild objective threats to which he attributes his emotional reaction; the term *free-floating anxiety* is used when the person feels overwhelmed with a nameless dread even though he realizes there is nothing to be afraid of. Such over-reactions, according to observations made in psychoanalytic interviews, are generally touched off by cues that arouse anticipations of inner dangers involving the possible loss of self-control over forbidden sexual or aggressive impulses that the person usually excludes from his consciousness. (See the discussion of neurotic anxiety and repression in Part II, pp. 371–76.) Freud emphasized that in order to diagnose neurotic anxiety we must observe and evaluate the person's reaction as "disproportionately . . . greater than in our judgment it ought to be. It is by this excess that the neurotic element stands revealed [Freud, 1926, p. 148]."

Most psychologists who specialize in personality research have followed Freud in distinguishing between normal and neurotic varieties of emotion, but many find it difficult to maintain the distinction in practice. Who is to say how much fear is "appropriate" or "proportionate" when a person is told by his doctor that he may have a serious disease? What constitutes "normal" arousal when a soldier is told he is going to be sent to a combat zone where casualty rates are high? Or when a student or job applicant is told that he will not be permitted to go on working in his chosen field if he obtains a low score on a qualifying examination? Granted that Freud's distinction is important, we must have additional criteria that will enable us to differentiate consistently between normal and neurotic reactions to external threats. What are the additional criteria that can be used for this purpose? A tentative answer to this question is given in an analysis of the concept of *reflective fear*.

Reflective Fear

The adjective "reflective" has been introduced (Janis, 1962) in order to avoid some of the misleading connotations of the synonymous term, "normal"; it also highlights two distinctive features of the nonneurotic type of emotional reaction, which are in line with Schachter's and Lazarus' emphasis on cognitive appraisal. First, the emotional state can be markedly influenced by thoughtful *reflection*; second, as a result of being mediated by conscious verbal responses, the emotion tends to increase or decrease in intensity as the signs of external threat increase or decrease. In other words, the emotion reflects like a mirror the environmental changes. Since the differences between reflective and neurotic fear have been most fully worked out, we shall examine and illustrate the outstanding characteristics of reflective fear and then consider briefly some equivalent characteristics of reflective shame and reflective guilt.

Four functional properties have been described that distinguish reflective from neurotic fear:

1. As a starting point, Freud's criterion of appropriateness is embodied in the foregoing statement about environmental changes being reflected by the emotional response. More precisely, a person's level of reflective fear is *highly responsive to environmental threat cues,* increasing with warnings that danger is becoming greater and decreasing with plausible reassurances that the danger is lessening. Neurotic fear, however, remains relatively unchanged even when the person is repeatedly informed that the danger is over or is given impressive assurances that there was no real danger in the first place. The main point is that the person's level of reflective fear will go up or down depending on the information he receives concerning his *personal vulnerability* to danger or deprivation, whether it involves anticipations of illness, career failure, or any other potential loss. Such anticipations are evoked in all of us whenever we are exposed to an effective warning communication. The content of these anticipations, as both Schachter and Lazarus have pointed out, is determined by the cultural norms and socializing experiences that shape our expectations of where, when, and how we could be affected by the given source of danger.

2. A second differentiating characteristic of reflective fear, which is also emphasized by Schachter and Lazarus, is an *increase in vigilance.* In Chapter 6 we discussed typical examples of increased vigilance in the surgical patients who became moderately fearful before the operation. They displayed a strong interest in obtaining information about what was in store for them, sometimes making it clear that they wanted to know the

truth even if the outlook was bad. Heightened vigilance affects actions as well as cognitive processes of perception, attention, and planning; that is, an individual becomes keyed up in a way that makes him more likely to execute precautionary actions.

3. Another important feature of reflective fear is that the person displays a strong *need to seek reassurances* in order to alleviate the unpleasant emotional state. Like heightened vigilance, this need leads to changes in both cognition and action. For example, when surgical patients are moderately fearful, they turn to the doctors and other staff members for reassurance and often focus their thoughts on the reassuring instructions given them for dealing with postoperative pain. If these attempts to gain reassurance do not succeed in alleviating intense fear, they may resort to an attitude of fatalism to bolster their sense of security. Sometimes the dominant attitude involves anticipations of total invulnerability. Such anticipations, referred to as "blanket reassurances," usually lead to a maladaptive lack of vigilance when the external danger is actually at hand. Nevertheless, these reactions are regarded as instances of reflective fear if we find that the person's unrealistic denial persists only as long as he lacks clear-cut information about the threat.

4. A fourth major characteristic of reflective fear is that its arousal increases the chances that the person will develop a new attitude constituting a compromise between vigilance and reassurance tendencies. If a compromise attitude does not develop, the conflict between the two tendencies may give rise to extreme vacillations. For example, a parachutist who is waiting for the jump signal feels at one moment that he must watch out for ever-present dangers; at the next moment he feels that he ought to relax and forget about the dangers because the jump will surely be safe. Sometimes one tendency almost completely dominates the other, and the person temporarily shows an indiscriminate all-or-none reaction. Either he becomes so excessively jittery (hypervigilant) that he can no longer distinguish very well between what is safe and what is dangerous, or he complacently ignores all signs of danger by clinging to the belief that even though others might be affected, he will remain immune to any harm (blanket reassurance). But when normal persons are repeatedly exposed to impressive warnings, they are likely to develop a *compromise attitude* that combines *discriminative vigilance* (seeking further information about the threat and remaining alert to signs of oncoming danger) with *discriminative reassurances* (expecting to be able to cope with it successfully, or to be helped by others, if the danger becomes extreme).

Outstanding examples of compromise attitudes are seen among victims of heart disease who learn to live with their illness. For instance, after his first heart attack a man may go about his business carrying in his pocket a clearly labeled bottle of the heart stimulant digitalis. A legible note in his wallet will state what dosage he should be given if he is ever found un-

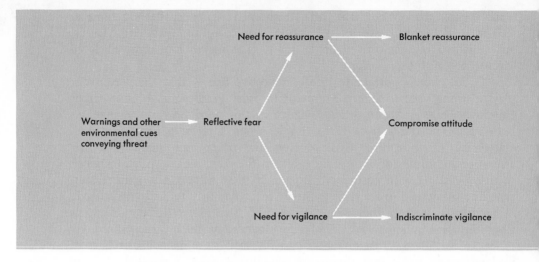

Figure 7-1 *Hypothetical consequences of the arousal of reflective fear.* (*Adapted from Janis, 1962*)

conscious. Such a person displays a mixed attitude: He remains *vigilant* to possible signs of a worsening of his illness and worries about being incapacitated or killed by it; yet he is able to gain some *reassurance* by adhering to a medical plan that could save his life in an emergency. Obviously, this type of attitude is likely to be much more adaptive than either indiscriminate vigilance or blanket reassurance.

Figure 7-1 diagrams the three alternative modes of adjustment to threat

Figure 7-2 *Normal psychological changes evoked by warnings or signs of external danger.* (*Adapted from Janis, 1962*)

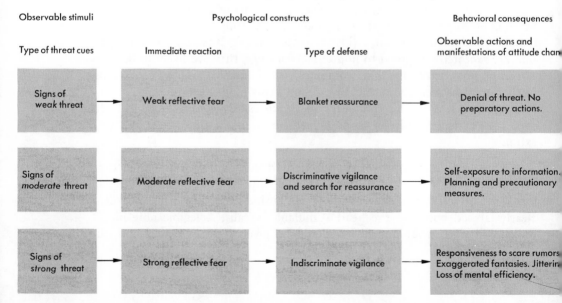

that have just been discussed. The three possible outcomes are shown on the right.

What determines which of the three types of reaction will be evoked by a warning? One important factor is the *magnitude of the threat*. The influence of this factor is represented in Figure 7-2, which shows the expected reactions of normal persons to weak, moderate, and strong threats. At one extreme, when the threat cues make the danger appear unlikely to materialize or so mild as to be unimportant, the person's reaction is likely to be dominated by an attitude of blanket reassurance, and his behavior will remain essentially unchanged. The behavioral consequences of this type of complacency are denial of the threat and absence of preparatory actions, as shown in the figure. At the other extreme, when very strong warnings are given, reflective fear mounts to a very high level, and indiscriminate vigilance is likely to become dominant. The resulting changes in attitudes and emotional symptoms (for example, responsiveness to scare rumors) are likely to be disruptive and maladaptive.

Between these extremes, when a person is warned about an impending danger that he judges to be potentially serious but manageable, he usually experiences a moderate degree of reflective fear, and the dominant attitude evoked is likely to combine discriminative vigilance with a search for reassurance. This sequence, depicted in the second row of Figure 7-2, represents what happens when a person successfully carries out the "work of worrying" (see pages 100–05). When a person engages in the work of worrying at a relatively moderate level of arousal, the compromise attitude he develops is usually sufficiently realistic so that he will remain vigilant and the reassurance component will not be undermined later on when he is confronted by the anticipated danger or deprivation. Thus, the resulting changes in attitude and action, as described in the figure, are much more likely to be adaptive if the danger materializes than are the changes resulting from very mild or very strong arousal.

Reflective Shame
and Reflective Guilt

The distinction between the *reflective* type of emotional response, which is influenced by new information, and the neurotic, relatively unmodifiable type probably can be applied to other negative emotions such as grief, guilt, and shame as well as fear (Janis & Leventhal, 1965, 1968). All reflective emotions can be regarded as an integral part of normal adjustment. Reflective guilt is one of the least understood of these emotions, although it seems subtly to pervade our daily feelings and actions.

At a cocktail party a young man is attracted by the appearance and charm of his friend's wife, and he wonders how he might make his sexual daydreams about her come true. But he halts this fantasy as soon as he becomes aware of a vague sense of self-disgust. The attractive wife, responding to the young man's attentive interest, may entertain similar fantasies until with a twinge of guilt she realizes that she is trying to punish her wayward husband by deliberately "turning on the charm" with his vulnerable friend. Meanwhile, an ambitious executive, standing nearby, cannot understand why he feels so dejected now that he has discovered that he can defeat his main rival for promotion simply by spreading the word about the man's drunken derogatory comments about the company. Next to him is a lively, talkative woman, who successfully maintains a cheerful front that masks her depressive feelings as she castigates herself for being a "bad mother" after having angrily decided to punish her indolent son. In each instance the guilt reaction sets in before any action is taken, at the mere contemplation of violating the person's internalized code of proper conduct.

Reflective guilt is usually aroused whenever we become aware of a personal wish, intention, or plan that we regard as morally wrong or unethical. Just as reflective fear leads us to increase our vigilance and to seek reassurance, reflective guilt leads us to watchful self-scrutiny and to special efforts to ward off the unpleasant emotion by renouncing the unacceptable action or turning to some other means of assuaging our conscience. Another similarity is the appropriateness of the reflective emotional reaction to the anticipated or actual transgression. For example, when we are about to take an action that could make others suffer, new information about the amount of potential suffering will markedly influence the intensity of our reflective guilt feelings. Neurotic guilt, like neurotic anxiety, is relatively unresponsive to new information. A skilled psychotherapist can readily diagnose the neurotic component in disproportionate guilt when a patient becomes profoundly dejected each time he merely indulges in a daydream about illicit sexual or hostile actions.

Erich Fromm, David Riesman, and other social critics concerned about the deteriorating moral standards of our times point to an insidious trend in modern society toward relying on "other-directedness" (avoidance of shame) rather than "inner-directedness" (avoidance of guilt) for the regulation of conduct. Among many men in powerful managerial and executive positions, deceit and exploitation are no longer shunned on the basis of the individual's moral code. The main deterrent is the threat of being caught, censured, and humiliated by others. Thus, shame rather than guilt governs many of their actions. As a point of contrast, Abraham Lincoln can be cited as an outstanding representative of the inner-directed type of leader that may have been more prevalent during the nineteenth century than at present. Lincoln expressed his readiness to ignore the threats that arouse social fears in order to ward off those that arouse guilt when he said to the critics of his administration in 1864: "I desire so to conduct the affairs of this administration that if at the end, when I come to lay down the reins of power, I have

"I'd *know*. That's who would *know!*"

Figure 7-3 Reflective guilt. (Drawing by F. B. Modell; Copyright © 1953 The New Yorker Magazine, Inc.)

lost every other friend on earth, I shall at least have one friend left, and that friend shall be down inside of me."

We know that one of the most effective reassurances for reducing reflective shame is the belief that "no one will ever know about it." That this belief does not alleviate reflective guilt is beautifully conveyed by the classic cartoon of the shipwrecked couple, shown here.

The crucial reassurances required for reducing reflective guilt are those that will restore the person's sense of his own moral worth. Among the most effective means are resolving to avoid future lapses, planning acts of expiation, and inflicting deprivations upon oneself as a form of self-punishment. Extreme examples are often seen among volunteers for dangerous jobs. Like the hero of Joseph Conrad's *Lord Jim*, some people devote themselves to making reparations for one or more guilt-laden action. In Conrad's story, the young naval officer abandons all his former career aspirations and devotes himself exclusively to self-sacrificing humanitarian acts among primitive people in a remote corner of the world. Conrad's account makes it clear that this fundamental change was a consequence of self-condemnation following an accident at sea, during which Jim panicked and impulsively abandoned his ship when he should have tried to save the passengers. Much more frequently, however, acts of reparation involve temporary changes, such as several weeks of increased attendance at church, self-imposed prohibitions against sexual gratification, or rejection of pleasurable leisure activities. Often these self-limitations have no apparent logical connection with the guilt-laden act, although upon close examination they may prove to be associatively linked in the transgressor's mind.

One means of warding off self-condemnation is the very hallmark of guilt: the urge to confess one's misbehavior to a parent-surrogate. This tendency and most other guilt-reducing efforts can best be understood as symbolic reenactments of the child's means of gaining the forgiveness of his parents during the formative stages of his moral development. (See the discussions of superego functioning in Part II, pp. 284–86, and of moral concepts in Part III, pp. 469–73.)

From the foregoing discussion it is apparent that reflective fear, reflective shame, and reflective guilt differ with regard to the type of vigilance that is evoked and the type of reassurance that is effective. Moreover, as we noted earlier in this chapter, the external cues that arouse and augment these emotions are also different: Reflective fear ensues when the external cues suggest the possibility of personal damage or deprivation; reflective shame is stimulated by anticipated or actual signs of social disapproval; reflective guilt arises when the threat cues point to an anticipated or actual deviation from one's personal standards of ethical conduct.

The details have not yet been worked out concerning the alternative consequences of different intensities of reflective shame and reflective guilt, but we would expect them to be roughly similar to those evoked by different intensities of reflective fear, as shown in Figure 7-2. For example, if reflective guilt is aroused to only a very slight degree, as when a person anticipates the remote possibility of committing a very minor lapse from his moral standards, one would probably ignore the threat, relying on a complacent attitude equivalent to blanket reassurance. The thought of wanting to commit a more serious misdeed that evokes a moderate degree of reflective guilt would motivate the person to avoid situations in which he might be tempted to carry out the misdeed. It might also induce a psychological process similar to the work of worrying. Thus, the person might start thinking about how he will be able to "live with himself" if he succumbs to the temptation, and he might thereby develop a compromise attitude that enables him to cope more effectively with a subsequent crisis involving a loss of self-esteem. A very strong threat of being on the verge of committing a crime, however, would arouse intense reflective guilt and would probably induce extreme efforts to avoid misconduct along with other reactions equivalent to indiscriminate vigilance. The resulting behavior might be disorganized and maladaptive, including symptoms resembling those listed in the bottom right-hand box in Figure 7-2. When intense reflective guilt cannot be promptly alleviated, the disorganized person may end up suffering irreversible losses as a consequence of maladaptive forms of self-punishment, such as ruining his chances for a successful career, becoming accident-prone, or—in the most extreme instance—committing suicide.

Some Unanswered Questions

A similar analysis might eventually be worked out for other types of reflective emotions and may help to clarify some of the current confusions concerning a number of overlapping emotional states, some of which probably should be distinguished from guilt because of their distinctive behavioral consequences. These include a variety of vaguely defined affective states that are variously designated as existential shame, feelings of inferiority, fear of losing love, humiliation, and despondency. The foregoing discussion of reflective emotions provides a framework for further inquiry into the nature of such affective reactions and enables sharper research questions to be posed concerning what happens to the person when one type of affective state is aroused rather than another.

Consider, for example, Helen Lynd's (1958) perceptive account of an affective pattern that arises when a person realizes he has made a *faux pas* or reveals a personal weakness that unexpectedly stirs up acute feelings of self-disparagement, even though the precipitating incident may be felt to be quite trivial. Lynd examines this reaction in the context of the search for identity ("Who am I?"), which Erik Erikson (1950) has so vividly highlighted as the strategic personal problem of our time, just as sexuality was in Freud's time. As Lynd describes it, the affect centers upon "a wound to one's self-esteem, a painful feeling or sense of degradation excited in the consciousness of having done something unworthy of one's previous idea of one's own excellence . . . in a situation that incurs the scorn or contempt of others [Lynd, 1958, p. 24]." Recognizing that many psychoanalysts treat this type of affect as a form of guilt, she argues that it should be given a distinctive label because of its unique qualities. (The term she selects is "shame," in the sense of being privately ashamed of oneself for failing to live up to one's expectations or ideals. But this label does not help to reduce the present jumble of contradictory terminology, because "shame" is frequently used by other writers in the way we have been using it in this chapter, to designate the response to threats of social disapproval, contempt, or humiliation.) Regardless of what one calls it, the traumatic type of shame reaction Lynd describes, and the ensuing changes in attitude and motivation, seem quite different from the common forms of shame and guilt we have been discussing. The person condemns himself and cannot be reassured by signs that he is once again accepted and admired by his friends. Nor can he counteract the shameful event by acts of repentance or expiation, which generally alleviate feelings of guilt. Rather, he is burdened with an almost hopeless feeling that the only way he can ever restore the damaged image of himself is to change his personality in some fundamental way—and somewhat dispiritedly he may set out to try to do so.

By making use of the conceptual schema presented in the discussion of reflective fear, we can take Lynd's description of unmitigated shame as the starting point for a number of researchable questions: Does this affective state have the functional properties of a reflective emotion? Or is it generally a disproportionate emotional reaction like neurotic anxiety, always remaining quite impervious to reassuring environmental events and information? Is the traumatic type of shame reaction the extreme point on a continuum of varying degrees of arousal, so that we can detect milder intensities of the same affect? Is this type of affect aroused as an anticipatory emotion, when a person is merely thinking about the possibility that he might behave in a shameful way in the future? If so, does such arousal lead to some form of vigilant activity and a search for reassurance? Are there any characteristic differences in the modes of response that ensue from weak, moderate, and strong intensities of this emotional state, comparable to those shown in Figure 7-2 for different intensities of reflective fear?

In seeking the answers to these questions, we may succeed in making new discoveries about some important aspects of the emotional life of normal persons and perhaps increase our understanding of the conditions under which anyone will strive to undergo a fundamental change in personality.

While much remains to be discovered about the distinctive consequences of different reflective emotions, psychological research also must continue the quest for understanding the basic functional properties that may characterize all reflective emotions. One major question that arises from the earlier discussion of Figure 7-2 pertains to the effects of varying intensities of emotional arousal. For every reflective emotion, we might expect to find a curvilinear relation—like that shown by the findings from the surgery research (Figure 6-2, page 97)—whenever we investigate how well a person is able to function at low, middle, and high levels of emotional arousal. This type of curvilinear relation between adaptive behavior and emotional arousal follows directly from the sequences shown in Figure 7-2. According to the figure, a moderate degree of emotional arousal leads to the most adaptive reactions (discriminative vigilance and reassurance), in contrast to weak arousal (which leads to inadequate vigilance for taking protective action) and very strong arousal (which leads to excessive vigilance and disorganized thought and action). Therefore we expect the peak of the curve to fall somewhere in the middle range of emotional arousal. In the next chapter we shall have a great deal more to say about this curvilinear relation, as we examine evidence concerning the ways people respond to warnings that try to motivate them to take precautionary actions by arousing reflective emotional reactions of fear, shame, or guilt.

"Why can't you tell him?" I said.

"Because he wouldn't believe me. This here is the kind of a thing you—a man has got to know his—himself. He has got to learn it out of his own hard dread and skeer. Because what somebody else just tells you, you jest half believe, unless it was something you already wanted to hear. . . . But something you don't want to hear is something you had done already made up your mind against, whether you knowed—knew it or not; and now you can even insulate against having to believe it by resisting or maybe even getting even with that-ere scoundrel that meddled in and told you."

"So he wouldn't hear you because he wouldn't believe it because it is something he don't want to be true. Is that it?"

"That's right," Ratliff said. "So I got to wait. I got to wait for him to learn it his—himself, the hard way, the sure way, the only sure way. Then he will believe it, enough anyhow to be afraid."

WILLIAM FAULKNER. The Town

CHAPTER 8
WHEN WARNINGS FAIL

I n this chapter we shall see what the evidence from systematic research tells us about the way warning communications influence the average person's behavior. Most of the evidence comes from research on the effects of emotional appeals in persuasive messages that attempt to induce people to adopt precautionary measures in order to avert the predicted dangers. Contrary to popular belief, this type of research gives very little information about how communicators can devise emotional appeals to persuade people. What we mainly learn is why warnings so often fail.

The Curvilinear Relation
Between Arousal and Performance

One of the main implications of the analysis of reflective fear in the preceding chapter is that we should not expect to find a linear relation between the probability of adaptive compromise defenses and the level of fear evoked by a warning or any other threat stimulus. (See Figure 7-2, page

116.) Specifically, the following three propositions should characterize the main changes in behavior that will occur as the intensity of reflective fear increases:

1. At very low levels of fear arousal, the probability that a person will be responsive to a warning is very low because of the tendency to remain indifferent and inattentive to mild threat cues.

2. As fear increases to a moderate level, the arousal of vigilance will motivate attention to and learning of the information contained in a warning, which, in turn, may lead the person to form an adaptive type of compromise attitude.

3. When fear mounts to a high level, the probability that the person will develop an adaptive compromise attitude in response to a warning will again decrease because of the disruptive effects of strong emotional stimulation, which results in indiscriminate vigilance, poor judgment, and extreme forms of defensive avoidance.

If all three hypotheses prove to be correct, the relation between intensity of fear and adequacy of performance will form a curve that is known as an "inverted U-shaped function" because it looks something like the letter U upside down. We noted earlier that an outstanding feature of this type of relation is that the peak of the curve—which represents the best possible performance that a person can achieve—will occur at some moderate level of arousal, rather than at either very low or very high levels of arousal.

The inverted U-shaped function has long been familiar to experimental psychologists who have investigated changes in performance produced by varying degrees of motivational arousal in animals and in man (see Levitt, 1967). At low levels of motivation the organism remains inattentive to the environment; at moderate levels the organism's attention increases and its performance becomes more efficient; at very high levels the organism is in a state of very strong drive, which is disruptive and leads to ineffective performance. The inverted-U relation has also appeared in the research reports of physiological psychologists, whose discoveries suggest that the cerebral cortex in men and animals may function more effectively when the amount of stimulation reaching the cortex from the ascending reticular system is at a moderate level, rather than at a very high or a very low level (Schlosberg, 1954; Hebb, 1955; Malmo, 1958).

These neurophysiological considerations make it plausible to assume that the relation between emotional arousal and adaptive reactions to threat cues will prove to be curvilinear. But it still remains an open question whether the inverted U-shaped function does in fact accurately describe the way in which the average person will react to warnings that arouse varying intensities of fear, shame, or guilt. Before trying to answer this question, however, we must take account of the various ways that people resist being influenced by warnings to such an extent that they fail to take adequate precautions.

Resistance to Warnings
and Persuasion

During recent decades, many self-styled experts in propaganda, advertising, and public relations have been promoting an image of modern man as highly gullible. Time and again we are told that the mass media have great power to arouse strong emotions and to manipulate, exploit, or brainwash the public. But evidence from systematic research indicates that mass communications seldom produce marked changes in social attitudes or actions (see Klapper, 1960; Janis & Smith, 1965). The slight effects that are produced by the press, films, radio, and television are usually limited to reinforcing preexisting beliefs and values. Campaigns that try to use emotional appeals and other motivating devices to persuade people to adopt public health precautions, to modify their social stereotypes, or to support a new political ideology generally mobilize powerful resistances in the public. The average man seldom heeds warnings or changes his mind unless he learns, as Faulkner put it, "out of his own hard dread and skeer."

Most of the research on the effects of persuasive communications has concentrated on factors that help to decrease psychological resistances when the recipients are exposed to the communications. Being exposed requires not only adequate physical transmission of the message but also *audience attention*. The audience will not be attentive if the communication is too distressing or is perceived as deviating markedly from group norms. If a persuasive communication that contains a warning evokes enough attention to surmount the "exposure" hurdle, its ability to produce results will then depend upon: (1) *comprehension*, that is, the extent to which the audience grasps the intended meanings and (2) *acceptance* of the communicator's recommendations, that is, the degree to which the audience is convinced by the arguments and responsive to the motivational appeals.

In an analysis of factors that influence attention, comprehension, and acceptance of persuasive messages, Hovland, Janis, and Kelley (1953) point out that the experimental findings indicate three types of resistances (interfering expectations) that decrease the degree of acceptance: (1) expectations of being manipulated by the communicator (for example, being made into a "sucker" by an untrustworthy source who has ulterior financial or political motives); (2) expectations of being wrong (for example, making incorrect judgments about the consequences of a recommended course of action or overlooking the opposing evidence that could affect one's decision); and (3) expectations of social disapproval (for example, from the local community or from a primary group whose norms do not agree with the communicator's recommendations).

When people are given warnings, all three types of resistance are likely to be evoked and to interfere with the success of the warnings. But, of course, warnings do not always fail. Obviously, people sometimes do pay attention to warning messages, modify their outlook, and take precautionary actions. The key question is: Under what conditions are resistances sufficiently overcome so that these results can occur?

In discussing this question we shall draw on evidence from field studies and laboratory experiments, some of which bears directly on the curvilinear relation between arousal and performance. We shall begin with findings that deal with the ways warnings about realistic threats affect mental efficiency— and hence affect attention and comprehension, the first two requirements for a successful communication. Then we shall turn to the third requirement, acceptance. We shall examine a series of experiments on emotion-arousing communications that help us understand the conditions under which warnings will evoke high or low resistance to acceptance of recommended protective actions.

Emotional Arousal
and Mental Efficiency

We have observed that indiscriminate vigilance accompanies states of intense fear and detrimentally affects a person's perceptions, judgments, and decisions. A prime example is the "trigger-happy" soldier who thinks he sees a sniper in the shadows and impulsively shoots at it, thereby giving away his own location to the enemy. Such instances suggest that when fear mounts to a very high level, the individual's mental efficiency is markedly impaired. A number of experimental investigations support this conclusion. They show that whenever a person's fear is strongly aroused, he will display a marked narrowing of attention, poorer judgment, and more errors on intellectual tasks (Beier, 1951; Osler, 1954; Easterbrooks, 1959; Berkun, Bialek, Kern, & Yagi, 1962).

Most of the experiments involve giving students one or more communications that describe plausible-sounding threats. For example, high school students are told that they are failing their courses, that their achievement scores on a college entrance examination are relatively low, or that their responses to a projective personality test reveal signs of serious personality weaknesses. During the period when the subjects presumably believe the psychologist's communications, they are given tests of their mental efficiency. Their performance during the period of emotional arousal is then compared with a control condition, when little or no stress is generated.

The subjects are of course carefully dehoaxed afterward. Nevertheless, this type of experimental manipulation of human beings poses the same ethical questions mentioned in the discussion of traumatic conditioning experiments (pages 41–44). Moreover, when these experiments are repeated, the results are not always the same the second time, probably because of differences in the degree to which the subjects were suspicious about being hoaxed.

If we limit ourselves to those experiments that appear to have been most successful in convincing the subjects that they were facing a genuine threat, we find fairly consistent evidence that a relatively high intensity of unpleasant emotion produces temporary impairment in cognitive functioning. For example, Osler (1954) arranged to have high school students told individually to report to the principal because a serious complaint had been made about their behavior, a summons that aroused fear combined with some degree of shame and guilt. Shortly after being given this information but before his appointment with the principal, each student was tested on various intellectual tasks. Compared with subjects in a control (nonarousal) condition, the subjects in the emotionally aroused state showed markedly poorer test performance. This study and a number of others support the conclusion that a temporary loss of perceptual and cognitive efficiency occurs when a person is exposed to communications that arouse anticipation of punishment.

That this conclusion applies to extreme threats of physical danger is indicated by an extraordinary series of field experiments carried out with Army recruits under conditions that parallel those of natural disasters (Berkun et al., 1962). In order to study the physiological as well as psychological changes induced by extreme emergencies, the investigators carefully rigged several "accidents" in such a way that the subjects would regard themselves as seriously threatened.

In one of the experiments a group of soldiers on a routine flight suddenly felt the aircraft lurch violently, and they could see that one of the propellers had stopped turning. Over the intercom they were informed that serious malfunctions required an emergency landing, and this warning was powerfully reinforced as the passengers heard a pilot-to-tower conversation about the impending crash landing. The experimenters arranged for fire trucks and ambulances to converge on the airstrip in apparent readiness for a crash; the emergency vehicles were placed so that they could be clearly seen by the subjects in the stricken aircraft as it circled above the airfield. Furthermore, the pilot announced that malfunctioning of the landing gear would make it necessary to ditch in the nearby ocean, which everyone aboard realized meant only a small chance for survival.

At this point a crew member administered tests of memory and mental efficiency, disguised as emergency data forms that would allegedly furnish proof to insurance companies that all emergency precautions had been properly followed. The subjects were informed that these papers would be jettisoned in a waterproof container and would survive the crash, even though the plane and all of its occupants might end up at the bottom of the ocean.

After sufficient time elapsed for these paper-and-pencil tests to be completed under the hectic conditions of preparing for a crash landing, the aircraft was safely landed. The investigators then obtained biochemical measures in order to study the men's physiological recovery from the stressful episode. All subjects were thoroughly informed about the purpose of the experiment; they were also interviewed to make sure that no one had seen through the deception, to calm any residual fears about the situation, and to repeat the explanation that they were put through the stressful experience in order to obtain research data needed for military planning. (Not all psychologists agree, however, that the military and scientific purposes of the research, however important they may be, make such a harassing experiment ethically justifiable.)

A routine flight procedure was followed for a control group of soldiers at the same air base, and no emergency was communicated to them at any time. At the equivalent time during the flight, just before landing, the control subjects filled out the same forms as the experimental subjects. In addition, a nonflying control group was given the same forms in a classroom situation.

As expected, the data from this study consistently showed that a very high degree of fear was aroused by the stressful condition. The men in the experimental group frequently spoke about having worried about being killed or injured and reported on mood questionnaires that they felt a high degree of emotional tension. In addition, a high degree of physiological arousal of the type that accompanies severe stress was revealed by a marked rise in the steroid level in urine samples collected from the men after the plane landed.

In their performance on the mental efficiency tests embedded in the emergency data forms the stressed subjects showed significantly more errors and markedly poorer retention of information than the controls, indicating a temporary impairment in cognitive functioning. Parallel results showing a marked decrease in mental efficiency were also obtained from other investigations in this series, including one in which intense guilt was aroused by making each subject feel responsible for an accident that seriously injured a fellow soldier.

From the accumulated evidence, it appears to be quite certain that at very high levels of emotional tension, the average person's perceptual and cognitive functions will be severely impaired. It still remains an open question, however, whether a relatively mild threat that arouses a slight or moderate degree of fear has any consistent effect on intellectual efficiency; the evidence is fragmentary and inconsistent. We must await further experimentation in which the level of fear arousal is systematically varied from very low to very high to find out whether the relation between cognitive efficiency and level of reflective fear turns out to form an inverted U-shaped curve.

Emotional Appeals
and Attitude Change

According to our analysis of modes of adjustment to threat, presented in the preceding chapter, the average person is most likely to become both vigilant and responsive to reassuring recommendations about how to cope with an anticipated danger when his level of reflective fear is aroused to a moderate degree, rather than when it is either very low or very high. We would expect this outcome for all types of warning communications—warnings of oncoming natural disasters; warnings by business or labor leaders that their stockholders or members must accept new policies in order to avoid financial losses; warnings in scare propaganda by politicians that the nation will collapse "if you don't support me"; warnings by public health authorities that dramatize the hazards of air pollution and other conditions requiring precautionary action; and so forth.

PREDICTIONS BASED
ON THE INVERTED U–SHAPED CURVE

If the theoretical assumptions in the preceding chapter are correct, we should find that audience acceptance of a communicator's main recommendations will not uniformly increase as the amount of fear stimulated by a warning increases. Rather, the relation should vary in the more complicated way depicted by the inverted U-shaped curve, as shown in Figure 8-1.

Beginning at the left-hand end of the curve, we see that an increasing level of fear brings a corresponding rise in audience acceptance of the communicator's recommendations. But no matter how cleverly the message is presented to overcome resistance and no matter how credible the source is, the curve eventually reaches a point of maximum stress tolerance. This is the point at which a person's fear is so intense that he is on the verge of "going to pieces." That is, if his extreme fear increases beyond this point of maximum stress tolerance, the person will become so jittery, so mentally inefficient, and so distraught that he can no longer attend to or comprehend adequately any communication. Nor will he be able to function well enough to execute any plan for protective action. Thus, at the extreme right of the curve there is a decline in acceptance, which results from inefficient thinking and extreme defensive efforts that interfere with judicious planning and action.

Later we shall see that there are good reasons for believing that the highest point of the curve (the optimal level of fear arousal for inducing maximum acceptance) will seldom be at the point of maximum stress

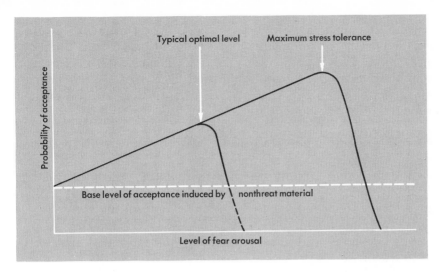

Figure 8-1 Hypothetical curvilinear relation between the level of fear arousal elicited by a warning communication and the degree of acceptance of the recommended attitude or decision. (Adapted from Janis, 1967)

tolerance; typically, it will fall somewhere in the middle range of fear arousal (as shown by the arrow labeled "typical optimal level" in the figure). We shall postpone further discussion of this point until we have examined some of the experimental evidence bearing on the relation between level of fear arousal and acceptance. For the present we shall merely note two main predictions that can be readily tested by controlled experiments if our assumptions are correct. The main assumption in question is that when people are given emotionally arousing communications, the optimal level of arousal usually falls well below the maximum level of stress tolerance. The two predictions are that when a communicator uses an emotional appeal or warning to tell about the dangerous consequences of failing to adopt his recommendations, (1) the average person will be *more* likely to accept the recommendations if his fear is aroused to a slight or moderate degree than if no emotional appeal or warning is used (represented in Figure 8-1 by the dashed "base level" line, which shows the amount of acceptance when fear is not aroused at all); and (2) the average person will be *less* likely to accept the recommendations if his fear is aroused to a high degree than if it is aroused to a more moderate degree.

DIMINISHING RETURNS
FROM STRONG EMOTIONAL AROUSAL

To what extent does evidence bear out the inverted U-shaped relation shown in Figure 8-1? When we compare the amount of attitude change produced by persuasive communications that vary in the amount of emotionally arousing material presented, can we confirm the two predictions? A number of communication experiments have been carefully designed, most of which bear on the second prediction concerning the diminishing returns from strong fear arousal. Unfortunately, the findings are not completely consistent. However, the research does increase our understanding of why fear-arousing warnings are likely to fail and provides suggestive leads about the conditions under which resistance might be overcome sufficiently to induce acceptance of the communicator's recommendations for warding off dangerous consequences.

We shall start off with evidence from several experiments indicating that strong threat appeals induce much stronger psychological resistances than do milder emotional appeals. In these experiments the strong fear-arousing communication motivated people to avoid thinking about the threat and to revert to blanket reassurances after an initial flurry of emotional excitement.

The First Experiment on Mild Versus Strong Fear Appeals

The diminishing returns of fear-arousing appeals in persuasive communications was initially suggested by a series of experiments involving public health recommendations (Janis & Feshbach, 1953, 1954; Janis & Terwilliger, 1962). The first experiment by Janis and Feshbach (1953) compared the effectiveness of three different forms of an illustrated lecture on dental hygiene, which were presented to different high school classrooms. An additional classroom of control subjects was given a similar communication on an irrelevant topic.

The strong fear-appeal version emphasized the threat of pain and disease; the recorded lecture was accompanied by color slides showing festering gums, decayed teeth, and other body damage that can result from neglect. The moderate-appeal version was presented in a more factual manner; the accompanying slides depicted milder tooth decay. The minimal-appeal version merely alluded to the unpleasant consequences of improper dental hygiene; the slides showed diagrams, rather than photographs, of tooth decay. The three versions, which contained essentially the same basic information and the same reassuring recommendations about how to avoid having decayed teeth and gum disease, were assigned at random to equivalent groups of students.

One week later, attitude changes were assessed. As shown in Figure 8-2, the minimal-appeal version was most successful in producing adherence to the communicator's recommendations, according to the students' descriptions of how and when they were brushing their teeth. The strong-appeal version failed to produce any significant change in dental hygiene practices, although it aroused more interest and vigilance. The same outcome was observed when all the subjects were exposed to a counterpropaganda statement a week after the original presentation. Students in the group exposed to the minimal-appeal version were least likely to be impressed by the new communication, which belittled the need for precautionary measures. They were much more inclined than the students who had received the strong-fear version to continue to accept the original warning communication and its reassuring recommendations. But what about differences in the personalities of the subjects? Would a relatively anxious person respond differently to the fear-arousing communication from someone whose anxiety level was normally low? One week before the original communication was given, the subjects all took a personality inventory test that indicated each one's usual anxiety level. The investigators later compared the reactions to the communication of subjects who had scored high or low on the inventory (Janis & Feshbach, 1954). The diminished acceptance of the strong fear-arousing communication was found only among the students whose personality test scores indicated that they were chronically most anxious. The results of this analysis fit the predicted inverted U-shaped curve nicely, as shown in Figure 8-3.

As expected, the level of arousal was found to depend on two factors: (1) the strength of the fear-appeal material presented and (2) the individual's anxiety predisposition (as assessed by high versus low scores on the personality test). Using these two factors in combination—and ignoring the middle range of both—we get four subgroups: the high-anxiety students exposed to the minimal-appeal message, the low-anxiety students exposed to the minimal-appeal message, the high-anxiety students exposed to the strong-appeal message, and the low-anxiety students exposed to the strong-appeal message. The level of fear arousal that was reached by each of these four subgroups immediately following their exposure to the dental hygiene communication is shown on the horizontal base line of Figure 8-3. (The numbers 5 to 8 represent a fairly wide range on the fear-arousal scale.) It will be noted that the two extreme groups, characterized by very low

Figure 8-2 Effect of fear appeals in an illustrated talk on dental hygiene practices. (Based on data from Janis & Feshbach, 1953)

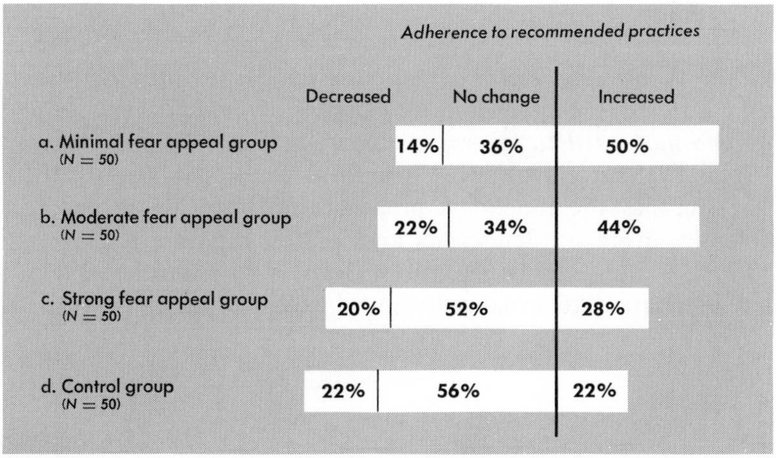

	Adherence to recommended practices		
	Decreased	No change	Increased
a. Minimal fear appeal group (N = 50)	14%	36%	50%
b. Moderate fear appeal group (N = 50)	22%	34%	44%
c. Strong fear appeal group (N = 50)	20%	52%	28%
d. Control group (N = 50)	22%	56%	22%

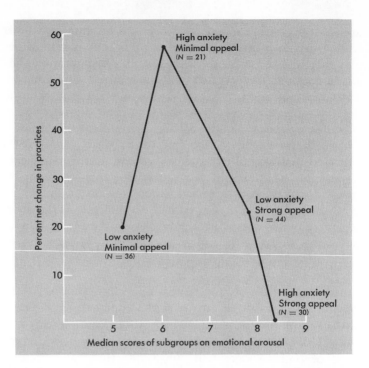

Figure 8-3   Observed relation between level of emotional arousal following the dental hygiene communication and acceptance of the recommendations. (Based on data from Janis & Feshbach, 1954)

and very high fear arousal, showed less acceptance of the recommended dental hygiene practices than did a group characterized by an intermediate level of arousal.

The Defensive
Avoidance Hypothesis   On the basis of the various findings from the initial experiment, including subjects' written responses to open-ended questions that indicated their objections and doubts (resistances), the investigators formulated the following general hypothesis: *When fear is strongly aroused but is not fully relieved by the reassuring statements contained in a persuasive communication, the audience will become motivated to ignore, minimize, or deny the importance of the threat.* This "defensive avoidance" hypothesis is compatible with the postulate that fear has the functional properties of a drive (see pages 49–53). The defensive avoidance tendencies arising after exposure to a strong emotion-arousing warning can be regarded as learned responses based on a newly acquired motivation to avoid subsequent exposures to those internal and

external cues, such as statements about the threat of gum disease, that were present at the time the fear was aroused.

In the sphere of human communication, the key theoretical assumption could be formulated as follows: If rehearsal of the reassuring statements contained in a communication fails to alleviate the emotional tension elicited by the use of a fear appeal, the audience will be motivated to continue trying out other (symbolic or overt) responses until one occurs which succeeds in reducing fear to a tolerable level. Thus, a strong fear appeal which is intended to motivate the audience to take account of a realistic threat of danger could have the paradoxical effect of motivating the audience to ignore the threat or to adopt "magical," "wishful" or other types of reassuring beliefs that are antithetical to the communicator's intentions. Moreover, according to the same theoretical assumption, when a communication produces a high degree of persistent fear, the audience will be motivated to engage in overt escape activities, some of which (e.g., acceptance of counterpropaganda) may prove to be incompatible with the protective actions recommended by the communicator. Unintended effects of this kind can be regarded as spontaneous "defensive" reactions which are motivated by residual emotional tension [Janis & Feshbach, 1954, p. 90].

The defensive avoidance hypothesis does *not* predict that the stronger of two fear-arousing appeals will always be less successful in producing acceptance of the recommended precautionary measures. Rather, the hypothesis predicts that the higher the intensity of induced fear, the higher will be the degree of resistance. And the higher resistance will tend to reduce acceptance if it is not outweighed by other motivating effects of arousal that can facilitate acceptance.

Several other experiments support the defensive avoidance hypothesis by bearing out the prediction that strong threat appeals will evoke more resistance than will milder appeals. The communications used in these experiments dealt with a number of different types of threat—the danger of developing lung cancer from cigarette smoking (Janis & Terwilliger, 1962); the threat of mental illness (Nunnally & Bobren, 1959); and the prospect of mass annihilation by nuclear weapons (Haefner, 1956). The last experiment used antiwar communications with varying intensities of guilt-arousing appeals as well as of fear-arousing appeals. One guilt-arousing version, for example, emphasized the enormous number of people killed by the American A-bomb attacks on Hiroshima and Nagasaki and the suffering unexpectedly inflicted upon Japanese fishermen exposed to radioactive fallout from American H-bomb tests in the Pacific. The high-guilt version of the communication evoked more resistance in American students and produced less attitude change than did the low-guilt version.

Similar findings concerning the effects of the arousal of guilt were found by Zemach (1966) in a field experiment carried out under the auspices of a civil rights organization that was trying to recruit male college students as volunteers. A recruitment pamphlet that used a medium level of guilt-arousing material and did not personalize the blame was found to be more effective in inducing the students to sign up for civil rights activities and in modifying related attitudes than either the version that aroused very high guilt or the one that aroused low guilt (see Figure 8-4).

WHEN HIGH–THREAT VERSIONS ARE EFFECTIVE

The findings from the communication experiments just cited are consistent with the curvilinear relation predicted from the theoretical analysis of reflective fear. But the issue is complicated by the findings from several other similar experiments that show more attitude change from a high-threat version than from a low-threat version.

One complicating consideration is that attitude changes depend partly on the *interest value* of a persuasive communication, and this is likely to be greater when a strong threat is presented in a provocative way. Whenever a low-threat version is regarded by the audience as boring and uninteresting, the inclusion of a high-threat type of appeal can facilitate acceptance of the recommendations; under these circumstances, the negative

Figure 8-4 Observed relation between level of guilt aroused in college men by civil rights pamphlet and participation in civil rights activity. (Adapted from Zemach, 1966)

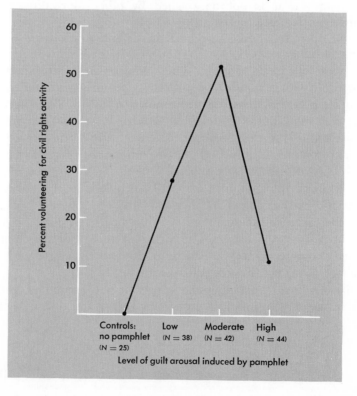

effects of defensive avoidance, if any, may be offset by an increase in interest value.

This conclusion is suggested by a communication experiment carried out by Berkowitz and Cottingham (1960), in which students were given illustrated talks urging them to use automobile safety belts. Among students who seldom rode in automobiles, more acceptance was elicited by a version of the communication that played up the risk of serious injury in an automobile accident than by a version containing the same arguments without discussing the threat at all after merely alluding to it. But in this experiment it appears likely that the so-called high-threat version aroused only a very low degree of fear, comparable to the minimal-threat appeal in the Janis and Feshbach experiment. If this interpretation is correct, the findings would support the prediction stated earlier, that when an emotional appeal is included that arouses a slight or moderate degree of fear, it will increase the audience's vigilance and will heighten their motivation for reassurance in a way that facilitates acceptance of precautionary recommendations.

In terms of Figure 8-1, which shows the inverted U-shaped function, this interpretation would assume that both versions of the communication would arouse levels of fear near the low end of the curve (at the extreme left). For most subjects the stronger of the two threat appeals would presumably still fall well within the moderate range of fear arousal (that is, to the left of the point labeled "typical optimal level"). A few other experiments can be interpreted in the same way (Leventhal, Singer, & Jones, 1965; Leventhal & Singer, 1966).

Sometimes even a strong appeal containing a great deal of threat material may fail to evoke any awareness of personal vulnerability and hence may fail to produce any significant degree of fear arousal at all. Moreover, a strong emotional reaction momentarily evoked by a disturbing image (for example, a picture of a mutilated corpse) may never become linked in any way with the particular threats and recommendations the communicator is talking about. Therefore, the question of how much fear is aroused by a given threat appeal cannot be answered merely by analyzing the communication stimuli; the answer must come from empirical observations of the recipients during or immediately after exposure to the threatening communication.

Niles (1964) provides evidence suggesting that under certain conditions fairly strong arousal can be more effective in modifying attitudes than mild arousal, despite whatever resistances are provoked. In this experiment, which compared different versions of a film on smoking and lung cancer, the strong fear-arousing version included a technicolor sequence showing the surgical removal of a young man's cancerous lung, with all the gory details. This version proved to be more successful in inducing college students to resolve to give up smoking than a milder threat version that included the same case study of a lung cancer patient but left out the surgical sequence. However, further analysis showed that this difference held only for a par-

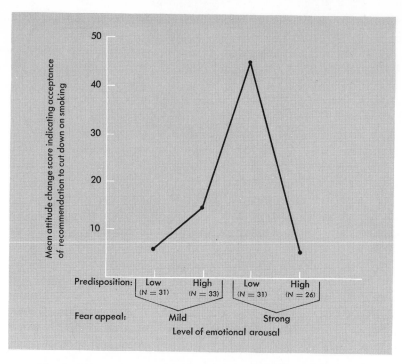

*Figure 8-5   Observed relation between level of emotional arousal
evoked by an antismoking communication and acceptance of the
recommendation. (Based on data from Niles, 1964)*

ticular subgroup of students who initially reported feeling relatively invulnerable to the threat and not for the subgroup that initially felt vulnerable and was located at the highest level on the arousal continuum. The
results of this predispositional measure were used to compare students who
would be expected to react with high, intermediate, and low levels of fear
arousal, in an analysis comparable to the one shown in Figure 8-3 (see Janis,
1967, pp. 201–02). The resulting curve obtained from Niles's data, shown in
Figure 8-5, again turned out to have a peak of acceptance at an intermediate
level of arousal, thus conforming to the inverted U-shaped function.

The Optimal Level
of Fear Arousal

We cannot expect to formulate any definitive rule specifying
the intensity of fear arousal that is most likely to induce people to accept
precautionary recommendations. Some of the experiments we have discussed
show more psychological resistance and less acceptance of the communicator's recommendations when strong fear appeals are used in warning mes-

sages than when milder ones are used. Others point to the facilitating effects of fear arousal. Attitude changes evidently depend on the relative weight of facilitating responses and interfering responses (resistances), both of which are likely to be evoked whenever a communication arouses fear. Consequently, we must expect the optimal level of fear arousal to vary for different types of warning communications and personalities.

The *optimal* level of fear is the level at which the facilitating effects of fear arousal are most powerful and outweigh the interfering effects. Above that level interference takes the upper hand, and acceptance of the communicator's recommendations will decrease. Figure 8-6, which is an expanded version of Figure 8-1, represents a three-dimensional model made up of a family of inverted U-shaped curves, each of which is similar to the ones shown by the data in Figures 8-3, 8-4, and 8-5. In the diagram of the three-dimensional model, each curve has a different peak (labeled A, B, C, D, and so on). The optimal level can fall at any of these peaks—anywhere along the fear continuum—depending on the trustworthiness of the communicator, the cogency of the recommended precautions, and any other factors that influence the relative strength of facilitating and interfering responses.

Suppose, for example, that we were to see in a newspaper advertisement or television commercial a persuasive presentation of the need for taking a new type of vitamin pill every day in order to prevent serious deficiency diseases. The optimal level of emotional arousal might be near the low end of the arousal dimension, as shown by curve A in Figure 8-6. But if the very same message were from a highly trusted source in a non-

Figure 8-6   A three-dimensional model for analyzing effects of emotional appeals. (From Janis, 1967)

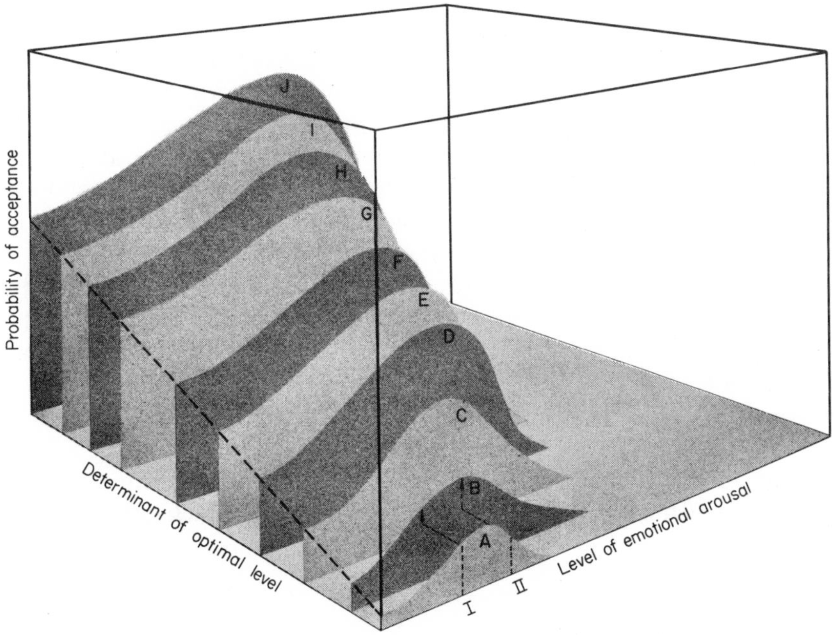

commercial medium (for example, in comments made by a well-known medical scientist on an educational television program), the optimal level of emotional arousal might be at point D in the figure, which is at a higher level on the fear dimension and results in a higher degree of acceptance. In this example the trustworthiness of the message, which is a typical determinant of resistance to a persuasive message, can be regarded as a third dimension that must be taken into account in order to predict the probability of acceptance. In Figure 8-6 this third dimension is labeled "determinant of optimal level." It represents any factor that helps to overcome the resistances discussed at the beginning of this chapter (pages 126–27), thus resulting in a shift in the optimal level toward the maximum level of stress tolerance. The trustworthiness of the message is one such factor. There are probably many others, some of which we do not know much about.

Whenever people are exposed to communications that stimulate strong fear, shame, or guilt, they are likely to scrutinize the communicator's arguments carefully, looking for obvious loopholes that can serve as excuses to dismiss the communicator's statements about threats that would require costly or unpleasant protective actions. These reactions make for a low optimal level of arousal. By introducing impressive new arguments that eliminate obvious loopholes and break down the usual efforts to evade distressing ideas, the communicator may be able to prevent the recipient from denying the personal relevance of what is being said and thus raise the optimal level. Similarly, the optimal level would tend to be higher when the communicator's recommendation is known to be a feasible, well-tested solution to the threat than when it has all the earmarks of guesswork that might not avert the danger.

Any such factor that determines whether the optimal level of arousal will be high or low can be conceptualized as falling on the third dimension of the model in Figure 8-6. This model enables us to reconcile some of the findings of past experiments that seemed to contradict each other (see Janis, 1967, pp. 203–15). It also allows us to state more precisely the expected outcomes when new experiments are designed to investigate interacting factors that determine the optimal level of arousal. We notice in the figure that if the optimal level were to be shifted from point A to point C, the probability of acceptance should be more than doubled; a shift from A to D should produce about five times as much acceptance; and a shift from A to J (the maximum level of stress tolerance) should produce more than ten times as much acceptance in the same audience. These statements illustrate an important type of prediction that follows from the three-dimensional model. Such predictions pertain to any communication device that helps people tolerate a high level of fear arousal without becoming so defensive and resistant that they reject the message.

One such device is suggested by recent experiments with a new psychological procedure called *emotional role playing*, which stimulates empathic reactions and seems to break through the individual's usual defensive façade in a way that makes him more receptive than before to precautionary recommendations made by public health authorities.

Experiments
on Emotional Role Playing

In biographies of eminent men and women we read of how a single dangerous event in adult life can have a profound effect on the individual's personality. Attitudes, values, and life goals may be suddenly transformed following a dramatic near-miss incident, as illustrated in the biblical account of St. Paul's conversion after being struck by lightning on the road to Damascus. At a more mundane level, similar transformations occur when green combat troops, disaster rescue workers, and medical personnel undergo their "baptism of fire." Research evidence on this point comes from a field experiment on fear and attitude change by DeWolfe and Governale (1964). Student nurses were given a 6-week assignment on the tuberculosis wards of a hospital, where they were in constant danger of being infected. The nurses showed a marked transformation in their attitudes: Most of them accepted wholeheartedly the precautions recommended by their nursing-school instructors, in contrast to a control group of comparable nurses who were given no direct experience on tuberculosis wards. At first the nurses exposed to the actual threat of the disease became extremely apprehensive about becoming infected. Gradually they developed some degree of emotional adaptation, but they nevertheless continued to follow, more rigorously than before, the safety precautions they were taught.

In contrast to verbal warnings, such direct confrontation with the threat seems to be extraordinarily effective in breaking through the defensive façade that normally enables a person to remain complacent. No longer able to feel invulnerable, the person replaces blanket reassurances by compromise defenses that embody a new attitude of healthy respect for the danger. Here again we are reminded of what the character in Faulkner's novel says in the passage quoted at the beginning of this chapter: When someone gives you a useful warning, you can "insulate against having to believe it by resisting or maybe even getting even with that-ere scoundrel that meddled in and told you"; a person has "got to learn it out of his own hard dread and skeer."

Are there any psychological devices that a counselor might use to achieve comparable breakthrough effects by preventing resistances from becoming dominant? An affirmative answer is strongly suggested by several recent experiments that show the effectiveness of a special role-playing device.

In the first in a series of experiments Janis and Mann (1965) set up a psycho-dramatic situation in which the subject plays the role of a medical patient who is suffering from the harmful consequences of cigarette smoking. Twenty-six young women served as subjects. All of them were smokers who were unaware of the purpose of the study and had expressed no intention to try to cut down on their smoking. In the experimental group each subject was asked to play the role of a patient in a doctor's office and to express her spontaneous personal responses, just as if she were really talking with a doctor. The experimenter played the role of the physician. He wore a white coat and used impressive props, such as an X-ray of the lungs, in order to make the situation as realistic as possible. Altogether, five different scenes were acted out. In one of them the "physician" pointed out the X-ray indications of a malignant mass in the patient's lung as he gave her the bad news that diagnostic tests indicate that she has lung cancer (see Figure 8-7). In the last scene the cancer victim was asked to think over the bad news while the physician arranged for her hospitalization for lung surgery and to soliloquize about her error in not having stopped smoking before it was too late. This role-playing procedure proved to be an extraordinarily disquieting experience for the subjects, generating plenty of "dread and skeer."

Half the subjects were assigned at random to a control condition in which they were exposed to the same information without engaging in any active role playing. These subjects listened to a tape recording of an authentic session that had been conducted with one of the subjects in the experimental group.

The results showed that emotional role playing had a marked influence

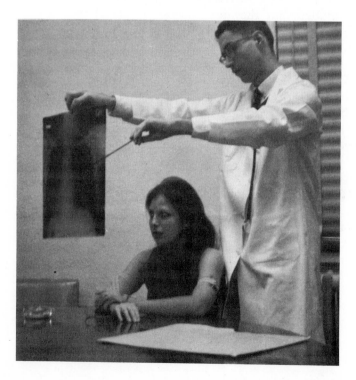

Figure 8-7 The subject ("patient") and experimenter ("doctor") in an emotional role-playing experiment dealing with smoking and lung cancer.

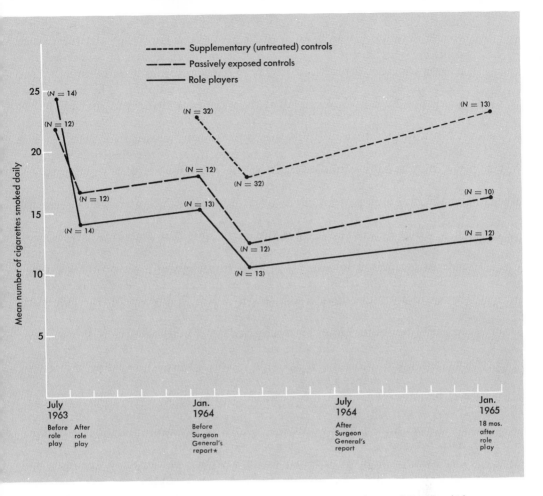

* This refers to the famous U.S. Public Health Service report on *Smoking and Health*, which was issued on January 11, 1964, and which states that "cigarette smoking contributes substantially to mortality from certain specific diseases and to the over-all death rate." The document is best known as the Surgeon General's report.

Figure 8-8 Long-term effects of emotional role playing on cigarette smoking. (Adapted from Mann & Janis, 1968)

on smoking habits and attitudes (see Figure 8-8). This technique of emotional role playing seems to provide unusual empathic experiences similar to those that occasionally lead to spectacular "conversions" among physicians, relatives, and friends of cancer victims. There are numerous indications that the high level of fear and vigilance aroused by the realistic quality of the experimental procedures may be a major factor in the increased antismoking attitudes and the changes reported in smoking habits.

In a follow-up study Mann and Janis (1968) found that over an 18-

month period the emotional role players continued to report a significantly greater decrease in the number of cigarettes consumed than did the passive controls. This outcome indicates that a one-hour session of emotional role playing can have a profound long-term effect on smokers who initially have no intention of cutting down on cigarette consumption. The results, diagramed in Figure 8-8, suggest that the significant changes in smoking habits may persist for years. Additional research (Mann, 1967; Nowlis & Janis, 1968) indicates that for both men and women, whether young or middle-aged, this type of emotional role playing is more effective than cognitive role playing (for example, enacting the role of a debater arguing against smoking). Mann also found that the amount of attitude change produced by this fear-arousing procedure increases when subjects are given increased opportunity to verbalize their own ideas while playing the role.

All these studies support the conclusion that emotional role playing can function as a device for "repackaging" information that is already available to the person in a way that leads to a change in his or her self-image of personal vulnerability to health hazards. In terms of the hypothetical curves in the three-dimensional model shown in Figure 8-6, the emotional role-playing procedure evidently reduces psychological resistances sufficiently so that the optimal level of arousal for the average subject is shifted from a relatively low level when the threat information is presented without any emotional role playing (for example, optimal level A); enacting the role of a victim may enable a person to tolerate a much higher level of fear without becoming predominantly defensive (for example, optimal level C or D). Thus, a person might be more likely to change his attitudes under these conditions than if he were shown a movie, a television program, or an illustrated magazine article that passively exposed him to the same fear-arousing information. Here we have an example of one of the most important implications of the theoretical analysis developed in the preceding chapter and elaborated in the discussion of Figure 8-6: Acceptance of a reassuring recommendation markedly increases whenever the communicator says or does something that reduces the person's resistances so as to overcome the psychological interferences. When these interferences no longer outweigh the facilitating effects of fear, shame, or guilt, warnings will no longer fail. The experiments on emotional role playing make this implication appear to be plausible. The findings encourage us to continue the search for psychological devices that can break through the average person's defensive façade. A long-standing attitude of complacency might thus be transformed into one of vigilance and heightened receptivity to precautionary recommendations that can function as effective forms of reassurance.

"You—you—don't know?" *mimicking my drawling manner of speech.* "What do you know? . . . The idea of you being a pilot—you! Why, you don't know enough to pilot a cow down a lane."

Oh, but his wrath was up! He was a nervous man, and he shuffled from one side of his [steamboat's] wheel to the other as if the floor was hot. He would boil a while to himself, and then overflow and scald me again.

"Look here! What do you suppose I told you the names of those points for?"

I tremblingly considered a moment, and then the devil of temptation provoked me to say:

"Well—to—to—be entertaining, I thought."

This was a red rag to the bull. He raged and stormed so (he was crossing the river at the time) that I judged it made him blind, because he ran over the steering oar of a trading scow. Of course the traders sent up a volley of red-hot profanity. Never was a man so grateful as Mr. Bixby was: because he was brim full, and here were subjects who would talk back. He threw open a window, thrust his head out, and such an irruption followed as I never had heard before. The fainter and farther away the scowmen's curses drifted, the higher Mr. Bixby lifted his voice and the weightier his adjectives grew. When he closed the window he was empty. You could have drawn a seine through his system and not caught curses enough to disturb your mother with. Presently he said to me in the gentlest way:

"My boy, you must get a little memorandum book; and every time I tell you a thing, put it down right away. There's only one way to be a pilot, and that is to get this entire river by heart. You have to know it just like A B C."

MARK TWAIN. Life on the Mississippi

CHAPTER 9
FRUSTRATION AND AGGRESSION

Is the pilot in Mark Twain's autobiographical account mad? Mad he certainly is in the slang sense of the term. But when a man's actions are so irrational, shouldn't we wonder whether he is suffering from "madness" in the ominous sense of the term? The question is only a fleeting one as we read the passage, because we recognize that the irrationalities displayed by the steamboat pilot on this occasion are all too human. We know perfectly well that each of us sometimes behaves in a similarly mad fashion—although our cursing is not always so noisy and may never, even during our most profane moments, reach such heights of virtuosity. We are all quite capable of boiling inside and of venting our fury on any fool who hasn't sense enough to avoid being an innocent bystander.

Our recognition of the normal human qualities of the pilot's reactions is a tacit acknowledgment of the reflective nature of his emotional state: For all his seemingly uncontrolled impulsiveness, he is nevertheless strongly influenced by information from the environment. We cannot make this judgment, of course, without knowing the context of the man's explosive outburst. If we merely saw the pilot run over the scow's oar and then castigate the poor boatmen who were his victims, we might indeed surmise that he is a madman—or is at least suffering from a neurotic character disorder—since he seems unable to tolerate even a very minor frustration, when he is himself at fault, without becoming uncontrollably enraged.

However, the passage preceding the one quoted makes it clear that the pilot's negligence and fury came after a buildup of frustrations. It began when the young apprentice incorrectly answered a few simple questions. A more thorough display of his ignorance followed, leading the conscientious instructor to believe that his painstaking efforts had been wasted. The pilot could not allow himself to discharge fully his intense anger on an inept youngster, but he could unhesitatingly do so when some grown men suddenly presented themselves as convenient scapegoats. After venting his boiling rage on the substitute target the instructor could return in a reasonably calm way to the distressing business of trying to educate the boy. Thus we place his behavior within the normal range, knowing that almost anyone exposed to provocative frustrations will display just such a buildup and displacement of anger.

In this chapter we shall examine some of the key psychological concepts embedded in this simple example: the *cumulative* effects of a series of frustrations, the *inhibition* of overt aggression toward an inappropriate target, the *displacement* of aggression to strangers or out-groups, and the *cathartic effects* of aggressive release that may enable the provoked person to deal more rationally with whatever obstacles are thwarting him.

Aggression is broadly defined as any action intended to harm or punish another person. In everyday social life such actions are generally the result of an aroused emotional state of anger. Occasionally, when anger is extremely intense, aggression takes the form of overt attack, destruction, or sadistic violence. Much more often it involves purely symbolic forms of hostility.

In the present discussion we shall not deal at all with the "cold" forms of aggression, such as those inflicted on local villagers in a war-torn country by the members of a military planning group who make a coolly calculated decision to use the destructive weapons at their disposal. Rather, we shall be concerned with the more heated acts of aggression in everyday life, acts that anyone is likely to carry out when he becomes "hot under the collar" after being frustrated.

The wide range of events that are designated as "frustrations" will soon become apparent as we discuss the conditions under which a frustration is most likely to instigate aggression. Most of the examples of frustration discussed in this chapter are less extreme instances of stress than those we have been considering up to this point, but they are nevertheless effective in provoking anger.

Reflective Anger

In Chapter 7 an important distinction was made between a *reflective* emotional reaction, which is capable of being modified by new information, and an *internally aroused* emotional reaction, which stems from a chronic neurotic predisposition and remains relatively unchanged despite new information. Reflective anger, like reflective fear, shame, and guilt, can be regarded as an integral part of normal behavior. Some outspoken social critics, such as Erich Fromm, argue that many of the worst features of modern society are perpetuated because most people complacently ignore the cues that should arouse their emotions.

> A man sits in front of a bad television program and does not know he is bored; he reads of Vietcong casualties in the newspaper and does not recall the teachings of religion; he learns of the dangers of nuclear holocaust and does not feel fear; he joins the rat race of commerce, where personal worth is measured in terms of market values, and is not aware of his anxiety. . . .
>
> If enough people become aware of their shared misery, they will probably effect changes. Anger may often be less sick than adjustment [Fromm, 1966, p. 30].

If our anger is aroused to some degree, as Fromm suggests, our actions may become more adaptive than if it is not aroused at all. When we speak of adaptive actions in this context, we mean circumventing or eliminating whatever obstacles are constantly producing frustration. A successful act of aggression may be physical, as when an angry crowd of demonstrators vigorously pushes its way through the surrounding guards who are spraying them with tear gas; or it may be purely verbal, as when a group of indignant employees asserts its rights to a person in authority in a way that induces him to withdraw his unwarranted demands.

When someone's anger mounts from a moderate level to a very high level, however, his actions tend to become somewhat disorganized, impulsive, and diffuse, resembling the indiscriminate vigilant behavior that occurs at very high levels of fear.

When this happens, aggressive action is no longer likely to be adaptive; it is regarded as maladaptive if the action results in more rather than less suffering either for the aggressor or for other persons with whom he is affiliated. A furious adult, like Mark Twain's steamboat pilot, may lash out indiscriminately against any person or physical object in his way, performing clumsily and showing poor judgment. All too often the enraged person succeeds only in antagonizing his frustrators and causing them to retaliate, thus increasing rather than decreasing his frustration. But even in the midst of seemingly uncontrollable rage the infuriated person is still capable of testing reality: His violence can be calmed by impressive conciliatory information conveyed by environmental events or by other people, if the information contradicts his initial beliefs about who is frustrating him and for what reason. Thus, the reflective character of anger is clearly revealed whenever we see a marked decrease in aggression immediately following receipt of new information about the removal of frustrating obstacles.

The Relation
Between Frustration and Aggression

Normal anger, as has just been suggested, is characterized by at least a rough proportionality between the severity of the provocative frustrations perceived by the frustrated person and the intensity of his aggressive reaction. This point was first made by Freud, who postulated that aggression would always occur as a basic reaction to frustrating circumstances— whenever pleasure-seeking or pain-avoiding behavior was blocked (1917). This postulate is widely accepted today by most psychologists; moreover, it is firmly established by both clinical and experimental evidence. (Few psychologists, however, accept Freud's later assumptions about the nature of aggression, such as his notion that aggression is primarily a self-destructive drive—a "death instinct"—that is diverted from the self to others when released by external frustrations.)

The Freudian postulate that frustration leads to aggression was called to the attention of experimental psychologists in 1939 in a seminal book that is now a classic of psychology: *Frustration and Aggression* by John Dollard, Leonard Doob, Neal Miller, O. Hobart Mowrer, and Robert Sears. In their elaborations on the frustration-aggression theme, these authors (known as the Yale group) showed how the methods and concepts of experimental psychology could be applied in studying highly significant aspects of the human personality, including the arousal, expression, and control of interpersonal hostility. The core of their theory can be summarized in two testable propositions based on Freud's postulate: (1) Whenever any organism is frustrated, it will always show an increased tendency to respond aggressively; and (2) whenever an organism is responding aggressively, the behavior is always a consequence of frustration.

This reformulation stimulated considerable critical comment and controversy, much of which turned merely on definitions of terms. For example, one eminent psychoanalyst, Karl Menninger, called the second proposition "nonsensical," because "anyone who has had his toe stepped on, which is certainly not a frustration, knows how inadequate such a formula is [1942, p. 295]." Having had their own toes stepped on in this figurative way, members of the Yale group were led to redefine "frustration" to include painful stimulation resulting from the apparent negligence of others. Unfortunately, there are other semantic issues that have still not been fully settled, as we shall see shortly.

Another widespread criticism takes as its point of departure the evidence of withdrawal, regressive fantasies, primitivization, and other nonaggressive reactions to frustration (see pages 150–53). Neal Miller answered this type of criticism by pointing out that much of the controversy stemmed from the ambiguous wording of the key propositions, which had been mis-understood as implying that frustration has no consequences other than aggression. He argued that the meaning should be understood as follows: "Frustration produces instigations to a number of different types of responses, one of which is an instigation to some form of aggression [Miller, 1941, p. 338]." This new formulation proved to be more acceptable and could be substantiated by systematic evidence.

The form of the frustration-aggression hypothesis that is most widely accepted today asserts that the probability of any person's displaying aggressive behavior is a function of the severity of the frustrations to which he is currently exposed, which is determined by three factors (in addition to the predispositions that influence the person's capacity to tolerate frustration):

1. the strength of whatever motive for reaching a goal is currently aroused and being blocked;
2. the degree of interference or blocking of the goal-directed response;
3. the number of motives currently or recently aroused that are being blocked.

When Is a Person Frustrated?
When Is He Aggressive?

The foregoing propositions linking frustration with aggression may at first sound consonant with our own daily observations and with common sense. However, they pose a number of definitional issues that must be solved before we can use these key concepts to predict how anyone will respond when he is thwarted.

We shall illustrate some of these issues by turning to two early experiments, one with young children, which highlights the primitivization of behavior that may accompany overt aggression, and the other with young adults, which reveals the more subtle or indirect ways that aggression may be expressed.

A STUDY OF FRUSTRATED CHILDREN

In a well-known experiment by Barker, Dembo, and Lewin (1941), young children were allowed to play for a time with a set of attractive toys, such as a large dollhouse and a play pond with sailboats. Then, as shown in Figure 9-1, a frustrating wire-screen barrier was introduced, preventing the children from reaching the toys.

As expected, many of the children showed furious aggressive behavior, kicking or shaking the barrier and threatening to hit the experimenter. Some of them spent an appreciable amount of time trying to circumvent the barrier—attempting to squeeze their hands through it and protesting to the teachers that they wanted to get at the playthings. Others quickly lost interest and withdrew from the barrier.

Careful ratings of the children's play activities showed that during the frustration period there was also a marked decline in constructive forms of play with the less attractive toys that were available. For instance, some children reverted to a monotonous, infantile banging together of the toys. The most primitive forms of play were shown by those children who were most persistent in their orientation toward the barrier, including the ones most aggressively determined to get at the more desirable toys.

PRIMITIVIZATION AND DISTRACTION

In the experiment by Barker et al. the physical barrier, which prevented the young children from reaching the attractive toys that they had just been allowed to play with, is regarded by most psychologists as a paradigm that illustrates the essential features of frustration situations. *Frustration*, according to the most widely accepted definition, is a condition that results from the interruption of an organism's habitual sequence of acts directed toward the attainment of a goal. Obviously, this definition requires that two key components be present, as depicted in Figure 9-2: (1) an aroused need, drive, or tendency to action (usually referred to as a *motive*) and (2) a *barrier* preventing the motivated organism from reaching the goal.

There is considerable disagreement among psychologists, however, as to how the behavioral observations of the frustrated children should be conceptualized. Clearly, the changes in their behavior induced by the presence of the barrier cannot be fully described merely by saying that the children became angry and more aggressive. In their report the investigators emphasize the increase in primitivization and the decrease in constructive play activity, which they regard as symptoms of a temporary disruption of personality functions—referred to as a "loss of differentiation"—resulting from the frustration.

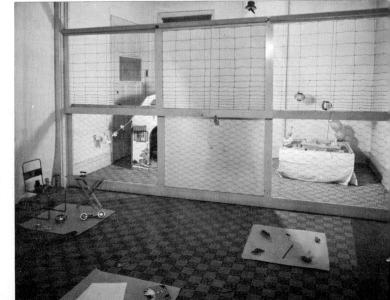

Figure 9-1 Frustration situation used in a study of young children. (From Barker, Dembo, & Lewin, 1941)

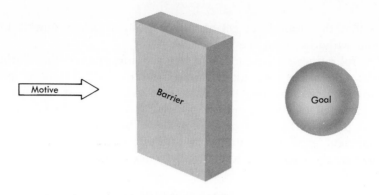

Figure 9-2   Schematic representation of a frustrating situation.

Commenting on this experiment, Child and Waterhouse (1952) have suggested two different types of interfering effects produced by frustration. These two types of effects can be formulated as general propositions concerning what will happen whenever a person is frustrated while carrying out a task that requires concentrated effort in order to produce a constructive piece of work:

1. The emotional upset evoked by any source of frustration will interfere with attention, thinking, planning, and other mental processes that make for constructive and imaginative performance.

2. When a barrier results in the frustration of an aroused motive that is irrelevant to executing the task, the frustrated person will try to continue the irrelevant activity that is being interfered with instead of working on the original task.

The first proposition ties in with the clinical observations, mentioned earlier, concerning the loss of mental efficiency and irrational activity that characterizes normal adults when they are being severely frustrated. At such times an adult is capable of reverting to relatively primitivized forms of action that resemble the infantile banging displayed by the frustrated children.

The second proposition highlights the distracting effects of frustration. In the experiment by Barker et al. the children became so distracted that they no longer worked on constructive tasks with whatever toys were at hand; instead, they devoted their efforts to seeking access to the highly attractive toys that had become unobtainable. This distraction effect, as specified in the second proposition, has important practical as well as theoretical implications. On the practical side, for example, the management of any large industrial organization can anticipate what would happen if they were to impose a new rule restricting smoking and coffee breaks in a way that would be frustrating to employees. According to the second proposition, the outcome would be a lowering of work output, because the workers would devote more and more time to finding ways of circumventing the new rule. But it would be difficult to tell, of course, whether this change in behavior was a form of aggressive retaliation, based on the anger generated toward the management as a result of the frustrating rule, or a distraction effect that is unrelated to aggression. This brings us to a theoretical issue that has not yet been settled.

Some psychologists regard the distraction effect as a special instance of a more general postulate that has been put forth by several experimental psychologists on the basis of careful observations of the behavior of thwarted animals—namely, that frustration has a general motivating effect, resulting in more vigorous goal-directed actions (Brown & Farber, 1951; Amsel, 1958; Wagner, 1959). For example, when a hungry organism is frustrated by a barrier that prevents it from reaching food, it will move toward the food more energetically than before, as though it had become hungrier. Similarly, when a thirsty organism is prevented from reaching water, the frustrating barrier evokes more vigorous activity that resembles an increase in the thirst drive; when a sexually aroused organism is prevented from mating, the frustrating barrier evokes more vigorous activity that resembles an increase in sex drive; and so on for any other drive or motive that is frustrated, whether innate or learned.

The increase in vigor might conceivably be a symptom of increased aggression. Or it might be an independent effect of frustration, influenced by various antecedent factors that are different from those determining the strength of aggression. Here again we shall have to await subsequent research on this unsettled issue.

A STUDY OF INDIRECT FORMS OF AGGRESSION

Some additional issues are highlighted in a study by Sears, Hovland, and Miller (1940), which revealed certain of the indirect forms of aggression elicited by a combination of different types of frustration. In this study a group of college students volunteered to stay awake for 24 hours. (Incidentally, we now know that 24 hours is a sufficiently short time for inducing frustration without producing the changes in brain functioning from sleep deprivation that give rise to disorganized behavior, as described in Chapter 2.) The subjects were told that the purpose of the experiment was to allow the psychologists to study the effects of fatigue on simple task performance and physiological functions. In addition to having their sleep interfered with, the men were subjected to a variety of unexpected frustrations. For example, all of them were habitual smokers, but no smoking was allowed; when the men began to converse with each other, they were told to remain silent; when they tried to amuse themselves by reading or playing games, they were told to stop. At the outset they had been promised that a number of amusing activities would be introduced before the night was over, but these were not forthcoming. They were also told to expect a meal toward morning, but when the time came they were told that the meal was canceled because of some unexplained difficulty.

Most of the frustrations inflicted on the men can be readily subsumed under the standard concept of frustration as represented in Figure 9-2. The barrier to the goal of obtaining much-needed sleep, however, was not physical (the men could quit the experiment simply by closing their eyes and dozing off); rather, it was a symbolic barrier, based on a social commitment (the men's promise to the experimenter that they would cooperate). Furthermore, some of the frustrations would have been less frustrating if the subjects' expectations had not been built up by the promise of a meal. The situation is similar to the sexual teasing that a young woman sometimes inflicts upon a male admirer, which may arouse the man's motivation to indulge in the consummatory act. If the strength of the barrier remains constant, the increasing strength of the motive makes for more severe frustration.

As predicted, the sleepless, disappointed subjects displayed numerous aggressive reactions in response to their accumulated frustrations. A few made openly critical remarks directed toward the psychologists running the experiment. Most of them, however, did not express their feelings directly, probably because of the inhibiting effects of the social norms in a university community. Nevertheless, they used indirect means for expressing aggression: For example, one man made a number of drawings of dismembered and disemboweled bodies in grotesque positions, stabbed, drowned, or hanged by the neck. When a fellow student asked him who was represented in the drawings, he immediately replied, "Psychologists!" Other subjects who saw the sketches burst out laughing, thus using humor as a socially acceptable mode of vicarious participation in a symbolic act of aggressive release.

In many real-life frustrating situations, similar indirect or symbolic ways of expressing aggression are likely to be observed, especially in circumstances where people realize they can get into serious trouble by expressing hostility openly. The subtle manifestations of hostility, however, may be missed entirely by an outsider who is unfamiliar with the subculture of a particular community, social class, or occupational group whose traditions may prescribe certain types of humor, playful needling, or cool indifference as the preferred means for expressing hostile feelings to one another. Their traditions may also prescribe somewhat different means for aggressing friendly and unfriendly out-groups. An outstanding example is the pattern of apparent self-effacement that grew up among Negroes in the Old South. In the presence of hostile white men, many Southern Negroes would act just as stupid, shuffling, and inept as the stereotype called for, while laughing to themselves about duping their unsuspecting oppressors. Similar forms of indirect attacks involving humiliating acts of self-aggression are encountered in any rigidly oppressive social hierarchy that punishes open expressions of aggression; additional examples will be given shortly, when we take a look at the reactions of frustrated trainees in the armed services and of frustrated workers in large industrial organizations.

CRITICISMS OF
THE FRUSTRATION–AGGRESSION HYPOTHESIS

Proponents of the frustration-aggression hypothesis assert that everyone will show an increase in one or another form of aggression—direct or indirect, overt or symbolic, open or disguised, real or imaginary—in response to any frustration. Their definition of frustration is essentially the one presented earlier in this chapter and represented in Figure 9-2. According to this definition, a state of *privation*—involving the lack of satisfaction of hunger, thirst, sex, or any other drive or motive—is *not* sufficient to constitute a frustration. For example, a man who has been separated from his wife for many months would not necessarily be regarded as sexually frustrated as long as his sexual desires are not aroused by the presence of erotic cues. Taking a different stand, other psychologists argue that it is difficult in practice to distinguish between privation and frustration without becoming involved in circular reasoning by calling a privation frustrating if we find that it evokes aggression. Buss (1966) points out that the blocking of motives is such a standard feature of the human condition that it is difficult to find any circumstance that does not meet the broad definition of frustration.

Still another criticism of the frustration-aggression hypothesis is that it offers at best an incomplete theory of man's aggressive impulses. For many years psychoanalysts have made the basic assumption that aggressive drives are part of man's instinctual make-up. Recently, some experimental psychologists have begun to take seriously the claims put forth by Lorenz (1964) and other biologists who view aggressiveness as an innate biological drive that is released in circumstances where fighting has adaptive value, that is, protecting the home territory from invaders and serving related functions that make for survival of the species. Homo sapiens, Lorenz tells us, is one of many species whose members are instinctively aggressive toward one another, so that if you put together two boys who have never seen each other before they will fight, just like two strange monkeys, rats, lizards, or stickleback fish.

At present very little research is concerned with the elusive search for some way of differentiating between the presence and absence of frustration when youngsters (or oldsters) seem to be fighting instinctively in the manner described by Lorenz. Most investigations on the effects of frustration are now focused on *determinants* that increase the probability that a mild, moderate, or strong aggressive response will occur.

Determinants of the Strength
of Aggression

Among the major factors that have emerged from recent research as important determinants of the strength of aggressive responses are:

1. the arbitrariness of the imposed deprivations;
2. the degree to which the amount of deprivation exceeds or falls short of the amount expected;
3. the anticipated social punishments or rewards from aggressive action.

In the remainder of this chapter we shall consider these factors and several subsidiary ones that influence both the arousal of reflective anger and the choice of the target of aggression. Other aspects of aggressive behavior are discussed in Part II (pp. 325–34, 358–65) and Part III (pp. 497–503).

ARBITRARINESS OF THE FRUSTRATOR'S INTERFERENCE

Whenever we are in a frustrating situation, our reactions are determined to some extent by our expectations and beliefs about the reasons for our being deprived of what we want. When a man is prevented by his boss from going home at the end of a hard day's work, for example, his cognitive appraisal of the demand for overtime will include consideration of the arbitrariness of the deprivation. Anger is much more intensely aroused if an interference is perceived as unreasonable or arbitrary than if it is regarded as an expected or inevitable barrier (Pastore, 1952).

Imagine a group of people who, after a long wait, see a bus go right past them without stopping, when no other bus is in sight. If the bus is empty and displays a sign stating "motor trouble—on the way to garage," little anger is likely to be evoked, since the bus driver's unwelcome action is perceived as reasonable and beyond his control. In contrast, considerable heat will be generated if the unavailable bus displays its usual sign and is half-filled with passengers. Pastore (1952) points out that in the sleep-deprivation experiment described earlier the subjects became aggressive, while the experimenters, who missed just as much sleep and underwent essentially the same physical deprivations, did not.

These considerations have led research psychologists to investigate systematically the hypothesis that people will react with a higher degree of aggression when they are frustrated arbitrarily than when they are given a reasonable explanation for the interference. Typical of the evidence that confirms this hypothesis is the outcome of an experiment by Fishman (1965) conducted with girls at a teachers college. In the arbitrary frustration condition the subjects were promised a $2.00 bonus if they succeeded on a routine assigned task. Then, after completing it successfully, they were informed that the bonus was being withheld, for a rather flimsy reason. ("Remember, I said it was important that you do your best, and I don't think you did.") In the nonarbitrary frustration condition the same bonus was promised to an equivalent group and then withheld on the grounds that the girls had not attained high enough scores to earn it. A control group was given the same task, but no frustration was introduced; there simply was no mention of a bonus nor of failure on the task.

The degree of aggression against the frustrator was ascertained by asking each subject to rate the competence of the student experimenter. The effects of the three different conditions on the incidence of negative ratings (verbal aggression) are presented in Figure 9-3. While both types of frustration were provocative, the arbitrary type elicited much more verbal aggression than the nonarbitrary type.

In a sense, the arbitrary type always involves a cumulative effect of at least two different sources of frustration: To the initial frustration (for example, loss of promised money) is added a *social* source of frustration (for example, unfair and insulting treatment by a professional person who is expected to be polite and helpful). Most people build up considerable tolerance for all sorts of frustrations imposed by representatives of large institutions: They will wait patiently for appointments, fill out endless forms, execute boring tasks, and even go without food, sleep, or sexual gratification in order to meet the apparently legitimate demands of a

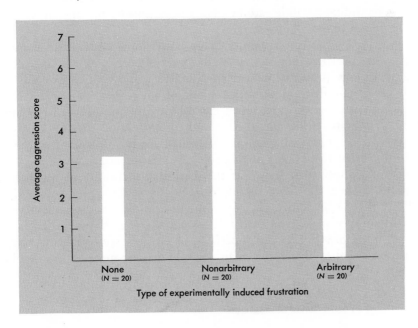

Figure 9-3   Aggression against the experimenter evoked by arbitrary and nonarbitrary frustrations. (Based on data from Fishman, 1965)

formal organizational hierarchy. But the very same people become incensed when the frustration comes as a personal affront or undisguised insult that cannot be subsumed under the cloak of legitimate or nonarbitrary necessity. Thus it is quite understandable that most experimental studies of frustration in college laboratories, as Buss (1966) points out, fail to evoke very much aggressive behavior unless the experimenter himself treats the subjects in an arbitrarily aggressive manner by being rude or insulting.

UNPLEASANT SURPRISES AND RELATIVE DEPRIVATION

Closely related to the factor of arbitrariness is the question of whether or not the frustration was expected. In general, anticipated frustrations give rise to milder emotional reactions than do unanticipated ones that come as unpleasant surprises. The importance of expectancies in frustration has been shown in a series of experiments by Berkowitz (1962). Pairs of college students were brought into the laboratory ostensibly for a study of the way people form first impressions. Each subject was first asked to rate his partner on several traits. Then the experimenter induced mutually unfriendly feelings by telling each subject privately that his partner had given him a negative or hostile rating. The experimenter was also able to manipulate the subject's initial expectations about these ratings by providing fictitious information about the partner beforehand. Near the end of the session (before the experimenter dehoaxed the subjects by telling them how and why he had rigged the earlier ratings) each subject made a final rating of his partner, which enabled him to express his aggressive feelings.

The findings showed that when a subject had been led to expect a hostile judgment from his partner, he reacted much less strongly to such a judgment than when he had expected a friendly reaction. This outcome adds further support to the view that frustration is a *relative* matter, depending on how rewarding or unrewarding the person expects his encounters with another person to be.

In everyday life we encounter many professional people and authority figures who obstruct our activities in one way or another. By simply doing their jobs properly, policemen, clergymen, and physicians are constantly preventing us from satisfying certain of our wishes, as is tacitly recognized in the well-known quip, "How can I have any fun when all the things I want to do are either illegal, immoral, or fattening?" If we know the frustrator to be functioning in a well-defined social role and if we expect him to be obstructive as part of that role, his interference is much less likely to evoke our anger than if we, as the frustrated victims, had no such expectations. Hence, the more sharply defined the role requirements are, the less likely the average citizen is to become hostile toward those members of the community who take on such roles as chronic frustrators. So too in any work organization: When the supervisor or chief is seen as being obliged to function at times like a policeman, his role may be more or less despised, but his thwarting actions will not come as unpleasant surprises and thus will have a less powerful emotional impact.

The importance of expectations was repeatedly emphasized in social psychological studies of attitudes and morale among American soldiers during World War II (Stouffer et al., 1949a). Many of the findings showed that the men's feelings of resentment and hostility toward the Army authorities were not always proportional to the objective amount of deprivation inflicted on them. For example, bitter complaints about poor living conditions, too little time off, and delays in promotion were more frequent in the Air Force than in other branches of the service; yet in the Air Force the men were given better living conditions, faster promotions, and more elite status than in any other military branch. At the other end of the spectrum, the Military Police, whose promotions were rare, expressed relatively few complaints about this situation. Thus there was an apparent paradox, in that anger and protests were expressed more frequently in units where these reactions were least warranted by the objective deprivations that the men endured.

In order to explain this paradox, a new explanatory concept was introduced—the concept of *relative deprivation*, which postulates that a man will generally evaluate his personal gains and losses by comparing himself with others whom he regards as being "in the same boat" (Stouffer, Suchman, DeVinney, Star, & Williams, 1949a). Thus, if a man is in a unit where he sees many others being more rapidly promoted, getting more time off, and living more comfortably than he, his level of expectation will be high, and he will therefore feel more frustrated by the deprivations he encounters than will a man whose comparative reference group is much worse off. Merton and Kitt (1950) point out that comparison with a reference group is likely to occur throughout society and is certainly not limited to Army life. As a person advances in his chosen career, his comparative reference group will tend to change with each change in status. If a man becomes a high-ranking executive or a specialist in his profession, he will no longer evaluate his gains and losses or his own achievements and failures in quite the same way he did at the outset of his career; his standards will be set by what he sees happening to his companions in the *new* boat he is now in. This is one of the ways in which a man can be "wrecked by success": The new reference group may raise his expectations so high that he becomes chronically resentful about minor deprivations he had formerly ignored, such as the inconvenient location of his office.

ANTICIPATED CONSEQUENCES
OF RESPONDING AGGRESSIVELY

As in all other spheres of human behavior, environmental signs of forthcoming rewards or punishments play an important role in controlling the release of aggression whenever a person is frustrated.

Instrumental Value:

Overcoming the Obstruction   One obvious type of anticipated reward involves the consequences of the aggressive act, or its *instrumental value,* with respect to overcoming the source of frustration. Everyone learns a great deal about these consequences from parents, teachers, and other authority figures who shape his standards of conduct during his formative years.

An experimental demonstration of the influence of positive feedback on aggressive action was recently reported by Buss (1966). In this experiment each college student who came to the psychology laboratory was given a frustrating partner who appeared to be a fellow student but was actually a paid confederate of the experimenter. The subject was told that it was his job to give electric shocks to the partner as part of a learning experiment. The partner then proceeded to make a series of errors that allowed the subject to carry out his assigned police function and mete out the punishment. Each time his partner made an error, the subject had to make a decision about how much of a shock to give him. By pressing the appropriate button, he could give shocks that supposedly ranged from very mild to excruciatingly painful. The subject had no way of knowing that the wires to the partner were disconnected. The partner, by behaving agitatedly, led the subject to believe he was actually receiving the shocks every time the button was pressed. The situation was made frustrating for the subject by telling him that his grade in the psychology course would be affected by his ability to perform as a good teacher. So each time the inept fellow student failed on the learning task, the subject—like Mark Twain's steamboat pilot—was severely frustrated in his role as instructor. But in this laboratory situation the frustrated instructor had the opportunity to vent his aggression directly against the pupil by inflicting painful shocks.

Two different conditions of frustration were compared. In the first the victim showed a marked improvement each time the intensity of shock was stepped up; in the contrasting condition his performance was unrelated to the intensity of the shocks he was given. This variation proved to have an enormous effect on the subjects' aggressive behavior. When the shock appeared to have no instrumental value for the subjects in improving the victim's poor performance, the subjects gave shocks so sparingly that they showed no more aggressive behavior than under control conditions (in which comparable subjects went through the same procedure but with no frustration involved). However, when the subjects could perceive that the shock had instrumental value in overcoming the frustrating behavior of the pupil, they inflicted a significantly greater amount of shock on the pupil. Thus, in this laboratory situation, frustration produced an increase in direct aggression only when the aggressive act was perceived by the subject as helping to attain the goal. In other words, when aggression was rewarded by removal of the obstruction—when it had instrumental value—it became a dominant response to frustration, but not when it had no such value.

Negative Feedback from the Victim

In addition to knowledge about the instrumental value of the aggression, another type of feedback from the victim was also found to be effective in Buss's experiment: When the victim showed only mild disturbance in response to the shock that he was supposedly receiving, the subject's aggression was much greater than when the victim vocalized pain and showed signs of acute discomfort. Such signs, of course, might influence expectations of instrumental value. The victim's howls of pain might cause a frustrated instructor to stop administering shock because he realizes that too much punishment can upset the student and lead to even poorer performance. But the instructor may, of course, become motivated to stop his punishment simply because he is humane: The victim's painful cries may arouse guilt about hurting a fellow human, as well as anticipatory shame about being censured as a sadist, even when the instructor's punitive role is legitimized. (It should be noted here that we know very little about the extent to which the experimental subjects continue to be emotionally disturbed about their own aggressive actions after they leave the laboratory, even when the experimenter has frankly discussed the purpose of the research and has tried to give reassurances to alleviate residual feelings of shame and guilt. This is one of the main reasons why the study just described and the one to be described next have provoked a widespread debate among psychologists and other interested parties. The debate centers on the criticism that it is ethically unwarranted to use procedures that induce human subjects to believe that they are performing punitive or hostile acts against fellow human beings.)

The same type of negative feedback from a victim has been found to be an effective deterrent in experimental studies of what might be called "malignantly blind obedience" (Milgram, 1965). The subjects were adult employees hired by a seemingly fly-by-night commercial research office and instructed by their work supervisor to give painful shocks to another person for the alleged purpose of carrying out research in human learning. Actually, as in the Buss experiment, the wires were disconnected, but the victim acted in such a convincing way that he looked as though he was really being hurt. Many of the subjects blindly carried out the supervisor's orders each time the learner made an error, even though they believed that he was being tortured and might be killed. This has been called the "Eichmann effect," after the notorious Nazi leader who solemnly justified his executive role in the torture and murder of thousands of helpless Jews on the grounds that he was merely carrying out his superiors' orders and was doing his duty as a subordinate.

Variations of the experimental conditions, which involved placing the

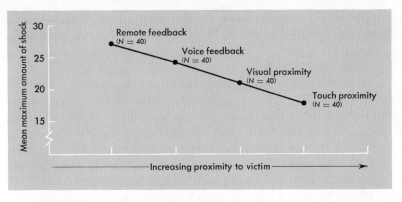

Figure 9-4 Amount of shock the subject inflicts on the victim as a function of his proximity to the victim: (a) remote feedback— the victim cannot be heard or seen; (b) voice feedback—the victim's protests are heard; (c) visual proximity—the victim is in the same room, less than 2 feet away; (d) touch proximity—same as visual, but the subject is required to put the victim's hand on the shock plate. (Adapted from Milgram, 1965)

subjects at varying distances from the victim, indicate that the more opportunity a man has to observe the suffering of the victim the less likely he is to display the "Eichmann effect." The main findings, summarized in Figure 9-4, show that increased proximity to the victim creates increased resistance to carrying out the punitive orders.

FEAR OF RETALIATION AND INDIRECT AGGRESSION

There is another important type of anticipated negative feedback from the frustrator that has not yet been considered: the threat of retaliation for aggressive treatment. Studies of military training provide clear-cut examples of the way men react to anticipated punishment for showing signs of anger in the presence of oppressive superiors. The norms of the military organization specify that an officer should punish severely any soldier who protests against an apparently frustrating order, no matter how arbitrary or humiliating he and his fellow soldiers may judge it to be. During basic training, the soldier is taught to expect immediate retribution for the slightest gesture of defiance toward any superior. Long afterward he retains his sensitivity to differences in military rank.

This sensitivity was nicely illustrated in an experiment by Thibaut and Reicken (1955). Air Force reservists, who were not on active duty, were exposed to a highly realistic situation in which they heard an officer in the Air Force giving another man orders in a highly insulting manner, deliberately calculated to evoke feelings of hostility in anyone who heard what was being said. Each subject was then given the opportunity to talk with the insulting officer. As expected, relatively little aggression was communicated when the insultor was of higher military rank than the subject, whereas a great deal was expressed when he was of lower rank. Here it is obvious that a simple cue of relative status in a social structure can exert a powerful influence on the expression of aggression. The same type of influence is to be expected in any school, business firm, or government agency, where people know that those in a superior position have the power to punish them for objecting to orders.

When collective verbal protests are prohibited, as in most military organizations, aggressive discharge is likely to be indirect, resulting in hidden forms of defiance. Observations of American soldiers during World War II reveal that the men displayed acts of indirect aggression whenever the offending officers' backs were turned (Janis, 1945). The observations were made in a strict training camp, where even a frown in response to a superior's orders might be punished by hard labor in the kitchen or confinement to the barracks during holidays. Four main patterns of indirect aggression appeared to be most frequent among the enlisted men: (1) *griping* to one another in exaggerated terms about the alleged stupidity and sadism of the officers; (2) *gossiping* in a derogatory manner about the officers' weaknesses and private foibles; (3) *mimicking* the on-duty speech and mannerisms of the officers as a form of ridicule of the way they barked out orders and threatened to discipline anyone who did not automatically obey; (4) playing the game of *goldbricking*, which involves seeing who can get away with the least amount of work (preferably, doing nothing at all) while pretending to be carrying out an assigned task.

Letting off steam by engaging in verbal or symbolic aggression in collaboration with fellow sufferers exposed to the same restrictions, whether in a civilian or military organization, probably serves as a form of catharsis. The aggressive fantasies accompanying an indirect act of aggression may momentarily reduce the strength of aggressive arousal, even if the action is purely verbal and totally ineffective in removing the frustrating obstacles. Some experimental studies suggest that after people have been angered by a frustrating authority figure, their aggression toward the frustrator can be markedly reduced if they are given the opportunity to express their feelings symbolically—for instance, by making up aggressive stories on the Thematic Apperception Test (Feshbach, 1955, 1961). This hypothesis of catharsis, however, has been called into question by other investigators (Berkowitz, 1962) and may require reformulations that specify the *conditions* under which aggressive fantasies will lead to a decrease or an increase in overt aggressive activity.

Although the evidence concerning cathartic effects remains equivocal, there is little question that whenever people are kept under strict authoritarian controls—whenever they are exposed to all the usual day-to-day frustrations and, in addition, are not allowed to express their grievances—they will show a marked increase in indirect forms of aggression, just as

Army recruits do in basic training. A high incidence of indirect aggression can be a serious problem to the management of any large organization, because, together with the previously discussed distraction effects, it can give rise to a marked deterioration in work performances. This problem frequently arises in schools, factories, and offices, whenever authoritarian superiors use threats of retaliation to block the aggressive responses evoked by their new demands or restrictions.

Displacement of the Target
of Aggression

Often when a person becomes angry he displays indirect rather than direct aggression against the frustrator because of anticipatory shame, guilt, or fear of retaliation. Under such conditions of partial inhibition there is also a marked tendency to displace aggression away from the frustrator toward a scapegoat, usually someone who appears to be *similar* to the frustrator. If a top administrator announces a new set of restrictions that disrupts every employee's vacation plans, one of his underlings is likely to become the butt of the employees' hostile ridicule and insulting remarks.

DISPLACEMENT TO SIMILAR OUT-GROUPS

In our everyday work groups and friendship cliques certain types of frustration regularly evoke aggression that is displaced to out-groups. This type of displacement pattern is illustrated by the combat soldier reacting to the dire frustrations engendered by confusing, arbitrary, and negligent actions on the part of comrades or highly esteemed leaders within his unit. Finding himself the victim of "snafus" committed in the confusion of battle, the individual may be burdened with burning indignation toward a commanding officer, a squad leader, or even his closest buddy. If these feelings of hostility are not rapidly dissipated, the man is at least dimly aware that his aggressive acts might disrupt group solidarity, and he is likely to be inhibited by feelings of guilt or shame. Thus he is in the market, so to speak, for a good scapegoat that can deflect his anger away from the group he depends upon for companionship, reassurance, and perhaps preservation of his life.

It might be expected that the enemy, as a real source of danger to all men in combat, would be a natural target for displacement. But evidence from World War II indicates that American combat troops felt relatively little hatred or vindictiveness toward the enemy (Smith, 1949). Instead, soldiers at the front tended to express hostility toward out-groups within the same military organizations, especially toward the authorities in remote headquarters who required the soldiers to bear the enemy harassments.

PARTIAL DISPLACEMENT OF THE AFFECT

Although the displacement mechanism may reduce hostility toward others in the in-group, it cannot eliminate all the animosity that arises when members of an in-group are in daily contact. As in most families, each individual becomes hostile and resentful from time to time. The hostility may result from his being pressured to conform with strong demands from the others, being humiliated by their unjustifiable complaints, or being unnecessarily deprived by their carelessness. Among American troops overseas during World War II, even more than in their training camps, the preferred mode of verbal aggression against comrades was playful *needling*. Men jokingly made gross criticisms and exaggerated accusations against one another, using satirical mimicry and mock threats of violence. In a variety of ways the needler made it clear, however, that he was "only kidding around." In such instances there was no displacement of the *target* but a partial displacement of *affect*, from genuine rage to mock rage, which was singularly lacking in the normal spirit of fun. This mode of discharging aggression, which has its counterpart in many civilian work groups, was described in the following way by Bill Mauldin:

> While men in combat outfits kid each other around, they have a sort of family complex about it. No outsiders may join. Anybody who does a dangerous job in this war has his own particular kind of kidding among his own friends, and sometimes it doesn't even sound like kidding [1945, p. 58].

Being permitted to indulge in the group's special form of kidding probably functions not only as a status reward but also as a shared device, along with displaced hostility, for safely discharging residual resentments toward others in the in-group.

The same dual pattern can often be seen in industrial plants. The members of a face-to-face work group, once they develop strong feelings of solidarity, regularly share in denouncing the central office and other out-groups within the same organization, even when the frustration stems from errors made by a member of their own in-group; but their intra-group aggression is generally restricted to playful needling.

SELECTING THE SCAPEGOAT

The selection of a scapegoat is influenced by several factors in addition to similarity to the perceived source of frustration. One of the prime determinants is cognitive awareness of the scapegoat's role in causing the frustration. Let us suppose that the same administrator who had restricted his employees' vacations subsequently cuts down on their coffee breaks—a restriction that the employees recognize as being justified because many have been abusing the privilege. The scapegoat who will have to bear the brunt of the aggression may be some lowly employee who is known to be a flagrant exploiter of the coffee break. Typically, in such cases, a person who is partly to blame for the frustration is treated as if he were entirely to blame. In this way hostility is deflected away from the powerful frustrator and also from highly valued members of the group who might be just as blameworthy as the isolated scapegoat.

Another determinant, which has already been alluded to several times, involves estimates of the scapegoat's capacity to retaliate. The persons or groups selected as scapegoats usually have little power to inflict social rewards or punishments and are not among those who are regularly encountered face to face in daily life. Thus, if a person belongs to a social or ethnic group that is disliked and segregated by the community at large, the chances are greater that he will be blamed when other members of that community are severely frustrated. This well-known truism about social prejudice has been repeatedly documented by observations of the scapegoating of minority groups during periods of economic and wartime deprivation.

SCAPEGOATING OF MINORITY GROUPS

Typical findings are reported by Bettelheim and Janowitz (1950) from a study of 150 civilians who were veterans of World War II. These investigators found that the men who had become "downwardly mobile" (whose postwar jobs were of lower social status than their prewar jobs) expressed more hostility toward Negroes, Jews, and other minority groups than did men who had not undergone a downward shift in social status. Although such findings might be explained in several different ways, they are consistent with the hypothesis that when people are chronically frustrated by downward shifts in their social status, they tend to direct their hostility toward disliked minority groups as scapegoats. Other studies also point to a relation between the person's dissatisfaction with his social or occupational status and his contempt for minority groups (Allport, 1954).

Experimental evidence indicating the readiness with which generally despised minority out-groups will be chosen to bear the brunt of a current frustration is provided by a social psychological experiment conducted by Miller and Bugelski (1948). These investigators studied a real-life frustration that was imposed at a vocational training camp for unemployed young men. One evening, when the men were expecting to go to the local movie house, they were confined to the camp and required to take a series of dull, difficult tests. Included among the tests were questionnaires asking them about their attitudes toward Mexicans and Japanese. Considerably stronger negative attitudes toward these out-groups were found right after the frustrating event than before.

Whenever the causes of frustration in a large organization or a nation remain somewhat ambiguous, as in periods of economic depression and pro-longed military stalemates and defeats, the stage is set for selecting a minority group—such as the Jews, the Negroes, or the Puerto Ricans in the United States—as scapegoats. Once people have begun to displace their aggression to an out-group target, they become inclined to rationalize and justify their hostility. Moreover, their provocative insults to members of the minority group may evoke counteraggressive threats of retaliation. These threats, coming from a relatively weak minority, are usually not powerful enough to inhibit aggression but may be taken as evidence that members of the out-group are truly vicious and deserve to be punished. Thus, any single act of scapegoating can lead to an escalation of intergroup hostility, which strongly reinforces the initial negative stereotypes.

This psychological analysis of the channeling of aggression against minority groups has been applied directly to the history of Nazi Germany during the decades between the two world wars.

> The Nazi party systematically and ruthlessly exploited the cumulative discontent that the German people had suffered since their defeat in World War I. Added to the hardship and humiliation of that military defeat were the devastating effects of economic depression and monetary inflation. Hence, when Hitler first raised his frenzied voice, a large segment of the German population was ready to listen and act.
>
> . . . Hitler probably would not have been nearly so successful had not the German people already possessed a propensity to employ the mechanism of displacement in dealing with the motive of aggression. . . . Thus, in the typical German household prior to World War II, the father was quite clearly the family "boss" whose authority was not to be doubted or disobeyed by his wife or children. Moreover, children were expected to show the utmost deference to their fathers and to refrain from any outward display of opposition or hostility toward him.
>
> . . . When encouraged by the Nazi leaders to destroy the Jews, the Germans were presented with a sacrificial lamb toward which they could fully and freely express the hatred that it had been unsafe for them to reveal to their own parents.
>
> Of course, it should be kept in mind that socio-economic conditions need not deteriorate as much as they did in pre-Hitler Germany in order to generate a reservoir of aggression which can be displaced against innocent victims. Nor are Germans the only people capable of displacing aggression in the form of destructive violence . . . [Sarnoff, 1962, pp. 245–46].

PERSONALITY PREDISPOSITIONS
AND THE CHOICE OF SCAPEGOATS

The constellation of attitudes described as characteristic of the members of a typical prewar German household represents an extreme form of what has been called *the authoritarian personality*. A number of psychological investigators cite evidence that this personality constellation is by no means limited to Germany, but occurs with sizable frequency within the United States, furnishing a hard core of Americans who are especially predisposed to develop social prejudices against Jews, Negroes, and other minority groups. The well-known study by Adorno, Frenkel-Brunswik, Levinson, and Sanford, *The Authoritarian Personality* (1950), which aimed at understanding in depth the psychological roots of social prejudice, pointed to a latent personality trend of repressed hostility among American men and women who are most ready to accept totalitarian ideas and hate propaganda. The most prejudiced persons appear to be those who cling to an overidealized view of their parents, bosses, and political leaders. Although extremely submissive toward all these authority figures, they are seething with hostility and defiance under the surface, but they cannot allow themselves to think about their hostility or to express it in any direct way. Because of their excessive fear of releasing their own forbidden impulses, they maintain a rigid personality organization that makes their overt behavior appear to be cool, detached, unspontaneous, and highly conventional. They are especially intolerant of deviations from conventional sexual norms. Signs of human "weakness" or "tenderness" in their fellow men evoke their contempt, whereas aggressiveness on the part of those in high positions evokes their admiration. Their own aggressive impulses are readily released against scapegoats—Negroes, Jews, aliens, communists, peaceniks, eggheads, hippies, or anyone who lacks power and appears to be an unconventional deviant. Thus, the outstanding characteristic of personalities who are most ready to adopt and adhere to social prejudices is their need to displace hostility away from authorities and toward apparently weak persons and out-groups of low status.

Although personality predispositions may play an important role in social prejudice and scapegoating, we must recall the experimental evidence cited earlier concerning the extent to which negative feedback can modify aggressive behavior (pages 161–63). However strong their inclination to interfere with the rights of minority groups may be, highly prejudiced people can still be deterred by impressive information about the unfavorable consequences of their aggressive actions. The changes in race relations in the United States during the 1960's have frequently been mentioned in this connection. They have been cited as a prime example of the way scapegoating can be reduced through well-organized political action and legal measures that threaten retaliatory punishment for interfering with full equality for black Americans or other ethnic groups. The codification of new social norms, embedded in civil rights legislation, may also help to foster new ethical values in America. In the long run this may lead to widespread internalization of the constraints against vicious forms of scapegoating.

Concluding Thoughts
on Intergroup Aggression

Although not intended as the sole explanation, the foregoing hypotheses concerning the dynamics of displaced aggression might help explain certain of the causes and consequences of intergroup conflicts and war. Intergroup hostility between labor and management, between rival political groups, and between rival nations is frequently built up by a series of aggressive and counteraggressive moves. From the hypotheses discussed in this chapter concerning the determinants of the target of aggression, we would expect the probability that members of one group will become hostile toward a rival group will be increased if the rivals are seen as: (1) responsible for a current source of frustration; (2) too weak and too lacking in support from any powerful allies to mobilize effective retaliation; and (3) morally reprehensible in the eyes of "right-thinking" people, so that inflicting punishment will be morally justified and will lead to little or no disapproval from onlookers. A great deal of current research in the social sciences is oriented toward finding out the extent to which governmental policies, international conferences, information campaigns, and persuasive appeals can change each of these three factors in order to reduce hostility between national groups (see Kelman, 1965).

'Tis not alone my inky cloak, good Mother,
Nor customary suits of solemn black,
Nor windy suspiration of forced breath—
No, nor the fruitful river in the eye,
Nor the dejected havior of the visage,
Together with all forms, moods, shapes of grief—
That can denote me truly. These indeed seem,
For they are actions that a man might play.
But I have that within which passeth show,
These but the trappings and the suits of woe.

WILLIAM SHAKESPEARE. Hamlet

And you, my father, there on the sad height,
Curse, bless, me now with your fierce tears, I pray.
Do not go gentle into that good night.
Rage, rage against the dying of the light.

DYLAN THOMAS. Do Not Go Gentle into That Good Night

CHAPTER 10
GRIEF

In this chapter we shall examine the emotional impact of two closely related sources of stress that recur throughout a normal person's life: temporary and permanent separation from loved persons. The most disruptive form of separation, of course, is the death of a loved one. We know that this is "common," as Hamlet's mother says, since "all that lives must die"; but though we accept the necessity, we cannot help being shaken, displaying "all forms, moods, shapes of grief" and suffering "that within which passeth show."

Profound grief is by no means found only in bereavement; grief reactions regularly occur whenever there is prolonged separation from loved ones, as when a young man or woman migrates to a distant country for a stay of several years. Many adolescents feel such grief when they go off to college. Even more frequent are the mild, transient grief reactions evoked by temporary separations from close friends. More intense reactions of mourning and depression occur if physical separation is accompanied by signs of rejection. When an intimate friendship or love affair is terminated by the cold withdrawal of one of the partners, the other is likely to experience intense grief. In all these circumstances of separation, just as in bereavement, the person suffers a profound sense of loss, which is the central feature of grief. During the time when the feeling of loss is most acute, the world appears "weary, stale, flat, and unprofitable," and the dejected person may even briefly share Hamlet's fantasy of violating the "canon 'gainst self-slaughter."

Separation Reactions
of Young Children

It is in young children that we can most clearly see the profound emotional impact of separation. Among the best-known investigations are the case studies of Robertson (1958) and Bowlby (1960), who observed more than 50 preschool children confined in a hospital to receive medical or surgical treatment or sent to a residential nursery so that the mother might take a full-time job.

THREE EMOTIONAL PHASES

According to Robertson and Bowlby, there are three main phases that characterize the emotional reactions of a young child during the period of separation from his mother:

Phase 1:

Protest   During the first day or two of separation, the average 2- to 4-year-old cries violently, screams, repeatedly calls out "I want my mommy," refuses to allow a maternal substitute to take over, and appears to be constantly vigilant for the return of his mother. After the most acute forms of protest die down, the child continues to complain about the mother's absence, is reluctant to comply with demands from the substitute, has temper tantrums, and continues to complain loudly and tearfully.

Phase 2:

Despair   After several days of protest the child usually begins to show characteristic reactions of grief—moaning, quiet weeping, and sad facial expressions. He no longer responds eagerly to any sight or sound that might signal the return of his mother. Observers are left with the impression that the child is in a depressed state.

Phase 3:

Detachment   From several days to about one week following the onset of the separation, the young child gradually begins to change in the direction of seemingly unemotional, bland response to his environment. No longer is there any apparent seeking of the mother or clinging to her if she comes to visit. The child also appears indifferent to mother substitutes, such as the nurses who take care of him in the hospital. He becomes increasingly more apathetic, as if he no longer cared about his mother or anything else in his environment. Sometimes the child directly verbalizes this feeling: "I don't care if Mommy isn't here; I don't need her."

The child's withdrawal from his mother and from maternal substitutes during the third phase is regarded as highly dangerous to his personality development, since it seems to lead to a permanent blocking of affection and a tendency toward superficial or exploitative relationships with other people; it may even dispose the person to become psychotically withdrawn or depressed later in life. According to Bowlby, the longer the period of separation, the greater the chances of entering the third, pathogenic phase. Furthermore, the longer the pathogenic phase continues before the toddler is reunited with his mother, the greater are the chances of permanent personality damage. The third phase may be attenuated, however, if a full-time mother substitute is available.

Even under the most favorable circumstances, a separation of more than a day or two is generally followed by a great deal of turmoil when the mother returns: At first the toddler is likely to be unruly, responding negativistically to discipline and acting as though he does not recognize his mother at all, even though he will readily recognize his father and others who may have been away even longer. Then his behavior shifts to the opposite extreme: He becomes extremely dependent on his mother, clinging to her constantly and screaming whenever she starts to go. The mother may have to put up with several weeks of this regressive dependency before a normal relationship with her child is reestablished. The same tearful protests about parting and similar spells of sullenness and sulking or wild, destructive play may occur when a 2-year-old starts nursery school, even though the period of separation from the mother is only a few hours each school day (Marjorie Janis, 1964).

When a mother must leave her toddler for a week or two to enter the hospital for surgery or just to take a needed vacation, the young child is unable to comprehend the repeated reassurances that his mommy will be back soon and that she still loves him. His reaction to the period of separation may induce as much despair and detachment as if his mother had died. Even children old enough to understand the reassurances are still prone to interpret their mother's temporary absence as abandonment or as withdrawal of love in punishment for their own misbehavior.

The three phases of separation reactions have been vividly portrayed in a film called A Two-Year-Old Goes to Hospital, prepared by James Robertson. Robertson had never before done any photography; he merely wanted a documentary record for research purposes. Quite unexpectedly, his film turned out to be one of the most effective psychological films ever made. In it we witness profound emotional changes during a period of one week

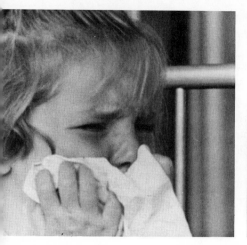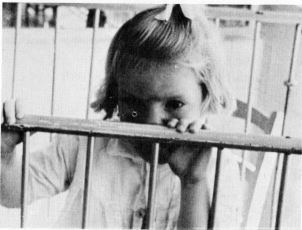

Figure 10-1 The despair phase (left) and the detachment phase (right). (Still photographs from a documentary film study, A Two-Year-Old Goes to Hospital, *by James Robertson)*

when a 2-year-old girl was hospitalized for a minor, only slightly painful operation. At the outset, the child displays clear-cut manifestations of protest, with much crying and screaming; then come reactions of grief and despair. The still photographs from the film in Figure 10-1 show the girl's characteristic facial expression during the second and third phases. At times she is distracted and begins to play happily, but then she suddenly drops the activity and looks very sad, as in the left-hand photograph.

Then we see the beginning of the third phase, which is marked by the child's distinctive reactions when her mother comes during visiting hours. Although greatly enlivened by her father's visits, she completely ignores her mother and actually turns away from her. On one occasion when her mother brings a picture book as a gift, she tears it up as soon as her mother leaves the room. These and other signs indicate that the child is beginning to develop a reaction of aggrieved detachment, as though she were trying to push her mother out of her life to avoid being hurt so deeply ever again.

THOMAS DE QUINCEY'S SYMBOLIC LADIES OF SORROW

When Robertson and Bowlby reported their observations of the three phases of reaction to separation, they were quite unaware that more than 100 years earlier Thomas De Quincey had delineated exactly the same three phases. De Quincey is best known for the revealing account of his drug addiction in *Confessions of an English Opium-Eater*. His childhood memories of intense grief over separation from his mother remained a source of painful preoccupation throughout his life. In an autobiographical essay, "Levana and Our Ladies of Sorrow" (1845), De Quincey tells how deeply impressed he was by his personal observations at Eton, a boarding school where boys started at six and were thus cut off from their families at an early age:

> Now, I am far from saying that children universally are capable of grief like mine. But there are more than you ever heard of who die of grief in this island of ours [when children are torn away from mothers and sisters]. . . . I speak of what I know. The complaint is not entered by the registrar as grief; but that it is.

In this essay De Quincey presents a poetic, allegorical account of "three ladies of sorrow," who personify certain of the "sufferings of man's heart" and strikingly parallel the three phases of separation described above:

> The eldest of the three is named . . . Our Lady of Tears. She it is that night and day *raves and moans*, calling for vanished faces.
> . . . [She] is often-times *stormy* and *frantic, raging* in the highest against heaven, and *demanding back* her darlings. But Our Lady of Sighs [the second sister of sorrow] . . . is humble to *abjectness*. Hers is the meekness that belongs to the *hopeless*. . . . Mutter she does at times, but it is in solitary places that are desolate as she is *desolate*. . . .
> [Our Lady of Darkness, the third sister] . . . is the mother of *lunacies*, and the suggestress of *suicides*. . . . [She] can approach only those in whom a profound nature has been upheaved by central convulsions; in whom the heart trembles and brain rocks under conspiracies of *tempest from without and tempest from within* [italics added].

In a final passage De Quincey explicitly recognizes the progression that begins with the protest phase (Our Lady of Tears), which sets the stage for the despair phase (Our Lady of Sighs), which in turn prepares the bereaved child for the ominous domination of Our Lady of Darkness, when the child permanently loses his capacity to be consoled by tender maternal care, when all hope and all love are forever banished from his life: "Suffer not woman and her tenderness to sit near him in his darkness. Banish the frailties of hope, wither the relenting of love, scorch the fountains of tears, curse him as only thou canst curse. . . ."

Here we have a prime example of the foreshadowing of modern psychological discoveries in the work of a literary genius; but we do not know whether nineteenth-century readers comprehended the meaning of this passage in the same way we do today. Perhaps it is only on the basis of recent research on grief reactions in children that we can fully grasp the psychological implications of De Quincey's symbolic imagery.

By the time the child has reached late adolescence, his reactions to separation from his mother differ markedly. He may even welcome the opportunity for independence from his family when he leaves home to go off to college. Nevertheless, the remnants of early childhood reactions might involuntarily reassert themselves, giving a melancholic coloring to the daily life of the first-year college student and generating persistent fantasies whose symbolic content centers on abandonment, rejection, and lack of personal worthiness of the affection of others.

In adult life we can sometimes see manifestations of protest, despair, and detachment when married couples or lifelong friends are separated for several months. The symptoms become most clearly visible in adults when death has entered the household. The intense grief so openly expressed in the words and facial expressions of the young child separated from his mother seems to reappear in the adult as he goes through the prolonged period of mourning. Nevertheless, the grief reactions of children may differ in some important respects from the comparable reactions of bereaved adolescents and adults.

A recent study conducted by Martha Wolfenstein (1966) in a guidance clinic for children and adolescents suggests certain points of similarity and difference between the child's stages of grief, as described by Bowlby and Robertson, and the emotional reactions of teen-age boys and girls who have lost a parent. The dead parent is usually idealized by the teen-ager; all his anger and protest is diverted toward the surviving parent or toward other adults (including the therapist) who try to help him. In the most mature adolescents, however, the reproachful feelings toward the dead ("abandoning") parent eventually emerge, and this phase is then followed by grief reactions that resemble the phase of despair. But the final phase of detachment in normal adolescents, just as in normal adults, seems quite different and does not lead to generalized withdrawal from all emotional attachments. Rather, the detachment seems to be narrowly confined to the memory image of the deceased, enabling the bereaved person once again to develop close relationships with friends and parent substitutes.

Wolfenstein suggests that this constructive type of mourning may be possible only after the adolescent has already gone through the process of developing a fair degree of emotional independence from his parents. She points out that during normal adolescence and postadolescence there is a period of several years when the young person is actively struggling to sever his emotional ties with his family, during which time he goes through "trial mourning" for his living parents. The result of this process is that he finally becomes able to renounce his childlike dependence on his parents. This emotional achievement during adolescence may then serve as a kind of model for handling separations and losses throughout the rest of his life, so that he becomes capable of facing up to the subsequent death of a loved one without becoming suicidal or resorting to the extreme forms of pathological detachment.

Comparison of Normal and Pathological Grief

Edith Jacobson, an eminent American psychoanalyst who has made a lifelong study of the clinical problems of treating depressed and grief-stricken adults, has given a detailed account of the psychological processes that differentiate normal mourning from pathological depressive reactions (1957).

A CASE OF NORMAL GRIEF

Jacobson describes a typical case of a middle-aged woman in a state of profound grief following the death of her husband.

This widow was not a patient for individual therapy but had come only for a brief consultation on family problems when her life was disrupted by bereavement. We do not know whether she went through an initial phase of protest, but at the time of the consultation she felt full of despair. She wept copiously and dwelt constantly on memories of her dead partner. One of the few times she expressed any joy in life was when she recalled the visits she and her husband had taken to beautiful places in the mountains. But even these memories made her weep. Despite her pervasive sadness, she managed to keep going in her work and gradually found that it was a source of consolation to her. Although her social activities were markedly reduced, she still saw a few old friends, particularly those who had known her husband and were willing to talk with her about him. At times she expressed feelings of guilt for not having done everything possible to help her husband or for having become angry with him when he did not deserve it.

A follow-up interview months later indicated that the phase of despair was followed by progressive detachment from her dead husband, with a corresponding increase of renewed interest in the existing social world, similar to the outcome of mourning in the most mature adolescents. Certain of her friendships had intensified, and her painful preoccupation with the activities she had shared with her husband had now given way to enjoyable pursuits of those same activities with friends. When she went to the mountains to look at the scenery, she felt as though she were doing it for both of them. She still had sad remembrances of her husband, and in the midst of an enjoyable activity she would think, "If only he were still alive and could experience this happy event with me"; but such thoughts no longer were so painful as to spoil her enjoyment.

She also developed new hobbies and skills in which her husband had shown a special interest. Thus, while gradually detaching herself emotionally from the lost love object, she took over certain of his values, as if to compensate for the loss. We shall return shortly to this form of "identification with the lost object" when we discuss Freud's hypotheses concerning the normal processes of mourning.

The despair followed by gradual detachment in the mourning reactions of this widow appears to be typical of the way many normal persons react to bereavement.

A CASE OF SEVERE DEPRESSION

Jacobson describes a contrasting case of another bereaved woman of approximately the same age in order to highlight the characteristics of pathological grief. This profoundly depressed woman was grieving over the death of her sister, but she showed little weeping or sadness; her main complaint was that life had become empty and that she was no longer interested in anything that used to please her. Now she felt restless, constantly seeking momentary pleasures but never succeeding. She suffered from vaguely defined painful emotions, which she tried to dispel by having affairs, just for the fun of it, with casual male acquaintances. But the fun never lasted very long.

At times she suffered from guilt feelings about her negligence and immorality, and yet, unlike the widow, she never felt any guilt with regard to the person for whom she was grieving. Her grief turned into a chronic state of depression, which led her to seek escape from external social reality as well as from her own inner reality of guilt and bereavement. Whereas the widow's acute grief gradually subsided and was followed by a more or less progressive return to normal activity, this woman's grief persisted unchanged over a period of years, and she continuously avoided the company of all her former friends. Depressive inhibitions affected her thought processes and her work, as well as her social life. Because of the seriousness of this woman's psychological disturbance she was given prolonged therapy, during which it became apparent that her underlying problem centered in ambivalent feelings toward her dead sister: Although she had affection for her, she also had intense feelings of hostility, which she was unable to acknowledge but which generated severe guilt feelings. Time and again the analyst noted in the patient's dreams, free associations, and transference fantasies the signs of intense guilt about her hostile wishes toward her sister; the guilt appeared to be central to her inability to end her grieving.

DIFFERENCES BETWEEN THE TWO TYPES OF REACTIONS

These two cases illustrate some of the major differences between normal and pathological grief reactions precipitated by bereavement. According to numerous clinical psychiatric surveys, the pathological symptoms of prolonged depression are most likely to occur in persons who have two main characteristics: (1) a history of long-standing emotional disorder and (2) unacknowledged hostility toward the lost person, which generates intense guilt. Thus, the loss of a loved one is merely a precipitating factor that touches off the acute symptoms of depression, such as the feelings of worthlessness, the detachment from friends, and the constriction of interests that were described in the case of the woman whose emotional disorder was precipitated by the death of her sister. The constellation of repressed hostility and guilt toward the lost person that was revealed during the psychoanalytic treatment of this depressed woman is often encountered in the treatment of other such cases and appears to be at the core of the pathological depressions evoked by bereavement. In the most extreme instances these depressed patients become preoccupied with feelings of worthlessness and suicidal thoughts, and there is usually some risk that they actually will commit suicide.

In contrast, normal grief does not produce such intense feelings of worthlessness and guilt that the person is impelled toward drastic self-punishment. Not only are the feelings of despair less self-condemnatory, but the period of acute emotional turmoil is much shorter. Typically, the normal grief pattern following the loss of a loved one begins with a period of numbness and shock. Upon learning of the death, the person reacts with disbelief. For several days his feelings may be blunted and he may be in a semidazed state, punctuated by episodes of irritability and anger. In some instances the protest reactions take the extreme form of outbursts of impotent rage, as when adult brothers and sisters bitterly blame one another for having failed to do something that might have prolonged the life of their elderly parent. This initial phase usually ends by the time of the funeral, which often can release the tears and feelings of despair that had been bottled up in the grief-stricken person. Thereafter, a very intense grief reaction ensues: The mourner weeps copiously, yearns for the lost person, and wishes he had been more helpful and considerate while the loved one was still alive. He may openly express a hopeless form of protest combined with despair, repeating over and over such phrases as "Oh God, why did this have to happen?" and "Why couldn't I have prevented it?" These attacks of agitated distress are likely to alternate with periods of more silent despair, during which the sufferer is preoccupied with memories of the dead person.

For many days and perhaps weeks the mourner remains somewhat depressed and apathetic, expresses a general sense of futility, and becomes socially withdrawn, although he still goes through the motions of carrying out his usual social obligations. During this period of despair, he is likely to suffer from insomnia, psychosomatic intestinal disorders, loss of appetite, restlessness, and general irritability. A tendency to deny the fact of the death may persist for many weeks; the mourner continues to think of the dead person at times as still alive and present in the house. There is also a tendency to idealize the dead person in memory and, as in the case of the widow described earlier, to seek companionship mainly with persons who are willing to limit their conversation to talking about him.

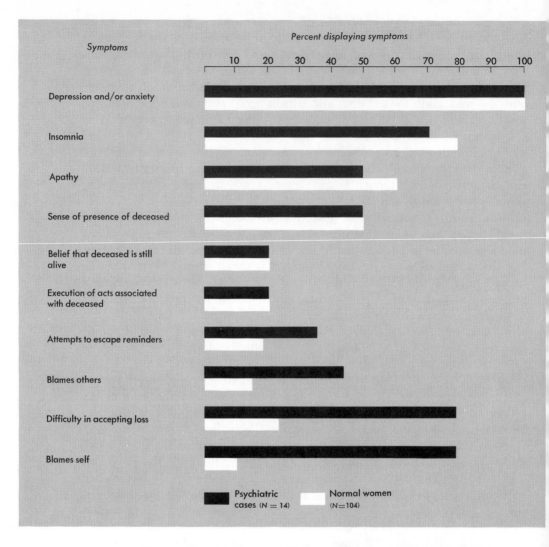

Figure 10-2   *Incidence of grief symptoms in two matched groups of bereaved women: psychiatric and nonpsychiatric cases of women under 60 years of age who had recently become widows or experienced the death of a blood relative. (Based on data from Marris, 1958 [data for normal women], and Parkes, 1965 [data for psychiatric cases])*

The mourner is usually able to return to work and resume other daily activities, such as talking with friends and relatives, after about two or three weeks. But he may continue to withdraw from certain types of social affairs that used to give him pleasure. After a month or two the most acute symptoms begin to subside, but there may still be residual sadness, yearning, and attacks of acute grief during the ensuing months.

The above description was drawn from a large number of clinical studies of bereavement. There are also a few systematic research investigations that highlight similarities and differences between normal bereaved persons and depressed psychiatric patients. Marris (1958), for example, obtained a random sample of widows living in one section of London by tracing their names through the official registers that reported the death of their husbands. He interviewed more than 100 widows, ranging in age from 25 to 56, in order to determine the percentage who had suffered, at least temporarily, from various symptoms of grief following the death of the husband.

A parallel study was designed by Parkes (1965) for the purpose of determining the extent to which normal bereavement resembles "reactive depression" in hospitalized psychiatric patients. Parkes was able to make systematic comparisons by selecting a small group of women who were hospitalized because of severe bereavement reactions and who matched, in age and social background, the nonhospitalized widows studied by Marris. The main findings are shown in Figure 10-2.

When we compare the main symptoms of emotional disturbance observed in both groups, we note that the percentages are almost identical for the first six symptoms listed in the figure but are different for the remaining four symptoms. The most pronounced differences are for the last two: The majority of the psychiatric patients showed difficulty in accepting the loss (which represents some form of denial) and blamed themselves for the death of the loved one; only a minority of the normal widows showed such symptoms. These findings help to confirm certain of Freud's observations and hypotheses, presented in his classic study, "Mourning and Melancholia" (1917): Normal grief, according to Freud, resembles abnormal grief, except that the latter involves much more latent hostility toward the deceased and consequently intense latent guilt, which gives rise to abnormal defenses—denial and a deflection of hostility from the dead person to oneself. It is this displacement of hostility that is regarded as a major impetus to suicide among persons suffering from pathological grief.

Sexual Promiscuity
as a Reaction to Bereavement

Another subtle bereavement reaction is the bereaved person's indulgence in sexual promiscuity or in other deviant activities that violate his earlier moral code. Since the deviant behavior ordinarily is kept secret, it is difficult to obtain systematic evidence on this point. Case studies suggest that many widows and widowers begin to engage in promiscuous sexual affairs for the first time in their lives after several months of mourning the loss of the spouse. In some instances these are loveless sexual affairs that appear to be a form of psychological narcosis to forget the past, but in others the indiscriminate sexual activity appears to be a first step toward reestablishing relationships with other persons and finding someone to replace the dead spouse. It seems that when a man loves his wife and she dies, he cannot contemplate replacing her except by a temporary sexual substitute. But for many months after his wife's death no substitute will satisfy his longing for his dead spouse, so each new sexual partner is quickly dropped. This period of promiscuity is often followed by the final selection of a woman who can be loved, and the widower is then likely to settle down and remain as faithful to her as he had been to his first wife. Paradoxically, then, the period of crude sexual promiscuity may be a step toward recovering from grief that enables the person to regain a normal love relationship.

The same process seems to occur in many widows, although they are less likely than men to be open about it. There are, of course, many popular jokes about the sexual availability of widows, but what is commonly overlooked is the fact that if they are promiscuous, it is generally during a painful period while they are still suffering from intense grief. This aspect of promiscuous sexual behavior in an emotionally upset widow is vividly conveyed in an autobiographical book by Caitlin Thomas, entitled *Leftover Life to Kill* (1957). The book is devoted largely to a subjective description of her mourning reactions during the first year after the death of her husband, Dylan Thomas, whose famous lines to his father about death are quoted at the beginning of this chapter. At the age of 39, his health ruined by chronic alcoholic intoxication, Dylan Thomas himself certainly tried not to "go gentle into that good night." His wife describes her own protesting rage and grief at the unexpected loss:

> Dylan and dying, Dylan and dying, they don't go together; or is it that they were bound to go together; he said so often enough, but I did not heed him. I was as foolish as women are supposed to be, the traditional woman, paid no attention, took him for granted, was only concerned with how to express my own aggressive, demanding, frustrated, vile, jealous self. And look what he had done to me! How brutally cruelly am I punished; surely out of proportion to my misdoing [p. 6].

In her attempt to give a complete, truthful record of what the death of her husband meant to her, she tells how deeply she resented the barren existence imposed on widows by the rigid dictates of her community, a small Welsh village whose foibles had been dissected in her husband's well-known play, *Under Milk Wood*. Unlike the widows who carefully conceal their promiscuous sexual behavior during the mourning period, Caitlin Thomas openly admitted the sordid details. From what she says, we can

see that her aggressive break with the community norms was partly a protest against the unsympathetic scrutiny of the townsfolk, but more than
that it was a hostile attack against her dead, deserting husband and against
her own guilt-ridden, depressed self:

> I did all the things a Lady should not do, and showed them, aggres-
> sively, just how unladylike a Lady can be. I gave myself up with selfless
> abandonment to being awful. . . .
> I stole their sons and husbands, doing violence to both our diversely
> raw feelings; violating purposefully my most precious holy vows to Dylan;
> saying his golden endearing words for me to them, making the same
> familiar sweet affectionate gestures . . . inciting a deliberate sacrilege, a
> shameful sacrifice of our love that was too stubborn to be put out.
> And all this fervour of destruction, to no, not one, flickering twinge of
> improvement, curative effect in my buried, unremitting black burning world;
> the ridiculous reverse; an increase in my inescapable dedication to Dylan
> and a mutilated, guilt-soaked, pride-stripped body [pp. 15–16].

Since Caitlin Thomas's flamboyant, emotional style shows so pervasively the influence of Dylan Thomas, one is led to wonder if she produced this diary-like account partly to work through her sense of loss. She
seems to identify with her dead husband by incorporating into her own
writing some of the salient attributes of his pungently ornamented poetry.

The Old Sergeant
and the Old Citizen Syndromes

Most of the observations of adult grief reactions we have considered so far come from studies of widows, but essentially the same patterns
of grief appear in bereaved men. Although no systematic research has been
carried out on the grief reactions of widowers, many observations have been
made of grief reactions among combat soldiers when they lose their close
friends. In some instances soldiers who have been suffering the miseries of
front-line duty a long time and have lost many comrades become depressed,
withdrawn, and apathetic. So frequent is this extreme reaction in wartime
that it has been given a special name: the "Old Sergeant syndrome" (Sobel,
1949). The soldiers' apathetic withdrawal might be a primitive effort to
ward off feelings of overwhelming grief and anxiety that would be too
painful to bear (perhaps resembling the final detachment phase of grief in
children described by Bowlby and symbolized by De Quincey as "Our Lady
of Darkness, the mother of lunacies").

The pattern of incapacitating detachment, anxiety, and depression has
been labeled the "Old Sergeant syndrome" by military psychiatrists because

the most striking cases have been found among conscientious noncommissioned officers who were "old" in combat experience. A similar pattern of affective disturbance is often encountered in elderly people who after a long, normal life are beginning to lose their sense of physical well-being, are neglected by members of their family, and are cut off from old friends. From a psychological standpoint many aged persons are in a stressful situation comparable to that of the infantrymen in combat, as they battle the infirmities, restrictions, and other harassments of old age. Those in homes for the aged—even when they have excellent facilities for social contact and distraction—undergo one crisis after another as they see members of their in-group become incapacitated by heart trouble, crippling arthritis, and muscular weakness or as they see their friends taken suddenly to the hospital for emergency surgery, never to return. As the casualties mount month after month and year after year, many senior citizens begin to develop chronic depressive symptoms. If, in addition, they experience the most dreaded event in the life of elderly married persons, the death of the spouse, they are especially likely to become despondent, apathetic, and utterly hopeless in their outlook, since it is no longer possible for them to conceive of any replacement for their lifelong companion. Their apathetic withdrawal parallels that of the soldiers who develop the Old Sergeant syndrome, and so we might well use a parallel term for them—the "Old Citizen syndrome."

Perhaps there is a tendency toward defensive detachment in response to repeated or prolonged loss of affectionate persons in all socialized human beings of whatever age—the young child sent to a hospital for many weeks, the mature man or woman relocated in a new city far from all former friends, or the elderly person outliving all those who had been closest to him.

The Psychoanalytic Theory of Mourning

Sigmund Freud's (1917) account of normal mourning emphasizes the process of recovery. During the initial stage of mourning, according to Freud, the bereaved person reminisces constantly about his past life with the dead person, becoming more and more aware of the painful disparity between the richness of the past, when the beloved was alive, and the emptiness of the present and future. The central postulate of Freud's theory is that as the person engages in this form of painful reminiscing, he gradually "works it through," so that eventually he is able to accept the changes in his life imposed by the loss. While carrying out this "work of mourning," as Freud labeled it, the bereaved person makes a variety of efforts to compensate for his loss. A number of psychological mechanisms are involved, and they are discussed in the sections that follow.

COMPENSATION THROUGH UNCONSCIOUS IDENTIFICATION

One of the main compensatory mechanisms described in case studies by Freud and other psychoanalysts is *unconscious identification*. Following the death of his father, for example, a man is likely to show a striking change in his physical appearance, mode of dress, and mannerisms, all of which begin to resemble those of the dead parent. (An instance is cited in Part II, pp. 364–65, of a man who grew a beard after his father died. The son thereby assumed his image of his father, who had gone unshaven for several days before his death.) More deep-seated characteristics are also likely to be assumed, including the ethical code, ideals, and values that the dead person is believed to have stood for. (An example is presented in Part IV, pp. 768–70.) The mourner may suddenly accept and rationalize parental attitudes and moral standards that he had rejected while his father was alive. Sometimes the acceptance will be so uncritical that the person comes into conflict with his wife and friends, who continue to reject the standards of the older generation. From the fantasies and free associations of bereaved patients, Freud inferred that this "postponed obedience" is based on unconscious imitation of the lost person, which represents an effort to retain him symbolically, to keep his image alive.

The mechanism of identification, together with other processes that enter into the work of mourning, may gradually enable the mourner to adapt to the loss. Thus, after a period of several weeks or months of mourning the grief-stricken person begins to regain his interest in daily life activities, to console himself in one way or another, and to seek substitutes with whom he can at least partially satisfy certain of the longings that were centered upon the dead person. Unless he is predisposed to develop pathological depressions, he will ultimately find one or more persons to replace the lost one.

We have had an example of prolonged grief and pathological detachment in the case of the middle-aged woman whose depressive symptoms were precipitated by the death of a sister toward whom she had always had intensely ambivalent feelings. This type of predisposition is thought to be most pronounced in persons who display signs of chronic conflict in dealing with members of their family throughout their lives. Such persons, from early childhood on, show frequent manifestations of strong dependent needs that no one can ever quite satisfy. Following the death of a close relative or spouse, their unconscious identification is likely to take a pathological form, involving imitation of physical defects or other undesirable traits that make the mourner suffer all the more. These mourning reactions are colored by the mixture of love and hate they had long felt while the person was still living. They may have frequently quarreled and even broken off relations in a stormy outburst of pent-up hostility. As one psychoanalyst put it, "Those who cannot live well with the living cannot live well with the dead."

At the beginning of the period of bereavement the normal mourner concentrates on reviewing his past life with the loved person, carefully contemplating all of the ways in which he will be missed. As he mentally rehearses each bit of past experience, he painfully acknowledges to himself that "here is another thing we did together, but now the two of us can never do it again." This distressing process is eloquently conveyed in a poem by Friedrich Rückert that forms the text for one of Gustav Mahler's most moving songs in his *Kindertotenlieder*. In the poem a father tries to appease his intense feelings of grief over the loss of his two children, who died from scarlet fever, by telling himself, "They must be back soon . . . there is nothing to worry about. They've been gone so long because they've decided to take a longer walk than usual." Later he sees his wife coming through the door and expects, as usual, to see her holding the hand of their younger child. But the child is not there; there is nothing at all where the child's hand should be. The bereaved father realizes once again that his little girl is no longer alive, and in his thoughts he speaks to the dead child: "From now on, when mother comes through the door, you will not be there."

This preoccupation with the harsh reality of death, partly accepting and partly denying it, is an essential step in the direction of resignation. Like the father in this poem, the mourner must resign himself to all the inevitable consequences of the death, every one of which must be worked through by the mourner before he can psychologically bury the dead (Caplan, 1961).

Although the bereaved person makes repeated efforts to prolong the "sweet sorrow" of parting by fantasying that the loved one is alive and will soon return home, he gradually faces up to the painful truth. Acceptance of the facts of the death is sometimes facilitated by the various funeral rituals and mourning customs that each society evolves for dealing with the problem of bereavement. At first grief is experienced only in very small doses; if it were to be released in its full strength, the person would feel overwhelmed with utter despair (Fenichel, 1945). Each memory of the loved person in a different context of daily life must be brought up and relived in the mourner's imagination before the work of mourning is completed and the full reality of the loss can be accepted. Only then can the person become free from his preoccupation with the loss and take an interest in his daily activities with other persons.

WHEN THE WORK OF MOURNING HAS BEEN DONE

Inadequate or incomplete mourning, which usually involves persistent denial of the death, is likely to lead to prolonged depression and some form of pathological identification with the dead person. In a survey of bereaved persons who were depressed enough to require psychiatric treatment, approximately 25 percent were found to have developed physical symptoms resembling those suffered by the dead person during his last illness (Parkes, 1964).

In contrast, when the person's symptoms of grief subside after he has completed the work of mourning, he manifests a more constructive type of identification, enriching his personality by taking over certain of the interests and values of the dead person that are compatible with his own. An example of constructive identification was cited in the case of the widow who became more interested in visiting places of great natural beauty in an effort to do some of the things her husband would have done with her. Augmented interests and activities of this kind seem to be motivated by an unconscious wish to triumph over death by continuing to live as though the loved person were not dead; but unlike the pathological forms of denial these efforts lead to appropriate actions that increase rather than decrease the person's overall satisfaction of recreational, esthetic, or social needs and help to maintain a high level of self-esteem.

Another constructive outcome that can ensue from the work of mourning arises from the mourner's tendency to have frequent daydreams in which he converses with the dead person. Particularly in children who have lost a parent, these imaginary conversations can be an impetus to creative imagination. It has been noted that a number of outstanding writers, such as Dante, Rousseau, the elder Dumas, Emily Brontë, Baudelaire, and A. E. Housman, lost their mothers or fathers when they were very young (Kanzer, 1953). Their writings, like De Quincey's, are pervaded with feelings of melancholy and contain many symbolic images of reunion with the dead.

Mourning Induced by Personal Disasters

The psychoanalytic theory of mourning implies that the same gradual process of working through that characterizes bereavement will occur whenever an individual loses any object of great symbolic value to him or fails in the quest for goals linked with his ego ideals, such as having good health, a happy marriage, and a successful career. Here again the stricken person reminisces and makes painful comparisons between the rich past and the empty present. And again the work of mourning must be completed before the person is able to accept the limitations imposed by the loss or failure, to resume his daily activities, and to find substitute satisfactions for the ones he has lost.

Thus, according to the theory, we should expect that any major disappointment in any important sphere of a person's life will have essentially the same emotional consequences as bereavement and separation, giving rise to intense grief that will persist until the loss is fully worked through.

For normal personalities, the intensity and duration of grief reactions generally are roughly proportional to the perceived magnitude and importance of the loss. It seems appropriate, therefore, to use the term *reflective grief* to refer to this normal type of emotional response to objective loss (see pages 114–22). During a period of separation, the more important the missing person is from the standpoint of fulfilling emotional needs, the greater will be the intensity of reflective grief. So, too, when a man undergoes a loss of status or of cherished possessions. If he is physically injured, the more he is incapacitated, the more intense will be his reflective grief.

From studies of what typically happens when a cancer victim finds out about his "death sentence," we learn that even the most profound feelings of despair can gradually subside if the victim is able to work through the anticipated loss of his own life and discover some limited ways of gaining compensatory satisfactions during his remaining days. Again the recovery process seems to be essentially the same as in bereavement, so that by the end of several weeks or months of mourning, the loss is no longer the dominating preoccupation of the stricken victim; the painful contrasts between the sunny past and the oppressive present are relegated to a corner of his mind, so that only on special occasions, such as commemorative ceremonies, will he momentarily dwell upon his loss and reexperience the pangs of sorrow.

Shands (1955) has described the marked changes in mood and outlook in a series of cancer patients, all of whom initially reacted to the traumatic information about their disease with dazed shock and apathy but gradually recovered their emotional equanimity sufficiently to go about their business again. The grieving phase appears to be an essential step in this development.

> Grieving is a response to the loss of a whole system of assumptions and expectations upon which human beings build a view of the world. In some manner the weeping reaction . . . serves to "dissolve" the old system in such a way that it can be replaced by a new. Where the grieving is blocked for any reason, the patient has to adopt some precarious defensive sort of adaptation rather than attempting, after clearing the site, to make a new construction with the materials at hand [Shands, 1955, p. 406].

The reorientation that follows these reactions of reflective grief is adaptive, in that it enables the patient once again to take an interest in the social world around him, to plan his actions in a realistic way that maximizes his chances for survival, and to take account of the limitations imposed by his illness. Certain situational factors, such as the availability of a sympathetic listener, can greatly facilitate the reorientation process, provided the personality of the patient is sufficiently mature.

Whenever a person is seriously ill or suffers any other misfortune, he becomes especially sensitive to any apparent sign of rejection or lack of sympathy from his relatives or friends. In part this sensitivity seems to stem from the arousal of deep-seated dependency needs and involves a reactivation of childhood fears of being abandoned (Janis, 1958). Thus, any failure on the part of a physician, nurse, or visitor to keep an appointment with an ill person, or any other apparent form of neglect, is likely to evoke an emotional reaction out of all proportion to the circumstances. Similarly, following any other type of major setback—an unsuccessful marriage, a career failure, or a humiliating loss of social status—any objective sign of rejection by a close friend or relative can add considerably to the burden and contribute to inducing depression.

The Emotional Aftermath of Large-Scale Disasters

Following large-scale disasters, a pattern of mourning reactions similar to those just described is often seen among survivors who escape intact.

THE DISASTER SYNDROME

So frequent is the sequence of dazed shock followed by grief and mourning in disaster-stricken cities that it has been called the "disaster syndrome." Wallace (1956, 1957) observed the syndrome among many survivors of a tornado that destroyed a large section of Worcester, Massachusetts. He concluded that whenever a person witnesses destruction within his own community, he goes through a process of assimilation that is identical with the work of mourning. He asserts that even when a survivor has not undergone any personal loss in a disaster, he is shocked by the "cultural damage": When he sees that a part of his culture is no longer intact, he reacts "as if a beloved object were dead."

> Again and again in the interviews the phrase "the end of the world" occurs to describe the phantasy of the survivors; the sight of block after block of ruined houses, of maimed and bleeding people, fallen trees, scarred and lifeless lawns, bedraggled wires, and everything covered with mud, aroused momentarily in many the thought that this was the earth's last hour, or that an atomic bomb had fallen, or that the whole city of Worcester was in ruins [Wallace, 1956, pp. 62–63, p. 24].

The dominant reaction during the initial stage, according to Wallace, is "stunned disbelief, inability to express emotion, [and] random movement." Two further stages again closely parallel mourning for a lost loved one: "A stage of passivity, dependence, acceptance of sympathy and help from family and friends; and finally a stage of joining with the community in burying the dead and of taking up a new life more or less free of disabling grief over the deceased [Wallace, 1957]."

THE STARING REACTION

A peculiar phenomenon follows every large-scale disaster and seems to be closely linked with the process of working through the cultural damage. People living nearby converge on the disaster site and stare, hour after hour, at the destroyed buildings. This staring behavior appears to be obsessional and is accompanied by disturbed feelings of morose perplexity. This is suggested by interviews following a disaster caused by the bursting of a frozen gas main, which produced a bomb-like explosion in a residential section of New Haven, Connecticut, completely demolishing a three-story house and killing or injuring all the occupants (Janis, 1965). A large number of silent spectators who lived in the immediate neighborhood spent the greater part of the daylight hours, day after day, standing outside in the bitter cold and staring fixedly at the black, gaping hole containing the charred debris from the house that was destroyed. (See Figure 10-3.) From interviews with these people it became apparent that although they had not

Figure 10-3 *An example of the staring reaction. The scene is in Worcester, Massachusetts, shortly after the city was hit by a tornado. (From Wallace, 1956)*

been close friends of any of the victims, their mood resembled that of grief-stricken mourners. Their thoughts were directed toward trying to comprehend the significance of the disaster, not in terms of its physical causes, which had already been explained to them, but in relation to their personal concepts of life and death. For example, a man who lived across the street and had seen the burning house suddenly crumble to the ground made the following comment:

> I just stand here all day long looking across the street, I don't know why. I can't get over it. To think that they could be so alive the night before, playing cards, talking to us. Then all of a sudden, for no reason, they are wiped out. A big house is there one minute and the next minute nothing is left of it at all. I just can't understand it [Janis, 1965, p. 217].

This man kept a silent vigil, standing outside all day long and staring at the destroyed house. He avoided speaking to anyone in the crowd of curious "outsiders," toward whom he expressed resentful feelings ("The police ought to keep them out"). On the whole, however, his mood was clearly depressive, and most of his comments, like the one quoted above, indicated an

Figure 10-4 Another example of the staring reaction. Government employees watch television after news of President John F. Kennedy's assassination, November 22, 1963.

inner struggle to assimilate the personal implications of the distressing disaster events he had witnessed.

In the interviews with others who lived in the same neighborhood there were similar indications that their staring behavior was part of a general preoccupation with the disaster as a distressing demonstration of the uncertainty of life. Their depressive tone and their quasi-philosophical expressions of perplexity about man's vulnerability to sudden disaster indicated an effort to work through a painful aspect of the human condition that could no longer be ignored.

Assimilating Bad News

The pattern of reactions just described seems to be characteristic of the individual's efforts to assimilate any bad news that has a disruptive effect on his life. If a man is fired from his well-established position in a business firm or if he discovers that his wife has been unfaithful, the blow will evoke essentially the same sequence of stunned shock followed by a state of dejection and obsessional preoccupation. Rage and protest usually enter into the emotional reactions to a greater degree in these interpersonal disasters than in impersonal ones, but after a time grief over the loss becomes dominant, and then the person starts to recover from the blow as he carries out the work of mourning.

To at least a mild degree, the same sequence is sometimes evoked in millions of people when there is bad news about a national or international crisis. This is what happened in the United States and in many European countries in November 1963, following the assassination of President Kennedy. Interviews of a cross-section of the American public (Sheatsley & Feldman, 1964) indicated that a large part of the population remained glued to their television sets, watching the last films taken of the President, the funeral, and other sights linked with the disaster, just as when people converge on a destroyed town and stare obsessively (see Figure 10-4). According to the poll results, the average adult in the U.S. cross-section reported having spent more than 8 hours every day for four days listening to the radio or watching the television coverage of the President's assassination and funeral; more than 25 percent reported having spent most of their waking hours watching the television coverage and talking about the assassination. The preoccupation was so strong that almost 50 percent of the U.S. cross-section had trouble falling asleep during the four days of national mourning. The authors conclude that the most frequent types of reaction to the President's death

> followed a well-defined pattern of grief . . . an initial phase of shock and disbelief; a developing awareness of the loss coupled with feelings of

sadness, sorrow, shame, and anger; the onset of physical symptoms such as tears, tenseness, sleeplessness, fatigue, and loss of appetite; and, finally, a gradual recovery in the course of which these symptoms disappeared and a normal state of well-being is reestablished [Sheatsley & Feldman, 1964, p. 207].

Implications
for Community Mental Health

Personal disasters pose a serious problem for the community, since they give rise to behavioral disturbances that prevent the afflicted person from functioning adequately as a parent, worker, and citizen. How frequently do people become grief-stricken by life crises of the type discussed in this chapter? A rough indication is provided by a study of 500 normal adult employees at Fort Detrick, Maryland, which showed that during the preceding year, *one out of every four* of these employees had undergone a major crisis—the death of a close relative, a serious illness, the breakup of their marriage, or some other disruptive event (Imboden, Canter, & Claff, 1963).

Preventive mental health measures that will decrease the intensity and duration of psychological incapacitation from such crises are actively being sought by many specialists in the field of mental health, with considerable government support. The goals are not only to reduce the amount of human suffering but also to reduce economic losses to the community resulting from absenteeism, from reduced work efficiency, and from overloading of the community's facilitie for providing psychiatric treatment and for taking care of children when their parents are unable to do so.

The observations and theory bearing on the work of mourning, discussed in the preceding sections of this chapter, support a relatively optimistic outlook with respect to the search for effective preventive measures. There are many indications that a normal person's recovery from the emotional impact of a personal disaster can be facilitated by appropriate environmental circumstances. Especially useful are those circumstances that enable him to obtain realistic information about available resources for coping with the loss, to correct his exaggeratedly bleak fantasies about the future, and, above all, to be in the presence of people who understand and are responsive to his emotional needs.

In recent years there have been many new developments in community mental health, some of which are intended to set up the appropriate conditions for helping grief-stricken people to carry out the work of mourning successfully and to regain their self-confidence. Three of the most promising developments entail establishing a therapeutic milieu, providing group therapy for the victim's family, and giving emotional inoculation to help people face impending crises.

A THERAPEUTIC MILIEU

Special efforts to create a supportive social environment are now being made in many general hospitals, nursing homes, old-age centers, and other institutions responsible for the care of incapacitated persons. The main goal is to relieve the symptoms of depression and anxiety that so frequently arise from the accumulated stresses of physical suffering, restricted daily activities, and separation from the family. In order to set up a favorable social milieu it is necessary to provide special training to all the aides, nurses, and physicians on the staff who are in daily contact with the patients. In recent years the training of nurses in particular has begun to reflect this new development by placing emphasis on meeting the emotional as well as the physical needs of hospitalized patients. Student nurses not only are made aware of the emotional problems they will encounter but are sometimes given supervised training in dealing with distressed patients. They are taught how to listen and respond appropriately and how to give reassurances that will help the patient overcome his intense feelings of apprehensiveness, anger, or grief without generating new sources of disturbance. But this type of training may not have the intended effect unless others on the staff share in maintaining an atmosphere that encourages the patients to speak freely. Moreover, new administrative policies are needed to provide the appropriate atmosphere and sufficient staff time for face-to-face discussions with the patients.

Another purpose of a therapeutic social environment, one that will also require drastic changes in the traditional approach to hospital management, is to promote active participation by the patients. This pertains most directly to encouraging the patients to participate actively in carrying out the necessary steps in their own convalescence, but it also includes contributing to the life of the institution—performing useful work when they are ready for it, visiting bedridden patients, and the like. Living arrangements for facilitating such participation must be specially designed to take account of the different types of social environments appropriate to the different stages of recovery. The intensive care units, where very ill and relatively helpless patients receive constant nursing care, might require modifications in architectural design to allow the patients to see for themselves that helpful persons are always at hand when needed. At the other extreme, the units for convalescing patients who can move about freely and start to take care of themselves might require a motel- or cottage-type arrangement of living quarters. Such a setup would encourage them to engage in normal activities—such as shopping trips—that would help restore their self-confidence in being able to handle the more independent way of life at home. It seems obvious, however, that at best this type of change will proceed very slowly. We cannot expect in the near future to see a rapid transformation of traditional hospital wards into a graded series of appropriate social environments for convalescing patients, since drastic changes are required in the architecture of the institutions as well as in the administrative policies and job functions of the staff.

GROUP TREATMENT FOR THE STRICKEN FAMILY

A second major development pertains primarily to the treatment of emotionally upset persons who are still living at home after being stricken by a personal disaster. This development is essentially an extension of the work of those psychiatrists, psychologists, social workers, and clergymen who are consulted by distressed individuals when they are bereaved or badly shaken by a catastrophic loss. Some therapists and counselors are beginning to use the special techniques of group therapy by working with the entire family during the crisis period. Their goals are usually quite modest: to increase the awareness of everyone in the family that they have mutual needs for emotional support and to open up channels of communication so that hitherto suppressed topics can be freely discussed. These family discussion sessions sometimes allow long-standing disagreements to be openly examined and at least partially resolved without generating the usual outbursts, recriminations, and mutual insults.

Family discussions conducted by a skilled psychological counselor are likely to be especially valuable when some members of the family are angry at the troubled person for having allowed the crisis to arise. For example, when an unmarried girl becomes pregnant, the parents may turn against their "wayward" daughter and treat her so harshly that they augment her suicidal depressive feelings; or else they and the older brothers and sisters may suppress their feelings but urge a hasty wedding or an abortion, which prevents the girl from working out her own solution and makes it difficult for her to work through her feelings of guilt, shame, and grief. In such circumstances a counselor may arrange for several group sessions with the adult members of the family. His intervention during these family discussion sessions may make a significant difference in enabling the girl to make her own decision and to recover her emotional equanimity. At the same time, the sessions allow other members of the family to ventilate their feelings in a way that does not lead to scapegoating or quarrels that would impair family relations in the future. This type of group treatment for the entire family is now being extended to many other types of personal crises, including those of students who are dejected about their course work and want to quit school against their parents' wishes and those of young men and women who have been arrested for smoking marijuana or for participating in other illegal acts.

The third development consists of interventions to help people prepare psychologically for a blow before it strikes, as in the case of a young person facing his first separation from his family, a married person whose spouse is fatally ill, or an older person who is being forced to retire from a gratifying career. Emotional inoculation is often worked into the treatment of disturbed personalities as part of group therapy or individual psychotherapy, but it is also given sometimes in special sessions for many people who ordinarily would not come to a clinic for psychological treatment.

The goal of emotional inoculation is to make the person aware of an impending crisis or disaster well in advance of the full confrontation. That way he has an opportunity to anticipate the loss, to start working through his anxiety and grief, and to make plans that might enable him to cope more effectively with the subsequent crisis. The technique consists of three steps, which are essentially applications of the research and theory on the work of worrying discussed in Chapter 6:

1. The first step is to give realistic information in a way that challenges the person's blanket reassurances so as to make him aware of his vulnerability. If the person perceives no threat at all or feels that the losses will be slight, he will be unmotivated to do the work of worrying or to plan preparatory actions for dealing with the subsequent crisis.

2. Once the person's anticipatory emotions are aroused, it becomes necessary to counteract feelings of helplessness, hopelessness, and demoralization. By discussing the person's image of the future, asking pertinent questions, and calling attention to certain of the known facts, a skilled counselor can help the person take account of reassurances that enable him to feel reasonably confident about surviving and ultimately recovering from the impending ordeal. When told about an oncoming disaster, many people become at least temporarily hypervigilant, and they over-react to the bad news with an exaggerated conception of the suffering in store for them. Their excessive fear and pessimism, however, can be corrected by reassuring information, particularly about the way other people can be counted on to help out. The success of emotional inoculation partly depends on providing a balance between arousal of anticipatory fear or grief on the one hand and authoritative reassurance on the other.

3. The final step is to encourage the person to work out his own ways of reassuring himself and his own plans for protecting himself. As a crisis approaches, many people tend to become passive and rely almost exclusively on the protective powers of authority figures or friends. If this tendency is not counteracted, they will later become bitterly disillusioned when some unavoidable suffering materializes. Furthermore, the emotional impact may be heightened by their sense of having been misled and aban-

doned. (This point was illustrated when we discussed the postoperative resentment of those surgical patients who felt relatively unworried before the operation. Many of them had relied on an almost religious faith in the doctors' powers to protect them from pain and suffering [pages 95–100].) Here again a delicate balance must be attained in order to gain the reassuring value that comes from having confidence in the good intentions and skills of the protective authorities without losing the additional gains that come from an attitude of self-reliance.

Conceivably, the amount of time and effort required for effective emotional inoculation might be reduced by the judicious use of films, recorded lectures, and pamphlets that are specially prepared to convey the essential preparatory information. The United States Peace Corps, for example, has developed a set of such communications for use in conjunction with group discussions. They are intended to provide emotional inoculation for volunteers who are about to leave for an arduous assignment overseas, where they will be separated from family and friends, subjected to cultural shock in an underdeveloped country, and probably exposed to a series of failures and other stresses that could make them feel depressed or demoralized. Unfortunately, we do not as yet have any systematic data from evaluation studies to indicate whether this program of emotional inoculation has achieved its objectives. In fact, there are only a few careful evaluative studies, such as the one on the successful emotional inoculation of surgical patients, that can be cited as a basis for extending the use of these preparatory techniques to large numbers of persons who are facing the prospects of surgery and comparable types of stress.

With regard to minimizing the disruptive emotional impact of separation and bereavement, there are some indications that when a normal person carries out the work of worrying before the loss actually occurs, he also begins to carry out the work of mourning (anticipatory grief) and can complete it more successfully afterward. But this hypothesis has not yet been adequately tested.

These remarks about the tentative status of emotional inoculation procedures and the need for systematic evaluation also apply to the other two new developments just described. So far, each of these developments has been carried out in only a few communities on a trial basis. If subsequent systematic research shows that they are effective and that they do not produce any seriously unfavorable side-effects, we can expect to see them applied on a wide scale in a large number of communities.

Along with the new practical developments in the field of community mental health, a broader conception of the problems posed by life crises has begun to emerge (Erikson, 1959; Caplan, 1964, 1965; Parad, 1965; Lazarus, 1966). The central theme is that any instance of bereavement, separation, failure, or suffering can be a turning point in the person's life, resulting either in emotional breakdown and sustained personality damage or a marked improvement in personality functioning. (Some examples of the latter type of outcome were presented in Chapter 6.) Crises are viewed as rare occasions when the person faces serious threats, losses, and demands that are near the limits of his resources for coping. But if the person solves adequately the difficult problems confronting him, his sense of self-confidence is greatly increased, and he may be able to overcome other difficulties that had been interfering with his adjustment in the past. This way of looking at episodes of stress and frustration, emphasizing the potentials for personality *progression* as well as regression, has been built into a general conceptual model of life crises by Gerald Caplan, a leading authority on problems of community mental health. Caplan (1964, 1965) applies this conception not only to stressful personal disasters of the type we have been discussing but also to the stresses arising from *changes in role* that occur during adolescence and adult life, such as starting college, getting married, having a baby, shifting to a new job, and taking on new responsibilities as a public leader in the community. The question of whether the outcome of any of these crises will be favorable or unfavorable from the standpoint of the person's mental health probably depends partly on his initial *personality strengths and weaknesses* and partly on certain types of *environmental circumstances*, like those discussed in this chapter and the preceding ones—circumstances that affect the person's cognitive awareness of vulnerability before the crisis materializes, his plans for coping with it, his opportunities for obtaining reassuring social support, and his attitude of self-confidence when he actually undergoes his worst moments of stress and frustration.

PART TWO
CONFLICT
AND DEFENSE

*Part Two is dedicated to Martha
and to Barbara and the rest of the next generation*

That which you have loved with youthful enthusiasm and admired with youthful ardor, that which you have secretly and mysteriously preserved in the innermost recesses of your soul, that which you have hidden in the heart: that you always approach with certain shyness, with mingled emotions, when you know that the purpose is to try to understand it.

SØREN KIERKEGAARD. Either/Or

Let them say he dared too much;
the audacity was beautiful.

CHARLES AUGUSTIN SAINTE-BEUVE.
Sonnet to Ronsard

CHAPTER 11
ORIGINS
OF PSYCHOANALYTIC
IDEAS

The first part of this book explored the psychology of external stress and frustration. The emphasis was on real crises, such as Don's near drowning, war, the death of a loved one, and a variety of external frustrations. Much of the material dealt with the critical variables in such extreme external dangers and with their usual behavioral effects, such as disruptive changes in normal behavior, escape and avoidance reactions, and methods of coping. The here and now —current reality and conscious experience or overt behavior—was the main concern. Since the criteria of stress and frustration are largely objective and since observable behavior is readily measurable, it was possible to draw heavily on field studies and laboratory experiments. Some individual case study material was also presented, largely as a source of insights and hypotheses for guiding the examination of systematic research or to illustrate the findings of such research.

In Part II we shift our attention to the causes of those behavioral disturbances that make up most of man's misery, to difficulties like those listed in Table 11-1. Internal, subjective factors, rather than extreme external dangers, are the causes of such disturbances. The subjective causes are nearly always unconscious. As Table 11-1 indicates, no aspect of man's re-

Table 11-1   Examples of Behavioral Disturbances

Behavior class	Minor disturbances	Major disturbances
Eating	Temporary loss of appetite or over-eating upon entering college.	Chronic inability to eat, resulting in extreme weight loss and even death. Chronic overeating, resulting in obesity.
Elimination	Temporary constipation or diarrhea when starting a new job.	Chronic constipation or diarrhea, resulting in physical illness.
Autonomic responses	Sweating or fast heartbeat on a first date or during an examination.	Sustained sweating or fast heart rate.
Sexual activity	Impotency or frigidity when first attempting intercourse, or with a particular person.	Chronic impotency or frigidity.
Affective reactions	Unexplained passing anxiety when talking with an instructor. Episodes of irrational anger with a close friend.	Chronic, intense anxiety. Chronic suspicious and angry behavior with everybody.
Perception	A student attending the funeral of a beloved teacher blots out the image of his dead body by "seeing" the open casket as closed. A student mishears his teacher's criticism as praise.	Hallucination that one's dead child still lives; a soda bottle wrapped in newspaper is experienced as the child. Hysterical blindness or deafness.
Memory	Forgetting the name of the speaker one is introducing to a seminar. Forgetting an appointment with a teacher one fears or dislikes.	Amnesia about long periods or critical events of one's life.
Thinking and learning	Inability to have thoughts and organize them for a particular part of a term paper. Temporary inability to learn about a particular subject or to develop a particular motor skill.	Chronic inability to study or think during examinations, resulting in academic failure by an intelligent student.
Speech	Temporary flustering and occasional slips of the tongue in everyday speech.	Severe stuttering. Loss of capacity for speech. Mutism.
Social relations	Brief disruptions in friendships.	Extreme isolation of "the loner" on the campus or of the hermit. The "social butterfly" or "hail-fellow-well-met" type who is unable to form close friendships.

markable range of behavior is immune to impairment by unconscious processes. His social life, cognitive functions, emotional behavior, and even his life-sustaining biological functions are all susceptible to such impairment.

Since we shall be concerned largely with unconscious processes, which usually originate in childhood, rather than with here-and-now crises, we shall draw primarily on psychoanalytic case studies and secondarily on experimental research. Most of what is known about the unconscious aspects of behavior has been learned through the use of the psychoanalytic method.

So far, the major contribution of systematic research to our knowledge in this area has been the occasional confirmation of hypotheses originating in clinical investigations, and this is likely to be true in the future. Experimental manipulation of "the unconscious" in the laboratory is extremely difficult, even if it were ethically justified.

Psychological conflict is the nexus of Part II. A state of conflict exists when the individual is prompted to respond simultaneously in different and incompatible ways. In the kind of conflict we will be dealing with here, the *approach-avoidance conflict*, the individual is prompted both to approach a goal and to avoid doing so. Unpleasant emotional states, such as anxiety and guilt, motivate the avoidance reactions. Sometimes external stimuli, usually unrealistically perceived, arouse these unpleasant emotions; but more often very human propensities, such as love and hate, do so, because people often anticipate that some danger will occur if they engage in sexual or aggressive behavior. Avoidance responses are methods of preventing the unpleasant emotions and anticipated dangers from materializing. Since the avoidance responses have this protective function, they are called *defense mechanisms* or, simply, *defenses*.

Persons under extreme realistic stresses, such as those examined in the first section, often use defenses to gain relief from their emotional distress. We saw in Chapter 5 that parachutists often *repress* their fear, in Chapter 9 that people may *inhibit* and *displace* aggression when frustrated, and in Chapter 10 that those bereft by the death of a loved one often *identify with the lost person* to ease their grief and *turn aggression around upon themselves* to avoid a sense of guilt for the rage they feel at their deprivation. One purpose of this part of the book is to examine a broader range of unpleasant external situations and to discuss in more detail the process of defense against them. But we shall be primarily concerned with the unconscious inner conflicts involving defenses against anticipated dangers.

Most psychologists agree that Sigmund Freud is the towering figure in the area of conflict and defense, and we shall discuss in detail the discoveries of Freudian psychoanalysis about conflict and the unconscious determinants of behavior. Thus, in the process of discussing conflict and defense we shall also be presenting elements of an introduction to Freud— the best of Freud, which in the writer's judgment consists of the many empirical phenomena Freud "discovered" and the concepts most immediately related to them, not his most abstract theory. Of course, "the best of Freud" also includes the example he set as a person and as an investigator, especially his everlasting commitment to understanding real people and to the science of psychology. A background knowledge of Freud is one component of a thoroughgoing grasp of the psychology of personality. While concentrating on Freudian findings, we shall also discuss some major contributions by psychologists with other theoretical or methodological orientations, such as Neal Miller and Kurt Lewin. Some important experiments by other research psychologists will also be considered in our discussion.

Freud's contribution to the understanding of human behavior has already been indicated in the first part of this book, as for example in the discussion of his concept of the belated mastery of trauma and his views on the work of mourning. But these are only fragments of his total contribution, much of which we shall consider. Yet some psychologists take an extremely negative position about psychoanalysis (for example, Wolpe & Rachman, 1960), maintaining that the clinical evidence and hypotheses put forth by Freud and other analysts are merely fanciful speculations that have no place in a "scientific" psychology. However, those findings that become generally accepted among psychoanalysts are grounded in careful and prolonged studies of people's lives. Such is the case for the findings with which we will be concerned.

In this chapter we shall review the origins of Freud's ideas about conflict and defense. In the next two chapters we shall discuss and illustrate different kinds of conflicts and formulate a general paradigm for the approach-avoidance conflict. Then in subsequent chapters we shall discuss some typical conflicts of childhood and adolescence in our Western culture and their influence on personality development and adult behavior. If childhood conflicts are unresolved and continue to exist unconsciously, they give rise to inappropriate, disturbed behavior in adulthood. We shall discuss several kinds of such inappropriate adult behavior: for example, unrealistic perceptions and inappropriate emotional reactions to innocuous external stimuli, and conflictful sexual and aggressive behavior. In the course of these discussions the kinds of dangers people anticipate, the situations in which they do so, and the kinds of unpleasant emotions that result will all be examined. Some defense mechanisms must necessarily be discussed as we proceed, but a systematic consideration of all the known defense mechanisms is postponed to the final chapters of this section.

If our discussions seem discursive, it is largely because of the nature of the subject matter and the limitations imposed by sequential, rather than simultaneous, presentation. It is impossible to present the subject matter of conflict and defense all at once or to present it in a neat series of steps. Instead, we shall take up some topics several times, drop them, and return to them again later. We do this largely because the intervening discussions would be disjointed if we postponed them or because they contribute to the background necessary for further examination of the topic. Our frequent use of case material may also add to the impression of discursiveness. This too is unavoidable. Freud's theories are based upon clinical case material; they are either incomprehensible or unbelievable without it. In addition, only case material conveys a sense of how psychological conflict *feels*. Without such a sense, *understanding* conflict is impossible.

The Historical Background

When we look into the origins of psychoanalytic ideas about conflict and defense, their empirical basis becomes clear. And by following Freud through his earliest discoveries, we come to appreciate the relationship between observation and inference in the clinical case study of a human personality. Although Freud's earliest concepts were subsequently modified because they were oversimplifications and grossly incomplete, they nevertheless included many key notions, such as unconscious motivation, conflict, repression, and other defenses.

When Sigmund Freud (1856–1939) started his neuropsychiatric medical practice in Vienna in 1886, he faced the problem of treating people who suffered from just the kinds of major disturbances presented in Table 11-1. Yet little was known about the causes of the disturbances or about effective ways to treat those patients. At first Freud used the conventional procedures, which were almost exclusively physical: baths, faradic electrical stimulation of various skin areas, massage, and rest cures. These failed, and toward the end of 1887 Freud turned to hypnosis, which was then moving to the center of psychiatric interest. In preparation for private psychiatric practice Freud had gone to Paris in 1885 and had seen the power of direct hypnotic suggestion demonstrated by Jean-Martin Charcot, the giant of French psychiatry. In Charcot's form of treatment a patient suffering from a functional (nonorganic) impairment was hypnotized by the therapist and simply told that he would no longer have his symptom even after the hypnotic trance ended. At Charcot's command, people in wheelchairs got up and walked, mutes started to talk, blind people saw, amnesiacs remembered who they were. After witnessing these and other dramatic results, Freud tried direct hypnotic suggestion when he began to use hypnosis. But gradually he realized that this method did not always cure the symptoms and that the removal of one symptom was frequently followed by the appearance of others. Furthermore, he became bored with direct hypnotic suggestion; he was not learning anything about the puzzling conditions he was trying to cure. Fortunately, he remembered what an older colleague and friend, Josef Breuer, had told him a few years earlier about a clinical experience in which hypnosis was used in a different way.

THE PATIENT WHO HELPED DISCOVER PSYCHOANALYSIS

During the winter of 1880–81, Breuer undertook the treatment of a now-famous patient, known in psychoanalytic literature as Anna O. When he first examined her, Breuer saw lying in bed in her home a 21-year-old unmarried woman. Anna O. had taken to her bed some weeks earlier, exhausted and very upset from five months of helping to care for her very sick father. When he died in April 1881, Anna's condition grew worse. During the course of her illness, she had a severe nervous cough, bad headaches, a noticeable cross-eyed squint, and many other symptoms. She often had strange visual experiences; for example, objects often looked bigger than normal. There was a spontaneous rhythm to Anna's daily life. In the afternoon she would be irresistibly sleepy and would sleep until sunset; then she would spontaneously pass into a deep trance state, which she called "clouds." At night she would become excited and have frightening hallucinations and fantasies. She might sleep a few hours, but upon awakening in the morning she would continue in this excited and hallucinatory state until she again entered the somnolent condition in the afternoon. As nearly as Breuer could determine, this "illness" first manifested itself, and then in only slight ways, as the weeks of nursing her sick father passed by.

Breuer treated Anna from the winter of 1880–81 until June 1882, a little over a year. He saw her every two or three days, at times daily. Apparently he started to treat her by prescribing narcotics and by generally ordering her routine. But a warm personal relationship developed between Anna and Breuer. They talked, much more than doctors and patients usually do. And here Anna O. made her own contribution to the psychology of personality. If Breuer visited her during her evening trances, or spontaneous hypnotic states, she would tell him of all the terrifying hallucinations and fantasies she had had that day. Breuer listened! Afterward all the excitement, anxiety, and horror created by her daytime hallucinations and fantasies temporarily ceased, and she was "normal" that night. But if something prevented Breuer from visiting for a few days, she grew more disturbed. She herself perceived the therapeutic value of their talks and came to call it "chimney sweeping" or "the talking cure." The beneficial effect of Anna's "chimney sweeping" took Breuer by surprise, but once he recognized it he deliberately and systematically used the method. He intentionally visited her in the evening, when she would be in her spontaneous hypnotic state. She would talk; he would listen. She would usually feel and function more normally after telling him of her frightening mental experiences of that day.

But then something else began to occur. As Anna spoke about her current symptoms, she would recall earlier emotional experiences that were obviously related to her current symptoms. These recollections usually were of previous emotional reactions that included some version of the current symptom. *When she vividly relived these past experiences, including especially the first one, the current symptom would disappear.* Since her illness started while she was caring for her sick father, it is not surprising that most of these symptom-creating emotional experiences occurred at that time. About Anna's nervous cough, for example, Breuer discovered:

> She began coughing for the first time when once, as she was sitting at her father's bedside, she heard the sound of dance music coming from a neighbouring house, felt a sudden wish to be there, and was overcome with self-reproaches. Thereafter, throughout the whole length of her illness she reacted to any markedly rhythmical music with a *tussis nervosa* [nervous cough]. [Breuer & Freud, 1893–95, p. 40]

Her cross-eyed squinting was a remnant of an incident when her father asked the time from his bed and she brought her watch very close to her nose to look at it as she fought back the tears and sadness she felt for him; the fact that things looked larger than usual was a repetition of the apparent increase in size of the watch dial. The spontaneous rhythm to her life—drowsiness in the afternoon and wakefulness at night—seemed to repeat her daily pattern when she was nursing her father: She would nap in the afternoon and sit up with him at night.

Once Breuer realized that her spontaneous hypnotic states facilitated the therapeutic recall of such significant experiences, he supplemented them with induced hypnosis. Through this combined use of spontaneous and induced hypnosis, Anna obtained relief from many of her symptoms. Thus, in the period from 1880 to 1882, patient and doctor collaborated in developing a new use of hypnosis for the investigation and treatment of psychological disturbances: cathartic, or abreactive, hypnotherapy.

Breuer did not apply his technique to other patients, but he told Freud about it in the fall of 1882. In 1888 or 1889, frustrated with the results of direct hypnotic suggestion, Freud tried Breuer's method and found it more satisfactory. It was just as effective and, more important, it seemed to shed light on the *causes* of the patient's symptoms. They *seemed* to be indirect expressions of forgotten memories of intensely unpleasant, overwhelming emotional experiences, for they disappeared when the memories were recalled with abreaction (reliving) of their emotional content. The memories were forgotten only in the sense that the individual was not aware of them; they still persisted "in the unconscious," fresh and dynamically pressing for expression and doing so in symptoms. This was a new hypothesis about mental aberrations—a brilliant searchlight penetrating the darkness for the curious, inquiring, and ambitious Freud. Little wonder that he now relied mainly upon abreactive hypnotherapy.

FREUD'S FIRST "PSYCHOANALYTIC" CASE STUDY

Soon, however, something happened that decisively influenced Freud's views about conflict and his therapeutic-investigative method. Freud found that he could not hypnotize every patient who came into his office. In view of his and Breuer's hypothesis, this posed only a practical problem. If he could enable the patient to recall the forgotten memories by some other means, the symptoms should still disappear. But how was he to do this? Here Freud recalled something he had recently observed in France in the clinic of Hippolyte Bernheim (1840–1919), another outstanding psychiatrist of the time:

> I was saved . . . by remembering that I had myself seen Bernheim producing evidence that the memories of events during [hypnosis] are only *apparently* forgotten in the waking state . . . . He had, for instance, given a woman in a state of [hypnosis] a negative hallucination to the effect that he was no longer present, and had then endeavored to draw her attention to himself in a great variety of ways, including some of a decidedly aggressive kind. He did not succeed. After she had been woken up he asked her to tell him what he had done to her while she thought he was not there. She replied in surprise that she knew nothing of it. But he did

not accept this. He insisted that she could remember everything and laid his hand on her forehead to help her to recall it. And lo and behold! she ended by describing everything that she had ostensibly not perceived during her [hypnosis] and ostensibly not remembered in her waking state [Breuer & Freud, 1893–95, pp. 109–10].

Freud coped with the unhypnotizable patients in a similar way and described the results for the first time in the case history of Lucy R. (Breuer & Freud, 1893–95).

Lucy R. was 30 years old, unmarried, and serving as a governess to the children of a widowed Viennese industrialist. She was referred to Freud primarily because she had lost her sense of smell and was bothered constantly by olfactory hallucinations. She smelled things that were not there. During her treatment with Freud, she hallucinated the odor of cigar smoke.

Freud unsuccessfully tried to hypnotize Lucy. When he decided to proceed without hypnosis and asked her to try to recall times when she had really smelled the odors of her hallucinations, she insisted that there were no such times. He insisted that there must have been, urged her to remember, insisted that she would remember (but not *what* she would recall), pressed on her head with his hands, and in general *pitted his will and efforts against her contrary insistence and desire.* As a result of a series of such clashes between herself and Freud, Lucy did recall several very painful emotional experiences that she had forgotten but that were obviously related to her olfactory symptoms. About cigar smoke, for example, she remembered an occasion when her employer had entertained two men from his factory at luncheon in the house. After lunch the men smoked cigars. As they were leaving for their offices, one of them, who was especially fond of the children, started to kiss them goodby. At this their father became angry and shouted, "Don't kiss the children!" This reaction upset Lucy very much. She was secretly in love with her employer and fantasied that she would marry him some day, but now she doubted that he was the right kind of man for her.

But this episode had also reminded her of a still earlier one, which she recalled next. A woman, an acquaintance of the father, had visited one day and had kissed the children on the lips. This too had infuriated their father. Afterward he released his anger on Lucy, saying that it was her responsibility to see that no one ever kissed the children's mouths and that he would discharge her if it ever happened again. It is easy to imagine the disappointment and heartbreak Lucy felt as she concluded from this outburst that he did not love her and as she was reminded of this episode by the other related one. Two days after Lucy recalled the earliest of these memories, her symptoms disappeared. She no longer had olfactory hallucinations, and her sense of smell returned. She was no longer depressed over her disappointment in love; she was reconciled to it, at least for the time being. Her treatment ended on this note.

We have called Lucy R. the first "psychoanalytic" patient because hers was the first treatment described by Freud that proceeded without hypnosis—that is, in which the essential tool for bringing unconscious thoughts and feelings into awareness was largely *verbal communication* between Freud and a patient *in the usual waking state* of consciousness. Although Freud later modified his method in many ways, as have other succeeding analysts as well, psychoanalysis still retains the goal of making conscious the unconscious, and it still relies exclusively upon interaction channeled through words. We put the term "psychoanalytic" in quotes because Freud guided and exhorted the patient in a specific direction: toward the recall of memories. *Free association* by the patient, which may lead in any direction, was not yet the basic feature in the treatment technique. It had become so, however, by 1900, when Freud's classic work *The Interpretation of Dreams* was published.

Key Concepts
from the Early Case Studies

When Freud found that he could force the recall of memories without hypnosis, he gradually stopped using hypnosis altogether. He tried out his new technique on a wide variety of symptoms in addition to hysterical ones affecting sensory experience. These included fears, compulsions, obsessional thinking and behavior, paranoid thoughts, and psychotic hallucinations.

REPRESSION

In all these cases the use of insistence, urging, and pressure on the head appeared to overcome the amnesia for memories. Freud felt that his effort overcame a resisting force in the patient. This subjective experience became a crucial datum stimulating his creative thinking. Freud hypothesized that *his use of force produced memory recall because it overcame a force that was preventing the spontaneous emergence into awareness of memories.* And, he hypothesized further, *this force that maintained the patient's amnesia had produced the amnesia in the beginning.* The "forgetting" of his patients, then, was not to be regarded as true forgetting at all. It was not like the usual fading of memory. Nor was it attributable to organic brain deficiencies or to any other type of physiological weakness. It seemed that the perceptions and thoughts of unpleasant emotional experiences were actively forced out of consciousness and actively kept out of consciousness; that is, they were *repressed.*

UNBEARABLE AFFECT
AS THE CAUSE OF REPRESSION AND CONFLICT

Why was the memory repressed in the first place? Because of the *unbearable affect,* or unpleasant feelings, stemming from it, Freud answered. The unbearable affect might be in direct response to real or imagined perceptions; Lucy's hurt and disappointment, for example, were direct responses to her employer's angry outbursts and to the shattering of her fantasy that he loved her enough to marry her. Or the unbearable affect might arise from the individual's moral standards, as it did in the case of Anna's guilt over her desire to be off dancing to the music she heard nearby instead of nursing her father. One of the basic laws of human experience, Freud maintained, was the *pleasure principle*. By this he meant that there is a basic tendency in human behavior to avoid unpleasant experiences and to seek out pleasant ones. Repression of the memory was in accord with the forces of the pleasure principle, for the expulsion of the memory from consciousness prevented the related unpleasant feelings from developing. For example, by repressing her memories Lucy spared herself the reliving of the painful feelings that were part of the original experiences. The basic function of repression, Freud hypothesized, was exactly this attempt at defense against experiencing the unbearable affect.

The preceding remarks cover only half the forces Freud thought were involved in neurosis. The other half consisted of forces inherent in the intense emotions themselves, in those urges toward expression or "discharge" that characterize emotions. Thus, at the time of the original repression the repressive forces were pitted against these expressive forces. And with the repression of the memory, Freud hypothesized, an emotional "charge" remained associated with the unconscious memory trace. This "charge," too, constituted a force tending toward "discharge." Thus, in sustained repression the repressive forces were continually pitted against the expressive or "discharge" forces of the pent-up emotions.

With such working hypotheses, which were based on concepts then popular in physics, Freud could account for many of his observations. Symptoms could be attributed to indirect "discharge" or expression of the pent-up emotional charge associated with the repressed memory trace. Freud's ability to produce recall of the repressed memory by his efforts of will and urging of the patient could be explained as the overpowering of the repressive forces inherent in the pleasure principle. And the abreactive recall was therapeutic, Freud argued, because with the emergence into consciousness of the repressed memory the pent-up emotional "charge" was now "discharged." With this, he thought, the necessary condition for symptoms was abolished.

From this historical sketch it is apparent that the concepts of conflict and defense were among the first developed by Freud. The sketch also shows the original empirical bases and behavioral referents for these concepts. Conflict and defense have remained principal concepts in psychoanalytic theory, although more precise formulations were given later, as we shall see. In fact, their specific content changed several times as Freud observed new instances of unconsciously motivated behavior, saw old and seemingly understood symptoms in a new light, and modified his conceptual scheme accordingly. Thus, the nature of the conflicting forces, the personality components involved, and the role of conflict and defense in adjustment are all viewed quite differently today than they were in this

Figure 11-1 Freud's "laboratory" in Vienna, where he made nearly all his discoveries.

While his patient lay on the couch, Freud sat in the armchair behind the head of the couch. The reclining position of the patient derived from the period when Freud had used hypnosis. He continued to use this position to facilitate relaxation and free association by the patient. Freud sat behind the patient to minimize the influence of his facial expressions and other visible reactions on the patient's flow of associations and to enable himself to relax, free from being watched by patients for many hours each day. Not having to be continually "on guard," Freud could thus listen more carefully, and respond more perceptively, to the patient's free associations. This general physical arrangement is now part of the standard psychoanalytic situation throughout the world.

initial phase of psychoanalysis. It is with the present meanings of these concepts, of course, that we will be most concerned. But these present meanings are better understood if we know their beginning.

FREE ASSOCIATION AS THE CENTRAL PROCEDURE

The historical sketch also shows Freud in action—observing keenly and attempting to understand and explain his empirical observations. To do the latter he drew readily on the ideas of others that appeared useful,

Figure 11-2 *Freud's study and desk in Vienna.*

Here Freud worked on his many papers and books. Here, too, he conducted consultations with patients, who sat in the armchair in the left foreground.

but he was not handcuffed by tradition or fashion. When old methods failed, he devised new ones. Freud soon realized, for example, that abreaction of unpleasant experiences was of limited therapeutic value and that the use of both psychological and physical force and pressure was fraught with both therapeutic and investigative dangers.

Accordingly, he modified his technique along lines mentioned earlier, making *free association* its cornerstone. In this procedure the individual abandons his customary conscious control over his behavior and gives free verbal expression to every thought, feeling, or impulse of which he becomes aware. Under these conditions the extent to which overt behavior is determined by unconscious conflicts increases, and the nature of those unconscious determinants is more accessible to observation. Thus, the *freedom* of *free* association means freedom from the conscious inhibition and other forms of control over *verbal* expression.

Largely through the use of free association, Freud saw things that others could not see or overlooked. Where explanatory concepts were lacking or inadequate, he invented new ones. Always, however, his speculation was geared to observation; his formulations derived from facts as he saw them and were maintained only as long as they seemed to account for the facts. He was never interested in idle speculation or in creating fairy tales.

Repression Investigated Experimentally

Freud often resorted to metaphors and failed to define precisely some of his principal terms, but that is often the case with pioneers who open up new fields of research. In the course of opening up research on human conflict Freud made basic clinical discoveries that stimulated a great deal of research by psychologists using the more rigorous techniques of experimental psychology. Even his earliest discoveries about the repression of unpleasant memories had this stimulative effect. For example, many systematic studies have now been performed by psychologists that clearly demonstrate that the memories of unpleasant experiences are "forgotten" more readily than others. This has been shown for spontaneous real-life experiences (for a review of such studies see Sears, 1943, and Cofer & Appley, 1964) and for unpleasant experiences induced experimentally by temporarily threatening subjects' self-esteem—for example, by telling them that they have failed in experimental tasks (Rosenzweig, 1943; Alper, 1948; Glixman, 1949, for example) or by arousing pain and fear reactions.

A study by Diven (1937) illustrates one way of investigating repression experimentally. Diven placed college students in an apparatus that made it appear that they were part of an electrical circuit originating in a wall socket. He presented a series of stimulus words to each subject and asked him to associate with as many words as he could for 12 seconds. Periodically *red* and next *barn* recurred in the list of stimulus words. Each time *barn* was presented, the subject was given a mild electric shock at the end of his 12-second association period. Although the shock was delivered only at these times, nearly half the subjects never became aware of the connection between *barn* and the occurrence of the shock. After periods of delay varying from 5 minutes to 48 hours this entire procedure was repeated, except that the shocks were now omitted. At the outset of this second test the subjects were asked to remember as many of the stimulus words in the first test as possible. Throughout the experiment, Diven recorded the electrical activity of the subjects' skin (the psychogalvanic skin response), which indicated how emotionally upset his subjects were.

The results? As a result of the experimental procedure, *barn*, *red*, and other words with a *rural* meaning produced changes in the electrical activity of the skin. Of particular interest was the finding that this occurred just as often in those subjects who were not aware of the fact that *barn* always preceded the shock as in those subjects who were. When the subjects tried to recall the stimulus words at the outset of the second test, they recalled many more "neutral" words than "traumatic" words—*red*, *barn*, *rural words*, or *whatever word had followed barn*. Furthermore, this temporary memory loss was greater for those subjects who were not aware of the timing of the shock than it was for those who were. Finally, some of Diven's results suggested that the longer the delay (he called it, aptly, "the incubation period") between the two tests, the greater were the effects of the shock in the "unconscious" subjects.

Diven's experiment was stimulated by Freud's early ideas about the repression of unpleasant emotional experiences. It shows the fruitfulness of these early ideas and the possibility of subjecting them to experimental scrutiny even though they represented only a fragment of the truth, as we shall see.

Our sketch of Freud does not reveal the whole complex man who developed a momentous new psychology, that Freud about whom Thomas Mann wrote as follows in celebration of his eightieth birthday:

> as physician and psychologist, as philosopher and artist, this courageous seer and healer has for two generations been a guide to hitherto undreamed-of regions of the human soul. An independent spirit . . . a thinker and investigator who knew how to stand alone . . . he went his way and penetrated to truths which seemed dangerous because they revealed what had been anxiously hidden, and illumined dark places . . . and made even his opponents indebted to him through the creative stimulus they derived from him. Even should the future remould and modify one result or another of his researches, never again will the questions be stilled which Sigmund Freud put to mankind [Quoted in Jones, 1957, pp. 205–06].

The reader interested in these aspects of Freud should see Jones's biography (Jones, 1953, 1955, 1957), which also covers much of the long, intricate history of Freud's ideas subsequent to the phase we have discussed.

Thomas Mann referred to the possibility that the future may require that various parts of Freud's thought be modified. Colby, in *The Skeptical Psychoanalyst* (1958), presents an extreme view of this possibility. He concludes that many of Freud's ideas, as was true of some of Darwin's and Newton's, will turn out to be wrong or so drastically changed that their future form will bear little resemblance to the original ideas. What about this possibility of change? What are its implications for the reader's attitude toward the rest of this section of the book?

Certainly psychoanalytic thought will change in the future. Any viable science changes. New facts will be discovered. They will give rise to new concepts. New ways of thinking about old facts will also emerge. Such evolutionary changes occurred repeatedly within Freud's own work. We have already seen signs of them in the historical sketch presented in this chapter. Although we cannot continue the historical approach throughout these pages, we shall pick up briefly the historical thread of Freud's thinking in Chapter 14. And throughout this section we shall refer to landmarks in the development of his observations and ideas. Other psychoanalysts have already carried Freud's thinking beyond the point it had reached when he died in London in 1939. (He was 83 when he died, a refugee from Nazi-occupied Vienna.) We shall refer to some of these.

All science is a process, not a dogmatic, static body of knowledge, and psychoanalysis is no exception. What the following chapters present is our current basic knowledge about conflict and defense—in particular, the part of our knowledge that is least likely to undergo radical change, for our focus is on empirical-clinical observations that have been repeatedly confirmed and on those concepts of Freud that are tied directly to these observations.

*Oh! To love a woman! To be a priest! . . . Oh, happy is
the man who is sawn in two or pulled apart by horses!*

VICTOR HUGO. The Hunchback of Notre Dame

*The younger girl with the braids was leaning out of the
window.*

"Goldmund!" she whispered. He stood and waited.

*"Are you coming back?" she asked. Her timid voice was no
more than a breath.*

*Goldmund shook his head. She reached out with both hands,
seized his head; her small hands felt warm on his temples. She
bent far down, until her dark eyes were close before his.*

*"Do come back!" she whispered, and her mouth touched his
in a child's kiss.*

*Quickly he ran through the small garden, toppled across the
flower beds, smelled wet earth and dung. A rosebush tore his
hand. . . . "Never again!" commanded his will. "Again! Tomorrow!" begged his heart.*

HERMANN HESSE. Narcissus and Goldmund

CHAPTER 12
TYPES
AND EXAMPLES
OF CONFLICT

B efore we examine conflict and defense in detail, it will be useful for us to take a broad, general view of the subject. As noted earlier, we speak of *conflict* when a person is prompted simultaneously by incompatible response tendencies.

The Four Basic Types of Conflict

Lewin (1931) and Miller (1944) have shown that there are four basic types of conflict situations. Since the types were first named with reference to tendencies to approach or avoid goals, they are most readily described in those terms. The term *goals* refers to external objects or to definite activities, such as specific thoughts or specific overt responses, around which behavior is organized. In this sense we may speak of both *positive* and *negative* goals. Positive goals are those objects or activities an individual is impelled to approach; negative goals are those he is impelled to avoid. For the sake of clarity, we shall assume that no more than two goals are involved in a conflict; actually, any number of goals may figure in a given conflict. We shall also assume that the incompatible response tendencies are of equal strength, although this is not always true.

THE FOUR TYPES DEFINED

Approach-Approach
Conflict
Here the individual is prompted simultaneously and to an equal degree to approach two desirable but mutually exclusive goals. The child who must choose between two equally attractive toys, the student who must select one of two equally valued courses, the adult who must pick one of two equally desirable jobs, are all in approach-approach conflict situations.

Approach-Avoidance
Conflict
Here the individual is prompted to approach a single goal at the same time that he is prompted just as strongly to avoid it. The child who wants to pet a dog he is afraid of, the adult who desires but fears intimacy, the student who is impelled yet ashamed to speak before his classmates, are in approach-avoidance conflicts.

Avoidance-Avoidance
Conflict
Here the individual is prompted to avoid two goals or two courses of action. The high school graduate who abhors going on to college and equally dislikes going to work, the individual who is equally ill at ease talking with both men and women at a party, the voter who dislikes the presidential candidates of both the Democratic and Republican parties, are in avoidance-avoidance conflict situations.

Double Approach-
Avoidance Conflict
In this case each of two goals or lines of action invokes an approach-avoidance conflict. Upon close examination, what appear to be simply avoidance-avoidance or approach-approach conflicts are frequently seen to be double approach-avoidance conflicts. Thus, it is very possible that the high school graduate just mentioned is in the more difficult position of wanting to go on to college and also to work at the same time that he dislikes each. Each of the two alternatives prompts approach and avoidance behavior. Anna O. was probably in this type of conflict situation as she sat by her father's bedside that night, both wanting and not wanting to stay there caring for him and at the same time wishing she were at the dance next door but feeling guilty about this desire and then repressing it.

General Principles:
Approach and
Avoidance Gradients

Many properties of behavior in these various conflict situations have been discovered through clinical and experimental observation. One of these properties is that *the approach and the avoidance tendencies become stronger and stronger the closer in time or space one is to the goal.* If a student wants to go to college, he becomes more interested and involved in preparing to go as the time for going approaches. If he wants to avoid it for any reason, all of his attempts to do so will increase in vigor as the time comes.

These variations in the strength of the approach and avoidance tendencies are conveniently known as the *approach gradient* and the *avoidance gradient.* Miller (1944) and Brown (1948) have proposed that *the avoidance gradient is steeper than the approach gradient.* Figure 12-1 illustrates these relationships. Clinical and experimental observations (for example, Miller & Murray, 1952; Murray & Berkun, 1955) strongly suggest that the facts of behavior fit this model very frequently. We are not concerned at the moment with the nature of this evidence or with the exceptions to the model. We shall examine the figure in more detail shortly. For the moment it should be noticed that both the approach and avoidance tendencies get stronger as a person nears a goal and that the avoidance gradient is the steeper of the two—that is, the avoidance tendency increases more sharply than the approach tendency as one gets nearer the goal. Of course, the directional "pull" of the two tendencies is opposite: the stronger the approach tendency, the stronger the pull *toward* the goal; the stronger the avoidance tendency, the stronger the push *away* from the goal. (This is what the arrows on the approach and avoidance gradients indicate.)

Lewin and Miller made clear how different the behavior is in the various types of conflict situations. These differences are due to the kinds of tendencies involved and to the gradient property of the tendencies.

Approach-Approach
Conflict

The approach-approach conflict is quickly and easily resolved. Assume that an individual is in a state of equilibrium: His two approach tendencies are equally strong. For a moment he will be unable to choose between two goals. Very soon, however, one or the other goal will become more desired than the other, even though ever so slightly. A shift in attention or some additional extraneous stimulation might produce this change. However it is produced, that change will be enough to tip the balance. At this point the individual will start to approach that goal. As he moves nearer, his tendency to move nearer still will become stronger, and this strengthened tendency will then

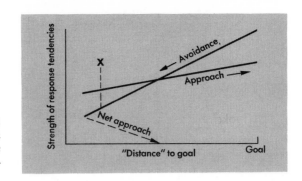

Figure 12-1 The approach and avoidance gradients in a simple approach-avoidance conflict. (Adapted from Miller, 1944)

move him still closer to that goal. Since there is no opposing avoidance tendency, a snowballing of approach behavior to the particular goal in question will occur, and the original state of conflict will cease.

Approach-Avoidance Conflict The introduction of avoidance tendencies alters the situation drastically, as an examination of the approach-avoidance conflict reveals. Remember that in this case the individual is prompted to approach and avoid the same goal, to make and to refrain from the same response. Remember, too, that in our model the avoidance gradient is steeper than the approach gradient. In this instance we are assuming that the avoidance gradient is of sufficient overall strength to cross the approach gradient.

Suppose an individual is at point X in Figure 12-1. At that point his approach tendency is stronger than his avoidance tendency. Thus, the individual will start to approach the goal. As he approaches the goal, however, his more sharply rising avoidance tendency eventually will be stronger than the approach tendency. At this point the individual will retreat from the goal. Soon he will reach a point where his approach tendency is again stronger than his avoidance tendency, and he will again start to approach the goal. And so he might continue oscillating. In general, we can say the individual would be trapped in the approach-avoidance conflict situation. His avoidance tendency would prevent him from reaching the goal he strives for; his approach tendency would prevent him from ever giving up that goal.

The "edge" the approach tendency has over the avoidance tendency is shown by the "net approach" line in the diagram. That edge decreases steadily as the individual approaches the goal, and it disappears at the point where two gradients meet—that is, where the two tendencies are of equal strength and there is neither a net approach nor a net avoidance. Net approach is simply a convenient quantitative way of representing the comparative strengths of the two opposing tendencies.

There is quite a difference between the approach-approach and the approach-avoidance conflict. The former is easily resolved and results in some form of satisfaction: One or the other goal is attained. The latter introduces negative factors (such as fear and guilt), which give rise to the avoidance tendency. It results in the frustration of both the approach and the avoidance tendencies, and it creates the distress of sustained conflict per se. We assume that approach-avoidance conflicts produce the kinds of chronic symptoms experienced by Anna O. and Lucy R., which we discussed in the preceding chapter. We saw there how Lucy, for example, loved her employer and at the same time was driven to suppress that love by her fear of being rejected and humiliated by him. Her constant preoccupation with cigar smoke appeared to be an indirect expression of these conflicting feelings, for the smell of it reminded her of him—both how attractive he was and how cruel he could be. Lucy was also chronically fatigued, which can be attributed to her prolonged state of conflict.

Double Approach-Avoidance Conflict

The double approach-avoidance situation also produces misery but of a somewhat different type. Remember that in the double approach-avoidance conflict the person is prompted to both approach and avoid two different goals simultaneously. To bring out the contrasting features of this situation, we shall again assume that the avoidance gradient is steeper than the approach gradient and also that it is of such overall strength that it crosses the approach gradient. The state of the individual in these circumstances is diagramed in Figure 12-2. As a result of the conflict over approaching goal A, the individual's net approach tendency for goal A progressively decreases as he comes nearer to it and becomes zero before he reaches the goal. The same state of affairs is true with regard to his net tendency to approach goal B.

What will the individual do if he is at point X? He will approach B, since the tendency to do so is stronger at that point than the tendency to approach A. Soon, however, the tendency to approach A will be the greater. When it is, he will start to approach A, retreating from B. And so on. This simultaneous action of the two incompatible net approach tendencies will prevent him from reaching either goal. Yet he will be trapped in the situation. The donkey who starved to death because he couldn't choose between

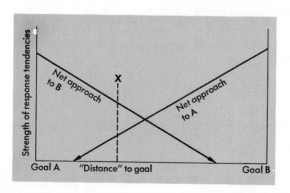

Figure 12-2 The net approach gradients in a double approach-avoidance conflict. (Adapted from Miller, 1944)

two equally attractive piles of hay was trapped in such a double approach-avoidance conflict. In his case it was greed that gave rise to the two avoidance tendencies. The thought of giving up one pile while he ate the other produced his eternal dilemma and his eventual starvation. The young man who cannot choose between a beautiful but stupid girl and a less beautiful but intelligent one is caught in the same kind of situation. The double approach-avoidance conflict situation is clearly a distressing one: In it are the aversive factors underlying the avoidance tendencies, the frustration of the four general response tendencies (two approach tendencies and two avoidance ones), and the tension created by the conflict itself.

Avoidance-Avoidance
Conflict   What about the avoidance-avoidance conflict? Since there are no approach tendencies to maintain the conflict, the individual will leave the field entirely, avoiding both goals. While momentarily distressful, this conflict permits of a ready solution and relief in a free-field situation. However, escape from the field may be, and very frequently is, blocked by physical or psychological barriers. (The latter are often additional avoidance tendencies.) If so, the individual is trapped in the conflict situation.

Our study of conflict psychology must return now primarily to the empirical discoveries and theory of psychoanalysis concerning the approach-avoidance conflicts. For convenience we shall generally use the simple term *conflict*, by which we shall always mean approach-avoidance conflicts. Nearly every human approach-avoidance conflict is part of a double approach-avoidance conflict, in fact part of a whole series of interrelated double approach-avoidance conflicts. But in our examples we shall focus on only the most salient *single* approach-avoidance conflict. This is sufficient for an exposition of the basic principles of conflict and defense.

We shall begin by considering real conflicts experienced by three different people. For now we shall discuss only those aspects of their lives that are directly relevant to the specific conflicts with which we are concerned. In later chapters we shall add further information about these three people and about the case studies of Freud that we shall cite.

Examples of Conflict

A PERCEPTUAL CONFLICT: DUANE

Duane, a man who is considered psychiatrically normal, had the following unusual perceptual experience at the time of his father's death. Dutifully present during the prescribed hours for the "viewing" of the body by friends and relatives, Duane spent much of the time virtually alone in the room. Several times he walked up to the open casket and looked for long moments at his father's body.

Duane knew and could see that his father was dead. He could see this from the grotesquely distorted mouth position produced by the clumsy mortician. He could see it from the pancake make-up on his father's face. He could see it from the utter stillness of his father's body. And yet, episodically, he saw his father alive, as if he were restfully sleeping. Especially vividly he saw the rise and fall of his father's chest as he breathed deeply, easily, and regularly. Why did Duane experience this perceptual conflict?

The death of his father was a very painful loss for Duane, as the loss of a loved parent is for anyone. But it also frightened him because it aroused fearful memories of three earlier deaths—the death of his mother in his early childhood, the death a few years later of his grandfather, who was in effect the boy's father (his own father having remarried and abandoned the boy to his grandparents until adolescence), and the death of his grandmother during his adolescence. A new and special instance now occurred with the death of his father. Thus, the sight of his dead father aroused an intensely painful and fearful sense of loss.

There were other reasons why the sight of his dead father was unpleasant. When Duane was told that his father was seriously ill and might die, he consciously hoped that he would. That would free Duane of responsibility for an ailing old man who would intrude on his life. And, at first, he was relieved to hear that his father had died. In both instances these thoughts and feelings made him feel guilty. This complex reaction had lasted very briefly when it first occurred, but Duane remembered it for a moment soon after he first saw his dead father. Then he banished such thoughts from his conscious thinking.

The sight of his dead father, then, was acutely unpleasant for this man: It aroused a painful *grief reaction* based on his love for him and a *fear reaction* based on a latent childlike need for him; but it also rearoused the *guilt* stemming from his wish that his father would die and from his sense of being relieved and freed by his father's death, and he saw before him the fulfillment of these guilt-laden wishes. It was as if he coped with the disturbing vision of his dead father by distorting the final perception— by seeing his father alive, not dead. To the extent that he saw his father alive, one could say that he *denied* the realistic perception that he was dead.

The behavioral processes are diagramed in Figure 12-3. With one exception (to be mentioned in a moment), the components diagramed are known, they are facts. The solid arrows represent inferred causal relations. The gray arrow is an arbitrary notation indicating that the inaccurate perception interferes with the occurrence of the accurate perception. The label "denial" is the technical psychoanalytic term for this type of substitution of an inaccurate perception for an accurate one.

But there were also reasons for Duane to perceive his father accurately, and these we have not yet discussed. One reason was the simple fact that Duane's perceptual processes, like those of other normal adults, would automatically tend to be accurate. There are, of course, *motives* for realistic perception. Thus, a desire to look at his father's body is listed in Figure 12-3 as one of Duane's approach motives. That he did want to look at his father can be inferred from his behavior. He was not physically forced to go to

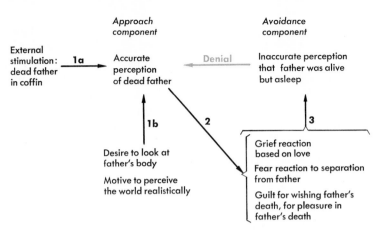

Figure 12-3 The approach-avoidance conflict instigated in Duane by his father's death.

The presence of Duane's dead father's body and the approach motives (the desire to look at his father and to perceive the world realistically) prompt the accurate perception of his dead father (1a and 1b). But this accurate perception produces a complex, unpleasant emotional state in Duane (2), which in turn prompts his inaccurate perception that his father is alive (3). This inaccurate perception replaces, or denies, the accurate perception. As a result, the intensity of the unpleasant emotional state is decreased. Thus, the perceptual denial defends Duane against painful emotional experiences. (In all of the schematic diagrams gray arrows and labels indicate defenses.)

the coffin, stand by it, and gaze on his father, yet he did just that. We infer that both his love and his thinly veiled pleasure at his father's death motivated him to approach the coffin and look at his father's body. And we can also infer that he wanted to perceive accurately, for nearly every adult learns that it is to his advantage to do so.

Diagrams like that in Figure 12-3 will be used throughout this section. Therefore, it might be worthwhile to focus attention on this first one to be sure it is clear how the diagram schematizes what we know about Duane's experience. Recall that we have singled out for explanation one aspect of his experience: his perceptual conflict. This was manifested in the oscillation between the accurate perception of his father as being dead and the inaccurate perception that his father was alive but asleep.

In terms of the approach-avoidance conflict model, we can regard the accurate perception of his dead father as both the goal and the approach behavior. The two black arrows numbered 1a and 1b represent diagrammatically the fact that this approach behavior was instigated by both the external stimulus of his father's body and by the two approach motives, his wish to look at his father and his desire to perceive it realistically. The black arrow numbered 2 represents the fact that the accurate perception of his dead father aroused in Duane a sense of grief, of separation fear, and of guilt over his wish that his father die. These unpleasant emotions in turn motivated Duane's inaccurate perception, as represented by the black arrow numbered 3. This misperception is defensive avoidance behavior in terms of the approach-avoidance conflict model, and the unpleasant emotions are avoidance motives. We can see that the substitution of the inaccurate perception for the accurate one would provide Duane with some temporary reduction of his sense of grief, fear, and guilt by obliterating momentarily the vivid reminder of his father's death.

In the remainder of this chapter we shall examine two additional examples of conflict. Then in the next chapter we shall present a general paradigm concerned with the elements of conflict and their interrelations common to all our examples.

A SEXUAL CONFLICT: ED

A young man, whom we shall call Ed, periodically attempted to find sexual satisfaction in masturbation and in premarital intercourse with his fiancée. However, in both circumstances he felt uneasy, tense, and sweaty, and a vague sense of impending doom engulfed him afterward. Hence, Ed avoided both activities most of the time.

Conscious guilt and shame were very important causes of Ed's discomfort. He did not want anyone to know about his masturbation, and, despite a boastful attitude toward his premarital intercourse, he preferred that no one know about it. Mere discretion or a sense of privacy was not his only motivation; he felt that both acts were sinful and relieved evil urges on his part. He discovered a still more powerful and previously unknown source of his discomfort as he explored his behavior day after day in psychoanalysis: He feared that his genitals would be cut off if he engaged in these activities. This fear was unconscious; it manifested itself most clearly in frightening dreams that only occurred following an increase in either masturbation or intercourse. After one such upsurge in sexual activity, for example, Ed dreamed that he had a fatal illness and was in a hospital. The doctors had removed an organ from his body and wrapped it up. It made a small, elongated package. As Ed told the dream to his analyst, the shape of the package reminded him of the shape of a penis.

Following another upsurge in sexual activity, Ed dreamed that one of his testicles was quite large owing to a tumor growing within it. A man, presumably a doctor, was going to cut it off. Ed's view of his sexuality as a fatal and evil cancerous process as well as his fear that he would be castrated were very thinly disguised in these dreams. While thinking about this dream, he remembered suddenly that he had dreamed something similar when he was about 7 years old: "A woman had cut off my penis and was starting to slice the end of it the way my mother sliced bananas for my cereal. This woman had cut the penises off all the little boys in the world. She looked like a witch."

The content of these nightmares, their close temporal correlation with active phases in his sexual life, and his associations to them strongly sug-

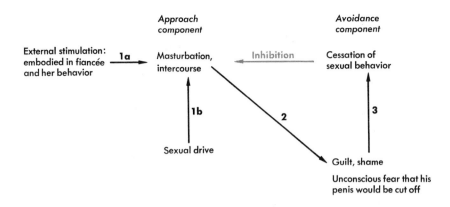

Figure 12-4   Ed's approach-avoidance sexual conflict.

The combined effects of his fiancée and his sexual drive prompt Ed to engage in sexual behavior (1a and 1b). But such activity arouses conscious guilt and shame and unconscious castration anxiety (2), which in turn motivate Ed to stop engaging in sexual behavior (3). He does so by actively inhibiting the actions he wants to perform. As a result, he no longer experiences the guilt, shame, and fear. Thus, the inhibition has defended him from very unpleasant emotional experiences, but at the expense of his losing full sexual gratification.

gest that Ed's uneasiness, tension, sweating, and sense of doom associated with masturbation and intercourse were surface manifestations of an unconscious fear of castration, a fear present in his childhood and still operative in his adult life. It appears that sexual behavior activated this fear and that he avoided the danger of castration by inhibiting his sexual behavior.

Recent experimental studies of dreams and sleep suggest that similar inhibition occurs even during dreams. Fisher, Gross, and Zuch (1965; see also Fisher 1965a, b) found that penile erections accompany more than 90 percent of the rapid eye movement periods of sleep, which indicate dreaming (see Part I, pp. 26–29). However, preliminary data suggested that nightmares involving disguised castration anxiety and conflicts over unconscious incestuous wishes caused the erections to disappear.

A diagram of Ed's sexual conflict, including the known behavioral components and the inferred causal relations, is presented in Figure 12-4. *Inhibition* is the psychoanalytic term for the type of cessation of sexual activity manifested by Ed. The term implies that this cessation functions *actively* to prevent such sexual behavior as masturbation and intercourse. It is distinct from passive cessation, such as that which follows sexual gratification.

AN EATING CONFLICT: EDIE

Edie was a young woman who periodically could not eat. When she tried to eat at such times, she would feel nauseated and would be afraid she might choke on a piece of food because it would be so big it would get stuck in her throat. Physicians could not find any medical basis for her difficulty, and there was nothing wrong with the size bites she took. Nor was anything wrong with her appetite. In fact, eating was one of her favorite activities. Furthermore, eating the foods she liked best bothered her the most. The whole picture is one of a psychological conflict of the approach-avoidance type. The ordinary human need for food, but particularly her special relish for it, strongly motivated her to eat. Yet her nausea and fear of choking motivated her to avoid it.

If Edie had ever actually eaten foul food, so spoiled that it made her sick to her stomach, or if she had ever actually choked on food, she could have had a conflict resulting from simple conditioning. But as far as she could remember, she had had no such experiences.

A retrospective view of her analysis shows that her eating conflict was based on another conflict. The nature of this other conflict and of its relation to the eating conflict will become apparent from some of the relevant information. We are going to reach a strange conclusion. To make that conclusion as credible as possible, we have selected the least inferential information available. Only close attention and fitting together of details of scattered descriptions and seemingly isolated episodes of Edie's life were required to formulate the following material, not "deep interpretations." To avoid giving the wrong impression, however, we must point out that the mutual relevance of these various items of information and the way we have fit them together are all part of a *retrospective account* of portions of Edie's psychoanalysis. During an actual psychoanalysis, separate items of information are embedded among many other items. They do not emerge in a logical sequence, and the meaning of each is not crystal clear at the time it occurs. But gradually the bits form a consistent pattern, converging on a unique formulation that appears to account for them.

The Origin and Early Form of the Eating Conflict

As a child Edie had always been an "eating problem" for her parents, but her present severe problem started in her adolescence. Following a high school dance, she and her date went to a local teen-age hangout, where they ordered cheeseburgers, one of her favorite foods. As she ate she felt nauseated. On a few subsequent dates, which also included a stop for cheeseburgers, she again felt nauseated and was afraid she might vomit and strangle on the vomitus or on a fresh bite of the cheeseburger. During this period, she was not affected this way if she ate with girls or at home; it only occurred with boys. Edie's discomfort and fear were so intense that she stopped eating with her boyfriends.

For the next 7 years, she avoided eating when in the presence of a man. This restriction prevented her from developing any sustained, intimate relationship with a man. She would date a man up to the point when he would ask her to dine with him, whereupon she would refuse without explaining why. That would be the last she would hear from some men. Those who took her out again would sooner or later again suggest a dinner date and would be curious about her rejections, which she still refused to explain. Eventually even these persistent men would stop calling her, or she would simply refuse all dates with them. Her reasoning then was that she was too ashamed to explain her fears about eating with them and that she could not cope with their curiosity about her unpredictability in accepting dates with them.

Two things are striking at this point: the specific relation between Edie's eating conflict and her heterosexual life, and the far-reaching effect it had on that life. This effect is especially curious if one stops to consider it. It seemed perfectly logical to Edie that her inability to eat with men and her reluctance to tell them why should preclude every potential intimate male relationship. But it is not logical. If Edie unconflictfully wanted intimacy, she could have obtained it in spite of her eating conflict. Many men would not have been driven away by it, and some would have been interested by it. People pursue love despite even more severe handicaps. The fact that she did not do so makes one wonder if she also had a sexual conflict, and if it might be intimately connected with her eating conflict.

Edie was, in fact, very conflicted in her sexual life, both during adolescence and for a long time after the onset of her eating conflict. Her sexual desires were strong, but so were her anxiety and guilt about them. Even during late adolescence her sexual life was minimal, and any kissing or necking and petting were sources of great anxiety and guilt. She had been raised to believe that any kind of sexual activity not immediately connected with having children was sinful and would eventually be punished harshly by her parents and God. The severity of Edie's upbringing is indicated by the fact that her parents never shared the same bedroom after her younger sibling was born when Edie was 3. Her parents always gave as the reason for this drastic step their decision not to have any more children. Previously, sexuality had been a necessary evil for them; now it was an unnecessary one, to be avoided at all costs.

Thus, the speculation that her sexual life was quite conflictful is correct. But we have not yet seen the further evidence that there is a relation between this and her eating conflict.

Concomitant Variation in the Eating and Sexual Conflicts

Lonely and frustrated in her early adulthood, desperate that she might never enjoy a normal life, Edie met a young man to whom she revealed her eating conflict. He mothered her with his own cooking and with a great deal of tolerance and sympathy. At the same time, she was waging a painful conscious struggle to overcome her sexual conflict. Finally she achieved a temporary and partial victory over both of her conflicts: She was able to eat with this man and to be sexually intimate with him. She was not completely free of discomfort in either circumstance, but at least she was able to achieve enough gratification to give her a new life. In fact, she soon married him.

The fact that both conflicts changed at the same time suggests that they might have been related. We could confidently conclude they were if we saw repeated instances of such covariation.

By the time Edie undertook psychoanalysis, her eating conflict had become sporadic and was no longer limited to the situation of eating in the presence of a man. The very frequent psychoanalytic interviews over a period of several years provided a unique opportunity to observe the psychological context of the fluctuations in severity of her eating conflict.

At the time she started psychoanalysis, Edie's sexual conflict had been intensified for a few months. For many reasons, which we will not go into, she was not enjoying a pleasurable spontaneous sexual life with her husband. At the same time, her eating conflict had flared up again. She complained especially of her inability to eat hamburgers, which were still among her favorite foods. Things continued in this way for nearly a year, but then she reached a point where there was a marked reduction in her conflict over sexuality. She was able for a while to tolerate her rich erotic feminine capacities. While this change affected many aspects of her life, it was most directly shown in frequent and enjoyable intercourse with her husband. What happened to her eating conflict now? It too disappeared. For the first time since she entered analysis she was eating hamburgers, and her general pleasure in eating was very great. This kind of thing happened again several times. When her sexual anxiety, guilt, and inhibitions decreased, so did her conflict over eating. Thus, there was clearly a relation between these two conflicts.

Can we go further and say what the nature of that relationship was? For example, was one conflict a necessary condition for the other? The most plausible answer seems to be that her sexual conflict was the cause of her eating conflict. Three types of observation suggest that this was the case.

1. Other information in her analysis very strongly suggested that her becoming an "eating problem" was the residue of a severe childhood neurosis around the ages of 5 and 6. This neurosis involved a severe childhood sexual conflict. Before the neurosis came about, she was a beautiful, rounded, feminine little girl with wavy hair; after it appeared, she became unattractively "stark" (to use her own word), dour, and thin, and she wore her hair in a straight, tightly drawn style.

2. We know that her sexual conflicts in adolescence preceded the eating conflict that emerged at that time.

3. In her analysis her sexual conflict always *appeared* to change before her eating conflict did. We can only speak of *appearance* here, for patients do not always let analysts know such things precisely when they happen.

We have seen that Edie's eating and sexual conflicts varied together. And we have reason to believe that they did so because her sexual conflict was the necessary condition for her eating conflict. Did her analysis bring to light any explanation for these two aspects of her eating conflict? It did.

Hunger and Eating as Substitutes for Genital Desires and Sexual Behavior

One day Edie and her husband were visiting a local museum; suddenly she was struck with an overwhelming wish to have intercourse with him. They rushed home, but something in the situation momentarily stimulated her sexual anxiety and guilt to a slight degree. Thereupon she was seized with an equally urgent hunger. For a moment she could not decide whether to eat and then have intercourse or vice versa, so equally balanced and peremptory were these two desires. The outcome was a quick bite of something from a refrigerator shelf on the way to the bedroom.

Notice that the arousal of a strong sexual wish and then inhibition of that wish *preceded* the appearance of her strong hunger. Notice also that eating was nearly as desirable as intercourse. It is as if hunger and eating were substitutes for sexual desire and sexual gratification.

If they were, that would explain the covariation of the two conflicts and the dependence of the eating conflict on the sexual conflict. When her sexual conflict was intense, leaving her sexual desires inhibited and frustrated, eating became a substitute activity and acquired a new meaning: it was *sexual activity* providing actual erotic gratification. This being true, it now became the source of anxiety and guilt. Thus, *this woman's eating conflict was a substitute for her sexual conflict.* This is "the strange conclusion" we mentioned in the beginning. It is strange, yet it seems inescapable in view of the evidence. Exactly the type of evidence we have cited led Freud and other psychoanalysts to construct their hypotheses about the unconscious motivational conflicts that underlie surface inhibitions, hysterical symptoms, and other forms of neurotic behavior.

Sexual conflicts have different effects in different people. Edie developed an *eating* conflict because her previously established attitudes or fantasies, of which she remained unaware, made eating and sexuality *equivalent* for her. Her eating conflict did not arise by chance that night she was eating cheeseburgers with her boyfriend after the high school dance. Nor was chance responsible for the fact that it retained its peculiar form for 7 years and kept her from becoming intimate with a man. Many other means could have been used to solve that problem. The eating conflict had to be the solution for Edie because of its sexual equivalence. It is in this sense that symptoms and their behavioral effects are psychologically determined and have a specific "unconscious meaning," in Freud's terms. (Why that equivalence came to be, we have not considered. We have only been concerned with showing that there was such an equivalence.)

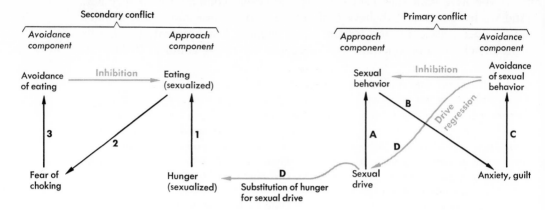

Figure 12-5   Edie's manifest eating conflict and her more basic, underlying sexual conflict.

Edie's sexual drive prompts her to engage in sexual behavior (A). But even the slightest tendency to do so, such as wishing to or thinking about it, arouses anxiety and guilt (B). These painful emotions motivate her to avoid sexual behavior by actively inhibiting it (C) and to regress to an earlier form of sexual desire—oral cravings. Thus, Edie not only inhibits her sexual behavior but also substitutes hunger for sexual desires (D). Hunger, now sexualized, prompts her to engage in highly sensual, sexualized eating (1). But to eat, especially in the presence of a man, produces in her a fear of choking (2). This fear motivates her to avoid eating, to actively inhibit it (3). In this way she defends herself against the fear of choking and, indirectly, against the primary conflict over sexuality.

The diagram in Figure 12-5 schematizes the basic processes that we have discussed in this example of conflict. *Drive regression* is the psychoanalytic term for the process of substituting a developmentally earlier drive and its resultant behavior for a developmentally later drive and its resultant behavior. In Edie's case hunger and eating were substituted for the sexual drive and sexual behavior. As we shall see in Chapters 14 and 22, there are good reasons to believe that oral stimulation constitutes an earlier form of sexuality than does genital behavior and that Edie had defensively returned to this earlier stage.

In this chapter we have presented three examples of approach-avoidance conflicts. In the example of Duane we focused on his perceptual conflict; he oscillated between "approaching" the realistic perception of his dead father and avoiding that painful experience by hallucinating that his father was breathing and thus still alive. Ed's conflict consisted of the oscillation between "approaching" sexual gratification and actively avoiding it. Edie suffered from two interrelated approach-avoidance conflicts: her sexual conflict and her eating conflict. Within each conflict she would oscillate between the relevant gratification and the avoidance of it. In addition, she oscillated between the two conflicts, now approaching sexual gratification, now avoiding it by regressing to eating, but then having to avoid that pleasure because of its sexual significance.

In each case, of course, we have focused only on certain aspects of what were highly complex situations. We saw, for example, that conflicting approach and avoidance motives operated behind the drama of the conflicting overt responses we have just mentioned. Thus, a wish that his father be dead and the conflicting guilt over this wish were among the underlying motives causing Duane's perceptual conflict. This motivational conflict produced many other effects on Duane's behavior that we did not discuss. The same was true in the other two examples.

In fact, I am no clever work of fiction;
I am a man, with all his contradiction.

K. F. MEYER. Hutten's Last Days

CHAPTER 13
BASIC CONCEPTS
OF CONFLICT
AND DEFENSE

I n the preceding chapter we became familiar with a few concrete examples of conflict. Now we can go on to discuss some important features common to all of them. The starting point of each example was an instance of impaired behavior—a faulty perception of reality, a sexual disturbance in a young man, an eating disturbance in a young woman.

Psychological Determinism

In each instance the behavioral impairment was caused by conflict, by psychological rather than biological processes. In this sense each instance was a special case of the most fundamental principle of psychoanalysis: the principle of exceptionless psychological determinism. This principle states that in a biologically intact human being every aspect of behavior is determined by psychological factors. It insists that there are no accidents or coincidences in human behavior and that there is no such thing as a meaningless pattern of behavior.

Although Freud did not create the idea of psychological determinism, he did make a revolutionary contribution to it: He extended the concept to include forms of behavior, such as hysteria, dreams, and many aspects of psychotic behavior, that previously had not been regarded as psychologically caused, and he relentlessly applied the principle to *details* of behavior that had been largely ignored. Slips of the tongue, memory lapses, and other forms of what Freud called "the psychopathology of everyday life," as well as "random" thoughts, including free associations, all appeared to him to be psychologically determined. Revolutionary at the time, this extension is still heatedly contested by biologically oriented psychologists and psychiatrists. However, the general principle of exceptionless psychological determinism is accepted at least implicitly by many behavioral scientists.

Not that psychoanalysis ignores the role of biological factors in behavior; on the contrary, they are assumed to be the ultimate basis of all behavior. The emphasis on *psychological* determinism merely means that many aspects of human behavior, including conflict and its results, cannot be attributed to biological aberrations. They seem to be caused by such psychological processes as motives, emotions, stable personality traits, fantasies, anticipations, and so forth.

Nor are sociological or cultural factors ignored. Indeed, psychoanalysis has always insisted that these factors play an important part in the development and functioning of the personality. Psychoanalysis does maintain, however, that society and culture influence behavior only through their impact on the psychology of the individual. These influences alter or mold psychological processes within the individual and thus become part of the "internal" psychological determinants of behavior.

The adjective "exceptionless" is redundant, of course, but it serves to emphasize that no behavioral detail is exempt from psychological causation. Thus, Edie's sexual conflict caused not only her eating conflict but also the specific conditions in which it arose and the specific form it took during the 7-year period. If we had examined the other two examples as minutely, we would have found that their specific details too had to be exactly as they were: that there were reasons why Duane hallucinated breathing movements on the part of his dead father rather than something else and why Ed's sexual fears were expressed specifically in medical terms. The relentless application of the principle of exceptionless psychological determinism as a working assumption greatly enhances the understanding of human behavior.

The Conflict Paradigm

We have examined several specific instances of conflict, but what are the patterns and principles common to all approach-avoidance conflicts? What is the essence of the psychological determinism of the results of conflict?

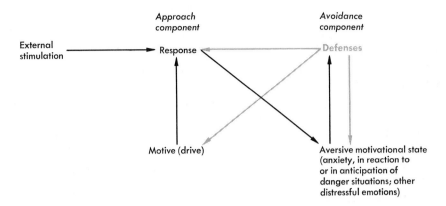

Figure 13-1   The general approach-avoidance conflict paradigm.

An external stimulus or an approach motive or, more often, a combination of the two instigates an approach response. In turn, the approach response evokes distressing emotions, which are usually some kind of anxiety—anticipatory fear, shame, or guilt. The distressing emotion motivates defenses, which have the effect of ending or preventing the painful emotion. Some defenses interfere with the approach motive or drive; some interfere with the approach response; and some are oriented directly against the unpleasant emotions.

We began our search for such generalizations in the last chapter, where we discussed the four basic types of conflict as categorized by Lewin and Miller: approach-approach, approach-avoidance, avoidance-avoidance, and double approach-avoidance. We saw that these categories are based on the kinds of competing response tendencies operating in the conflicts. We then discussed some general principles of conflict behavior: the approach and avoidance gradients and their behavioral consequences in the four classes of conflict.

We can now arrive at a general model, or paradigm, of conflict by extracting the common features from the schematic diagrams used earlier to describe specific conflicts. What we obtain is the following formulation, which is also illustrated in Figure 13-1. Approach-avoidance conflicts involve opposing response tendencies. One of these tendencies, conveniently called the "approach" tendency, is instigated by external stimulation (for example, Duane's perception of his dead father), by internal motives or drives, or by the combined action of external stimulation and internal motivation. This response (the approach tendency) in turn gives rise to an aversive motivational state in the individual. An aversive motivational state is an internal condition, such as pain or fear, that impels a person to bring it to an end. At times this aversive state is a direct response to the perceptions of the external situation. The grief and sense of painful loss experienced upon seeing the dead body of one's parent is such a direct response. In most human conflicts, however, there is no such current basis in reality for the aversive motivational state. Yet the individual is acting *as if* some *dangerous situation* actually did exist or as if he will suffer some dangerous consequences because he has responded as he has. He appears to be *anticipating a danger situation.* Ed was clearly doing this, for example, when he feared that someone would cut off his penis because he was intimate with his fiancée. So was Edie when she feared her parents' and God's punishment for her sexual behavior.

The aversive motivational state also includes from time to time other distressing feelings that we cannot so readily describe as anticipations of danger situations, such as the fear of being separated from a loved one, the guilt and shame that appeared in the examples, and other distressing affects, such as disgust and depression, that did not appear in our examples. But closer inspection in later chapters will show that it is possible to conceptualize these aversive states as reactions to or anticipations of danger situations.

Once produced, the aversive, unpleasant state motivates the individual to respond in ways that enable him to avoid it and the anticipated danger situation. Since these responses have this protective effect, they are called *defense mechanisms,* or simply *defenses.* There are many different kinds of defenses. Even our limited number of examples illustrated several different kinds. In the first example Duane distorted his perception of his father by *denial.* The other examples involved *inhibition* of actions that would have been instrumental in obtaining satisfaction: Ed was inhibited in his sexual behavior, and Edie was inhibited in both eating and sexual behavior. Another defense mechanism, *regression,* in this case from genital to oral-alimentary desires, was also involved in Edie's conflict. In Ed's case we saw still another defense, *repression,* in his obliteration from awareness of the ideational content of his fears—that he would be castrated. Repression very commonly involves obliteration from consciousness of the approach motives as well as the avoidance motives. Later we shall examine the whole array of known defenses; the important point right now is to realize that there are different kinds and that the process of defense can affect different aspects of behavior—such as the perceptual, the ideational, the motoric—and different components of the conflict paradigm.

All the defenses, however, have the same result of avoiding or decreasing the aversive motivational state, of avoiding or mitigating a perceived or anticipated danger situation. Some defenses do so by altering perceptions that cause distress; others do so by altering the drives or responses that indirectly bring about the aversive state; still others do so by interfering with the aversive states themselves. The three gray arrows of Figure 13-1 depict such various orientations of defenses.

Do Conflict and Defense
Ever Concern Trifling Matters?

At first glance, the products of conflict and defense often seem trivial and foolish. It is a temptation to view in this light such events as the transitory perception of respiratory movements in a dead body and an outbreak of anxiety over eating a cheeseburger—a temptation often yielded to by experts in human behavior as well as by the layman. But this appearance is deceptive. Death, ambivalence composed of love and hate for a father, sexual desires, fear of parents and of God, shame and guilt—all these and more of the most significant aspects of human life lie behind such seemingly insignificant phenomena as the surface events. Our examples are not exceptional; the investigation of any product of conflict and defense leads to the same order of vital factors in life and to the same degree of complexity.

Conscious and Unconscious Conflict

The examples make clear the extent to which unconscious processes are involved in conflict; we saw that the very fact of there being a conflict may not be known to an individual. While Ed was aware of having a sexual conflict and of some of the conflicting motives, he was not aware of the very important fear that his penis would be cut off. That fear manifested itself only in disguised form in his nightmares. Edie knew, of course, by the time she started analysis that she had a sexual and an eating conflict, but she was not aware of the relationship between them or of the key factors involved in each. Obviously, some of the most significant aspects of the lives of these people were unconscious. Consciousness and significance are not equivalent in human psychology.

One can place conflicts on a continuum representing the extent to which conscious and unconscious processes are operative. No conflicts are completely free from unconscious influences, but some are relatively free; in such instances the person is aware that he is in conflict and knows what his conflict is essentially about. And such conflicts, too, may involve very significant aspects of life. The conflict of the frightened but honorable soldier and that of the parent who must punish the child he loves are familiar examples.

It makes a great deal of difference, however, just how free a conflict is from unconscious influences. This difference is shown in three ways: (1) the degree to which the conflict is realistic or appropriate, (2) the process by which the conflict is resolved, and (3) consequences of the conflict.

APPROPRIATENESS

Conscious conflicts are usually appropriate to the external or internal situation, while unconscious conflicts seldom are. (See the discussion of reflective versus neurotic emotional reactions in Part I, pp. 113–17). The conflict of the normal soldier about to enter battle is highly realistic and appropriate; Edie's conflict over eating was highly unrealistic and inappropriate. Conflict is highly appropriate if one is knowingly about to commit an opprobrious act but not if one is merely daydreaming; yet daydreams greatly disturb people whose unconscious wishes are gratified by this means.

RESOLUTION

To resolve most conscious conflicts, people think, reason, and make decisions. Furthermore, they do these things to a degree appropriate to the seriousness and complexity of the issues. Thought and decision making play little or no part, however, in the resolution of unconscious conflicts. Instead, the individual resorts automatically and unknowingly to the defense mechanisms. This is what occurred in each of our examples.

Sometimes people do engage in a great deal of thought when unconscious conflict is involved, but in a manner that is quite inappropriate. The thinking has a ruminative quality, and decisions are very late in coming or never come at all. And the amount of thinking bears no relation to the issue at hand. When her eating conflict was activated, Edie would often spend a great deal of time considering whether, and what, to eat. She did this briefly that day she and her husband rushed home from the museum. That rumination and indecision was due to a momentary, unconscious increase in her sexual conflict. In extreme cases of this kind of inappropriate thinking people cannot decide such simple things as whether to say Yes or No to the simplest question, whether to turn right or left, or which shoe to put on first. Freud speculated that Hamlet's indecision about avenging his father's death was due to a conflict over his unconscious hostility toward his father.

CONSEQUENCES

Of course, conscious conflicts do not always have a happy ending, even though they are more easily resolved than unconscious ones. Sometimes we choose not to do something we desire to do. We feel regret, but we are able to tolerate our frustration or disappointment. Often we sympathize with ourselves, comforting or rewarding ourselves with a substitute satisfaction, or we let our friends and family do so for us.

The outcome of unconscious conflict resolution by defense mechanisms is quite different. Defenses impair behavior, as we have already seen. But still more disadvantages follow. They prevent a person from becoming aware of the true nature of his anxieties and thus from modifying them through reappraisal and relearning. Moreover, they provide for no real gratification of needs and thus leave the individual in a frustrated, pent-up state. There is a price, then—often a very great price—for the relief of anxiety and the security from imagined dangers achieved through the process of defense. The relief is particularly expensive because this is not the end of the matter, especially where internal needs are the primary instigators of the conflict. They still motivate the individual, usually driving him with even greater intensity. The opposing motives are unchanged. The result is perpetuation of the conflict, in the same or disguised form, and further defense. An endless process of conflict and defense is the typical outcome of unconscious conflict.

When Edie resolved her sexual conflict in adolescence with repressions and inhibitions, her sexual needs continued at a high level of intensity, partly because they were completely unsatisfied by even indirect means and partly because of the physiology of adolescence. They were then transposed from her sexual apparatus and functions to her alimentary system and functions. Eating became a substitute for sexual behavior. But eating now became the source of conflict and the target of defense. At first this "new" conflict was a restricted one, only a step removed from her sexual conflict: She became panicky and unable to eat cheeseburgers whenever she was with a boy. Her specific phobic avoidance of this situation was a temporary resolution of conflict by means of a defense that did not alter the unconscious conflict. She then developed a conflict over eating anything in the presence of a man and resolved this by phobic avoidance. Finally, eating under any circumstance became embroiled in conflict. And she still had her sexual conflict! The defensive attempt to resolve her adolescent sexual conflict thus initiated a repetitive process that continued for many years and that involved progressively larger segments of her behavior. Whenever she decreased her defensive resolution of her sexual conflict, gradually in her developing relationship with her future husband or episodically in her analysis, her eating conflict vanished.

The differences between conscious and unconscious conflicts that we have been discussing and illustrating are generally observable phenomena. They rank among the most significant discoveries made by Freud.

The Role of the Past

As the facts about the conflicts unfolded in our examples, they led in each case to significant events in the remote past of the individual's life. The causes of the present manifestations of conflict included behavioral components stemming from the past. The series of painful losses of "parents" that started in Duane's early childhood gave a special quality and intensity to the "pain" caused by his father's death. The young man who dreamed that his penis was cut off had had very similar dreams in his child-hood. Edie's eating and sexual conflicts in adulthood were related to con-flicts in early adolescence and to her situation at the age of 5 or 6, when she started to change from a vivacious, plump little girl into a thin, stark person, fleshless and sexless. These are but some of the connections between the later conflicts and the earlier experiences of these people.

Past experiences significantly influence all present behavior, including conflict behavior. Generally speaking, present behavior has *evolved* from past behavior and experience into its current form. The speech of the adult, for example, has developed from the early vocalizations of the infant. Here past is to present behavior as the seed is to the plant. In the case of conflict, however, the usual progressive transition is arrested. Memories of old ex-periences remain fresher, more susceptible to arousal by current events, and thus more important as determinants of present behavior. Needs and wishes of childhood, fears related to their fulfillment, and the resulting conflicts all persist into the present, only slightly disguised and modified as a result of the inevitable maturation and socialization of the individual. Earlier de-fenses, too, tend to persist with relatively little change. The phrase *repetition of the past* is more descriptive of conflict behavior, and the phrase *develop-ment from the past* is more descriptive of unconflicted behavior.

Freud discovered that the past has these consequences when it has been excluded from consciousness. *Unconscious* memories, fantasies, fears, conflicts, and defensive patterns of response all remain relatively *unchanged with the passing of time*. (This is one of the things Freud meant when he said "the unconscious is timeless.") Being unconscious, they are cut off from the psychological growth of the individual, which is largely tied up with con-scious experience. When these unconscious remnants of the past become conscious, their present influence is greatly diminished. Memories frequently recalled lose their impact on behavior; fears consciously experienced can be reassessed in view of the current external reality; old modes of behavior cease to be automatic when the person becomes aware that he is following them.

The Adaptive Value
of Conflict and Defense

When they find themselves unable to control and tolerate their emotional distress, many people attempt to avoid it as quickly and directly as possible. This is the essence of the process of defense. While it tem-porarily relieves the person from his unpleasant affect, defense is usually ultimately ineffective, because it does not change the real sources of the emotional distress. Duane's perceptual denial, for example, did not change the fact of his father's death or his pleasure over it. In one sense, Duane did not even perceive his father realistically. But these maladaptive features are of no consequence from the standpoint of the process of defense so long as its essential goal is achieved—the quickest attainment of the maximal degree of emotional equanimity possible under the circumstances. Our major emphasis has been and will be on the maladaptive results of conflict and defense, because these are the most thoroughly investigated ones. But conflict and defense can be of adaptive value.

ADAPTIVE CONFLICTS

We have indicated that some conflicts may be realistic and appropriate; they may also be useful. For example, the soldier who goes into battle after coming to grips with the realistic conflict between his loyalty to his comrades and devotion to the cause of his country on the one hand and his fear of death on the other is quite likely to be more resolute and courageous than the soldier who had no such trial conflict in thought. Because he is also consciously frightened, the soldier who has the conflict is motivated to protect himself. He will be attentive to his own performance, alert for signs of danger, and effective in battle—all for his own safety as well as for the success of the mission. (The operation of similar principles in realistic conflicts associated with the threat of impending surgery is discussed in Part I, pp. 95–105.) It seems fairly clear, then, that realistic conflict can be adaptive.

ADAPTIVE DEFENSES

Defenses, too, can be adaptive. For example, an accurate perception of an external situation completely beyond the individual's control would overwhelm him and render him incapable of action. Perceptual distortion by denial could enable this individual to function temporarily, perhaps long enough for the external danger situation to pass.

Another example is that in which external reality is accurately perceived but the anxiety it evokes is repressed and inhibited just long enough for the individual to perform adequately. Epstein and Fenz (1965) found that skilled parachutists experienced considerable anxiety prior to the time of jumping but repressed this anxiety just before and at the critical moment of jumping. If they did not do this, the act of jumping might be seriously interfered with and even be impossible for some individuals. (This research is discussed in detail in Part I, pp. 88–90.)

Still another instance where defenses serve an adaptive function is that in which basic drives are suddenly intensified in a situation where their gratification would be highly maladaptive. Puberty in a member of modern society is a case in point. For example, the early adolescent in our culture must resort to some degree of defense against his rekindled, intense sexual and aggressive urges. Otherwise he becomes a "delinquent" and is treated as a "misfit." Society does not tolerate him, and he is cut off from the established avenues for further growth and development, such as school and relatively unsupervised participation in peer groups.

In all these instances the defenses operate unconsciously and add to the unconscious forces operating in the individual. Thus, they pose a risk for the individual in addition to providing him with adaptive mechanisms. To be adaptive, the defenses must be elicited selectively, used to the minimum degree and for the minimum time necessary for the purpose of adaptation. And eventually the unconscious forces created or maintained by the defenses must be temporarily diminished by catharsis or gratification. Epstein and Fenz observed just this process. After completing their jumps, the experienced parachutists' repressions ceased, and they *then* experienced anxiety.

It is a temptation to say that unrealistic conflict could never be useful or adaptive, but here we must be cautious. Impaired functioning can indeed always be traced back to unrealistic conflicts, but it is not a foregone conclusion that all unrealistic conflicts result in maladaptive behavior and in only impaired functioning. We shall soon discuss, for example, how sons often feel jealous of the relationship their fathers have with their mothers. In these circumstances the sons usually repress their rivalrous anger because of unrealistic fears of their fathers' retaliation and because they also love their fathers. Thus, this is an unrealistic conflict. Yet it promotes the sons' identification with the moral standards of their fathers; this identification is essential for the sons' psychological growth. As another example, many outstanding creative achievements in art and science seem to be related to unrealistic conflicts.

Heinz Hartmann (1939, 1950, 1952, 1955), one of the leading contemporary psychoanalytic theorists, has proposed still another adaptive result of defenses with his concept of the "change of function" of defenses. This concept holds that defenses, which originate in conflict, may later be used for reasons that have relatively little to do with conflict. Thus, Hartmann suggests, defenses may become *autonomous* from conflict, "conflict-free." He refers to some of the same types of changes that Gordon Allport (1937, 1961) has described in his discussion of the "functional autonomy of motives." A girl who represses her sibling rivalry, for example, and resorts to excessive loving of her sister in order to maintain that repression is simultaneously learning how to get along affectionately with another female. As she grows up, she may come to enjoy warm, close relationships with other women, including her sister, for their own sake, not because she is still struggling with hatred for her sister. In Chapter 18 we shall present some clinical observations about a woman whose life approximated this pattern.

In the meantime, we shall examine more closely some of the other characteristics of conflict and defense that we have been discussing. Since one of the most important is the childhood origin of many conflicts appearing in later life, we shall now turn to certain aspects of the emotional life of children. In this way we shall more completely understand such conflicts as the one Duane experienced when his father died, the one that disturbed Ed's sexual life, and those involved in Edie's unusual attitudes about eating.

*Welcome is every organ and attribute of me, and of any
man hearty and clean,*
*Not an inch nor a particle of an inch is vile, and none
shall be less familiar than the rest.*

WALT WHITMAN. Song of Myself

CHAPTER 14
CHILDHOOD
SEXUALITY
AS A SOURCE
OF CONFLICT

We have all heard that Freud discovered that our sexual life starts in childhood, not with puberty and adolescence. But we may not all have a clear idea of exactly what it was he discovered or of the kinds of observations that led to his discovery. The next two chapters present Freud's major discoveries about childhood sexuality and the ways it influences adult life. They also illustrate the kinds of observations that led to these insights about human behavior. Before we begin, we must make clear the limited aims of these chapters: We shall be discussing only one dimension of childhood, albeit one of the most significant ones, and even the treatment of this dimension will be incomplete. Our focus on childhood sexuality will enable us to see more clearly the nature of the persisting conflicts and defenses that underlie behavioral disturbances in many adult men and women. The larger context—the total development of the child—is the subject of Part III.

A Return to History

Childhood sexuality and the associated aggression due to sexual frustration and jealousy were not products of Freud's imagination, nor were they his a priori assumptions. Rather, the existence of sexual and aggressive impulses, wishes, fantasies, anxiety, and conflicts in childhood and their significance for the behavior of the adult were *forced upon* Freud's attention by his clinical observations and the attempt to understand symptoms to which they give rise.

We saw in Chapter 11 that Freud's earliest view was that neurotic symptoms were caused by *unconscious memories of real experiences,* which consisted of intolerable emotional responses to external stimulation. This was his explanation for the symptoms of Anna O. and Lucy R., for example. Freud had no sooner stated this theory than he started to modify it. First he extended it along its original line to what seemed a necessary conclusion. He had been impressed from the beginning with how frequently the repressed memories were of traumatic *sexual* experiences and with the fact that a *series* of overwhelming experiences extending back into the person's early life seemed to be involved. Many of his patients abreacted memories of sexual experiences dating from their childhood. So it seemed then. Consequently, only a few years after *Studies in Hysteria* started to appear in 1893, Freud published several papers (1896a, 1896b, 1896c) in which he stated that the basic overwhelming experience involved in neuroses was always a sexual one incurred before puberty at the hands of an older person. Memories of having been sexually aroused or abused in childhood by nursemaids, older siblings, or other adults, for example, seemed to be at the source of hysterical symptoms. Thus Freud arrived at his *seduction theory of neuroses.*

FREUD'S DISCOVERY OF CHILDHOOD SEXUALITY

Four years later, in *The Interpretation of Dreams* (1900), Freud maintained instead that conflicts involving childhood sexual and hostile *wishes,* not memories, were the basic causes of neuroses. He had reevaluated the likelihood that adults seduced or sexually stimulated children as frequently as his patients' accounts of their childhood indicated. More important, he had discovered that what had seemed to be repressed memories of real, externally imposed childhood sexual experiences were actually *unconscious fantasies* elaborated in the service of the child's *internal* sexual impulses and conflicts. Often these impulses and conflicts involved the child's own parents, as we shall see. Fantasies of sexual stimulation by adults could serve as wish fulfillments of the child's own desires, analogous to the function of conscious daydreams. These fantasies might also serve as "defensive fictions," the function of which was to conceal from the person himself conscious knowledge of his own still earlier, childhood masturbatory and other erotic actions. The individual could feel relieved of responsibility for his sexual excitement and "misbehavior," for example, by fantasying that adults had caused it. These discoveries were related to something else Freud had come to realize: Reality and fantasy, truth and fiction, are not distinguished in unconscious thinking. Unconscious fantasies, memories of such fantasies, and unconscious memories of real events all seem equally real when one becomes conscious of them. By all these interrelated observations and realizations, then, Freud had discovered by 1900 that conflicts over sexual and hostile impulses dating back to childhood were crucial in the causation of adult conflicts. At the root of many conflicts in the adult man was an unconscious childhood desire to have sexual satisfaction with his mother and to eliminate his father as a rival. In adult women, like Anna O. and Lucy R., unconscious sexual wishes for the father and jealousy of the mother were involved. Freud named this constellation of forbidden desires and fantasies the *Oedipal complex*.

It was not easy for Freud to make these discoveries. The major difficulty, of course, arose from the pioneering nature of his work. He was one of the few people studying these problems, and all of his colleagues considered neurosis to be a disease of the nervous system. There were also personal difficulties. To make these discoveries, he had to admit to himself that his seduction theory had been wrong. To publish his discoveries, he had to publicly acknowledge his earlier error. It is easy to imagine how distressing this admission was for a physician still trying to establish himself professionally and scientifically; a physician, furthermore, who, with Breuer, had proposed a radical new theory and published his new discoveries.

From a study of Freud's letters to his friend Wilhelm Fliess, one senses another obstacle to his discovery of childhood sexuality, an obstacle repeatedly encountered even today in the training of analysts—a disbelief, or a reluctance to believe, in its validity. As early as the spring of 1897 Freud doubted his seduction theory, and he nearly abandoned it in the fall of that year. But then he appeared to hesitate for over a year before he was finally convinced in the belief that "to the question: 'what happened in earliest childhood?' the answer is 'nothing.' But the germ of a sexual impulse was there . . . [Freud, 1892–99, Letter 101, p. 276]." An important aspect of his reluctance to recognize the importance of the person's *own* childhood sexuality must be attributed to the fact that this discovery stemmed in a large part from the first psychoanalysis in history—his own self-analysis. Thus, in addition to the usual obstacles on the path to momentous insights, Freud had to overcome his own conflicts, without the help of another analyst, in order to discover childhood sexuality.

Now we must see what Freud meant when he said of childhood, "the germ of a sexual impulse was there." However, we shall not limit ourselves to what he meant at that time, although the germinal ideas for much that follows were then in his mind.

The Psychosexual Life of the Child

In a very broad sense Freud discovered that the human being's erotic, sensual life starts in childhood, and he delineated a sequence of developmental stages of childhood eroticism (1905b). He also recognized that the child's erotic life has extensive psychological ramifications, which go far beyond simple bodily pleasure and include his inner mental life and his early relations with other members of his family. The term *psychosexual* refers to these two aspects of the child's emotional life.

THE THREE STAGES OF CHILDHOOD EROTICISM

During the first year or so of life, childhood eroticism is dominated by the pleasures caused by stimulation of the mucous membranes of the mouth. This is the *oral stage,* and the passionate thumb-sucking of many very young children is one typical manifestation of it.

In the second year, according to Freud, the child's erotic life comes more and more under the dominance of his anal membranes. Now his chief sensual delight is derived from rectal stimulation provided primarily by his own excretory activities but also by such forms of stimulation as his own touching of his anal region, cleaning and bathing by his parents, and enemas. The preoccupied pleasure of the defecating child and his contentment after he has just evacuated a large stool, often after a period of deliberate retention designed to increase its size, is typical of this *anal stage.*

Sometime during the third year or the first part of the fourth, genital stimulation and excitations start to provide the child with his most intense sensual pleasures. This is the *childhood genital or phallic stage.* Phallic or clitoral masturbation is now a typical occurrence. No observant adult can help seeing this either in open and unmistakable behavior or in more covert forms, such as rubbing against people and objects in play or rhythmical thigh-pressing.

Aggressive Aspects There is an aggressive aspect to each of the stages, too. In the oral stage, after he has teeth, the child delights in biting. As he is developing bowel control, and often afterward, the child enjoys defying his parents by defecating according to his desires, not theirs. He can now be especially willful and stubborn and cruel in many ways. The phallic stage is usually accompanied by delight in penetrating and destroying things, but the most prominent feature of the child's aggression in this phase involves his parents, in ways to be discussed shortly.

The oral, anal, and phallic eroticism of childhood, Freud reasoned, are different, age-appropriate manifestations of the same eroticism characteristic of postpubertal life. Many people have claimed that Freud thereby widened the meaning of "sexuality" to include all pleasure-seeking behavior and that "sexuality" in psychoanalysis lost its usual meaning. On the contrary, Freud was insisting that we recognize the *sexual* quality of all three stages of childhood eroticism. The oral and the anal are just as sexual as the genital, and the childhood genital pleasures are just as sexual as those of adulthood.

Freud based this conclusion on several converging empirical observations and lines of reasoning that render it less mysterious or bizarre than it seems to be at first glance.

The Biological Similarity of the Three Zones

To begin with, the biological structure and functioning of the various zones are similar. The mouth, anus, and genitals are all lined or covered with mucous membranes and are richly supplied with blood vessels and sensory receptors. When stimulated from within or without, they become engorged with blood and give rise to intense sensations. Sensations in the various zones do differ, but they have a common quality Freud often described as an "itching," which is usually experienced as a craving for further stimulation in the form of rhythmical, abrasive contact with some object. This stimulation may be provided by rhythmical thumb-sucking, rubbing of the anus with the fingers or the passing of a stool, or various kinds of masturbation of the genitals. All these activities may be regarded as masturbatory. A commonly observed phenomenon also indicates that excitations in the various zones are closely related: In baby boys, erections frequently accompany oral and anal stimulation.

The Relationship Between Childhood Eroticism and Adult Sexuality

Freud supported the sexuality of the three stages with a second group of observations and inferences. These concerned an apparent relationship between the eroticism of childhood and the sexual life of adults—normal adults, perverts, and psychoneurotics. In the complexities of the adult sexual life of these three groups Freud perceived the operation of oral, anal, and, of course, genital eroticism, and he concluded that the sexual significance of such eroticism in adulthood was either a residue, a continuation, an unconscious persistence, or a return of the sexual significance of this same eroticism in childhood.

Thus, he noted that pregenital eroticism plays an important role in the sexual foreplay or byplay of the normal adult. Sensual kissing is a familiar instance. Childhood oral eroticism appears here as a residual, subordinate process. The fact that intercourse is the major goal of adult sexual activity Freud called *genital primacy*. The usual fate of pregenital sexuality is to become a preliminary to the main goal.

In many perversions, however, oral or anal eroticism is paramount. Orgasm is possible for many perverts, for example, only by sexual union via the mouth or anus or only if there is a great deal of oral and anal stimulation. Such a condition, where childhood pregenital eroticism continues to play the dominant role it played in the pregenital phases of development, is an example of *fixation*.

The situation of psychoneurotics was perceived by Freud as somewhat more complex. A typical configuration here is: inhibition of overt genital eroticism, substitution of unconscious fantasies centered in fixated oral and anal eroticism, and overt symptoms caused by the wishes expressed in these unconscious fantasies and by defenses against such wishes. The unconscious fantasies involve the same wishes experienced consciously and gratified openly in the sexual perversions. If he had no conflict about these wishes and fulfilled them in overt behavior, the psychoneurotic would engage in the same kinds of sexual activity enjoyed by perverts. But of course he does have conflicts about them and thus is markedly different from perverts. As Freud explained, the psychoneuroses are the negative of the perversions.

The configuration just outlined operated in the example of the eating conflict presented in Chapter 12. Eating was a substitute for genital behavior for Edie. But the conflict over eating, as became clear in her psychoanalysis, was a conflict over unconscious fantasies of sucking, biting, and feeding on a penis. While these fantasies never became fully conscious, derivatives of them did. Thus, she one day said that one of the happiest moments in her life was a particular time when she was eating a hot dog a boy had given her. As she ate it and the small group of peers about her were silent, she felt an intense state of peaceful bliss. On another occasion late in her analysis the nausea she experienced upon eating reminded her of a strong bout of nausea and feelings of disgust she had experienced in adolescence when a boy told her he had "creamed his jeans." Eating was such a sensual experience for this patient because it was a disguised gratification of her unconscious desires to suck, bite, and feed on a penis, but by the same token it was the object of severe inhibitions.

In addition to discovering that pregenital eroticism was of sexual significance in the adult lives of psychoneurotics, Freud also discovered that these forms of eroticism had been especially prominent in their childhoods. It appeared that they had returned to earlier forms of sexual eroticism when frustrated in their genital behavior by external circumstances or by their own internal conflicts. When we discuss the Oedipal complex, it will be apparent how that aspect of childhood sexuality, which subsumes a great deal of the child's genital eroticism, is also often continued into adulthood and becomes the source of neurotic conflict.

**The Interchangeability
of the Excitations**   A third reason for regarding oral and anal eroticism as sexual is that excitations in the oral, anal, and genital zones, and their related gratifications, are interchangeable. This property of interchangeability is at the basis of the psychoneurotic phenomena that we have just discussed, but it manifests itself in other ways as well, which would not be regarded as neurotic. For example, adults who have been accustomed to normal genital gratification frequently manifest an upsurge in oral and anal interests if they are deprived of intimate contact with members of the opposite sex. Perhaps without realizing it, most of us become more interested in food and eating or our bowel functioning—depending upon our individual make-up—when there are occasional interruptions in our genital sex life. We do in miniature and without conflict what many psychoneurotics wish to do on a grand scale but cannot do. The normal limits of such behavior are often exceeded in situations of prolonged deprivation. Men in all-male schools and army camps and in prison often become intensely involved with their food, even to the point of strongly protesting about it on unrealistic grounds. And they often become excessively preoccupied with bowel movements and flatus. The prominence of "latrine humor" is a typical derivative expression of this preoccupation.

In *Ulysses*, James Joyce portrays the flow of Leopold Bloom's subjective experience after finishing his breakfast. As the episode begins, Bloom is in a reverie about his youth stimulated by a letter from his daughter, Milly, in which she mentions the attentions of some young men.

> Seaside girls. Torn envelope. Hands stuck in his trousers' pockets . . . singing. . . .

> *Those girls, those girls,*
> *Those lovely seaside girls*

Milly too. Young kisses: the first. . . . Mrs Marion [Bloom]. Reading lying back now, counting the strands of her hair, smiling, braiding.

A soft qualm regret, flowed down his backbone, increasing. Will happen, yes. Prevent. Useless: can't move. Girl's sweet light lips. Will happen too. He felt the flowing qualm spread over him. Useless to move now. Lips kissed, kissing kissed. Full gluey woman's lips.

. . .

The cat, having cleaned all her fur . . . stalked to the door. . . . Wants to go out. . . .

He felt heavy, full: then a gentle loosening of his bowels. He stood up. . . .

. . .

A paper. He liked to read at stool. Hope no ape comes knocking just as I'm.

. . .

He kicked open the crazy door of the jakes. . . . The king was in his counting house. . . .
Asquat on the cuckstool he folded out his paper turning its pages over on his bared knees. . . . No great hurry. Keep it a bit. . . .
Quietly he read, restraining himself, the first column and, yielding but resisting, began the second. Midway, his last resistance yielding, he allowed his bowels to ease themselves quietly as he read, reading still patiently. . . . Hope it's not too big bring on piles again. No, just right. So. Ah! . . . He read on, seated calm above his own rising smell [1961, pp. 67–69].

In the latter part of this excerpt Joyce portrays succinctly and honestly the anal pleasures many adults secretly experience. The excerpt also shows the close association that may exist between sexuality and anal eroticism. Notice how quickly Bloom's desire to defecate follows upon his sexual reverie and how the reverie is toned with the nostalgic regret that he will never again experience the excitement of those first young kisses. Could Bloom be turning from his disappointing sexual reverie to a substitute, anal form of pleasure? Did Joyce knowingly and deliberately juxtapose the sexual reverie and the sensual defecation because he, the perceptive artist, knew of the frequent close connection between sexuality and anality? Or did his own unconscious thought associate these two images? Or is the anal episode to be simply attributed to the fact that Bloom had finished breakfast a short while before? And are we to regard it as mere coincidence that the pleasurable anal episode so closely follows the sexual reverie? Only a rigorous study of the associative context of all excretory episodes in *Ulysses* and probably in Joyce's other works as well, and of Joyce himself, would enable us to answer these questions. The mere fact that we can ask such questions, however, illustrates the stimulative effect of Freud's ideas about pregenital sexuality and of the relentless application of the principle of exceptionless psychic determinism. Incidentally, Joyce's use of the image "The king was in his counting house" in this anal context is an artist's recognition of a symbolic unconscious equation of feces with money that Freud frequently observed operating in his patients and in dreams of normal people.

The Development of Object Relations

The three psychosexual stages are defined by the regions of the body dominating the child's erotic life, and the progression from one stage to the other is defined by changes in the dominant erotogenic zone. There is another aspect to the child's sexual life, which Freud also discovered. The important people in the child's life—including the child himself and his parents—necessarily become involved in his erotic life. The emergence of this interpersonal dimension, which is called in psychoanalytic writings the *development of object relations,* makes the child more than a biological assemblage of erogenous body parts. It contributes greatly to his becoming a social creature, and specifically a *human being.*

NARCISSISM

The Greek myth about Narcissus epitomizes a very important aspect of human object relations: self-love. Upon seeing his reflection in the water, Narcissus sat transfixed in self-adoration and self-absorption. Unable to give up looking at his image, he eventually died of starvation.

Self-Love and Feelings of Omnipotence Young children love themselves nearly as much as Narcissus did, frequently manifesting their narcissism in the same way when they look in the mirror with unabashed, shameless admiration. But the most important expression of the child's self-love is the cherishing of his body and its parts, his good bodily sensations, and his body products. All those things he conceives of as his—toys, clothes, bed, parents—are also loved in an extended narcissism. When he forms a concept of himself, probably in the second half of his first year, he loves *himself* too. One indication of this is his love of his own name and his angry hurt in any teasing play with his name.

Another aspect of the child's narcissism, in addition to his self-love, is his sense of omnipotence. Much of the time he acts as if he feels in control of the world about him, as if he believes that his wishes, gestures, and cries *in themselves* determine events in the external world. He does not seem to realize that his behavior is effective only because his parents are disposed to react to it.

Narcissism as the First Stage of Object Relations When Freud developed the concept of childhood narcissism and incorporated it into psychoanalysis (1914a), he also speculated that it was the first developmental stage of human object relations. The most important reason for this speculation was his observation that severely disturbed psychotics who have abandoned normal adult love relationships react in ways that resemble the narcissistic behavior of very young children. Daniel Paul Schreber, who was a German judge before he became mentally ill, described his own paranoid schizophrenia in his memoirs, which Freud studied (Freud, 1911). Schreber lost interest in the people about him (they seemed to constitute a shadow world) and at the same time acted as if he loved himself and as if he felt omnipotent. He would pass the time standing half-naked in front of his mirror, all the while experiencing erotic, voluptuous bodily sensations. His sense of omnipotence revealed itself in his delusion that God had selected him alone as a love object and was gradually transforming him into a woman. He was going to bear a new race of men, fathered by God. Such phenomena of schizophrenia are associated with the abandonment of normal human relationships, with the loss of close human contact in old-fashioned "insane asylums," and with a great deal of oral and anal activity resembling that of very young children. Hence Freud thought it plausible that the narcissism of cases like Schreber was a result of regression to a stage of object relations that preceded relationships with other people, to the stage of loving only oneself.

Later Manifestations of Narcissism

While we cannot say exactly how and when narcissism develops in childhood, it seems certain that it does. It also appears that as we grow up we lose most of our narcissism. But we never give it up entirely. Adults, too, like to look at themselves in mirrors, literally and figuratively. The pride we feel in recognizing in ourselves something worthwhile, or in having our accomplishments recognized and reflected in the attitudes of other people, can be considered a normal, healthy bit of narcissism. Freud also noted several other manifestations of narcissism: the usual concern we feel for ourselves when we are sick, the satisfaction of knowing we are loved, and some of the pleasure parents derive from loving their children, who are extensions of themselves. It is just as certain, of course, that the child comes to love others too, a development that is correlated with decreasing narcissism. It is time now to consider this aspect of the child's life.

In nearly all that we shall say about the child's love of others, we shall be speaking about the child in our Western civilization—a monogamous, patriarchal culture in which the basic social unit, the *family*, consists of the biological (as well as psychological) mother and father and their children. It is in such a child that we are naturally most interested, and the emotional relationships and conflicts of just such a child have been more thoroughly studied than those in other cultures.

SEXUALITY IN FAMILY RELATIONSHIPS

The parent-child relationships in our culture involve erotic feelings in both parent and child. We shall discuss only some of these feelings operative in the child.

Preoedipal Attachments to the Mother

The Oedipal complex is one of the most important results of the child's passionate feelings for his parents, but it is a relatively late phenomenon of childhood. Freud regarded it as one aspect of a developmental process starting in earlier, preoedipal erotic attachments of both the girl and the boy to the mother. Freud reasoned that the early erotic attachments developed because the child obtained erotic stimulation from the mother in the course of the biologically necessary activities in which they engage—nursing, bathing, comforting, toileting, and so forth. In nursing, for example, the child not only is fed but also experiences the erotic pleasures of sucking and of being warmed against his mother's body, rocked, and murmured to. It seems quite plausible that children should come to long for erotic oral stimulation from their mother as well as to long for food from her. This type of erotic longing is reinforced and expanded in content. Each step in the child's psychosexual development, outlined earlier, introduces new kinds of erotic gratifications into the changing mother-child relationship.

Toileting After weaning, the most intense interaction between mother and child is focused around toileting and toilet training. This involves a great deal of physical contact between the mother and the child's excretory organs. From this interaction children may develop a longing for anal stimulation by their mothers and often by their fathers, too, for the father is likely to share in this aspect of child rearing. The parents' interest in bowel training contributes further to an anal-erotic current in the parent-child relationship. Parents are pleased with and proud of signs that the child is developing bowel control, and they transmit these feelings to the child, who comes to share in them and to learn that a bowel movement brings him his parents' love. His excretory process becomes an important medium for expressing his love for his parents as well as for obtaining their love. Thus, what is very pleasurable for autoerotic reasons takes on an interpersonal meaning and becomes even more pleasurable and object related.

Erotic-Genital Stimulation As the boy and girl enter their third or fourth year, they long for erotic-genital stimulation by their parents, especially by the mother, and they express interest in her genitals. This change in the primary form of erotic attachment to the mother reflects the fact that the child's genitals are becoming his primary source of erotic pleasure and the child's related growing awareness, however primitively conceived, that his parents have a genital love life.

Soon boys and girls start to follow separate lines of development. A boy continues his primary erotic attachment to his mother. Indeed, he develops a passionate, though childlike, genital love for her that is a forerunner of his heterosexual loves of adolescence and adulthood. At the same time, his filial love for his father becomes complicated by jealousy and hostility toward him because he is a rival, and more successful, lover of his mother. In this way the boy typically develops his positive Oedipal complex. Although the little girl never gives up all her sexual attachments to her mother, she does turn away from her mother as a primary erotic love object and comes to focus her sexual longings upon her father. She too develops an Oedipal complex—passionate love for her father and jealous hostility toward her mother.

In the next chapter we shall discuss the Oedipal complex in detail, but first we shall discuss the little girl's turning to the father to keep our developmental portrayal intact. Freud often said that the emotional life of women was an enigma. It was not until the middle 1920's that he thought he might have discovered the most significant cause for the girl's turning to the father—a constellation of thoughts and feelings that he called *the female castration complex* (Freud, 1924, 1925b).

THE FEMALE CASTRATION COMPLEX

While still erotically attached to her mother, the little girl discovers that boys have penises and that she does not. This discovery is a severely traumatic experience that threatens her narcissism and is experienced as a painful loss of her self-esteem, as a sense of inferiority. Common results of this mortifying blow are the development of penis envy (to be discussed in Chapter 16), a repression of clitoral eroticism and an associated aversion to masturbation, and the change in object relations with which we are concerned now. The girl usually blames her mother for the fact that she does not have a penis, and she turns to her father in the hope of getting a penis substitute from him, a baby.

The female castration complex thus consists of the girl's loss of self-esteem and a sense of inferiority because she does not have a penis, usually the angry blaming of her mother for this "defect" in herself, and the longing for a penis substitute to restore her lost self-esteem. The female castration complex provides the motivations for the development of the girl's positive Oedipal complex.

A Clinical
Example
The following excerpts from observations made by a female analyst illustrate the appearance of the castration complex in one of her little daughters. The parenthetical remarks are quoted from the original source; bracketed comments have been added by the present writer.

A little girl of three years old whose upbringing had presented no difficulty in her first year and little serious difficulty in her second and third years, suddenly began to shew signs of trouble. She was heard one day saying to herself, "Mummy has smashed me up." At about the same time it happened that when her mother was drying her after her bath the little girl displayed great anxiety every time the mother approached her genitals with the towel.

.   .   .

Some months before this episode, this child and her [somewhat older] sister . . . had seen a little boy naked when they were playing on the beach. Probably this was the first time that they had noticed the difference between the sexes.

. . .

It happened that, at about the same time that she made the remark I have recorded and displayed anxiety lest her mother should touch her genitals, the children's father went into the nursery and tried to shake hands with them. The younger of the two refused to give him her hand, saying, "I won't give you my hand, I will only give you my finger." When her father asked in amazement why she did so, she replied, using her own childish terms, that it was because he had a penis and "a little bag." [Is the little girl substituting her finger for the penis she fantasies she has lost? She may be defensively *denying in action* that she does not have a penis.] (Her knowledge of the scrotum could only have been derived from the incident on the beach several months previously; it had never been mentioned in the conversations between her elder sister and the grown-ups.) It is true that she only said this once. Only a few hours later, when her father, hoping to elicit the same reply, again asked her to give him her hand, she refused, as she had done before, but gave as her reason, "because you've got an apron." [Has she now made her father into a woman, who wears an apron instead of a penis? This might be a *denial in fantasy* of her father's masculinity.] . . .

From that time on, certain difficulties arose which might perhaps be called symptoms. At meals the child did not want to have her meat cut up and wished to take all her food only in large pieces, not divided up in any way, so that in fact it was impossible for her to eat them. For instance, she would not allow anyone to break off a piece of cake for her, and so forth. A dog which she knew was once brought to see her when it had just been shaved and the effect was to give her a shock. [All these details are symbolic substitutes for her concern with the integrity of her own body. We can surmise, for example, that she does not want to see food cut up because it stimulates her thoughts that her genitals had been cut up.] She became more and more preoccupied with the idea of "big and little" until she could think of nothing else. . . . She also evolved a theory that she had once been big and had only just become little.

. . .

The little girl also developed a transitory symptom in the shape of a tic. On one occasion she took hold of her nose and asked if it was a big one. This gesture very soon became a tic: every moment she put her fingers to her nose. [Now her nose seems to be a symbolic substitute for a penis. By touching her nose constantly she may be again *denying in action* the perception that she does not have a penis.] At this point her mother intervened with an interpretation and gave a suitable explanation that nothing had been taken away from the child, that all boys and men were from their birth like the little friend whom she had observed, that all girls and women, including her mother, were like herself and that the one form was just as nice as the other and that some day she would have children. At first this interpretation had no effect, but its effect was instantaneous when it was repeated by the other child, the [older] sister. . . . The tic vanished the same day.

Finally the child developed a habit of blaming her mother for everything disagreeable which happened. If she dropped anything, it was her mother's fault, although the latter was often nowhere near: she should have looked after her better. The same explanation applies here—the child was reproaching her mother, who was really "to blame for everything," seeing that she had not borne the little girl as a boy [as reported to Waelder, 1937, pp. 453–56].

A Baby
as a Fantasy Substitute
for a Penis

The idea that having a baby is a fantasied substitute for having a penis is at first very strange. But psychoanalytic evidence leaves little doubt about this equivalence in unconscious thinking, especially that of many women who have been psychoanalyzed.

Most women will admit to, or give evidence of, a wish that at least their first child be a boy. Many have the same wish but keep it a secret. The present writer observed five women before, during, and after pregnancy in either psychoanalysis or long-term, intensive psychotherapy. In one case the writer observed a second pregnancy as well. In each instance the woman secretly preferred to have a boy. The emotional depth and importance of this preference was strikingly shown in the woman with two pregnancies.

> She maintained until just before delivery of her first baby that she was impartial, in spite of the fact that she used to assert that the world regarded females as "second-class citizens." But the moment she gave birth to a girl she was aware of a sense of disappointment. For an instant she consciously wished her baby were a boy. When she heard the next day that a friend of hers had just given birth to a boy, she felt extremely jealous and angry. That little boy immediately became severely ill. She was then horrified by a fleeting awareness that she was glad of it, for he might die and her jealousy would be satisfied. Because these thoughts were so alien to her conscious values and attitudes and guilt-producing, she repressed them. Within two months she was in the throes of a severe depression that had a paranoid quality. The guilt produced by her reactions to having had a girl instead of a boy was a very important determinant of that profound disturbance. Subsequently she gave birth to a boy. During the pregnancy she was nearly incapacitated with anxiety, but with the birth of a boy there was no postpartum reaction. Instead there followed a long period of an equanimity she had never previously shown in a 7-year period of analytic and psychotherapeutic observation.

This preference for boy babies cannot be attributed solely to the women's internalization of our cultural evaluation of the male, for another type of evidence emerges in psychoanalyses of women. Their dreams and associations concerning their babies often show the unconscious phallic meaning of the baby, as in the following example. Another young woman had the following associations and dream during a 10-day period in her fifth month of pregnancy. (Significantly, the dominant theme of her conscious everyday life at this time was her competitiveness with men, typified by a minor automobile "accident" in which she angrily cut in front of a man who was about to pass her in an adjoining lane of a one-way street.)

One day the patient's free associations included an image of an *erect penis* seen in profile. As she described it, she thought of the profile of her nose and her embarrassment that it turned up at the end. [Compare the nose–penis equation in the example of the little girl.] Her next thought was of how her "*belly is really beginning to stick out now.*"

In her next analytic hour, as she was wondering whether her analyst's *penis* was *erect*, she felt her abdominal muscles contract. Then she said that she was actually actively doing this. She then realized that lately she had been contracting her stomach muscles to *make* her "*belly into a hard, protruding ball . . . to make the baby stick out hard.*" Her *competitive driving* and the auto "accident" occurred 2 days later. This was the only auto mishap in 6 years of analytic observation.

Two analytic hours later she reported the following dream: She was lying down and was looking down her body at her abdomen. She saw her pregnant abdomen sticking up. The baby inside was moving rapidly and extensively, causing the wall of her abdomen to be pushed way out in places as though the baby was pushing out with a leg here, a leg there, an arm here and then there.

Then a place on her abdomen was pushed out, making a protuberance a few inches long, about the size of a thumb. This protuberance was either from her navel or near it.

Her associations to the dream were that the baby might have had an erection, which was causing this protrusion near her navel. Then she recalled that as a little girl she had thought her navel was her penis. She further recalled that in the previous two hours of her psychoanalysis her competitiveness with men had been discussed. She realized that she did compete with men and needed to "cut them down to size."

The unconscious equating of parts of the female body and especially of a baby with a penis has been observed in many women during psychoanalysis. Evidently this equation in fantasy, together with her castration complex, leads the girl in her transition from her preoedipal attachment to her mother to her choice of her father as her primary love object. Freud assumed that the boy and the girl reach the Oedipal stage of their psychosexual development around the fourth year. The girl reaches it in the manner we have discussed. The boy reaches it as a result of the involvement of his developing phallic eroticism in his already positive attachment to his mother, which dates back to his first awareness of her as a distinct person. In the next chapter we shall take a close look at the Oedipal complex and its impact on adult life.

If the little savage were left to himself [and had] the violent passions of a man of thirty, he would strangle his father and lie with his mother.

DENIS DIDEROT. Rameau's Nephew

CHAPTER 15

THE OEDIPAL CONFLICTS AND THEIR EFFECTS

D iderot's striking statement, which was also quoted by Freud (1915–17), epitomizes the positive Oedipal complex. This complex is an emotional constellation of two components: (1) an intense conflict over erotic love for the parent of the opposite sex and (2) an intense conflict over jealous, rivalrous hatred for the parent of the same sex. The Oedipal conflicts significantly influence children's emotional and fantasy relationships with their parents at around the ages of 3 to 6. What kind of evidence led Freud to the discovery of the Oedipal conflicts? How is the Oedipal complex manifested in the behavior of the child and the adult?

Manifestations of the Complex

We shall devote most of this discussion to the Oedipal complex in the male, taking account of the fact that nearly all of Freud's published observations concerned the male. Three basic lines of evidence can be extracted from Freud's writings on the Oedipal complex: (1) direct observations of childhood behavior and fantasies, (2) childhood memories recalled by patients in psychoanalysis, and (3) observations of themes or events in adult behavior that can best be understood as indirect results of a persisting repressed, and thus unconscious, Oedipal complex. In the following paragraphs we shall sample these three classes of evidence.

MANIFESTATIONS OBSERVED IN CHILDREN

In 1909 Freud reported the observations made by the father of a 5-year-old boy, whom Freud called Little Hans (1909a). The father, who was a layman sympathetic to Freud's ideas, made these observations as he tried to help Little Hans overcome an intense fear of horses. His method was psychoanalysis, modified in keeping with Little Hans's age and the father's inexperience, and aided by occasional consultations with Freud. This was the first "child analysis" in history. (Nowadays, a father would not be encouraged to try to treat his own child but would be helped in finding a suitable specialist in child therapy.)

Many of the father's observations concerned things Little Hans did and thought as a result of his Oedipal complex. For example, the boy enjoyed getting into bed with his mother, where they would hug and caress each other. He also asked her to touch his penis because "it's great fun." He would masturbate and have sexual fantasies about his mother and playmates as he did so. He described one such episode as follows. (His opening remark refers to masturbation, and the events he describes as he masturbated were taking place in fantasy. Grete is a female playmate.)

I put my finger to my widdler just a very little. I saw Mummy quite naked in her chemise, and she let me see her widdler. I showed Grete, my Grete, what Mummy was doing, and showed her my widdler. Then I took my hand away from my widdler quick. . . . the chemise was so short that I saw her widdler [p. 32].

Little Hans also enjoyed being in the bathroom with his mother when she went to the toilet. "He goes on pestering me till I let him," she said. He had fantasies that he would some day marry his mother and that they would have children.

Little Hans's Oedipal jealousy and hostility took such forms as being inappropriately aggressive in roughhousing with his father, defying his father's occasional attempts to keep him from getting into bed with his mother, fantasying that he, and not his father, was married to his mother, and wishing that his father would be dead so that he could have his mother all to himself.

These are some of the least inferential observations about Little Hans's Oedipal complex. Many child analysts have replicated these findings.

Using doll-play materials similar to those illustrated in Figure 15-1, Pauline Sears (1951) and a group of colleagues observed how normal boys and girls—3, 4, and 5 years old—expressed aggressive fantasies concerning their mothers and fathers. More than 100 lower-middle-class and upper-lower-class children from the Midwest were given the opportunity to play freely with the doll family, which consisted of a father, mother, boy, girl, and baby. Observers recorded everything the children did in this projective play. (The theoretical rationale for using projective assessment techniques is discussed in Part IV, pp. 623–27.) Later the researchers carefully defined criteria for judging whether play behavior was aggressive and then counted the number of times aggressive behavior had occurred in the doll play. They also determined how frequently the aggressive behavior was directed toward the various members of the doll family.

The results that interest us concern the mother and father dolls. As Figure 15-2 shows, the girls directed much more aggression toward the mother doll than toward the father doll; the boys expressed more aggression toward the father than toward the mother doll. Such results cannot be explained simply as reactions to how the children were disciplined and frustrated (in the usual sense of that word) by their parents. These results are highly consistent with the pattern of aggression one would predict if he assumed that these young children were in the throes of their Oedipal complex.

Sears included a sample record of the play of a 4-year-old boy named Mike. The following excerpt from the record shows the vividness with which Mike fantasied that all sorts of misfortunes should descend upon his father:

Figure 15-1 *The doll house and part of the doll family used in Sears's study of children's aggressive fantasies concerning their parents.*

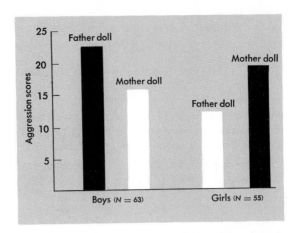

Figure 15-2 Results of the doll-play aggression study. (Based on data from Sears, 1951)

chair goes on top of the old man . . . Mother kicks him [father] backward out of house . . . the girl kicked him back again . . . toilet sits on F [father] . . . someone goes phooey on the old man . . . he [father] falls . . . F has to go to jail . . . table smashed on top of him . . . the house is burning . . . Daddy is going to stay in and burn . . . F falls in fire . . . chair smashes his head in . . . [Father] lying in bed and burning . . . someone piles furniture on top of him [father]. He's all smashed up . . . [Father has] to sleep in tub—pokes his head down—jams him in [Sears, 1951, pp. 40–41].

Neither Diderot nor Freud exaggerated the intensity of the hostile designs the little boy has on his father.

MANIFESTATIONS REVEALED BY CHILDHOOD MEMORIES: THE RAT MAN AND THE WOLF MAN

Freud's adult patients recalled doing and thinking in their childhood the same kinds of things that were directly observed in Little Hans.

The Rat Man (Freud, 1909b), for example (so named because of his obsessional thoughts about rats), recalled that in his fourth, fifth, and sixth years he begged his governesses to let him engage in sexual play with them and enjoyed crawling under their nightgowns, undressing them, and touching their genitals. He could recall that he had erections in these early years, too. The governesses, of course, were maternal substitutes, for they took care of him. He could also recall a thinly disguised Oedipal death wish directed toward his father: In his childhood he feared that if he thought about his strong wishes to see some of his little girl friends naked, *his father might die.*

Another patient, called the Wolf Man because of a childhood phobia of certain pictures of wolves and a nightmare about wolves, recalled similar childhood events, after painstaking work in his analysis. (The study of the Wolf Man is the best published example of Freud's analytic work [Freud, 1918].)

Like the Rat Man, the Wolf Man was cared for largely by governesses and maids rather than by his mother, so his Oedipal behavior, too, was directed toward them. Once, in the middle of his third year, he saw a nursery maid named Grusha, whom he loved very much, on her hands and knees scrubbing the floor. When he saw her he urinated in front of her, an act Freud interpreted as the effect sexual excitement had on him at that time. The psychoanalysis of the Wolf Man produced a mass of indirect evidence that he had seen either animals having intercourse or his parents in the same position, which Freud believed was why the sight of Grusha in that position, with her buttocks prominently raised, had such a stimulating effect. He reasoned that it must have triggered an overt, displaced expression of the boy's early Oedipal longing for his mother. (We shall consider this inference further in a moment.) When the Wolf Man was nearly 4, his sister, who was two years older, seduced him into sex by-play and handled his penis. As she did this, she said that his nurse, Nanya, used to do this with other men. The boy loved Nanya as much as any woman in his life at that time, so within a few weeks he tried to repeat the erotic experience with Nanya by masturbating in front of her.

The recapturing of memory fragments from the Oedipal period similar to those of these two patients of Freud is a very common occurrence in psychoanalyses. Individuals differ, of course, with respect to the clarity of recall, the explicitness of the erotic and hostile dimensions of their childhood behavior, and the extent to which adults had encouraged their overt sexual behavior. Sometimes the memories are of real events; sometimes they are memories of fantasies.

INDIRECT MANIFESTATIONS OBSERVED IN ADULTS

The fate of the Oedipal complex is repression, which usually starts in the fifth or sixth year. But many themes and events in the later life of almost any person can best be understood if one assumes that there really was an Oedipal complex in childhood and that it continues to influence behavior after its repression. These later forms of behavior become evidence, or manifestations, of the Oedipal complex to the extent that one accepts the validity of such explanations. And, as we shall see, the full significance of the early experiences or fantasies recalled in fragmentary fashion in adulthood, as in the case of the Rat Man and the Wolf Man, is fully realized only retrospectively, following a careful study of their aftermath in later life.

Actually, observations of indirect manifestations in adult behavior were primarily what led Freud to his discovery of the Oedipal complex. One form of behavior, dreaming, was especially important in this regard.

By the time he wrote *The Interpretation of Dreams* (1900), Freud had studied a large number of dreams—his own, his patients', and other people's as well. He observed that many adults reported dreaming of the death of their parents. When he examined these dreams, he detected a pattern: "that men . . . dream mostly of their father's death and women of their mother's [p. 256]." He also observed at this time that "many men dream of having sexual relations with their mothers, and speak of the fact with indignation and astonishment [p. 264]." These dreams, he thought, must be produced by repressed Oedipal wishes, both the hostile and the erotic, that originated in childhood but persisted into the dreamer's adult unconscious mental life. Since they are defended against in everyday behavior, they find expression in the wish fulfillments (which are usually disguised) of dreams.

At the time he was making these observations and inferences about dreams, Freud was observing in the symptoms and behavior of his patients what he thought must also be indirect results of repressed Oedipal wishes or memories.

The Rat Man and the Wolf Man as Adults The Rat Man's and the Wolf Man's later lives clearly illustrate this phenomenon. We mentioned that when he was a boy, the Rat Man had sexual fantasies and feared that his father would die if he had such fantasies. The Rat Man's later sexual life remained closely tied to the theme of his father's death.

1. When he fell in love in adolescence, he had the obsessive wish that his father would die. Then, he fantasied, his girlfriend would love him because she would feel sorry for him.

2. A few years later, when he was again in love, he used to imagine that if his father died he would have enough money to marry.

3. When he first engaged in intercourse, the obsessive thought flashed through his mind, "This is glorious! One might murder one's father for this! [Freud, 1909b, p. 201]."

4. His father died when the Rat Man was 21, whereupon he experienced an uncontrollable upsurge of desires to masturbate.

This pattern seems best explained as a manifestation of persisting, repressed Oedipal wishes. The recalled childhood fear that his father would die if the boy had sexual fantasies would then be viewed as but a fragmentary manifestation of the Oedipal complex.

The diagram in Figure 15-3 illustrates how we can conceptualize adult manifestations of the hostile component of the Oedipal complex as the results of an unconscious approach-avoidance conflict.

Turning to the Wolf Man, we should remember the childhood scene with Grusha: The little boy saw this nursery maid on her hands and knees,

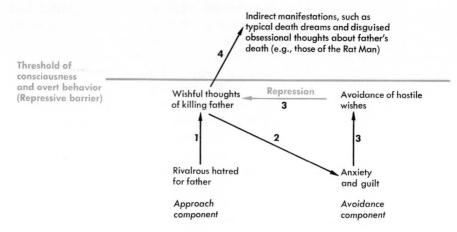

Figure 15-3　How adult manifestations of the hostile component of the unconscious Oedipal complex might result from an approach-avoidance conflict.

Most adult men have repressed the unresolved residues of their childhood conflicts involving their Oedipal jealousy of their fathers. The heavy gray line represents this fact. In the case of unconscious conflicts, the "threshold of consciousness and overt behavior" is a barrier resulting from the active process of repression; it is not a simple threshold analogous to sensory thresholds, which may be crossed merely by increasing the intensity of the stimulus. When intensified for any reason, the individual's rivalrous hatred for his father can make him unconsciously wish to kill his father (1). Even though unconscious, such a wish evokes unconscious anxiety and guilt (2), which motivate the intensification of the repression of such death wishes (3). At this point the individual is left with very strong wishes to kill his father, but they are blocked from becoming conscious by a very strong repression. Such "dammed-up" death wishes frequently produce strange conscious experiences, such as dreams about the death of the father, or simply of an older man, and isolated, bizarre thoughts about one's father's death when one has intercourse or engages in some other sexual behavior (4).

with buttocks made prominent, scrubbing the floor; he then urinated in front of her, which Freud interpreted as a sign of Oedipal sexual excitement. In judging the significance of this episode and its relation to his adult sexual life, one is bound to be influenced by these further facts in the Wolf Man's life:

1. "From his puberty he had felt large and conspicuous buttocks as the most powerful attraction in a woman; to copulate except from behind gave him scarcely any enjoyment. [Freud, 1918, p. 41]."

2. Early in adolescence he was attracted to a servant girl working in his home, but he kept his distance from her. One day, however, he was overwhelmed with love for her when he saw her kneeling on the floor scrubbing it.

3. Late in his teens he came upon a peasant girl kneeling by a pond as she washed clothes. He fell violently in love with her on the spot, before he even saw her face. He had intercourse with her at some time not specified in the case report. Freud noted that the Wolf Man was unusually secretive about this girl's name, which had a "motherly ring" to it—Matrona.

4. Freud states that the Wolf Man's "final choice of object," by which we presume Freud meant his wife, was determined by the same factors operating in the preceding scenes and in the Grusha episode. Freud does not give details, however, perhaps to protect the identity of the patient or out of consideration for the patient's wife.

Thus, the Wolf Man showed a pattern of sexual excitement by stimulus situations similar to that of the sight of the kneeling Grusha. The pattern is highly compatible with Freud's hunch that the boy was sexually excited when he took out his penis and urinated in front of Grusha.

The adult individual free of severe neurosis rarely shows such clear-cut manifestations of his Oedipal complex as we have seen in the Rat Man and the Wolf Man. The neurotic behaves as if he is repeating nearly the same stimulus-response patterns that were characteristic of his childhood; he seems to be *fixated* in unconscious Oedipal object relations. Many of his symptoms are manifestations of his conflictful, still-operative Oedipal wishes, as illustrated by the Rat Man's obsessive, intruding, "inappropriate" thoughts of his father's death and by the particular form of the Wolf Man's impulsive sexual behavior.

Other Evidence of the Continued Oedipal Complex The sexual and related aggressive behavior of the normal adult usually shows evidence of having *evolved from* the Oedipal complex. The exciting sexual attributes of one's spouse or adult lover are less similar to those of the Oedipal object than were the Wolf Man's; one's hostility toward one's father or everyday rivals is less intense and less tied to sexuality than in the Rat Man. In psychoanalytic terminology, the normal adult has sublimated his Oedipal complex through greater displacement, instead of remaining fixated in it.

Nevertheless, the behavior even of the person who has achieved considerable sublimation of his Oedipal complex seems to retain distinct traces of it, suggesting that the Oedipal complex may never be completely overcome. Remarkably often one discovers that a friend has found a mate who resembles his parent in some special characteristic. A man "suddenly" realizes long after he has married that his wife taught school for a few years before they met, as his mother had done before she married. Or a woman "finds" that her husband likes the outdoors, as her father did. It is as if the same process of displacement seen in neurotic patients is simply extended further.

An example from the analysis of a hysterical female patient is typical of this displacement process. (The displacement to the analyst is a characteristic event in analysis. It is part of the phenomenon Freud called *transference*. In transference, the patient reenacts in his relationship with the analyst repressed wishes and experiences involving his parents or other significant people. Thus, he "transfers" from them to his analyst.)

Each time this patient's analyst had his hair cut, she acknowledged it, even if only by remarking, with a smile, "I see you got your hair cut." There was nothing unusual about his haircuts, and none of his other patients mentioned them. This patient's interest stemmed from a favorite game she had played with her father between the ages of 5 and 10: "barbershop." She would be the barber and he the customer.

That game derived from a still more exciting activity they had shared. Regularly, until she was 6 or 7, she used to sit on the toilet and urinate while her father was shaving in the bathroom. It is presumed that she was sexually excited at that time, for the need to urinate regularly accompanied her sexual excitations in adulthood.

The displacements here are: bathroom activity with father → barber game with father → special interest in analyst's haircuts.

Figure 15-4 illustrates the way we can apply the approach-avoidance conflict paradigm to indirect manifestations of the sexual component of the unconscious Oedipal complex, such as the *sexual over-reactions* of the Wolf Man to kneeling women and the special interest of the woman just mentioned in her analyst's haircuts. Her special attentiveness to them is clearly a form of perceptual vigilance. (For a discussion of perceptual vigilance see Part I, pp. 114–17.)

Traces of Oedipal hostility, as well as of Oedipal sexuality, can be found in the average adult. Freud referred to a common instance of this when he said, "A physician will often . . . notice how a son's grief at the loss of his father cannot suppress his satisfaction at having at last won his freedom [1900, p. 257]." In Chapter 12 we saw just this kind of reaction by a normal person, Duane.

Freud always emphasized that another aspect of adult life provided further evidence of a still active, though sublimated, Oedipal complex: the creation and enjoyment of great myths and literary works built upon Oedipal themes. He cited, at various times, the myth of Zeus castrating his father and replacing him as ruler, Sophocles' *Oedipus Rex*, Ibsen's *Rosmersholm*, and Shakespeare's *Hamlet*. Freud ascribed Hamlet's inability to decisively avenge his father's murder to a conflict over a latent wish for his father's death. Freud reasoned that the widespread impact and appeal (as well as the creation) of such masterpieces must depend on the residual, unconscious Oedipal complex in every man.

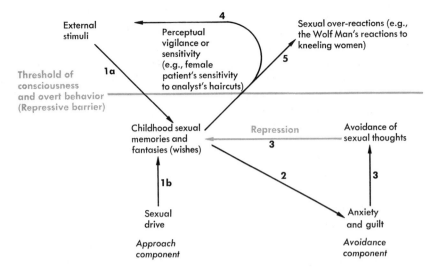

Figure 15-4   How adult manifestations of the sexual component of the unconscious Oedipal complex might result from an approach-avoidance conflict.

Most adults have repressed the unresolved residues of their childhood conflicts involving their Oedipal love. The combined action of one's repressed sexual drives and the presence of a person who resembles one's Oedipally loved parent may activate repressed childhood sexual memories and fantasies (1a and 1b). These repressed memories and fantasies will then arouse unconscious anxiety and guilt (2), which in turn motivate the intensification of their repression (3). Thus, the individual is left with enlivened memories and strong fantasies or wishes that are blocked from becoming conscious or from overt expression by a very strong repression. Such "dammed-up" sexual memories and fantasies frequently produce strange overt behavior, such as a special perceptual sensitivity to minor characteristics of other people that remind the individual of his loved parent (4), or impulsive sexual reaction to such people (5).

IS THE OEDIPAL COMPLEX UNIVERSAL?

Freud assumed that the Oedipal complex and its repression in men and women were universal phenomena. Since the relevant controlled scientific investigations have not been carried out, this must still be regarded as a tentative hypothesis. How seriously should it be taken?

The idea that the complex may be universal in Western civilization seems fairly plausible if one merely considers the great range of literary works and individual life histories in which Oedipal manifestations have been found. We have noted that such literary expressions date back to the

Greeks. As for individuals, Freud encountered the Oedipal complex in all his patients, regardless of the subculture in which they grew up. Many of his patients were reared in middle-class Viennese homes, but some were not. The Wolf Man, for example, was of a wealthy Russian family. He had spent his childhood on country estates surrounded by the opulence of the pre-revolutionary culture. Some form of the Oedipal complex is typically found by every contemporary American or European analyst in his patients, regardless of differences in subcultural origin. And we should recall the doll-play aggression study: Normal boys and girls from the contemporary Midwest displayed just those aggressive fantasies characteristically detected in the psychoanalysis of adults.

Evidence from Cultural Anthropology

The hypothesis that the Oedipal complex is universal receives additional, though indirect, support from cultural anthropology. Anthropological literature describes the widespread incidence among primitive peoples of taboos against incest and also against killing totemic animals, which are regarded as ancestors of the people. Freud reasoned (1913) that such taboos would not be required if there were not strong unconscious motivation to do the very things proscribed by them. Thus, the incest taboos indicate that strong unconscious incestuous wishes must be operative in widely scattered primitive peoples. The totemic taboos, he argued, were displacements—disguised taboos against unconscious wishes to murder the father. In short, Freud saw in the prevalence of both taboos evidence that the repressed Oedipal complex was just as active in members of these widely scattered societies as it was in his own patients.

Murdock's cross-cultural study (1949) of 250 primitive societies extended knowledge about incest taboos. Three of Murdock's findings are directly relevant to the Oedipal complex. First, in every one of the societies, incest taboos existed proscribing sexual relations between all persons of the opposite sex within the nuclear family, except of course between the parents. (In a few societies, royalty was exempted.) Second, taboos against incestuous relations with relatives outside the nuclear family tended to be less intense than taboos against incest within it. Third, Murdock noted that a "peculiar intensity and emotional quality [p. 288]" is associated with incest taboos, which he felt could be accounted for only by assuming that they were related to unconscious Oedipal conflicts.

Condominas (1957), a French anthropologist, observed at first hand those unique emotions associated with incest taboos. One day, while he was living among the Montagnards of Vietnam, disaster struck: Tieng and Aang, a man and woman of their clan, had been detected having sexual intercourse. Even though the last common ancestor of Tieng and Aang had lived 15 generations earlier, and even though both were mature adults whose mates had died, the tribesmen responded with the greatest alarm. Tieng and Aang's violation of the incest taboo was certain to bring forth calamitous events: dragons, tigers, and elephants would kill all the important members of the clan; torrential rains, landslides, and flooding from within the earth would threaten everyone's life. Drastic measures, prescribed by ritual custom, were taken to forestall the doom. Animals were sacrificed and their blood mixed and drunk, and prayers were said before an altar (Figure 15-5). Tieng and Aang had to lick excrement of pig and dog, which was painted on their chins. Finally, the community as well as the immediate families of Tieng and Aang were cleansed of evil and stain. These procedures, which occupied an entire day, relieved the distress of everyone but Tieng. His was too great: He hanged himself that night.

Anthropologists have often pointed out that prohibiting incest has many adaptive consequences: By preventing sexual rivalry it guarantees the integrity of the family unit, which is so necessary for sheer survival under primitive conditions; it prevents societies from breaking up into family-centered clans, which might happen if sexual relations and marriage within the family were permitted; it ensures greater cultural homogeneity within a society by guaranteeing that one family's skills, knowledge, and habits will be mixed with those of other families as a result of extrafamilial marriage; and so forth. The fact that incest taboos may have such adaptive consequences is regarded by some social anthropologists as an argument against connecting taboos with the Oedipal complex. Psychoanalysts argue, in turn, that if these consequences do in fact have anything to do with the existence of the taboos, they simply constitute some of society's implicit, but practical, reasons for strongly prohibiting the incestuous Oedipal wishes.

Lindzey (1967) has recently summarized evidence that inbreeding results in biological inferiority in successive generations. He proposes that in

Figure 15-5 "Early in the ceremony at riverside to expiate the incest, Aang's brother Toong-Biing prays before a small altar." (From Condominas, 1957)

its long history mankind has learned that it must prohibit inbreeding that would result from the Oedipal complex in order to remain biologically strong and to survive. He also emphasizes the rarity of any psychological phenomenon being as widespread throughout the world's many cultures as is the incest taboo. He too infers that the Oedipal complex is "universal."

Without minimizing the significance of early life experiences, Freud (1905b) believed the Oedipal complex was universal because its essential ingredients were innate. While there is a good deal of evidence that the Oedipal complex is widespread in Western civilization, and some evidence that it is manifested in many other cultures throughout the world, there is no evidence that the conflict is, or is not, innate. Its wide distribution, in the boy at least, could be the inevitable result of the close physical and emotional attachment between mother and child throughout the world and of the fact that the parent of the same sex is a real rival for the affection of the other parent. In other words, the conflict could be learned; and it could be extremely widespread because certain elemental aspects of child rearing are widespread. If child-rearing conditions do give rise to the Oedipal conflict, the conflict should be different in cultures with highly distinctive ways of caring for and socializing their children. We shall discuss this point further in Chapter 22.

Repression of the Oedipal Conflicts

Few of us, as adults, feel an erotic attachment to our parent of the opposite sex or jealous hatred for our parent of the same sex. And few of us realize that children are serious when they say they will marry Mommy or Daddy and that they are expressing genuine hostility when they push away the other parent or wish he were dead. Nor do we realize how much enjoyment children get out of pretending these things in their play. Psychoanalysts point out several reasons why the Oedipal complex seems unreal to us. First, we did not fully comprehend our own Oedipal complex when we were children. Second, what we did comprehend we energetically repressed almost as soon as we became aware of it. Third, by having gradually and unknowingly accepted our culture's prescription for our sexual and aggressive life, we have transferred most of those energies, especially the sexual, to our extrafamilial peers. Fourth, the need to keep our own Oedipal complex repressed interferes with our capacity to fully appreciate what we see in the behavior of children.

As we have noted, the fate of the Oedipal complex is repression. Why? Parents expend a great deal of effort helping their children regulate their nonincestuous sexual life, while they exert relatively little pressure, judged by external criteria, against the childhood incestuous wishes. Yet, remarkably, all of us share in "the horror of incest [Freud, 1892–99, p. 257]," and incest taboos have that "peculiar intensity and emotional quality" noted by Murdock.

The reasons the complex is repressed arise in part from the reactions of adults to manifestations of childhood sexuality. Most parents discourage whatever signs of sexual behavior they observe in their young children. And Oedipal behavior inevitably arouses jealousy in the parent of the same sex, especially since the other parent usually unwittingly reciprocates the child's attachment, if only to a slight degree. This jealousy is transmitted to the Oedipal child.

However, the repression derives not only from parental reactions but also from the psychology of the child. Psychoanalytic observations strongly suggest that neither the parents' threats of punishment or loss of love because of the child's sexual behavior nor the signs of their jealousy fully account for the repression. Parental threats seem, rather, to provide the ingredients for the child's fantasy elaboration, which occurs largely outside of awareness and in which the child's own Oedipal hostility plays a significant role. The principal evidence is that children fear a monstrous retribution, which bears no necessary relation to the actual overt behavior of the parent. The hostility that the child imagines will be vented against him appears to be proportionate to, and to derive from, his own hostility toward the hated Oedipal parent. In his fantasy the child *projects* his own intense hostility onto his parent. Fear of a largely fantasied retribution by his parents motivates the child to repress his Oedipal complex. Both boys and girls repress the Oedipal complex, and the general cause of that repression is the same, but the specific content of the fears differs in ways that we shall now discuss.

REPRESSIVE MOTIVES IN THE GIRL

The girl typically *fears that her mother hates her* for her Oedipal attachment to her father and for her rivalry. Consciously or unconsciously she expects her mother to bear a deep-seated malevolence toward her, which threatens her with the loss of her mother's love and may even cause her mother to actually abandon her or to harm her physically. The witch in the Sleeping Beauty fairy tale is a prototypic rendition of the fantasied image the young girl has of her mother, as revealed by women's memories of their childhood view of their mothers when that view is recalled in analysis.

The patient who played barber games with her father is an example.

She recalled her discomfort as a little girl when her mother combed her hair. In her subjective experience she sensed that her mother resented her blonde, curly hair and that she meanly tried to hurt her by deliberately combing her hair hard and pulling on it to straighten it out. In later years she formed a more abstract idea based on her childhood perception: She thought, in looking back, that her mother was trying then to destroy her femininity. She also feared then that her mother would destroy her in a more literal sense, for once when she was recalling those early years she dreamed of a woman who came into her analyst's office during one of her sessions. This woman, "looking daggers" and with hands outstretched, walked toward the patient as if she were about to choke her. Her associations to the woman led directly to her mother. This dream image, the memory of how her mother seemed as she combed her hair, and the more abstract idea of her mother's enmity toward her femininity are all indications of this woman's childhood conviction that her mother resented her Oedipal relationship with her father and entertained evil intentions toward her because of that relationship.

Since her childhood conception of justice was based on the talion principle—an eye for an eye—she could easily imagine that her mother was deliberately trying to hurt her when combing her hair. What more appropriate punishment situation could there be for a girl who obtained erotic pleasure from combing her beloved father's hair?

An adult woman can cope with a jealous, angry rival without sacrificing her own passionate interests. The little girl, however, cannot do so. Compared to her mother, she is weak. Also, she loves her mother, and she needs her. Thus, the possibility that her mother hates her forebodes *several* kinds of dangers, including the possibility that her mother might harm her or abandon her. To avoid those dangers she represses her Oedipal thoughts and affects and inhibits their behavioral expression.

THE CASTRATION COMPLEX IN THE BOY

The specter of an additional danger looms in the thoughts of the Oedipal boy: He fears that his penis will be cut off or damaged. Typically, he fears that his father will do this, but if his mother is dominant in the family and is more the disciplinarian, she may be the imagined perpetrator. This was so in the case of Ed, the young man described in Chapter 12. He used to dream that a witch cut off the penises of all little boys.

The danger of castration is terrifying on several counts. It threatens extreme pain and damage to the integrity of his body; the child may regard it as the equivalent of being killed. Freud speculated that man's conscious fear of death in later life was a derivative of his fear of castration. Castration also threatens to deprive the child of a highly prized part of his body, the part that he narcissistically may love most. It also threatens to turn him into a girl, with the loss of all the privileges and advantages he has been taught that men have.

How the Complex Arises

How does the fear of castration usually arise? The most meaningful data have come from psychoanalyses of boys and men, where the necessary detailed observations can be made. Freud concluded that two experiences typically antedated the appearance of castration anxiety: explicit or implicit *castration threats by the parents* and the *sight of the female genitals*, which give these threats substance and meaning. Freud's observations about Little Hans and the Wolf Man illustrate the empirical basis for his conclusion:

1. Little Hans's mother and the Wolf Man's nurses made castration threats or allusions as these boys were engaged in erotic-genital play. But no sign of castration anxiety was apparent immediately.

2. Some time later, both boys saw their sisters' genitals.

3. Following this observation, each child developed what seemed to be thinly disguised castration fears. (We shall describe some of these in a moment.)

When Little Hans saw his sister naked, he *denied the perception that she did not have a penis.* He said that she did have one but that it was small and would grow bigger. The Wolf Man also denied what he saw, for he called his sister's genitals her "front bottom."

Apparently, when they saw their sisters' genitals, both boys for the first time registered the fact that a girl does not have a penis. Yet they had to deny the reality of what they saw. Perhaps they imagined that the girls once did have penises but had lost them and that the castration threats the boys had earlier received represented a real danger. If so, the boys would be denying perceptions that aroused a distressing affect in them—castration anxiety. The paradigm would be the same as for Duane's denial of the perception of his father's dead body, which was described in Chapter 12.

If what has been said so far is valid, the subsequent anxiety of the boys should give some clue of being related to frightening thoughts of being castrated. These clues must necessarily be indirect, for castration thoughts are so disturbing that they are defensively distorted. Both boys gave such clues, and of a very similar kind.

Little Hans first developed general, free-floating anxiety, which very rapidly changed into a phobia of horses, particularly the fear that they would bite his fingers. These and other associations indicated that for Little Hans horses were displacement-substitutes for his parents and that his fear of being bitten by a horse was a disguised fear that his father would bite off or cut off his penis. Hans's fear of being bitten by a horse was derived partly from an experience he had in the country, when he heard the father of a little girl say to her "Don't put your *finger* to the white *horse* or it'll *bite* you [Freud, 1909a, p. 29]." Hans had been threatened that if he masturbated (that is, put his *finger* on his penis, as in his description of his masturbation fantasy presented on page 263), Doctor A would be called to cut off his penis. There were associative links between his father and biting horses. He used to play *biting* games with his *father*, and once when the boy and his father were talking about Hans's wish that his *father* were dead, Hans "accidentally" knocked over a toy *horse* he was playing with.

The Wolf Man gave similar indications of castration anxiety.

A picture of a wolf in a story book terrified the Wolf Man each time he saw it as a child, and a childhood nightmare was about wolves. As he later recalled this nightmare during his analysis with Freud, he pictured the scene shown in Figure 15-6. In the dream all the wolves were sitting in a tree outside his nursery window and were silently staring at him. His associations about wolves included several fairy tales in which wolves lost their tails and were also aggressors against small animals. It appeared that one of the reasons the wolves' picture and dream image frightened the boy was that they represented a disguised form of, and stimulated, both his castration fear and the fear that his father would do the castrating.

We shall mention only one of the many bits of evidence that supported this idea. In his early analytic interviews the Wolf Man used to repeat a stereotyped pattern of behavior: He would look at Freud and then turn to look at a grandfather clock in the room. The Wolf Man himself later came to realize that he had been reenacting a scene from one of the fairy tales in which a little goat had avoided being eaten by a wolf by hiding in a grandfather clock! Even as an adult, then, he was unconsciously under the influence of his childhood fantasy. The relationship between himself and Freud reminded him of the helpless little goat that was in danger of being eaten by a wolf. It was as though the Wolf Man had generalized his castration anxiety from his penis to his entire body. The wolf would get his entire body, including his penis.

Another childhood experience of the Wolf Man was an indirect manifestation of his castration anxiety. Some time after he had been threatened with castration by his nurses and had seen his sister's genitals, the idea of castration was reinforced when he was told of a female relative who had been born with six toes, only to have the extra one chopped off with an axe. The Wolf Man was almost 5 years old when he heard this news; shortly thereafter he became terrified while he was cutting on the bark of a tree with a pocket knife, and he hallucinated that his little finger was cut nearly off and was hanging by the skin.

The behavior of both boys, then, contained indirect manifestations of their castration anxiety. These indirect manifestations—which included the denial of their perceptions that girls have no penises, their animal phobias, and the hallucinatory experience of the Wolf Man—illustrate the kind of

Figure 15-6 Wolf Man's drawing, made during his analysis in adulthood with Freud, of the dream scene in his childhood nightmare. (From Freud, 1918)

clinical evidence that led Freud to the discovery of the boy's castration complex. Similar clinical data characteristically emerge in the psychoanalyses of other men, indicating that castration anxiety is not unique to Little Hans and the Wolf Man.

The reader interested in Freud's full account of Little Hans and the Wolf Man should see *Analysis of a Phobia in a Five-Year-Old Boy* (1909a) and *From the History of an Infantile Neurosis* (1918). Freud's later formulations about these two cases are contained in *Inhibitions, Symptoms, and Anxiety* (1926). The reader may also be interested in these reports for reasons going beyond what we have discussed here, particularly because they pertain to the historic controversy between Freud and Carl Gustav Jung. Jung was one of Freud's earliest colleagues, but he later formulated his own theories of depth psychology. One of the reasons he did so was his belief that many of the things patients reported as memories of sexual experiences or fantasies of childhood were really later fantasies of adolescence or adulthood. Nor did he attribute the same significance to childhood sexuality that Freud did. The patients, Jung believed, unconsciously and erroneously attributed later sexual fantasies to their childhoods. Freud wrote the report of Little Hans before the break between Jung and himself occurred during the years 1912–14. It is interesting to see that the direct observations of this small boy's behavior and fantasies were essentially identical with those recalled from childhood by adult analysands. Freud wrote the report of the Wolf Man in rebuttal of Jung's belief. For this reason, he subjected the childhood memories of the Wolf Man to what he considered to be rigorous analysis and questioning. He concluded that the crucial memories were not fantasies of later life but rather memories of actual childhood experiences or of childhood fantasies. And he remained unshaken in his belief in the reality and significance of childhood sexuality. (We have touched here on only a few aspects of Jungian depth psychology. Further discussions of it, as well as references to Jung's basic writings, are contained in Hall and Lindzey [1957] and Munroe [1955]. Both of these books also review other schools of depth psychology and "neo-Freudian" psychodynamic views. These include such systems of thought as those of Alfred Adler and Karen Horney, who were also followers of Freud who later disagreed with him on various essential postulates, and those of Harry Stack Sullivan, one of America's great psychiatrists. We shall discuss some of the views of Adler and Sullivan in the next chapter.)

An Experimental Study of Castration Anxiety

General clinical experience suggests that intense castration anxiety in childhood is often followed by a recurrence of castration anxiety in adulthood when one thinks, feels, or behaves sexually. This appeared to be the case in the example of Ed in Chapter 12. Ed used to have frank castration dreams as a boy, and as a young man his sexual behavior was followed by nightmares in which he became fatally ill or in which doctors were going to remove his genitals. As we have said earlier (page 276), Freud proposed that such a fear of having a fatal illness is a characteristic derivative of repressed castration anxiety.

Sarnoff and Corwin (1959) conducted an experiment that bears on the validity of this psychoanalytic proposition. They reasoned that if such a formulation is valid, it should be possible to demonstrate experimentally that sexual arousal will increase the fear of death in men who are characterized by high levels of castration anxiety. These psychologists recruited more than 50 college men for their experiment. They measured the subjects' preexperimental fear of death by means of a scaled questionnaire. Then they measured the degree of unconscious castration anxiety to which each person was susceptible by asking the subjects to look at one particular cartoon from the "Blacky Test" (Blum, 1949), so named because a black dog, with whom the subject identifies, is a recurrent figure in the whole series of cartoons. In the particular cartoon they used Blacky is watching a scene in which a large knife hovers above the tail of a blindfolded dog, who is unaware of the disaster about to befall him. (Compare this with the castration significance for the Wolf Man of fairy tales in which wolves lose their tails.) The subjects were asked to indicate on a scale the degree of anxiety that they imagined Blacky felt as he witnessed the threatened tail amputation. The subjects' ratings were taken as an indication of the degree of unconscious castration anxiety that the scene aroused in *them.*

A few weeks later came the experimental arousal of sexuality, followed immediately by postexperimental measurement of the intensity of fear of death. Sexual arousal was accomplished by having subjects look at and describe photographs of nude women. Immediately afterward the postexperimental measure of fear of death was obtained by readministering the original scaled questionnaire.

And now, the results. As illustrated in Figure 15-7, sexual arousal produced a significant increase in the fear of death measures in the subjects with high castration anxiety, but not in the subjects with low castration anxiety. Other subjects who were shown only magazine pictures of fully clothed fashion models, and thus were less likely to be very sexually aroused, did not show any significant difference between their two fear of death measures. These control findings make it quite probable that the change following exposure to the pictures of the nude women was in fact due to sexual arousal, not merely to looking at pictures.

The results of this study by Sarnoff and Corwin are consistent with several psychoanalytic propositions concerning castration anxiety—its existence in varying degrees in young men, its relation to sexual arousal, and its indirect manifestation in the fear of death. The study is perhaps most important in demonstrating that systematic experimentation with this aspect of psychoanalytic theory is possible.

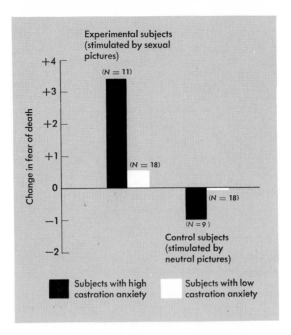

Figure 15-7 Average results of the experiment on castration anxiety in college men. (Based on data from Sarnoff & Corwin, 1959)

The subjects' fear of death was measured before and after they were either sexually aroused by pictures of nude women or presented with pictures of fully clothed women. Subjects with high castration anxiety became significantly more afraid of death after being stimulated by sexual pictures than did subjects with low castration anxiety.

THE OEDIPAL COMPLEX
AND ITS REPRESSION: A SUMMARY VIEW

Now let us return to the psychoanalytic theory of "the passing of the Oedipal complex." The typical consequence of the castration anxiety in the average young boy is assumed to be analogous to what we observed in Ed, the young man with the castration dreams. Motivated primarily by his fear of castration, the boy represses his Oedipal sexual desires and his hostile jealousy of his father. In doing so, he is behaving as if he thought he would thereby avoid the danger of castration, typically at the hands of his father. Other motives, such as the child's fear that his parents will stop loving him and will abandon him, which play the primary role in the girl, supplement the impetus for the boy's repression.

In Figure 15-8 the essential features of Oedipal conflicts are dia-

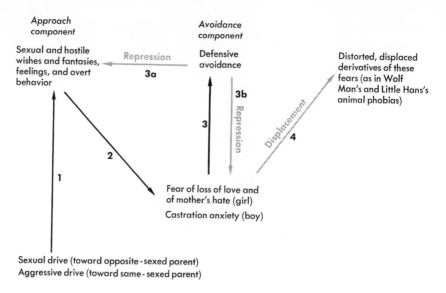

Figure 15-8   The child's Oedipal conflicts.

(1) *Under the pressure of his Oedipal sexual and aggressive drives, the child experiences corresponding sexual and hostile wishes, feelings, and fantasies and often engages in corresponding overt behavior (as in Little Hans, the Wolf Man, and the Rat Man when they were children). (2) Because he does such things and has such wishes, feelings, and fantasies, the child fears the loss of love of the same-sexed parent and also some form of active retaliation. (3) These fears motivate the child to engage in various defensive responses, which have the effect of reducing the fears. The child may repress his sexual and hostile wishes, fantasies, feelings, and overt behavior (3a). He may also repress the fears themselves (3b). These repressions produce a state of "dammed-up" sexual and aggressive tendencies and of "strangulated," unexpressed fears. The "dammed-up" sexual and aggressive tendencies may be expressed indirectly in the manner illustrated in Figures 15-4 and 15-5. (4) The unexpressed fears may be expressed in such distorted, disguised forms as the childhood animal phobias of the Wolf Man and Little Hans. The animals in such phobias appear to be symbolic substitutes for the feared parents, and the feared behavior of the animal appears to be a symbolic substitute for the feared retaliation by the parent. (Thus, Little Hans's fear that a horse would bite off his finger appeared to be a symbolic substitute for his fear that his father would cut off his penis.) Therefore, it is as if the child displaced his fear from his parent to the animal.*

gramed. Included in the figure are not only the repression of the sexual and hostile components (the approach component) of the conflicts but also the defensive process oriented directly against the anxieties themselves—fear of loss of love and of the mother's hate in the girl and castration anxiety in the boy. In other words, the child strives for emotional peace both by repressing his Oedipal wishes, which end in distress, and by defending against the unpleasant emotions themselves.

Aftermath of the Oedipal Conflicts

The child represses the Oedipal complex—both the sexual and the hostile conflict components—in the fifth or sixth year. But the influence of the Oedipal complex on his life obviously does not stop here. We have already seen evidence of this in our discussions of castration anxiety in college students, of incest taboos, and of the continued influence of the Oedipal complex in the life of the adult. This continual influence may be manifested in the relatively unchanged repetitions of the neurotic, such as the Wolf Man's adult sexual reactions and the Rat Man's adult death wishes for his father. Or it may be manifested in the more remote displacements of the normal individual, such as in choosing a mate who resembles the parent to some degree. Part of the significance of the repression of the Oedipal complex is that it initiates processes that continue into later life and that have the effect of freeing the person from this complex. Psychoanalytic observations and theory point to many ramifications of the repression of the Oedipal complex, however, some of which will be discussed briefly.

CHILDHOOD AMNESIA

The child's drastic repression of the Oedipal complex seems to serve as a nucleus for a widely generalized repressive process. Freud speculated that it was just such a process that caused the general amnesia almost everyone has for most events of childhood. This possibility suggests that our inability to recall much, if anything, about our childhood sexual life has an entirely different meaning from the one we customarily see in it. Rather than being a basis for refuting the reality of early sexual activities, our childhood amnesia might very well be an inevitable consequence of such activities. To be sure, the extent of childhood amnesia differs greatly from one person to another.

INFLUENCE ON THE LATENCY PERIOD

The generalized repressive process has still another consequence. It contributes to the onset and maintenance of the latency period of childhood, which separates the Oedipal and the pubertal phases of life. With the repression of the Oedipal complex, according to Freud, there is a *relative* decrease in all manifestations of childhood sexuality—pregenital and genital—and in the intensity of aggressive behavior in general. The average child becomes generally "better behaved," and, consequently, he is usually then able to participate constructively in formal schooling. While this developmental phase may also be determined in part by a decrease in the intensity of sexual and aggressive drives, it seems highly likely that the repressive process makes an important and regular contribution to it.

The clearest indications of repression are found in the exaggerated symptoms of neurosis that often appear for the first time during the latency period. It was just such a repressive process that caused Edie, the woman with the eating conflict, to change from a lively, happy, plump, feminine girl into a little spinster. Such extreme transformations in latency frequently take the form of clear-cut, severe, obsessive-compulsive neuroses in which the child strives defensively to be "very, very good": very clean, very obedient, very kind and considerate, very asexual, very moralistic, and so forth. Such a child is defending against being just the opposite because he fears the consequences of being "very, very bad." Both the Rat Man and the Wolf Man, incidentally, manifested just such neuroses, with a strong emphasis on religiosity, in their latency periods.

Recently a number of psychologists have reported that there are fewer manifestations of inhibitions in children of this age, and they suggest that the latency period may be less severe now because of more lenient handling of the child's sex behavior on the part of parents. Further studies obviously are needed on this issue.

CONTRIBUTION TO THE SUPEREGO

It is now clear that the child's repression of sexual and aggressive wishes is not an incidental aspect of personality development. It is associated with many impressive changes in the total behavior of the child. It will not be surprising, therefore, to hear that Freud attributed still another extremely important step in life largely to the repression of the Oedipal complex: the formation of the nucleus of the child's superego.

Fear of parental retribution motivates the child to repress his Oedipal complex. But the most varied kinds of psychoanalytic evidence (to which we shall refer in Chapters 20, 21, and 22) suggest that the child accomplishes that repression by internalizing a set of parental functions. (Parental functions mean here not only personality traits of the parents but also certain behavior in which every parent engages with his child. We shall mention these in a moment.) *Internalizing* connotes that he not only learns them but takes them "inside" and makes them part of himself. Foremost among these functions are the parents' own moral values in the domain of sexuality and aggression. The parents' moral values serve as internal standards of behavior with which the child struggles to comply.

If the child is to be successful in this struggle, however, the internalization of *other* parental functions must also occur: parental observation, evaluation, and moral judgment—that is, the evaluative comparison of the child's behavior against moral norms resulting in parental punishment or praise. When the latter functions have become internalized they are transformed into self-observation, self-evaluation, and self-punishment and self-approval.

The moral values and ancillary functions adopted from the parents constitute the core of the superego. While both parents are sources of such functions, the core of the child's superego consists of selective internalizations from the parent most feared in the Oedipal phase. In this sense the child is said to *identify with the aggressor* in forming his superego (A. Freud, 1936). Since the girl typically has most fear of her *mother's* retribution, the nucleus of her superego consists of her mother's values and her mother's mode of observing and judging, and punishing or approving. Since the boy typically has most fear of punishment by his *father*, the nucleus of his superego consists of his father's values, and so forth. In Chapter 20 we shall discuss identification with the aggressor in considerable detail.

Identification with a lost love object (discussed in Part I, pp. 185–87) also contributes to the formation of the child's superego. When a child represses his Oedipal love, he is also losing a love object through his own renunciation. (We shall discuss this matter more completely in the next chapter.) He is in a psychological position analogous to the college student who still loves someone whom he has decided to stop dating. In this situation the child also internalizes some of the attributes of the parent whom he had loved in the sensual, Oedipal sense. Often these attributes are the positive ideals of that parent, which now become important ideals of the child. Even when the attributes are not parental ideals, the child may elevate them from seemingly incidental traits of the parent into major ideals or goals for himself. In this way the ideal of becoming an artist may develop in a man whose mother was only mildly interested in art. However, it is often possible in such cases to demonstrate that the "mild interest" of the parent actually derives from an intense unconscious interest that is transmitted by various slight cues to the child. We shall discuss identification with a lost love object in more detail later. The important point here is that this form of identification also contributes to the child's superego. Although it is somewhat of an oversimplification, we will say that a person's positive ideals start with his identification with the parents he loved intensely as a child and that a person's restrictive, harsh moral values start with his identification with the parent he most feared as a child. By processes like these, a person's superego usually blends the characteristics of both parents. Even so, the identification with the parent of the same sex, which is primarily identification with the aggressor, gives the superego its dominant characteristics.

Freud suggested that the degree to which parental values are internalized, and thus the extent to which a person's standards of right and wrong, good and bad, and appropriate and inappropriate are his own inner ones, depends in part on how frightened children are when they identify with their parents. No childhood anxiety, Freud reasoned, equals castration anxiety in intensity. Therefore, he concluded, *internal* moral standards are much more firmly consolidated in men than in women, while women are more likely to be concerned with *external* standards. These are provocative statements, which Freud asserted but did not document, and they have been vehemently challenged.

The results of several studies, however, are relevant, although none were concerned with testing Freud's hypothesis. Lunger and Page (1939) found that a much higher proportion of women than men worried about "not being popular socially" (71 percent versus 49 percent) and about "the possibility that no one cares for them" (32 percent versus 14 percent). Two studies in the 1950's also reported such differences. Gough (1952), whose subjects were high school and college students, found that girls were socially more sensitive and restrained than boys. The adolescent girls studied by Moss (1955) were more concerned with courtesy, neatness, and the inhibition of *public* displays of romantic and aggressive behavior than were boys. In a study of the dynamics of friendship in eighth graders (Berlin, 1966), girls were found to have greater nurturance needs and concern that their best friend would desert them for someone else than boys had. One study (Pintner & Lev, 1940), however, failed to demonstrate such differences.

The theme in most of these studies of greater concern on the part of women with external appearances, with the social effects of behavior and with being liked is consistent with Freud's view that women's standards for behavior are not as thoroughly internalized as men's. The results of the studies may also be interpreted as simply indicating greater social sensitivity in women and as not bearing on Freud's hypothesis. However one interprets the results, they do not mean that men are more "moral" than women. They do, however, imply sex differences in the extent to which one's personal standards regulate one's behavior, in the consistency with which those standards are applied in varying interpersonal contexts, and in the reasons for conforming to norms of behavior. We are speaking of average tendencies, of course; some women have a strongly internalized, severe conscience, and some men are very other-directed (Riesman, 1950).

EFFECTS DURING ADOLESCENCE

The quiescence of latency, whether it be the relative, "choppy" calm of the normal child or the ominous stillness of neurosis, comes to an end with the onset of *puberty* and the ensuing, often stormy, adolescence.

Rearousal of the Childhood
Oedipal Conflicts   Biological changes intensify the adolescent's sexual urges and his propensity for aggression. In turn, the rudimentary superego and the defenses established in

latency, which constitute many of the child's character traits, are severely strained by these intensified drives. The result is a rearousal of the childhood conflicts over sexuality and aggression, as well as their displacement outside the family to peer groups and other social arenas, where the conflicts continue.

Much of the adolescent's stormy behavior is a result of the intensely renewed childhood conflicts. Thus, the adolescent girl is likely to erupt in hostile explosions with her mother, and the boy with his father, but then be on the best of terms with the parent a moment later. Manifestations of deep love for the parent of the opposite sex will oscillate with avoidance of any intimacy. Sibling rivalry and affection succeed one another in bewildering fashion. Temptations to have physical contact with a brother or sister are counteracted by prudish, standoffish reactions. Periods of ascetic abstinence separate sprees of masturbation, especially in boys. One of the major tasks the adolescent must accomplish is the further resolution of his childhood conflicts. Especially he must, and typically does, free himself from the grip of both the erotic and the hostile components of the Oedipal complex. Often, however, this freeing process is not complete until after the young adult has married and established himself in a vocation.

The Struggle with Values

Another aspect of adolescent turmoil is the young person's struggle with values—his own, his parents', and his society's. The upsurge of his drives seems to be one of the key causes of this struggle, for it puts his previously developed values to a severe test. This unstable state of affairs is further complicated by the beginnings of liberation from his childhood emotional ties to his parents, for this liberation affects his identifications with his parents as well as his drive relations with them. As he becomes somewhat estranged from his parents as real people, so too he becomes estranged from the main internal representations of them—from his superego. Until adolescence the average American and European child takes his moral standards for granted; indeed, he is hardly aware of them. But in adolescence he becomes painfully aware of them and treats them almost like objects. He "looks" at his standards and values, talks about them, likes or dislikes them, and so forth. During all this, the typical adolescent is also exposed to, becomes aware of, and is freed to experiment with an array of moral alternatives provided by his culture. Some resolution of his struggle with values is another task the adolescent must accomplish.

The two processes of adolescence we have discussed—the renewed struggle with the sexual and aggressive drives and the explorations of value systems—are obviously interrelated. We might call these major tasks, together with the establishment of an *ego identity* (discussed below), "the work of adolescence."

Sexual Identity   One outcome of these developmental processes is the determination of the *sexual identity* of the individual. While the seeds of this identity were planted in childhood in relation to the Oedipal conflict, the final outcome is not determined until the work of adolescence is completed. Nor need it be, in our society. As adolescence progresses, however, one's sexual identity is relentlessly shaped by external and internal forces. Whether one is to be a masculine man or a feminine woman, in what ways one is masculine and in what ways feminine, how comfortable and free of conflict one is with one's sex roles, the depth of intimacy one desires or tolerates—these are some of the important attributes of sexual identity. They reflect issues that must be more or less settled by the close of adolescence if one is to progress to adulthood and participate fully in marriage and parenthood.

Ego Identity   The consolidation of one's sexual identity is the central aspect of a still larger process that comes to the fore in adolescence: the crystallization of one's *ego identity* (Erikson, 1950, 1959), the definition of who and what one is. Our sexual identities, occupational or career choices, shared group identities, preferred defenses, and significant personal identifications become organized into a coherent pattern that defines each of us as a unique individual. Obviously, one's identity formation does not begin and end in adolescence. It begins with birth and ends with death. But it is typically a focal task of adolescence in our culture. During the high school and college years, the individual "decides" what kind of person he is going to be in certain crucial respects. Severe identity conflicts often arise at this time. Keniston's (1965) study of the uncommitted Ivy League college student illustrates such conflicts with concrete case material. (For a further discussion of identity formation, see Part III, Chapter 26.)

Those who cannot remember the past are condemned to repeat it.

GEORGE SANTAYANA. The Life of Reason

CHAPTER 16
PAINFUL EXPERIENCES AND OVER-REACTIONS OF DISTRESS

In the last two chapters we focused on childhood conflicts over sexuality and aggression, on their repression, and on the influence of such repressed conflicts on the later behavior of the adult. We discussed, for example, the childhood conflict of the Rat Man over his jealousy of his father and the way this conflict, after it became unconscious, continued to influence his behavior in sexual situations in adulthood. We also discussed the childhood sexual conflict of the Wolf Man and the way this conflict, after it became unconscious, caused him to over-react sexually in adulthood to kneeling or squatting women. Our emphasis in those chapters may have created several false impressions, such as: (1) that conflict and defense involve only inner wishes, such as sexual or aggressive ones; (2) that only sexual or aggressive over-reactions result from unconscious processes; and (3) that a person's emotional life, especially in childhood, consists only of sexual and aggressive feelings and the fears associated with them. In this chapter we shall begin to correct any such false impressions. We shall also expand on aspects of conflict and defense that we have mentioned only briefly so far. We shall do this by shifting our attention to some of the "objective" *painful experiences* nearly all children and adults undergo and by considering three of the ways such painful experiences might result in *over-reactions of distress* to innocuous stimuli. Chapters 14 and 15 have provided the background for proceeding in this way. At the same time we discuss these immediate issues, we shall be laying the foundation for further discussion in Chapters 20, 21, and 22 of the kinds of conflicts and defenses that were introduced in the preceding chapters.

We shall begin our discussion by examining major types of "objectively" unpleasant stimuli.

Six Categories
of Objectively Unpleasant Stimuli

The following set of characteristics is very useful for classifying unpleasant external situations:

1. Frustration
2. Threats to physical integrity
3. Loss of a love object
4. Separation from a protector
5. Loss of love
6. Loss of self-esteem

Most unpleasant events share the properties of two or more of these categories. The death of Duane's father represented both separation from a protecting parent and loss of a loved and loving person (as well as the realization of Duane's wish that his father would die). The danger of castration threatens not only the boy's physical integrity but also his self-esteem. Hence, the examples that we shall use to illustrate a category will be events that typically and predominantly, but not exclusively, belong to that category. The dominant features of the emotional reactions to an event will be the basis on which we shall categorize it. It should be noted at the outset that these categories may not be universal but do apply to our Western culture.

EXTREME FRUSTRATION

Frustration is an unpleasant state that can produce marked changes in behavior ranging from anger and aggression to regression and withdrawal (see Part I, Chapter 9). The reports of people in psychoanalysis suggest that a *sense of helplessness* is an important ingredient in the unpleasant feelings accompanying frustration. When we are frustrated, we feel helpless in the face of our *ungratified desires*. As we sense these desires becoming stronger, we feel our capacity to tolerate the mounting tension being severely strained. Our self-control seems endangered. We also feel helpless in the face of the frustrating *external obstacles,* especially those that are arbitrarily enforced. (Experimental findings that the increasing arbitrariness of frustrations imposed by other people leads to greater aggression are described in Part I, pp. 156–59.)

THREATS TO PHYSICAL INTEGRITY

Near-miss experiences that constitute threats to physical integrity include such general disasters as floods, tornadoes, and wars and such great personal disasters as a near-drowning and the stress of major surgery. (Both types of disasters are discussed at length in Part I.)

Near-misses experienced by almost all children include castration for the boy and the mother's evil, witchlike, retaliatory jealousy for the girl. While these are largely fantasy experiences, there is often some real basis for them in the signs of anger displayed by the parental rival. These experiences are very important instances of *perceived threats* to physical integrity and welfare.

LOSS OF A LOVE OBJECT

The loss of a loved person through death or a long separation is the most obvious instance of this stress. Grief—a complex blend of a painfully sad, helpless sense of loss and an anguished longing for the loved one— is the dominant emotional reaction. Even very young children are capable of complex grieving reactions, especially when they are separated from their mothers. (Chapter 10 in Part I fully explores this and other aspects of grief.)

Loss of a love object may also occur through an undesired yet active *renunciation* by the subject or through a failure or refusal by the object to fulfill that role. Imagine an intimate, deep love relationship that has become platonic because one partner decided on moral grounds or out of fear that he must renounce the other as a lover. Each of the people has lost a love object, and each experiences something very similar to grief and bereavement. These emotions are usually so painful that the couple either become lovers again or give up even the platonic relationship.

Oedipal
Renunciations   The Oedipal boy and girl, whom we discussed in Chapter 15, go through an analogous experience. They unwillingly renounce their parents as love objects, and the parents, except in rare instances, fail to fulfill the role of sexual love objects. Although the matter requires systematic research, there are reasons to believe that this childhood renunciation or imposed loss is just as painful as the more familiar adult versions.

One reason is that during the Oedipal phase—from age 3 to age 6— children long to spend every possible moment with the parent of the opposite sex, and they feel that any deprivation of this wish is a major tragedy. Little Hans, for example, showed many signs of painful longing for the close contact and the rather erotic relationship he had enjoyed with his mother (Freud, 1909a).

Second, when adults reexperience their childhood renunciations during psychoanalysis, the affects of sadness and anguished longing often become very intense.

> One woman first expressed all this in a disguised manner: in the way she experienced her relationship with her analyst. As often happens during psychoanalytic treatment, she felt that she had fallen in love with her analyst and fantasied that he was in love with her. But she also fantasied that both of them were refraining from having an affair and from eventually divorcing their spouses to marry each other out of loyalty to their spouses and on general ethical grounds. Thinking and talking about this self-denial left her tearful, filled with sadness, and overwhelmed by a hopeless yearning for what she was losing by renunciation.

Although phenomenologically it was utterly real to her, this entire experience was one of *transference love* (Freud, 1912, 1915a). In every important detail she was *repeating* love fantasies that she used to have about herself and her father (Freud, 1914b). One such fantasy had occurred on her wedding day, when she interpreted the tearful looks exchanged between herself and her father as a mutual recognition that their love for each other inevitably had to be renounced.

There is a third reason for comparing these childhood Oedipal renunciations with the loss of a loved person through death or long separation. *Identification with the lost object* plays a prominent role in the subject's attempts to cope with each kind of loss. (The discussion of bereavement and mourning in Part I, pp. 183–89, applies equally well to children's struggling renunciation of their parents as love objects.) Freud observed this process frequently. Dora, an hysterical patient, repressed her Oedipal love for her father and later developed a nervous cough that persisted for years (Freud, 1905a). This was evidence that she had identified with him, for he had coughed persistently from tuberculosis during Dora's childhood "love affair" with him.

SEPARATION FROM A PROTECTOR

Very young children typically react with intense anxiety to being separated from their mothers. So characteristic is this reaction that it has been given a special name: *separation anxiety*. Because they are so vulnerable and helpless, young children conceive of such a separation as very dangerous and are more disturbed by it than by conditions that actually threaten their lives. During World War II, psychologists found that the youngsters of London who were separated from their mothers during the large-scale evacuation of children to the country were more emotionally disturbed than those who remained in London with their mothers, even though the latter were subjected to extensive bombings by the Germans (Pritchard & Rosenzweig, 1942; A. Freud & Burlingham, 1943). Being separated from their mothers was more real and dangerous than the possibility of their being killed, which is in any case a scarcely conceivable idea to young children.

Even brief separations from their mothers frighten young children. Sleeping alone or being left with strangers while mother goes out to shop, visit, or work are typical of such disturbing separations and bring on the normal form of childhood separation anxiety. Ordinarily, separation becomes less and less frightening as the individual grows older, but a person may experience some degree of separation anxiety at any age. The object may be a parent or a parental substitute. (Studies of separation anxiety are presented in Part III, pp. 504–09.)

LOSS OF LOVE

This type of universally experienced stress differs from grievous loss of a loved person and separation anxiety in two ways: in the kinds of situations that may produce it and in the content of the emotional experience. The impact a sibling's birth has on a young child is prototypical of this kind of experience. Commonly, the older child has been accustomed to the nearly exclusive devotion of his mother and to being the center of attention for both parents. Suddenly he finds his position usurped and his accomplishments seemingly unnoticed. In his eyes, his parents do not love him any more.

In adult life, a broad spectrum of events can produce the state and sense of loss of love:

Not being noticed by people we care about.
A decrease in their underlying emotional interest and attention.
Decreases in the amount of overt affection and care they give us.
Disapproval and punishment for an error or oversight, which are interpreted as signs of loss of love.
Outright rejection.

The state or sense of being unloved has several exceedingly unpleasant effects (though the adult victim typically tries not to show his hurt). One effect is grief. Another is frustration. The victim neither receives the love he wants nor has the satisfaction of actively loving in return. This amounts to a frustrating disruption of one of man's basic ways of relating to others, *getting and giving* (Erikson, 1950).

Self-esteem may fall painfully with a loss of love, especially in children and in "other-directed" adults, since their sense of self-worth is highly dependent on the reactions of other people to them. They may *feel* worthless, inferior, or bad and may even conclude that they *are* these things and have been ignored or rejected because of these qualities.

Rejection, punishment, and other signs of loss of love frequently arouse separation anxiety, because they stimulate fantasies that one will be abandoned and left utterly helpless if he is unloved. For example, after a teacher has criticized a student, the student may feel that the teacher will not want to supervise his work any more. An employee who has been criticized may become convinced that he is about to be fired. Children are very susceptible to such fantasies. In fact, Freud (1926) hypothesized that fear of loss of love developed out of separation anxiety through a displacement of anxiety from separation experiences to signs of loss of love.

Finally, there is loneliness. Feeling unloved cuts a man off from meaningful relations with others and leaves him feeling alienated and actually estranged. Though the exact nature of loneliness is unknown at present, it seems to blend loss of love, separation anxiety, and frustration.

In summary, the loss of love arouses varying degrees of grief and despairing longing, frustration, lowered self-esteem, separation anxiety, and loneliness.

LOSS OF SELF-ESTEEM

Rejections are not the only stimuli that lower our self-esteem. Indeed, they are not even necessary. Once we have formed our ideals, we criticize ourselves whenever we judge that we have fallen short of them. These self-criticisms can damage our self-esteem as effectively as criticisms by others. Many of these painful self-appraisals involve a comparison of ourselves with some other person whom we have taken as an ideal.

Like the other stressful experiences we have discussed, loss of self-esteem has childhood as well as adult versions. We have already discussed the narcissistic mortification experienced by most little girls when they perceive the difference between their own bodies and those of boys. Another prototypical experience of the loss of self-esteem is produced by parents' derogatory reactions to their children's strivings to be little men and women. A mother's making fun of her little daughter's physical appearance or a father's criticism of his son's handmade model airplane may severely bruise the child's self-esteem.

Another prototypical experience is familiar to most children of minority groups: the realization, provided by some form of social discrimination, that they are different from other people and are (unjustifiably) despised or regarded as inferior because of that difference.

Should any of the childhood wounds we have discussed be repeatedly and deeply inflicted, they may never heal or may lead to a badly scarred adult personality. A more or less chronically low sense of self-esteem sometimes develops because the person internalizes the attitudes that idealized people express to him about himself. Without being aware of it, he comes to regard himself as others regarded him when he was a child—that is, at that time in his life when the opinions of others really were crucial for his well-being.

The concept of self-esteem is a junction point connecting Freudian psychoanalysis with the diverging views of two other well-known theorists: Alfred Adler and Harry Stack Sullivan. Adler parted ways with Freud in 1911 largely on the theoretical grounds that a sense of inferiority, as he termed feelings of low self-esteem, was the prime mover in much human behavior, especially social behavior and neurosis. The sense of inferiority, Adler argued, caused the individual to compensate for it by engaging in various kinds of assertive or power behavior. This he termed the *masculine protest*. Such views led Adler to conclusions about any given behavior that were quite different from those reached by Freud. As Ernest Jones says in his biography of Freud, "Sexual factors, particularly those of childhood, were reduced to a minimum: a boy's incestuous desire for intimacy with his mother was interpreted as the male wish to conquer a female masquerading as sexual desire. The concepts of repression, infantile sexuality, and even that of the unconscious itself were discarded . . . [Jones, 1955, p. 131]." Adler and his followers went on to develop an independent school of thought known as *individual psychology*. It is actually a psychology that places great emphasis on social aspects of behavior.

Harry Stack Sullivan developed his views, known as the *interpersonal theory of psychiatry*, in the United States between 1925 and 1945, approximately. He too placed great emphasis on the human need for a solid sense of self-esteem and attributed many forms of interpersonal behavior to the attempt to regulate one's self-esteem by what he called *security operations* (which closely resemble what we call *defenses*). The cruel domination of a child by a mother, for example, might be the mother's attempt to make herself feel worthwhile or powerful. Usually, this viewpoint holds, people intimately involved with each other develop reciprocal security operations. Thus, the child of such a mother might very well learn to be submissive to her because she rewards such behavior. She does this, of course, to perpetuate an interpersonal relationship pattern that maintains her self-esteem. The child continues in his reciprocal behavior because his self-esteem is raised by her rewards. These remarks only touch upon a few of Sullivan's basic ideas, which are set forth in his *Conceptions of Modern Psychiatry* (1947). The surveys by Hall and Lindzey (1957) and Munroe (1955) discuss both the Adlerian and Sullivanian viewpoints in detail and contain references to the important original writings of these two men and their followers.

We have now examined the six classes of unpleasant external stimuli and the characteristic emotional reactions to them. All these emotional reactions are painful. If a person does not learn to adapt to the situations, the emotions will naturally persist and the person will then resort to defenses, to less adaptive ways of avoiding the painful emotions. Before we can discuss these defense mechanisms, however, we must deal with another issue: the arousal of unpleasant emotions by innocuous stimuli.

Transformation of Innocuous Stimuli into Noxious Stimuli

"INNOCUOUS" AND "NOXIOUS" STIMULI

No stimulus is inherently innocuous or noxious: Distress arises from the *interaction* of an external stimulus and the organism. Even elemental physical pain requires a contribution from the organism, if only in the form of pain receptors, an intact nervous system, and sensory thresholds. And an experience that most of us would find painful might be pleasant to someone else. Yet all of us in a given culture agree in considering and labeling certain stimuli "noxious" or "stressful" and certain emotional reactions to them "realistic" or "appropriate." Such labels can be used because the people in a given culture are similar physiologically and psychologically and so react in roughly the same ways to these stimuli. We call stimuli "noxious" or "stressful" when they elicit unpleasant emotions in all, or nearly all, of us. We call unpleasant emotions "realistic" or "appropriate" when all, or nearly all, of us experience them in response to the same stimuli.

The part psychology plays in determining the "appropriateness" of responses may be doubted. Are there not "objective" dangers—death or bereavement, for example—to which all people react in the same way? Consider the following historical example. During World War II, crashing on the deck of a Japanese battleship was "objectively" an extremely stressful situation for American combat pilots; fear and attempts to avoid doing so were "realistic" and "appropriate" responses. But hundreds of Japanese kamikaze pilots deliberately crashed on American ships. For them, such a death was an honorable entry to a glorious afterlife (Grinker & Speigel, 1945), not an "objective" danger. Fear would have been an inappropriate and unrealistic response. This is dramatic evidence that psychological factors, in this case internalized cultural definitions of the meaning of a "reality" event, determine and define "noxious" stimuli and "realistic" emotional distress.

Just as cultures differ from one another, so do individuals within a given culture. Most American men, for example, are only momentarily startled by the loud report of a backfiring engine. But the same stimulus may terrify a combat veteran who had once been severely wounded by an exploding shell. We shall call such inappropriate emotional responses *over-reactions of distress* to external stimuli. (See also Part I, pp. 20–27.)

What kinds of stimuli elicit such over-reactions? Why? What psychological processes transform innocuous stimuli into noxious ones?

SIMPLE CONDITIONING AND STIMULUS GENERALIZATION

If we review the discussion of conditioning in traumatic neuroses in Part I (pp. 39–59), we realize that the simplest types of stimuli causing over-reactions of distress are *conditioned stress stimuli* and *generalized conditioned stress stimuli*. The former are innocuous stimuli that have been associated with noxious ones; generalized conditioned stress stimuli resemble the originally innocuous, conditioned stimuli. The discussion in Part I showed how combat experiences produce such conditioned and generalized stimuli. Actually, any stimulus situation significant for the organism, such as the six we discussed at the beginning of this chapter, can generate conditioned or generalized stimuli. If a child has been frightened by separation from his mother, merely seeing her put on her coat or hearing her say she is about to go or seeing her leave may come to frighten him. All these stimuli have been associated with her past absences and have become conditioned stimuli for him. If his own separation experiences have been unpleasant, the mere sight of another mother leaving her child may function as a generalized conditioned fear stimulus and also frighten him.

Perpetuation of Childhood Reactions

Most adults outgrow the unpleasant situations of childhood. Maturation and further learning modify their original unconditioned responses, and their early conditioned emotional responses become extinguished. Obviously, a college-aged person will rarely become frightened at being separated from his mother. But in extreme cases the adult remains disturbed in essentially the same way by essentially the same childhood situations. For example, the adult may remain tied to his mother's apron strings by a separation anxiety that he was never allowed or helped to outgrow because of his mother's overprotectiveness. Or he may never have gotten over the effects of intense separation experiences. Such prolonged separation anxiety takes specific forms at various stages of life. The "school phobias," for example, are usually caused by intense separation anxiety in children of school age. A relatively undistorted fear of separation from parental protection keeps many young adults tied to the home, a family business, or the town where their parents live. Usually the separation anxiety combines with other anxieties—such as fear of parental disapproval at signs of independence—and with unconscious libidinal attachments.

The adult who was a spoiled child may still feel unloved and jealous whenever his parents pay any attention to his brother or sister. And the man who was never guided appropriately by his father along the paths of achievement may feel just as worthless when his father criticizes his present work performance as he did as a boy, when the only things his father noticed about the birdhouse he built were its imperfections.

In less extreme cases of immaturity the disturbing adult situations resemble those of childhood less closely. For example, some adults who have been able to leave their parents displace their separation anxiety to other people or even to institutions, openly experiencing anxiety at the prospect of leaving a protective employer, government bureau, university, or hospital where they have been long-term patients. Similar displacements of the sense of being unloved cause many commonplace conditions to be transformed into ones of acute distress, for example, not always being the center of attention, being appropriately criticized, seeing others being recognized for their achievements, and not being the sole concern of one's employer or spouse.

The following fairly common instance of the same general process may be less familiar. Most women outgrow their girlhood unhappiness about lacking a penis and come to enjoy their femininity and men's maleness. Some women, however, continue to experience a sense of humiliation, worthlessness, and envy of the male whenever they perceive their femaleness and the difference between men and women.

One woman, for example, told her analyst how a veil of gloom surrounded her if she happened to touch her breasts in the process of dressing, or if a man touched them. When she and her husband made love, and especially at the point of intromission, a sense of humiliation would frequently sweep over her, together with an urge to "smash" him. Another woman who also felt humiliated and hostile when she made love with her husband had the same feelings for her analyst following each analytic hour in which she referred to her clitoris. In these same interviews her free associations frequently concerned "defects" in herself and her children. She finally realized that she regarded herself as defective for having a clitoris instead of a penis.

Perceptions or thoughts about their feminine attributes and men's contrasting attributes, and indeed the situation of sexual intimacy with their husbands, devastated the self-esteem of these women. They reacted with a sense of deep humiliation, just as they had when they were little girls comparing their bodies with those of little boys. They had not developed a positive feminine identity.

The similarity between these adult situations and the comparable childhood ones is analogous to the similarity for the combat veteran between the noise of a backfiring engine and the sound of the gunshot that had severely wounded him in battle. All of them are instances of stimulus generalization and generalized responses.

The Conditioned Response Paradigm

We have just been describing various kinds of observable relations: the close timing of unconditioned and conditioned stimuli, the similarity of certain stimuli, and the temporal relation between a stimulus and the response to it. The paradigm for these relations is presented in Figure 16-1. It states simply that

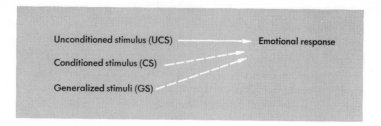

Unconditioned stimulus (UCS) ⎯⎯⎯⎯⎯⎯→ Emotional response

Conditioned stimulus (CS) ⎯ ⎯ ⎯ ⎯

Generalized stimuli (GS) ⎯ ⎯ ⎯

Figure 16-1   The conditioned response paradigm.

conditioned and generalized stimuli produce essentially the same emotional response that the original unconditioned stimulus produced. The dashed arrows represent learned stimulus-response relations; the solid arrow represents either innate or earlier learned relations that have become highly automatic and reflex-like. Applying this paradigm to the "over-reactions" of separation anxiety we have discussed, we get the diagram shown in Figure 16-2.

Some Unanswered Questions

Psychologists are still struggling with many of the questions implicit in these diagrams. For example, do conditioned responses result simply from the close temporal association of the unconditioned stimulus and the conditioned stimulus, as Pavlovian theory maintains? Or must there be a close temporal association of the conditioned stimulus-conditioned response sequence and drive reduction or need satisfaction, as Hullian learning theory assumes? Are more complex theories, involving cognitive concepts and language, required to explain the complex human behavior we have been describing? For example, can a mother's leave-taking preparations frighten a child who has not yet developed memory and a general capacity to anticipate the future? Does the appearance of this anticipatory anxiety reaction depend on the development of a capacity to *actively* reproduce in miniature the more intense anxieties the child experienced *passively* during past absences of the mother? A fuller discussion of such complicated issues would take us too far afield from the topic of over-reaction, but the interested reader should see Freud's monograph *Inhibitions, Symptoms, and Anxiety* (1926), Dollard and Miller's *Personality and Psychotherapy* (1950), and Hilgard and Bower's *Theories of Learning* (1966).

Another question is the nature of the internal processes mediating the over-reactions to conditioned and generalized stimuli. Some psychologists insist that psychology is a science of directly observable stimulus-response relationships and should not be concerned with this issue. Most psychologists, however, prefer to investigate the intervening mediating mechanisms as well. Some psychologists focus on the intervening physiological

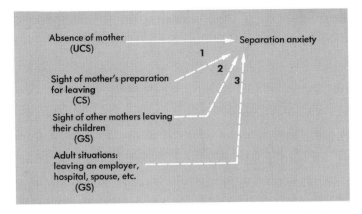

Figure 16-2   Over-reactions of separation anxiety in the child and the adult, according to the conditioned response paradigm.

The reactions produced in instances 2 and 3 are clearly over-reactions. If the reaction in 1 were intense in a very young child, or if it were present much beyond the age of 4, it too would be an over-reaction.

processes, especially brain functioning. Others focus on intervening psychological processes. Among learning theorists, Dollard and Miller, who were greatly influenced by psychoanalytic theory, have been most concerned with the mediating function of slight internal reactions, thoughts, and other intervening cognitive factors.

Every time an instance of over-reaction is observed through the microscope of the psychoanalytic technique, *it appears as if over-reactions to innocuous stimuli—conditioned, generalized, or any other kind—are mediated by memories, fantasies, wishes, and conflicts involving those stimuli.* In the rest of this chapter we shall discuss in detail the role of unconscious memories and fantasies in over-reactions.

Transformation Through Unconscious Memories: A Case of Separation Anxiety

In Chapter 11 we reviewed Freud's early work on hysteria and the role of memories of traumatic experiences. We also noted that subsequent systematic studies have demonstrated that most people selectively "forget" memories of unpleasant experiences. That is, the more unpleasant an experience is, the more likely most people are to "forget" it. Psychoanalytic case studies tell us that such "forgetting" is an active process of repression, not simply the gradual fading away of memory, and that repressed memories of unpleasant experiences often cause us to over-react with emotional distress to current events. We saw how the Wolf Man over-reacted sexually to scenes resembling those that had excited him in childhood. The process we are discussing now is analogous, but it involves distressing memories and experiences instead of, or in addition to, pleasant ones.

Memories affect everyone's reactions to external stimuli at some time or other. We may "over-react" by taking an immediate dislike to a stranger we pass on the street. Later we may realize that the person reminded us of someone else about whom we had very unpleasant memories. Some of these memories may even have spontaneously appeared in our stream of consciousness after we passed the stranger. Essentially the same phenomenon can be observed in psychoanalysis, with important differences: The process can be observed more completely there, more important over-reactions are involved, and the over-reactions may at first seem quite strange because they spring from unconscious memories.

Let us consider over-reactions of separation anxiety. In any psychoanalysis the continuity of the nearly daily analytic sessions is inevitably interrupted by holidays, vacations, trips, or illness by the person in analysis or the analyst. Many analysands react to these interruptions with separation anxiety. This in itself is evidence of an over-reaction determined by something within the analysand, for the interruptions do not inherently produce separation anxiety. Other analysands, for example, react with feelings of being unloved, or with a loss of self-esteem, or with a sense of frustration. And some are glad to be "free" for a while. When the analysand reacts with an over-reaction of separation anxiety, his thoughts at the time contain clues of the inner processes, of the activation of memories of previous separations.

THE MEMORIES
ACTIVATED BY IMMINENT SEPARATIONS

A married woman in her late twenties suffered from intense separation anxiety. Four brief separations from her analyst occurred during the first 8 months of her analysis. She reacted to three of them with a good deal of anxiety, and each time the separation from her analyst became imminent, memory fragments of previous separations, or of closely related experiences, crept into her associations. The fragments from her associations in one analytic session preceding each separation are listed below. When these occurred, they were embedded in a larger context that rationalized them and disguised their relevance to separation anxiety from the analysand. She did not realize that the current separations were activating the memories that were creeping into her associations. This process of memory activation is quite different from active, intentional recall of the past. It is an automatic, involuntary effect of current stimulation. We shall use the word "remember," in quotes, to stand for the process.

1. A Separation
of 5 Days

As she sat in the analyst's waiting room just prior to the last session before the separation, she had an anxiety attack. For a moment she felt disoriented spatially: The analyst's office seemed to be on the wrong side of the waiting room, and the windows of the waiting room seemed to be located in the wrong side of the building. This perceptual experience was accompanied by panic.

Memory fragment 1. Shortly after describing that experience, she "remembered" an episode at college when she drank too much and was disoriented. She did not speak of her anxiety attacks at college, which she had previously described as having been accompanied by a similar perceptual distortion, of the walls of her room closing in on her. But the striking similarity of those anxiety reactions and the present one suggests that memories of her separation from home when she went to college had also been activated but had not directly emerged into consciousness. She "remembered" being disoriented at college, but not her separation anxiety.

Memory fragment 2. Later in the session she "remembered" a question, and her answer, on a psychological test she had taken 2 months earlier. The question was, "What would you do if you were *lost and alone* in the woods?" She had said she would sit down and wait for someone to find her.

Memory fragment 3. Still later in the session, she "remembered" an episode of a few nights before: She was *by herself* in a dark hallway in the tenement where her apartment was. She was trying to find her way and had banged her head on a door while searching for the light switch.

2. A Separation
of 3 Weeks

This was the first lengthy separation and occurred 4 weeks after the first one. In addition, she was faced with the possibility of having to go with her husband to a distant ocean resort during the interruption. If she went, she would be leaving her parents, who lived nearby, and her home. Thus, she anticipated a double separation—from her parents as well as from her analyst. In the end, she and her husband stayed home; she was too frightened to leave. Two nights before this separation she had a *nightmare,* in which her father appeared as a reassuring figure. This was a manifestation of her very intense anxiety in response to this separation and of her wish to remain with her analyst and parents. Her associations to the nightmare included memories of previous separations, extending back to her early childhood.

Memory fragment 1. She "remembered" times several years earlier when she had walked *alone* in a tunnel associated with the building in which her analyst's office was located. She was scared; she always felt calmer if other people were walking there too.

Memory fragment 2. She "remembered" a frightening scene she had observed a year before when she and her husband had *gone away* from home to a nearby ocean resort: The breakers had been exceptionally high, four people had been *swept away* by them and drowned, and lifeguards had been on hand to rescue people from drowning.

Memory fragment 3. Later in the hour she "remembered" a related childhood incident. Her parents had taken her to the beach for a picnic. She became *separated from them* (when they ignored her) and had tried to swim to a small island just off the shore. She was panicked by the time her mother found her on a sand bar.

Memory fragment 4. She "remembered" another traumatic separation experience in her childhood. She and her brother, she said, used to exasperate their parents by cutting up at the dinner table. On one such occasion her mother and father got up, put on their hats and coats, and walked out of the house, saying *they were leaving forever.* As she recalled this, she said, "*Just picture two little kids sitting there white with fear.*"

3. A Separation
of One Week

This separation occurred during the eighth month of analysis, 6 months after the preceding 3-week separation. She and her husband were about to go on a week's trip of several hundred miles, during which they would stop overnight with several different friends and relatives. She was *terrified about the sleeping arrangements* they might encounter—so much so that she was not sure she could go. This time she finally went.

Memory fragment. In associating to a dream expressing her conflict over going on this trip, an image of herself as a little girl with pigtails formed in her mind. Then she "remembered" how, as a child, she often used to be *afraid when alone in bed at night.* She would leave a hall light shining into her room when she went to bed to ease her *fear of being alone in the dark.* When the adults came to bed later, they would turn off the lights. And often she would wake up in terror, thinking that kidnappers were after her. With that, she continued to "remember," she would run and jump into bed with her big, fat grandmother. She would lie very close to her grandmother, where she would feel secure.

Her further thoughts drifted on to how she would miss sleeping in her own bed and being in her own home for a week and, later, to how comfortable she felt now in her analysis. She specified that she was no longer distressed at coming for her sessions, even at lying silently on the couch. This associative drift from the memory fragment to thoughts of feeling comfortable on the couch, where the analyst was nearby, suggested that leaving the analyst for a week was specifically reminiscent of her nighttime terrors upon being separated from her big, fat grandmother. She provided some evidence giving additional support to this inference: A short time before this separation, she dreamed of a big, cuddly, chubby, loving, and lovable cat that, according to her associations, represented her analyst.

The fact that all these memories were caused by the imminent separations is suggested by another observation: Her stream of thoughts during a "control" sample of the hours immediately following the three separations included no memories whatsoever of earlier separations.

These observations illustrate several important features about memories and their place in current behavior that are quite typically revealed by psychoanalysis. One striking feature is the abundance of memories lying ready to be activated by current stimuli. In only 150 minutes of "free-association time" (three 50-minute periods) this woman "remembered" eight clearly identifiable separation experiences. And she was not even trying to remember them. Another feature: A given stimulus may activate not just one memory but *sets of related memories*. The woman's first separation, for example, activated three memories tied together by the theme of being lost or disoriented in space. The second separation activated two memories dealing with the dangers of swimming in the ocean and the safety provided by protectors, as well as two memories sharing the theme of separation from her parents. One memory, that of being separated from her mother as she swam, was common to both sets, which hints at the intricacy of the way memory traces are organized. As we have seen, an especially important characteristic of memory sets is that they extend far into the past, back to intense emotional experiences of childhood. Thus, the observations included childhood memories of very frightening separation experiences: the time she swam off by herself, the time she thought her parents were abandoning her, and the nightmares she had when she slept alone.

COVARIATIONS IN SEPARATION STIMULI, MEMORIES, AND ANXIETY REACTIONS

The abundance of memories, their organization into sets, and their extension back to childhood do not shed much light on the process of over-reaction per se. Another phenomenon illustrated by the observations does exactly that: the covariation in the three variables—the current separation stimuli, the nature of the memories, and the current separation reactions.

Let us consider first the covariation on the dimension of sheer *intensity*. As the intensity of the current separation stimulus increased, so did the intensity of the anxiety in the "remembered" experiences, and so did the intensity of the current separation anxiety. *The three separations can easily be ordered into different degrees of intensity.* The *most intense* separations were the second and third ones. The second was to be a long one, and the distance from home and the analyst was to be considerable. The third was to take her a considerable distance away too, but its intensity also stemmed from the subjective meaning of the analytic relationship, which by now had taken on a special quality for her that had not been present earlier. In contrast, the first separation was of *moderate intensity*. While it was nearly as long as the last one, she would not be leaving home and she did not perceive the analyst as going far away. Nor had her relationship to her analyst yet taken on quite as special and personal a meaning for her. There was another very brief separation of 2 days during the period we have studied, and it was the least frightening of all. *The intensity of the "remembered" anxiety closely parallels the severity of the current separations and the intensity of the current anxiety reactions.*

Equally important, and nearly as clear-cut, are the covariations in the qualitative or substantive *content* of the current stimuli, of the memories, and of the current reactions. By contrasting the first and last separations, we can demonstrate these phenomena most fully. The first separation occurred one month after this woman had started her daily analytic sessions. Her relationship to the analyst was more impersonal than personal, so the separation could only be somewhat impersonal. And, in fact, she voiced no such personal feelings as she did later. The same impersonal quality permeated her memories. She "remembered," for example, the question about being "lost and alone in the woods" and the experience of being by herself in a dark hallway. And she "remembered" being slightly disoriented when somewhat tipsy in college. There were no references to people, except to the "someone" who would find her waiting in the woods. Her anxiety reaction, too, bore this stamp of her being lost and disoriented in an impersonal world: As she sat in the waiting room, her orientation in space seemed out of kilter, not her relationship with the analyst. The match, or fit, between the quality of this separation, her memories, and her anxiety reaction is impressive.

Now let us look closely at the last separation, which had a much more personal and special meaning for her. Instead of being separated from *an* analyst with *a* couch in *an* office in a large building, she was about to be separated from a very *real*, warm *person*, toward whom she had all the feelings expressed in the dream of the big fat cat. And now *the couch* was a place on which she could lie quietly and feel safe and at ease. What she now "remembered" were the nightmares she used to have as a child when sleeping alone in the dark and the wonderful safe feeling that would come over her as she ran and climbed into bed with her big, fat grandmother. Further, the specific content of her intense anxiety about the separation shows the imprint of these memories, for what she feared was that the strange bedrooms in which she would be sleeping while she was away would be so located in the houses that she would not be able to get out of them easily and rapidly in the middle of the night. Here again the meaning of the current separation, the content of her memories, and the content of her current anxiety are strikingly similar.

Finally, our brief description of the second separation suggests that the same "good fit" existed there as well.

MEMORIES AS MEDIATORS IN OVER-REACTIONS

What does the precise covariation in the nature of the current separation stimuli, of the memories, and of the anticipatory reactions to the current separations tell us about over-reactions? It very strongly suggests that the memories mediate the over-reactions. *Innocuous conditioned and generalized emotional stimuli appear to activate memories of past emotional experiences, which appear, in turn, to determine the intensity and content of the over-reactions.* Very often these memories emerge from repression only during free association. Even if they have not been repressed, the individual is usually not aware of their influence on his over-reaction. The woman, for example, was not aware that her memories of her nighttime terrors in childhood played any part in her fears about the sleeping accommodations she would encounter during her separation from the security of her analyst's couch. Nor was she aware of all the details of the covariations we have described. In other words, the mediation by memories is an unconscious process, and usually the memories themselves are unconscious.

Memories may mediate any kind of over-reaction; we have merely chosen to illustrate the process in detail for over-reactions of separation anxiety.

If we incorporate what we have inferred about memories into Figure 16-1, we get the scheme shown in Figure 16-3. This new diagram places the conditioned and generalized stimuli and the over-reaction above the "threshold of consciousness and overt behavior (repressive barrier)" because those variables are consciously experienced or overtly displayed by the subject. They are also apparent to the outside observer. We have placed the memories at and below the threshold of consciousness because they are not ordinarily conscious to the subject and he is not aware of the important part they play in his experience and behavior. The threshold of consciousness in instances like these is different from the ordinary sensory thresholds, which may be passed simply by increasing the intensity of a stimulus—as when we notice a sound simply because it becomes louder. Instead the threshold of consciousness in such instances is determined largely by the active repression of the crucial memories. (Thus, the threshold may be termed the "repressive barrier.") When the repressive efforts are decreased, as during free association, the memories emerge into consciousness. The case material presented above illustrated these aspects of Figure 16-3. The woman was conscious of the fact that the separations were imminent, and she consciously experienced her anxiety reaction. Any outside observer would also have been aware of these matters. But it was only during the process of free association that the memories emerged into consciousness.

Figure 16-3   The memory mediation of emotional over-reactions to relatively innocuous conditioned and generalized stimuli.

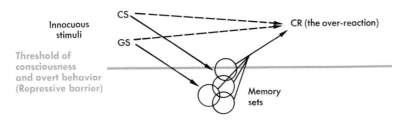

The diagram shows memory *sets,* and it depicts them as *intersecting.* We illustrated these characteristics of memory organization in the case material. The diagram also portrays the memory sets as being at varying depths below the threshold of consciousness. This represents the fact that some memories appear to be more strongly repressed than others. The woman, for example, readily "remembered" the test question about being lost and alone in the woods. In marked contrast, however, the memory of her parents' pretended abandonment, which left "two little kids sitting there white with fear," was so strongly repressed that it first found indirect expression in a nightmare and then slowly emerged in her associations to the dream.

The dashed arrows in the diagram represent the direct causal relationship that the "purest" stimulus-response psychologist would infer. The solid arrows represent some of the relationships that the psychoanalyst would infer. He believes that unconscious, repressed memories mediate many over-reactions of distress to innocuous stimuli. The precise nature of the memories appears to determine the nature of the over-reaction—the kind and intensity of the felt emotion and the nature of the accompanying thoughts. In our example, the observations of the covariation in the current separation stimuli, in the woman's memories, and in her concurrent anxiety reaction illustrate the basis for these psychoanalytic inferences.

One final comment about Figure 16-3: It does not portray everything we observed in the case material dealing with separation anxiety. It does not show, for example, the changing feelings of the woman for her analyst or her conflicts over those feelings. The presence of such conflicts appeared to influence what the meaning of the various separations was for her and which memories were activated. But the figure does diagram what appears to be the essential process in many over-reactions of distress: the relatively direct activation of repressed memories of painful experiences.

We shall now discuss the way in which unconscious fantasies of painful experiences often produce over-reactions of distress.

Transformation
Through Unconscious Fantasies

INFLUENCE OF CONSCIOUS FANTASIES ON BEHAVIOR

A normal person walking down a dimly lit street may be preoccupied with fearful fantasies that a robber or a "sex maniac" might be lurking in the darkness. Under these circumstances the person may freeze in terror at the mere sight of the moving shadows of swaying trees. A student's fantasies of how poorly written his last essay was and of how displeased his teacher must be with it can transform the teacher's minor criticisms into very harsh ones. A surgical patient may panic before her operation because she suddenly fantasies that her surgeon will fiendishly mutilate her. (Such cases are described in Part I, pp. 101–02.)

Murray (1933) conducted an experiment with 11-year-old girls that showed how fantasies can influence reactions to external stimuli. When the girls were in a relaxed state of mind, Murray asked them to look at some photographs of strange men and to rate how malicious the faces appeared to them. Then he had the girls play a game of "murder." Playing games is a special form of fantasy activity for children, and doing so stimulates still further fantasies. After the game the girls rated the faces as much more malicious. The child who had been most frightened by the game woke up the next morning screaming with fear, saying she had seen a "bad man" coming into her room. In the confused state of awakening she falsely perceived the external world to be in line with the scary fantasies of the preceding night.

These girls took their perceptions of men's faces as representations of *reality*, and the surgical patient was convinced that her perception of her doctor also reflected a real situation. Why? Basically because they did not know that they had distorted their perceptions. External stimuli and internal mental and emotional processes, operating *automatically and unconsciously*, combined to produce their perceptions. And they took their perceptions for reality, regardless of their objective validity. They were merely doing what all of us do when we dream and accept the wildest perceptions arising almost completely from our fantasies as absolutely real. And they were doing what many of us do to a lesser extent in our waking life, when we see things the way we need to or want to.

MASS FANTASIES IN THE IVY LEAGUE

A good example of seeing things the way we want to—or living in a fantasy world—was provided by Hastorf and Cantril (1954). Following a bitterly fought game between the Princeton and Dartmouth football teams, the two psychologists made a survey of students at both schools who had attended the game. It turned out that the two groups "saw" the game quite differently: The Princeton students were nearly unanimous in seeing it as "rough and dirty" and the Dartmouth team as much "dirtier" players than their own. Most of the Dartmouth students thought the game had been "rough and dirty," more than one-third of them thought it had been "rough and fair," and one-tenth of them thought it had been "clean and fair." They did not think the Dartmouth players had been "dirtier" than the Princeton players. Judging from the objective evidence—the incidence of serious injury on both sides and the official penalty statistics—both teams played a rough game, and about equally so.

This episode involved conscious fantasies. Unconscious fantasies can have analogous effects on behavior.

A MARITAL RELATIONSHIP
BEDEVILED BY UNCONSCIOUS FANTASIES

Situations that directly arouse heterosexual wishes and sensations very commonly end up producing conscious experiences of anxiety, shame and humiliation, or guilt. The role of unconscious fantasies and conflict in such instances is especially clear when the persons involved are married adults with no external, realistic reason for not enjoying sexuality. Again, the unconscious conflicts often date from childhood. They are usually Oedipal, but frequently they involve conflictful incestuous fantasies about brothers or sisters.

Ed, the young man with castration dreams who was described in Chapter 12, had attacks of anxiety and guilt and occasional castration dreams when he and his wife made love. One reason he responded this way was that *any* sexual arousal and gratification were by now adequate activators of his unconscious castration anxiety. But there was another particularly important reason: Ed had conflictful incestuous fantasies as well.

As a boy Ed had loved one of his sisters dearly. He had frequently played sexual games with this sister, and he had been terrified that his mother would cut off his penis if she ever found out. This was one reason he had castration dreams at the age of 7. His boyhood fear manifested itself in yet another way during this period of his incestuous play with his sister: Once when he was being examined by his doctor, he became so frightened that he doubled up his knees over his abdomen so that she would not be able to examine his scrotum and groin. It seemed that he was afraid that the doctor would be able to divine what had happened between him and his sister and would then tell his mother, whereupon the two would castrate him. This boyhood castration fantasy caused Ed to inhibit his sexual play with his sister and to repress his love for her. The fantasy was also recorded in Ed's memory just as though it were an objectively real experience, and the unconscious memory of this fantasy experience continued to affect his adult behavior. Its influence can be detected in Ed's castration dreams as an adult, which were cited in Chapter 12: There too, doctors were castrators.

Ed's early experiences with his sister had a significance transcending the arousal of castration anxiety. His erotically toned attachment to her served as a model for his later relationships with women. Eventually, as the Wolf Man had done, Ed "just happened" to marry a woman who resembled his childhood incestuous love object and substituted for her. There were several details—such as age, intellectual interests, and emotional attitudes—in which the two women resembled each other, but they were insignificant compared to one major attribute. The woman came from a cultural background that was despised by Ed's parents. His marriage to her was a tabooed act in their eyes, and to some extent in his own. It was in being a "tabooed female" that his wife most clearly resembled his sister.

There was a good deal of other evidence that his wife represented his sister. For example, once, when his sexual conflicts were prominent, Ed dreamed he saw a brother and a sister sitting in front of a television set and thought to himself that they were emotionally disturbed. Earlier that night he and his wife actually had sat in the front row of a theater watching a sensuous play. Ed had become sexually excited by the play and had felt guilty about it. When the analyst pointed out the similarity between the real scene with his wife and the dream scene, Ed realized that recently he had been thinking that living with his wife was like living with a sister. Later he commented that all his wife did when he was home in the evening was watch television. During other periods in his analysis, Ed found that for several days in a row his sister's name would come to the tip of his tongue in place of his wife's. And visits with his sister intensified his anxiety over his sexual intimacy with his wife. It is reasonable to conclude that his wife was a "generalized sister stimulus."

Making love with his wife, then, often made Ed feel tense, uneasy, and sweaty because it activated conflicting unconscious fantasies that resembled the conscious sexual conflict of his childhood. Sexual intimacy with a woman who resembled his sister stimulated repressed incestuous fantasies and, in turn, his unconscious castration fantasies. His adult conscious experience of anxiety was simply *the emotional component of these castration fantasies stripped of the castration thoughts themselves.* These he continued to repress, but they manifested themselves in his castration dreams. Such *isolation* of affective and ideational components—a particular defense mechanism, which we shall discuss further in Chapter 21—is a common mechanism in over-reaction.

Ed's anxiety motivated him to avoid sexual intimacy with his wife until his own sexual needs, his wife's demands, or his "need to be masculine" became imperative.

If we incorporate what we have inferred about Ed's unconscious fantasies into Figure 16-1, we get the scheme shown in Figure 16-4. The clinical data strongly suggest that the over-reaction, though it appears to be directly elicited by the generalized stimulus, is actually mediated by the unconscious fantasies. The dashed and solid arrows and the "threshold of consciousness and overt behavior (repressive barrier)" shown in Figure 16-4 have the same significance as those of Figure 16-3.

Over-reactions to many different kinds of stimuli are mediated by intervening unconscious sexual fantasies and conflicts in essentially the same way as in the case of Ed. Edie's fear of eating, which we discussed in Chapters 12 and 13, is another example. The opportunity to dine with an attractive date thrills nearly every young woman. Yet this stimulus situation frightened Edie because of the unconscious sexual-oral fantasies it triggered. Casual contact of her breasts with her hand or a piece of her clothing rarely brings about a feeling of depression in a woman. But we saw earlier in this chapter that this can happen if this stimulus activates an unconscious fantasy that to be a woman is to be an inferior human being. Walking down the street to the grocery store in broad daylight frightens some women so much that they are unable to continue once they have started, if indeed

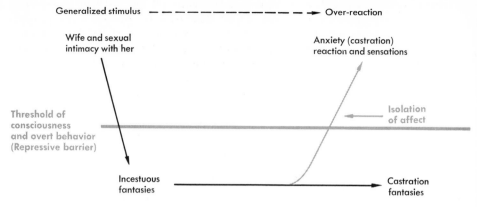

Figure 16-4   *The mediation of an emotional over-reaction to a generalized stimulus through the activation of unconscious fantasies.*

they are even able to leave their doorstep. Very commonly, unconscious wishful fantasies of exciting some man into picking them up are stimulated by this "street-walking." And these fantasies, in turn, arouse frightening fantasies of various kinds stemming from childhood. As with Ed, however, only the emotional component of these fantasies may become conscious and overt and thus result in over-reactions of distress.

In the next chapter we shall discuss how somewhat different processes also produce such over-reactions.

*The Captain was a tall man of about forty, grey at the temples. He had a
handsome, finely-knit figure, and was one of the best horsemen in the West.*

He had never married . . . .
*To his orderly he was at first cold and just and indifferent . . . . Then the
change gradually came.*
*The orderly was a youth of about twenty-two, of medium height, and well
built. He had strong, heavy limbs, was swarthy, with a soft, black, young
moustache. There was something altogether warm and young about him. . . .*
*. . . He could not get away from the sense of the youth's person. . . . It
was like a warm flame upon the older man's tense, rigid body, that had become almost unliving, fixed. . . . And this irritated the Prussian. He did not
choose to be touched into life by his servant. . . . He now very rarely looked
direct at his orderly.*

. . .

*In spite of himself, the Captain could not regain his neutrality of feeling
towards his orderly. . . . Sometimes he flew into a rage with the young
soldier, and bullied him.*

. . .

At last he slung the end of a belt in his servant's face. . . .
*. . . His own nerves must be going to pieces. He went away for some days
with a woman.*
*It was a mockery of pleasure. He simply did not want the woman. But
he stayed on for his time. At the end of it, he came back in an agony of
irritation, torment, and misery. He rode all the evening, then came straight
in to supper.*

. . .

*The orderly took his hands full of dishes. . . . As he was crouching to
set down the dishes, he was pitched forward by a kick from behind. . . . And
as he was rising he was kicked heavily again and again.*

. . .

*The officer, left alone, held himself rigid, to prevent himself from thinking.
. . . He stood there for an hour motionless, a chaos of sensations, but rigid
with a will to keep blank his consciousness, to prevent his mind grasping.*

D. H. LAWRENCE. The Prussian Officer

CHAPTER 17
PROJECTION, OVER-REACTIONS, AND UNCONSCIOUS HOMOSEXUAL CONFLICTS

With the keen eye and sensitive skill of the artist, D. H. Lawrence has portrayed the Prussian officer's agonized attempts to cope with his conscious attraction to his orderly. Each reaction —his reluctance to look at the orderly, his episodes of increasing conscious hatred of him, his flight into heterosexuality, and his final supreme struggle to rid his mind of all thoughts and feelings— was part of a defensive effort to ward off homosexual feelings and the inner distress they evoked.

Suppose the Prussian officer had succeeded in obliterating this homosexual conflict from his consciousness. By this repression he would have achieved relief from the conscious misery of frustrated desires and of the shame, guilt, and self-criticism those desires provoked. But the repression would have left him with an unconscious homosexual conflict. If this unconscious conflict were to be intensified in the future, it might again become conscious. Suppose the officer was later faced with the danger of such a rupture of his repressive barrier as he was becoming acquainted with a new orderly. He might then resort to another defense that could help to maintain his repression. He might perceive this orderly as being attracted to him, rather than himself being attracted to the orderly. The officer would then have been using a defense mechanism called *projection*. In this mechanism the person protects himself from becoming aware of repressed impulses, feelings, and thoughts by attributing them to others. If he had projected his homosexual wishes onto his orderly, the officer could have remained unaware of his own homosexual wishes and thus could have protected himself from the torment those wishes caused him.

Projection of unconscious wishes causes one to live in a perceptually distorted world. The projectively transformed people now evoke in the subject all the unpleasant emotional reactions his own wishes would evoke if they were to become conscious or to be expressed in overt behavior. At other times the subject may project his negative reactions to his own wishes and thus be confronted with projectively created people who seem to view him just as negatively as he unconsciously views himself.

Thus, the projective distortion of reality is another way in which unconscious conflicts cause over-reactions of distress. It was primarily in attempting to understand homosexual conflicts that Freud discovered projective patterns. Hence we shall illustrate the two patterns described in the paragraph above with two examples of over-reactions based on homosexual conflicts.

Male Companionship Spoiled by an Unconscious Conflict

PROJECTION OF UNCONSCIOUS HOMOSEXUAL WISHES

Ray, a young, married attorney, went camping with his family. His long-standing goal had been to climb a high mountain in the area. Although Ray was not a sociable person, he did manage to seek out and find another camper who appeared to be an ideal companion for the difficult overnight climb: a congenial young doctor whose family, like Ray's, did not relish the hike. On the eve of the climb the two men sat by the fire, talking over their final plans. Suddenly the doctor stood up, adjusted his underwear, and scratched his groin, all the while smiling at Ray. An alarming thought struck Ray: "He's a homosexual." Ray suddenly saw standing before him a man who was excited at the prospect of spending a night in a lean-to on the trail with him and who was crudely but seductively hinting at what he had in mind. Ray now felt only scorn and contempt for the doctor, and making many excuses the next day, he set off on the hike alone.

Ray's perception of the doctor that night might conceivably have been correct, but he certainly lacked sufficient evidence for the sense of conviction he had. When he recounted this episode in analysis and later reconsidered it, Ray was not even sure that the man's "smile" had not really been a grimace. And the scratching was not so unusual, especially since no women were present. Many relevant thoughts were stimulated by his recounting of this episode in his analysis, so we can reconstruct what probably happened. Ray's behavior was an over-reaction to an ordinary stimulus situation that had triggered an unconscious conflict in him.

In childhood Ray had occasionally initiated and participated in homosexual play, as many a boy does. Usually it occurred with friends but occasionally with new buddies with whom he wanted to develop a close relationship. For example, at the age of 7, Ray moved into a new neighborhood. The boys there played "soldiers," using homemade tents in their backyards. One boy and Ray had "played with each other" in their tent. Ray's last overt homosexual behavior had occurred when he was 13. He and a friend had shared a bed in a bunkhouse on an overnight Boy Scout hike. Ray became excited and masturbated his friend. This boy acquiesced to Ray's masturbating him until he had an orgasm but did not reciprocate in any other way. Ray then disappointedly masturbated himself and fell asleep. To his great shame, a fellow scout taunted him the next day by saying that he had overheard the activity of the night before. From this moment his homosexuality became a source of greatly increased conflict for him. He first consciously suppressed it and later unconsciously repressed it. In fact, he went on to achieve a fairly satisfactory heterosexual adjustment, although he was occasionally preoccupied with homosexual fantasies, fears, and suspicions about himself as well as others. But his heterosexual life and his defenses against his homosexual inclinations maintained those inclinations in a latent, but not dormant, state.

The hiking situation with the doctor disturbed this balance. In its budding intimacy and the details of the physical setting—the tents, the outdoors, sleeping in the lean-to—the situation with the doctor was very similar to those of the "tent game" and the Boy Scout hike. It was a generalized stimulus that, together with Ray's latent homosexual wishes, activated memories of those experiences and the fantasy of repeating them. But these memories and wishful fantasies as to what might happen if he and the doctor were to camp out overnight in a lean-to could not become conscious, for they were in direct conflict with Ray's adult masculine values and superego, and they were opposed by self-scorn and self-condemnation. Yet there was a very real danger that the memories and fantasies would become conscious, for Ray's homosexual desires were intensified. This was made perfectly clear by the excitement (warmth in his genitals, for example) that accompanied the fantasies when they were expressed in his analysis. Some defensive effort was necessary, beyond his customary repression, so Ray's unconscious solution was to project his unconscious homosexual wishes and thoughts onto the young doctor. The doctor now evoked the critical, scornful emotional attitudes Ray had about his own homosexuality. That is, Ray displaced these attitudes from himself to the doctor. He actively avoided the opportunity for enjoyable companionship. In avoiding intimacy with the doctor Ray removed himself from the stimulus situation that had upset the original equilibrium between his homosexual wishes and his opposing masculine values. Figure 17-1 schematizes this process.

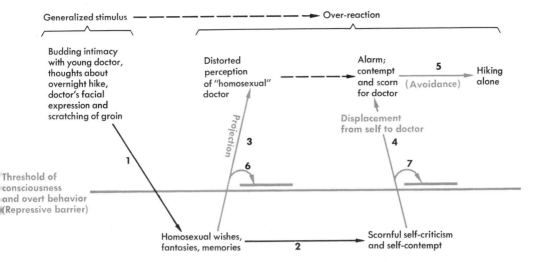

Figure 17-1 *Ray's over-reaction to the prospect of hiking in the mountains with a young doctor.*

The *"threshold of consciousness and overt behavior"* distinguishes between those aspects of Ray's behavior that were conscious or overt (above the line) and those that were unconscious (below the line). Since it is determined largely by the active resistance of repression, the threshold is also termed a *"repressive barrier."* The dashed arrows indicate the apparent stimulus-response relationships. The solid arrows represent the causal relationships inferred from clinical evidence to be the actually important ones. (1) The interaction between Ray and the doctor stimulated Ray's unconscious homosexual wishes, fantasies, and memories. (2) These, in turn, evoked unconscious self-criticism and self-contempt. At this point Ray's unconscious homosexual conflict was so intensified that it could have become conscious. (3) But Ray projected his homosexual wishes onto the doctor and (4) displaced his self-criticism and self-contempt to the doctor. (5) As a result, he hiked alone. By hiking alone Ray avoided further stimulation of his unconscious conflict. By projecting his homosexual wishes and displacing his self-criticism and self-contempt he reinforced the repressive barrier. This is represented by the curved arrows and the double line (6 and 7). (These reinforcements consist of the distorted perception and the displaced criticisms themselves, not of the acts of projection and displacement. For example, the thought "He's a homosexual" prevents the subject's own homosexual wishes from coming into his consciousness.)

PROJECTION OF NEGATIVE REACTIONS
TO UNCONSCIOUS HOMOSEXUAL WISHES

In the episode in the mountains Ray projected his homosexual wishful thoughts to prevent them from agitating his conscience into such intense self-criticism and self-condemnation that he would have felt worthless. At other times he created a dangerous reality out of very ordinary situations by projecting the unconscious self-criticisms and self-condemnations. Some of Ray's lunchtime experiences illustrate this point.

As one might expect, Ray did not enjoy easy, comfortable relationships with men. He was a "loner." Habitually, for example, he ate lunch by himself at his desk instead of making his lunch hour an occasion for comradeship. To ease his loneliness, he would occasionally go to a nearby businessmen's restaurant, where at least there would be other men present. Every once in a while, however, something happened to spoil these ventures. When he would start to open the door of one of these restaurants he would look in at the men already there and be seized with the thought, "I can't go in there. They will all look at me and think to themselves, 'Look at that fellow. He looks like a woman. He must be a fairy.'" Feeling sickened and worthless, Ray would turn away. (Incidentally, Ray's appearance was quite masculine.) One day this experience was repeated every place he went until his lunch hour was gone, and he still had not eaten.

When Ray was discussing this episode in his analysis, his thoughts drifted to a memory of an experience he had had in late adolescence. He was attending an out-of-town convention and had gone to a restaurant. He asked the waitress for directions to the house where he was to be quartered. In a few minutes, a man came to his table and said that he had overheard Ray's question and offered to give him a lift. On the way this man told Ray that he was an overt homosexual and tried to seduce him. Although he did not succumb, Ray had difficulty falling asleep that night and then had a disturbing dream with homosexual overtones. When this dream woke him up, he was not sure for a moment whether or not he actually had refused the man's advances the night before.

Shortly after recalling this experience, Ray "remembered" that the Boy Scout hike when he was 13 had occurred in winter and that the bunks had been set up in a large, heated mess hall. Thus, that homosexual experience had involved an eating place. The businessmen's restaurant can be regarded as a generalized stimulus similar to these earlier eating places.

From all we know about Ray, it is possible to reconstruct the chain of events resulting in that intensely unpleasant experience at the door of the restaurant. Although his isolation from male company was caused by his unconscious conflict over homosexuality, the loneliness it produced only intensified this conflict. Eating in a businessmen's restaurant could have been a good solution, relieving his loneliness and providing a sublimated gratification of his homosexual longings. But the combined action of his unconscious wishes and the generalized stimulus—the sight of the restaurant —activated those two unconscious memories of homosexual experiences and

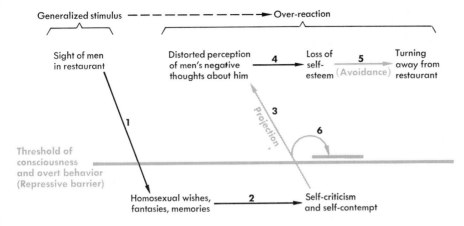

Figure 17-2 Ray's over-reaction at the restaurant door.

The dashed arrow indicates the apparent stimulus-response relationship. The solid arrows represent the causal relationships
inferred from clinical evidence to be the actually important ones.
(1) The sight of the men in the restaurant stimulated Ray's unconscious homosexual wishes, fantasies, and memories. (2) These,
in turn, evoked unconscious self-criticism and self-contempt. At
this point Ray's unconscious conflict might have become conscious. (3) But Ray projected his self-criticism and self-contempt
onto the men in the restaurant. Now he saw them as judging him
harshly and negatively. (4) This distorted perception lowered his
self-esteem and (5) caused him to turn away from the restaurant.
By doing this he avoided a situation that stimulated his unconscious conflict. The projection of his self-criticism reinforced the
repressive barrier. This is represented by the curved arrow and the
double line (6). (The distorted perception prevented his repressed
self-criticism from becoming conscious.)

fantasies of doing something similar now. These in turn instigated unconscious, harsh, negative self-criticism, which he projected onto the men eating
in the restaurant. Having done so, but without realizing it, Ray could only
feel inferior and worthless and turn away from the door. This experience
was very painful. But awareness of his unconscious conflict would have been
more painful. The projection and the reaction to the "reality" constructed
by it prevented this awareness. Figure 17-2 represents the main aspects of
our reconstruction.

PARANOIAC PROJECTIONS OF JUDGE SCHREBER

The episodes in the mountains and at the restaurant door illustrate some common causes of social isolation among men. The former
involved projection of unconscious homosexual wishes and displacement of

the self-criticism prompted by those wishes; the latter involved projection of the unconscious self-criticism. Frequently the defensive pattern also includes a defensive hatred by the subject of the man toward whom he is attracted, which helps to keep his desire for contact with the other man out of consciousness. The Prussian officer in Lawrence's story reacted this way. The reactive hatred is often repressed and projected. Projection of the hatred occasionally leads to frankly paranoid reactions toward one's fellow men and an eventual withdrawal from them.

When Freud analyzed Judge Schreber's memoirs (1911), which we mentioned in Chapter 14, he discovered essentially the same basic pattern illustrated by Ray's experience.*

> At one time or another Schreber projected his unconscious homosexual wishes, his unconscious defensive hatred, and his unconscious self-criticism. But he differed from Ray in two very important ways: Schreber projected continually and his capacity to test the reality of his projective perceptions was severely impaired, whereas Ray seldom projected and his sense of reality was largely intact. As a result, Schreber lived in a delusional and hallucinatory world, a condition that is designated as a psychosis. In his untested, projected reality, God loved him and wanted to copulate with him (projected homosexual wishes); doctors were intent on persecuting him and emasculating him (projected defensive hatred for man and projected wish to be a woman); and, in his auditory hallucinations, he heard derogatory accusations about himself (projected self-criticism). In the latter, he heard mocking and jeering voices say such things as "*Miss* Schreber" and "so this sets up to have been a (Judge), this person who lets himself be f——d!" and "Don't you feel ashamed in front of your wife [Freud, 1911, p. 20]."

Incidentally, these auditory hallucinations of Schreber are of great historical significance to psychology, for they stimulated Freud's concept of the superego. Freud conjectured that they were created by the distorted externalization of processes operating within us all the time, whether we are aware of them or not (1914a). These are the processes of self-observation, self-evaluation, and self-approval or self-criticism—many of the processes fused in the concept of conscience. Freud saw the similarity between these and comparable parental functions of watching over, evaluating, and praising or scolding the child. He reasoned that these parental functions were internalized along with the parents' values in the course of the child's growing up. Here was the kernel of his later theory (Freud, 1923, 1933) of superego content, function, and development: moral values, self-observation and self-assessment, and the resulting self-approval or self-criticism—all developed by identification with the parents.

Experimental Studies
of Projection and Paranoia

Several psychologists have systematically or experimentally investigated some of the behavioral mechanisms that we have been discussing and that Freud originally inferred from his clinical observations. One question that has been investigated is whether the basic phenomenon of projection can be demonstrated by methods more "rigorous" than clinical observation. This is an extremely difficult question, but some suggestively affirmative results have been obtained.

PROJECTION ALONG FRATERNITY ROW

A study by Robert Sears (1936) illustrates both the suggestive findings and the difficulties. Sears asked members of college fraternities to rate themselves and their fraternity brothers on the traits of *stinginess, obstinacy, disorderliness,* and *bashfulness*. The extent to which a person actually manifested each of these traits was estimated by averaging the ratings all his friends gave him for that trait. Each person's self-awareness was determined by comparing his self-rating with the average of the ratings others made of him. A person who rated himself low in stinginess while

Figure 17-3 Average trait scores assigned to fraternity brothers by subjects high in the traits and with or without insight about themselves. (Based on data from R. Sears, 1936. In this figure Sears's data have been changed to comparable scores that equal his average ratings.)

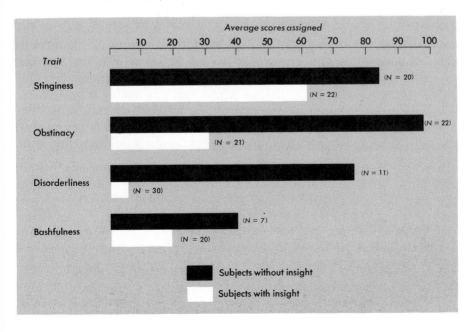

being rated high by his fraternity brothers, for example, possessed little awareness of his own tendency to be stingy. If projection occurs, those students high in a presumably "undesirable" trait but unaware of being so should attribute more of that trait to other students than would those who were high in the trait and aware of it.

The key results are shown in Figure 17-3, which contains averages of the rating scores assigned to their friends by subjects who lacked insight into themselves and by subjects who had this insight. Those subjects who were stingy but did not realize it rated their fraternity brothers as being more stingy than did those subjects who were stingy and knew they were; and so on for the other traits. These subjects were acting somewhat like Ray did in the episode in the mountains and then later in psychoanalysis. When the traits he felt were contemptible (latent homosexual inclinations) were stimulated to a "high" level and he was not aware of it, he thought his friend was homosexual. But when he became aware that he himself had been homosexually aroused, he was no longer certain that his friend had been.

Another finding of Sears illustrates some of the difficulties of validating psychoanalytic hypotheses by simple rigorous methods. The students attributed "good" qualities to their friends just as readily as they did "bad" qualities. The "good" traits of generosity, flexibility, and orderliness, for example, were attributed in the same way as their "bad" counterparts. These findings would not have been expected on the basis of general psychoanalytic theory about projection, which emphasizes its defensive function. There would be no defensive gain in projecting "good" traits. These results could be produced, however, by man's general tendency to conceive of the world as a reflection of his own nature, as it is assumed people do during projective testing (see Part IV, pp. 624–27), and this might offer a simpler explanation. But it is possible that both tendencies entered in: Sears's subjects may have *defensively projected* their "undesirable" traits and also indulged in the more general *nondefensive attribution* of desirable characteristics. (See Holt [1951] for another study and further discussion of this issue.) One way of testing whether both tendencies were involved would be to see how upset subjects become as you "undo" these two kinds of projections. They should be much more upset when the presumably defensive projections are interfered with than when the presumably more general, nondefensive tendency to attribute one's own qualities to others is interfered with. But this type of experiment has not yet been carried out, perhaps because it is too difficult to find an appropriate and ethically justified situation for such interference.

HOMOSEXUAL CONFLICTS IN PARANOID MEN

Another group of studies has been concerned with the proposition that paranoid men—that is, men who project hatred extensively—do in fact have homosexual conflicts. Zamansky (1958) showed paired pictures of men and women to male paranoid schizophrenics and to a control group of male nonparanoid schizophrenics and measured the amount of time the subjects looked at the male picture and at the female picture of each pair of pictures. The paranoid men spent much more time looking at the pictures of men than at those of women. The nonparanoid men looked longer at the female pictures. Sternlaff (1964) obtained similar results when he presented pictures of men or women singly to male paranoid schizophrenics and to psychotically depressed men. In addition, Sternlaff fused his pictures of men and women, making a series of ambiguous pictures. The paranoid men perceived more of these as pictures of men than did the depressed men.

Wolowitz (1965) also showed single pictures of men and women to paranoid schizophrenic men and to nonparanoid schizophrenic men. His pictures, however, were graded for the "powerfulness" of the faces in them. Both the male and female faces ranged from weak, ineffectual-looking ones to powerful or potent ones. And instead of measuring the amount of time the subjects looked at these faces, Wolowitz measured the distance at which the subjects placed the pictures from their eyes by asking them to slide each picture back and forth in a specially designed viewing box until it "looked best." The paranoid men, when compared with the nonparanoid men, placed the male faces farther away than the female faces. This difference was not quite statistically significant when the "power" factor was disregarded. However, there was a significant effect of the power factor. The more "powerful" the faces of the men in the pictures, the farther away from themselves the paranoid men placed them. They did not respond this way to differences in the women's faces, however. But the nonparanoid men did, and, at the same time, they were unaffected by the power factor in the men's faces.

Here, then, are three experiments in which pictures of men produced special reactions in paranoid schizophrenic men, just as one would expect if these pictures activated an unconscious homosexual conflict in these men. In Wolowitz's study the paranoid subjects apparently felt less threatened by the male pictures if they moved the pictures slightly away from themselves, and this was increasingly so the more "powerful-looking" the faces were in the pictures. We cannot be sure, however, why the more powerful faces were more threatening. Perhaps they were more attractive and hence more conflictful, or perhaps they could more easily be projectively distorted into critical or persecutory images. Perhaps the reason differed for different subjects. Only the study of each subject in depth would enable us to answer this kind of question.

The paranoid men's selective perception of ambiguous figures and their preference for looking at the pictures of men in Sternlaff's and Zamansky's experiments could also have resulted from two different consequences of the unconscious homosexual conflict we have assumed was triggered by the pictures. On the one hand, seeing male figures in ambiguous pictures could have been wish-fulfilling perceptions, and looking at pictures of men could have been pleasing because of unconscious attraction to them. In principle, such behavior would be no different from that shown by hungry subjects in other perception experiments. Several investigators, for example, have shown that normal people, when hungry, will see more food-related things in ambiguous pictures than will people who are not hungry (Sanford, 1936, 1937; Levine, Chein, & Murphy, 1942; McClelland & Atkinson, 1948).

On the other hand, the paranoid men tested by Sternlaff and Zamansky could have been especially attentive to male pictures because of the anxiety and guilt components of the conflict. In this respect they would be showing the same general kind of perceptual vigilance for unpleasant stimuli shown by people under stress (see Part I, pp. 114–17).

The fact that several explanations are possible is not unusual in science. And people, after all, regularly do the same thing for different reasons. But much of the uncertainty in experiments such as those we have been discussing might be eliminated through more intensive observation and measurement of other details of behavior, such as muscle tension, autonomic responses, and free associations. For the time being, we can either leave the question about Sternlaff's and Zamansky's results open or attribute them to the aversive component of the homosexual conflict, which seemed to account for Wolowitz's findings. Regardless of all these details, however, the results of the three experiments fit very well with Freud's hypothesis of the significance of unconscious homosexual conflicts in paranoia and with the clinically based explanations of "over-reactions" such as Ray's. The special responsiveness to men's pictures resembles Ray's sensitivity to men in the real-life episodes in the mountains and at the restaurant door.

Oh, what may man within him hide,
Though angel on the outward side!

WILLIAM SHAKESPEARE. Measure for Measure

CHAPTER 18
OVER-REACTIONS AND UNCONSCIOUS CONFLICTS ABOUT AGGRESSION

One major theme unites this chapter with the preceding two and with the following one: *Any unconscious conflict has the potential of producing a distressing over-reaction.* In Chapter 16 we saw how a young woman over-reacted with intense anxiety at the prospect of separations from her analyst; her separation anxiety was produced by the activation of unconscious memories of childhood separation experiences. In the same chapter we saw how Ed's unconscious castration and incestuous fantasies were responsible for his over-reaction (intense castration anxiety) to sexual intimacy with his wife. In Chapter 17 we saw how Ray's unconscious homosexual conflicts triggered such over-reactions as his alarming, distorted perception of and scorn for his proposed hiking companion and his turning away from businessmen's restaurants in a state of extremely low self-esteem. In this chapter we shall discuss certain over-reactions resulting from unconscious conflicts over aggression. In the next chapter we shall conclude our focused discussion of over-reactions with an examination of the distress caused by interference with defenses and with other controls over unconscious processes.

Conflicts over aggression produce a variety of over-reactions: in one instance, an excessive anger far out of proportion to the ostensible provocation; in another instance, too little aggression, or even excessive affection, when there is every reason for anger; in another, very unpleasant emotional experiences such as guilt, anxiety, or depression. The case study that is the heart of this chapter provides a striking example of this last kind of over-reaction, on which we are focusing in this chapter: a severe depression that was precipitated by the loss of a pet. The case study also illustrates all of the other over-reactions that arise from unconscious conflicts over aggression, except excessive anger. However, we have already seen examples of this: Duane's reaction to his father's death, discussed in Chapter 12, and the dreams of the death of the same-sexed parent and the Rat Man's hostility, discussed in Chapter 15. To dream wishfully for the death of one's parent and to feel even fleeting pleasure when this actually happens are both excessive reactions. And so is the gleeful contemplation of killing one's father, such as the Rat Man experienced when he had sexual intercourse for the first time. Such intensely hostile thoughts accompanied by malicious pleasure are obviously not commensurate with anything parents do. Instead, they are caused by the unconscious, hostile component of the Oedipal complex.

A common instance of the over-reaction of excessive anger is the displacement of inhibited aggression resulting from frustration. (See Part I, Chapter 9, "Frustration and Aggression.") Scapegoating and many other everyday incidents of excessive anger may arise in this way. This is very often what causes a man to shout angrily at his wife and children after an irritating day at the office. All day he has been inhibiting the anger provoked by one frustration after another, and now he takes it out on his family at the slightest provocation. Frequently an individual realizes later what has happened in such incidents, but the scapegoating represented by social prejudice, such as anti-Semitism, remains largely unconscious.

Now we shall turn to the other over-reactions produced by unconscious conflict over aggression. Most of what follows is based on a clinical paper by a famous psychoanalyst, Helene Deutsch. Her report (1965) deals with the life history of an unmarried woman who became so severely depressed in her late forties that she was hospitalized and treated with psychoanalytic therapy by Deutsch. As will become apparent, this case study is instructive on many counts and reveals in extreme form some of the psychological mechanisms that occur in normal persons when they become temporarily depressed.

An Example of Over-Reactions
to a Minor Loss

At the time Miss Eaton (our name for this patient) started treatment with Deutsch, she suffered from three kinds of symptoms: (1) She was *deeply depressed*; (2) she had *frightening delusions* that people were going to throw her naked into the street and leave here there to die; (3) her thoughts were replete with *self-accusations* that she deserved this horrible fate, though the only transgressions she could cite to justify such thoughts were trivial. One of Deutsch's first discoveries was the immediate cause of her patient's condition: the death, 3 years earlier, of her pet dog. At the time, her dog had been her constant and closest friend, perhaps her only friend. Even so, her reaction was clearly excessive. (Such pathological reactions to loss are discussed in Part I, pp. 177–81.)

During treatment, it became obvious that an unconscious conflict over aggression was the primary cause of this and other over-reactions Miss Eaton had experienced from childhood on. We shall describe all of these over-reactions, because each sheds light on the others and because they illustrate a variety of emotional reactions produced by variations on the same theme: *an unconscious struggle against hatred for her sister* that, like other conflicts we have examined, arose in childhood. In this account the formulation of some of Deutsch's observations has been changed slightly, and aspects of Miss Eaton's emotional life not essential for our purposes have been omitted. But Deutsch's empirical observations and basic formulations have not been altered.

Miss Eaton's struggles began when she was 8 years old, with the birth of her "very beautiful and talented" sister. For a few years she was intensely and openly jealous of her sister. She hated her and wished she were dead. Exactly why her sibling rivalry was so intense is not reported, but her having been an only child for so long may have been an important factor. Perhaps, too, her parents had wanted another child for some time and now doted over the new baby at Miss Eaton's expense. In any case, the inappropriate emotional reactions with which we are concerned proceed from the basis of Miss Eaton's jealous hatred of her sister.

Adolescent Defense Against Sibling Rivalry

The first inappropriate emotional reactions appeared a few years after her sister's birth. When Miss Eaton was 12 her mother died. She now began to respond to her 4-year-old sister with excessive love and tenderness. This dramatic change did not come about because her sister ceased being a rival, nor because her jealousy had vanished; it occurred primarily because her jealousy was banished from consciousness and overt behavior. Indeed, the primary reason for this excessive love was that it helped her to repress her hatred and the guilt and anxiety the hatred provoked in her. An attitude of this kind—one that is the direct opposite of how one really feels about a person—is a specific defense mechanism called *reversal of affect*. Miss Eaton's loving thoughts, actions, and feelings crowded hating thoughts, actions, and feelings out of consciousness and overt behavior. And, of course, she now had no rational reason to feel guilty. It is quite likely that this reversal also served two other important functions dealing with the two sides of her feeling about her mother.

(1) The reversal relieved her pain at losing her *beloved* mother by enabling her to *identify* with her mother. In loving and caring for her little sister, she no doubt fantasied that she was in fact her mother. Identification with the lost object, as noted earlier, is one major defense against grief. (2) The reversal, again by enabling her to identify with and "replace" her mother, fulfilled her unconscious Oedipal wishes. She was now the little woman of the house.

Development
of an Obsessional Symptom

A balanced situation such as this one rarely lasts forever; sooner or later unconscious conflicts erupt. This happened when Miss Eaton was 18, while she was still living with her father and her sister, who was 10 years old at the time. Miss Eaton now became obsessed with the frightening thought that something harmful might happen to her little sister unless she repeated all her actions a number of times. As long as Miss Eaton did this she felt at ease and was certain that she was protecting her sister from an evil fate.

What was happening here? Many actions Miss Eaton performed were stimuli to which she responded with the unrealistic fear that something harmful might now happen to her sister; this fear could be reduced if she then repeated the action a magical number of times. Here was inappropriate behavior compounded: an unrealistic fear in response to the most innocuous stimulus, followed by nonsensical, superstitious behavior. Such experiences are classical obsessive-compulsive symptoms. ("Obsessive" refers here to the *thoughts* that evil would come to her sister and to her *lack of control* over these thoughts. They would suddenly intrude into her consciousness, and, once there, would preoccupy her. "Compulsive" refers here to the ritualized *acts* and to the fact that she felt *compelled to perform* them. Such symptoms occasionally occur in normal persons and evidently have the same psychological basis as when they appear in such a severe or persistent form that the person is regarded as suffering from an obsessional neurosis.) Symptoms like these are frequently found to be caused by unconscious conflicts over aggression. The basic fact was that her sister was not in any real danger. Only Miss Eaton entertained evil wishes for her; only Miss Eaton knew of these wishes; only Miss Eaton felt frightened and guilty because of them; and only Miss Eaton had to be relieved of this fear and guilt. All this was true with one qualification: We have been describing her unconscious conflict. Her conscious experience and behavior consisted of *derivatives* of this unconscious conflict and the defense known as *undoing*, which consisted of her repetitious, protective actions. We shall refer to these again in a moment.

For some reason not specified in the case report, the balance Miss Eaton had achieved between her hatred for her sister and the defenses against it was disturbed at this time. Possibly something happened that intensified her hatred. Perhaps there was a weakening of her reversal of hate into love. Perhaps both these things happened. Whatever the reason, this disturbance caused both components of her unconscious conflict—both her hatred and her guilt and anxiety—to become conscious in an indirect way. Minor, everyday actions were now expressions of her hatred, and her unconscious guilt and fears were now expressed in the vague conscious sense that these actions would somehow result in great harm to her sister. By repeating these actions, Miss Eaton was attempting to undo any possible effect of her unconscious hatred. She was engaging in superstitious behavior.

OBSESSIONAL SYMPTOMS
AND THE DEFENSE OF UNDOING: THE RAT MAN

In his clinical paper about the Rat Man (1909b) Freud reported some cogent illustrations of obsessional derivatives and the defense mechanism of *undoing*.

The Rat Man was very much in love with an attractive young woman, but like all people afflicted with severe obsessional neuroses, he hated her as much as he loved her. Naturally this hatred was a source of conflict for him, because it produced distressful emotions (anxiety and guilt in his case). The hatred, as part of such a conflict, was largely unconscious. As was true of Miss Eaton, a broad range of the Rat Man's daily activity was invaded by his unconscious conflict. One summer he and the young woman were staying at the same resort. Once, when they were out boating and a strong breeze was blowing, a command popped into his conscious thoughts that "nothing must happen to her." And because the sentence was completed in his unconscious thoughts with the words "for which [I] might be to blame [p. 189]," he forced her to put on his cap. Another time, they were together during a thunderstorm. He was compelled to count to 40 or 50 between each lightning flash and thunderclap to protect her from being harmed.

The day she was to leave the resort, he was out walking a few hours before her departure. As he was walking along, his foot knocked "accidentally" against a stone in the road. He picked up the stone and put it off the road, but after walking on for a short while he returned and put the stone back in the middle of the road.

Why did he act so oddly? When he kicked the stone, he immediately thought that the carriage in which his friend would be leaving would hit the stone and overturn. So he put it off the road. But then he thought this was a foolish idea, so he put the stone back. His kicking against the stone and the thoughts that followed it were derivations of his repressed hate and his unconscious guilt; his removal of the stone was an *undoing*, which undid the danger and wish of the first act and thus reduced his guilt and anxiety; but then his unconscious hate drove him to put the stone back in the road. Of course, he *rationalized* this latter action, ascribing it to a thought acceptable to his conscious image of himself (that he was not a foolish man), rather than to his repressed hate, which was intolerable to his conscious self. His behavioral oscillation with the stone is a classic example of the oscillation of approach-avoidance conflicts, which was mentioned in Chapter 12. The Rat Man's "goal" here was expression of his hatred. The approach drive was his hatred itself; the avoidance drive consisted of the guilt and anxiety that hatred produced.

The same basic phenomenon had a drastic effect on his nightly prayers, only here the unconscious hatred was very directly expressed. Although he consciously wanted to pray, "May God protect her," his unconscious hostility would cause him to make a slip of the tongue and say, "May God *not* protect her." Naturally, this curse against his loved one would arouse the most intense guilt in him. Thus he would try to repeat the prayer very rapidly so that the "not" could not slip into it. He might have to repeat it several times before an uncontaminated version would come from his lips. At other times he tried to shorten his prayers to prevent this kind of thing. Finally he was driven to replacing ordinary prayers with a nonsense word made up of the initial letters and syllables of his favorite prayer phrases, to which he added "amen." And he uttered this "prayer" as rapidly as possible. But even this defensive effort was unsuccessful. His unconscious wish to curse his loved one caused him to select such letters and syllables that the total "nonsense" word now contained her name and the word *semen*. Without realizing it, he still insulted her, expressing at the same time a sexual wish. It is not surprising that he often had to spend several hours praying and finally gave it up entirely—a striking case of unconscious conflicts over aggression transforming an innocuous situation into a most unpleasant one.

When we discussed Miss Eaton's repetitious actions, we did not specify their nature. It is possible that they followed the same pattern as the repetitive prayers of the Rat Man; that is, the first occurrence of the actions may have been "spoiled" by some expression in them of her unconscious anger at her sister, and the repetitions of the actions may have been attempts to perform those actions "perfectly," without having them "spoiled" in this way. But the symptoms are not described in sufficient detail in the case report to draw any such inference.

Although Miss Eaton's obsessional behavior appears to have been less severe than the Rat Man's, it did persist for the next 20 years or so. Yet because she so successfully concealed it, no one but herself knew about it until she confessed it to her psychoanalyst.

Altruistic Surrender in Adulthood

We shall now return to the case study of Miss Eaton, because the later events in her life help to illuminate several additional psychological mechanisms.

When she was 21, her father died, leaving his two daughters poor and virtually alone in the world. Miss Eaton had seriously hoped to pursue a writing career, but she now had to postpone that goal in order to support herself and her younger sister. It is easy to imagine how severe was the internal conflict with which she now struggled: She must set aside all her own interests and hopes and take a safe, steady job in order to care for a little sister she had hated from the day she was born. Miss Eaton, showing the strength of many "neurotics," did what she had to do and mothered her sister into young womanhood. She took a menial job as a typist, masochistically subjecting herself to a humdrum career. She bestowed on her sister even more tenderness and loving care than before.

Indeed, this reversal of feelings became a *general character trait* of kindliness. When this further development of a reversal occurs, the defense is called a *reaction formation* (see Chapter 21). Miss Eaton also fostered her *sister's* ambitions to become a writer. She was able to do this because in her unconscious fantasy life she and her sister were the same person: She had achieved a *projective identification* with her sister. She would become a writer through her sister's achievements, just as many parents fulfill their own thwarted desires through their children's accomplishments. By means of three defenses—a projective identification, a masochistic turning of her hatred for her sister against herself by working at menial jobs, and a reaction formation—she was able to contain her aggressive response to the frustration she had to endure.

Anna Freud (1936) pointed out that the general behavior pattern based on projective identification, which she called *altruistic surrender*, has an important adaptive function as well as a defensive one: It enables the individual to maintain a meaningful emotional relationship with another person where this might not otherwise have been possible. The altruistic surrender enabled Miss Eaton to live relatively happily with her sister for the next 25 years, first raising her and then supporting her so that she might develop her writing talents. And she came to love her sister in a quite genuine way, while still hating her so much that her relationship remained basically *ambivalent.*

Incubation and Triggering of the Severe Depression

The years passed, but Miss Eaton's sister did not become a successful writer. Perhaps Miss Eaton could have tolerated this disappointment, but then something even more drastic happened. Unexpectedly, her sister, who was then about 37, married and moved to a distant country. At first Miss Eaton repressed her intense feelings. Instead of becoming angry or depressed, she "bore the parting with quiet dignity, even appeared to be pleased at her sister's happiness, and remained behind alone [Deutsch, 1965, p. 148]." *Soon she obtained a small dog, which substituted emotionally for her sister.* For more than a year they were constant, close companions. Then one day the dog was lost. Miss Eaton became severely depressed and began to experience the persecutory ideas and self-accusations mentioned earlier.

The loss of the dog was a symbolic repetition of the loss of her sister. Miss Eaton's over-reaction to the loss of the dog was mediated by all the feelings and wishes she had repressed when her sister abandoned her. Her depression was primarily a displacement of all her repressed grief over the loss of her sister. It would be quite understandable if Miss Eaton had now become very angry at her sister for deserting her. But she didn't—because she couldn't. And not because she wasn't angry, as Deutsch's report, here quoted, shows:

> In the further course of the treatment the patient's so reasonable attitude at the separation from the sister was soon succeeded by bitter reproach against the ungrateful one, by the return of the most intensive sadistic vindictiveness against the once-hated, afterward loved, and finally so faithless sister.
>
> What had this sister done to her? For the sake of a strange man she had betrayed her self-sacrificing love and ruthlessly left her to a life of loneliness. This was the thanks she got for having reached the little orphan a helping hand at the time when she was completely helpless. The clearer the picture of her own loss became in the analysis, the louder grew her reproaches against the sister until they took the form of wishing her to be thrown out into the street, where she would have landed in any case if she had not had mercy on her [Deutsch, 1965, pp. 148–49].

Miss Eaton could not tolerate consciously thinking, feeling, or expressing her rage until her treatment enabled her to feel less guilty about it. Instead she repressed it. The loss of her dog, however, was like putting a match to a fuse on a bomb: It threatened an explosion of her unconscious rage. New and renewed defenses were now necessary.

Miss Eaton's new defense was *projection* of her hatred, which contributed to the production of her persecutory delusions: Others might throw her into the street to starve, as she unconsciously wished she had done to her sister. Her renewed defense was a further *turning of the hatred against herself*, which helps to account for her self-reproaches. The critical evidence that these two processes took place is the observation that the content of her persecutory ideas (delusions) and self-reproaches was identical with the content of her furious wishes and thoughts about her sister. Only the subject and the object of these wishes were changed. These were, of course, drastic changes that transformed an easily understandable over-reaction of depression into a bizarre, delusional one.

How were the changes brought about? By the combined action of the defenses and the preexisting identification with her sister. We can best appreciate what happened by recalling that in her unconscious thinking she was, to a significant degree, her sister. Thus she was a potential target of her own hatred. When she then projected onto others her wish to throw her sister into the street, she (now identifying with her sister) became the object of these "others," these projectively created tormentors. She did not project her reproaches against her sister. They were directed against herself. Something else was also involved in the production of her self-reproaches: Her hatred for her sister was first transformed into self-criticism and guilt. In Miss Eaton's case the empirical basis for these concepts is the moralistic, judgmental quality of her self-criticisms. They were self-*accusations* and self-*reproaches* accompanied by a sense of being a guilty, worthless person, deserving of punishment. In short, the stamp of conscience was plain. In fact, the self-reproaches of extremely depressed and delusional patients, such as Miss Eaton, formed the second major empirical basis for Freud's concept of the superego (1917). The first, noted earlier, was the observation of the critical, derogatory nature of Judge Schreber's auditory hallucinations.

This discussion of Miss Eaton's over-reaction to the loss of her dog concludes our discussion of her lifelong struggle with her hatred for her sister. It is also our last example of over-reactions mediated by unconscious conflicts over aggression.

Other Unconscious Conflicts

Unconscious conflicts over aggression mediate over-reactions to just as broad a range of stimuli as do sexual conflicts. The episodes in Miss Eaton's life and the obsessive activities of the Rat Man give a sense of this range. Many other examples could be cited, some of which may occur temporarily in very mild form in normal persons who ordinarily are free from neurotic symptoms: the mother who is afraid to use a butcher knife in the kitchen because she unconsciously fears she will kill her child with it; the man who panics as he drives his automobile because his unconscious urge to run over pedestrians is so strong; the brilliant scientist or student who becomes very anxious or guilty as he writes a paper because he fantasies that his considered evaluation of another man's ideas will destroy that person's scholarly status.

Most of our examples of over-reactions based on unconscious conflicts have involved aggression and genital sexuality. *Any* conflicted wish, however, may mediate an over-reaction to an innocuous stimulus, for linked to any such wish is the unpleasant emotion that either forms the main ingredient of the over-reaction or leads indirectly to it. Since many children in our culture are punished severely for enjoying their oral and anal activity and their voyeuristic and exhibitionistic tendencies, they develop conflicts over such wishes that may lead to over-reactions. Thus, the act of defecating or the sight of a speck of dirt may upset the person who has repressed his anal eroticism and his wishes to be messy. A person driven by strong but conflicted voyeuristic desires may be unable to look at the person he is talking to; a person with an unconscious conflict over oral eroticism may become very uneasy as he watches a diner smacking his lips out of sheer pleasure at the taste of his food; and so on. The theme announced at the beginning of this chapter also concludes it: Any unconscious conflict has the potential of producing a distressing over-reaction.

I lost all sense of the place in which I had gone to sleep, and when I awoke at midnight, not knowing where I was, I could not be sure at first who I was; I had only the most rudimentary sense of existence . . . and out of a half-visualized succession of oil lamps, followed by shirts with turned-down collars, [I] would put together by degrees the component parts of my ego.

MARCEL PROUST. Swann's Way

CHAPTER 19

INTERFERENCE WITH DEFENSES AND REALITY CONTACT

I n the discussion of over-reactions in Chapters 16, 17, and 18, we emphasized one general mechanism: that in which an objectively innocuous external stimulus situation has influenced unconscious processes in such a way that they have burst into consciousness, even though frequently disguised. Thus, we first discussed the way in which innocuous stimuli (such as a brief separation from the analyst) may activate repressed unpleasant memories and thereby result in over-reaction (such as acute separation anxiety). This process of memory activation appears to be analogous to the arousal of a person who is half-asleep. Then we discussed the way in which innocuous, or even very pleasant, stimulus situations (such as approaching a restaurant door or making love with one's wife) may similarly activate the approach component of an unconscious conflict—the wish or impulse and relevant memories and fantasies (such as repressed homosexual wishes or repressed incestuous wishes and fantasies). Sometimes the external stimulus functions more like a triggering device that fires a loaded gun or like a puff of air that causes a smoldering fire to burst suddenly into flames. This appeared to be the case when the loss of her little dog triggered Miss Eaton's repressed hatred for her sister, who had deserted her. In either case, as we saw, the intensification of the approach component arouses some kind of aversive unpleasant emotion, such as Ed's unconscious castration anxiety, Ray's unconscious self-contempt when he was at the restaurant door, or Miss Eaton's intense unconscious guilt. Sometimes these emotions become conscious and constitute the over-reaction, as in Ed's anxiety when he made love with his wife or Ray's loss of self-esteem or Miss Eaton's unrealistic feelings of guilt. But they may also motivate such defensive actions as phobic avoidance, projection, identification, undoing, turning of aggression against oneself, and reaction formation, all of which have been illustrated in the last few chapters. Sometimes these defenses contribute very significantly to the distress of the over-reaction, as they did when Miss Eaton's projection of her self-criticism, turning her aggression against herself, and identification with her sister combined to produce her terrifying delusion that other people were going to throw her into the street naked to starve. While the defenses do not always eliminate unpleasant emotional experiences, they do minimize the intensity of these experiences. That is why they are learned in the first place, and that is why they persist.

It follows that any stimulus situation that interferes with the operation of defenses will produce the very emotional experience that the defense normally prevents. In this chapter we shall discuss two such situations. One is the *interference with defenses*. The other is the *interference with contact with reality*. As we shall see, the latter situation can be very unpleasant, because it results in a marked change in defense effectiveness and in many of the other ways people control the expression of their unconscious wishes and thoughts.

Interference with Defenses

Forcing or persuading an individual to give up his defenses only makes him miserable. If Miss Eaton's father, for example, had coerced her into stopping her ritualized repetitions, she would only have suffered greater anxiety. If a boy has developed a hand-washing compulsion that relieves his guilt over masturbating, any attempts by his parents to stop him—reasoning, pleading, threatening, or hiding the soap—will only leave him intensely guilty. Unless his guilt is resolved, it will drive him to secretive hand-washing or to some other defensive action.

Psychotherapy has identical effects if the therapist resorts to the same tactics.

One "victim" of such a strategy was a man in his early twenties. He was a passive, dependent person, afraid to function away from the protective security of his parents. Since he became very frightened at being away from home, for example, he was not able to hold a steady job. He finally learned that he could venture outdoors if he had enough to drink. Drinking, then, was his defense; it was motivated by his anxiety, and it relieved that anxiety. But, of course, this was a maladaptive defense, which led his family physician to refer him to a mental health clinic.

He came quite regularly for psychotherapy interviews for several months without improving. Always arriving slightly intoxicated, he passed most of the time talking about that fact: apologizing for it, berating himself for it, complaining that he could not do otherwise, and so forth. The well-meaning but inexperienced therapist impatiently concluded that psychotherapy would be worthless if the man could not come sober, whereas if he did come sober his underlying anxieties and conflicts might become so uncomfortable that they would properly become the focus of attention. Accordingly, the therapist abruptly suggested one day that at the next interview the young man would start a new conditioned response treatment. The treatment, he explained, consisted of ingesting a chemical together with a drink of whiskey. The chemical would make him violently sick to his stomach. After one, two, or three such experiences the sight of a glass or even the thought of taking a drink would nauseate him. Soon the young man would be coming for his interviews completely sober, and they could then get down to what was really troubling him. The young man agreed to all of this. But he did not show up the next time. He later sent word to the clinic that he had gotten a job that did not allow him time off for his interviews. And, anyway, he felt he could get along without more psychotherapy.

Five years later he reappeared at the clinic and was interviewed by the same therapist. The patient explained that for the last three years he had been in a state hospital, where he had voluntarily gone, hoping to get over his anxiety and drinking. Both had actually increased after the earlier efforts at psychotherapy. Now he was trying life again outside the hospital and in coming to the clinic was following the advice of his doctor at the hospital. He had broken off his earlier psychotherapy, he explained, because he had been frightened by the therapist's plans to stop his drinking and make him talk about his emotional problems. The threatened premature and forcible interference with his defense had mobilized the very anxiety he was trying to relieve himself of by drinking. His psychotherapy was transformed into a noxious situation, to which he over-reacted with anxiety and flight.

This is a typical clinical experience when techniques are used that do nothing more than forcibly interfere with defenses and leave the underlying conflict unresolved. Even when a "cure" has apparently been achieved, it is likely that the old symptoms will reappear or that new ones will arise. As we pointed out earlier, this was the main reason Freud abandoned the use of direct hypnotic suggestion.

The reader who is familiar with behavior therapy derived from conditioned response theory (see Part I, pp. 55–59) might wonder how much of what we have just asserted applies to behavior therapy. We are, frankly, uncertain, and prefer to leave this issue open for careful investigation in the future. It should be noted, however, that behavior therapy as formulated by Wolpe and his followers attempts to reduce the anxiety behind symptoms and not simply to abolish the symptoms. Nor do experienced behavior therapists deal with their patients as abruptly and impatiently as the therapist did in the instance we have discussed.

THE NEGATIVE THERAPEUTIC REACTION

Effective psychoanalytic psychotherapy includes interference with defenses, but in a quite different way from the procedure described above. Rather than blocking them, the therapist strives to identify what defenses a person uses, what kind of distressing affect motivates them, and what "approach" tendencies are eliciting this distressing affect. He also helps the patient work through the developmental history of the conflict. As the patient becomes aware of his defenses, they become less automatic and less effective. He begins consciously to experience the unpleasant emotions—for example, anxiety, guilt, shame, and disgust—that had been motivating the defenses and to recall and reexperience the childhood situations in which his conflicts developed. All of this can be very unpleasant and disturbing, even to the point where the patient consciously suffers more than he did before treatment started. But the patient is usually "getting better"—he is enjoying life more and functioning better than he did when he suffered less, before treatment started. This paradox is part of what is referred to by the term "negative therapeutic reaction."

The negative therapeutic reaction includes another seeming paradox. As the person becomes aware of the nature of his conflicts and their past history, he indulges more in the approach components of his conflicts because the intensity of the competing aversive emotional reactions eventually decreases. Yet he experiences greater emotional distress than he did before treatment started! If one follows Miller's reasoning, it becomes clear that this *must* happen, according to the dynamics of approach-avoidance conflicts (Miller, 1944; Dollard & Miller, 1950).

Let us take a specific example of a man with a sexual conflict and follow Miller's argument with the aid of part A of Figure 19-1. The approach and avoidance gradients in part A of the figure represent the strengths of this man's tendencies to approach and to avoid a certain woman, and these are motivated, respectively, by his sexual desires and by his sexual anxiety or guilt. As we saw in Chapter 12, the avoidance gradient is steeper than the approach gradient. Thus, at any point beyond the intersection of the two gradients, avoidance is stronger than approach, and the person will retreat from the goal. The point of intersection of the approach and avoidance gradients represents how close the man gets to the goal of complete psychological and physical intimacy with the woman. In other words, the closest a person in an approach-avoidance conflict will get to the goal is the point of intersection of the approach and avoidance gradients. The man's situation at the outset of treatment is represented by the combination of the "approach" gradient and the "strong avoidance" gradient. That is, he desires intimacy, but his opposing anxiety is so strong that he cannot come closer to her than the idle talking stage (intersection 1). After many weeks of psy-

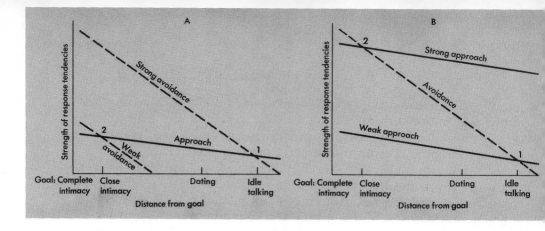

Figure 19-1   *Effects of changing the strengths of avoidance and approach gradients. (Adapted from Miller, 1944)*

Part A demonstrates that, within the limits in which the two gradients cross, decreasing the strength of the avoidance gradient moves the intersection closer to the goal and at the same time raises the height of the intersection. Thus, decreasing the strength of the avoidance gradient has the paradoxical effect that the man will engage in more intimate sexual behavior than formerly and at the same time will experience greater anxiety and conflict over doing so than he did when the avoidance gradient was higher. Part B demonstrates that increasing the strength of the approach gradient also moves the intersection closer to the goal and, in addition, places it higher on the avoidance gradient. Thus, decreasing the avoidance gradient results in less intense conflict and avoidance at intersection 2 than does increasing the approach gradient. This difference is reflected in the difference in the heights of intersections 2 in the two diagrams.

chotherapy he may be in the dynamic situation represented by the "approach" and the "weak avoidance" gradients. That is, his underlying anxiety may now be sufficiently reduced so that he can not only date but also be somewhat intimate with the woman (intersection 2). (Miller assumes that such reductions in anxiety lower the overall height of the entire avoidance gradient.) Yet he will be experiencing greater anxiety at this point than he did earlier, when he could only engage in idle talking with her. (That is, the point on the "weak avoidance" curve at intersection 2 is higher than the point on the "strong avoidance" curve at intersection 1.) He can come closer to her, but he experiences greater conflict—greater desires *and* greater anxiety—than he did earlier. His torment is greater but also more pleasurable. The hopeful outcome, of course, is a further weakening of the avoidance gradient through the combined action of more therapeutic self-exploration, learning from the actual experiences of increasing intimacy that his anxieties are groundless, and outright extinction of his anxieties.

Freud and other psychoanalysts gradually learned empirically that the most effective way to resolve conflicts was to follow the detour just de-scribed—to "analyze the defenses" first. It might seem more expedient to start by interpreting the unconscious wishes and actively urging a person to gratify them in spite of his conflicts over them. Indeed, Freud often did this early in his career. But this direct method leads to such great conflict that it is doomed to failure. Part B of Figure 19-1 may explain why this is so. This direct method leaves the strength of the avoidance motives and re-sponses unchanged; its only effect is to increase the strength of the approach drives and responses. A comparison of the two intersections within part B shows that this method will cause the person to experience very great anx-iety—and he will still not reach the goal. Comparing the strengths of the avoidance tendencies at intersection 2 of both parts A and B makes it clear that the first method—decreasing the defenses and their underlying avoidance motives—brings the person just as close to the goal, with less in-tense anxiety and conflict. Being less miserable, he is less likely to flee therapy and can more easily progress in unlearning his irrational anxieties. Throwing people into deep water is not a very good way to help them learn to swim; most of them will have to be rescued and will refuse to try again. Increasing the approach gradient is simply a way of trying to over-power one's defenses. The result is the same as any other direct interference with defenses—an over-reaction of anxiety or renewed defensive efforts.

A complete discussion of the negative therapeutic reaction would lead us into the masochistic gratification of an unconscious need for punishment and suffering many people obtain from their neuroses, and their resulting negative reactions to what seems to be technically correct therapy. But we have been mainly interested here in those aversive events in therapy that are related to the direct interference with defenses.

Interference with Reality Contact

Imagine yourself floating in a balloon at 60,000 feet or lying in bed, halfway between wakefulness and sleep. Or picture yourself suspended for hours in a tank of water maintained at the same temperature as your body. The light level is constant, and no noise reaches you. You are alone, attached to the outside world by an oxygen line and a microphone cable over which you can report how you feel. All these situations represent an *interference with reality contact*: an absence of direct human contact and a marked decrement in sensory stimulation. Furthermore, the small amount of sensory input that exists is monotonously constant and of very low in-tensity.

Many people—among them Arctic explorers, astronauts, prison wardens and inmates familiar with solitary confinement, physicians caring for patients isolated in hospital beds, and psychotherapists—have long known that *sensory deprivation*, or *interference with reality contact*, has marked effects on be-havior.

The pioneering experimental investigations started in 1951, when Hebb, Bexton, Heron, and Scott paid college students to spend time in a condition of sensory deprivation (Bexton, Heron, & Scott, 1954). The subjects lay on comfortable beds in a lighted, semisoundproof chamber (see Figure 19-2). They wore translucent goggles, which passed a uniform, diffuse light to their eyes but prevented patterned *vision;* cotton gloves and long cardboard cuffs decreased their *tactile perception. Auditory perception* was reduced by means of the semisoundproofing, by a U-shaped foam rubber pillow, and by the masking noise of the air-conditioning equipment. *Time perception* was also curtailed; as far as possible, the subjects were prevented from finding out the time.

At all times the experimenter on duty could observe the subjects through the observation windows, and the subjects and experimenter could converse when absolutely necessary over microphone-speaker systems. The subjects were fed in the chamber and were allowed to go to the toilet in an adjacent room. On the average, the subjects had only 2 to 3 hours a day of these interruptions in the sensory monotony. (Figure 19-2 also shows wires leading from the subject's scalp. These recorded the electrical activity of the brain.)

Few subjects could endure this situation for more than 2 or 3 days. Sooner or later they became bored and *craved stimulation.* And they very frequently had *intense emotional experiences,* including anxiety. Since

Figure 19-2 The kind of experimental situation used in Heron's (1961) studies of sensory deprivation, as it would appear from above with the ceiling removed. The air-conditioning unit is above the foot of the bed.

arousal of anxiety is our chief interest in these experiments, we shall discuss only those aspects of sensory deprivation experiments that are relevant to it.

ANXIETY-PROVOKING EXPERIENCES

The decrease in reality contact is not inherently noxious; some people even enjoy it. Yet many subjects in many subsequent experiments have also become extremely frightened. Some have been unable to tolerate the situation for more than a few hours. Interviews reveal why: The interference with reality contact produces a variety of other experiences that, according to many subjects, arouse anxiety. The following are examples of the most extreme reactions; effects vary greatly from one experiment to another.

**Loss of Control
of the Thinking Process** Many subjects report an inability to concentrate. Instead they experience a "jumble of thoughts with no rhyme or reason [Smith & Lewty, 1959]." Some are unable to "think about anything to think about [Heron, 1961]." Many are frightened by such changes in their self-control because they feel they are becoming insane (Smith & Lewty, 1959; Cohen, Silverman, Bressler, & Shmavonian, 1961).

Images and Hallucinations One subject saw objects moving toward his face and was observed jerking his head back in response (Heron, 1961). Others reported seeing "a face covered with horrible red spots and lumps," "a large wheat field waving in the wind," and a "burning tree [Zubek, Aftanas, Kovach, Wilgosh, & Winocur, 1963]." Most of the hallucinations are visual, but other senses may be involved. One subject, for example, "heard" someone breathing and walking about the isolation room and panicked when she *smelled* something burning (Zuckerman, Albright, Marks, & Miller, 1962). Another subject heard her sisters' voices speaking, often to each other (Azima, Vispo, & Azima, 1961).

**Changes
in Body Image** This kind of perceptual distortion is very frequent. One subject said "My arms aren't here sometimes. . . . They feel to be in the back of my body . . . my head seems to be floating . . . parts of my body keep missing and coming back . . . [Azima, Vispo, & Azima, 1961]." Another subject felt herself getting "smaller and smaller [Zuckerman et al., 1962]"; another feared that his body parts would disappear and disintegrate (Cohen et al., 1961); others felt that their bodies were floating or revolving in space, that their arms or legs were rising, or that one limb was much shorter than another (Zubek et al., 1963). Another felt that his arm was "like a ton-weight and feels fatter than my body [Smith & Lewty, 1959]." Some subjects feel they cannot control their muscles. Thus, one young man was afraid he could not speak when he wanted to and later feared he was unable to move (Cohen et al., 1961).

These alterations in self-perception may even reach the point of depersonalization, where a person perceives his body, or part of it, as an external object. One subject saw his head before him protruding from a purple cloud (Zubek et al., 1963).

Fantasies   Fantasies—pleasant and unpleasant—frequently dominate the subject's stream of experience, and they may become so vivid as to be nearly delusional. Sometimes the person's most cherished wishes are represented as fulfilled. One subject who longed to be a missionary in Africa became deeply engrossed in a vivid fantasy that she was drifting in a rocking boat along a jungle river (Zuckerman et al., 1962).

Unpleasant fantasies also occur. One 20-year-old woman started to imagine that she was locked in the experimental room. While she knew this was not true, she could not get rid of the idea. She became so unnerved that she had to stop participating in the study (Smith & Lewty, 1959). In another study (Cohen et al., 1961) two female subjects imagined that the oxygen in the room would be used up and they would suffocate. A male subject in the same study fantasied that he was continually being watched, although the room was dark and the observation window was covered with black board, and he imagined that he was somehow in danger. When he then heard a slight variation in the noise of the ventilating fan, he fantasied that someone was scooting about the chamber seated in a captain's chair and was rapidly turning some dials that "had something to do with the chamber."

The fantasies may reflect the person's characteristic concerns. In one experimental setup (Mendelson, Kubzansky, Leiderman, Wexler, & Solomon, 1961) the subjects fed themselves whenever they wanted food by sucking nourishing eggnog from a glass tube. One subject took a sip shortly after entering the isolation chamber. It tasted cool to him, yet he fantasied that bacteria were growing in the eggnog that was trapped in the feeding tube, that these bacteria were poisoning him, and that his body then started to produce a counterpoison. This very vivid fantasy was one reason he quit the experiment after about 3½ hours. The fantasy was a continuation of trends present in his everyday experience. Thus, when he smoked cigarettes he became preoccupied with thoughts of getting lung cancer, and when he entered a building housing tuberculosis patients he feared that he would develop tuberculosis. Apparently he could normally control such thoughts; but with the decrement of external stimulation they became very prominent.

**Emergence
of Conflicted Wishes**   Some subjects acknowledged that very disturbing wishes dominated their thoughts during sensory deprivation. After 2 hours of sensory deprivation, one sub-

ject told an interviewer that he was panicky. But he could not admit the cause of this intense anxiety until the following day, when another interviewer was very supportive and reassured him that the condition itself often produced bizarre effects in many people over which they had no control. The man then told how he had been overwhelmed by homosexual fantasies when he was in the chamber by himself. Furthermore, these fantasies had persisted into the first interview and involved his feeling for the first interviewer (Cohen et al., 1961).

The experiences that have been described here are not limited to experimental situations or to real-life situations in which sensory deprivation is *imposed from without*. They may also occur when contact with reality is reduced by a withdrawal of attention and interest from it. The hermit's seclusion, the hospitalized patient's psychosis, the drug addict's "trip," and the neurotic person's daily sessions with a psychoanalyst at times exemplify the condition. A more common instance of a decrease in reality contact is the transition between sleep and wakefulness.

THE TRANSITION BETWEEN SLEEP AND WAKEFULNESS

Most of us can recall lying half-awake in the middle of the night, preoccupied with a vivid fantasy in which we have imagined satisfying all kinds of sexual and aggressive wishes that we did not care to admit to ourselves the next day. And in that twilight state we have all been caught up in fantasies in which the day's frustrations have been overcome or some harrowing experience has been relived so vividly that our hearts pounded and we were brought to our feet wide-awake.

Many people experience at night the kinds of changes in the body image that subjects experience during the sensory deprivation experiment. One young woman occasionally felt that her body was many times larger than its actual size and that her flesh was puffy and spongy. As there, the alterations in body image may extend to the point of depersonalization. This young woman recalled vividly an experience she used to have when she was 8 years old: While falling asleep she used to "see" her body, in the form of an amorphous, gelatinous shape, in the corner of the room. Federn (1952) reported that one of his psychoanalytic patients had an unusually pleasant, vivid sexual dream and felt, on suddenly awakening, as if his body was lying beside him and did not belong to him.

Many other alterations in body image seem to be just as intimately related to the subject's sexual life.

One young man reported frequently lying in bed with a sensation that his right leg ended at his knee. The "disappearance" of the lower part of his leg appeared to be related to a repressed memory of an early childhood experience. Once he had slept with his father after a long separation. He awoke in the night to find that he was touching his father's erect penis with his foot, which had slipped inside his father's pajamas. He fell back to sleep in that position, feeling that it was wonderful to be with his father again. The body-image distortion occurred at a point in his psychoanalysis when his love for his father was especially intense but repressed. It was as if, at these times, he longed to relive that remembered experience of touching his father's penis with his foot, an episode of intimacy and of directly experiencing his father's strength. But it was as if he also had to withdraw his attention completely from his foot and leg in order to keep the memory repressed.

The change the young woman felt in the size of her body was also related to her sexual life. It would occur when she became exceptionally aroused and then suddenly repressed her voluptuous sensations.

Vivid imagery, approaching hallucinatory intensity, is not unusual during the sleep-wakefulness transition. One instance of this was the young girl's terrifying perception that a "bad man" was coming into her bedroom to get her (page 309).

Difficulty in concentrating, in controlling one's train of thought, may also occur. When we try to think through something logically as we drop off to sleep, our thoughts eventually ramble. Sometimes we suddenly realize that our thoughts have been jumping wildly about for some time and that we cannot retrace their sequence.

Many people do not enjoy these experiences. Some are so frightened by them that they avoid the transitional stage and thereby develop insomnia. Some resort to sleeping pills or alcohol, not only in order to sleep but to avoid the transitional stage of the decrease in reality contact. Others compulsively read themselves to sleep, clinging to a tenuous contact with reality as they pass through the transitional stage.

WHY LOSS OF REALITY IS DISTURBING

What is so disturbing about the interference with reality contact? The observations that have been presented here suggest two sources of discomfort.

Weakening of Defenses   The first is a weakening of defenses. Inherently frightening memories and fantasies may emerge from repression, as do sexual and aggressive sensations, memories, and wishful fantasies. When they do, the anxiety and guilt prompted by them, which normally motivate mitigating defenses, are intensely experienced. So far we are in familiar territory: This source of discomfort stems from the subject's unconscious conflicts because of an interference with his defenses. But we have also encountered something new: the realization that *normal contact with reality (a normal kind and amount of sensory input) is an important condition for the maintenance of defenses.*

The second source of discomfort is the loss of the *mode,* or *form,* of thinking and perceiving that is characteristic of normal waking life. The inability to concentrate, the perception of the world largely from an egocentric point of view, the loss of an integrated body image, and the intrusions of hallucinations or images that allow forbidden wishes to emerge into consciousness—all these represent a shift from a more or less logically organized, modulated style to a primitive form of behavior, thought, and experience. In psychoanalytic terminology, there is a shift from a more *secondary process* to a more *primary process* mode of functioning (Freud, 1900, Chapter 7). "Secondary process modes of functioning" refers to the way we usually think and act when we are awake: with words, with a logical organization, and with our emotions kept within reasonable bounds. "Primary process modes of functioning" refers to more primitive forms of behavior, such as that found in dreams: thinking in the form of sensory images like pictures, in an illogical manner, and with emotional controls largely removed. Freud called the latter "primary" because he considered them to be characteristic of the conscious behavior of infancy and also of the unconscious processes of adults. He called the former "secondary" because he regarded them as developing during the course of life and also as characteristic of the conscious thinking and behavior of adults. In other words, he believed that adult unconscious functioning retained the characteristics of conscious childhood functioning.

Rapaport (1958) made the general formulation that *continued contact with reality is a prerequisite for maintaining the more mature secondary process mode of functioning and, indeed, for keeping all our behavior relatively free from domination by our basic drives.* Developments in neurophysiology complement this formulation nicely. Magoun and others (whose work is reviewed in Lindsley, 1961) have identified a system in the brain known as the *reticular activating system,* which "alerts" or "arouses" the cortex of the brain in the presence of sensory input to the sense organs. The brain-wave pattern this system arouses is characteristic of the waking, alert state only; sleeping or drowsy animals show a different pattern. Stimulation of the reticular system will make a sleeping animal alert and also improves the actual capacity of the brain to make fine stimulus discriminations. It thus appears that behavior during normal wakefulness and during sensory deprivation have different neurophysiological counterparts.

The shift in the *form* of functioning and experiencing—from the more secondary process to the more primary process modes—itself distresses some people greatly when they experience it. Present knowledge indicates that this shift is distressing when the person cannot, or feels that he cannot, control it. At such times people may be terrified that they are losing self-control, going insane, or experiencing disintegration of their personalities. This type of anxiety is called *fear of the loss of one's ego organization* (Waelder, 1930; A. Freud, 1936). (It is closely related to the concept of fear of personal vulnerability, which is discussed in Part I.) It appears to be just as disturbing and just as potent a motive for defense as any of the other anxieties and unpleasant affects we have discussed.

Formulations such as these, especially Rapaport's, suggested an interesting study to Goldberger and Holt (1961). They reasoned that a measure of the extent to which a shift toward the primary process disturbed an individual in one situation—in this case the Rorschach Test (described in Part IV)—should be related to the degree of emotional disturbance experienced by the same individual in the sensory deprivation experiment. They began by administering the Rorschach Test to a group of college students. They measured the amount of primary process functioning during the test performance and the extent to which each student was disturbed by such functioning. These measures were obtained by a special Rorschach scoring system Holt had devised previously (Holt, 1956). Next they ranked the subjects according to the *ease* with which they could tolerate shifts to the primary process mode. Top ranks were given to those students who could readily engage in primary process functioning without becoming anxious or defensive; low ranks were assigned to those subjects who frequently shifted to primary process functioning and became very disturbed because of it; middle ranks were assigned to students who rarely engaged in the primary process. Presumably these last students were also afraid to do so, but were able to avoid it in the testing situation.

The experimenters then observed the students in the sensory deprivation situation. They found that the more disturbed a student was by primitive perceptions, thoughts, and drive expressions in the Rorschach Test, the more likely he was to react to sensory deprivation with unpleasant affect and with thoughts about quitting the experiment. He was especially more likely to avoid going to sleep. Perhaps the partial loss of reality achieved by the experimental procedure was frightening enough, and the subjects did not want it intensified by the further sensory isolation of sleep.

In any event, this study demonstrated that the *formal* shift to primitive modes of functioning is very disturbing for some people, less so for others, and pleasant for still others. It strongly suggests that when this shift is induced by decreased reality contact, it frightens the same people who are also frightened by it under other conditions. Perhaps the tolerance for the shift to primary process is a general personality attribute that determines how disturbed a person will become in many types of situations that involve sensory deprivation. If so, measures of this tolerance may prove to have practical value in the selection of pilots, astronauts, or other skilled technicians for jobs that involve prolonged exposure to monotonous conditions.

> "Well! my dear Pangloss," said Candide, "when you were hanged, dissected, stunned with blows and made to row in the galleys, did you always think that everything was for the best in this world?"
>
> "I am still of my first opinion," replied Pangloss.
>
> V O L T A I R E . Candide

CHAPTER 20
DEFENSE AGAINST UNPLEASANT EXTERNAL SITUATIONS

W e have discussed a variety of stimulus situations
that produce unpleasant emotional reactions
in most people in our Western culture.
We began, in Chapter 16, by describing
the six categories of "realistic," or objective,
external dangers. To recapitulate, the categories were as follows:

1. Frustration of basic drives
2. Separation from a protector
3. Loss of love (rejection by a loved person)
4. Loss of a love object (separation from a loved and loving person through death, long-term separation, or renunciation)
5. Loss of self-esteem
6. Threats to physical integrity

Then we added "unrealistic" external dangers to the list:

7. Innocuous stimuli that have been associated with or resemble "realistic" external dangers (Chapter 16)
8. Innocuous or potentially pleasant stimulus situations that produce an inner conflict by

a. arousing conflictful unconscious fantasies or wishes (Chapters 16–18) or

    b. interfering with the functioning of defenses (Chapter 19)

9. Interference with reality contact (Chapter 19)

Man's behavior in these situations ranges from adaptive mastery to domination by unpleasant emotions and utter helplessness, with the process of defense falling between the two poles.

As we saw in Chapter 13, some defenses prevent unpleasant emotional experiences by interfering with the impact or perception of the external stimuli that give rise to them. We have mentioned most of these defenses already, but in this chapter we shall discuss them systematically and in detail.

Escape and Simple Avoidance

Reflexive withdrawal of one's hand from a hot stove is the simplest way to stop the pain and the tissue damage. The withdrawal reflex is simultaneously an innate adaptive mechanism and also the simplest known defense. This reaction, like all withdrawal reactions, *halts an unpleasant experience.* All defenses share precisely this experiential effect; they differ only in the means of achieving it. In this example an elementary motor act removes the sense organs from the external stimulus source, thereby disrupting at its origin the chain of events leading to the experience of pain.

But withdrawal reflexes are inadequate and even irrelevant under most circumstances: those circumstances in which man's inner needs and special capacities are very important in determining the danger. Frustration, separation from a nurturant figure, and permanent loss of a loved one can produce a state of *continual* and intense *inner* drive stimulation. These internal states give rise not only to distressful physical sensations (for example, feelings of thirst, hunger, and cold) but also to a sense of unrelieved tension and even a sense of helplessness. Furthermore, man's capacities to learn and anticipate, to remember and imagine, to engage in inner conflict, and to develop highly organized patterns of behavior create an order of external dangers rarely involving physical pain—for example, separations devoid of actual distressful needs and helplessness, loss of love, and innocuous stimuli that trigger inner conflict. To cope with all these experiences, man must and does develop other mechanisms of defense.

The withdrawal reflex is the prototype for the simplest of these additional mechanisms: *escape and physical avoidance* achieved by motor behavior that is more complex than mere reflexes. Since this defense is so elementary, it is especially characteristic of children. When the small child becomes frightened at being separated from his mother in the middle of the night, he runs into her bed. He literally *escapes* an unpleasant stimulus situation and creates a new, pleasant one, and his anxiety subsides. He can also learn to *avoid* separation perceptions and thus to avoid separation anxiety. For example, he soon learns to cling tenaciously to his mother as she is about to leave him, if she rewards this behavior by not leaving him alone.

Older children may develop "school phobias" to avoid separation from their mothers. There are even many adults who refuse more promising jobs with new, young, aggressively liberal employers to avoid the anxiety of separating from benignly paternalistic, autocratic ones. Erich Fromm (1941) presented a substantial discussion of this "escape from freedom."

Escape and avoidance may be used to defend against any unpleasant situation, not just that of separation. Ed avoided sexual intimacy with his wife to prevent the castration anxiety produced by the incestuous significance of making love with his wife. Many subjects escaped from the sensory deprivation experiments when that interference with reality contact frightened them. People often break off a close but unsatisfying relationship to escape from frustration. A student may avoid having conferences with an especially critical teacher who threatens his self-esteem. Other examples of flight from "realistic" and "unrealistic" danger situations are familiar to everyone.

THE PROBLEM OF INTIMACY AND ISOLATION

Erikson (1959) has underscored the importance of the capacity for physical and psychological intimacy—for *personal intimacy*, let us say. *Isolation* and *self-absorption*, Erikson points out, are the fate of the person who cannot enter into intimate relationships with other people. He believes that this capacity is a prerequisite for the *ability both to love and to work well* (abilities that Freud once proposed as the basic, empirical criteria of normality). But intimacy *is* a danger for many people. The list of danger situations presented at the beginning of this chapter and the examples that have been cited show why: Nearly all of them are strictly interpersonal, and, generally speaking, their intensity varies directly with the degree of intimacy involved. A person will never experience any stronger separation anxiety, any deeper hurt or fear of loss of love, any sadder grief, or any humiliation so painful as that which might arise out of intimacy. Furthermore, intimacy brings with it the *potential* for *all* the unpleasant experiences we have discussed.

Many young people flee from intimacy because they experience in it one or more of those dangers. As a result, they enter adulthood without the capacity for intimacy. A few gradually discover that human closeness is not so dangerous, and they belatedly develop the capacity. Social isolation is the fate of the others. "Loners" may appear to be strong, contented, and self-sufficient, even to themselves. But this is a deceptive image. This defensive escape from intimacy brings with it all the misery that a loss of love entails.

Marriage and family life and some other patterns of interpersonal relationships may camouflage an escape from intimacy. Flighty, superficial, and ritualized social interaction—epitomized by the "cocktail hour" of executive suburbia (and some academic and professional circles)—is a sham intimacy, a pretentious togetherness concealing a defensive aloneness. A married couple may one day realize that they are actually strangers. They discover that they spend very little time together (one or both of them always have "homework" that simply must be done). They may not even sleep in the same room, let alone the same bed ("I can't sleep with all that snoring and tossing and turning," or "I'll sleep in the other room again, dear, because I'll be late coming to bed again tonight"). Of course, the sheer quantity of time spent together is no gauge or guarantee of intimacy; even a small amount of the right quality can suffice.

Denial

Escape and avoidance achieve their defensive effects by removing the sense organs from the effective action of external stimuli. In this way they interrupt the chain of events leading to unpleasant perceptions and distressful emotional experience. But perception is an active process, controlled in part by internal processes.

The *distribution of attention* determines whether or not we perceive physical stimuli impinging on our sense organs. If we concentrate on carefully reading a difficult book, we do not hear a song being played on the radio. By withdrawing our attention from noises, we can stop hearing them and go to sleep. The stimuli may be *registered* in our nervous system, but we do not *perceive* them. The same withdrawal and shifts in attention can and usually do occur unconsciously. All day long we unconsciously *selectively* perceive the world about us. Man can prevent unpleasant perceptions by varying his attention and by wishful perceiving or thinking. Unconscious distortion of perception of external stimuli that arouse unpleasant emotions is called *denial*. Denial is a *nonverbal* reaction that alters the *perception* of external stimuli. (Another defensive process, called *negation*, is verbal and cognitive. A person is using this defense when he says or thinks to himself, "No, I don't hate you" or "I don't love you" when his unconscious feelings are just the opposite.)

The simplest form of denial is blotting out the perception by withdrawing our attention from it. In this way we may fail to see a snake in the middle of a trail or an angry facial expression or fail to hear a criticism or our mother's loving tone when she mentions our brother's name. We may fail to perceive sexually attractive qualities in a person who is the object of an unconscious approach-avoidance sexual conflict. If we have an unconscious conflict over responding aggressively, we may fail to perceive another person's provocations to anger. Withdrawal of attention, then, may produce *"perceptual blanks."*

People frequently *"fill in the blanks"* with wish-fulfilling perceptions. Duane did this in his transitory perceptions of his father, as we discussed in Chapter 12. The most extreme outcome of this process is the wish-fulfilling hallucinatory world of psychosis. In his first published discussion of denial (1894) Freud wrote of a woman who had fallen in love with a man who frequently visited her home.

> She thought he came to see her out of love for *her*. But he had really been using her to gain access to another woman in the household. When that other relationship failed, he stopped coming. We can imagine that the woman suffered greatly—frustration, a sense of rejection, humiliation, grief, and intense conflicted anger at the man. Eventually she hallucinated that he was continually there with her. She was denying on a grand scale the perception of a tormenting reality.

Filling in the blanks with wish-fulfilling perceptions increases the defensive effectiveness of denial. It dissolves the tension of ungratified wishes and evokes pleasant affects. It also provides an obstacle to the reappearance of the unpleasant blanked-out perceptions. Life's unpleasant facts keep knocking at the door of consciousness, but our attention does not go to open the door and help them across the threshold. It is preoccupied, preempted by the pleasant perceptions that have already forcibly entered the mind's room. The price of this defensive gain can be high: an inability to live in the real world. But denial usually stops short of the hallucinatory extreme of psychosis: In the adult, wishful thinking and even the tendency to it are usually restricted by being tested against reality. Not so with the child, however, whose behavior conforms more to the pleasure principle than to the reality principle. Children, then, give us our clearest examples of *denial in fantasy and action.*

DENIAL IN CHILDREN

Children often resort to denial in fantasy and action, according to Anna Freud (1936), when they are confronted by any unpleasant situation. Little Hans (Freud, 1909a), whom we discussed earlier (pages 263, 277), provides an example of how children may deny in fantasy stimuli that arouse a feeling of being unloved.

> Little Hans was 3 years old when his sister Hanna was born. Previously his only rival for his mother's love had been his father. Now he had to share it with Hanna, too. He witnessed many unpleasant scenes that made him long for the "good old days." Often he watched Hanna being bathed, toileted, and caressed by his mother. Eventually he denied such distasteful sights by fantasying that he had many children of his own, whom he cared for lovingly. In the fantasy he participated in the kind of pleasant experiences enjoyed by Hanna and his mother.
>
> Because of his Oedipal love for his mother, Little Hans also found it very

disagreeable to see reminders of his father's relationship to his mother. Hans denied this situation with a fantasy in which he was married to his mother, she was the mother of *his* children, and Hans's father was married to *his own* mother.

Hans also used fantasy to ease his fear that his father would castrate him. He imagined that his father, who was disguised as a plumber in the fantasy, robbed him of his little penis *but* replaced it with a big one. This fantasy denial so relieved Little Hans of his castration anxiety that it appeared to have brought his fear of horses—which was partly a disguised fear of being castrated by his father—to an end. Here we have a vivid demonstration of the defensive effectiveness of denial in fantasy.

We have discussed how inferior, worthless, and envious little girls feel when they recognize that they do not have a penis. Many girls relieve themselves of this painful loss of self-esteem by denying the perceptions of their female physical characteristics. One lovely 3-year-old girl, having seen little boys urinating while they ran wildly around the yard, pretended to do the same thing at home. She would take off her clothes, press back her labia with her fingers so as to expose her clitoris, and run excitedly around the room, screaming in frantic elation, "Look at my tinkler. Look at me tinkling." Later, in a touching conversation with her mother, she sadly admitted that she wanted a "tinkler like Timmie's." Following several discussions in which her loving and sympathetic mother expressed pride in the little girl's femininity and made it clear that they both had bodily things little boys didn't have, the episode of frenzied elation and perceptual denial subsided.

Some girls continue into adolescence and adulthood feeling humiliated and worthless and envying maleness upon perceiving their own femaleness. Two such women were described in Chapter 16. Another, in adolescence, dressed in boy's clothes and bore a short stick inside one trouser leg in order to appear to have a penis. She no longer did this as a young adult, but she still walked with a marked mannish gait and carried her head and body in the characteristic fashion of her father.

We shall now consider some other uses of denial.

EXPERIMENTAL STUDIES OF DENIAL

One of the most devastating results of social discrimination is that members of minority groups may internalize the derogatory values and attitudes of the majority and regard themselves as inferior or worthless. When they do, the perception in themselves of characteristics singled out by the majority for derogation is the basis for a marked loss of self-esteem. One way out is to deny the perceptions of these characteristics in oneself. An experiment by K. B. and M. P. Clark (1958), prominent Negro psychologists in New York City, showed clearly how Negro children denied their own skin color. This was one of the psychological studies cited in the

1954 decision by the U.S. Supreme Court that racial segregation in public schools is unconstitutional (United States Reports, 347).

The Clarks administered a Dolls Test to 253 Negro children ranging from 3 to 7 years of age. In this test the Clarks presented the children with both brown dolls and white ones and asked the children to answer a series of questions by selecting the appropriate doll. The questions fell into three categories. The first category determined if the children perceived accurately the racial, skin-color characteristic—for example, "Give me the doll that looks like a white child, . . . a colored child, . . . a Negro child." The second category determined the affective attitude toward the dolls—which one was a "nice doll," which was a "nice color," which "looks bad," and which they would like to play with or liked best. Finally, the children were asked, "Give me the doll that looks like you."

The results were all too clear-cut. Most of the children accurately perceived the racial characteristic of skin color; they could select correctly the doll that looked like a white child or a Negro child. Table 20-1 sum-

Table 20-1   Affective Responses and Self-Perceptions of Negro 3-Year-Olds and 7-Year-Olds in the Dolls Test

Instruction and Choices	Responses	
	3-Year-Olds	7-Year-Olds
"Give me the doll that looks bad."		
Colored doll	68%	43%
White doll	19	17
No choice	13	40
"Give me the doll that looks like you."		
Colored doll	36	87
White doll	61	13
No choice	3	0

Based on data from K. B. & M. P. Clark, 1958.

marizes the results that primarily concern us. The prominence of an internalized, negative self-image is clearly shown: 68 percent of the 3-year-olds saw the *brown* doll as looking "bad"! The bottom group of numbers reveals the frequency of denial at this age level: 61 percent saw the *white* doll as resembling *themselves*. These data strongly suggest that the majority of the younger Negro children denied their *own* skin color in order to avoid the painfully low self-esteem associated with its accurate perception. The following observations by the experimenters support this inference.

> Some of the children who were free and relaxed in the beginning of the experiment broke down and cried or became somewhat negativistic during

the latter part when they were required to make self-identifications. Indeed, two children ran out of the testing room, unconsolable, convulsed in tears. . . . A northern five-year-old dark child felt compelled to explain his identification with the brown doll by making the following unsolicited statement: "I burned my face and made it spoil." A seven-year-old northern light child went to great pains to explain that he is actually white but: "I look brown because I got a suntan in the summer" [K. B. & M. P. Clark, 1958, p. 611].

The data for the 7-year-olds show the decrease in denial with increasing age: 43 percent of these children still judged brown skin to be "bad," but only 13 percent denied their own skin color. Even this, of course, is a high percentage.

The fact that 3-year-old Negro children had internalized values should not surprise us, for the general phenomenon of internalization in small children has already been discussed. The white man's world touches such young children in many ways that could transmit the negative attitude of the majority of white people toward the Negro. But it seems quite likely that the parents of the Negro children had themselves internalized the white man's attitude that dark skin is "bad" and had passed it on to their children. In his recent autobiography, *Manchild in the Promised Land*, Claude Brown, a Negro, portrays his father's negative view of dark skin and how he explicitly transmitted that view. We can be sure that there is also a great deal of implicit communication of the same value from the time the child is born.

Papa used to make me mad with, "Who was that old boy you was with today, that old tar-black boy?" . . .

I knew that Pimp [Brown's younger brother] was at an age when he'd be bringing his friends around, and Papa would be talking that same stuff about, "Who's that black so-and-so?" If you brought somebody to the house who was real light-skinned, Papa would say, "They're nice," or "They're nice lookin'." . . .

I remember one time when Papa was telling his favorite story about how he could have passed for white when he first came to New York and moved down on the Lower East Side. He became a janitor of a building there. He said everybody thought he was white until they saw Uncle McKay. . . . Papa said if it wasn't for McKay, he could have passed for white. This story used to get on my nerves, and I thought it was probably bothering Pimp now too. Sometimes I wanted to tell him, "Shit, man, why don't you just go on some place where you can pass for white, if that's the way you feel about it? And stop sitting here with all us real colored niggers and talkin' about it." . . .

I wondered if it was good for him to be around all that old crazy talk, because I imagined that all my uncles who were dark-skinned—Uncle McKay, Uncle Ted, Uncle Brother—felt that Papa didn't care too much for them because they were dark-skinned, and I supposed that Pimp might have gotten that feeling too [Brown, 1965, pp. 276–77].

Anyone who reads this remarkable book will realize that Claude Brown's awareness of the devastating effects of the transmission of the negative self-image by Negro parents, and of course by white people, and his protest against it were intimately involved in his victory over such effects.

Why do some Negro parents add to the misery their children must bear in a generally white society? Claude Brown's father had to maintain his own self-esteem in a world bent on devastating it. This is what he was doing when he unconsciously internalized the white man's negative attitude toward black skin. (We shall discuss this process in more detail in a moment.)

The Mark of Oppression by Kardiner and Ovesey (1951), psycho-analysts especially interested in the relationship between man and society, shows by the case study method the extent to which the self-esteem of their Negro subjects was damaged by the social climate in America. That climate, of course, is now changing so rapidly that the presently available studies will soon be outdated. American Negroes are developing an intense pride in their black color and culture. If they continue to do so, and if the attitudes of more and more white people change, future Negro parents and children should be quite different from those reflected in Claude Brown's book and in the studies by the Clarks and by Kardiner and Ovesey.

A study by Tagiuri, Bruner, and Blake (1958) suggests that denial of perceptions of being disliked by the people around us *may* be a more wide-spread process than we realize. These investigators asked sailors, summer campers, and students to express their likes and dislikes for their associates and also to state how they thought their associates felt about them. The subjects' accuracy in perceiving negative attitudes about themselves was poor. This outcome could be due to defensive denial.

Identification

IDENTIFICATION WITH THE AGGRESSOR

We discussed in Chapter 15 how the Oedipal boy defends against his anxiety that his father will castrate him: He adopts his father's moral values and punitive attitudes, applies them to himself, and consequently represses his Oedipal complex. In the process, the boy takes a giant step along the path of superego development. We have just seen how Claude Brown's father had internalized the loathing many white people have for black skin, and we saw indirect evidence that a large number of Negro children had done the same thing by the time they were 3 years old. These are instances of identification with the aggressor.

Anna Freud (1936) relates the following story.

One day a male teacher consulted August Aichorn, a former colleague of Miss Freud and author of a well-known book, *Wayward Youth* (1935). The boy the teacher had brought along with him made odd faces whenever the teacher scolded him in class. The other pupils laughed uproariously at this, and the teacher was at his wits' end: Was the boy intentionally ridiculing him, or was it just a nervous habit? Aichorn noticed that the boy grimaced involuntarily during the interview whenever the teacher became angry. Furthermore, the grimaces were a caricature of the teacher's angry look. Frightened by the facial expression, the boy had unconsciously imitated it.

Anna Freud gives another example of the same process.

A little girl was afraid to cross a hall in the dark for fear she might meet a ghost. She resolved this fear by gesturing peculiarly as she ran across the hall. "There's no need to be afraid in the hall," she explained to her little brother, "you just have to pretend that you're the ghost who might meet you [1936, p. 119]." Copying the aggressor's *physical characteristics* made the fear go away.

In the following example the identification took a slightly different form.

One day a 6-year-old boy in therapy with Anna Freud was noticeably cross and unfriendly with her, and he played very aggressively, cutting into pieces with his knife everything he could lay his hands on. Why? He had just been to the dentist and this "aggressor" had hurt him. The identification here was with the *aggression* of the aggressor, not with his physical characteristics. The boy did not play at being a dentist; he played only at being aggressive, but he did that with a vengeance.

This same child demonstrated still another form of identification with the aggressor—the unconscious adoption of symbols representing *idealized attributes* of the aggressor to bolster his self-esteem as well as to increase his courage. We quote Anna Freud's succinct account of this episode:

On another occasion this little boy came to me just after he had a slight accident. He had been joining in an outdoor game at school and had run full tilt against the fist of the games-master . . . . My little patient's lip was bleeding and his face tear-stained, and he tried to conceal both facts by putting up his hand as a screen. I endeavoured to comfort and reassure him. He was in a woe-begone condition when he left me, but the next day he appeared holding himself very erect and dressed in full armour. On his head he wore a military cap and he had a toy sword at his side and a pistol in his hand. When he saw my surprise at this transformation, he simply said, "I just wanted to have these things on when I was playing with you." He did not, however, play; instead, he sat down and wrote a letter to his mother: "Dear Mummy, please, please, please, please send me the pocket-knife you promised me and don't wait till Easter!" Here again we cannot say that, in order to master the anxiety-experience of the previous day, he was impersonating the teacher with whom he had collided. Nor, in this instance, was he imitating the latter's aggression. The weapons and armour, being manly attributes, evidently symbolized the teacher's strength and . . , helped the child to identify himself with the masculinity of the adult and so to defend himself against narcissistic mortification or actual mishaps [A. Freud, 1936, pp. 120–21].

These episodes of identification with the aggressor share an underlying pattern:

1. Somebody threatens or distresses a person.
2. The "victim" identifies with some aspect of the "aggressor's" behavior that was involved in the aggression: values and consequent criticism, physical features, aggression, a symbol of the strength of the aggressor.
3. Concomitant with or following such identifications the victim's emotional distress disappears.

How does identification with the aggressor provide this relief? Probably by a combination of factors.

When Freud thought about episodes in children's play resembling those we have described, he noticed that they involve the *active* reenactment of a *passive* unpleasant experience (1920a, 1926). The boy with the knife, for example, "hurt" other things by cutting them up after he had been hurt by the dentist. The change from helpless passivity to doing something, anything, always makes one feel better. This relief produced by activity does not necessarily have a realistic basis. The grimacing boy, for example, infuriated his teacher. Realistically based or not, the relief seems to come about from internal changes. Activity releases or dissipates the physiological and psychological tension produced by traumatic stimulation. But probably more important is the *change in self-perception* brought about by actively identifying with the aggressor. Bodily sensations of helplessness and passivity cease. One perceives in one's own behavior qualities of the aggressor—a facial expression, articles of clothing, aggressiveness. Most important, one perceives oneself as the aggressor, not as the victim. This is only possible because one is *fantasying* that he is the aggressor. The little girl deliberately and overtly imagined she was the feared ghost; others do the same thing unconsciously.

A blatant example of this phenomenon in adults is the "you can't fire me, I quit" stereotype. Fearing he will be fired, the employee turns the tables. The student who suffers at the hands of a strict and critical teacher frequently acts the same way in class discussions or when he writes his term paper. Now *he* tears to shreds the work of leading thinkers.

IDENTIFICATION WITH THE AGGRESSOR
IN EXTREME SITUATIONS

The same defensive mechanism we have been discussing produces one of the most insidious consequences of organized hostility and sadism in prisons and other authoritarian situations: It induces detrimental personality changes in the victim. Such identifications, however, may enable the victims to cope with their immediate, extreme situations.

In 1938 the Nazis imprisoned Bruno Bettelheim, a Jewish Viennese psychoanalyst who is now one of the leading analysts and child therapists in America. Bettelheim endured a year at Dachau and Buchenwald, two particularly notorious concentration camps. Partly to help ward off the disintegration of his personality, he carefully observed how the victims reacted to the extremely cruel, inhuman conditions of these camps (Bettelheim, 1943). One outcome of his observations is a vivid picture of how "old" prisoners—those confined at least 3 years—eventually came to identify with their cruel Gestapo jailers. This was an insidious, unconscious process—a last desperate measure to cope with their extreme condition. The identifications involved the physical attributes of the Gestapo, their aggression, and their values.

When speaking angrily to other inmates, the old prisoners came to use the vocabulary of the Gestapo. They wore old pieces of Gestapo uniforms or tried to alter their own prison clothes so they would resemble Gestapo uniforms. The old prisoners often treated other inmates just as cruelly as the guards treated them. The Gestapo got rid of "unfit" prisoners—the complainers, those who could not adjust, and those who disobeyed orders or could not work in the labor gangs. Sometimes the old prisoners collaborated with the Gestapo in this weeding out of the unfit. Some prisoners turned traitor, and the others decided it was necessary to kill them if the others were to survive. Identification with their own Gestapo torturers caused the old prisoners to kill these traitors slowly, torturing them for days.

Clearly, the old prisoners had internalized Gestapo values, and some came to share the Gestapo's anti-Semitism. (Bettelheim closes his account with the reminder that identification with the Gestapo was but one part of the picture. At times the very same prisoners also acted with extraordinary courage in defying the Gestapo.)

The growing literature about the Negro contains many references to a very similar phenomenon. Kenneth Clark gives many examples of it in *Dark Ghetto* (1965), ranging from hair straightening and skin bleaching to an abandonment of Negro values and culture for the white man's. Friedman (1966) describes a young Negro woman who had completely identified with the white man's values and racial attitudes, even to the point of unknowingly referring to Negroes as "they," unconsciously accepting the concept of "black gorilla," which her parents had called her as a child, and avoiding most pleasures in life because they seemed "niggerlike." The journalist Jack Newfield (1966) tells of a Negro kitchen worker at the store in Greensboro, North Carolina, where the first sit-in occurred. She spoke like some white Southerners when she called the original sit-inners "a disgrace to their race" and "ignorant." According to Newfield, many parents of Negro leaders in the nonviolent civil rights movement expressed the same attitudes about them. Several presidents of southern Negro colleges suspended students who participated in the growing movement. Those who take this stand, of course, are regarded as "Uncle Toms" and as "white man's niggers" by many Negro parents and educators who take pride in the civil rights activities of young Negro adults. Much of the meaning of their epithets lies in their allusion to the tendency of the more conservative Negroes to identify with the white aggressors. (Sarnoff [1951] indicates that the same process may be involved in the psychodynamics of the anti-Semitic Jew.)

IDENTIFICATION WITH THE AGGRESSOR
AND SUPEREGO FORMATION

We are now in a better position than we were in Chapter 15 to discuss the hypothesis that identification with the aggressor plays an important part in superego development.

Defensive identification with the aggressor consists essentially of unconsciously imitating attributes of a feared person—his values, his aggression, and the form of his aggressive expression, for example—and the consequent relief from distressing affect. The internal regulation of behavior by one's superego involves not only the internalization of values (notably those of parents) but also the "awakening" of those values by one's wishes and feelings, the subjugation of these to one's values, and self-criticism for transgressions. Thus, it is a big jump from the relatively simple phenomenon of defensive identification with the aggressor to self-controlled, conscience-regulated behavior. If this hypothesis—that identification with the aggressor plays an important role in superego development—is valid, identification with the aggressor in childhood should reflect the transition. We shall cite here some illustrative observations indicating that the transitional forms do occur, and we shall suggest their nature.

Anna Freud (1936) describes a curious pattern of behavior shown by a boy who lived in a children's home.

He used to ring the entrance bell very loudly and then, while waiting for the housemaid to let him in, would become frightened that she would scold him for making so much noise. When she finally came to the door, *he would angrily scold her,* ostensibly for taking so long to answer the bell. Actually, he was identifying with the aggression he anticipated from her. He was scolding her as he feared she would scold him for his misbehavior.

The following observation, also from Anna Freud, shows that the same anticipation and externally directed aggression can be set in motion even by sexual *thoughts and wishes.*

A 5-year-old boy who was in child analysis with Jenny Waelder in Vienna was usually docile and passive, but episodically he would become "fiercely aggressive." Pretending he was a lion, he would roar and attack Mrs. Waelder. Or he would carry a stick with him and hit everything in sight, pretending he was *a devil who punished naughty children*. He would try to hit his mother and grandmother in the face, and eventually he threatened them with kitchen knives. Mrs. Waelder noticed that each of these outbursts occurred whenever the theme of masturbation was about to come out in his therapy. The outbursts ceased when these tabooed thoughts and feelings did come out and were openly discussed by Mrs. Waelder and himself. In his aggressive episodes he was treating others as his parents had treated him when they had caught him masturbating—they had shouted at him, slapped his face, and beat him with a rod. And he fantasied that they might even cut off his penis with a knife. But his identification was anticipatory, in two senses: Thoughts and wishes that were *about* to become conscious and overt evoked identification *before* any actual punishment occurred.

Both of these observations reveal transitional stages in the step from defensive identification with the aggressor to adult superego functioning. In neither instance is the child simply defending against a past or present external aggression, as in the first observations that were presented on page 359. He is, instead, identifying with an *anticipated punishment*, and this anticipated punishment is *linked with his own behavior*—actual misbehavior or only "bad" thoughts and wishes, even unconscious ones. The child has become a "self-starter" with respect to *his* punitive behavior. But his punitive behavior is not yet directed against himself or even against another guilty person. It is directed only against an external "aggressor."

One can observe children in other additional transitional stages as well. Often they scold other people for projected misdeeds or wishes, for the very things they are beginning to feel anxious and guilty about themselves.

We have discussed here the role of identification with the aggressor in superego formation and functioning. But it is not *only* fear that is involved in these matters. *Love for our parents, especially when we renounce them as sexual love objects, also contributes to identifications that produce many of our ideals.*

IDENTIFICATION WITH THE LOST LOVE OBJECT

We have already seen that people defend against the pain of object loss by identifying with the loved person. Identification with a loved one who has died was described in Part I (Chapter 10). In Chapters 15 and 16 we discussed identification when there is active renunciation of a love relationship. The object loss need not be permanent, as it is in death and Oedipal renunciation, for identification to occur. It need only be painful. People often temporarily identify with the loved one when *unwanted* transient separations are forced upon them.

We shall now consider some important questions about the process of identification that we have not yet discussed.

THE BASIC MECHANISM
OF IDENTIFICATION: AN HYPOTHESIS

"Identification" is a descriptive concept denoting the tendency of one person to acquire personality attributes of another person. Its relationship to object loss and to encounters with aggressors is grounded in empirical, clinical observation. The nature of the mechanism or process that produces identifications is a different matter. Frequently the terms *internalization, incorporation,* and *introjection* are used as though they indicated the nature of the process, but they are little more than metaphors. Some people do have conscious and unconscious fantasies of eating their loved ones, and others have subjective experiences of fusing with other persons, even of complete bodily identity. But, obviously, no one actually takes another person inside himself. The nature of the *mechanism* of achieving an identification is still an open question. Basic ingredients in this process may be our memories of the other person and the matching of our behavior to those memories by carefully observing and correcting ourselves. Such a process would be analogous to that by which children *unknowingly* adopt the precise speech patterns of their parents. There, too, memory traces of someone else's behavior and self-monitoring and self-regulation based on sensory feedback from one's own behavior (the preconscious hearing of one's own speech, for example) are crucial. According to this hypothesis, the identification mechanism is patterned after what Wiener (1948, 1950) calls a *negative-feedback process*. In such a process feedback signals result in the minimizing of any deviations from a preset pattern. The development of speech is a good example.

One real-life example will illustrate the hypothetical process.

A middle-aged man grew a beard for the first time a few months after his father died in a distant part of the country. The son had been told that his father had gone unshaved for several days just before he died, and one relative had emphasized to him the shock she had felt when she had beheld the father's helpless, whiskered face instead of his usual robust, cleanly shaved cheeks and chin. Hearing this, the son pictured clearly how his father must have looked. Then the image vanished. A few weeks after this experience he decided to let his beard grow—"just for kicks." But for days, each time he washed and saw his whiskery image in the mirror, a vision of his dying father's unshaved face flashed before his eyes and he experienced a welling-up of grief. After more than 2 years he shaved the beard off, ostensibly because he had "had his kicks." Actually, it was because his most intense period of mourning had ended. One feature of his behavior illustrates the self-observation and correction—the negative feedback process—mentioned above. He felt comfortable only when he had his beard very short—to match his memory image of his dying father's unshaved face.

Such a process pertains only to the mechanism of identification that might be set in motion by the distress of object loss and threatening aggressors. It does not account for the *relief* of emotional distress provided by identification. We have already discussed on page 360 how identification with the aggressor might provide this relief.

Why does identification with a lost love object ease the grief of object loss? Probably because we unconsciously fantasy that we *are* the lost person and carry on a largely unconscious emotional relationship with the inner replica of the lost object. Miss Eaton unconsciously hated herself in precisely the same way and on the same grounds as she hated her sister. People can love themselves (as identified with the lost object) in much the same way they love any memento or facsimile of the lost object—his picture, clothing, or favorite chair, for example. The man with the beard bestowed all the tender care and affection on his whiskers that he wished he had been able to give his dying father. In fact, his conscious emotional attitude toward his whiskers varied with his unconscious fantasy relationship to his dead father. He loved or hated them (and his father) one day, pitied them another, admired them frequently, and finally gave them up. Like this man, Dora, who developed her father's coughs, and women who adopt their husbands' professions after their deaths all find relief from their grief because unconsciously they have not suffered the loss. In their unconscious fantasies things are still the same.

Ego Restriction

When a person perceives that his accomplishments are inferior to someone else's, his self-esteem is lowered. Many people who cannot tolerate such a situation bring it to an end and prevent it from arising again in the future by simply abandoning the activity involved. Anna Freud first delineated this defense and named it *ego restriction*. The following episode, which occurred during her psychoanalytic treatment of a small boy, illustrates the phenomenon. In her own words,

> One day, when he was at my house, he found a little Magic Drawing-Block, which appealed to him greatly. He began enthusiastically to rub the pages, one by one, with a coloured pencil and was pleased when I did the same. Suddenly, however, he glanced at what I was doing, came to a stop and was evidently upset. The next moment he put down his pencil, pushed the whole apparatus (hitherto jealously guarded) across to me, stood up and said, "You go on doing it; I would much rather watch." Obviously, when he looked at my drawing, it struck him as more beautiful, more skillful or somehow more perfect than his own and the comparison gave him a shock. He instantly decided that he would not compete anymore, since the results were disagreeable, and thereupon he abandoned the activity which, a moment ago, had given him pleasure. *He adopted the role of the spectator, who does nothing and so cannot have his performance compared with that of someone else. By imposing this restriction on himself the child avoided a repetition of the disagreeable impression* [Anna Freud, 1936, p. 101; italics added].

Escape and avoidance of an unpleasant stimulus situation, then, is the essential feature of this defense. But whereas other forms of escape and avoidance usually physically remove the person from an unpleasant situation, ego restriction entails the subject's stopping an *activity* he himself is performing. The abandonment of the activity then becomes permanent and constitutes a restriction in one or more areas of life.

Ego restriction may occur in connection with any activity. The intelligent student who does not study because he is mortified if he does not get an A is engaging in ego restriction. The wife who never entertains at home because she feels her cooking and table-setting are inferior to those of the people she would invite is doing the same thing. Many potential talents lie fallow simply because people cannot tolerate the inevitable imperfections in their first efforts.

Ego restrictions differ from what is commonly meant by *inhibitions,* such as the "stupidity" or ineffectiveness of the intelligent student who *does* study or the chronic stammering and loss of voice of the person who *does* keep trying to speak in public. Unconscious conflicts over sexuality or aggression cause such disturbances, just as they caused the avoidances discussed in Chapters 16–19. Some students, for example, become sexually aroused when they study—either because of the subject matter or because of intellectual activity per se. When this happens, they become anxious or feel guilty, and the stage is set for various kinds of disturbances of studying and learning. Sexual thoughts and feelings can be distracting. Anxiety and guilty feelings can disrupt learning. Or they can motivate defenses, such as a general inhibition of intellectual functioning. Stammering is frequently caused by the inhibition of the urge to speak aggressively. One patient in psychotherapy stammered severely in those interviews when she was afraid to vent her anger at the therapist and the world. But the stammering itself turned out to be an indirect expression of her anger: She admitted to taking a malicious pleasure in the fact that her stammering prevented the therapist from understanding her.

Anna Freud suggested a useful criterion for distinguishing ego restrictions from inhibitions resulting from unconscious conflicts. In ego restrictions the person is perfectly satisfied to give up the activity and turns readily to other activities in which he does not experience insults to his self-esteem. In inhibitions, however, the person does not give up the activity in spite of all the suffering it causes him. In fact, he cannot give it up for the same reason he cannot complete it effectively: because of its sexual or aggressive meaning to him. We might say that he is trapped by his approach-avoidance conflict. In ego restriction, however, there is no *hidden* sexual or aggressive gratification in the abandoned activity. Here the approach gradient is so weak that it never rises above the avoidance gradient. As a result, the individual turns with relief to another activity.

Major Aspects of Defense
Against External Dangers

Summarized here are the major aspects of processes of defense oriented toward external dangers—the danger situations listed at the beginning of this chapter.

1. The interaction of external stimuli and internal motives gives rise to perceptions of the unpleasant external stimuli and to disturbing perceptions of oneself.

2. These perceptions evoke corresponding unpleasant emotional experiences, either for realistic reasons or because they activate unconscious memories, fantasies, or conflicts in the manner illustrated in Chapters 16–19. Motivated by these unpleasant emotions, one can reduce their intensity by adaptive coping or by various defenses. We are concerned here only with defenses.

3. Physically *escaping or avoiding* the relevant external stimuli can terminate any of the various unpleasant emotions previously discussed in this section of the book, ranging from the intense pain of frustration, through separation anxiety, to fear of ego disorganization.

4. *Denial* prevents the realistic perception of unpleasant external stimuli by simply blotting out or distorting the perception. Alterations in the distribution of attention and the substitution of fantasies or hallucinations for the realistic perceptions achieve these results. Denial, too, can terminate any of the unpleasant emotions.

5. *Identification with the dreaded stimulus*, which is nearly always another person, can terminate all the unpleasant emotions. *Identification with an aggressor* who is threatening one's physical welfare is the paradigm of this defense mechanism. In this defense the subject perceives himself to be like the threatening person and thereby perceives that person as less threatening. The subject's conscious and unconscious fantasies, as well as related changes in his overt behavior, form the bases for these changes in perception of self and of external stimuli.

6. *Identification with a lost or renounced love object* eases the pain of loss. Unconscious fantasies that he is the lost person, and related changes in overt behavior, alter the subject's self-perception. In his unconscious fantasies he is now both himself and the lost object and perpetuates within himself the emotional relationship that existed between himself and the object.

7. *Ego restriction* protects one from the loss of self-esteem. By abandoning his attempts at achievement, which he or others may evaluate negatively,

the subject brings the mortifying stimulus situation to an end and prevents its recurrence.

8. Escape and avoidance, denial, ego restriction, and identification with the "aggressor" and with the lost love object all achieve their defensive effect by interrupting and modifying the chain of events leading from external stimuli to the unpleasant emotional reactions. These defenses are oriented toward the external danger situations.

9. A person can also avoid experiencing the unpleasant emotions by orienting defenses toward these very reactions. He can, for example, repress or project fear or guilt. Such processes were not discussed in this chapter because examples of them have already been shown and because these additional defense mechanisms will be dealt with in the next two chapters.

Every man has reminiscences which he would not tell to every-one, but only to his friends. He has other matters in his mind which he would not reveal even to his friends, but only to him-self, and that in secret. But there are other things which a man is afraid to tell even to himself, and every decent man has a number of such things stored away in his mind.

FYODOR DOSTOEVSKY. Notes from Underground

CHAPTER 21
DEFENSE AGAINST DRIVES AND AFFECTS

L ife would be reasonably easy if the only sources of emotional turmoil were external stimuli. But many people are frightened or feel guilty because of their own natural sexual and aggressive drives, and when this happens they often try to avoid having sexual or aggressive feelings or thoughts or engaging in overt sexual or aggressive behavior. We have discussed many examples of such conflicts, ranging from those of Ed, Duane, and Edie, described in Chapter 12, through Miss Eaton's guilt-ridden conflict over her hatred for her sister, which we examined in Chapter 18. Our primary concern in these two final chapters is to discuss systematically the nature of such conflicts. Most of this chapter is devoted to the nature of the defenses against sexuality and aggression. Of the ten such defenses we shall discuss, the first six—repression, projection, reaction formation, negation, isolation, and undoing—all result in a *damming up* of a sexual or aggressive drive or emotional state and consequent relief from the anxiety and guilt evoked when those drives are aroused. The last four—turning around upon the self, reversal, regression, and sublimation—all change the *nature* of the drive itself and serve both to relieve the anxiety and guilt and to provide some gratification of the now transformed drive. Our discussion will consolidate and summarize the main points illustrated by our cases, and it will also include new material. The last chapter will consider some additional points about conflict and defense.

The Motives
for Defense Against Drives

In Chapter 13 we noted that when people defend against their sexual and aggressive drives, they act as if they are anticipating dangerous consequences if they express those drives. The dangers are the ones we discussed in Chapters 16–19.

FEAR OF EXTERNAL DANGERS

Some people anticipate that if they engage in sexual and aggressive behavior, the people they depend upon for security will leave them or the people they care about will reject them. Others think they will be shamed or ridiculed; still others think they will be physically harmed. Some even unconsciously believe their own anger or sexual excitement may kill the people they love.

When people anticipate such dangers as being abandoned, rejected, or castrated, they are not engaging in cool, cognitive expectations like predicting tomorrow's weather. They are experiencing *anticipatory fear reactions*. In these reactions the bodily changes and distressing sensations of fear blend with specific memories and thoughts that define the nature of the particular danger situation anticipated. *Our anxieties consist of just such specific anticipatory fear reactions.* For example, Ed's castration anxiety, as expressed in his dreams, was not simply the bodily reaction and feeling of fear. It included ideational content: that his penis would be cut off by a "witch" or a doctor if he engaged in sexual behavior. The woman suffering from separation anxiety, discussed in Chapter 16, experienced fear too, but her memories and thoughts about separation specifically defined that fear as separation anxiety.

FEAR OF INTENSE DRIVES

Many people anticipate that if they become sexually excited or angry, they will be *helpless in the face of intense urges* for which there is no relief or that they will lose control of themselves, that *their usual personality organization will disintegrate*. For example, some subjects fled from the sensory deprivation experimental situation as their sexual feelings and thoughts became intense and they began to fear that they were losing self-control.

FEAR OF CONSCIENCE

When the child internalizes his parents' moral standards and their observing, evaluating, and punitive functions, he begins to scold and punish himself for violating standards that are now his own. Such self-directed aggression produces *feelings of guilt* and of *lowered self-esteem;* the extreme intensity such feelings can reach was shown in the case of Miss Eaton, among others. Most people will do anything to avoid guilt and lowered self-esteem, including defending against the sexual or aggressive thoughts, feelings, or overt expression that instigate them.

Before we develop a superego, we feel safe from external censure as long as we do not actually *do* bad things and as long as no one, especially our parents, *knows* that we are wishing to do them or are thinking about them. Adults whose morality depends on what they can "get away with" are still functioning this way. After we develop a superego, however, *we* observe, judge, convict, punish ourselves, and feel guilty or worthless for mere *intentions*, even *unconscious* ones, that conflict with our personal moral code.

The motives for defense against sexual and aggressive drives, then, are the various anxieties we have discussed, plus lowered self-esteem and guilt. In *inner* conflict, these unpleasant affects are stimulated internally by drive arousal and as anticipatory reactions, not by external events. The slightest trace of such an unpleasant affect, an emotional "signal," instigates defenses (Freud, 1926). It is quite probable that such a pattern of internal regulation—the drives producing emotional signals, which then instigate defenses—is a product of learning (Dollard & Miller, 1950). In a moment we shall examine the defenses that are used against sexuality and aggression.

Direct Defense
Against Unpleasant Affects

In addition to defending against the external stimuli or the internal drives that arouse anxieties and guilt, people also defend directly against these distressing emotions. Clinical observations have shown that the defense mechanisms used for this purpose are the same as those used against sexuality and aggression. Ed, for example, not only repressed his incestuous wishes; he also repressed his castration thoughts and sometimes

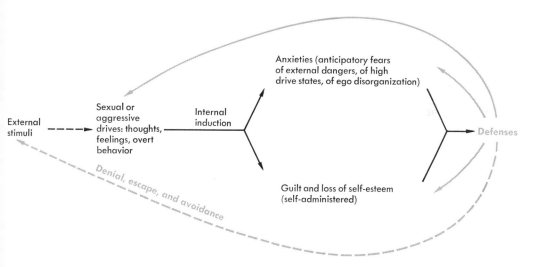

Figure 21-1 *Internal conflict: the relation between external stimuli, drives, motives for defense, and defenses.*

Since external stimuli are not essential for internal conflicts, their role and the defenses against them are represented by dashed arrows. In internal conflict the person's drives induce anxiety, guilt, or loss of self-esteem, which in turn instigate defenses. The defenses may be directed against the drives or the unpleasant emotional reactions or both.

the anxiety associated with them. In the discussion of the defenses used against the sexual and aggressive drives we shall occasionally illustrate their use against the distressing emotions themselves.

Figure 21-1 schematizes the relation between the sexual and aggressive drives, the motives for defense, and the defenses in internal conflicts. The diagram also represents the influence of external stimuli in internal conflicts. Generally speaking, external stimuli are not essential for internal conflicts, although they may trigger such conflicts, as we saw in Chapters 16–19. One way they trigger inner conflicts is by "releasing" drive thoughts, feelings, and tendencies to action when the individual is in a high drive state, as most adults know from encounters with members of the opposite sex, especially after a period of abstinence. In such situations, some people reduce their drive-aroused anxiety or guilt by using the "stimulus-oriented" defenses of denial or escape and avoidance. Ed avoided sexual intimacy with his wife, and Ray avoided close male companionship to relieve the conflict over his unconscious homosexual wishes (see Chapters 16 and 17). Since these defenses have already been discussed in detail, they will not be considered here.

Flight and Barricades

Man does gain control over his sexuality and aggression, his anxieties and guilt, but he cannot obliterate them from his life. Yet this is what he attempts to do in the process of defense against drives and affects. Figuratively speaking, he tries to run away from his own sexual and aggressive, anxious and guilty thoughts, feelings, and action tendencies. But his own internal workings and the inevitable provocations of the external world see to it that his drives and distressing emotions keep chasing him in hot and close pursuit. Continuing in his futile attempt to escape them, man tries to build barricades between himself and his drives and affects. As Edie's eating difficulty showed, a single barricade does not work. So he builds another, and another.

The process of defense nearly always utilizes two tendencies analogous to flight and the erection of barricades. We have already seen these two tendencies at work in the defenses against unpleasant external stimuli. In denial, for example, they took the form of withdrawal of attention from unpleasant perceptions and the substitution of wishful fantasies or perceptions for them. In a similar fashion, many of the defenses against drives function as barricades against "the return of the repressed," as Freud noted (1915c, 1937). But even repression utilizes these two tendencies.

It is important to remember that *all defenses operate automatically and outside of awareness.* Defenses are motivated, but they are not executed voluntarily. The average person does not know what defenses he is using, nor can he voluntarily stop using a defense if its presence is pointed out to him.

The following discussion consolidates and summarizes the main points about each defense mechanism, some of which could not be made explicit earlier when examples of their use were presented.

Repression

The basic empirical evidence of repression is an *inappropriate under-reaction* to a relevant situation and *indirect evidence that the repressed tendencies are actually present.* A nasty insult usually evokes some response—a flushed face, a clenched fist, an angry thought or retort, or all of these. A sexy picture or story, or the intimacy of the wedding night, usually arouses sexual reactions—widespread autonomic changes, localized ones in the genitals giving rise to sexual feelings, wishes to make love or fantasies of doing so, actual lovemaking. Repression prevents these reactions. *Repression* is the exclusion of drive thoughts and feelings from consciousness and the inhibition of related overt activity and autonomic bodily changes.

These effects are achieved by the twofold process noted earlier. The "flight" can be observed very clearly when it occurs during free association. The patient's "blank mind" indicates that he has *withdrawn his attention* from his thoughts and from the sensations arising within his body. One can even sometimes observe the body go limp, especially when people are repressing anger.

If this were all that happened when a strong drive is repressed, the repressed thoughts, feelings, and action tendencies would soon reappear. But the drive is still there, producing thoughts and feelings that attract attention again and threaten to burst forth in behavior. So the "barricade" process also occurs. Perhaps its simplest form is a shift to an active immobility—a not-thinking, not-feeling, not doing anything. At these times, patients in psychoanalysis frequently report such sensations as, "My jaws feel like they are wired shut," or "I am beginning to feel like I *won't* think, not just that I can't think of anything." A common form of repressive barricade is to shift attention to some *external* stimulus, the more "insignificant" the better. But perhaps the most common type of repressive barricade is *focusing attention and interest on displacement substitutes* for the repressed. Even the "insignificant" external stimuli that a person might "just happen to notice" usually prove to be displacement substitutes. One young man, for example, suddenly became preoccupied with a spot of peeling paint on the ceiling; he was repressing the wish to shake hands with and contaminate his analyst. The peeling paint "reminded" him of a spot of ringworm he had noticed on his hand that morning. The Wolf Man's sexual reactions to kneeling and squatting women (Chapter 15), Ed's marriage to a "tabooed" woman (Chapter 16), and a husband's angry reaction to his wife after a frustrating day at the office are all examples of displacement substitutes.

It is the presence of repressed, unfulfilled wishes and urges that produces displacement substitutes. But once produced, they serve as repressive barricades, provided they do not resemble the repressed too much. In time the substitutes take on more and more of the qualities of the repressed, and further repression involving the substitute occurs. Ed's sexual relationship with his wife illustrates a common sequence. (1) When he first met his future wife, Ed had repressed his incestuous memories and wishes. Furthermore, Ed felt that he had found a girl who was markedly dissimilar from his sister, especially because of her tabooed ethnic origin. His sister always came off the loser in his frequent and emotionally involved comparisons of the two. Not realizing his wife-to-be was a partial substitute for his sister, Ed became very involved with her and was able to enjoy all aspects of their relationship to a certain extent. (2) By means of his involvement in this relationship and the satisfaction of his sexual urges, he was able to keep his "sister complex" repressed. But as time went by, his unconscious thinking endowed her more and more with the qualities of his sister until his sister replaced his wife in his dreams, as was illustrated in Chapter 16. He finally found himself thinking that living with his wife was like living with his sister. (3) During this development, his sexual life with his wife became the target of defense too.

Ed's experiences illustrate two other important features of repression. The first is a distinction Freud made between *after-repression* and *primal repression*. If something "reminds" a person of his repressed memories or wishes, it too will often be repressed. A common example would be forgetting the name of someone because it is the same as the already "forgotten" name of someone else about whom we have many repressed feelings and memories. The "new forgetting" is an instance of after-repression; the "old forgetting" was the primal repression. Ed's eventual repression of his wishes, feelings, and behavior toward his wife was after-repression; his childhood repression of his incestuous sexual desires and fantasies was primal repression. The second feature of repression emphasized by Freud and illustrated by Ed is that childhood repression is a prerequisite for later repression and predisposes the individual for this fate. Thus, the primal repressions are the childhood repressions.

We have been talking about repression of drives and the feelings and memories that accompany them. But the anxious or guilty thoughts and feelings generated by those drives and feelings may also be repressed. Sometimes only the anxious or guilty thoughts are repressed; sometimes the anxious or guilty feelings are repressed; sometimes both. In Chapters 12 and 16 we described Ed's repression of his castration *thoughts*, which were manifested in his dreams. While he had repressed those thoughts, he did not repress his feelings of anxiety. Therefore he experienced an objectless anxiety when his sexual impulses were aroused. Other males might have repressed *both* their castration thoughts and feelings of fear. Little Hans and the Wolf Man did this. They were afraid of being castrated by their fathers, but they were able to tolerate and even enjoy the company of their fathers. This was possible because they had repressed both their *thoughts* and their *fears* that their fathers would castrate them. These repressed complexes were then expressed indirectly in their over-reactions of fear of large animals.

Guilt feelings and thoughts may also be repressed. An example is the adolescent who masturbates, seemingly without guilt, but then experiences such extreme guilt about his "dirty" hands that he must wash them every half-hour.

Projection

Another way to barricade against the reemergence of repressed thoughts, feelings, and action tendencies is to attribute them to another person. This is defensive *projection*. We have observed it as a defense against both drives and guilt (see Chapters 17 and 18) and as a prominent element in homosexual conflicts (Chapter 17). The present discussion will therefore be limited to two general considerations.

The projective attribution of unconscious qualities to another person is not a barren intellectual act. It creates a "perceptually real" world for the subject. Ray did not merely *think* his potential hiking companion was homosexual; he *saw* a leering and crudely seductive homosexual before him, and he responded with shock and alarm. The paranoid psychotic may spend years and thousands of dollars in a legal battle with an enemy who is perceptually real, even though only projectively created to maintain the repression of the subject's own hatred.

How does projection come about? Freud (1922) observed that the projector does not create tormentors "out of the blue." He seizes upon tiny clues in the other person's behavior, *minor* indications of the same unconscious wishes the projector is defending against. Then the projector magnifies their significance unrealistically by focusing all of his attention upon them and discounting all the *major* personality characteristics of the other person. It is analogous to the way a spot of dirt on the door changes the appearance of a new car. Suppose Ray's companion did have unconscious homosexual wishes, which caused him to act as he did. Most people would not rivet their attention on those transitory actions and elevate them into major traits. Only someone driven by unconscious homosexual wishes himself and the need to reinforce their repression would do that. Since every human being shares the same classes of unconscious wishes, which are inevitably betrayed in very slight indications, the vigilant projector has ample opportunity to find suitable victims.

Reaction Formation

In her adolescence Miss Eaton (discussed in Chapter 18) repressed her jealous hatred of her younger sister. To maintain this repression she also *reversed* (see "Reversal," below) her dominant feelings toward her sister: She exaggerated her love for her. Then, over the next few years, she developed a *general attitude of kindness* toward everyone, including her sister. This attitude became a general *personality trait*, which persisted for at least 20 years. Its major function was to maintain the repression of all her aggression. Such general personality traits with a defensive function are called *reaction formations*. They are the epitome of behaviors that oppose "the return of the repressed," for they consist of deeply ingrained attitudes that are the direct opposites of the repressed ones.

Reaction formations take various forms, depending on the nature of the drives that must be kept repressed. The general trait of orderliness and cleanliness as a defense against repressed desires to be messy and dirty is a classic example discovered by Freud (1908). Generosity is often a defense against unconscious stinginess. The asceticism developed by many adolescents often becomes an extreme reaction formation, a defense against all drive gratifications—all pleasures of the flesh, even eating, sleeping in a comfortable bed, or being warm (A. Freud, 1936).

Some people use reaction formations to *ward off repressed distressing affects*. The chronic daredevil, in every arena of life, for example, is often behaving that way to keep deep-seated anxieties repressed. His condition is called "counterphobic." Many generally unscrupulous people are actually warding off an unconscious sense of guilt. Unrelieved cheerfulness is often a reaction formation against underlying depression.

Since most reaction formations consist of socially desirable behavior, the temptation is strong to attribute them to social approval rather than to relief from anxiety and guilt over sexuality and aggression. The psychoanalytic view is that both "gains" are important but that the internal relief from anxiety and guilt is the "primary gain" and external social approval is a "secondary gain." Psychoanalysis takes this view for several reasons. One is that not all reaction formations—defensive unscrupulousness, for example—are sociably desirable. Also, many of the "socially desirable" reaction formations are carried to such an extreme, for defensive purposes, that they become socially undesirable and socially or economically disadvantageous to the individual. Yet such traits persist. The compulsively clean housekeeper makes herself work hard all day long and makes visitors so uncomfortable that they avoid her; and the compulsively orderly office worker often falls so far behind in getting his work done that he loses his job.

Such exaggeration of what is normally simply a socially desirable way of behaving is, in fact, a reliable clue that a reaction formation exists. But even reaction formations do not succeed completely in blocking the repressed impulses. Miss Eaton's kindliness, for example, was not a completely successful defense against her repressed hostility toward her sister. Throughout her twenties and thirties she still suffered from her secret ritual of repeating minor acts several times. Thus her repressed hostility still found indirect symbolic expression in very insignificant actions, and she had to magically undo the effects she superstitiously attributed to them. This coexistence of reaction formations and hidden islands of expression of the repressed impulses is a common phenomenon. The overly generous person is always a miser in some respect. And the compulsively fastidious person is very likely to have dirty toenails or underwear. Furthermore, reaction formations are likely to break down at times (when a person is drunk, for example), whereupon the repressed tendencies suddenly erupt, as in Somerset Maugham's well-known story, "Rain," about the prudish clergyman who suddenly began violently making love to the prostitute whom he thought he was trying to save from a life of evil.

Freud thought the distinction between primary and secondary gain applies to all defenses and symptoms, a possibility worth keeping in mind, especially in these days when so much emphasis is placed on the external causes of mental distress.

Negation

The comical stereotype of an angry man shouting "Who's angry? I'm *not* angry!" illustrates this defense. In *negation* a repressed thought is expressed in its negative form (Freud, 1925a). The repressed content is conscious, but with a "negative sign" attached to it.

As in repression, the individual using negation is not aware of the nature of his repressed thoughts and thus feels relieved of anxiety or guilt. But when negation is the defense, the informed onlooker can immediately tell the nature of the thoughts being defended against. He simply deletes the negative words in such statements as "I'm *not* angry"; "I *don't* think I like you"; "I *don't* remember *ever* loving my sister."

Psychoanalysts' refusal to accept negations at face value is the source of a common complaint about them: that they automatically translate a patient's "no" into a "yes," and vice versa. Actually, to determine if negation is really being employed, the psychoanalyst draws upon a variety of information. In the first example, he would notice that the person *angrily shouts* "I'm not angry!" And the patient would no doubt forcefully repeat the assertion several times. This is especially impressive when no one has asked him if he was angry. The total context and style of negation causes the analyst to think to himself: "Who says you are angry—who except another part of yourself? Why do you need to convince me and your conscious self that you aren't angry, unless you really are? Aren't you protesting too much?" After such a negation is called to the patient's attention, he often confirms its validity by acknowledging his anger.

It is easy to confuse the concepts of denial and negation. They are quite distinct both in regard to what is defended against and in behavioral content. *Denial* substitutes pleasant for unpleasant perceptions of external stimuli. *Negation* consists of negated thoughts and negated perceptions of internal states.

"I'm *not* afraid"; I'm *not* sad"; "No sir, I *don't* feel guilty or ashamed that I did it"; "I *don't* miss you"; "My feelings are *not* hurt" are all familiar examples of *negations of unpleasant affect*.

Isolation

When conflict is not intense, drive thoughts, feelings, and impulses to action blend to produce a unitary conscious experience. The defense of *isolation* shatters this experience: The individual components remain conscious or overt, or potentially so, but split apart, isolated from one another. The person who isolates has, at one moment, relatively undisguised sexual and aggressive thoughts but without feelings. Another time he will be seized with sexual or aggressive feelings without any clear thoughts, such as about the person toward whom they are directed. At another moment a relatively "cold" impulse to action will overtake him. As we shall show, selective, transitory repression of components is basic to the phenomenon of isolation.

Imagine talking with someone and suddenly having the thought of breaking his arm flash into your mind, or having an angry feeling surge up, or an urge to grab his arm and start twisting it. Many people have just such upsetting experiences, in which the drive components occur individually— robbed of their total context. These different forms of expression of the underlying anger are examples of *obsessional thoughts, obsessional feelings,* and *compulsions.* It was no accident that Freud first clearly delineated the defense of isolation in his report about the Rat Man's obsessive-compulsive neurosis (1909b), for isolation creates many of the symptoms of that neurosis.

One of the Rat Man's most troublesome thoughts arose when he was a Reserve Army officer on summer maneuvers. A fellow officer described an Oriental punishment in which a container of rats was fastened upside down on the buttocks of the criminal. The rats bored into the victim's anus. The *thought* of this happening to the woman he loved flashed through the Rat Man's mind. This thought embodied a disguised wish, and most people would have repressed it. But it became fully conscious to the Rat Man for a moment, because he isolated his pleasurable sadistic feelings from it by momentarily repressing them. His conscious experience was of an *idea* stripped of its affect. Freud saw the emotion, however, in the expression of horrified pleasure on the Rat Man's face as he described that experience.

DISPLACEMENT

Isolated feelings may occur in relatively pure form, as in sudden surges of anger with little thought content or in surges of genital sensations. Usually, however, they are *displaced* or transferred (generalized, in the language of conditioned response psychology), often onto very insignificant events. Several examples of such displacement were given in Chapter 18.

ISOLATION OF TENDER FEELING FROM SENSUAL LOVE

Isolation takes many forms, two of which will be cited here. One concerns love. Many people cannot simultaneously experience tender, loving feelings and sensual feelings without becoming anxious or guilty, but they can tolerate those feelings in isolation. As a result, they often lead double love lives. A man, for example, may carry on an intimate, tender, loving relationship with the kind of woman he idolizes and wants to marry. He cannot tolerate any sensual feelings for her, nor successfully engage in any overt sensual behavior with her. Yet he is able to enjoy sexual relations with another woman whom he looks down upon. Why does blending the sensual with his idealized love life make him anxious or guilty? Because the idealized love relationship resembles the "cleansed" relationship of the boy to his mother (Freud, 1910b). To introduce sensuality into it makes it all the more Oedipal and thus all the more anxiety-provoking and guilt-ridden.

INTELLECTUALIZATION

An exaggerated emphasis on thought, called *intellectualization,* is another frequent form of isolation. We all try to minimize our emotions when we are trying to think logically about a practical or intellectual problem. The isolator carries this process to an extreme for defensive purposes. He will talk about the most blatant sexual and aggressive matters in a highly abstract, logical manner, devoid of the feelings most people would experience if they talked about the same themes. Many adolescents use intellectualization in their struggle with their sexual and aggressive turmoil (A. Freud, 1936). A common result is the "bull session," in which questions involving sexuality and aggression are talked about in the abstract and sexual excitement or angry feelings are experienced only slightly, if at all. In this case the defense may have adaptive value; such "bull sessions" obviously help most adolescents resolve their conflicts and develop their philosophies of life.

Many people can talk about the impact of separations, bodily threats, and other unpleasant events without experiencing any feelings. Then, some time later, they will suddenly experience "free-floating," objectless anxiety. They have *isolated their distressing feelings* from the relevant memories and other thoughts.

Undoing

A person who hurts someone's feelings and then tries to make up for it, or someone who has gone too far in flirting with someone and then becomes quite indifferent or even slightly "cool" to that person, is showing normal behavior that is the prototype of undoing. The second action "undoes" the first one and thus minimizes the person's anxiety and guilt over having committed the first one. The defense of *undoing* is simply an unconscious exaggeration of this normal process. Undoing, as illustrated by the Rat Man and Miss Eaton in Chapter 18, often attempts to "undo what isolation has already done." The Rat Man's kicking the stone loose in the road, for example, gave direct expression to his angry wish that his girlfriend's carriage would hit it and turn over. The act of kicking the stone loose from the road's surface was not accompanied by angry thoughts and feelings about her. They and the act had been isolated from each other. When he then removed the stone from the road, he was undoing the "isolated" act. The pairing of isolation and undoing is especially noticeable in obsessive-compulsive disorders.

Inhibition is the ultimate effect of the defenses we have just discussed—of repression, projection, reaction formation, negation, isolation, and undoing. They exclude from consciousness and overt behavior either wishes, bodily changes and feelings, or impulses to action that would bring drive gratification or emotional discharge. When directed against painful affect, these defenses also have the ultimate effect of inhibition. A "dammed-up" drive or emotional state is the net result.

The defenses we shall now discuss change the *nature* of the drives, rather than simply *blocking* them. This drive transformation has two consequences. First, the person gains *relief* from the anxiety or guilt prompted by the original form of the drive. Second, *gratification* of the transformed drive does occur, within limits.

Turning Around upon the Self

One way of defensively transforming a wish or impulse is to change the person toward whom it is directed. We have already seen several examples of such displacements from one person to another. In a more radical displacement the person himself becomes the object; the drive gets turned around upon the self (Freud, 1915b).

TURNING AGGRESSION AROUND UPON THE SELF

Turning aggression around upon the self is a very common instance of this defense. Its simplest form is the "unintentional," but open and direct hurting of oneself instead of the other person. Many self-injurious "accidents" are caused this way. One patient in psychotherapy frequently cut himself shaving, nearly always when he was obviously repressing anger toward his wife. Many people scratch themselves with their fingernails when they are inhibiting anger. One young female analysand did this so frequently and vigorously that both forearms became badly infected from her wrists to her elbows (Mahl, 1968).

Frequently, the self-directed aggression stops at the level of thoughts and compulsive urges of self-destruction. The Rat Man had many symptoms like these. Once he was seized with the impulse to rush to his razor and cut his throat; he was very angry that his girlfriend had gone away to nurse her sick grandmother, and he had just repressed the wish to kill the old woman. On another occasion, during the visit he and his girlfriend made to the mountain resort (Chapter 18), an inner command ordered him to jump off a cliff upon which he was standing; the turning around of a repressed desire to kill another man who was paying a lot of attention to his girlfriend prompted this suicidal impulse.

Miss Eaton's self-accusations that she was guilty of serious offenses and her self-deprecatory thoughts and feelings of being worthless illustrate more disguised forms of turning aggression around upon the self. As her treatment with Helene Deutsch revealed, these behaviors consisted of repressed hostile thoughts about her sister, which she was now directing against herself.

Turning aggression around upon the self accomplishes two important things. First, it provides relief from the sense of guilt prompted by the original, outwardly directed anger. Second, it provides some gratification of the repressed anger, albeit in a different form. Children feel better when they have been punished by their parents for misbehavior. Having paid penance and been forgiven, they are relieved of their guilt. Adults seem to operate by the same principles in relation to their own conscience, to their internal representation of their parents. The role of conscience and guilt in this defense accounts for its prominence in obsessive-compulsive and severely depressed people, such as the Rat Man and Miss Eaton, for such people suffer from an especially severe conscience.

TURNING LOVE AROUND UPON THE SELF

Turning love around upon the self also occurs, although it is usually referred to as a "return to narcissism" or a "regression to narcissism." This is misleading, for not all instances of turning love around upon the self are regressive. The self-concern of the sick person, for example, is not always accompanied by regressive, childish helplessness. Nor is the loving of oneself that is mediated by the identifications of normal mourning. At least one instance of turning love inward is "progressive": the self-love produced by internalizing our parents' ideals (Loewald, 1962, 1964). Originally, we admire our parents and all they stand for. When we internalize their values and make them our own, we cherish these aspects of ourselves just as we did our parents.

Reversal

When a person uses *reversal*, he shifts from the wishes, feelings, and impulses that make him anxious or guilty to directly opposite kinds. There are two types of such reversals (Freud, 1915b): changing from loving to hating (or vice versa) and changing from active to passive modes of obtaining sensual pleasure (or vice versa), as in shifting between sadism and masochism. Reversals bring relief from anxiety or guilt over one kind of aggressive or sexual impulse and simultaneously provide for some type of alternative gratification.

Let us consider first the activity-passivity reversals, using sadism and masochism for illustrative purposes. Overt sadism blends sexual and aggressive satisfaction: The fully developed sadist must humiliate and inflict pain on his partner in order to become sexually excited and have an orgasm. Sadism starts in childhood. In one expression of it the child masturbates while consciously fantasying that another child is being beaten by that child's parent or a parent substitute. Such wishes and experiences arouse so much guilt in some young sadists that they defend themselves by turning into overt masochists, but they remain unconscious sadists. They achieve this reversal by turning their sexualized aggression around upon themselves and then taking one more step. They seek out some other person to inflict the sexualized pain upon themselves.

The child masochist will usually provoke his parents into beating him, mainly for erotic satisfaction. The Wolf Man (Freud, 1918) did exactly this when he was about 4 years old. He would deliberately misbehave in front of his father in order to be spanked. That he wanted to be spanked is shown by the fact that at times he would even get as physically close to his father as possible when he misbehaved. Most boys, of course, stay as far away from their fathers as possible under such circumstances. As an adult the Wolf Man got great pleasure out of beating fantasies, especially ones in which he pictured boys being beaten on their penises. The adult masochist, of course, insists that his or her lover inflict the pain and humiliation on him. Consciously, he enjoys being hurt; unconsciously, he also enjoys the fantasy that he is the sadist.

Having become a masochist, the conflicted person may then revert to sadism because he can no longer tolerate the passive situation. It may arouse his castration anxiety, for example, or lower his self-esteem. But when he does behave sadistically, he now gets a great deal of secret masochistic gratification, too, for he projectively identifies with the partner he is now hurting and humiliating. This seems to involve the same type of empathy that enables us to "feel" the pain when we see someone being hurt. That is a normal prototype of what the reconverted sadist does on a grand scale.

The sadist and the masochist enjoy the same blend of sexuality and aggression. Only the overt—passive or active—form is different. If one form is enjoyed consciously and overtly, the other form is enjoyed inwardly through projective identification with the partner and unconscious fantasy.

Other defensive reversals involve love and hate, as was noted above. Miss Eaton's adolescent reaction to her sister was an example of the use of love to defend against guilt-ridden hate. The same kind of reaction is one of the many causes of homosexuality. Thus, Freud (1922) found that some homosexual men had started out hating their brothers and fixed on homosexual love because their hatred made them feel so guilty.

Hate may be used to defend against love. A person who is afraid of unconscious heterosexual wishes may hate members of the opposite sex; a person who fears homosexual wishes may hate members of the same sex. Paranoid delusions of persecution arise from the projection of such defensive hatred, which keeps homosexual wishes repressed, as we saw in Chapter 17.

Reversals of the unpleasant emotions resulting from conflict—anxiety and guilt—are analogous to reversals of love and hate. Many people, for example, repress their anxiety and "whistle in the dark"; acting brave helps them to avoid fear. And the nonchalant flouting of one's ideals can help a person to defend against a sense of guilt.

How do reversals differ from reaction formations? The main distinction is the *degree of generality* of the opposing feelings and behavior. In reversal, the defensive behavior is fairly specific. For example, the type of homosexual who turned to homosexual love because hatred of a brother brought on great guilt can hate in many areas of his life. When Miss Eaton first reversed her hatred for her sister, she undoubtedly could express anger toward many other people. It is only when a reversal becomes generalized to all people and to all areas of one's life—only when a characterological change occurs—that we call it a reaction formation.

Regression

Let us recall what happened to Edie the day she and her husband, feeling sexually aroused, rushed home from the museum. She became anxious and felt guilty and momentarily repressed her sexual desires. Then she experienced intense hunger and delayed her lovemaking long enough to eat something. And we saw many indications that eating was an intensely erotic experience for her. We also saw that early in her childhood she had enjoyed eating but had then become a chronic "eating problem-child." Here in a nutshell is an example of the defensive regression of drives. To avoid the anxiety and guilty feelings about her *heterosexual* wishes, Edie repressed them and regressed to the developmentally earlier stage of *oral eroticism*. Put another way, she regressed to an early *fixation* point in her psychosexual development.

The minor episode the day of that museum outing encapsulated what had happened on a major scale late in her adolescence. The night of the senior prom in high school she had become sexually excited but had repressed her sexual wishes. She became ravenously hungry and was all set to eat a juicy cheeseburger. But something happened that did not occur that day of the museum trip. As she was about to eat with her boyfriend, she became afraid she would choke to death. In her unconscious thinking, eating was a sexual act. She anticipated the same danger upon eating that she anticipated from her mother in retribution for her Oedipal love for her father. (In Chapter 15 we discussed a woman whose fear that her mother would choke her was expressed in her first dream in analysis. Edie had identical unconscious fears.) Her new anxiety necessarily motivated still a further defense: the inhibition of eating with a man, the repression of her oral eroticism. This further defense against even the regressed wishes is a common outcome. It is, as noted earlier (pages 250–51), the *immediate* cause of most hysterical symptoms.

To round out this account of Edie, it should be noted that her transition from adolescence into young adulthood repeated the same defensive trend of oral inhibition that she showed earlier in her childhood, when she changed from a fleshy little girl of 5 to a "stark" beanpole by the age of 7.

It is possible and useful to distinguish between regressions of erotogenic zones, of wishes, and of objects. Edie's regression involved only a retreat from the genital to the oral erotogenic zone. From her fantasies and free associations it appeared that her wishes and their object were unchanged: Unconsciously, she wanted to have oral intercourse with a man's penis. This specific wish was the target of her inhibition of eating with a man. Another woman might have regressed in all three aspects, ending up wanting to be fed like a baby by her mother. The Wolf Man regressed on all three counts, as the next chapter will show.

Some regressions involve reversions from adult loves to childhood ones, as in the frightened bride who longs to be back home with her Oedipal father and the guilt-ridden bridegroom whose thoughts turn to his Oedipal mother. Other regressions involve retreats from sensuous relations with other people to autoeroticism. Still others are to pregenital psychosexual stages, as in the Wolf Man.

In the most marked regressions of schizophrenia the person retreats to the pregenital pleasures of being cared for like a baby by maternal figures, to narcissism like that of Judge Schreber (discussed in Chapter 14), or to a level of experience in which they feel fused with parental surrogates, usually horribly distorted by psychotic thought.

Sublimation

Sublimation, often called a "normal" defense (A. Freud, 1936), also provides for the expression of repressed drives and affects. But the forms sublimation takes are highly displaced and resemble only slightly the raw, unconscious emotional urges and feelings from which they derive most of their impetus.

Helene Deutsch (1965) reports the following "absolutely true anecdote":

> One early summer morning many years ago, the inhabitants of a small . . . university town . . . made the horrifying discovery that all the dogs which had been running loose during the night in a certain point of the city had

lost their tails. They learned that the medical students had attended a drinking bout that night and that when they left the party one young man had had the highly humorous inspiration to cut off the tails of the dogs. Later he became one of the most famous surgeons in the world [p. 304].

This anecdote illustrates not only how alcohol "dissolves the super-ego" and releases repressed sadistic urges but also how such repressed sadistic urges may be expressed in very constructive, socially valuable activities such as surgery—in other words, they may be sublimated.

One nurse recalled that her favorite game in childhood had been to pretend that her dolls, who were "sister" and "mother," were dead and that she was bringing them to life again. From the case material it appeared that her childhood conflict between her unconscious jealous hatred of her mother and sister and her defensive undoing in the rescue fantasy was sublimated in her adult occupational role.

Freud (1910a) noted a remarkable parallel between Leonardo da Vinci's "Madonna and Child with St. Anne" (Figure 21-2) and Leonardo's own childhood. "He had had two mothers: first, his true mother Caterina, from whom he was torn away when he was between three and five, and then a young and tender step-mother, his father's wife, Donna Albiera [p. 113]."

Figure 21-2 Leonardo's "Madonna and Child with St. Anne."

Freud noted several unusual things about the painting. Few Italian painters portrayed St. Anne, Mary, and Jesus together as a trio; and the few other European artists who had painted the trio never had a mature Mary sitting on her mother's lap while she reached out to the child on the ground. Furthermore, St. Anne here has a youngish, beautiful, radiant face—very similar to Mary's—not the face of an old woman. Finally, the blissful smile —so famous from "Mona Lisa"—appears on the faces of both women. Freud concluded that this picture (and many other Leonardos of the same period that featured the same smile) must be a derivative expression, or sublimation, of Leonardo's repressed Oedipal memories and feelings, for the existence of which Freud adduced a great deal of indirect evidence. The painting could be viewed as a condensed recapitulation of Leonardo's childhood: As a baby he had been cared for by a loving young "mother" and before that by a second, perhaps slightly older, loving mother.

Freud also thought that Leonardo's painting of so many women like Mona Lisa and the women in "Madonna and Child with St. Anne" was as much a sublimation of his unconscious painful longings for his lost mothers as it was of his simpler Oedipal desires. One can appreciate how this might happen by putting oneself for a moment in Leonardo's position and imagining what inward emotions one might feel spending hour after hour completely absorbed in creating stroke by stroke all those mysteriously marvelous mother-faces. Freud's inferences can be questioned, of course, by both Leonardo scholars and psychoanalysts on the ground that unconscious meanings cannot adequately be determined from biographies of dead people who cannot give the analyst their own free associations. Granted; but the general mechanism of sublimation is commonly observed in artistic creativity (Kris, 1952).

The intellectual curiosity of the adult, Freud proposed (1905b), was in part a sublimation of the child's "sexual researches." And the inhibitions of creativity that he observed in adults seemed to derive from the strong repression of childhood sexual curiosity.

In Chapter 15 we discussed the way in which the child begins to establish his ideals by renouncing his Oedipal sensuality and by identifying with his Oedipal love objects. This, too, is regarded as a sublimation.

The differences between adult phenomena of sublimation, such as those mentioned above, and the presumably related childhood sexual-aggressive drives and experiences reflect the critical mechanisms of sublimation. All the adult sublimations show a marked displacement away from the childhood sexual or aggressive aims and targets. In addition, the adult behavior serves a socially constructive function. Where a young man might obtain sadistic pleasure and master his own castration anxiety by cutting off the tails of dogs and symbolically castrating his father, the surgeon cuts up sick people in order to save lives. The child Leonardo may have reveled in his sensuous intimacy with his two mothers; Leonardo, the middle-aged artist, might have become absorbed in painting the biblical scene partly to symbolically relive this intimacy and partly for the enjoyment it would provide his fellow men and posterity. The child starts to form his ideals out of adoration of his parents, the need to cope with giving up his Oedipal relationships, and the need to relieve his castration anxiety; the adult man of principles is relatively free of parental ties and fits into the value system of society.

The "goodness of fit" between the childhood and adult phenomena is one reason for taking the concept of sublimation seriously. But there is an even more compelling reason. Sublimations sometimes lose their adjustive value by becoming invaded by the sexual or aggressive drives from which they stem. When this happens, the sublimations become the target of severe inhibitions. Intellectual activity, for example, sexually excites some men who devote themselves to scholarly pursuits; they eventually lose their keenness. One male psychotherapy patient avoided libraries and eventually all serious reading because studying in the library stacks regularly aroused him to the point of masturbating on the spot. Painters, doctors, and nurses occasionally become unable to carry on their vocations for similar reasons.

This completes the discussion of defenses against sexual and aggressive drives. The brief final chapter touches on a few important aspects of conflicts and defenses that have not yet been considered.

A Word About Freud's Terminology

Readers who plan to study Freud's original papers may profit from a few preliminary words about the changes in some of his concepts and terminology. The bit of history presented in Chapter 11 demonstrated that defense and repression were among his original psychoanalytic discoveries. Each subsequent paper in his long life, regardless of its principal topic, dealt with some aspect of these processes. In addition, he wrote general or theoretical discussions of defense and repression during three different periods of his work—1893–96, 1914–17, and 1923–37. But he meant different things at these different times by "defense" and "repression."

In the early phase of his work "defense" was a general concept subsuming a wide variety of specific defenses. "Repression" was regarded as one of many defenses, along with most of those mentioned in this chapter (Breuer & Freud, 1893–95; Freud, 1894, 1896b). Freud's next general discussions of defense and repression appeared in some of his "metapsychological papers" of 1915 (1915b, 1915c, 1915d), which presented his then-current psychological theory in a highly condensed form. Here he referred to nearly all the various defense mechanisms as simply "repression." What he had earlier thought of as different mechanisms of defense—repression, projection, reaction formation, and so forth—he now viewed as mechanisms of "repression." He also spoke of other mechanisms—such as turning aggression around upon the self—as "defenses," and he referred to defenses as "vicissitudes" of instincts.

In these same papers Freud insisted that "repression" (synonymous

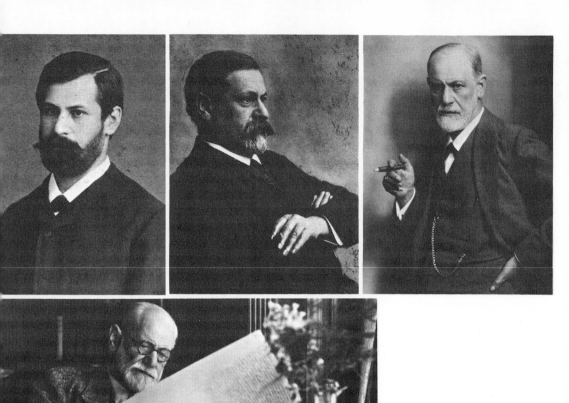

Figure 21-3 Sigmund Freud.

Top left: Freud in 1891, at age 35. Freud was just beginning to discover the far-reaching effect of unconscious memories and emotions on conscious behavior and thought. Top middle: Freud in 1906, at age 50, one year after the publication of one of his most important monographs, Three Essays on the Theory of Sexuality. *Top right: Freud in 1922, at age 66. A year later Freud will have published his new model of the personality in* The Ego and the Id. *Much of this monograph was devoted to his discoveries and new theoretical ideas about the superego. Bottom: Freud in 1938, at age 82, after having emigrated from Vienna to London. Here Freud is reading his manuscript for* Moses and Monotheism, *which would soon be published in English. Freud died in 1939.*

with "defense") applied only to *ideas*; at other times he spoke of repression of an instinctual *impulse*. And the "vicissitudes" altered drive *behavior*, as in the change from sadism to masochism.

Furthermore, in the years from 1893 to 1923, Freud held two different views on the relation between anxiety and defense. On the one hand, he claimed that anxiety motivated defenses, which, in turn, minimized anxiety. On the other hand, his "official" theory of anxiety held that it was transformed, repressed sexual affect; that is, defense ultimately produced anxiety. Moreover, in some passages he asserts that anxiety motivates defenses, while in other passages he asserts that the "self-preservative instincts" do so. Freud does not make the relation between the two very clear.

There were probably two main reasons for all these terminological inconsistencies and conceptual difficulties. First, from 1900 to 1923 Freud's main goal had been to clarify the role of drives, especially sexual wishes, in normal and neurotic behavior. He believed that the biological drives were the basic source of all behavior. In keeping with this goal, he was very specific about drives but became less specific about defenses. Thus, he differentiated all the forms and stages of sexuality we mentioned in Chapters 14 and 15 at the same time he was indiscriminately referring to all the defenses as "repression." Also in keeping with this goal of explaining *all* aspects of behavior in terms of biological drives, he adopted as a working hypothesis the assumption that the "self-preservative *instincts*" supplied the motivating force for repression. Second, he was in the process of developing a general psychological theory concerning as yet unstudied aspects of human behavior. He realized this and explicitly acknowledged several major difficulties with his theory (1915d).

At the same time, Freud gradually increased his empirical and theoretical study of "ego" psychology. With the writing of *The Ego and the Id* (1923) and, especially, *Inhibitions, Symptoms, and Anxiety* (1926) he arrived at essentially the theory of conflict and defense that has been presented here. Anna Freud restated it especially clearly and amplified it considerably in *The Ego and the Mechanisms of Defense* (1936). In this third phase (1923–37) Freud returned to the general concept of defense. Abandoning the view that repression produces neurotic anxiety, he concluded that anxiety is anticipatory fear and that the various anxieties we have mentioned (as well as guilt) motivate the defenses. Defenses, he now made clear, can interfere with ideas and with feelings and their underlying bodily changes, as well as with overt behavior. And he returned to his early distinction between various defense mechanisms. In his last major paper, *Analysis Terminable and Interminable* (1937), however, he gives repression a special place and regards the other defense mechanisms as supplementary to it.

So, to the uninitiated reader about to plunge into the middle of Freud's collected papers: Beware! But go ahead and jump. The swimming is fine, but you have to work to keep your head above water.

There was a child went forth every day,
And the first object he looked upon, that object he became,
And that object became part of him for the day or a certain part of
the day,
Or for many years or stretching cycles of years.

The early lilacs became part of this child,
And grass and white and red morning-glories, and white and red
clover, and the song of the phoebe-bird. . . .

. . .

His own parents, he that had fathered him and she that had con-
ceived him in her womb and birthed him,
They gave this child more of themselves than that,
They gave him afterward every day, they became part of him.

The mother at home quietly placing the dishes on the supper-table,
The mother with mild words, clean her cap and gown, a wholesome
odor falling off her person and clothes as she walks by,
The father, strong, self-sufficient, manly, mean, angered, unjust,
The blow, the quick loud word, the tight bargain, the crafty lure,
The family usages, the language, the company, the furniture, the
yearning and swelling heart,
Affection that will not be gainsayed, the sense of what is real, the
thought if after all it should prove unreal. . . .

. . .

These became part of that child who went forth every day, and who
now goes, and will always go forth every day.

WALT WHITMAN . There Was a Child Went Forth

CHAPTER 22
ORGANIZATION OF DEFENSES AND INDIVIDUAL DIFFERENCES

I n this final chapter we shall discuss briefly two additional aspects of conflict and defense: the patterning and organization of multiple defenses and individual differences in conflict and defense. Why have these topics been left until the end, and why are they discussed so briefly? Partly because they take us beyond the goal of dealing with basic concepts, and partly because little is known about them. This chapter, especially the discussion of individual differences, raises questions whose answers lie in the future.

Patterning of Multiple Defenses

For the sake of clarity, the discussion in the last two chapters focused on one defense at a time. Actually, defense mechanisms do not operate singly. From three different perspectives we can speak of a *patterning of multiple defenses.*

1. *Multiple defenses against each single target.* Defense against any single "target" in the conflict paradigm—a perception of an external stim-

ulus, an approach component (such as a drive), or an avoidance component (such as an unpleasant affect)—nearly always involves repression and at least one other defense that reinforces the repression.

2. *Multiple defenses against multiple targets.* There is always defense against more than one target in the paradigm, and these multiple defenses are not always the same. In his experience at the restaurant door Ray was repressing both his homosexual wishes and his self-criticism for having such wishes, but in addition he projected the unconscious self-criticism. A similar patterning of multiple defenses was demonstrated for most of the over-reactions discussed in Chapters 16–18.

3. *Correlated defenses.* Clinical experience suggests that there is some correlation in the use of certain defenses. Thus, obsessional people seem to use isolation, undoing, regression, and reaction formation. Repression and denial seem to be characteristic of hysterical individuals. Identification seems to be correlated with projection and denial in schizophrenia. (These statements do *not* mean, of course, that all people using these defenses suffer from a neurosis or a psychosis.) However, these clinical impressions have not been verified by careful, systematic research.

Hierarchical Organization of Defenses

Most conflicts have discernible "natural histories"; they are seldom, if ever, resolved by a single defensive effort. The discussion of Edie in the last chapter (pages 385–86) illustrated the "succession of movements" over time that constitutes the dynamic history of conflicts. Just as influences from previous historical periods continue into the present so, it seems, many of the earlier stages in the process of defense continue to exist and operate unconsciously in the present. Thus, a concept of a *hierarchical organization of defenses*, of a "layering of defenses," seems necessary to account for the behavior of an individual at the last stage in the historical process. Indeed, this theoretical necessity was one of several weaknesses Freud saw in his early model of the personality, which consisted of an Unconscious and an opposing Preconscious or Conscious. It was one of the reasons he replaced the earlier model with the Ego-Id-Superego model in 1923.

We shall draw upon the clinical observations Freud made during his psychoanalysis of the Wolf Man to illustrate this concept of the hierarchical organization of defenses. Figure 22-1 summarizes and illustrates the main points of the discussion. The bottom entries in this figure summarize some of the facts about the Wolf Man's childhood that were mentioned in Chapter 15:

He was sexually excited about his nursemaids, first Grusha and then Nanya, but he repressed these sexual desires when he developed castration anxiety. These repressed desires, however, continued to affect his sexual behavior as an adult,

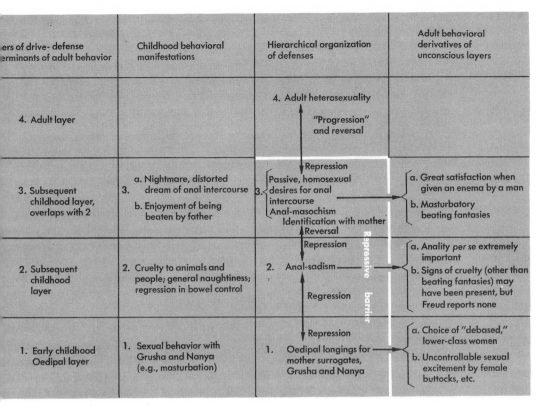

...ers of drive- defense ...erminants of adult behavior	Childhood behavioral manifestations	Hierarchical organization of defenses	Adult behavioral derivatives of unconscious layers
4. Adult layer		4. Adult heterosexuality ↑ "Progression" and reversal	
3. Subsequent childhood layer, overlaps with 2	3. a. Nightmare, distorted dream of anal intercourse b. Enjoyment of being beaten by father	↑ Repression Passive, homosexual 3. desires for anal intercourse Anal-masochism Identification with mother ↑ Reversal	a. Great satisfaction when given an enema by a man b. Masturbatory beating fantasies
2. Subsequent childhood layer	2. Cruelty to animals and people; general naughtiness; regression in bowel control	↑ Repression 2. Anal-sadism ↑ Regression	a. Anality per se extremely important b. Signs of cruelty (other than beating fantasies) may have been present, but Freud reports none
1. Early childhood Oedipal layer	1. Sexual behavior with Grusha and Nanya (e.g., masturbation)	↑ Repression 1. Oedipal longings for mother surrogates, Grusha and Nanya	a. Choice of "debased," lower-class women b. Uncontrollable sexual excitement by female buttocks, etc.

Figure 22-1   Hierarchical organization of defenses in the Wolf Man.

as is indicated by his preference for women who were socially inferior to him and by his sexual over-reactions to women's buttocks and to kneeling women.

But repression was not the Wolf Man's only childhood defense. He also regressed to the anal stage of relating to people. Soon after his Nanya threatened him with castration if he "misbehaved" sexually, he became generally naughty and cruel. He took great delight in killing and torturing insects and small animals, in fantasying that he was beating large animals, and in teasing and disobeying Nanya. He also reverted to incontinence of his bowels.

Soon other changes appeared in the boy's behavior. He misbehaved so as to elicit beatings from his father, as we saw in the previous chapter, and he started to fantasy that boys were being beaten, especially on their penises. He also made a peculiar complaint about his loss of bowel control, saying that he "couldn't go on living like that." Since there was convincing evidence that he had heard his mother make just this remark about *her* intestinal troubles, it appeared quite likely to Freud that the little boy had unconsciously identified with his mother. About this time, the Wolf Man had his nightmare of the wolves staring in at him through his bedroom window, and he also developed his phobia of pictures of wolves standing and walking on their hind legs. His free associations to this nightmare (which he reexperienced in his transference relationship with Freud), the evidence that he had identified with his mother and that he liked to be spanked by his father, and many other facts led Freud to conclude that this dream scene was a disguised picture of a scene the boy had witnessed earlier—either his father and mother having intercourse from behind or animals having intercourse. In either case, the male was up on his hind legs. Collectively, these items strongly suggest that the boy had defended against his anal sadism (which was itself a defense by regression) and his repressed erotic feelings about Nanya by developing passive, masochistic erotic desires for his father. It was *as if* the boy now unconsciously wished that his father would have intercourse with him.

But it was also *as if* this wish was extremely frightening to him; otherwise his dream would not have been a nightmare. Since the theme of castration emerged in all the many free associations about wolves, the most plausible reason for the boy's terror of the nightmare and the pictures was that he thought he would have to be castrated if his erotic feminine wishes for his father were to come true. He knew women did not have penises. This *rearoused castration anxiety* appears to have caused repression of his anal masochism. Later, under the pressure of puberty, his heterosexual desires again became predominant. The term "progression" can be used for this change, which contrasts with the childhood regression. His repressed, passive anal eroticism, however, still operated. One bit of evidence was that he indulged in beating fantasies when he masturbated. The most striking evidence, however, was that he developed a severe obsessional neurosis after he contracted a venereal disease. It was as if this disease had reactivated his castration anxiety, which in turn had intensified his repressed anal masochism, especially his unconscious feminine desires for his father. That this was the case is most clearly indicated by one of his adult symptoms: *One of his greatest pleasures was to be given an enema by a man.* But, in fact, his entire obsessional neurosis was caused by conflicts over his intensified, unconscious anal eroticism.

(Any reader interested in the detailed clinical data that emerged in the Wolf Man's analysis and gave rise to the formulations presented here should study Freud's original case report [1918], which is also, as we said earlier, the best sample of Freud as a clinical investigator.)

Figure 22-1 depicts the hierarchical organization of defenses just described. The third column summarizes his defensive movements starting, at the bottom, with the repression of his Oedipal longings for his mother surrogates, Grusha and Nanya. The second column cites the major behavioral manifestations of the earlier, childhood movements. The singular features of the Wolf Man's adult behavior are noted in the fourth column. Such observable symptoms provide the major *empirical* basis for assuming that there is a hierarchical organization of defenses. Note that two defensive "layers"—the regression to anal sadism and the reversal to anal masochism or passive homosexuality—are unconscious. Here we see concrete examples of the fact that defenses are unconscious.

Another important empirical reason for assuming such hierarchical organizations is a general timetable that characterizes most psychoanalyses. At first the analysand talks primarily about aspects of his life concerned with the "top layer." But his associations include slight, disguised indications of even the lowest layers, showing that those "deep layers" are active at that moment but are being defended against. As the analysis progresses, the analysand talks increasingly and more directly about the "lower layers" and their influence on his present life.

Individual Differences
in Conflict and Defense

We are now going to open Pandora's box, without being able to sort out all that pours forth from it and without closing the lid.

The clinical experience of psychoanalysts and psychotherapists strongly suggests that people differ from one another in the three major variables in the conflict paradigm: the kinds of drives that disturb them, the kinds of unpleasant affects that plague them, and their preferred defenses (Freud, 1926, 1937; A. Freud, 1936). All we shall do here is indicate the nature of these apparent individual differences and discuss briefly how they *might* originate.

We shall start with *drives*. Few people develop inner conflicts over the basic, life-sustaining biological drive behavior, such as eating, drinking, excretion, and breathing. But some people do, when those behaviors become the means for sexual or aggressive gratification. Individual differences become more prominent within the realm of sexuality and aggression. Aggression is the *primary* source of conflict for some people, for example those suffering from severe depression and obsessional behavior. With others, the paramount source of conflict is some kind of sexual wish. Every adult with a sexual conflict seems never to have resolved his childhood incestuous attachments. But, beyond this core conflict (which in itself varies in intensity from person to person), different aspects of sexuality stand out in the conflicts of different people. Some people's misery stems primarily from heterosexual conflicts, that of others from homosexuality or from their oral or anal eroticism or even from self-love. Other powerful motives, such as autonomy or dependency strivings, may also be subject to conflict in any given person.

People also appear to differ in regard to the *motives for defense*. Where one man's predominant anxiety is fear of disorganization of his personality, another's is separation anxiety, another's is fear of loss of love, and still another's is castration anxiety. Still others find their nemesis in shame or in other forms of lowered self-esteem or in hypertrophied consciences and the resulting sense of guilt.

All the *defense mechanisms* discussed here and others that will undoubtedly be discovered in the future are probably used by everyone at one time or another. But some people seem to be predominantly "repressors and deniers," others "projectors and identifiers," and so on. Furthermore, each individual appears to use his "preferred defenses" against all the instigators of those defenses. If a person is a "projector," for example, he is likely to project his sexual and aggressive thoughts, his corresponding feelings, and his anxiety or guilt.

The whole enterprise of diagnostic testing within the framework of psychoanalytic theory (presented in Part IV) stands largely on the premise that the kinds of individual differences mentioned here can be observed and assessed by psychological tests.

Determinants
of Individual Differences

Freud (1905b, 1926, for example) consistently took the position that innate determinants and environmental influences interacted to produce each of the individual differences we have discussed. He distinguished two kinds of innateness. First, he believed that an innate ground plan, or biological schedule, present in all people, determined both psychosexual development (described in Chapters 14 and 15) and the progressive emergence of the anxieties and guilt we have described. He believed that the latter appeared in this order: the original fear and sense of helplessness of the newborn child (evoked by the high levels of inner and outer stimulation to which he is subjected), separation anxiety, fear of loss of love, castration anxiety and low self-esteem (all of which intimately involve the parents and parental surrogates), and, finally, the impersonal conscience of the adult. Biological schedules of maturation, he believed, also influence the sequence in which defenses appear. Projection and identification, for example, might be used by the very young infant and contribute to the formation of his self-concept. Repression might not develop until later in childhood, when controls over attention and drive behavior have developed. Such controls are required in repression—to block conscious perceptions of inner or outer excitations and to inhibit autonomic and skeletal activity. This first kind of innateness is general, common to all people. It would make people alike.

The second kind of innateness Freud referred to was specific to individual people. Freud held that there were such unique, organically based dispositions as innate differences in drive intensity, in the readiness to develop anxiety, and in precursors of the specific defense mechanisms.

Freud believed that experience, environmental influences, and learning had definite effects on the potentialities provided by the unfolding biological ground plan. He emphasized two kinds of experiences: traumatic ones and those producing the identifications with our parents, especially the identifications resulting in superego formation. The latter, in his view, provided the primary means of cultural transmission.

Although he clearly believed that "nature and nurture" interacted to determine individual differences, Freud did not always seem to appreciate the full impact of the environment. Anybody who reads the Little Hans paper (1909a) today, for example, will be struck by the erotic stimulation of Little Hans by his mother and her inconsistent castration threats. But Freud minimizes the significance of her behavior. In assessing Freud's attitude three things must be remembered. Freud, like the other thinkers of his age, was profoundly influenced by Darwin's theory of evolution, including Darwin's acceptance of Lamarck's idea that acquired characteristics are inherited (Ritvo, 1965). Such a heavy emphasis on heredity meant a corresponding lack of emphasis on environment. Also, the behavioral psychology of Freud's day was largely an "instinct psychology"; learning theory was practically nonexistent. Finally, cultural sociology and anthropology had not yet developed into the powerful disciplines they are today.

Among Freudian psychoanalysts, Karen Horney was one of the first to take strong exception to Freud's relatively heavy *theoretical* emphasis on innate biological determinants of behavior. One of her major books, *The Neurotic Personality of Our Time* (1937), opened and closed with chapters focusing on the cultural definition and determination of neuroses. Horney believed that "nurture" was far more important than "nature" in determining the conflicts people have. For example, she thought that the Oedipal complex was a product of the child's family environment. In fact, she believed that the Oedipal complex was not found in children raised in a family atmosphere of healthy warmth and security. Instead, she thought it was a neurosis itself, a response of the child to such parental behavior as sexual overstimulation of the child, emotional withdrawal from him, or severe hostility toward him.

Many factors have since combined to bring into better balance the present-day psychologist's views concerning the roles of innate and environmental influences. The view that today appears most valid and productive holds that individual differences in conflict and defense result from equally important variations in innate and environmental influences, especially those of family life. In its broadest form, this view holds that the behavior of any individual is the resultant of cultural forces and systems interacting with his biologically provided potentialities, a resultant that guarantees the "adaptive fit" between himself and society (Hartmann, 1939; Erikson, 1950; T. Parsons, 1964). Adaptation between the individual and his immediate family, as a representative microcosm of society, is a crucial link in this process.

This broad view faces in two directions, toward individual differences within a culture and toward cultural differences in "national character." According to this view, individual differences in conflict and defense within a culture would result from the interaction of the individual's unique innate endowments, the uniqueness of his family with respect to the drives and defenses it promotes or stunts, and the kind of emotional distress the family fosters in doing so. Cultural differences in the world at large would result from the interaction of genetic differences in racial stock, if they exist, and the uniqueness of the cultures with regard to the drives and defenses they promote.

CROSS-CULTURAL VARIATIONS
IN THE OEDIPAL COMPLEX

The Oedipal complex can serve to illustrate some of these general propositions, especially the assumptions that (1) an individual's conflicts are influenced by social institutions as these are mediated through the family, and (2) the outcome is an "adaptive fit" between the individual and his society.

The child's erotic and mental capacities and the social conditions of child rearing guarantee his forming erotic attachments to maternal figures and ambivalent relationships with people he sees as frustrating those attachments. In our patriarchal Western culture the child develops these relationships with his mother and father—that is, he develops a positive Oedipal complex. But in different social systems this complex may take different forms. In a matrilineal society such as that of the Trobriand Islanders (Malinowski, 1927; A. Parsons, 1964) the "psychic father" is the boy's maternal uncle. In this culture conception is attributed to action by spirits; the father is simply the mother's husband and is not considered to be related to the boy. The boy becomes a member of his mother's kin group, in which the maternal uncle holds authority over him and his mother. The mother, in turn, shows a great deal of respect to her brother. Furthermore, the myths of the Trobrianders are highlighted by brother-sister incest themes, suggesting that strong unconscious incestuous attractions draw the mother and her brother to each other. In fact, the strongest incest taboos in the society concern the brother-sister relationship. It is not surprising that the young boy appears to develop a "nuclear complex" somewhat different from the Oedipal complex we are familiar with. The best-known variation is that the "Oedipal" hostility and ambivalence are directed at his psychic father, his maternal uncle. What we have said so far pertains to the conditions for the development of the Trobriander's variation on the Oedipal complex.

There is another important point about all this. By being disciplined and frustrated by his maternal uncle, the young boy presumably identifies with him the way boys in our culture identify with their fathers, and in the process he internalizes the intense taboos against brother-sister incest. This identification is crucial. It guarantees not only that the boy will grow up avoiding incest with his sister but also that he will later be able to fulfill the maternal uncle role for his sisters' children. Thus, the net effect of his Oedipal conflict and its resolution is that he will fit into and perpetuate the kinship system, the basic social organization, of his culture. (This discussion of the Trobriand Islanders is based on Anne Parsons' reevaluation [1964] of Malinowski's anthropological field data [1927]. Parsons' paper also discusses another version of the Oedipal complex in the "madonna culture" of southern Italy.)

VARIATIONS WITHIN A CULTURE

What holds for cross-cultural variations probably also holds for "*cross-family*" *variations* within our own culture. Families with distinctive needs and organizations of their own foster particular conflicts, anxieties, and defenses in the children. One of Freud's own early discoveries in this area (1920b, 1922) concerned those heterosexual conflicts that are resolved by a defensive homosexuality. He found that this particular conflict-resolution combination is produced by an unusually intense, intimate relationship between a mother and son in a family where the father is "psychologically absent or weak." More recent research—such as that by Lidz, Fleck, and Cornelison (1965) on family dynamics in schizophrenia, Keniston (1965) on adolescent alienation, and Myers and Roberts (1959) on family structure, social class, and mental illness—has begun to extend our knowledge about cross-family variations. Lidz and his co-workers, for example, studied the families of schizophrenic patients. They intensively interviewed family members and made first-hand observations of how the family interacted both at home and in group meetings. Their observations led them to hypothesize that personality deficiencies in the parents and related disturbed marital interaction had profoundly influenced the children. The parents appeared to deprive their children of adequate nurture, to provide them with faulty models for forming a healthy sexual identity, to stimulate conscious incestuous fantasies that bound the children to them in guilt- and anxiety-ridden relationships, and to transmit irrational modes of behavior—irrational ways of thinking and disordered ways of handling interpersonal relationships. Setting aside the question of the cause of schizophrenia, this research suggests that family dynamics and organization influence significantly the kinds of conflicts and defenses found in the offspring.

Family structure reflects social-class values as well as the idiosyncratic dynamics of the individual family members. So the question naturally arises: Do individual differences in conflict and defense vary with social-class membership and participation? A pioneering study by Hollingshead and Redlich (1958) and another by Srole, Langer, Mitchell, Opler, and Rennie (1962) suggest that this *might* be the case. Both studies demonstrated that the general forms of mental illness (psychosis versus neurosis, for example) differ markedly in the various social classes. Psychosis, for example, is more prominent in the lower classes; neurosis, in the upper classes. *If* different emotional distresses and different defense processes determine the form of mental illness, these studies obviously suggest that the *life differences* of the various social classes in America promote different conflicts and defenses. More direct studies of social class and of specific conflicts and defenses characteristic of members of different social classes are clearly needed. Psychologists, sociologists, and psychiatrists are beginning such investigations (for example, Miller & Swanson, 1958). Indeed, there are many indications that the energetic efforts now being made in community mental health programs and centers will stimulate many people to do the clinical and systematic research that will greatly increase our understanding of the ways social conditions influence the dominant conflicts and defenses of people in different sectors of present-day society.

PART THREE
PERSONALITY
DEVELOPMENT

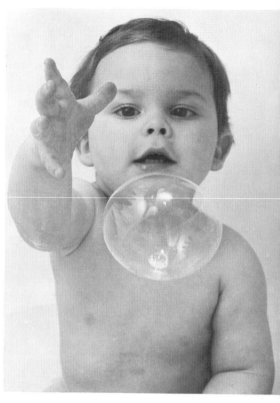

Every man has three characters: that which he exhibits, that which he has, and that which he thinks he has.

ALPHONSE KARR

CHAPTER 23
WHAT IS PERSONALITY DEVELOPMENT?

T he phenomena of growth fall into two patterns: enlargement and change. The leaf expands as it grows, but it does not alter its essential form. The butterfly, on the other hand, passes through dramatically different stages of change en route to adulthood. Man illustrates both kinds of development. Bone, muscle, and fat become larger and heavier, but like the leaf they retain essentially the same structure throughout life. Man's psychological processes and overt actions bear a closer kinship to the butterfly, for they undergo major changes during the first dozen years of life. The development of an individual personality furnishes a classic example of how *changes* in organization characterize the growth process.

Personality can best be conceptualized, in terms of mental processes and overt actions, as the relation between thinking, wishing, and feeling on the one hand and behavior on the other. Both the child and the adult have expectancies of events that might happen, beliefs about the world, motives and wishes, standards, emotions, anxieties, and defenses against unpleasant feelings. Each person also has a large collection of responses designed to maintain beliefs, gratify motives, express or inhibit emotion, and protect himself against anxiety. The task of a theory of personality development is to trace the connections between the personality of the child and that of the adult—to understand how the adult organization of psychic processes and behaviors was derived from that of the child. In other words, how does the butterfly emerge from the caterpillar? A look at the case of a moderately disturbed personality will help to illustrate the nature and complexity of the problem.

Personality Development:
A Case Study

Louise was a member of a research group that had been studied since birth. At 22, when she appeared for an interview with the author, she was attractive, unmarried, and recently graduated from college with a major in biology. She was initially cooperative and superficially relaxed, but bursts of inappropriate laughter and hostility eventually began to punctuate the interview. Louise was often unable to answer questions directly, and she became entangled in long strings of tangential associations that had little to do with the original question. She was excessively preoccupied with danger and with the integrity of her body. When asked about her major area of study in college, she replied:

> I had gone up with my zoology professor and seven other girls, and we went through the lab and saw the medical technologists at work. At the hospital up there I saw the apparatus and understood that there are three or four different fields of medical technology, and I was always worried about my eyesight a little bit because I always heard there was quite a bit of microscopic work and, ah, then I talked to my optometrist about that and he said that I needn't have to worry—he wore glasses—and that if I ever go into a hospital that I planned to work on for any, any length of time that they grind the top lens for you according to your eyes and so, ah, that sort of abolished that and I felt free to go into the field as far as my eyesight was concerned.

Louise showed a deep suspicion of others. She spoke repeatedly about the jealousy of other women and said that she maintained a wall between herself and the social environment. As the interview progressed, she became increasingly icy and hostile to the interviewer until she suddenly turned on her heel and left without a comment.

During the two days of assessment, she had shown serious disorganization in her thinking, a tendency to attribute hostility to others, and generally inappropriate behavior. She was easily threatened, and the subsequent anxiety disrupted her behavior and thinking. How had this personality structure developed? In search of an answer, let us look briefly at Louise as a child.

Observations on Louise and her mother during the first 10 years revealed that Louise was an extremely irritable baby. During the first 2 years of her life, she had wild tantrums, which her mother did not know how to handle. The mother was cold and critical and as early as 2 years of age placed excessive demands on Louise's development. Louise's irritability subsided after age 2; by the time she was 5 she was described as a shy, withdrawn, and frightened child. It was sometimes difficult to understand her speech, and she appeared suspicious of adults and other children. However, after she entered elementary school her behavior changed markedly. The school situation seemed to provide Louise with a way to contain her basic conflicts. She became more friendly, seemed happier, and was less concerned with potential danger than she had been during the prekindergarten years. She was an excellent pupil, highly motivated to do well. She got A's and B's, and her teachers regarded her as a relatively mature, intelligent, self-contained child who was not conspicuously different from her peers. Louise's behavior remained essentially the same until she went to college, when the stress of leaving home and adjusting to new people began to reveal itself in open signs of anxiety and behavioral disruption. The time of the interview was a relatively anxious period, for she had just graduated from college and now faced the problem of deciding what to do with her life.

Louise was an irritable infant, a shy, withdrawn 5-year-old, a composed and motivated 10-year-old, and an anxious, suspicious adult. How did she get to be that way? How are we to explain the changes? These are the questions that a theory of personality development attempts to answer.

Why Study the Development of Personality?

There are three reasons why the gradual establishment of adult personality deserves close attention. First, understanding how a structure develops aids in understanding how the structure functions in its mature form. This is true in spite of the fact that the laws that govern the functioning of an organism, group, or institution are often different from the laws that explain the gradual growth or establishment of that organism, group, or institution. For example, the sociological laws that describe the functioning of contemporary American cities are not the same as the laws that describe how these cities grew to their current size. An understanding of the current social problems of Detroit is facilitated if one knows that part of the labor market in Detroit is composed of migrants from Southern cities.

Similarly, understanding the personality of an adult is facilitated if one knows how that personality was formed. Consider two women, similar in temperament, both of whom have decided to become professional economists. One woman is the daughter of a famous statesman who has encouraged her to enter the field of economics ever since she was in elementary school. Her father spent many evenings reading to her and often took her on trips with him. He led his daughter to believe that if she became a scholar in economics he would be very pleased with her. As the daughter approached maturity, she realized that if she became an economist she would retain her father's affection; since she wanted this goal, she was highly motivated to succeed in graduate school. Her desire to be an economist was based primarily on her desire to please her father and thus to retain his affection.

The second woman initially wanted to be a physicist because a teacher suggested early in her adolescence that she would be good at physics. Her parents were neither pleased nor displeased with this choice. However, after two years of college she decided that physics was too difficult a study to pursue and shifted her interest to economics. She had no strong desire to be an economist but chose this area because it held some interest for her, and it allowed her to capitalize on her background in mathematics.

These two life histories give us valuable information for predicting the future behavior of the two women. The first woman should be expected to persist more strongly in her studies than the second in the face of unusual hardship or frustration, because economics was a primary choice, closely linked with her family relationships. The second woman's choice was a compromise and is, therefore, potentially less stable. We must, of course, know the history of the two women's choices of career in order to understand their different behaviors.

A second rationale for the study of development is that the organization of motives, beliefs, fears, skills, and defenses is different at different ages. Psychological development is not like the growth of muscle, during which a strand merely becomes stronger and larger with time but never changes its basic structure. At 4 years of age anxiety over possible loss of parental affection is usually the most intensely felt fear. At 1 or 18 years of age, however, this fear is weak in relation to other sources of anxiety. The 1-year-old is most afraid of strange situations; the 18-year-old is anxious over his self-image. In order to understand why a child of a given age behaves as he does, it is necessary to know the specific organization of motives and fears that exists at different ages.

A third reason for inquiry into development is born of the practical need to predict adult personality—and personality disturbance—from knowledge of the child's life experiences and personality. A basic assumption of developmental psychology is that the child is father to the man, that responses learned early in childhood guide and direct the adoption and practice of future behavior, thus giving a sense of continuity to human behavior. Although boys do not seriously select a vocation until late adolescence, they typically begin to adopt sex-typed interests and traits between 5 and 10 years of age. If the boy fails to adopt traditional masculine characteristics during this early stage, he is less likely than those of his peers who do develop these characteristics to select the traditionally masculine vocations of medicine, law, engineering, professional athletics, or business when he is 18. The adoption of one set of responses at age 10 reduces the chances of selecting a new set of responses at age 18. It is often of practical importance that we be able to predict occupational choice, performance in high school and college, or future creativity from behavior displayed during the early school years.

The prediction of adult behavior is also important for prevention of adult personality disturbances. Most of the psychological ills that plague man and, in turn, society as a whole are difficult to modify in the adult. Schizophrenia, suicidal depression, drug addiction, criminality, and alcoholism are each the result of a long history of specific experiences. Many psychologists assume that the critical events that predispose the adult to develop any one of these disorders occur at different stages in childhood. During various critical—or sensitive—periods in human development, specific psychological processes are developing most rapidly. An intrusion during one of these periods is most likely to alter the course of a particular pattern of behavior developing at that time. It is during the critical periods that patterns that lead to psychological disturbances in the adult may best be altered.

Critical Periods in Development

The term "critical period," then, refers to those time periods during which a particular type of environmental event has its most dramatic influence on a specific developing organ, physiological process, or behavior. During each critical period, the effect of a particular event or experience on a behavior is maximal.

It is common knowledge among students of biology that changing the location of a few cells of a recently fertilized egg will have one effect during the early hours after fertilization and a much different effect 48 hours later. Castration of a newborn male rat during the first 5 postnatal days leads to the display of female mating behavior in adulthood, because the presence of testicular androgens during the first 5 days is necessary if the hypothalamus of the rat is to take on normal male functioning. Castration of the male rat *after* the fifth day minimizes the likelihood of female mating responses in adulthood, because the androgens have had a chance to masculinize the central nervous system (Young, Goy, & Phoenix, 1964).

Examples of critical-period phenomena in human development are not so easily isolated as they are in animal development. One example comes from information on the child's physical growth. The first 3 years of life constitute the period of most rapid growth in stature; it is also at this time that quality of diet exerts its maximal effect on the adult's final height. In fact, improved diet is probably one reason that second-generation American children are taller, on the average, than their parents. Thus, there is a clear relation between the time during which a particular attribute—in this case, stature—is developing most rapidly and the time when it is most vulnerable to environmental processes—in this case, diet.

Another example of the critical-period phenomenon in human physiological development involves a rare form of mental deficiency called phenylketonuria. The child with this disease lacks an enzyme that is necessary for normal physiological functioning of the brain. In effect, the child becomes poisoned because he cannot metabolize certain substances that are in most

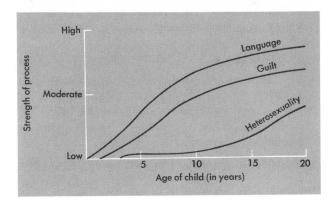

Figure 23-1 Relation of growth of response processes to age of child.

foods and his brain becomes permanently damaged. However, if a special diet excluding these substances is instituted during the early months of life, a critical period for the development of the brain, the child can be prevented from becoming a mental defective.

Let us consider an example at a more speculative level, involving psychological development. The first 3 years are regarded as a critical period for the establishment of trusting relationships with adults. Some theorists assume that the young child's failure to develop a trust in his mother or a substitute caretaker during this critical period leads to the development of a withdrawn, detached, or extremely aggressive personality.

Note that when the term "critical period" is applied to psychological, as opposed to biological, development, the analogue for anatomical structure or physiological process is either a particular behavioral response or a covert mental process such as an affect, anxiety, a standard, a motive, a skill, or a defense. It is assumed that these responses or mental processes in the adult generally began to develop at different times in the child and that each is most vulnerable to modification during that period when it is developing at its most rapid rate.

It is possible to view psychological development as a series of curves, in which each curve represents a different type of process. Figure 23-1 illustrates this idea for three kinds of processes: language ability, capacity for guilt, and ability to interact successfully with the opposite sex. The vertical axis measures the strength of the process; the slope of the curve indicates the rate at which the process is being acquired; and the horizontal axis denotes the age of the child. The critical-period concept assumes that the age at which the slopes of the curves are maximal will differ according to the process. The curves in Figure 23-1 are all hypothetical but are based on existing evidence from many types of observations. The slope for language ability is considered to be greatest between ages 2 and 6; the slope for capacity for guilt is greatest between 4 and 10; and the slope for heterosexual behavior is greatest between 13 and 17 years of age.

The critical period for language development, for example, is between 2 and 6 years because the curve is steepest for those years. At that time the rate of acquisition of language skills in family-reared children is most rapid; modifications in the environment during this 4-year span should have a major influence, either positive or negative, on the quality of the child's language at maturity.

This discussion has centered on the reasons for studying personality development. However, it also contains the essential rationale for the existence of the discipline called developmental psychology, which is concerned with mental as well as personality growth. In the past, developmental psychology consisted chiefly of a collection of norms for motor and mental performance: The 1-year-old child should have two or three words; the 15-month-old child should be walking; the 24-month-old child should be able to run and should have a vocabulary of 30 words. The contemporary bases for developmental psychology, however, are more theoretical and are held together by the fundamental ideas implied earlier:

1. There are critical periods of development during which certain responses and processes develop rapidly.
2. Motives and anxieties learned early in life guide and direct the adoption and maintenance of future behavior.
3. The organization of thoughts, beliefs, and behavior is different at different ages.

These three ideas are central to an understanding of the development of adult personality.

Patterning in Development

The establishment of an individual personality from the first hours of life to adulthood bears a particular resemblance to the development of an animal embryo. Both processes involve the emergence of new components in a specific order. For example, the central nervous system begins to develop before the organs of reproduction in all mammalian forms; similarly, the emergence of speech always precedes the appearance of reciprocal play with other children. In some cases the order of emergence is fixed so that one structure permits the development of a succeeding one. The vertebral column appears before the rib cage in embryological development, for the ribs must be attached to a solid structure. Similarly, the child must develop some anxiety over the possible loss of his parents' affection before he can experience the affect of shame, for shame is derived from the anticipation that other people might disapprove of his behavior.

The second parallel between the growth of the embryo and the psychological development of the child is the existence of the critical periods referred to earlier. The belief that adults are sources of pleasure is acquired most intensively during the first 4 years of life. Removing the child from adults or exposing him to minimally affectionate people during this period may impair his ability to relate to people during later childhood and adulthood.

An orderly emergence of each of the component parts of the whole during particular time periods is one way to conceptualize development. Two problems confront us: What are the essential components, and how can we understand their changes over time? The chapters that follow consider these questions.

The Need
for Theoretical Terms

The sciences of biology, chemistry, and physics have developed over the years a vocabulary that is shared by most of the scientists in these disciplines. Biologists agree that the gene, glucose metabolism, and selective mutation are central concepts; physicists agree that wave length, force, speed of light, and electromagnetic energy are basic to understanding physical phenomena. Unfortunately, psychology is not as mature as these sister sciences, and there is no agreement as to which phenomena are most important and which concepts are most useful. Too often each theorist consults his own prejudices when he initiates research on personality development. But selection of a working vocabulary is essential and frequent reference will be made to such concepts as expectancy, motive, standard, belief, affect, anxiety, and defense throughout this section. Detailed discussions of these concepts appear in those chapters of the section where they seem most appropriate.

Let us begin our journey now by turning our attention, appropriately, to the infant.

. . . man's education begins at birth; before he can speak or understand he is learning. Experience precedes instruction; when he recognises his nurse he has learnt much.

JEAN-JACQUES ROUSSEAU. Emile

CHAPTER 24
THE FIRST
CRITICAL PERIOD:
BIRTH
TO 18 MONTHS

This chapter delineates the major psychological acquisitions associated with the first 18 months and the environmental events that appear to be most influential in promoting these acquisitions. At a general level, the infant is acquiring (1) perceptual representations of the significant people and objects that surround him; (2) an attachment to the person or persons who care for him; (3) conditioned associations between feelings of pleasure or displeasure and certain human beings; and (4) expectations of being gratified or not gratified when in distress. In addition, he acquires increasingly mature coordination of eye, hand, head, trunk, and limbs, as well as the early rudiments of language. Before considering these first four psychological acquisitions—those that are most essential for understanding personality—we shall examine briefly some of the significant events that occur at various periods in the opening year and a half of life.

Important Stages
in the First 18 Months

THE NEWBORN PERIOD OF REFLEX ACTIONS

The newborn period is considered to cover the first 5 to 7 days. During this time, the infant is recovering from the physiological trauma of delivery and is only beginning to establish an equilibrium with his environment. Many of the behaviors that the newborn displays, such as sucking, searching for the nipple, or visual pursuit of a moving light, do not involve the cerebral cortex and are mediated by the older portions of the brain. Nevertheless, the newborn is a remarkably capable organism from the moment he begins to breathe. He can see, hear, and smell, and he is sensitive to pain, touch, and change in position. He is biologically ready to experience most of the basic sensations of his species from the moment he is born. This is not true of all mammals—puppies, for instance, are both blind and deaf at birth.

The newborn's behavioral equipment is also well developed. After only 2 hours he will follow a moving light with his eyes, if the velocity of the light is optimal; he will suck a finger or nipple inserted in his mouth; he will turn in a direction in which his cheek or the corner of his mouth is touched. He can cry, cough, turn away, vomit, lift his chin from a prone position, and grasp an object placed in his palm. His body will tense to a loud sound; he can flex and extend his limbs, smack his lips, and chew his fingers. Contemporary psychologists view the newborn with considerably more respect than did the scientists of the sixteenth century, who regarded the infant as a relatively insensitive vegetable. The myth of newborn insensitivity and incompetence has been dispelled by modern scientific observation.

Is a Baby's World
Confusing?

A second myth concerning the young infant is depicted in the oft-quoted belief that the world of a baby is a "blooming, buzzing confusion." This idea developed from the bias that regarded the infant as a passive, helpless animal with little power to cope with his environment. The belief that the world is a confusing place is a reasonable conclusion for an urban-dwelling scientist; it is understandable that the scientist would conclude that if his world is a noisy place, it must be even more intrusive for the obviously more helpless infant. Recent research on attentional processes suggests, however, that the infant's world may actually be quieter than the adult's.

Human beings typically attend to only one sensory channel at a time. For example, when we are listening intently to a bird's call in a forest, we do not feel the touch of a leaf or see a grazing deer. We choose the sensory event to which we wish to attend and are temporarily blinded or deafened to other sensory events. We *think* we can attend to so many channels of information at once, because we shift our attention rapidly and frequently from one event to another. The rapid shifting of attention gives the impression of continuous perception of many events simultaneously. This rapid oscillation of attention is analogous to the electric current in the light bulb that goes on and off 60 times a second. We perceive continuous rather than discontinuous light because the shift in current is so rapid that we cannot detect it.

It is possible that the newborn cannot change his focus of attention as rapidly as can the older child. When the baby is watching his mother, he may not hear sounds around him; when he is attending to a hunger pain, he may not feel his mother's touch. His world may be made up of single perceptions and, therefore, may be less confused and noisy than that of the adult.

CHANGES AT 2 TO 3 MONTHS

From 1 to about 12 weeks of age the infant is gradually developing a rhythm of eating and sleeping. His ability to focus on visual stimuli improves considerably, and his cerebral cortex gradually assumes control of his actions. However, he still seems to be in a semistuporous state and does not always appear alert when his eyes are open. Four important changes occur between 8 and 12 weeks of age that mark the end of this semialert state and the beginning of a new phase. These changes include the appreciation of depth in visual perception, increased vocalization and play, the disappearance of the Moro reflex, and the display of satiation or boredom to a repetitive visual stimulus.

Prior to 8 weeks two- and three-dimensional representations of human faces or objects elicit from the infant the same amount of smiling and the same duration of looking. However, by 10 to 12 weeks he will look longer and smile more frequently at the three-dimensional stimulus, which suggests that he now appreciates depth. A second change is that the amount of time spent crying decreases dramatically, and the amount of time spent cooing, babbling, and playing with fingers increases. The third change is the disappearance of the Moro reflex. This reflex involves the whole body and occurs when the infant experiences a sudden change in head position, for example when his head and trunk are lowered abruptly. The infant throws his arms out to the side, then brings them back to the mid-line as if he were embracing someone. One interpretation of the disappearance of the Moro reflex at this time is that the infant's behavior is now being controlled by the cerebral cortex, which inhibits and modulates the lower brain stem centers that are responsible for the Moro reflex.

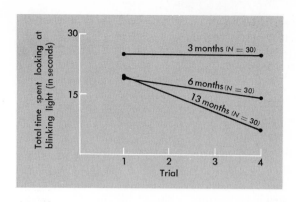

Figure 24-1   Effect of age on infant attention. (Adapted from Lewis, 1967)

Infants display major differences in the rate at which they become bored with or habituated to a repeated event. Habituation is the tendency to give diminished responses to repetitions of the same stimulus. This is usually manifested in decreased looking, but it can involve decreased autonomic reactivity or decreased babbling or smiling to a visual or auditory stimulus. Prior to 10 to 12 weeks of age infants do not typically show decreased attention to repeated presentations of a face, a bull's-eye, or a point of light that blinks on and off once every 2 seconds. However, at about 3 months of age the infant begins to pay decreased attention to a repeated stimulus, and the rate at which his attention drops off increases as he grows older.

Figure 24-1 illustrates the results of a study in which infants of different ages were shown a single blinking light for four 30-second trials. The 3-month-old infants showed a slight decrease in attentiveness over the four trials. The 6- and 13-month-old infants, however, showed a dramatic decrease in attention over this short period of time; the older the child was, the more rapid was his rate of habituation.

Differences among infants in the rate at which they habituate to events may have important implications for personality; this issue will be considered in the last section of this chapter.

THE INCREASE IN SMILING AT 3 TO 5 MONTHS

One of the most predictable developments in the first year is the marked increase in smiling to human faces and voices during the period 3 to 5 months. The peak age for this social smile typically is 4 months in many different child-rearing environments. The smile at 4 months seems to be one way the infant can signify that he has recognized a familiar event; in Figure 24-2 it is the face. The smile is his "Aha!" reaction and resembles the smile adults show when they have resolved a puzzling situation.

Gewirtz (1965) studied the smiling of three groups of infants raised under different conditions in Israel. One group of infants lived in residential institutions, rarely saw their parents, and received routine institutional care. Kibbutz infants lived in collective settlements. They were raised in large houses with professional caretakers but were fed frequently during the first year by their mothers. The family-reared children were raised in typical Western apartments by their mothers. The peak for smiling for the kibbutz- and family-reared infants was a few weeks earlier than the peak for the infants raised in the institution (see Figure 24-3). But in general the peak for all infants was very close to 4 months of age.

As with most behaviors, there are major differences among children in the frequency of smiling. Mothers generally misinterpret the meaning of a smile and assume that a smiling baby is happier than a nonsmiling one. The frequency of smiling—which need not have anything to do with how happy the child is—can affect the mother's attitude toward the infant. The mother of a smiling baby will be persuaded that her infant is happy and content and may feel satisfied with herself and with the effectiveness of her maternal practices. The mother of an infant who is less

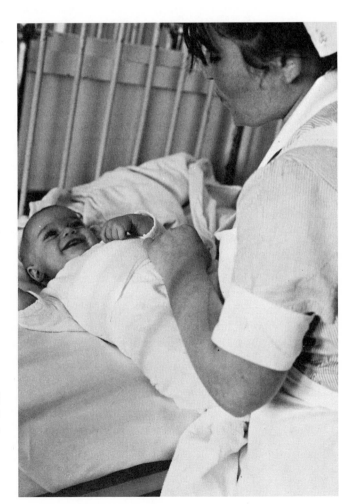

Figure 24-2 Four-month-old institution infant smiling to caretaker. (From Gewirtz, 1965)

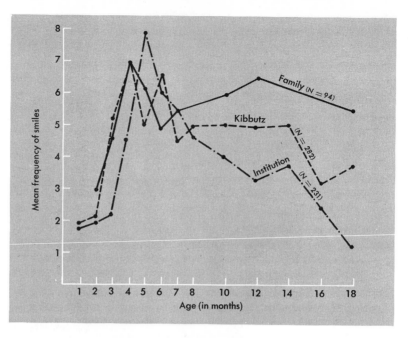

Figure 24-3 Frequency of smiling in infants of different environments. (Adapted from Gewirtz, 1965)

disposed to smile may feel threatened; she may begin to doubt her effectiveness and wonder if she should be handling her infant in a different way. The American mother is prone to believe that she is the primary cause of her baby's well-being; if she considers her infant's lack of smiling to be a reflection of her inadequacy rather than a constitutional characteristic of her baby, she is likely to become anxious or angry and behave in ways detrimental to the infant's development.

THE EMERGENCE OF ANXIETY AT 6 TO 12 MONTHS

During the latter half of the first year, the infant behaves as if an event that is a bit unfamiliar is frightening. He becomes vigilant, apprehensive, and upset when he confronts a strange person or when he is in an unfamiliar environment without his mother. The first anxiety is called *stranger anxiety*; the second is called *separation anxiety*. Even presentation of a mask of a distorted human face (shown in Figure 24-4) or speech sounds that deviate somewhat from normal speech can elicit crying and other signs of fright in 8-month-old infants.

The likelihood of open display of fear is increased if the infant cannot interpret the strange stimulus or if he is unable to act when the strange event occurs. Thus: The infant is most likely to show signs of fear when (1) he encounters a person, object, or situation that is slightly different from that to which he is accustomed (called a discrepant stimulus) and (2) he is unable to act upon or interpret the strange event. The importance of action in inhibiting fear is illustrated in the following sequences.

1. A 10-month-old infant playing in a room with his mother seated in one corner shows no signs of fear or upset. When the mother leaves the room, the baby watches her go and then returns to playing with his blocks and pail. As long as he is preoccupied with the blocks he seems content. However, once he drops the blocks and is inactive and not attentive to any other stimulus in the room his behavior suddenly changes. After a few seconds of inactivity he may look toward the door where the mother had left several minutes earlier, and he may begin to cry. Although the child noticed the mother's departure at the time she left, as long as he was occupied he did not cry. The upset that leads to crying is most likely to occur when his attention is not occupied—when the system is psychologically open.

2. If a 10-month-old child is placed in a strange room alone, he typically cries within 1 minute. If the same child is placed with his mother in a room that adjoins the strange room in which he cried earlier, the infant will crawl into the strange room, out of sight of his mother, but he *will not cry*. He will look around the unfamiliar room and then crawl back to the room where the mother is sitting. He does not cry in the strange room because he has a response to make in the unfamiliar context: He can crawl back to the more familiar room where his mother is (Rheingold, personal communication).

3. A 13-month-old is allowed to play with toys while his mother sits in a corner of the room. After 20 minutes of play the child is put on one side of a transparent barrier, with his mother and the toys on the other side. Some children begin to cry immediately or after 1 or 2 minutes. As in the separation situation described above, the crying typically occurs when the infant is not involved in any activity. However, if he begins playing with the barrier or tries to climb over the barrier, the crying is inhibited. When he stops playing with the barrier, crying is likely to recur. Some children display alternate crying and contentment, depending on whether they are

Figure 24-4 Clay mask shown to infants at 8 months of age.

inactive or occupied. For instance, in one sequence a child was pushing on the barrier and was relatively content. He then stopped pushing, stood with his arms at his sides and began crying. A moment later, as he started to push once more on the barrier, he stopped crying.

This cyclic pattern of activity and the cessation of crying followed by inactivity and the resumption of crying gives strong credence to the idea that fear and distress can be inhibited by active preoccupation with an object or event. Unpleasant feelings, resembling fear, dominate behavior when the infant—and probably the adult as well—is not distributing his attention to other matters.

**The Relation
of a Schema to Fear**   The displays of fear described in the discussion of separation and stranger anxiety above involve two of the most important characteristics of the first 18 months of life: the development of a schema for familiar stimuli and the acquisition of both cognitive and overt reactions toward familiar objects and events. The infant learns perceptual structures that allow him to recognize those people, objects, and locations that he has encountered in the past. Such perceptual structures are called *schemata*. Once a schema is established, the child becomes unusually sensitive to events that deviate or are discrepant from the familiar stimuli on which the schema was based. Discrepant events alert the infant. If he has no response to make, he is likely to cry; if he does have a way to interpret the event or is able to behave toward it, he is less likely to become upset. He may even signify his ability to deal with the strange event by smiling or laughing.

These basic reactions are remarkably similar to the ways adults function. An adult in a strange situation usually becomes alert and tense. If he can interpret his presence in the situation or feels he can predict what will happen to him, he is not likely to become afraid. However, if he does not understand why he is in the situation, is unsure of the immediate future, and, in addition, does not know how to respond, he will probably become afraid. The basic cause of anxiety and its inhibition may be remarkably similar in both infant and adult. The major difference between the infant and the adult may lie in the specific events that are perceived as strange and the nature of the responses the individual makes to deal with the unfamiliar.

12 TO 18 MONTHS

The fifth period of infancy—from 12 to 18 months—is witness to the onset of walking and the beginning of language comprehension and expression. The infant is able to understand simple requests, to use language to obtain desired goals, and—what is most critical—to react to objects on the basis of their symbolic names rather than such physical characteristics as color, shininess, or capacity for being slapped or mouthed.

The 12-month-old can crawl or walk, can manipulate toys, and shows a form of purposefulness in his play. For instance, he will put blocks in a pail for 20 to 30 seconds and then take them out. He will pile blocks into a tower and then knock them over. He will remove a set of quoits one by one from a shaft and replace them one by one. A striking difference between the 6- and 12-month-old child is that the older child actively manipulates the objects and explores their potential uses. The younger infant makes the objects conform to the basic responses he has already developed. He will suck or slap blocks rather than build towers. The most significant development, however, is the symbolic approach to objects. The 18-month-old infant may treat a doll as a baby, or a pillow as a rocking horse. He has begun to conceptualize his world.

The Development of Attachment
to a Caretaker

We have considered the infant's acquisition of a schema for the caretaker and its role in the experience of anxiety to discrepant events. Let us now examine the learning of an emotional attachment to the mother or to the person who cares for the infant. The infant's eventual emotional tie to the mother is learned because the baby begins life with no specific emotional reactions to other people. He has no innate tendencies to love, to hate, to fear, or to value people. His experiences with them during the first year lay the foundation for these future attitudes.

THE NECESSITY OF BEHAVING

From the moment the baby is born, he acts. Some of these actions are spontaneous; others are reactions to biological needs. Some of the actions are necessary for survival, others are not. The baby spontaneously scans the environment, listens to sounds, vocalizes, sucks, smiles, thrashes, and cries. As he approaches the third month of life, he begins to cling to people and objects, and he manipulates his fingers, his mother's hair, his blanket, and his toys.

What is the role of the caretaker, particularly the mother, in this complex set of actions? Since the mother is an interesting stimulus object to look at, listen to, and manipulate, the infant typically spends long periods of time scanning her face, babbling when she speaks, and smiling when she smiles. The nursing infant also makes sucking responses to the mother and assumes a definite posture during feeding. Even when the child is bottle feeding, he is usually cradled in the mother's arms, and the relaxed posture is associated with the person feeding him.

Crying is an important response of which the infant is capable from the first hours of life. If the infant is separated from his mother by a few feet or more, the crying response acts as an effective signal to the mother to retrieve or attend to her baby. This is exactly what happens among animals; there is every reason to believe that the squeal of a young puppy performs the same function as the infant's cry. This cry guarantees that the infant will not be in distress for too long a time. When the caretaker comes to relieve the distress, the infant typically relaxes his muscles and, when held upright, rests his head on the mother's shoulder and holds her neck.

Thus, most reactions of the young infant that occur spontaneously (looking, babbling, smiling, crying, sucking, clinging) are directed to the adult caretaker rather than to a rattle, the crib, or a bottle. As a result the infant becomes attached to the caretaker, whether the location is a city apartment, a suburban home, or a hut in the mountains of Guatemala. Attachment is defined here as *the degree to which the infant is predisposed to initiate reactions toward the caretaker.*

ATTACHMENT AS THE BASIS
FOR THE VALUE OF THE MOTHER

The Traditional View   The concept of attachment is relatively new in our theorizing about personality development, but it has recently taken on an important connotation that was missing from earlier theoretical discussions about it. The classic interpretation of the close relationship between infant and mother assumed that the relationship was due to a conditioning of pleasure (that is, positive reward value) to the mother as a stimulus. This interpretation was usually stated in the following way: Any new stimulus that is associated with a reward (a pleasant state, for example) acquires reward value in and of itself. Thus, the mother, as a stimulus, gradually comes to signify pleasure and contentment. The mother becomes a stimulus signaling pleasure, in much the same way that the buzzer became a signal of food for Pavlov's dogs. The infant learns that if he approaches this source of pleasure he will be gratified with minimal delay. He learns the important response of looking for and approaching his mother when he is hungry or in distress. The mother's value, according to this theory, rests primarily on her ability to reduce pain and provide pleasure.

If the initial feeding experience was not rewarding because the mother was tense, held her baby in an awkward manner, or handled him roughly, the infant would experience some discomfort in association with the stimulus of the mother and the sensations of hunger. If these events occurred frequently enough, the mother would acquire negative or anxiety-arousing value. She would then become symbolic of discomfort rather than comfort. Since an organism's innate reaction to discomfort and pain is withdrawal and avoidance, the infant would learn to avoid rather than approach the mother.

In sum, the traditional theoretical view assumes that because the mother reduces pain and imparts pleasure she begins to represent a valuable object—a sign of comfort and security. These assumptions are still regarded as valid. Recent observations, however, have suggested that the tie between mother and infant is more complicated and involves—in addition to the conditioning of pleasure to the mother—the dynamic process of attachment. To this end, Professor Harry Harlow (1959, 1966) and his colleagues at the University of Wisconsin have conducted an important series of studies on attachment in monkeys.

**Attachment
in Monkeys**   In Harlow's experiment infant monkeys grew up with artificial "mother" monkeys constructed of wire mesh. Some of these infants were fed from a bottle attached to the "chest" of a plain wire-mesh mother. Other monkeys were similarly fed by a wire-mesh mother that differed in only one respect from the other one—it was covered by terrycloth (see Figure 24-5). When the monkeys were given the choice of going to either mother, the animals, regardless of which one had fed them, usually chose the terrycloth mother and spent more time clinging to it than to the plain wire-mesh mother. This preference for the cloth mother persisted for many months. Even if the bottle were only attached to the wire mother and the infant could never feed from the terrycloth mother, the monkey would still spend much more time on the terrycloth than on the wire mother. The infant monkey would go to the wire mother only when hungry; it would feed until satisfied and then return to the terrycloth mother for most of the day.

Moreover, the terrycloth mother more effectively reduced the infant monkey's fear than did the wire mother. When a fear-provoking stimulus (such as the large wooden model of a spider shown in Figure 24-6) was placed with the monkey, its initial reaction was to run to the terrycloth mother rather than to the wire-mesh mother. After a while, if the terrycloth mother was present, the young monkey was likely to venture out to explore the fear-arousing stimulus. However, if only the wire-mesh mother was present, the monkey remained fearful and was less likely to explore the open space around the strange stimulus.

Other studies stimulated by Harlow's original work suggest the following conclusions. If the young monkey is to develop normally, it must have some interaction with an object to which it can cling during the opening months of life. Another monkey is best as a caretaker, but a terrycloth surrogate allows the infant to cling and is therefore better than a wire surrogate. The clinging response is as natural to the monkey as perhaps scanning and vocalizing are to human infants. In time of stress the monkey runs to the object to which it normally clings.

The opportunity to cling and grasp, a behavior that young monkeys normally display at birth, seems to be important to the development of the infant monkey's attachment to the mother and to the mother's power to

Figure 24-5 Wire and ter-
rycloth mother surrogates.
(From Harlow, 1959)

allay fear and distress. There appears to be a strong similarity between this
clinging behavior in the monkey and that of a 1-year-old human child who
runs to his mother and hides his face in her skirts if a strange person enters
the house or an unexpected noise is heard.

Since the pain associated with a hunger need is reduced by the wire
but not by the terrycloth mother, the traditional theory would predict that
the wire mother, which supplies the food, should be the object of attachment and more capable of reducing the infant's fear. But the fact that the
monkey spends more time on the mother that allows him to cling forces
us to reassess our basic hypothesis about those events that cause an infant
to become attached to the mother.

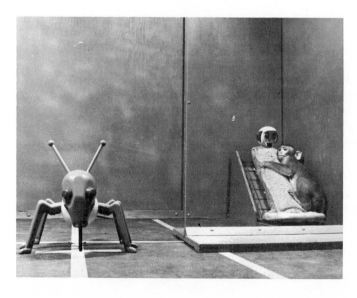

Figure 24-6 Typical re-
sponse with terrycloth mother
to fear-provoking stimulus.
(From Harlow, 1959)

A New View
of Attachment

The present assessment of attachment is based on the hypothesis that each organism is provided with a special set of responses that it can emit at birth or soon after. These responses are like reflexes, but they are more complex. The infant emits these responses to the first appropriate stimulus that the environment supplies; this stimulus is likely to become an object of attachment for the infant.

In the natural context of the jungle the young monkey clings to the hairy undersurface of his mother for several months after birth. Because nature has supplied the infant monkey with a strong grasping reflex, the monkey becomes attached to those objects that allow it to display this response. The mother is the most effective stimulus for this reaction. Upon hatching, the duck or chicken typically follows a moving object; under natural conditions the mother is the first moving object the young bird encounters. The chick becomes attached to the mother because the mother allows the natural response of following to occur.

The human infant scans, smiles, babbles, sucks, manipulates, and holds, among other things. The mother is often the stimulus that elicits these responses. She talks and stimulates the baby to babble; she moves her face and stimulates the child to scan it; she allows the baby to play with her hair and fingers and permits the manipulative responses to appear. As a result, the baby gradually becomes attached to the mother.

If, in addition to allowing these responses to occur, the mother provides food, alleviates pain, and supplies pleasant tactile stimulation, then we have *three* mechanisms that will lead the child to value a human adult: the reduction of discomfort due to hunger, thirst, or pain; the receipt of pleasant sensations; and the attachment process, in which the adult becomes the stimulus object for the infant's early behaviors.

CONSEQUENCES OF ATTACHMENT

There are two important consequences of these early experiences of attachment and pleasure with the caretaker. First, the responses the infant makes to the caretaker will generalize to other people. Second, the infant will develop the fairly articulated schema for the caretaker's face, form, and voice that is necessary for separation anxiety to occur. Let us consider each of these consequences in detail.

Generalization
of Responses

The principle of generalization states that if the infant makes a set of responses to one class of objects he is likely to make them to similar objects, but not to objects that are very dissimilar to the original. Perhaps the best support for this principle comes from a study of monkeys that were raised under a variety of conditions (Sackett, Porter, & Holmes, 1965).

One group was initially reared by a human for 3 weeks, and then each monkey in the group was placed in a wire cage with no physical contact with any other monkeys until it was 1 year old. The monkeys in a second group were reared by their natural mothers until 1 year of age. Each of the monkeys in a third group was placed in isolation at birth and could neither see nor touch humans or other monkeys until it was 6 months old; then they were each put in wire cages until 1 year of age. During the second year of life, all the monkeys lived in wire cages but had daily opportunities to play with other monkeys.

When the monkeys were between 2 and 3 years of age, each was placed in a circular chamber with a human on one side and a monkey on the other. The monkey could approach either side or stay in the center and approach neither the human nor the monkey. The monkeys who were reared by a human for the first 3 weeks and then isolated in wire cages for the rest of the first year spent more time with the human than did any other group. The early experience with the human apparently led to a preference for a human. The monkeys reared by their mothers spent most of their time approaching another monkey. The monkeys reared in complete isolation for the first 6 months spent most of the time in the center of the chamber, approaching neither monkey nor human.

This generalization of approach responses from the earliest object of attachment to a similar object is also true for the human infant. Rheingold (1956) has demonstrated the generalization of an infant's social responses from a mother substitute to other people in a rigorous experimental study. The investigator selected sixteen 6-month-old infants who were living in an institution in which many volunteers cared for each child. For eight of these infants (the experimental babies) the investigator herself played the role of mother 8 hours a day, 5 days a week, for 8 consecutive weeks. During this time, she bathed and diapered them, played with them, smiled at them, and generally tried to be as good a substitute mother as possible. The other eight infants (the control babies) were cared for in the typical institutional fashion, with several women performing the motherly duties for each child in a routine fashion. Moreover, the experimental babies received more nurturance than the control babies during the 8-week period. Thus, the experimental babies differed from the control babies in two ways: They had one person care for them consistently and they received more caretaking during the 8-week period.

All infants were tested each week during the 8-week experimental period and for 4 weeks following the termination of the experimental treatment. The tests administered included tests of social responsiveness to three kinds of people—the experimenter, an examiner who administered the tests, and, at the end of the 8-week period, a stranger. As Figure 24-7 illustrates, the eight experimental infants who had been cared for by the surrogate

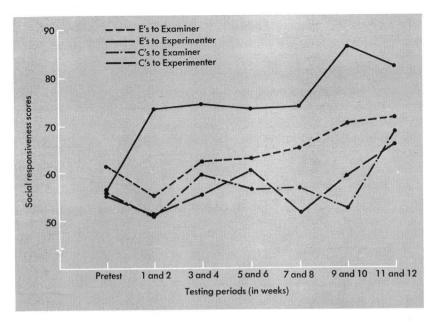

*Figure 24-7   Average social responsiveness of the 8 experimental
(E) and 8 control (C) infants to the experimenter and examiner
over 12 testing periods. (Adapted from Rheingold, 1956)*

mother showed much more social responsiveness to her and to the examiner
than did the control children. Although these data are not shown in the
figure, the experimental babies also exhibited greater responsiveness to a
stranger than did the control babies. The results show that when the three
kinds of adults smiled or talked to the children, the experimentally treated
infants were more likely than the control infants to smile back or give some
facial reaction, the effect being most marked in response to the experimenter.
These results support the notion that social acts learned in response to a
nurturing and socially stimulating caretaker will generalize to other people.

Separation Anxiety   One of the indexes of a strong attachment
to a caretaker and the consequence of
acquisition of schema about the caretaker is the display of separation anxiety
—crying when the child is separated from his mother. There are major differences among children in the age at which this reaction first appears and
in its intensity and persistence. For example, American infants usually
exhibit separation anxiety at 10 months of age, whereas Ugandan infants
typically show this reaction at 6 months of age (Ainsworth, 1967). What
causes this difference? Let us compare the experiences of a typical middle-
class American infant with those of an infant from Uganda.

The American infant spends most of his time in a crib in a room separate from his mother. During at least half of his waking hours he is alone scanning the room, manipulating his fingers, watching shadows on the wall, studying a mobile, playing with his crib, looking at the curtains. The mother comes to her baby primarily when he cries, when she thinks he is hungry, or when she thinks he needs a diaper change. The single human being he comes to know better than any other is his mother. However, since his mother is not always near him, he also learns to make responses to objects, such as pieces of blanket and stuffed animals in his crib. Many American infants become intimately attached to their furry animals or pieces of blanket.

Let us now consider a baby raised in a small hut in Uganda, a small country in east central Africa. Ugandan babies typically are nursed until they are 2 years old and are often fed on demand. American infants either are not nursed or are weaned from the breast before they are 5 months old; they are then fed on a schedule. Second, toilet training is begun early and is initiated by the mother supporting the baby in a squatting position while the baby holds on to her. Thus, the infant makes clinging responses to his mother early in the first year during bowel training. The American mother usually lets her baby soil his diapers during the first year, and the baby lies passively in the crib while he is being changed. Finally, the Ugandan mother is always available to her child. She carries her baby with her most of the day, either straddled across her hip or held in place on her back by a sling of cotton cloth. Since the baby is with his mother most of the day, he does not experience the perception of the mother leaving him, an event the American baby experiences many times each day. In sum, the American baby spends much of his first 6 months alone in a crib; the Ugandan baby spends most of his time being held by someone.

These differences in child rearing permit several possible interpretations for the fact that Ugandan infants show separation anxiety 4 months before typical middle-class American infants show this reaction. One interpretation involves the notion, discussed earlier, that a discrepancy from a schema elicits anxiety. Since the Ugandan baby is with his mother almost continually, we would expect him to have a schema that includes the mother as an essential part of every situation. The perception of the mother leaving him would be an obviously discrepant event and would elicit anxiety. If he can make no other response to it he will cry.

Because the American infant is not with his mother continually, he requires more time to develop a schema in which his mother is an essential stimulus element of the immediate situation in which he finds himself. As the infant matures and the mother becomes a more distinctive object, it becomes increasingly more likely that if she is in the room where he is playing, she will be an essential part of his schema for the "room." It is reasonable to assume that the more regular the presence of the mother, the earlier the infant will reach the point where he includes the mother as part of his schema. The typical American infant does not reach this stage until 10 months of age.

A second possible interpretation is closely related to the earlier discussion of the process of attachment. The infant, like the older child and adult, learns specific responses to particular stimulus situations. After many repetitions of the same stimulus-response chains, they become habitual. The adult typically sits in the same chair at breakfast every morning, despite the availability of three other chairs. The 3-year-old child always takes the same furry toy to bed with him, despite the availability of newer and more colorful ones. If a person is prevented from making his habitual response he may become upset. If the 3-year-old is not allowed to take his favorite furry dog to bed he is likely to cry, even though other toy dogs are available. It appears, therefore, that when a response to a particular situation or object becomes very strong (that is, habitual), disruption of the response can lead to anxiety.

Let us see if this hypothesis applies to separation anxiety. Consider the baby who is continually making a small set of responses toward his mother. He looks at her, smiles, vocalizes, and clings to her. Moreover, the frequency of these actions increases when he is mildly distressed. When the mother leaves, the child is aroused but cannot make these habitual responses. As a result, he may cry. Since the Ugandan baby, who is continually with his mother, builds up stronger responses earlier than the American infant does, he should show separation anxiety earlier.

Both interpretations of separation anxiety imply that the more frequent the contact between baby and mother is, the earlier and more intense the separation anxiety will be. Separation anxiety should vanish when the mother's absence is no longer a discrepant event or when the child can do something about the mother's absence. Both of these changes occur with age. As the child grows he experiences more frequent separations from his mother, and he gradually becomes able to interpret her absence and reassure himself of her return.

THE MINIMALLY ATTACHED INFANT

The Ugandan infant seems to be maximally attached to his mother; the American baby also is attached, but not to so great an extent. Let us now consider infants raised in institutional environments under conditions of minimal contact with a caretaker. A child who does not have a primary adult devoted to his care will generally not become attached to an adult.

It is known, through research with monkeys, that the absence of any close relation with a living object has grave consequences for the infant. If a monkey is placed in isolation for the first 6 months of its life, its behavior is extremely abnormal when it is removed from isolation. It avoids all social contact, appears very fearful, clutches at itself, and crouches (see Figure

24-8). If the period of isolation is less than 6 months, the monkey usually recovers and gradually begins to show normal behavior. But if the isolation lasts for 6 to 12 months, the social and sexual behavior of the adult monkey is abnormal indeed. Some of these monkeys do not recover and never interact appropriately with others. They show extreme fear and occasionally extremely labile aggression.

Even the monkeys who were raised with the terrycloth mothers described earlier and who seemed secure with them were initially fearful with other monkeys and did not display normal social or sexual behavior in adulthood. After a year of living with other monkeys they gradually begin to approach normalcy. But absence of a living mother with whom the infant monkeys could interact seriously affected their social behavior. We do not yet know all the critical actions that a live mother performs that produce normal psychological growth. Movement is probably one of the critical factors. Monkeys raised with a terrycloth mother that was attached to a motor so that it moved irregularly in the cage were less fearful and socially more responsive than monkeys raised with stationary terrycloth mothers (Mason, 1967).

However, no human child is raised in total isolation, so the closest the investigator of the effect of lack of a caretaker can come is to study infants raised in an institution. A child raised in an institutional environment, even a clean and conscientious one, has dramatically less opportunity than a family-reared child to become attached to an adult. Because the institutionalized infant generally does not have a well-articulated schema of a caretaker or of one familiar adult face, he can be expected to show relatively little anxiety when an adult leaves or when he encounters a stranger. Because this infant does not have the opportunity to engage in reciprocal face-to-face vocalization or smiling, he should show minimal babbling and smiling. Finally, because his crying rarely brings anyone, he should gradually decrease the frequency of crying and protesting.

Figure 24-8 Typical behavior of monkey deprived of attachment to a living object in its first 6 months of life. (From Harlow & Harlow, 1966)

Provence and Lipton (1962) observed 75 American infants living in an institutional environment in which nutrition and care were adequate and the infants were in good physical health. The following description of this environment gives an idea of the conditions under which these infants lived.

> The younger group of infants (age 4 days to 8 months) occupied cribs placed singularly in glass partitioned cubicles. The room was clean, cheerful, and light, with adequate heat and ventilation. The infants were fed in their cribs with bottles propped. When cereals, fruits, and vegetables were added to the diet they were also given in a propped bottle with a large holed nipple rather than given by spoon. . . . sometimes a stuffed toy was placed in the crib for the baby to look at. After about 4 months of age, simple rattles, beads, and so on were placed on a string suspended across the crib sides and the single playpen which contained other age appropriate toys. . . . Each infant in this group shared the time and attention of the attendant with 7 to 9 other infants in the same age range for the 8 hour period of the day when she was present. For the remaining 16 hours of the day, there was no person in the nursery except at feeding time when an attendant who also had similar duties in other nurseries heated formulas, propped bottles, and changed diapers. Not only were the infants fed without an adult present, but there was minimal variability in their experience. There were no vocalizations from other people, no reciprocal play, no close relationship between a child's crying and the reaction of someone else [Provence & Lipton, 1962, p. 26].

Let us consider how these babies differ from those raised in families. It should first be noted that there are no major differences between family-reared and institutionalized babies prior to 3 or 4 months of age. Only after 4 months do the differences become apparent.

The institutionalized babies vocalized very little; they showed no cooing, no babbling, and little crying. Moreover, they did not adapt their postures to the arms of an adult: "They felt something like sawdust dolls; they moved, they bent easily at the proper joints, but they felt stiff or wooden [p. 56]." Because these infants were not picked up very often, they did not make the kinds of postural adjustments made by babies who are often picked up. By 8 months of age, most of these infants were markedly uninterested in grasping or approaching toys, and they began to lose interest in their external environment.

During the second half of the first year, body rocking became very common and was more frequent than would be observed among family-reared babies. Stranger anxiety was rare, and the babies' facial expressions were bland and clearly not as expressive as those of family-reared infants. If they were frustrated they would cry passively or turn away, but rarely would they make an attempt to conquer a frustration. Finally, language ability was delayed. There were no words at all at 1 year of age; vocalization and language were the behaviors that were most seriously depressed. The following is a description of one of the institutionalized babies near the end of his first year.

> Outstanding were his soberness, his forlorn appearance and lack of animation. The interest that he showed in the toys was mainly for holding, inspecting, and rarely mouthing. When he was unhappy he now had a cry that sounded neither demanding nor angry—just miserable—and it was usually accompanied by his beginning to rock. The capacity for protest which he had earlier was much diminished. He did not turn to adults to relieve his distress or to involve them in a playful or pleasurable interchange. He made no demands. The active approach to the world, which had been one of the happier aspects of his earlier development, vanished. As one made active and persistent efforts at a social interchange he became somewhat more responsive, animated and motorically active, but lapsed into his depressed and energy-less appearance when the adult became less active with him [Provence & Lipton, 1962, pp. 134–35].

Two descriptive comments by observers convey the impression the subject made at this time: "The light in Teddy has gone out" and "If you crank his motor you can get him to go a little, he can't start on his own [p. 135]."

In sum, lack of a consistent interaction with a caretaker, which is one of the major deficits in an institutional setting, leads to depressed and abnormal social behavior and retarded language development. All the behaviors that were most likely to be learned as a result of interaction with an adult, such as clinging, crying to distress, approaching adults for play, and vocalization, were clearly retarded or absent in the institutionalized children. In general, social responsiveness, emotional involvement with others, and motivation to perform for adults were found to be vulnerable to deprivation of interaction with others. Institutional living, however, does not retard all aspects of psychological development. These children do eventually develop motor skills, and their memory and drawing performances are at least satisfactory.

The Mother-Infant Relationship

THE RELEVANCE OF FEEDING PRACTICES

So far this discussion has emphasized the attachment of the child to the mother and the complex social interaction of the two. The significance of the specific feeding practices the mother uses, such as whether she nurses or uses a bottle, has not been considered. This deemphasis on the mode of feeding represents an important theoretical change in the psychologist's view of what is important in the mother-infant interaction during the first year.

There have been major shifts over time in the proportion of mothers from particular social, ethnic, or personality groups who choose to breast or bottle feed. During the period from 1930 to 1940, lower-class mothers nursed and middle-class mothers used bottles. In the current decade the situation is the reverse: Middle-class mothers prefer to nurse, and lower-class mothers use bottles almost exclusively. However, the major psychological differences between children of the lower and the upper-middle classes have not changed very much. The mother's attitude toward the child and the kinds of social interaction that occur during feeding are more critical factors than whether the baby is nursed or fed by bottle.

MATERNAL ATTITUDES TOWARD THE INFANT

The mother's attitudes toward her infant are major determinants of her overt actions with the baby. If she likes him she will spend time with him; if she considers him bright she will stimulate him; if she thinks he is biologically defective or too irritable to calm she may ignore him. If she resents the infant's interference with her career, she may reject him.

An intriguing study of the important role of attitudes compared 30 Japanese and 30 American mothers and their 3- to 4-month-old first-born infants (Caudill & Weinstein, 1966). The Japanese child typically lives and sleeps in the same room with the mother and father; thus the Japanese mother is always close to her infant. When the infant cries, the mother is apt to respond quickly and feed him soon after he begins to fret. In contrast, the American child usually has a room of his own, and the mother often lets him cry for a few minutes before she comes to feed him. Another difference is that the Japanese mother feels the need to soothe and quiet her baby, whereas the American mother more often wants to stimulate him and make him vocalize and smile. Since the Japanese baby is typically less active and less vocal than the American baby, there seems to be an association between the mother's practices and the child's behavior.

The differences in maternal behavior apparently derive from different philosophies, or attitudes, about the infant. The American mother believes that her child is basically passive and dependent and that she must mold him into an active, achieving, independent child by stimulating him. Thus she plays with him, makes him babble, and does not attempt to soothe him at the first cry. The Japanese mother believes that her infant is basically independent and that she must soothe him as quickly as possible and make him dependent on her and the family. She sees the infant as a separate biological organism, which from the beginning, in order to develop, needs to be drawn into interdependent relationships with others. This study presents a clear example of the important effects of cultural attitudes on the rearing practices of the mother and, consequently, on the behavior of the infant and older child.

Behavioral Differences
Among Infants

During the 30 years between 1920 and 1950, most psychologists assumed that all healthy infants were basically similar in temperament and ability and that the differences observable at age 5 were the product of differential experience. However, in the past ten years careful study of the human infant has revealed that these immature organisms differ dramatically along several dimensions. It is possible that these differences, real as they are during the first 6 months, are short-lived and exert minimal influence on behavior during the preschool or early school years. The answers to this issue must be left to the research of the decades to come. There is value, nevertheless, in noting some of the behavior patterns that differentiate infants during the first 6 months, for it may be that these patterns help shape important developmental processes.

VIGOR OF ACTIVITY

The intensity of motor activity is one of the most striking characteristics that differentiate young infants. Some infants move their arms and legs with great force, others with minimal vigor. Some vocalize lustily; the babbling of others is soft. Some bang toys or strike their cribs with much energy; others are more placid. It is tempting to speculate that these vigorous infants will be more energetic or lively when they are 10 years old than their placid counterparts. What evidence we have is congruent with this expectation, but there is not yet enough information to be completely confident of it.

IRRITABILITY

A second obvious difference among infants refers to the ease with which they cry and whine and the amount of effort required to placate them. Some infants become irritable at slight or no external provocation, whereas others do not cry unless pain and discomfort are relatively high. Moreover, some infants appear to possess an inhibiting mechanism that brakes the spiraling character of irritability. These infants typically will fret for half a minute and then stop spontaneously with no external interference, behaving as though they possessed mechanisms that inhibited the buildup of extreme upset. In other infants crying increases rapidly in intensity until it reaches a maximum and either the mother placates the infant or he falls off to sleep, exhausted. These infants seem to lack the capacity to inhibit the growth of a tantrum; when fretting begins, the reaction goes to completion.

It is easy to imagine the differential impact of these two types of infants on a mother. The hyperirritable infant is more likely to vex and puzzle a parent. Initially, this infant will elicit care from the mother as she attempts to placate her crying baby. However, if the mother's attention is not effective in quieting her child, his irritability may begin to provoke anger and lead to less maternal affection. The extremely irritable baby therefore experiences patterns of maternal reactions different from those the more contented child experiences, even though the basic personality of the mother is the same.

STIMULUS SATIABILITY

Although most normal infants begin to show habituation when they are 3 months of age (see page 417), there are some quite dramatic differences among children of the same age in the *rate* at which they become bored with—or habituate to—a particular pattern. Often children who are vigorous in their movements show faster rates of habituation than more placid infants, and large, chubby boys show slower rates of habituation than small, wiry boys.

Figure 24-9 illustrates the differential rates of habituation to clay faces of two children at 4, 8, and 13 months of age. Baby S did not readily become bored and continued to look as long or almost as long on trials 9 through 12 as he did on the opening 4 trials. Baby P rapidly became satiated with the visual stimuli and spent much less time looking at them on the

Figure 24-9   Differential rates of habituation in two infant boys.

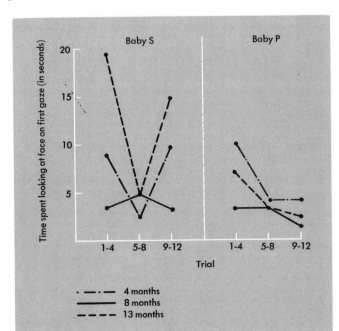

last 4 trials than he did in the opening 4 trials and less than Baby S did in the closing part of the series.

The fact that a tendency for slow or fast habituation may be stable during the first year suggests that the rate of habituation could be a critical aspect of the child's psychological organization and perhaps an important predictor of his future behavior and temperament. We might speculate that Baby S will develop into a child who is able to become deeply engrossed in an activity and who shows a reflective attitude. Baby P may be more likely to develop into a restless, energetic child who is unable to spend long periods of time quietly involved in one activity. This prediction is partially verified by some behavioral observations that were made on Baby S when he was 13 months of age. He was in a room with his mother when he discovered a plastic quoit. For almost 10 minutes he gently rolled the quoit around the room, watching it carefully after each push that he gave it and issuing a small laugh as it rolled to a stop. During most of this period the child was deeply engrossed in this activity and perceptually addicted to the rolling quoit. Most of the observers felt that the child's attention to the rolling quoit was so intense that he would have been virtually insensitive to any other stimulus changes that might have occurred around him.

Other observations indicate that infant boys who show a rapid rate of habituation tend to invest short periods of sustained attention to a particular toy or activity. For instance, they will put blocks in a pail for 10 seconds and then quickly skip to another activity for 10 to 15 seconds. Boys who show a slow rate of habituation are likely to spend a minute or two putting blocks in a pail before shifting to another activity. Thus the speed with which an infant becomes bored with a visual stimulus during the opening months of life seems to be associated with a faster tempo of play during the latter half of the first year.

Evidence from other investigations suggests that behavioral tempo continues to be relatively stable from the preschool period to the school years. School-age children differ markedly in their tendency to make decisions quickly, as opposed to brooding a long time before deciding to act, and in their tendency to skip restlessly from activity to activity, in contrast to investing long periods of time on a particular task. It is possible that these differences in 6-year-olds are related to the differences in rate of habituation and tempo of play observed during the first year.

THRESHOLD FOR ATTENTION CHANGE

Infants also differ in the intensity of stimulus energy and in the uniqueness of a stimulus necessary to attract their attention. Some babies orient to minimal changes in visual or auditory input and appear to be alerted by slight changes in their surroundings. Others require more perceptible changes before their attention is elicited. This threshold of attention variable has been called "perceptual sensitivity."

It is not clear whether social responsivity is biologically based or is developed entirely through experiences in the early weeks of life. It is clear, however, that by 16 weeks of age there are dramatic differences among infants in the degree to which they elicit positive, affectionate, socially responsive overtures from adults. The socially attractive child smiles, babbles frequently, and becomes very responsive (laughing, cooing) when an adult talks to him, tickles him, or picks him up. The socially unresponsive infant is generally quiet, is less likely to smile or babble when adults look at or talk to him, and tends to fret or stiffen when someone picks him up.

Obviously, these two types of babies will elicit different degrees of social stimulation from adults. The responsive baby should become even more responsive as a result of increasingly frequent interaction with others, whereas the initially unresponsive baby is likely to become even more withdrawn and quiet, since adults will be less inclined to play with him.

These five attributes are some of the most obvious differences observed among young infants. It is not yet possible to state what relation there may be among the manifestations of these attributes or what their power to predict a personality in later years may be. It may even be that dispositions less obvious to an observer are more critical for future development than the ones outlined above.

How Behavioral Dispositions in the Infant Influence Personality Development

At the present level of knowledge it is reasonable to suggest that there are some unlearned behavioral dispositions present at birth. Some of these dispositions are stable over time and may facilitate or impede the acquisition of particular motives, anxieties, and instrumental acts either directly or indirectly as a result of the special reactions these dispositions evoke in the caretaker. There are two complementary ways by which temperamental dispositions of the infant might influence the later personality of the child.

The simplest mechanism operates under the assumption that a particular temperamental trait—vigor, let us say—leads the infant to behave in ways that predispose him to learn special reactions and to encounter special experiences. A vigorous 1-year-old is likely to lash out and knock down physical obstacles when frustrated. As a result, he may learn how to deal with obstacles early. The vigorous infant also may encounter frequent parental punishments and pressures because he gets into more "mischief" than a less vigorous infant. The rationale for these predictions rests on the assumption that the vigor (or any disposition in the infant) is a more or less fixed entity that has certain constant consequences in the environment (a vigorous infant will attack obstacles and will encounter restriction). This general—and rather simplistic—point of view is partially responsible for the belief that inactive infants will become shy and pensive 10-year-olds and active infants will become sociable and active 10-year-olds.

A second and more plausible mechanism by which infant temperament might influence later personality development engages a subtle set of interactions; it operates under the assumption that the parent categorizes the infant along selected dimensions. These categorizations are determined in part by the infant's actual characteristics. The parent's pattern of reactions toward the infant then corresponds to some extent with the label or category applied to the child.

Take, for example, two mothers, each of whom has a highly irritable baby. Both babies cry incessantly, cannot be satisfied easily, and do not respond positively to affection. One mother interprets this behavior as indicative of the infant's dislike for her. She feels threatened by her inability to placate the infant, and she begins to treat him as a hostile and irritating child. The other mother interprets the irritability as a sign of illness (colic, perhaps) and nurtures the infant more than she would a less irritable child. Since she views her infant as fragile and sensitive, her behavioral reaction is increased solicitousness. These different reactions to infants with identical behavioral attributes derive from the mothers' different interpretations of these attributes.

One important attribute that influences a parent's categorizing process is the sex of the child. There is some evidence that mothers react differently to boys and girls as early as 12 weeks of age. For instance, a mother is more likely to let her son cry longer than her daughter. She may rationalize this behavior by asserting that she does not want to "baby" her son: "He has to learn to take stress," she may say. A mother is more likely to imitate the vocalizations of her daughter than of her son but more likely to stimulate and amuse her son than her daughter through flexing and manipulating his muscles and touching him (Moss, 1967). Some of the differential handling is, of course, a result of different behaviors in the infants. But some of it is due to the mother's automatic reactions that result from the implicit labeling of the sex of her child. The mother-infant relationship is a sensitively tuned interaction in which the mother's unconscious image of the ideal adolescent boy or girl directs her caretaking actions.

Thus, we should not expect any constant personality structure to develop from specific infant characteristics alone. Mothers differ in their interpretations of a given infant attribute, and maternal reactions are based in part on that interpretive label. The child's emerging behaviors will be shaped in accordance with the interaction between these maternal reactions and his particular early behavioral dispositions.

First, children (earlier perhaps than we think) are very sensible of Praise *and* Commendation. *They find a Pleasure in being esteemed, and valued, especially by their Parents, and those whom they depend on. If therefore the Father caress and commend them, when they do well; shew a cold and neglectful Countenance to them upon doing ill; And this accompanied by a like Carriage of the Mother, and all others that are about them, it will in a little Time make them sensible of the Difference; and this if constantly observed, I doubt not but will of it self work more than Threats or Blows, which lose their Force, when once grown common, and are of no use when Shame does not attend them. . . .*

But Secondly, To make the Sense of Esteem *or* Disgrace *sink the deeper, and be of the more weight, other agreeable or disagreeable Things should constantly accompany these different states; not as particular Rewards and Punishments of this or that particular Action, but as necessarily belonging to, and constantly attending one, who by his Carriage has brought himself into a State of Disgrace or Commendation. By which Way of Treating them, Children may, as much as possible, be brought to conceive, that those that are commended, and in Esteem for doing well, will necessarily be beloved and cherished by every Body, and have all other good Things as a Consequence of it; and, on the other Side, when any one by Miscarriage falls into Dis-esteem, and cares not to preserve his Credit, he will unavoidably fall under Neglect and Contempt; and in that State, the Want of what ever might satisfie or delight him, will follow.*

JOHN LOCKE. Some Thoughts Concerning Education

CHAPTER 25
INITIAL SOCIALIZATION: 18 MONTHS TO 3 YEARS

The second critical period, from 18 months to 3 years, is characterized by three major developments: the ability to walk and run about, the ability to understand and speak language, and the encounter with the first major socialization demands made by parents. As the child grows during this period, he learns instrumental effectiveness—that is, he becomes capable of exerting an effect on his world of objects. The child also learns a set of expectancies connected with his development. He learns to anticipate that if he sees a desired object a few feet away, he will be able to obtain it; he learns to expect that if he uses language to tell his parents of his needs or to make a request, he will be understood; he learns to expect that if he acts in the face of a problem or frustration, it is more likely that the problem will be solved or the frustration minimized than if he does nothing or merely cries.

Motor Abilities

As the child masters the crawling, walking, and running sequence, he is able to obtain desired goals and overcome frustrations. He can apprehend a toy that catches his attention rather than cry or squeal to his mother to bring it to him. He can reach for cookies, push open doors, crawl around obstacles, and climb up and down stairs and chairs.

The child seems to enjoy using his motor skills and often derives more pleasure from practicing a new response than from obtaining a prize with it. In a recent study in the Harvard laboratory, children early in the second year were presented with a clear plastic box that contained an attractive toy. The box could be opened only by manipulating a pair of latches on the door of the box. Those children who succeeded in opening the latches paid little attention to the toy but spent their time opening and closing the latches and the door of the box. Manipulation of the latches and the door, not the attractive toy, was the prize.

Language Ability

The growth of language during the ages 18 months to 3 years is extraordinary. In this period the child learns the differential meaning of No and Yes; the intent of requests, demands, and prohibitions; and the connection between a word and its referent (such as look at the dog, drink the milk, see the moon).

The typical 1-year-old rarely uses meaningful speech. His spoken vocabulary is usually limited to a few words like "Dada," "Mommy," and "Hi." By age 2, however, the average child has a respectable vocabulary of 100 words and can recognize and label pictures of familiar animals, household objects, silverware, furniture, and parts of the body.

Two of the most important words the child learns at this time are *bad* and *good*. He discovers those actions that his parents regard as undesirable and bad or as desirable and good. The collection of attributes and actions that he eventually comes to regard as "bad" or "good" constitute his indoctrination into the values of his society. This process of indoctrination is called *socialization.*

Socialization Demands

Socialization is the process by which the child acquires the dominant beliefs, values, motives, and behaviors of his culture and gradually becomes more similar to other members of a particular cultural, ethnic, or religious group. Socialization is the basis for the typically shy, quiet behavior of a Chinese boy, in contrast to the boisterous, exuberant behavior of his counterpart in California. The acquisition of culturally appropriate behaviors, beliefs, and values involves recognition of the ideal traits a person should possess, as well as the undesirable traits he should be free of or should inhibit.

WHAT BEHAVIORS AND VALUES ARE SOCIALIZED?

The major psychological entities that are socialized include:

1. Acquisition of desired behaviors, such as learning the skills of reading, arithmetic, cooking, social poise, and talking to a large group without being anxious.

2. Inhibition of undesirable behaviors, such as aggression, destruction, dependency, crying, tantrums, and spontaneous urination or defecation.

3. Acquisition of culturally approved values, such as sincerity, altruism, cleanliness, honesty, conscientiousness, dominance, and ambition.

4. Suppression of undesirable values, such as hate, narcissism, idleness, and sexual infidelity.

Because socialization of behaviors and values is a dynamic and constantly changing process, the child alters both values and actions as he grows. For example, the 2-year-old boy has not yet learned that it is inappropriate to cry for help when he has a problem; the 10-year-old boy, on the other hand, believes strongly that it is childish and inappropriate to ask for help with problems, and he will inhibit crying and requests for aid when faced with a difficult task.

The specific behaviors and values that are regarded as desirable or undesirable will differ across cultural groups. The Mayan Indian peasant boy in Guatemala is taught that he must learn to help his father work the coffee plantations, remain close to his family, and contribute to their financial stability. The son of a Chicago lawyer is taught to do well in school and to become independent of his family. Although the content of what is socialized differs with the culture, psychologists believe that the mechanisms of socialization are the same for all cultures.

MECHANISMS OF SOCIALIZATION

Socialization is accomplished through four basic mechanisms: (1) the desire to obtain the affection, regard, acceptance, and recognition of others; (2) the motive to avoid the unpleasant feelings generated by punishment or rejection by others; (3) the desire to be similar to particular people the child has grown to respect, love, and admire (a process called identification, which will be discussed in Chapter 26); and (4) a general tendency to imitate the actions of others. Acquisition or inhibition of overt actions is most readily accomplished through social rewards and punishments, supplemented by observations of the behavior of others. Acquisition or suppression of values and beliefs is less likely to be facilitated by watching others behave and more likely to be the product of identification with a desirable model.

Each of these four mechanisms—desire for reward, fear of punishment, identification, and imitation—is strongest at different periods of development and facilitates different aspects of the socialization process.

FIRST STEPS IN SOCIALIZATION

During the second and third years of life, the child's joint desires for parental acceptance and for avoidance of punishment are the major mechanisms in socialization. The child is too young to identify with his parents or other adults, and, although the 2-year-old child does observe others and imitate some of their actions, observational learning is not a major basis for socialization during the second year of life.

This discussion will be restricted to the behaviors and values that are typically socialized in *Western* society during this age period, because social scientists have acquired the most valid information about our own culture. These behaviors and values include learning to inhibit spontaneous bowel and bladder evacuation, regressive crying, destruction of property, and open aggression to others. All four classes involve *inhibition of a behavior that is relatively strong in the child's repertoire.* American parents generally do not regard the child as mature enough to learn positive values like honesty, sincerity, persistence, and altruism, or behavioral skills like reading, painting, or tying shoelaces. In most American homes the first socialization attempts are directed at stamping out undesirable behaviors. The primary instruments used for this task are reward for successful inhibition and punishment for failure to inhibit the prohibited actions.

Toilet Training:
An Example of Early Socialization

The socialization of toilet training is discussed in detail below not because it is the most important response that is socialized but because (1) all cultures socialize this behavior, (2) it provides a good example of the inhibitory mechanisms that are involved in early socialization, and (3) there is more research on toilet training than on other aspects of socialization during this early period. It should be noted, however, that aggression, destruction of property, or regressive crying could just as well have been chosen to illustrate the process of socialization.

INHIBITION LEARNING

The essential characteristic of toilet training is the learning of an inhibition—that of spontaneous evacuation. The degree to which anxiety over punishment, observation and imitation of others, or reward dominates the learning of this inhibition depends on the age when the toilet training is initiated. If a parent waits until the child is 3 years old, anxiety is less important than if training is started at 12 to 15 months of age. Let us consider, first, the role of anxiety in motivating the inhibition of spontaneous evacuation in a child under 18 months old.

Anxiety as an Inhibitory Mechanism   The mother is able to elicit anxiety in the child through (1) physical punishment of the prohibited response and (2) gestures or communications that symbolize loss of nurturance. The following is a hypothetical analysis of this sequence, using defecation as the response to be inhibited.

Internal stimulus → response of → imposition of → experience
for defecation (*elicits*) defecation punishment of anxiety
  (or potential (with its
  loss of distinct
  nurturance) noxious
  properties)

These events occur in close temporal succession. For the inhibition response to take place, the anxiety must gradually move forward in the temporal sequence so that it is eventually elicited by the stimulus that signals defecation. In that case the prevailing response to anxiety will be temporary inhibition of the response originally elicited by the stimulus (see Part I, Chapter 3).

Internal stimulus → Experience → Inhibition of
for defecation of anxiety response of defecation

In short, if the anxiety that was originally based on punishment moves forward in the temporal sequence so that it occurs to the stimulus for defecation, the normal sequence of stimulus → defecation will be interrupted. The child might signal to his mother to indicate that he has to defecate (using postural or language signs), or he might go to the bathroom himself (assuming he is able to walk and has learned the connection between defecation and that particular room).

If the anxiety elicited by the urge to defecate was originally based solely on painful physical punishment, no additional assumptions are required to explain the learning of correct toilet habits. But if the anxiety was based primarily on the caretaker's gestures of disapproval that symbolized a possible withdrawal of acceptance, then an extra cognitive component must have been established prior to the socialization training. The child must have had a set of experiences that made the caretaker a valued person and led the child to anticipate anxiety if the caretaker gave signs of possible disapproval or withdrawal of nurturance.

It is reasonable to assume that the 18-month-old is conceptually mature enough to have learned the value of an affectionate relationship with another person, primarily the mother. A mother can manipulate her relationship with her child to produce the desired toilet training, because anxiety over loss of maternal acceptance or nurturance, like anxiety over punishment, can become anticipatory, disrupt the automatic defecation sequence, and lead to inhibition of the defecatory reflex. The greater the child's awareness of the response desired by the mother, the easier the inhibition training will proceed.

To sum up: (1) If there is a nurturant relationship between caretaker and child so that anxiety over anticipation of loss of nurturance can be an incentive to learning, (2) if the child is given instructions about the proper responses and the appropriate place to evacuate, and (3) if the child is sufficiently mature to be aware of what behavior is required of him, then relevant cognitive links will occur simultaneously with the arousal of anxiety over defecation and will facilitate successful inhibition.

Other Mechanisms for Learning Inhibition

Although anxiety learned to punishment, disapproval, and anticipated loss of nurturance seems to be the primary incentive for learning to inhibit spontaneous evacuation in the child under 2 years of age, it is theoretically possible that the mechanisms of identification, observation and imitation, and simple reward can mediate the learning of this inhibition. For example, as a consequence of his desire to strengthen his identification with his parents, the child might learn proper toilet habits. However, identification with a parent is not strong during the second year of life; it generally does not begin to grow until the child is 3 to 4 years of age.

The child might spontaneously watch and imitate the parents' or an older sibling's habits, as he does when he picks up his father's pipe or applies his mother's lipstick. But if imitation is to mediate toilet training, the child must have the opportunity to see the action that is to be copied; the stimuli he experiences when he has the urge to evacuate must be associated with the actual behavior of a model. However, inhibiting spontaneous defecation is not a public response, for most adults close the bathroom door behind them. Although the child can observe where he is to go to evacuate, he cannot observe the private act of inhibition of evacuation. For the most part, the learning of toilet habits by the 18-month-old through observation and imitation alone is not very likely.

Finally, it is possible for a child who understands language and who has been given verbal instructions on what to do when he feels he must defecate to become trained through consistent reward of inhibition every time he goes to the proper toileting place. In practice, however, most parents find it extremely difficult to refrain from a punitive statement or punishing action when the child has an accident. It is likely, therefore, that in most cases anxiety over physical punishment or parental disapproval, in differing intensities, is involved in the acquisition of appropriate toilet habits.

Comparison of Two Forms of Inhibition Learning: Evacuation and "Dangerous" Exploration Basically, the child learns to inhibit unrestrained exploration of his environment and "destruction" of household property in a manner similar to the learning of inhibition of spontaneous evacuation. For example, when the parent punishes the child for tearing a new curtain, anxiety becomes interposed between the sight of the curtain and the urge to pull on it. The major difference between the inhibition of evacuation and that of property destruction or exploration lies in the distinctiveness of the stimuli with which the anxiety becomes associated. The stimuli for evacuation are internal, intense, and relatively distinct. The stimuli that incite the child to explore something (curtains, drawers, vases, pots) are external and relatively indistinct. If the child is punished for pulling pots from the kitchen cabinet, it is unlikely that an inhibition resulting from this punishment will immediately generalize to the sight of clothes in a bedroom closet. A new set of punishments is required for the child to learn to inhibit exploration in this new situation.

Thus, the learning of inhibitions over exploration requires more time than does the inhibition of evacuation—and is more tenuous. The urge to defecate occurs only three to four times daily, whereas the child's urge to explore attractive objects can be aroused a hundred times a day, depending on the variety of attractive objects in his environment. Since the parent cannot be present to punish each "dangerous" exploration, the child has many opportunities to extinguish the anxiety reaction to exploration and potential property destruction.

CONSEQUENCES OF OVERLY SEVERE TOILET TRAINING

The intense anxiety that often accompanies toilet training can lead to the development of other dispositions unrelated to inhibition of evacuation. If it is agreed that an adult should have the capacity for attaining satisfying sexual and interpersonal relationships, then certain consequences of overly severe toilet training can be labeled as undesirable or maladaptive because they interfere with the development of those relationships. (The criteria for judging behavior as "maladaptive" are, of course, arbitrary and reflect to some extent the particular biases of our culture.)

"Overly severe" training refers to the use of excessively punitive procedures that generate strong anxiety. Five of the consequences of overly severe toilet training during the second and third year of life that can have lasting effects on the child's personality are (1) hostility toward and fear of the training agent (usually the mother), often accompanied by excessive resistance to any limitation on autonomy; (2) anxiety over sexual thoughts and behavior and over the body's anal and genital area; (3) anxiety over dirt and disarray; (4) conception of the self as dirty and bad; and (5) inhibition of spontaneity and novel activity. Each of these consequences is treated in detail below.

Hostility Toward
and Fear of the Mother

Hostility Toward and Fear of the Mother   A mother who is excessively punitive or threatening in her training will become a cause for anxiety arousal in the child. Excessive punishment of toilet accidents may generate urges to resist maternal coercion and perhaps result in aggressive behavior toward the parent in the form of kicking, pushing, biting, and, if language is available, verbal attacks. These violent discharges are not like the aimless rage of an 8-month-old but are directed attacks on a specific person.

A more impersonal method of expressing hostility is resistance to the training itself. This resistance is apt to be expressed by refusal to evacuate while sitting in the bathroom. Often the mother will sit with the child for half an hour and finally, in exasperation, remove him, only to encounter immediate evacuation on the floor. When the mother displays her obvious upset at this event, she provides the child with gratification for his hostile motives. The parent who displays extreme upset in similar situations rewards the child's resistant disposition and lays the foundation for a personality that resists any curbing of autonomy.

Anxiety over Sexuality   The 3-year-old does not clearly differentiate among the acts of evacuation, the organs involved, and the products. He tends to apply the same simple word or phrase to the three referents, maximizing the similarity among them. The close proximity of the external genitals, the urethra, and the anus makes it likely that anxiety over evacuation will generalize to sexual functioning when the 7-year-old learns words for the unique stimulation derived from the genitals. If the strong anxiety linked to the genitals persists into adolescence, the young adult is likely to experience conflict in sexual behavior.

The close semantic link between bowel and bladder functioning and the genital-sexual complex is supported by data from an intensive interview study with middle-class American mothers. These mothers could not keep the topics of sex training and toilet training separate. The interview questions kept the topics separate, but the mothers' answers did not. "When we were discussing the modesty standards [actually referring to sex and nudity], mothers would describe their efforts to train their children not to urinate outdoors [Sears, Maccoby, & Levin, 1957, pp. 107–08]." In the minds of many mothers, and in the minds of children, there is an intimate association between urination and defecation on the one hand and exposure of genitals and sex modesty training on the other. It is not surprising that the separate anxieties associated with each of these areas support each other.

Anxiety over Dirt and Disarray

If the mother tells the child "You are dirty" every time he soils and accompanies these statements with punishment, anxiety will become attached to the word "dirty" and in time will extend to the child's environment—to dirty fingers, dirty rooms, dirty floors. One defensive response the child may adopt that attenuates the anxiety is to remove and avoid dirt compulsively and to maintain an aversive posture to any kind of disarray. Of course, a child also learns to avoid being dirty as a result of direct punishment for dirty fingers or clothes.

Anxiety over the Self-Concept

The stigma of "You are dirty" or "You are bad" applied by parents to the child each time he soils eventually may affect the child's self-concept. The parents' reactions toward the child and their verbal evaluations of him are basic sources of his attitudes toward himself, for the child views the parents as omniscient and is prone to believe that their evaluations are accurate. Repetition of the charges, "You are dirty, smelly, naughty," and so on, persuades the child to believe in the truth of these accusations. When he learns during the preschool years that people avoid dirty objects, his behavior may begin to reflect the expectation that people will avoid him.

Inhibition of Spontaneous Responding

Inhibition of a response to a particular stimulus or situation is a major component of socialization, and our culture regards appropriate inhibition as characteristic of maturity. But undesirable consequences may arise if a tendency to inhibit behavior gains too much strength too quickly. It is possible that the association of an urge to act and strong anxiety, as experienced in toilet training, may lead to the tendency to "inhibit responding" *whenever* anxiety is experienced.

For example, the inhibition of the urge to explore a new toy is a possible consequence of excessively fearful punishments surrounding toilet training. Similarly, the inhibition of an aggressive outburst in response to the mixed stimuli of anger and anxiety, or the inhibition of sexual behavior in response to the combination of erotic excitement and apprehension, might result from severe toilet training. The generalization of inhibition to actions other than those involved in the original toilet training is suggested by clinical observations and is theoretically reasonable.

Although the possible consequences of severe training described above seem reasonable, they are still only theoretical possibilities. There is not a large body of research that either proves or disproves these ideas. Moreover, research into the effect of various toilet training methods is methodologically weak and subject to multiple interpretations. We shall consider only the most relevant work here.

Psychologists generally agree that toilet training should be delayed until the child's locomotor and conceptual abilities allow for it. He should be able to sit up comfortably over a period of time and understand simple communications about the task required of him. These qualifications suggest that learning of bowel and bladder control is not facilitated until the child is well into his second year. An interview study of more than 300 American middle-class mothers (Sears, Maccoby, & Levin, 1957) found that the majority initiated toilet training at between 9 and 14 months but completed it at approximately a year and a half. As might be expected, the mothers who started the training later required less time to train the child than did those who started earlier. It was found that toilet training was accomplished with most ease when it was initiated after 20 months of age.

Maternal attitudes toward toilet training are not independent of attitudes toward a cluster of other behaviors that are to be socialized. If a mother is severe in her toilet training, she tends to make strict demands in the areas of table manners, orderliness, control of noise, school performance, obedience, and inhibition of aggression to parents. Moreover, mothers who practice harsh toilet training procedures are minimally permissive of masturbation and social sex play. In one study it was noted:

> We get the impression of a rather pervasive quality of strictness in the mothers who are most severe in toilet training. They seem to have been seeking to achieve more mature standards of conduct at a faster pace than other mothers. They had more of a tendency to drive rather than to lead their children and they used a more punitive kind of discipline [Sears, Maccoby, & Levin, 1957, pp. 121–22].

The clinical literature is marbled with correlational studies implying that early and severe toilet training is associated with future mental illness in the child. There are several obvious difficulties inherent in these studies. First, mothers who are strict in toilet training tend to be severe and punitive in other areas. Therefore, the critical set of causal factors may have been the mother's general punitiveness rather than her specific toilet training practices. Moreover, the child who had difficulty learning to inhibit evacuation (and this difficulty might arise for a variety of reasons) possibly engenders more punishment and hostility from the mother; a continuing friction between the child's resistance and the mother's punitiveness could eventually create the conditions necessary and sufficient for the development of symptoms of mental illness. Thus, although the empirical associations are consistent, the interpretations of these data are still equivocal.

The Importance of Rules for the Child

Socialization is essentially the acquisition of the rules of social living. This process is important not only because it provides for a more harmonious society—the reason for which parents generally believe they socialize their children—but also because it gives the child *rules* to reduce the uncertainty of each day. Children, as well as adults, become apprehensive when they are not certain of what is permitted and what is prohibited. Rules provide that certainty.

Parents who are consistent in the acts that they punish provide their child with a degree of certainty to guide his actions. If a parent is inconsistent—that is, occasionally punishing a certain act but occasionally allowing its expression—the child will experience an uncomfortable state of uncertainty. He will be unsure as to whether dirtying his clothes, for example, will be punished or permitted. He will not feel that he is in control of future punishments. One common reaction to this uncomfortable feeling of uncertainty is to commit the inconsistently punished act and perhaps even announce the violation to the parents.

Consider these observations made in the home of a 27-month-old boy. The boy had put some freshly ironed clothes into the toilet bowl. When his mother discovered this violation, she became upset and spanked him hard for several minutes. He cried for a long time and was clearly both afraid and in pain. His mother was often inconsistent in her punishments of rule violations. Sometimes she would punish an act with vigor, but on other occasions she would ignore it. The next day the boy put a new set of freshly ironed clothes into the toilet, walked into the kitchen, announced to his mother what he had done, and then stiffened his body as if to prepare himself for a spanking.

Why did he commit an act that he knew would bring painful punishment? One explanation is that he had a stronger desire to be certain of his punishment than he did to avoid being punished. By committing that violation he was controlling when a punishment would be administered. He would not be in the uncomfortable state of not knowing "when the knife would fall." The learning of rules for appropriate beliefs and behaviors fills an important human need for certainty and structure. Socialization is as necessary for the child's psychic health as it is for the health of society at large.

The Affect of Anxiety

It has been suggested in this chapter that anxiety over possible punishment or parental rejection is one important force in socialization. The previous chapter argued that fear of the unfamiliar was a common experience during the first year of life. Two of the child's frequent responses to the emotion of fear or anxiety are crying and withdrawal. Let us now consider more directly the relation between crying or withdrawal on the one hand and the emotion of fear or anxiety on the other. Before delving into this issue we must first examine the meaning of the word *emotion*, or, as it is termed in psychology, *affect*. (These concepts are discussed in more detail in Part I, Chapters 7–10.)

CHARACTERISTICS OF AFFECTS

The concept of affect defies precise definition. The popular and traditional view assumes that there are some basic internal physiological changes—such as increased heart rate, motor discharge, or sweating—that either accompany or cause the emotional states that we label anger, excitement, fear, and so on. These internal physiological states are presumed to have consistency within an individual and, perhaps, universality across mankind.

Recent research developments suggest the need for some modification of this traditional view. An affect is now thought to involve an interpretation of a combination of three sets of conditions: (1) perception of internal bodily sensations, called visceral afferent stimulation (referring to perceived change in the level of stimulation coming from heart, intestine, stomach, muscles, skin, and other internal organs), (2) the immediate external situation or context of the individual (home, beach, office, or classroom), and (3) the thoughts and images the individual is having at the time. Sadness, fear, happiness, anger, and other affects are names for combinations of these three sets of conditions.

During most of the child's waking day, he is acting, thinking, and imagining in a variety of environmental and interpersonal situations or contexts, such as playing with a sibling, talking with a parent, or fighting with a playmate. These contexts are not regarded as affect situations until one necessary ingredient is present: The child must perceive a change in the quality or intensity of the internal sensations originating in his muscles, stomach, intestines, heart, skin, and so on. When he feels different in some respect from the way he usually feels, he is in an "emotional" situation.

Thus, an affect is experienced when a person recognizes a discrepancy between the intensity or quality of the internal stimulation he feels and that which is normal for him. Some affects are marked by a perception of internal sensations that are very strong or intense, and therefore noticeable, to the person. Excitement, rage, joy, and fear belong to this class. Other affects are characterized by bodily sensations less intense than a person's normal sensations. Sadness, apathy, and lassitude are included in this class.

Generalized Excitement in Infants Versus Specific Affects in Older Children

When the older child or adult experiences a change in the quality or intensity of his internal feelings, he *interprets* the change. The immediate context and his thoughts are used as the basis for explaining why he feels different. The interpretation specifies the affect.

Specifically, this interpretation is influenced by (1) the direction of the discrepancy the individual notices (that is, higher or lower intensity of stimulation), (2) the content of his images and thoughts, (3) his immediate context, and (4) the language labels available to him. For instance, a perception of decreased arousal level combined with thoughts about missing one's family while in a strange hotel room is likely to be labeled depression or loneliness. The same level of decreased arousal combined with thoughts about the hard day at the office while on the late bus home at 7:30 p.m. is likely to be labeled fatigue.

Because the infant has no language ability, he cannot interpret and label his discrepant feelings. When he experiences changes in sensations, he usually exhibits only states of generalized excitement. He cries, laughs, or thrashes to external events or internal sensations directly, not as a consequence of interpretation. The 6-month-old infant who sees his mother smile and feels her tickle may laugh; when he feels a cramp or sees a strange face, he may cry. But 6 years later the child's laughter or crying is marbled with meaning and is more closely linked to certain contexts. The 6-year-old has learned to evaluate his feelings; the infant has not. An infant does not experience disgust, pride, joy, or guilt, in the adult sense of these words, for he does not have the thoughts about himself and other persons that are an integral part of these adult emotions.

The Role of the Social Environment in Development of Affects

One mechanism that facilitates the development of states of infant excitement into the more differentiated affects of the older child is the labeling of the child's emotions by parents and peers. For instance, by taking away a piece of candy a mother may cause her 2-year-old child to stamp his feet and scream. If the mother then says, "Don't show your anger to your mother" or "Don't get mad," she gives the child a connection between the word "angry" or "mad" and the visceral afferent stimulation he is experiencing in the context of the loss of a valued object. Suppose the mother said, "Don't be sad because I took away your candy," and consistently used the word "sad" in situations in which the child experienced upset after having lost a prized object. It is presumed that when the child later experienced the same visceral afferent stimulation in a context of loss of an object, he would label his feelings as "sadness"; whereas another child might label them "anger." The specific word chosen to label the visceral sensations is important because the child's overt behavior is linked, in large measure, to what the word connotes.

The *context* of the social environment also has been found to have a definite effect on how a person interprets the visceral afferent stimulation and associated cognitions that accompany the context. Empirical support for this view has come from experiments conducted by Schachter and his colleagues (Schachter & Singer, 1962; Schachter & Wheeler, 1962). They found that adults with the same induced state of bodily feelings reacted differently depending on the context in which they were placed and whether or not they had an explanation for their visceral sensations. The subjects were injected with adrenalin, which led to perceived bodily changes in heart rate and tactile sensations. Subjects who watched a funny movie reacted to these bodily changes by labeling their feelings as "humor" and "joy." Subjects who watched a sad movie reacted by labeling their feelings as "depression." In both instances the subjects were being aroused by the adrenalin and were aware of a discrepancy from their normal state of feeling.

These experiments indicate that the richness and appropriateness of an emotion are governed as much by the person's labeling of his feelings according to the context as by the raw feelings themselves. In an adult or older child there is an increased tendency for behavior to reflect the affect interpretation that is applied, in contrast to the infant and the very young child, whose behavior is more directly controlled by, or conditioned to, the visceral afferent stimuli. Thus, the cry of a 15-month-old is likely to be a direct reaction to the pain of being spanked or to the experience of the unfamiliar. The cry of the 3-year-old could be a direct reaction to visceral afferent stimulation, but it is just as likely to be a reaction to the expectation of being sent to his room, or a strategy of obtaining sympathy when he feels "persecuted" by restrictive parents.

THE NATURE OF ANXIETY

Anxiety is an affect because it always has a cognitive aspect. Anxiety is present when the child experiences unpleasant visceral sensations in a context in which he anticipates that something painful or uncomfortable might occur. Thus, the 3-year-old who cringes from his mother when she warns him of his father's reaction to a toilet accident is probably experiencing the affect of anxiety. The response of cowering or crying in this particular context is the result of anxiety. On the other hand, the crying of the 5-month-old to a strange face is probably not a reaction to anxiety. The infant of this age is too immature to interpret his visceral sensations. The crying is a direct reaction to a discrepant event, not to the anticipation of some painful experience.

The condition that is most likely to produce the affect of anxiety in a child of 3 years or older is uncertainty about a future event. Major sources of uncertainty are possible loss of nurturance or affection, anticipation of physical harm, and lack of congruence between a rule or socialization standard the child has learned and his evaluation of his current beliefs or behaviors. Refinements, elaborations, and subtle combinations of these sources of anxiety give rise to such unpleasant affects as helplessness, depression, guilt, and shame, which appear during the later preschool and the early school years.

Although psychologists agree that anxiety is an important affect in childhood, there is no agreement as to how to measure it or how to distinguish among the specific sources of anxiety. There has been no lack of effort in this direction; psychologists have tried interviews, questionnaires, inkblot tests, and measures of palmar sweating and heart rate, but none of these is a completely satisfactory means of measurement. The concept of anxiety continues to be discussed because it is believed to be an essential idea; hopefully, social scientists will eventually devise an exact method for measuring its presence and intensity.

A Review of the Major Processes

The period from 18 months to 3 years is witness to three major processes: (1) the development of the locomotor and perceptual-motor coordinations that allow the child to learn that he can have an instrumental effect upon his environment, (2) the emergence of speech and of language comprehension, and (3) the acquisition of socially appropriate inhibitions on toileting, exploration, property destruction, excessive dependency, tantrums, and crying.

The sequence of responses in early toilet training has received detailed consideration not only because it is important for future development; it also provides a good model of the mechanisms of early socialization, which can also be applied to the socialization of exploration, property destruction, and genital manipulation. There is a core sequence in which the child feels an urge to commit a prohibited act, experiences anxiety, and subsequently inhibits the act he was about to perform. This sequence is replicated many times during the first 10 years of life in the course of establishing those socialization standards that the culture considers characteristic of a mature and responsible person.

Children have more need of models than of critics.

JOSEPH JOUBERT. Thoughts

We are, in truth, more than half what we are by imitation. The great point is, to choose good models and to study them with care.

LORD CHESTERFIELD. Letters

CHAPTER 26
THE PERIOD OF IDENTIFICATION: 3 TO 6 YEARS

T he years from 3 to 6 are characterized by several important developments. The child begins to orient his actions and motives away from his mother and toward his father, his brothers and sisters, and his peers. He seems less concerned with obtaining his mother's attention, recognition, and approval for his actions and less anxious about her absence. On the other hand, he now experiences guilt and shame for violation of socialization standards, rather than just the fear of being punished, and he inhibits prohibited actions in order to avoid these painful states. He shows more active involvement with toys and activities and derives much pleasure from constructive play. The child learns that he is called a boy or girl, and he becomes aware of the appropriate dress, actions, play activities, skills, and motives of the ideal boy and girl.

One of the most important developments of this period is the child's perception of the powers and competencies of his parents and his desire to be more similar to them. This new development is closely associated with the process of *identification* of child with parent. Since the child's identification is such an important aspect of his self-image and his expectations of the reactions of others, much of this chapter will be given to a discussion of this process. The chapter will conclude with a consideration of the role of identification in acquisition of standards, including a description of the guilt and shame that occur as a result of violation of standards during the pre-school period.

The Concept of Identification

A 5-year-old boy feels proud as he watches his father defeat a rival in tennis or sees his brother hit a tie-breaking home run. A young girl feels the elation of being "grown up" as she puts on her mother's apron and attempts to bake a pie. A young boy feels ashamed when authorities arrest his father or commit his mother to a mental institution. In each of these cases the child behaves as if he possessed some of the characteristics of another person to whom he feels similar. The proud 5-year-old boy feels as if he had won the tennis match and not his father. The girl who prepares to bake a pie behaves as though she had her mother's culinary skills; the boy suffers as if he, not his parent, had been arrested or institutionalized. The concept of identification is used to explain the phenomenon of vicarious sharing in the emotional states of others. (See Part II, pp. 358–67.)

Identification is, in part, the belief of a person that some attributes of a model (for example, parents, siblings, relatives, peers, and fictional figures) are also possessed by the person. A boy who realizes that he and his father share the same name, notes that they have similar facial features, and is told by relatives that they both have lively tempers develops a belief that he is similar to his father. *When this belief in similarity is accompanied by vicarious emotional experiences in the child that are appropriate to the model, we say that the child has an* identification *with the model.*

HOW IDENTIFICATION
IS ESTABLISHED AND STRENGTHENED

Children do not develop strong identifications with everyone they share some similarity with, but they do develop identifications with more than one model. The conditions that determine the strength of the identification are, therefore, important. Four related processes must be examined in order to obtain an understanding of how identification works.

Process 1. The person (P) believes that he and a model (M) share particular physical or psychological attributes. P believes that some of the characteristics of M also belong to him. The more distinctive these shared attributes are, the stronger is P's belief.

There are three major ways that the child may perceive similarity to the model: (1) by adoption of the model's attributes, (2) by believing others who tell him that he shares similarities with the model, and (3) by initially recognizing some fundamental similarities, including surname, basic affective states (such as anger, joy, and disgust), and physical characteristics (genitals, special skin markings, color of eyes or hair). As a result of these accumulated similarities, the typical 6-year-old believes that he is more similar to his parent, specifically the parent of the same sex, than he is to any other adult he knows.

Process 2. P experiences vicarious affective reactions that are appropriate to events that M is experiencing. The identification is present when P feels as though events that happen to M are happening to him. He often behaves as if the world will react to him as he believes it will react to M.

The assumption that a child vicariously experiences the affect that he believes the identification model would feel has not been proved, but it has been demonstrated in the laboratory. One such attempt was made in a study by Kagan and Phillips (1964). Boys and girls (age 5½ to 8½) were brought to a laboratory with either the father (for boys) or the mother (for girls). Each child was told he was going to watch a contest between his parent and an adult stranger of the same sex. The contest involved the identification of blurred pictures projected on a screen. Both the parent and the stranger had been prerehearsed to fail or pass specific pictures on the test. It was expected that the child would show greater elation when his parent was successful or the stranger failed than when the parent failed or the stranger succeeded. These results would indicate greater vicarious emotional involvement with the parent than with the stranger.

After the child was told how the contest worked and after electrodes for measuring his heart rate were attached to him, all communications were directed toward the two adults and the child was ignored. His overt behavior and his heart-rate reactions were studied while the adults were trying to solve the problem and after the examiner announced whether the adults had passed or failed the item. It was found that the child smiled much more following parent success or stranger failure than after parent failure or stranger success. The child behaved as if he were elated by his parent's success. Moreover, he showed the greatest excitement, as measured by increase in heart rate, following parent success and stranger failure than after the other conditions. Although there are several ways to interpret the results, they are consonant with the suggestion that children are likely to share vicariously in the affective states of the models with whom they perceive basic similarities.

Process 3. P wants to acquire the attributes of M that he perceives to be desirable; P wishes to have access to the positive goal states that he believes M to possess.

The child perceives that adults, especially his parents, are stronger, more powerful, and wiser than he is, and they have special privileges and easy access to desirable goals. The child wants these privileges and goals for himself. For instance, he wants to be strong, to be able to order other people around, to decide what and when to eat and where and when to go to bed, to drive a car, to swim in deep water, to pick up heavy things. In short, the child would like to possess the skills and privileges of adults.

The attractiveness of an identification model seems to be based both on the model's nurturance of the child and the degree to which the model seems to possess desirable attributes, especially power over the child and over other adults, competence at tasks the child considers important, receipt of affection from the parent of the opposite sex, and acceptance by others.

Process 4. P adopts and practices attitudes and behaviors that M displays, because he believes that by increasing his similarity to M he might command M's desirable attributes.

The child assumes that since he possesses some of the tangible, external characteristics of the model, he might also possess the model's desirable psychological properties—power, affection from others, and instrumental competencies. In effect, the child seems to believe that objects appearing alike on the outside have similar internal properties. Thus, the greater the overlap of external similarities between himself and the model, the greater he considers the possibility that he will possess the model's power, affection, and competence—the intangible psychological qualities he wishes to command. The desire for those qualities leads him to adopt and practice the model's characteristics.

The Interrelation of the Four Processes

These four processes combine to yield two causal sequences. The first two processes, whereby the child believes that he shares unique and distinctive attributes with the model and, therefore, experiences vicarious emotional reactions appropriate to events the model experiences, lead to the establishment of an identification. Their joint occurrence defines identification.

The second causal sequence involves the last two processes. As the child adopts additional attributes of a model, in the service of a desire to possess the model's goals, he will perceive that he, in fact, shares more attributes with the model. Consequently, he will experience even more intense vicarious emotional reactions and a stronger identification.

The four processes are thus interrelated because each time the child imitates the behavior of the model or adopts an attitude of the model, he perceives an increased similarity to the latter. This perception strengthens his belief that he must also possess the model's covert characteristics and allows him to share vicariously more of the positive affects of the model. The more desirable the model (process 3), the greater the degree to which the child will strive to adopt the model's attributes (process 4). The adoption of these behaviors leads the child, in turn, to perceive increased similarity to the model (process 1), which promotes more intensive vicarious affective reactions in the child (process 2).

THE EFFECT OF IDENTIFICATION
ON BEHAVIORAL DEVELOPMENT

The processes surrounding identification with and imitation of a model are as influential in determining behavioral differences among children as are differential reward and punishment of specific acts. Consider, for example, the lower-class child whose teachers reward him for studying and punish him for poor school performance but whose parents do not display any personal interest in the acquisition of knowledge. This child is not as motivated to master school tasks as is the child whose parents display an active interest in his education. A child places special value on those behaviors practiced by desirable models.

Aggressive, dependent, and sexual behaviors also assume different strengths in the child's behavioral repertoire, according to the extent to which these behaviors are displayed by the models the child has chosen for identification. When the pattern of adult reward and punishment agrees with the models' overt behavior, the child is most likely to practice that action. For example, a girl whose mother rewards dependent responses and is herself dependent on her husband is likely to become strongly dependent on her parents and friends. Prediction of the child's behavior is less certain, however, if these two conditions act antagonistically. For instance, if a father rewards his son's aggression toward others but is rarely aggressive himself, the frequency and style of aggressive behavior in the son is difficult to predict. However, consistency between the pattern of reward and the model's behavior is more likely than inconsistency, because parents are likely to reward explicitly those behaviors they themselves manifest most frequently.

THE EFFECT OF IDENTIFICATION
ON SELF-LABELS

Identification not only is important for the sculpting of overt behavior but is also critical for the development of the ambiguous process of self-definition, which is sometimes called a *self-concept.* The child's self-concept consists, in part, of his evaluation of the degree to which his attributes match those that the culture has designated as desirable. The critical dimensions for Western culture include, among others, virtue, honesty, strength, size, attractiveness, intelligence, autonomy, wealth, and power. To some extent the child's evaluation is determined by his social experiences. For instance, his self-conception of his power is based to some extent on his ability to defeat a rival, demonstrate his strength on an athletic field, or achieve good grades. But the child is also prone to label himself on the basis of his identification with a model. The boy who has developed an identification with an intelligent father begins to regard himself as intelligent. A girl who is identified with a beautiful mother views herself as more attractive than she would if her parent were not beautiful.

Negative self-evaluations can be established in a similar manner, if a model's attributes are undesirable. One critical antecedent of psycho-pathology is the child's belief that he shares basic similarities with a nega-tively valued parent. Intensive interviews with seriously disturbed adults, including those with schizophrenic reactions, have provided evidence that many of these people feel unworthy, incompetent, or basically evil because they believe that they are fundamentally similar to a parent whom they regard as unworthy, incompetent, or unloving. The severely disturbed and unhappy person does not want to possess these undesirable traits, but the identification that has taken place has caused these beliefs.

A 5-year-old, confronted with the fact that he is more similar to his parents than to any other adult he knows (because they share the same sur-name, body build, and often the same features), must inevitably develop some minimal identification with them. This minimal identification develops regardless of how undesirable or how unattractive the parents may be. As the child begins to recognize the negative qualities of the parental model, he also begins to believe that some of these qualities are part of his own set of per-sonal characteristics.

FURTHER IMPLICATIONS OF IDENTIFICATION

The development of beliefs, motives, and behaviors that reflect the dominant or expected standards of a culture are easier to explain than those that deviate from the norms. In most instances it is possible to explain normative behaviors without resorting to the concept of identification. The child sits in school, runs on the playground, talks at the school lunch table. These behaviors are appropriate in those contexts and do not require the concept of identification to explain them. Neither does the child's con-scientious making of his bed each morning necessarily involve identification. More likely than not, the child is motivated in this task to avoid parental punishment. Most of the behaviors that the child displays during the day either are habitual responses to a particular context or are motivated by a desire for positive reward or a desire to avoid punishment.

These mechanisms will not, however, explain why a child whose parents praise good grades and punish poor school performance obtains poor grades; why a 10-year-old boy who is told his grandfather won a Nobel Prize suddenly shows a spurt of motivation; or why a 30-year-old woman whose mother became psychotic at age 31 becomes tense and apprehensive as if she believed that she, too, were about to become psychotic. These behaviors are not appropriate to any particular context, nor do they bring praise or post-pone social punishment. Many of these actions are derived from beliefs about one's attributes established as a result of perceived similarity to a model. Others are attempts to strengthen a beginning identification. The child will imitate the parent of the same sex in order to maximize similarity to him and thereby increase his identification with the parent. The child is predisposed to imitate the parent of the same sex because he initially perceives more similarity to that parent than to the parent of the opposite sex.

During the years 3 to 6, the child identifies primarily with his parents, for they are the adults whom he knows best and whom he respects and admires. As he grows older, his parents' power and competence wane as he becomes aware of other adults who possess qualities and skills that surpass those of his parents. He meets local heroes or heroines; he hears about great athletes, astronauts, and scientists. Often the extreme motivation that is required to work on a scientific discovery or a novel requires either an identification with a model who has played this role or an attempt to maximize similarity to such a model. One reason for the relative paucity of outstanding women scientists and artists is the lack of available role models for young girls. The child is more likely to believe he can command power, glory, or greatness if someone of his own sex, ethnic, religious, or racial group has done so in the past. The perception of similarity, which is one of the necessary conditions for identification, facilitates attempts to imitate the model.

The adolescent and young adult establish identifications with groups (clubs, colleges) and with ideas (liberal attitudes, civil rights beliefs, philosophical positions). As he grows, he develops partial identifications with many different people. Some of these identifications are strong, and some are weak. Each identification contributes to his image of himself. The test for the presence of identification is relatively simple. If a person experiences positive feelings (joy or elation) when good things happen to the model and negative feelings (sadness or shame) when bad things happen to the model, an identification is present. The beliefs about the self are derived, to some extent, from the models with whom the person has developed identifications.

Theoretical Views on the Adoption of a Model's Behavior

The fact that children imitate behavior they have observed adults perform, without the intrusion of direct reward and punishment, is not generally disputed. However, there is serious disagreement as to how this phenomenon should be interpreted. Some psychologists emphasize the love relationship between child and model, suggesting that the child imitates the model's behavior because the model has acquired reward value through nurturance of the child (Mowrer, 1950). The boy presumably adopts the father's interest in cars, for example, because this activity has become attractive as a consequent of its link to a nurturant adult. The practice of this behavior, then, is motivated by the desire to reproduce a valued response. Mowrer's view suggests that—other things being equal—the child will adopt the behavior of the more affectionate and nurturant parent.

One pair of studies (Payne & Mussen, 1956; Mussen & Distler, 1959) supports Mowrer's emphasis on the importance of a nurturant relationship between father and son in facilitating imitation of the former. High school boys and their parents filled out a questionnaire assessing their motives, attitudes, and behaviors. The 20 boys whose answer patterns were most similar to those of their fathers were compared with the 20 boys whose answers were least similar. The 40 boys were then given a first part of a story and asked to complete it. The boys whom the questionnaire found to be most similar to their fathers told stories that contained more frequent evidence of warm father-son relationships and a perception of the father as more nurturant than did the stories of the other subjects. Moreover, these boys displayed more masculine behavior and attitudes than did the boys who were unlike their fathers (Payne & Mussen, 1956).

In a similar experiment (Mussen & Distler, 1959), the degree of adoption of sex-typed masculine interests was assessed in kindergarten boys. The 10 most masculine and the 10 least masculine boys were asked to make up stories using dolls to represent family members. The stories of the masculine boys contained more evidence of a perception of the father as affectionate than did the stories of the less masculine boys, which suggests that adoption of the father's attributes is facilitated when he is seen as nurturant to the child.

Bronfenbrenner (1960) suggests that there is no generalized motive to become like one or the other parent. But Maccoby (1959) believes that the child does have a motive to imitate adult models; according to her, frequency of exposure to the model's behavior and the degree to which the model commands power are the two major determinants of imitation of the models' behaviors. Bandura (1962) treats imitation and identification as synonymous and suggests that a sufficient condition for the learning of a response displayed by a model is exposure to that response.

Bandura and his colleagues (Bandura, 1962; Bandura, Ross, & Ross, 1963a, 1963b) in their experiments typically place nursery school children in laboratory situations with a variety of adult models, whose degree of reward, power, or nurturance is manipulated by the experimenter. The models display unique postural, motor, and verbal responses. For example, the model might put on an absurd hat at a rakish tilt and shout, "March, march, march!" as he walks around the room. Subsequently, the child is observed and the differential imitation of the various models is assessed. The more nurturant the model was to the child, the greater was the child's imitation of him. Children exposed to models who displayed aggressive behavior were more likely to display aggression than were children exposed to nonaggressive models. Not surprisingly, the child was more likely to express aggression in a subsequent session if the model's aggression led to rewarding goals than if aggressive behavior was punished.

In one ingenious experiment (Bandura, Ross, & Ross, 1963a) different groups of preschool children were exposed one by one to male or female adults who either dispensed or received toys and other desirable objects. Following the child's exposure to this situation, problem tasks were given to the adults, to which they displayed unique responses. For example, an adult would pick up a special colored cap, place it upon his head at an odd angle, and display unusual behaviors. The models then left the room, and the child was asked to perform these problems. The tendency for the child to imitate the unique responses of the models was assessed. The model who dispensed the desirable objects was imitated more frequently than was the adult who received them. However, the male in the control or power position of dispensing objects was imitated more frequently than the female in the identical power role. And boys who watched a female dispense desirable objects in a situation in which the adult male was ignored *imitated the ignored male rather than the female.*

The children's verbalizations indicated that they felt sorry for this man. This finding suggests that a model's sex, as well as his power, influences the child's differential imitation of adults; boys are more likely to imitate men than they are women, even though most 6-year-old boys have had much more exposure to the behavior of women (mother, babysitter, nursery school teacher) than to that of men. Support is thereby given to the importance of a child's perceived similarity to the adult model.

THE IMPORTANCE OF PERCEIVED SIMILARITY

A major difference among theorists in their interpretation of identification and imitation involves the emphasis placed upon the child's initial perception of similarity to the model. This similarity can be based on concrete physical attributes (short hair, trousers, dresses) or merely on the fact that the model and the child are called by the same categorical name (such as, boys, men, ladies, Christians). The child wants consistency and order in his world. All objects or people with the same name should have the same characteristics. Once he learns what he is called—be it boy, Quaker, or Negro—he acts to elaborate that definition.

Many theorists acknowledge the relevance of the model's power over the child in governing the degree of identification or imitation of the model. But some do not place heavy stress on whether the child believes in some initial basis of similarity to the model. However, it does seem reasonable to expect that if the child felt that he shared neither attributes nor categorical similarities with the model, he would doubt his ability to share vicariously in the model's goals. As a result, he would not strive to increase behavioral similarity to that model.

The relevance of perceived similarity to imitation has been demonstrated in several experiments. In one study young children who were normally impulsive in their behavior were taught to become more reflective (Kagan, Pearson, & Welch, 1966). One group of first graders was taught to be reflective by a warm and friendly trainer (a woman for the girls and a man for the boys) using normal tutoring conditions. A second group was trained under identical conditions, except that prior to training the trainer took time to persuade each child that he or she shared basic attributes with the child. For example, the trainer would ask the child how many siblings he had and would then comment that he had the same number as the child. Questions about interests and favorite animals were answered first by the child, followed by the trainer noting the similarity between the child's choices and his own. The actual training to make the children more thoughtful and reflective was identical in both groups, and for both groups the trainers announced that they were thoughtful when they solved problems and that they valued this trait.

If the child's desire to maximize similarity to a model is enhanced by an initial perception of similarity to the model, then the children trained by the adult who emphasized similarity to the child should have become more reflective after training than the children in the other group. This prediction was confirmed for the girls but not for the boys. There was no difference between the boys trained under the two conditions. However, although the boys in this study were trained by a male adult, they were tested by a female; whereas the girls were both trained and tested by a female adult. Thus one would expect the tested effects of training to be more striking for the girls.

Perceived similarity to the model also facilitates imitation in older children. Young adolescent boys were told that they would be given a gamelike task to solve after they watched a boy in a film work on the same task. Some of the subjects were led to believe they were similar to the model boy portrayed in the film; others were led to believe they were different from the model. After viewing the film each boy was allowed to work on the task for 7 minutes. The boys who believed they were similar to the film model imitated many more actions of the film model than did the other group of boys (Rosenkrans, 1967).

A perception of similarity is capable of increasing feelings of empathy. Boys and girls in the first grade were shown a series of slide sequences depicting 7-year-olds in different emotional situations. Some of them involved happy events (a birthday party, winning a television contest); other slides displayed sadness (a lost dog or social rejection), fear (a lost child or a frightened dog), and the emotion of anger (a false accusation). After the child was shown the slide, a short narration was read so that he would understand clearly what the picture was about. Some children saw girls depicted in the slide sequences, and other children saw boys. Immediately following each slide sequence the child was asked simply to state how he felt. The boys were much more empathic when they were observing boys in the pictured situations, whereas the girls were more empathic when they were observing girls. Thus, a perception of similarity, in this case similarity in sex, facilitated empathic responses (Feshbach & Roe, 1968).

A perception of similarity to a model has also been found to increase the probability that the child will attend closely to what the model says or does. This conclusion has important implications for learning and school performance. It is supported by an experiment on the relation between perceived similarity and attention in two groups of college women who had been previously classified as highly involved either in obtaining good grades or in leading a social life (Chang, 1965). The women were told that they were to judge the creativity of a pair of poems that two other female students had written. Each of the two hypothetical poets was described as being concerned with either good grades or an active social life. Thus, the subjects who were motivated to obtain good grades perceived themselves as resembling one poet; the socially motivated subjects perceived themselves as similar to the other poet.

The subjects heard the poems read on tape and then, instead of being asked to comment on the creativity shown in the poems, were asked to recall as much as they could of both poems. Since they had not expected to be asked to recall the poems, differences in the amount recalled should reflect differential attention to the two models. The subjects who were concerned with grades recalled more of the poem read by the model described as academically motivated, whereas the socially motivated girls recalled more of the poem read by the model who was more concerned with social life. It seems that perceived similarity to a model oriented the women to attend more closely to that model.

Further support for the central role of perceived similarity comes from the fact that children do not imitate the behavior of every person to whom they are exposed or identify with every model who has power. Psychiatric reports suggest that sons with excessively powerful and competent fathers often fail to identify with them. One possible explanation of such a failure is that the boy may perceive no major bases of similarity to the father (that is, they may differ in body build, in frequency and intensity of affective states, in occurrence of failure at tasks). When the child cannot perceive some basis of similarity to the parent, he may be discouraged from attempting to establish an identification and consequently not strive to adopt the model's characteristics.

In the current civil rights struggle the Negro leaders recognize that the Negro child has a difficult time perceiving similarity to the white majority and thus identifying with the white culture. It is reasonable that they would request to have a totally black community, which would make the Negro child's task of identifying with appropriate black models easier than if he were in an integrated one. A Negro child is apt to feel less regret when a powerful Caucasian boy in his class is hurt than if the same misfortune befalls a less privileged Negro peer 100 miles away. The phenomenon of vicarious sharing in the affective states of a model appears to require a perception of similarity to another.

The Role of Identification
in Acquisition of Standards

One of Freud's most significant statements is, "The superego is the heir of the Oedipus complex." Freud meant that the child's major defense against the anxiety created by the Oedipal conflict is identification with the parent of the same sex. The primary consequence of this identification is the adoption of the parents' standards regarding those behaviors and wishes that the society values.

The discussion of the socialization of standards was introduced in Chapter 25, with special reference to the child under 3 years. That chapter stated that the major forces behind the 2-year-old's adoption of standards on toilet training, aggression, and destruction of property were the desire for affection from the parents and the need to avoid their punishment or rejection. During the preschool and early school years, a new motivational force supplements the purely external goals of social reward or avoidance of punishment. The 5-year-old realizes that certain standards of behavior and thought characterize "grown-up" children and adults, especially the adult model that is represented by the parent. Since the child wants to be like the adult models he has selected, he begins to adopt their behavior, attitudes, and values.

Thus, the acquisition of standards is based not only on fear of external punishment but also on the belief that these standards are appropriate for the child to possess. For instance, if the father is kind to other people and if the child wishes someday to be like the father, then he should come to believe that kindness is an appropriate characteristic to display. It should be one of his defining characteristics, just as his eyes, arms, and legs are part of his anatomical attributes.

HOW STANDARDS OPERATE: A CASE STUDY

Standards operate as if they were judges to whom decisions about beliefs and behaviors are referred for final approval or veto. This is a fortunate development, for socialization of the child would be exceedingly difficult if the only bases for inhibition of undesirable behavior were fear of external reprisal and desire for nurturance and acceptance. Sears, Maccoby, and Levin (1957) provide an excellent illustration of the early operation of a standard in a girl under 2 years old.

Martha's parents brought her along one Sunday afternoon when they came for a visit. She was 17 months old, full of curiosity and mischief. While we had coffee and cookies, she thirstily drank down a glass of milk, ate half a cookie, and began an eager exploration of her surroundings. Toddling most of the time, crawling occasionally, she left trails of crumbs and tipped over cups wherever she went. One of the floor lamps fascinated her especially. It was tall and straight, made of a single, glossy round of wood, just the right size for Martha to get a good grip on. When she stood up against it, clutching happily, the lamp teetered and swayed in what was obviously an entrancing fashion for Martha.

Twice her father had to put down his cup and leap across the room to prevent a crash. Twice he said, clearly and distinctly, "Now, Martha, don't touch." Each time he took her by the hand and led her over to some toys. These distracted her only briefly.

After the second interruption, Martha began a general exploration of the room again. Now she went a little more slowly, and several times glanced at her father. As she came closer to the lamp, however, she stopped looking his way and her movements were all oriented toward the lamp. Deliberately she stepped toward it, came within a couple of feet of it, and lifted her arm partly, a little jerkily, and then said sharply, commandingly, "Don't touch."

There was an instant of struggling silence. Then she turned and stumbled across the room, flopped down on the floor, and started laughing excitedly. Her father laughing with her, and obviously adoring, reached out and hugged and snuggled her for minutes.

Why was this a beginning of conscience? Why not assume, more simply, that Martha was afraid her father would punish her if she touched the lamp again? The difference between fear and conscience lies in the self-instruction and the incorporation in the child herself of the values expressed by the parents. Martha was playing the parental role when she said sternly to herself, "Don't touch." Had she continued to look furtively at her father as she got close to the lamp— had she oscillated back and forth in her approach—had she been whimpery or silent and withdrawn after the moment of decision—we would have said she was responding to the dangers of the situation by simple avoidance. But at the crucial moment, she did not have to look at her father; she looked to herself for guidance and the behest she followed was her own [Sears, Maccoby, & Levin, 1957, pp. 365–66].

CONSEQUENCES OF DEVIATION FROM STANDARDS

Standards are, in one way, like the perceptual schema for objects that were discussed in Chapter 24. Once a child acquires a schema for a face, an encounter with a discrepancy from a face elicits fear and a sense of discomfort. Similarly, once a 5-year-old believes that kindness is an appropriate characteristic for him to possess, he will experience discomfort if he recognizes that he deviates from this standard—if he sees a discrepancy between the standard and his behavior. Consider the 4-year-old who has been exposed repeatedly, 20 times a week for several years, to descriptions from his parents as to how he should behave if he is going to be grown up! He hears repeatedly such commands as, "Wash your hands, do not yell at your mother, be kind to your sister." A point will come when these statements will harden cognitively and become accepted as the appropriate way for him to act. Behavior or thoughts that are discrepant from a standard are liable to provoke guilt or shame.

At a superficial level, guilt and shame seem
similar, for both are characterized by an unpleasant feeling that results from violating a standard. At a somewhat deeper level, however, one finds that there are means of differentiating between the two. The *behavioral manifestations* of shame and guilt are one means of differentiation. Shame is commonly, although not always, accompanied by blushing or lowering of the head and eyes. Guilt does not typically lead to any characteristic set of behaviors that are quite so public.

The *conditions* that elicit guilt and shame provide another basis for differentiation. The unpleasant feelings called shame are elicited by an expectation that *other people* will be disappointed in the fact that a standard has been violated. The unpleasant feelings called guilt are caused by expectations that the *self* will disapprove. (See Part I, Chapter 7.) The child is likely to feel shame when he believes he has violated a standard that someone has held for him. Shame is therefore tied to anticipation of disapproval from others for violation of a standard that the child accepts. Guilt, on the other hand, is more independent of the expectation of disapproval from another person. The child experiences guilt when he anticipates reprisal from his own conscience for violation of a standard he has set for himself, rather than of one he believes other people have set for him.

Shame typically occurs before guilt in the developmental process, for the learning of standards is fostered by the exchange of social acceptance for the practice of appropriate actions. Initially, many standards are set by other people. Although the child is aware of the standard and accepts it as appropriate for himself, he has not necessarily decided that it should be one of his defining attributes. The role of judge still resides in the external world. However, when the child himself eventually becomes the judge, the punishment is meted out by the self and guilt is experienced.

This subtle distinction between shame and guilt can be appreciated by considering the following question: Does the child believe he has a choice with respect to initiating a certain act? There are some responses for which society gives the child little freedom of choice. He feels a pressure to behave in a particular manner because his family and friends expect it. It is as if society demands this behavior and he has no choice but to obey. Under these conditions, if the child does not behave in accordance with these standards he feels ashamed. He anticipates disapproval from parents, friends, or teachers because he has violated their expectations of how he should behave. If the child believes he has a choice regarding a particular action, he perceives that the expectations of his social environment are not explicit. Under these conditions, he is more likely to experience guilt if he violates a standard. Guilt is a reprimand to the self for a mistake, for selecting the wrong alternative.

Let us consider some specific behavioral examples to illustrate this point. If a child's parents expect him to help his younger brother in a crisis, the standard "help your brother" is fully defined and allows no choice. The child would then feel shame if he did not aid his brother. If, on the other hand, the child felt that he had a choice, if he felt that his parents might not punish him for not being helpful, he would probably experience guilt for not coming to his brother's aid.

For the standard of nurturance, as indeed for most standards of conduct, the cultural requirements seem to be clearer and more commanding for girls and women than they are for boys and men. A girl typically orients to her parents, to her boyfriend, to her husband, and to the wider social community for guidelines as to how to behave. As a result, she is more likely to feel shame than guilt when she violates a standard. In her view of the world she has no choice. The boy is more likely to feel guilt over violation of a standard because as he matures he comes to see that the source of authority for moral judgments must be himself. He is more likely to recognize that he has a choice. It is in a moral situation where choice exists that the conditions for guilt—that is, self-reprimand—are bred.

WHAT STANDARDS ARE ESTABLISHED?

Dependence, aggression, sexuality, and task competence are some of the major behavioral areas around which standards develop during the period from 3 to 6 years of age. The order in which these specific standards are established during these years is not known in detail and depends in part on the child's family background.

A primary determinant of the rate of establishment of standards is the frequency with which specific behaviors and their associated affects are given unambiguous verbal descriptions. It is likely that hostile feelings and resentful and angry thoughts will be frequently labeled as such by persons in the social environment. Aggressive postures, words, and behaviors are public. American parents, for example, often label the child's pouting face, foot stamping, or verbal barbs by remarking, "Don't be angry" or "Stop being so mad." In addition, parents display signs of anger that are appropriately labeled by others. The child's sexual excitement, urges for mastery, or feelings of dependence or helplessness, on the other hand, are not as frequently and unambiguously labeled by the adult community. It follows, therefore, that standards concerning aggression and anger should emerge earlier than standards dealing with dependency, sexuality, or task mastery.

An important standard adopted during the latter part of the preschool period involves task competence. The 5-year-old may cry when he loses a competitive game, smash his fist on the parts of a puzzle that he cannot fit together successfully, or withdraw sheepishly from a rope he cannot climb. These signs of disappointment, anger, and shame are consequences of the child's recognition that he has deviated from the standard that represented what he felt was the appropriate level or quality of performance.

The articulation of this standard is one reason that children become increasingly inhibited in school and reluctant to risk a guess or offer an answer of which they are unsure. The 2-year-old, in contrast, is still innocent of a well-defined standard of competence and, as a result, feels free to try anything and to ask any question, regardless of how silly it might seem. As a child gradually accepts the burden of the standard that says he is "supposed to be correct and knowledgeable," he avoids placing himself in situations where the standard might be violated. As a result, he appears less inquisitive and less eager to try new tasks. If at the same time a child is aware of what is incorrect and believes that incorrectness is a violation of a standard, then he is driven to protect himself from exposure—and from possible shame and guilt.

Main Trends in Development During the Preschool Years

The preschool years are characterized by a symbolic labeling of the self. The child becomes aware of both the attributes he wants to possess and those that are his psychological inheritance, whether he desires them or not. The process of identification plays a central role in this evolution of the self. This self-definition is aided also by acquisition of standards for actions and beliefs. An awareness of how *right* and *wrong* one's attitudes and wishes are is as important in defining what a person is as his physical appearance or overt behavior. A man is defined by his form, his actions, and his thoughts.

The articulation of standards leads necessarily to the capacity for the uncomfortable feelings of shame and guilt that occur when the child recognizes a discrepancy between the standard and his actions or thoughts. If the shame or guilt is too intense, the child will be forced to defend against his uncomfortable feelings, and psychological symptoms may develop. The emergence of irrational fears, odd rituals, or excessive timidity in the 5- or 6-year-old is often the product of a burden of shame or guilt that became too heavy for the child to bear.

The child's increasingly socialized behavior passes through stages. Initially, the desire for acceptance and the fear of punishment or rejection motivate the process. By age 3 the child has learned that he is called by certain symbolic names (big boy, brave, good girl), and he tries to ensure that his characteristics match the name assigned to him. Finally, he attempts to increase similarity to identification models; in so doing he acquires additional responses, motives, and standards. These four forces—desire for acceptance, avoidance of punishment, elaboration of his symbolic labels, and identification—continue to operate throughout the life span to supply each member of the social community with a collection of goals and standards, and behavioral rules for their implementation.

Higgins: . . . I find that the moment I let a woman make friends with me, she becomes jealous, exacting, suspicious, and a damned nuisance. I find that the moment I let myself make friends with a woman, I become selfish and tyrannical. Women upset everything. When you let them into your life, you find that the woman is driving at one thing and you're driving at another.

Pickering: At what, for example?

Higgins: . . . Oh, Lord knows! I suppose the woman wants to live her own life; and the man wants to live his; and each tries to drag the other on to the wrong track.

GEORGE BERNARD SHAW. Pygmalion

CHAPTER 27
SEX TYPING DURING THE PRESCHOOL AND EARLY SCHOOL YEARS

Although cultures differ in the degree to which they promote standards on aggression, dependency, and sexual modesty, all cultures promote different standards for males and females in certain psychological areas. Most of the psychological differences between adult men and women are the result of these different standards for the sexes. In our culture, men are supposed to be aggressive and women dependent when attacked or frustrated. Men are expected to inhibit signs of strong fear, emotion, and weakness; women are expected to cry if stress is intense and to display their emotions overtly. Men should be interested in athletics, mechanics, science, and mathematics; women in the arts, cooking, gardening, and literature. These assumptions about the appropriate behaviors for men and women in our culture are called sex role standards and are impressed upon the growing child through the process of *sex typing.*

This process refers to the tendency for each culture to promote the adoption of different behaviors for boys and girls and to establish different attributes as desirable for the respective sexes. The child generally learns these values between 3 and 10 years of age. Although the effects of sex typing are most apparent during the school years, the process commences during the preschool period.

The concept of sex typing and the related concepts of sex role standard and sex role identity have achieved much prominence among psychologists during the last decade. It is surprising, however, that this prominence has been so late in coming, for the behavioral differences between the sexes are public and have an ancient and transcultural heritage. Sociology and anthropology have not been neglectful of these concepts; more than a quarter of a century ago Linton (1936) wrote, "The division and ascription of statuses with relation to sex seems to be basic in all social systems. All societies prescribe different attitudes and activities to men and to women."

The process of sex typing first requires the learning of behavioral standards that are different for boys and girls.

The Sex Role Standard

As the last chapter brought out, a standard is a belief about the appropriateness of a characteristic—be it an attitude, a motive, an affect, an external attribute, or a response. Children attempt to develop and maintain a belief system about the self that coincides with those attributes they have learned to regard as "good" and to renounce and avoid attributes regarded as "bad." The bases for the evaluations of "good" or "bad" are culturally derived; they include for the Western community the belief that a person should be valued by and attractive to others, should develop the necessary instrumental skills and competencies to deal with selected problems, should possess the attributes and skills that the majority of the culture judges to be appropriate for his sex, should be rational, coherent, independent, and responsible, and should not engage in behaviors or become preoccupied with thoughts prohibited by the primary reference group (such as violence, aggression, disobedience, dishonesty, selfishness, and open sexuality).

Thus, the Western middle-class child believes he should tell the truth, speak and think coherently, and behave in a way appropriate to his sex role. Many standards are of approximately equal importance for boys and girls. But the standard that is called a "sex role standard" sets different values on a particular attribute depending on whether the child is male or female.

The child's learning of the content of a sex role standard resembles his learning of the meaning of any concept. He learns that a glass is clear, has a cylindrical shape, and is used to hold liquid. A ball is round, made of rubber, and bounces. Similarly, the child learns the definitions for boy and girl by noting what boys and girls do and how they look and by listening to what adults and such sources as television tell him are the respective critical attributes of the words "boys" versus "girls," "men" versus "women," "fathers" versus "mothers."

The early discrimination of persons into these distinct classes is facilitated by the presence of a variety of clearly discriminable cues that include dress, bodily form and proportion, strength, distribution of hair, depth of voice, posture at the toilet, typical interactive behavior with another person, and characteristic behavior in the kitchen, the garage, or the backyard. The definitions of the words "boy" and "girl," "male" and "female," compose what is known as the sex role standard, and these standards dictate the adoption and practice of motives, attitudes, and behaviors that are appropriate for the respective sexes.

THE CONTENT OF THE SEX ROLE STANDARD

The characteristics that define the sex roles of male and female fall into one of three classes: physical attributes, overt behaviors, and covert attributes such as feelings, attitudes, motives, and beliefs. Although the characteristics differentially associated with maleness and femaleness among most adults in our culture are not clearly crystallized in the mind of the 6-year-old, there is considerable overlap between the standards of the first grader and those of the adult.

Physical Attributes   Analysis of the representation of males and females by the public media and the results of studies of preadolescent and adolescent youngsters reveal that American girls regard an attractive face, a hairless body, a small frame, and moderate-sized breasts as the most desirable physical characteristics for girls; boys regard height, large muscle mass, and facial and bodily hair as the most desirable characteristics for boys. A girl should be pretty and small; a boy should be large and strong (Frazier & Lisonbee, 1950; Jersild, 1952; Cobb, 1954; Nash, 1958; Harris, 1959).

Overt Behaviors   Although the culture's differential standards regarding behavior are not as clearly delineated as are the standards for physical attributes, they are strongly felt nonetheless. The following paragraphs describe some of the overt behaviors that help define the sex role.

Aggression. One of the primary classes of sex-typed behavior involves aggression. The standard for this behavior requires inhibition of verbal and physical aggression among girls and women but grants boys and men license—and even encouragement—to express aggression when attacked, threatened, or dominated by another male. Various data support the expectation that American males are more likely to display aggressive behavior than are American females. It is difficult to find a sound study on American preschool or school children in which aggressive behavior is not found to be more frequent among boys than among girls (as in Bach, 1945; Muste & Sharpe, 1947; Sears, 1951; Maccoby & Wilson, 1957; Emmerich, 1959; Kagan & Lemkin, 1960; Bandura, Ross, & Ross, 1961; Bandura, 1962).

This differentiation is also evident in the make-believe stories children tell to dolls or to pictures and in the child's perception of adult males and females. If children are asked which parent is more dangerous or more punitive (that is, aggressive), both boys and girls agree that the father is more aggressive than the mother. This perception of the male as dangerous also holds when aggressive and nonaggressive animals are used to represent the sexes. A 6-year-old who is shown a picture of a rabbit and a tiger will say that the tiger is more like a man, the rabbit more like a woman (Kagan, Hosken, & Watson, 1961). Adults as well as children regard men as more aggressive than women (Jenkins & Russell, 1958; Bennett & Cohen, 1959), and parents hold differential standards for their children, for they expect more overt aggression from boys than from girls (Sears, Maccoby, & Levin, 1957; Kohn, 1959).

Dependency, passivity, and conformity. A second class of sex-typed behavior includes the correlated trio of dependency, passivity, and conformity. Girls and women in America and most European countries are allowed license to express these behaviors, but boys and men are pressured to inhibit them. The data on sex differences in these areas are less consistent than those for aggression, but most studies report greater dependency, conformity, and social passivity for females than for males at all ages. (See, for example, Crutchfield, 1955; Hovland & Janis, 1959; Kagan & Moss, 1962.)

Affiliative and nurturant behavior is generally regarded as more appropriate for females than for males; a majority of investigations of overt behavior or storytelling responses reveal more frequent occurrence of affiliative and nurturant behavior and greater preoccupation with people and harmonious interpersonal relationships among girls than among boys (Whitehouse, 1949; Winker, 1949; Honzik, 1951; Lansky, Crandall, Kagan, & Baker, 1961).

Not surprisingly, children view women as more nurturant than men, and adult women see themselves as more nurturant than their male counterparts (Bennett & Cohen, 1959).

Other sex-typed behaviors. Additional sets of sex-typed responses include the boy's display of interest and skill in gross motor and mechanical tasks and the girl's display of interest in clothes, dolls, and babies (Tyler, 1947; Honzik, 1951; Kagan & Moss, 1962). During the adolescent and early adult years some refined derivatives of the sex-typed patterns established in childhood are added to the sex role standard. Female behavior reflects submissiveness with males, inhibition of overt signs of sexual desire, and cultivation of domestic skills (Douvan & Kaye, 1957; Harris, 1959). Male behavior is marked by independence and interpersonal dominance with both men and women, initiation of sexual behavior, sexual conquests, competence at some skill, and acquisition of money and power (Douvan & Kaye, 1957; Walters, Pearce, & Dahms, 1957; Bennett & Cohen, 1959; Harris, 1959).

Game preferences as an index of sex-typed behavior. The games, toys, and fantasy heroes chosen by young children corroborate the behavioral sex role standards outlined above. The large body of research on children's game and toy preferences indicates that boys choose objects related to sports, machines, aggression, speed, and power; girls select objects associated with the kitchen, the home, babies, personal attractiveness, and fantasy roles in which they have a subordinate relationship to a male (such as a nurse or secretary). Thus, knives, planes, trucks, and cement mixers are regarded by school children as masculine; dolls, cribs, dishes, and nurses' equipment are regarded as feminine (Foster, 1930; Vance & McCall, 1934; Honzik, 1951; Rosenberg & Sutton-Smith, 1960).

Investigations in which the child is asked about his preferences directly or indirectly indicate that as early as 3 years of age boys show preference for masculine games and that this preference increases with age. Among girls, however, preferences may vary until they are 10 years of age. Many girls between 3 and 10 show a strong preference for masculine games, activities, and objects, whereas it is unusual to find many boys who prefer feminine activities during this age period. Many girls between 5 and 10 years of age state a desire to be a boy or to be a daddy rather than a mommy when they grow up (Brown, 1957).

Rosenberg and Sutton-Smith (1960) tested children in grades 4, 5, and 6 for game preferences. The results suggest that in 1960 girls were more masculine in their game choices than they were in 1930. The wall separating male and female recreational activities is cracking, and some of the traditional differences in sex-typed game choices are undergoing change. It is not really surprising, however, that girls should show preference for some masculine attitudes. Our culture assigns greater freedom, power, and value to the male role; it is understandable that a girl might wish for this more attractive role. The devaluation of the female role is probably one reason that the typical woman regards herself as less adequate and more fearful than most men (Bennett & Cohen, 1959).

Finally, it should be noted that there are social class differences in the sex-typed game preferences of children. Rabban (1950) asked children aged 3 to 8 from two diverse social groups to select the toys they liked best. The choices of lower-class boys and girls conformed more closely to traditional sex-typed standards than did the choices of middle-class children, suggesting that the differentiation of sex roles is sharper in lower-class families. This finding agrees with the fact that lower-class mothers encourage sex typing more consistently than do middle-class mothers (Kohn, 1959).

The difference in sex typing between the classes is greatest for girls (Rabban, 1950). Apparently the middle-class girl, unlike the middle-class boy, is much freer to express an interest in toys and activities of the opposite sex. Among girls, the higher the educational level of their families, the greater is the involvement in masculine activities (Kagan & Moss, 1962).

Covert Attributes　　　The covert sex-typed attributes consist of feelings, attitudes, motives, and wishes that are appropriate to the respective sexes. The feminine attributes include the ability to elicit sexual arousal in a male and to gratify a love object, the desire to be a wife and mother, the correlated desires to give nurturance to one's children and affection to a love object, and the capacity for emotion. For males, the primary covert attributes include a pragmatic attitude, sexual prowess and the ability to gratify a love object, suppression of fear, and a capacity to control expression of strong emotion in time of stress (Parsons, 1948; Jenkins & Russell, 1958; Bennett & Cohen, 1959). Although the data in support of these covert attributes are less systematic than they are for the overt behaviors listed above, clinical studies (Bieber, Dain, Dince, Drellich, Grand, Gundlach, Kremer, Rifkin, Wilbur, & Bieber, 1962) and self-ratings by adults (Bennett & Cohen, 1959) generally support these contentions.

In sum, females are supposed to inhibit aggression and open display of sexual urges, be passive with men, be nurturant to others, cultivate attractiveness, and maintain an emotional, socially poised, and friendly posture with others. Males are urged to be aggressive in the face of attack, independent in problem situations, sexually aggressive, instrumentally competent, in control of regressive urges, and suppressive of strong emotion, especially anxiety. Parsons' (1955) dichotomy of masculine and feminine roles into instrumental versus expressive is consistent with the attributes assigned above to those roles. Instrumental roles require skills at solving environmental problems; expressive roles require skills in dealing with people.

This list of masculine and feminine attributes may strike readers as unrealistically traditional and not representative of contemporary values. However, existing data indicate that despite a common adult assumption that sex role standards are changing at a rapid rate, children continue to believe that aggression, dominance, and independence are more appropriate for males and that passivity, nurturance, and the ability to get along with others are more appropriate for females (Parsons, 1948; Hartley, 1960).

HOW SEX ROLE BEHAVIOR
IS ESTABLISHED AND MAINTAINED

The learning of sex role standards for behavior is mediated by desires to identify with the same-sex model, to gain acceptance from parents and peers, and to avoid rejection. Parents punish aggression and open sexuality more consistently in daughters than in sons; they punish passivity, dependence, and open display of fear more consistently in sons than in daughters (Aberle & Naegele, 1952; Sears, Maccoby, & Levin, 1957; Kohn, 1959). Moreover, children are aware that their parents want them to adopt sex role attributes (Fauls & Smith, 1956). Thus, parental reward of sex-appropriate behavior and punishment of inappropriate responses facilitate the adoption of sex-typed traits. Furthermore, the typical child's desire for the acceptance of parents and peers predisposes him to shun sex-inappropriate activities and choose responses that are congruent with sex role standards.

It is conceivable, of course, that a child might have a parent of the same sex who displayed sex-appropriate behavior but a parent of the opposite sex who did not reward—and perhaps punished—sex role attributes. This child should be ambivalent about the display of sex-typed traits. Thus, in order to predict with maximal accuracy the occurrence of sex role behavior one must assess (1) the degree of identification with the parent of the same sex, (2) the degree of sex-typed behavior displayed by each parent, and (3) each parent's pattern of rewards.

It is interesting to note that most of the girl's overt sex-typed responses require reactions from other people. It is almost impossible for a girl to assess whether she is attractive, socially poised, or passive with others without continued interaction and feedback from the social environment. The girl is forced to be dependent on people and to court their acceptance in order to obtain those experiences that help to establish her sex-typed behaviors. In addition, the critical significance of adult and peer acceptance for girls probably contributes to the greater degree of conformity and concern with socially desirable behaviors typically found among females (Crutchfield, 1955; Hovland & Janis, 1959).

The boy, on the other hand, develops many important sex-typed behaviors on his own. Quite a few sex-typed skills involve solitary mastery; for these the boy does not require the reactions of others in order to assess whether he has reached an adequate level of mastery. Perfection of gross motor or mechanical skills are examples of such mastery. Consider the 10-year-old boy shooting baskets in his backyard or fixing his bicycle. The boy receives confirmation from these solitary endeavors that he is acquiring masculine attributes. Moreover, independence of the attitudes and opinions of others—which implies relative independence of the wishes of others—is in itself a sex-typed trait. The typical boy, therefore, suppresses anxiety over social rejection because this concern is not regarded as masculine in this culture.

Sex Role Identity

A sex role standard has been defined as a belief shared by the members of the culture regarding the characteristics that are appropriate for males and females. But the abstracted concept of the ideal male or female as viewed by the culture is to be distinguished from a particular individual's conceptualization of his own degree of masculinity or femininity. The degree to which an individual regards himself as being masculine or feminine determines his sex role identity. Although this identity is but one component of a complex, interlocking set of beliefs that make up his complete self-concept or self-identity, it is mandatory that the individual assign himself a value on the dimension of masculinity versus femininity. Although a person can be indifferent to some specialized attributes that might make up a self-identity (for example, a knowledge of photography or an ability to prune trees), he cannot be indifferent to his sex role identity.

How can a person determine how masculine or feminine he is? The degree of match or mismatch between the culture's sex role standards and the individual's assessment of his own overt and covert attributes provides him with a partial answer to this question. It is a partial answer because the belief system that is labeled sex role identity is not completely conscious. There is an imperfect correlation between possession of accepted sex role attributes and the integrity of one's sex role identity. A man who possesses many masculine traits might not necessarily regard himself as highly masculine. But it is unlikely for a man who possesses none of the culturally approved sex-typed attributes to regard himself as highly masculine. Possession of some sex-typed traits is necessary, but not necessarily sufficient, for a firm sex role identity.

Unfortunately, there is little empirical information that deals with how a child establishes his sex role identity. Since only broad inferences are possible, the discussion that follows should be regarded as conjectural.

THE ESTABLISHMENT OF A SEX ROLE IDENTITY

At least three kinds of experiences determine the degree to which the child regards himself as being masculine or feminine: (1) differential identification with mother, father, parental surrogates, older siblings, and special peers, (2) acquisition of sex-typed attributes or skills, and (3) social interaction that reveals how other people regard the individual's sex role behavior.

Identification   Part of the process of establishing a sex role identity is voluntary, for a boy can decide if he wants to develop athletic skills or write poetry and a girl can decide whether she wants to try to be popular with boys. However, the development of a sex role identity is not completely in the child's hands. Failure to develop an identification with the parent of the same sex who possesses the appropriate sex-typed attributes or the development of an identification with a parent who does not possess these attributes can impair a sex role identity. It is necessary to assess the strength of the child's identification with the parent of the same sex as well as the parents' actual sex-typed behaviors in order to predict the strength of the child's sex role identity.

A strong identification with the parent of the same sex in the early school years can facilitate the establishment of an appropriate sex role identity. For instance, the girl who strongly identifies with a nurturant and competent mother begins to adopt the mother's attributes. Each time she successfully imitates a behavior or adopts an attitude of the mother she perceives an increased similarity to her. The perception of increased similarity strengthens the child's belief that she possesses some of the mother's femininity or characteristics symbolic of femininity.

What of the children who have minimal identifications with the parent of the same sex? If these children adopt the sex role behavior displayed by peers, siblings, or relatives, they will possess some basis for an appropriate sex role identity. But it is possible that a weak identification with the parent may prevent the child from developing the confidence to master many sex-appropriate skills.

The appropriateness of the sex-typed behavior of the parent is an important factor in establishing a sex role identity through identification. Does the parent display behavior that is congruent with sex role standards? Does the father, for instance, have masculine interests, or is he passive, non-aggressive, withdrawn, and uninterested in athletics, machines, boats, or planes? The boy with a nurturant and competent father who does not display masculine sex-typed behaviors will confront the societal standard for masculinity when he enters school. Since his overt behavior is likely to be less sex-typed than that of his peers, he will soon perceive a discrepancy between his attributes and those of the other boys. He will be tempted to conclude that he is less masculine than his peers because his behavior does not match that of the group and because he may be the target of remarks implying he is a "sissy." These experiences are likely to weaken his sex role identity.

The girl who identifies with a mother who does not manifest traditional feminine attributes is not likely to have adopted such sex role characteristics as passivity and submissiveness with boys, inhibition of aggression, the cultivation of personal attractiveness, and an interest in domestic and nurturant activities. She too may begin to question her femininity when she confronts the values of the peer group, and her sex role identity will also be weakened to some degree. Thus, the child's sex role identity is based not only on identification with a masculine father or feminine mother but also on the child's perception of similarity between his attributes and the societal sex role standard as displayed by his peers.

Acquisition
of Sex-Typed Attributes

Sex role identity may be strengthened as a result of the acquisition of desirable sex-typed attributes. The boy who learns to be dominant with peers, sexually aggressive with girls, or competent on the athletic field often begins to regard himself as being masculine. The girl who becomes popular with boys, socially poised with adults, or capable of giving nurturance may conceive of herself as more feminine.

It has been suggested that the strength of a sex role identity is at least partly a function of the discrepancy between the inventory of actual sex-typed attributes and the ideal attributes prescribed by the culture. It is assumed that the acquisition of appropriate attributes acts to reduce this discrepancy and leads to corresponding modifications in the self-label. The opposite effect is also possible. Loss of attributes that are essential to the self-label "I am masculine/feminine" can widen the gap between actual and ideal attributes and make a sex role identity more vulnerable. For instance, loss of athletic prowess or being forced into a passive role can make an adolescent male feel less "masculine."

Social Interaction Sex role identity may also be established through social interaction. By this process other people's opinions of an individual's sex-typed attributes may cause him to alter his self-labels. If men and women react toward a young man as though he were dominant and strong, any discrepancy between that young man's idealized model and his existing self-concept will become smaller. If a girl continually hears compliments on her attractiveness, she may gradually alter her conception of herself to agree with her sex role standards. However, since the identification with each parent is presumed to form a basic foundation for a sex role identity, there is no guarantee that such social experiences will lead to marked changes in the self-labels that characterize the sex role identity.

THE SIGNIFICANCE
OF THE CHILD'S SEX ROLE IDENTITY

The child's continuing desire for a stable and firm sex role identity is central to his development, for this desire imposes strong constraints on future behavioral choices. The sex role identity has special significance for two psychological developments that occur in the preschool and early school years: (1) stability of behavior over time, and (2) differential mastery of academic skills.

The Effect on Stability
of Behavior The stability of human behavior touches an issue of both practical and theoretical significance. Knowledge of that period of development during which an intimation of future behavior can be obtained is important for teachers, psychiatrists, and psychologists as well as for other practitioners who wish to initiate preventive or early treatment procedures, whether the situation requiring attention is delinquency, excessive fears, or academic problems. It is generally acknowledged that asocial behavior, sexual deviations, and academic retardation in a 14-year-old are often resistant to conventional psychiatric treatment. Knowledge of the period during which these behaviors are being established would justify initiation of procedures at that time in-

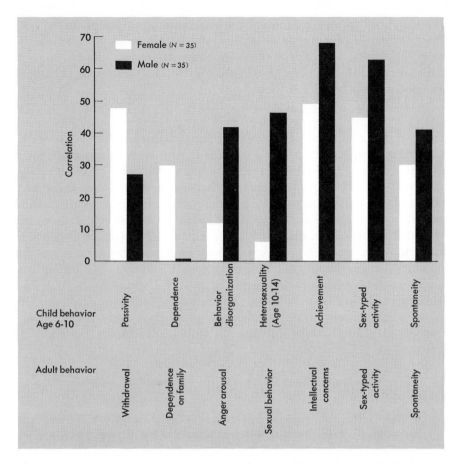

Figure 27-1   Summary of correlations between selected child be-haviors and similar adult behaviors. (Adapted from Kagan & Moss, 1962)

tended to prevent the early forms of personality disorder from becoming firmly entrenched. This knowledge would also be theoretically useful in pinpointing the developmental period during which investigations into the learning of deviant responses would be most profitable.

A study of the long-term stability of behavior from birth to adulthood in a group of middle-class subjects from the Fels Research Institute's longitudinal population suggested some important conclusions regarding the relation of sex role identity to behavioral stability (Kagan & Moss, 1962). Briefly, the procedure involved study of the relation between two independent sets of data on the same individuals: (1) ratings of adult behavior based on interviews when the subjects were between 20 and 30 years of age and (2) independent ratings of their behavior during the four developmental periods from birth to age 3, from 3 to 6, from 6 to 10, and from 10 to 14.

The childhood ratings were based on behavioral observations in the home, nursery school, day camp, public school, and interviews at the Institute. The major behavioral variables studied included aggression, dependency, passivity, intellectual achievement, anxiety over social interaction, heterosexual behavior, and sex-typed activities.

There was a strong association between the occurrence of a certain class of behaviors during age 6 to 10 and the occurrence of a similar behavior during young adulthood. The strongest correlations held for behaviors that matched sex role standards (see Figure 27-1). If a sex role standard required inhibition of a behavior, the continuity from childhood (age 6 to 10) to adulthood was minimal. To illustrate: According to what we know of sex role standards, childhood passivity and dependence in stress situations should correlate with passivity and dependence for adult women but not for men. Since these traits violate masculine sex role standards, a passive or dependent boy would experience considerable pressure both from his parents and from the outside environment to inhibit overt passive behavior. For instance, one subject in this investigation showed a marked shift from dependence to independence during late childhood. His father placed unusually high value on autonomy of action and as the boy approached early adolescence, he experienced strong family pressure to inhibit dependent behavior. The change in his behavior can be traced in his case history.

At 2½ years of age the subject (S) was described as unusually passive and cautious:

> S spent an unhappy week at nursery school. He cried a great deal and looked ready to cry even when he was not actually doing it. He drew away when other children approached him and he seemed afraid of them. Usually he stood around and looked lost.

At 4½ years of age, passivity was still a characteristic response for the boy:

> This was one of the group's most isolated members. He was non-competitive, unassertive, and sedentary. He shrank from actual physical contact with others, and his relationship with peers was a long distance verbal one. When he was verbally rebuffed he smiled weakly and put his hands behind his back. S was the most eclipsed member of the group because of his apprehension, shyness, and inhibition.

By age 8, some shift toward independent behavior had occurred. There was a forced independence and swagger, and S had learned to use his intellectual skills as a weapon of power over others. He lectured and bragged to his peers; the fear that was manifest at age 4 was more disguised. He became less dependent on his family and more committed to hard work in school.

As a late adolescent the conflict over being passive had swelled in intensity, and his standards did not permit retreat from potential failure situations. At age 16, for example, he realized that he was still afraid of dating girls and decided that there was only one effective way to conquer this fear. He invited to a dance the most popular girl in the school, even though he had never been out with her before. He admitted that the primary reason for inviting her was to test his ability to conquer his fears. When he was asked if he ever went to his parents for advice, he replied, "My father was not approachable and I didn't gc to him for advice. In fact, he used to tell me to solve my own problems by myself and I felt uneasy about going to him for help. My mother wouldn't know what to tell me anyway."

The expression of aggression and the initiation of sexual behavior, unlike passivity and dependency, are acceptable responses for males but not for females. The data from the longitudinal population revealed that aggression toward adults and heterosexual behavior during childhood was related to frequency of anger arousal and sexual behavior in adulthood for men but not for women.

An intense concern with good grades in school and mastery of intellectual skills is appropriate and encouraged for both sexes among the middle class; sex role standards do not dictate strong inhibition of intellectual mastery for either sex. As a result, concern with intellectual skills should be relatively stable for both sexes. The results of the study affirm this expectation, with the degree of continuity slightly higher for males than for females.

Finally, the child's tendency to practice sex-typed behaviors is highly stable from early childhood to adulthood. The correlations between practice of sex appropriate activities during the period from 6 to 10 and adulthood were .63 for men and .44 for women. This finding is supported by data from the Oakland Growth Study (Mussen, 1961, 1962), which revealed a moderately high relation between degree of masculine interests in males in adolescence and adulthood.

In sum, childhood behaviors that are congruent with sex role standards are likely to remain strong and display continuity from childhood through adulthood. Behavior that deviates markedly from sex role standards will be inhibited as a result of the child's desire to avoid social rejection and to model himself after culturally approved role models.

The Effect on Intellectual Mastery

Although competence in intellectual and academic tasks is not as clearly a consequence of sex role identity as is the expression of aggression or dependency, it appears that the degree of involvement in challenging intellectual problems is greater for adolescent and adult males than for females. Particularly well documented is the fact that mastery of problems requiring analysis and reasoning (primarily those involving spatial and mechanical reasoning, science, and mathematics) is viewed as more appropriate for boys than for girls. When adolescent or adult subjects were presented with problems involving primarily mathematical or geometric reasoning, males consistently obtained higher scores than females. Moreover, there was a low positive relation between interest in culturally approved masculine activities (athletics and mechanics) and the quality of problem-solving scores for both sexes.

The female who rejected traditional feminine interests performed better on mathematical and geometric problems than did the girl who had adopted traditional feminine behaviors. On problems dealing with feminine interests, such as cooking and gardening materials, the females scored better than on problems dealing with guns, money, and geometric designs, even though the logical steps and computations were identical. It seems that the typical female believes that the ability to solve problems involving geometry, physics, logic, or arithmetic is a uniquely masculine skill, and her motivation to attack such problems is low. This decreased involvement may reflect the fact that the girl's self-esteem is not at stake in such problems. Or she may feel threatened by the possibility that she might perform with unusual competence on such tasks, for excellence on such tasks might be equated with a lack of femininity.

Boys are more likely than girls to adopt an analytic approach to natural events in the environment and to formal problems. Smith (1933), for example, reported that preschool boys spontaneously asked many more "how" and "why" questions; girls preferentially asked questions about social rules and the conventional labels to be applied to objects. Milton (1958) gave problems to men and women and asked them to state whether their preference would be to analyze the situation, go for help, or adopt a trial-and-error approach in the solution of this problem. Males were much more likely to select the analytic approach. The masculine preference for analysis is also present in the male's tendency to break down visual stimuli; 8- and 9-year-old boys are more likely than girls to analyze a complex design into its component parts.

Other sex differences in the problem-solving approach relate to the qualities of autonomy and persistence. McDavid (1959) had children 3 to 9 years of age observe an adult perform a task. When the children were later asked to perform the same task, the girls were more likely to imitate the adult than the boys. Crandall and Rabson (1960) gave children two puzzles, one of which they solved and the other of which they failed. When the children were asked subsequently which one they wished to take up again, more boys than girls chose the puzzle they failed.

The sex-typed character of domains of knowledge is most evident in the vocational choices of young adolescents. A recent national survey of thousands of high school students conducted by Project Talent (Flanagan, unpublished) asked students about their planned majors in college and future occupational choices. The sex-typed character of their choices was already evident in the ninth grade. For example, 25 percent of the boys and only 3 percent of the girls selected the physical or natural sciences or engineering, whereas 3 percent of the boys and 13 percent of the girls chose elementary or secondary school teaching as future vocations (Flanagan, unpublished).

Another reason for a girl's lower motivation and poorer performance in science and mathematics—in addition to her belief that females are not supposed to be competent in these areas and her reluctance to analyze problems—is the fact that a girl's sex role identity is more dependent on her ability to attract and maintain a love relationship than on her academic skills. For many males, however, academic excellence is considered necessary for vocational success, an essential component of the male's sex role identity. The adolescent male would be expected to be more highly motivated to master those tasks linked to his vocational aspirations. It is also possible that the girl more often works to obtain the acceptance and approval of her teachers and parents, whereas the boy is more likely to view mastery as a test of his personal adequacy.

Although an intense involvement in academic mastery is more characteristic of the adolescent and adult male than his female counterpart, this is not the case in the primary grades. From kindergarten through grade 4 the girl typically outperforms the boy in all areas, and the ratio of boys to girls with reading problems ranges from 3 to 1 to 6 to 1 (Tyler, 1947; Bentzen, 1963). Why is there a developmental shift between the ages of 6 and 17? One reason has been mentioned above: among late adolescent boys academic proficiency becomes linked to vocational success, and their motivation is stronger than it was during the early years of school. Moreover, the girl's motivation toward mastery decreases with age as a result of anxiety over feeling intellectually more competent than the boy. She also may experience conflict over excessive intellectual competitiveness. It is not uncommon for an adolescent to view competitive intellectual striving as an aggressive behavior. Since the typical female acquires stronger anxiety over aggressive and competitive behavior than the male, she experiences greater conflict over intellectual competition (Buss, 1961; Kagan & Moss, 1962). This conflict can lead to inhibition of intense strivings for academic excellence.

Another reason boys gradually increase in academic superiority is that their perception of the sex-typed character of school and academic work changes. The average American boy perceives the primary school atmosphere as excessively feminine: His introduction into school is conducted by female teachers, who usually initiate the activities of painting, coloring, and singing. Moreover, most teachers place a premium on obedience, decorum, and inhibition of aggressive and restless behavior—values that are clearly more appropriate for girls than for boys.

Recent studies with second graders confirm the suggestion that the school situation is viewed as more feminine than masculine. The children were taught different nonsense syllables to stand for maleness and femaleness. They were then shown pictures of school-related objects, such as a blackboard, a page of arithmetic, a book, a school desk, and a library, as well as nonacademic stimuli, such as a lion, a bird, and a cup, and were asked to label them with one of the "masculine" or "feminine" nonsense syllables (see Table 27-1). The results indicated that the second graders were more likely to label the school objects feminine than masculine (Kagan, 1964). This tendency diminished with age, especially for boys. The labeling

Table 27-1   Percentage of Second Graders Labeling Objects Masculine or Feminine

Stimulus	Boys		Girls	
	M	F	M	F
Pencil	79%	15%	61%	36%
Tree	8	4	8	1
Blackboard	29	69	18	78
Lion	26	5	29	1
Library	50	42	38	59
Rabbit	11	9	7	5
Painting	43	16	41	33
Boat	85	2	86	3
Book	38	52	24	75
Bird	10	12	7	7
Arithmetic page	36	60	26	72
Apple	18	12	17	25
School building	42	49	43	51
Alligator	25	4	22	1
Desk	40	51	34	61
Cup	32	57	30	62
Map	68	16	75	13
Carrot	7	3	8	11
Boy and girl at desk	37	56	21	77

Adapted from Kagan, 1964.

of the nonacademic objects was as expected—that is, the children called a cup feminine and a lion masculine.

Since the typical 7-year-old American boy perceives the school atmosphere as "feminine," he is likely to resist complete involvement in its activities and should be expected to fall behind in academic areas. As indicated earlier, more boys than girls in American schools are classified as seriously retarded in reading ability. However, if this argument has merit, then in a community with a large proportion of male teachers there should not be a larger proportion of boys than girls with serious reading problems. The island of Hokkaido in northern Japan is such a community. In grades 1 and 2 close to 60 percent of teachers are men and 40 percent are women. The occurrence of reading difficulties is not more frequent among boys than girls. In fact, the percentages are equal—about 9 percent of each sex are considered to have problems with reading.*

Thus, it seems that during the opening years of school, the boy's motivation to master academic skills is partly dependent on his view of its appropriateness for his sex role identity. However, during the adolescent years a more sophisticated differentiation of academic work occurs. This differentiation turns on the schism between the sciences and the humanities. The

* These data were supplied by Dr. Kuzuo Miyake.

adolescent begins to classify knowledge on three related dimensions: Is it practical or impractical? Does it have an important effect upon the world, or is it unrelated to instrumental changes in the environment? Does it deal with machines or words? Since a pragmatic, instrumental, and mechanical orientation to nature is important in the sex role standard for males (Parsons, 1948), some adolescent boys are highly motivated to master the sciences but poorly motivated to master "impractical" subjects that involve only words and ideas, such as language or history. Similarly, the girl who has chosen a masculine career, such as law, medicine, or science, may experience anxiety over exerting effort in an activity that is not traditionally feminine. There is an implicit association between subject matter and sex role standards.

It appears that for most adult members of Western culture there are strong semantic associations between the words "masculinity" or "femininity" and specific areas of knowledge. This is an unfortunate connection, for one would hope that knowledge would retain neutrality amid the warring factions of the mind. There is, however, cause for some optimism. American elementary and secondary schools—long the exclusive domain of female faculty—now contain a larger proportion of male teachers, especially in the high schools. The Massachusetts Institute of Technology, among other institutions, has decided recently to emphasize the humanities in its program for engineers and physical scientists, and women are beginning to win Nobel Prizes in science and medicine and to attain executive positions in business. It may be possible to change dramatically the associational link between specific domains of knowledge and the sex roles through appropriate modifications in the procedures and atmosphere of the elementary and secondary schools.

The meaning of sex role identity is not without its ambiguity, and one could argue for its fragmentation into several better-articulated terms. Its retention as a descriptive and explanatory concept rests on the assumption that the concepts of male and female and the dimensions of maleness and femaleness are basic to our language and culture.

The 3-year-old has already dichotomized the world into male and female people, and he is concerned with sex differences. By the time he is 7, he is committed to molding his behavior in accordance with cultural standards appropriate to his sex; he shows uneasiness, anxiety, and even anger when he is in danger of behaving in ways regarded as characteristic of the opposite sex. The appellation of "sissy" to a boy or "tomboy" to a girl usually has a strong negative affective charge.

It has been pointed out in this chapter that the desire to behave in accordance with sex role standards extends far beyond an interest in sports for boys and cooking for girls. The desire to establish a sex role identity touches many important behavioral areas, including schoolwork, sexual behavior, and vocational choice, and has a strong effect on behavioral continuities in development.

Not always actions show the man: we find
Who does a kindness is not therefore kind.

ALEXANDER POPE. Moral Essays

CHAPTER 28
MAJOR MOTIVE-BEHAVIORAL SYSTEMS IN THE YOUNG CHILD

B etty is often very angry at her mother but rarely raises her voice and never strikes her. Paul, on the other hand, slams doors with vigor almost every time his mother criticizes him. Bill feels strong jealousy toward his brother but is always friendly with him; John likes his younger brother but occasionally slaps his arm or teases him when he is around. These examples indicate that there is no simple or direct relation between the strength of a child's hostile motivation and the frequency or quality of his aggressive behavior toward the disliked person.

This imperfect relation between motive strength and the occurrence of motive-related actions holds for most motives, including hostility, dependence, dominance, sexuality, and mastery. The presence of a motive is no guarantee that the child will display a relevant behavior directed at gratifying the motive. Moreover, the occurrence of a response (such as teasing a brother) that looks like it is an attempt to gratify a particular motive (such as aggression) may actually be the product of a motive other than the one that seems so obvious. Teasing may be an attempt to obtain the brother's attention, rather than an attempt to annoy or anger him. Neither presence nor absence of a particular behavior is a faithful index of the strength of the motive.

The Nature of a Motive

The concept of a motive must be kept distinct from the concept of a biological drive. A drive is a state of deprivation or discomfort caused by a disturbance in the basic physiology of the organism. Hunger, thirst, cold, and pain are the classic biological drives. Each drive leads to the activation of particular central nervous system structures and sensory receptors and often, but not always, produces internal sensations that are felt as unpleasant. Although these drives play a significant role in development, this chapter is primarily concerned with motives.

In simplest form, a motive is a wish. It is a set of images or thoughts that represents events or things the individual desires to experience or to possess. Motives, then, are cognitive processes and have no necessary relation to overt behavior. One may have wished for many years to go to Tahiti but may have taken no steps toward attaining that goal. Moreover, motives are learned as a result of experience and are not part of the infant's inborn equipment, as are drives.

POTENTIAL AND ACTIVE MOTIVES

Motives have two states—potential and active—much as energy has a potential and a kinetic state. Most of the time a child is not experiencing a set of images or thoughts related to a desired goal. At these times the motive is regarded as being in a potential state. Motives are transformed from a potential to an active state when an event—either in the external environment or in internal thought or feeling—arouses the motive. This arousing event is called an *incentive*. Thus, the sight of a well-tanned young lady in Boston in late January may activate the wish to take a winter holiday.

Individuals differ dramatically in the ease with which an incentive provokes a motive. Some children are easily provoked to wishes to have their mother hug them; others rarely have such thoughts. Some children respond to the slightest frustration with hostile thoughts; others require excessive frustration before they experience hostile wishes. In general, the easier it is for an incentive to elicit or activate a motive, the stronger is the motive. A child whose wishes for his mother are activated whenever he is alone for more than an hour has a stronger motive for his mother's presence than the child who does not wish for his mother until she is gone for more than a day.

CHANGES IN MOTIVE STRENGTH

The strength of a motive can change with experience: some motives get weaker, others stronger. As the child grows, his desire for his mother's presence becomes weaker and his desire to dominate his peers becomes stronger. Psychologists do not understand all the conditions that control the waxing and waning of motive strength. One hypothesis is that motives grow in strength to the degree that frequent preoccupation with a set of goals (the motive in an active state) is not accompanied by gratification of the motive. The motive is then aroused but is not satisfied. If a person rarely experiences the motive in an active state, it is likely that it will not grow in strength. The truth of this statement is recognized implicitly by those who are in love with someone but cannot gratify this motive. The standard cure is for the person to arrange that he will not encounter the loved one who activates the motive—"out of sight, out of mind."

On the other hand, if the motive is gratified every time it is activated, it probably will not increase in intensity. A motive is most likely to grow when the person becomes aware of a goal he cannot attain. Frustration of a desired goal leads to an increase in the intensity of the motive. This view of motive intensity is illustrated in the context of the contemporary civil rights movement. Society is creating an active motive for power and dominance among Negroes and other disadvantaged minorities by increasing active preoccupation with these goals. The motive grows stronger each day because the wishes are thought about more frequently but are not gratified.

The Relation
Between Motives and Behavior

Since motives are cognitive in nature, there is no necessary link between a motive and an overt action. A child may have a desperately strong wish to care for his younger sister and yet display no overt attempt to gratify that wish. A 10-year-old may have a strong desire for a close friend but fail to show any behavior that would bring him into a closer relationship with another. What determines whether the motive will produce goal-related actions?

First, the child must have learned responses that effectively gratify the motive. If a 6-year-old who has a strong desire to control his older brother has not learned how to effect this control, there will probably not be much evidence of this motive in his everyday behavior. The child acquires these goal-gratifying actions through direct reward and punishment, through exposure to models who display the actions, and through books, radio, and television, which describe effective ways to gratify motives. The 3-year-old learns that resisting his mother's requests upsets her, and this experience leads him to use this behavioral tactic more regularly every time he feels hostile toward her. Whenever the mother indicates how upsetting her child's stubborn resistance is, she unwittingly rewards his resistant behavior and increases the likelihood that he will continue to behave this way. The child also learns ways of gratifying motives by watching the successful goal-related behavior of others. For instance, he may see a boy successfully dominate another by pushing and verbal threats. When the child is motivated to dominate his peers, he may imitate that response because the result he witnessed matched the goal that he is striving to attain.

A second factor governing the probability of a motive leading to a related behavior is the child's expectancy that the action will be successful in obtaining the desired goal. A 5-year-old who has been in three foster homes, none of which responded to his requests for affection and help, is likely to stop displaying such requests and become sullen and withdrawn. His desire for adult affection may still be present, but his behavior does not reveal it. The lower the child's expectancy of gratifying a motive, the less likely will he be to direct his behavior toward attainment of a goal.

Anxiety over displaying the goal-related behavior is a third factor that controls the link between motive and action. A motive in a 2-year-old is likely to lead immediately to behavior aimed at direct gratification, because children of that age have not yet learned to delay or inhibit gratification of most of their strong motives. The 5-year-old, by contrast, has learned that he must delay gratification of many of his desires and must inhibit certain actions because of guilt or anxiety over parental rejection. The stronger the child's anxiety over commission of a goal-related act, the less likely will he be to display that act when he experiences the motive in an active state.

A final determinant of the probability of goal-directed behavior is the immediate situation or context in which the child becomes aroused. The child who feels strong hostility toward his mother is not likely to behave in a way that will gratify the motive if he is sitting in a classroom, although he would be likely to behave that way if he were home.

In sum, acquisition of acts that gratify motives, expectancy of goal attainment, anxiety over display of goal-directed responses, and the immediate context all influence the probability that the child will actively attempt to gratify a strong motive.

The rest of this chapter considers some of the relations between four classes of motives and their goal-related behaviors: sexuality, aggression, dependency, and mastery. The emphasis will tend to be on the behaviors, because as a child grows older it becomes increasingly difficult to infer motive from behavior. Moreover, the available research has focused on the child's behavior rather than his motives. Finally, as far as parents, peers, and teachers are concerned, the young child's behavior is of prime consideration. The social environment reacts to and classifies the child primarily on the basis of his actions rather than his motives, and it is through his behavior that other people initially come to know the child. Indeed, society generally cares more about whether a child hits other children than about his hostile thoughts; it cares more about whether a child is able to inhibit crying when he is afraid than about his wishes for help and comfort; it cares more about his overt sexual modesty with peers than the quality of his sexual fantasies.

Anger, Hostility,
and Aggressive Behavior

ANGER

There are certain classes of incentive stimuli that have a common effect on the person: They thwart, block, or threaten his attempts to act out preferred behaviors or work toward attainment of goals. In the most general sense, these incentive conditions frustrate the person, but the word "frustration" should be understood to include not only the blocking of goal-directed activity or the interruption of a frequently practiced chain of behaviors, but also the potentiality of thwarting preferred actions in the future. The central characteristic of these events is that desired action sequences are not allowed their normal expression, and the person must alter his behavior. In such situations a child or adult normally becomes affectively aroused; this affect is labeled *anger*.

A second set of incentive stimuli are slightly different in quality but have a similar effect. These events threaten the beliefs or values of the person; they imply that his standards are incorrect, invalid, or, more seriously, morally reprehensible. Name calling is a classic example of this type of incentive. The state of emotional arousal experienced in this context is also labeled *anger*.

Anger, then, is the affective state that is characterized by a specific visceral arousal in a context in which (1) goal-directed or preferred action sequences are thwarted or potentially thwarted or (2) the standards of the person are threatened by another person or group. (See Part I, Chapter 9.)

HOSTILITY

The affect of anger should be differentiated from the motive of hostility. Hostility is a wish for a specific class of goals: to cause pain, distress, or anxiety to another person or a surrogate of that person. The person to whom the hostility is directed is the one who is believed to be the thwarting agent or the one who threatens the valued standards.

Although the affect of anger and the motive of hostility often occur together, each can take place separately. The 5-year-old who cannot open the screen door to enter the house becomes angry and may stamp his feet on the porch, but he may not have any hostile wishes toward anyone at that moment. The 10-year-old girl who is chronically teased by her brother may consider how she would like to throw him off the roof of the house, but she may have these hostile thoughts without being emotionally aroused. One need not experience the affect of anger while entertaining hostile wishes.

DETERMINANTS OF ANGER AND HOSTILITY

Psychology does not possess sensitive procedures for determining when the child is angry or when he is having hostile thoughts. Thus, most of what is written is conjecture and must be studied cautiously. The actual situations that are likely to arouse the affect of anger change rather dramatically as the child grows. During the first 2 years of life, the response disruptions most likely to arouse anger are restrictions of the child's natural tendency to explore his environment. The parents' propensity to force the child to sleep, to stay within fenced areas, and to keep away from attractive but fragile objects often elicits an increase in emotional arousal and motor protestation—signs of the affect of anger.

During the preschool years, when the child is given more mobility and freedom to explore his environment, deprivation or postponement of specific goals are chiefly responsible for eliciting anger. The parents forbid candy, playing in the dirt, watching television through the dinner hour, or playing too roughly with the baby. These disruptions of goal-directed behavior often anger the child. During the school years, even more freedom is granted to the child, but standards regarding instrumental competence, sex role identification, passivity, autonomy, and acceptance by others are well articulated. Events that violate or threaten these standards elicit anger and hostile thoughts toward the person who is viewed as the source of the violation or threat. These values can be threatened by someone who implies that the child has an undesirable set of characteristics or by a person who is salient and holds a set of values different from the one held by the child.

The 10-year-old who believes that good grades require prolonged study is angered by and hostile toward the child who obtains an A but rarely studies. The presence of this peer is a threat to the child's standard. The 9-year-old who wants to believe that she is her father's favorite is threatened when she perceives her 11-year-old brother receiving more attention. The brother's presence threatens the validity of the girl's belief and engenders anger.

In sum, restriction of ongoing behaviors, deprivation or postponement of desired goals, and threats to dearly held values are the major instigators of anger and hostility. Whether these covert forces lead to aggressive behavior and what form the behavior will take depend on certain factors that will be taken up in the following section.

AGGRESSIVE BEHAVIOR

The definition of an aggressive action is the subject of considerable controversy. It is reasonable to suggest that any behaviors that follow from or are caused by the affect of anger are aggressive. The problem with this view is that children who have acquired anxiety over their angry feelings inhibit behavior when they are angry. It does not seem reasonable to label restriction of action as aggression. A second possibility is to call any action that is in the service of hostile motivation an aggressive act. However, a child who has strong hostile wishes toward his father but is afraid that his father is aware of his resentment may become excessively obedient and deferential to his father in order to disguise his hostility. Again, it does not seem reasonable to label passive obedience as aggression.

A third possibility—the one that is most popular in contemporary psychology—is to judge only the effects of the behavior on the social environment. If the action causes pain, anxiety, or upset to another, if it destroys the integrity of objects, or if it is an extremely vigorous response, it is called aggressive, regardless of the child's intention or affect. However, there are problems with this definition also. If a 7-year-old touches his younger sister's face and accidentally makes her cry, we would have to call the playful tickling aggressive because it caused distress to another. Similarly, the child who rode his bicycle up and down the driveway with extreme vigor and as a result damaged a wheel would have to be called aggressive, even though his intention was not to damage the toy.

A Definition
of Aggression

A single-criterion definition for aggressive behavior seems theoretically unsatisfactory. A two-criteria definition intuitively seems more reasonable. Aggression is an act that (1) causes pain, anxiety, or distress to another person (or damage to an object), and (2) is in the service of a hostile wish or the affect of anger. The advantage of this definition of aggression is that it allows us to reject acts that unintentionally hurt others but to include acts that, on the surface, appear to be kind or culturally valued but that intentionally cause anxiety to another.

Consider a family situation in which the father, an autocratic and rejecting man with only 8 years of education, is threatened by the enormous school success of his 16-year-old son, who is planning a career in law. The father becomes upset every time the boy brings home a very good school report or discusses his plans for college. The boy, who feels hostile to his rejecting father, is gratifying his hostile motivation by hard work in school. That is, one of the motives behind his academic involvement is his intention to hurt his father, and the behavior successfully accomplishes its goal. Another example is the 10-year-old girl who decides to be excessively obedient to her parents in order to displace her older sister's preferred role with the mother. She is behaving aggressively, even though the act of obedience to her parents does not appear to be in the service of causing harm to another.

In these cases, studying hard in school and obedience are aggressive acts by the two-criteria definition. It is clear, however, that one cannot decide that these behaviors are aggressive without knowing the motives behind them. Most children who study hard in school and who obey their parents do *not* do so out of hostile motivation.

　The definition of aggression given above allows us to omit from the category of aggressive acts certain behaviors that do not arise from anger or hostility. Sex role standards for maleness dictate that "roughhouse" behavior is masculine. Boys who value the standard for masculinity may be prompted to push a playmate, grab another's toy, or tease a teacher. These behaviors do not necessarily reflect a desire to hurt anyone but may be the boy's way of announcing to his social environment that he is behaving in accordance with a masculine standard. Although poking a peer is often regarded as an aggressive act, some boys strike each other on the arm as a way of greeting and not as an expression of resentment. Girls, however, are less likely to display this type of aggressive behavior, and poking a peer is more likely to be prompted by hostile motivation in girls than in boys.

Another common cause of behavior that is often mislabeled aggressive is the child's desire to attract the attention of an adult. For instance, a 3-year-old might get in the way of his mother while she is busy in the kitchen in order to obtain her attention, not to cause her distress. Although this behavior is usually aimed at attracting the mother's attention, it is susceptible to misinterpretation. If the mother assumes the child is acting out of hostile motives, she may punish him severely.

There is a third way that behavior not inspired by hostility may be labeled aggressive. Our society tends to equate the high intensity or vigor of an act with aggressiveness. We are prone to consider a loud yell and the vigorous striking of a desk as aggressive, but low-intensity versions of these acts are less likely to be so judged (Walters & Parke, 1964). This association between the vigor of a reaction and aggression has special consequences in social interactions. A mother who interprets her child's vigorous pounding of the table as an aggressive act may punish him, whereas she would think nothing of his merely tapping the table.

　The child's tendency to display particular aggressive acts is determined by at least three factors: (1) the intensity of hostile motivation or anger, (2) the amount of anxiety, guilt, and inhibition associated with the aggressive act, and (3) the degree to which the aggressive act has become an effective way to gratify hostility. (See Part I, pp. 156–68.)

In general, the stronger the hostility or anger, the greater the probability that aggressive behavior will be expressed. But this positive relation between the intensity of motive or affect and overt behavior can be altered in two ways: first, by the degree to which the child is anxious or guilty over expressing aggression. If he has been consistently punished for aggressive behavior or has acquired a standard that dictates inhibition of aggressive acts, the child is less likely to react to hostility with aggressive responses. Second, a particular aggressive act is not likely to be expressed if it is not successful in achieving its intention of hurting someone. A child may cease misbehaving if his mother does not become as upset or anxious as the child intended. Thus, strong motivation, minimal anxiety, and an expectancy that the act will achieve its goal increase the likelihood of a particular aggressive act being expressed.

The preceding theoretical discussion led to the suggestion that an aggressive act should be defined in terms of a hostile intention or anger state and the effect of the act on another person. According to this definition, it is not possible to tell from an act alone whether it is aggressive.

However, most if not all of the psychological research on aggression —in children or adults—has not used this definition. Because it is extremely difficult to infer intention from behavior, psychologists have made some arbitrary decisions in order to facilitate their study of aggressive behavior. They have decided either that any action that hurt another or injured property was aggressive or that any act that was vigorous and demanded a reaction from another was aggressive (Patterson, Littman, & Bricker, 1967). These definitions are not concerned with the motive or affect state present at the time of the behavior.

More specifically, these investigators have focused on a small set of behaviors that they have called aggressive: verbal or physical attack on parents and peers, disobedience and resistance to adults, destruction of property, making up of stories to pictures or acting out themes with dolls that refer to injury to people or property, and, finally, extremely vigorous motor responses. As a result, most of our knowledge in this area concerns the determinants or the correlates of these classes of behavior, some of which are clearly in the service of hostility and anger but others of which are probably not so motivated.

The Learning of Aggressive Acts Research findings show that aggressive behaviors are generally learned as a result of one of two factors. First, they can be learned through the realization that these acts are an effective way to elicit some response from the environment —such as an attention response from the mother or a passive or submissive response from a peer. Second, they are learned through watching or copying the behavior of another adult or child who displays the same behavior. It has been found through studies of children's behaviors in natural settings that although frustrating situations occur very frequently in the daily life of a normal child, these events do *not* often lead to aggressive behaviors (Fawl, 1959).

Bandura and Walters (1963) have shown that a child who observes aggressive behaviors displayed by a model tends to behave more aggressively thereafter, but it is likely that many of these behaviors are associated neither with hostile motivation nor with the affect of anger. The tendency to imitate a model suggests that boys with older brothers would be more likely to display assertive and aggressive behaviors than boys who have no siblings; in general, this prediction is confirmed (Koch, 1960).

In an important study of naturalistic behavior (Patterson, Littman, & Bricker, 1967), continuous observations were made of 4-year-old children. The researchers dictated their observations onto magnetic tape and recorded a total of 2,583 aggressive acts and their consequences. In general, the more structured the nursery school setting, the fewer were the aggressive responses. When children were allowed permissiveness and freedom, they were apt to behave more assertively. If a particular child's aggressive behavior was successful (that is, his victim gave up a toy or became passive), it was likely that the child would increase his level of aggressiveness. If he was not successful or if he met with counteraggression, the child was less likely to behave aggressively in the future.

The child who was highly aggressive and assertive at the beginning of the nursery school sessions continued to be aggressive over a period of several months. The major reason for this stability is that the child's aggressive behaviors were successful. The aggressive children were generally more active and, as a result, were more likely to be targets for aggression and instigators of counteraggression. It appears that a typical nursery school contains, on the one hand, some very active, aggressive children who also meet the aggression of others and, on the other hand, relatively inactive children who initiate little aggression and do not encounter much aggression from others.

The effect of adoption on aggressive behavior. It is generally assumed that adoptive parents are less closely identified with their children than natural parents and consequently may be less affectionate, frustrating the child's need for affection. The adopted child who is told that he is adopted often develops the belief that he was not loved by his biological mother because she gave him up for adoption. This belief is likely to make the child angry and hostile at adults in general and increase the likelihood that he will express aggressive behavior.

This hypothesis was verified in a study of 10-year-old children, all of whom had gone to a psychiatric hospital with some form of problem behavior (Menlove, 1965). One group of children had been adopted; a second group, matched with the first on sex, social class, and age, were not adopted. The children's behaviors were evaluated in the psychiatric hospital. Of the 9 kinds of symptoms that might be called aggressive, 7 were more frequent in the adopted children: setting of fires, impulsive behavior, delinquency, sexual misbehavior, hyperactivity, disobedience to others, and negativism.

The effect of parental punishment. In general, boys who are seldom punished for disobedience, as well as those who are frequently punished, display more aggressive behavior than do boys who receive moderate punishment. Moreover, boys who receive minimal punishment direct their aggressive behavior toward their parents; those who receive frequent punishment are likely to behave aggressively with peers. This latter fact could be a result of the frustrating quality of punishment. It could also reflect the fact that the more frequently the parent displays aggression to the child or spouse (and this includes the physical and verbal displays that accompany punishment), the greater the likelihood of aggression in the child as a result of imitation of the parents as models.

The relation between parental punishment and aggressive behavior in the girl is simpler: The more frequent the punishment for aggression, the less aggressive behavior displayed to parents or peers. This sex difference may be attributed in part to differential sex typing for aggressive behavior. As previously noted, the models girls choose for imitation are generally not aggressive, and most girls possess the sex role standard that calls for inhibition of aggression. Among girls, therefore, exposure to an aggressive model has less of a facilitating effect on overt aggressive behavior than it does among boys (Bandura, Ross, & Ross, 1963b).

How Aggressive Behavior Changes in Meaning

Aggressive behavior takes on different meanings at various times during the preschool period. A 3-year-old who acts aggressively with his peers will not necessarily be a highly aggressive 5-year-old. As a matter of fact, he is likely to be more extroverted and masculine, rather than directly involved in such aggressive activities as grabbing toys or hitting.

This conclusion comes from a study in which 22 boys were observed in a nursery school when they were 3 and 5 years of age (Byram, 1966). The observers watched each child for a series of 5-minute periods and recorded everything the child did during each period. The boys who were overtly aggressive at age 3—that is, who teased their peers, tattled on them, grabbed their toys, or called them names—were rated neither high nor low on similar aggressive behaviors at age 5. The correlation between direct aggression to peers at age 3 and age 5 was only .08. However, the correlation between aggression at age 3 and extroversion at age 5 was about .50. The aggressive 3-year-old boys were at age 5 more involved in traditional masculine sex role play than were their nonaggressive counterparts. That is, they were more likely to play cowboys and Indians, to climb, to play with hammers, or to be interested in racing games. They also tended to be more outgoing and to initiate more social contacts with other children.

Thus, it appears that a mild degree of aggression at age 3 is a good predictor of extroversion and masculinity but a poor predictor of aggression at age 5. Transformations of this kind are not uncommon during the first 6 years of life, and this is one reason why the attempt to understand development resembles the decoding of a complex cryptograph.

Anxiety, Affiliation,
and Dependent Behavior

The hypothetical relations among affect, motive, and behavior that seemed reasonable for anger, hostility, and aggression are also appropriate for another set of psychological processes—those associated with the desire for supporting relationships with other people.

ANXIETY

There are certain classes of incentive events that have the common effect of creating serious uncertainty about the future. The uncertainty can be created by an encounter with an unfamiliar situation, object, or person; doubt about the effects of one's actions; or an unclear expectancy about such matters as being loved or rejected, passing or failing a test, being robbed on a dark street, functioning effectively away from home, and being fired or promoted.

The common psychological components in these situations are that the child or adult (1) either is in an unfamiliar situation or is uncertain about the likelihood of various events and (2) either is not sure what response to make or has no response to make in the unfamiliar situation. At such times the child is likely to experience the affect we call *anxiety*. Unlike anger, which occurs when incentives block a well-articulated sequence of behavior, anxiety is most likely to occur when the person does not know how to behave. Anxiety is an unpleasant experience that is phenomenologically different from anger and is accompanied by different physiological reactions (Ax, 1953).

AFFILIATIVE MOTIVES AS REACTIONS TO ANXIETY

As with anger, there are often direct and immediate motor responses to anxiety. Some of these responses are learned; others are more reflexive. For instance, a person who is anxious may freeze or may display motor trembling. However, one of the most important classes of cognitive reactions to anxiety is the motive (or wish) that accompanies the affect. In some children and adults anxiety is likely to elicit a wish for another person to intervene and reduce the anxiety by giving affection, reassurance, advice, money, or a letter of introduction. This wish has been called by various psychologists a motive for succorance, dependent gratification, or affiliation (the term that will be used here). *The motive of affiliation is a wish for the supporting intervention of another in order to alleviate or reduce anxiety.*

As we have noted, anger does not always lead to hostility, and anger and hostility can occur separately. Similarly, anxiety does not always lead to the wish for affiliation, and each can occur separately. When he is anxious, a child may wish to be alone, away from others. Conversely, he can wish to be with his friends even though he is not anxious. However, anxiety and the affiliation motive often occur together, especially in the child who has learned that other people effectively reduce his anxiety.

DEPENDENT BEHAVIOR

Those specific behaviors directed toward other people that are characterized by requests for affection, help, support, or the establishment of physically or emotionally close relationships have been labeled dependent. Dependent behaviors need not be the product of affiliative wishes or anxiety. A boy who always plays with a particular group of peers and rarely plays alone could be motivated by a need for power and dominance rather than anxiety, if the boy were a leader in the group and the group had high status in the school he attended. A 12-year-old girl may continually ask her boyfriend or father for help with minor problems because she regards this behavior as appropriate to her sex role standard for femininity, not necessarily because she needs help or is anxious. An 8-year-old may establish a close relationship with a crippled boy in the neighborhood because he has a motive to help others rather than to have a friend.

A Definition
of Dependency
It is not possible to know the motive behind the behaviors that are normally called dependent. As with aggression, it seems wise to use a compound definition of dependency behavior. Dependent responses are those in which the person establishes close, supportive, affectionate, or soliciting relationships with other people as a function of anxiety or an affiliative wish for help, advice, support, or affection.

This definition allows us to reject those behaviors characterized by close relationships with others that are not caused by affiliative wishes, and to include actions that do not, on the surface, appear to be desires for help. For example, a 7-year-old who complains that he is ill will probably receive care and support from his mother, but the announcement of illness was not necessarily serving an affiliative motive. The college student who is anxious and lonely may write a suicide note to a close friend announcing that she plans to take sleeping pills at 7 p.m. on the following evening. The note, sent 24 hours ahead of time, can be a disguised request for companionship and not a serious declaration of suicidal intentions.

Determinants
of Dependent Behavior
The probability that a child will behave dependently (as defined above) is a function of the same factors that control aggressive behavior: the intensity of anxiety or of affiliative motives, the degree to which anxiety and guilt over

overt dependency lead to inhibition of these responses, and the degree to which the dependent behavior has been successful in the past in gratifying the child's affiliative motives.

The stronger the motive, the greater the likelihood that dependent actions will occur. However, if the child has learned to regard these actions as childish, inappropriate, or in violation of his sex role standards, he may inhibit them. Dependent behavior tends to be more stable over the period from 10 to 20 years in girls than in boys, because dependency does not violate the girl's sex role standards. A highly dependent preadolescent girl is likely to continue to behave in this manner when anxious or buffeted by affiliative wishes. The behaviorally dependent 10-year-old boy is likely to be teased for these actions because they violate sex role standards for masculinity. For this reason, these responses may disappear from his behavioral repertoire, and he may appear to be relatively independent as an adult. Finally, dependent overtures toward others will be maintained only if they are met with positive and helpful support that alleviates anxiety. If the child's continual requests for support, whether open or disguised, are not answered, he will eventually inhibit such overtures and become cold, aloof, and cynical of the belief that warmth is a basic human attribute.

As with aggression, most investigations of dependency in children have focused on a small set of behaviors in an attempt to establish the correlates of these behaviors, apart from the varied motives that might have produced them. An exception to this generalization are the studies in which the child's anxiety over his relationship with a strange adult was manipulated experimentally. In a typical experiment of this kind, children played a simple game of dropping marbles in a hole. The experimenter played the role of the stranger who rewarded each child and took note of the rate at which he worked at this task. At this point in the experiment some children were left alone in the room for a short period of time to allow both anxiety over their relationship with the adult and a motive for adult contact and approval to be established. The rest of the children never experienced any isolation from the adult. When the adult returned to the isolated children, their behavior in the marble game was observed again. In most cases, the children who were left alone worked harder at the game than did those who were not isolated (Gewirtz & Baer, 1958; Walters & Ray, 1960). A favored interpretation is that the isolation from the adult elicited the child's anxiety over the uncertain relationship with him and motivated the child to seek adult reassurance and approval by working harder at the game.

The hypothesis that dependency is likely to occur when the child is anxious is also supported by a study of preschool girls (Rosenthal, 1965). The child's dependent behavior toward the mother or toward a strange female was observed under conditions in which the children were either minimally anxious or highly anxious. The group that had been made highly anxious entered a room containing a slow-burning alcohol lamp standing on a steel tray. Next to the tray was a pair of scissors, some tissue, and a pencil. The pictures on the wall were dreary, and a phonograph was playing a record consisting of loud banging sounds on a metal object and a child's high-pitched shrieks. After 12 minutes, following a loud, continuous shriek, a red door opened very slowly and a hand wearing an arm-length black glove reached in slowly, put out the lamp, and withdrew. The anxious children were much more likely to stay near and cling to the adult than were the children who had not been made anxious.

This result matches a finding of an experiment with adult women who were told either that they might be given a strong shock or that they might receive a mild shock at some point in the experiment (Schachter, 1959). Each woman was asked whether she would like to wait alone or wait with other students who were strangers. The women who expected a strong shock were more likely to choose to wait with others than were the women who were told they could expect a mild shock. Anxiety generated by uncertainty led both the 4-year-old girls and the 21-year-old women to seek proximity to others. These effects resemble those produced when a mother leaves her 1-year-old alone. The child cries and seeks proximity to the mother upon her return. (See the discussion of attachment and separation anxiety in Chapter 24.)

Children with wishes for affiliative contact will generally behave in a way that will increase contact with others. If one assumes that children who are deprived of adult contact wish more for it, these children should behave in a way to gratify that motive. In one study (Zigler, 1961) two psychologists examined the case histories of institutionalized retarded children and rated them according to the degree of deprivation of social contact they experienced. Some children were regarded as highly deprived of contact with adults, others minimally deprived. The highly deprived children spent a much longer time working at a marble task for which adults praised their performance than did the children who were minimally deprived.

Thus, anxiety generated by uncertainty, as well as conditions causing a child to have strong motivation for affiliative contact, may each lead to behaviors classified as dependent.

Parental Influences on Dependent Behavior

A mother who consistently rewards and rarely punishes dependent behavior produces a highly dependent child. A child reared in an extremely neglectful institutional environment, on the other hand, is less likely to behave dependently because dependent actions are not rewarded (Spitz & Wolf, 1946). In studies with more representative groups of American children (Sears, Maccoby, & Levin, 1957; Kagan & Moss, 1962), it was found that consistent maternal reward and inconsistent punishment of dependent actions were each associated with a high degree of overt dependent behavior in the child. However, maternal acceptance did not of itself foster dependent actions in the child, because if the mother valued and rewarded independence, the child would inhibit direct dependent overtures to others.

Young boys who are independent have parents who show consistent discipline, expect mature behavior, encourage independent contacts, and do not restrict or coerce the child. Independent girls have mothers who demand obedience and adoption of maternal values but do not use coercive power. In general, parents who set consistent and firm standards for their children and who strive to socialize them properly have the most independent children. Because the American middle-class culture tends to value responsibility and independence, middle-class parents who take the socialization process seriously urge independence on their children (Baumrind & Black, 1967).

Parental influences may help account for the developmental changes in dependency from age 2 to 6. There is a decrease during this period in overt direct dependency requests to other people in anxiety-arousing situations (Shirley & Pointz, 1941; Heathers, 1955; Martin, 1964). This decrease is probably a function of the fact that mothers begin to encourage and reward independent behavior during the preschool years, and they become increasingly impatient with direct requests for reassurance, help, and support, which are often punished. By the time the child is 5 years old, his mother expects him to dress himself, go to the toilet, and solve minor problems autonomously. The typical 5-year-old has strong tendencies to behave both independently and dependently; as a result, he may display both types of responses.

Dependency Conflict The longitudinal study by Kagan and Moss (1962) found that children who were extremely passive and dependent during the ages 6 to 10 appeared to have less conflict about their passive and dependent behavior as adults than did children who were only moderately passive during the early school years.

More girls than boys are extremely dependent and minimally conflicted about their dependency. When scenes depicting men or women in a dependent posture were shown at rapid speeds (tachistoscopically) to young adults, the women recognized these pictures much earlier than the men, which suggests the women had less conflict over reporting and recognizing such scenes. The more conflicted the men, the greater difficulty they experienced in recognizing the scenes. In general, boys and men are more conflicted about dependency than are women, and dependent behavior is more stable in females than in males.

**Concluding Comments
on Dependency** As indicated earlier, dependency is a global and ambiguous concept; Maccoby summarizes this state of affairs well:

> dependency is too global a concept to be useful in the analysis of behavior beyond the first year or two of life. There seems good reason to speak of a unitary, primary, affectional system in infancy and early child-

hood. The term attachment seems a good choice to designate the behavior involved at this age, and the parallels between the development of this behavior in the human infant and subhuman primates lends force to the view that the behavior has an instinctual base. At the very least, we can say that some species show attachment in infancy while others do not, and mankind is one of the species in which the probabilities are great that the behavior will develop in any given individual. . . . By the age of 3 or 4, specific learning and general cognitive growth have brought about a considerable differentiation of attachment and dependent behavior with respect to its topography, its targets, and its eliciting conditions, and new clusters of behavioral dispositions have become organized which incorporate elements of the formally unitary system. Different cultural settings differ, of course, and the nature of the learning experiences they provide can differentially affect the rate and course of this development. [Maccoby, 1969].

There are many parallels between the development of aggressive and dependent behavior. Both behaviors to a certain extent have built-in conflicts between the child's desire to display these acts and standards that dictate their inhibition. The child wants to be helped and to be close to his parents, just as he wants to express his anger, but he may be anxious about openly displaying each of these behaviors because of fear of punishment, loss of love, or guilt following violation of standards. Consistent parental reward of each of these classes of behavior should increase their occurrence, consistent parental punishment should decrease their occurrence, and inconsistent reward or punishment should lead to a high frequency of occurrence. There are important sex differences in the degree to which anxiety is attached to aggressive or dependent behavior. Girls are more conflicted over the expression of aggressive behavior; boys have more conflict over dependent behavior. But for both systems there is always ambiguity in the overt response. Even extreme behavioral examples of aggression or dependency, such as homicide or chronic illness, can be disguised expressions of other motives: "Who does a kindness is not therefore kind."

Sexual Motives and Behavior

The third motive-behavioral system to develop during the preschool years is usually classified under the heading of sexuality. This heading is perhaps too general, because it includes many different motives. The bond of similarity among them rests on the fact that a primary incentive stimulus for the relevant affects and motives is the genitals of the self and others. The child has both a motive to see and explore the genitals of others and a motive to manipulate his own genitals in order to experience the pleasant sensations that accompany masturbation. According to psychoanalytic theory the child has an especially strong sexually based desire for close physical contact with the parent of the opposite sex (see Part II, Chapter 15).

CURIOSITY ABOUT
AND MANIPULATION OF THE GENITALS

The child's motive to view and explore the genitals of others does not seem always to be tied to a specific affect, as is the case with anger and anxiety. The curiosity about the genitals derives in part from the child's desire to study all events that are discrepant from the familiar (see Chapter 24). The discrepancy in physical appearance between his own genitals and those of the opposite sex elicits a strong motive to understand and to comprehend the difference. Just as the 1-year-old fixes his gaze for long periods at a face that is different from the faces with which he is familiar, so the 5-year-old wants to study those anatomical areas that are different from those to which he has become accustomed. This motive might be as much a desire to satisfy intellectual curiosity as it is a desire for sexual excitement.

The motive to manipulate the genitals is initially based on a different rationale. Many preschool children have discovered that touching of the genital area produces pleasant sensations, and they wish to repeat this experience. In one study (Sears, Maccoby, & Levin, 1957) about half of a group of 379 mothers reported observing sex play in their children. Since many mothers are reluctant to report this information and children are hesitant to display genital exploration openly, these figures are undoubtedly conservative estimates of the frequency of genital manipulation in young children.

ANXIETY OVER THE GENITAL AREA

Curiosity about the sexual anatomy of others and genital play lead to punishment and subsequently to anxiety. According to Sears, Maccoby, and Levin (1957) only 5 percent of the mothers they studied reported complete permissiveness about masturbation; less than 15 percent permitted the child to run about the house naked. Thinking about the genital area is thus capable of eliciting anticipation both of the uniquely pleasant sensations and of punishment and anxiety. This combination of pleasure and anxiety, added to the child's natural curiosity about the genitals of others, heightens his preoccupation with the genital area.

Since the young child is punished for sexual curiosity and genital manipulation, he often inhibits the behavior that will gratify these motives. As a result, the motive becomes much stronger than it would if the social environment were permissive. The motives that grow strong are those that are frequently aroused but are not permitted regular gratification.

It is common for the young girl 4 or 5 years of age to fail to appreciate the fact that the anal orifice is separate and distinct from the urethral and vaginal orifices. Many young girls call the entire genital area by one name, despite conscious attempts by some parents to teach the child distinctive names for urine and feces and for the anal and vaginal orifices. Since considerable anxiety is associated with bowel accidents, it is theoretically reasonable that during the few years when the girl regards these areas as similar, anxiety associated with bowel functioning may become linked with the genitals. It is more common for young girls than boys to regard the genitals as unclean and to be anxious about genital exposure. The young boy is less susceptible to this conflict because the penis is a distinctive stimulus and it is clear that urine and feces emerge from distinctively different anatomical places.

It is important to realize that the preschool child's preoccupation and anxiety are centered on the genitals, not on the romantic interactions that adults label sexual love. However, the anxiety that is attached to the genitals and to the sensations to which they give rise may become attached to the acts surrounding heterosexual behavior when the child is 11 or 12 and recognizes the close relation among the genitals, sexual excitement, and heterosexual behavior. In this way one basis for adult sexual anxiety can be established during early childhood.

Effectance Motivation and Mastery Behavior

The fourth motive-behavioral system to be considered is different in at least two respects from the first three systems. First, unlike aggression, dependency, and sexuality, there is no clearly perceived affect state that elicits behavioral attempts at mastery. Second, behaviors aimed at gratifying hostile, affiliative, or sexual motives can be delimited in some reasonable way: There is a strong tendency for anger to lead to motor discharge and for anxiety over uncertainty to lead to the seeking of proximity to familiar people. But the desire to master a task tells very little about the particular task that will be chosen. Typically, the tasks chosen to gratify this motive are more arbitrary than the behaviors chosen to gratify the other three motives.

Effectance motivation is defined as the desire to master a new skill or perfect an old one—to improve one's proficiency at a task. Mastery behavior is the behavioral attempt to gratify that motive. These definitions imply that an attempt to master any skill is an illustration of mastery, whether the skill be reading, baseball, dancing, harmonica playing, social poise, fighting, or collecting match boxes. Unfortunately, however, psychologists have arbitrarily decided to study only two areas of mastery—intellectual and athletic skills, with more emphasis on the former than the latter. Before examining the research on the mastery of academic or intellectual skills, let us continue our theoretical discussion of the effectance motive.

Why should a child want to perfect a skill, complete a difficult task, learn a new ability? We know from our earlier discussions (Chapters 25, 26, and 27) that the child could strive for mastery because he wanted to gain approval from his parents, to reduce anxiety over possible adult rejection, or to make himself similar to a desirable model. He might also strive for mastery to gratify hostility toward a peer, to facilitate dominance of a brother, or to increase congruence between his attributes and his sex role standards. The motives of approval, affiliation, recognition, hostility, power, and sexuality provide many dynamic bases for learning to read, to swim, to speak clearly, or to build a kite. Why then do psychologists feel forced to assume still another basis for mastery behavior?

The main reason derives from the child's behavior. A 2-year-old boy sitting alone in his room, carefully building a tall tower of blocks, appears intensely involved in the task and shows behavioral upset if the tower falls. It does not appear that the child is involved in this activity because he wants approval, because he is trying to be masculine, or because he is attempting to gratify any of the other motives listed above. He seems motivated by mastery *for its own sake*. This phenomenon—and others like it—have prompted psychologists to postulate the effectance motive. An especially vocal spokesman for the position is White (1959), who argues that mastery of some skills is the result of an intrinsic motive to perfect those skills.

The domains of mastery behavior, according to this hypothesis, are arbitrary. Any response can be perfected, even in such idiosyncratic domains as raising gerbils, pruning Japanese yew, and playing musical melodies on partially filled glasses of water. There are an infinite number of tasks that can be mastered, and there is a variety of motives that can serve that mastery, one of which is effectance—a desire to achieve mastery for its own sake.

There seem to be several bases for effectance motivation. One basis is seen, during the first 3 years of life, in the child's desire to match his actions and the products of his actions to an internal standard, or an acquired schema. As early as 4 months of age the infant is likely to smile when he studies a stimulus that almost matches his acquired schema for a face. This act of recognition releases the smile. It is as if the dynamic process of matching was a pleasant experience.

Similarly, the 2-year-old who builds a tower may smile as the tower becomes taller. It appears that the child has an internal schema for the tower he wishes to build, and as his product comes closer to matching that schema, he smiles. The 5-year-old acquires a schema for the successful riding of tricycles by watching other children; he then tries to master this skill so that he can experience the match between the product of his actions and his schema for successful tricycle riding.

A second basis for the effectance motive may come from the desire to be able to predict and control events. When the 1-year-old discovers that hitting the keys of a toy xylophone produces varied sounds, he is likely to repeat this action many times. He is controlling the feedback from the keys. When he can predict the outcome of his behavior every time, however, he becomes bored and less motivated to master the task. The involvement generated by a challenging task seems to rest on the fact that challenge entails uncertainty of prediction. This uncertainty evokes attempts at mastery in order to be able to make successful predictions.

The challenge of many school-age games is maximal when the child is not sure what will happen. When he knows all the permutations of the game and can predict the outcome before it happens, he is likely to become bored and to abandon the game. The more varied and unpredictable the outcome, the more interesting a game will be. Perhaps that is why games of chance are so addicting: They are unpredictable by their structure, and they never permit a person to arrive at a point where he can guess the outcome.

A third possible basis for effectance motivation is characteristic of the school-age child and concerns the desire for self-definition—the wish to know one's attributes and the collateral need for believing that one is unusually competent in at least one skill. An attribute has salience for the child if it is somehow distinctive and is not possessed by everyone. Possession of two eyes, hair, and fingers is of minimal relevance for the child's self-image, for these attributes are characteristic of all the children he knows. If, however, the child lost his hair, he would possess a distinctive attribute that would have a strong influence on his self-identity. Similarly, learning to read is irrelevant to a child's self-identity if all the children he knows possess this skill. If the child is competent at ice skating, however, and most of his friends do not ice skate, then this attribute, acquired through mastery, helps the child's self-definition.

In sum, the bases for the effectance motive may rest on three rather fundamental processes: (1) the desire to match actions and products of actions to a schema, (2) the desire to predict and control events, and (3) the desire to acquire an articulated self-identity.

MASTERY BEHAVIOR

Mastery behavior that is in the service of an effectance motive can be psychologically different from mastery in the service of other motives (for example, approval or sex role congruence). As with aggression or dependency, a variety of actions can gratify the effectance motive. Unfortunately, we can learn only a limited amount about this motive from existing research because that research has focused on mastery of intellectual skills, regardless of the motive.

Mastery
of Intellectual Skills

The rate of mastery of academic skills is one of the most stable aspects of a child's behavior. Children who are motivated to acquire knowledge and to perfect academic skills during the early school years retain this motivation during adolescence and early adulthood (Kagan & Moss, 1962). Two factors seem to be important in facilitating the development of mastery behavior and its stability. One factor is the amount of encouragement and reward given by parents and the degree to which the parent of the same sex is an effective identification model. For example, children of mothers who encouraged walking and talking during the first 2 years of life had higher mastery levels in school than did children whose mothers were less encouraging of mastery of these early maturational tasks. There is, of course, a positive correlation between the social class of the mother and her acceleration of the child's intellectual or gross motor development (Moss & Kagan, 1958; Kagan & Moss, 1962). The second factor is that mastery of intellectual skills is not subject to strong prohibitions for either sex; consequently there is apt to be a close relation between the preschool child's behavioral attempts in this area and his motivations.

There are distinct sex differences in overt mastery of intellectual tasks. For example, boys are more likely than girls to choose difficult problems. In an experiment by Crandall and Rabson (1960) young children were allowed to complete a first puzzle given them but were made to fail a second one. Afterward the children were asked whether they wanted to try to finish the puzzle they had failed or to complete the easier one again. Among preschool children there were no striking sex differences between those who requested the failed task and those who requested the easier one. With increasing age both sexes showed an increased desire to undertake the failed puzzle, but boys showed a greater tendency to do so than did girls.

The Role
of Expectancy

As with the motives of sexuality, aggression, and dependency, the probability of mastery behavior occurring in the service of effectance motivation is a function of the intensity of the motive, the degree to which anxiety and inhibition are associated with behavioral expression, and the expectancy of gratifying the motive. Because our culture has no strong sanctions against mastery behavior (unlike sex, dependency, and aggression), conflict becomes less important than the child's expectancy of gratifying his motive, which has come to be called expectancy of success.

Expectancy of success. If a child feels he will be able to successfully solve a puzzle, climb a rope, ride a bike, or read a book, his mastery attempts become more intense. For example, a child's I.Q. score may rise if his teacher is led to believe that the child is smarter than she had thought. The teacher's greater confidence in the child probably increases his expectancy of success, which in turn increases the quality of his performance on the intelligence test. In Rosenthal's provocative experiment (1966) all the children in a public elementary school were given a group intelligence test, which was disguised as a test that singled out those children who would dramatically improve in academic ability during the coming school year. Each teacher was given the names of a few children in the class who "would show unusual academic development." Although these children were actually no different in academic ability from the other children in the classroom, the teacher was led to expect that they had greater potential. At the end of the school year all the children were given the same group intelligence test they had taken earlier. The children in grades 1 and 2 (but not in the higher grades) whose teachers expected them to gain in academic ability showed larger gains in I.Q. than did the remaining children. Rosenthal writes: "If teachers can, then probably healers, parents, spouses and other ordinary people also can affect the behavior of those with whom they interact by virtue of their expectations of what that behavior will be [Rosenthal, 1966, p. 412]."

There are positive relations among expectancy of success, motivation for mastery, and quality of mastery behavior. In one investigation (Crandall, Katkovsky, & Preston, 1962) boys and girls 7 to 9 years of age were asked to state whether they thought they could solve problems of varied difficulty. Afterward the children were observed in a free-play situation to see how long each played with various intellectual games and puzzles. The children who had a high expectancy of success on the intellectual problems approached the intellectual playthings more frequently.

As might be expected, there is a consistent positive relation between the child's expectancy of obtaining good grades and his actual report card grades. However, girls' estimates of success are consistently lower than boys', despite the fact that girls and boys have equivalent I.Q. scores and grades (Crandall, Katkovsky, & Preston, 1966).

Expectancy of failure. If a child expects to fail, he is unlikely to make behavioral efforts at mastery. The extreme vulnerability of mastery behavior to expectancy of failure can be observed in the 2-year-old who is just beginning to establish standards of correctness. It is not difficult to engage the young child's involvement in a puzzle or an interesting game that requires persistence in order to obtain success. The child shows interest and mastery behavior as long as he is successful. But after one or, at the most, two failures he abruptly abandons the task. The desire to master new skills hangs on a thread that snaps easily when the child fails and believes he cannot succeed.

It is difficult to explain why the expectation of failure is so strong a force in governing the Western child's behavior. It appears that failure leaves the child with no response to make to the task. Prior to failing, he had been issuing behaviors that were accepted and led to positive outcomes that he could predict. When these responses suddenly are no longer accepted, the child feels pressured to behave but is uncertain about what to do. The prevailing reaction in such a situation is task withdrawal. The child in the Western culture is strongly driven to avoid failure, and the quality of his mastery attempts on any task is continually monitored by his expectancy of success or failure at that task.

Common Themes

The preschool and early school years are witness to a flowering of motives and behavioral systems that are linked with different degrees of anxiety and different degrees of expectancy of gratifying those motives. By the time a child is 6 or 7 years of age, motives for affiliation, genital stimulation, instrumental aid, affection, mastery, and the wish to hurt another are active components of his personality structure.

Several common themes characterize these motive-behavioral systems. In the first place, the possession of behaviors that can gratify a motive, the degree of anxiety associated with those behavioral attempts at gratification, and the expectancy of gratification all exert a powerful influence on the child's goal-directed behavior, even though motivation for a goal is strong. Further, a behavior that seems intended to gratify a particular motive might be aimed instead at gratifying one of several other motives. Depending on the child's experience, a particular motive—be it sexuality, affiliation, hostility, or effectance—can lead to a variety of behaviors.

It is difficult, therefore, to make absolute statements about the meaning or intention of particular goal-oriented behaviors or to predict what kinds of behaviors will result from a particular motive. Each person has his private code, and more must be learned about the way he thinks if his actions are to be interpreted correctly.

To judge how high a child's talent will reach, do not attend so much to his greater and smaller facility for assimilating technical notions, but watch to see whether his eyes are occasionally clouded with tears of enthusiasm for the work.

RÉMY DE GOURMONT. Dust for Sparrows

CHAPTER 29
PERSONALITY AND INTELLECTUAL DEVELOPMENT IN THE SCHOOL-AGE CHILD

T here are dramatic changes among Western children in their overt behavior and in the form and quality of their intellectual functioning between 5 and 8 years of age. The popular explanation attributes these changes to the varied experiences associated with school attendance. However, many cultures institute formal changes in responsibilities and expectations for task mastery between the fifth and eighth year, and these changes may not be the sole result of school attendance. For example, English common law typically did not regard the child as responsible for his actions prior to the eighth year, and the Catholic Church does not ask a child under 7 to confess his misbehaviors. Thus, there is a general recognition, spanning cultures and time, that something special happens to the child at this time. It is likely that basic biological and psychological changes transpire during these years. These changes, which are recognized by most cultures, provoke the society to institutionalize the mastery of specific skills and the acceptance of certain social responsibilities when the child is about 6 or 7 years of age.

Behavioral and Cognitive Changes

Several of the critical responses established during the early school years have been discussed in preceding chapters: anxiety and guilt over aggression, dependency, and sexuality; adoption of sex role standards; and the crystallization of a sex role identity. In addition, children in Western society acquire attitudes about intellectual mastery, especially expectancy of success and failure; standards of performance and competence; attitudes about teachers; tendencies for active versus passive behavior with peers; attitudes toward self; preferences for particular defenses to anxiety; and standards for rational thought and autonomy.

THE IMPORTANCE OF STANDARDS

A major transformation occurring during the preschool and early school years is the decreasing importance of motives for specific external goals and the increasing importance of standards. The 5-year-old has motives for genital stimulation, hostility, effectance, affection, affiliation, and praise. These motives are satiable and are typically aroused by a trigger stimulus in the environment or by a thought. Standards, on the other hand, being beliefs about the ideal attributes the child feels he should possess and the ideal goal states he feels he should be achieving, are not easily satisfied, nor are they easily changed in intensity by introducing a particular incentive stimulus. One can easily arouse the child's desire for a chocolate bar or a checkers game with his father by merely suggesting that goal to the child. It is not easy to change the child's standard about his sex role attributes just by suggesting that he should be more masculine or that he is more masculine.

The establishment of standards during the preschool years gives rise to a special motive—the desire to think, feel, and behave in ways that are maximally similar to the standard. The goal of this special motive is a thought, the child's evaluation of the degree to which his attributes match his standard. As the child grows older, this desire for congruence with the standard increases in strength and subordinates earlier learned motives that were satiated directly by external events. For instance, a 4-year-old girl may have a motive to be kissed by her parents, which is gratified by receipt of that kiss. Several kisses may satiate the wish for several hours or days. The 7-year-old girl has generally acquired a standard that states, "I should be valued by my parents." In searching for ways of fulfilling this standard, she may or may not require kisses. Moreover, in the 7-year-old's case the critical event would not be the kiss but her interpretation of it.

A motive for an external goal may differ from a motive to maximize congruence with a standard, yet each may lead to the same action. For example, a teacher who sees a 10-year-old girl ask a boy for help with a problem may wonder if that act was impelled by the wish to fulfill a feminine sex role standard of dependence or by a desire to get the boy's attention. It is difficult to pinpoint the basis for this particular response because the primary incentive for the behavior could have been either a desire to maximize congruence with a standard or a motive for an external goal.

PREDICTING ADULT BEHAVIOR

Because crystallization of major standards, motives, anxieties, expectancies, and defenses occur during the early school years, this period offers a preview of the personality of the late adolescent and young adult. The bases for dramatic individual differences among adults can be discerned by the time the child is 10 years old. At this age motives for affiliation, mastery, hostility, and sexuality, as well as for dominance, affection, acceptance, and recognition, can be seen to exist in different hierarchies in a group of children, and the standards for sex role behavior, rational judgments, and autonomy of action have been formed. The major sources of anxiety, such as anticipation of physical harm or social rejection and violation of standards, have been operating for several years. Moreover, preferred defensive reactions to these sources of anxiety have become more automatic and predictable.

SYMPTOMS OF THE SCHOOL-AGE CHILD

The early school years produce a broad array of maladaptive symptoms, including extreme fearfulness, nightmares, physiological disturbances with psychological causes (ulcerative colitis, asthma, headaches, repeated vomiting, skin disturbances), stereotyped repetitive rituals (hand washing, postures at bedtime, or obsessional thoughts), motor tics (blinking of the eyes, twitching of the face), aggression, and delinquency.

It will probably be more profitable to discuss these symptoms according to their presumed causes rather than their similarities in form.

Anxiety over Loss of Parental Nurturance and Guilt over Violation of Standards
Anxiety over possible loss of parental acceptance and affection makes the child overly susceptible to conforming to the parents' demands. This conformity is an effective way for the child to maintain his belief that the parents still value him. He must inhibit violation of parental wishes in order to keep his anxiety over potential loss of nurturance at a low level. If he does violate or contemplate violating these wishes, his anxiety over loss of affection predisposes him to develop symptoms. If he is at a point of maturity where he begins to blame himself for these violations, he will experience the affect of guilt.

Nightmares, ritualistic behaviors, or acts intended to invite punishment may be signs of guilt or fear of reprisal following the violation of standards. The exact source and intensity of the anxiety or guilt is a function of the specific behaviors or thoughts that the child has initiated. Hostile wishes and aggressive actions, sexual curiosity and masturbation, selfish intent, dishonesty, excessive dependency, and lack of perseverance with difficult tasks are responses most heavily socialized during the ages 4 through 10 and are primary sources of anxiety and guilt during the early school years.

Reactions to guilt. Children often display three major reactions to guilt feelings. One type of reaction can be regarded as restitutive in intention: The child accepts the guilt as applicable to himself and behaves as though he should be or is about to be punished for his misdemeanors. In this reaction the child is likely to express self-deprecatory statements, commit violations that will lead to punishment, or develop fears of death, illness, or mutilation.

A typical example of the development of such fears is the case of an 11-year-old girl who suddenly developed an intense fear of dying following an accident in which she almost choked to death on a piece of food. Badly scared by this freak experience, she later told her parents that she had rabies and was going to die. After she was talked out of this belief, she became convinced that she had cancer and would soon die. Psychological study of the child and the family revealed that socialization of hostile thoughts and aggressive behavior was unusually severe in the family; there were constant verbal reminders of the inappropriateness of hostile feelings. The girl admitted strong resentments toward her mother and younger siblings but felt that she had no right to them. She stated that she must be a "bad girl" if she had these thoughts. The belief in imminent death appeared to be a direct consequence of the guilt she experienced over her hostile thoughts toward her family.

There are less dramatic modes of self-punitive action. It appears that poor school performance and inciting peers to rejection might sometimes be the products of a need for punishment to relieve whatever guilt the child is experiencing.

A second set of defensive reactions to guilt involves the tendency to attribute the blame for the prohibited act to other people. Why some children choose this reaction whereas others choose a self-punitive route is not well understood, although it appears that the less intense the guilt, the more likely the child will be to attempt to minimize it through direct means. The most common direct defense against guilt is to project the blame for the prohibited action onto another person. The familiar cry of the accused 6-year-old, "I didn't hit him; anyway, he started it," is a clear example of guilt projection. Other forms of this response include blaming the teacher for school failure and blaming a particular peer for failure to be invited to join a club.

Finally, the child may attempt to reduce guilt directly through intellectual analysis of the transgression or rationalizing the action. When a group of 10-year-olds talk about their resentments toward their parents, they reduce one another's guilt by providing justifications for their hostility.

The parental milieu that seems to be associated with high guilt is one in which an affectionate relationship between parent and child has existed for several years and threat of withdrawal is the main method of socialization. Under these conditions the child who values the mother's nurturance is led to believe that he has the power to maintain the affectionate relationship by inhibition of selected acts. In the case that he feels the responsibility for his actions, he experiences guilt if he anticipates violating or actually violates a standard.

Hostility
Toward Parents

Strong hostility toward parents can generate maladaptive symptoms in the child. Often the intent of the symptom is to cause anxiety in whoever is the source of the child's resentments. The forms of expression depend in part on the models of aggressive behavior to whom the child has been exposed. The most direct form is physical aggression toward the parents. However, since instances of homicide are rare among young adolescents and are virtually absent in children under 10 years of age, the most common behavioral consequence of hostility during the early school years is direct verbal aggression. This response, though subject to strong punishment, allows the child to gratify his hostile feelings immediately.

Many of the maladaptive responses occur when the child is not able to express his hostility verbally and is forced to choose more indirect means. These indirect strategies typically involve a behavior that will cause the parent anxiety but is not obviously aggressive. The few responses that fit this requirement are often frustrations of strong wishes the parent has for the child, such as school success, honesty, social poise, and responsibility. By failing in school, violating parental standards for social conduct, or regressing, the child elicits the anger and emotional upset in his parents that gratifies his hostile wishes. The child is, of course, unaware of the intent of his actions and must suffer the very real pain and anxiety that accompany school failure or peer rejection.

Conflict
over Sexual Wishes
and Behavior

Anxiety over masturbation, desires to view the genitals of the parents, or urges for close physical contact with the opposite sex (kissing, petting, intercourse) can lead to behavioral symptoms. For example, anxiety over sexual motives toward peers of the opposite sex may lead to public avoidance of the other sex. The strict voluntary sexual partitioning of play groups during the preadolescent years is one evidence of this anxiety. School-age girls show a sudden increase in modesty. At age 5 a girl may readily dress and undress in her father's presence; by age 10 she may insist on closed doors and blushingly demand that the father leave the room while she dresses or prepares for bed. Anxiety over masturbation, as with aggression, can lead to nightmares, rituals, and self-punitive procedures.

The appearance of tics—repetitive involuntary muscle movements— is sometimes a product of sexual anxiety. Some of the more frequent tics include eye blinking, rolling of the lips, movements of the muscles of the lower face, and jerky movements of the fingers or wrists. It is thought that the muscular form of the tic may be symbolic of the action that causes conflict and arouses anxiety. The blinking tic, for example, is thought by some to be related to anxiety over seeing the opposite parent unclothed. However, the meaning of tics is still unclear, and these interpretations are conjectural.

Anxiety over Sex Role Identification

A final source of conflict and related behavioral symptoms derives from the pressures a school-age child feels to conform to the standards for sex-typed behaviors. Some of these pressures were described in Chapter 27 (pages 475–91). During the school years, anxiety over violating male sex role standards often leads boys to inhibit open displays of emotion (crying, exuberance, and depression, for example) and to avoid any sign of passivity. These behaviors are considered inappropriate to a masculine ego ideal. For the girl, inhibition of intense intellectual efforts, especially in mathematics and the sciences, can be a consequence of anxiety over violating sex role standards.

This discussion of symptoms in the school-age child has suggested the value of discussing symptoms according to their causes rather than manifest similarities in form. Thus, failure in school can be the product of strong hostility to a parent or a self-punitive act resulting from guilt over masturbation. A nightmare can stem from guilt over hostile feelings toward a sibling or anxiety over sexual fantasies about a parent.

External Versus Internal Symptoms

There is, however, a clustering of symptoms that seems to divide those symptoms that are direct, undisguised violations of society's standards from those that are characterized by extreme inhibition, anxiety, and guilt (Achenbach, 1966). Psychologists have examined the symptoms children possess when they are referred to a clinic or hospital for psychiatric or psychological care. There is a strong tendency for symptoms such as disobedience, stealing, lying, fighting, cruelty, destructiveness, vandalism, and setting fires to appear together in one cluster—usually called an externalizing or acting-out cluster. There is a second cluster, at the opposite pole, that consists of symptoms like phobias, fears, stomach aches, social withdrawal, obsessions, shyness, and insomnia; this cluster is usually called internalized guilt.

The symptoms in the externalizing cluster seem to reflect minimal anxiety over social prohibitions; the symptoms in the second cluster seem to reflect excessive anxiety. Children with internalized symptoms were found to be living more frequently with both natural parents, who had fewer overt social problems than the parents of children with externalized symptoms. Furthermore, the parents of internalizers were more involved with and less resentful of their children. The internalizers had fewer previous social problems and significantly better school performance than the externalizers. It is assumed that a stable family organization is more likely to produce guilt than a disorganized, unstable family in which parent-child relationships are not close and affectionate.

The School Situation

For most children, school entrance marks the first continuous separation from their mothers for a large part of the day. In school the 6-year-old is presented with a new adult whom he must obey and whose acceptance he is encouraged to court. This adult requires the child to learn and practice responses that are not continually pleasant or exciting.

The school's major responsibilities are to facilitate the development of a motive to be intellectually competent and the development of specific intellectual skills, including the ability to persevere in problem solving and to formulate long-range goals. The school also provides the child with special opportunities to establish relationships with his peers. Recently educators have decided that improving the quality of peer relationships is indeed part of the pedagogical enterprise.

THE ROLE OF THE TEACHER

In almost every instance the child's first teacher is a woman who praises what she regards as good behavior, punishes what she regards as bad, and nurtures the child when he is anxious. The teacher's appearance, attitudes, and actions are usually so similar to those of the child's mother, especially if teacher and mother are from the same social class, that it is not surprising that many children react to the teacher as though she were a substitute mother. The motives, attitudes, fears, and behaviors that the child has developed in relation to his own mother often generalize to the teacher. Since mothers are generally viewed by young children as more nurturant and less fearsome than fathers, there is some advantage in having a woman as the child's first adult contact in school.

However, there would be advantages for boys if primary grade teachers were men. As we have seen, the typical 6-year-old boy is in the process of establishing an identification with his father and other male role models; the boy's attempt to increase similarity to adult males predisposes him to rebel against the mother and other female figures. In addition, most boys regard the father as the dominant figure in the household and are indoctrinated by such media as television to deemphasize the power and competence of adult females. The fact that academic retardation and conduct problems are more frequent among boys than girls in the first 5 years of school suggests that boys enter school with greater resistance to it and are less anxious than girls over potential rejection by the female teacher for misconduct.

If elementary grade school teachers were men, the boys might resist school less, be more concerned with acceptance by the teacher, and be more likely to identify with him. The children would also be more likely to associate the act of acquiring knowledge with masculinity (see Chapter 27, page 490). The degree of masculinity or femininity associated with any one activity is primarily a function of the sex of the person who normally performs the behavior. Thus, cooking, sewing, and caring for children are feminine; repairing fences, mowing the lawn, and fishing are masculine. Since elementary school classes are usually conducted by women, children tend to view schoolwork as more closely related to femininity than to masculinity and, therefore, as more appropriate for girls than for boys (Kagan, 1964). This attitude increases the girls' motivation to master reading and spelling but inhibits deep involvement for some boys.

SOCIAL CLASS DIFFERENCES IN SCHOOL PERFORMANCE

It is an established fact that children of middle-class, well-educated parents are more highly motivated and perform better in the early years of school than do children of lower-class, poorly educated parents. The reasons for this social class difference in performance are not puzzling. School success is more important in maintaining social class membership for those in the middle class than for those in the lower class. The middle-class child recognizes that most vocations to which he might aspire depend heavily on the acquisition of academic skills. Moreover, middle-class parents actively encourage their children to work hard in school and to develop an interest in intellectual hobbies in the home. The child of a doctor, lawyer, or architect has the opportunity to watch his father read books and journals and display a personal interest in intellectual problems. Middle-class parents, then, are identification models who not only reward mastery of intellectual tasks but also display an active involvement in intellectual mastery, which indicates to the child this goal is valued. In addition, in the United States and Europe the teacher's values are typically middle class in content, for she rewards neatness, obedience, cooperation, and cleanliness and she punishes waste, lack of responsibility, lying, aggressiveness, and idiosyncratic behaviors.

The child's motivation for scholastic success can also be strengthened or reduced according to the values of his peers. In many middle-class groups scholastic success is highly valued by the children, and the best students are the most popular children. Among lower-class and particularly slum children scholastic achievement is of less value, and the possibility of peer acceptance is not enhanced by school success.

Davis (1948) pointed out that the middle-class child learns a socially adaptive fear of receiving poor grades in school, being aggressive toward the teacher, fighting, cursing, and having early sex relations. The slum child learns to fear quite different social acts. His peer group teaches him to have a fear of being taken in by the teacher. To study homework is literally a disgrace, and instead of boasting of good marks in school one conceals them.

The lower-class child typically has a lower intelligence test score than the middle-class child (15 to 20 points difference). This fact can be used as a focus for summarizing the differences in experiences with family and peers that lead the lower-class child to get poorer grades in school, drop out of school earlier, and have lower expectancies of success on intellectual problems. Because the intelligence test score is a fairly sensitive index of a child's motivation for mastery of intellectual skills, its correlates help to explain the forces that produce the dramatic class differences in school performance. Let us begin by discussing the concept of intelligence.

Intelligence and the Intelligence Test

The concept of intelligence and the intelligence test have gained more acceptance and allegiance from Americans than any other psychological trait or dimension. The typical American parent is anxiously concerned about his child's intelligence test score—the I.Q.—and attributes more value to a high I.Q. score than to any other individual characteristic. How can we explain this zealous, often fanatical, belief in the power and fundamental character of the I.Q.?

WHAT IS I.Q.?

Let us first consider the mystique of the I.Q. Most people believe that a person's intelligence is inherited, that the I.Q. does not change very much over the course of a lifetime, that psychologists can measure the I.Q. in the first year of life, and that high I.Q. is associated with a large financial income, mental health, and a generally happy life. These assumptions are not uniformly true, and there is a great deal of misunderstanding about the meaning of intelligence both among the public and among psychologists.

At a general level, intelligence may be defined as the ability to benefit from experience and is related to the ease with which a person learns a new idea or response. Since most children are capable of learning something as a result of experience, the I.Q. has come to mean the capacity or limit to which a person might profit from experience. It has been assumed that a child has a learning ceiling, a point above which he will not be able to acquire more information or profit from more experience, and that this ceiling is governed by his heredity. Except for children with known brain damage or obvious biological defects, there is no definitive evidence available to support this assumption. The intelligence test contains few questions that require the child to learn any new responses or ideas. Most questions on the test measure a knowledge or skill that the child already possesses. The I.Q. test, therefore, does not evaluate the essential component of the popular conception of "intelligence."

I.Q. AND SCHOOL PERFORMANCE

The I.Q. test was initially constructed to solve a practical problem. Because the public schools in Paris were overcrowded at the turn of the century, the city fathers decided that they needed some useful way to determine which children would benefit most from public school. They commissioned a psychologist, Alfred Binet, to construct a fair test that would be a sensitive predictor of the child's ability to profit from academic instruction in the public schools. Thus, the test was constructed with a specific goal in mind: to predict the child's success in school. This goal was to a large extent accomplished, and changes in that I.Q. test constructed more than half a century ago have been minimal; the test that clinical psychologists use today strongly resembles the earlier test.

It should be apparent by now, then, that the intelligence test that gives rise to the I.Q. is a good measure of what a child knows and of what he has taken from his culture, and it is a moderately good predictor of how well the child will do in school. The child with high standards for intellectual mastery and a strong motivation to improve the quality of his intellectual skills is likely to have a higher I.Q. score than the child who has low standards and is not highly motivated. The strongly motivated child is also likely to show important increases in his I.Q. score during the early years of school, for intense motivation has a beneficial effect on I.Q. test performance. Since middle-class children are more consistently encouraged than lower-class children to learn and master reading, spelling, arithmetic, and writing, it is not surprising that a child's intelligence test score, social class, and school grades are all positively related to one another. Moreover, the personality traits associated with academic success, such as persistence, nonaggression, and responsible behavior, are similar to the traits associated with a high I.Q. and with increases in I.Q. That is, children who show large increases in I.Q. during the early school years tend to work hard in school, obtain good grades, and appear to care about intellectual mastery. Thus, one can use the amount of increase in I.Q. as a rough index of the child's motivation to master academic skills.

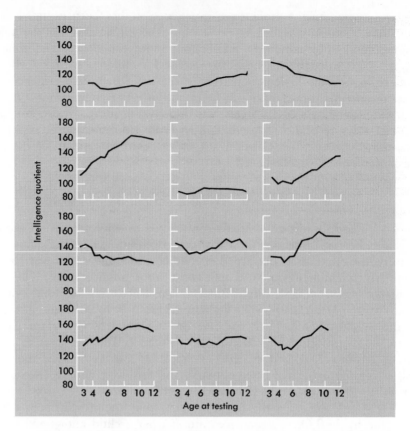

Figure 29-1   Twelve cases illustrating changes in I.Q. (Adapted from Sontag, Baker, & Nelson, 1958)

RESEARCH ON I.Q. LEVEL AND I.Q. CHANGE

The correlation between a child's I.Q. at age 6 and at age 10 approximates .70, suggesting that although the later I.Q. can be predicted fairly well from the earlier one, some children are capable of major changes in intelligence test scores between the first and the fifth grades. Investigations at the Fels Research Institute have revealed several interesting correlates of an increase in I.Q. (Sontag, Baker, & Nelson, 1958). The subjects were 140 boys and girls for whom annual intelligence test scores and behavioral observations were available from the preschool years through early adolescence. Some children's scores remained stable, others decreased, and still others increased (see Figure 29-1). Twice as many boys as girls showed major increases in I.Q.; the I.Q. scores of girls were more likely to drop. The children whose I.Q.'s increased were more independent, competitive, and verbally aggressive than those whose I.Q.'s decreased, but there was little relation between I.Q. increase and the degree of affiliative behavior with peers.

The child's I.Q. score is in part a function of his desire to master and improve his problem-solving skills, and this motive, in turn, is related to the degree of parental encouragement the child receives and the availability of appropriate parental models. Some mothers were rated with respect to the degree to which they encouraged their children to talk and walk during the first 3 years of life (Kagan & Moss, 1962). There was a positive relation, among girls, between maternal concern with the child's early progress and the amount of I.Q. increase the girl showed during the ages 6 to 10. The correlation for boys was also positive, but it was lower. This sex difference can be attributed to two factors. First, the girl is more likely to identify with the mother and is therefore more highly motivated to adopt the mother's values. Second, it is sometimes assumed that the motive to retain the mother's affection is more important for the girl than for the boy. A mother's pressure for the child to improve his or her intellectual skills in return for continued parental acceptance will be more effective with the girl than the boy. Since college-educated mothers are more likely to urge intellectual mastery than are mothers who never attended college, we would expect a higher association between level of maternal education and the child's intellectual level for girls than for boys. This expectation is verified: A mother's education is a better predictor of girls' than of boys' I.Q. scores at 3, 6, and 10 years of age (Kagan & Moss, 1959).

Components
of Intellectual Activity

Intellectual performance is composed of a complex set of factors: elemental cognitive units, cognitive processes, motives, standards, expectancies, and sources of anxiety. Examination of these factors will facilitate our understanding of the differences among children in quality of performance on intellectual problems.

ELEMENTAL COGNITIVE UNITS

A primary requisite for the learning of new information, for problem solving, or just for the enjoyment of playful thought is a previously acquired set of cognitive units. These units consist primarily of images, symbols (words and numbers), concepts, and rules. The child must have mental images of past experiences and he must have a vocabulary to understand speech and the written word and to report orally what he is thinking. The child must also learn certain rules that represent combinations of concepts. He should know by age 10, for instance, that 2×3 is 6 and $2 + 3$ is 5. He should know by age 12 that cities generally develop where means of transportation are plentiful. Later, he should learn that the area of a circle is πr^2 and that acts considered illegal at one time in history may be regarded as appropriate 100 years later. Some of these rules, like the πr^2 formula, are formal and always yield the same answer. But rules may also be informal and not consistently yield the same answer—for example, angels are usually white, men are usually taller than women, and cities generally develop where transportation is available.

The elemental cognitive units the child possesses are the basic tools with which he interprets the world and does mental work. He is able to understand only the information that either matches or is slightly in advance of his own sets of images, symbols, and rules. If a new idea, equation, or word does not have some connection with his available cognitive units, he will learn very little. A primary cause for the dramatic differences in quality of thinking among preschool children is the basic differences among the children in richness of symbol and rule resources. Although this richness continues to be important, motivational factors also contribute to differences in quality of cognitive performance during childhood and early adolescence.

Most tests of intellectual aptitude and achievement simultaneously assess knowledge of images, symbols, concepts, and rules. Since these tests confound all four factors, they cannot determine the specific deficit that might have led the child to make a mistake. For example, a typical problem in a sixth grade arithmetic book reads: "The circumference of a lake is 200 miles. What is the distance a swimmer must swim from any point on the shore to the exact center of the lake?" The child who fails to obtain the correct answer to this problem may have done so because he did not know the meaning of the word "circumference." Or he may have failed because he did not know the rule that the circumference equals $2\pi r$. Or perhaps he knew neither the concept nor the rule. It is important that the exact cognitive deficit be diagnosed if the teacher is to help the child most effectively.

WAYS OF DECODING EXPERIENCE
AND PROCESSING INFORMATION

Children label and interpret experience differently. These differences are dramatic for children of different ages, and they may also be observed in less dramatic fashion among children of the same age. Let us consider, first, some of the differences that are products of development.

**Age Differences
in Decoding
and Processing** The child naturally and spontaneously decodes and interprets information that is presented to him, but children of 1, 3, 5, and 10 years perform these processes in slightly different ways. How are these differences to be explained? One might decide that they are caused by the nature of the structural units that will do the decoding. We know, for instance, that a bee sees a flower much differently than a hummingbird

does, because the nature of their receptors is different: The bee has ommatidia whereas the bird has a retina. The difference in the structure of the receptors could explain why the final decoded message to the nervous system is different. But since infant, child, and adolescent all have the same receptor, it is necessary to look further to determine why the infant and the older child decode an identical stimulus in different ways. The answer lies in the cognitive units that perform the interpretation. These units might be described as local currency into which the new coin of experience is converted.

In the language of computers, the units are the program code. There are four basic translation codes: images, symbols, concepts, and rules. In general, the infant and the young child translate experience into images; the older child translates it into words, concepts, and rules. For example, consider this figure: ⊃ . A 2-year-old is likely to code this figure as an image, for he has no other way to interpret it and this is his natural bent. It is likely that the image may be distorted a bit and actually be registered in his thinking as a ⊃ or even a ▭. The 6-year-old is likely to code it verbally: "It looks like a finger" or "It looks like a pencil." If asked to reproduce it or to select the figure from a list of similar ones, he might make an error that would reveal that he perceived it more like a finger or a pencil. He might draw it as ⊃ or ⟩ . The 6-year-old thus assimilates the original figure to his language label. The college freshman might label the figure a parabola, and if he were a math major he might even code it as $y = x^2$—the generalized equation for a parabola.

The point is not that one of these codes is better or poorer than another, but rather that each one is different. The image is the most faithful representation of the original stimulus; the mathematical formula $(y = x^2)$ is the least faithful, for it says nothing about the orientation of the figure, its size or color, the materials out of which it was made, the paper upon which it was drawn, or whether the lines were dotted or solid. The mathematical formula merely tells us the general shape of the line. However, the formula has tremendous power and flexibility, because it can describe the shape, *regardless* of its color, size, or materials. In general, the more symbolic the code is, the more power it has to describe a variety of events that have a common form but the less faithful it is to the original event. A good example of this generalization is the natural law that the momentum of an object equals its mass times its velocity. This law is highly general and therefore powerful, but it is minimally faithful to the image of what an observer might see watching a collision between a new Ford convertible and an old Chrysler on Route 1 outside of Baltimore on a rainy day.

This principle of different codes for different ages aids our understanding of cognitive development. In general, at 2 years of age a child begins to shift from images to symbols, and at 5 he begins to incorporate concepts and rules into his translation system.

Although words lend an efficiency and public communicability to experience that is not characteristic of images, they provide only one basis for understanding. It is important that the child not become overly dependent upon one class of units. Many educators have begun to use Cuisenaire rods with first grade children to teach the fundamentals of arithmetic and numeration. The rods are wooden sticks of different lengths and colors. The number 1 is represented by a colored stick one unit long; number 2 is represented by a stick of a different color that is twice as long as the stick for unit 1; and so on. The advantage of this method of teaching is that it gives the young child a concrete introduction to the concept of number as a magnitude estimator. If the mental units given the child for decoding numbers are rods of different lengths and colors, the child will quickly develop a strong tendency to translate all numbers and number problems into these rods, which have become his mental currency. But consider how troublesome and disadvantageous this system will be when long division or multiplication problems are confronted. The young child must be weaned from the Cuisenaire representation of numbers before he becomes addicted to it and is unable to shift to a new translation system.

The mind is vulnerable to such addiction to codes and, consequently, to rigidity in translation systems. If the child overlearns one method of

TRAINING   TEST

Figure 29-2 *Pairs of stimuli that children had to associate in an experiment on overlearning.* (From Gollin, 1966)

understanding or decoding a problem, it is that much more difficult for him to see the problem in a different perspective. In a recent experiment (Gollin, 1966) children had to learn to guess the object that was represented by a set of fractionated lines (see Figure 29-2). Some children were given only a few trials in which both the entire object and its fractionated representation were paired; other children were given many trials. When the children were tested later, the quality of their performance depended on whether the order of presentation of the original items remained the same or was changed. If the order was the same, the children who had many trials performed better; but if the order was changed, the children with fewer trials did better, presumably because they had not overlearned a particular order and were still flexible.

Intellectual development is, in part, the learning of codes for events. Since it is helpful for the child and adult to be able to shift codes for different events and different problems, he must be given practice with diverse ways to decode his experiences.

Different Strategies of Decoding and Processing

All children do not label or decode experience in the same way; they have different strategies for processing stimuli and for selecting ideas for thought. Some children typically are global as they scan a visual stimulus; others are more detailed and analytic. The analytic child would see the trees where the global child would see the forest. Both types of strategy are important; depending on the specific problem the child is facing, one strategy may be more appropriate than the other.

The reflective versus the impulsive child. One difference in the way information is processed concerns the child's tempo of responding—the speed with which he decides on the correct label for an object or the correct formula for a problem. Some children decide quickly and impulsively; those who are more reflective brood for a long time before deciding on a solution. A means of measuring a child's tendency to be reflective or impulsive is illustrated in Figure 29-3. In this test the child is shown a card with figures, such as the teddy bears or the trees. The child must select the one figure (out of six) that is exactly like the single figure in the first row. The impulsive children point to one of the figures in less than 10 seconds, but they are often incorrect. The reflective children wait 30 seconds or so before deciding the answer and are usually correct.

Let us consider how this dimension of reflection and impulsivity might apply to the problem involving the circumference of the lake mentioned earlier. Imagine two children—one reflective and one impulsive—who are given the circumference problem; each is not sure whether the formula for the circumference of a circle is $2\pi r$ or πr^2. The impulsive child typically would quickly select one formula without giving the matter much consideration. The odds are 50-50 that he would select the correct rule. The reflective child would pause and evaluate the differential validity of each of these formulae. During this pause, the reflective child might remember that the area of a square involves the square of a side and conclude that πr^2 must apply to the area of a circle. Thus, he would conclude by process of elimination that $2\pi r$, not πr^2, must be the correct formula for the circumference.

The tendency to be reflective or impulsive is an essential characteristic of the *evaluation* phases of the problem-solving process. Evaluation occurs at three points in the process of solving a problem. During the first phase, the child reads or listens to a problem and decodes the language of the problem. Some words may have double or ambiguous meanings. The reflective child pauses to evaluate his comprehension; the impulsive child is less likely to consider whether his classifications are correct. As a result, the impulsive child often misinterprets problems.

A second phase of evaluation occurs when the hypothesis is selected. Consider a typical arithmetic problem for a fourth grader. "Four children have 16 pennies. Each one wants to have the same number of pennies. How many does each get?" The 9-year-old child has learned a rote rule that you either add, subtract, multiply, or divide whenever you have two numbers. The child has two numbers, 4 and 16. What operation should he perform? The impulsive child may quickly decide that adding 4 and 16 is the correct rule to use and decide on an answer of 20. The reflective child pauses to consider the validity of each rule for this problem.

A final opportunity for evaluation occurs when the child has to report his solution to someone, either by speaking it aloud or by writing it down.

Figure 29-3   Examples from Matching Familiar Figures Test for reflection-impulsivity. (From Kagan, Pearson, & Welch, 1966)

The impulsive child is less likely than the reflective child to pause at this point to consider the plausibility of his answer, which claims that each child gets more than the total number of pennies. A last check for validity would give him a chance to rethink the problem and correct his error.

Since the tendency to be reflective or impulsive in intellectual tasks is stable over time and applies to a variety of tasks, we should ask: Why is a child reflective or impulsive? It appears that the reflective child is afraid of making a mistake. His unusually high anxiety over making an error causes him to brood a long time before acting. The impulsive child cares less about error and so imposes weaker inhibitions upon action.

The very young child (3 through 8) tends to generalize the tendency to be impulsive or reflective across different areas of functioning. However, as the child matures and has a chance to conquer specific fears, he is able to distinguish among different sources of anxiety. Thus, many children who are reflective on tests measuring intellectual skills may not be reflective on the athletic field because they have minimal anxiety over error in the latter situation. Similarly, a child who is reflective in social situations because he has high anxiety over making a mistake may not be anxious or reflective in schoolwork. There is, therefore, less generalization of a reflective tendency across varied areas of functioning in the older adolescent and the young adult.

Changing a child's tempo. Although the tendency to be impulsive or reflective when faced with a problem-solving situation is often a basic attribute of the child's personality, it is not so firmly entrenched that it cannot be changed to some degree. It is possible to make an impulsive child more reflective either through direct training or through exposure to people who have a different tempo. In one investigation (Kagan, Pearson, & Welch, 1966) a group of impulsive first grade children were instructed to think about their answer while they were solving a problem and to inhibit the first response that occurred to them. Each child was told that he could not offer an answer until 15 seconds had passed, at which time the examiner told him he could give the answer if he wished. After only 2 hours of such training, distributed over several days, the impulsive children showed a spontaneous tendency to be more reflective when they were faced with problems similar to those shown in Figure 29-3.

Another study demonstrates the importance of exposure to the tempo of the teacher (Yondo & Kagan, 1968). A group of first grade teachers were tested to determine if they tended to be reflective or impulsive; some of the children in their classes were also tested in the beginning and at the end of the first year in school. The children who spent their first year with a reflective teacher were more reflective in June than in September, whereas the children who were taught by an impulsive teacher proved to be more impulsive.

MOTIVES, EXPECTATIONS, AND SOURCES OF ANXIETY

A trio of processes that exert considerable influence over the quality of the child's intellectual performance concerns the *motives* that prompt him to acquire new segments of knowledge and to utilize those he has obtained, his *expectancy of success,* and the *anxiety-based inhibitions* that oppose new learning and effective performance.

Motives The motives that impel a child to memorize the Gettysburg Address or to work at a difficult mathematics problem are similar to the motives that impel most of his behavior. Let us examine the goals of a typical 10-year-old that might facilitate learning academic skills:

1. Affection and praise from significant adults and peers; signs from people he values indicating that he is positively regarded by parents, teachers, peers.

2. The belief that he is becoming more similar to desirable adult models.

3. Support for the belief that he is competent (congruence with a standard for mastery—the effectance motivation).

4. Responses from peers and adults signifying that he is "superior" on some dimension (social recognition).

5. Power over peers.

6. Support for the belief that he is behaving in congruence with sex-typed values (sex role identity).

If the child believes that mastery of academic subject matter will increase the likelihood of gratifying one or more of these motives, he will work hard at learning these academic skills. Some children choose academic competence as a route to these goals; others choose other means of obtaining them. The major forces influencing the child's choice are (1) the degree to which the child's parents value academic skills and use parental acceptance to motivate the child, (2) the degree to which the models the child has chosen for identification display an active interest in intellectual mastery, and (3) the child's expectation of success in intellectual work.

**Expectation
of Success** As indicated in Chapter 28, the child wishes to avoid failure at all costs. The strength of his motive to master academic skills is governed in large measure by the degree to which he expects he will be successful. If the child believes he will not be able to learn geometry, he will probably become less motivated to work at this goal. The typical high school dropout says that he is bored with school and has no desire to attend classes; in most instances, this apparently

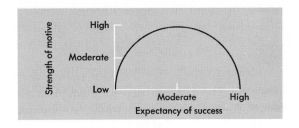

Figure 29-4   Relation of motive strength to expectancy of success.

low motivation is the end result of a long succession of school failures that led to the feeling he could not learn effectively. The low expectation of success produced the minimal level of motivation.

An unusually high expectation of success, however, often has a similar effect on motivation. A student who believes he will have no trouble mastering algebra frequently is not optimally motivated in class. He does not view the work as challenging. It is not uncommon for college students to avoid subjects that they are intrinsically interested in because they consider the subject matter too easy to master. This kind of student has a strong motive to prove that he is intellectually competent; he feels he cannot prove this to himself by studying easy subjects.

It appears that when a person is slightly unsure of his ability to learn something, his motivation is highest. In more formal terms, when expectancy of success is moderate, motivation is highest. Figure 29-4 illustrates the relation between the strength of the motive and the expectancy of gratifying that motive. This is a curvilinear relation, in which the highest value of the motive dimension is correlated with a moderate value of the expectancy of success dimension.

If the motive remains low for a long period of time—because of either too high or too low an expectancy of success (or for other reasons)—the person may stop thinking about the goal, and the intensity of the motive will be reduced.

Sources of Anxiety and Conflict

Expectancy of failure is one source of anxiety that can block investment of effort in intellectual work. Various kinds of conflict constitute other sources of anxiety. For example, if a child considers school success to be in conflict with sex role standards, his efforts will be low. A second conflict concerns the child's hostility toward his parents. If the child perceives that his parents value intellectual mastery but he happens to feel strong resentment toward them, an excellent way of gratifying this hostility is to fail to perform in the way the parents wish, causing them to display obvious signs of anxiety and upset.

A third conflict, less common than the other two, is caused by anxiety over excessive competitiveness. In our rank-order culture the child who wishes to be at the top of his class usually entertains competitive and hostile wishes toward his classroom rivals. If the child feels that these hostile wishes violate his standards, he may become anxious and inhibit intense effort.

A fourth conflict involves anxiety over peer rejection. In many communities the child's friends promote academic mediocrity, and they are likely to reject the child who too obviously excels in school. The taunt "teacher's pet" is common among young children. The child who wants to be accepted by his friends and who is anxious about potential rejection may inhibit effort at academic mastery in order to retain peer acceptance.

A final conflict that provokes anxiety concerns the child's assumption of a passive role vis-à-vis the teacher. In the primary grades the child is supposed to do what the teacher says and conform to her wishes. However, since most boys of this age are in the midst of developing an assertive identification with masculine role models, a dominant posture with women becomes important. Anxiety over assuming a passive role, which violates this standard, can block involvement in schoolwork.

How Learning Takes Place

Some of the factors that facilitate or retard efficient learning of new intellectual skills and the use of new knowledge in problem solving have been described above. But *how* does a motive for approval, for example, make the learning of a speech more likely; how does fear of failure make learning less likely? It is not sufficient to say that a motive helps learning unless it can be explained how it does so. For example, man thought that the moon affected the tides long before he suggested that the mechanism might be gravitational force between moon and earth. In a similar fashion, psychologists today are searching for the psychological concepts—analogous to "gravitational force"—that will explain how motives, expectations, and anxiety influence ease of learning and quality of performance. This explanation of the process of learning is a central problem in psychology.

CONTIGUITY AND REINFORCEMENT

There has been a long-standing debate between two schools of thought regarding the conditions necessary to produce learning. The simpler position states that if two stimuli or events occur close together in time or space, learning will occur, and that is all that is required. This approximate simultaneity of two events is called *contiguity*. But a majority of psychologists feel that contiguity alone is not enough. For instance, we look at the dial on a telephone every day, but despite hundreds or thousands of exposures to the pairing of letters and numbers, most of us have not yet learned what letters and numbers are in the first, second, and third holes on the dial. We do not learn an association between every single pair of stimuli that we experience. Another ingredient is needed that might catalyze learning when contiguity exists. The most widely accepted point of view is that learning takes place when there is contiguity between two events, accompanied by a *reinforcement*. (See Part I, Chapter 3.)

It would be convenient if reinforcement were unitary and could be easily defined. Unfortunately, "reinforcement" is a term applied to a wide variety of events that at a manifest level have little in common. Consider the following examples.

When a dog learns to flex his paw to a tone through pairing the tone with electric shock to his paw, the shock is the reinforcement.

When a rat learns to press a bar to get food, the food is the reinforcement.

When a child learns to subtract two numbers and is rewarded by his teacher saying "Good boy," the phrase "good boy" is the reinforcement.

When a child learns to stay out of the cookie jar because his mother raps him on the fingers, the rap on the fingers is the reinforcement.

A shock, food, praise, and a rap on the fingers are all called reinforcements. Although they seem to have little in common among themselves, they each promote and facilitate learning. Rewards (desirable goals) are considered to function as positive reinforcers, and punishments (aversive stimuli) are regarded as negative reinforcers. Some argue that the common attribute of reinforcements is a function not of what they are but of their effect on the organism.

It is suggested that one reason learning is helped by reinforcements is that some of the reinforcing events act to attract the *attention* of the organism and focus it on the stimuli surrounding the "reinforcement" and on any response the organism made in the recent past. The shock to the paw forces the dog to attend to the tone and his paw; the food pellet attracts the rat's attention to the bar; the adult's praise focuses the child's attention on the adult and the task. The equation "contiguity + reinforcement = learning" might turn out to be "contiguity + attention to relevant stimuli = learning."

Any event that is called a positive reinforcement often has the additional characteristic of representing a desirable goal. Food, praise, and affection are desirable events. In this way the concept of reinforcement becomes intimately related to the concept of motivation: Reinforcements are most effective in producing learning if the child is motivated to obtain the goal that is inherent in the reinforcement. Furthermore, when the child is motivated to obtain something he wants, he pays more attention to the learning situation.

THE ROLE OF ATTENTION

The demonstrated effect of motives and anxieties on ease and efficiency of learning is mediated, in part, by attention—increased atten-

Figure 29-5 A teaching machine. (From Skinner, 1961)

tion to a task if the child feels his motive will be gratified, decreased attention if he is preoccupied with a motive or source of anxiety that is irrelevant to or conflicts with the task.

If the child has a strong need for adult approval and believes he can obtain this goal by learning his multiplication tables, then he will focus more attention on the learning. If a girl is afraid she will not be meeting her sex role standards if she does too well in geometry, her attention to the task will be decreased accordingly. Intense anxiety or fatigue makes learning difficult, because attention becomes focused on the internal sensations associated with the anxiety or fatigue. It is difficult to attend with equal effectiveness at the same time to several different kinds of stimulation.

Attention plays a part in the effectiveness of the teaching machine, a new device being used increasingly in the elementary school curriculum (see Figure 29-5). This machine presents the child with questions to which he must respond. If he is correct, the machine tells him so at once and allows him to proceed to the next phase of the learning. If he is incorrect, he is also told at once and is drilled again on that phase of the problem. Apparently the novelty of the machine attracts the child's attention and increases his involvement in the whole learning situation, enabling him to master the material more rapidly.

Attention appears to be a process central to all learning. Future research may reveal precisely how the degree of attention to a task explains the effect that motives and conflicts have on how new skills and ideas are learned. Unfortunately, we do not now have attention meters that can furnish us with an instant measure of how much attention the child is devoting to a particular task or set of stimuli, and it is usually difficult to infer the attention value from his overt behavior. Daydreaming, for instance, can be mistaken for thoughtful concentration. Perhaps someday each school desk will be equipped with an attention meter that will enable the teacher to monitor through a machine on her desk the level of attention of each of her pupils; this would give her a rational basis for encouraging Johnny to pay more attention to his work.

*Busy with the ache of their own growing-pains, his brothers
and sisters had little time for him: he was almost six years younger
than Luke, the youngest of them, but they exerted over him the
occasional small cruelties, petty tormentings by elder children
of a younger, interested and excited by the brief screaming in-
sanity of his temper, when, goaded and taunted from some deep
dream, he would seize a carving knife and pursue them, or batter
his head against the walls.*

*They felt that he was "queer"—the other boys preached the
smug cowardice of the child-herd, defending themselves, when
their persecutions were discovered, by saying they would make
a "real boy" of him. But there grew up in him a deep affection
for Ben who stalked occasionally and softly through the house,
guarding even then with scowling eyes, and surly speech, the
secret life. Ben was a stranger: some deep instinct drew him to
his child-brother, a portion of his small earnings as a paper
carrier he spent in gifts and amusement for Eugene, admonishing
him sullenly, cuffing him occasionally, but defending him before
the others.*

THOMAS WOLFE . Look Homeward Angel

CHAPTER 30
PEER
AND SIBLING
INFLUENCES

T he child's parents constitute the most important social influence on his psychological development during the first 5 years of life. But in the next 5 years interactions with peers and siblings become critical factors in molding his personality. This chapter considers how these influences affect the expectancies, motives, conflicts, anxieties, and standards of the young child.

The Peer Group

The child typically wants acceptance from his peers, particularly those of the same age and sex as himself. This desire motivates him to adopt the standards of the peer group, which are so strong they often prevail over conflicting standards of parents and teachers. There are several reasons for the enormous influence of peers.

WHY IS THE PEER GROUP INFLUENTIAL?

First, the peer group fosters rebellion against the socialization demands of the adult community. The peers promote discussion of sexuality and some sexual exploration, and they give license for aggressive play and venting of hostility. With peers the child feels safe discussing and expressing prohibitive actions. Friends function as mutual psychotherapists for one another; a child who suffers intense anxiety over his resentment toward his parents may feel less guilt when he hears that his friends also experience strong hostility toward their families.

A second reason the peer group is so influential is that it can communicate its evaluation of the child—positive or negative—by giving or withholding group acceptance. Evaluation by parents functions in the same manner, but the child seems to prefer the group's positive evaluation and constant signs of acceptance. Why is parental acceptance insufficient? The child trusts the group's evaluation and often mistrusts that of adults. The child may feel that parents and teachers are either overly accepting of his undesirable qualities or overly critical of him and thus are not capable of an accurate evaluation of his attributes. The child behaves as if he believed in the greater validity and inherent wisdom of peer evaluation.

The child needs other children his age to evaluate his degree of competence at diverse skills and his attractiveness to others. The typical 10-year-old does not have absolute measuring rods to help him evaluate how bright, handsome, wise, honest, capable, or likeable he is. There are no absolute definitions for these qualities as there are for height, weight, or skin color. The child naturally and spontaneously uses his immediate peer group as the reference for the qualities he wants to measure. His evaluation is partially dependent on the size and psychological quality of the reference group and is thus highly relative. Specifically, the larger the peer group, the less likely will the child be to conclude that he is high in the rank order and therefore the less likely will he be to decide that he is unusually smart, handsome, or capable of leadership.

Let us consider an example of how this principle works. Astronauts are chosen partly for their self-confidence and capacity to tolerate stress. Although almost half our population lives in three large urban areas, the vast majority of the astronaut candidates grew up in rural or semiurban areas. One interpretation of this fact is that these astronauts were able to perceive themselves in childhood as more skilled, cool-headed, and inventive than most of their peers because they grew up in small towns where few boys were as talented as they. If one of these astronauts had grown up in Chicago, for example, he would have encountered many boys as brilliant as or more brilliant than he, and he might not have developed the belief that he was exceptional. The child's evaluation of his intelligence is less a function of his absolute I.Q. than of his perceived rank relative to his peers.

To illustrate this point, imagine two boys, Jack and Bill, each with identical I.Q. scores of 130 and identical profiles on the best standardized tests of mental ability. But Jack lives in a small town with a population of 2000, attends a fifth grade class of 25 children, and interacts with a group of 10 boys his own age. Bill lives in a city of one million and attends one of 100 fifth grade classes with an immediate peer reference group of perhaps 200. Jack is likely to perceive himself to be the brightest in his immediate peer group; Bill may perceive himself to be only near the top of his group. Jack's expectancy of success with intellectual tasks should be greater than Bill's, and his behavior in the face of difficult problems should reflect less anxiety over possible failure.

It is important to emphasize the critical function of the peer group in the self-evaluation process. The child implicitly recognizes his dependence on peers for this evaluation and realizes he cannot obtain it from adults. This dependence is one reason that peer acceptance is courted and peer rejection is feared with such intensity.

A third factor in peer group influence is the provision of role models for identification. Some peers are respected and command power positions, so that the child is predisposed to adopt the leader's standards and behaviors in the hope of eventually commanding the same power and competencies.

Finally, peers teach the child a role to play in a group. Unlike the typical small family with two adults and two or three children of different ages and sexes, the same-sex peer group has no obvious differentiation by age and sex. But it is natural for any members of a group to organize and to differentiate. The differentiation in the peer group involves assignation of different roles to various members. Three roles that seem to be essential to the group are the leader, the leader's closest advisor, and the scapegoat. Other roles, which may or may not be present, are the intellectual, the clown, the rebel, the athlete, and the "ladies' man." The children who are cast in these roles take them seriously and behave in a manner dictated by the role given to them. One reason for adopting the behavior appropriate to the role is that the group gives acceptance and even distinction to the child who plays the role properly. Thus, the child can derive some satisfaction from his behavior in the group.

In sum, the peer group acts as a psychotherapist, helps the child evaluate himself on critical attributes, provides him with role models with whom he may identify, and gives him a role to play. The peer group exerts major control over the child because it represents important resources that the preadolescent requires.

FACTORS AFFECTING PEER ACCEPTANCE

Since the peer group is critical to the child for self-evaluation, there are significant consequences that accrue to youngsters who are accepted or rejected by peers. It is important, therefore, to understand the factors that promote or militate against peer group acceptance. A popular way of measuring the degree of peer acceptance involves asking children to name the children in their class whom they like and do not like and to rate those children according to a list of specific attributes, such as friendly, smart, dominant.

Bonney (1943) used this technique to differentiate the personalities of popular and unpopular fourth grade children in three schools. In this study classmates and teachers rated the 20 most popular and the 20 least popular children on a battery of 20 variables. Popular children were rated much higher in socially aggressive and outgoing characteristics. These children manifested two personality syndromes: The first was represented by strong, positive, aggressive characteristics, including leadership, enthusiasm, and active participation in events. The second involved a cheerful disposition and a friendly attitude toward others.

There were, of course, sex differences in the traits that led to peer acceptability. Among first grade girls, popularity was associated with a docile temperament. In the fifth grade, however, physical attractiveness and friendliness were more influential in determining a girl's acceptability with her peers. Among first grade boys, physical prowess and daring were critical attributes, whereas fairness in play and leadership ability were the most important attributes among third grade boys. Although the characteristics of popularity vary with age, they follow closely the sex-typed standards for boys and girls.

The child's social class background is a major factor in determining his prestige among his peers. In socially mixed communities lower-class children are likely to have the poorest reputations, because these children have less command of the desirable resources that the wider cultural community values. There is some interaction between social class and sex-typed traits with respect to popularity. Lower-class boys respect two masculine types: the aggressive, belligerent boy and the outgoing, sociable boy who is not necessarily aggressive. The effeminate boy who is conforming, passive, and uninterested in masculine activities is always rejected by lower-class children. A lower-class boy who excels in schoolwork risks alienation from his peers. Lower-class girls are willing to accept both the verbally aggressive girl who shows a strong interest in boys and the friendly, pretty, and studious girl who is not necessarily a leader. A lower-class girl can be a good student without alienating her friends. Middle-class boys accept peers who are skilled in competitive games but are not blatantly aggressive. Friendliness and studiousness are also accepted. As in the lower class, the frightened, passive, and conforming boy is rejected. There is only one acceptable stereotype for middle-class girls—the attractive, friendly, and socially vivacious girl.

The child's status among his peers strongly affects the course of his socialization and contributes to his ability to exercise influence over others. One investigation team studied 8 groups of boys and 8 groups of girls, age 11 to 15, in a summer camp (Polansky, Lippitt, & Redl, 1950). The observers recorded all interactions that involved attempts to influence others either directly or indirectly. They also noted all instances of behavior contagion (spread of excitement) initiated by any child. Each child's influence in his group was assessed in terms of frequency of initiation of behavior contagion and successful direct attempts to influence others. Children who had high status were found to be aware of their position, to feel more secure and accepted by the group, and to be able to sway the behavior of others by both direct and indirect techniques.

DOMINANT VERSUS PASSIVE ORIENTATION WITH PEERS

The initial tendency to adopt a passive-submissive or an active-dominant approach to peers is a remarkably stable disposition from age 10 through adulthood, especially for females. The dominant child characteristically initiates social contacts with peers, suggests activities for the group, and resists pressure to conform to the demands of others. The passive child typically is quiet with peers and follows the suggestions of others.

This orientation, which is so obvious when one watches children, is determined by many interacting factors. An important one involves the degree of the child's identification with a dominant versus a passive parent. Another factor concerns the degree to which the child *expects* acceptance or rejection by his peers. If the child believes he possesses the attributes that peers value, such as attractive physical appearance, strength, physical skills, and verbal facility, he will expect acceptance.

A third determinant concerns the degree of parental restriction of the child's autonomous behavior—that is, the degree to which the parent punishes attempts at domination and rewards submissiveness. There is much evidence to support the hypothesis that a restrictive parent promotes the learning of passivity, whereas a permissive parent promotes a more active, dominant disposition in the child (Radke, 1946). A longitudinal study of children at the Fels Institute (Kagan & Moss, 1962) showed that maternal restrictiveness during the child's first years of life predicted high conformity and low dominance in the older child. This study also found that social passivity during the ages 6 to 14 predicted high social anxiety during early adulthood.

Finally, there may be biologically determined dispositions that promote a tendency toward passivity. The Fels study (Kagan & Moss, 1962) revealed that boys who were extremely passive during the first 2 to 3 years of life were more likely to be passive and dependent later in life with their girlfriends and wives than were boys rated as nonpassive. Moreover, the degree of passivity displayed by a child was moderately stable over the first 6 years of life. Thus accumulated evidence indicates that biological forces—as yet unspecified—may cause a child to be extremely passive when attacked or frustrated, but this idea remains to be validated.

The Stability of Passivity: A Case Study   An excerpt from the case history of one of the children in the Fels Institute study documents the continuity of social passivity.

S was the second-born child of a lower middle-class family. He usually showed distinct signs of fear when he came to Fels for a physical or mental examination, or for the nursery school sessions. When he came for his examination at 2 years of age, the following summary was written.

> S gave the appearance of being frightened at first. When taken downstairs for the physical examination following the mental test, S would not allow the doctor to take his hand to guide him. He was shy and remained very timid throughout the procedure. He cried when the examination began and cried at new items in the procedure. He was suggestible and responded to distraction. He recovered quickly from his tears, was attentive to the toys given him, and was interested in their construction. Although the mother was present during the mental test that preceded the physical exam, S was shy and apprehensive.

At 4 years of age S attended the Fels nursery school for the first time. His initial reactions to this new setting were characterized by timidity and caution. The following notes were written after the three-week period.

> This was S's first visit to the nursery school and probably his first time away from home for any length of time. S was very apprehensive and insecure during his first days. He cried a lot and stood about looking sad in the interim between his howls. Once at the school he stood about weeping or sobbing and followed the teacher around for comfort. For the first two weeks S made no attempts to get into any of the groups.

One year later, at 5 years of age, S again attended the nursery school for a three-week period. His behavior continued to reflect caution and apprehension.

> S was one of the gentlest creatures in the group. He seemed to be like a delicate plant in the vivid world of the nursery school, meekly and solemnly acquiescing to whatever other children or adults suggested. At times S would stand helplessly crying and shielding his face while he was pelted with snowballs. S spoke in an exceedingly low voice, barely above a whisper, and never really laughed outright or came near a shout. He would hang his head and edge off when any strange adult was present or give apprehensive glances toward the children in the other groups. He was slow to warm up to the materials and would look at them from a distance, gradually

finger them, and when the sanction for their use was established, he would then use them. During one experimental session, when he was taken from the room, he came back and saw the nursery school room deserted. He began to cry, but once I got him playing contentedly with me, he came up willingly again to the experimental room. He was not frightened as long as I was with him.

At 8 years of age S attended the Fels day camp.

S is still a shrinking violet, avoiding any situations where he might be hurt, by physical contact with others, hard objects, high places, etc. He seems to show a social diffidence and an unsureness. He was continually ignored or shoved around by the more energetic and outspoken children. In any close contact situation, such as a crowded car, S completely withdrew and became self-effacing.

When S was 10 years old, he was interviewed by a staff psychologist, who wrote the following summary.

S was very quiet and very cooperative during the physical examination and hardly said a word. He warmed up a little afterwards and talked in a friendly way but still without much spontaneity. He talked about school and had a bright smile when he mentioned his teacher, whom he likes very much. He prefers English and has a desire to become a school teacher. His general behavior during the interview was placid and rather feminine.

At 16 years of age S was again interviewed.

E: "What are some ways in which you would like to be different from the way you are now, some of the things you would change about yourself?"
S: "I'd like to be more forward, I mean, to be able to meet people and talk."
E: "Any other ways that you would like to change?"
S: "I'd like to feel like I could take on responsibilities, which I don't. I don't feel like—I don't feel self-confident. *That's it in a nutshell,* self-confidence."

S was 20 years old when he was seen for the adult interview. He was thin and slight of build, with a bony, pale face. He looked more like an adolescent than a young adult. He spoke in a very low, high-pitched voice, and he was uneasy and tense during the three interviews. He was restless and very eager to please and to cooperate with the interviewer. At the time of the interview he had completed several years of college. As he had indicated during preadolescence, he was still interested in becoming a teacher. He had made few friends at college, and he habitually expected rejection and aloofness from authority figures as well as peers. He was tense in his interactions with others, and he had intense feelings of personal inadequacy. Excerpts from the adult interview reveal his extreme social anxiety.

E: "Did you tend to be afraid of your boss on the job when he came around?"
S: "Yeah, I was kinda afraid of him."
E: "What about this fellow you are working with now? Do you feel relaxed with him, or tense?"
S: "No, I don't feel relaxed with him. I just as leave he's not around."
E: "You feel tense when he's around?"

S: "I'm not afraid of him, see; I just don't like to have him around. That other guy down there; at first I couldn't talk to him, ah—not at all, but it's getting a little bit better now."

E: "What about Dr. ———, the man that you worked for in college? Did you feel tense when you were with him?"

S: "It's a funny thing; I wasn't exactly at ease with him, but he was nice and I really liked him and I still do. I think I am in awe of him. You know, he was a big professor, something that I'd like to be, and I was really never friendly with professors. Well, I was really never friendly with any schoolteachers."

. . .

S: "I never knew professors, any professors that you would say personally, except Dr. ———. Well, of course, I asked him things 'cause I worked with him, but, ah—not any of the others, like Dr. ———. I wanted to talk to him, and I think if I had talked to him, my problems would have been solved."

E: "Why didn't you talk to him?"

S: "I don't know; I couldn't. He had such a way about him that I couldn't get my point across. He would persuade his opinion on me. He would, and I don't want his opinion. I mean he would try to tell me that he was right and I'm wrong and believe me he's right. He had a way about him that my opinion had no value. It was like going in and talking to a blank wall. He would have such a better argument than I would that I would lose, that's what I thought anyway."

The remarkable degree of continuity of a passive disposition over a 20-year period displayed by this individual is not typical, but it illustrates that, in extreme cases, childhood dispositions can persist into adulthood with remarkable stability.

This case also illustrates that the tendency to be passive in time of stress is moderately associated with the tendency to be an introvert as opposed to an extrovert. It is relevant to note that as long as man has written about human nature, he has usually included a descriptive dimension concerning the degree to which a character shuns active social interchange and prefers solitude (the introvert) in contrast to the character who actively seeks and enjoys social interaction (the extrovert). The stability within an individual of a tendency toward passivity and the historical concern with the dimension of introversion-extroversion implies that this general segment of behavior is a fundamental component of an individual's personality.

Siblings

The psychological influence of siblings on the child's personality development is felt most keenly when the child is between 3 and 9 years of age. The arrival of a sibling at this time represents the greatest threat to the first-born's relationship with his mother. For the second-born it is the time when the older sibling is perceived as an omnipotent and invulnerable competitor, with special privileges and status. Thus, each position in the family has its own set of advantages and disadvantages. Perhaps the best way to systematize the developmental correlates of birth order is to specify some of the unique experiences associated with a particular position and the behavioral consequences of these experiences.

DIFFERENTIAL CHARACTERISTICS
OF FIRST-BORN AND LATER-BORN CHILDREN

The critical experiences associated with being a first-born child are (1) the tendency to orient to the parents for values and to identify with parental rather than peer models, (2) anxiety over loss of parental nurturance when the second-born arrives, and (3) a perception of the privilege that parents usually accord the first-born because of his status and age. These experiences are likely to lead to certain psychological outcomes, described below.

Standards First-born children have higher standards than later-born children about competencies and attributes that are positively valued by the parents. Occasionally these standards are likely to be excessively high. The child must discover for himself the standard of how "good" he is supposed to be at a task. The first-born is forced to use his parents as a reference for the level of competence he should try to attain. The later-born child, however, is exposed to less competent performance, since he looks both to his older siblings and to his parents for guidance in setting a standard of excellence. The later-born child generally has more realistic standards because his reference includes the performance of adults *and* children.

Identification Because the first-born has only adult models available to him, he is prone to identify primarily with them and as he grows older to choose them as models. Since adults, in fact, have more power and competence than children, the first-born is likely to pass through a period of more intense identification than is the later-born child. The fact that the later-born child has an older child as an available model dilutes the younger child's motivation to identify with adult models.

**Orientation
to the World** The first-born is more likely to experience an orderly world, for he can usually obtain from his parents coherent and orderly answers to his questions about events that puzzle him. Moreover, his parents do not impulsively snatch his toys or irrationally interfere with his play. Consider, however, the situation of a typical second-born child. When he is playing with a toy, his older brother

may suddenly race toward him and grab the toy without explanation. If he asks his older brother why it is raining, he may receive one answer the first time and a different answer the next. The world should appear less orderly, less predictable, and less rational for the later-born child. In the extreme case a later-born child may develop a picture of a predatory world in which one must vigilantly protect one's possessions against the onslaughts of the unpredictable older sibling.

Anxiety over Loss of Affection

The three attributes discussed above are usually regarded as "advantages" of being the first-born child. There are some consequences of this status, however, that might be viewed as disadvantageous. The first-born is subjected to anxiety over loss of parental affection in a more traumatic way than is the later-born child. The first-born becomes accustomed to the exclusive affection of his parents; since he is not required to share this resource, he comes to expect a certain amount of intense attention. The inevitable attenuation of attention that must occur when the next child is born represents a dramatic loss of parental nurturance, over which he is likely to become highly anxious. Furthermore, since he normally received nurturance from adults, he tends to continue to turn to them for help when he is anxious. In short, he is likely to be overtly dependent in time of stress if an adult is around. The later-born child is not so severely affected by potential loss of affection because he enters a world in which he is always sharing his parents with his older siblings; he grows up expecting and accepting this situation.

Guilt

The first-born child is predisposed to experience more guilt, especially over hostility, than is the later-born child. This expectation is based on the assumption that the first-born is naturally jealous of the new baby and his special status but has no way to rationalize his hostility. Because he knows and is told repeatedly that babies are entitled to extra attention, he perceives that his hostility is not appropriate and cannot be justified. The inability to justify his resentment leads to guilt (for he has violated a standard) and self-derogation. The later-born child is better able to justify any hostility toward his older sibling, because the first-born is, in fact, aggressive toward him and does enjoy privileges he does not possess. Being able to rationalize his resentment makes him less likely to experience strong guilt over these hostile thoughts.

Sense of Inadequacy

A unique attribute of the later-born child is the sense of inadequacy he may feel when he compares himself with his older sibling, especially if the age differential between the two is small—say, 2 to 4 years. The later-born child typically sees himself as physically weaker, intellectually less competent, and socially more awkward. He does not excuse these inadequacies by acknowledging the obvious age differential between himself and his older sibling. Because he compares himself to the older sibling as if they were the same age, he can only conclude that he is less adequate.

SOME CONCLUSIONS ON SIBLING DIFFERENCES
BASED ON ORDER OF BIRTH

The set of attributes ascribed above to first- and later-born children is conjectural but consistent with existing theory and data (see Altus, 1966; Warren, 1966). If these hypotheses are generally correct, several conclusions can be drawn. First-borns, in contrast to later-born siblings of the same sex, should be more concerned with social acceptance and rejection, less likely to break the rules imposed by authority, more ambitious and hard-working, more cooperative, more prone to guilt and anxiety, and less openly aggressive. First-borns should view the world as an orderly and essentially knowable place, rather than as a chaotic jungle where social predators lie waiting at every turn.

Research findings suggest that first-born children are more likely to be anxious over potential rejection from adult figures, to choose adult models as figures for identification, to view events that happen to them as the product of their own actions, to be willing to cooperate with adults conducting psychological experiments, and to be more anxious and more dependent on others in time of stress. This greater anxiety among first-borns is indicated by evidence that first-borns respond with more fear to the prospect of physical harm (Helmreich & Collins, 1967) and report an electric shock to be more painful than do later-borns (Nisbett & Schachter, 1966). First-born college men are less likely than later-borns to participate in dangerous sports like football, soccer, and rugby (see Figure 30-1) but are just as likely to participate in less dangerous sports like crew (Nisbett, 1968). One hundred adult men and women who were staying in a New York hotel during a power blackout in November 1965 were asked the question, "How nervous or uneasy did you feel during this experience?" The first-borns admitted to slightly greater anxiety than did the later-borns (Zucker, Manosevitz, & Lanyon, 1968).

First-born children of parents who value school success adopt and practice this value with greater vigor than do later-born children, as indicated by the disproportionately high percentage of eminent men who are first-born or only children. First-borns, for example, are predominant among Rhodes scholars (Apperly, 1939), listings in Who's Who (Jones, 1954), and distinguished scientists (Roe, 1953). There seems to be a disproportionate number of first-born children who attain very high scores on intelligence and aptitude tests and who matriculate at colleges with high admission standards (Altus, 1966). Moreover, middle-class first-born and only children are sub-

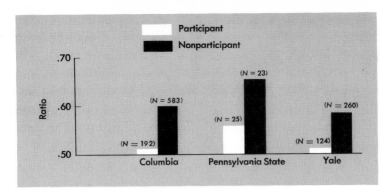

Figure 30-1   Ratio of first-borns to second-borns as participants in dangerous sports. (Adapted from Nisbett, 1968)

jected to more restrictiveness, greater acceleration, and more intense induction of guilt over violations of standards than are later-born children.

First-born children, in contrast to later-born children, tend to adopt more idealistic philosophical positions and prefer single unifying principles in moral codes or in science to schemes that are expedient or have many qualifications. In a recent study (Stein, 1966), 54 Harvard freshmen were interviewed; 27 were older sons with a younger brother and 27 were younger sons with an older brother. Each student was presented with a series of philosophical statements that either condoned or criticized three points of view:

1. The search for truth is good and, regardless of the consequences, should be pursued, in contrast to a point of view that states that one must take into account the outcome of an inquiry.

2. Man is essentially good, in contrast to a point of view that says that man is essentially bad.

3. The role of science is synthesis in contrast to analysis.

Each student had to state his understanding of each philosophical statement and to indicate his degree of agreement or disagreement with it. The difference between first- and second-born sons held only for those 16 freshmen who admired and felt similar to their fathers—that is, for the young men who seemed to have identified with their fathers. Among this group, the 9 first-borns were more likely to value man and his creative works, to endorse the importance of human freedom, to regard the formulation of a general and unitary theory as the most important aim of science, and to favor a morality that is based on principles rather than expediency. For example, the statement that produced the greatest difference between the first- and second-borns was this:

In striving toward ends that he finds morally acceptable, man must not resort to methods that violate other acceptable principles. Arguments of "expediency" are invalid and cannot obscure the fact that an immoral act is immoral regardless of whether it is used to achieve a final state that is just or one that is unjust.

None of the first-borns disagreed with this item, whereas more than 40 percent of the later-born group did. This commitment to moral standards and reluctance to sway from principles on the part of the first-born agrees with our theoretical description of the different relationships of first- and second-born children with their parents.

INTERACTING EFFECTS OF SEX, BIRTH ORDER, AND SPACING OF SIBLINGS

The most comprehensive empirical study of the effect of siblings on personality development has been reported by Koch (1956a, 1956b), who studied sex, birth order, and spacing of siblings in 384 families. The four types of sibling combinations—older boy–younger girl, older girl–younger boy, two sisters, and two brothers—were equally represented, and there were groups of siblings separated by 1 to 2 years, 2 to 4 years, and 4 to 6 years. The teachers of these children observed and rated them on a variety of behaviors. The results indicated that all the major variables—sex, birth order, and spacing—interacted in producing differences in the children's behaviors.

The sex of the older sibling was found to be an important determinant of the adoption of sex-typed behavior by the younger child. Girls with older brothers, as compared to those with older sisters, were more masculine in their behavior (that is, they were more ambitious and aggressive and performed better on tests of intellectual ability). Boys with older sisters were less masculine (less aggressive, less dominant) than were boys with older brothers. These results support the hypothesis that the younger child identifies to some degree with the older sibling and imitates his behavior because the older child is perceived to possess desirable attributes and resources.

When birth order alone was considered, Koch found that the first-born children generally had stronger and more consistent standards regarding honesty, responsibility, and aggression than did the second-born children. However, the effect of birth order was dependent on both the sex of the siblings and spacing. When the siblings were of the same sex and separated by less than 2 years, there were few behavioral differences between them. When the spacing increased to 4 years and the siblings were of different sexes, behavioral differences were most marked. Koch concluded that a 2- to 4-year age difference between siblings provided the most threatening situation to the older child. If the first-born was 3 years old when the new baby arrived, he was very likely to become anxious over possible withdrawal of nurturance. If the first-born was only a year old, on the other hand, his self-image was still diffuse enough so that he probably did not regard the baby as a major threat to his bond with his mother and, therefore, not a competitor for his mother's affection. If the older child was 8 when the sibling arrived, he was already on the road to independence from his parents and was less threatened by the newcomer. In general, it is difficult to speak of the influence of birth order without acknowledging the effect of the other two variables, sex and spacing.

It appears that sibling position is an important psychological variable, because it presents a microcosm of the significant social experiences of adolescence and adulthood. To be first or second, to be dominant or submissive, to side with authority or to rebel against it, to feel guilt over hostility or to be able to "place the blame" are tendencies that begin to be differentially strengthened during early childhood as a result of the child's sibling position.

The consistent personality correlates of sibling position serve to remind us that despite the importance of parental rewards and punishments, the mere existence of a younger or older sibling in the family can be an active force in the psychological development of a child. Every child and adult lives in a social structure and perceives his position in that structure. That perception molds his attitudes about himself, his vulnerability to anxiety, and his beliefs about others.

Just as in agriculture the operations that precede planting, and the planting itself, are certain and easy, but once the plant has taken life there are a variety of ways of cultivation and many difficulties; so with men, it requires little skill to plant them, but once they are born, training them and bringing them up demands care of a very different kind, involving much fear and tribulation.

MICHEL DE MONTAIGNE. Essays

CHAPTER 31
THE
INFLUENCE
OF PARENTS

T he preceding chapters in this part have described the major motives, expectancies, standards, anxieties, and behaviors learned during the first decade of life. These dimensions contribute to the dramatic individual differences in behavior noted in most 10-year-olds. This chapter will consider the maternal attitudes and behaviors that help to shape these differences. The reason for concentrating on maternal reactions is simply that there is very little sound information on the father, in contrast to the wealth of information available on the mother. However, some of the more general statements probably hold for both parents.

So that the significance of this discussion may be appreciated, it is well to emphasize the place that parents occupy among the many agents that influence a child. Parents exert the greatest influence, followed by siblings, peers, teachers, and public media (television, books, films, and so on), in that order. This hierarchy of influences also shows a chronological order, according to when each agent exerts its maximal effect. Parents and siblings have their major effect during the first 6 years, peers and teachers during the preadolescent period, and the public media during early adolescence.

Modes of Parental Influence

Parents can mold the behavior of the child in four ways: through reward, punishment, instruction, and as a consequence of their role as models for the child. Let us consider each of these mechanisms separately.

If parental nurturance, acceptance, and praise are valued, as they commonly are, they can be used as reward to establish and maintain selected responses. The early vocalizations and primitive speech of the 2- and 3-year-old commonly are rewarded by adult praise and recognition. These reactions from adults act as incentives to elicit more vocal and language behavior. The 5-year-old who is praised for tying his shoes, holding his fork correctly, or learning to write his name is strengthened in these dispositions.

Punishment is a second method of effecting changes in behavior. Whether the punishment be spanking, threat of rejection, or deprivation of goals, the anxiety generated by anticipated punishment usually leads to inhibition of the undesirable response and, in many cases, to substitution of an acceptable act. Inhibition of immediate evacuation, direct aggression, or open masturbation are attributable, in part, to the anxiety attached to the stimuli originally eliciting the response.

Parents also influence behavior through modeling, which facilitates imitation and identification, and through tutoring and explanation.

There is a developmental perspective to these four mechanisms. The infant's behavior is molded through the reward of nurturance and affection; punishment first appears as an instrument of socialization during the second year, and modeling and instruction first assume significance during the third year.

Types of Maternal Behavior

It is difficult to specify the maternal behaviors that are of primary consequence to a child's development, and the effects these behaviors have. First, one must make a distinction between specific maternal behaviors, such as spanking, verbal chastisement, and kissing, and the more abstract attitudes commonly labeled rejection, acceptance, permissiveness, and so on, that influence the child. A second and related problem is that it is not always possible to determine precisely what attitudes lie behind the mother's behavior. Her behavior is, at best, an indirect reflection of her attitude, and there is a considerable gap between attitude and behavior. The theoretical and methodological problems that make it difficult to assess the extent and nature of maternal influence are illustrated in the following discussion of some of the aspects of maternal behavior.

REJECTION AND ACCEPTANCE

Some examples of what *appears* to be maternal rejection are presented below. They illustrate the difficulties in inferring rejection from parental behavior.

1. Mothers in the isolated rural areas of northern Norway rarely ask their children to move when they find them blocking a doorway. The mothers simply pick them up silently and move them out of the way with an indifference that is characteristic of the treatment shown a pair of shoes that are out of place. An American psychologist would be prone to label such "aloof" behavior as rejecting if it were observed in a middle-class mother in Chicago. But this behavior in the rural Norwegian setting is normative and does not necessarily reflect an attitude of rejection.

2. An uneducated unwed mother slaps her 4-year-old boy across the face when he does not come to the dinner table on time. The intensity of the mother's act tempts an observer to conclude that the mother hates or at best does not like her child. However, during an interview conducted by the observer, the mother says that she cares about her child and only wants to ensure that he does not grow up to be a delinquent. She believes firmly that physical punishment is the most effective way to socialize him. In this case her behavior seems motivated more by love than hate.

3. A 20-year-old girl from a blue-collar family talks feelingly about the severe restriction and punishment she experienced as a child but adds that she now appreciates her parents, for they helped her develop the character she has today. In another part of the city, the 20-year-old daughter of a free-lance writer evidences hatred for her parents, who she claims were too permissive. She is convinced that their laissez faire attitude reflected a lack of concern for her welfare. Can we say for certain which set of parents were rejecting?

These examples suggest the conceptual problems surrounding the word "rejection." It should be clear from the examples above that there are three different meanings of the word. It can be defined in terms of the parent's behavior, the parent's attitude, or as a belief held by the child. Let us examine the last two meanings.

The Parental Attitude

A parental attitude of rejection is defined as one of dislike for and resentment of the child. However, it is not obvious which specific behaviors are most likely to reflect that attitude at various ages. Neglect of the child's needs for food, warmth, and comfort; open and direct criticism; and expressions of rage at the child are popular and even reasonable indexes of a rejecting attitude. But mothers with a rejecting attitude may not express these overt behaviors, and there is no general agreement on what might constitute more subtle behavioral indexes of a rejecting attitude. Moreover, a mother who was not rejecting but who had high standards for her child might display signs of rejection if the child violated these standards.

It is generally assumed that an attitude of rejection is one end of a dimension, the other end of which is usually labeled acceptance. As with rejection, acceptance is an attitude that may find varied expressions in different mothers. Psychologists often assume that physical affection is the obvious expression of maternal acceptance, but there is some reason to question the validity of this assumption. Mothers who are aware of their hostile feelings toward the infant may display intense physical affection to reduce their guilt and to attenuate the anxiety elicited by recognition of their basic resentment. Some mothers may not initiate close physical contact with their children because they believe it is not good for them or because of anxiety over the sexual associations that affectionate behavior arouses. Middle-class mothers in certain parts of the Netherlands, for example, put their young infants in an unheated room, away from the heated rooms in which they work, and do not go to their babies until they decide it is time for them to be fed, regardless of how intensely the babies may cry. Although these mothers value and love their infants, they believe that aloof treatment is good for young babies.*

It is not easy, therefore, to tell whether a mother loves her baby by noting how often she displays a particular set of behaviors toward the baby. As noted earlier, mothers of different cultural and subcultural groups express their accepting or rejecting attitude in different actions, and a mother's behavior is not always an accurate reflection of her attitude.

In spite of these difficulties, there has been considerable study of behavioral indexes of parental rejection and acceptance. Schaefer (1959) studied the variables used in many independent investigations of maternal behavior and found the results remarkably similar. He concluded that a fundamental characteristic of maternal behavior is the rejection-acceptance continuum. It is possible, however, that the conceptual heritage of Western-trained psychologists demanded this result. For example, Western prose and poetry, as well as empirical work in the social sciences, deify the dimension of love-hate. These attributes are typically the first ones evaluated when a parent is observed. Moreover, since Western thought dictates that a loving mother never treats her child harshly, an American psychologist generally *expects* to find the two variables of acceptance and rejection at opposite ends of a continuum.

The common belief that attitudes of rejection or acceptance can be identified by objectively watching the mother perform certain acts is in need of revision. Moreover, there is a second and much different definition of rejection that originates with the child's perception of his value.

* Personal communication from Dr. Freda Rebelsky (1968).

The Child's
Concept   The child's view of acceptance is based
on the degree to which he believes the
parents value him. The child arrives at this conclusion on the basis of
the quality and frequency of the parents' sacrifices for him and of his perception of the enjoyment they derive from being with him. The child of
9 is fully aware of the resources that a parent can give with no hardship
and those that he is reluctant to share with the child. If the parents have
little money, a gift of a one-dollar toy is viewed as a sign of great affection
by the child, for he realizes he has been given a scarce resource. However,
the wealthy executive who brings home a five-dollar toy after each four-day
business trip may not be credited by the child with a great deal of affection.
On the other hand, a long walk on Sunday morning by the executive father
and his son, an event the child rarely experiences, probably has the value
of the dollar toy given to the less privileged child.

Thus the child's feelings of being valued or accepted must take into
account his idiosyncratic perceptions of the value of various gifts. The
resources that he evaluates as scarce are the major tokens of affection, and
these evaluations may vary from child to child. This situation is not, however, completely relative. Most parents, regardless of their finances, are unwilling to make the sacrifices of very expensive gifts, long periods of uninterrupted attention, and reciprocal friendship either because of sincere
efforts to avoid spoiling their children or because of their own narcissistic
needs. Thus, many children come to regard the same resources—such as
uninterrupted attention and extravagant gifts—as symbolic of love and positive evaluation.

The psychologist's task is first to assess the range of resources that the
parent commands and then to measure the child's differential evaluation of
each of these resources. This information permits categorization of the degree of rejection or acceptance felt by the child and, by inference, the
rejecting or accepting quality of the parent's behavior. This concept of rejection and acceptance is relative, not absolute, for it rules out the possibility of deciding that any particular parental reaction *always* is viewed
as rejection by the child.

Of course, the child's belief concerning his value has no validity for
the infant; it is true only for the child 3 or 4 years of age or older. It takes
several years to develop the conceptual maturity necessary for a child to
evaluate his worth in the eyes of another; the definition of rejection based on
the child's concept is appropriate only for the child who thinks symbolically.

In short, then, in considering the behavioral dimension of rejection
and acceptance it is necessary to distinguish the following three meanings
of these words: (1) the quality and frequency of particular acts that are
presumed to reflect rejection or acceptance, (2) the parent's attitude toward

the child, and (3) the child's assessment of his value in the eyes of the parent. Since a particular set of behaviors does not always reflect a rejecting parental attitude for all caretakers, whoever they may be, and is not always perceived as rejecting by the child, the term rejection takes on a relativistic definition.

It is probably not a coincidence that this relativistic attitude toward the concepts of parental love and rejection coincides with similar theoretical changes in the areas of sensation and perception. Many psychologists are arguing for a relativistic concept of the stimulus. They suggest that the person's adaptation level (that is, the stimulus situation to which he is accustomed) must always be taken into account in order to understand what stimuli he attends to and what stimuli will register. As a result, the notion of an absolute stimulus with an absolute effect is becoming archaic. These developments in psychology are occurring about 50 years after Einstein's dramatic postulates concerning the relativity of physical events. "It depends on your point of view" has become a unifying principle not only for the physicist and the contemporary moral philosopher but also for the psychologist.

RESTRICTION AND AUTONOMY

The dimension of restriction and autonomy concerns the mother's tendency to control or restrict her child, as opposed to following permissive, laissez faire practices. The restriction-permissiveness continuum conforms more to specific maternal behaviors than does the acceptance-hostility continuum and thus presents fewer methodological problems. A controlling mother punishes deviations from her standards, prevents the child's explorations of new areas, and punishes excessive independence of action. The mother who gives relative autonomy allows the child more freedom to express some of his idiosyncratic tendencies. She does not punish all the child's explorations, and she allows some assertion of independence.

Although a mother's restriction and autonomy conform more to specific behaviors, the degree to which she is restrictive or permissive with her child shows less stability over the first 10 years than does the degree to which she is affectionate or hostile toward him. That is, an American mother who behaves as if she loved her 1-year-old child is likely to remain affectionate through the first decade of the child's life. However, a mother who is overly permissive with her infant may be either highly permissive or highly restrictive when the child is 10 years old. This difference seems to be due to the fact that the degree to which a mother restricts or grants freedom to her child is a function of the degree to which she feels he *requires* control.

The mother of a 6-year-old boy who has suddenly become unruly may increase her degree of restrictiveness in order to control her son. The mother who has been so overcontrolling that her 9-year-old daughter has become excessively shy may become concerned and ease up on her restrictions. The typical parent adjusts the tightness of control to match the child's behavior. As a result, the degree of restriction and permissiveness is not very stable over the first 10 to 12 years.

This intimate and reciprocal relationship between mother and child can be seen even during the opening weeks of life. Moss (1967) has observed mothers and infants when the latter were 3 and 12 weeks of age in the natural setting of the home. The infant's crying was a major determinant of the mother's behavior. If the infant cried a lot, the mother spent a lot of time with the child, holding him, picking him up, and talking to him. If the child was unusually quiet and nonirritable, the mother was likely to spend much less time near him and playing with him. The infant's behavior was a major determinant of the degree to which the mother demonstrated nurturant acts toward him. In effect, the infant was partly shaping the mother's behavior. This causal chain tends to contradict the popular myth that the degree to which a mother cares for her child is entirely a function of her internal motives and conflicts.

RESEARCH ON THE REJECTION-ACCEPTANCE AND RESTRICTION-AUTONOMY CONTINUUMS

Numerous studies have attempted to relate maternal affection, hostility, permissiveness, and control to the child's behavior. Most of these investigations have been cross-sectional, have used children between 3 and 15 years of age, and have implicitly assumed that the mother's attitude or behavior caused the child's behavior. This implicit assumption may, however, be fallacious. The mother's attitude toward her child, as we have noted, can be a reaction to his behavior at that time or during the previous months, rather than an antecedent of the behavior he is displaying. Moreover, many studies have used parental interviews to assess maternal acceptance or restriction and rarely supplement these data with direct observations of the mother to determine the validity of the mother's verbal report.

Schaefer (1959) has suggested that the rejection-acceptance and restriction-autonomy continuums are independent of each other and that mothers should be categorized into one of four major types: accepting and controlling, accepting and permissive, rejecting and controlling, and rejecting and permissive (see Figure 31-1). Schaefer further suggests that each of these four maternal types is linked to a specific syndrome in the child.

The antisocial child who displays his aggression directly is hypothetically linked to a mother who is both rejecting and permissive. This linking implies that the rejection creates strong hostile feelings in the child and reduces his motivation to inhibit his asocial behavior, which is not punished because of the mother's permissiveness. However, it is possible that the child's aggression led the mother to become hostile to her child. The accepting and permissive mother presumably produces a child who is confident and relatively uninhibited.

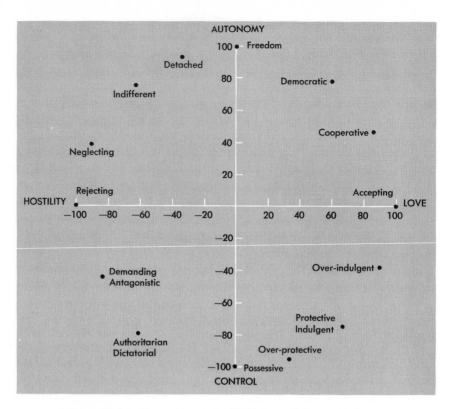

Figure 31-1 Types of maternal behavior. (Adapted from Schaefer & Bayley, 1963)

The combination of acceptance and control in a mother supposedly causes signs in the child of excessive guilt, phobias, tics, obsessive thoughts, academic problems, or ulcerative colitis. However, acceptance and moderate control, especially a control that demands independent and responsible behavior, seems to produce mature, self-reliant children. In a study by Baumrind and Black (1967) more than 100 preschool children were observed in nursery school in order to arrive at descriptions of their personalities. During the same period, the behavior of the children and their parents was observed in the home, and each parent was interviewed separately. Approving and affectionate parents were found to have the most autonomous boys. In addition, parents who made demands for maturity and self-reliance and were approving had children who were independent and responsible in the nursery school.

The psychotic child is assumed to be the product of maternal rejection and excessive control acting on the child's deviant biological dispositions.

The rejection presumably creates feelings in the child of self-hatred and strong hostility toward the mother. However, the mother's control prevents the child from expressing his feelings and leads to fear of prohibited behaviors. The combination of a negative self-image, extreme guilt, and failure to learn how to retaliate can lead to serious and persistent withdrawal, which in the biologically predisposed child can lead to psychosis.

This scheme is admittedly oversimplified, for it omits the influence of the father and does not consider the biological variables that might make the child susceptible to particular pathological syndromes, but it is an initial attempt to classify parental actions and should not be rejected out of hand.

OTHER MATERNAL VARIABLES

Maternal variables other than acceptance, rejection, restrictiveness, and permissiveness may affect the child's behavior. One such factor is the degree of consistency the parents display in their behavior toward the child. Rejecting mothers are, of necessity, inconsistent in their ministration of comfort and affection. Perhaps it is this inconsistency that contributes to those behaviors in the child that have been regarded as a consequence of a rejecting atmosphere.

The degree of verbal discipline and the regularity with which a rationale for discipline is offered are variables that might affect a child's behavior. A mother who is arbitrary in her restrictiveness is apt to confuse the child and generate strong hostility, in contrast to the mother who sets limits in a context in which her actions are explained. The coherent and rational quality of the mother's communications to the child is another dimension that needs further study. The period of infancy, when the child is most dependent on the nurturance of the mother, provides a setting for another variable—the delay between the onset of need in the child, as evidenced by his crying, and the administration of some nurturance that will satisfy the need.

The parent's behavior as a model represents still another variable. Since the parent is a model, the attitudes and acts he or she exhibits are likely to be adopted by the child. When the parent's behavior matches the content of a parental socialization demand, the child is faced with a consistent socialization situation. However, the child is confronted with an inconsistent situation when the parent speaks aggressively to the spouse, strikes the child, and insults friends but consistently punishes all such displays of aggression in the child. It is likely that the effect of the parent as a model for aggression in the above situation is as critical for the child's behavior pattern as is the degree of punishment of aggressive behavior (Sears, Maccoby, & Levin, 1957).

Cause and Effect Sequences
in the Mother-Child Interaction

Maternal actions toward a child do not always have an immediate effect on the child's behavior; some maternal behaviors display a "sleeper" effect. For example, a mother's attempt to accelerate her child's intellectual skills at age 5 may have a profound influence on his level of intellectual mastery at age 10. The Fels Institute longitudinal investigation gives evidence that sleeper effects can occur (Kagan & Moss, 1962). A hostile and overly critical maternal attitude toward daughters during the first 3 years of life, for example, was predictive of adult mastery in the daughters, whereas a hostile or a critical maternal attitude during the preschool or early school years showed a negligible relation to the daughters' adult mastery behavior. Similarly, maternal protection and nurturance of daughters during the first 3 years predicted a tendency toward withdrawal from stressful situations in adulthood; maternal protection during the preschool years showed no relation to adult passivity in time of stress.

These results give credence to the assumption that the reciprocal nature of the mother-child interaction changes with time. Not only does the mother's effect on the child vary at different ages, but the child's ability to provoke relatively permanent changes in specific maternal reactions increases with age. The 6-year-old is more likely to produce a major alteration in the mother's characteristic behavior toward him than is the 2-year-old.

The mother typically has expectations as to what the child's conduct should be like, or to what standards his behavior should conform. The greater the discrepancy between her expectations and her evaluation of the child, the greater the likelihood that she will either modify her expectations or modify her behavior, and exert pressure on the child in an attempt to direct him according to her expectations. Because the infant's personality is relatively amorphous, the discrepancy between the mother's standards and what she perceives in the infant is necessarily small; the mother sees the infant as she would like to see him, as an object primarily to be acted upon. The form and content of maternal behaviors toward her child, therefore, are not as contaminated by the effects of the infant's behavior as they are by the behaviors of the more complex 10-year-old.

A mother's concern with the intellectual development of her 2-year-old is more likely to be an index of her own basic needs and values than is her degree of concern with the performance of her 10-year-old daughter who is failing in school. Mothers change their expectations and values as the child develops, and the lack of concern with the 10-year-old's school grades could be merely a defensive maneuver the mother recently acquired to protect herself from excessive disappointment. Similarly, encouragement of independence, a critical attitude, or overprotection toward a 10-year-old may be lately developed reactions to the child's excessive dependence, rebelliousness, or fragile defenses.

It is possible, therefore, that certain maternal practices—such as nurturance, restrictiveness, and hostility—that are manifested during the first 3 years provide the most sensitive index of the mother's basic attitudes toward the child and, perhaps, of her lasting effect on his future behavior. The further elucidation of cause and effect sequences in development may require longitudinal study of parent and child. For example, a cross-sectional investigation of the relation between maternal protection and passivity in a 10-year-old might yield a negligible association between these variables, but if the maternal behavior had been assessed when the child was 3 years old, a strong positive relation with the child's behavior when he was 10 might have emerged.

Certain parent-child interactions are particularly vulnerable to the sleeper effect. Maternal behaviors that are likely to change in frequency and intensity over the first decade, such as kissing, reward of dependency, and physical punishment, are more likely to display this effect than are the relatively stable attitudes (for instance, about sexuality or about the appropriateness of traditional sex-typed traits). Furthermore, maternal reactions that are unique to the child's behavior during the school years, such as concern with grades or punishment of overt aggression, may give misleading correlations between contemporaneous assessments of both maternal and child behavior.

Factors Controlling Maternal Reactions

THE CHILD'S ATTITUDES
AND THE MOTHER'S TEMPERAMENT

There is a danger in inferring cause and effect sequences—especially the effect of a maternal practice on a response of the child—merely from an association between a particular type of parental attitude or behavior and the child's personality. Close observation of the mother-infant and mother-child interaction indicates that the mother's reactions are governed to some extent both by the child's attributes and by her own temperament. If the child is irritable, she reacts with more anger than if he is content; if he is vigorous, she treats him with either more or less restriction than if he is lethargic; if he is frail and appears helpless, she is more protective than if he is robust. Even in the opening weeks of life, the mother's behavior is governed by the characteristics of the baby. Irritable babies tend to receive more nurturance than quiet, placid, happy ones. Boys, being generally more irritable than girls, tend to elicit more maternal handling (Moss, 1967).

The mother's reactions to her child's behavior are also affected by her own temperament. Some of the mothers in the study by Moss (1967) had been interviewed prior to the birth of their infants, at which time their dispositions to be affectionate and nurturant to the infant were assessed. The mothers who were regarded then as more nurturant were indeed more responsive to their infants at 3 weeks and 3 months of age than were those who were regarded as more hostile to the unborn baby. Thus, it is not surprising that the most frequent interaction will occur between the irritable child and the basically affectionate and nurturant mother, and that the placid child with a nonnurturant mother will receive the least handling.

THE MOTHER'S INTERPRETATIONS

The mother's behavior toward her child is governed to some extent by her *interpretation* of the child's attributes. The mother typically pins a label on the child, based initially on his sex, activity level, vigor, size, health, and irritability, and she reacts to this label. As a result of the initial labeling mothers usually will let 16-week-old infant boys cry longer than girls of the same age, for they feel boys have to learn how to take stress. They are generally more protective to small, light babies, because they feel these infants require more care. As the child approaches preschool age, his attributes become more complex, and his parents often must revise the labels they give him. At this stage the labels are based on the child's intellectual competence, attractiveness, and popularity; favorable and unfavorable labels will elicit different maternal reactions to the child.

The child's sex is a major determinant of a mother's reactions. Rothbart and Maccoby (1966) describe an experiment in which mothers and fathers listened to the tape-recorded voice of a 4-year-old whose voice could have been perceived as either male or female. Some parents were told the voice was a boy's; others were told it belonged to a girl. After the experimenter described a typical family situation, the parents heard the taped voice make such remarks as, "Daddy, come look at my puzzle," "Help me," "I don't like this game—I'm gonna break it." After each statement the experimenter stopped the tape, and the parents wrote down what they would say or do in response to the statement. Mothers were more permissive for the boy's voice and fathers more permissive for the girl's voice. Moreover, fathers allowed more aggression toward the parent from the girl than from the boy; mothers allowed more aggression from the boy than from the girl.

Mothers do not assign the same labels and do not react uniformly to the same set of attributes. One mother may regard her son's motor vigor and resistance to sleep as a sign of autonomy and high spirits and be pleased that he will probably develop into an active, masculine boy. Another mother, with a different value system and a different set of conflicts, may consider that these same attributes are indicative of future violence and delinquency and should be punished. Two mothers might interpret extreme irritability in their daughters in different ways: one as a sign of the child's sensitivity, the other as a sign of her own incompetence. In the latter case the irritability would be threatening to the mother, causing her to withdraw from involvement with her daughter.

The child's basic characteristics, therefore, rarely evoke a constant or invariant response in a mother. The child's attributes are cryptic messages that the mother decodes and acts upon. If she misreads the message, she may take the wrong action. Since mothers have different standards, motives, and conflicts, they use different criteria to decode the infant's behavior. As a result, similar child behaviors may evoke dramatically different interpretations and reactions.

THE MOTHER'S EXPECTATIONS

Mothers have an initial set of expectations about how their children will grow, and they typically act on the basis of these predictions. A mother who decides that her infant will probably not perform well in school may not read to him when he approaches preschool age. A mother who believes her daughter will be popular will arrange to surround her with friends as she grows up.

There are striking differences among mothers in the nature of the expectations they have for their children. Some of these differences are attributable to social class, others to the sex of the child, still others to the mother's unique conflicts and motives. As part of a continuing study of a large group of parents and infants, mothers of 16-week-old babies were asked to predict what their children would be like when they were 10 years old. Some mothers in the group had never graduated from high school, some were high school graduates, and the others had either attended or graduated from college.

Figure 31-2 *Social class differences in mothers' expectations of their children's behaviors.*

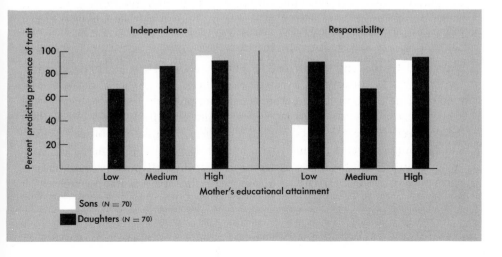

For some traits, such as popularity, there were no important differences among the mothers of the three educational levels or between mothers of sons and mothers of daughters. However, traits such as cautiousness, responsibility, and stubbornness produced interesting differences. The poorly educated mother was more likely than the better-educated mother to say that her daughter would be stubborn, cautious, not very interested in music, and poor at arithmetic. Among mothers of sons, the less well-educated parent was more likely to predict that her child would be athletic, not cautious, not responsible, and likely to jump from one activity to another.

Lower-class parents predicted more independence for their daughters than for their sons, but upper-middle-class mothers in general expected more independence from both sons and daughters than did lower-class mothers. Similarly, the upper-middle-class mother expected more responsibility from her son than did the lower-class parent (see Figure 31-2).

These expectations closely match reality. For example, 10-year-old sons of parents with little education are, in fact, less responsible than are 10-year-old sons of college-educated parents. And lower-class boys are less cautious and more impulsive than are middle-class boys. It is likely that the mothers' expectations played an important role in shaping the final outcome.

The Importance
of the Parental Role

If one reflects on the discussion in this chapter, it becomes clear why it is so difficult to attain a comprehensive understanding of human personality development and why we know so little of each person's individual growth. For a comparable situation, consider what the discipline of chemistry would be like if the chemical compounds reacted differently according to the vessel in which they were placed or the laboratory in which the experiment took place. The parent-child relationship is a continual dialogue involving messages the child sends that the parent interprets and messages the parent sends that the child interprets. The interpretations govern the parent's and the child's next set of reactions, and so the dialogue continues, like a well-practiced ballet.

There is a small minority of parents, of course, who are relatively unresponsive to the child's attributes. Their reactions to the child are more chronically and consistently a function of their own particular motives and sources of anxiety. Such parents often are responsible for pathology in the child, because the child is cast in a definite role from which he cannot escape, even if the role does not fit him. For example, a mother who has strong conflict over sexuality may restrict her daughter's activities with boys, regardless of the girl's attractiveness or her attitudes toward heterosexual behavior. The parent who must have his son become a scientist or doctor, regardless of the boy's skills or interests, is likely to create strong hostility in the child that is manifested either in withdrawal or in open rebellion toward the parent. In these cases the dialogue has become a monologue.

If we are to understand personality development, we must discern the standards, anxieties, and motives of each parent, the roles they force the child to play, and the degree of responsiveness and flexibility they display to the child's attributes.

Personality Development:
An Afterword

This part has provided an introduction to the psychological growth of the typical child and has described the approximate time of emergence for selected responses. Much of the discussion has necessarily been conjectural, for there is very little substantiated information on the *mechanisms* of development and the ways in which environmental events influence personality organization.

The major theme has been that the establishment of the components of the primary psychic systems—motives, standards, expectancies, affects, sources of anxiety, and actions—takes place at different periods in development. The discussion has been more descriptive than theoretical; its rationale is similar to that of Piaget's scheme for intellectual development. Piaget (1957) delineates stages of cognitive functioning so that one may predict that a 9-year-old, for instance, will show signs of conservation of volume or space and will be able to deal with some hypothetical problem conditions. Similarly, from the delineation of stages of personality development one can expect most 9-year-olds to have identified with a parent, to be concerned with their sex role, and to have incorporated the standards of their community. But just as Piaget has not been able to provide statements explaining how a child passes from the stage of intuitive to concrete operations or how environmental experiences facilitate or obstruct this passage, so those who study personality development have had difficulty detailing the mechanisms of how dominant mothers influence the behavioral development of their children.

Theories of cognitive and behavioral development lack the tight net of interlocking theoretical propositions that permit satisfactory explanations. The constructs of identification; anxiety over loss of affection; motives for power, autonomy, mastery, affection, hostility, and sexuality; and standards for sex roles have assumed a heavy burden of explanation in this section. The results of empirical work in the next two decades will determine the wisdom of these choices and the utility of these ideas.

Two conclusions seem reasonably correct: (1) The organization of motives, expectancies, standards, and anxieties changes as the child grows, and (2) the meaning of the child's overt behaviors becomes increasingly ambiguous. The task before us is to map the child's public responses on those internal, dynamic processes that function to adapt the child to his environment and to make sense of his experiences.

PART FOUR
ASSESSING PERSONALITY

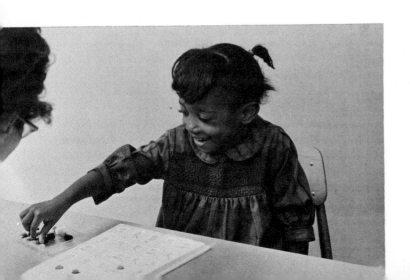

As the weaver elaborated his pattern for no end but the pleasure of his aesthetic sense, so might a man live his life, or if one was forced to believe that his actions were outside his choosing, so might a man look at his life, that it made a pattern. . . . Out of the manifold events of his life, his deeds, his feelings, his thoughts, he might make a design, regular, elaborate, complicated, or beautiful. . . . In the vast warp of life . . . a man might get a personal satisfaction in selecting the various strands that worked out the pattern.

W. SOMERSET MAUGHAM. Of Human Bondage

CHAPTER 32
THE WHAT
AND WHY
OF PERSONALITY
ASSESSMENT

E verybody routinely spends a great deal of time assessing the personalities of others, for in its first and basic sense, personality assessment means an *informal* process of getting to know and understand people and describing them. This same term also refers to a scientific and professional specialty, which applies a *formal* discipline of analyzing and measuring personalities. Both kinds of assessment will interest us here. Although the formal assessment of personality is young both as a science and as a profession—still very much a skill or even an art—studying it can help sharpen anyone's capacity to size people up informally. And the professional psychologist can improve his own results by investigating how the good natural judge of men operates. In the chapters that follow, therefore, the term "assessment" will be used broadly to refer to all the complex processes of perceiving and observing personalities, analyzing them, measuring their components with tests and other instruments, and understanding them.

The Nature of Personality
and Its Assessment

BEHAVIOR PATTERNS

People behave in organized, recognizable ways. That is the basic fact on which the whole psychology of personality is founded. At least two levels of organization, or patterning, can be distinguished: the *trait* and the *personality*. As soon as we begin to use adjectives to describe someone's behavior, we are talking trait language. To say someone is clever implies not just a single clever remark on his part, for almost anyone may occasionally say something delightfully witty; rather, it implies some regularity: Clever acts and sayings must be a recurrent feature of the clever person's behavior. Since recurrence is the paramount property of recognizable pattern, a trait is a simple behavioral pattern—a disposition to behave in a describable way. And a first approximation to a working definition of personality, for the purposes of the assessor, is that it is a pattern of traits.

What is meant by the phrase "a pattern of traits"? Surely more than just a list. Indeed, the pattern of deeds, feelings, and thoughts in a person's life makes up a design far richer and more complex than that of the Persian rug to which Maugham's hero compared his own life. Just as two weavers may take identical batches of threads but make from them markedly different designs, so too the uniqueness we always associate with personality is mainly to be found in the pattern rather than in the elements.

The uniqueness of pattern arises in part because the same traits have *different strengths* in two people. Both Henry and Herbert are to some degree strong, friendly, tidy, anxious, and effeminate; but Henry's friends notice in particular that he is both very strong and markedly effeminate, less friendly than average, and neither very tidy nor very anxious, while Herbert's friendliness and anxiety stand out, his effeminacy is near average, and the amount of strength and tidiness he possesses are slight. These hypothetical examples can illustrate another type of patterning, the *causal*. Because of his effeminacy, Henry has concentrated on keeping down anxiety by building up his muscles, at the expense of cultivating friendships. Though Herbert's effeminacy is slightly above average, it is unrelated to his anxiety—a fear of being rejected that leads him to be unusually friendly to others. Traits may conflict with one another; ambition, for instance, sometimes gets in the way of friendliness. Sometimes the traits alternate in their manifestation. Traits differ not only in strength but in the degree to which the person is conscious of them. Out of these relations (and others) is the unique pattern of a personality made.

Even the hypothetical examples given above clearly imply that the patterning of behavior in a personality must take place over time. Murray (1938) has said that the psychology of personality is the study of human lives, implying that the full pattern of a person's behavior becomes manifest only across the span of his entire life. The *genetic method* of studying life histories is therefore centrally important to personality. Getting a person to tell his life story is a basic method of formal assessment. It is the most natural way of intensifying informal assessment in pursuit of deeper understanding.

Most of the time when we talk about personality, however, we use the term in a cross-sectional, or contemporaneous, rather than a genetic sense. Fortunately, at any one time a person does have a complexly patterned set of dispositions to behave in particular ways, which can be assessed by tests and interviews; otherwise personality assessment would be limited to developmental studies over unmanageably long periods of time. A formal assessment of personality may include some direct observation of behavior patterns, but the observation is generally done in such a brief period of hours as to be like a stop-action snapshot. Nevertheless, it is good to be reminded that the ultimate subject matter of a science of personality is entire lives.

A DESCRIPTIVE DISCIPLINE

The key terms *personality* and *trait* have been defined in two apparently different ways: in terms of observable patterns of ongoing behavior and in terms of inferred dispositions to behave in patterned ways. Though dispositions refer to future actions and sound somehow more intrinsic to a person than do behavior patterns, the difference is only verbal. To say that a person is disposed to be punctual or that he has been observed to show up promptly time after time amounts to the same thing. A trait, therefore, is a descriptive, not an explanatory, concept. The failure to grasp this point exposes us to the dangers of two fallacies—that of *tautology*, or thinking in circles, and that of *reification*, taking an abstraction as if it referred to something concrete. To say that a person is prompt because he has the trait of punctuality is an excellent example of a tautology in which what looks like an explanation adds nothing to the original observation. The attempt to give the concept more solidity by thinking of traits as real structures somewhere inside the person is a clear reification.

To be sure, there *are* real structures inside people that determine their behavior in lawful ways. Two main classes of such structural determinants may usefully be distinguished. First, the kind of gross structure we call *physique* has some causal influence on behavior; for example, a man may be a good athlete partly because he has a sturdy skeleton and well-developed muscles. Second, a finer but more pervasively important type of structure is the *organization of the central nervous system*. The good bodily coordination that the athlete needs seems to be to some extent an inborn capacity, which in some unknown way is "wired in" as a property of his brain.

Most psychologists believe, however, that the brain influences behavior primarily because it contains an ever-changing record of the modifications of

578   *The What and Why of Personality Assessment*

its innate programs produced by *learning*. A person is characteristically generous not so much because he was born that way but because a complex pattern of experience taught him how to be generous and how to get gratification from generosity. In ways that are only beginning to be understood, learning causes submicroscopic structural changes in the brain, probably in the organization of its biochemical substance.

If such structural determinants of behavior patterns exist and if they constitute causal, not merely descriptive, concepts, why should we be concerned with traits? In part, it is a matter of necessity. Eventually, psychologists may be able to find out which characteristics of the body— especially in the fine structure of the brain and its electrical and biochemical processes—determine specific aspects of behavior. At present, that is only an interesting possibility; even if it becomes an actuality, we shall never escape from the need to identify recurrent patterns of behavior, so that we may specify the personality traits of interest to us and for many other reasons. Furthermore, behavior is an interesting and significant kind of reality worthy of being studied on its own level without attempting to reduce it to something presumably more basic. Sometimes psychology is criticized on the grounds that behavior is too evanescent and impalpable to be objectively studied; such criticism often comes from those who wish to replace behavior patterns with physiological concepts, which they feel to be more substantial. To be sure, it is not as simple and objective a matter to assess traits of behavior as it is to make many kinds of physical measurements. Nevertheless, we can measure the extent to which different people agree on their ratings of a personality trait after independently studying a person, and the agreement is often quite good. Moreover, when this kind of reliability proves poor, we know a number of ways to improve it. There is nothing more mysterious about the ability to perceive consistency, or patterning, in behavior than there is about the ability of a person with a trained ear to listen to a few minutes of music and describe its musical form.

There is a final, more important, reason to retain and respect the descriptive concepts of personality assessment. They perform a necessary task, for which they were designed; and even when a causal theory can explain such a phenomenon as hesitancy, the explanation cannot be substituted for the description of trait. Suppose we knew that impulses from brain area x to area y caused indecisiveness; suppose also that we could measure them. The personality assessor would have a splendid way of assessing an important aspect of behavior that would be vital in, for example, selecting executives, but he would report his findings not in terms of the frequency of impulses but as an estimate of how decisive the man would be.

For the reasons given above, personality assessment is almost entirely a descriptive discipline. Nevertheless, good description can yield a great deal of understanding and can enable us to predict and—to some extent—control behavior.

An analogy with metallurgy will illustrate how a descriptive discipline can make possible a great deal of practical application. During the middle ages, alchemists and more practical men learned much about metals by working with them. In time, they learned to make precise measurements of a metal's melting point, its density, hardness, and other descriptive properties—long before there was an explanatory theory to show how these properties were interrelated. As it became possible to classify metals and measure their descriptive properties, a complex technology of working with metals grew up; indeed, much of the Industrial Revolution was based on it. Today, metallurgists know that the "traits" of metals are determined by their crystalline molecular structure, which in turn depends on the structure of the metallic atom. Yet measurements of a given metal's ductility, hardness, conductivity, and the like, have not been replaced by statements about free electrons in its atomic shell, nor could they be.

PERSON VERSUS PERSONALITY

Notice that *person* and *personality* are not identical terms; the second is more restricted. A person is an individual human organism. He has not only a personality (a distinctive and characteristic pattern of traits) but also a physique, an anatomy, a physiology, a social role, and a status; he expresses and transmits a culture, performs such operations as spending and investing to keep an economy going, and, in short, is the concrete embodiment of that grand generalization, man. The psychology of personality is only one of the sciences relevant to persons, the principal subject matter of all the behavioral, social, and medical sciences. A person is so complex and many-layered that many disciplines can be brought to bear on the physiochemical, fleshly, ideological, spiritual, or other aspects of his being. The student of personality must know something about all these aspects of persons, for they affect the patterns of behavior, which are his special concern.

What Are the Uses
of Informal Assessment?

In order to interact with people, even in the simplest ways, we have to be able to understand them and to predict what they will do. Most of the time it is relatively easy to do so because much behavior is conforming and a great deal of the patterning in personalities is contributed by society and culture. Nevertheless, it is a happy fact that no one conforms completely to social *norms* (including laws, customs, and other standards for conduct). If we are to know what to expect from a specific person, one of the first things we must learn is the extent of his conformity and conventionality.

ASSESSMENT OF NONCONFORMITY

There are three principal types of nonconformity to major social norms: criminal, psychotic, and creative nonconformity. Each type has quite different implications for action toward the deviant person.

Criminals, psychopaths, or, more generally, people who are poorly socialized and narrowly self-seeking often break laws and other norms because they think they can do what they want and get away with it. Of course, everyone has *some* minor antisocial trends, but people differ tremendously in this respect. Clearly, honesty or integrity is one of the first qualities we look for, consciously or not, in sizing a person up.

If we saw someone driving down the wrong side of the street or taking a short cut across a busy airfield, we might be tempted to yell, "What's the matter, are you crazy?" Sometimes such a nonconformist is, for it is a hallmark of psychosis that the affected person loses touch with the social reality of norms; his deviant behavior may endanger himself or others. Hence the degree of *contact with reality* is another absolutely basic dimension of assessment. These two fundamental decisions about other people—the degree to which they are reasonably ethical and sane—are usually tacit. We are not aware of making them and probably could not explain how we do so, but someone has only to raise the issue for us to be quite emphatic in our judgments.

Creative nonconformity is the kind we have in mind as needed when we deplore the conformity of modern life. It represents a questioning of norms and an attempt to improve on them. Sometimes the questioning is more negativistic and rebellious than constructive, and violent disagreement can arise about what constitutes improvement. For example, many persons would be reluctant to classify social and political rebellion as creative. Sometimes, however, progress requires revolutionary change. In the long run, society's most valuable members are those who contribute new ways of doing things; we must, therefore, be able to distinguish creative nonconformists from destructive types in assessing personalities. In some cases the three forms of nonconformity may be intricately combined. Raskolnikov, the protagonist in Dostoevsky's *Crime and Punishment*, was a psychotic who committed a crime that he thought of as an act of creative nonconformity.

ASSESSMENT
OF OTHER INDIVIDUAL DIFFERENCES

In most everyday situations, you want to know a good deal more about a person than the extent to which he can be counted on to behave like most other people. There is a great deal of latitude for individual variation *within* the general framework of the norms in many areas of life, and people do differ from one another in interesting and important ways. One reason we are concerned with such differences is simply that they are inherently fascinating—perhaps because of the universal tendency to assume that everyone else is essentially like us, which makes each discovery that someone else can behave or view things differently something of a surprise. Indeed, personal idiosyncrasies are the favorite topic of gossip, if not of most conversation.

Another reason to assess these differences is the need to know how others will respond to things, for all kinds of decisions at every level of human enterprise hinge directly on this knowledge. For example, your strategy against an opponent in any kind of competitive situation (love, war, business, play) will be determined by your evaluation of him and his probable aggressiveness, courage, wiliness, tractability, or intelligence. Or if you are looking for someone to marry, it is not much help to know that, on the average, the men or women you encounter in your everyday social life would probably be satisfactory: You want to find the *best* combination of qualities. The same reasoning holds for finding a good adviser, choosing a secretary, or seeking a compatible business partner or professional collaborator. Although everyone is subject to the same general laws of behavior, there is a great range in ability, disposition, emotional make-up, and other behavioral tendencies. One would be crippled in interpersonal relationships without some ability to assess individual differences in personality.

In these few examples, it should be apparent that informal assessment is the rule. Even though computer-arranged dating is proving acceptable on many college campuses, it would be highly inappropriate to try to use formal procedures of assessment in serious courtship or in business competition (although there would be no objection to a person's sharpening his native wits by the extracurricular application of scientific principles). In choosing an employee, however, most organizations of any size have found that it is good business to replace or supplement informal assessment by such formal means as tests of stenographic and typing skills.

SELF-ASSESSMENT

Perhaps the most important, and surely the most interesting, subject for a person's informal assessment is himself. As soon as self-awareness is possible, a child begins to evaluate himself and to form expectations about what he can do compared to others. The self-assessing process is closely connected with ambitions, ideals, and levels of aspiration, as well as with feelings of self-respect, inferiority, shame, guilt, or pride. Learning more about both informal and formal methods of assessing personality *can* help a person to know himself better, though it cannot be guaranteed to do so.

THE MECHANISMS OF INFORMAL ASSESSMENT

Once we realize that informal assessment begins as soon as a child starts to form expectations and conceptions about himself, his parents, playmates, and the other people in his world, it is apparent how involuntary and essentially nonverbal an operation it is. Informal assessment is one of the best examples of what the eminent philosopher Polanyi (1964) calls *tacit knowing*. That is, informal assessment does not generally operate by means of a highly conscious, rational, explicit drawing of inferences; it typically happens outside the spotlight of our fullest (or *focal*) awareness. A child knows far more about his mother—her moods and impulses, how to get around her, how far he can trust her, how much she will do for him— than he can begin to put into words.

Expectations Based on Experience   In part, informal assessment is the building up of expectations on the basis of experience. There is little basic difference between learning to recognize a mother's face and learning to recognize her quick temper: Both are abstractions, or concepts, formed gradually. The process involved may be illustrated by an experiment in concept formation conducted by Rommetveit and Kvale (1965). They taught their subjects to recognize complex geometrical patterns indicating "good luck" and "bad luck" on a wheel of fortune; the payoff was in fact controlled by the experimenter. After repeated trials with the wheel, the subjects began to learn the types of patterns that paid off—long before they could correctly verbalize the difference between the "lucky" and "unlucky" designs. For example, certain subjects were told that they would be tested on their ability to tell the lucky from the unlucky patterns by choosing the correct verbal description of this difference from among various formulations. As their ability to recognize the lucky and unlucky patterns improved, as shown by increasing "success" on the wheel, they selected the correct description *less* often. Such a capacity to perform better than one can verbalize is part of what we mean by tacit knowing. Even though the abstractive process of forming concepts or expectations usually takes place automatically and without any necessary involvement of deliberate intent, it nevertheless can be shown to have a logical structure.

Empathy   A process of tacit knowing of people that is less rational than building up expectations, but is nevertheless fundamental to informal assessment, is *empathy*. As usually defined, empathy is a process of feeling what another person feels, but exactly how it happens is still unclear. It has been repeatedly observed, however, that a very young baby will grow tense and restless if the mother holding him is herself anxious; this process has been called *emotional contagion*. In an experimental demonstration, Campbell (1957) studied two groups of mothers and babies at a well-baby clinic, where the children are brought for routine injections. Some of the mothers were given preliminary instructions that emphasized the possible dangers and difficulties surrounding the injection; the others were given neutral instructions. Significantly more mothers in the first group became noticeably anxious, and significantly more of their babies cried *before* getting their shots.

Empathy, the mature version of emotional contagion, makes it possible for one person to know some things about another on rather brief acquaintance. Like all other capacities, it is not present in everyone to the same extent, nor is it infallible. The main information empathy gives us is emotional; it can tell us nothing about how intelligent a person is and can give no specific facts about his background or history (though we may sense such general events as that he has been deeply disappointed at some time in the past) and little information about the way his thinking is organized. But through empathy it is possible to tell how friendly or hostile, tense or relaxed, interested or bored, open or defensive, hopeful or bitter, self-confident or doubtful a person feels; how much he enjoys life; and even how sick he is. Empathy cannot always provide this information; nor does it work for everybody with complete accuracy; but the fact that so much information *can* be picked up by this effortless opening of oneself to impressions of another person means that it is important to consider how empathy becomes impaired and what can be done to improve it. It seems to be at the center of what is commonly called intuition, though that ill-defined term probably refers to all the processes of tacit knowing. Further discussion of empathy may be found in Chapter 33.

The Basic Steps   Effective informal assessing presupposes that you *care* about people. It is likely that the more interested you are in other human beings as individuals, the better you will be at assessing them. The objective ideal of a completely mechanized assessment will be impossible until computers can be taught to feel, to judge, and to care about people. Having an interest in a person and a desire to get to know him is, then, the first step in informal assessment; next we obtain immediate impressions through empathy; and finally we continue to observe his behavior until we notice invariances in it—persistent, recognizable trends. There is more to the process, as will be seen in the next chapter, but these are the basic steps.

THE PLACE OF INFORMAL ASSESSMENT
IN MODERN PSYCHOLOGY

There has been a curiously antipsychological tradition within the discipline of psychology, which makes a kind of fetish of skepticism and iconoclasm so far as the main processes of informal assessing are concerned. According to this view, intuition, empathy, judging personality from facial or bodily expression, are all unscientific mysticism. So eager were generations of leading psychologists to separate themselves from quacks and charlatans that they indoctrinated their students with the belief that the processes by which we directly come to know and understand one another are completely untrustworthy and sources of self-deception. Moreover, they produced a sheaf of apparently good experimental demonstrations of their indictments. In study after study it was shown that judges could not recognize emotions from photographs, could not distinguish geniuses from idiots by their portraits or their handwriting, and so forth. The proponents of this view held that psychologists should be laboratory scientists, not skillful gypsies, and that they should be concerned not with understanding individual people but with seeking the general laws of behavior. Once you had learned enough of these laws, you might then be able to apply that basic knowledge to everyday affairs; but since psychology was a young science, it could not yet be expected to have wide applications.

A few psychologists held out against the tide. Most psychoanalysts were unaffected by this "know-nothing" orientation, which chiefly characterized behaviorism, though many of them were a little too impressed with Freud's theories as a short cut to understanding by means of formulas and not aware enough of his own practice, which relied on his intuitive feelings about people, enriched by a deep literary culture. Within academic psychology, G. W. Allport (1937) was expounding a different but equally humanistic approach. In one of the experiments Allport stimulated, Estes (1938) studied various people's ability to judge personality from watching a brief movie of subjects doing such things as taking off a shirt and putting it on again. Unhappily, he found that psychologists were poorer judges than artists, thus unintentionally providing evidence that studying the psychology of the 1930's had apparently produced a "trained incapacity" to size people up.

In recent years, however, the tide has begun to turn. As part of the study of "social perception," social psychologists have begun to elucidate the processes by which people form impressions of one another. And within the philosophy of science, the superobjectivists have simmered down as it has become apparent that no scientist actually worked in the ways they had described. There is a large element of skill or art (know-how) in scientific theorizing and experimenting, which must be recognized and respected before we can begin the laborious job of studying scientific inquiry and formulating parts of it in explicit rules. All psychologists can agree that a science of human behavior must eventually establish lawful relationships by objective methods, but in *discovering* psychological principles (as opposed to nailing them down in scientific laws) and in applying them to everyday life, we should not hesitate to make use of empathy and to rely on our own feelings.

What Are the Uses
of Formal Assessment?

Those who are involved in formal assessment must supplement the tacit processes of informal assessment by a number of technical procedures for obtaining data about people and reaching conclusions about them. Even within the field of personality assessment there are those who strive to eliminate all human judgment and other nonmechanical processes from their work; typically they rely upon "objective" tests. They often deny that they make any use of the intuitive methods of the ordinary man. But they do continue to rely on them, anyway, because they must, if only to recognize when a mechanically-arrived-at assessment is so implausible as to indicate that the system has broken down.

The techniques of gathering data in formal assessment include interviewing, testing, obtaining personal documents (such as autobiographies and letters), and making observations in specially controlled situations. The technical procedures for reaching conclusions may be summarized as clinical and statistical inference, processes that will be explained in Chapter 34.

Formal assessment is undertaken for the most part by five types of professional people: psychologists of several specialized kinds, psychiatrists, personnel workers, social workers, and guidance counselors. (To a lesser degree, anthropologists, criminologists, and sociologists also assess personalities.) The settings in which the work goes on also can be classified into five groupings, though these do not precisely correspond to the five types of professions.

CLINICAL SETTINGS

Clinical settings include hospitals, mental-health clinics, and private offices of psychodiagnosticians and psychotherapists of various kinds (including psychoanalysts). People being assessed in these settings suffer from the personal problems and difficulties in living that are often called mental illnesses, emotional disorders, or types of psychopathology. The tradition of regarding these as "health problems" is understandable because until recently most psychotherapists have been psychiatrists, who have received full medical training and who use medical treatments as well as psychotherapy. (Nonmedical therapists, such as clinical psychologists, use only psychological methods of treatment such as psychoanalysis, psychotherapy, and behavior therapy.) Because of the traditional conception of mental health and mental disease (see Szasz, 1961), the suffering individual often takes himself to medical institutions or practitioners and is called a patient. In this context assessment goes by the name of diagnosis. The focus of assessment in clinical settings is to find out just what is wrong with the person and to measure the strengths or assets that are relevant to helping him, so that the most effective plan of treatment may be devised. A private practitioner of psychotherapy or psychoanalysis may conduct a diagnostic assessment by means of a single, unstructured interview, relying on his empathic impressions and the other methods of informal assessment.

In institutional clinical settings, such as hospitals for severely disturbed people, the task of assessment is often divided up between clinical psychologists, social workers, and psychiatrists. The psychologist concentrates on administering and interpreting tests; the social worker conducts interviews, obtaining a *social history* from the person and from members of his family; and the psychiatrist may supplement his own interviewing by such physical procedures as testing reflexes in a neurological examination or by such laboratory procedures as X-rays or studies of blood biochemistry or of brain waves (the electroencephalograph). All this information is brought together in case conferences where the participating members of the clinical team construct a picture of the personality pattern—how the person got that way, his assets and liabilities, and his future prospects. They then plan what to do to help him. A similarly elaborate assessment is sometimes used to gauge the effects of a course of treatment, although more usually the patient is merely reinterviewed by one person and retested.

LEGAL SETTINGS

Professionals of the types described above often assist judges, prison officials, and other legal authorities in assessing the personalities of people accused of crimes. To some extent—especially in the most enlightened legal systems—the purpose of the assessment is to decide on a plan for treating, rehabilitating, or otherwise helping the prisoner change his behavior. Often, however, this forensic assessment is conducted for the scientifically less meaningful purpose of deciding whether the accused is "sane" and may thus be held legally responsible for his acts. At times the assessment may be used to help the judge decide on the nature of punishment or duration of imprisonment. Also, when it is necessary to decide on a person's eligibility for parole, the resources of formal assessment are sometimes called upon to help predict the man's behavior.

EDUCATIONAL AND VOCATIONAL GUIDANCE

The people who offer themselves (or who are referred by teachers or administrators) for assessment at schools, colleges, or vocational-guidance centers are looking for advice in deciding what to do with themselves educationally or vocationally. Should this young woman go to a junior college or to a university? Does this young man have what it takes to become a linotyper, or a lawyer, or a laundromat operator? Perhaps the person is confused about his own abilities and interests or knows too little about the spectrum of possible jobs to make up his own mind about a career. Vocational counselors are usually psychologists, but they are sometimes social workers. Educational counselors generally have had training in education or psychology. Interviewing and testing are the most common methods of assessing personality for purposes of advisement.

EDUCATIONAL AND VOCATIONAL SELECTION

The prospective student or employee is not the only one concerned with the question of who is to fill which slot in schools, businesses, and government: Whenever they can, educational institutions and employers *select* from among applicants those most likely to succeed. Thus, students who have been carefully tested and advised to apply to, let us say, medical schools find themselves subjected to a further assessment by application form, credentials (transcripts of grades and letters of recommendation), and often more tests and personal interviews before they are admitted. An employer too may have a personnel department where specialized workers (who are sometimes industrial psychologists) screen and evaluate applicants for each job.

Sometimes such selection is for special assignments in the government —as, for example, Peace Corps projects and, during World War II, the undercover operations of the OSS; in these cases elaborate programs of assessment may be employed. By extension of this logic, the armed forces are also employers trying to select the most suitable workers, even when the latter "apply" only after receiving a notice from a draft board. The medical and psychiatric examining and the psychological testing of recruits have constituted the largest personality-assessment programs in history.

RESEARCH SETTINGS

Research on assessment is conducted in university, government, and commercial laboratories or research centers. Psychologists do most of this work, but psychiatrists and other behavioral scientists are also involved. Whether the research has a primarily applied and practical or a purely scientific emphasis, assessment has to be sufficiently formalized to make it possible to collect data about the personalities of adequate numbers of subjects and to relate facts about characteristic patterns of behavior to some other aspect of a person.

For example, suppose you were interested in the problem of high school drop-outs who are intelligent enough to handle the academic work. It would be reasonable to study the possibility that—among other causes— something about their personalities was related to dropping out. If you happened to know a drop-out personally, you would already have some ideas about what he was like from your informal assessment of him, which would probably suggest leads for systematic study. Perhaps you knew that your friend had constant battles with his parents and you suspected that in some way this struggle interfered with his schoolwork. You might be right, and yet there are others who make the grade despite similar family crises. To settle the question you would have to get good information on performance in school and relationships with parents from a large enough sample of both failures and successes in high school. For this purpose you would probably use a focused interview or a test, or both. Groups of students who are alike in intelligence but who differed on dropping out could then be compared on the quantitative measures or scores obtained from the systematic assessment. Thus you could check on the validity of the initial inference about the effect of the family struggle on schoolwork.

Formal assessment in these different settings, carried out for different purposes, focuses on different aspects of personality. Just as no set of abilities is relevant to any and all jobs, there can be no single scheme of personality variables that should be measured in every formal assessment. Nevertheless, the general principles that are presented in the chapters that follow are useful, no matter what specific facets of personality may be appropriate for a particular assessment enterprise.

This initial survey of the field of assessment has necessarily been just a quick introduction. In the next three chapters, we shall take a closer look first at informal assessment and then at clinical and "objective" formal assessment. In Chapters 36–40, we shall see the various methods and approaches at work on a concrete example, a man whom we shall study in some depth. Finally, in Chapter 41, we shall appraise the field of assessment and some of its controversies.

I do not love thee, Dr. Fell;
The reason why I cannot tell,
But this alone I know full well:
I do not love thee, Dr. Fell.

THOMAS BROWN

CHAPTER 33
MAJOR
PROCESSES
OF INFORMAL
ASSESSMENT

The process of informally assessing personality begins the moment one person claps eyes on another, in the formation of a first impression. Much of what can go right and wrong in informal assessment can be seen operating during this initial phase. Insights or misconceptions acquired during a first meeting can have a lasting effect on a relationship and may heavily weight a person's final assessment of another. An important part of initial impressions is the perception of affects, or emotions; empathy plays a large role in the assessment of these states. This chapter surveys the present state of knowledge about all these matters, concluding with a discussion of the methods by which informal understanding of personalities is deepened and systematized.

First Impressions of Personality

A large proportion of the systematic psychological research on informal assessment has dealt with the formation of first impressions, since these are relatively easy to investigate. We are therefore beginning to learn something about the subtle and complicated processes involved in what is rather misleadingly called "social perception" or "person perception." True, a first impression of a personality is largely a perceptual event, but it also involves judgment, inference, and various other processes, among which emotion plays a surprisingly large role.

Recent research on forming impressions of personality has confirmed a fact we know from direct experience: The process begins with a vague but total impression (a *Gestalt*), which has a strongly evaluative or affective character. This impression later takes on greater clarity and specificity as well as increased organization, always remaining the percept of a *person*. We never form an impression by perceiving a few isolated traits, nor do we build up an overall concept of someone the way a child builds a block tower, piece by separate piece. Typically, a first impression of a stranger—a "Dr. Fell"—is poorly differentiated and hard to put into words; yet it often yields a distinct emotional flavor of liking or dislike. This affective reaction may be a source of both useful information and error. Yet remarkably enough, most people learn to pick up a modicum of truth about one another on very brief acquaintance. As it happens, however, most of the research on forming impressions of personality has focused on uncovering ways in which first impressions are faulty. Such informal assessments may be erroneous because the observer gets mistaken impressions (for any of a number of reasons shortly to be surveyed) or because the person being judged is inscrutable.

SOURCES OF ERROR IN THE OBSERVER

Hearsay Very frequently, we form impressions of people from *hearsay*. Even a brief description may affect our expectations about someone so markedly that when we do meet him our perception and judgment of what he actually does and says is selective and biased. In a controlled experiment on this topic, Kelley (1950) met a class after arranging for their usual instructor to be absent. He gave the students a brief note describing a stranger who was to be their substitute teacher. This description included the following information: "He is 26 years old, a veteran, and married. People who know him consider him a rather cold person, industrious, critical, practical, and determined." On half the notes, the words "rather cold" were replaced by "very warm." After the substitute instructor had conducted a 20-minute discussion and left, the students rated him on 15 traits. On related variables (consideration of others, informality, sociability, popularity, humor) students who had been told the teacher was warm gave him significantly higher ratings than did those whose notes had described him as cold; on unrelated traits like intelligence the difference was negligible. This experiment also showed that the hearsay effect could affect overt behavior, for students in the "warm" group were noticeably more likely to participate in the discussion than were students in the "cold" group.

The Halo Effect   Kelley's experiment demonstrates not only the power of hearsay and the organized nature of first impressions but also the power of a generally positive or negative impression to affect more specific judgments about a person. This spread is usually called the *halo effect*. If you like a person, you will probably consider him "a good guy" in most respects, and if he rubs you the wrong way, you are likely to rate him low on any trait that is evaluatively tinged.

One result of the halo effect is to wash out most of the potential differentiation, or particularity, in a first impression, leaving just a general feeling of liking or dislike. Even in a formal assessment situation, when professional people are trying to make relatively specific behavioral ratings after extensive contact with a subject, they may be unable to come up with anything more meaningful than a general sense of how good a man they are dealing with. In an experimental attempt to find ways of selecting young physicians for psychiatric training (Holt & Luborsky, 1958), supervisors were given careful instruction on evaluating the performance of psychiatric residents on 20 aspects of work; they also rated each resident on how well they liked him after guiding his work for several months. A factor analysis of these ratings showed that liking and *all other* variables were highly loaded on one general factor. The impression of general competence pervaded every rating and was closely related to the supervisors' affective feelings about the residents.

The halo effect tends to produce an unnaturally consistent impression of a person, which is most marked when the contact is brief and not focused on a particular aspect of behavior. Yet the halo effect is not necessarily all error; because it is the outgrowth of a complex emotional and empathic response to a person, it may contain valuable information.

The Leniency Effect   Another emotional effect on first impressions is called the *leniency effect*; it also primarily concerns evaluative aspects of personality. When a person adopts the policy of always giving the other fellow the benefit of the doubt in order to maintain a picture of himself as a benign and decent person, the leniency effect is operating. The converse error is the sour or suspicious assumption that "people are no good unless proved otherwise," an orientation that implies a deeply injured, often paranoid, person.

Stereotypes   *Stereotypes* and folk theories about personality tend to give a bias to first impressions. For instance, if the stranger differs from the perceiver in any immediately obvious way, that difference is likely to be noticed first and to bring to mind the set of standard notions the perceiver has about "that kind" of person. Such foci of stereotypes include, of course, ethnic-group membership with all the prejudicial clichés that entails; nationality; unusual or perceptually salient physical characteristics, such as marked beauty or ugliness, height or weight, prominent facial features ("weak chin," "intellectual forehead," and so on), physical deformity, or handicaps of any sort; and anything out of the ordinary about a person's voice or expressive movements. Most cultures are full of such misinformation, and though we may become aware of prejudices and try to disregard them, their effects are insidious. Even members of minority groups often cannot escape from prejudice against their own kind.

A stereotype or folk theory has the logical structure of an inferential rule and can be translated into one, as in these examples: "If anyone is a Negro, infer that he loves rhythmic music and loud colors"; "if a person has red hair, infer that he has a hot temper." Signs of irritation that would not be noticed in a brunette are more readily noticed in a redhead because the prejudiced person is set to perceive them; such a person can then protest that it's not just a theory because he has actually seen it work out most of the time. Such theories also operate, in R. K. Merton's words, like "self-fulfilling prophecies" in that they lead us to act toward people in a way that brings out the traits we expect them to have. Thus, if a person believes that those who come from a higher socioeconomic class than he does are generally haughty and condescending, he may very well approach such people with a chip on his shoulder and provoke rejection.

The obvious unfairness of prejudice and such oversimplifications as expecting all fat people to be jolly should not blind us to the fact that folk theories often do contain a germ of usable truth. As long as we do not fall into the trap of assuming that "all Jews are alike," we can make cautious use of a set of expectations that arise from cultural uniformities: Jewish traditions of hospitality are such that it is safe more often than not to assume that a middle-aged Jewish hostess will be pleased by a guest's over-eating. (See also the discussion of constitutional psychology in Chapter 35.)

Stereotypes exert their biasing effects on formal as well as on informal assessment. Recent research (summarized by Masling, 1966) shows that clinical psychologists are influenced in their formal assessments by such variables as ethnic-group membership and socioeconomic status whether they realize it or not. A similar effect showed up in a study of the attempts of psychiatrists to select people for psychiatric training on the basis of a brief interview (Holt & Luborsky, 1958). It turned out that a particular interviewer's impression of poor voice quality was completely unrelated to the subsequent performance of the interviewees during residency training; and the interviewer himself said that he did not think it was a very relevant variable. Nevertheless, an examination of his comments about the men he interviewed showed that he had noted "poor voice" for 75 percent of the men he expected to do badly and for only 21 percent of the men he predicted would do well.

There are only two ways to prevent first impressions from being influenced by stereotypes and extraneous characteristics such as physical appearance: by becoming fully aware of these effects and trying to allow for them or by avoiding direct contact with the person being appraised, lest his personal attributes prejudice us. Since the latter course would cut us off from most of the valuable sources of information about personality, it is best to follow the former.

Moods and Need States

Our *moods* and *need states* can also bias perception and judgment when we encounter another person. All the world may seem to love a lover in part because his elation acts like a pair of rose-tinted glasses, and in part because his mood may be infectious and bring out the best in others. On the other hand, an anxious or depressed person is likely to perceive others with one of two distortions: He may see others as exaggeratedly frivolous or carefree in contrast to his own misery, or he may project his own mood and find it reflected all around him. In an ingenious experiment involving a house party of young girls, Murray (1933) showed that in the overwrought state following a scary game of Murder his daughter's guests rated men's faces as significantly more "mean" and threatening than they did in a calm and relaxed condition. More recently, Kleiner (1960) was able to bring about an increase in the rated attractiveness of a person who made a special contribution to the success of a small group in solving problems. In each of his experimental trios (whose members were previously unacquainted with one another), one person was always a confederate who knew the solution to puzzles in advance; the more threatened the group felt and the larger the improvement in the group's performance produced by the stooge, the more he was rated as someone the other members wanted to get to know better.

Depending on the situation and the nature of the need state, there can be other types of distorting effects on the formation of impressions. In general, the presence of an active, unsatisfied need tends to make a person especially attentive to the presence of a gratifier or goal object: Hunger will alert the eyes of the berry picker, sometimes even making him momentarily mistake a pebble for a berry. A young man who is longing for a girlfriend will often wishfully endow with great virtues any passably attractive girl who expresses an interest in him. A frightened, lone sentry more easily forms the impression that a stranger is hostile or dangerous than he would if he were to meet the same man on a city street under civilian circumstances.

Defenses and Blind Spots

Everyone has blind spots in appraising others, which are generally caused by the operation of his own defenses. A hysterical person who follows the model of the famous three monkeys may be able to see and hear no evil in others as part of his struggle to speak—and do—no evil himself. Put more technically and less moralistically, when a person defends himself against hostile impulses by denial, he may have difficulty perceiving hostility in other people. Conversely, self-knowledge can help to overcome the distorting effects of defenses in the formation of impressions.

**Projection, Empathy,
and the Self-Concept**   One defense, *projection*, is of special interest as a source of error in impressions of personality. The term is understood here in the sense Freud used it to explain paranoia (not in the broader and looser sense he and a number of others have used it, to refer to any distorting or selective effect of a person's inner world on his perception or conception of the outer world). In its narrower meaning, projection is a distortion of reality that occurs when a person's desires conflict with his moral values and when his self-concept is too rigid to admit any frailties. Almost everyone uses this defense mechanism at times, but its use is especially pronounced in some seriously disturbed people.

Projection is a kind of opposite to empathy. In empathy, a person perceives the anger that is actually another's by allowing some of that emotion to develop within himself but attributes it to his percept of the other (see page 606). In projection, as a person's anger arises, he attributes it to his percept of another in order *not* to recognize that it originated in himself, since that would be intolerable to his righteous picture of himself. There are more complicated forms of projection, such as when a person begins to imagine that other people suspect or accuse him of having the evil thoughts he finds so intolerable. (Further discussion of projection and additional examples may be found in Part II, Chapter 17.) Obviously, anyone who uses this defense very extensively will make many errors in his informal assessments of others, though it should be added that paranoid people are often shrewd enough to fasten their suspicions on people who do have somewhat more anger (or whatever quality is in question) than average, even though it may not be obvious on the surface.

Projection and empathy are two forms of one basic process in the perception and judgment of other people, but projection distorts the accuracy and depth of understanding, whereas empathy enhances it. The basic process might be called subjectivity, or egocentricity; whatever name we give it, it is the almost universal tendency to judge everyone else in relation to the self-concept. A person inevitably compares everyone else to himself. He himself is, after all, the person he knows best and longest and for whose welfare he makes the most continuous efforts.

In an experiment on the effects of subliminal stimuli on thought, Fiss (1966) showed how the self-concept of his subjects (college girls) affected even their perception of nonhuman figures. Before showing each subject abstract linear designs for .33 sec. in a mirror tachistoscope, he briefly flashed (for .01 sec.) either the word ANGRY or just a blank card; the subject then rated the "angriness" of each design. Under the conditions of the experiment only the longer-exposed image was visible. There was no significant difference in the average ratings given the drawings that were preceded by the word and those preceded by the blank, so at first the experiment appeared to have failed. But the subjects were also asked to rate themselves on a scale of interpersonal hostility, and this rating correlated significantly with the tendency to judge in accordance with the subliminal suggestion. In other words, only girls who were willing to describe themselves as having hostile thoughts and feelings rated the figures as if they were influenced by the subliminal stimuli.

From experiments like those described above we are only beginning to learn something about the extent to which perceptions and judgments of personal and emotional qualities are made with reference to the self-concept, and no doubt the process is a complicated and subtle one in many people. Yet the involvement of the self-concept in perception is a working hypothesis that brings together quite a number of observations, particularly those concerning errors in first impressions that are induced by the emotional and motivational states of the observers. The experimental findings also suggest that people are capable of unconsciously using subtle cues in making judgments of personality; indeed, such use of unnoticed evidence may have something to do with the "uncanny" skill of some diagnosticians.

Lack of Abilities   Errors in forming first impressions may arise from a lack of various clearly relevant abilities, including general intelligence, observational ability, and sensory acuity. The observer's interests and values obviously determine what he pays attention to and how he judges it; and anything that interferes with effective cognition, from brain damage to faulty education, can affect informal assessment.

**Oversimplification
and Tolerance
for Ambiguity**   First impressions are necessarily incomplete and fragmentary, for any personality is too complex to be completely grasped in a brief time. Naturally, the most common sort of error in such informal assessments is *oversimplification*. The danger of oversimplification is obvious, yet some people find it inordinately difficult to suspend judgment and to live with the realization that they cannot possibly know another person thoroughly on brief acquaintance. As a result, they jump to conclusions, prematurely crystallize their judgments, and are rigidly impervious to new information. An important dimension of people, therefore, is the degree to which they can hold back their need for a perfectly clear view of the world. Psychologists call it *tolerance for ambiguity*; it is one dimension of cognitive style, or one way of taking in and processing information about the world.

The concept of tolerance for ambiguity was first suggested by Else Frenkel-Brunswik (1949). In studying authoritarian personalities (see also Adorno, Frenkel-Brunswik, Levinson, & Sanford, 1950), she found that persons with an exaggerated deference to authority tended to have a highly simplified view of the world about them and the people in it; they described their parents, for example, in stereotyped and usually laudatory terms. Only students who had relatively democratic ideologies were able to describe personalities in balanced terms, seeing both good and bad.

In a well-controlled experiment, Scodel and Mussen (1953) demonstrated the relevance of authoritarianism to one kind of oversimplification—the direct attribution of aspects of the self-concept to others. They gave several hundred college students the F scale, the main instrument used in research on authoritarianism; this scale measures "protofascist" or radical-right attitudes. From this population the investigators chose 2 groups of 27 (each containing 12 women and 15 men), one having the highest and the other the lowest scores. The subjects were studied in pairs, each of which was made up of a high scorer (authoritarian) and a low scorer (nonauthoritarian). The members of each pair were introduced and were asked to discuss radio, television, and movies for 20 minutes. Each subject was then taken into a separate room and given a fresh copy of the F scale to fill out as he thought the other member of his pair had done. As was expected, the authoritarians saw the nonauthoritarians as being like themselves and predicted for them significantly higher F scores than they actually had. The low scorers correctly predicted that the high scorers had authoritarian attitudes, though less extreme ones than the high scorers had actually attained. Thus, the high-scoring group naively assumed that the low scorers were not significantly different from themselves, and the low-scoring group saw their authoritarian acquaintances as prejudiced but not as much as they actually were.

SOURCES OF ERROR IN THE PERSON JUDGED

Characteristics That Make a Person Hard to Know Personalities differ in almost every way imaginable, including what might be called transparency versus inscrutability—how easy or difficult it is to form correct impressions of them. In addition there are several types of inscrutability. Some people are like turtles, so withdrawn into a shell of reserve and inhibition that it is hard to guess whether their inner experience is rich with sensitive perceptions and vivid fantasies or whether it is as drab as their shy exterior. Others are like porcupines, so bristling with suspicion and defensive hostility that it is hard to get close enough to them to learn more than this obvious fact. Then there are the lions, the nonintrospective men of action who are so much more complicated than they realize that they can give relatively little useful information about themselves. Chameleon personalities also lack insight and are hard to know because, not having a stable sense of identity, they adopt different

roles in every context. Brief observation may thus give an entirely misleading impression of them, as it may also of those sly foxes who deliberately
mislead others to throw them off their scent. And some people are so color-
less that they do not even bring to mind a zoological analogy to help us
caricature them; such a nondescript "average man" blends into the crowd,
standing out too little from his background to make it easy to find anything
distinctive to say about him.

Paradoxically, we also find it difficult to form correct first impressions
if a person is *too* different from ourselves. For example, it is proverbial that
all members of another ethnic group tend to look alike: we are often more
impressed by characteristics that a member of another nationality shares
with his compatriots than by the traits that set him apart from them.
Moreover, we may find that our usual inferential rules do not work, that we
lack appropriate concepts to make sense of his behavior and discern the patterns in it, and that our expectations are violated so often that we become
confused and disoriented.

The "Best Foot Forward" Error

Most people intuitively recognize that it is
possible to bias first impressions in their
favor by good grooming, smiling rather than scowling, and the like, and so
there is an almost universal tendency to try to take advantage of these effects. The result is what might be called the *best foot forward error* in first
impressions. This error is especially important if the observer's behavior or
the context is such as to arouse the subject's suspicion, hostility, or anxiety
and thus to make him defend himself by dissembling in this way. The observer may also contribute to the best foot forward error by giving cues about
the kinds of words or actions that will win his approval.

Deception

A certain amount of mild deception is involved when a person tries to be judged in
terms of his most attractive side, but most people—not just the "foxes"
spoken of above—go further. Voltaire was not the first cynic to note that
men use speech to conceal their thoughts; nor was Freud the first to see
that the person from whom a man wants most to hide his true feelings on
many topics is himself. Psychoanalysis has taught us, however, that these
processes are mostly involuntary self-defensive operations, not conscious dis-
simulations. We all engage in unconscious (as well as some conscious)
duplicity, at least occasionally deny our true motives, and lie about our
intentions or our reactions, hiding whatever would expose us to ridicule,
scorn, or other forms of social rejection. To be sure, we typically anticipate
more rejection than we would get if our dreadful secrets came to light,
because most people are not only tolerant but blessedly indifferent, having
many of the same secrets themselves and being more concerned with the

impression *they* are making on others than with sitting in judgment on them.

In any event, deceptive maneuvers greatly complicate the task of formal and informal assessment. Study and practice can, however, make it possible to penetrate some defensive smoke screens and to grasp part of the truth, even in initial contacts. Here is an area where the study of psychology can pay off in an increased ability to understand other people and deal with them effectively.

FURTHER IMPLICATIONS
OF ERRORS IN FIRST IMPRESSIONS

Because personalities are far more complex than first impressions of them, it is obviously easy for two people to disagree completely in their view of a third man and yet for both of them to be right. Cartwright and French (1939) demonstrated this point experimentally, showing that the validity (agreement with an assessment in depth) of two judges' impressions of a person exceeded their reliability (agreement with one another) because they were struck with quite different aspects of their man. In a way, this is the story of the blind men and the elephant all over again—each of the blind men had hold of part of the truth of what an elephant was like, though there was no overlap in their impressions because each came into contact with a different part of him.

What causes two people to form different impressions of the same personality? They may approach him with different sets or expectations based on hearsay, looking through the variously hued spectacles of different moods and needs, subject to the interferences of different defenses—in short, all the sources of error in first impressions also turn out to be determinants of variation in impressions from one observer to another. Not everyone is equally prone to such biasing influences as the halo effect or projection—seeing oneself in others. This last fact has a dual significance: It helps to explain observer-to-observer variation in first impressions, but it also suggests that the assessor of personality might do well to pay attention to the sources of error reviewed above as they operate in people who are themselves being assessed. Man is a social creature, and a subject's ability to size up others, as well as his susceptibility to various types of error in perceiving people are aspects of behavior worth noting.

This survey of the sources of error in first impressions has repeatedly brought out how intimately the process of impression formation involves emotion. So far, we have been concerned with the emotional reaction of the perceiver; let us turn now to the complementary point that a good deal of what we notice first about another person has to do with the latter's emotional state.

Perceiving Emotions
in Face and Voice

Much of the early research on the expressions of emotions and how well they are recognized proceeded on implicitly atomistic, rather than configurational (*Gestalt*), assumptions. It seemed not only a reasonable procedure, but the only proper one, to begin by asking subjects to match drawings or still photographs of people with the names of the emotions they were attempting to express. Although in these studies some subjects judged facial expressions with great accuracy and others did badly indeed, the overall results were positive—significantly better than chance. Consider, for example, the two poses in Figure 33-1; Feleky (1914) found that one of them was called *surprise, astonishment,* or *wonder* by 74 of her 100 judges and the other was called *disgust* or *repugnance* by 50 percent. Moreover, there was hardly any overlap in the lists of adjectives applied to the two pictures. Yet, as Davitz (1964) pointed out, textbook writers who have cited such work have often concluded that emotions *cannot* be judged from facial expressions. Perhaps they came to this conclusion because they were looking for uniform laws of behavior and considered individual differences an uninteresting nuisance. The differences among people are the main subject matter of personality assessment, however, so let us consider what seem to be the main sources of variability in the accurate judgment of emotions. Because the experimental evidence deals only with mien or voice (or both), it will be necessary to disregard posture, gait, gesture, and such physiological signs as pallor or flushing, trembling, and perspiring, though these cues obviously can tell an observer much about emotions.

THE PERSON JUDGING

Almost all the relevant research has indicated a great range of ability in judging the emotions expressed by face or voice. The ability to assess emotions from tape-recorded voices is significantly (but not highly) correlated with verbal I.Q. (Davitz, 1964). Usually there is no consistent

Figure 33-1 Pictures from an experiment on judging emotions. (From Feleky, 1914)

superiority of one sex over the other, but when a difference is found it is in favor of the females.

Clearly, the ability to interpret facial and vocal cues correctly is learned, for it can be improved by specific training and practice and improves with age, at least from age 5 to age 10 (Dimitrovsky, 1964). Even so, the youngest children who have been tested have performed significantly better than chance. Gates (1923) found that children under 3 years of age can recognize laughing faces in still photographs; and that at 5 to 6 years they can recognize pain, although the subtler emotions like contempt are seldom accurately identified from pictures by preadolescents.

THE PERSON BEING JUDGED

Some people have impassive, "wooden" faces and monotonous voices; others are highly expressive. If an experiment requires the subjects to simulate emotion in facial expression or in voice, those who are trained in emotional communication—actors—are generally more effective than nonactors in getting a message across, although ordinary college students do remarkably well (Thompson & Meltzer, 1964; Levitt, 1964). In a Russian experiment (Kalina, 1960), where nonactors and actors posed for photographs of various emotions, the superiority of the professionals showed up only in the more complex emotions.

Not a great deal of research has been done on the characteristics of the "sender" of emotional communication, but it has been demonstrated that the facial expressions of 10-month-old babies are less recognizable than those of children and that emotions enacted by members of one's own culture are usually (though not in all studies) easier to recognize than emotions that are transmitted across cultural barriers. Much depends, however, on the emotion in question, and cross-cultural recognition of emotions has been found to be consistently better than chance in studies involving Americans and the supposedly inscrutable Chinese (May, 1938—photographs), and Americans, Israelis, and Japanese (Davitz, 1964—voices).

THE CONTEXT AND AMOUNT
OF EMOTIONAL COMMUNICATION BEING JUDGED

An emotion is not a static, detached state but a fluid and literally *moving* process that is part of a situation. Thus, in everyday life we rarely base our judgment of how someone feels on a momentary expression; we observe the total pattern of his behavior in the context of some situation. Several experimenters, realizing this point, demonstrated that accuracy and agreement among observers increased when they had information about the *situation* of the pictured person. Such findings were at first widely interpreted in a negative way: Emotion could not be judged from facial expression; it was all a matter of inference from knowledge of the situation. According to this theory, we learn that dangerous situations arouse fearful behavior; therefore, we perceive fear in the expression of a person who is in danger, no matter what his expression may be.

There is good evidence against this theory in the data of a well-known experiment (Munn, 1940) in which college students were shown candid pictures of people experiencing various emotions. First, they saw enlargements of the faces only; a week later they saw pictures of the entire person in the natural setting. When the feelings in question were joy, terror, pain, anxiety, surprise, or disappointment, correct judgments on the initial showing ranged from 65 percent to 99 percent, and performance was *not* improved when the context was added.

Other studies show that the overall accuracy with which emotions are recognized from facial expression alone increased when still photographs were replaced by short movies (Frijda, 1953) and that adding a sound track to silent movies of faces increased accuracy in judging fear and surprise (though not other emotions), even though the voices were merely reciting irrelevant, neutral material (Levitt, 1964).

THE NATURE OF THE EMOTION BEING JUDGED

In several of the investigations mentioned above, it was clear that the results varied greatly depending on the particular emotions involved. If the affective state is basic and elemental—that is, if a person is laughing heartily, weeping with sorrow, in agonizing pain, or ragingly angry—very little visual or auditory information is necessary to convey the message to the beholder. When it is a question of such extremes, particularly the unpleasant emotions like sadness and anger, communication is good despite cultural differences, lack of context, the age of either person involved, or the intelligence of the judge (Levy, Orr, & Rosenzweig, 1960). The more subtle, complex, and weakly expressed emotions—for example, nostalgic, quizzical, or ambivalent feelings—are correspondingly harder to identify because they are expressed in less dramatic and less uniform ways by different people; success in these cases depends more on the skill of the judge and on completeness of information about the behavioral situation.

INNATE FACTORS AND CULTURAL LEARNING
IN EMOTIONAL COMMUNICATION

It is difficult to obtain good evidence from human subjects about the degree to which emotional expression and recognition are inborn, biological endowments. Smiling and laughing are universal expressions of pleasure, and anguish of any sort tends to produce weeping in all cultures and at all ages. Obviously, however, it is difficult to determine just when in infancy we become able to recognize the emotions of others around us.

Some suggestive evidence comes from work with subhuman primates.

Miller, Murphy, and Mirsky (1959) found that monkeys clearly avoided color slides of other monkeys in a frightened state, discriminating them from pictures of calm monkeys. Another experimenter (Sackett, 1966) strikingly demonstrated that the ability to recognize emotion is innate, though not completely developed at birth. Eight rhesus monkeys were reared in individual, enclosed cages from birth to 9 months, during which time they saw no other living creatures. One wall of the cage was a translucent screen on which color slides were projected daily. Most of the pictures were of monkeys in various positions and emotional states, but some were control slides of human beings, landscapes, and miscellaneous scenes. The experimenter observed the monkeys' reactions to each picture through a one-way vision screen. All pictures of monkeys consistently stimulated more responses than did the control slides, indicating an innate "species identity," but two types drew most responses of all types: pictures of other monkey infants and of threatening adult monkeys. Typical responses to pictures of babies were attempts to play with them and exploratory behavior. The threatening expression of an adult monkey seemed to be innately meaningful, for the threat pictures caused more responses of almost all kinds at each age level, and had a specific effect that peaked at 3 months: The baby monkeys would squeal, rock, huddle, and shrink back in obvious fear on seeing the threat pictures. These negative responses were not called forth by any other slide.

It is possible that evidence may someday be found that human beings also have some inborn capacity to respond differentially to expressions of basic emotions in others. Surely the emotional expressions found in man and other animals have survival value as a means of direct, nonverbal communication among members of the species and, often, across species. The creature who is innately able to tell at a glance whether he is confronted by an angry or a contented specimen of his own or of some other kind is more likely to survive and pass along this ability to descendants than is his less sensitive brother.

It is equally evident that emotional expression is heavily influenced by culture. A young Chinese girl, for example, is taught not to show her teeth when she smiles; the gestural expansiveness of many Mediterranean peoples contrasts with the stolidity and impassiveness proverbially associated with American Indians and Orientals, who probably have as much depth of inner feeling as anyone else.

The cultural standards for emotional expression that constitute a vocabulary of nonverbal language are perhaps most clearly expressed in the theater. Actors develop a good deal more uniformity and clarity of facial expression than do nonactors, just as they tend to enunciate words more clearly. Most cultures teach the language of facial expression in their graphic arts, too. Since a painter must convey his message with a single momentary expression, it may not exactly match any one frame of a motion picture of a person who is realistically experiencing the same emotion, yet it may communicate feeling equally well. These pictorial standards of expression, epitomized and sharpened by the caricaturist and cartoonist, constitute a constant and pervasive indoctrination in ways to express our feelings. It is no wonder, therefore, that the first experimenters in this field assumed that still pictures were perfectly adequate material for studying the recognition of emotion.

Rival theorists in psychology once advanced extreme theories claiming that some aspect of behavior was innate *or* that it was determined by learning. We are now beginning to recognize that there are important genetic contributions to behavior up and down the line; at the same time there are hardly any aspects of behavior that do not show some shaping by the cultural environment of the individual. At this time more is understood about learning than about behavioral inheritance, although recent developments in the biochemistry and biology of heredity may reverse the situation. Psychologists stress environmental determinants because it seems that more can be accomplished currently by training, re-education, and therapy than by genetics, at least in human beings.

Empathy and Understanding

An important means of understanding the emotions of others goes by the somewhat abused term *empathy*. This concept was first introduced around the turn of the twentieth century by the German psychologist-philosopher Lipps, who based an esthetic theory on the observation that many people made small involuntary movements when observing certain works of art. He claimed that the sagging, drooping lines of a funereal sculpture (as shown in Figure 33-2) or of a weeping willow appear to us that way because they evoke similar dejected postures in us, while the linear qualities of a monumental building convey a sense of heroic strength by stimulating us to throw back our shoulders and stand more fully erect. We are not aware of our own movements and stance, said Lipps, because the evoked qualities are perceived as *in* the work of art or nature.

Such observations contain a clue to the way perception sometimes works: through a kind of identification or subjective merging of self and non-self. Although processes of this kind have been difficult to approach by means of systematic research, they play a major role in informal assessment and therefore deserve our attention. Despite their relative lack of control, the observations of psychoanalysts and other clinicians have a good deal to teach us about empathy (see, for example, Schafer, 1959).

There are five kinds of phenomena to which the concept of empathy is applicable. Besides the *esthetic empathy* mentioned above, there is the closely related process of what Murphy (1947) calls *autistic* (or magical) *participation*, more familiarly known as "body English." Golfers try to help push the ball into the hole by involuntarily leaning in that direction. If you have ever fed a baby or watched anyone else do it, you know how irresistible

Figure 33-2 *What are your empathic responses to this study by Rodin for his "The Burghers of Calais"?*

is the irrational impulse to get that little mouth to open by opening your own (see Figure 33-3). Behind all responses of the types mentioned is the automatic and unconscious identification of every normal human being with any other he encounters, which seems to be part of a phenomenon called *basic species identity*. In the infant, the first observable form of empathy is the direct transmission of emotional arousal by *emotional contagion*. Finally, the healthy human adult is capable of *mature empathy*. We will look most closely at the last three of these types.*

* Deliberately omitted is any discussion of the recent experimental literature that purports to deal with empathy but is actually concerned with predicting another person's test responses. What at first looked like a promising approach to measuring empathy turned out to be subject to many methodological complications and flaws.

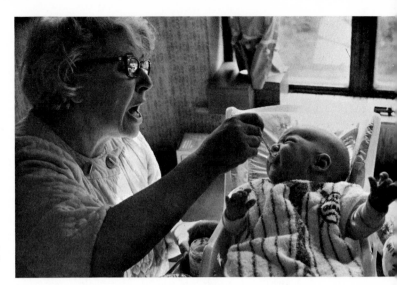

Figure 33-3 "Open wide, please!" An example of autistic participation.

BASIC SPECIES IDENTITY

The ability to recognize a member of one's own species is widespread among the higher animals. It is rather remarkable, when you stop to think about it, that a cat acts toward her kind as if she *knows* that she and they are all cats. A story like Hans Christian Andersen's "The Ugly Duckling" seems to say that animals have an inborn knowledge of what they are: The forlorn hero of that tale ultimately responded appropriately when he encountered other swans and no longer felt like a substandard duck. Indeed, an experiment summarized above (Sackett, 1966) seems to show that monkeys do respond innately to their own in this way. Much recent research by students of animal behavior indicates, however, that whether a hatchling feels itself to be a duck or a swan depends on which species it happens to encounter in a precisely determinable, short period of time during the first days of life. By managing to be the only moving thing in sight during such a critical period, Lorenz (1952) imprinted a jackdaw chick with a permanent interest in human beings, to the exclusion of other members of the bird's own species. Even when the jackdaw became sexually mature, it heard no "call of the wild" that lured it off to an appropriate romance; instead, it gave every sign of having fallen in love with the German naturalist and courted him by tenderly stuffing his ears with tasty worms.

No direct evidence exists as yet of either an innate sense of humanness or a critical period of imprinting in the human infant. Nevertheless, the sense of species identity somehow gets inculcated. It is surely part of being human to recognize every other member of the species *Homo sapiens* as fundamentally like yourself. Furthermore, the greater cognitive complexity of man means that we are likely to attribute to other people a great deal of what we know about or experience within ourselves. Inevitably, much of what we attribute to others will be true of them (many philosophers and psychologists have argued that we are all more alike than we are different), but much will be false, also. If I scratch you where you don't itch, it is likely to be because I *do* itch there. Even the paranoid's overalert sensing of hostility all around him is the pressing of an originally nonpathological capacity into the service of defense (see page 596).

EMOTIONAL CONTAGION

In Chapter 32, the concept of emotional contagion was introduced with an experimental demonstration that babies cry more when their mothers are anxious. In the first year, an infant has no way of resisting the emotions of others, no barriers to prevent their spread; his smile in response to his mother's is as helpless as his squeals when she tickles him.

There is good observational evidence that emotional responsiveness to others depends greatly on the child's experience of being loved, having his own feelings perceived and responded to appropriately, and developing close relationships to his parents. Institutionally raised babies are less responsive to people than are babies who have been cared for by their mothers, particularly if no one worker in the institution serves as foster mother. According to Harlow (1962), even infant monkeys show similar effects when they are taken from their mothers and raised without contact with their kind. After they grow up, such monkeys never develop fully normal social responsiveness, and have disturbed sex lives. If a socially deprived female monkey does succeed in becoming pregnant, she seems devoid of mother love and is unable to care for her own young (see Figure 33-4).

From a developmental point of view, the significant fact is not so much that the infant responds directly to his mother's fright or loving warmth but that the older child grows out of this emotional contagion stage and can learn to be relatively indifferent to the emotional states of others. For to do so he must have a clearly differentiated sense of self, a feeling of his own separate identity and where its boundaries are; this sense is acquired only gradually during the first couple of years. When he does learn that every one of us is, to some extent, an island, he does not have to make a separate discovery that these other creatures in the world also have feelings; he has only to separate out of the welter of his own emotional states the ones that originate with himself and those that are to be attributed to the other person.

Redl (1966) has used the term *contagion* to refer to the rapid spread of a mood or a form of expressive behavior in a group of preadolescents or adolescents. For example, sometimes a boy who has no particular prestige in a group will impulsively yell at a teacher or throw a plate in a mess hall, and at once the whole place gets in an uproar as the others unexpectedly follow suit. According to Redl's analysis of such instances, the group takes over the emotional state and the acts of one of its members when he ex-

Figure 33-4 Typical behavior of an unmothered mother monkey toward her infant. (From Harlow, 1962)

presses something that is latent (but usually not conscious) in all of them. The more mature the members of a group are, the more difficult it is for this kind of emotional contagion to take place and the more controlled its manifestations are. Emotional contagion seems, then, to be a developmental stage preceding the controlled awareness of the feelings of others that we call true empathy.

PREREQUISITES FOR MATURE EMPATHY

The difference between the passive emotional contagion of animals and children and adult forms of empathy can often be seen in cases of schizophrenia, the most common form of psychosis. A preschizophrenic or schizoid person may sometimes be sensitive to others in a mature way, in that he is able to detect the feelings of others in a socially useful manner and without losing distance or objectivity. But after a psychotic break, some schizophrenics display the vulnerability to contagion by their emotional surroundings that characterizes a baby. Such sensitivity is too passive and involuntary to constitute usable empathy, although at times it can make a severely psychotic and apparently withdrawn person astonishingly responsive to concealed feelings and impulses in the doctors and nurses who try to work with him. For example, Stanton and Schwartz (1954) found that when the staff of a mental hospital had internal disputes that they tried to suppress, the schizophrenic patients seemed to sense it and became more disturbed and upset than they were at any other time. This openness to emotional contagion accompanies other evidences of breakdown in the boundaries of the self, such as these patients' bizarre difficulties in drawing pictures of people (see Figure 33-5).

A long process of social learning must take place before empathy works smoothly and automatically. A typical nursery school tussle exemplifies the process in miniature: Bill won't let Barbara have the tricycle. He is in good contact with part of the emotional truth, for he can see very well that she wants it as much as he does. But the teacher tries to introduce a new set of considerations: "How would *you* feel, Bill, if she had it and wouldn't share it with you, even for a little while?" Here is a homely example of the ways children are taught to imagine as fully as possible the feelings of the other person—as sociologist G. H. Mead (1934) put it, to "take the role of the other."

A Secure Sense
of Identity

Paradoxically, mature empathy presupposes a clear separation of self and other and a secure sense of identity. To be willing to let go of his own immediate interests and to participate imaginatively in someone else's world, a person must have the security of knowing that he can slip comfortably back into his own skin. Mature empathy also requires the ability to tolerate enough delay in getting satisfaction of one's own needs to be able to consider those

Figure 33-5 *Drawings of a man and a woman by a paranoid schizophrenic man. (From Machover, 1949)*

of others, which in turn means being able to imagine the future. Anyone who lives only in the present is bound to the urgency of getting what he wants when he wants it; overcoming this impatience is an important part of growing up. Freud expressed this aspect of maturing as the change from the pleasure principle (acting only for immediate gratification) to the reality principle (deferring momentary pleasure so as to attain lasting and important goals).

Genuine
Communication Mature empathy is not only an active but an interactive process; it is trained and refined by the interplay of communication. When young children first play together, they are more properly described as playing *alongside* one another. Piaget (1926) called their conversations "collective monologues." Some people never wholly outgrow this phase; although they may seem to be animated conversationalists, they do not listen, so that genuine interaction with them is not possible. The attempt to talk with such a person, even if it is merely to pass the time of day, can be extremely frustrating and annoying. Why should that be? Apparently, a normal person feels a need to establish some emotional contact with anyone he meets and to communicate, if only by exchanging conventional symbols of friendliness and of caring about one another's welfare. By failing to supply the expected feedback, an unempathic person thwarts this need.

An understanding person does not have to be an intuitive wizard who knows exactly what is going on inside you before you say a word; indeed, he may be preoccupied with his own concerns when the exchange begins and greet you cheerily when you are in pain. But he shows his empathy by noticing that you do not react in the way his gaiety presupposes, and by becoming appropriately serious and concerned.

Practice The ordinary principles of learning are adequate to account for the development of empathy in a person who is not blocked in some way from being interested in others, from listening to them and to his own inner response, and from giving the other person a chance to talk about himself in the true sense of a dialogue. In the process of consistently attempting to respond appropriately to what the other person is trying to communicate, we become more and more alert to subtle cues to complex states of mind and feeling. Indeed, it takes practice to maintain the empathic skills. Marooned sailors and other involuntary hermits typically find it difficult on first reentering society to participate in ordinary social interchange, and they often make social blunders because their empathic capacities are rusty. By the same token, one of the early signs of the emotional withdrawal characteristic of schizophrenia is the appearance of inappropriate language and emotion and a resulting awkwardness and eccentricity in social behavior.

Caring

About Other People   Clearly, affection and empathic perception are closely connected. Whoever lacks the capacity to care about others will be sealed off from understanding them fully. An example of such a person is the psychopathic personality or sociopath, who has the kind of character disorder often found in criminals. These people are usually wholly self-centered and interested in others only for what they can get out of them. Psychopaths may be very shrewd in spotting a victim who can be easily deceived and in exploiting his weaknesses, yet it is an old saying among policemen that a really honest person seldom gets exploited in a confidence game. The apparent cleverness of the psychopath in assessing personality is limited to recognizing those qualities that he himself can experience (such as greed and willingness to cut moral corners) or that he can exploit (such as naive gullibility).

The Ability

to Experience Emotions   Since empathic understanding is based on a person's *re*-experiencing within himself what he sees the other person undergoing, empathic range is limited by the extensiveness of a person's experience. If you have never lost a person who was very dear to you, you may find it impossible to empathize fully with someone whose mother has just died. Yet this principle does not necessarily operate in a literal way: To have loved a pet that died may enable you to build in your imagination a sense of what the bereaved person feels so that you can respond in an appropriate and helpful manner.

Another clinical observation illustrates some conditions limiting mature empathy and some prerequisites for it. People whose defensive make-up is so rigid as to shut them off from fully experiencing their emotions lack the empathy that would enable them to get along with others easily. A common example is the dry, overly intellectual, compulsive person who isolates emotion and tries to live a life of dispassionate fact. He tends to treat people like objects and is unaware of their nonverbal signals of distress. Capability in informal assessment, therefore, requires that a person be aware of what goes on inside himself; in particular he must be in touch with his own feelings. Not that an empathic person spills over with emotion; he may be restrained in his outward expressions while still being very much in tune with his own affective life, and thus with that of other people.

Several psychoanalysts who have observed and pondered mature empathy agree that it is a process of temporary and controlled partial identification, similar to the process by which the self is formed (see Schafer, 1959). It must be partial, or the empathizer loses his distance, and instead of (or in addition to) perceiving the other person as anxious, he feels the anxiety as his own. People who are learning to become psychotherapists often go through a phase of just this type. They must open themselves to the emotional states of their patients; and until they learn to control the process of identification, they become overidentified with them and experience considerable personal turmoil. Indeed, research on the training of psychiatrists has shown that the men who eventually become the best therapists tend to go through such a phase, whereas those who from the beginning are unruffled by contact with disturbed people tend to be too closed off by their own defenses to develop much empathy (Holt & Luborsky, 1958).

How We Develop
an Understanding of a Person

METHODS OF INFORMAL ASSESSMENT

As we get beyond first impressions, we use three main methods in getting to understand a person: (1) observing his behavior in a variety of situations, (2) conversing with him, and (3) getting information about him from other sources.

Observation In the process of learning to know a friend thoroughly, we scrutinize him carefully and repeatedly in his home, at work, at parties, and so on. By seeing for ourselves how he behaves in a variety of situations, we automatically winnow the aspects of his conduct that are situational and are left with the enduring dispositions that make up his personality. In addition, we can increase the range of our information about him by calling *more* of these personal dispositions to the surface. Thus we can overcome the unrepresentativeness of the sample of behavior from which we formed our first impressions.

Conversation It is the exception rather than the rule when, in getting to know a person well, our observations occur in any way other than through interacting with him. Verbal interaction, or conversation, is especially valuable, since it enables us to find out rather directly our friend's feelings about things and people, his thoughts, his organization of his world, and especially his subjective sense of what he wants and is striving for. The primary means of comprehending behavior is through learning about a person's motivation—how behavior is organized by the attempt to attain goals of all kinds; therefore, to understand a person it is essential to know his ambitions, his aims in life, and the values he holds dear. There is hardly any substitute for personal discussion as a way of finding out about these matters; indeed, even though we can learn a great deal by watching what a person seems to be trying to accomplish and by piecing together the observations of others, our understanding is incomplete if we do not know how he thinks and feels about these matters himself. The very fact that he might not know or be willing to admit that he consistently tried to attain social status, for example, would be important for understanding his behavior and might illuminate aspects of his motivation that would otherwise remain obscure or puzzling.

To be sure, there are pitfalls in the conversational method; it has the drawbacks of subjectivity and personal involvement. Fortunately, however, the very attempt to keep up a series of conversations with a person tends to be somewhat self-correcting. As long as we remain open and do not intrude too much nor rigidly shut off the feedback from our successes and failures at communicating, we can continue to learn more and more about a friend, thereby deepening and enriching our understanding of him.

Information from Others No matter how long one person has been acquainted with another, it is always possible to learn new things about him from other persons, who see him in different contexts and relationships. A person reveals somewhat different faces depending on the situation, and whatever is known about the informants themselves adds to the meaning of the behavior and conversations they report. The dangers of hearsay are reduced when the opinions of one informant can be checked against those of others and against personal knowledge. The range of observations from others can be enormously increased to the point where they cover almost all the subject's life.

FORMING A SCHEMA FOR UNDERSTANDING

These three methods of getting data constitute only half the story of informal assessment; a conceptual and integrative step must follow as separate facts are woven together to form a schema for understanding. It is possible to collect a great deal of information about a person, and even to predict aspects of his behavior successfully, without any sense of understanding him. Common metaphors provide clues to just what is meant when we talk about understanding someone: We speak of wanting to know "how he is put together," or "what is his game," or "what makes him tick." These are causal and configural questions, which point to the existence of something like a theoretical model as the basis for understanding a particular person—a set of facts linked by causal propositions to yield expectations. This formulation unfortunately sounds excessively abstract, verbal, and intellectual, whereas it should give the idea of an implicit and affective understanding of someone we know well. In place of "theoretical model," let us borrow Piaget's term *schema* to refer to the basis for this affective understanding.

Ask a friend to tell you what sort of person his father is, and you may be surprised by his difficulty in finding things to say that convey more than one layer of feeling about a man he has known as long and as closely as anyone. To be sure, the very fact that such intense and conflicting emotions are centered on a parent makes it difficult to talk about him analytically. He is likely to be the focus of so many desires and such an important obstacle to, or means for the fulfillment of, others that his own son cannot be expected to come up with a disinterested, objective appraisal. Nevertheless, your friend knows a great deal more than he can put into words—an instance of Polanyi's *tacit knowing*. He knows "how to work the old man" for something he wants in the same way that he knows how to ride a bicycle, for an intimate familiarity is there that is readily available to guide behavior, though not in a verbal form. Psychologists assume that a complex schema is built up about every person we know well; this schema guides behavior in relation to the person and need not be verbal in order to be effective.

The Systematization of Informal Assessment

It should be clear by now that the methods of informal assessment used in everyday life are subjective, empathic, and even intuitive; yet they *can* be subjected to rigorous, objective investigation. We can study the validity of these methods; for example, we can check the extent to which the statements one person makes about another's personality are true by comparing them to some independent standard (or *criterion*) or, more indirectly, by translating them into explicit predictions, which can then be checked against future behavior. We can select people who are good natural judges of men and investigate the ways in which they differ from others who are ineffective. And we can attempt to train people in order to improve their skill.

As soon as the methods of science are applied to an informal, everyday process, it begins to turn into a discipline, perhaps eventually into a technology, and even a science. The first attempts to systematize informal methods of understanding personalities produced clinical assessment, to which we shall turn in the next chapter.

Roger Chillingworth scrutinized his patient carefully, both as he saw him in his ordinary life, keeping an accustomed pathway in the range of thoughts familiar to him, and as he appeared when thrown amidst other moral scenery, the novelty of which might call out something new to the surface of his character. He deemed it essential, it would seem, to know the man, before attempting to do him good. . . . [So he] strove to go deep into his patient's bosom, delving among his principles, prying into his recollections, and probing everything with a cautious touch, like a treasure-seeker in a dark cavern. Few secrets can escape [such] an investigator. . . . If the latter possess native sagacity, and a nameless something more,—let us call it intuition; if he show no intrusive egotism, nor disagreeably prominent characteristics of his own: if he have the power, which must be born with him, to bring his mind into such affinity with his patient's, that this last shall unawares have spoken what he imagines himself only to have thought; if such revelations be received without tumult, and acknowledged not so often by an uttered sympathy as by silence, an inarticulate breath, and here and there a word, to indicate that all is understood; . . . then, at some inevitable moment, will the soul of the sufferer be dissolved, and flow forth in a dark, but transparent stream, bringing all its mysteries into the daylight.

NATHANIEL HAWTHORNE. The Scarlet Letter

CHAPTER 34
FORMAL ASSESSMENT: THE CLINICAL APPROACH

C linical assessment, the effort "to know the man before attempting to do him good," began as an application of the common-sense methods of informal assessment to the problems presented by psychiatric patients. Thus the early practitioners of clinical assessment focused on direct methods. For example, the nineteenth-century German psychiatrist Kraepelin interviewed each patient and his relatives, observed the patient's behavior in the mental hospital over a prolonged period of time, and followed up to learn what became of him. He made limited use of somewhat formalized medical diagnostic methods, but primarily he relied on his eyes and ears and information supplied by other staff members of his hospital to discern so-called pure cases of what he thought were "diseases" and to describe their essential characteristics. He succeeded so well that recent attempts to isolate types of mental patients by statistical methods (for example, factor analysis) have substantially confirmed his work (Wittenborn & Holzberg, 1951; Lorr, O'Connor, & Stafford, 1957).

Since the time of Kraepelin, clinicians have added special, indirect methods of their own. The pages that follow will focus first on the direct methods of gathering data used in clinical assessment and then on the indirect methods, a discussion of which will lead into an analysis of means of interpreting data and integrating everything into an explicit schema.

Direct Methods
of Clinical Assessment

THE INTERVIEW

An important characteristic of the psychiatric approach to assessment is that it has always (but especially since the work of Freud) been concerned with the most important crises of human lives, and the diagnostic interview has always focused on the problems that troubled patients the most. Therefore, the psychiatric tradition has the great merit of looking first at the main issues in a person's life, regardless of whether they lend themselves to accurate appraisal or not, but it also has the possible drawback of a medical orientation to symptoms and disease.

As the process of talking with another person to learn about his personality has moved from conversation toward something technical enough to be called interviewing, it has been formalized in two quite opposite ways. These formal techniques are the *structured interview* and *free association*.

Structured Interviews

An interviewer generally introduces some degree of structuring by means of questions. To be sure, it is possible to interview someone by informal, relaxed, and normally discursive conversation, without specific questioning. Sometimes the subject's anxiety, wariness, or the like makes unstructured interviewing necessary; but it requires much discipline and experience to be effective, and it takes much time. At one extreme, interviewing approaches testing when the interviewer uses a list of set questions in fixed sequence and even a set of "canned" answers from which the subject chooses (as in the case of certain public-opinion interviews that use multiple-choice questions). Most clinical assessors distrust the rigidity of such set methods and prefer to structure interviews according to *objectives*, or goals. Suppose, for example, the interviewer decides ahead of time that he wants to find out about the subject's home life; he will make himself a set of notes to cover the main facts about the family (what persons lived together at various times in his past, whether the family was broken, the ages of brothers and sisters, and so on), the nature of the emotional relationships that existed in the family, and the subject's informal assessment of his principal relatives.

The main problem for the interviewer is managing to steer the best course between oversubjectivity and overobjectivity. Too great subjectivity involves several kinds of dangers: The interviewer may get so emotionally involved that he forgets his goals or injects too much of his own personality into the interaction; he may reword questions so that they no longer get at what was intended or so that they suggest certain types of answers. He must take particular pains not to influence what the subject says, beyond pointing him in the appropriate direction and encouraging him to speak freely, for the whole point of an assessment interview is lost if the information elicited is seriously biased in any way.

The dangers of overobjectivity, on the other hand, are that the interviewer may become clinically insensitive and mistake rigidity for consistency. A uniform procedure is highly desirable, but the interviewer cannot assume that using the same words with all subjects will automatically bring about the same understanding of what he intends. It is being overobjective, also, to plod through a list of questions, disregarding the subject's signals that he is interested in a particular area and ready to talk about it even though it does not happen to be next on the schedule, or to ignore indications of anxiety, embarrassment, or guilt—signals that the interviewer should tactfully change the topic and approach the sensitive area later in a different way.

Whatever the technique of interviewing may be, it can sometimes yield a great wealth of information and, at other times, merely huge quantities of words with little in the way of useful fact. In any case, a major part of the interviewer's job is not just to elicit the subject's words but to record them in some way—in writing, on tape, or in his memory. The tradition in clinical interviewing has been to rely on memory, though in research settings electrical recordings are increasingly being used.

Free Association The unique type of interview Freud developed has been used for diagnostic as well as therapeutic purposes. Freud became convinced that because most neurotics did not consciously know what was bothering them, direct questioning had limited value. At the same time, the conflicting motives underlying neurosis, as he understood it, were capable of steering the course of thought and talk when external formal structuring was removed. Therefore, he encouraged his patients to speak their thoughts freely, to talk about anything that came to mind whether it seemed relevant or not, while trying not to censor their words by any polite conventions or by the desire to please him through saying "the right thing." To minimize his own influence on the "free associations," he refrained from direct questioning and sat behind the patient (who lay on a couch), so as not to allow even his facial expression to give cues about what was wanted or expected.

The resulting method, free association, is unexcelled for providing data about the inner longings and fears that impel people, particularly data from which their unconscious motives may be inferred. Although the process of free association sounds easy, few people can immediately relax their conscious and unconscious defenses enough to do it, so learning the method usually takes many hours. Moreover, the analyst needs extensive training not only to interpret the subject's wanderings but to cope with the emotions that are often released: The subject may find himself unexpectedly faced by such painful thoughts and wishes that he needs not just acceptance and reassurance but skilled psychotherapeutic help.

Because Freud listened to his patients talk about anything they chose to over months and years of interviews, which were held four or five times each week, he grew to know and understand them better than any therapist had before him. Because of his conviction that all behavior was lawfully determined by conscious and unconscious motives, he listened when the neurotic men and women who came to him told him about their dreams and fantasies, instead of impatiently dismissing such stuff as irrelevant. In this way, the interview became to a great degree an *indirect* method of assessment. (Free association is not included among the indirect methods discussed later in the chapter, because it is little used in psychodiagnosis, except by psychoanalysts.)

TESTS

Some tests strongly resemble the highly structured interviews in which the questions are all written out. The Eysenck Personality Inventory, for example, consists of 57 questions, the first of which is: "Do you like plenty of excitement and bustle around you?" A place is provided for the subject to check his answer, Yes or No, by each question. Other such tests usually consist of many separate items, each of which is stated as a question that either might be asked in an interview or could easily be turned into one. (This and other direct, nonprojective tests will be discussed further in Chapters 35, 37, and 39.)

An intelligence test is the prototype of another sort of nonprojective, direct test that relies less on conversational means and more on setting the subject tasks to perform. Any test of abilities is generally presented in a straightforward manner. Thus it is a direct method of gathering data, even though it has to be administered and scored according to technical rules and even though it is not always obvious how an item should be solved. So-called group intelligence tests, of the self-administered type, exist in considerable variety, but clinical assessment usually relies on individual tests of intelligence administered by a skilled psychologist. The best known examples are the Stanford-Binet Scale, the Wechsler Intelligence Scale for Children (WISC), and the Wechsler Adult Intelligence Scale (WAIS). These are actually compound tests with many varieties of items testing relatively specific abilities; thus, they yield general intelligence quotients (I.Q.'s), but they also enable the experienced examiner to assess many qualitative aspects of the way a person thinks, reasons, solves problems, and copes with objective demands.

OBSERVATION

Any contact between assessor and subject is an opportunity for many interesting types of observable behavior to emerge, which are concrete instances of a variety of the behavioral dispositions or traits making up the subject's personality. Since observation yields the most direct type of evidence, it is a cardinal rule of formal assessment to take advantage of every opportunity to observe a subject's behavior during testing and interviewing or at any other time. The assessor must observe as sharply (though inconspicuously) as possible and record the observed behavior, with its context, as soon as he can.

An assessor's notes might include, for example, the observation that the subject became red in the face and perspired freely when asked to disrobe for a physical examination. Or they might contain a report of a subject's conversation with one member of a clinic's staff while the subject waited for an appointment with another, including observations of his attempts to ingratiate himself and get some information about how he was doing. Valuable as such incidental observations are, they must be interpreted with some caution and with the realization that they are based on a small sample of behavior, often in an atypical situation.

PERSONAL DOCUMENTS

Autobiographies When the subject is cooperative and intelligent enough to carry out the assignment, an excellent method is to have him write an autobiography. If no specific instructions are given, a good deal can be learned by his choice of topics and by the kinds of things he omits, such as any mention of a much disliked brother. The usual procedure, however, is to suggest general areas for the subject to cover, so that the assessor may have direct information on the topics that concern him most. The structured extreme of this procedure is the *biographical inventory*, an instrument that contains a series of specific questions and, sometimes, sets of alternative answers, one of which is to be checked.

For example, Siegel (1956) developed a biographical inventory containing 372 items of the following kinds, which fall into ten clusters. Here are 5 items exemplifying five different clusters; the subject checks True or False for each:

Father has taught me to fish or enjoy some other individual sport. (Action)
I have taken a trip of more than 100 miles with friends. (Social Activities)

I never have dates. (Heterosexual Activities)
Mother is active in a political group. (Political Activities)
Father is active in a church group. (Religious Activities)

Such inventories have proved useful in large-scale research on selection of personnel.

Diaries   Diaries are personal documents of the greatest interest to the clinical assessor if they are something more than bare records of external events. Yet even a set of appointment books can yield objective, direct evidence about the breadth of a person's acquaintance, his pattern of work, his orderliness, his involvement in community activities, and so forth. Sometimes researchers will ask subjects to keep special types of diaries recording a form of behavior under study, such as dreams (Schonbar, 1959) or fantasies (Singer, 1966).

Personal Letters   Although personal letters can be extremely revealing, they are difficult to obtain and are not usually asked for in routine clinical assessment. If a collection of letters does become available, it may be an invaluable source of information about a personality that is otherwise inaccessible for assessment. For example, Sigmund Freud wrote a series of letters to a close friend and colleague, Wilhelm Fliess, during the years when he was forming his basic psychoanalytic ideas; most of the letters, discovered about 50 years later, have been published (Freud, 1887–1902). They give a sense of direct acquaintance with a genius during an important phase of his life, and they have been of great value to his biographers.

Without the evidence of these letters, even so close a disciple as Ernest Jones might not have known that Freud suffered from a moderately severe neurosis during the 1890's, and he surely would have been ignorant of the subjective nature of Freud's symptoms. Jones quotes a letter of December 6, 1897, in which Freud described "spells where consciousness would be greatly narrowed . . . with a veil that produced almost a twilight condition of mind [Jones, 1953, p. 306]." And it is only because Freud's letters to his fiancée some years earlier were preserved that we have a glimpse of the intense, romantic love he was capable of feeling; without them, we

> could easily have formed the impression that his marriage had been a simple affair of two people suited to each other being drawn together and deciding to marry. . . . How different was the truth, as revealed in the love letters! There we are confronted with a tremendous and complicated passion, one in which the whole gamut of emotion was evoked in turn, from the heights of bliss to the depths of despair with every grade of happiness and misery being felt with unsparing intensity [Jones, 1953, p. 99].

Letters from Jenny, edited by G. W. Allport (1965), shows how a collection of letters may be subjected to several kinds of systematic psychological analysis.

The direct methods that yield the most valuable results in some cases tell little in others; but this is characteristic of clinical assessment as a whole. For every great diarist or letter writer, there are hundreds of people whose personal documents are scanty, impersonal, and even misleading in the impression they give of a prosaic or shallow person. The same is true of any method in which subjects have any degree of freedom to respond, including tests and interviews. It is not difficult to learn through conversation, observation, or personal documents if a person is in fact taciturn, constricted in his thinking, or secretive, but it is often hard to learn more about his inner life of feelings and desires. As we saw in Chapter 33, people differ greatly in their openness, or transparency. The more defensive or otherwise inscrutable a person is, the less can be learned by direct methods. The *indirect* approach therefore plays a leading role in the clinical tradition of assessment.

Indirect Methods
of Clinical Assessment

The special methods involved in the indirect approach are the *projective techniques* of studying personality; but the indirect approach is also an orientation and a way of using data that can be applied to virtually any sort of information about a person—even to the results of objective tests.

It was Freud, again, who originated indirect assessment. He soon discovered that the dark stream of free associations is not always transparent, and because of the technique's permissiveness, a good deal more than the painful mysteries of the patient's suffering emerges. His dreams, daydreams, and the trivial mistakes of everyday living often have no obvious bearing on the problems that brought the neurotic into treatment, but Freud found that they constitute valuable indirect data when examined for their latent, rather than their manifest, content.

Freud learned to interpret dreams through studying his own. As he unravelled the tangle of determinants that brought a dream into being, he found that the same principles unlocked many of the mysteries of neurotic symptoms. After turning his attention to the psychological causes of slips of the tongue, momentary lapses of memory, and other types of seemingly unimportant errors, he was able, with the aid of the subject's free associations about such a slip, to reveal the impulses and defenses that brought it into being. In doing so, he laid the foundation for projective techniques and for all indirect methods of studying personality, and he provided the main interpretive rules.

HOW PROJECTIVE TECHNIQUES
AND OTHER INDIRECT METHODS WORK

The assumption underlying both the specific techniques and the whole indirect approach to interpreting assessment data is that *when a person can respond relatively freely, his total behavior betrays many of the determinants that brought it about.* Let us take a closer look at this highly condensed formulation.

Freedom to Respond Freedom to respond does not imply freedom of the will in the metaphysical sense of an absence of determinism. Rather, it simply acknowledges the fact that behavior is sometimes highly constrained by the requirements of a situation, and at other times a person has many more behavioral options open to him. The more freedom to act a person has, obviously, the less are the particulars of what he does and says dictated by forces external to him and thus the more is his behavior determined by the tendencies within him that make up his personality. Thus, the question, "What type of job are you looking for?" offers far less scope for personal dispositions to affect the answer than does "What are your main goals in life?"

"Total Behavior" The phrase "total behavior" in the formulation calls our attention to the fact that at any one time a person is actually doing many things. Consider someone who is taking an intelligence test and simply responding correctly to the question, "How much are $5 and $4?" He may say "$9" in a straightforward, bored, haughty, tentative, or supercilious manner, indicating that he finds the question gratifyingly easy, or insultingly so, or that he suspects a trick, and so on. Or his answer, while technically correct, may be so peculiarly stated that it suggests a serious disturbance. The following example came from a nearly psychotic doctor: "That's 500 pennies and 400 pennies. Shall I add them?—A total of 900 pennies.—Oh, I guess you want me to say $9."

The subject's reaction time will often be significant: He may be so eager to show his skill or his contempt for the test that he blurts out his reply before the examiner stops speaking, or he may be so fixed in a pattern of caution that he ponders the question and checks his answer before responding. At the same time, he may display a characteristic posture: He may sit bolt upright, his stiff spine never touching the back of the chair, or slumped down in an attitude of overcasualness; or he may fidget in unconcealed anxiety. He may also spring up and pace the floor while replying, or he may crane his neck to see what the examiner is writing down. Meanwhile, his facial expression may be appropriately relaxed and calm, tense, depressed, frozen, smirking, or angry.

Although this by no means exhausts the range of behaviors that may occur while a subject is giving a routine, correct answer to a question that seemingly allows him very little leeway, it should be enough to suggest the wealth of diagnostically significant behavior that may be going on simultaneously. Some questions do in fact tend to constrict response, and the very situation of taking an intelligence test exerts subtle restraints on behavior to which most people unconsciously respond. Nevertheless, a human organism has many channels of response, and what seems to be a one-dimensional measurement provided by an arithmetic test is actually the result of ignoring most of the behavior that goes on. If you put a schizophrenic patient into a bare little room where there is a lever he can press, as some operant conditioners have done, he may bang his head on the walls, shout incoherent delusional speeches, or have murderous fantasies; but by concentrating your attention on just the number of times per hour he presses the lever, you can act as if the single aspect of behavior you are measuring is all that is really going on. The tradition of clinical assessment, by contrast, emphasizes sharp observation and accurate recording of *all* the subject's important behavior patterns.

The point about accurate recording deserves some emphasis. If the tester does not write down every word the subject says as nearly verbatim as possible and if he does not make notes on any behavior that deviates from the normal, most of the richness of his observation will soon vanish in the welter of impressions left by a session of testing. If he just records a plus for the arithmetic question, he will have only that single bit of information to work with later on when he is surveying and interpreting all his data; the residue of unverbalized understanding may then continue to resist translation into words.

**The Multiple Determinants
of Behavior** A major implication in the statement of assumption we are discussing is that any given act, mannerism, or personal characteristic has many determinants. Freud was struck by the superficiality of the answers people would give to such questions as "Why did you do that?" and in particular by their blindness to the unconscious motives their actions often expressed in addition to the conscious intention by which they sincerely tried to explain them. The fact that an act or thought had more than one motive Freud termed "overdetermination."

The principle of overdetermination may be generalized far beyond the realm of motivation, however. At a minimum, the following classes of determinants operate in bringing about any single answer given by a person who is being assessed: (1) the general situational context; (2) the immediate perceptual impact of the stimuli to which the person is responding, including the personality of anyone he is speaking to; (3) the directing sets that steer his attention and thought according to preconceptions about what is going on, what is wanted, what it is appropriate to do under the circumstances, and so on; (4) the processes of identification, which greatly affect the way the subject responds to other persons actually present or pictured in test materials; (5) the whole hierarchy of motives that are more or less active in the person at the time; (6) the defenses that control these motives; (7) the cognitive elaboration of response, as it draws on various kinds of information stored in his memory (his own life history, his self-concept and identity, his attitudes and values, and his store of general information); (8) the enabling and limiting effects of abilities, including not only general intelligence but also specific capacities that are relevant to the immediate task or situation; (9) the internal climate of moods and affects that give emotional flavor to the cognitive process; (10) the personal style of the subject's cognitive organization and of the words and gestures he uses to express his thoughts and feelings.

Several of these ten headings could be further broken down, and the whole list could be supplemented by looking at the behavior in question not psychologically but from the point of view of the other behavioral sciences and disciplines relevant to understanding man. A subject's behavior in answering questions put by a tester or interviewer can be viewed from the vantage point of the ethnologist, who would point out the extent to which the behavior is culturally determined; from that of the sociologist, who would stress the role relationships of the two persons and their relative places in a social structure; from that of the economist, who would remind us that part of the subject's motivation is the money he is being paid or is paying for services rendered in the context of a capitalist, free-enterprise system; from that of the biochemist, who would inquire into the chemical composition of the subject's blood and perhaps relate his fast reaction time to a momentarily high secretion of adrenalin because of stress; from that of the physical anthropologist, who can expertly analyze the subject's physique and relate it to his behavior; and so on. Much of the information that would be developed by the work of these and other specialists might be integrated into a broad conception of personality, but much would simply be too peripheral. For the most part, therefore, we assess personality with a psychological orientation. Nevertheless, we should not lose sight of the fact that many other sciences are concerned with behavior and that it is determined on many levels other than the one that may interest us at the time.

The "Betrayal" of the Determinants

The final assertion made by the italicized formulation a few pages back is that an action or verbal statement *betrays* many of its determinants. The metaphor is intended to suggest that a full understanding of behavior presupposes a process like the penetration of a disguise. Few of the many factors responsible for the detailed structure of behavior are visible to the untrained eye, yet the content and style of what a person says and does contain many subtle indicators of what motivates him. To change the figure of speech, the instruments of thought often leave their toolmarks on the final product, enabling the trained observer to discern and infer what the important determinants were. This last process is *clinical interpretation* (or clinical inference), which plays a central role in projective techniques and in the indirect analysis of most other kinds of data. The process is described later in this chapter and is illustrated in later chapters with an actual case. Likewise, the nature of projective techniques will become much clearer in Chapter 37, as we examine one man's responses to two standard projective tests (the Rorschach and the Thematic Apperception Test).

Projective techniques differ from direct methods in that they do not depend on the subject's willingness to give information about himself. They are designed to encourage freedom of response so that the material the subject produces will have the most opportunity to reveal its own determinants; they yield information about the person only by enabling him to furnish a thought product that we can interpret by reconstructing the determinants that brought it about. For some years clinical assessors assumed that the essential feature of projective techniques was the ambiguity or unstructuredness of the test materials, the immediate stimuli to which the subject responded. It has become clear from theoretical analysis and from research data that the pictures about which the subject tells stories in the Thematic Apperception Test, for example, may be quite clear and specific with no loss in the test's effectiveness; the task itself, making up an imaginative story, permits so much freedom in responding that the answers are not unduly constrained by the specificity of the pictures.

A BRIEF SURVEY OF PROJECTIVE TECHNIQUES

All of a man's behavior expresses his personality to some extent, and almost any observations can be useful. Nevertheless, the great advantage of working with relatively fixed and standardized methods is that they provide a constant backdrop against which the individuality of each subject may stand out in bold contrast. A projective test presents the subject with a standard set of inkblots (the Rorschach Test or the Holtzman Inkblot Test), a standard set of pictures about which to tell imaginative stories (Thematic Apperception Test, or TAT), a standard set of incomplete sentences to be finished (Sentence Completion Test) or of words to which the subject is to respond with the first word that enters his head (Word Association Test), a standard group of toys the child is invited to play with (World Test), a standard set of pictures of people out of which the subject must select those he likes and those he dislikes (Szondi Test), or a standard set of geometric figures to be copied (Bender Gestalt Test). The procedure is the same for everyone, the instructions are relatively fixed, and the examiner tries to maintain the same attitude of unbiased readiness to hear and record whatever the subject wants to say. The test's materials are usually varied enough so that they present a variety of challenges, or bring to mind a full range of generally important topics or situations, or otherwise elicit as rich a sample of reactions as possible.

Without the degree of constancy provided by standardized methods, it would be much more difficult to compare the subject's behavior with that of others. But by holding the stimulus situation constant, the examiner hopes to be able to account for the variation of responses in terms of differences in the internal organization of his subjects. Even graphic techniques that lack structured stimuli, like figure drawing (the Draw-a-Man Test or House-Tree-Person Test), easel painting, or finger painting, follow the same rationale.

Clearly, there is no limit to the types of standardized materials a person might be confronted with and asked to talk about, manipulate, construct something with, or the like. During the first decade after World War II, the heyday of projective techniques, clinical psychologists turned their ingenuity to the development of many more instruments of this type than can be listed here, a number of which have their staunch advocates. Those who have retained their enthusiasm for projective tests tend to place more emphasis now on building up better norms and a stronger base of clinical experience with a small range of instruments with established usefulness rather than on trying out new ones.

The subject's freedom to respond, which enables him unwittingly to reveal so much about himself, is also a weakness of this type of test. A Rorschach or TAT protocol (the record of a subject's responses and behavior) may allow a skilled clinician to make inferences about almost any facet of personality—abilities, motives, defenses, past history, pathological trends, values and attitudes, and much more—but there is no guarantee that he will be able to make *valid* statements about any one of these areas for any particular subject. One man's figure drawings will tell worlds about his inner experience of his own body; another's drawings will tell little beyond the fact that he is a conventional and guarded person.

An Introduction to Interpretation
in Clinical Assessment

Projective techniques, and the methods of clinical assessment generally, are no better than the man who interprets them. They have little, if any, intrinsic validity, since they are not direct measures of any one aspect of personality. Instead, they are devices to scoop up samples of thought and behavior, which must be interpreted before they can be of value; and interpretation of this kind of material is an expert performance requiring a blend of art, experience, native shrewdness and intuition, and science, or at least technology. Science is included because interpretation demands a thorough knowledge of personality theory and a disciplined way of handling evidence—by forming and verifying hypotheses—which closely resembles the scientific method.

To interpret clinical data properly, one must be able to form hypotheses or to make inferences freely, drawing on experience, empirical rules about what means what (statistical inference), and hunches, but ideally deriving hypotheses (possible interpretations) from a theoretical understanding of how the test responses come about. This is the creative or inspirational phase of the job. It must be followed by a hard-headed and dispassionate scrutiny of each hypothesis, when one tests it against as many kinds of data (other than the fact it was based on) as possible. No single test, not even the most elaborate projective technique, can be a sufficient basis for statements about an entire personality. The best clinical assessment, therefore, is *multiform*; that is, it draws on as many different sources of information as can be practically obtained. The best tradition of clinical assessment emphasizes the use of a balanced set, or *battery*, of tests, including both objective and projective types.

By the same token, the clinical assessor generally uses both direct methods, such as the interview, and indirect methods, in which the subject is baffled about how his responses can be of any value. He observes behavior directly, gets reports of what his subject has done in the past, and makes inferences from the content of test responses and from formal features of these responses. To illustrate this last process, one can infer conscientiousness (1) from TAT stories about people who are scrupulous in living up to their obligations (that is, from content) and (2) from a subject's serious, orderly approach to the job of telling stories of just the kind specified by the examiner (a formal aspect of the TAT).

Much of the task of interpretation, therefore, consists of putting together a theory about a particular person, which accounts for as much as possible of what is known about him. The examiner forms a schema, just as in informal assessment; but in formal clinical assessment he has the additional task of making explicit what is usually in large part implicit and of setting his formulation down in well-chosen words so that it makes sense to someone else. Sometimes (chiefly in research contexts) part or even all the output will be ratings on a set of personality variables; usually there will be a prose report of manageable length.

Like much of the rest of the material in this chapter, the general remarks on interpretation above will become more meaningful when applied to the concrete data of one subject, treated in Chapters 37 through 40. First, however, we must take a close look at a very different way of gathering and working with data in the formal assessment of personality—the "objective" method.

Better to measure cloth ten times and cut it once than the other way around.

Yiddish proverb

CHAPTER 35
FORMAL ASSESSMENT: THE OBJECTIVE APPROACH

T he attempt to make the measurement of abilities and other personality traits a rigorous, objective discipline led to the development of a new specialty, *psychometrics*. This science of psychological measurement relies heavily on statistics and has its own technical vocabulary. Only an introduction to this subject can be given in this chapter, for it would be virtually impossible to present in a few pages a treatment of the objective, psychometric approach that would be simultaneously clear to the uninitiated and comprehensive in its coverage of the major issues. Because clinical assessment is closer to the informal ways of getting to know people, it is easier to present and to understand than objective assessment. It would be a mistake, which the reader should resist, to conclude from this irrelevant fact that the objective approach is less intrinsically interesting or less worth studying.

However it is done, assessing personality is in large part a matter of measuring various kinds of traits—dispositions to behave in specifiable ways. Precise, objective, quantitative measurement is certainly preferable to vague, sloppy, ambiguous description, as long as it does not get in the way of more important considerations. Good measures of personality traits facilitate both the research that tests psychological theory and the applied, more im-

631

mediately usable kind (like research to establish methods of selecting students or employees). Some psychologists, unfortunately, make such a fetish of numbers and objectivity that they care more about getting quantitative measures than about what the numbers mean or whether they contribute to understanding. The difficult task for a science of personality is to find a path between the swamps of oversubjectivity and the deserts of overobjectivity. Nevertheless, those who have zealously pursued the ideal of objective measurement have learned a great deal that can and must be adopted by those who are more clinically oriented, if the latter are to translate their insights about individuals into transmittable scientific knowledge.

This chapter briefly surveys the contributions of the "objective" approach to assessing personality. The quotation marks (which will hereafter be dropped) are a reminder that the ideal of entirely eliminating clinical judgment and interpretation is unattainable. Even when a testing device manages to do without a subjective rating or report by anyone, its relevance to personality has to be established ultimately by reference to someone's judgment, whether that of an expert, the subject, or his friends. And, as we shall see, most objective techniques involve subjective estimates even more directly.

The pursuit of objectivity has led to the gradual crystallization of two very useful ideals of measurement, along with ways of finding out how close any particular technique of assessment approaches those ideals. A perfect measuring instrument would be completely *reliable* and completely *valid*.

Reliability and Validity

The term "reliable" primarily means "consistent"; but since there are several kinds of consistency, reliability is an ambiguous word unless the type of consistency is specified. The two most important types are internal consistency and consistency in time (repeat reliability). In the first of these senses, a test is reliable if its components all measure the same trait; in the second, a test is reliable if it continues to give constant results when it is repeated after a lapse of time.

Common usage can be a confusing guide here. We generally say that something is reliable if we can rely on it to do what it is supposed to do; but this rather vague merit encompasses both reliability and validity, as they are understood in the technical terminology of psychometrics. A test, rating, or other measure is "valid" to the extent that it demonstrably measures what it claims to measure. Since there are various ways of demonstrating a claim, validity too can have several different meanings, as we shall see later.

In addition, the two concepts of reliability and validity are interdependent. If a test happened to give a valid measure of a trait at one time but at another time its score fluctuated for unknown reasons, this lack of repeat reliability would lower the validity. Also, if a test proves internally consistent and stable over time, it must measure something (even if not necessarily what it purports to assess); on investigation it may turn out to be a useful measure of some aspect of behavior.

Let us pause for a moment to consider how a test measures a trait of personality, using the example of an ability—say, immediate memory for symbolic units, such as numbers. An examiner reads strings of digits aloud (for example, 4, 7, 2, 9, 1, 5) and then the subjects write them down. One subject may have been able to retain and reproduce 9 digits in correct order, another only 5. We assume that, in some way, the brains of these two people differ, so that one is generally better at taking in and recalling units like letters or numbers. If the test is repeated a week later, a few of those who did badly the first time will do much better, some of the original top performers will stumble, but most subjects will get approximately the same scores. The more the scores differ from one week to the next, of course, the poorer the reliability. But why should scores change? Does the ability—the assumed although unknown property of the brain—itself fluctuate? The standard psychometric assumption has been that it does not; all abilities tend to improve up to about age twenty, after which a very gradual decline begins, becoming noticeable only a few decades later. The mathematical theory of probability, on which statistics is based, encourages the assumption that there is a "true score" for everyone, which does not change in the short run, but that there is also a certain amount of random error in measuring it. An "error of measurement" should be carefully distinguished from indeterminancy; it does not imply at all that the test scores fluctuate for no reason, only that we do not usually know what the causes are and that in the long run they tend to be distributed in a certain fashion (according to the normal curve of errors).

In the case of the digit-span test just described, it is not difficult to imagine some extraneous determinants of the score. The sound of distant music drifting through a window may be ignored by all the subjects except one girl to whom the song has special meaning; a fly may light on another subject at a critical moment, distracting him from the numbers; a third may be in unusually good spirits for personal reasons and may be functioning better than usual. None of these particular small influences on performance is at all likely to operate in the same way a week later: The last subject may have lost sleep the night before and perform below par, and the formerly dreamy girl may now be on her toes. Hence, scores change more easily than brains do. Among the distractions that have been found to interfere with digit-span performance, one of the most common, anxiety, is of interest in itself. Rapaport, Gill, and Schafer (1945) divided a group of unselected highway patrolmen into an anxious and a nonanxious group on the basis of a psychiatric interview and then found that though the anxious policemen were not generally less intelligent, they got significantly poorer digit-span scores than the nonanxious ones.

If we could know *all* the determinants of all aspects of performance on a test, we would be able to say how much of the variance (the man-to-man variation in score) was attributable to a specific form of immediate memory, how much to anxiety, how much to a variety of trivial external influences, and so on. There would then be no need to distinguish between reliability and validity, and in fact we should have solved the problems of interpretation as well. At this time, however, we must make do with coefficients of reliability and validity.

Reliability is never perfect. We can never get rid of every unwanted influence and concentrate only on the degree to which a test score is determined by—and therefore measures—the enduring aspects of personality in which we are interested. Nevertheless, anything short of total confusion or psychotic delusion is unlikely to cause a person to change his answers to some questions (for example, "Are you male or female?"). The aim of those who construct self-report tests is to write items that have this degree of stability.

There is less agreement about the ideal of internal consistency, or homogeneity. Probably the disagreement arises because some tests attempt to measure simple, unitary concepts, in which case a high degree of homogeneity is desirable, but others aim at broad, general aspects of personality and can be validated only by predicting some form of behavior (see Cronbach, 1960, and Cattell, 1964). Tests of general intelligence, which are usually validated against performance in school, are a good example of the latter type; as we shall shortly see, Binet long ago found that very homogeneous tests of conceptually simple functions were inferior to more complex tests as predictors of grades.

Any test that is not scored in a completely objective, mechanical way is subject to another kind of unreliability—disagreements between scorers. The more clinical judgment is involved, the more difficult it is to get scorers or judges to agree, which is one of the good arguments for objective tests. All too often, however, the kinds of simplifications that are necessary to achieve objectivity undermine validity. We shall return to some of these issues in Chapter 41, where the relative strengths and weaknesses of the various techniques of assessment are considered further.

Intelligence Testing
and the Psychometric Tradition

The concept of a "mental test" was developed by Galton in the last quarter of the nineteenth century, and J. M. Cattell was using 50 tests (measures of sensory sensitivity and the like) by 1890. The first practically useful test, however, was constructed shortly after the turn of this century by Alfred Binet, a Frenchman of wide interests and catholic curiosity. He is known as the man who figured out how to do what all the other testers had wanted to accomplish—to measure an aspect of human capacity that had practical and social significance.

Given the task of separating the bright students from the dull for the Paris school system, Binet had the insight to start with miniatures of real-life problems, not with "elementary functions of the mind." Thus, instead of measuring how quickly a child could press a telegraph key when a signal light went on, as Cattell was doing, he asked his subjects to follow a set of orders or to state the ways objects were similar. He saw also, with practical eclecticism, that tests of various types would be needed (tests of memory, attention, comprehension, and seven other functions) and that they would have to be appropriate to the levels of attainment characterizing children of different ages. His scale grouped items according to the ages at which a majority of normal children could pass them, so that a child who could perform at a given level was said to have that mental age. These practical considerations, and the administrative need for a single score, overruled Binet's convictions about the manifold nature of intelligence, which might otherwise have led him to provide several scores (Guilford, 1967).

William Stern, a German pioneer in the study of individual differences, contributed the insight that if mental age (as Binet measured it) were divided by chronological age, the resulting quotient might remain relatively stable as the child grew up. When, in 1916, a group at Stanford led by Terman issued the American translation and revision of Binet's test, which was to become the American standard for the next 20 years, they called this ratio by the name that has stuck ever since: the intelligence quotient, or I.Q.

USES OF INTELLIGENCE TESTS

Testing caught on in the United States because tests like Binet's were useful in predicting how well a child would perform at school. It also quickly became apparent that intelligence tests could be used in vocational guidance and selection, because different occupations required different levels of measured intelligence.

The First World War caused a great spurt of growth in the testing movement. A man had to have certain basic abilities even to be a foot soldier, and the mentally defective had to be eliminated as quickly as possible from huge numbers of recruits. Therefore, a group of Army psychologists who were familiar with individual intelligence tests invented the first group test of intelligence, the Army Alpha. This test and its successors have been useful not only in screening out the unfit but in identifying those capable of complex and responsible jobs.

The years following the war saw a rapid increase in the variety and popularity of tests. Many kinds of performance tests were used in vocational selection; some attempted to measure generalized motor abilities, and others were frankly miniature standardized samples of the kind of work a man would have to perform on a job (for example, putting together a disassembled lock). As the number of tests grew, their content differing for different purposes, it became apparent that a number of more or less independent abilities must exist. But just how many were there, and just how independent were they?

FACTOR ANALYSIS

Such questions as those above could not be answered by theoretical analysis alone; special statistical techniques were required, especially *factor analysis*, which came to its first great flowering in the 1930's. The first step in a factor analysis of several tests is to give them all to a group of subjects and find out to what extent the scores achieved on any one test can be predicted from a knowledge of scores on any other. Through the statistical method of *correlation*, invented by Galton and Pearson, his student, it is possible to calculate precisely the degree to which doing well or poorly on a given test is related to performance on another test. This relation is expressed as a number between 1.00 (perfect positive correlation) and −1.00 (perfect negative correlation), the midpoint being .00 (total absence of any relation). If the people who obtain high scores on one test uniformly get low scores on a second one, and the low scorers become high scorers, there is a high negative coefficient of correlation. As a rule, however, tests of abilities tend to be positively correlated, and negative coefficients are exceptional.

Let us assume that we have persuaded several hundred high school students to take 12 tests of intellectual abilities, which we wish to factor analyze. We would compute the 66 coefficients of correlation, arranging them in a matrix, which makes it easy to see how each one is correlated with the others. If the numbers were all close to zero, each test would then measure a separate and independent ability. By the same token, if all the coefficients were very highly (and positively) intercorrelated, it would be reasonable to conclude that the tests were alternative measures of one ability. The more usual case, however, is that subgroups of tests form clusters that are more highly intercorrelated than any of their components are with the other tests—yet the clusters usually overlap somewhat. In such a state of affairs, common sense is no longer much help. We need a method by which we can comb through the tangled skein of interrelationships and find the smallest number of independent abilities that could account for the results. Factor analysis is a mathematical method that does just this. It extracts from a correlation matrix a set of independent (or orthogonal) dimensions, called factors, which account for the clustering of the tests (or other variables). It seems reasonable to identify the factors in aptitude tests as abilities.

There is more than one method of factor analysis, however, and the various methods give somewhat different results. The first factor analyst,

Spearman, developed a method that always yielded one major general factor; working with intellectual tests, he called this factor *g* (for general intelligence). For several years, many psychologists did not understand the fact that Spearman's "discovery" of *g* was a necessary consequence of his mathematical method, and so accepted the conception that intelligence was basically one unitary ability, of which vocabulary was an excellent test. The controversy is by no means over, but a rival conception vigorously advanced by Guilford (1967) seems to be gaining favor. According to this point of view, many independent intellectual abilities exist, a fact that could not have been foreseen from the early factor analyses of small groups of tests.

This discussion so far has focused on intelligence tests because the first great advances in psychometric method occurred in the testing of abilities and intellectual achievements. But factor analysis was only one of many technical advances in psychometrics. Other refinements of method have been developed that make it possible to produce ever more precise, reliable instruments to measure psychological variables. The goal of psychometrics is not to understand the complex patterns of behavior that constitute personality, but to find a way of measuring one thing at a time with maximal precision and objectivity. To this end, psychometricians have invented techniques of item analysis (ways of finding out which items in a test are best) and scale construction (ways of putting together groups of items that apparently measure the same construct or aspect of personality).

Objective Tests of Personality

We shall next consider a few representative examples of objective tests of personality developed in the psychometric tradition. They are called objective because the subject responds by bits of nonverbal behavior, like checkmarking pre-set answers, which can be scored according to mechanical rules. The scores may then be subjected to various statistical manipulations, which do not require any human judgment, subjective estimate, or the like. Since subjectivity always opens the door to bias and since it is not as constant in its operations as a machine, there are undeniable advantages to objective tests, at least in principle.

THE DIRECT APPROACH

Personality Inventories The first objective tests to be developed were adjustment inventories. As part of the effort to save time in processing recruits for World War I, Woodworth invented the first personality inventory, which he called the Personal Data Sheet. Essentially a self-administered psychiatric interview, it presented the subject with 116 questions about common physical and mental symptoms to be answered with checkmarks by the appropriate answers (Yes or No). The total number of Yes's was taken as a measure of general maladjustment. The approach is perfectly straightforward, obvious, and *direct*.

In the surge of testing that followed the war, the authors of many other adjustment inventories followed in Woodworth's footsteps, usually revising and extending his items. Sometimes the revisions amounted to little more than changing an item from one format (Do you daydream a great deal? *Yes   No   ?*) to another (I daydream—*Almost always   Frequently   Occasionally   Rarely   Almost never*). In the attempt to measure the trait of adjustment, all such inventories list personal problems, worries, or symptoms. If a person attains a *critical score*, this is considered an indication of a need for counseling. A critical score is one chosen in such a way that most members of a group of psychiatric patients (such as neurotics) score that high or higher, but most members of a normal group obtain lower scores.

The number of similar self-report tests of various traits mushroomed in the 1920's and 1930's. Some, like the Bernreuter Personality Inventory, included a measure of adjustment, among other traits, which were scored on a logical or theoretical basis: The author thought about a trait like introversion, drawing on what the concept's originator wrote about it (Jung, 1921), and made up a set of items describing various aspects of introverted behavior. When Flanagan (1935) subjected Bernreuter's test to factor analysis, however, he found that all the information it provided could be accounted for by two independent factors, which he called measures of sociability and confidence. This example shows one of the shortcomings of the logical (theory-based) method of constructing scales, as well as the apparent superiority of the factor-analytic technique.

Guilford, Thurstone, and R. Cattell are among the best known of the psychologists who followed with other personality inventories constructed by the aid of factor analysis. A recent example, "How Well Do You Know Yourself?" (Jenkins, 1959), provides factorial measures of 17 variables; it is a shortened version of an unpublished, longer form (described in Jenkins, 1962) measuring more than 100 interrelated traits, as well as two independent, general "superfactors" (superordinate factors derived from the intercorrelations of the trait scales). Because it covers many aspects of personality in a relatively short time, such an instrument can be useful in personality research with subjects who are motivated to describe themselves as well as they can.

The validity of direct and undisguised self-report tests depends greatly on the subject's honesty and self-knowledge, since these tests are generally quite transparent and thus susceptible to the strategy of "faking good" and "faking bad"—that is, of presenting yourself as either less or more troubled than you really are. Even when a person is trying to be completely honest, his particular problem may not be covered. Despite these disadvantages an inventory can be useful in such situations as military selection, because it takes very little time of a psychiatrist or a psychologist; the inventory can be given and scored by a clerk, and the few men who do admit to many symptoms can subsequently be interviewed.

As an example of what can be achieved by a relatively simple self-report questionnaire, consider the Neuropsychiatric Screening Adjunct (NSA) developed by the Army in 1944 for use in induction centers during World War II (Star, 1950). The objective of this questionnaire was to identify men who might later break down and thereby to reduce the necessity for psychiatrists to interview every draftee. The 23-item questionnaire contained 15 questions dealing with psychosomatic symptoms to detect neurotics (for example, "Have you ever had spells of dizziness?") and 8 additional "stop items" to pick up nonneurotic conditions such as psychosis ("Did you ever have a nervous breakdown?"), addiction ("Do you ever take dope?"), and psychopathy ("Were you ever sent to reform school?").

In a preliminary study, the test was given to a group of hospitalized neurotics and a group of ordinary working soldiers; a *critical score* was found, which correctly identified 90 percent of the neurotics. True, 30 percent of the "normal" soldiers scored this high or higher on the test and thus looked like potential psychiatric casualties (a kind of error called "false positives"). It was judged important, however, to keep the number of "false negatives" (actual neurotics undetected by the test) as low as 10 percent even at the cost of having to interview many men who would make satisfactory adjustments. This is the nature of a screening instrument: If it is to be useful, it must identify for more intensive study almost all the potential breakdowns ("true positives"); and if it can cut down the amount of interviewing significantly, there is a net saving in scarce psychiatric man-hours, even with many false positives.

A test of the NSA's effectiveness was made in induction centers all over the country in July 1945, when more than 100,000 men were given the questionnaire and were also interviewed by psychiatrists. (The latter could see the scores on the test if they wanted to, and it is not known just how much they used or were influenced by them.) The results of applying the critical score from the preliminary study as a cutting score are shown in Table 35-1. Even under the hurried, stressful conditions of induction, the test agreed well with psychiatric judgment. For example, the psychiatrists judged 57.7 percent of the total sample to be acceptable for service (left column of the table); of this group, 21.8 percent got a critical score on the test as potential psychiatric casualties, which means that test and doctor agreed on 78.2 percent of them. Likewise, the great majority (80.8 percent) of the small number rejected by psychiatrists as neurotic were also picked out by the test's critical score. Furthermore, the rates of rejections (and specific diagnoses) by psychiatrists varied far more widely from station to station than did the test scores. A longer test with less obvious questions might conceivably have worked even better, but this performance was good enough to justify the routine, official use of the NSA.

Table 35-1 Effectiveness of U.S. Army Neuropsychiatric Screening Adjunct (NSA) in Agreeing with Psychiatric Judgments

Categorization of draftees by psychiatrists (with proportion of total)	Percentage of each category picked out by test as potential psychiatric casualties
Men judged acceptable for service (57.7%)	21.8%
Men rejected for medical reasons (27.1%)	30.3
Men rejected for all psychiatric reasons (14%)	69.5
Men rejected as neurotics (5.6%)	80.8
Men rejected as psychopaths (3.9%)	68.2
Total (100%)	31.9

Based on data from Star, 1950.

Tests of Vocational Interests   In 1927 the first of a new type of test appeared—the Strong Vocational Interest Blank, followed 7 years later by the Kuder Preference Record. These remain the best known and most widely used tests of vocationally relevant interests. Both are self-administered, pencil-and-paper questionnaires composed of many small items that present specific topics or foci of interest; the subject indicates how he feels about each item by making a mark next to his choice from a set of possible answers.

More than 50 scoring keys for Strong's test are available; each is the result of administering the test to hundreds of people in a given vocation. Strong compared the average answers of any one occupational group, such as lawyers, with those of a large miscellaneous group of subjects and retained for a key only the items that discriminated lawyers, say, from men in general (see Table 35-2). This procedure is known as *empirical keying*. The scoring method gives a quantitative expression of the similarity of a subject's pattern of answers to those of people in each of the keyed occupations.

Kuder's test was built quite differently, by the method of *homogeneous keying*. He made up many forced-choice items; each requests the subject to indicate the one possibility in three that he likes most and the one that appeals to him least. The following is an example from the Kuder Preference Record—Vocational (1948):

a. Collect autographs
b. Collect coins
c. Collect butterflies

Table 35-2   *Example Using the Item "To Be an Actor" **

Showing How Scoring Weights Are Derived for

Occupational Scales in the Strong Vocational Interest Blank

Occupational groups tested	Responses of occupational groups			Responses of men in general			Differences			Scoring weights		
	L	I	D	L	I	D	L	I	D	L	I	D
Artists	40%	30%	30%	21%	32%	47%	19	—2	—17	2	0	—1
Chemists	16	34	50	21	32	47	—5	2	3	0	0	0
Carpenters	11	32	57	21	32	47	—10	0	10	—1	0	1
Ministers	42	33	25	21	32	47	21	1	—22	2	0	—2
Musicians	34	48	18	21	32	47	13	16	—29	1	1	—3

* To which the subjects responded Like (L), Indifferent (I), or Dislike (D). Adapted from E. K. Strong, Jr., 1943.

Kuder intercorrelated items and by means of factor analysis identified groups of them that represent the same type of interest. In this way he put together 10 general dimensional scales (Scientific, Artistic, Mechanical, and so on), giving an easily surveyed profile of interests, which is useful to a counselor in guiding a person into occupations to which his profile is known to be relevant.

Neither of these tests is particularly successful as a means of *selecting* suitable people for a job, because a person can easily fake his answers in order to be hired. The items are on the whole too transparent; the responses that can make one "look good" are too obvious. The tests are, however, of proved usefulness in vocational guidance and counseling.

THE INDIRECT APPROACH

In this approach, any kind of item on an objective test is worth using as long as it can be reliably measured and it is statistically associated with one type of person only. The item does not have to make much sense or be intuitively meaningful to the tester. This conclusion follows clearly enough from the logic of indirect measurement in the realm of personality: If a psychologist cannot measure a trait directly in a way that is convenient enough to constitute a practical test, he can try to find some other form of readily measured behavior that happens to be highly correlated with what he is really interested in and that will serve as an indicator of it. The correlation coefficient takes the place of understanding, so an item can be anything that works.

Notice two points about such objective indirect assessment. First, a measure of this type can never be any better than its correlation with something different in kind, and it is unlikely therefore to have very good validity. Second, its rationale is similar in several ways to the logic of projective techniques (or of any other indirect assessment), for they too rely on a correlation between easily accessible test behavior and relatively inaccessible behavior of greater intrinsic interest. The difference is, first, that each bit of information a projective test provides is not treated mechanically but is interpreted clinically by means of a theoretically illuminated understanding of the inner relation between test response and the aspects of personality that determine it. Second, projective techniques have the disadvantage that they typically do not yield precise, objective measures, or at least do not do so as easily as objective tests.

Personality Inventories

After the example of the Strong Vocational Interest Blank, an indirect type of objective inventory has been introduced, which relies less than early inventories did on the face validity of the items and on the subject's ability to report his own feelings and behavior accurately. It uses, instead, the method of empirical keying. The best-known example is the Minnesota Multiphasic Personality Inventory (MMPI), published by Hathaway and McKinley in 1943 after considerable preliminary research. It comes in a group form with printed answer sheets and in an individual form in which the 550 items are printed on separate cards, which the subject sorts into three slots in a box (marked True, False, and Can't Say).

A typical item is a statement that might have been taken from a psychiatric interview; indeed, many of them were. Some are frank statements of rather extreme, psychotic symptoms ("My soul sometimes leaves my body"; "I see things or animals or people around me that others do not see"); some represent milder psychological and physical symptoms ("I have a great deal of stomach trouble"; "I brood a great deal"; "I feel weak all over much of the time"). Some items describe past history ("In school I found it very hard to talk before the class"); and some are statements of belief or attitude ("I like science"; "I am entirely self-confident"; "Horses that don't pull should be beaten or kicked"). Many are quite innocuous, whichever way one answers them ("I used to keep a diary"; "I enjoy detective or mystery stories").

The original aim of the authors of the MMPI was to create an aid to psychiatric diagnosis. Accordingly, they administered their items to groups of patients with known psychiatric diagnoses and compared the answers of each group of patients item by item with those of a large group of non-hospitalized persons (relatives and other visitors at a hospital); only those items that distinguished the schizophrenic patients, for example, from the nonpatients were retained for the schizophrenia (Sc) scale. Eight of the basic nine clinical scales are named after types of psychopathology (see Figure 39-1, page 740).

In practice, the examiner rarely looks to see whether a subject answers any one item True, False, or Can't Say. Instead, he scores the answers on the empirical scales and then draws inferences from the resulting profile. Even at that point, he does not rely on his understanding of the nature of the diagnostic categories that give the scales their names, for the test happens not to have been notably successful when used in the way it was originally intended. That is, if a person's highest score is on scale 2, depression (D), it does not necessarily mean he is clinically depressed, even if the score is above 70 (which is presumed to be in the pathological range for each scale); and if he is depressed, that scale alone will not indicate whether the condition is of neurotic or of psychotic degree. Instead, the test's authors recommend taking into account the rest of the profile and interpreting the meaning of each scale in terms of accumulated clinical experience with the kinds of people who tend to get high or low scores on it.

Hathaway and his collaborators made a determined effort to enhance the usefulness of the MMPI by providing several correction keys to alert the user that a subject's answers may not be taken at face value. Anyone who does not want to commit himself on an item, does not understand it, or feels that neither True nor False is the right answer for him can omit the item in the group form or sort it Can't Say in the individual form (scored "?"). Because some subjects will overuse this escape hatch, the simplest control score is just a count of these ?'s; if as many as one-fifth of the items are answered this way, the test is considered invalid.

Another possible cause for invalidity of the test is that the subject may deny all difficulties so as to look as normal as possible. It should be possible, Meehl and Hathaway (1946) reasoned, to distinguish such a subject from a genuinely untroubled normal person by measuring his tendency to deny some "symptoms" that most normal people will actually admit to (for example, "I get angry sometimes"). About a dozen such items were included, constituting the L (lie) scale. The F (false) scale is somewhat similar; it consists of 16 items very rarely answered in the scored direction, which for the most part is pathological. Thus, both a person who is trying to look as "sick" as possible and a careless or inattentive subject may get a high F score.

The K control scale was derived from the common answers of a special group of people—psychiatric patients whose scores on the scale most appropriate to them were not high enough to fall in the pathological range. These items are taken to measure a kind of defensiveness or denial that anything much is wrong. Fixed proportions of the subject's K score are therefore added to his raw total on five of the clinical scales to correct directly for the tendency toward defensive understatement.

Although the idea behind such special keys is excellent, they have often proved disappointing in practice. Some recent work on another test suggests the reason. Norman (1963b) hoped to develop a test of five personality factors (see page 659) that would be valid even when a subject was trying to put his best foot forward. He administered the test twice to a large group of college men, first with the usual instructions to answer as frankly and accurately as possible and then again with instructions to answer so as to make the best impression for getting into Officer Candidate School. From the differences in responses under these two conditions, he was able to develop a special key, or scoring method, to detect faking. When he repeated the dual procedure with a similar group the key correctly identified 94 percent of the faked tests while erroneously tagging only 6 percent of the "frank and accurate" ones as phony. Later, a third group of students took his test twice, the second time as each thought would maximize his chances of being accepted by the Peace Corps. The faking key, which had worked so well before, now did a very poor job of distinguishing the new set of faked answers from the subjects' honest answers, because the subjects' conception of the ideal Peace Corps trainee was quite different from the conception of a promising Officer Candidate. It is therefore dangerous to assume that subjects will respond in only one way in an effort to look as good as possible, for their definition of good will vary according to the nature of the situation. (Further data on the reliability and validity of the MMPI are given in Chapter 39.)

The problem of response sets. In discussing the problem of how to assess motives, long before the first work on the MMPI was begun, Murray raised the possibility that

> we might solve our problem by getting the subject to state his desire. We might ask: what are you trying to do? Here, however, we are confronted by more problems; for the S [subject] is often unconscious of his motives or, if conscious, is unwilling to reveal them. The S may have a host of secondary conflicting motives. He may want to show himself in the best light, to be consistent, to exhibit independence, to be different, to give the normal response, to mislead or please the E [examiner], to amuse himself, and so forth [Murray, 1938, p. 245].

About twenty years later, psychologists interested in objective assessment began to take these problems seriously. Today, under the name *response sets*, rather than "conflicting motives," they are widely recognized as limiting the questionnaire approach (which is, in effect, simply asking the subject, "What are your desires, and how do you usually behave?").

A response set is an enduring disposition that helps determine a subject's answers to a questionnaire but one that is different from and usually irrelevant to the kinds of traits the questionnaire is intended to measure. The sets generally assumed to be most important and troublesome are *acquiescence* and *social desirability*. The majority of items in tests like the MMPI make their points straightforwardly; hence, if a person was susceptible to the traditional medical student's disease of imagining that he has a symptom as soon as he reads about it, or if he had a habit of being obliging, or a trait of suggestibility, he might answer Yes indiscriminately, and through this acquiescent behavior end up with a set of pathological scores. On the other hand, if a person was concerned (consciously or unconsciously) about how he was "coming across" to the examiner, if he wanted "to show himself in the best light" and "to give the normal response," his answers to questions might be heavily determined by his idea of what most people would consider the good, right, or socially desirable response. Few of us are wholly immune to the effects of such secondary conflicting motives; yet obviously some people are much more prone to behave in one or both of these ways than others are. Therefore, the effects of response sets are widespread but not uniform, which makes it more difficult to cope with them: Any correction has to be differential, not uniform.

When the importance of response sets became apparent a few years ago, they were overemphasized at first. With the alleged discovery that most of the variance in the MMPI scales could be traced to acquiescence (Couch & Keniston, 1960; Messick & Jackson, 1961) and social desirability (Edwards & Heathers, 1962), many workers with the MMPI jumped to the conclusion that this test was best interpreted in terms of response sets rather than in terms of the content, or meaning, of its items. One step in the disillusionment of the psychometricians who had been the MMPI's main supporters was the repeated demonstration that in the bewildering variety of scales that had been developed, only two factors of any size were to be found (for example, see Messick & Jackson, 1961; Block, 1965). In a series of ingenious analyses, however, Block (1965) has shown that the meaning of the items remains the most important determinant of people's responses to the MMPI and that acquiescence and social desirability play insignificant roles. By balancing the number of responses keyed True and False, he constructed acquiescence-free scales; he then showed that these scales contained the same two factors, one of which had been widely interpreted as a measure of acquiescence. Likewise, he eliminated items with strongly positive or negative social desirability and again showed that the resulting scales had these two factors. Finally, he explored the meaning of the two factors in five different samples of subjects who had been intensively and independently assessed. He found that the first and largest factor seems to measure psychological health, or adjustment versus maladjustment—a conclusion also reached by several other investigators (for example, Tyler, 1951; Kassebaum, Couch, & Slater, 1959), though Block prefers to term this factor Ego-Resiliency. The second factor, which Welsh (1956) had called repression and Kassebaum and his colleagues (1959) had identified with introversion-extroversion, Block labels Ego-Control. At one extreme, this factor measures overcontrol—an excessive delaying of impulse and gratification; at the other extreme, undercontrol—"insufficient modulation of impulse and an inability to delay gratification [Block, 1965, p. 115]."

The final chapter of the MMPI story has yet to be written, and it may turn out to contain more interpretable variance than Block's impressive researches would seem to allow. Meanwhile, the developers of new inventories will do well to eliminate the unwanted and unnecessary effects of the principal response sets.

The ethics of personality testing. It should be clear from experiments cited above that self-report inventories can easily be faked. Yet the whole point of such tests is lost if they are given in a context in which the subject cannot feel confident that he is acting in his own best interests by telling the truth. It may be that the development of empirical keying and other indirect methods got some test constructors off on the wrong foot, so that they conceived of their job as outwitting the subject and getting from him information he did not want to give. However it started, the fact is that in recent years inventories like the MMPI, which contain many highly personal questions and which try to get information indirectly, have been used in contexts where the subject's answers may expose him to some danger, like that of not getting a job for which he is applying.

The question has therefore been raised whether such use of personality tests is ethical. Members of the American Psychological Association subscribe to a Code of Ethics, which is designed to give guidance in all aspects of their work. One principle from the code states:

> The psychologist's ultimate allegiance is to society, and his professional behavior should demonstrate an awareness of his social responsibilities. The welfare of the profession and of the individual psychologist are clearly subordinate to the welfare of the public. . . . in service, the responsibility of most weight is the welfare of the client with whom the psychologist is working.

In the judgment of many members of the profession (Lovell, 1967), the client whose welfare must be protected is the person being tested, even when the psychologist is hired by a company to select employees. It is therefore an ethically questionable practice to ask people to take tests and answer questions that they might consider an invasion of their privacy in situations where they have little effective freedom to refuse.

Not surprisingly, such abuses led to a rash of books attacking the MMPI and similar personality tests (for example, Whyte, 1956; Gross, 1962; Packard, 1964) and finally to senatorial and congressional investigations in June 1965. Our society offers all too many examples of the unwarranted invasion of privacy by government and business, by politicians and market-research firms; and recent years have seen the rise of "thought reform" (misleadingly called brainwashing; see Holt, 1964) and other authoritarian attempts to use psychology to invade and control the innermost thoughts of citizens.

Is personality testing an invasion of privacy? The main issue of invasion of privacy grew out of the application of the MMPI to the selection of people for government employment, but the use of such tests in research has been attacked as well. Because the issue can easily be overgeneralized, we need to see clearly that in the matter of privacy, context makes all the difference. Thus, when a lawyer asks his client personal questions in order to prepare a defense, the accused person is likely to react quite differently to the probing than he does when the same questions are put to him by the prosecuting attorney in open court. What is necessary and helpful in one context is an intolerable breach of privacy in another.

Let us consider what is meant by "privacy." If someone comes into your home, inspects the premises, looks at the titles of the books on the shelves, and asks you questions about various possessions you have scattered around, is that an invasion of your privacy? If he is a friend, surely not; you may even have "conversation pieces" just to stimulate such inquiries. Or if he is an expert you have asked to appraise your furniture, by coming into your home he is doing you a service for which you will pay. If, however, you go to the door to answer an unexpected ring, and a stranger demands to come in, inspects your belongings, and asks you questions about them, the whole situation changes, and you are likely to feel that your privacy is being invaded.

The psychologist's role is like that of the expert appraiser—he appraises personality when he assesses it by means of tests. If he does so in a clinical setting where a client has gone to seek help with personal problems, it is appropriate for him to ask personal questions; in this situation the confidences of the client are protected by the ethics of the psychologist's profession. If a girl applies for a job as a typist, she will expect to be asked about her familiarity with office procedures or to have her typing speed tested; but she may understandably resent being asked her views about religion and sex.

For these reasons, official representatives of the American Psychological Association made it clear in their testimony at the 1965 hearings that tests like the MMPI were not intended for this kind of selection and that such use violated the Code of Ethics. They also pointed out that when personality tests are given to a subject in a research project, his answers remain anonymous and are used only in the attempt to increase scientific knowledge about personality. A subject in such a study always has the option of refusing to answer a question that upsets him; on the other hand, if he records his response honestly he can be certain that his confidence will not be abused and that his cooperation in research will be appreciated. Ironically, the MMPI is often scored by machines or by other impersonal means so that the psychologist does not see any particular person's answer to any specific question; he is generally concerned only with the summed answers to many questions in scoring keys.

Nonverbal Tests   There is no intrinsic reason why the method of empirical keying should be confined to verbal items (see page 640); it can be applied to many other kinds of behavior, and has been. The results have not been impressive, however, and few such tests have achieved much currency. Most of the existing nonverbal indirect tests of the objective type have been constructed by an alternative strategy, that of factor analysis: The investigator finds clusters of covarying scores from nonverbal tests and interprets them by examining their correlation with verbal tests of known significance.

The leading exponent of indirect, nonverbal testing of personality is R. B. Cattell (1957), who has declared that the ultimate goal of assessment should be to do away with self-report inventories and rely entirely on objective tests made up of motor, perceptual, or even physiological items. He has published batteries of Objective Analytic tests, as he calls them, based on factor analyses of more than 200 scores derived from such tests. To establish the significance of his performance-test factors, he does not use empirical keying but depends rather on correlations of his test factors with behavioral ratings and with factors from tests of the self-reporting type.

Eysenck (1960) has pursued a program of research along somewhat similar lines, using objective tests of conditionability and the effects of various drugs as well as sensory, perceptual, and motor tests similar to Cattell's.

These indirect nonverbal tests have been criticized on the grounds that (1) the results bearing on validity are not impressive; (2) the approach is clumsy and time consuming; and (3) though the tests are not subject to faking, they are not satisfactorily reliable (Vernon, 1964). The underlying difficulty seems to be that if a test is to measure an important aspect of personality, the performance that produces a score must itself be rather directly determined by the personality trait in question. And since, as we saw in Chapter 32, a trait is a disposition that is inferred, ultimately, from a person's behavior in real-life situations and is not itself an entity with an independent physical existence, it is not surprising that the approach has had little success.

Cattell is under no illusion that self-report inventories are about to be made obsolete, therefore; indeed, he works actively with them. The sort of variable his factor analyses of inventories and judges' ratings has led to is typified by his factor E: dominance versus submissiveness; or C: Ego-Strength versus neuroticism. These are complex patterns of behavior, which are ultimately dependent on some kind of stable anatomical-physiological patterns in the body and nervous system. In apes and monkeys, for example, dominance versus submission is an obvious behavioral pattern, which is much affected by the animal's hormonal status (Clark & Birch, 1945) and which can be drastically changed by electrical impulses to certain regions in the midbrain (Delgado, 1966). At present, however, it is impossible to assess a personality by studying the brain in any direct manner; even if experimenters could practically and ethically undertake such a study, they would not know what to measure. For the time being, therefore, investigators must rely on behavioral indexes of traits, and the sorts of measures Cattell has provided (for example, his 16 P-F Test) have been found useful by many workers in assessment.

Objective Measures
from Physical Anthropology and Biology

Some psychologists are convinced that an excellent angle from which to approach personality assessment is that of the body, long studied by physical anthropology. Almost as long as there has been interest in personality, people have been struck by the association of certain temperamental traits with aspects of physique: The fat man is traditionally supposed to be easygoing, the muscular man vigorous, the thin man contemplative. The German psychiatrist Kretschmer (1921) gave such observations an apparently scientific basis, though his methods were too casual and slipshod to be convincing. He described three main types of physique and claimed to have found a predominance of *pyknics* (stout builds) among manic-depressive patients and a dearth of them among schizophrenics, whom he classified as either muscular (*athletic*), thin and weak (*asthenic*), or disharmonious mixtures of the principal types (*dyplastic*).

SOMATOTYPING

Sheldon (1940), the best-known recent worker in the field of physique and personality, attempted to follow up Kretschmer's work. First he replaced Kretschmer's typology with three variables or components of physique, which he called endomorphy (fat), mesomorphy (bone and muscle), and ectomorphy (leanness). Using a standardized photographic technique and a method of inspection backed up by various objective measurements, he rated each of the three components on a 7-point scale and found 76 combinations, or somatotypes (types of body build). Figure 35-1, for example, presents a standard picture of a 4 5 1—that is, this young man's

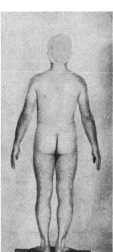

Figure 35-1   Standard photograph of a 26-year-old man with somatotype 4 5 1. (From Sheldon et al., 1940)

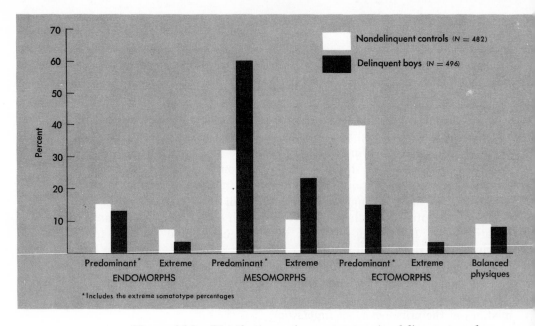

Figure 35-2 Distributions of somatotypes in delinquent and nondelinquent adolescents. (Based on data from Glueck & Glueck, 1950)

body is rated at the midpoint (4) on endomorphy, just above the middle of the scale on mesomorphy, and at the minimum on ectomorphy. He would thus be classed as a mesomorph, since the second component is predominant, though he is by no means an extreme mesomorph.

Sheldon then published a study (Sheldon & Stevens, 1942) in which he claimed to have isolated three components of temperament, each of which was correlated very highly with one component of physique. But critics (such as Adcock, 1948) have pointed out that he made no effort to get objective, independent measures of physique and temperament; he rated everything subjectively, a procedure that makes bias inevitable when the rater has an expectation about how the variables ought to be related. In a study of state-hospital patients, Sheldon (1949) claimed to find equally strong relations between somatotypes and three components of psychosis: Roughly, the bulkier the patient, the more he was inclined toward affective exaggeration; the more lean but muscular, the more paranoid hostility he showed; and the frailer, the more hebephrenic characteristics he had. Another study by Sheldon in the same book found a disproportionate number of overdeveloped muscular and fleshy physiques among delinquent adolescent boys. Again, however, he presented no satisfactory control data, and his conclusions cannot be taken at face value.

A number of Sheldon's claims have been checked by others, with mixed results. The better-controlled study of delinquents by Glueck and Glueck (1950) did tend to confirm Sheldon's last finding, for they found twice as many mesomorphs among their 500 delinquents as they found among 500 controls (see Figure 35-2). Bellak and Holt (1948) found that the somatotypes of a sample of schizophrenics differed significantly from Sheldon's published norms based on college students—though not, as he had reported, by containing an overrepresentation of frail ectomorphs. Rather, they contained a disproportionate number of wiry (slender but secondarily bony and muscular) somatotypes and a dearth of pronounced mesomorphs (the brawny "Mr. America" types). Moreover, the schizophrenic patients were *not* significantly different from a matched control group of patients with paresis, an organic psychosis resulting from syphilitic infection (see Table 35-3). To some extent, the findings could be accounted for, if

Table 35-3   Distribution of Somatotypes Among Schizophrenics, Paretics, and College Students

	Proportions having these somatotypes		
Groups of somatotypes	Schizo-phrenics	Paretics	Sheldon's college students
The stout (all endomorphs, endomorphic mesomorphs, and endomorph-meso-morphs)	16%	21%	27%
The brawny (predominant mesomorphs and ectomorphic mesomorphs)	8	3	22
The wiry (mesomorphic ectomorphs and mesomorph-ectomorphs)	50	58	13
The frail (predominant ectomorphs, endomorphic ectomorphs, and ectomorph-endomorphs)	16	15	19
Balanced physiques (no component predominant)	10	3	19
Totals	100%	100%	100%
Number of cases	50	33	4000

Adapted from Bellak & Holt, 1948.

it could be proved that psychosis caused a wasting away of muscles through inactivity and a loss of interest in food.

Despite Sheldon's claims, some investigators have found that somatotype measures change with age and with nutritional status. On the other hand, well-controlled studies, in which physique has been measured by objective physical measurements or else by somatotyping and personality by means of self-report tests and inventories, have often found small but positive correlations in the direction of Sheldon's hypotheses. Psychologists tend to discount Sheldon's claims because of their dogmatic and undemocratic tone and because of his faulty experimental designs. Nevertheless, his conclusions seem to contain some valid insights, which need to be verified by more truly objective methods (see Chapter 37).

BIOCHEMICAL MEASURES

It has often been suggested that measures of physique are persistently, though never very strongly, related to personality because of some third factor that is more directly related to both, such as the operation of the endocrine glands. This hypothesis gains plausibility from repeated clinical observation of the marked changes in personality that accompany known endocrine disorders. For example, in Addison's disease the cortex of the adrenal gland is progressively destroyed, so that the production of its hormones is cut down; as this occurs, apathy, negativism, and paranoid attitudes often appear. Similarly, when the blood contains more than the normal amount of cortisone (a hormone produced by the adrenal cortex) as a result of treatment for such conditions as arthritis, other marked changes in behavior and mood often occur, most notably euphoria. Despite such observations, there is little evidence that normal variations in mood are related to changes in amounts of hormones. Moreover, both a deficiency and an excess of some biochemical substances can produce similar effects, and the same hormonal abnormality can be associated with very different personality changes in different people.

The situation is similar in other biological branches of psychology. Exciting discoveries are occurring—the effects on behavior, thought, and emotion of direct electrical stimulation of the brain or of introducing small amounts of various chemical substances—and the relations usually turn out to be more complicated than they look at first. Although more is being learned about, for example, the significance of certain parts of the brain for emotions and motives, more detailed findings are needed to throw light on stable individual differences. The important advances made in recent years in endocrinology and biochemistry may eventually help to illuminate the biological basis of some aspects of the human personality, but most psychologists who are experts in assessing personality and who follow these developments feel in no immediate danger of being thrown out of work by endocrinologists or biochemists.

PSYCHOPHYSIOLOGICAL MEASURES

In the past, great hopes have been pinned on such psychophysiological measures as the galvanic skin response (GSR), which indexes the activity of part of the autonomic nervous system by measuring sweating. Since many chronically anxious people tend to perspire freely, which changes the electrical properties of their skin in a way that is measured fairly easily, psychologists have assumed that the GSR and other similar measures of autonomic function, such as the rate of the heartbeat or of respiration, might make good objective tests of emotionality, anxiety, or the like.

Ultimately, some measures of this type may prove to be useful methods of personality assessment. At present, however, the available measures seem related to aspects of personality in ways that are too complicated to be useful. As one of the leading workers in the field of psychophysiology has put it:

> The relationship of the autonomic nervous system to behavior in general, and to the problems of neurosis and psychosis, is a vast and controversial field. . . . the autonomic response is a part of the total behavior of the subject . . . the "meaning" of the somatic response must be *interpreted* in terms of the transactions of the individual with his environment, and in terms which involve judgments, or at least statements, of "molar" psychological states and behavior [Lacey, 1959, pp. 160, 174, 178].

He reached this conclusion after a thorough review of many attempts (mostly unsuccessful) to find objective, external, physiological measures of some of the intangible changes in personality accompanying psychotherapy. Nevertheless, Lacey is quick to add that psychophysiological investigations can contribute greatly to research on psychotherapy when they are used interpretatively and not in an attempt to avoid dealing with psychological phenomena by direct psychological means.

Objective Measures
of Cognitive Style

A rationale often offered for projective techniques is that everyone has his own personal world—his peculiar way of looking at reality, conceptualizing things and people, and organizing experience. Psychologists of personality such as Klein (1951) and Witkin (1954, 1962), whose earlier research was in the experimental psychology of perception, saw that their standard methods of analyzing visual and kinesthetic phenomena could tell something about the subject's personal world if they were used in a new way. Formerly, experimental psychologists were interested only in group averages, because they wanted to learn the laws of perception in general. If, however, you ask how far any individual subject deviates from the average, you can measure rather directly an aspect of his unique way of viewing things, his cognitive style. By the logic of indirect measurement, this might also give clues to related and less strictly cognitive aspects of personality, as indeed it did. Thus, the recent emergence of tests of cognitive controls or styles constitutes a promising development in assessment.

Leveling versus sharpening. Consider, for example, a dimension of cognitive style that Holzman and Klein (1954) call leveling versus sharpening. Working with certain classical psychophysical methods, in which subjects estimated the sizes of squares or the heaviness of small weights, they found first that people tended to be consistent in their perceptual judgments, some (sharpeners) making sharp discriminations and following closely any changes in the nature of the stimuli, others (levelers) tending to miss changes in the level of stimulation because their memories of what they had just experienced became confused. An interpretation in terms of memory—that is, how well a person can keep records of successive similar experiences separate rather than letting them blend into one another—was suggested to Holzman, Klein, and their co-workers by the results of a larger study in which they gave many cognitive tests to a group of subjects and then did factor analyses of the results (Gardner, Holzman, Klein, Linton, & Spence, 1959). Leveling-sharpening emerged as a factor made up of scores not only from the perceptual tests just mentioned but also from such tasks as giving free associations to the word "dry"; levelers used a good many words in talking about each topic that came to mind but stayed quite close to the starting word, while sharpeners flitted about quickly from one idea to another, ranging far afield.

The general cognitive sluggishness of levelers was shown also in their slowness to recognize the effect of distorting spectacles and to name the colors of ink in which rows of asterisks were printed. More clinical data suggested that the levelers tended to have repressive, hysterical defenses (see Chapter 39). A number of experimenters have taken up the dimensions of cognitive style that Klein and his co-workers developed and have suggested that these may have many other ramifications in emotional as well as cognitive behavior.

Field independence, or psychological differentiation. Like Klein, Witkin has headed a team of investigators who have spent more than fifteen years developing measures of cognitive style and relating them to many aspects of their subjects' lives. Witkin's group has concentrated on a dimension of cognitive style that he called first *field independence* and then *psychological differentiation.* The impetus to this work came from the armed services' concern about the fact that some pilots, after flying into a cloud and losing sight of the ground, would fly out the other side with one wing up, or even upside down. They literally did not know which way was up. Through experimental studies of how people told "up" from "down," Witkin found that two kinds of information played a role in this orientation—the visual field and the inner experience of the pull of gravity on the body.

Let us suppose you have suddenly found yourself in a chair inside a small room. You were blindfolded when you took your seat; with the blindfold off, you can see that your chair is tilted, at least in relation to the room. But the room is devised so that it too can be tipped one way or another from the true vertical; and the chair can be tilted quite independently of the room (see Figure 35-3). If you were asked to operate a control that changed the position of your chair, would you be able to "fly by the seat of your pants" until you were *actually upright*, even though the appearance of the room would make it seem that you were out of line? People differ greatly in the extent to which they can perform such tasks, depending on how much of the two kinds of information (external and internal) they use.

One reason Witkin changed the name of the dimension was that when he gave various other cognitive tasks to his subjects, the "field-dependent" ones showed a general difficulty in articulating, or differentiating, complex stimuli, such as the puzzle pictures of the Gottschaldt Test. (An example from a similar test is shown in Chapter 39 in Figure 39-4.) Subjects who had been able to select the bodily sensations of gravity out of a total mass of stimulation also proved best able to select the simple design out of the complex figure in which it was embedded. Moreover, they seemed to have more differentiated body images; Witkin found large and significant correlations between field independence and such aspects of figure drawings as the amount of realistic detail (see Figure 35-4). When the subjects were clinically assessed, largely by means of projective techniques, the less differentiated proved to be significantly more passive in coping with their life situations, less insightful, and more afraid of their own impulses (Witkin et al., 1954). Linton (1955) found less differentiated subjects to be more easily influenced by suggestion than more differentiated, or field-independent, subjects. Though these relationships are interesting, cognitive styles are important to assessment for their intrinsic interest rather than as indirect measures of other traits.

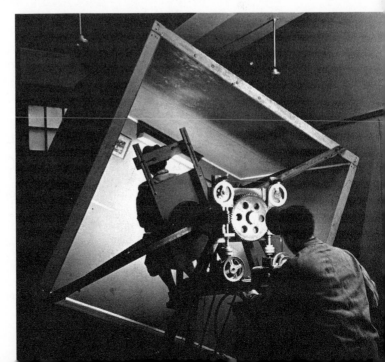

Figure 35-3 Tilting-Room–Tilting-Chair Test.

Figure 35-4 Left, figure drawings by a field-dependent man. Right, figure drawings by a field-independent woman. (From Witkin et al., 1954)

Criticisms of cognitive-style research. Critics (for example, Postman, 1955; Gruen, 1957) point out that much of the work of Witkin, Klein, and other exponents of cognitive style concentrates on extreme groups, when in fact most people fall somewhere nearer the middle. They also object that the links of perceptual and other cognitive phenomena to what is usually thought of as personality are vague, analogical, or just empirical correlations —for instance, it is known that field-dependent people are often passive in social situations, but it is not understood *why*, or where the causal connection is. Researchers on cognitive style have been accused of claiming findings of general validity more quickly than the small and selected samples of subjects in their experiments would allow. Undoubtedly it will take years before enough research has been done to answer these objections. The issues that have been raised by both sides are important ones, and the effort to answer the questions of the critics is advancing the psychology of personality.

Judgments of Personality
as Objective Measures

Some psychologists take the position that personality is purely a matter of social perception—that it is meaningless to speak of anyone's personality apart from the particular people who interact with him, get impressions about him, and use trait terms in describing him. The weakness of this position, as Allport (1937, 1961) pointed out for thirty years, is that it neglects the problem of how a person's friends could get a consistent conception of him as, let us say, warm, if there were no actual consistency in his behavior. As we have seen, first impressions can be biased by hearsay and prejudice, but in the long run a specious judgment is unlikely to be held by more than a few rigid people who have need to maintain a fictional view about someone for some personal reason.

The purely social conception of personality may partly account for the profusion of research studies using inexpert judges to provide measurements of personality. Regardless of one's definition of personality, there is value in such judgments, and they do have the great advantage of being far easier to obtain than expert (clinical) judgments. Most of the published research on ratings of personality deals with inexpert judges, because there are so many more of them than of highly trained and skilled assessors of personality. Understandable though this imbalance is, it has the regrettable effect of concentrating research on the most superficial aspects of personality, which *can* be fairly adequately rated by amateurs.

HOW TO OBTAIN JUDGMENTS OF PERSONALITY

Who could give the most accurate picture of your personality? You may perhaps think of close relatives, those people you have lived with and who have been able to observe you under the greatest variety of conditions for the longest time; perhaps close friends, in whom you confide inner thoughts and feelings, some of which you might be reluctant to tell even a parent, brother, or sister; or perhaps someone with whom you have had a long-term loving relationship, who undoubtedly knows you better in many ways than anyone else.

Obviously, these people are well qualified in many ways to assess your personality; yet one fact immediately casts doubt on their usefulness as informants—they are biased. Anyone who loves you is going to have a hard time being objective, particularly when the assessment touches on socially valued aspects of behavior—and there are extraordinarily few aspects of personality that are not to some degree considered admirable or base, good or bad, attractive or unattractive. To ask a man's mother or wife to rate his personality is doubly dangerous; not only would the judgments, if you could get them, probably be biased but the very attempt to do so would violate the privacy of both the subject and the informant. For such reasons, personalities are rarely assessed by obtaining judgments from the people who know a person best, although they are used as informants whenever possible.

But if a person has only casual contacts and is not emotionally involved with the subject, does he know him well enough to judge his personality? It all depends on the *aspects* of personality in question. Students who live together in a dormitory for months or years may not know one another's deepest longings and ultimate goals in life, but they may know more than anyone else about one another's patterns of everyday social behavior.

The judgments of a person's acquaintances are classified under objective methods of measuring personality as *peer ratings*. Objectivity in this context properly refers to intersubjectivity; in other words, if a consensus of apparently normal adults agrees that something is true, it can be accepted as true unless there is good reason to believe that they are all laboring under a common handicap. One such handicap is the lack of any opportunity to form independent judgments by direct contact with the facts, in which case prejudice or some form of reliance on the judgments of other people may operate or the judge may try to infer the truth through use of some theory. The crucial point, then, is to *have an acquaintance rate or judge only those facets of a subject's behavior that he has had the best opportunity to observe directly and not those he has not observed.*

One of the best ways to get useful quantitative measures, which are substantially equivalent to judgments or ratings, is to ask members of a group of acquaintances to choose or nominate "one of the four best leaders" or "the five kindest members" of the group, or the like. This technique, called *sociometry*, was developed by Moreno (1953), who has based a branch of social psychology on it.

PERSONALITY VARIABLES BEST RATED BY PEERS

What aspects of personality are best assessed by the ratings of acquaintances? Clearly they must be overt patterns of behavior. A leading figure in the objective approach to assessing personality, R. B. Cattell, decided that the psychology of personality would be much aided by having available a comprehensive, clearly intelligible vocabulary for describing observable behavior, the outermost layer of personality. Allport and Odbert (1936) had started the job by pulling out of the largest unabridged dictionary all words that could be used to describe personality—18,000 of them, of which just over 4500 clearly denote traits, or consistent and stable modes of behaving. Cattell (1957) sifted through this latter list, grouping words that were essentially synonyms; he found 171 clusters, from each of which he selected one term that seemed to express its core meaning.

At this point, Cattell called on the services of a large group of people to rate their acquaintances on each of the 171 traits. Cattell thought it likely that the judges would be able to make a much smaller number of real discriminations. He intercorrelated the ratings, therefore, and found 36 clusters of traits that were so highly correlated they seemed to be expressing the same judgments. As expected, for example, the terms *talkative* and *silent* proved to be highly, but negatively, correlated; the other clusters also contained such logical opposites. Cattell thus obtained a set of paired (or *bipolar*) trait names, which he subsequently expanded slightly to a total of 46 pairs by drawing on the special terminologies of personality theorists.

Many personologists (psychologists who specialize in research on personality and its theory) have used this comprehensive list in a variety of re-

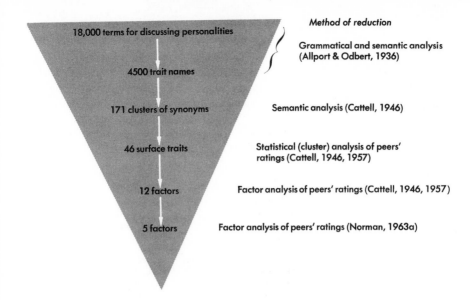

Figure 35-5   *The attempt to achieve a manageable vocabulary of traits.*

searches. A number of them, including Cattell, decided to examine the set of paired traits further by factor-analyzing sets of ratings using the list. At this point, the story becomes quite technical, for as was pointed out earlier (page 636) there are quite a number of different techniques of factor analysis, which make different assumptions and give different results. Cattell himself claims that in his 46 overt traits he finds "twelve very stable and two or three less definite primary personality factors [1957, p. 73]." Other workers (such as Norman, 1963a) have analyzed some of Cattell's data as well as their own and just as repeatedly find only 5 factors (see Figure 35-5). Meanwhile, yet another team (Glueck, Meehl, Schofield, & Clyde, 1964) have started all over again with Allport and Odbert's 4500 terms, which they have supplemented from 72 other sources to make a total of 6682 items. After going through rather similar procedures of clustering the terms, they came up with a list of 329 phenotypic items, or overt traits, defining 176 factors, and 101 genotypic items (similar to what Cattell calls source traits).

Let us take a look at the smallest list, that of 5 dimensions. These factors seem to be suitable for acquaintances to judge, for they have emerged from studies in which the ratings were made by small groups of casual friends —fraternity brothers, college-dormitory friends, graduate students of clinical psychology who spent a week together while being assessed, and U.S. Air Force officer candidates. Each factor name in Table 35-4 is followed by the 4 specific bipolar ratings that best express it (that is, have the highest loadings on that factor).

*Table 35-4   Five Major Factors
in Ratings of Personality*

1. Extroversion

talkative	vs.	silent
frank, open		secretive
adventurous		cautious
sociable		reclusive

2. Agreeableness

goodnatured	vs.	irritable
not jealous		jealous
mild, gentle		headstrong
cooperative		negativistic

3. Conscientiousness

fussy, tidy	vs.	careless
responsible		undependable
scrupulous		unscrupulous
persevering		quitting, fickle

4. Emotional stability

poised	vs.	nervous, tense
calm		anxious
composed		excitable
not hypochondriacal		hypochondriacal

5. Culture

artistically sensitive	vs.	artistically insensitive
intellectual		unreflective, narrow
polished, refined		crude, boorish
imaginative		simple, direct

Adapted from Norman, 1963a.

WHO ARE THE BEST JUDGES?

Whenever a group of friends rate one another's personalities, some are bound to come consistently closer to the consensus than others. Therefore, if we single out those whose judgments are closest to the mean (comparing them with the most deviant ones) and examine the ratings they have *received*, we have a quick formula for a study on the characteristics of the good judge of personality. There has been a good deal of research along these lines, from which much can be learned if the inherent limitations of this kind of data are kept in mind. In the better studies, the qualities of good judges are determined by other means as well, usually by tests. The fact that the various studies converge on the findings outlined below increases the likelihood that these generalizations are meaningful.

Not surprisingly, the better judges are generally more intelligent and more mature than the poorer ones. Their tendency to excel in social skills and to be warm and socially adjusted may indicate that their ability at judging is attributable simply to the fact that they see people the way most of their friends do, for the socially successful should be most in touch with the group's ways of perceiving and judging. It is just as plausible, however, to argue that possessing such abilities as accurate judging is a distinct social asset.

In forming judgments, it helps to be similar to the people being rated: The best judges resemble their subjects in sex, age, and ethnic and cultural background, a finding that again may be partly valid (for we can understand best those whose experiences have been like our own) and partly an artifact (Bruner & Tagiuri, 1954; Taft, 1955). The latter may be true because a person who was actually like most others in the group he had to rate and who proceeded almost entirely on the basis of naive projection, assuming that everybody was like himself, would show up as an apparently shrewd judge of men.

A hint that some very general kind of sensitivity may be involved in rating personalities comes from the repeated finding that judging ability is related to literary and artistic interests and skills. The good judge has a relatively complex and differentiated set of concepts for thinking about people rather than a set of simple stereotypes. Such a statement comes very close to saying that the good judge should be psychologically minded (in Murray's term, *intraceptive*)—concerned with the subjective and interpersonal dimensions of experience. This quality has been found to be lacking in the authoritarian personality, as measured by tests of prejudice against minority groups, notably by the California F-Test of fascist-like attitudes. A couple of studies have found that authoritarianism does in fact show up more strongly in people who are poor judges of others. So does reliance on the defense of projection, which is part of the authoritarian syndrome.

There are some data available on the characteristics of the best *expert* judge of personality. In the original explorations of personality at the Harvard Psychological Clinic (Murray, 1938), groups of 12 to 24 subjects at a time were studied intensively by teams (or diagnostic councils) of 6 expert judges, who rated them on the needs and other variables developed and defined by Murray. In one experiment, the diagnostic council had been working together long enough to rate one another on the same variables of personality that they had been using to express their understanding of the subjects. When the ratings an expert had given were compared with the ratings given him, a general tendency to judge subjects in terms of contrast became apparent; that is, an expert who was rated as highly orderly tended to give ratings of the need for order that were low on the average, while the judges who were considered somewhat disorderly by their colleagues rated the same subjects as higher on this need. Even a highly trained judge will tend to take himself as the standard. In addition, the results showed that the experts tended to do the best job of rating subjects who were most like themselves and who had similar cultural backgrounds, and to mark inaccurately those who least resembled them. The best judges were generally more experienced in assessing personalities. On the whole, these findings have been upheld by subsequent research and are congruent with the findings from the research on inexpert judges.

Judgments of personality have brought us full circle, back to clinical assessment. The clinical and the objective traditions do overlap, for both approaches can be used together, and often are—as they were in the study of Morris Brown, with whom we shall now proceed to become acquainted.

All that a man does is physiognomical of him. You may see how a man would fight by the way in which he sings; his courage, or want of courage, is visible in the word he utters, in the opinion he has formed, no less than in the stroke he strikes. He is one; and preaches the same self abroad in all these ways.

THOMAS CARLYLE . Heroes and Hero-Worship

CHAPTER 36
MR. MORRIS BROWN: AN ILLUSTRATIVE CASE STUDY

So far, we have been considering assessment in the abstract, the general case. The issues will become much more meaningful as we look at a case study of a real person and examine how he was actually assessed. As we saw in Chapter 32, personalities can be assessed in a number of different settings. Though the aim of assessment in almost any context is to understand a person, the extent and focus of understanding does differ a good deal from one setting to another. Therefore, to be most useful, the example chosen cannot be taken from routine practice of diagnostic testing or of any other kind; it should come as close as possible to satisfying the ideal requirement of *complete* understanding. Before considering the actual case of Morris Brown, which is by no means ideal, it may help to take a close look at what is meant by "complete understanding" of a person.

Specifications
for an Ideal Assessment

VARIABLES TO BE ASSESSED

First we will want to know, What is he like? An ideal understanding of a person requires a *comprehensive description* of his personality at some point. It will include:

1. Physical, biological personality—appearance, physique, and physiological characteristics.

2. Temperament—characteristic level of energy and emotional states (moods, affects, strength of drive), especially the frequency and intensity of anxiety, guilt, shame, helplessness and hopelessness versus enjoyment of life, zest, hope, and buoyancy.

3. Stylistic, expressive aspects of personality, including gesture and voice.

4. Manifest traits of other types by which people who know him classify and recognize his characteristic behavior. (See Table 35-4, page 660.)

Such a description does not so much provide understanding in itself as help us frame more penetrating questions. We begin to approach understanding when we can ask, *Why* does he act this way? This question reflects the desire to ask our subject what he is trying to do, what he is aiming for, and what his intentions are. Yet we should recognize that just asking him alone will not suffice, because he cannot be expected to know all the answers. We must include in our description some consideration of *personality dynamics:*

5. Conscious and unconscious motives, their sources, and the sources of the affects listed above (2), such as anxiety.

6. Values, ideals, interests, and attitudes.

The *organizational* (configural) approach to understanding is another way to go beyond description. This approach has two distinct though related objectives: On the one hand, we are interested in the enduring inner conditions that make behavior possible and set limits to what a person can or will do; and on the other, we want to know how the pieces fit together, how a person is organized. Implied, then, are:

7. Defenses and controls, in relation to impulses.

8. Thought organization, cognitive style.

9. Abilities and achievements.

10. Identity—self-attitudes; sense of competence; self-concept; insight; sense of integration with his occupational role, social group, and culture.

To understand a person, we must not limit ourselves to studying the processes and organizations inside him, even though (as in 10) they have outward reference; we must also know about the actual *relations between him and his environment.* Involved here are the enormous issues of the person's relations to society and culture and the large question of his adaptation. The following variables are particularly important:

11. Situational origins and setting—cultural tradition, family background (ethnic, religious, ideological) and the degree of the subject's rootedness in it; significant persons who have helped shape his personality; present ecological context; major "press" (opportunities for gratification, frustrations and demands upon him, types of stress).

12. Adequacy of his adaptation to situational origins and setting— pathological trends and potentialities, conflicts, symptoms.

13. Nature of his principal relationships to people and feelings about them.

In the process of attaining understanding, we sooner or later want to ask, *How* did he get that way? The *genetic* approach to personality thus requires that we learn:

14. Major facts of his past history and the chronological development of main trends.

Finally, we come back to organizational considerations, for everything has to be put together into

15. *An integrative synthesis,* linking the separate pieces into a coherent whole that, in Carlyle's words, "preaches the same self abroad in all these ways."

METHODS OF ASSESSMENT

An ideal case study would provide all the kinds of understanding described above; obviously, in order to do so, it would demand the use of many methods (multiform assessment), since no single technique can provide all the necessary information. An ideal study, then, ought to make use of the following types of methods for gathering data:

1. Application forms, face sheets, objective public records.

2. Interviews, ranging from highly structured to free-associative.

3. Autobiographies and other personal documents (letters, diaries, biographical inventories).

4. Self-descriptive inventories and questionnaires, direct and indirect; self-ratings.

5. Projective techniques.

6. Physical and physiological measurements, as well as other biological approaches.

7. Judgments by others (behavioral observations and ratings, sociometric ratings by peers).

8. Objective and situational tests, such as tests of cognitive style.

9. Tests of intelligence and other abilities.

10. Sociological and anthropological techniques of studying the person's societal and cultural origins and setting.

All this makes up a rather tall order, especially when we add to it the stipulation that the data should be gathered and interpreted by experts who have optimal talent and training for the job.

The case study chosen for presentation below is far from ideal in a number of ways. The data were initially gathered by two graduate students without prior experience in assessing personality (one was studying sociology, the other psychology).* In addition, there are gaps in the coverage of variables assessed; therefore, no claim is made for anything like a complete understanding of the subject. But the case of William Morris Brown has two unusual qualifications to exemplify multiform assessment: First, a wide variety of methods was used, which represented each of the 10 categories listed above and resulted in a great mass of data. Second, the relatively rare opportunity of a long follow-up was presented when the subject allowed himself to be reassessed after a lapse of 26 years.

An Informal Assessment

The two assessors began their report with the following description, which conveys the general impression Morris Brown made in casual social and business contacts around 1940.

If you were to meet William Morris Brown, you would probably find him likable and eager to please, although not very unusual. He talks with apparent relish, racing along from one thing to another with a naive sort of eagerness at once disarming and refreshing. His face is alert and mobile, and in spite of a smile that seems a little too ready, you would probably put him down as a happy extrovert who would fit into the local service club with ease and satisfaction. At 26, Morris looks like any other energetic young businessman, well satisfied with himself, the world, and all the good "business prospects" in it.

Morris is large and compact, without much excess fat, although he is beginning to have trouble keeping his weight down to 194 pounds. The fat is starting to cover a strong and uniformly well-muscled body, creating the impression of a sort of surface softness. He carries his 6-foot frame well and easily, however, with a trace of the athlete in his walk. The same softness shows in his face and at times gives a juvenile look to what is otherwise a quite mature appearance. Not handsome, he is not hard to look at either, with features that are smooth and regular, although slightly heavy. Morris is overly aware of a hardly noticeable Jewish cast to his full lips and long broad nose and sometimes worries about being mistaken for a Jew (he is not Jewish).

His well-fed look of stability and maturity is probably a help to Brown in his business. He is a securities salesman and is quite successful for his age. He carries around with him a mimeographed office periodical sheet showing that he led his agency in business volume one month. Since graduation Morris has been

* The student of sociology was Robert F. Bales, now Professor of Sociology at Harvard and a distinguished contributor to his field. The psychology student, Robert R. Holt, is the author of this section.

living in the eastern city where the large and well-known university he attended is located. At present he lives alone in an inexpensive rooming house near the college; he makes a considerable proportion of his sales to members of the university community, including undergraduates. Within the last few months he bought a new Studebaker from the fellow who was his roommate before leaving the city, but, on the whole, Morris does not spend much money. He appears prosperous; recently a credit report on him rated his income and his total worth at, he says, about double their real value.

His present life goes along pretty smoothly, to outward appearances. He works hard and takes an afternoon off every few days to play golf, at which he excels. Almost every weekend he gets away for a while to work on a cabin he is building in the country. On these trips he almost always takes along at least one companion, usually of college age, to help with the work. He has a rather large number of friends whom he sees with about equal frequency, but no intimate ones. Morris rarely goes to a movie because he says movies hurt his eyes, but he likes to read, mostly biographies. He seldom has a date and knows few girls.

HOW THE ASSESSMENT WAS MADE

This assessment relied in part on observation during numerous informal contacts. For example, the investigators gave a large party and invited the subject; he came by other evenings for casual chats and parlor games; the psychology student spent a day with Morris in the country helping him build his cabin; and there were occasional meals, rides in Morris' car, and visits to his apartment. These were, then, more than first impressions. Let us try to reconstruct how these contacts resulted in the characterization above.

Interest in the Subject

The assessors would not have learned much about Morris if they had been unable to get *interested* in him. The very first assertion in their description—that he was likable—attests to the fact that they did not try to remain "scientifically detached," wholly unmoved by their subject. Although their original motivation was to carry out an assignment for academic credit, before long both students were much more deeply engaged by the intrinsic interest of the task—learning about another human being in as much depth as possible—and by a growing friendly interest in Morris himself.

One component of this interest may have arisen from the subject's tendency to define the situation implicitly as one in which the graduate students were experts who could see into mysteries that were closed to him. His relationship with them was characterized by friendliness, deference, and extraordinary cooperation; he went out of his way to satisfy all their requests for information and personal documents and made an honest effort to be as frank and open as possible in answering their probing questions. The investigators explained in the beginning that they would want to inquire into all aspects of his life, including matters that were most secret and private; after agreeing, Morris never complicated the investigators' task by conscious withholding or distortion.

It would have been difficult not to like someone who clearly wanted so much to be liked and who did all he could to satisfy the investigators' demands. Nevertheless, it might be added that Morris was in a number of respects quite different from other members of the graduate students' circle of friends, in whom intellectuality and a kind of sophistication were prime values, which Morris lacked.

Empathic
Perception

The investigators learned a fair amount about their subject *empathically*, without doing so deliberately or being focally aware of it. His eagerness to please, for example, was a characteristic they directly perceived; it was not inferred, nor did he state it about himself in so many words. In fact, the first three sentences of the assessment above (up to the "happy extrovert" characterization) are primarily based on direct, empathic perception. To be sure, the description required no particular depth or subtlety of interpersonal perception. The levels of species recognition and emotional contagion (see Chapter 33) were sufficient to tell the assessors that this was a smiling, nonhostile fellow man. Only the observation that his smile was over-ready suggests anything like mature empathy. To make such a point, the assessors needed an implicit set of standards by which to judge the appropriateness of common affective expressions, and a modest capacity for simultaneous detachment and responsiveness.

On the whole, however, neither of the graduate students had great natural empathic ability or any training in its use. Both were bookish and studious rationalists, committed more to attaining knowledge by the exercise of reason than to enriching their affective lives by cultivating an emotional sensitivity. Close examination of their work shows how many times they missed empathic communications or suppressed awareness of what was going on in the interpersonal relationship instead of recognizing and using it. For example, when we examine Morris' TAT stories, we shall see evidences that beneath his overt effort to cooperate seriously there was a level of teasing, almost mocking, resistance. Being wholly unskilled in handling resistance, the examiners not only did not deal with it but remained unaware of it.

Direct
Observation

The third channel through which the informal assessment operated was *direct observation*, both of behavior and of the subject's physical personality. The latter aspect might have been less emphasized had the psychology student not been enrolled in a seminar on constitutional psychology with W. H.

Sheldon (whose work on somatotypes and temperament was reviewed in Chapter 35, pages 649–52); the study was also serving to satisfy one of that seminar's assignments. The kind of observation encouraged in Sheldon's seminar is exemplified by the remarks on Morris' carriage and athletic walk and indeed by all of the second paragraph of the description except for its final sentence. In general, the majority of the assertions made in the description are factual and are derived either from direct observation or from essentially public and objective information readily provided by the subject.

CRITICISM OF THE ASSESSMENT

If we turn from analysis of this informal assessment to criticism, perhaps we can agree that it is hardly remarkable in any way. It does mention a few traits, some interests and activities, and some (though not all) vital statistics. It may at least help you to form an image of the man, a concrete nucleus for the schema you will build up as you read on. Although this assessment shows no obvious signs of being seriously inept, it is perhaps disappointing because it says so little. It drops only a hint or so that there may be more to the subject than appears on the surface, but this is hardly surprising, since the authors' intent was precisely to present Morris' social front before penetrating to a psychologically more interesting level.

They made no attempt to exhaust the possibilities of informal assessment or even to raise questions for more systematic exploration. To be sure, in their informal contacts with the subject the investigators did form a host of impressions that are neither recorded here nor explicitly set down in any other part of the original case study—the written product of the first assessment. These impressions may be sensed throughout the document, however, for they are an integral part of the schema formed by the complex interaction of formal and informal processes of assessment. Such a schema operates like a frame of reference or a group of orienting sets, anticipations, and guiding assumptions; it helps in choosing material to present, judgments and evaluations, and causal and organizational hypotheses. In this sense, informal assessment operates behind the scenes in every situation where it is given a chance.

Notice how much the attempt to depict the surface of Morris Brown's personality emphasizes his conformity and conventionality. It is as if the authors consciously intended to say to the reader, "This man can be counted on in many respects to behave predictably." They are, in effect, establishing a level of expectation against which deviations will stand out sharply. The amount of conformity is also an important initial fact about any personality (see Chapter 32, page 581); it is regrettable that the level is so vaguely indicated, without any quantitative indication of the extent to which Morris' behavior was conventional.

Let us see how the sources of error in informal assessment described in Chapter 33 operate here. The examiner's emotional reaction to the assessed subject is usually feared and minimized because of the dangers of the halo effect, the leniency error, and need-fulfilling distortions of perception and judgment. The assessors in this case had been alerted to these dangers, and they made conscious efforts not to fall into any obvious traps. They also safeguarded themselves against these types of error by using many methods, including objective ones, and by prolonged study, which tested prejudgments against a constantly accumulating body of evidence.

In spite of their precautions their own somewhat antiphilistine value system can perhaps be sensed in the slightly snide tone of the second half of the first paragraph: If Morris had proved to be nothing but a happy, extroverted young businessman, they would have been disappointed. A slightly prejudicial stereotype of the typical member of the Junior Chamber of Commerce was operating here. (At this point we cannot evaluate how far it may have biased the assessment, but let us keep it in mind, along with the other sources of error just mentioned, as we go further into the case study.)

A Clinical Assessment

The assessors led into their attempt to provide a deeper understanding of Morris Brown by discussing next in their assessment the inconsistencies in Morris, the ways he was nonconforming and violated expectations:

> Morris doesn't like to think of himself as "having problems with a capital P," but suggested himself that the case study be undertaken when he learned that the writers were looking for a subject. He was most eager about the study from the start, frankly admitting that the idea of finding out about himself fascinated him. He has a friend who is a vocational tester and has taken all the tests he could get his hands on. Morris declared that he can't figure himself out and ventured that he would make an interesting, though normal, case. He has "turned inside out" psychologically "in the last five years or so," he said, and there are aspects of his personality now that are "just silly—don't make sense." It was the hope of clearing up some of these puzzles, then, as well as a characteristic desire for a new experience, that impelled Morris to submit himself for study, promising not to hold anything back intentionally.
>
> Morris feels independent, yet he has a strong need to have others around. "Apparently I'm the most independent bastard ever made," he writes in his autobiography; "you're supposed to tell me why. I have made many friends in the last five years but have never felt too close to or too dependent on any one of them." A fear of being alone, a desire for sympathy and response, is matched by

a fear of becoming too closely involved. Morris has a feeling that he is engaging in too many "extracurricular activities," referring to community enterprises like the Red Cross Drive. A fundamental conflict that has not reached a satisfactory solution may be seen here.

There is another basic clash of tendencies in Brown, with even more implications. He has a deep aversion to being hampered or tied down in any way. "You get in a rut, but not in the right things. Besides, I don't *want* to get in a rut." "I never have followed any pattern in my life . . . I don't want a settled married life—it would drive me crazy." "I would go crazy working for someone else: my work has to be something I can do on my own." Related to this theme is a certain lack of moral sensitivity, which Morris recognizes when he admits: "I don't think I have very much moral sense." Deception of his mother (she thinks his car was borrowed from a friend), keeping some of the money he has collected in fund drives, unconventional sexual practices—these are commonplaces of Brown's life; and though he wonders why he doesn't feel guilty, he says, "I just think about the nice angle on it."

Despite his impatience with restraint, Morris declares that his deepest desire is complete control of himself: "My greatest victory would be to go for a month for 24 hours a day doing what I decide to do. Keeping on schedule—even if it called for getting drunk every night. Doing what I *planned* to do." To this end, he involves himself in as many external constraints as possible, such as appointments. "What I need is a job where somebody will control me—help my self-control—the army would do me good for a year." Even when controls of this sort are self-imposed, he has the feeling that it "would be swell to have a whole day of appointments and then just say 'to hell with it,' and yet I don't." As recently as a year ago, he used to decide "that I wanted to take a trip and start off somewhere, not caring where." This idea of flight persists in constant plans and fantasies of travel.

Though he declares he does not really worry about it, Brown is concerned about his sex life. "Another thing I'm interested in is sex: Why isn't it more important to me? . . . I don't think I'm normal in this respect." "Maybe I worry about masturbating too much, but nothing particular about that. I don't want you to get the idea that I think I'm going insane or anything like that. I'm brutally callous. But I wonder why I've never been in love—but once." He has had at least as much homosexual as heterosexual experience and shows no signs of changing his ways.

The conflicts and inconsistencies described above, together with his puzzled lack of insight into them, form the outstanding problems in Brown's life.

We are now clearly beyond the realm of informal assessment and into the considerations with which a clinical assessment often starts—a person's problems. It is not so much the fact that conflict and inconsistency have entered the picture that takes us into formal assessment as it is (1) the explicit use of special techniques (in this instance, the autobiography) and (2) the nature of some of the problems, which involve socially taboo areas about which even a close friend might not know. (In fact, even his roommate was not aware that Morris engaged in any homosexual activity or that he lacked "moral sense" about money entrusted to him.)

As we saw in Chapter 34, the term "clinical assessment" covers a variety of processes, using several sorts of methods. Following Meehl's breakdown of clinical prediction (1954), we can usefully simplify this variety by distinguishing two major phases, or levels, of clinical assessment (see Table 36-1).

Table 36-1   *Two Main Phases of Clinical Assessment*

	First Phase	Second Phase
General character	factual	interpretive
Systematic emphasis	conscious content—events and meanings	latent structure—organization and causal relationships
Methods used	interview, autobiography, other personal documents	projective techniques, free association

Though the student-investigators made a stab at the second phase, they devoted most of their time and efforts to a first-phase clinical assessment, supplemented by a number of objective approaches. The remainder of this chapter will therefore concentrate on the methods and results of their first-level clinical assessment; Chapter 37 will focus on the objective assessment and the second phase of clinical assessment; and Chapter 38 will present an attempt to integrate these and all the remaining data.

FIRST-PHASE METHODS

The case study written about Morris Brown in 1940 was primarily his life story, based for the most part on more than two dozen interviews. The examiners took turns conducting these sessions, during which they wrote down in longhand as much of Morris' responses as possible. Before deciding what questions to ask they consulted several systematic guides, such as those contained in Young's *Personality and Problems of Adjustment* (1940) and Murray's *Explorations in Personality* (1938). These are outlines of major topics to be covered in a psychological life history; Morris' first assignment was to look them over briefly before writing his six-page autobiography. The inexperienced investigators at first felt the need to have written lists of questions at hand, but the interviewing quickly developed into a somewhat more natural process of following up topics the subject himself introduced.

The methods used here approach those of more sophisticated clinical assessment, which generally relies heavily on the interview as the fundamental method; and in research contexts, an autobiography of the kind obtained from Morris is often standard procedure. The assessment of Brown was unusual in two respects: A good deal more time than usual was spent in interviewing, and the subject provided much more information than is generally available by way of *personal documents*. On a visit to his home town, he collected the "baby books" and infant diaries his mother had kept, her genealogical tables and records, a sample of letters he had written to her during the summers of his adolescent years, his own diaries covering the years 1929 to 1939, themes and a few short stories he had written in high school and college, photograph albums giving a complete record of his growth and appearance up to maturity, a scrapbook filled with newspaper clippings about himself, expense accounts, maps of his home town, and records of results on vocational and similar tests he had already taken. The examiners gave him a list of questions concerning his birth and early development; he put them to his mother and wrote down her answers. The account of his first years is based on this indirect interview and on Mrs. Brown's records; hence, it tells something about her as well as about Morris.

Clinical assessment, even of an ambitiously multiform variety, does not require anything like this profusion of personal records. The assessors did go through all the material, however, using it largely to check facts and dates. During two brief periods of his life, Morris' diaries became full and introspective and thus psychologically useful; they are quoted in the life story that follows.

This story is the assessors' synthesis of the data gathered by the methods just listed; it is presented substantially as it was originally written. Quotations from the autobiography, when not specifically identified, may be recognized by Morris' characteristic preference for dashes as his principal punctuation.

FIRST-PHASE RESULTS:
THE STORY OF MORRIS BROWN TO 1940

Infancy   Morris was born in the spring of 1914, 11 days before he had been expected. He weighed 7 pounds and appeared hardy from the first.

During his infancy, his mother reports, Morris was never sick, aside from a case of baby jaundice shortly after birth and a little constipation in his first year, which apparently was not painful. He was breast-fed until he was 10 months old; his appetite was so great that he developed the habit of waking up in the night and crying until fed to his capacity. The doctor advised Mrs. Brown to continue with the night feeding when Morris could not be broken of the habit. Weaning took place gradually, and the transition to more solid foods was made by easy stages. Toilet training was a simple and objective matter, without punishment, and Morris was out of diapers in a year. Other sources of conflict in many infancies, such as enuresis and autoeroticism, were not present, if Mrs. Brown's reports are accurate. From all indications, Morris was a happy baby and thrived. His physical development was normal, except that he was always tall and heavy for his age.

In one respect, however, the course of his development differed significantly from the norm: At age 2, he would say only "bow-wow," "no," and "mama," although the average size of a child's vocabulary at this age is nearly 300 words. His mother wrote in January 1916, "he shakes hands, waves and grunts his way thro' conversations, but will not speak a word." Later, "at 2¾ years, he learned all his letters, then slowly began talking—'aw pick up' being his first real attempt to express an idea,"—referring to his blocks, with which he played actively and constructively.

His father had an explanation: Morris, he said, was long learning to speak intelligibly (note that he did vocalize indistinctly, "grunting") because he did not need to. His mother had some ability as a teacher and was devoted to her child; she was able to understand what he meant and wanted without his having to learn the strict conventions of language.

The first few years present a picture, on the one hand, of normal development of locomotion and dentition, and, on the other, of the formation of certain definite personality traits and problems. At 22 months, Morris' mother wrote in the diary she kept sporadically for him: "He is usually good, but very positive and determined, but will do as I wish in the end . . . loves to play with his sisters,—takes an old doll to bed with him, builds blocks, and plays with everything he can get hold of." Again, at age 2, "he is a real boy, cunning, sweet, spunky, determined, lovable." Looking back on the early years now, she remembers him as lively, very talkative (he was speaking distinctly by the time he was 3 years old), sociable; he liked attention and interrupted a lot. Little Morris was very headstrong, she says, and her greatest problem with him was his tantrums.

Mrs. Brown had a deep pride in her family and was determined not to let it down. Both paternal and maternal branches of her family had been in this country for a century and a half and settled in her home town as leading citizens. It was a shock, then, when her father, a well-to-do clothing manufacturer, was financially ruined through no fault of his own and died soon after, when she was 14. A short time later she became a teacher and a governess. In 1912, Nathan Brown, a widower who had married her best friend, asked her to marry him. She was 33 and may have thought this her last chance; in addition, her brother was about to marry Nathan Brown's sister. At any rate, she accepted him. They settled down in a large house in a nice residential area of a small city in the northeastern part of the United States, and she undertook to bring up her stepdaughters, Nancy and Marcia, 6 and 4 years old respectively. Morris was born the following year.

As Morris says, "Father and Mother were made so differently it was impossible for them to get along." She was practical, "nervous," concerned with the observance of the amenities; he was enthusiastic, impatient, independent, and irresponsible. There was, in addition, the difference in age—Morris' mother was 34 at the time of his birth, his father 50. Mr. Brown's speculative bent asserted itself in a characteristic way just before Morris' birth. He borrowed $50 of the money his wife had been saving to pay the doctor and went west to see some oil wells. He had previously made a considerable fortune from speculation in real estate and oil but had gone bankrupt just a month before Morris was born.

Mr. Brown "was no long-time worrier or planner," and as "he would dodge unpleasant things rather than get ruffled," he left the small city where they had settled and got a job selling insurance in a big city. He came home only on weekends; he refused a $50-a-week job in a bookstore there when it was offered to him, to the great disappointment of his wife. The job wasn't "his kind of life—steady hours, etc.," Morris explained. Mrs. Brown simply "couldn't *understand*" his refusal to take a steady job when his wife and three children at home were in such desperate need of money. She viewed it as a "cardinal sin." Her only means of support was the income she got from renting the top two floors of their house.

This state of affairs—conflict over economic arrangements and Mr. Brown's never holding a job long, never staying at home for any length of time—continued until 1923 (when Morris was 8), at which time Mr. Brown left permanently for another state. Mr. Brown never contributed to the support of the family after 1924 and made overtures about a divorce some years later. The idea of being a divorced woman, however, was too much for Mrs. Brown to bear; Morris thinks also that she always hoped he would come back and be a real father to his children.

In addition, during Morris' early years, his mother had several physical difficulties: poor eyesight, internal disturbances from Morris' birth and from an earlier injury, and a major operation in 1923. Nevertheless, she worked hard, too hard—she not only had to make ends meet but had to keep up appearances. As the business section of the city grew up around her and her friends moved farther away, she apparently grew more determined that her children were not going to go down in the social scale.

Childhood   This overworked, unhappy woman did not have the time that she would have liked to devote to bringing up her son, whatever her theories of child guidance were. She grew less and less able to handle him. From "spunky" Morris grew to "very headstrong." When thwarted, he would go into a screaming tantrum, and all Mrs. Brown could do was remove him to some place where he would not be heard too loudly; she did try throwing water on him, too, but with slight success. Morris claims that his frequent spankings worked. Nevertheless, he continued to cry to get his own way when angry or disappointed. His mother tried repeatedly to get his father to punish him; Morris thinks that his father applied a reluctant hairbrush no more than two or three times and then only after her demands grew insistent. Morris' early memories of his father are mostly pleasant; in one recollection they are walking together through a cemetery while the father explains to the son about the different kinds of trees.

During his early years, Morris got along fairly well with people, at least when he was having his own way. He started to read at an early age and liked to read to the roomers who rented the upper floors. He had a few friendly contacts with them but made no particular friends there. He often quarreled with the few other children that there were to play with. A succession of most of the childhood diseases, severe pneumonia, removal of his tonsils and adenoids (twice), and a serious ear infection may have contributed to a rather marked social isolation during Morris' childhood.

Morris says that the two things he will always remember about his early life were "its extreme poverty and complete loneliness." What was an upper-class neighborhood on the edge of the thriving business section when Mr. Brown and his wife moved into their house became a disorganized rooming-house area during Morris' early childhood. The business section spread until the busiest corner was only a few blocks away, and the well-to-do families moved farther out. The large houses were converted into rooming houses, as Mrs. Brown had converted hers.

The people who lived in the area no longer knew one another. The neighborhood organization disappeared, and with it went most of the children, most of the intimacy, and most of the control that people in a neighborhood group exercise over one another's behavior.

These statements can be made with some confidence, because the sociologist member of the assessment team made a sociological study of the community in which Morris Brown grew up. Morris provided a good map of the city, and a library book on its recreational facilities and city plans yielded information about the location of industrial areas, new homes, business and other areas, all of which were marked on the map. From information Morris provided, it was possible to locate his parents' home, his schools, his church, the residences of his friends and his mother's friends, and various pertinent institutions. From this composite map, and from Morris' verbal characterization of various sections, the several *ecological zones* of the city could be located—the business area, the area of slums and rooming houses, the middle-class workingmen's homes, and the upper-class homes. Nationality groupings were also located. The graphic summary of all this information, partly subjective and partly a matter of objective record, made it possible to check some of Morris' statements about socioeconomic status relationships and to gauge more accurately the social status of his own neighborhood and play areas.

Morris' dominance and resistance to control continued, especially as his sister Nancy and his mother tried to enforce obedience. His sister Marcia was tactful, however, he says, and handled him by explaining why he should do what was required.

At the age of 4, Morris was sent to a Catholic kindergarten next door, which he attended for two years. He remembers that they had chapel once in a while, but apparently any religious teaching that he might have received there did not leave a noticeable residue of piety. When he was about 5, he and another neighborhood boy worked out a system of stealing the money from milk bottles. They bought soda pop with the money, but he was not otherwise close either to this boy or to the one other he knew. There was no neighborhood gang or play group; and this one episode, for which he was punished by his mother, is the only record of any behavior approaching delinquency.

When he was 6, Morris was enrolled in a grade school several blocks beyond the main business avenue, on the edge of the city's Polish section. Most of his classmates were the children of Polish mill workers. Morris regarded them as "very dumb." He made friends with one big Jewish boy by helping him with his lessons. Apparently he received admiration from this one boy, but he was constantly annoyed by two Polish boys who would tease him, wash his face with snow, and lie in wait for him as he went to and from school. Morris used to go several blocks out of his way to avoid these tormenters.

However hesitant Mrs. Brown may have felt about sending her boy to this school, she could not afford to send him to a private school as her family and friends did their children. It was all she could do to put the girls through private school. She tried to make up for this and to give Morris contact with "friends who were good enough for him," as she put it, by giving him piano lessons and sending him to the dancing classes attended exclusively by the children of her upper-class friends. Morris felt that he had nothing in common with them, hated dancing school, and on occasion merely pretended to go.

These efforts to do her best for him only widened the gap between Morris and his mother. "I never was one to hang around her," he reported. "She always visited school and so on—that drove me crazy." She wanted him to go to Sunday school and say his prayers, but after the age of 7 or 8 Morris gradually left off the prayers. A little later, he told the investigators, "I was going to build a houseboat, and asked the woman next door to go with me. I wasn't going to ask mother because she would make me do things I didn't want to."

Nancy, who was in high school at the time Morris was about 8 years old, was extremely embarrassed by her lack of suitable clothes and by other signs of poverty. She was nervous and cried a good deal. One day after she had visited her aunt, Mrs. Brown's brother came to the house for a talk. He told Mrs. Brown that she "wasn't fit to keep the girls," and he took Nancy to live with them. "Stabbed in the back," Mrs. Brown felt that nobody appreciated her efforts. For two years she was likely to cry at unexpected times. Morris himself does not recall being particularly sorry to see Nancy go.

Mrs. Brown's relatives were also vociferous in their condemnation of Mr. Brown for leaving his family in hardship while he lived elsewhere in comparative luxury. Mrs. Brown was in a dilemma—she wanted him to come back and play the part of the proper father, and yet she could not help condemning him. Morris did not defend his father, but "didn't exactly blame him," as his uncle and the rest of the family did. Morris does not believe that he imitated his father or identified with him, but in another interview said spontaneously, in contrasting his mother's "practicalness" about money with his father's attitude, that he has "taken more after" his father.

During his childhood Morris had little contact with girls other than his sisters. In his eighth year, he and the two little girls who lived next door were caught behind a woodpile, engaged in mutual display. He was put to bed without food for the rest of the day, which he considered "an awful punishment." On one or two occasions, Morris played "doctor" with his sisters. Once, when he was about 8, he looked through the keyhole of a locked door and saw his parents in the act of intercourse. He didn't realize the significance of it until years later, he says.

Morris did very well in school and was repeatedly moved ahead of others. Always much younger than his classmates, he had a sense of his own brilliance, which was appreciated neither by his teachers nor by the other boys in the school. He was also overweight, a poor athlete, and regarded as a "sissy" by most of the boys. To show that he was not a sissy he took a dare the March of his tenth year: He plunged into an icy pond and swam around.

Conditions did not improve much when Morris started going to another school in a middle-class area at the beginning of the seventh grade. He did well in his studies but still did not gain a single close friend. He sat under a tree with the teacher when the boys played baseball at the annual school picnic. He developed an interest in big-league baseball. He learned to play tennis and began to dream about being a really "big-time" player. He spent a great deal of time reading; biography and travel were his favorite topics. He asked his teacher to go to a movie with him and was very disappointed when she refused.

At the age of 10, just about the time he finished grade school, Morris decided to gratify his desire to travel. He took the money out of his savings account and bought a train ticket to a nearby city. Arriving there, he walked around a couple of hours and came back. In spite of his mother's objections, Morris learned to hitchhike the next year and made many trips to neighboring cities; one trip to play in a tennis tournament involved a considerable distance. His father, who was living in this city, gave him a couple of $5 tennis lessons and let him hitchhike back. Morris greatly enjoyed this form of being independent but not alone; his companions were often other boys he knew at the YMCA.

Adolescence In high school Morris began to get fair but inconsistent grades. He cut class often and did not care especially how he did his assignments. His philosophy when grades turned out lower than he liked was, "What's the sense of *worrying* about grades— if you do, you do, if you don't, you don't. Let somebody else piddle around with the details—hell, there are always plenty of $18-a-week clerks." The "Y," only two blocks from his house, became a growing interest for Morris; it gave him the contact with other boys that he so much desired. He swam, played basketball and ping-pong, and continued with tennis, his best game. He made the high school team and played in a number of boys' tournaments, but his social techniques were still not satisfactory. He says he was "a lousy competitor—always folded at the wrong time." Outside of sports, he rarely participated in high school activities.

By the age of 11 there was a quickening of sexual desire, which manifested itself in several ways. After hearing some boys talking about masturbation, Morris "gave it a try. It was fun, so I kept it up, and have ever since." About two months later, in the gym after tennis and showers, he says, he and another boy masturbated together with no idea that they should not. In the next few years a number of incidents occurred similar to the following. One afternoon when Morris was about 13, his mother came home early from a club meeting and knocked on the bedroom door, behind which he and a boy friend were engaged in mutual sex play. She had to wait until they dressed before they unlocked the door; suspecting what had been going on, she reproached Morris in spite of his attempt to "brazen it out." He was ashamed of himself, but not overly, and he was not further punished.

At about age 12, Morris began to think of girls sexually. There was a pretty blond girl in some of his classes whom he admired from afar and thought of regularly when masturbating, but he never approached her. He was always un-aggressive with girls, and the very few formal dates he had were duties imposed by his mother in return for invitations to parties that he didn't like anyway.

Another major manifestation of sexual development in adolescence was the appearance of a "terrific case of hero worship," directed at a boy of 17 or 18 at a "Y" camp. Morris engineered his hero into taking his Sunday school classes and "used to think he was pretty near God. It almost broke my heart once when I heard him tell a dirty joke."

Beginning at about age 14, Morris made "one after another, a series of very close friendships, almost passionate, altho never any desire for sex relations of any kind. I couldn't stand the thought of that."

Morris grew very rapidly at puberty; at 13 he was a big, mature-looking boy, 5 feet 6 inches tall, weighing 147 pounds. When he was a sophomore in high school, his mother wrote that he "plays tennis, swims, and eats, all heartily . . . is a fine-looking boy, broad and straight, and usually very good." From what he says now of his disobedience and aggressive attitude toward her, that last thought must be considered in the light of an apparently wishful one: "He and I are alone now, so are everything to each other."

Morris' own view toward his mother was much the same as it had been earlier: "I've always done what I wanted; what she said didn't have any effect. I used to have battles with her until she saw it was useless." By the time he was 12, Morris came and went pretty much as he pleased: "What could she do? I had control of my own money."

At the age of 15½, Morris graduated from high school, with little idea of what he wanted to do next. He got a job as usher in a nearby movie theater that he had often attended, where he worked for the rest of the year (1929). In non-working hours he did postgraduate work at high school. His spare time was taken up with athletics, reading, and playing around with the "crush" of the moment. He began to be a very good athlete; a scrapbook contains newspaper notices from the winter of 1927–28 on, in both swimming and tennis. In August, he won second place in the YMCA tournament and was one of the city's outstanding tennis players. Public notice and approval were just what Morris wanted; he was considerably happier in these years than he had been in childhood.

Morris kept a very full and introspective diary at the time, almost entirely concerned with his ups and downs with George, another usher and a "crush" for months. He speculates for half a typed page about George's motive in insulting him—which was evidently not difficult to do, for he wrote: "I can't stand any kind of razzing." Resolutions to punish George by being cool to him are followed the next day by descriptions of the great time they had together, for example, hitchhiking. Morris indignantly rejects the idea that there was anything sexual in this friendship, or in any of his relationships of this sort. There was, instead, continuous aggression between the two boys, with occasional tussling. The mutual masturbation affairs continued all through this period, but, Brown stresses in the autobiography, "never with anybody I liked." Even so, several instances of overt sex play with a real friend have come up, each of which Morris characterizes as the only thing of that kind he ever did with anyone he liked.

Brown knew few girls; in his marginal social position the daughters of his mother's friends were superior to him and the Polish girls inferior to him. Although Mrs. Brown got him, much against his will, to go to some dances, "the effort on her part to get me social wore her out—we had some awful battles." At the time he did begin to find himself socially, he attracted friends by his athletic prowess and by slavish devotion, qualities that apparently got him friends among boys rather than girls. There was one girl whom he went to see frequently the summer he was 15, just "hanging around her house." He had dates with her off and on for two years. But his initial sexual experiences were all with boys; he had had no instruction from his mother in the facts of life, which he picked up around the "Y." It was a few years before he learned of the stigma that is attached to homosexuality, but even then he did not cease homosexual activities. Instead, he isolated them in his mind into a sort of neutral category, along with masturbation; he put disgusted rejection of "fairies" in another, and emotionally fraught friendships in still another compartment.

In the spring of 1930, Morris and his mother bought a used car, of which he was quite proud. After he got a job as clerk in a rayon mill in the summer, he took out a few of the mill girls who were reputedly easy marks but to his surprise was unable to get anywhere with them sexually. Morris complained: "Women can be so illogical!"

When the mill moved, shortly before he turned 17, Morris decided to go back to high school for four months to prepare for admission to college. He took on a heavy schedule; in June he got honor grades in college-entrance examinations. This time his social life in school was happier:

> for the first time I was in a gang—about 8 of us—and I loved it—two of those fellows are now the only friends I have in the home town, and I see them every trip home—I didn't get into any messes during that time for a change—(all through high school I had a series of fights with teachers, was always in trouble for doing one thing or another,—although my marks were always good).

This year was the height of Morris' tennis career, and he was kept busy winning the city championship and finishing among the first four in the state tournament. He was now at last captain of the school team and attracted wide notice.

Ever since he became old enough to start finding odd jobs, Morris was resourceful in earning his own money. With what money he saved, he began at age 15 to speculate in stocks. This was the year of the stock-market peak, when everyone was dabbling in the market. Despite the crash, Morris was shrewd or lucky enough to make some money; he kept it up for several years. It is interesting to note that in 1931 he wrote a school theme in which he made an impassioned defense of the stock market, with the most exaggerated claims for the moral nature of stock manipulators' motives.

At this time Morris was doing an increasing amount of small-time gambling, too. It became one of his most time-consuming interests and continued throughout college. The summer he was 15 years old he went to a famous nearby resort where he spent four seasons, first as a golf caddy, then as an assistant professional. He rapidly took to the game of golf and soon learned to like it as much as tennis. "I gambled incessantly the first two years, then had a well-rounded life the last two."

Morris still has many of his neat and careful expense accounts from these years, which give evidence of moderate expenditures that were well within his means. His gasoline record for his cars has the cost per mile to six decimal places. The problem of controlling himself was worrying him then as now, and this meticulous record-keeping appears to have been a means he took to discipline and get a grip on himself. A similar motive underlies the sporadic, usually brief, and almost always objective diaries that he has kept from 1928 to the present [1940]; they are filled with factual accounts of when he went to bed and when he got up, what he saw, makes of cars in which he hitched rides and the distance he traveled in each. His letters to his mother from the resort are of the same type. After the first few he wrote: ". . . please keep all the letters I send you, so that when I'm thru, they will be sort of a diary." Another quite typical letter ends:

> Write as often as you can—I always like to hear anything you like to say. Send me something like a big sticky gingerbread or some kind of cake. I'm eating everybody else's, so I've got to hit back some way. I would like my typewriter & topcoat; please *don't* send any more *old* sweaters; my old Hi-Y *red* and that old green sweater are no good—I need good clothes.
>
> Write,
>
> Morris.

College Years   In July of the summer he passed his entrance exams, Morris suddenly decided to go to college in the fall without waiting another year, as he had planned. He and his mother decided on a school of notably high and venerable reputation. He was given a small scholarship and got a job waiting on tables. This assistance, the money he had saved from working, and the philosophy that "things would work out" were enough to get him through the first year.

Though he was entering college at 17, Morris had attained his full 6 feet and weighed about 175 pounds; he looked hardly less mature than he did nine years later.

"I must make the right kind of friends, and use them to advantage," Morris wrote in his diary soon after arriving. "A freshman . . . is given every chance to go in for any form of athletics; and I'm going to take advantage of every opportunity . . . I might just as well start trying to leave a mark now." (Though he made no freshman teams, he often took advantage of the opportunity to play golf inexpensively on the university's course.) "I'll be taking the regular freshman course in every respect, which at least gives me an even chance, to get some good marks and high standing." "I like . . . the fellows. Some, it is true, are awful snobs, but the greater part will turn out to be nice fellows once we get acquainted."

Up to this time, there had been only one new development in Morris' sex life. Largely on a home-town girl's initiative, he had an evening of sex play. He enjoyed it enough to take the girl out several times afterward, hoping for more intimacies, but she did not permit them. After this experience, he began to seek lower-class "pick-ups" occasionally with some friend. He continued to find other boys who enjoyed mutual masturbation, and he made more intense, crush-like friendships, with the usual aggression and tussling, but apparently no overt sexuality. One difference at this point was that Morris was becoming aware of his overdependence on particular friends and began trying to prevent such extreme emotional involvement.

He had one date all freshman year. A month or so later he wrote in his diary:

It's very peculiar the difference between me and say, Dick, or any of the other fellows. I get no real pleasure from a casual date or from the company of a woman: it seems a very ineffectual way to waste time, and one that costs a lot of money, or if you don't spend money on a girl, it should make you feel cheap.

Morris summarized his undergraduate days in his autobiography: Freshman year was "the most fruitful I have ever spent in my life—I ended up with 2 A's and 2 B's, and felt that I had done a good job. . . . The next three years show what college can do for a guy with no self-control—marks down each year, more and more time playing cards, going out chasing women, etc., etc.— . . . 3rd year—lost my scholarship and my job." He was then supported by money from his mother and by some contributions from his uncle.

My roommates made other arrangements for my last year, and I moved into a single. There I managed to get studying again, wrote a good thesis and got a *cum laude*—was not present at graduation—had no desire to be—because I was with 3 other fellows sailing a boat—Played golf religiously, made the varsity my senior year.

Not excelling in stiffer tennis competition, Brown dropped it for golf, at which he has continued to improve, until he has now [1940] been state champion in his class. He had said, "My real goal is to make Phi Beta Kappa some time," at the beginning of sophomore year, but this goal apparently fell by the wayside.

The growing caution of becoming too involved with friends was sharply reinforced during his junior year by what Morris regards as a "traumatic" experience. That year he got in with a gambling gang, one of whom was a sophomore named Henry. The two soon became fast friends, playing ping-pong together, picking up girls for casual necking and petting, and "wasting a lot of time." Then one night everything went wrong. Walking home from an evening on the town, Henry proposed that they break the whole thing up. Morris was stunned. "That whole business was the greatest shock I ever had in my life." He broke down and cried when he was alone. Henry had been criticizing him a lot and calling him "Hoiman," because he knew Morris disliked being thought Jewish, but Morris was still very fond of Henry and had no intimation that their friendship was going to end that way.

The upshot of this crisis was to make Morris take a new attitude toward friendship. In its extreme form this attitude is a professed preference for doing things with people he doesn't know, getting to know strangers, but not too well. His friendships have become more and more extensive, rather than intensive, and there have been no more crushes. Looking back on those early affairs, Morris is confused and incoherently uncomfortable. He remembers many of the boys as "awful dopes," a fact that he even occasionally recognized at the time but with no effect on his attachment. "It was all so silly . . . usual at that age, but I really did overdo it."

Early Adult Years   College widened Morris' interests considerably. He began to be aware of the world of ideas, a process of growth that is still continuing; he is attaining some degree of intellectual sophistication but still lacks subtlety of response and is ill at ease with persons he considers intellectuals; such people have a good deal of prestige with him. An interest in concert music, which he traces back to his early adolescence, was stimulated and grew. Surgery began to fascinate him, and he began both to witness and read about it.

During his first postcollege summer, when Morris was 21 and was working as a lifeguard, a homosexual of the most obvious kind propositioned him. Morris was willing, four or five times in fact, though he declares himself disgusted by the man's entirely feminine reactions, affectations, and the like. Then why did he do it? His answers are all inconclusive and more or less evasive:—well, it was something new, he'd never known a guy like that, there weren't many people to talk to there anyway. But he also remarked, "I didn't care—just as soon; there wasn't any moral degradation about it."

In spite of at least half a dozen homosexual affairs, Brown has never admitted to himself their implications, nor has he seriously faced the question of what their nature was. It was a satisfaction; he accepted it and had no regrets. In his view it did not amount to anything. "If there's anything that disgusts me—a fairy, I just don't understand it—not getting any pleasure out of a woman . . . I can't imagine it—it just doesn't make sense, silly," he protested in an interview. "I'm absolutely sure I'm not a fairy, no matter what you decide."

The fall after graduation Morris returned to the city where his university was located, after only a few days at home. He soon became interested in the idea of selling securities, took a training course, and got a job. At the same time he was approached about working with the Boy Scouts, and he agreed to become a scout-master. Almost at once he experienced success, for he had always been able to get along well with boys younger than himself. After a few years of active interest and work both in camp and in the troop, he became one of the city's outstanding young scouters. Then one day the mother of one of his scouts accused him of making sexual proposals to her son. Morris denied the charge and had a scout executive investigate it. Nothing could be proved one way or another; Morris believes that the boy probably misunderstood one of his "filthy jokes." He could only make an issue of it or resign; realizing how he could be ruined if the accusation were made public, he chose the latter alternative and got out of scouting completely four years after he had begun.

This episode was a severe shock to Brown, but it did not have the effect of forcing on him a realistic view of his sex life. As recently as this fall [1940] he had an evening of extensive homosexual activities with a young man who was a good friend. Brown was embarrassed in telling about this (it was the only time he manifested such a reaction) because of the obvious connection of friendship and sex, which he strives to keep separate.

The same separation of "the sacred and the profane" is to be seen in his attitudes toward women. On the one hand, he mentions a desire for a wife, a distant romantic feeling that he has seldom felt with any vividness, and he has had a couple of instances of companionship with women, one with a woman older than himself. During the summer of 1940 he met Alison, his closest friend's girl; when the friend left the city Morris began seeing her occasionally. As his recent roommate said, "he never really saw much of her; it was just an idea he got . . . He never stood too much of a chance with her." However, Morris speaks of Alison as the one girl with whom he has been in love or has thought of as a possible wife. His fantasies about her have never gone further than thinking about her "in a bathing suit—I've never touched her, kissed her only twice." This idealized and rather tenuous affair was broken up by a misunderstanding about a date, which depressed and worried Morris for a month or so, but not seriously.

On the other hand, when he goes out with a girl Morris usually has hopes of some sexual fun, preferably with only a minimal prelude or aftermath. None of these dates has ended in intercourse; he says that the girl has always thwarted him at the last moment. Indications are, however, that he has no very active desire for heterosexual genital relations: "I'd rather stop at second base than at third, where it's no fun, when I know I can't have a home run. I do develop a feeling of shame after I've been messing around third base—wash my hands, etc." He has had intercourse twice, both times in his junior year at college, and with prostitutes. He went to a brothel with his pal Henry the first time, with neither much success nor enjoyment. After going back again within a week and definitely "proving his man-hood," he was quite disgusted and resolved never to have anything more to do with prostitutes.

A dream he had during the period of the interviews expresses several of Morris' attitudes about girls. He was walking up to an altar with Ethel Merman, who turned into a girl whom he has taken to a couple of dances but does not like much. They kneeled and a priest, "trying to calm me down," went through a marriage ceremony. After it was over, he thought: "What am I going to do with a wife?—I didn't expect this; how am I going to adjust all the little details of my life?" Ethel Merman, a "singer of hot songs in Broadway shows," who usually appears as a frankly and pleasantly bawdy wench, seems to represent Morris' sexual ideal in this dream; instead of attaining this, however, he gets involved in the constraints of marriage and with a less desirable but more probable sort of girl.

Morris has reached no consistent or satisfactory sexual adjustment. In the post-college years there have been occasional "streaks of taking four different girls out in five days," some seeking of pick-ups, and sporadic homosexual adventures; masturbation has continued unabated. Even in his autoeroticism, no emotion is connected with sex; the act is casually performed and usually with no fantasy that Brown can recall. At the most, he will think of voluptuous female forms or "a few male genitals," but in neither case are they personalized.

Of the years between the ages of 21 and 26, Morris said little except that he did a great deal of growing up. He has the theory, which he got from a friend, that a person has a certain amount of growing up to do, and he considers himself to have done it almost all in the last year and a half. It is interesting to note that in trying to define growing up, Morris, after a little incoherence, identified it with "whether or not you acted, governed your emotions with your reason."

About five years ago he heard a talk by a psychiatrist, which made a considerable impression on him. The man held that (1) it was most important to do what you planned to do and (2) you should "think *there*, not *here*." The latter advice Morris interpreted as meaning "think about what you are doing, don't introspect or analyze yourself." It was the first idea, however, that was most important to him. In the last five years Morris has been trying to plan his days and control his activities in this way. "I don't like responsibility, but I go after it now because I think it's good for me."

The first year away from the regulating power of either school or home, with a business that made few rigid demands by way of schedule, "I gambled hard, lived crazily . . . proved myself in everything I undertook very unreliable—as I always had. The next four years I have been gradually growing up—have tried the system of always doing anything I was asked to." To the end of "transforming his personality" he fills his day with appointments, makes himself speak at meetings, goes to parties where he doesn't know anyone. He keeps three marbles in his left coat pocket, and each time he makes a serious effort to sell a man some securities, he transfers one marble to the right coat pocket. His firm calculates that to be successful a man should make at least three such efforts per day.

In the autobiography, Morris wrote:

> I have a yen for community activities—apparently I want to be a big man in town before I have proved my right to it—I have a good reputation as a guy who gets things done—if they only knew! . . . I have made many friends in the last five years, but have never felt too close to or too dependent on any one of them. And I feel a disdain for anyone who is not pretty self-sufficient— I keep myself busy all the time, often on very trivial things.

Scout work put him in touch with philanthropic and civic organizations, and he soon began taking part in them. It was hard at first; having always avoided parties and social affairs of a genteel sort, Morris was afraid of these social situations. It occasionally came out in interviews that he still fears meeting people, that he feels greatly relieved to get away to the country where he is not under the tension of selling to strangers. Experience has proved to Morris, however, that he can sell, he can make a speech, and he can get people to do things; and so most of the reluctance and fear has gone.

At present, Morris has worked his way to the top of such organizations as the Red Cross Roll Call, Junior Chamber of Commerce, and Community Chest, holding important executive positions in each. He is also the president of a businessman's athletic association that he organized and president of a business association in his office. A couple of other clubs claim him as a member. All these activities were undertaken gradually while he was learning to sell stocks and bonds, and though Brown has devoted a great deal of time to these nonbusiness activities, they have proved to be financially rewarding by getting him much publicity and favorable notice. Two years ago he resolved to get his name in the paper at least once every two weeks for six months—and he did. Usually he appears not to have been greatly affected by his public recognition, but when he gets drunk he has a tendency to recount his achievements and ask what it is about him that makes people want to honor him so signally.

Morris Brown is jolly, tells jokes fairly well and often, and has a ready laugh. But his approach is without the appeal of an original style; he once said, "I never made up an original joke in my life." He also says that he "seems to rub people the wrong way sometimes" and wonders why. Yet he says, without apparently seeing any connection, "If there's anything I'm not, it's tactful. Oh, I've learned a certain amount of superficial tactfulness, but dealing with people is still a new thing for me; I say things that are all wrong." For example, his attempts to use flattery at times fail from lack of subtlety.

In the past year or so, Morris has become quite interested in the Catholic church. He thinks he has read more than a score of books on it—"everything from the Catholic Question Box up" to Newman's *Apologia*. "If I get myself all screwed up mentally, I'll go sit in a Catholic church somewhere—just sit, not pray." Yet he will not join and could not imagine taking the step of accepting everything the church says. His most frequent condemnation of things is not a moral judgment, but a rational objection: "it's silly . . . just doesn't make sense."

He has many liberal views, but hates to hear an idea or an institution challenged. "Martin Luther was one of the greatest criminals who ever lived, because he shook the faith of thousands of people." "In college you see a lot of Goddamn free souls wandering about with their own ideas—it's so crazy." "I don't like to be around skeptical people, it makes me doubt."

Morris' attitude to immortality is perhaps indicative of the function that his established beliefs have and that he would like the church to have, in his mental economy. "It's no use discussing it with someone who doesn't think we're immortal. . . . If you don't have such a belief, it takes the brakes off what you may do here—encourages the idea of living hard, fast, and loose."

Brown's gambling, referred to above, continued after college for a few years; and he went from speculating in stocks to taking fliers in the commodities market. In 1937 he bought a lot of wheat for a rise; but the price fell, and all of a sudden he had lost $1000. For a couple of days he was almost dazed by it, but he quickly determined never to gamble seriously again and has in the main lived up to his resolve. Occasionally—once a month or so—he will take a hand in a poker game, but not for high stakes.

Morris prefers to live in the present or plan, at most, for only a short time ahead. When asked what his goals are, he beat around the bush a little, then said that they were

> not very well thought out—always sort of immediate. I have a desire to be a big man around town. Most men have ideas about getting married, having a nice home, doing things for Mother with a capital 'M.' I know I owe her a lot, but never thought about setting her up. I hadn't thought of this—I'm changing my goals. . . . I want to be a really good golfer. I think it's silly of me to think of what I'll be 20 years from now. People who have their life all planned out bother me.

Morris feels that he has about reached the ceiling of prestige and status in his community activities; it is now a question of whether he seems to other people to be a success. Money, beyond enough for a modest level of comfort, means nothing to him. He is a little unsure about what he wants in the way of friends. The idea of knowing many different kinds of people, particularly important people, appeals to him: "I love it—you can *learn* something from them." He expressed no desire for intimate friends. The fact is that he has three or four reasonably close friends, but he is judging these relationships in the frame of reference of his former intense involvements.

Though he has a conventional wish for a wife he could get along with and for "a good crop of boys," he admits it is "beyond immediate possibility—I don't have plans for when I'm fifty." Brown does not have much interest in ordinary social affairs; he likes to dance, but he is poor at it and seldom attends dances. He does have occasional dates and goes to a cocktail party now and then. He is vaguely aware of a certain lack of knowledge and sophistication in himself, due to his pre-college background, and so would like to study, meet "smart people," and acquire polish in whatever ways he can.

It would be a mistake to leave an impression of Morris as a completely calculating person, either consciously or unconsciously, as some of the foregoing material may suggest. A final appraisal must mention his genuine desire to please, his fresh interest in people and things about him, his perennial good spirits, his willingness to help and to cooperate, and his quite charming naive frankness, without which it would not have been possible for the investigators to write this story of his life.

So ends the case history written in 1940. The next two chapters will present additional data on Morris Brown gathered at that time, to serve as illustrative material for a detailed consideration of objective and projective tests of personality.

So we sometimes espy a bright cloud formed into an irregular figure; when it is observed by unskilful and fantastic travellers, it looks like a centaur to some, and as a castle to others; some tell that they saw an army with banners, and it signifies war; but another, wiser than his fellow, says it looks for all the world like a flock of sheep, and foretells plenty; and all the while it is nothing but a shining cloud.

JEREMY TAYLOR. Holy Living and Holy Dying

CHAPTER 37
OBJECTIVE AND PROJECTIVE TECHNIQUES OF ASSESSMENT

Now that we have a grasp of the main facts in Morris Brown's life up to the time of his formal assessment in 1940–41, we are in a position to appreciate the kinds of contributions to understanding him that both projective and nonprojective (or objective) techniques can supply. In the process, some of the general points about these types of assessment made in previous chapters may become more concrete as they take on relevance.

Objective Techniques

QUESTIONNAIRES

As we noted in Chapter 35, self-administering tests and inventories are a major resource of objective assessment. Eight such tests were taken by Morris Brown in 1940, a good sample of the instruments available at the time. Of these eight, we shall examine here only two, which are still used today.

689

The A-S
Reaction Study The A-S (Ascendance-Submission) Reaction Study, by G. W. and F. H. Allport (1928), was one of the first trait measures. It has only moderate retest reliability (measured by a correlation coefficient of .74 for men), and the evidence for its validity is even weaker: Correlations of about .45 (but ranging from .29 to .74) have been reported, the criteria being ratings by self and others. It can hardly be regarded as a precise or highly trustworthy measuring stick for *ascendance-submission* (the tendency to dominate others or to give way to them), yet most of its content seems meaningfully relevant to that trait. Here is a sample item:

> You are at a mixed party where about half the people are friends of yours. The affair becomes very dull, and something should be done to enliven it. You have an idea. Do you usually
> take the initiative in carrying it out———————————
> pass it on to another to put into execution——————
> say nothing about it———————————————

The subject merely checks the answer he considers most self-descriptive. Morris attained a score of +11, which the authors express as A2, or moderately ascendant, on a scale ranging from A4 through Average to S4. This score agrees reasonably well with the informal and clinical assessment of Morris, who was clearly not a shy or self-abasing person in most situations, particularly since he had begun to take on positions of leadership, to speak at meetings, and to work successfully at an occupation demanding a good deal of persuasiveness on his part. The score would be more valuable if there had been more work on norms (see page 696).

The Study
of Values The Study of Values, by G. W. Allport and P. E. Vernon (1931), gives scores on half a dozen variables and is based on the theory of personality of the German psychologist, E. Spranger. In his book *Types of Men* (1928), Spranger proposed that six major foci attract the interest of adults: Theoretical, Economic, Aesthetic, Social, Political, and Religious values. Because these values represent relatively conflict-free areas of experience, in which defensiveness and concealment are not expected, the authors constructed a test of a few dozen transparent items relevant to these six categories of personal values.

The test has enjoyed wide use in research and, to some extent, in other types of assessment, such as vocational guidance and selection; in its recent revision (which will be discussed in Chapter 39), it has taken a new lease on life. The reliabilities of the six scores from the original form vary, but they are generally satisfactory: On retest after three months, correlation coefficients range from a distinctly poor .39 (Social) to a good .87 (Religious) and, for internal consistency, from .49 (Social) to .84 (Aesthetic and Religious). A respectable degree of validity is indicated by the differences between the scores of occupational groups; for example, ministers and seminary students do score higher on the Religious interest than men in general.

The test is ingeniously constructed so that it gives a purely *relative* measure of the strength of a person's values. Each item pits two to four values against one another, as in the following examples (taken from Lindzey's 1951 revision). In the first type of item, the subject is to distribute 3 points between two possible answers:

> Which of the following branches of study do you expect ultimately will prove more important for mankind? (a) mathematics; (b) theology.

By awarding 2 points to the first alternative, Morris contributed that much to his score on the Theoretical value; the single point for (b) was chalked up to his score on the Religious value.

In the second type of item, the four possible answers are to be ranked in reverse order. In the example below, Morris' answers are given, along with the value measured by each (which does not appear in the actual item):

> To what extent do the following famous persons interest you—
> a. Florence Nightingale (2) (Social value)
> b. Napoleon (4) (Political value)
> c. Henry Ford (3) (Economic value)
> d. Galileo (1) (Theoretical value)

In these answers, Morris indicated that his strongest interest was in Napoleon, the political figure, his least in Galileo, who embodies the Theoretical value.

As can be seen from the profile of values for Morris in 1940 (Figure 37-1), his strongest value was the Political, on which his score exceeds that of 90 percent of the normative group of college students. This finding implies a primary interest in power, not necessarily within the field of politics as such; it suggests that he is motivated by a desire to be a leader, to dominate others, and to gain influence and renown.

The next rank was shared by the Economic and Social values, both at the 70th percentile. The economic man, according to Spranger, is interested in what is *useful;* but the Economic value also includes self-preservation, all the practical concerns of business, and the gaining of wealth. The Social value was defined by Spranger as love for people in all its manifestations; it was the most diffuse of the values. The social man is kind, sympathetic, and unselfish; or, at least, someone with a strong Social value rates such qualities high as ideals.

The Aesthetic value, at the 20th percentile, was quite low; unlike Spranger's aesthetic man, Morris did not prize form and harmony above all

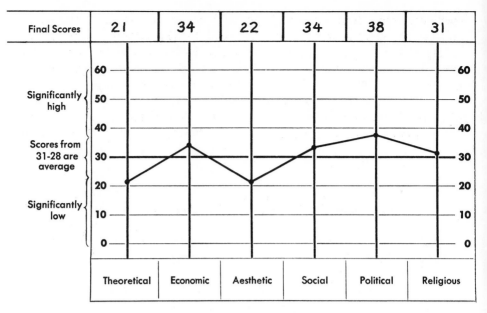

| Final Scores | 21 | 34 | 22 | 34 | 38 | 31 |

Figure 37-1   Morris Brown's profile of values (Allport & Vernon, 1931).

else, nor did he tend to judge things in terms of grace, symmetry, or fitness. Morris' weakest value—the Theoretical—showed a slightly lower score, but was also at the 20th percentile. The dominant concern of the theoretical man, Allport and Vernon tell us, is the discovery of truth; his interests are cognitive, empirical, critical, and rational.

This ordering agrees well with the assessors' impressions on the basis of interviews and other data. To quote the original report: "One of them predicted at the beginning of the study, on the basis of only a few casual contacts, that the Political, Social, and Economic would be the leading interests." The Study of Values provided confirmation, true, but just what else did the test provide? In defense of the test's authors it must be added that their manual suggests only the following types of use with individuals: "to secure an initial impression . . . and as a basis for subsequent interviews."

INTELLIGENCE TESTING

Terman and Merrill's 1937 revision of the Stanford-Binet Scale was long the standard individual test of intelligence for subjects of all ages. (Today, as Chapter 39 will point out, the Wechsler Adult Intelligence Scale has supplanted it in work with adults.) In 1940, the Stanford-Binet existed in two forms (L and M), with unusually good alternate-form reliability (.91) and excellent stability over time. One group of 11-year-olds was retested after 1 year, 2 years, and finally after 6 years; the later I.Q.'s were correlated with the earlier set to an equally high degree (.93, .93, .92). As the direct lineal descendant of the original Binet test that virtually defined intelligence in 1905, the Stanford-Binet had almost unquestioned validity in 1940. It is heavily weighted with verbal skills and is a particularly good predictor of academic achievement, which is what Binet intended it to be in the first place. But the test also predicts life achievement; for example, children with I.Q.'s in the mentally defective range (65 and lower) can be expected never to enter college or to succeed in professional or managerial occupations, unless the I.Q. is temporarily lowered by an emotional disturbance that is later alleviated. Terman and Oden (1947) made a special study of those at the other extreme, following up 730 persons whose childhood I.Q.'s were 140 or higher. By age 40, they had published 67 books, more than 200 plays and short stories, and over 1400 professional or scientific papers; they tended to be in occupations with the highest levels of prestige and remuneration.

Form L was administered to Morris Brown in 1940 by a graduate student who had had enough experience to feel comfortable in giving it. Morris' I.Q. was determined to be 146, Very Superior; he was able to perform practically every task that was put to him. This score was a quantitative measure of considerable interest in light of Morris' tardiness in learning to speak. To be sure, that he graduated with honors from one of the country's most respected colleges suggests that he must have had at least superior intelligence, as does his history of rapid advancement in primary school and his early graduation from high school. Casual contact and even extended conversation, however, would not have led the investigators to predict such a high intelligence quotient. Despite his *cum laude*, Morris seems to have been somewhat of an underachiever for most of his college career and was still not using the full extent of his ability in his activities as of 1940.

CONSTITUTIONAL ANALYSIS

Somatotype Morris' *somatotype* was determined according to the judgmental system of W. H. Sheldon and under his supervision. Sheldon took a standardized photograph, from which the somatotype was rated 4½ 5 1½. These numbers mean that Brown's physique was just above the theoretical midpoint of a 7-point scale of endomorphy, slightly higher on mesomorphy (which was thus the dominant component), and only a fraction of a point above the theoretical minimum for ectomorphy. This somatotype is a member of a family of rather common ones; Sheldon (1940) describes its closest relatives as follows:

The 452 is the commonest of the overwhelmingly massive physiques . . . These are solid, heavy people, of great strength and energy [p. 201].

The 451 is a massive, compact physique, of short stature [not true of Morris], and usually of tremendous energy. It is a body built for an active, strenuous life. The endomorphic 4 supports the predominant mesomorphic

5 to produce a highly efficient machine as long as the first component is kept in check by vigorous activity, but given an opportunity, the endomorphic 4 will produce a laying-on of fat which rises like the tide and soon swamps the athletic outline of the physique. . . . [Athletic slenderness] is predominant only as long as a vigorously active life is maintained, or a rigid diet established. Under ordinary circumstances, especially after marriage, the first component suddenly asserts itself and for a time seems to run rampant. These people can sometimes gain 30 or 40 pounds within a year. Likewise they can lose this weight relatively easily, if they are willing to diet rigidly, but usually they are not [pp. 212–13].

The 4 5 1 somatotype is illustrated in Figure 35-1, page 649.

Brown did not deviate markedly from the norms for his physique in the secondary variables, also rated on 7-point scales. His scores were gynandromorphy (resemblance to the other sex), 2; texture (fineness of structural detail), 2½; dysplasia (inconsistency between regions), 5 (Morris' rather moon-shaped face, for example, made his head considerably more endomorphic than his hard-muscled legs).

Temperament
Typing

Sheldon's method for the analysis of temperament is basically clinical: It relies upon interviewing and direct observation to collect facts, which are processed by means of ratings, again on 7-point scales. Temperament, Sheldon believes, is best conceived of as varying on three dimensions (or *components*), which are defined in terms of three somewhat heterogeneous lists of separately rated traits. The 20 ratings for each component are averaged to arrive at the final scores, expressed in a formula similar to the somatotype: 5 5 3.

Morris' overall rating of 5 on *viscerotonia* indicates a considerable liking for comfort, eating, and relaxation, with attendant good fellowship, and dependence on expressed affection, particularly when in trouble. This above-average rating also reflects warm and readily expressed emotions and the ability to get along with people easily and well. The equally high rating of 5 on *somatotonia* reflects Morris' characteristically high level of energy, activity, and exercise. The rating was earned also by his loud extroverted characteristics—his aggressive leadership, his insensitivity to others, and his maturity of appearance (one of Sheldon's odd variables of "temperament" that guarantee high correlations with measures of physique). On each of those traits Morris was moderately strong, and he was particularly strong on having "sharp cleavage between conscious and unconscious." He was rated below the midpoint on *cerebrotonia*, a tense, inhibited hyperattentionality that is revealed both physiologically and socially.

Sheldon's variables did not, however, fit Brown without internal contradictions. With his high degree of viscerotonia, he should have been a better sleeper and a more ceremonious person. Greater love of adventure and danger and a much more aggressive and active response to both trouble and alcohol should go with a rating of 5 in somatotonia. And, finally, Brown was more cerebrotonic than his 3 rating implied, in that he had difficulty making habits, resisted disease well, and was often rather tense.

A COMMENT ON THE OBJECTIVE ASSESSMENT
OF MORRIS BROWN

In spite of some attempts to interpret his scores on a few of the questionnaires, it can hardly be argued that the objective assessment, except for the I.Q., contributed very much to our understanding of Morris. With one further exception (see next paragraph), the objective assessment did not provide concepts that would help us pull facts together in ways that are not already obvious, nor does it deepen our sense of knowing him as a person. Even the quantitative precision apparently given by numerical scores is vitiated by their only moderate validities.

For the most part the scores could be taken at face value, and the test results seemed to make far better sense than might have been expected from the meager evidences of validity accompanying most of the questionnaires. Consider, for example, the Humm-Wadsworth Temperament Scale, a then-popular multitrait test that is no longer widely used; it brought out his lack of ambition, his deficiency in what Morris himself called "moral sense," and his tendency to be below average in fantasy, imaginativeness, and schizoid traits. His highest scores were on the "cycloid component" scales of both manic and depressive tendencies. This finding had the value of suggesting that his fluctuating moods—his generally high level of energy and cheerfulness, which were sometimes replaced by considerable self-doubt and feelings of uneasiness—could be seen as expressions of cyclothymic temperament.

A moment's reflection can provide us with a hypothesis to explain both the surprising "validity" of the tests and their failure to add much to the picture of our man. In both interviews and tests, Morris made a conscientious attempt to present himself honestly. Indeed, his only motivation—the wish to gain more self-understanding, perhaps in the service of self-control—operated to minimize conscious faking of any kind and helped to make the tests valid in his case. It is not surprising that a consistent picture emerged in both interviews and questionnaires—two types of assessment that had in common their directness of approach. Because the interviews were so comprehensive, the tests did not cover much new ground.

We have thus seen exemplified a point already made about inventories: If a subject is willing and able to describe himself truthfully, they allow him to present himself rather faithfully and efficiently (at least in terms of the investigator's time), even if in a less personalized and individualized way than the methods of direct clinical assessment permit. The main advantage these inventories have over free self-description is the opportunity they give for systematic coverage and interindividual comparison: It is possible to see to what extent other people have answered the same questions in a similar way. But *what* other people? It makes little sense to compare a 26-year-old college graduate with high school seniors on a questionnaire like the Wrightstone Test of Civic Beliefs (another test Morris took, which is now defunct), because even the data of that test's author showed that the average score on liberalism rises steadily during the high school years, and it might surely be expected to go up even more during the college years (as subsequent research has shown to be true; see Sanford, 1962). The moderately liberal Brown looked like an extreme radical in comparison to the only available norms.

Projective Techniques

By turning now to projective tests, which are widely used in the interpretive phase of clinical assessment, we can go beyond the point to which the objective tests have brought us. The Thematic Apperception Test and the Rorschach Test given to Morris Brown exemplify the uses to which these techniques can be put.

THE THEMATIC APPERCEPTION TEST

The TAT (Morgan & Murray, 1935) was devised in the course of a research program at the Harvard Psychological Clinic and was published after some years of development (Murray, 1943). The test consists of 30 pictures and a blank card, onto which the subject is encouraged to project his own imagined picture. The pictures are marked in such a way as to indicate four overlapping sets of 20 each: one for boys, one for girls, one for males over 14, and one for females over 14. Thus, card 6BM is to be used both for boys and for older males, 13MF is for older males and females only, and card 1 is used with all subjects. The subject tells a story about each picture, following instructions similar to those given two paragraphs below.

The investigators used a set of the TAT pictures that were then current, most of which were either identical with or very similar to the ones generally available today; see Figure 37-2 for two of the pictures. Being untrained and inexperienced in the use of projective techniques, they made just about every mistake possible in administering the test to Morris; nevertheless, they obtained a great deal of usable material. In three sessions, Morris told stories about 22 pictures; 7 of these stories are quoted below and 2 are summarized briefly.*

* In the old series, the first 10 pictures were used with all subjects; only one of these, card 1, carries the same number in the current, published test. The investigators also got Morris to tell stories about 9 of the 10 pictures used with men only (which were designated M-11 through M-20), and 3 of the 10 pictures for women (F-11 through F-20). To minimize confusion, the stories will be numbered here sequentially as they were given, and where possible the pictures will be referred to by their current code numbers.

Figure 37-2   Illustrative TAT pictures (numbers 8 and 10 in an unpublished series).

Administration   As it is used today, the TAT is introduced by instructions like the following:

This is a story-telling test. I am going to show you some pictures, one at a time, and your task will be to make up as dramatic (or interesting) a story as you can for each. Tell what has led up to the event shown in the picture, describe what is happening at the moment, what the characters are feeling and thinking; and then give the outcome. Speak your thoughts as they come to your mind. Do you understand? Here is the first picture.

The instructions given to Morris were essentially the same, except that they specified that the test was "a test of imagination, one form of intelligence." The examiner today records the length of time before the subject begins and the total time he takes for each story.

**Sample Stories
from Session 1**

1. [A young boy is contemplating a violin, which rests on a table in front of him.]

Probably this boy has just taken up the violin and is looking at it wondering how he is going to make anything out of it. His teacher wasn't very encouraging. It's not his first lesson, I see now—all this music, he wouldn't have it in the first few weeks. Could be Yehudi what's-his-name at the time he made his first concert appearance. Reminds me of a story about a boy who went to hear Kreisler, came home and broke his violin. Thereafter he wouldn't go watch good tennis.

5. [Card 10 in the present, published series: A young woman's head against a man's shoulder.]

Can you explain what this is? (points; E [Examiner] shakes head) It suggests something similar to the idea of *Ladies in Retirement*—the woman is similar to Flora Robson in that, or the servant in *Rebecca*. She's devoted her whole life to the boy; this is one of the few times she's let herself go. He's home from school on holidays, about 15 or 16. Thinking about how much she has and is going to do for him; her whole life is wrapped up in him, yet he's probably going to turn out something like the boy in *My Son, My Son*. (At this point Morris complains about how he keeps thinking about other books, plays, and so on.) I have seen that somewhere in some play. Anyone can see—it's obvious to look at the boy that he'll never be worth a damn—he's pudgy, soft, and sort of weak.

8. [See Figure 37-2.]

This could be in a primitive Indian civilization in Central America. It's hard to put in any specific atmosphere; faces are so different. (He may have said "indistinct.")

Down in Yucatan, Mayans or Incas—where family life was different from what we know—more like in India today, where marriages are apart from the wishes of the participants or anything like that, this young couple about 17–18 years old—the man's a very sensitive sort, an artist; therefore, he must have been . . . very much in love with this very charming girl. Since custom . . . Well, the idea is, somehow they got together, she had a baby—but since the marriage hadn't been sanctioned, the elders of the tribe were outraged. They couldn't have the baby, since they had violated all the taboos, etc. It would be taken by the boy's mother, who felt worst about it, to be reared by a priest in one of the temples. The couple were driven out of the place and were never heard of again. This is where the baby's being taken away. The girl's pretty much crushed; he'd like to do something about it, but there's nothing he can.

10. [See Figure 37-2.]

(laughs) It suggests Sinbad and the sailor—I could be very trite and tell that. I must have a very trite brain. (long pause; turns it several ways)

This is a copy of a drawing found on the wall of a cave in Arabia by Burton. He had the idea of getting down all the old Arabian legends. He went all over Arabia, eating their food, living with their women, trying to run down all the stories that were told by night around the fire. This was the first time anybody had heard of a cave in Arabia—why the mouth wasn't closed by sand, nobody could imagine. He went in, found the walls covered with drawings; there was a whole series of caves, and he could recognize a lot of the drawings because they illustrated stories he'd found. He went further back, found some he couldn't recognize; this was one of them. Then he noticed this same gaunt, weary figure was in many of the other pictures, representing many adventures this same man had gone through—trials and tribulations. Burton had found that opium smoking helped in this work so he decided to settle down and try it to see if he couldn't get some interpretation of the picture. They camped outside, and for the next week he spent 24 hours a day lying on a couch in the cave looking at the pictures. Gradually he saw in this gaunt old man a curious portrayal of all the difficulties the human soul must undergo. The idea of everyone bearing his own cross: Sinbad carrying this old man on his shoulders. When Burton got back to England after this, people found him changed. He had been knighted and had great honors. He was very different now, liked more and more to sit alone, smoke, and read. He was a man of great wealth and lacked for nothing. It came to be that he had to be watched, because his mind wasn't just right. He would wander around the room shaking himself as if trying to get rid of this burden. They say that when he died he was alone in his big old castle in an ornate room clutching at his throat trying to tear the old man's hands away.

It is usually not desirable to administer more than 10 pictures in one session, since the subject—particularly if he is as productive as Morris—is likely to become too tired to do the job properly. A new set of instructions was given at the second session one week later, in accordance with the procedure Murray recommended at that time. Current practice does not require different instructions.

Sample Stories from Session 2   Brown had a bad headache during this whole session. He was instructed as follows:

The procedure today is the same as before, only this time you can give freer rein to your imagination. Your first ten stories were excellent, but you confined yourself pretty much to the facts of everyday life. Now I would like to see what you can do when you disregard the commonplace realities and let your imagination have its way, as in a myth, fairy story, or allegory.

11. [6BM: A short elderly woman stands with her back turned to a tall young man. The latter is looking downward with a perplexed expression.]

(Before starting, Morris said that he could make up an unusual one, about murder, and also the obvious one. *E* asked for the latter.) The obvious thing is that this fellow has just told his mother that he is going away on a trip, won't be back for several years; she's obviously all broken up about it, thinks it's not necessary, is foolish. His mind was made up; nothing she said or thought could change it, so he's getting ready to go. There's nothing especially dangerous, about where he's going—just different sort of work. She doesn't like to see the settled order of their life broken up. This is the end of a couple of weeks of talking and worrying about it; he has told her what he's going to do; they've had a lot of trouble about it.

14. [12M: A young man is lying on a couch with his eyes closed. Leaning over him is another man, his hand stretched out above the face of the reclining figure.]

This is about a couple of roommates in prep school, one of whom thought he was pretty hot stuff as a hypnotist, other thought it was a lot of crap, that it was impossible for anyone to hypnotize him, for his will to be subject to another's. Wright explained that only a strong will could be hypnotized and then if he were willing, so they agreed to try it out. The picture represents just about when the subject is getting completely under the control of Wright, the other boy. Of course, there's no need for Wright to use his hands and gestures, it's not an essential part; but it fits in with the usual picture and he was that kind of fellow, wanted to be spectacular about it. The main reason Wright was interested in this work was he knew that in the state of hypnosis a subject will do nothing against his fundamental nature, and he wanted to find out a few things about his roommate. So as soon as everything was fixed he asked him to walk over to his—Wright's—bureau, take some money that was there, put it in his pocket, which Bill did. He came back and sat on the edge of the couch, took one of the pillows, put it between his legs and started screwing it, faster and faster until he went off and came out of the state of hypnotism at once. The problem is, whether the act was something repugnant to him or whether it was a reaction to his nervous state that made him snap out of it. This is a problem story, sort of like the Lady and the Tiger.

Came from a little incident I heard about 13 years ago; never thought of it since. A fellow in prep school hypnotized his roommate, had him screw a pillow; the fellow who told me about it was named Wright. From the general situation, I don't think it was a true story.

(Brown asked if it were true that one would do only what he really had no objections to; said he had learned about hypnotism only here and there, partly from Poe's story "Mesmerism.") I was brought up on five volumes of Poe—do you want them lurid? I could probably drag sex in by the heels all over the place, a few dead bodies and so on.

16. [17BM: A naked man is clinging to a rope. He is in the act of climbing up or down.]

The man is a eunuch in Ethiopia—I've just been reading in *Days of Our Years* a chapter about it. At 14, he was captured by a slave trader who at one blow cut off not only his balls but his prick—that's the way the Arabs liked 'em. He was bought by this Arab chief who very peculiarly had a castle— would have to because of the picture—and there this man Ahab, as he was called by the Arabs, lived for 20 years, as servant in the chief's harem. Surprisingly, instead of developing the usual lackadaisical castrated attitude that comes to eunuchs (laughs)—oh, yes!—this Ahab was constantly tormented by the presence of all the women and his complete inability to do anything about it. Thinking the thing over, trying to reason it out, he decided he must escape, come what may. Since the harem was kept in the tower of this peculiar castle and he never did get outside for a minute, there was only one way to do it: by means of a rope. So early one morning just as the sun was coming up, he threw a rope out of the window, tying it to a post inside the room, and let himself down. As in most such rash acts, fate was against him. He got to the bottom; four of the servants of the Arab chief were there, ready to grab him. So Ahab failed in his attempt to gain freedom. He died in the most unique way the chief could think up. Do you want to know the way? They put him in a room with a couple of colonies of red ants: one of the quaint Ethiopian customs I've just been reading about.

Sample Stories
from Session 3

A week after the second session Morris told stories about some more pictures to the other investigator. Two of these stories are summarized below.

21. [18GF: A woman has her hands squeezed around the throat of another woman whom she appears to be pushing backwards across the banister of a stairway.] "That's a beaut! Oh boy! One woman murdering another one." A younger woman served as personal secretary to an older one—"it's coming from a story," he interpolated—and they got involved in a lesbian relationship. The secretary eventually turned on her employer and choked her; the latter fell, hit her head, and died. "The girl had a good time on the swag she had gotten away with." Apparently pleased with his surprise ending, Morris remarked that it wouldn't do for Hollywood.

22. [13MF: A young man is standing with downcast head buried in his arm. Behind him is the figure of a woman lying in bed.] "I've got to cut loose on this one. Jesus, what a shape! Positively indecent! Looks like a Gibson girl!" His first thought was that the man was "going to the bathroom to make sure he doesn't catch anything!" He then said the scene was in Hawaii, where a man and girl were "sitting and drinking on a terrace." After "six drinks, they stagger upstairs and land on the bed"; a couple of minutes later, the man goes to the bathroom to throw up.

Inquiry

One of the investigators conducted an inquiry into the sources of the stories, asking Morris where he got the ideas for each. For the most part, he attributed them to various books he had read; but the following responses (quoted just as recorded in the investigator's handwritten notes) are more personally revealing:

1. From a story he read in a tennis book. Tennis doesn't fit in naturally around here. Did want to be a famous tennis player. Never got any definite goal. Golf now. Either going to be good or leave it alone. Hates to think he is wasting his time.

5. Had a job figuring out the sexes. Came from the stories mentioned. Does think of himself as pudgy and soft as a kid; didn't then.

11. No special source. Ties back to own experience probably. Overdrawn. Resistance she didn't express.

16. Directly from *Days of Our Years*. Escape—something I've read some-where—*Thief of Bagdad*—or Arabian Nights story where hero cut villain in two. (Couldn't believe Arab actually cut off members.) Escape, from *The Three Musketeers*.

The Process of Interpretation

How should one interpret a projective technique like the TAT? There is no one correct way. Experts differ in their procedures, and few of them use any formal system of scoring. Analyzing a TAT is not a complicated technical process of counting certain kinds of words or making quantitative ratings on many variables and entering formulas of any kind.

Rather, the general practice is, first, to approach the stories with a background of general knowledge about the person (the more knowledge the better), which helps orient the investigator to what is relevant and helps him to rule out various obviously inappropriate hypotheses that might otherwise cause him to waste time. To take an extreme example, there is no point in trying to figure out from a set of stories whether the author was a man or a woman; there are easier and more valid ways of finding that out. The task of the interpreter is to develop hypotheses about what caused the person to tell just these stories in just these ways—hypotheses about the determinants of all aspects of the test data—in order to help develop a picture of the storyteller's personality.

Second, as the skilled interpreter makes himself more and more thoroughly familiar with the stories, he begins to notice divergences from what would be expected on the basis of experience with the stories most people tell about any given picture and divergences from the subject's own baseline. Divergent material, which is unusual through being rare, or repetitive, or very intensely stated, or accompanied by signs of strong emotion, is the main basis for inferences, or interpretive hypotheses. After putting these hypotheses together and checking them against other evidence (which causes some of them to be dropped or modified), the interpreter finally writes his report.

In making his interpretations the investigator may use such procedures as *empathic perception, statistical inference,* or *inference based on theory.* Statistical inference simply means reasoning that if one aspect of a test has often been associated in the past with a personal characteristic, such as a kind of symptom, it will continue to have the same significance whether or not there is any intelligible connection between the two. In inference based on theory (or clinical inference), a theory of personality, or a more specific theory of a particular kind is used to establish a meaningful connection, which makes it understandable that some feature of a test performance is determined by some aspect of personality. These forms of inference are not mutually incompatible; ideally, a hypothesis suggested by theory is verified by statistical data, so that the interpreter can have a known degree of confidence in the inference.

Whatever the procedures the interpreter uses, they amount to *generalizing from particulars*. He translates the test responses as raw data into statements about aspects of personality, which he then treats as if they are characteristic. If he is prudent, he will use as wide a base as possible for such generalizations; therefore, he will test hypotheses from the TAT against other types of information.

By now it should be evident that projective techniques differ sharply from self-reporting questionnaires as techniques of assessment. It is misleading to group them all together as "personality tests," because they contribute to the assessment of personality in quite different ways. Projective techniques provide raw data of special value and richness, which the psychologist must then *interpret* before he can obtain measures of any variables of personality; the scores of inventories give immediate measures of personality variables. Thereafter, the psychologist may or may not decide to draw interpretive inferences from the profile, or configuration of scores, on a multidimensional test like the MMPI; in any event he does not have to. In a test like the TAT or Rorschach, however, the most commonly used scoring schemes merely count salient features of the subject's responses and are not direct measures of any one variable. It is impossible, therefore, to escape the necessity of interpreting projective test data. Some of the worst abuses of projective techniques have resulted from attempts to bypass clinical judgment and to use them as if scores derived from them were comparable to those of an inventory.

The lack of immediately meaningful scores also means that it is difficult to pursue the standard psychometric ideals, which presuppose such scores as the only yield of tests. That does not imply that reliability and validity are irrelevant. Validity remains an overriding consideration, and reliability concerns us in the following ways: We do not want to make the mistake of interpreting an aspect of a story in terms of some semipermanent feature of the personality if it actually resulted from a purely temporary mood (like Brown's headache) or a recent but unimportant experience like a movie the subject saw the night before. Furthermore, it is highly desirable for more than one assessor to be able to reach the same conclusions about the subject through interpreting his projective test results. The more the process of interpretation is structured and systematized, and the more common experience of training and working over the same data that two judges have, the better one can do in attaining reliability of this latter kind ("observer agreement").

The account given above deliberately avoids treatment of the more detailed steps, commonly found in texts on interpretation. Such accounts of orderly procedure give a false impression: Experts do not operate that way. Interpreting complex qualitative data, like any other exercise of expertise, is largely a tacit process. The interpreter concentrates his attention on the *person*, trying to catch glimpses of him through the medium of his test responses, which are not of interest in themselves. Even less prominent in his awareness are his own methods of processing the data. To be sure, in the early stages of learning, things are quite different: Just as when you are learning to drive a car, you are vividly conscious of where you put your hands and feet at every moment and how you move them, so also when you are mastering the craft of interpreting clinical data you must do it with slow, awkward laboriousness. With practice and experience, performance of these steps merges into performance of the whole act and recedes from awareness, which makes it possible to become aware of much more about the person.

How Inferences Were Drawn from the Stories   The most this account can do to illustrate interpretation is to consider a few interpretive hypotheses about Morris and relate them to the TAT data. Since Morris' stories suggest a tremendous number of possible hypotheses, let us concentrate on a few areas—the problematic ones raised at the end of Chapter 36 and restated below:

1. What had been going on in Morris during the years since college when he "turned inside out"?
2. What can we learn about his conflict over dependence and independence?
3. How can we understand his problem of controlling himself?
4. What can we make of his confused sexual adjustment?

From each question, we hope to learn something of the *unconscious* meanings of these conscious conflicts by the indirect method of the TAT. The underlying assumption is that the same unconscious needs, anxieties, and defenses that shape a person's everyday behavior will affect his cognitive products during the test in such a way that they can be discerned through interpretation. The very indirectness of the approach—the fact that the subject himself was in the dark about the personal significance of his stories, beyond the superficial parallels to his experience he pointed out in the inquiry—means that if dynamic factors within the subject did in fact determine the test responses, they were unconscious ones.

Inferences about sexual adjustment. To take these questions in reverse order, let us see what light the stories can throw on Morris' sexual problems. Why was he so little interested in girls? Why did he get involved in homosexual contacts? What did it all mean to him? An answer to any such focused set of questions requires that we examine all the stories that contain direct or circuitous reference to sex and to intimate relationships between actual or possible sexual partners. In doing so, we will be guided by certain normative expectations: To most people, the scene shown in picture 13MF (story 22) is an overtly sexual one, although many will knowingly avoid this interpretation of the relationship in their stories. Number 8 in the old series (Figure 37-2) had at least as strong a "pull" for a heterosexual interpretation. But tender and intimate relations between partners are also commonly seen in picture 10 of the present series, so we should examine story 5 as well. Since the other pictures do not directly suggest anything heterosexual, a story told about one of them should be examined with particular interest if erotic material crops up (see stories 10 and 16). The only picture that is at all often responded to as if there might be a homosexual relationship between the characters is 12M (see story 14; in the old series the characters' ages look more comparable than they do in the present, redrawn version); the emergence of the homosexual theme in story 21 is therefore of particular note.

One noteworthy element that is common to stories 8, 10, 16, and 22, where there is heterosexual content, is that they all take place in remote locations—Hawaii, Arabia, Ethiopia, and even ancient Yucatan. A fairly conservative interpretation would be that Morris found it difficult to imagine or at least to describe a sexual involvement with a girl in a "here and now" setting. Perhaps that would be so close to home as to make him anxious. Another possibility is that his heterosexual desires are repressed and thus can find only relatively remote expression. By contrast, note that the one explicitly homosexual theme (in story 21) and the implicit one (in story 14) came out in settings that seem to be contemporaneous and American.

In story 22, there is no suggestion of love, nor of any relationship at all other than a strictly sexual one, which takes place in a virtually anesthetic state of intoxication. The pseudo-enthusiastic exclamation about the woman's exposed breasts ("Positively indecent!") is a curious mixture of pleasure and rejection, and disgust with heterosexuality is strongly suggested by the man's throwing up. This reaction, however, could have been anticipated from Morris' remark about disgust and shame after heavy petting (see Chapter 36, page 684); the question remains: *Why* did Morris feel this way? The story contains two hints in associations he tossed off at the beginning and did not develop: first, that the woman looked "like a Gibson girl"—the equivalent of a pin-up girl in his mother's generation; and second, that the man might be afraid of venereal disease. From these hints come two possible inferences to be checked against other data: Morris may have been inhibited heterosexually (1) because a girl was unconsciously equivalent to his mother and (2) because he feared damage to his genitals. These are familiar elements of the Oedipus complex; psychoanalytic experience has taught us that a boy often develops a homosexual orientation because of the incest taboo and castration anxiety (see Part II, Chapter 15). Neither of these themes is at all directly expressed, yet the symbolic translation used here is not a far-fetched one in psychoanalytic practice.

As it happens, however, one of Morris' stories (16) does contain an unusually graphic and explicit reference to castration—and it is a story that also contains heterosexual material. This story is an interesting combination of common and unusual, original and borrowed elements: The interpretation of the picture (Daumier's lithograph "The House Painter") as one of a man escaping by climbing down a rope is quite usual; most of the rest of the content stands out by being highly infrequent, if not unique. Although the immediate source of much of this shocking content was a current best-selling travel book, the story is twisted around to highly personal ends. The fact that Morris could so easily disavow responsibility for having made up these improbable events undoubtedly made it possible for him to talk about them without anxiety—indeed, with a teasing kind of relish—for surely the events had nothing to do with *him*.

An interpreter of such a story always looks first at the central character (usually the one depicted in the picture), or *hero*, and makes the trial assumption that the teller expresses various feelings about himself through what he says about the hero. Moreover, older male figures—particularly those in positions of authority—are often symbols of the subject's father. Adopting these two assumptions, we can translate the underlying theme as an unconscious fantasy that says something like this: "Father castrated me and made me a powerless slave because he liked me better that way; if I showed sexual interest in mother or sisters [the chief's harem], with whom I was forced to be in close contact, he would torture me to death—escape would be impossible."

Before we turn to other stories for corroborative evidence or refutation, notice that the reaction of the hero to the (presumably sexy) women of the harem was not disgust but a tormenting conflict between sexual desire and "complete inability to do anything about it." Perhaps the attitude of disgust (which Morris consciously felt, for example, about prostitutes) was a cover for a more terrifying unconscious feeling of impotence, a fear of being castrated if he should make a move toward *any* woman (for, in Ahab's world, all the women belonged to the powerful father-figure and were thus taboo), or a feeling of already having been castrated. Indeed, Morris was impotent on his first visit with Henry to the brothel. Too much, however, must not be made of this as corroborative evidence for the deep and complicated interpretation being developed here, since for many reasons boys quite commonly react with both impotence and disgust on a first encounter with prostitutes.

Picture 8 (Figure 37-2), which virtually guarantees a story with sexual content, is the one that Morris made most remote, placing it in the Yucatan and verbalizing a feeling that the people were entirely alien ("faces are so different"). The embarrassed, almost euphemistic tone and the lack of any direct reference to sex are in striking contrast to the crudity and Anglo-Saxon explicitness of story 16, told when he was urged to let himself go. Moreover, in story 8 Morris spoke about love, the love of a man for a "very charming girl." Though the lovers had their baby taken away and incurred the wrath of all the parental figures for their explicitly taboo relationship, their punishment was to be banished and "never heard of again." The contrast of attitudes expressed in these two stories is an ancient one in Western culture and a familiar one in this case history: sacred love versus profane sex, the madonna versus the prostitute. In the dream about Ethel Merman (Chapter 36, page 684), as in this story, sacred love led to consequences Morris experienced as unpleasant, but not to any of the agonizing fates imagined in story 16.

The other stories mentioned above contain bits of corroborative evidence. In picture 5 (10 in the present numeration), typically seen as an embracing, mature couple, Morris saw a mother and a son with whom he identified. Notice that he did not refer explicitly to an embrace or to any feelings; it would have been helpful if the examiner had asked what he meant by saying "she's let herself go." Morris did mention the mother's devotion and all that she had done and would do for the son. Again, he could conceive of a tender relationship with a woman, but only a maternal (tabooed) one, and his conception primarily emphasized getting, not giving.

This picture is the only one in which Morris misperceived the sexes, but he got them both wrong, seeing the upper, comforting (male) figure as the mother and the soft, feminine, lower figure as the boy, whom he took to be much like himself at age 15 or 16. This misperception is a formal aspect of the test that strongly suggests a confusion in Morris' sense of sexual identity. That inference is quite consistent with his feeling of having been castrated in some sense, which was inferred from story 16.

In story 10, the hero is said to have sought to learn the Arabs' culture by "eating their food, living with their women" (note the close relation of these two ideas). Morris tossed off this remark in a casual, man-of-the-world tone, as if for him sex was a gratification to be taken as lightly as a good meal. Yet at the end of the story, we see that this same hero comes to a very bad end: For unexplained, mysterious reasons, he loses his mind and dies under the delusion that he is being choked by "the old man"—another unmistakable father figure. In Morris' story, the Old Man of the Sea (Morris was correct in so identifying him, for the picture *was* an illustration for *Sinbad the Sailor*) becomes a symbol of the conscience; the religious metaphor (the cross) strengthens this interpretation. Psychoanalysis teaches us that the main constituent of the conscience is an image of the punishing father and that this superego is the source of self-punishment, the burden of guilt, and the inability to enjoy worldly success. Perhaps the unconscious message here is: "If I gratify my desires with other men's food and women and if I pry into secret cavelike places, that bad, punitive father will eventually kill me, even if he is far away or dead, for I carry him around inside me."

Story 14 is not obviously homosexual, but one boy has an orgasm while performing a sexual act in the presence of his roommate, who has him in a hypnotic state, which is conceived largely in terms of dominance and submission. This is about as thin a disguise for a homosexual fantasy as one could hope to find. The story is further notable for its curiously illogical quality; it remains unexplained why Bill started acting out a sexual impulse after having been told only to take some of his roommate's money. Morris apparently felt a need to explain this non sequitur by the reference to an allegedly true story, but that did not succeed in making his own story plausible. It is as if the sexual fantasy stirred up by the dominance-submission relationship clearly stated in the picture had to break through, following an associative link that makes sense only in terms of unconscious (anal) symbolism.

Morris managed to put story 21, which does contain an explicit homosexual reference, at some distance from himself by describing a relationship between two women. Note that, as in story 14, there is a close relationship between stealing and homosexuality; and again he had to push the theme away from himself by parenthetically noting, "It's coming from a story." Interestingly enough, guilt seems connected with heterosexual activity (disgust or drastic punishment), but not with homosexuality; the initiators of the latter relationship in both stories come through unscathed, and only the partner gets hurt.

Summary of additional TAT interpretations. Limitations of space make it impossible to continue to present the process of interpretation in this much detail. The interpretive summary that follows draws on all the stories (not just the ones quoted above) and uses their formal aspects and the subject's behavior during the test as well as thematic content, which has been heavily emphasized up to this point. This summary also continues to make frequent use of the historical data from Chapter 36.

It seems that Morris as a little boy may have been confused about the sexual identity of his parents and at times may have conceived of his mother as the one who wore the pants. He may also have been sexually attracted to his father and frightened by closeness to him. His parents conveyed to him a strong incest taboo and castration anxiety, not necessarily by overt threats but more likely by their own emotional attitudes. As a result (and, of course, because of his father's absence), he lacked a strong sense of masculine identity at a time in adolescence when he was overweight and was far outstripped by his older classmates in physical, athletic manifestations of virility. The blow to his self-esteem was so great that at age 26 he had not yet gained an inner sense of being an adult, competent man, but unconsciously doubted his capacity to cope successfully with life's demands. Heterosexuality was altogether too frightening; but he was quite ambivalent about homosexuality too, for that threatened to undermine his feeling of manliness.

The unconscious picture of Morris' father that emerges from the TAT stories is a split image of a remote, terrifying castrator and a lovable, harmless man who, however, could not inspire respect. Perhaps quite early in

Morris' life Mr. Brown was impatient and punitive with the demanding, poorly controlled infant, and at a later stage he seemed more appealing but fumbling and ineffectual.

An equal degree of ambivalence, or simultaneous positive and negative feelings, about his mother may be inferred from Morris' stories. A rejecting conscious attitude of impatience with her covered a deeper feeling of dependence and respect for her strength and competence. He saw her as having considerable influence on his father and as having done a great deal for himself; she was someone whose strength and generosity he could rely on, without having to give much love in return.

Lacking a strong sense of identity and inwardly confused and insecure because of an identification with both his father and his mother, neither of which was integrated with his conscious picture of himself, Morris did not have a firm inner base of operations for self-control.

An important sub-issue of self-control was what Morris felt to be a lack of moral sense in himself. Signs that he had not achieved a well-integrated conscience (superego) are plentiful in the TAT: On the one hand, he portrayed self-destructive behavior and severe, cruel punishments for relatively slight offenses; on the other hand, more serious crimes went unpunished in some stories. He seemed preoccupied with thoughts about crime and troubled by the feeling that he had a hidden, immoral self. It would be easy to infer from these signs that the internalized parental images that make up the core of the unconscious self-regulating agency, the superego, were too harsh and punitive to be of much help in controlling his day-to-day behavior and would operate only to make him dissatisfied and self-destructive; compare the classical pattern of the "criminal out of a sense of (unconscious) guilt" described by Freud (1916).

But this pessimistic formulation would overlook several important, common-sense facts: Morris was quite self-critical without being self-defeating in any obvious way—he was not accident prone, nor addicted, nor involved in serious crime, but was *actively striving* to gain self-control. The TAT shows us what he had to fear in himself—the temptations and dangers from his own superego if he yielded too much; the stories tell little about his everyday behavior, especially those of the second and third sessions, when he was urged to let his fantasy roam as unrealistically as he liked. When a person is in conflict, as Morris Brown was, it is not unusual for apparent contradictions to result from analyses of data about the conscious and the unconscious levels of personality. This very lack of internal consistency and integration is an important fact about Morris in 1940; neither the apparent adjustment of his manifest behavior nor the indications of strong impulses for immediate gratification with only ineffective and oversevere superego controls on the unconscious level give a complete picture, and neither level can be properly understood without the other.

The conflict of dependence versus independence looks somewhat different from the perspective of the TAT. According to his conscious picture of himself, Morris was already completely independent of parents and friends; he was an adult, on his own. In his stories, there is little evidence that he felt able to succeed unaided, even though his heroes do often lack support from others. When (as in story 5) a hero depends on a parent to do things for him, he turns out to be weak and worthless. Thus, though Morris had little confidence in his own ability to strive manfully and independently and little ambition to attain distant goals, his stories suggest a sense that he had to break away from his mother if he was ever to be a man. There are repeated themes of rebellion, revolution, and violation of the rules set by "the elders of the tribe," which are common in the TAT's of late adolescents who are trying to free themselves from the emotional hold of the family, which they feel to be infantilizing.

Morris wanted money, prestige, fame, and power; but these goals seemed impossibly remote, and at the time he took the test he was discouraged, tempted to chuck them in favor of more easily obtained immediate gratifications. Nevertheless, there were some slight signs of the beginnings of an identification with the positive and admirable aspects of his mother's personality. The stories do not suggest that he felt very close to, or dependent upon, friends, but that they were a natural part of his life.

We come now to the first question, concerning what had been going on inside Morris during his first five postcollege years. This actually requires an overall diagnostic formulation, which we will not be ready for until we have looked into the Rorschach Test and then back over all the data. Meanwhile we can examine the TAT for signs of possible psychopathology. Could it be that Morris' state of relative turmoil, inner confusion, and implicit reaching out for help (which may have motivated him to offer himself as a subject for study) was part of a decompensation ("breakdown") into a neurosis or other such condition?

In regard to his characterological diagnosis (also called ego structure and defensive style), Morris' TAT gives evidence of a primarily *compulsive* kind of organization: his attempts to infer the story from details of the picture, his frequent display of his large fund of general information, his marked ambivalence, his severe superego, and his use of isolation as a defense. Without the capacity to isolate feelings from ideas, Morris would never have been able to speak so freely about the deeply disturbing matters that occur in his stories. Indeed, he seemed relatively cut off from experiencing genuine emotions, despite the presence of superficial displays of shallow affect in his exclamations about the pictures, none of which was deeply felt.

Morris' way of handling emotions at times went beyond isolation and suggested the callous, flippant, avoidant style of persons with a character disorder. Such people have little tolerance for anxiety or inner tension; they keep themselves busy (by "acting out") rather than permit themselves any moments of introspection and self-scrutiny. Consistent with this pattern was the teasing, tantalizing role Morris tended to play during the test, using trick or puzzle endings and attempting to shock or upset the examiner by "dragging in sex by the heels, a few dead bodies" and other sadistic details. Despite his attempts to be cooperative, Morris was evasive; and running away or escaping (as a way of reacting to an unpleasant conflict) is a frequent theme in his stories.

Nevertheless, Morris' generally good contact with reality and orderly thinking, together with his ability to flaunt conflict-laden ideas without getting noticeably upset, would be very surprising characteristics in a seriously disturbed man. Despite his insecurity, he did not appear especially anxious or on the verge of a breakdown.

THE RORSCHACH PSYCHODIAGNOSTIC
INKBLOT TEST

Rorschach's test (1921) is the oldest and most widely used of projective techniques. The subject's task is to look at inkblots on 10 separate cards and say in each case everything that the blot could resemble. The examiner then conducts an inquiry in which he asks enough questions about the responses to enable him to score them in terms of location (where seen on the card), determinants (the aspect of the blot that suggested the content, such as its shape, color, or shading, or an impression of movement), and the accuracy of the forms. Even when fully scored, however, this test—like the TAT—cannot be used without expert interpretation. The responses to the blots, which may be seen in as many ways as Taylor's "shining cloud," betray the perceiver's interests (as the seventeenth-century divine surmised) and a good deal more.

Morris Brown's
Rorschach Test Protocol Two years after his initial assessment, the Rorschach Test was given to Morris by a graduate student of psychology who had had only a year or so of training and who wanted to supplement her experience with the test. She was kind enough to make the data available, even though the original case study had been finished. Because the tester was a Swiss girl whose English was somewhat imperfect, the following scored protocol, taken from her notes, is almost certainly not a verbatim transcript of all that Morris said; but it is good enough for our purpose: to illustrate the type of data this technique of assessment provides and the general procedure of interpretation. (The scoring symbols, in the left column, will be explained shortly.)

	Responses	*Inquiry*
Card I. 5″ *		
W F+ A P	1. This looks like a bat, prehistoric.	
W M+ (H)	2. Fantasia monster, hands upraised; early crude attempt at flying, tying bat wings to his body. That's about all.—1′30″ [total time]	2. Belt and clasp; hands and arms and bat wings attached. Smooth brown umbrella-silk material.

* The subject's reaction time, from presentation to first scorable response.

	Responses	Inquiry

Card II. (laughs) 10″

W MC+ H P

1. Can-can dancers playing pattycake. Peculiar kind of head-dress and red stockings . . . That's all. That's just very queer.—50″

1. Cigarette; hairdo. Fluffy petticoat business down here. Impressionistic. Gaité Parisienne satin dresses.

Card III. 5″

W MC+ H P
(FC′ tendency)

1. Two waiters bowing to each other. Each one carrying a basket of candy or something. . . . They have high heeled shoes on. The rest doesn't seem to be important.—1′5″

1. I always go back to concrete things I have seen. White wing collar, high shoes.

W M± H

2. [an additional response made during inquiry] ∨ * Aviator with goggles, upraised hands.

Card IV. 7″

W FCh+ Ad P

1. Bear skin rug.—30″

1. Fuzzy side turned back on edges.

Card V. 7″

W F+ A P

1. Same as first one. Some kind of a bat or an insect with antenna up here and leg down to the side.

D F+ Hd

2. A girl's leg minus the foot over here, her knee here.—1′35″

Card VI. 5″

D FCh+ Obj

1. The only thing I see in that is a certain Navajo Indian design and

1. Woven rug.

D FCh+ Ad P

2. bear skin underneath—that's—that's all.—1′30″

2. Peculiar skin of an animal at the top; it got woven.

Card VII. 5″

D M+ H P

1. Little boys making faces at each other.

D F± Map

2. All four of these upper bodies look

D F± Map

3. like a map of South America.

W M+ H
(FC′ tendency)

4. Two women with hairdo gadget in back looking at each other . . . Curved back chair, curving in the back. Sitting perhaps with their knees touching.—1′35″

4. Nondescript gray clothes on.

Card VIII. 5″

Ws MC(C)— H

1. Fu Manchu: Tartar with a beard and a triangular hat on with his bloody hands raised like this. A fur collar on. Some kind of chain around his neck. Looks pretty, disemboweled himself.

* The subject may turn the card any way he wishes; the position of the card when he gives a response is indicated by this ∧-sign, the point indicating the top of the blot.

D→W FM+ A P	2. > Perfect little mammal of some kind, a weasel or mountain animal jumping from one cliff to another on different ledges of rock.	
Dr→D F(C)± Hd, Obj	3. < Eurasian with fur cap, mouth wide open, short nose. An arrow has just been shot into his mouth. I don't know why I didn't think of turning them around like this.	3. (part of blue and darker center Dr).
Ds FC± At (CF tendency)	4. ∨ Vertebrae—skeleton of a woman's body; these are the 2 lungs and the vertebral column all through. —4'15"	4. pinky, fleshy mass (lungs).

Card IX. 20"

D F+ Ad	1. ∨ Elephants with their trunks together.	
D F± Pl (FC?)	2. Some trees.	
S F± At	3. In between, a skull.	
D F± Obj	4. In the center is an elephant hook. < ∧ Those same eyes I noticed the other way in the skull.—50"	
D M+ H P		5. [additional] Two old Chinamen with long fingernails looking at each other.

Card X. 10"

D FMC+ A	1. (laughs) Couple of mice holding up	1. Sort of mouse color.
D F+ Pl	2. a corn stalk.	
D F± Ats	3. Down here a section of a large intestine. < (laughs) These could be a whole bunch of medical diagrams:	3. (in area usually seen as a green worm)
D F+ Obj	4. Wishbone,	
Dr F∓ Ats (FC?)	5. Liver,	5. Doesn't look so much like a liver (side red)
Dr F∓ Ats	6. Appendix.	6. (tiny detail, outside lower end of worm)
D F± A	7. Double bodied caterpillar.	7. (green worm)
D F+ A (FM?)	8. Sheep—a ram with his horn, sitting down. ∨ That's about it. [E did not record the total time for card X.]	8. (upper green)

Morris' final comment on the test was: "It let me down completely. I thought I was not being original; annoyed me. I didn't see anything."

Scoring and Interpreting the Rorschach

The responses have been scored in the left-hand column of the protocol above according to the system worked out by Rorschach himself, as revised and extended by Rapaport (Rapaport, Gill, & Schafer, 1968). Though the scores are not necessarily the most important features of

Table 37-1 Rorschach Summary ("Psychogram")

Locations			Determinants				Content			Popular (P) Responses and Ratios	
W	8	} 9	F+	7			A	6	} 9	P	9
Ws	1		F±	7			Ad	3		(1 on each card except X)	
			F∓	2			H	7	} 10	P%	29
D	16	} 18	F−	0			Hd	2			
Ds	1		Total F	16			(H)	1			
D→W	1		FM+	2			Obj	3	(4)	Other Ratios	
Dr→D	1	} 3	M+	6	} 8			Map	2		$M:\Sigma C = 8:2.5$	
Dr	2		M±	1			At	2	} 5	F%	52/100
S	1	(3)*	M−	1			Ats	3		F+%	87
	31		FC+	(3)	} 1	(5)	Pl	2		A%	29
			FC∓	1				31		H%	32
			FC−	(1)						AT%	16
			FCh+	3						W%	29
			F(C)+	1	} 1	(2)				D%	58
			F(C)−	(1)						DR%	13
				31							

R (total number of responses) = 31

* Parenthetical numbers indicate frequency of secondary determinants. Thus, the MC(C)— on card VIII is tallied as M—:1, but also as FC—:(1) and F(C)—:(1).

KEY TO SYMBOLS

Locations

W Whole blot
D Large, common detail
Dr Rare detail
S, s White space (large or small portions)

D→W A response primarily based on one detail but extended to include the entire blot

Dr→D From a small part to all of a large, common detail

Determinants

F Form
FM Animals seen in movement
M Human movement

C Chromatic color
C' Achromatic color
Ch Chiaroscuro (gray shading)
(C) Shading in a chromatic area

Note: Form may be combined with the color or shading scores, the order of the symbols indicating which predominates in determining the response. Thus, in FC the form is definitive; in CF form is vague and the color impression strong; and in C form plays no part.

Form Level (accuracy of match between the subject's concept and the blot area he chooses)

+ Sharp, accurate match between concept and blot, easily seen by E
± Reasonably good fit with some weakness of perceptual organization (included in F+%)
∓ Poor match but with some redeeming features
− Arbitrary response with little or no convincing resemblance between concept and blot

Content

A Animal
Ad Part (detail) of an animal
H Human being
Hd Part of a person
(H) Quasihuman beings (monstrous, mythological, or the like)

Obj Object
At Bony anatomy
Ats Soft anatomy
Pl Plant

Ratios (those not explained are self-evident)

DR%   Percentage of all responses to unusual areas (including *Dr* and *S*)

AT%   Percentage of all anatomical responses (including both *At* and *Ats*)

F%   The first figure is the proportion of all responses determined by form alone; the second is the proportion of all responses in which form is predominant.

M:ΣC   This ratio of the number of M responses to the weighted total of color responses is always written thus, not as a percentage. FC responses are weighted ½, CF 1, and C 1½.

the responses, they form a conventional starting point for the interpreter; Table 37-1 summarizes the scores in what is usually called a *psychogram*.

There are 31 responses, fewer than might have been expected from Morris' very superior I.Q. and his verbal productiveness in part of the TAT. But Morris is an extrovert who does not feel particularly at home in tasks requiring imagination; for example, his final, self-critical comment about his lack of originality is similar to complaints in the TAT ("I must have a very trite brain"). Actually, the responses are an interesting mixture of the original and the banal. He is capable of such a well-observed, integrated whole response as the second one to card I and of a couple of highly original but pathological-sounding ones (card VIII, 1 and 3), yet he seems to push himself to produce, and often comes out with relatively "cheap" responses, giving a rather high proportion (about 30 percent) of interpretations that are very commonly seen, or *popular* (scored P). This mixture parallels the pattern that emerged in his TAT stories, and represents the quality of Morris' thought rather well. He certainly has the common touch, which is probably more important for his work than creative originality. And the accuracy of his form perception ($F+\%$ of 87) implies good contact with reality.

Location. The first letter in the string of symbols that constitutes the full score of a response (W, D, *Dr*, and so on) indicates where Morris saw whatever he reported. On the first four cards, he responded only to the whole blot (W), which is not uncommon for people of his intelligence who are not highly productive; when he got the idea that he could use the large, easily segregated details (D), he responded mostly to them, and occasionally to rare details (*Dr*) or parts of the white space (S). The distribution of his location scores altogether is not remarkable, being roughly within average expectations; perhaps the 13 percent of all rare details he reacted to is enough above the average expectation (about 5 to 10 percent) for a record of this size to lend weak support to the TAT indication of a basically compulsive defensive style. This interpretation is based on statistical inference as well as on theoretical expectations: Part of the compulsive style is meticulousness, a concern for fine points. Although that quality is not obviously characteristic of Morris, it is present to a noticeable degree if one looks for it; recall his tendency to pick out details of the TAT pictures and infer story content from them, as in his first story, and his detailed expense accounts (Chapter 36, page 681).

Determinants. The second group of letters in the full scores represent the determinants. Half the responses were determined by form (*F*) alone, which is somewhat below the average; on the other hand, there was not a single response in which form or shape was not the primary determinant. Otherwise put, Morris described only things that have definitive shapes, instead of including vaguely shaped content like clouds or blood spots, or offering amorphous responses like "sky" or "springtime," in which color or some attribute of the blots other than shape sets off the association.

According to the tradition of Rorschach interpretation, Morris' pattern suggests tight control under an appearance of easy responsiveness. Again, we know this to be characteristic of him: Morris was much concerned about self-control and the task of striving for it, despite a superficial appearance of easygoing, ready responsivity. Such an effort for control is another Rorschach indicator of a compulsive ego structure, and his large number of human-movement (*M*) responses supports the inference. When Morris responded, with moderate frequency, to the color of the blots, it was only in a controlled way; the color impression was subordinated to and controlled within the framework of a definitive form (*FC*). This suggests a socially adaptable, compliant, and cooperative person; again, to us, for what we know of Morris supports the traditional interpretation. The fact that two of his five *FC* responses were inaccurately seen is consistent with the occasionally forced quality of his social adaptation.

Content. The third column of symbols consists of abbreviations for content, the general class of things seen. The most frequent content category in Morris' responses is the human (*H*, *Hd*, and (*H*) for the monster on card I); a third of his responses are of this kind. The implication here is congruent with his fairly high score on the Social value (Allport-Vernon): He is strongly interested in people. Other frequent scores are for animals (the percentage of *A* is 29, about average) and for anatomy (16 percent or more—some would include two extra scores on card VIII). The rather high *AT* percentage suggests an underlying bodily concern, which is given particular point by the content of three responses that did not happen to be scored either *At* or *Ats* (hard or soft anatomy)—the "girl's leg minus the foot" on card V, a classical symbol of castration anxiety, and the two gory images of deadly wounds to human beings on card VIII, the first of them self-inflicted.

Sequence analysis. Let us consider the series of responses to card VIII in a little more detail and sequentially, a technique of interpretation called *sequence analysis.* Card VIII presents the first blot to be made up entirely of colored inks; it therefore produces a strong visual impact. The prevailing assumption is that people tend to react to such a vivid, "compelling" stimulus in the same way they cope with the inner impact of impulses and affects. Morris was not slowed up; his excellent intellect immediately supplied him with a highly original, strong, though quite inaccurate, integration of the disparate parts of the blot. Fu Manchu, a fictional character in a series of novels, represents a literary association that has a distinctly lower-middle-class flavor and thus reflects the intellectual limitations of Morris' precollege milieu. This rather frightening, sinister figure with upraised bloody hands was controlled, not realistically (the form level is minus), but in a way familiar to us from Morris' TAT—by being put at a great distance in terms of geographic location, ethnic identity, and level of reality.

Then an even more pathological-sounding defensive attempt ensued: Morris saw the sinister figure as just having disemboweled himself. This sequence is reminiscent of his own development from an aggressive, pugnacious child to a timid older boy who turned his aggression against himself. The inappropriate attempt to laugh it off ("Looks pretty") has the same quality as his laughter in story 16 of the TAT, where the hero was also the victim of bodily mutilation; again, this reaction suggests a defense that protects Morris from fully experiencing his own affects.

Despite his poor control of this masochistic response, Morris was able to make a quick recovery and give a good popular response, which he obviously enjoyed. Immediately afterward, he returned to the realm of pathological fantasy, using again the defense that made the person he visualized— a Eurasian with an arrow shot into his mouth—quite remote from himself. This third response, like the first one, is strikingly original; but it is better justified by the form of the blot, and it was handled more calmly. It suggests an underlying homosexual preoccupation as well as the same self-directed aggression; this interpretation is somewhat supported by the final response, a safely intellectualized and disguised image of aggression turned against a woman. There is, of course, nothing about lungs or vertebrae to indicate sex, yet he said that they were part of a woman's body. (Perhaps it is relevant to note here that the examiner was a very attractive young woman.)

Another point that is well to keep in mind, particularly with reference to responses 1 and 3, is that the Rorschach was given just before Morris was inducted into the armed services, at a time when America was involved in a bloody war that was precipitated by an attack by an oriental power. The thoughts of young men of draft age at that time often dwelt on the possibility of severe bodily injury.

An Overview of the Rorschach

Some of the main ways a Rorschach is interpreted have been exemplified above. Clearly, when the responses are treated as if they were comparable to dream symbols, as was just illustrated, speculation may soar. So long as it is regarded as a source of hypotheses to be checked against other data, such speculation can be useful to an assessor of personality. He must guard, however, against a tendency to become enchanted with his own ingenuity and to treat such shaky extrapolations as true findings.

On the whole, the Rorschach furnished many bits of evidence corroborating points inferred from the TAT. Most of what it rather directly suggests is confirmed by the case history and the other tests; but it adds little that is new, at least on the issues of major interest. What shows up more clearly here than in the TAT is the somewhat sloppy cognitive style that limited Morris' intellectual achievements: a quality of slipperiness, a slight fluidity, and an occasional tendency for ideas to interpenetrate (for example, the two responses to card VI—or is it just one?), all of which made it difficult to pin him down precisely. From the perspective of the test alone it is difficult to evaluate this quality of cognitive style properly, but it contributes to the impression given by many of the responses, when closely examined, that the subject was to some extent seriously disturbed.

FREE ASSOCIATION

The therapeutic and investigative technique of free association, developed by Sigmund Freud, can be a valuable form of assessment, though it is rarely used outside the context of professional psychoanalytic treatment. With some stretching, it may be classified with projective techniques because many of the interpretive principles and methods used in the analysis of free associations, TAT stories, and Rorschach responses are the same. The procedure is deceptively simple. The subject is asked to stretch out on a couch in a softly lighted room; the examiner sits out of his line of sight. The instructions to the subject are to let his thoughts move freely and to say everything that comes to mind, without censoring it on any grounds.

Many psychoanalysts use the first session of psychoanalytic treatment for purposes of additional diagnostic assessment (beyond the appraisal of the patient that always precedes the start of treatment).They rightly object to the use of free association by psychologists who have not been trained in psychoanalysis, because it may release powerful emotional reactions with which the examiner is unprepared to deal as a therapist may. In the case of Morris Brown, the investigators' very ignorance encouraged them to try it; and they were fortunate in that Morris was able to go through two such sessions of approximately an hour each without becoming particularly upset and without the development of unmanageable emotional reactions to themselves.

Examples of Data
and Interpretation
The data (which were written down in longhand notes as faithfully as possible) are not presented here in full; but certain passages can provide corroboration of hypotheses drawn from the TAT stories.

In the first session, Morris moved from thinking about the process of free association to the idea of being able to read minds: "It would be an awful power, wouldn't want anyone to have that power over me. (pause) Something in the sex business is sort of funny." He related a conversation he had had with a busboy at a bar, about (hetero-) sex, adding two thoughts about him:

> 1. Raise his sights a little, get him a good job; 2. If I wanted to make a pass at him I could—comes up when I've had about 5 drinks—never done anything about it, never would. Because if I had inclinations I think I sometimes have on that stuff I wouldn't hesitate. Conscience stirring within you— two weekends ago, up at the cabin—it would have been so damn nice to have Alison there. When I get it built I've got to get a woman for it: after finishing the cage, get a bird for it. Do you ever do any sailing?

He then spoke about a recent sailing trip: "Don't know why I got so seasick. I came close to chucking up" (laughs).

Notice here that the theme of power and domination makes him think of sex and a homosexual impulse he has been restraining. It is closely related to a nurturant, parental kind of concern for a younger man. Then his conscience objects and he thinks (presumably as he knows he should) of Alison, the focus of his distant, romantic ("sacred") love fantasies, but he comes back to the theme of domination in the metaphor about the bird and the cage. The next thought concerns a physical manifestation of disgust. (Compare this sequence with the similar one in TAT story 22.)

A similar sequence of themes came out toward the end of the same session:

> Morris first spoke of a man he knows: "just got married—birth control—cesspool," whereupon he sat up and said loudly, "Boy, if you tie those up you're a hot one!" After a pause, he mentioned "sugar" and some other kinds of food, then: "playing tag at the 'Y' pool. Jim, hot shower Saturday night. Swimming practice. George, poor guy, what a damn fool he was when he married."

The close association of heterosexuality with the disgusting image of a cesspool (perhaps mediated by the "messiness" of birth control) was too obvious for Morris himself to miss, but he reacted as if it were only a surprising concatenation of unrelated ideas. An oral wish then obtruded itself, followed by an indirect (perhaps sublimated) homosexual thought about one of his favorite activities, where he sees many men in the nude. The reversion of thought to marriage was followed once again by a strongly rejective sentiment.

In the second free-association hour, Morris' thoughts were preoccupied with two seemingly unrelated topics—money and sex (but see TAT story 14); he also mentioned travel several times. On this occasion, there was much less evidence of homosexual desires; the relations with men he mentioned were competitive and unsuccessful. As in the second TAT session, he had a headache. He seemed to feel under considerable pressure about his debts (a theme that had appeared in the earlier hour) and cast about for a source of funds:

> "So much money—Red Cross—no. Blood transfusion—no, last one hit me. Home." A moment later, "where you gonna get any money this time of year. I don't know. Communism—amputation." After more stewing about possible securities sales: "That's the trouble—I sit around and think about the big clients I could get instead of getting out and working my ass off."

Although the themes of money and of girls who might be possible sexual objects wove in and out throughout this session, it is hard to see just how they were connected in his mind; perhaps it was through the common theme of *getting* something. The experience of being pressured by external demands on him for money may have stirred up aggressive feelings, which were then turned against himself (the headache and the castrative theme of an amputation), because he was feeling a lack of self-confidence and competence. He was struggling with a conflict between the knowledge that he should force himself to go after some big deals and the frequently expressed wish to travel—to escape into irresponsibility.

A COMMENT ON THE PROJECTIVE ASSESSMENT OF MORRIS BROWN

The case of Morris Brown is an excellent example of what is at once a characteristic strength and weakness of projective techniques: They tend to highlight pathological trends. At times, that is a useful property, particularly when an attempt is made to diagnose a person who is very guarded but is suspected on other grounds of being seriously maladjusted. At other times, however, this property can lead to serious overestimation of the degree to which a person is disturbed, especially if diagnosis is based entirely on projective tests analyzed without the benefit of a clinical history.

In this instance, the facts as they could be learned through extended and fairly intimate conversation and through objective tests were deliberately presented before the projective techniques. Treated in this order, these techniques can contribute a useful increment of hypotheses, and other knowledge can act as a protection against jumping to conclusions that the subject must have been very "sick" at the time.

In the presentations of the objective tests used with Morris Brown, quantitative data were given on the reliability and validity of their scores, but no such figures appear in the sections on projective techniques. One reason is that the scores themselves play a much less prominent role in the latter; another reason is that both scores and qualitative data lend themselves to a great range of interpretations. Properly speaking, each interpretive principle or inferential hypothesis used to interpret the TAT and the Rorschach should be the subject of a validation study, but obviously such research would be difficult (see, however, Lindzey, 1952). Without some sort of time machine we cannot get direct observations to verify some of the developmental hypotheses, and it is virtually impossible to get direct data for the many interpretations that deal with unconscious configurations. The best we can usually do is to look for the convergence of independent sources of data, as in the parallels between projective test data and free associations that have just been pointed out. Seeking such convergences is the first step in the *synthesis* of a case history, to which the next chapter is devoted.

He . . . overhauled his room, wrote out resolutions, mar-
shalled his books up and down their shelves, pored upon all kinds
of price lists . . . tried to build a breakwater of order and ele-
gance against the sordid tide of life without him and to dam up,
by rules of conduct and active interests and new filial relations,
the powerful recurrence of the tides within him.

JAMES JOYCE. A Portrait of the Artist as a Young Man

CHAPTER 38
THE SYNTHESIS OF DIVERSE DATA ON PERSONALITY

N o matter how large a file of tests, personal documents, interviews, and what-not is compiled on a person, and no matter how well the sources agree, the data do not pull themselves together. To synthesize such materials is something of an art, and doubtless always will be.

How Data on Personality
Are Synthesized

The basic procedure is to look for agreements and disagreements on the level of primary inferences from the various individual procedures. When agreement, or convergence, emerges, our confidence in the validity of the indicators increases. When there are seeming contradictions, we may first examine the validity of the conflicting indicators with a skeptical but open mind; occasionally we will simply discover that one is right and the other wrong. More usually, both will be partly right, but they may be operating under the confusing influence of some condition that we had not paid enough attention to before. Or other kinds of hypotheses may suggest ways to reconcile both points of view in a larger synthesis.

As we start our synthesis, we enter the realm of *secondary inference*. We are no longer reasoning directly from test scores or the subject's statements but from our previously (although tentatively) established primary inferences about his personality traits. The process of fitting the pieces together shows us gaps to be filled by going back to the raw data or by making changes in some of the more dubious primary inferences, so that they fit the emerging schema. If the synthesis is well done, a very high proportion of the primary inferences can be used directly or can be fitted in, sometimes in surprising ways.

Of course, it takes more than cleverness to develop a schema of secondary inferences: The process must be guided by a theory of personality. Of currently available theories, psychoanalysis is the richest with relevant principles and generalizations; it is the theory that will be drawn on most heavily in this chapter.

What follows is a synthesis of the case of Morris Brown, in which we may be able to see how the data and inferences developed to this point from both objective and subjective procedures can be put together. Although many of the formulations will be more or less factual, and although others will come from the confluence of several streams of evidence, this sketch is still largely constructed of hypotheses. Some of the most important ones, in terms of their function of bringing together several disparate kinds of facts about Morris and making common sense of them, will be plausible speculative constructions for which there is no *direct* evidence. But that is the nature of personality assessment: At best, it is a matter of obtaining a closer approximation to a receding, never securely attained truth.

An Integrative Summary
of the Case of Morris Brown at Age 26

THE RAW MATERIALS

**Physique
and Constitution**   One of Morris' great assets is his tough, solid, manly, and well-coordinated body. Morris' constitutional endowment seems to include natural athletic ability as well as sheer strength and sturdiness, and great energy and endurance. He was thus automatically protected from many of the troubles that beset boys with weaker frames. He appears to have been naturally resistant to most diseases and rugged enough in bone to have gone through a good deal of rough and tumble without incapacitating accidents. In general, he was endowed with natural competence in bodily matters, and as he was neither strikingly handsome nor ugly, he was spared the problems that accompany a very deviant physical appearance.

Abilities   In regard to the most important ability, general intelligence, Morris Brown was also well endowed: His I.Q. of about 145 easily surpasses that of 99 people out of every hundred in the general population. This intellectual gift supplemented his outstanding physical abilities as a guarantee of competence; it assured him educational and vocational success, unless he were seriously crippled in some other way.

Morris had no other obvious and outstanding abilities or talents, nor was he notably lacking in any special ability that might have played a role in his general adaptation.

Temperament   Temperament is considered to be a person's largely innate endowment of emotional and energetic characteristics. It is difficult to summarize because just what personal qualities constitute this endowment has not yet been determined. Nevertheless, Sheldonian analysis and some of the questionnaires agree in finding the cycloid (or cyclothymic) characteristics typically associated with his kind of physique: He tended to be outgoing rather than withdrawn, extroverted rather than introverted, and in general exuberant, energetic, and buoyant, but he also suffered periods of mild depression. His friendliness, readily available warmth, and emotional display, though they seemed shallow, were all cyclothymic qualities. Morris' temperamental (as well as constitutional) qualities seem definitely masculine. Certainly his mother's description of his stubbornly persistent, aggressive, and generally rambunctious behavior in his preschool years is that of a very boyish little boy.

Cultural Tradition   The raw materials for the formation of a personality that are contributed from cultural sources are among the most elusive to a person working within the same culture. We know, however, that Mrs. Brown had a sense of identity with "a fine old family," that she treasured certain ideals of gentility, *noblesse oblige*, integrity, and altruism. It is clear that she struggled to maintain these ideals and to prevent Morris from slipping in the class hierarchy as he grew up in a deteriorating neighborhood. That he was a WASP Yankee was an important fact about Morris in the same kind of quiet, almost negative sense as was his freedom from serious medical problems: For a boy growing up in a small city in eastern America, it was the least troublesome kind of ethnic and cultural identity to have.

Mrs. Brown's marginal position and her fight against downward mobility, however, inevitably contributed to a conflict between the boy and his mother and caused her to try constantly to block his natural social impulses, which were to play with and identify himself with the children in the neighborhood. Moreover, in grade school Morris' self-esteem probably suffered more than it was enhanced because of his cultural identity: His Polish-

American classmates rejected him for belonging to a group considered socially "superior" to them.

Family Members   It would be ideal to have direct information about Mr. and Mrs. Brown instead of having to rely on what can be pieced together from their son, who certainly could not be disinterested or impartial. Fortunately, the very circumstances of their lives tend to confirm most of what Morris said directly or indirectly about their personalities.

The major facts about the father were that he was so unreliably present for Morris' first eight, crucially formative, years, and that he thereafter deserted the family. Information available only recently reveals that he was brilliant: He earned a Phi Beta Kappa key at a fine university and graduated later from an equally well-known Protestant seminary. Yet the elder Brown refused both a fellowship for advanced study and a congregation; he was a YMCA secretary for a number of years but tended to drift from job to job. His marriage to Morris' mother seems to have been motivated by expediency on both sides rather than by any depth of love; they needed each other for external reasons rather than for what they could give each other emotionally. The father, at least, seems never to have been deeply committed to the marriage or to his children. His image is that of a self-centered seeker after easy money and direct gratifications.

The following is a list of his father's traits that also seem to have been present in Morris at age 26:

> Enthusiastic, impatient, independent, lacked closeness to family, little capacity to give love, tended to avoid difficulties, footloose (loved travel), disliked long-term planning, self-centered, highly intelligent.

In addition, Morris was struggling to control the following tendencies, which were prominent in his father's personality:

> Impractical about money, speculative, undependable and irresponsible, unconscientious (hated routine).

Mrs. Brown was an anxious, hard-working, often tearful woman who was forced to bear heavy burdens and who must have had extraordinary inner strength to persevere and achieve as much success as she did. Despite poor health and three children to care for, one of whom (Morris) was difficult to manage, she supported the family by converting her home into a rooming house. She provided private schooling for the girls, gave Morris as many cultural advantages as she could to afford him contact with his peers of a class higher than that in the neighborhood, put him and the younger of his two sisters through colleges with the highest prestige, and in general kept up appearances despite many rebuffs to her self-esteem and to her feeling of being lovable. She seems to have possessed a unique mixture of masochism and strength, which may have been transmitted in subtle ways to her son.

The following traits, clearly discernible in the Morris Brown of 1940, he shared with his mother:

Concern about money, concern about appearances (present in Morris' projective tests though not superficially obvious), insecurity, sensitivity to rejection, anxiety about maintaining status identity (in Morris' case, about how to avoid having other people think he was Jewish).

GENETIC HYPOTHESES

If we put the elements above together, guided by what we know from the historical facts in Chapter 36 and the insights afforded by the interpretation of clinical data such as the TAT, it becomes possible to construct some plausible theories about what caused Morris to develop as he did. For lack of adequate data, it will be necessary to pass much more quickly over the earliest years than psychoanalytic theory would suggest.

The Maternal Relationship   The very fact that Mrs. Brown made so many careful entries in Morris' baby books and that she kept them so long are evidence both of her compulsiveness and of her devotion. It is easy to imagine how precious the first months of nursing and of Morris' complete dependence must have been to this woman, who for years may have longed to have a baby and who probably had given up even the hope of marriage. His delay in talking suggests that this early *symbiotic* relationship (that is, one of great mutual involvement and dependence) was unusually prolonged by her slavish devotion. This hypothesis would also help account for his pattern of resisting his mother and trying to push her away, which began early and was still strong at age 26.

Yet by satisfying his wants so completely in the first period of life, Morris' mother laid the foundation for his sense of basic trust (Erikson, 1959), his feeling that the world is ultimately a pretty good place and likely to yield satisfactions. We can never know how much of Morris' optimism and energy is attributable to this good start in the oral phase and how much is genetically determined, but surely these qualities go back very far. The history also shows us that from the beginning he had strong oral needs; apparently the basic mode of *getting* was strongly reinforced and pervaded much of Morris' subsequent life.

At a fairly early age, Morris began to have tantrums. A small child's tantrums are an exhausting ordeal for him as well as for his mother. In light of this fact, Mrs. Brown unwittingly failed Morris by her inability to cope with his tantrums and to give him an external model of control and calmness, from which he in turn could borrow strength. His tantrums and their consequences probably laid a foundation for Morris' fear of his own anger and for his inability to let himself go in later childhood when he could have gained self-respect by becoming the rugged scrapper he was otherwise cut out to be. These hypothetical constructions also help us to understand better the projective test indications of a savage, primitive superego and unconscious masochistic fantasies in a man of 26 who was still struggling to complete the task of getting control over himself: If a child's tantrums are uncontrolled, the exhaustion and pain that result forcibly demonstrate that when anger is aroused it turns against oneself.

The Paternal
Relationship

Mrs. Brown's intuitive feeling that her husband should have been more active in controlling Morris may have been correct. As Morris grew older and needed to develop more of a sense of what it was to be a male person, his father was simply not there enough to set the example of strong masterfulness that our culture calls for a man to aspire to.

According to Morris' conscious recollections, his father was easygoing, companionable, certainly not punitive. And yet his projective test productions consistently present images of frightful, remote, overwhelmingly evil father figures, which one would expect to be the residue of terrifying experiences of sudden, arbitrary, and severe punishment in early childhood. If we consider what we know about the father—his self-indulgence and disinclination to accept the more distasteful aspects of familial responsibility— it is easy to understand how he must have resisted being the awesome authority figure who meted out just punishment for the day's sins when he arrived home each night. But is it not also probable that such a man would have had little patience with a demanding, noisy, highly active, and headstrong little boy during the second and third years, when Morris had less inner control and a more effective motor apparatus for causing trouble than most boys his age? Although Morris himself did not remember such experiences, the unempathic Mr. Brown may well have lost his temper easily, doling out unpredictable cuffs and slaps, which might have hurt all the more coming from a father who was seldom around.

Undoubtedly, one of the most important events in Morris' life was being abandoned by his father. It must have been a major blow to his developing a feeling that he could be loved, a traumatic experience that was rekindled with every subsequent rejection by anyone he cared about. Each such episode thus became an occasion of poignant grief. To take the place of a man about whom he had mostly fond conscious memories, he started turning to father substitutes: the Sunday school teacher who was his hero, the boys (generally older than himself during adolescence) on whom he had crushes, and finally, at about the time of the assessment in 1940, a Catholic priest with whom he had many long talks. (Curiously, though he mentioned a recently developed strong interest in Catholicism, he did not at that time tell the investigators about this "father.") The urge to travel may have been in part an identification with his father and in part an effort to find him (which he actually succeeded in doing on one occasion). It is worth mentioning in passing that he had no living grandfathers, and none of his several uncles assumed a supportive paternal role that might have substituted for the loss of his father.

Sexual Behavior During the preschool years, Morris was in a dangerous situation: He was the dominant member in a household with three females, where the father's presence was unpredictable and infrequent. Proper as she was, Mrs. Brown must have transmitted the incest taboo clearly enough, discouraging too intrusive or bodily a closeness but at the same time inevitably trying in subtle ways to make her son stand in the place of his father. Ideally Morris would have given her great quantities of devoted but quite desexualized affection to help fill the void left by her uninterested husband. Instead, it seems likely that he fought off her enveloping tenderness and showed some openly sexual interest in her and in his sisters.

We do not know the timing of Morris' two operations, for tonsils and adenoids, but if either of them happened to come at a time of awakened sexual intrusiveness, which is normal in little boys, it might very well have been the sort of real event that can leave the lasting scar of castration anxiety. (See Part II, pp. 276–83.)

From what we know of it, Morris' sexual behavior in childhood seems to have been normal, with enough emphasis on peeping to suggest that his sexual curiosity was quite active. Psychoanalysts generally find that when people easily recall having seen their parents in the act of intercourse during childhood, as Morris did at age 8, the memory is a screen for an earlier, repressed, and more traumatic instance of this *primal scene*. The feeling of not understanding what was going on, attached to the conscious memory, may be a displaced and toned-down version of a more intense bewilderment and anxiety from an earlier exposure. Memories of such episodes, according to psychoanalytic clinical observations, may often cause the later behavior of mutual display. In addition, the child typically interprets the memories in sado-masochistic terms; that is, he believes that the parents are hurting each other in this strange act. This interpretation can cause considerable fear of heterosexual intercourse and of the intimacies leading up to it.

From these speculative inferences, it is possible to formulate the following theory about the development of sexual patterns in Morris. His native endowment seems to have been essentially masculine; his lack of effeminate prettiness or weakness of frame and his temperamentally active and hardy bent for such manly activities as sports may have saved him from becoming a confirmed, overt homosexual. Yet there are strongly feminine elements in his make-up, derived from identification with his mother in the absence of his father. At the same time, Morris became fearful of making sexual approaches to girls because of the combination of fearing his father's unpredictable wrath, learning that the women of the family were all sexually taboo (despite the seductiveness implied in his mother's need for him and in his sisters' playing doctor with him), and developing a deep anxiety about bodily mutilation that unconsciously probably meant castration.

Although it is not known at what point Morris learned to control his temper, it was not a secure control that enabled him to use aggression in the service of manliness. In fact, his struggle to control his anger seems to have ended in his turning it against himself. One result was probably a generalization to heterosexual impulses of the anxiety Morris felt about hostile impulses. The lack of easy opportunities to be with eligible girls and the availability of boys helped to initiate his pleasurable sexual activity with persons who were reassuringly like himself in having penises.

During childhood Morris' superior intelligence undid the advantage his superior physique might have given him, pushing him ahead so that for a time he was no match for his classmates either physically or socially. His inferiority and anxiety, both bodily and social, caused him uncharacteristically (though temporarily) to become a sissy and to withdraw socially at around the time of his father's final departure. This pattern, and the fact that he had been somewhat isolated from other children, prevented him from developing social skills.

Not to paint too black a picture, we should keep in mind that Morris' feeling of worth and competence must have been bolstered by the recognition he no doubt received for being a good student most of the time. And with adolescence, his bodily prowess began to assert itself, so that he was able to attain even more self-respect and esteem from others through his outstanding performance in sports. He still had a strong need for autonomy, which helped him fight back against feelings of desertion by going places quite on his own.

MORRIS BROWN'S PERSONALITY PATTERN
(AS OF 1940–41)

Defensive Organization
("Ego Structure")

Morris' major defenses are a variant form of obsessive-compulsive reactions. His main goal was self-control; and he was beginning to attain it relatively late, using compulsive, ritualistic devices to aid himself, just as Joyce's hero did in *A Portrait of the Artist as a Young Man*. Because of his ability to isolate feelings from ideas, Morris was able to talk easily about very disturbing matters. His unusual defense against homosexuality also relied on isolation: He knew what homosexuality was, he knew its socially condemned status, and he knew what kinds of acts he had performed with men; but somehow he was able to keep these pieces of knowledge rather confusedly unintegrated, so that he never looked squarely at the total pattern and hence never saw himself as a homosexual. His emphases on reason and rationality and on using his good mind to collect information were parts of an intellectualizing and rationalizing defense.

There were, as we have seen, paradoxes and inconsistencies in his use of these defenses. Certainly they were not developed to a high degree of elaboration: He was not erudite, ruminative, rigid, or especially orderly. The compulsive's concern with time and his proclivity for delaying gratification did not fit in with Morris' impatience for quick action in sexual contacts and his wish to get rich quick by speculation. Moreover, his style of intellectualizing was somewhat roughhewn, not what one would have expected of an average Ivy League graduate; he would have liked to seem an urbane intellectual sophisticate and occasionally made some efforts in this direction. These intellectualizing aspects of the compulsive ego structure had developed late in Morris, for he had not grown up in a home that especially valued ideas, conceptual and verbal precision, and subtle distinctions. As a result there was some strain and inappropriateness in his efforts to be *au courant* culturally.

Part of the reason for the atypical organization of his compulsive defenses was the early development of another, somewhat contradictory, set, based on his physical attributes rather than on his mental prowess. In adolescence, Morris found that he could escape anxiety and boredom through action, especially adventurous activity that took him into the teeth of the dangers he feared. He had a capacity for introspection but tended to turn away from it, to rely on his extroverted interest in the actual world of things and activities to take him out of himself. The result was a mixture of acting out, counterphobic defense (mastering anxiety by taking pleasure in what had been feared), evasion, and avoidance, which together tend to eliminate the subtleties and depths of emotional experience in favor of immediate excitement. His self-centeredness, his tendency to be flippant or inappropriately jocular in the face of unpleasant feelings like sadness, and his inclination to exploit others while giving little in return, all fitted in with the acting-out defenses to suggest the personality pattern of someone with a narcissistic character disorder. Yet none of these trends were very strongly developed or rigidly applied.

Thus, two antithetical defensive organizations were present in Morris, alternating in prominence. The second, narcissistic pattern stressed quick gratification of rather selfish impulses (getting something for nothing), cynicism about moral values, an avoidance of anxiety, and evasion of responsibility. The first pattern, which seemed to be in the ascendant, included a conscientious effort at self-improvement and hard work, an attempt to prevent anxiety by organizing his life, an effort to work out and live up to a rational moral code of his own, and a seeking of responsibility. It is tempting, though perhaps oversimple, to connect the compulsive pattern to his identification with his mother, the narcissistic to his paternal identification.

Finally, some signs of a cyclothymic ego structure are evident—in his temperament, in his rather strong defense of denial, and in his tendency to turn aggression against himself. The latter defense did at times produce some depressive symptoms, but his tendency to deny depressed affect produced a generally prevalent *hypomanic* pattern (manic-like cheerfulness, energy, and activity, but within normal limits).

Organization of Thought and Speech

Though covered to some extent in the preceding section, Morris' cognitive style has some further features. He gave no sign of obsessional thinking; his thoughts tended toward the practical rather than toward highly abstract concepts. His thinking was for the most part orderly; but under the pressure of anxiety or conflict it often became somewhat fluid and elusive, and his use of words could become mildly confused and momentarily incoherent (apparently as part of a defensive maneuver to keep himself from confronting the source of his anxiety). He could at such times become aware of surprisingly gory, unrealistic ideas derived from unconscious sado-masochistic fantasies, taking rather gleeful pleasure in shocking others by means of them.

His style of talking was casual and informal to the point of occasional coarseness and poor taste; his conversation included a heavy admixture of slang and a light peppering of words from the upper reaches of a superior vocabulary. He did not use the latter in a pretentious way; because he knew them more from his reading than from conversation, such words not infrequently came out haltingly and mispronounced. Brown's speech tended to be rapid, often trailing off into swallowed or dangling phrases, spoken in a light baritone voice of mellow, rather than deeply resonant, timbre. But he had a ready flow of ideas and words, so that he could be persuasive with another person and effective as a public speaker. He was a pleasant if not a remarkable conversationalist.

Affects and Impulses

Morris readily displayed cheer and extroverted friendliness. He could—as his work required—easily meet people and impress them as "a good guy," normal and easygoing. He was, however, unwilling to take the risk of a full emotional investment in a close relationship. The fact that obligingness was a deliberate policy with him gave his adaptability a forced quality. For the most part he expressed appropriate feelings in predictable ways, while giving the impression of a somewhat limited emotional range. He would occasionally act out impulses, yet on the whole kept himself under rather tight control.

Motives

Morris had not yet made a number of important choices as far as his principal conscious and unconscious goals were concerned—another indication that he was in a transitional phase of development. Much as he strove to please and to be liked by everyone, he seemed to be leaning toward recognition, power, and money as substitutes for love. Voyeuristic conflicts and fixations in childhood sometimes stimulate an adult drive for learning and discovery; sometimes, however, they stimulate more of a concern about appearances, prestige, and status in the eyes of others—the outcome in Morris' case. Yet, paradoxically, his interest in recognition and acquisition did not result in a strong need for achievement. Perhaps the lack of a family tradition along these lines—that is, his father's spotty and erratic career and his mother's contentment in maintaining the status quo rather than advancing toward a higher status (directly or vicariously through pushing her son)—accounted for Morris' never having developed the typical businessman's insatiable drive.

As he saw it, Morris' main motive was to gain control over himself—a kind of power drive turned inward. His sexual drive was, as he recognized, stunted. He had an above-average urge to travel and seek adventure and excitement, which fitted in well with his constitution (though his degree of castration anxiety probably restrained him from becoming markedly counterphobic and going in for such dangerous thrills as skiing, shooting rapids, and the like). His urge to engage in vigorous bodily activity seemed a natural outgrowth of his physique, and in the direct competition of tennis and golf he found an adaptive outlet for his generally closed-off aggressive needs. Perhaps these needs were also expressed in the form of dominance in his drive to assume positions of leadership and to exercise his organizational talent. They contrasted with his interest in music and his enjoyment of nature.

Attitudes and Values

Like the great majority of his contemporaries, Morris was not ideologically committed. Nor was he actively engaged in working out a conscious philosophy of life for himself. He had liberal attitudes on most social issues, although he was sufficiently identified with the commercial world to have fairly conservative attitudes as well (for example, he opposed increased governmental control over business). He belonged to no political party, no religion, no organized social movement of consequence. In general, the Allport-Vernon test summed up his values rather well.

Relationships to Principal Figures

On the surface, Morris was impatient with his mother and felt like pulling away from what he considered to be her wishes to control and change him. But there are other signs of considerable underlying respect and affection for her and a growing identification with her. The letter written from camp when he was an adolescent (quoted on page 681 in Chapter 36) gives evidence of more positive feeling than he would have verbalized as such; he usually thought of her consciously in terms of what he could get from her. But in his mid-20's, Morris was beginning to assume for himself her role of controlling and attempting to improve him.

By this time, he seemed to have recovered from the wound of losing his father, who receded into a shadowy, still wistfully admired and pitied figure. Morris was more empathic and more willing to understand and forgive his father than a more bitter man might have been. In addition, he was no longer obviously seeking father substitutes. Though his occasional homosexual contacts may still have had some unconscious meaning of a search and propitiation, he was beginning to adopt a more parental role (recall the combined nurturant and sexual interest in the busboy, brought out in the free-association interview).

Morris' relationships to male and female peers have already been touched on; they were friendly, somewhat competitive, and occasionally exploitative, but not intimate.

Identity Who and what was Morris in 1940? It is not possible to give a very clear answer to such questions, because he was not sure himself. At the root of his insecure sense of identity was his confused sexual identification. In addition, he had little feeling for his home town, where he had few friends, and he had no regional loyalty to speak of. In his latest locality, he had no roots, was only on the fringe of the academic world, and had not yet established a place for himself in a circle of friends.

His concern about being taken for a Jew signified a lack of a firm self-definition in ethnic, religious, or cultural terms; his family's marginal status, their clinging to the remnants of a lower-upper- or upper-middle-class position, which might be lost at any time, left him a heritage more of insecurity than of positive identity. As an outstanding young leader in civic affairs and in the business community, he hoped that others regarded him with respect, but he felt too newly arrived to believe in himself. He felt like an impostor with a secret, dirty, and shameful self—"if they only knew!"

Yet he believed in his athletic talent; his conception of himself as a good, perhaps someday an outstanding, golfer was a source of considerable self-esteem. It probably did not contribute much to his sense of maturity, however. Inwardly, Morris remained an adolescent at the age of 26, still on the threshold of the adult world, wondering if he had what it took to be accepted among the mothers and fathers, and half ready to cut loose and move on rather than let himself get thoroughly committed to anything.

Diagnostic
Formulation The state of confusion and turmoil Morris was in does not approximate any standard diagnostic category, but it brings to mind the kind of condition described by Erikson (1959, 1963) as a *postadolescent identity crisis*. Morris was chron-

ologically in the time of young adulthood when his peers were rapidly finding life partners with whom to share an intimacy for which he was not
yet ready, partly because he lacked an inner solidity from which to reach
out to another. Instead, he was still grappling with the task of self-formula-
tion his peers had mastered in adolescence. As Erikson and Anna Freud
(1958) have taught us, a young man or woman who develops outside the
mainstream in this way may go through a period of upheaval in which alarming signs of serious pathology are likely to appear—antisocial acting out, self-
damaging sexual escapades, the temporary emergence of depersonalization
and other near-psychotic symptoms, all of which may get the youth into
serious trouble. Yet these same young people, if properly treated or if merely
given a moratorium from having to assume the burdens of an adult role, may
straighten out astonishingly well.

Morris' conflicts were typical of this condition: dependence on his
mother versus rejection of her, need for the approval of others versus fear
of involvement, resistance to external constraint and a deficiency in moral
restraints versus a seeking for his own form of self-control and morality,
and a deep confusion about himself growing out of his basic uncertainty
about his sexual identity—am I a man? a woman? some kind of sexually
deficient eunuch? All these problems were, as he vaguely realized, related
to "growing up." And there was intuitive wisdom in his own sense of the
priorities: It did make most sense for him to concentrate on getting himself
in hand by building up his compulsive defenses before thinking about long-
term goals and plans.

We should remember, too, that the historical era was one of considerable uncertainty and growing uneasiness for young men. World War II
was a year old when our study of Morris Brown began; at the time he was
given the Rorschach Test in 1942 America was already involved in the war
and he himself was waiting until some minor medical matters were taken
care of so that he could join the Navy as an officer candidate. These were
troubled years, not a time when a physically fit man in his 20's could realistically plan many months ahead. The prospect of active participation in the
war was something unknown, with great potentialities for making or breaking
him, or even snuffing him out completely. Small wonder that Morris was inwardly at sea and rather desperately groping for the tiller!

This summary completes the first assessment of Morris Brown. The
next two chapters will pick up his story and the evaluation of his personality
after a lapse of 26 years.

Mankind is made up of inconsistencies, and no man acts invariably up to his predominant character. The wisest man sometimes acts weakly, and the weakest sometimes wisely.

LORD CHESTERFIELD. Letters to his son

CHAPTER 39
RECENT DEVELOPMENTS IN NONPROJECTIVE ASSESSMENT

D uring the past two decades—the period of clinical psychology's most dramatic growth—a number of new, nonprojective approaches to the assessment of personality have been developed by research psychologists in an effort to broaden the scope and to improve on the validity of existing tests. By mid-1964, there were at least 800 English-language tests in print that were of interest to assessors of personality. In addition to hundreds of tests of intelligence, other abilities and aptitudes, and vocational interests, there were 312 personality tests, of which about a third were projective techniques (Buros, 1965).

Among the nonprojective personality tests developed since the first assessment of Morris Brown were questionnaires such as the MMPI, the Eysenck Personality Inventory, and Lindzey's revision of the Study of Values; among intelligence tests, the Wechsler Adult Intelligence Scale. Tests of cognitive style (for example, leveling-sharpening and field articulation) and new types of rating scales such as Gough's Adjective Check List and various types of Q sorts (a rating technique described later in this chapter) also appeared. In contrast to the earlier tests, which were often put into use before being carefully appraised, many of the new instruments have received a sophisticated evaluation with respect to reliability, norms (the average performance of large, unselected samples of people), and to some extent, validity.

New Tests in a New Assessment

In this chapter, each of the techniques listed in the paragraph above will be described in some detail. Recently gathered data from a follow-up reassessment of Morris Brown will be used to illustrate some of the problems involved in evaluating the test results. First, however, an explanation should be given for the resumption of the case study of Morris Brown 26 years after the first assessment.

Shortly after World War II, Morris reestablished contact with one of the investigators * by means of Christmas cards, which were exchanged off and on thereafter. Notes on these cards related that Morris had seen combat in the Pacific with the Navy, had returned to the same city and the same securities business, was now concentrating on selling mutual funds, and in spite of one intense involvement had remained a bachelor. When he went into politics, he sent a piece of campaign literature, on which the smiling, plump face looked much as it had before the war. It seemed at the least that he had attained enough success and was now sufficiently well adjusted to be able to undergo an unusual experiment in self-confrontation.

Early in 1966 the investigator proposed that it would be fascinating for him and perhaps of interest to Morris if he would cooperate once again in an assessment of his personality. He would be given new tests and some of the old ones, and they would have long talks; he would see what was written and of course would have to give his approval before anything was published. Morris responded with alacrity and enthusiasm and evinced some of the old curiosity to see what he could learn about himself. He completed the inventories and questionnaires and mailed them before flying in for a weekend of intensive clinical assessment.

With his unusual pattern of assets and liabilities, which might have resulted in either good adaptation or severe maladjustment, Morris exemplifies Lord Chesterfield's remark: His inconsistent performance on the new tests and procedures is such that it is difficult to describe him or fit him into any general set of types.

The attempt made below to relate Morris' test findings to the standard procedures used in evaluating them will bring out quite clearly some of the weaknesses as well as the strengths of the nonprojective techniques, and the problems in interpreting them. The discussion starts off with the MMPI and some of its modifications and focuses attention on general problems in interpreting even the most intensively developed objective tests, when they are used in accordance with recent practice. Each of the other new techniques will then be examined in turn.

* That investigator is the author of this section.

Personality Questionnaires

THE MINNESOTA MULTIPHASIC
PERSONALITY INVENTORY

The MMPI, by S. R. Hathaway and J. C. McKinley (1943), is the most widely used of all personality questionnaires today and has been the object of extensive and continuing developmental efforts. As was pointed out in Chapter 35, the original MMPI has four "validity" scales and nine clinical scales concerned with pathological trends. Many of the approximately 1400 titles that would appear in a complete bibliography of this test report the development of new scales; over 200 are current, and more are being produced every year.

The MMPI's original claim to attention among inventories purporting to measure several traits (hence, "multiphasic") was the nature of its scales. They were derived by the method of empirical keying described in Chapter 35 (pages 640–42). Their names (see Figure 39-1) suggest direct and simple diagnostic use: Presumably, if the scales had been well constructed, a known schizophrenic's profile would peak at the Sc scale, and conversely anyone whose highest score was Sc (and was 70 or over) would be found to be a schizophrenic. What is more, since the items in any one scale were derived purely empirically and were embedded in many diverse statements, the test should give a correct diagnosis despite the efforts of subjects to put up a bold front or to conceal their true feelings. It was hoped that the correction keys would compensate for whatever the indirect method of empirical keying did not accomplish. The problems of interpretation will be treated below. First, however, let us take a look at Morris' profile so that reference may be made to it as we proceed in the chapter.

Morris Brown's
MMPI Profile

Morris took the group form of the test, following the standard printed instructions. His answers on the four validity scales, the nine clinical scales, and three additional scales were then scored by the use of punched answer keys. The results were plotted as T scores on the profile (see Figure 39-1). T scores are standard scores obtained by converting the raw scores into deviations from the mean of the original normal group (in this case, predominantly rural Minnesota men and women who were visiting relatives in hospitals). On these scales, scores of 70 (two standard deviations above the normal mean of 50) and over are considered of pathological significance.

Because research has not given strong support to the MMPI's attempts at spotting invalid records, the validity scores of ?, L, F, and K will not be described in more detail than was devoted to them in Chapter 35 (pages

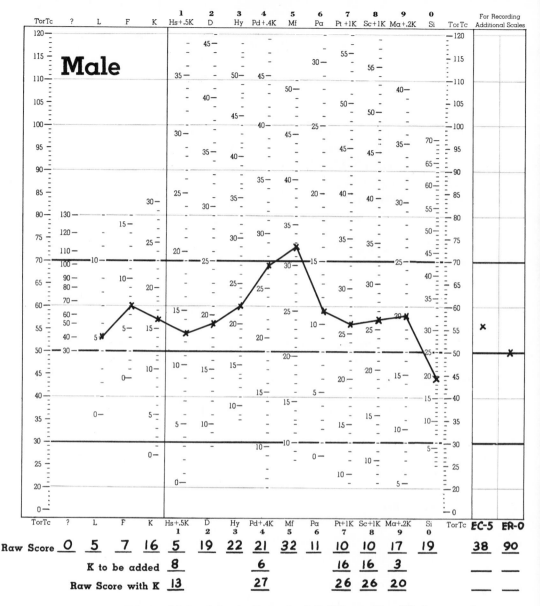

TorTc	?	L	F	K	1 Hs+.5K	2 D	3 Hy	4 Pd+.4K	5 Mf	6 Pa	7 Pt+1K	8 Sc+1K	9 Ma+.2K	0 Si	TorTc	EC-5	ER-0
Raw Score	0	5	7	16	5	19	22	21	32	11	10	10	17	19		38	90
K to be added					8			6			16	16	3				
Raw Score with K					13			27			26	26	20				

Figure 39-1 Morris Brown's MMPI profile (Hathaway & McKinley, 1943).

Key to Symbols

T or Tc	The T scale of standardized scores. (Tc means T score with K correction.)
?	The "Can't say" validity scale (number of omitted items).
L	The "Lie" validity scale (denial of trivial faults and symptoms).

F	The "False" validity scale (admission of rare, serious symptoms).
K	Correction score added to certain clinical scales to compensate for defensive understatement.

Clinical Scales

1	Hs	Hypochondriasis—multiple complaints of somatic symptoms without organic basis.
2	D	Depression—a sad, self-disparaging, apathetic, even suicidal, state.
3	Hy	Hysteria—a neurosis characterized by anxiety or blandness, naiveté, ready displays of emotion, and certain bodily symptoms.
4	Pd	Psychopathic deviate—a character disorder with impulsive, antisocial acting out.
5	Mf	Masculinity-femininity (based on responses of male overt homosexuals).
6	Pa	Paranoia—a rigid, suspicious, vengeful condition, which at its psychotic extreme includes delusions of persecution or of grandeur.
7	Pt	Psychasthenia—obsessive-compulsive neurosis, with vacillation, indecisiveness, over-conscientiousness, overintellectuality.
8	Sc	Schizophrenia—the most common psychosis, marked by withdrawal, inappropriateness, peculiar thinking, even delusions and hallucinations.
9	Ma	Mania—an overactive, excited, elated, driven condition; at its psychotic extreme, often alternating with depression.
0	Si	Social introversion.
	EC-5	Ego control (Block, 1965), the first factor in analyses of all scales.
	ER-0	Ego resiliency (Block, 1965), the second factor. (See text discussion of these two factors, page 645.)

643–44). Suffice it to say that Morris' validity scores are safely within normal limits, allowing the rest of his scores to be interpreted according to usual principles.

If we look at the profile quite naively, we notice that most of the pathological scales (even *Ma* and *D*) are less than one standard deviation above the mean and hence are not interpretable. Only *Si*, social introversion, is slightly below 50, indicating a moderate degree of extroversion. We should, therefore, disregard all the clinical scales except the high scores on scale 5 (*Mf*, masculinity-femininity) and scale 4 (*Pd*, psychopathic deviate). The MMPI manual tells us that "males with very high *Mf* scores have frequently been found to be either overt or repressed sexual inverts," though it goes on to warn that homosexuality must not be assumed without independent confirmatory evidence. Scale 4 (*Pd*) "measures the similarity of the subject to a group of persons whose main difficulty lies in their absence of deep emotional response, their inability to profit from experience, and their disregard of social mores." These statements are reminiscent of rather well-established features of Morris Brown as we knew him in 1940: Certainly he was inclined to seek overt homosexual experience, seemed relatively shallow in his emotional experience, and was prone to disregard social mores if they seemed silly or pointless to him. If he still had these characteristics, we might be tempted to conclude as well that he was not susceptible to learning from experience. The manual warns, however, that the scales should not be interpreted so simply and directly. Let us see, then, what other interpretive approaches add.

Pattern analysis. Research and clinical use
quickly showed that the MMPI did not
work as simply as originally intended. Its authors and proponents have been
forced to abandon the attempt to make diagnoses by a literal interpretation
of the scales and to adopt the configurational approach—that is, they now
say that the profile must be taken as a complex piece of clinical information
consisting of patterns to be interpreted only by someone with professional
experience and trained judgment. There has come into being, therefore, a
kind of "MMPI expert" who can at times perform dazzling feats of describing an "entire personality" on the basis of the profile alone. These
clinicians generally report that they interpret any one scale quite differently
in different contexts (that is, when certain other scale values are high or
low), though there is little hard evidence that they actually do so in practice
(Goldberg, 1968).

The development of profile interpretation has brought about a rather
anomalous and unstable situation. The one great advantage of the MMPI
is that it takes little of the clinician's time and requires no judgment to obtain a fully scored profile. Moreover, the original aim was to reduce psychiatric diagnosis to a simple clerical operation, eliminating the need for
clinical judgment in the test's interpretation also. Yet after much initial
work with the MMPI, its proponents declared that it had to be clinically
interpreted, in a way much like the "scatter analysis" of Wechsler's intelligence tests (to be discussed later in this chapter) or the interpretation of a
projective technique's quantitative scores.

Objective rules and ratios. In their research, Meehl and Dahlstrom
(1960) have pursued the original goal of eliminating the need for clinical
judgment. They sorted through the test profiles of hundreds of diagnosed
mental-hospital and clinic patients and devised a set of objective rules and
ratios by means of which a file clerk could classify an MMPI profile as
psychotic, neurotic, or indeterminate, in about a minute. When cross-
validated on 988 male patients, this procedure yielded a total correct classification of 53 percent, which is significantly above chance (50 percent)
but not impressively so. If one disregards the 30 percent of profiles that were
indeterminate, the rate of success ("hits") was 76 percent. It is especially
noteworthy that these rules worked better than the pooled weighted judgments of 29 Minnesota clinicians who used all their skills at pattern
analysis.

These rules, however, classify Morris Brown's profile as psychotic—
an implausible diagnosis. Clearly, such a system is not suited for clinical
use with individuals if any better method is available.

The "cookbook" approach. Halbower (described in Meehl, 1956) developed an original approach to interpreting the MMPI without clinical

judgment. He constructed what he called a cookbook with four recipes; the recipes correspond to four of the five most common types of MMPI profiles. More than half of the patients seen at the Veterans' Administration Mental Hygiene Clinic in Minneapolis, where the research was done, fell into one of these four categories. From these patients, he selected 9 from each profile type and asked their therapists (or another qualified clinician who knew the case well) to describe each subject on a 154-item Q sort made up of statements taken from diagnostic reports. The 5 subjects in each group of 9 whose Q sorts intercorrelated most consistently were taken as representative; their Q sorts were averaged to get a description of the personality type represented by that MMPI profile.

The next step was to select 8 new patients, 2 with each of the four types of MMPI profile. Their therapists described them by means of the Q sort, providing a criterion. When the Q sort description from the four-recipe cookbook was correlated with the criterion sorts, the results were quite good, for the median (validity) correlation was .69. Moreover, when clinical psychologists who were quite experienced in the use of the MMPI described the same patients on the Q sort after studying their MMPI profiles, their validities were significantly and impressively lower; not once did the clinical integration of the profile information produce a correlation as good as that of the cookbook. (We shall return to the implications of this finding and other aspects of Halbower's study in Chapter 41.)

Again, however, this approach yields nothing of value for our understanding of Morris Brown. It may persuade us that there probably is little to the claims of the enthusiasts for pattern analysis of the MMPI, but Morris' profile is not one of the four described in the "cookbook." Instead, his is quite an unusual collection of scores: for example, profiles like Morris' with the highest scores on Mf, followed by Pd, occurred among only 1.5 percent of a group of 136 midwestern male adults. There was not a single similar score among 100 male Iowa college students, and only .7 percent of 2551 North Carolina prisoners produced this type of profile (Dahlstrom & Welsh, 1960). Consequently, it will be a long time before enough data have accumulated for statistical analysis to provide a ready-made interpretation of even the most outstanding parts of Morris' profile.

Development of new scales. Another line of research, unlike the studies just described, has not assumed that the original nine clinical scales are necessarily the best way to score the MMPI. These researchers assume rather that, using the same basic questionnaire, or pool of items, more directly meaningful scoring keys could perhaps be devised. A number of new empirical keys have been developed, some of which have attracted wide interest and are widely used—for example, Barron's Es or ego-strength scale (1953), originally made up of the items distinguishing patients who improved after brief psychotherapy from those who did not.

Other psychologists have used factor analysis to clarify the nature of the existing scales and construct new ones. Welsh (1956) is one of over a dozen workers who have factor-analyzed the original empirical scales, and several others, and have found that only two main factors account for most of the information in the profile. For a while, many psychometricians (such as Jackson & Messick, 1958) tended to assume that these factors were themselves mainly measures of response sets (see Chapter 35). Block (1965) has recently shown, however, that these same two factors emerge even when the scales are first purified by (1) eliminating items that are contained in more than one scale and which thus produce spurious correlations, (2) eliminating the effect of any tendency of the subject to agree or disagree with an item indiscriminately (the *acquiescence* response set) by including in each scale equal numbers of items keyed positively and negatively, and (3) suppressing the *social desirability* response set by excluding all items with too obvious a degree of rated desirability or undesirability.

The first factor Block calls ego control (*EC*), a measure of how tight, constricted, and overcontrolled a person is, rather than being loose, impulsive, and undercontrolled. He calls the second factor ego resiliency (*ER*); high scorers seem to bounce back after frustration or stress, and low scorers admit to having many neurotic and other symptoms. Most of the traditional clinical scales (and Barron's ego strength) are heavily loaded with *ER*. Block also reports independent data from the clinical assessment of several samples of subjects in the form of correlations with ratings, which tend to support the validity of his interpretations based on the content of the items. As Figure 39-1 shows, Morris scored just above average on both *EC* and *ER*. He could be described as being slightly on the reserved side and as admitting to about as many symptoms as the mean of several groups of healthy men considerably younger than himself.

Improvement of scales by means of factor analysis. It seems wasteful to ask a subject to respond to 566 items to get measures of only two constructs. Surely more than this meager crumb of information about rather general traits is contained in so many responses. Block himself points out that the factorial structure of the MMPI is much more complex if one begins with the intercorrelation of items, not scales; unfortunately, even with the aid of modern computers it is difficult to work with the entire pool of items at once.

Several researchers (such as Comrey, 1957, 1958) have factor-analyzed the intercorrelations of items *within* scales and have found each scale to contain two or more quite independent clusters of items. This is not surprising, because coefficients of internal consistency for the empirical scales have been reported to range all the way from $-.05$ (for *Pa*, the paranoid scale) to .81 (for *Pt*, the psychasthenia scale). These analyses tend to separate the "obvious," face-valid items from the subtle and indirect ones contributed by empirical keying; one study (Dempsey, 1964) suggests that the direct admission of relevant symptoms may be the principal determinant of the test's validity. The shortened but more useful scale for depression (D) resulting from his factor-analytic investigation consists entirely of items like "I cry easily" and "I wish I could be as happy as others seem to be." With the help of factor analysis, it looks as if shorter but homogeneous and more easily interpretable scales may be developed, which may considerably enhance the MMPI's usefulness.

Construction of scales other than by empirical keying. Might it not be that some other strategy of building scales to summarize the answers to many separate questions would yield better results than has empirical keying? Hase and Goldberg (1967) decided to compare several strategies of constructing inventory scales, using the item pool of the California Psychological Inventory (Gough, 1957) and working with the test responses of 201 freshman college girls. (The CPI is an attempt to modify the MMPI for use with normal college populations; of its 468 items, about 200 are drawn from the MMPI.) Since Gough's manual describes 11 scales built by the method of *empirical keying,* they constructed three additional sets of 11 scales each, one by *factor-analytic* methods (based on item intercorrelations) and two by other methods that they call intuitive. One intuition-based method involved the judgments of three advanced graduate students, who constructed *theoretical* scales by selecting items that seemed to measure 11 of Murray's needs (1938). The other method, used in making *rational* scales, also involved judgment: One person selected items that seemed to measure various traits; then, by statistical means, inconsistent items were eliminated. In addition, for a baseline against which to evaluate the validity of the other scales, Hase and Goldberg used 11 measures of the response sets of social desirability and acquiescence (in various combinations) and 11 purely random scales of 25 items each, selected and the direction of scoring keyed by use of a table of random numbers.

The scales were tested for reliability by the usual psychometric measures of internal consistency (fairly good for the four major strategies, fair for the response-set, or "stylistic," scales, and nil for the random ones) and by retest after a four-week interval. The four main strategies gave mean repeat correlations of from .81 to .87, which is satisfactory and slightly better than the usual retest reliability of MMPI scales; the two sets of control scales made a distinctly poorer showing.

To test validity, Hase and Goldberg put together 13 criteria, which included behavioral measures of social conformity, peer ratings on five traits, objective measures of academic achievement and dropping out of college, and so on. Several ways of analyzing the data all led to the same conclusion: Scales made by the four major strategies *all performed equally well* (with mean validity correlations of approximately .30) and significantly better than the stylistic and random scales, which did not differ from each other.

Another finding by Hase and Goldberg constitutes impressive evidence that much of the psychometric ingenuity that has gone into such complex strategies of scale construction as empirical keying has been wasted. The subjects' self-ratings on such traits as dominance, sociability, and femininity were *better* predictors of their friends' ratings than the most elaborate statistical manipulations of any CPI scales. This is not an isolated finding; Peterson (1965) and Carroll (1952) report the same superiority of simple, direct self-ratings over inventory-scale scores.

It seems, therefore, that the vaunted method of empirical keying has not made any special contribution to the measurement of personality by means of self-report inventories. It still remains true that a good deal can be learned about a cooperative person by asking him directly to tell you about his usual behavior, express his agreement or disagreement with statements of attitudes, rate himself on various traits, or the like. In the absence of frankness and some insight, no amount of manipulation of numerical scores can extract much useful information from an inventory.

In summary, the MMPI is a collection of many interesting and potentially useful items; the study of these items, however, has been too much neglected in favor of the nine empirical scales, which have not stood the test of time very well. There is no convincing proof that they are highly valid measures of anything very meaningful, and they will probably give way to other, more directly intelligible ways of summarizing answers to the items.

THE EYSENCK PERSONALITY INVENTORY

The inventory by H. J. and Sybil B. G. Eysenck (1963) is a recent offshoot of a long-established line of screening devices for neurotic tendencies, stretching back to Woodworth (see page 637) and World War I. The Eysenck inventory is brief and to the point; its 57 questions give stripped-down but reasonably reliable and statistically independent measures of Extroversion and of Neuroticism, a rather generalized willingness to admit symptoms of no great severity. These variables are the cornerstones of Eysenck's theory of personality, as they are the persistently recurring pair of independent dimensions that crop up in the great majority of self-descriptive questionnaires. The test itself is a recent, only slightly modified version of the Maudsley Personality Inventory (Eysenck, 1962), which has had retest reliabilities of from .70 to .90 and internal-consistency coefficients ranging between .75 and .90. The few figures on reliability available on the present form are of the same order of magnitude. The test incorporates a brief *L* scale adapted from the MMPI, which is intended to detect invalid records. Eysenck has done a great deal of work on the construct validity of the two factors measured by these tests; this work is impressive but difficult to summarize.

The results of Morris' test (Table 39-1) show us that he still comes across as a clear-cut social extrovert, and that he is below average on

Table 39-1 Morris Brown's Scores on the Eysenck Personality Inventory

Scale	Score	Classification
E (extroversion-introversion)	18	93rd percentile
N (neuroticism)	7	41st percentile
L (lie)	1	negligible; valid result

neuroticism. Eysenck's test admittedly has little clinical use, and for our purposes its contribution is minimal. Nevertheless, it is fair to say in summary that its aims are modest and its performance good within those limitations.

A STUDY OF VALUES

The revised form of the Study of Values (Allport, Vernon, & Lindzey, 1951) was given to Morris partly to see how closely the 1966 profile would correspond to the 1940 profile (described in Chapter 37). The revision is a better test; its items are more discriminating, it is more reliable, and the Social value has been redefined and sharpened. That value is now restricted to altruism and philanthropy, rather than taking in all manifestations of

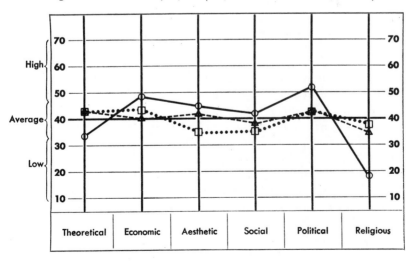

Figure 39-2 Value profiles (Allport-Vernon-Lindzey, 1951).

○——○ Profile for Morris Brown, 1966

△----△ Average profile for male students at Morris' college

□••••□ Average male profile

affection for people, as before. Internal-consistency correlations now range from .73 (Theoretical) to .90 (Religious); repeat reliability after one month, from .77 (Social) to .92 (Economic). The old and new forms are reasonably equivalent for the Economic and Religious values (inter-form correlations are .74 and .75); as would be expected, the Social value shows the poorest correlation between the two versions (.31), and the others are only fair, ranging from .45 to .55. Just the changes in the test itself, therefore, might give rise to a good deal of the difference in the two profiles.

Compare Figure 39-2 with Figure 37-1, on page 692, and you will quickly see that there are at least two points of similarity: The Political and Economic values are still the two strongest. His scores on those are quite significantly above those of a group of 264 students who attended the same college (but who were about 20 years younger than Morris at the time of testing). The greatest rise has been in the Aesthetic value (as it later turned out, this is attributable almost entirely to Morris' love for music, which had grown considerably since 1940); though the Theoretical value has risen, it is still below average. The Social value is down, but it rests at just about the general mean. The big drop has come in the Religious value, which is extremely low by any standard. Recall, however, that in 1940 Morris had recently been under the influence of a Catholic priest; and even though his Religious value was not strong then, it may have been temporarily inflated. At any rate, Morris' 1966 value profile is that of a secular man of affairs; it is not unusual for a businessman.

So much for questionnaires; the other nonprojective instruments used with Morris at the time of the reassessment were of several different types— an intelligence test, self-rating devices, and tests of cognitive style.

Intelligence Tests

THE WECHSLER ADULT INTELLIGENCE SCALE

David Wechsler's WAIS (1955) is now the most widely used individual test of intelligence for adults. When Morris was assessed in 1940, its predecessor, the Wechsler-Bellevue, had just been published but had not yet displaced the Stanford-Binet. The WAIS follows the same general design as the Wechsler-Bellevue: There are 11 subtests, each consisting of items graded in difficulty. The subject is repeatedly given "breathers," since each subtest starts with easy items, and he then is repeatedly required to exert the upper limits of his ability. In all tests modeled on Binet's, by contrast, the subject takes several sorts of tests at one level of difficulty before going up to another level to encounter another mixture of tasks.

The WAIS I.Q. does not have the same meaning as the Stanford-Binet I.Q., since the latter is predicated on the continuous increase in scores with development in childhood. All tests give point scores (such as the number of items passed); to compute a Stanford-Binet I.Q., this score is converted into a mental age—that is, the score is expressed in age units that serve as the numerator of the I.Q. formula

$$I.Q. = \frac{Mental\ age}{Chronological\ age}$$

By the same reasoning, Wechsler argued, the denominator could be viewed as the expected or average point score expressed in age units. But if the numerator was kept a point score, rather than translated into age units, the I.Q. would have the same meaning if the denominator was the one translated—that is, converted into the expected point score for the person's age. This ingenious argument is the basis of his tables for converting raw (point) scores into I.Q.'s. Since there are separate tables for ages 20–24, 25–34, and thereafter for decades until ages 65–69, 70–74, and over 75, a person's Wechsler I.Q. tends to stay constant despite the tendency of point scores to decline after about age 30.

Correlations with other tests of intelligence range from the .50's through the .90's, depending partly on the adequacy of the other tests. The WAIS also meets the standards for a valid intelligence test set by other available criteria (correlation with ratings, appropriate age curves, selection of mental defectives, and differentiation of occupational groups). The split-half internal consistency of the total I.Q. (in which scores on half the test are correlated with scores on the other half) is .97; its repeat reliability has been reported to be almost as good—.90. The individual subtests have poorer reliability, and the reliability of differences among them is even worse, a point that has often been raised in criticism of scatter analysis (interpretation of the pattern of abilities measured by the different subtests). Curiously enough, however, this same point never seems to be raised in criticism of profile interpretation on the MMPI, the component scores of which are hardly more reliable than WAIS subtests and are about as highly intercorrelated. Nevertheless, unevenness in the pattern, when interpreted by an expert, often gives diagnostically useful leads (see Rapaport et al., 1968). Morris' pattern, or scatter, was not particularly noteworthy, except for a weakness in the Picture Completion subtest.

In clinical use, the importance of the WAIS goes beyond its quantitative scores. The verbalization of answers, qualitative features of the subject's approach to the tasks, and his behavior during testing are all recorded by the well-trained examiner and are weighed along with other qualitative data in the interpretive phase of clinical assessment. Though the contribution of the WAIS is not singled out in the next chapter, it did play a part in the clinical assessment in 1966.

To save time, and because Morris had been given the same test several years before, some results of which were available, he took only 7 of the 11 subtests. His estimated total I.Q. from these subtests taken in 1966 is 145, well up in the top 1 percent of men Morris' age. This figure happens by chance to coincide almost exactly with the Stanford-Binet I.Q. of 146 obtained in 1940. Measurement of this sort is not usually that exact, and the shift from one test to the other ordinarily results in greater discrepancies, even when they are taken in immediate succession. The correlation between the two tests varies with the samples, but it is generally about .85.

Self-Rating Devices

THE ADJECTIVE CHECK LIST

This instrument, by Harrison Gough (1960, 1965), takes us back to self-description as a means of getting data for assessment, but with a difference. In the earliest type of inventory, the subject's self-report was taken at face value, and the trait measures were built directly on the answers to questionnaires, which were treated as valid reports of behavior. Our examination of the MMPI has shown that this direct approach has considerable value if the subject is motivated to reveal himself frankly; but if he is not, any such technique of assessment is hazardous. The Adjective Check List is presented as a way of getting at the subject's self-concept rather than as a way of measuring 300 traits; because it is self-description taken as such, it can be presumed valid unless there is reason to believe the subject is motivated not to reveal what he actually thinks of himself. This technique of measurement is simplicity boiled down. The test consists merely of 300 adjectives, and the instructions are: "Please put a check by each adjective that applies to you."

The Adjective Check List has been extensively used at the Institute for Personality Assessment and Research at the University of California, where Gough developed it, and elsewhere. It has proved empirically valuable in that independently defined groups of subjects differ in terms of the frequency with which their members check different adjectives. For example, results of one experiment singled out a group of subjects who were easily swayed by group influence, and another group who stuck to their guns despite the (manipulated) consensus of a group. The yielders significantly (p = .01) more often checked the adjectives *optimistic, kind, obliging,* and *patient,* and also *determined* and *efficient.* The uninfluenced subjects (at the same level of significance) described themselves as *artistic, emotional,* and *original.* These findings contributed to a meaningful picture of the self-concepts of people who are and are not easily swayed by a group, a picture that fitted well with other data on their personalities (Barron, 1952).

The terms Morris chose to describe himself are grouped below into clusters, which have been numbered and arranged to bring out apparent relationships; the arbitrariness of such grouping is obvious. Words in parentheses indicate other possible classifications.

1. adaptable, capable, versatile, practical, realistic
2. alert, curious, interests wide, sensitive, clear-thinking, thoughtful

3. active, adventurous, enthusiastic
4. cheerful, contented, optimistic, good-natured
5. appreciative, friendly, generous, sympathetic, understanding, warm, outgoing (thoughtful, tolerant)
6. cooperative, dependable, loyal, responsible, honest, sincere, tolerant, steady
7. informal, natural, unaffected
8. independent, individualistic, unconventional
9. attractive, good-looking
10. healthy, robust

Whether or not Morris really *is* as he describes himself, the self-descriptions above provide quite a lot of information and in many ways reinforce what we already know about him. Groups 5 and 6 perhaps contain the most surprises, for they suggest that he has taken a definite turn toward close and friendly relationships with people (instead of holding back from involvement) and toward morally proper behavior. The markedly favorable tone of the adjectives chosen indicates that he feels generally good about himself. We might expect, therefore, that the internal confusion Morris so freely expressed in 1940 has been replaced by a good deal of self-acceptance.

At least one negative fact ought also to be brought out: The total check list contains 14 adjectives expressing shades of hostility ranging from *cruel* and *aggressive* to *stern* and *intolerant,* but Morris did not check one of them. The preceding sentence provides an example of what Gough calls analysis by means of rational scales; it is also possible to make use of empirically derived scales. For instance, the assessment staff of the Institute for Personality Assessment and Research described 40 graduate students in various fields, half of whom had been chosen by their departments as outstandingly high, half as outstandingly low, on research originality (Gough, 1960). The assessors checked the following adjectives significantly more often to characterize the *more* original students:

adventurous	fair-minded	original
alert	foresighted	quiet
civilized	imaginative	rational
clear-thinking	intelligent	reliable
clever	interests wide	responsible
curious	inventive	shy

These adjectives significantly characterized the *less* original subjects:

confused	prejudiced	stubborn
conventional	restless	suggestible
defensive	sentimental	thrifty
emotional	simple	trusting
polished	slow	

By assigning a plus to every adjective in the first list and a minus to each in the second, we get an empirical scale ranging from +18 to −14. Morris' score would be +6, from which we could conclude that his self-concept tends to resemble the personalities of graduate students who were considered original, although he did not describe himself as *original*. In these ways, a great variety of rational and empirical scales can be derived from the Adjective Check List.

Such an all-or-none judgment as a check by an adjective is, of course, crude. Though psychologists have sometimes used the Adjective Check List to record an assessment staff's judgments, they usually prefer to rate on a scale with more than two points (that is, more than a Yes and No). For example, on the MMPI, Morris said True to, "I get mad easily and then get over it soon." Assuming that this is an accurate self-observation, if he were asked to rate his temper on a 10-point scale, how would he weigh the two considerations of threshold and duration of anger against each other? And they are only half the considerations here. Logically, a person should be higher on a scale of temper (1) if the trait has a low threshold—if he gets mad easily, (2) if the trait is extensive—if he loses his temper in a wide variety of situations, (3) if the trait is intensive—if he typically explodes instead of getting moderately annoyed, and (4) if the trait's operation is prolonged—if his temper is slow to subside rather than, as in Morris' case, likely to simmer down quickly.

There are even further complications to rating traits. As another example consider the trait of adventurousness. The daily life of Morris, like that of most people, offers fewer opportunities for him to act adventurously than to act, say, irritably. This fact would make it difficult to compare these traits on the same kind of rating scale; it also raises the question of the time period when the trait is displayed. Morris went rock climbing in the West ten months before he described himself as adventurous, and it is quite possible that he had not done anything equally bold and exciting since then. Should he have checked the adjective or not? Most of us would agree that he should have; but what if the last opportunity for adventure had arisen ten years earlier instead of ten months? Even though a person had seized the opportunity eagerly then, we would hardly think that he was being accurate a decade later to continue to describe himself as adventurous.

The issue of absolute versus relative measurement as determined by one's reference group also comes up in ratings: A member of a parachute-jumping club knows that his occasional weekend adventures are tame compared to the activities of the professional stunt man in the movies, yet they are enough to make him outstandingly adventurous compared to the population as a whole. But is that the proper base for comparison? There is no easy answer. Surely we should try to find out what a person's reference groups are, for his self-ratings to be most useful. It is important to know whether a person tends to compare himself primarily with people in general, members of his own occupational group, fellow townsmen, others in a close but extended family, people with the same ethnic or religious background, or what not. Everyone belongs to many groups simultaneously, and his status may change drastically as he goes from one to another. To anticipate his recent history a bit, Morris is an outstandingly successful politician in the small town where he lives, having been elected the equivalent of mayor for a dozen years; but the year he lost his reelection to the state legislature he was a small frog in the large pond of state politics. To rate himself well in relation to any group means also that a person has to be able to assess the same traits equally well in himself and in others.

Because of these vexing problems in *normative* rating (using other members of a group as the standard), many workers in personality assessment have begun using *ipsative* scaling—rating a trait high if it is outstanding or important for the subject compared with his own other traits, not with the same trait in other people. To be sure, all the other problems of rating remain, but this device has the important advantage of enabling the assessor to consider only one subject at a time. In addition, the frame of reference for self-ratings and ratings by experts can be kept the same more easily in this way. This feature of ipsative scaling is part of a special technique of rating traits known as the Q-sort technique and will become clearer as we proceed.

THE Q-SORTING METHOD

The particular form of Q-sorting technique used with Morris was the California Q Set (Block, 1961). It consists of 100 statements printed on separate cards. When it is used for self-description (as was done with Morris), the subject is instructed to sort through the randomly ordered cards and make a preliminary decision about each statement, putting it in one pile if it seems to describe him, in another if it seems wrong or misleading as applied to him, and in between if it does not apply at all. Then he reexamines the cards in the first pile and picks out the five that seem most to hit the nail on the head and bring out the main points about him: These cards are called 9's. From the remainder of this pile, he selects the eight cards that best describe him (called 8's), and then the next twelve (7's); at this point, he may find it easiest to go to the group of uncharacteristic statements and select the five that are most wildly off the mark (the 1's), then another very uncharacteristic group of eight (2's), the next twelve (3's), and so forth. When he finishes, he should have nine piles with the distribution shown in Figure 39-3.

This forced distribution is usually approximately normal, as in Figure 39-3, but it can be any shape that an investigator chooses. The great advantage of the forced distribution is that it controls such response sets as hugging the mean or giving extreme ratings and thereby eliminates a good deal of unwanted variance. Its disadvantage is that it forces every subject into the same mold, regardless of how well it fits: Some subjects complain, for example, that they cannot find exactly five statements that are highly apt.

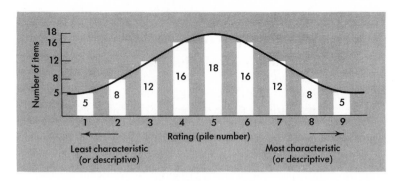

Figure 39-3   The California Q-Sort distribution, with a normal curve superimposed.

The California Q Set is not so much a test that could have reliability, or validity, as it is a language for describing a personality. As such, it is quite useful to assessors, who can use it to record a first impression or a more considered set of judgments. It was used in both ways with Morris: Two of the staff of the New York University Research Center for Mental Health, who had only brief encounters with him while administering some of the tests of cognitive style, Q-sorted their impressions, and the investigator close to Morris used the Q sort after having studied *all* the assessment data. The procedure also makes it easy to correlate two or more sets of ratings on the same person, as shown in Table 39-2.

Table 39-2   Correlations Among Q Sorts by Morris Brown, Raters, and Psychologists' Consensus on Optimal Adjustment

| | MB | Raters | | |
		RRH	DW	NI
RRH	.52	x		
DW	.33	.33	x	
NI	.32	.45	.31	x
Optimal Adjustment	.68	.39	.32	.35

Another feature of the Q sort is that it can be used to develop scales of various types, with which a subject's sort can be correlated. For example, Block had nine clinical psychologists describe "the optimally adjusted personality" by means of the Q set; he then made up a composite sort based on their ratings, which can serve as a standard with which to correlate other ratings. Thus, the bottom row of correlations in Table 39-2 may be taken as measures of how closely this conception of the well-adjusted man corresponded to Morris Brown's self-description (MB), and to the description of him given by the psychologist who knew him best (RRH) and by the other two assessors (DW and NI). The *absolute* sizes of coefficients like the ones in the table are not particularly meaningful, since they depend a good deal on the properties of the Q set. The ratings by the three judges do not appear very reliable, but it is surprising that the agreement is as good as it is, considering that judges DW and NI saw Morris for less than an hour each and had virtually no opportunity to talk with him. Block reports that well-trained observers who have had the opportunity to study a person can attain good agreement, with "typical reliabilities of .8 or .9 [Block, 1961, p. 91]."

Table 39-3 lists the 13 items Morris considered most characteristic of himself and the 13 items he considered least characteristic. These items, together with the Adjective Check List, give a good picture of his *self-concept*; by comparing his ratings with those given by the psychologists we can form some hypotheses about the nature of his insight.

Of the five most characteristic items (pile 9), only item 3 was given particularly discrepant ratings by Morris and by the psychologists. The two who had had brief contact with him had little basis for any direct knowledge about the breadth of his interests; the other psychologist's rating may have been affected by normative considerations: Knowing many people who have even broader interests, he may have been influenced to rate Morris lower than he deserves. Yet it is also possible that Morris considers this one of the most characteristic things about himself in part because he *values* breadth and would like to think of himself as more universal in his interests than he actually is.

This example brings out one of the ambiguities of ipsative scaling. What does it mean to say that items 19 and 96 are both true of Morris, but that the latter item, dealing with valuing independence, is more "characteristic" than the former, the issue of seeking reassurance? As we have just seen (page 752), there are many ways in which a behavioral tendency can be considered "strong," and they apply just as much to intraindividual comparisons among traits as to interindividual rankings or ratings.

When items are rated according to their *salience*, as Block calls the ipsative dimension, psychologists are likely to emphasize any items dealing with inferred inner constructs that seem to have explanatory relevance (such as item 86: "Handles anxiety and conflicts by, in effect, refusing to recognize their presence; repressive or dissociative tendencies"—rated 9 by both RRH and NI), even though—as in this case—the item may not precisely formulate Morris' individual blend of defenses. The subjects themselves, on the other hand, are likely to emphasize items that *describe* behavior or inner feelings to which they have direct access. Notice, for example, that all three psychologists put item 14 near the middle of the distribution, because of his unusual compliance and willingness to do whatever was asked of him, whereas Morris himself gave it a rock-bottom rating—which is probably more valid.

Table 39-3   Items from the California Q Set Sorted in Extreme Positions by Morris Brown

Most Characteristic (pile 9)

Item No.

3. Has a wide range of interests. (6, 7, 4) *
5. Behaves in a giving way toward others. (8, 4, 9)
8. Appears to have a high degree of intellectual capacity. (5, 9, 6)
35. Has warmth; has the capacity for close relationships; compassionate. (8, 6, 7)
96. Values own independence and autonomy. (9, 8, 5)

Highly Characteristic (pile 8)

2. Is a genuinely dependable and responsible person. (9, 8, 7)
19. Seeks reassurance from others. (8, 5, 7)
26. Is productive; gets things done. (7, 6, 8)
28. Tends to arouse liking and acceptance in people. (7, 6, 7)
44. Evaluates the motivation of others in interpreting situations. (5, 6, 6)
59. Is concerned with own body and the adequacy of its physiological functioning. (8, 5, 6)
77. Appears straightforward, forthright, candid in dealing with others. (9, 9, 8)
93a. *Behaves in a masculine style and manner.* (4, 5, 4)

Least Characteristic (pile 1)

14. *Genuinely submissive; accepts domination comfortably.* (5, 5, 6)
36. Is subtly negativistic; tends to undermine and obstruct or sabotage. (3, 2, 1)
48. Keeps people at a distance; avoids close interpersonal relationships. (3, 4, 3)
78. Feels cheated and victimized by life; self-pitying. (2, 7, 3)
90. Is concerned with philosophical problems; religions, values, the meaning of life, etc. (2, 6, 6)

Highly Uncharacteristic (pile 2)

6. Is fastidious. *(5, 7, 4)*
34. Over-reactive to minor frustrations; irritable. (4, 3, 2)
49. Is basically distrustful of people in general; questions their motivations. (1, 4, 1)
63. Judges self and others in conventional terms like "popularity," "the correct thing to do," social pressures, etc. (5, 3, 7)
68. Is basically anxious. (6, 7, 5)
80. Interested in members of the opposite sex. (1, 5, 2)
97. Is emotionally bland; has flattened affect. (3, 2, 4)
99. Is self-dramatizing; histrionic. (6, 1, 7)

* Numbers in parentheses following items (Block, 1961) are ratings given by the three psychologists; RRH's ratings are given first (see also Table 39-2). Italics used in items are Block's.

Only he himself knows how comfortable he is when accepting domination; apparently his very strong need for autonomy makes him not at all genuinely submissive. His warmth (35), helpfulness (5), and need to be liked (19) are so strong, however, that he forces himself to accept a certain amount of domination. This is a good example of the importance of getting the subject's own introspective point of view in any thorough assessment of personality. (For further discussion of these issues, see Holt, 1951.)

Some other items on which there are discrepancies seem more plausibly to represent limitations in Morris' insight. He thinks of himself as more masculine in his manner and style of behavior than do the psychologists, all of whom rate this item (93a) at or just below the midpoint. At the same time, it is noteworthy that the matter of his masculinity did not seem salient one way or another to the two observers who had had very brief contact with him and knew nothing of his sexual history. In three other items, discrepancies similarly arose because they deal with ways the subject comes across to an outside observer: Morris appears to be more fastidious and more conventional (items 6 and 63) than he realizes. And though he is a genuine person who does not appear histrionic in the sense of displaying phoniness or deliberate dissimulation, he does tend to dramatize himself (item 99) more than he is aware of doing.

Finally, Morris quite strongly rejects the conception of himself as basically anxious (item 68), although he endorsed several MMPI items that support the psychologists' judgments—for example, "I am anxious about something or other most of the time." His evident need to be liked would be interpreted by many psychologists (as it was by the three who rated him) as indicating a moderate degree of basic anxiety, in Karen Horney's sense of a fear of rejection. Perhaps if he had been given a definition of "basically anxious," he might not have rated it so low in his sorting. In all fairness, it should be pointed out that the California Q Set was not designed for the average subject to use for self-description, however helpful it proved in this case.

Tests of Cognitive Style

LEVELING-SHARPENING

The schematizing test (Holzman & Klein, 1954; Gardner et al., 1959) is one of the first measures to be used in the recently developed area of cognitive style, and it remains one of the most studied. (See Chapter 35, pages 654–55, for a brief description of the test.) For this test, Morris came to the laboratory of the Research Center for Mental Health, where he was introduced to the experimenter and was taken into a large room. He sat facing a screen, with a record sheet in front of him, containing spaces numbered from 1 to 75.

The experimenter gave the following instructions:

> We're going to show you a number of squares on the screen and I want you to tell me how big they are. The squares may range anywhere from 1 inch to 18 inches. This doesn't mean you will necessarily get a square that is 1 inch or 18 inches, though you may. The squares will always be somewhere within this range. To help you judge the size of squares, we will show you what a 1-inch square looks like—the smaller end of the

range—and what an 18-inch square looks like—the larger end of the range. [These two squares were then projected for about 3 seconds each.] You will see 75 squares, and you have 75 numbered spaces on your sheet. Write your estimation of the size of each square in its own numbered space. Thus, for square number 1, record its size in inches next to number 1, etc. You will see each of the squares for only a few seconds. Look at the square all the time it is on the screen and make your estimation when it disappears. The next square you see will be number 1.

At first, the squares were all near the smaller end of the scale. Soon, however, the smallest of the initial group of 5 was dropped out and a larger one was added; after the slightly changed group of 5 had been reexposed in random order, the smallest was again omitted and a slightly larger one added. As this process continued, the average size of the squares steadily increased until they were about twice the original magnitude. The test thus provides a measure of incremental error, which reflects how closely the subject follows the gradually changing sizes. Subjects who estimate accurately are called sharpeners; those who lag behind, paying less heed to the changes in the squares, are called levelers.

Morris' performance was an extreme example of leveling: Throughout the series of 75, he gave his judgments only in terms of 3, 4, or 5 inches. The mean of his final 15 guesses (3.87 in.) was just one-fifth of an inch larger than the mean of the first 15, although the last 15 squares were actually from 5.5 to 11.4 inches wide. This shows a truly extraordinary capacity to cling to a fixed conception despite the fact that the situation is undergoing drastic, though gradual, change. Morris remarked after the test that he thought he had fouled it up; he was vaguely aware that something had gone wrong, that he had gotten into a rut and did not know how to get out of it.

What does the test measure and what does such a performance mean? First, it should be realized that Holzman and Klein were not trying to develop a "personality test." Their aim was to explore consistencies in cognitive behavior, and this test proved to be one that successfully predicted other ways of dealing with sequences of stimuli. A factor analysis showed that a leveling-sharpening factor included, besides the scores from the schematizing test, measures of tendencies to overestimate the size of hand-held discs, to talk for a long time on one topic in free association before going to another, to be slow in recognizing the effect of special (aniseikonic) eyeglasses in distorting the visual world, and to be influenced by an interpolated weight (which is supposed to be disregarded) when judging which one of a pair of weights is heavier. As the experimenters summarized it, "In levelers, successive perceptual impressions were assimilated to each other, so that distinctions among them were blurred. Memories of past impressions were also less available to them, presumably because of the general lack of differentiation of their memory schemata [Gardner et al., 1959, p. 105]."

Several other studies have found a close relationship between leveling and a tendency to rely on the defense of repression, as judged from the Rorschach Test. This finding suggests that the process that allows someone like Morris to disregard changes in the external world is repression or is closely related to that defense mechanism. The analogue of repression, when applied to external stimuli, is the defense of denial; as we saw in the last chapter, Morris' cyclothymic (hypomanic) pattern included the tendency to use denial as a defense. The present finding connecting leveling and repression supports that interpretation, therefore. It also helps us understand Morris' relatively mediocre performance on the Picture Completion subtest of the WAIS: His defenses evidently interfere at times with his capacity to take in and to process information, especially visual information.

FIELD ARTICULATION

The Hidden Figures Test was given to Morris as a measure of the other widely studied dimension of cognitive style—field dependence versus field independence, or field articulation (see Chapter 35, page 655). The development of that concept and the methods for measuring it was the work of H. A. Witkin and his collaborators. Witkin developed what he called the Embedded Figures Test (Witkin, 1950) out of a demonstration of a *Gestalt*-psychological point by Gottschaldt (1929). This in turn was modified by Educational Testing Service, shortened, and made into a group test, which is used here.

A sample problem, like that given in Figure 39-4, can give a better idea of these tests than can mere description. The test presents 16 such problems, and the subject has 15 minutes to solve as many as he can; his score is the number correct. Morris got 10 items correct (and 1 wrong), which is a good enough score to put him in the field-independent classification.

In his original research Witkin found that his experimental measures of field independence, or psychological differentiation, were correlated with several general personality dispositions. Thus, Morris' performance on the test would lead us to expect him to be active rather than passive, not to be anxious about controlling his bodily impulses, and to have a high level of self-esteem. Those expectations seem to be consistent with the picture emerging from the other objective tests. Two other dispositions that would be expected of high scorers—an awareness of an inner life and a mature body image—were *not* characteristic of Morris, judging from his own description of himself as nonintrospective and from his rather crude and unelaborated figure drawings. He is not, therefore, a "pure culture" field-independent type, as might have been predicted from the fact that his score on this test was only moderately high.

But why was Morris able to do a better-than-average job on this test, if he is weak in "taking in and processing visual information"? Apparently that formulation was too sweeping; we must restrict our generalization to situations involving a gradual change in the stimuli or the detection of

This is a test of your ability to tell which one of five simple figures
can be found in a more complex pattern. At the top of each page in this test
are five simple figures lettered A, B, C, D, and E. Beneath each row of
figures is a page of patterns. Each pattern has a row of letters beneath it.
Indicate your answer by putting an X through the letter of the figure which
you find in the pattern.

NOTE: There is only one of these figures in each pattern, and this
figure will always be right side up and exactly the same size as one of the
five lettered figures.

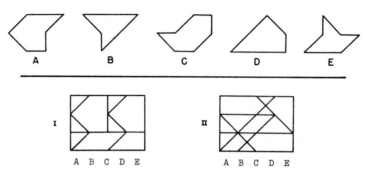

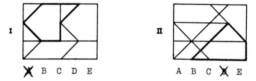

The figures below show how the figures are included in the problems.
Figure A is in the first problem and figure D in the second.

*Figure 39-4   Sample items from the Hidden Figures Test. (From
Messick, 1962)*

something missing. (If Morris still has some unconscious concern about his
own bodily integrity—castration anxiety—the Picture Completion task might
be especially likely to arouse his defenses.) It will take a good deal more
research, exploring the range of tasks that involve various kinds of visual
processing, before we can be confident about just how far we can generalize. It has been demonstrated in several research studies (for example,
Gardner et al., 1959) that leveling-sharpening and field articulation are
separate factors, despite apparent similarities in the tasks, and Guilford
(1967) indicates that many more independent factors exist in the content
domain of processing information about visual figures.

Judging from the two samples of tests and other devices used with
Morris Brown in 1940 and in 1966, nonprojective approaches to assessing
personality have far more to offer today than they did 25 years ago. Especially good progress has been made in assessing the subject's self-concept
and in developing cognitive tests—both of abilities and of the closely related
area of cognitive style. The goal of a truly objective test of personality, which

can be scored and interpreted by a clerk or a computer, as yet seems far away. Despite all the work that has gone into the pursuit of this ideal, it still takes a highly trained and intelligent person to interpret even the best of the currently available tests, if more than the simplest information is to be extracted from them.

Morris took a number of other objective tests and self-administering questionnaires in 1966, but they do not add a great deal to the information presented above. As was true of the 1940 assessment, it has been impossible to discuss even these nonprojective test findings without some exercise of clinical judgment or without drawing on some clinical observations. Let us see, then, how Morris appeared to the clinical eye in 1966.

To say that man is a compound of strength and weakness, light and darkness, smallness and greatness, is not to indict him, it is to define him.

DENIS DIDEROT. Supplement to Philosophical Thoughts

CHAPTER 40
THE MATURING
OF A PERSONALITY

A fter the tantalizing glimpse in the last chapter of a contemporary Morris Brown, so much the same and yet seemingly so different, the reader will probably want to know the intervening chapters of his life story and something about what the most recent clinical assessment reveals of its unconscious side. In the process of learning these things, we shall see some more facets of assessment in practice and find out what assessment can teach us about personal maturity.

Results of the 1966
Clinical Assessment of Morris Brown

In late 1942, Morris passed the Navy's medical examinations, went through communications training, and was put to work on the initial (or shakedown) cruises of small vessels destined for the European theater of the war. When the focus of the naval war shifted to the Pacific, he at last had a chance at regular sea duty and earned his battle star. He served honorably and well, staying in six months longer than required. Moreover, during nearly four years of active duty he developed an abiding affection for the naval service and a fondness for the sea.

On returning to the states, therefore, he decided to settle on the Eastern seaboard in a large city where he could be close to a weekend place on the water; Boston and Cape Cod seemed an ideal solution. He found a town on nearby Cape Cod—let us call it Inlet—which was convenient for both sailing and golf, and he bought several acres of land and a house there. Even with its very considerable growth since then, the town still has not exceeded a population of a few hundred and has remained off the tourist track. Morris spent his weekends in Inlet and the rest of the time in Boston, where he associated himself with a reputable securities firm and made an adequate living.

He started cultivating his golf game intensively. Golf is a sociable game, which mixes well with Morris' kind of business; he found that it brought him back into contact with a number of old golfing friends, some of whom had moved into the Boston area. Moreover, his prowess at golf gave Morris many opportunities to travel to invitational tournaments, and he saw a good deal of the South that way. More important, however, he became fast friends with a coterie of other good players and their wives, who followed the same circuit year after year. Through sailing, tennis, and bridge, he made still other groups of friends.

William Morris Brown (as he now regularly calls himself) rapidly became the best-known man in Inlet, where he had his legal residence. Soon he was elected to the local-government position equivalent to being mayor of a city, a post he has held for over a dozen years. He is particularly fond of this responsibility, for it puts him above the battle: He is responsible for chairing the town meetings and the sessions of the Board of Selectmen, where he casts a vote only in case of a tie. In each situation he tries to moderate disagreements and help disputing factions find compromise solutions. His is a middle-of-the-road political philosophy, with an emphasis on negotiating solutions and bringing warring parties together.

After several successful years in this role, Morris found himself (through a kind of "political fluke," as he put it) in the state legislature for a term. He enjoyed the one session in which he participated, but he disliked being forced to take a stand on every issue. Following a close defeat for reelection after a redistricting that forced him to run in an area where he was much less well known, Morris was happy to take a part-time civil-service job in the State House. This position keeps him in close contact with the legislature, but out of its hurly-burly, and enables him to continue to be well known to members of the lawmaking body. He now has political friends all over the state. He is being urged [as of 1966] to run again for state office, and he believes that his ever-widening circle of friends and acquaintances is a solid enough foundation for a fairly sure victory; at the moment, however, he is not certain that he wants the job.

The story of the last years of Morris' father has a touch of poetic justice to it. The elder Mr. Brown, alone and ailing, had again lost his speculatively gained substance and wrote to his wife asking if he could come home again. Certainly not, she replied; but he returned to the city anyway and took up residence in a nursing home. Several months later, taking pity on the feeble old man, now over 90, Mrs. Brown relented; he lived out his last six months in the same house where he had taken her as a bride. Morris had the opportunity to see his father again and to help his mother at the end.

After the war Morris and his mother had begun to be on increasingly good terms. Perhaps because she now accepted him as an adult (and a man of whom she could be proud), she made no efforts to interfere in his life. She continued running the rooming house, where she acted as informal foster mother to many a single woman. She and Morris began spending part of their vacations together, and he settled into a pattern of writing to her almost daily and talking to her by long distance every Sunday evening. When she died, a few years before the recent assessment, he could feel considerable satisfaction in the realization that he had been just the kind of devoted, good son she needed. He did not have to reproach himself, as did so many of his friends, for lack of consideration toward an elderly parent.

His stepsisters made good marriages to successful professional men and have families of their own with whom Morris keeps in touch. Nancy (the older sister) lives at some distance, but Marcia is close enough so that he has become her children's favorite uncle.

Morris has an unbroken record in the Naval Reserve; he has reported for summer training every year since his discharge and has carried through effectively every task he has been asked to perform. He is proud of the fact that he now has papers making him subject to call for active duty in an emergency; these papers are ordinarily held only by much younger men in the reserve. Moreover, through the excellence of his record and through friends now high in the Navy hierarchy, he has been called upon for special advisory assignments that have brought him into direct contact with famous persons in Washington and have given him very gratifying prestige.

The center of Morris' social life is his rambling Cape Cod house, which has been added onto so much it can now accommodate at least ten adults; a crib and a ready supply of disposable diapers are among its permanent amenities for family entertaining. In dozens of households all over New England and further south, people are accustomed to saying, "Let's run over to the Cape for a weekend at Morris' place." Uncle Morris is an almost legendary figure to the boys in these families—he swims and sails a boat as well as any teen-ager, licks most of them at tennis and all their fathers on the golf course, chops down trees, and is well-versed in the outdoorsman's lore of the Cape. The mothers are comfortable with him too, and his friends know that the latchstring is always out for them. Every weekend brings an interestingly different assortment: The husband in one couple was a member of Morris' old scout troop; another was a wartime buddy; there are always golfers when the weather permits a game (which is more than half the year in that location); occasionally a rebellious late adolescent will arrive without his family for a chance to have some long talks with a man who knows how to make him feel accepted for whatever he is.

Some of the younger members of his entourage became acquainted with Morris through his foster son Dave, now in his mid-20's. Morris had known Dave's father, who might have been a good golfer if alcoholism had not destroyed him. The widow found that she could lean on Morris and that her son took to him. Before she died, which was not long after her husband, she asked Morris to be the father Dave needed. Morris took him under his wing and feels that he helped get a rather mixed-up boy reasonably well straightened out. Although Dave is now on his own and lives in a different city, his relationship with Morris remains close.

Three years ago, Morris found that he was experiencing odd spells of fatigue and that he was losing much of his energy. He learned that he had diabetes.

Rather than make a more radical change in his style of life, Morris chose to lose 25 pounds and take insulin regularly. He can now eat anything he wants, but he has to keep his weight in the 170's. (His appearance is considerably the better for it; without the old rounded contours and with his now graying hair, his erect posture, and a spring in his step, he looks like a distinguished, vigorous executive.) The only way he could adhere to his new regimen was to give up his shared Boston apartment and constant commuting and live full time in Inlet. Morris proudly reports that his doctors have told him not 1 percent of diabetics hold to the necessary routines as well as he does, even though the patients know that carelessness will ultimately be fatal. Morris has gone into insulin coma twice, it is true, but he believes that he now knows the signs well enough to take the needed sugar promptly, and (to the relief of his friends) he has someone living with him—a foreigner who was offered a job in a city not far from Inlet but who had nowhere to stay. On hearing of the man's plight, Morris offered to take him in; though the two of them have no interests in common and virtually never converse, they get along amicably.

How should Morris' adjustment be described today? Is he happy? He surely seems to be; he claims to have found real peace since living in the country full time. In his own estimation, he has finally attained maturity since his mother's death. He sees himself as a contented man capable of frequent moments of high delight, even ecstasy:

> evenings of having the record player going and the dogs over in the corner and a good book to read and looking out and seeing all that snow and thinking, "Thank God I don't have to go anywhere!" Or now that it's getting to be spring, going out and chopping wood, staggering back and then taking a long hot shower, followed by a few beers. Those are the things that I love. And I really get ecstatic about 'em. The wonderful simple life.

At the same time, he noted that his (cyclothymic) mood swings have leveled out; both his highs and lows are less extreme.

In addition, he enjoys his work and is good enough at it to make a comfortable living. But he is content to work only enough to earn about $10,000 a year, and thus has more time for golf, sailing, tennis, and general outdoorsmanship than the great majority of more affluent men can enjoy. He is assured of financial security now: His savings, inheritance, and assured retirement pensions from the Navy, the investment firm, and Social Security enable him to look forward to a secure old age. In both work and sport he has attained positions of unusual recognition. He has hosts of friends, some of whom are young men who look up to him "as if I were Jesus Christ," as he puts it. He is fortunately situated where he can maintain a subscription to the Boston Symphony Orchestra and see his Boston bridge cronies regularly, while living the simple life in a rural community where he is the most respected of the town fathers. True, he has a chronic illness of some seriousness and a few other bodily complaints, but the diabetes is well controlled and on the whole his health and physical condition are far better than could be expected of the vast majority of men his age.

The one thing that is missing, as Morris himself is frank to point out, is love:

Whatever's wrong I have no idea, but people don't love me. They may like me very much—I'm not saying I'm a poor lost lonesome soul—but most of the people I know have somebody who is just absolutely wrapped up in them, and I never seem to have engendered that feeling. I have had plenty of gals who have made a first move. Maybe my trouble is I shove 'em away. I complain about not being loved but I'm not sure it's a complaint. Maybe I'd rather be more independent. . . . Is it possible that I'm so afraid of being hurt that I don't want to get involved?

So far in the second half of his life Morris' erotic life has remained fundamentally unchanged. He has had sexual affairs with both women and men, discreetly and rather infrequently, and usually without much tenderness and affection. His friends have for years introduced him to eligible and more or less attractive girls (by now they are mostly widows); he is polite, friendly, but rarely interested.

There was one major exception during a two-and-a-half-year period when Morris was about 35. His principal friends at the time were a group of men 10 years younger than himself, who were dating college girls; through them he met Sally, a sophomore at that time. When this beautiful young girl fell in love with him, Morris came closer to marriage than at any other time in his life. Yet, "as I finished with it, I was such an emotional wreck that I couldn't see, what is this business of being in love? I mean, it's just a torture—there was nothing good about it. We just badgered each other, killed each other—ecstatically happy for one moment and then made miserable for 24 hours. . . . There was just no peace in it," he concluded, observing that most of the happily married couples he is in constant contact with also have very little peace two-thirds of the time. He maintains that on a sexual level it was a highly satisfactory relationship, yet he spoke without nostalgia or any trace of unfulfilled yearning in his voice.

Recently, his main sexual contact has been with a younger man, who outwardly appears to be happily married but who has no moral scruples about taking any form of extramarital gratification he can get. Because he knows and likes the wife and children, Morris declares that he would have nothing to do with the man if he thought that there was any danger to the marriage. Neither man seeks the other out particularly; as Morris likes to put it, at times when they see each other something just happens spontaneously.

The encounter during the summer after graduation from college when he was a lifeguard (described in Chapter 36) is the only time Morris has had contact with an identifiably overt homosexual. There are colonies of such men on the Cape, but he avoids them; on the few occasions when he has been solicited, Morris says he has "run like hell in the opposite direction." He has thus managed to live a bachelor's life with only a minimum of gossipy suspicion and without a breath of scandal.

For the most part, however, Morris confines his sexual outlet to autoeroticism. Having close friends and much recognition, he has been able to renounce love without becoming a sexual prude. It is not an ideal life, but perhaps Morris has demonstrated (like many another unmarried man and woman before him) that it is possible to be reasonably well adjusted and socially effective without love, though cut off from the deepest of human satisfactions, which mature persons prize the most.

Some Reflections on Growing Up

Out of an unhappy family situation and a childhood most memorable for poverty and loneliness, we saw a confused young man grow, struggling to find himself and to control his impulsive, somewhat destructive behavior. A quarter of a century later, he had attained a large measure of happiness, peace, and adjustment, albeit in an atypical way.

Was he unusually slow to mature? Not nearly so much as one might think at first, for maturity is a continuous process rather than a state that should automatically set in at age 21 or any other time. Moreover, as White (1966) and Erikson (1963) tell us, maturation is a slower and more protracted process than is generally assumed, and many of the typical conflicts of adolescence do not subside in normal people until after the age of 30.

We should not, of course, overestimate Morris' achievement. His body is not functioning as well as could be desired; despite his good adjustment to the diabetes, it is a legitimate cause for anxiety. His sexual adjustment leaves a good deal to be desired, and there are other weak spots in his adaptation. The major problem of psychological interest, however, is how to explain his ability to get along so well by himself, quite without professional assistance.

The following explanation is a mixture of facts (elicited by interviews) and hypotheses, which are based on all the available data but especially on his projective test responses in the 1966 assessment.

HOW MORRIS BROWN ATTAINED MATURITY

The War Years:
A Moratorium

The Second World War, destructive though it was for millions of others, came at a fortunate time in Morris' life. It took him out of a situation containing almost as many temptations as supports and provided a temporary reprieve from his lonely effort to gain self-control. Such a period of time-out from the main game of life Erikson (1959) calls a *moratorium*, and he finds that it is often necessary for young people who are going through the kind of identity crisis Morris was enduring when he was first assessed. It takes off the pressure to make a major commitment, so that unconscious conflicts can simmer down and patterns of defense can be consolidated. The Navy replaced many burdensome responsibilities of civilian life with relatively manageable obligations within a tightly organized framework of external control. It was a common clinical observation during the war that military service was an unusually good environment for men who lacked inner controls, even for those with a psychopathic streak: The combination of absolute security, a strong institutional parent-substitute on which one could lean unobtrusively, and socially approved outlets for aggression provided a form of social control that allowed impulses to be expressed in acceptable ways. When Morris had to take command of a landing craft on its shakedown cruise, he could do it well (we saw in the preceding chapters that he had the necessary abilities) and therefore could legitimately feel he was becoming a man.

The service also gave him a sexual moratorium, freeing him from the social pressure to find a girl to marry while giving him occasional opportunities for condoned heterosexual adventures. And it threw him together with men in situations where his natural talent for friendship could manifest itself and his preference for close contact with men could be satisfied.

Thus, the war years took away opportunities for many elements of the more potentially pathological of Morris' two possible identities and ego structures to show themselves; and they strengthened important elements in the compulsive pattern. A major threat carried by the compulsive alternative was the danger of a predominantly feminine identity if he became too much like his mother. During the war and afterward, however, he was able to develop in himself the most adaptive and socially desirable aspects of his mother's heritage while being in many ways more masculine than his father had ever been.

Development of His Identity

When he first got out of the Navy, Morris experienced a short period of restlessness—he toured the national parks with four friends for several months before he settled down to work. During that period the paternal pattern seemed to be asserting itself one final time before subsiding. The strengthened compulsive defenses proved staunch, especially when Morris' athletic prowess began to emerge again. (Note that this important aspect of his personality owes little to either parent.) Thanks to his sturdy body and his extraordinary physical talents, Morris has always been outstanding in the "man's world" of sport. His travel in tournament competition seems to have satiated his wanderlust to the point where he seldom feels the old itch to get away.

But though he has been able to maintain an appropriately manly personality in many respects, it would probably have taken considerable psychotherapeutic help for Morris to have worked through the incest taboo, his anxiety about the masculine sexual role (basically, castration anxiety), and other unconscious hindrances to a sustained intimate relationship with a woman. Because that possibility was shut off, and because he had established a pattern of finding some sexual gratification with men, there was a distinct danger of overt homosexuality. In another situation and another vocation, and with various other changes, someone still recognizably similar to our man might have taken this route; but it was obviously impossible for

Morris. A political career, for example, would have been out of the question, as would many of the other important elements of his pattern of adjustment.

Thanks to Morris' unusual defenses—a blend of isolation, denial, and repression—he has been able to keep the door to sexual activity with males ajar, but not enough to bring against himself the accusation of being a "fairy," which he clearly is not, according to his own definition. Most people would probably agree. He has been able to develop an identity in which there are both masculine and feminine elements. And the latter are mainly qualities that were the source of his mother's *strength*—her moral backbone, her compulsive orderliness and organizing ability, and her kindly nurturance. The role Morris plays with so many of his young friends (and of course most literally with his foster son) is a parental one, just as his preferred role in politics is that of a just, impartial parent who empathically settles the children's squabbles without getting drawn into taking sides.

Morris' most recent projective test responses show none of the gory, self-directed destructive imagery that was so blatant in the Rorschach and TAT of 1940. The explanation may lie in one of Erikson's insights (1963): A strong sense of identity is a bulwark against the superego. As Morris grew more sure of himself and realized that he was a socially esteemed and estimable person, he was able to get control over the savagely self-punitive superego elements reflected in such images as the self-disemboweling Fu Manchu. The more his conscious values and role led to behavior that was acceptable to the primitive elements of his earliest identifications with his parents, the less unconscious guilt he had and the more he could consolidate a reasonable and useful nucleus of unconscious self-control. To be sure, this change, accomplished through the aid of more identification with his parents (particularly his mother), has also led to a degree of solidarity with all sources of authority that many would consider excessive. Morris feels so much at one with the controlling powers that he is overly ready to comply instantly with any authoritative requirement. At the same time, he has not developed an ideological authoritarianism; unconsciously, he seems to be more a good boy than a tyrant.

The Effect of His Environment

The importance of Morris' environment should not be overlooked as we try to understand how he made his adjustment. His being able to get away from the big-city pressure and competition to a small country town where he could live an outdoor life was a weekend safety valve for years, while he began to develop rootedness in the little community. His longtime position of public trust and leadership there has greatly strengthened his fatherliness and his sense of responsibility. It has made mature, moral integrity far more rewarding than any kind of opportunistic attempt at self-serving shortcuts could possibly be.

Morris Brown's life history is a good example of an important principle in understanding personality: Early traumas and other unhappy experiences and the growth of such defenses as isolation and denial do not necessarily imply a disturbance of the adult personality. These elements can constitute unsuccessful or successful personalities—people crippled by neurosis or solid citizens like Morris. Endowments of ability and strength (like our man's intelligence and physique) and how the person fits into his social setting probably tip the balance toward a socially desirable or undesirable personality.

Clinical psychologists and psychiatrists, who are accustomed to dealing only with people who have given up trying to make it on their own, often tend to overlook the positive role a defense like denial can play in a healthy adjustment. In some such colleagues, the presence of recognizably hypomanic elements in Morris' very happiness would bring on dark looks and ominously wagging heads. To them only this can be said: Let the one among you who is without this defense (or one of an equivalent and equally "pathological" type) cast the first stone. Good adaptation is not so much a question of the kind of defense as of the total biopsychosocial configuration in which it operates.

Concluding Thoughts
on Morris Brown's Assessment

It would be a mistake to leave the impression that this case study has been a typical application of personality assessment, or that it is being offered as a model for the practitioner to emulate. In many ways, it has been a unique opportunity and a special application of techniques. The very fact that so many hours were spent gathering and analyzing data of so many kinds makes this case history atypical. For most of the practical applications of personality assessment listed in Chapter 32, it would be a highly uneconomic procedure.

Much more abbreviated and limited approaches to personality assessment are not only more common but are more desirable, in a number of situations. When Morris served as a subject in an experiment, the quantitative data from objective assessment proved more useful than the qualitative understanding, for the group method called for uniform measures across all subjects. Most research projects are of necessity designed in that way, and if clinical assessments are to play a part they must be expressed in the form of quantitative ratings, like the criterion Q sort for Morris. The focused approach of objective tests of personality will continue to be the most useful one, particularly in research on the kinds of changes induced in personality by life conditions of stress or frustration, on the relationships between personality and ideology, and in general on any topic for which one (nonpersonality) variable must be quickly and accurately measured in large numbers of persons.

Let us turn, in the next chapter, to a reconsideration of the relative merits and uses of the two principal approaches to the assessment of personality.

He that judges without informing himself to the utmost that he is capable, cannot acquit himself of judging amiss.

JOHN LOCKE. Essay Concerning Human Understanding

CHAPTER 41
THE EVALUATION
OF PERSONALITY
ASSESSMENT

An attempt has been made in the preceding chapters to present research evidence bearing on assertions made there about personality assessment, but most of what is known about the topic, and about clinical assessment in particular, is the heritage of a tradition. Although this body of knowledge has been subjected to constant confrontation with empirical data and intermittent theoretical refinement, it remains true that assessing personality is the application of a science that is not yet fully developed.

One hallmark of a scientifically based discipline is that it tries to evaluate its practices as carefully and dispassionately as possible in a search not for self-justification but for the truth, which alone makes progress possible. Though there undeniably are elements of art and craft in assessment, its practitioners strive to put it on as sound a scientific basis as they can. In the course of this attempt, they have generated a fair amount of evidence, a large controversy, and some useful thinking about how so manifold an undertaking as personality assessment may be evaluated. This chapter is devoted to a survey of these topics.

How Should Personality Assessment
Be Evaluated?

We have seen that the first types of formal assessment were clinical and that they were little more than an extended attempt to apply the methods of informal assessment with relatively little systematization (Chapter 34). These clinical methods were evaluated in correspondingly informal ways, usually without any focused intent to question their worth and effectiveness—that is, they won social and institutional acceptance, so that it became possible to earn a living by assessing personalities in the variety of settings we examined in Chapter 32. It is difficult to believe that specialists in assessment could have won and retained the respect of their professional colleagues if they actually had nothing valid to contribute.

A few notorious impostors have demonstrated that a charlatan can practice even so concrete a discipline as surgery undetected, for a while, with no assets other than an impressive, assured manner, an ear for shop talk, and some shrewdness and common sense in handling practical situations. The criterion of cure is much less clear-cut in psychotherapy, so that a private practitioner of this healing art may survive for years without any valid knowledge or skill, simply because his work is not observed and checked by colleagues and because people in need of treatment tend on the average to get better anyway. But a lack of clinical competence cannot be concealed for very long from anyone who has participated in the daily work of a "mental-health team" in a clinic or hospital. The method of evaluating clinical assessment implicit in such vocational success is sometimes called "clinical validation"; its evidence is surely fallible, and it would be dangerous to put sole reliance on it, but it is real and important evidence. The personality assessment practiced by psychiatrists, social workers, and other non-psychologists is generally subjected to no more searching evaluation than the judgment of colleagues that it is worthwhile.

The psychometric tradition has won a respected place within psychology, in part because psychometricians have stringently evaluated their own techniques and have produced both principles and methods for doing so. Their first evaluative ideals were reliability and validity, as we saw in Chapter 35. Today, it is being recognized that these touchstones are not as automatically applicable as had once been thought. A test should surely be reliable, but it is difficult to lay down any handy, generally useful set of guidelines. For example, a statement that "repeat reliability must be .85 or better if the test is to be used with individuals" must be hedged about by so many definitions, explanations, and exceptions that it is of very little value. There is no consensus among psychometric experts on the degree of internal consistency a test should have, and obviously a test that did not reflect a real change in a subject on being readministered would be "reliable" in the narrow sense, at the cost of usefulness—like a stopped clock that always tells the same time.

Nevertheless, the ideal of reliability is undeniably relevant both to the psychometric approach and to personality assessment as a whole. It is meaningful to ask how well assessors can agree among themselves when they examine the same person (consensus), how well each one can agree with his own previous conclusions when he reanalyzes the same body of data about a person after a lapse of time (stability, a form of repeat reliability), and how well various techniques of assessment agree among themselves or lead to common inferences (convergence).

Before these questions can be answered, two important limitations on their applicability must be stated. First, only by requiring assessors to express their statements about their subjects in a common language, preferably in the form of quantitative ratings, can precise information about each of these points be obtained. Since most professional practitioners of personality assessment do not use Q sorts or other forms of numerical rating but express their findings in verbal reports, and since they may use quite varied conceptual vocabularies, their routine work cannot easily be evaluated for any of these forms of reliability. Second, personality assessment is a sprawling, heterogeneous discipline, practiced by different kinds of people in different settings for a variety of purposes. It therefore cannot be meaningfully evaluated as a whole, just as we cannot sensibly ask, "On the average, how reliable are psychological tests?" We have seen in earlier chapters that some tests are highly reliable by several kinds of criteria, others seem worthless, and many others occupy positions all up and down the scale. In almost all branches of personality assessment, there have been reports that most kinds of assessment *can* be carried out with good reliability in all three of these senses. Most of the published evidence, however, suggests that although clinical assessors tend to agree fairly well with themselves over time (stability), they agree far less well with one another (consensus), and most of the evidence on convergence is discouraging (Goldberg, 1968).

With respect to the issue of validity the situation is even more confusing. Recent critics like Ebel (1961) and Vernon (1964) have seriously questioned the old dogma that validity—at least, as expressed in terms of correlation coefficients—is necessarily the most important criterion for evaluating tests. The traditional method of measuring validity assumes that there exists an intrinsically valid criterion against which a test score can be measured—when in fact such a criterion exists only in exceptional cases, and almost never in the general realm of personality traits. It is worthy of note, however, that those who have attempted to validate tests of personality have quite generally assumed that the best criterion available is ratings from intensive, multiform, clinical assessment. It is difficult indeed to imagine a wholly different and better approach to a criterion measure of traits.

In terms of the traditional approach to the validity of specific techniques of assessment (correlation with a criterion), the results are much the same as in the case of their reliability, except that correlations run much lower and the best are only moderately good. In place of reliance on "validity coefficients," Ebel suggests that the following list of criteria for determining the value, or quality, of a mental test or measurement procedure be adopted.

1. The importance of the inferences that can be made from the test scores [or, more generally, from the test data]
2. The meaningfulness of the test scores, based on
   a. An operational definition of the measurement procedure
   b. A knowledge of the relationships of the scores to other measures, from
      i. Validity coefficients, predictive and concurrent
      ii. Other correlation coefficients or measures of relationship
   c. A good estimate of the reliability of the scores
   d. Appropriate norms of examinee performance
3. The convenience of the test in use [Ebel, 1961, p. 646].

These standards were designed for the evaluation of tests, and they are not as directly applicable to entire enterprises of assessment. Nevertheless, they may be of some value as guides. Suppose we look back over the assessment of Morris Brown presented in earlier chapters and ask whether clinical or objective tests and methods were more useful in our attempt to grasp what sort of man he is and what sort of sense his life pattern makes. Judged in this way the clinical approach seems an easy winner. Such an evaluative approach is close in spirit to Ebel's first principle, for (compared with the objective procedures) clinical methods led to a wider range of inferences and observations, which touched on deeper and more important issues. Objective tests do tend to be more convenient (Ebel's third criterion) in that they take less time and skill to administer and score than projective techniques, and they have the advantage of yielding quantitative scores—which are necessary to make Ebel's second, complex criterion workable. A word of caution about the first criterion, however, is in order: The mere fact that it is possible to make inferences about important aspects of personality from the TAT, for example, does not mean that those inferences can be trusted, nor that they convey much useful information. Ultimately it remains necessary to find some external or independent way of evaluating the same aspects of personality, against which we can check interpretations based on any one test or procedure.

A simpler approach to validation has been proposed and has been widely accepted by psychologists. The ultimate aim of psychology is to predict human behavior, the argument begins; therefore, let us aim any particular method of assessment toward some specific behavioral *prediction* and judge the validity of that method according to just how correct the prediction is. Later in this chapter we shall take note of several ways in which this argument is not wholly acceptable and shall continue the discussion of how to evaluate approaches to assessment. First, however, let us examine in more detail the predictive approach—the controversy (clinical versus statistical prediction) it has aroused and the sorts of data it has generated.

Clinical Versus
Statistical Prediction

THE NATURE OF THE CONTROVERSY

A recurrent theme in the preceding chapters has been the objective versus the subjective tradition within personality assessment. It has surely become clear that this section has a bias—that personalities cannot be understood or even meaningfully measured without the necessarily subjective processes of the clinician as he perceives, empathizes, intuits, makes judgments, integrates and synthesizes information, and constructs a theory, or schema, of a person. It would not be fair to the reader, however, to imply that this view is widespread among American psychologists or to minimize the many important advances in personality assessment made by those whose ideal is objectivity and who hope eventually to eliminate the clinician altogether as an assessor of personality.

The origins of the controversy over prediction go back to the 1920's and '30's, when a small group of prominent psychologists challenged proponents of statistical methods to try to predict behavior as well as the clinical case-history method could do. It was said (for example by Allport, 1942) that statistical methods had severe, inherent limitations in their applicability to the behavior of unique individual personalities. This point of view derived from a number of fallacious theories about the nature of science as applied to personality (described in Holt, 1967) and perhaps also from an emotional rejection of the idea that mechanical systems could predict the acts of live human beings. These critics knew little about the refined techniques being developed by statistical workers, and some of the most vocal were not themselves practitioners of the clinical assessment they upheld.

It is important to realize that advocates of the clinical and the objective traditions of assessment have almost always been involved in rather different kinds of work. Clinical assessment is practiced predominantly in hospitals and clinics where the emphasis is on intensive study of individuals to gain an understanding of them that can facilitate decisions about how to help them and guide a psychotherapist in his initial approach.

Objective assessment of personality is the main work of a smaller number of psychologists, mostly researchers interested in developing tests, and it has been a sideline of persons interested in educational advisement, personnel selection, and criminology, who have relied for the most part on ability tests and measures not generally considered within the realm of personality assessment. The objective assessor is usually called upon to make a simple decision about accepting a person for some kind of education, training, or employment, or paroling a prisoner.

The clinical assessor does make similar judgments (for example, should a given patient be treated by a particular method or not?), but for the most part his task is the evaluation and understanding of a person's problems, his major patterns of behavior, and the nature of his development. In the normal course of events, therefore, there was little direct competition between these different approaches.

Behind the two traditions there is a good deal more, however. They are offshoots of different and conflicting ideologies and schools of psychology (and perhaps, ultimately, of different temperaments). Psychologists of personality generally respect the divergent ideals of scientific rigor and human relevance, but some emphasize the one, some the other. Despite the desire of many—perhaps most—people in the field to maintain some integration and balance between these often conflicting standards, there has been an escalating tendency toward dichotomous thinking. The resulting attitude has been this: If there are two ways of approaching the assessment of personality, one must be right or at least superior; therefore, let us pit one approach against the other and see which is better.

Clearly, there is no way of telling whether it is "better" to be a valued member of a clinical team or a successful constructer of objective tests. Some common ground had to be found on which the issue could be joined. That ground was the *prediction of behavior*, and the issue was formulated as "clinical versus statistical prediction." The result was a controversy that picked up steam right after World War II and has been one of the most conspicuous features of the psychological scene for over a decade.

SOME TERMS DEFINED

There is less agreement than one might expect on what is meant by the two types of prediction. As we shall shortly see, predicting behavior is a complicated matter that involves half a dozen steps, in any of which clinical judgment may play a role. But the prevailing tendency has been to focus on only the final step, when the data—however they may have been gathered and processed—are put together to yield an actual prediction. Sawyer (1966) says: "Whether *prediction* is called clinical or mechanical typically depends on how the data were *combined*." Meehl (1954) is somewhat more specific: "By *mechanical* (or statistical), I mean that the prediction is arrived at by some straightforward application of an equation or table to the data." This latter definition will become more meaningful after we have examined some concrete examples of how predictions are made by means of equations and tables.

Notice that clinical prediction appears to be defined residually; that is, it seems to be any kind of prediction that does *not* rely on mechanical rules and procedures. This failure to give clinical prediction as positive a definition as statistical prediction has introduced a subtle bias into the research on this topic: Almost anyone is considered a "clinician," whether he has any training in clinical assessment or not, as long as he does not follow some formula; and "clinical" has tended to become synonymous with "unsystematic," "casual," or "haphazard." It would seem a foregone conclusion that if predictions are considered "clinical" only when they are made by people who are selected without regard for their degree of clinical skill or training and who follow no definite procedures, the statistical approach will surely appear superior.

Nevertheless, the crux of the matter seems to be the degree to which objectivity is achieved by diminishing the role of clinical judgment, replacing it at the final stage by a set of predetermined rules that may be applied by a person with minimal training. If we consider stages other than the final one, the problem no longer looks so simple. Sawyer (1966) urged that we also consider whether a clinician was involved in gathering the data:

> Data collection is mechanical if rules can be prespecified so that no clinical judgment need be involved in the procedure. Thus, on the one hand are all the self-report and clerically obtained data: psychometric tests, biographical data, personnel records, etc.; on the other hand are the usual clinical interview and observation [and projective techniques]. [Sawyer, 1966, p. 181]

Further distinctions can usefully be made among other types of predictions, but in order to grasp them we shall first have to consider in more detail just what statistical prediction is and what some of its accomplishments have been.

METHODS AND ACHIEVEMENTS
OF STATISTICAL PREDICTION

From its beginning, the psychometric tradition has been concerned with prediction. Binet, you will recall, invented the first successful intelligence tests in what was essentially an attempt to predict educational achievement. In the next four decades, the predictive task widened from weeding out defectives in elementary schools to selecting students who would be most likely to profit from college or postgraduate education. One of the best predictors was essentially a descendant of Binet's test, via the line of group intelligence tests: the Scholastic Aptitude Test (SAT), developed by the College Entrance Examination Board. Its total score was correlated about .50 with achievement in freshman courses; average grades in secondary school also were correlated with the same target, or criterion, variable (freshman grades) at about the same level. A statistical combination of SAT scores and high school grades by means of multiple correlation was somewhat better than either alone, but more than half the variance in freshman grades remained unaccounted for.

Prediction by the Experience Table

During the decade just before World War II, sociologists and criminologists doing research on marital adjustment and on the violation of parole made active and successful use of a predictive device known as the *experience table*. This method is called *actuarial* because in setting rates for life insurance an actuary proceeds in much the same fashion. For this reason, the nonclinical approach in general has come to be called either actuarial or statistical prediction, the two terms being used interchangeably by most authors. Another commonly used synonym for statistical in this context is "mechanical."

An experience table is a summary of experience with a group of subjects, which is broken down according to background data, their answers to a questionnaire, or the like. The group should be as large as possible. For example, a criminologist may classify past parolees from a prison system according to a large number of available items of information about the prisoners, looking for those items that create a significant difference in the rate of parole violation. Thus, Burgess (1928) found that although the general rate of violation among 3000 men paroled from the Illinois prisons was just over 28 percent, the rate was less than half that among men whose records showed that they had worked regularly before imprisonment—a statistically significant finding. This then became one of 21 items associated with success, to each of which Burgess assigned a value of 1. He next tabulated the percentage of nonviolators of parole in 9 groupings of men according to their total scores on these items; the result of this tabulation is shown in Table 41-1.

Table 41-1   Rates of Success on Parole,
According to the Burgess Experience Table

Experience Table Score Group	Number of Cases	Percentage of Nonviolators of Parole
A (16–21)	68	99
B (14–15)	140	98
C (13)	91	91
D (12)	106	85
E (11)	110	77
F (10)	88	66
G (7–9)	287	56
H (5–6)	85	33
I (2–4)	25	24

Adapted from Gough, 1962.

Two considerations must be kept in mind in evaluating any figures like those in Table 41-1, promising though they may appear. First, there is the problem of *cross-validation shrinkage*. This is a technical way of saying that one cannot expect everything to work out exactly the same with another group of subjects, and in fact if any of the original findings are attributable to chance (as they always are to some extent), cross-validating on a new sample will give poorer results. The larger the original group, the less likelihood there is that there has been much capitalizing on chance; but notice that although Table 41-1 is based on 1000 cases, the actual percentages in 5 of the 9 score groups are based on less than 100 men.

Second, there is the question of what is called the *base rate*—here, the proportion of persons who succeed in the total population of prisoners. Suppose that 95 percent of the men in a given prison tend to succeed in parole; obviously, we would very seldom be wrong if we *always* predicted nonviolation (assuming that the base rate remains stable, for variations in the base rate are one source of cross-validation shrinkage). Even when the base rate of violation is as high (28.5 percent) as it was in Burgess' original sample, Gough has shown that

> At only two cutting points, levels F and G, does the Burgess table improve over the flat assertion that no one will fail, and at the *optimum* point of dichotomy (predicting parole success for all men with scores of 7 or more) the error figure . . . is only 4.2 percentage points under that found when one simply forecasts that everyone will succeed [Gough, 1962, p. 563].

Indeed, Meehl and Rosen (1955) have shown that when the base rate of anything we are interested in predicting goes much above or below 50 percent, it is increasingly difficult to beat it. How can these statements be true, when it seems clear from Table 41-1 that if only those men with scores of 12 or more (groups A through D) were paroled, 9 out of 10 would be nonviolators? The hitch is that this is considering only what are technically called "valid positives" and "false positives," neglecting the "valid negatives" and especially the "false negatives"—in this example, the 338 men who would not violate parole if they got a chance but who would be refused it. Since almost as many subjects would be false negatives as valid positives (correctly predicted nonviolators) if the cut were made between D and E, this is a large group to overlook.

This example brings out another important point that has been learned from actuarial prediction: A predictor may be useful even when it has a relatively low validity, or success, rate attached to it, if the *selection ratio* is low—that is, if it is possible to skim off the cream by taking only the best applicants, or diagnosing only the clearest cases, or releasing only the best bets for parole. Where it is necessary, however, to predict for an entire population and to minimize both kinds of errors (false positives and false negatives), it becomes very important to know the base rate. "In order for a positive diagnostic assertion to be 'more likely true than false,' the ratio of the positive to the negative base rates in the examined population must exceed the ratio of the false positive rate to the valid positive rate [Meehl & Rosen, 1955]." This means that if only a small proportion of a total population actually belong to the predicted class (let us say, suicides), then if an indicator does not pick up virtually all of them (valid positives) and only a very small proportion of the great majority who are actually nonsuicidal (false positives), the latter will exceed the former. This is true whether the indicator is a test score, an objective fact of life history, or a clinical judgment by a team of investigators.

Prediction by Multiple Regression

Multiple regression is a complex statistical method of combining several variables in order to predict a quantitative criterion. It is an outgrowth of the method of correlation, a mathematical technique of expressing the degree of relation between two sets of numbers. If one set is a group's scores on a psychological test and the other set is their ratings on some kind of criterion behavior, a high correlation means that the first variable may be used to predict the second. Suppose that the same group has been given several tests, each of which is appreciably correlated with the criterion—how do we go about using all of them to improve the predictions that could be made with one test? If all the tests were measures of the same trait (for example, various intelligence tests), each would be highly correlated with all the others and any one of them would serve almost as well as the whole battery. But if the intercorrelations among the tests were low, there would be a good chance that they measured different traits and thus could supplement one another. Multiple regression is a statistical technique for extracting, from the web of interrelationships among a group of predictors and a criterion, a set of weights for each test score and a formula for combining them to yield the best possible prediction of the criterion.

This method will become clearer with an actual example. During World War II, the technique of multiple regression was brought to a high state of development in the Army Air Force. A battery of 20 tests (14 self-administering questionnaires and 6 tests requiring apparatus) was used to select men for the various jobs on a military plane—as pilots, navigators, tailgunners, and so on. Scores on the tests were put together by slightly different formulas for each aircrew job. When applied to new samples of recruits, these formulas repeatedly yielded predictions that correlated from .50 to .60 with passing versus failing the training course (DuBois, 1947).

How were such results obtained? (See the "pure actuarial" column in Table 41-2, page 787.) First, the army's psychologists made a "job analysis"—detailed studies of just what a pilot, for example, did and what the student had to learn. They next tried to determine what personal qualities—abilities, temperamental traits, and so on—a person must possess to carry out these functions. Assembling the existing tests of these characteristics, they made up others and put together a large battery, which was given to many hundreds of flight trainees. Records of these men's success or failure provided the criterion, with which every test's scores were correlated in a preliminary validation trial. Many tests immediately failed to show any promise and were dropped; others were modified, and the best were kept unchanged in the new battery. The statistical method of multiple regression helped the psychologists find the best ways of combining the separate test scores to predict a pass-fail criterion. Once the formula was found, it provided a statistical, or mechanical, rule for combining test data; the clerk who used it needed no special psychological knowledge. This formula was then put through further trial by cross-validation (being checked on a new group of subjects). The entire process was repeated until it looked as if the battery of tests had reached the limits of its effectiveness.

RELATIVE SUCCESSES
OF CLINICAL AND STATISTICAL PREDICTION

Emboldened by ignorance and by the encouragement of prestigious spokesmen, many clinical assessors of personality stuck their necks out in research projects that were set up—usually by the statisticians—to compare the "two kinds of prediction." The clinicians either did not notice or did not think it important that they were being asked to function in unfamiliar ways and to make statements about matters they understood poorly. Perhaps they thought there was nothing to be lost by such extracurricular adventures, which were, after all, sidelines for them. Most clinicians spent by far the greater part of their time in diagnostic and therapeutic work with patients, where they earned their livings and made their reputations.

Results of Surveys   The highly influential book *Clinical Versus Statistical Prediction* (Meehl, 1954) was the first of several surveys of the comparative performance of clinical and statistical predictors (Cronbach, 1956; Gough, 1962; Sawyer, 1966). Meehl reported finding "from 16 to 20 studies involving a comparison of clinical and actuarial methods, *in all but one of which the predictions made actuarially were either approximately equal or superior to those made by a clinician* [1954, p. 119]."

Just over a decade later Meehl (1965) wrote, that he had tallied 50 studies, in two-thirds of which the statistical predictions were superior and in the other one-third of which the two methods were substantially equal. He noted that the one exception he had found earlier demonstrated the apparent superiority of the clinician only by virtue of an invalid use of statistics, but he hailed a study by Lindzey (which will be described later in the chapter) as the first clear example in which the clinician was superior. Sawyer

(1966), in a slightly more recent survey tallying 75 comparisons in 45 different studies, is extremely discouraging in regard to both clinical measurement and clinical prediction: He reports *no* comparisons in which the clinical method was significantly superior to the mechanical (statistical) and many instances in which the latter approach *was* significantly more successful.

A Critique
of the Surveys

Before looking at some of the successes of clinical prediction, let us note some of the flaws of these surveys. Meehl wrote in 1954:

> The ideal design [for a study comparing clinical and statistical predictions] is one in which the same basic set of facts is subjected on the one hand to the skilled analysis of a trained clinician, and on the other hand is subjected to mechanical operations (table entry, multiplication by weights, or the like) [pp. 89–90].

A good many other writers (for example, Hoffman, 1960; Gough, 1962) take essentially the same position. Note, however, that this design allows the clinician no data beyond a string of numbers, supplemented at best by a few simple objective facts like marital status. Only a clinical psychologist who had been trained primarily in the profile analysis of the MMPI would consider this to be material on which he could properly exercise his talents. With nothing more to work with, the clinician is perforce a second-rate calculating machine, and the only surprising result of such comparisons is that the clinicians occasionally do as well as the formulas. If there was any issue here, it is settled: In any situation where only objective data are available and statistical prediction is possible, there is no point in wasting clinical time and talent in an attempt to outdo statistical methods.

Second, both Meehl and Sawyer have apologetically included a good many studies in which predictions by multiple regression used statistical weights that were worked out and validated on the same group of subjects—that is, without cross-validation. Such investigations should be included only if the clinicians, too, have the benefit of seeing the answers and then revising their predictions accordingly. The invalidity of the latter procedure points up the inescapable need to carry a rational predictive study through all six steps outlined in Table 41-2. Even when the original sample includes more than 1000 subjects cross-validation is necessary, because there is no guarantee that the next group will continue to be similar: Unexpected sampling fluctuations do occur frequently when we are dealing with human subjects.

Third, as Meehl (1954, p. 122) pointed out, the researches he collated "all involve the prediction of a somewhat heterogeneous, crude, socially defined behavior outcome." That is to say, if a psychologist attempts to predict the usual criterion, like grades in some kind of school, the *behavior* being predicted is not that of the subject who has been tested, interviewed, or the like—it is grade-giving behavior by unassessed and unknown people. Moreover, they evaluate the subject's behavior in future situations unforeseeable at the time of the assessment (or even rate what they believe his behavior to be, which itself may be more of a prediction than an observation).

To a clinician whose idea of predicting behavior is anticipating patients' responses to psychotherapeutic maneuvers, the kind of prediction tested in the published research is more like prophecy. As Meehl demonstrates, the criterion in a typical predictive study is so complexly determined, being the cumulation of so many individual acts, that

> in order to predict this outcome by clinical understanding it would be necessary to formulate an extremely detailed conceptual model of personality structure [and of the situation, or "press"]. . . . Now it is obvious that in none of the studies cited did the clinician have an opportunity to "formulate the personality" or to determine the *press* in anything like the detail indicated [1954, p. 123].

But instead of concluding that the studies in question were not reasonable tests of the clinician's ability, Meehl indicates only that the latter should have refused to attempt nonstatistical predictions. He may be right, but judgment about when to cooperate and when to refuse is of a different order from that involved in combining data to make predictions and should not be confounded with it.

It is doubtful that much can be learned about the value of clinical assessment by having clinicians attempt to predict college grades, success in some kind of vocational training, violation of parole, officers' ratings of their men, the winning teams in football, or the number of live children that will be born to certain couples in the 20 years following assessment. Yet a majority of the studies tabulated in the most recent of the detailed surveys (Sawyer, 1966) used criteria of these kinds. It *would* make sense to try to predict some form of behavior or some behavioral outcome in which a major role is played by personality traits, motives, defenses, and other such inner dispositions of the kind clinicians are trained to assess, but very few studies have used such criteria.

Fourth, it is misleading to compare the effectiveness of clinical judgment with that of a mechanical rule at the final stage of combining data unless in all five of the preceding steps (see Table 41-2) the competitors are on an equal footing. And in none of the 20 studies Meehl cites was this requirement met. Instead, the statistical predictions were usually being cross-validated, and the clinical ones never were.

Most of the published studies pitted examples of *pure actuarial* against *naive clinical* predictions (Table 41-2; see also Holt, 1958). A pure actuarial predictive system is one that uses objective data to predict a clear-cut criterion with the help of statistics. The role of judgment is held to a minimum, and full use is made of psychometric know-how throughout the six stages.

Table 41-2   An Outline of Three Types
of Predictive Systems

Steps in Prediction	How Steps Are Carried Out in Three Predictive Systems		
	Naive Clinical System	Pure Actuarial System	Sophisticated Clinical System
1. Analyze the criterion (study what is to be predicted)	Omitted or left to guesswork	The criterion actually used to test predictions is studied, yielding a description of relevant kinds of behavior (job analysis)	
2. Discover intervening variables to be measured (personal and situational)	Left to intuition or guesswork	Often bypassed; sometimes done by factor analysis	Done by careful study of known criterion groups and of their working situations
3. Choose tests or other means of assessment	Interviews and/or projective tests are used (largely because of familiarity with them)	Objective tests (self-administering questionnaires or apparatus tests) are preferred; many are assembled or invented	Instruments (both objective and subjective) are chosen or devised in terms of their suitability for assessing the relevant variables
4. First stage of validation: preliminary trial	Omitted	All test scores are correlated with the criterion; those that do not work are dropped or modified	Where possible, the same procedure as in the actuarial system is used; also, qualitative data (such as from the interview) on known subjects are studied to see how they relate to the criterion, and scoring keys or manuals to guide analysis are developed and tried out
5. Final validation: Gather and process data for measures of intervening variables	Clinical experience and judgment are used exclusively to process clinical data	A relatively simple, routine procedure, done by subprofessionals who administer and score tests	A combination of the other two, plus specific guidance in making primary inferences, by prior study of known cases' data
6. Final validation: Combine data for crucial predictions and test statistically	Unguided intuition and clinical judgment are used to construct a schema of each personality, from which the clinician tries to guess the criterion	Statistics are used to combine scores mechanically (for example, by multiple correlation with the criterion), applying the same formula to all cases	Clinical judgment, disciplined by the previous steps, is used to construct a schema of each personality, considering its functioning in expected situations and ending with case-by-case quantitative prediction

In a naive clinical study, the qualitative data are processed intuitively by rule of thumb without any prior study of the criterion or of the relation of the assessment data to it. Clinical judgment is relied on from start to finish not only as a way of integrating data to produce predictions but also as an alternative to acquaintance with the facts.

Yet a third type of prediction is also possible: *sophisticated clinical* prediction. This approach tries to combine the best of both traditions. It uses the refinements of experimental design from the actuarial side, with job analyses, pilot studies, item analyses, and successive cross-validations; but it also includes a full use of qualitative data and the clinician's personal as well as intellectual resources. With the discipline of scientific method, the latter can be an even more sensitive instrument than he is when he is allowed to run wild, and he is surely more organized and balanced. It would be a perverse clinician indeed who claimed that a casual, informal, uncontrolled approach was necessarily better than a disciplined, unbiased one. It is not being "more clinical" to give tests in a slipshod fashion than to do so precisely and carefully. Why, therefore, should it be assumed that prediction is clinical only when the person doing the predicting does not have the benefit of well-organized procedures?

Table 41-2 makes it plain that clinical judgment can be used in the predictive process at any of several points, and each time in either a disciplined or an undisciplined way. Sawyer (1966) made a start in the right direction by tallying studies separately, depending on whether the measurement as well as the prediction was clinical or mechanical, but this classification is still a long way from being adequate. The three categories of naive clinical, pure actuarial, and sophisticated clinical systems are also far from exhaustive. The research literature is still too variegated and the different components of predictive systems are combined in too many ways for nose counting to be very meaningful.

The irony of these classification attempts is that some clinical research has been tallied as evidence for actuarial prediction. This was the case for the research of Wittman (1941), which shows what can be accomplished in selecting patients for shock treatment by applying clinical judgment to the qualitative information in case files in a systematic, controlled way. Here the measurement was clinical, and the data were processed subjectively by highly trained clinicians, albeit only to the point where the intervening variables were quantified by means of ratings, which were then added up to yield the predictive score. This score correlated well with response to shock treatment while the predictions of that same criterion made in routine case conference in a state hospital were ineffective. The study is therefore classified in all the surveys as evidence for the superiority of *statistical* prediction. The investigation does not fit readily into any simple category, but it is surely misleading to tally it in a way that implies that clinical theories and techniques have once again been shown to be invalid.

The case for prediction based on clinical assessment turns out to be not as bleak as the recent surveys would have us believe, if we look at the few studies of appropriate kinds of problems and note (as we have just done) where and how clinical judgment was used.

The kind of prediction at which clinicians are generally best is diagnosis, which is not "prediction" in the usual sense but generalization: From a relatively small body of facts about a person, a clinician infers the results of processing a large body of facts. Thus, from reading a few TAT stories, a clinician may attempt to infer the presence of overt homosexuality in the storyteller, which may be established by the scrutiny of a larger (or at least different) body of clinical observations.

Lindzey (1965) demonstrated that two experienced clinical psychologists who knew a good deal both about the TAT and about male homosexuality could distinguish homosexual from heterosexual protocols significantly better than chance. With a group of undergraduate subjects, the first judge made a correct diagnosis in 95 percent of the 40 TAT's, while an attempt to analyze the same data according to a list of signs that had distinguished heterosexual from homosexual students in previous research failed to do better than chance. It was possible to construct a formula that apparently did almost as well as the clinician (on the sample it was based on, it identified 90 percent of the cases correctly); but when it was cross-validated on a new sample, this time of 30 prisoners, the new check list did only slightly better than chance (57 percent accurate), a level that could not be improved by any after-the-fact juggling. The original judge performed at about the same lower level of accuracy (60 percent) with the prison subjects, but a second judge's accuracy was 80 percent. The study has some flaws; it does not, for example, consider the base-rate problem, for the subjects were matched pairs of homosexuals and heterosexuals; but it does demonstrate that trained and experienced clinicians can perform better than cross-validated "objective" processing of the same data.

Another investigation, aimed at developing methods of selecting men for training in psychiatry at the Menninger Foundation, attempted to make a fair comparison of all three types of predictive systems (Holt & Luborsky, 1958). In this instance, predicting success in psychiatric training was a reasonable undertaking for clinical assessment, because being a good psychiatrist involves much more of the personality than does learning to fly or getting good grades in college. Reasonable chances of success were assured also by the facts that the study was restricted to one large school in Topeka, Kansas, and the predictive judges all worked in this one setting and were acquainted with its intangibles.

The first system experimented with was a *naive clinical* design. Experienced psychiatrists and psychologists assessed the personalities of young physicians at the time they applied to the Menninger School of Psychiatry, without any prior job analysis, study of criterion groups, or the like. One of the advantages of this design was that the clinicians functioned in a routine fashion, using their favorite methods (interviews and diagnostic tests) in the usual way, with the opportunity to use empathy as well as inference.

Each applicant was interviewed by three psychiatrists and took a balanced battery of tests. After the hour-long interview, each psychiatrist wrote a qualitative report, rated the man on a 10-point scale, and recommended his acceptance or rejection for the training program. The clinical psychologist made similar ratings and recommendations after analyzing and writing a report on the Wechsler-Bellevue, Rorschach, and Word Association tests. An Admissions Committee made the final decision on each man after discussing the reports and ratings.

All these predictive decisions (those of the committee and of the individual assessors) had impressive and statistically very significant validities (p < .001) against the psychiatric profession's main pass-fail criterion— passing the certifying examination of the American Board of Psychiatry and Neurology. Out of a total of more than 400 subjects who were assessed from 1946 through 1952, twice as high a proportion of those accepted by the Admissions Committee (as of those who were rejected) had the Board's certification by 1956 (71 percent versus 36 percent).

These naive clinical evaluations were less successful in predicting relative standing within the group of accepted trainees. The predictive ratings of the tester and the mean rating of the three interviewers both had correlational validities of about .25 against ratings by the psychiatric resident's supervisors after two or three years of training. These validities are less significant; but from a practical standpoint, the important criterion to be able to predict is passing versus failing.

In a second experimental design, the Menninger team tried to make *sophisticated clinical* predictions. First, the experimenters made a job analysis of the work done by psychiatric residents; that is, they tried to specify the attributes of personality that would help or hinder a man in carrying out each of the psychiatric functions. They did so partly by collecting opinions from experts with long experience in training psychiatrists and psychoanalysts, and partly by making an intensive study of a small sample of both excellent and ineffective residents, using interviews and many types of tests. In an attempt to guide and objectify the analysis of projective tests and the interview, they prepared manuals listing cues that discriminated the best from the worst residents in the small sample; they then cross-validated these cues on one class with encouraging results, making revisions in an attempt to learn from the predictive successes and failures.

As a final step four psychologists acted as judges in a predictive study with 64 new applicants to the school. Each judge scored tests or interviews according to the manuals, but they also made free clinical judgments based on increasing amounts of data. The analyses were done "blind"—that is, from files of tests, credentials, and a recorded interview, with all identifying information removed. The manuals proved a disappointment; different judges using the same manual did not agree well, for a good deal of clinical judgment was still required to score them, and the validities were on about the level of the naive ratings. But the free clinical predictions yielded considerably better results, especially for the two psychologists who digested the entire file of data on each subject and then made predictions: Their validities against various criteria were at about the level of r = .5. Both judges were able to predict a sociometric criterion (the residents' ratings of one another's competence) better than they could predict the supervisors' evaluations; and in general one judge did somewhat better than the other. But both performed at a level considerably above that of either naive clinical prediction or the mechanical combination of clinically judged cues.

The exigencies of research may have caused the judges to approach each man's data in a more intellectual and inferential spirit than they would have shown in a normal clinical situation. Nevertheless, they did tend to develop some emotional reaction to the schema of a human being they built up out of the fragments of data; they recorded this in the form of a rating of *liking*, with the thought that it might be a source of error. Surprisingly, this rating turned out to be the best predictor of all criteria, yielding better validities (from .25 to .64) for both judges. In retrospect, this anomaly seems a reminder that the clinician's own affective reactions, of an empathic rather than an inferential nature, are one of his most valuable sources of information about another person. To be sure, this finding has to be used with great caution and cannot be taken simply as encouragement to allow one's prejudices to take over.

The *pure actuarial* approach to prediction failed completely in this study. A number of test scores were correlated with criterion evaluations of the residents in a group of 64; the scores that seemed most promising were the verbal I.Q. from the Wechsler-Bellevue scale, the Lawyer key to the Strong Vocational Interest Blank, and two scores from the Rorschach—the number of rare details seen and the number of human-movement responses. The multiple correlation of this group of scores was .56 on the original sample; when cross-validated on 100 new cases, the validity dropped to .13—completely negligible. Another actuarial prediction was made possible by the work of Strong and Tucker (1952), who developed a Psychiatrist key through a statistical analysis of tests filled out by thousands of psychiatrists certified by the American Board. This key failed to predict any of the criteria at a statistically significant or practically promising level. To be sure, greater effort over a longer period of time might have produced a slightly better actuarial system, but the conditions for successful actuarial prediction did not exist.

The first condition that is necessary is a *stable world*, one that will not change in relevant particulars. The fact that a statistical formula or actuarial table is rigid is one of its merits: It plays no favorites, does not get sleepy or change its standards, does not forget its principles or abandon them for some exciting new intellectual fad. But by the same token, it has no way of allowing for the growth of a population, for changes in the meaning of test items, for new institutional policies, for changed social conditions, or for anything else that may affect part of the process. Such a system requires frequent revision, therefore, if it is to be used for long.

Second, actuarial prediction demands certain *resources*: the development of the system requires the services of a highly skilled technical staff and is usually both expensive and time consuming. The payoff in potential applicability must be large to justify it as a practical matter. If the numbers of people about whom predictions are being made in any one place are only moderate, the negative consequences of failing to predict have to be severe, as they are in situations where errors are costly in terms of money or lives.

Third, in order to establish an adequate statistical base, there must be *large numbers* of subjects—preferably thousands of them, available in samples of at least several hundred at a time and again not undergoing any important changes. Otherwise, the originally obtained relationships between predictors and criteria are likely to be misleading. Even a carefully developed system could prove useless when put into effect if a different type of person presents himself for testing, a type for which the previously established relationships among variables no longer hold.

Fourth, in actuarial prediction there must be an objective, reliable, and unvarying measure of the *criterion*—what it is you are trying to predict. Passing or failing in a school or training program usually meets this specification; but the faculty may suddenly change its standards with an increase in enrollments or with the advent of a Sputnik. It would be difficult to set up a statistical formula to predict the outcome of psychotherapy, since the only criteria available are judgmental and are of unknown reliability, or stability of meaning, when used by different judges.

In the Army Air Force example (see pages 783–84), all these conditions were almost ideally met: For several years conditions were stable enough and the numbers of men involved were large enough to make a very expensive system highly economical. The amount of money invested in each man who was dropped from training was considerable, even if he did not crash any planes and endanger any lives. The criterion (pass-fail) was objective, easy to obtain, and stable. And the whole process of training to this point took only a few weeks. Compare this situation to medical school selection, for example: To find out whether the men admitted to medical school make good doctors, it would be necessary to wait at least five years while they got their minimal basic training, plus one to five more years for those who took advanced (residency) training. This is the point reached by the Army Air Force psychologists a few weeks after the subjects started training.

It may be objected that in both situations what is important is not just graduating from medical or flight training school but becoming a good physician or becoming an ace under combat conditions. Did the Air Force not care about predicting criteria like that? They did, but little is said about it, partly because good criterion measures proved hard to obtain and partly because the actuarial success story has such an anticlimactic ending. For *the composite test predictor that did so well in selecting men who could get over the first hurdle was totally unable to predict any criterion of competence under military conditions*—such as the number of missions completed, the number of enemy planes downed, or the number of decorations or promotions received. Of course not. The tests were carefully tailored to an entirely different criterion; it would have taken many more years to have gone through the necessary steps to develop accurate predictors of combat behavior. By that time the age of the missile and the helicopter would have arrived, and the whole process would have had to be revamped again.

By comparison with this failure, the modest success of the OSS (Office of Strategic Services) teams, who selected secret agents by means of clinical assessment, looks much more impressive. They had even more difficulty getting good criterion measures, but the average validity of their predictive assessments against independent ratings and other measures of success in the field was about .25, p < .01 (OSS Assessment Staff, 1948; see especially Table 31, p. 423).

It seems fair to conclude from the research on prediction that the six-step approach, developed in the statistical tradition, has proved its value and should be incorporated as much as possible into any serious effort to set up a predictive system. Should clinical judgment be admitted into the final process of combining data to generate predictions? If the necessary conditions for a pure actuarial system exist, that system should certainly be tried, for it has often yielded excellent results. If such conditions do not prevail and if good clinical talent is readily available, a clinical method should be tried. It may not always work, but often it is the only possible approach. Clinicians need not be intimidated when someone cites impressive figures attained by actuarial prediction where it has worked well; there are no necessary implications that what the diagnostic tester or the vocational counselor is trying to do could be accomplished better by a formula.

THE STATUS OF THE THEORETICAL ISSUES

Despite the many deficiencies of the surveys, all of which have been conducted by persons identified with the statistical, psychometric approach, it is nevertheless possible to reach some conclusions about clinical and statistical prediction. Only a few theoretical issues have been at stake in the controversy, though its practical, professional, and educational ramifications have been many and important.

The Epistemological
Issue

Does the clinician have some unique access to truth? The claim that individual behavior could be predicted only from qualitative case studies did lead to the hypothesis that clinical prediction would always be superior to actuarial, a claim that has now been decisively refuted. Whatever else one may think about the evidence, it has been clearly established that statistical prediction *is* applicable to unique individuals and that for many socially important kinds of "behavior" it can do as good a job as that done by trained clinicians, sometimes better.

Even so, the claim that statistical prediction is inherently limited is refutable on logical and philosophical grounds alone (Holt, 1961, 1967; see also the theoretical sections of Meehl, 1954). The theoretical position on which the hypothesis was based is held by few clinicians, and its demolition in no way undermines the logic of clinical assessment as presented here.

The Cognitive
Issue

Is clinical inference only informal statistical inference? This problem, most closely associated with the name Sarbin (1943; see also Sarbin, Taft, & Bailey, 1960), is even less related to data than the first issue. Sarbin claims that the clinical assessor can in principle predict *only* by statistical inference. He rejects the claim that building a theoretical schema is a genuinely creative act and holds that all expectations of the future can be nothing more than extrapolation from past experience. Since in Sarbin's original experiment (1943) the clinicians did not in fact do any better than systematically accumulated and statistically manipulated experience, he believed that his point was proved. Meehl (1954) adequately demonstrated that this was a non sequitur and that even when clinical predictions are incorrect, they do not necessarily consist only of informal statistical inferences, guesses, and speculations. (See the discussion of clinical and statistical inference in Chapter 34, page 629.)

The Conceptual
Issue

Are the clinician's concepts and theories any good? While this issue has not been explicitly posed by many writers on clinical and statistical prediction, it may well underlie a good deal of the heat that has been generated. Clinical psychologists tend to overlook the influence of the situation in determining behavior, and among determinants within the individual they tend to be most interested in unconscious needs, conflicts, fantasies, defenses, pathological trends, identifications, and the like. Since such variables are usually assessed by means of indirect clinical inference and by methods (like projective techniques) that lack the usual psychometric credentials of demonstrated reliability and validity, many nonclinicians look askance at the whole enterprise of clinical assessment. They often feel that common sense, plus the application of the laws of learning, would probably do a much better job of psychodiagnosis and psychotherapy; and the simple, nontheoretical approach of statistical prediction appeals to them.

The ultimate test of the usefulness of any theory is whether it contributes to man's knowledge of and his ability to manage his world and his life more effectively through understanding. Yet there are too many other possible sources of error in the success or failure of clinical predictions for them to constitute a rigorous test of the clinician's theories. This does not mean that his concepts have too little relevance to reality, either. The concepts may be good, bad, or indifferent, but if a poorly trained person applies the measuring instruments ineptly, or if he lacks good normative information about how his tests operate in the population being studied, or if he makes incorrect assumptions about the situations in which future behavior will take place, or if he lacks information about some critically important ability—to give just a few examples—he may predict very badly. Likewise, he may predict correctly for reasons he does not understand, and he may erroneously attribute his success to a fallacious theory. It is impossible to conclude anything about the value of clinical assessment's conceptual underpinnings from the results of predictive studies.

The Real Issue: Not Theoretical but Emotional

There are probably no remaining theoretical issues to be tested by further competition between clinical and statistical predictions. Nor is it possible, in light of the many types and mixtures of clinical and statistical methods, to reach many meaningful conclusions of *any* kind from surveys of this highly miscellaneous literature. In the case of a particular predictive study, it is always possible to argue that different clinicians would have done either better or worse, since all studies show considerable individual variation in predictive ability, and that different formulas too could have performed either better or worse. What is being tested is "the state of the art" in two different technologies, and the procedure of simply tallying the studies that happen to have been published and discovered at some particular time is an extremely poor way of sampling the prevailing level of clinical and statistical prediction.

The argument that some empirical evidence is better than none, even though the sample is admittedly not in any way random or representative, is demonstrably weak. Before the scientific sampling of public opinion was invented, newspapers and magazines tried to predict American presidential elections by "straw ballots." One such magazine (the *Literary Digest*) collected literally millions of statements of voting intentions in 1936 and predicted

Roosevelt's defeat in an election that turned out to be the greatest landslide victory in United States history. This episode laid the *Literary Digest* to rest for all time and should have a similar effect on the notion that just collecting and tabulating available information is a reliable substitute for scientific sampling.

The competition between clinical and statistical prediction is both theoretically and practically useless. The main importance of the controversy is that the failure of clinicians to predict such complex social outcomes as school grades and success on parole any better than statistical methods has been used as a stick to beat the clinicians with. Because personality assessors have not surpassed statisticians on the latter's territory, they are being accused of incompetence in their own domain and are called smug and complacent when they fail to present convincing quantitative evidence that clinical assessment (and psychotherapy) is valid and effective.

The controversy has been going on during a time when clinical psychology has been coming under increasingly critical scrutiny. A widely publicized survey by Eysenck (1952) of research on the effectiveness of psychotherapy concluded that psychotherapists have not provided convincing quantitative evidence that their methods of treatment are effective. In the years following World War II, the number of clinical psychologists grew at a rate far greater than did the older, traditional branches of academic psychology; as a result, applied psychologists now vastly outnumber pure researchers and teachers. The latter group began to be distressed by the "professionalization" of psychology—by, for example, the need for the Central Office of the American Psychological Association and its officers and governing bodies to concern themselves increasingly with nonscientific problems and issues, mostly arising out of the work of clinical psychologists. Within the universities, too, there was rising dissatisfaction. Professors trained mostly in academic branches of psychology were called upon to train graduate students who wanted mainly to learn how to assess personalities and help troubled people. Partly, it was a clash of theoretical and pragmatic value systems, partly a matter of theoretical differences: As we have just seen, the theories that clinical psychologists tend to find useful in their work differ from those favored by experimental psychologists, who often consider the psychoanalytic, personalistic, or existentialist orientation of clinicians not really scientific.

There has, therefore, been a good deal of pressure on clinical psychologists to demonstrate the validity of their diagnostic and therapeutic techniques by the usual kinds of experimental evidence, or else to give up teaching and practicing a body of lore that for the most part is not even codified into the appearance of a coherent theory. It just happens, however, that there is hardly a research task within psychology so complex and difficult as the evaluation of assessment and treatment. In the judgment of most qualified members of the profession, there has never been a truly adequate study of either; a proper one would take great resources of money, time, personnel, subjects, statistical sophistication, and research creativity. The working clinician himself, spending most of his time trying to understand and to help people in distress, can hardly be expected to take careful stock of his theories and practices under such circumstances. As a result, the research that has been done has tended to be either what could be accomplished as a sideline by clinicians, or projects set up by persons more knowledgeable about experimental design than about the nature of clinical assessment and how it might be meaningfully studied.

Against this background, it is understandable how such excellent scientists as Meehl greatly overgeneralized the results of the surveys of research on clinical and statistical prediction and overlooked some of the data reviewed above (pages 789–91). Indeed, Meehl (1954) admits that his well-known conclusion—that the clinical psychologist should turn from diagnostic assessment to concentrate on therapy and research—"is my personal hunch, not proved by the presented data or strongly argued in the text [p. vii]."

THE PLACE OF THE STATISTICAL APPROACH
IN PSYCHODIAGNOSIS

Critics of clinical assessment often speak as if a great deal of the clinical psychologist's daily work consists of making predictions that could just as well (or better) be done by statistical methods. In a paper with a characteristically provocative title, "When Shall We Use Our Heads Instead of the Formula?" Meehl (1957) actually comes to a number of moderate and reasonable conclusions, but his very wording of the question implies that clinicians are frequently faced with such choices. In fact, however, "the formula" remains to be worked out in all but exceptional instances. Meehl admits as much: "Mostly we will use our heads, because there just isn't any formula." But he is optimistic about the prospect of developing one if clinicians will only shake off what he elsewhere calls "their dogmatic slumbers [Meehl, 1965, p. 27]." "In his daily decision-making," Meehl goes on to complain, "the clinician continues to function, usually quite unabashedly, as if no such book [as *Clinical Versus Statistical Prediction*] had ever been written." Yet nowhere does he demonstrate by specific job analysis that any large part of ordinary clinical work could be handled by formulas. Twenty years earlier, Chein (1945) argued eloquently that clinicians are mainly concerned with control, not prediction, putting the burden of proof on the critics to demonstrate the contrary. They still have not done so.

The misconception that clinical assessment is a predictive enterprise may arise partly from an overestimation of the importance of prediction in science. Some statistically minded psychologists argue that understanding does not signify anything different from predictive efficiency. The point of view presented here is that science is primarily concerned with understanding, which usually aids but is *not* identical with the ability to predict. It is easy to predict accurately that many a baby will bang his head against his crib if he awakens during the night, but it is difficult to know why. To understand such a form of behavior requires insight into its inner and outer causes, as instances of general laws or principles. Such insight will, it is true, usually lead to better prediction than could be attained without it, and also to more effective control. Yet it is not uncommon in science for prediction and even control to outstrip understanding. In medicine, for example, most of the effective drugs in use (at least until a few years ago) were discovered by trial and error and were put into use simply because they worked, long before the mechanism of their action was understood. That is still the case with aspirin, the most widely used and effective drug of all.

The expectation that clinical assessment ought to be reducible to a routine operation for clerks and computers may grow from a misconception of the nature of psychodiagnosis: Doesn't the clinical psychologist or psychiatrist simply check the diagnostic data on any new patient against a memorized list of the signs of each mental illness, to find the one that best fits the case?

In medicine, such an approach is actually being developed by collaborating teams of diagnosticians and computer experts. The computer's memory can store descriptions of thousands of diseases, many more than a physician can keep in his head and more than any single doctor can ever have personally seen in a patient. But its main usefulness is precisely in suggesting possibilities that might otherwise be overlooked, *not* in reaching a final diagnosis. Even in the field of internal medicine, where there are such relatively clear-cut conditions as measles, with a known germ, typical symptoms, and standard therapy, diagnosis remains an art. A computer is equipped with neither common sense nor judgment, and its program is no better than the human intelligence that produced it.

In the field of "mental illness" there are very few true diseases after the model of measles. Instead, there are people with problems. True, both the people and the problems may be sorted into categories of various kinds; there are types of personalities, and there are recurring types of difficulties they have in living satisfactory and socially constructive lives. Some clinicians object to the very idea of psychodiagnosis because they are so impressed with the rarity with which they encounter textbook cases of manic-depressive psychosis or psychopathic personality or hypochondriasis. To abandon diagnostic concepts would be like discarding the compass because one's city did not contain any streets running precisely north or west. True, as orienting points, the standard psychiatric diagnostic groups are a great deal less clearcut and simple than geographic directions; they are more like the church steeple and big red barn pointed out by the farmer giving directions to a traveler. Nevertheless, landmarks have served mankind well in helping people to get about, and generations of psychiatrists and clinical psychologists have found diagnostic ideal types useful in much the same way.

To use diagnostic conceptions like hysteria as orienting points, not as boxes into which to drop people, means to describe *in what ways* and *to what extent* a person is hysterical. Any other such diagnostic landmark that may locate the particular subject under consideration is then used in a similar way. Clinical assessment of normal people also very often finds the diagnostic typologies helpful, as was demonstrated in the case of Morris Brown.

In the best psychodiagnostic practice, the psychologist describes the person's ingrained pattern of coping with his impulses and with environmental pressures, which developed from the interaction of constitution and formative influences during his childhood. Then the clinician judges how far (if at all) this style of adaptation has broken down and relates it to the kinds of symptoms that have emerged. A good diagnostic report for clinical use will describe as many aspects of personality as seem relevant to understanding and helping the person—in the end putting the pieces together in a dual diagnostic formulation of the sort just described.

The "cookbook" approach of Halbower (see Chapter 39, page 743) was advocated by Meehl (1956) not as a way of putting patients into pigeonholes but as a means of arriving at general descriptions of their personalities. Nevertheless, this ingenious approach has two serious drawbacks. First, it is applicable only to persons whose test scores fall into a common type, or pattern. Yet *in most clinical contexts, the only cases referred for testing are the atypical ones, the diagnostic puzzles*. It would thus be inherently quite difficult to extend Halbower's cookbook approach enough to make it helpful in everyday practice. Second, the output or result of this essentially statistical method is a Q sort—a rehash of a set of statements made about other patients. To submit such a list of standard sentences, hierarchically organized though it is, as a report on every patient would be a sure recipe for getting the psychologist's contribution disregarded. For a diagnostic report is a *communication* to someone who has therapeutic or administrative responsibility, and it will be worthless, no matter how valid it may be, unless the information is transmitted in readily usable, intelligible form.

Other statistical enthusiasts have developed computer programs that write test reports when given an input of test scores. The process is actually a simple one: A sentence written by a psychologist expressing a primary inference in terms that therapists use is stored by the computer for each possible test score; the machine prints out as many such sentences as it is fed scores. Not surprisingly, the result sounds as if it was written by a machine, and it is a pretty good simulation of the unimaginative reports turned out by a conscientious but plodding novice who knows just enough to copy out sentences from books on testing. It is hardly any better than a Q sort as a substitute for a lively, individualized picture of a person, with causal hypotheses about genetic and other relationships among trends and traits, which a good diagnostic tester can turn out.

Nevertheless, these forms of automated test analysis may have a limited role in the preliminary processing of objective tests—an extension of machine scoring, as it were. The best-fitting Q sort can be used as a source of hypotheses and formulations for the final report, but not as a substitute for it.

Assessment Assessed

How shall we evaluate personality assessment, if not by the methods suggested so far? Let us make clear what we are evaluating: We can look at assessment as the work of a number of people at particular times and places or as a body of knowledge and technique. Taking the first of these standpoints, we can say that the situation is much the same as with any kind of professional practice. For example, despite the dramatic advances of medical science and technology, there is no way a person can know what level of care he will get if he consults a physician chosen at random from the telephone book. There are probably many more mediocre dentists than expert ones; surely the same is true of personality assessors. From society's standpoint it is very important to measure the general level of any professional practice and then to try to raise it; but in many ways it makes more sense to investigate the scientific underpinnings of a profession, as embodied in its best practitioners.

Viewing it from this vantage point, then, we can say in retrospect that the field of personality assessment is undergoing a good deal of needed development and improvement through research. Not very much is firmly established and universally accepted, yet much is known. At its best, the technology can be extremely useful; multiform, intensive assessment is the best available ultimate criterion of what a person truly is and remains the best way of gaining a deep understanding of him. Yet there is still a gap between understanding a person and understanding personality, a gap that is not likely to be filled by accumulating case studies. By such means one may learn wisdom about human nature, but science demands explicit hypotheses and their verification. Many psychologists of personality believe that significant research on personality, which will ultimately lead to a body of laws, can be done only by people who have some degree of such wisdom and unformulated (or poorly articulated), intuitive insight.

Progress in this field will depend both on improving assessors and on strengthening their science. That is, we must first select better people and give them more thorough training than has been generally available so far. Personality assessment needs people with a variety of gifts: Ideally, they should be capable of rigorous scientific research and should have a humanistic and humane outlook. In examining a projective test protocol, for example, the interpreter should be free to draw on intuitive insights from thorough self-knowledge and from a rich literary culture, but he should also be stern in testing his hunches and ruthless in discarding them if they cannot be supported by evidence. In short, the best assessor is capable of both tough-mindedness and tender-mindedness.

Clinical assessment can be greatly aided by sympathetically informed but relentless inquiry into all of its aspects. We need to know much more about the base rates of all the relevant variables in the populations most frequently studied, not just diagnostic syndromes but all their constituent elements. As new forms of psychotherapy and other ways of helping people with problems are invented, there must be systematic study of the kinds of people who are helped and not helped by each. Much research could be usefully focused on collecting statistics to convert hunch-based inferential rules to statistical inferences. An inference may be based on a fairly good theory, but we can never know how far to trust it until actual experience has been tabulated. Thus, clinical assessment will be advanced by first explicating and then testing out all kinds of inferential rules, whether they are applied to life-history data, objective test scores, projective techniques, or whatever.

Likewise, objective assessment can learn from the clinical tradition. Progress in the use of inventories will depend less on complex statistical manipulation of scores than on a clear understanding of what the basic data are and how they can be improved. There is no bypassing judgment; in an objective test, the examiner relies on the subject to observe and report on his own behavioral patterns. Objective measurement will be advanced, therefore, when the subject is helped to do as good a job as possible. That can be accomplished, first, by earning his trust and confidence (not just by "building rapport") so that his defensiveness will be minimal. This means *not* trying to trick the subject or pry into his inner life without his consent; it means respecting his confidence meticulously and being completely candid about how the results are used. The next step is to make the test items clear, interesting, and unambiguous. The format and instructions of tests need more work so that taking them will be less burdensome and more attractive and so that a set, or orientation, may be created in the subject that will aid him in taking the test seriously and reporting or rating accurately.

Many techniques of assessment exist that have not been adequately covered in this book. It may well be that some of the best methods of future assessment lie in the area between tests and interviews. Most workers in the field agree, however, that progress depends less on the invention of more ingenious methods than on the development of a better theory of personality. To be sure, in the testing of any theory or method, there must be ultimately a resort to statistics, as Meehl (1954) has insisted. Just as inevitably, however, there is no escape from the necessity of interpreting the results of any test, whether the word is used in the sense of an objective or projective test of personality or a statistical test of a theory-generated hypothesis. Any way we look at it, then, the future of personality assessment belongs to those who can combine the best from the objective and the clinical traditions.

REFERENCES AND INDEX TO AUTHORS OF WORKS CITED

The numbers in **bold face** following each reference give the text pages on which the paper or book is cited. Citations in the text are made by author and date of publication.

Preface and Introduction

LAZARSFELD, P. *The American soldier:* An expository review. *Public Opinion Quarterly,* 1949, 13, 377–404. **xxxi, xxxii**

LAZARUS, R. *Adjustment and personality.* New York: McGraw-Hill, 1961. **xxviii, xxix**

MISCHEL, W. *Personality and assessment.* New York: Wiley, 1968. **vii**

SANFORD, N. Personality: The field. In D. L. Sills (Ed.), *International encyclopedia of the social sciences,* Vol. 2. New York: Free Press, 1968. Pp. 587–606. **xxiv**

Part One

ABERD, D., *see* Cramond & Aberd (1954).

ADORNO, T. W., FRENKEL-BRUNSWIK, E., LEVINSON, D. J., & SANFORD, R. N., *The authoritarian personality.* New York: Harper & Row, 1950. **168**

ALFERT, E., *see* Lazarus & Alfert (1964).

ALLPORT, G. W. *The nature of prejudice.* Reading, Mass.: Addison-Wesley, 1954. **166**

AMSEL, A. The role of frustrative nonreward in noncontinuous reward situations. *Psychological Bulletin,* 1958, 55, 102–19. **153**

ARCHIBALD, H. C., & TUDDENHAM, R. D. Persistent stress reaction after combat. *Archives of General Psychiatry,* 1965, 12, 475–81. **34, 35**

ASERINSKY, E., & KLEITMAN, N. Regularly occurring periods of eye motility and concomitant phenomena during sleep. *Science*, 1953, *118*, 273–74. **27**

ATKINSON, R. C., *see* Hilgard & Atkinson (1967).

BACKER, R., *see* Sheffield, Wulff, & Backer (1951).

BANDURA, A., & WALTERS, R. H. *Social learning and personality development*. New York: Holt, Rinehart and Winston, 1963. **57**

BARKER, R. G., DEMBO, T., & LEWIN, K. Frustration and regression. *University of Iowa Studies in Child Welfare*, 1941, *18*, No. 1. **150, 151**

BARR, H. L., *see* Klein, Barr, & Wolitzky (1967).

BARTLETT, M., *see* Egbert, Battit, Welch, & Bartlett (1964).

BATTIT, G., *see* Egbert, Battit, Welch, & Bartlett (1964).

BEIER, E. G. The effect of induced anxiety on flexibility of intellectual functioning. *Psychological Monographs*, 1951, *65*, No. 9. **127**

BERKOWITZ, L. *Aggression.* New York: McGraw-Hill, 1962. **158, 163**

BERKOWITZ, L., & COTTINGHAM, D. R. The interest value and relevance of fear-arousing communications. *Journal of Abnormal and Social Psychology*, 1960, *60*, 37–43. **137**

BERKUN, M., BIALEK, H., KERN, R., & YAGI, K. Experimental studies of psychological stress in man. *Psychological Monographs*, 1962, *76*, 1–39. **127, 128**

BETTELHEIM, B., & JANOWITZ, M. *Dynamics of prejudice*. New York: Harper & Row, 1950. **166**

BIALEK, H., *see* Berkun, Bialek, Kern, & Yagi (1962).

BOBREN, H. M., *see* Nunnally & Bobren (1959).

BOWLBY, J. Grief and mourning in infancy and early childhood. *Psychoanalytic Study of the Child*, 1960, *15*, 9–52. **172**

BRADLEY, A., *see* Grinker, Willerman, Bradley, & Fastovsky (1946).

BROWN, J. S. *The motivation of behavior.* New York: McGraw-Hill, 1961. **52**

BROWN, J. S., & FARBER, I. E. Emotions conceptualized as intervening variables with suggestions toward a theory of frustration. *Psychological Bulletin*, 1951, *48*, 465–95. **153**

BROWN, J. S., KALISH, H. I., & FARBER, I. E. Conditioned fear as revealed by magnitude of startle response to an auditory stimulus. *Journal of Experimental Psychology*, 1951, *41*, 317–28. **52**

BUGELSKI, R., *see* Miller & Bugelski (1948).

BUSS, A. H. Instrumentality of aggression, feedback, and frustration as determinants of physical aggression. *Journal of Personality and Social Psychology*, 1966, *3*, 153–62. **155, 160**

CAMERON, N. *Personality development and psychopathology*. Boston: Houghton Mifflin, 1963. **27**

CAMPBELL, D., SANDERSON, R. E., & LAVERTY, S. G. Characteristics of a conditioned response in human subjects during extinction trials following a single traumatic conditioning trial. *Journal of Abnormal and Social Psychology*, 1964, *68*, 627–39. **41, 44, 53**

CANTER, A., *see* Imboden, Canter, & Claff (1953).

CAPLAN, G. *An approach to community mental health*. London: Tavistock Publications, 1961. **186**

CAPLAN, G. *Principles of preventive psychiatry*. New York: Basic Books, 1964. **197, 198**

CAPLAN, G. Community psychiatry: Introduction and overview. In S. E. Goldston (Ed.), *Concepts of community psychiatry: A framework for training*. Washington, D.C.: U.S. Department of Health, Education, and Welfare, 1965. Pp. 3–18. **197, 198**

CHAMPION, R. A. Studies of experimentally induced disturbance. *Australian Journal of Psychology*, 1950, *2*, 90–99. **67**

CHAPMAN, D. W., *see* Janis, Chapman, Gillin, & Spiegel (1955).

CHILD, I. L., & WATERHOUSE, I. K. Frustration and the quality of performance, 1: A critique of the Barker, Dembo, and Lewin experiment. *Psychological Review*, 1952, *59*, 351–62. **152**

CHODOFF, P. Late effects of concentration camp syndrome. *Archives of General Psychiatry*, 1963, *8*, 323–33. **36**

CLAFF, L., *see* Imboden, Canter, & Claff (1963).

CLARK, R. L., JR., *see* Cobb, Clark, McGuire, & Howe (1954).

COBB, B. C., CLARK, R. L., JR., MC GUIRE, C., & HOWE, C. D. Patient-responsible delay of treatment of cancer: A social psychological study. *Cancer*, 1954, 7, 920–26. **102**

COBB, S., & LINDEMANN, E. Symposium on management of Coconut Grove burns at Massachusetts General Hospital: Neuropsychiatric observations. *Annals of Surgery*, 1943, *117*, 814–24. **48**

COHEN, S., see Titchner *et al.* (1957).

COLBERTSON, W., see Titchner *et al.* (1957).

CONDRY, J. C., JR., see Kelley, Condry, Dahlker, & Hill (1965).

COTTINGHAM, D. R., see Berkowitz & Cottingham (1960).

COTTRELL, L., JR., see Stouffer *et al.* (1949b).

COWETT, A., see Titchner *et al.* (1957).

CRAMOND, W., & ABERD, D. Psychological aspects of uterine disfunction. *Lancet*, 1954, *2*, 1241–45. **102**

DAHLKE, A. E., see Kelley, Condry, Dahlke, & Hill (1965).

D'AMATO, M. E., & GUMENIK, W. E. Some effects of immediate versus randomly delayed shock on an instrumental response and cognitive processes. *Journal of Abnormal and Social Psychology*, 1960, 60, 64–67. **67**

DAVISON, L. A., see Lazarus, Speisman, Mordkoff, & Davison (1962).

DEMBO, T., see Barker, Dembo, & Lewin (1941).

DEMENT, W. C. The effects of dream deprivation. *Science*, 1960, *131*, 1705–07. **27**

DEMENT, W. C., see also Fisher & Dement (1963).

DE QUINCEY, T. Levana and our ladies of sorrow. *De Quincey's works*. Vol. XVI. *Suspiria de profundis*. Edinburgh: Adam and Charles Black, 1884. **175**

DE VINNEY, L., see Stouffer *et al.* (1949a).

DE WOLFE, A., & GOVERNALE, C. Fear and attitude change. *Journal of Abnormal and Social Psychology*, 1964, *69*, 119–23. **141**

DILLON, H., see Leopold & Dillon (1963).

DOBBS, D., & WILSON, W. P. Observations on persistence of war neurosis. *Diseases of the Nervous System*, 1960, *21*, 686–91. **34**

DOLLARD, J., DOOB, L., MILLER, N. E., MOWRER, O. H., & SEARS, R. R. *Frustration and aggression*. New Haven, Conn.: Yale University Press, 1939. **149**

DOLLARD, J., & MILLER, N. E. *Personality and psychotherapy*. New York: McGraw-Hill, 1950. **51, 53**

DOOB, L., see Dollard *et al.* (1939).

EASTERBROOK, J. A. The effect of emotion on cue utilization and the organization of behavior. *Psychological Review*, 1959, *66*, 183–201. **127**

EGBERT, L., BATTIT, G., WELCH, C., & BARTLETT, M. Reduction of postoperative pain by encouragement and instruction of patients. *New England Journal of Medicine*, 1964, *270*, 825–27. **103, 104**

EPSTEIN, S., & FENZ, W. D. Theory and experiment on the measurement of approach-avoidance conflict. *Journal of Abnormal and Social Psychology*, 1962, *64*, 97–112. **77**

EPSTEIN, S., & FENZ, W. D. Steepness of approach and avoidance gradients in humans as a function of experience: Theory and experiment. *Journal of Experimental Psychology*, 1965, *70*, 1–12. **77, 88, 89**

ERIKSON, E. H. *Childhood and society*. New York: Norton, 1950. **121**

ERIKSON, E. H. Identity and the life cycle. *Psychological Issues*, 1959, *1*, No. 1. **197**

FARBER, I. E., see Brown & Farber (1951); Brown, Kalish, & Farber (1951).

FASTOVSKY, A., see Grinker *et al.* (1946).

FELDMAN, J. J., see Sheatsley & Feldman (1964).

FENICHEL, O. *The psychoanalytic theory of neurosis*. New York: Norton, 1945. **65, 68, 186**

FENZ, W. D. Conflict and stress as related to physiological activation and sensory, perceptual, and cognitive functioning. *Psychological Monographs*, 1964, *78* (No. 8, Whole No. 585). **77, 79, 81**

FENZ, W. D., see also Epstein & Fenz (1962, 1965).

FESHBACH, S. The drive-reducing function of fantasy behavior. *Journal of Abnormal and Social Psychology*, 1955, 50, 3–11. **163**

FESHBACH, S. The stimulating versus cathartic effects of a vicarious aggressive activity. *Journal of Abnormal and Social Psychology*, 1961, *63*, 381–85. **163**

FESHBACH, S., see also Janis & Feshbach (1953) (1954).

FISHER, C., & DEMENT, W. C. Studies on the psychopathology of sleep and dreams. *American Journal of Psychiatry*, 1963, *119*, 1160–68. **27**

FISHMAN, C. G. Need for approval and the expression of aggression under varying conditions of frustration. *Journal of Per-*

sonality and Social Psychology, 1965, 2, 809–16. **156, 157**

FRASER, R., LESLIE, I., & PHELPS, D. Psychiatric effects of severe personal experiences during bombing. *Proceedings of the Royal Society of Medicine*, 1943, 36, 119–23. **24**

FRENKEL-BRUNSWIK, E., *see* Adorno, Frenkel-Brunswik, Levinson, & Sanford (1950).

FREUD, A. The ego and the mechanisms of defense. London: Hogarth Press, 1937. **66**

FREUD, S. (1917) Mourning and melancholia. *Standard edition*, Vol. 14. London: Hogarth Press, 1957. **149, 181, 184**

FREUD, S. (1921) Group psychology and the analysis of the ego. *Standard edition*, Vol. 18. London: Hogarth Press, 1957. **66**

FREUD, S. (1926) *The problem of anxiety*. New York: Norton, 1936. **65, 112, 113**

FRITZ, C., & MARKS, E. The NORC studies of human behavior in disaster. *Journal of Social Issues*, 1954, 10, 26–41. **23, 25, 85**

FROMM, E. Lecture to the American Orthopsychiatric Association, April 13, 1966 (reported in *The New York Times*, April 14, 1966). **148**

GANTT, W. H. Autonomic conditioning. In J. Wolpe, A. Salter, & L. J. Reyna (Eds.), *The conditioning therapies*. New York: Holt, Rinehart and Winston, 1965. Pp. 115–26. **41**

GILLIN, J., *see* Janis, Chapman, Gillin, & Spiegel (1955).

GLADSTONE, A. I., *see* Janis, Lumsdaine, & Gladstone (1951).

GLASS, A. Problem of stress in the combat zone. In *Symposium on stress*. Washington, D.C.: National Research Council and Walter Reed Army Medical Center, 1953. Pp. 90–102. **92**

GLOVER, E. Notes on the psychological effects of war conditions on the civil populations, Part 3: The blitz. *International Journal of Psychoanalysis*, 1942, 23, 17–37. **92**

GLUECK, B., *see* Hastings, Wright, & Glueck (1944).

GOTTSCHALK, L., *see* Titchner *et al.* (1957).

GOVERNALE, C., *see* DeWolfe & Governale (1964).

GRINKER, R. R., & SPIEGEL, J. P. *Men under stress*. Philadelphia: Blakiston, 1945a. **23, 68, 69, 70, 92**

GRINKER, R. R., & SPIEGEL, J. P. *War neuroses*. Philadelphia: Blakiston, 1945b. **68, 92**

GRINKER, R. R., WILLERMAN, B., BRADLEY, A., & FASTOVSKY, A. A study of psychological predisposition to the development of operational fatigue, 1 and 2. *American Journal of Orthopsychiatry*, 1946, 16, 191–214. **70, 102**

GUMENIK, W. E., *see* D'Amato & Gumenik (1960).

HAEFNER, D. Some effects of guilt-arousing and fear-arousing persuasive communications on opinion change. Technical Report No. 1, Office of Naval Research, Contract No. Nonr 668 (12), 1956. **135**

HAGGARD, E. Psychological causes and results of stress. In *Human factors in undersea warfare*. Washington, D.C.: National Research Council, 1949. Pp. 441–61. **67**

HARLOW, H. F. Motivation as a factor in the acquisition of new responses. In M. R. Jones (Ed.), *Current theory and research in motivation*. Lincoln: University of Nebraska Press, 1953. Pp. 24–49. **51**

HASTINGS, D., WRIGHT, D., & GLUECK, B. *Psychiatric experiences of the Eighth Air Force, first year of combat (July 4, 1942–July 4, 1943)*. New York: Josiah Macy, Jr. Foundation, 1944. **25**

HEBB, D. O. Drives and the c.n.s. (conceptual nervous system). *Psychological Review*, 1955, 62, 243–54. **125**

HERTZMANN, M., *see* Witkin *et al.* (1954).

HILGARD, E. R., & ATKINSON, R. C. *Introduction to psychology*. (4th ed.) New York: Harcourt, Brace & World, 1967. **42, 50**

HILL, A. H., *see* Kelley, Condry, Dahlke, & Hill (1965).

HOLT, R. R. Ego autonomy reevaluated. *International Journal of Psycho-Analysis*, 1965, 46, 151–67. **51**

HOVLAND, C. I., *see* Sears, Hovland, & Miller (1940).

HOVLAND, C. I., JANIS, I. L., & KELLEY, H. H. *Communication and persuasion*. New Haven, Conn.: Yale University Press, 1953. **126**

HOWE, C. D., *see* Cobb, Clark, McGuire, & Howe (1954).

IMBODEN, J. B., CANTER, A., & CLAFF, L. Separation experiences and health records in a group of normal adults. *Psychosomatic Medicine*, 1963, 25, 433–40. **193**

ISTEL, J. Statistical report. *Parachutist*, 1961, 3, 11–12. **77**

JACOBSON, EDITH. On normal and pathological moods. In R. S. Eissler *et al.* (Eds.), *The psychoanalytic study of the child*, Vol. 12. New York: International Universities Press, 1957. Pp. 73–113. **177**

JACOBSON, EDMUND. *Progressive relaxation.* (2nd ed.) Chicago: University of Chicago Press, 1938. **55**

JAMES, W. *The principles of psychology.* New York: Holt, Rinehart and Winston, 1890. **109**

JANIS, I. L. Psychodynamic aspects of adjustment to Army life. *Psychiatry*, 1945, 8, 159–76. **163**

JANIS, I. L. Objective factors related to morale attitudes in the aerial combat situation. In S. Stouffer, A. A. Lumsdaine, R. Williams, M. B. Smith, I. L. Janis, S. A. Star, & L. Cottrell, Jr., *The American soldier*. Vol. 2. *Combat and its aftermath*. Princeton, N.J.: Princeton University Press, 1949a. Pp. 362–410. **25**

JANIS, I. L. Problems related to the control of fear in combat. In S. Stouffer, A. A. Lumsdaine, R. Williams, M. B. Smith, I. L. Janis, S. A. Star, & L. Cottrell, Jr., *The American soldier*. Vol. 2. *Combat and its aftermath*. Princeton, N.J.: Princeton University Press, 1949b. Pp. 192–241. **67, 90**

JANIS, I. L. *Air war and emotional stress.* New York: McGraw-Hill, 1951. **23, 25, 92**

JANIS, I. L. *Psychological stress.* New York: Wiley, 1958. **13, 23, 71, 92, 95, 97, 100, 189**

JANIS, I. L. Psychological effects of warnings. In G. W. Baker & D. W. Chapman (Eds.), *Man and society in disaster*. New York: Basic Books, 1962. Pp. 55–92. **110, 114, 116**

JANIS, I. L. Psychodynamic aspects of stress tolerance. In S. A. Klausner (Ed.), *The quest for self-control*. New York: Free Press, 1965. Pp. 215–46. **190, 191**

JANIS, I. L. Effects of fear arousal on attitude change: Recent developments in theory and experimental research. In L. Berkowitz (Ed.), *Advances in experimental social psychology*. New York: Academic Press, 1967. Pp. 167–225. **131, 138, 139, 140**

JANIS, I. L. Group identification under conditions of external danger. In D. Cartwright & A. Zander (Eds.), *Group dynamics: Research and theory*. (3rd ed.) New York: Harper & Row, 1968a. Pp. 80–90. **93**

JANIS, I. L. When fear is healthy. *Psychology Today*, 1968b, 1, 46–49, 60–61. **93, 97, 100**

JANIS, I. L. *Contours of fear: The psychological impact of disasters, war, illness, and experimental stress.* In preparation. **109, 131**

JANIS, I. L., *see also* Hovland, Janis, & Kelley (1953); Mann & Janis (1968); Nowlis & Janis (1968); Stouffer *et al.* (1949b).

JANIS, I. L., CHAPMAN, D. W., GILLIN, J. P., & SPIEGEL, J. P. *The problem of panic.* Washington, D.C.: Federal Civil Defense Administration, Bulletin TB-19-2, 1955. **66**

JANIS, I. L., & FESHBACH, S. Effects of fear-arousing communications. *Journal of Abnormal and Social Psychology*, 1953, 48, 78–92. **132, 133**

JANIS, I. L., & FESHBACH, S. Personality differences associated with responsiveness to fear-arousing communications. *Journal of Personality*, 1954, 23, 154–66. **132, 133, 134, 135**

JANIS, I. L., & LEVENTHAL, H. Psychological aspects of physical illness and hospital care. In B. Wolman (Ed.), *Handbook of clinical psychology*. New York: McGraw-Hill, 1965. Pp. 1360–77. **102, 117**

JANIS, I. L., & LEVENTHAL, H. Human reactions to stress. In E. Borgatta & W. Lambert (Eds.), *Handbook of personality theory and research*. Chicago: Rand McNally, 1968. **117**

JANIS, I. L., LUMSDAINE, A. A., & GLADSTONE, A. I. Effects of preparatory communications on reactions to a subsequent news event. *Public Opinion Quarterly*, 1951, 15, 487–518. **94**

JANIS, I. L., & MANN, L. Effectiveness of emotional role playing in modifying smoking habits and attitudes. *Journal of Experimental Research in Personality*, 1965, 1, 84–90. **141**

JANIS, I. L., & SMITH, M. B. Effects of education and persuasion on national and international images. In H. C. Kelman (Ed.), *International behavior: A social-psychological analysis*. New York: Holt, Rinehart and Winston, 1965. Pp. 190–235. **126**

JANIS, I. L., & TERWILLIGER, R. An experimental study of psychological resistances to fear-arousing communications. *Journal* of Abnormal and Social Psychology, 1962, 65, 403–10. **132, 135**

JANIS, M. G. A two-year-old goes to nursery school: A case study of separation reactions. London: Tavistock Publications, 1964. **173**

JANOWITZ, M. see Bettelheim & Janowitz (1950); Shils & Janowitz (1948).

JONES, S., see Leventhal, Singer, & Jones (1965).

KALISH, H. I., see Brown, Kalish, & Farber (1951).

KANZER, M. Writers and the early loss of parents. Journal of Hillside Hospital, 1, 1953. **187**

KARDINER, A., & SPIEGEL, H. War stress and neurotic illness. New York: Hoeber, 1947. **23, 29, 30, 33**

KELLEY, H. H., see Hovland, Janis, & Kelley (1953).

KELLEY, H. H., CONDRY, J. C., JR., DAHLKE, A. E., & HILL, A. H. Collective behavior in a simulated panic situation. Journal of Experimental Social Psychology, 1965, 1, 20–54. **67**

KELLY, G. A. The psychology of personal constructs. New York: Norton, 1955. **40**

KELMAN, H. (Ed.) International behavior: A social-psychological analysis. New York: Holt, Rinehart and Winston, 1965. **169**

KERN, R., see Berkun, Bialek, Kern, & Yagi (1962).

KILLIAN, L. M. Evacuation of Panama City before Hurricane Florence. Washington, D.C.: National Academy of Sciences–National Research Council, Committee on Disaster Studies, 1954. **91**

KITT, A., see Merton & Kitt (1950).

KLAPPER, J. T. The effects of mass communication. New York: Free Press, 1960. **126**

KLEIN, G. S., BARR, H. L., & WOLITZKY, D. L. Personality. Annual Review of Psychology, 1967, 18, 467–500. **40**

KLEITMAN, N., see Aserinsky & Kleitman (1953).

LAVERTY, S. G., see Campbell, Sanderson, & Laverty (1964).

LAZARUS, R. S. Psychological stress and the coping process. New York: McGraw-Hill, 1966. **40, 94, 111, 197**

LAZARUS, R. S., & ALFERT, E. The short-circuiting of threat by experimentally altering cognitive appraisal. Journal of Abnormal and Social Psychology, 1964, 69, 195–205. **94, 95**

LAZARUS, R. S., SPEISMAN, J. C., MORDKOFF, A. M., & DAVISON, L. A. A laboratory study of psychological stress produced by a motion picture film. Psychological Monographs, 1962, 76, 1–35. **94**

LEOPOLD, R. L., & DILLON, H. Psycho-anatomy of disaster: Long-term study of post-traumatic neuroses in survivors of a marine explosion. American Journal of Psychiatry, 1963, 119, 913–21. **36**

LESLIE, I., see Fraser, Leslie, & Phelps (1943).

LEVENTHAL, H., see Janis & Leventhal (1965) (1968).

LEVENTHAL, H., & SINGER, R. P. Affect arousal and positioning of recommendations in persuasive communications. Journal of Personality and Social Psychology, 1966, 4, 137–46. **137**

LEVENTHAL, H., SINGER, R. P., & JONES, S. The effects of fear and specificity of recommendation upon attitudes and behavior. Journal of Personality and Social Psychology, 1965, 2, 20–29. **137**

LEVINE, M., see Titchner et al. (1957).

LEVINSON, D. J., see Adorno, Frenkel-Brunswik, Levinson, & Sanford (1950).

LEVITT, E. E. The psychology of anxiety. Indianapolis: Bobbs-Merrill, 1967. **125**

LEWIN, K., see Barker, Dembo & Lewin (1941).

LEWIS, H. B., see Witkin et al. (1954).

LINDEMANN, E., see Cobb & Lindemann (1943).

LORENZ, K. Ritualized fighting. In J. D. Carthy & F. J. Ebling (Eds.), A natural history of aggression. New York: Academic Press, 1964. Pp. 39–50. **155**

LUMSDAINE, A. A., see Janis, Lumsdaine, & Gladstone (1951); Stouffer et al. (1949b).

LYND, H. On shame and the search for identity. New York: Harcourt, Brace & World, 1958. **121**

MACHOVER, K., see Witkin et al. (1954).

MALMO, R. B. Measurement of drive: An unsolved problem in psychology. In M. R. Jones (Ed.), Nebraska symposium on motivation, Vol. 6. Lincoln: University of Nebraska Press, 1958. Pp. 229–65. **125**

MANDLER, G. Emotion. In R. Brown, E. Galanter, E. Hess, & G. Mandler, New directions in psychology, No. 1. New York: Holt, Rinehart and Winston, 1962. Pp. 267–343. **57**

MANN, L. The effects of emotional role playing on smoking attitudes and behavior. *Journal of Experimental Social Psychology*, 1967, 3, 334–48. **144**

MANN, L., *see also* Janis & Mann (1965).

MANN, L., & JANIS, I. L. A follow-up study on the long-range effects of emotional role playing. *Journal of Personality and Social Psychology*, 1968, 8, 339–42. **143**

MARKS, E., *see* Fritz & Marks (1954).

MARRIS, P. *Widows and their families.* London: Routledge & Kegan Paul, 1958. **26, 180, 181**

MASLOW, A., & MITTLEMAN, B. *Principles of abnormal psychology.* New York: Harper & Row, 1951. **23**

MAULDIN, B. *Up front.* New York: Holt, Rinehart and Winston, 1945. **26, 165**

MC GUIRE, C., *see* Cobb, Clark, McGuire, & Howe (1954).

MEISSNER, P. B., *see* Witkin et al. (1954).

MENNINGER, K. *Love against hate.* New York: Harcourt, Brace & World, 1942. **149**

MERTON, R., & KITT, A. Contributions to the theory of reference group behavior. In R. Merton & P. Lazarsfeld (Eds.), *Continuities in social research: Studies in the scope and method of the American soldier.* New York: Free Press, 1950. Pp. 40–105. **159**

MILGRAM, S. Some conditions of obedience and disobedience to authority. *Human Relations*, 1965, 18, 57–76. **161, 162**

MILLER, J. C., & TREIGER, N. Management of dependency under preoperative stress. Mimeographed prepublication report, 1969. **105**

MILLER, N. E. The frustration-aggression hypothesis. *Psychological Review*, 1941, 48, 337–42. **150**

MILLER, N. E., *see also* Dollard et al. (1939); Dollard & Miller (1950); Sears, Hovland, & Miller (1940).

MILLER, N. E., & BUGELSKI, R. Minor studies of aggression, 2: The influence of frustrations imposed by the in-group on attitudes expressed toward out-groups. *Journal of Psychology*, 1948, 25, 437–42. **166**

MITTLEMAN, B., *see* Maslow & Mittleman (1951).

MOORE, H. E. *Tornadoes over Texas.* Austin: University of Texas Press, 1958. **71, 84**

MOORE, S. C. Editorial. *Parachutist*, 1963, 4, 5–7. **78**

MORAN, P. A. *An experimental study of pediatric admission.* Unpublished Master's thesis, Yale University School of Nursing, 1963. **105**

MORDKOFF, A. M., *see* Lazarus, Speisman, Mordkoff, & Davison (1962).

MOWRER, O. H. *Learning theory and personality dynamics.* New York: Ronald Press, 1950. **51, 53**

MOWRER, O. H., *see also* Dollard et al. (1939).

NATIONAL SAFETY COUNCIL. *Accident facts.* (final condensed ed.) Chicago: NSC, 1967. **37**

NILES (KAFES), P. The relationship of susceptibility and anxiety to acceptance of fear-arousing communications. Unpublished doctoral dissertation, Yale University, 1964. **137, 138**

NOWLIS, G., & JANIS, I. L. Factors influencing the effectiveness of emotional role playing in modifying attitudes and actions. Mimeographed prepublication report, 1968. **144**

NUNNALLY, J. D., & BOBREN, H. M. Variables governing the willingness to receive communications on mental health. *Journal of Personality*, 1959, 27, 38–46. **135**

OSLER, S. F. Intellectual performance as a function of two types of psychological stress. *Journal of Experimental Psychology*, 1954, 47, 115–21. **127, 128**

PARAD, H. J. (Ed.) *Crisis intervention: Selected readings.* New York: Family Service Association of America, 1965. **197**

PARKES, C. Effects of bereavement on physical and mental health. *British Medical Journal*, 1964, 2, 274–79. **187**

PARKES, C. Bereavement and mental illness, Part 1: A clinical study of the grief of bereaved psychiatric patients. *British Journal of Medical Psychology*, 1965, 38, 1–12. **180, 181**

PASTORE, N. The role of arbitrariness in the frustration-aggression hypothesis. *Journal of Abnormal and Social Psychology*, 1952, 47, 728–31. **156**

PAVLOV, I. P. *Conditioned reflexes.* New York: Oxford University Press, 1927. **41**

PERVIN, L. A. The need to predict and control under conditions of threat. *Journal of Personality*, 1963, 31, 570–87. **67**

PHELPS, D., *see* Fraser, Leslie, & Phelps (1943).

RABBIE, J. M. Differential preference for companionship under threat. *Journal of*

Abnormal and Social Psychology, 1963, 67, 643–48. **93**

RADO, S. Pathodynamics and treatment of traumatic war neurosis (traumatophobia). *Psychosomatic Medicine*, 1942, 4, 362–68. **71**

REICKEN, H., see Thibaut & Reicken (1955).

ROBERTSON, J. *Young children in hospital.* London: Tavistock Publications, 1958. **172**

SANDERSON, R. E., see Campbell, Sanderson, & Laverty (1964).

SANFORD, R. N., see Adorno, Frenkel-Brunswik, Levinson, & Sanford (1950).

SARNOFF, I. *Personality dynamics and development.* New York: Wiley, 1962. **167**

SCHACHTER, S. S. *The psychology of affiliation.* Stanford, Calif.: Stanford University Press, 1959. **92**

SCHACHTER, S. S. The interaction of cognitive and physiological determinants of emotional state. In L. Berkowitz (Ed.), *Advances in experimental social psychology,* Vol. 1. New York: Academic Press, 1964. Pp. 49–81. **109, 110**

SCHACHTER, S. S., & SINGER, J. E. Cognitive, social, and physiological determinants of emotional state. *Psychological Review,* 1962, 69, 379–99. **40, 110**

SCHLOSBERG, H. The relationship between success and the laws of conditioning. *Psychological Review,* 1937, 44, 379–94. **53**

SCHLOSBERG, H. Three dimensions of emotion. *Psychological Review,* 1954, 61, 81–88. **125**

SCHMIDEBERG, M. Some observations on individual reactions to air raids. *International Journal of Psychoanalysis,* 1942, 23, 146–76. **68, 69**

SEARS, R. R., see Dollard et al. (1939).

SEARS, R. R., HOVLAND, C. I., & MILLER, N. E. Minor studies of aggression, 1: Measurement of aggressive behavior. *Journal of Psychology,* 1940, 9, 275–95. **153**

SELYE, H. *The stress of life.* New York: McGraw-Hill, 1956. **52**

SHAFFER, L. Fear and courage in aerial combat. *Journal of Consulting Psychology,* 1947, 11, 137–43. **25**

SHANDS, H. C. An outline of the process of recovery from severe trauma. *American Medical Association Archives of Neurology and Psychiatry,* 1955, 73, 403–09. **188**

SHEATSLEY, P. B., & FELDMAN, J. J. The assassination of President Kennedy: A preliminary report on public reactions and behavior. *Public Opinion Quarterly,* 1964, 28, 191–215. **192, 193**

SHEFFIELD, F. D., WULFF, J. J., & BACKER, R. Reward value of copulation without sex drive reduction. *Journal of Comparative and Physiological Psychology,* 1951, 44, 3–8. **51**

SHILS, E., & JANOWITZ, M. Cohesion and disintegration in the Wehrmacht in World War II. *Public Opinion Quarterly,* 1948, 12, 280–315. **92**

SILVER, H., see Titchner et al. (1957).

SINGER, J. E., see Schachter & Singer (1962).

SINGER, R. P., see Leventhal & Singer (1966); Leventhal, Singer, & Jones (1965).

SKINNER, B. F. *The behavior of organisms.* New York: Appleton-Century-Crofts, 1938. **53**

SMITH, M. B. Combat motivations among ground troops. In S. A. Stouffer, A. A. Lumsdaine, R. Williams, M. B. Smith, I. L. Janis, S. A. Star, & L. Cottrell, Jr., *The American soldier.* Vol. 2. *Combat and its aftermath.* Princeton, N.J.: Princeton University Press, 1949b. Pp. 105–91. **90, 92, 164**

SMITH, M. B., see also Janis & Smith (1965); Stouffer et al. (1949b).

SNYDER, F. New biology of dreaming. *Archives of General Psychiatry,* 1963, 8, 381–91. **28**

SOBEL, R. Anxiety-depressive reactions after prolonged combat experience: The "old sergeant syndrome." *Bulletin of the United States Army Medical Department,* 1949, 9, 137–46. **183**

SPEISMAN, J. C., see Lazarus, Speisman, Mordkoff, & Davison (1962).

SPENCE, K. W. A theory of emotionally based drive (D) and its relation to performance in simple learning situations. *American Psychologist,* 1958, 13, 131–41. **52**

SPIEGEL, H. Psychiatric observations in the Tunisian campaign. *American Journal of Orthopsychiatry,* 1944, 14, 381–85. **92**

SPIEGEL, H., see also Kardiner & Spiegel (1947).

SPIEGEL, J. P., see Grinker & Spiegel (1945a) (1945b); Janis, Chapman, Gillin, & Spiegel (1955).

STAR, S. A. Psychoneurotic symptoms in the Army. In S. Stouffer, A. A. Lumsdaine, R. Williams, M. B. Smith, I. L. Janis,

S. A. Star, & L. Cottrell, Jr., *The American soldier.* Vol. 2. *Combat and its aftermath.* Princeton, N.J.: Princeton University Press, 1949b. Pp. 411–55. **25**

STAR, S. A., *see also* Stouffer *et al.* (1949a) (1949b).

STOUFFER, S., SUCHMAN, E., DE VINNEY, L., STAR, S. A., & WILLIAMS, R. *The American soldier.* Vol. 1. *Adjustment during Army life.* Princeton, N.J.: Princeton University Press, 1949a. **159**

STOUFFER, S., LUMSDAINE, A. A., WILLIAMS, R., SMITH, M. B., JANIS, I. L., STAR, S. A., & COTTRELL, L., JR. *The American soldier.* Vol. 2. *Combat and its aftermath.* Princeton, N.J.: Princeton University Press, 1949b. **92**

SUCHMAN, E., *see* Stouffer *et al.* (1949a).

TAYLOR, J. A. Drive theory and manifest anxiety. *Psychological Bulletin,* 1956, 53, 303–20. **52**

TERWILLIGER, R., *see* Janis & Terwilliger (1962).

THIBAUT, J., & REICKEN, H. Authoritarianism, status, and the communication of aggression. *Human Relations,* 1955, 8, 95–120. **162**

THOMAS, C. *Leftover life to kill.* Boston: Little, Brown, 1957. **182**

THURMOND, C. Last thoughts before drowning. *Journal of Abnormal and Social Psychology,* 1943, 38, 165–84. **5**

TITCHNER, J., ZWELING, I., GOTTSCHALK, L., LEVINE, M., SILVER, H., COWETT, A., COHEN, S., & COLBERTSON, W. Consequences of surgical illness and treatment: Interaction of emotions, personality and surgical illness, and treatment, convalescence. *American Medical Association Archives of Neurology and Psychiatry,* 1957, 77, 623–34. **102**

TREIGER, N., *see* Miller & Treiger (1969).

TUDDENHAM, R. D., *see* Archibald & Tuddenham (1965).

TYHURST, J. S. The role of transition states —including disasters—in mental illness. In *Symposium on preventive and social psychiatry.* Washington, D.C.: Walter Reed Army Institute of Research, 1957. Pp. 149–69. **23**

WAGNER, A. R. The role of reinforcement and nonreinforcement in an "apparent frustration effect." *Journal of Experimental Psychology,* 1959, 57, 130–36. **153**

WALLACE, A. *Tornado in Worcester.* Washington, D.C.: National Academy of Sciences–National Research Council, Committee on Disaster Studies, 1956. **189, 190**

WALLACE, A. Mazeway disintegration: The individual's perception of socio-cultural disorganization. *Human Organization,* 1957, 16, 23–27. **189, 190**

WALTERS, R. H., *see* Bandura & Walters (1963).

WAPNER, S., *see* Witkin *et al.* (1954).

WATERHOUSE, I. K., *see* Child & Waterhouse (1952).

WELCH, C., *see* Egbert, Battit, Welch, & Bartlett (1964).

WILLERMAN, B., *see* Grinker, Willerman, Bradley, & Fastovsky (1946).

WILLIAMS, R., *see* Stouffer *et al.* (1949a) (1949b).

WILSON, W. P., *see* Dobbs & Wilson (1960).

WITKIN, H. A., LEWIS, H. B., HERTZMANN, M., MACHOVER, K., MEISSNER, P. B., & WAPNER, S. *Personality through perception.* New York: Harper & Row, 1954. **40**

WOLFENSTEIN, M. *Disaster.* New York: Free Press, 1957. **70, 85**

WOLFENSTEIN, M. How is mourning possible? *Psychoanalytic Studies of the Child,* 1966, 21, 93–123. **176**

WOLITZKY, D. L., *see* Klein, Barr, & Wolitzky (1967).

WOLPE, J. The comparative clinical status of conditioning therapies and psychoanalysis. In J. Wolpe, A. Salter, & L. J. Reyna, *The conditioning therapies.* New York: Holt, Rinehart and Winston, 1965. Pp. 5–200. **55**

WRIGHT, D., *see* Hastings, Wright, & Glueck (1944).

WULFF, J. J., *see* Sheffield, Wulff, & Backer (1951).

YAGI, K., *see* Berkun, Bialek, Kern, & Yagi (1962).

ZEMACH, M. The effects of guilt-arousing communications on acceptance of recommendations. Unpublished doctoral dissertation, Yale University, 1966. **135, 136**

ZWELING, I., *see* Titchner *et al.* (1957).

CORWIN, S. M., *see* Sarnoff & Corwin (1959).

DEUTSCH, H. *Neuroses and character types.* New York: International Universities Press, 1965. **327, 332, 333, 386**

DIVEN, K. Certain determinants in the conditioning of anxiety reactions. *Journal of Psychology*, 1937, 3, 291–308. **214**

DOLLARD, J., & MILLER, N. E. *Personality and psychotherapy.* New York: McGraw-Hill, 1950. **300, 339, 372**

EPSTEIN, S., & FENZ, W. D. Steepness of approach and avoidance gradients in humans as a function of experience: Theory and experiment. *Journal of Experimental Psychology*, 1965, 70, 1–12. **243**

ERIKSON, E. H. *Childhood and society.* New York: Norton, 1950. **288, 294, 399**

ERIKSON, E. H. Identity and the life cycle. *Psychological Issues*, 1959, 1, No. 1. **288, 352**

FEDERN, P. *Ego psychology.* New York: Basic Books, 1952. **345**

FENZ, W. D., *see* Epstein & Fenz (1965).

FISHER, C. Psychoanalytic implications of recent research on sleep and dreaming, Part 1: Empirical findings. *Journal of the American Psychoanalytic Association*, 1965a, 13, 197–270. **227**

FISHER, C. Psychoanalytic implications of recent research on sleep and dreaming, Part 2: Implications for psychoanalytic theory. *Journal of the American Psychoanalytic Association*, 1965b, 13, 271–303. **227**

FISHER, C., GROSS, J., & ZUCH, J. A cycle of penile erection synchronous with dreaming (REM) sleep: Preliminary report. *American Medical Association Archives of General Psychiatry*, 1965, 12, 29–45. **227**

FLECK, S., *see* Lidz, Fleck, & Cornelison (1965).

FREUD, A. (1936) *The ego and the mechanisms of defense.* New York: International Universities Press, 1946. **285, 332, 348, 354, 358, 359, 360, 362, 365, 378, 381, 391, 397**

FREUD, A., & BURLINGHAM, D. *War and children.* New York: International Universities Press, 1943. **294**

FREUD, S. (1892–99) Extracts from the Fliess papers. *Standard edition*, Vol. 1. London: Hogarth Press, 1966. Pp. 175–280. **248, 274**

FREUD, S. (1894) The neuropsychoses of defence. *Standard edition*, Vol. 3. London: Hogarth Press, 1962. Pp. 43–61. **354, 389**

FREUD, S. (1896a) Heredity and the etiology of the neuroses. *Standard edition*, Vol. 3. London: Hogarth Press, 1962. Pp. 141–56. **247**

FREUD, S. (1896b) Further remarks on the neuropsychoses of defence. *Standard edition*, Vol. 3. London: Hogarth Press, 1962. Pp. 159–85. **247, 389**

FREUD, S. (1896c) The etiology of hysteria. *Standard edition*, Vol. 3. London: Hogarth Press, 1962. Pp. 189–221. **247**

FREUD, S. (1900) The interpretation of dreams. *Standard edition*, Vols. 4 and 5. London: Hogarth Press, 1953. **210, 247, 266, 270, 347**

FREUD, S. (1905a) Fragment of an analysis of a case of hysteria. *Standard edition*, Vol. 7. London: Hogarth Press, 1953. Pp. 3–122. **293**

FREUD, S. (1905b) Three essays on the theory of sexuality. *Standard edition*, Vol. 7. London: Hogarth Press, 1953. Pp. 125–243. **249, 274, 388, 398**

FREUD, S. (1908) Character and anal erotism. *Standard edition*, Vol. 9. London: Hogarth Press, 1959. Pp. 167–75. **378**

FREUD, S. (1909a) Analysis of a phobia in a five-year-old boy. *Standard edition*, Vol. 10. London: Hogarth Press, 1955. Pp. 3–149. **263, 277, 279, 293, 354, 399**

FREUD, S. (1909b) Notes upon a case of obsessional neurosis. *Standard edition*, Vol. 10. London: Hogarth Press, 1955. Pp. 153–249. **265, 267, 330, 380**

FREUD, S. (1910a) Leonardo da Vinci and a memory of his childhood. *Standard edition*, Vol. 11. London: Hogarth Press, 1957. Pp. 59–137. **387**

FREUD, S. (1910b) A special type of object choice made by men. *Standard edition*, Vol. 11. London: Hogarth Press, 1957. Pp. 163–75. **381**

FREUD, S. (1911) Psycho-analytic notes on an autobiographical account of a case of paranoia. *Standard edition*, Vol. 12. London: Hogarth Press, 1958. Pp. 3–82. **254, 320**

FREUD, S. (1912) The dynamics of transference. *Standard edition*, Vol. 12. London: Hogarth Press, 1958. Pp. 97–108. **293**

FREUD, S. (1913) Totem and taboo. *Standard edition*, Vol. 13. London: Hogarth Press, 1955. Pp. 1–161. **272**

FREUD, s. (1914a) On narcissism: An introduction. *Standard edition*, Vol. 14. London: Hogarth Press, 1957. Pp. 67–102. **254, 320**

FREUD, s. (1914b) Remembering, repeating, and working-through. Further recommendations on the technique of psychoanalysis, 2. *Standard edition*, Vol. 12. London: Hogarth Press, 1958. Pp. 145–56. **293**

FREUD, s. (1915a) Observations on transference love. *Standard edition*, Vol. 12. London: Hogarth Press, 1958. Pp. 157–71. **293**

FREUD, s. (1915b) Instincts and their vicissitudes. *Standard edition*, Vol. 14. London: Hogarth Press, 1957. Pp. 109–40. **382, 383, 389**

FREUD, s. (1915c) Repression. *Standard edition*, Vol. 14. London: Hogarth Press, 1957. Pp. 141–58. **374, 389**

FREUD, s. (1915d) The unconscious. *Standard edition*, Vol. 14. London: Hogarth Press, 1957. Pp. 159–204. **389, 391**

FREUD, s. (1915–17) Introductory lectures on psychoanalysis. *Standard edition*, Vols. 15 and 16. London: Hogarth Press, 1963. **263**

FREUD, s. (1917) Mourning and melancholia. *Standard edition*, Vol. 14. London: Hogarth Press, 1957. Pp. 237–58. **334**

FREUD, s. (1918) From the history of an infantile neurosis. *Standard edition*, Vol. 17. London: Hogarth Press, 1955. Pp. 3–122. **266, 268, 278, 279, 384, 396**

FREUD, s. (1920a) Beyond the pleasure principle. *Standard edition*, Vol. 18. London: Hogarth Press, 1955. Pp. 7–64. **360**

FREUD, s. (1920b) Group psychology and the analysis of the ego. *Standard edition*, Vol. 18. London: Hogarth Press, 1955. Pp. 67–143. **401**

FREUD, s. (1922) Some neurotic mechanisms in jealousy, paranoia, and homosexuality. *Standard edition*, Vol. 18. London: Hogarth Press, 1955. Pp. 221–32. **377, 384, 401**

FREUD, s. (1923) The ego and the id. *Standard edition*, Vol. 19. London: Hogarth Press, 1961. Pp. 3–59. **320, 391**

FREUD, s. (1924) The dissolution of the Oedipus complex. *Standard edition*, Vol. 19. London: Hogarth Press, 1961. Pp. 173–79. **257**

FREUD, s. (1925a) Negation. *Standard edition*, Vol. 19. London: Hogarth Press, 1961. Pp. 235–39. **379**

FREUD, s. (1925b) Some psychical consequences of the anatomical distinction between the sexes. *Standard edition*, Vol. 19. London: Hogarth Press, 1961. Pp. 243–58. **257**

FREUD, s. (1926) Inhibitions, symptoms, and anxiety. *Standard edition*, Vol. 20. London: Hogarth Press, 1959. Pp. 77–172. **279, 295, 300, 360, 372, 391, 397, 398**

FREUD, s. (1933) The dissection of the psychical personality. In New introductory lectures on psycho-analysis. *Standard edition*, Vol. 22. London: Hogarth Press, 1964. Pp. 57–80. **320**

FREUD, s. (1937) Analysis terminable and interminable. *Standard edition*, Vol. 23. London: Hogarth Press, 1964. Pp. 209–53. **374, 391, 397**

FREUD, s., *see also* Breuer & Freud (1893–95).

FRIEDMAN, N. James Baldwin and psychotherapy. *Psychotherapy*, 1966, 3, 177–83. **361**

FROMM, E. *Escape from freedom*. New York: Holt, Rinehart and Winston, 1941. **352**

GLIXMAN, A. F. Recall of completed and incompleted activities under varying degrees of stress. *Journal of Experimental Psychology*, 1949, 39, 281–95. **214**

GOLDBERGER, L., & HOLT, R. R. Experimental interference with reality contact: Individual differences. In P. Solomon, P. E. Kubzansky, P. H. Leiderman, J. H. Mendelson, R. Trumbull, & D. Wexler (Eds.), *Sensory deprivation*. Cambridge, Mass.: Harvard University Press, 1961. Pp. 130–42. **348**

GOUGH, H. Identifying psychological femininity. *Educational and Psychological Measurement*, 1952, 12, 427–39. **286**

GRINKER, R. R., & SPIEGEL, J. P. *Men under stress*. Philadelphia: Blakiston, 1945. **297**

GROSS, J., *see* Fisher, Gross, & Zuch (1965).

HALL, C. S., & LINDZEY, G. *Theories of personality*. New York: Wiley, 1957. **279, 296**

HARTMANN, H. (1939) *Ego psychology and the problem of adaptation*. New York: International Universities Press, 1958. **244, 399**

HARTMANN, H. Comments on the psychoanalytic theory of the ego. *Psychoanalytic Study of the Child*, 1950, 5, 74–96. **244**

HARTMANN, H. The mutual influences in the development of the ego and id. *Psycho-*

analytic Study of the Child, 1952, 7, 9–30. **244**

HARTMANN, H. Notes on the theory of sublimation. *Psychoanalytic Study of the Child*, 1955, 10, 9–29. **244**

HASTORF, A. H., & CANTRIL, H. They saw a game: A case study. *Journal of Abnormal and Social Psychology*, 1954, 49, 129–34. **309**

HERON, W. Cognitive and physiological effects of perceptual isolation. In P. Solomon, P. E. Kubzansky, P. H. Leiderman, J. H. Mendelson, R. Trumbull, & D. Wexler (Eds.), *Sensory deprivation.* Cambridge, Mass.: Harvard University Press, 1961. Pp. 6–33. **342, 343**

HERON, W., *see also* Bexton, Heron, & Scott (1954).

HILGARD, E. R., & BOWER, G. H. *Theories of learning.* (3rd ed.) New York: Meredith, 1966. **300**

HOLLINGSHEAD, A. B., & REDLICH, F. C. *Social class and mental illness.* New York: Wiley, 1958. **401**

HOLT, R. R. The accuracy of self-evaluations: Its measurement and some of its personological correlates. *Journal of Consulting Psychology*, 1951, 15, 95–101. **322**

HOLT, R. R. Gauging primary and secondary processes in Rorschach responses. *Journal of Projective Techniques*, 1956, 20, 14–25. **348**

HOLT, R. R., *see also* Goldberger & Holt (1961).

HORNEY, K. *The neurotic personality of our time.* New York: Norton, 1937. **399**

JONES, E. *The life and work of Sigmund Freud.* New York: Basic Books, 1953 (Vol. 1), 1955 (Vol. 2), 1957 (Vol. 3). **215, 296**

JOYCE, J. *Ulysses.* New York: Modern Library, 1961. **252, 253**

KARDINER, A., & OVESEY, L. *The mark of oppression: Explorations in the personality of the American Negro.* Cleveland: World, 1951. **358**

KENISTON, K. *The uncommitted.* New York: Harcourt, Brace & World, 1965. **288, 401**

KOVACH, K., *see* Zubek et al. (1963).

KRIS, E. *Psychoanalytic explorations in art.* New York: International Universities Press, 1952. **388**

KUBZANSKY, P. E., *see* Mendelson et al. (1961).

LANGER, T. S., *see* Srole et al. (1962).

LEIDERMAN, P. H., *see* Mendelson et al. (1961).

LEV, J., *see* Pintner & Lev (1940).

LEVINE, R., CHEIN, I., & MURPHY, G. The relation of the intensity of a need to the amount of perceptual distortion. *Journal of Psychology*, 1942, 13, 283–93. **324**

LEWIN, K. Environmental forces in child behavior and development. In C. Murchison (Ed.), *A handbook of child psychology.* Worcester, Mass.: Clark University Press, 1931. Pp. 92–127. **218**

LEWTY, W., *see* Smith & Lewty (1959).

LIDZ, T., FLECK, S., & CORNELISON, A. *Schizophrenia and the family.* New York: International Universities Press, 1965. **401**

LINDSLEY, D. B. Common factors in sensory deprivation, sensory distortion, and sensory overload. In P. Solomon, P. E. Kubzansky, P. H. Leiderman, J. H. Mendelson, R. Trumbull, & D. Wexler (Eds.), *Sensory deprivation.* Cambridge, Mass.: Harvard University Press, 1961. Pp. 174–94. **347**

LINDZEY, G. Some remarks concerning incest, the incest taboo, and psychoanalytic theory. *American Psychologist*, 1967, 22, 1051–59. **273**

LINDZEY, G., *see also* Hall & Lindzey (1957).

LOEWALD, H. Internalization, separation, mourning, and the superego. *Psychoanalytic Quarterly*, 1962, 31, 483–504. **383**

LOEWALD, H. On internalization. Paper presented before the Western New England Psychoanalytic Society, New Haven, Conn., 1964. **383**

LUNGER, R., & PAGE, J. O. Worries of college freshmen. *Journal of Genetic Psychology*, 1939, 54, 457–60. **286**

MAHL, G. F. Gestures and body movements in interviews. In J. M. Shlien (Ed.), *Research in psychotherapy*, 3. Washington, D.C.: American Psychological Association, 1968. Pp. 295–346. **382**

MALINOWSKI, B. (1927) *Sex and repression in savage society.* London: Routledge & Kegan Paul, 1953. **400, 401**

MARKS, C., *see* Zuckerman, Albright, Marks, & Miller (1962).

MC CLELLAND, D. C., & ATKINSON, J. W. The projective expression of needs, 1: The effects of different intensities of the hunger drive on perception. *Journal of Psychology*, 1948, 25, 205–22. **324**

MENDELSON, J. H., KUBZANSKY, P. E., LEIDERMAN, P. H., WEXLER, D., & SOLOMON, P.

Physiological and psychological aspects of sensory deprivation: A case analysis. In P. Solomon, P. E. Kubzansky, P. H. Leiderman, J. H. Mendelson, R. Trumbull, & D. Wexler (Eds.), *Sensory deprivation.* Cambridge, Mass.: Harvard University Press, 1961. Pp. 91–113. **344**

MILLER, D. R., & SWANSON, G. E. *Inner conflict and defense.* New York: Holt, Rinehart and Winston, 1958. **402**

MILLER, G., *see* Zuckerman, Albright, Marks, & Miller (1962).

MILLER, N. E., *see* Dollard & Miller (1950).

MILLER, N. E. Experimental studies of conflict. In J. McV. Hunt (Ed.), *Personality and the behavior disorders.* New York: Ronald Press, 1944. Pp. 431–65. **218, 220, 221, 222, 339, 340**

MILLER, N. E., & MURRAY, E. J. Conflict and displacement: Learnable drive as a basis for the steeper gradient of avoidance than of approach. *Journal of Experimental Psychology,* 1952, 43, 227–31. **220**

MITCHELL, S. T., *see* Srole *et al.* (1962).

MOSS, H. A. Standards of conduct for students, teacher, and parents. *Journal of Counseling Psychology,* 1955, 2, 39–42. **286**

MUNROE, R. *Schools of psychoanalytic thought.* New York: Dryden Press, 1955. **279, 296**

MURDOCK, G. P. *Social structure.* New York: Macmillan, 1949. **272**

MURPHY, G., *see* Levine, Chein, & Murphy (1942).

MURRAY, E. J., *see* Miller & Murray (1952).

MURRAY, E. J., & BERKUN, M. M. Displacement as a function of conflict. *Journal of Abnormal and Social Psychology,* 1955, 51, 47–56. **220**

MURRAY, H. A. The effect of fear upon estimates of the maliciousness of other personalities. *Journal of Social Psychology,* 1933, 4, 310–29. **309**

MYERS, J. K., & ROBERTS, B. *Family and class dynamics in mental illness.* New York: Wiley, 1959. **401**

NEWFIELD, J. *A prophetic minority.* New York: New American Library, 1966. **361**

OPLER, M. K., *see* Srole *et al.* (1962).

OVESEY, L., *see* Kardiner & Ovesey (1951).

PAGE, J. O., *see* Lunger & Page (1939).

PARSONS, A. Is the Oedipus complex universal? The Jones-Malinowski debate revisited and a South Italian "nuclear complex." In W. Muensterberger & S. Axelrod (Eds.), *The psychoanalytic study of society,* Vol. 3. New York: International Universities Press, 1964. Pp. 278–328. **400, 401**

PARSONS, T. *Social structure and personality.* New York: Free Press, 1964. **399**

PINTNER, R., & LEV, J. Worries of school children. *Journal of Genetic Psychology,* 1940, 56, 67–76. **286**

PRITCHARD, R., & ROSENZWEIG, S. The effect of war stress upon childhood and youth. *Journal of Abnormal and Social Psychology,* 1942, 37, 329–44. **294**

RACHMAN, S., *see* Wolpe & Rachman (1960).

RAPAPORT, D. The theory of ego autonomy: A generalization. *Bulletin of the Menninger Clinic,* 1958, 22, 13–35. **347**

REDLICH, F. C., *see* Hollingshead & Redlich (1958).

RENNIE, T. A. C., *see* Srole *et al.* (1962).

RIESMAN, D. *The lonely crowd.* New Haven, Conn.: Yale University Press, 1950. **286**

RITVO, L. Darwin as the source of Freud's neo-Lamarkianism. *Journal of the American Psychoanalytic Association,* 1965, 13, 499–517. **399**

ROBERTS, B., *see* Myers & Roberts (1959).

ROSENZWEIG, S. An experimental study of "repression" with special reference to need-perspective and ego-defensive reactions to frustration. *Journal of Experimental Psychology,* 1943, 32, 64–74. **214**

ROSENZWEIG, S., *see also* Pritchard & Rosenzweig (1942).

SANFORD, R. N. The effects of abstinence from food upon imaginal processes: A preliminary experiment. *Journal of Psychology,* 1936, 2, 129–36. **324**

SANFORD, R. N. The effects of abstinence from food upon imaginal processes: A further study. *Journal of Psychology,* 1937, 3, 145–59. **324**

SARNOFF, I. Identification with the aggressor: Some personality correlates of anti-Semitism among Jews. *Journal of Personality,* 1951, 20, 199–218. **362**

SARNOFF, I., & CORWIN, S. M. Castration anxiety and the fear of death. *Journal of Personality,* 1959, 27, 374–85. **280, 281**

SCOTT, T. H., *see* Bexton, Heron, & Scott (1954).

SEARS, P. S. Doll play aggression in normal young children. *Psychological Monographs,* 1951, 65, No. 323. **263, 265**

SEARS, R. R. Experimental studies of projection, 1: Attribution of traits. *Journal of Social Psychology*, 1936, 7, 151–63. **321**

SEARS, R. R. Survey of objective studies of psychoanalytic concepts. *Social Science Research Council Bulletin*, 1943, No. 51. **214**

SHMAVONIAN, B. M., *see* Cohen, Silverman, Bressler, & Shmavonian (1961).

SILVERMAN, A. J., *see* Cohen, Silverman, Bressler, & Shmavonian (1961).

SMITH, S., & LEWTY, W. Perceptual isolation using a silent room. *Lancet*, 1959, 2, 342–45. **343, 344**

SOLOMON, P., *see* Mendelson *et al.* (1961).

SPIEGEL, J. P., *see* Grinker & Spiegel (1945).

SROLE, L., LANGER, T. S., MITCHELL, S. T., OPLER, M. K., & RENNIE, T. A. C. *Mental health in the metropolis: The midtown Manhattan study*. New York: McGraw-Hill, 1962. **401**

STERNLAFF, R. Differential perception in paranoid schizophrenics and depressives. Unpublished doctoral dissertation, University of Oklahoma, 1964. **323**

SULLIVAN, H. S. *Conceptions of modern psychiatry*. Washington, D.C.: William Alanson White Psychiatric Foundation, 1947. **296**

SWANSON, G. E., *see* Miller & Swanson (1958).

TAGIURI, R., BRUNER, J. S., & BLAKE, R. R. On the relation between feelings and perception of feelings among members of small groups. In E. E. Maccoby, T. M. Newcomb, & E. L. Hartley (Eds.), *Readings in social psychology*. (3rd ed.) New York: Holt, Rinehart and Winston, 1958. Pp. 110–16. **358**

UNITED STATES REPORTS. *Brown et al. v. Board of Education of Topeka et al.*, 347, 483–96. **356**

VISPO, R., *see* Azima, Vispo, & Azima (1961).

WAELDER, R. (1930) The principle of multiple function. *Psychoanalytic Quarterly*, 1936, 5, 45–62. **348**

WAELDER, R. The problem of the genesis of psychical conflict in earliest infancy. *International Journal of Psychoanalysis*, 1937, 18, 406–73. **259**

WEXLER, D., *see* Mendelson *et al.* (1961).

WIENER, N. *Cybernetics*. Cambridge, Mass.: MIT Press, 1948. **364**

WIENER, N. *The human use of human beings*. Boston: Houghton Mifflin, 1950. **364**

WILGOSH, L., *see* Zubek *et al.* (1963).

WINOCUR, G., *see* Zubek *et al.* (1963).

WOLOWITZ, H. Attraction and aversion to power: A psychoanalytic conflict theory of homosexuality in male paranoids. *Journal of Abnormal Psychology*, 1965, 70, 360–70. **323**

WOLPE, J., & RACHMAN, S. Psychoanalytic "evidence": A critique based on Freud's case of Little Hans. *Journal of Nervous and Mental Diseases*, 1960, 130, 135–48. **205**

ZAMANSKY, H. An investigation of the psychoanalytic theory of paranoid delusions. *Journal of Personality*, 1958, 26, 410–25. **322**

ZUBEK, J. P., AFTANAS, M., KOVACH, K., WILGOSH, L., & WINOCUR, G. Effect of severe immobilization of the body on intellectual and perceptual processes. *Canadian Journal of Psychology*, 1963, 17, 118–33. **343, 344**

ZUCH, J., *see* Fisher, Gross, & Zuch (1965).

ZUCKERMAN, M., ALBRIGHT, R., MARKS, C., & MILLER, G. Stress and hallucinatory effects of perceptual isolation and confinement. *Psychological Monographs*, 1962, 76, No. 30. **343, 344**

Part Three

ABERLE, D. F., & NAEGELE, K. D. Middle-class fathers' occupational role and attitudes toward children. *American Journal of Orthopsychiatry*, 1952, 22, 366–78. **480**

ACHENBACH, T. M. The classification of children's psychiatric symptoms: A factor analytic study. *Psychological Monographs*, 1966, 80(6). **523**

AINSWORTH, M. D. S. *Infancy in Uganda*. Baltimore: Johns Hopkins Press, 1967. **429**

ALTUS, W. D. Birth order and its sequellae. *Science*, 1966, 151, 44–49. **552**

APPERLY, F. L. A study of America's Rhodes scholars. *Journal of Heredity*, 1939, 30, 494–95. **552**

AX, A. The physiological differentiation between fear and anger. *Psychosomatic Medicine*, 1953, 15, 433–42. **504**

BACH, G. R. Young children's play fantasies. *Psychological Monographs*, 1945, 59(2). **477**

BAER, D. M., *see* Gewirtz & Baer (1958).

BAKER, C. T., *see* Lansky *et al.* (1961); Sontag *et al.* (1958).

BANDURA, A. Social learning through imitation. In M. R. Jones (Ed.), *Nebraska symposium on motivation*, Vol. 10. Lincoln: University of Nebraska Press, 1962. Pp. 211–68. **465, 477**

BANDURA, A., ROSS, D., & ROSS, S. A. Transmission of aggression through imitation of aggressive models. *Journal of Abnormal and Social Psychology*, 1961, 63, 575–82. **477**

BANDURA, A., ROSS, D., & ROSS, S. A. A comparative test of the status envy, social power, and secondary reinforcement theories of identification learning. *Journal of Abnormal and Social Psychology*, 1963a, 67, 527–34. **465**

BANDURA, A., ROSS, D., & ROSS, S. A. Vicarious reinforcement and imitative learning. *Journal of Abnormal and Social Psychology*, 1963b, 67, 601–07. **465, 503**

BANDURA, A., & WALTERS, R. H. *Social learning and personality development.* New York: Holt, Rinehart and Winston, 1963. **501**

BAUMRIND, D., & BLACK, A. E. Socialization practices associated with dimensions of competence in preschool boys and girls. *Child Development*, 1967, 38, 291–328. **508, 564**

BAYLEY, N., *see* Schaefer & Bayley (1963).

BENNETT, E. M., & COHEN, L. R. Men and women: Personality patterns and contrasts. *Genetic Psychology Monographs*, 1959, 60, 101–53. **478, 479, 480**

BENTZEN, F. Sex ratios in learning and behavior disorders. *American Journal of Orthopsychiatry*, 1963, 33, 92–98. **489**

BIEBER, I., DAIN, H. J., DINCE, R. R., DRELLICH, M. G., GRAND, H. G., GUNDLACH, R. H., KREMER, M. W., RIFKIN, A. H., WILBUR, C. B., & BIEBER, T. B. *Homosexuality.* New York: Basic Books, 1962. **480**

BIEBER, T. B., *see* Bieber *et al.* (1962).

BLACK, A. E., *see* Baumrind & Black (1967).

BONNEY, M. E. The constancy of sociometric scores and their relationship to teacher judgments of social success and to personality self-ratings. *Sociometry*, 1943, 6, 409–24. **545**

BRICKER, W., *see* Patterson *et al.* (1967).

BRONFENBRENNER, U. Freudian theories of identification and their derivatives. *Child Development*, 1960, 31, 15–40. **465**

BROWN, D. G. Masculinity-femininity development in children. *Journal of Consulting Psychology*, 1957, 21, 197–202. **479**

BUSS, A. H. *The psychology of aggression.* New York: Wiley, 1961. **489**

BYRAM, C. A longitudinal study of aggressive and self-assertive behavior in social interaction. Unpublished senior honors thesis, Radcliffe College, 1966. **503**

CAUDILL, W., & WEINSTEIN, J. Maternal care and infant behavior in Japanese and American urban middle-class families. *Yearbook of the International Sociological Association*, 1966. **435**

CHANG. B. The relation between identification with a model and attentiveness to verbal information from the model. Unpublished senior honors thesis, Harvard University, 1965. **468**

COBB, H. V. Role wishes and general wishes of children and adolescents. *Child Development*, 1954, 25, 161–71. **477**

COHEN, L. R., *see* Bennett & Cohen (1959).

COLLINS, B. E., *see* Helmreich & Collins (1967).

CRANDALL, V. J., *see* Lansky *et al.* (1961).

CRANDALL, V. J., & RABSON, A. Children's repetition choices in an intellectual achievement situation following success and failure. *Journal of Genetic Psychology*, 1960, 97, 161–68. **488, 514**

CRANDALL, V. J., KATKOVSKY, W., & PRESTON, A. Motivational and ability determinants of young children's intellectual achievement behaviors. *Child Development*, 1962, 33, 643–66. **515**

CRUTCHFIELD, R. S. Conformity and character. *American Psychologist*, 1955, 10, 191–98. **478, 481**

DAHMS, L., *see* Walters *et al.* (1957).

DAIN, H. J., *see* Bieber *et al.* (1962).

DAVIS, A. *Social class influences upon learning.* Cambridge, Mass.: Harvard University Press, 1948. **526**

DINCE, R. R., *see* Bieber *et al.* (1962).

DISTLER, L., *see* Mussen & Distler (1959).

DOUVAN, E., & KAYE, C. *Adolescent girls.* Ann Arbor: Survey Research Center, University of Michigan, 1957. **478**

DRELLICH, M. G., *see* Bieber *et al.* (1962).

EMMERICH, W. Young children's discriminations of parent and child roles. *Child Development*, 1959, 30, 403–19. **477**

FAULS, L. B., & SMITH, W. D. Sex role learning of five-year-olds. *Journal of Genetic Psychology*, 1956, 89, 105–17. **480**

FAWL, C. L. Disturbances experienced by children in their natural habitats: A study in psychological ecology. Unpublished doctoral dissertation, University of Kansas, 1959. **501**

FESHBACH, N. D., & ROE, K. Empathy in six- and seven-year-olds. *Child Development*, 1968, 39, 133–45. **467**

FLANAGAN, J. C. Project Talent. Unpublished manuscript. **488**

FOSTER, J. C. Play activities of children in the first six grades. *Child Development*, 1930, 1, 248–54. **479**

FRAZIER, A., & LISONBEE, L. K. Adolescent concerns with physique. *School Review*, 1950, 58, 397–405. **477**

GEWIRTZ, J. L. The course of infant smiling in four child-rearing environments in Israel. In B. M. Foss (Ed.), *Determinants of infant behavior*, Vol. 3. New York: Wiley, 1965. Pp. 205–60. **418, 419, 420**

GEWIRTZ, J. L., & BAER, D. M. The effects of brief social deprivation on behavior for a social reinforcer. *Journal of Abnormal and Social Psychology*, 1958, 56, 49–56. **506**

GOLLIN, E. S. Serial learning and perceptual recognition in children. *Perceptual and Motor Skills*, 1966, 23, 751–58. **532, 533**

GOY, R. W., *see* Young *et al.* (1964).

GRAND, H. G., *see* Bieber *et al.* (1962).

GUNDLACH, R. H., *see* Bieber *et al.* (1962).

HARLOW, H. F., & HARLOW, M. K. Learning to love. *American Scientist*, 1966, 54, 244–72. **425, 433**

HARLOW, H. F., & ZIMMERMAN, R. R. Affectional responses in the infant monkey. *Science*, 1959, 130, 421–32. **425, 426**

HARLOW, M. K., *see* Harlow & Harlow (1966).

HARRIS, D. B. Sex differences in the life problems and interests of adolescents, 1935 and 1957. *Child Development*, 1959, 30, 453. **477, 478**

HARTLEY, R. D. Children's concepts of male and female roles. *Merrill-Palmer Quarterly*, 1960, 6(a), 83–91. **480**

HEATHERS, G. Emotional dependence and independence in nursery school play. *Journal of Genetic Psychology*, 1955, 87, 37–57. **508**

HELMREICH, R. L., & COLLINS, B. E. Situational determinants of affiliative preference under stress. *Journal of Personality and Social Psychology*, 1967, 6, 79–85. **552**

HOLMES, H., *see* Sackett *et al.* (1965).

HONZIK, M. P. Sex differences in the occurrence of materials in the play constructions of preadolescents. *Child Development*, 1951, 22, 15–35. **478, 479**

HOSKEN, B., *see* Kagan *et al.* (1961).

HOVLAND, C. I., & JANIS, I. L. (Eds.) *Personality and persuasibility.* New Haven, Conn.: Yale University Press, 1959. **478, 481**

JANIS, I. L., *see* Hovland & Janis (1959).

JENKINS, J. J., & RUSSELL, W. A. An atlas of semantic profiles for 360 words. *American Journal of Psychology*, 1958, 71, 688–99. **478, 480**

JERSILD, A. T. *In search of self.* New York: Teachers College Press of Columbia University, 1952. **477**

JONES, H. E. The environment and mental development. In L. Carmichael (Ed.), *Manual of child psychology*. New York: Wiley, 1954. Pp. 631–96. **552**

KAGAN, J. The child's sex role classification of school objects. *Child Development*, 1964, 35, 1051–56. **489, 490, 525**

KAGAN, J., *see also* Lansky *et al.* (1961); Moss & Kagan (1958); Yondo & Kagan (1963).

KAGAN, J., HOSKEN, B., & WATSON, S. The child's symbolic conceptualization of the parents. *Child Development*, 1961, 32, 625–36. **478**

KAGAN, J., & LEMKIN, J. The child's differential perception of parental attributes. *Journal of Abnormal and Social Psychology*, 1960, 61, 440–47. **477**

KAGAN, J., & MOSS, H. A. Parental correlates of child's I.Q. and height. *Child Development*, 1959, 30, 325–32. **529**

KAGAN, J., & MOSS, H. A. *Birth to maturity: A study in psychological development.* New York: Wiley, 1962. **478, 479, 485, 489, 507, 508, 514, 529, 546, 566**

KAGAN, J., PEARSON, L., & WELCH, L. The modifiability of an impulsive tempo. *Journal of Educational Psychology*, 1966, 57, 359–65. **466, 534, 535**

KAGAN, J., & PHILLIPS, W. The measurement of identification. *Journal of Abnormal and Social Psychology*, 1964, 69, 442–43. **460**

KATKOVSKY, W., *see* Crandall *et al.* (1962).

KAYE, C., *see* Douvan & Kaye (1957).

KOCH, H. L. Attitudes of children toward their peers as related to certain characteristics of their siblings. *Psychological Monographs*, 1965a, 70, No. 426. **554**

KOCH, H. L. Some emotional attitudes of the young child in relation to characteristics of his siblings. *Child Development*, 1965b. 27, 393–426. **554**

KOCH, H. L. The relation of certain formal attributes of siblings to attitudes held toward each other and toward their parents. *Monographs of the Society for Research in Child Development*, 1960, 25(4, Whole No. 78). **502**

KOHN, M. L. Social class and parental values. *American Journal of Sociology*, 1959, 64, 337–51. **478, 479, 480**

KREMER, M. W., *see* Bieber *et al.* (1962).

LANSKY, L. M., CRANDALL, V. J., KAGAN, J., & BAKER, C. T. Sex differences in aggression and its correlates in middle-class adolescents. *Child Development*, 1961, 32, 45–58. **478**

LANYON, R. I., *see* Zucker *et al.* (1968).

LEMKIN, J., *see* Kagan & Lemkin (1960).

LEVIN, H., *see* Sears *et al.* (1957).

LEWIS, M. Infant attention: Response decrement as a measure of cognitive processes, or what's new, Baby Jane? Paper presented at the meeting of the Society for Research in Child Development, symposium on The Role of Attention in Cognitive Development, New York, March 1967. **418**

LINTON, R. Status and role. In R. Linton, *The study of man: An introduction*. New York: Appleton-Century-Crofts, 1936. Pp. 113–31. **476**

LIPPITT, R., *see* Polansky *et al.* (1950).

LIPTON, R., *see* Provence & Lipton (1962).

LISONBEE, L. K., *see* Frazier & Lisonbee (1950).

LITTMAN, R. G., *see* Patterson *et al.* (1967).

MACCOBY, E. E. Role taking in childhood and its consequences for social learning. *Child Development*, 1959, 30, 239–52. **465**

MACCOBY, E. E. Attachment and dependence. In P. H. Mussen (Ed.), *Manual of child psychology*. New York: Wiley, 1969. **509**

MACCOBY, E. E., *see also* Rothbart & Maccoby (1966); Sears *et al.* (1957).

MACCOBY, E. E., & WILSON, W. C. Identification and observational learning from films. *Journal of Abnormal and Social Psychology*, 1957, 55, 76–87. **477**

MANOSEVITZ, M., *see* Zucker *et al.* (1968).

MARTIN, W. Singularity and stability of profiles of social behavior. In C. B. Stendler (Ed.), *Readings in child behavior and development*. (2nd ed.) New York: Harcourt, Brace & World, 1964. Pp. 448–66. **508**

MASON, W. A. Motivational aspects of social responsiveness in young chimpanzees. In H. W. Stevenson, E. H. Hess, & H. L. Rheingold (Eds.), *Early behavior*. New York: Wiley, 1967. Pp. 103–26. **433**

MC CALL, L. T., *see* Vance & McCall (1934).

MC DAVID, J. W. Imitative behavior in preschool children. *Psychological Monographs*, 1959, 73, No. 486. **488**

MENLOVE, F. L. Aggressive symptoms in emotionally disturbed adopted children. *Child Development*, 1965, 36, 519–32. **502**

MILTON, G. A. Five studies of the relation between sex role identification and achievement in problem solving. Technical Report No. 3, 1958. Yale University, Department of Psychology, Department of Industrial Administration. **488**

MOSS, H. A. Sex, age, and state as determinants of mother-infant interaction. *Merrill-Palmer Quarterly*, 1967, 13, 19–36. **440, 567, 568**

MOSS, H. A., *see also* Kagan & Moss (1959) (1962).

MOSS, H. A., & KAGAN, J. Maternal influences on early I.Q. scores. *Psychological Reports*, 1958, 4, 655–61. **514**

MOWRER, O. H. Identification: A link between learning theory and psychotherapy. In O. H. Mowrer, *Learning theory and personality dynamics*. New York: Ronald Press, 1950. Pp. 573–616. **464**

MUSSEN, P. H. Some antecedents and consequents of masculine sex-typing in adolescent boys. *Psychological Monographs*, 1961, 75(2, Whole No. 506). **487**

MUSSEN, P. H. Long-term consequents of masculinity of interests in adolescence. *Journal of Consulting Psychology,* 1962, 26, 435–40. **487**

MUSSEN, P. H., *see also* Payne & Mussen (1956).

MUSSEN, P. H., & DISTLER, L. Masculinity, identification, and father-son relationships. *Journal of Abnormal and Social Psychology,* 1959, 59, 350–56. **465**

MUSTE, M. H., & SHARPE, D. F. Some influential factors in the determination of aggressive behavior in preschool children. *Child Development,* 1947, 18, 11–28. **477**

NAEGELE, K. D., *see* Aberle & Naegele (1952).

NASH, H. Assignment of gender to body regions. *Journal of Genetic Psychology,* 1958, 92, 113–15. **477**

NELSON, V. L., *see* Sontag et al. (1958).

NISBETT, R. E. Birth order and participation in dangerous sports. *Journal of Personality and Social Psychology,* 1968, 8, 351–53. **552, 553**

NISBETT, R. E., & SCHACHTER, S. S. Cognitive manipulation of pain. *Journal of Experimental and Social Psychology,* 1966, 2, 227–36. **552**

PARKE, R. D., *see* Walters & Parke (1964).

PARSONS, T. Age and sex in the social structure of the United States. In C. Kluckhohn & H. A. Murray (Eds.), *Personality in nature, society, and culture.* New York: Knopf, 1948. Pp. 269–81. **480, 491**

PARSONS, T. Family structures and the socialization of the child. In T. Parsons & R. F. Bales (Eds.), *Family, socialization, and the interaction process.* New York: Free Press, 1955. **480**

PATTERSON, G. R., LITTMAN, R. G., & BRICKER, W. Assertive behavior in children: A step toward a theory of aggression. *Monographs of the Society for Research in Child Development,* 1967, 32(Whole No. 113). **501, 502**

PAYNE, D. E., & MUSSEN, P. H. Parent-child relations and father identification among adolescent boys. *Journal of Abnormal and Social Psychology,* 1956, 52, 358–62. **465**

PEARCE, D., *see* Walters et al. (1957).

PEARSON, L., *see* Kagan et al. (1966).

PHILLIPS, W., *see* Kagan & Phillips (1964).

PHOENIX, C. H., *see* Young et al. (1964).

PIAGET, J. *Logic and psychology.* New York: Basic Books, 1957. **571**

POINTZ, L., *see* Shirley & Pointz (1941).

POLANSKY, N., LIPPITT, R., & REDL, F. An investigation of behavioral contagion in groups. *Human Relations,* 1950, 3, 319–48. **546**

PORTER, M., *see* Sackett et al. (1965).

PRESTON, A., *see* Crandall et al. (1962).

PROVENCE, S., & LIPTON, R. *Infants in institutions.* New York: International Universities Press, 1962. **433, 434**

RABBAN, M. Sex role identification in young children in two diverse social groups. *Genetic Psychology Monographs,* 1950, 42, 81–158. **479**

RABSON, A., *see* Crandall & Rabson (1960).

RADKE, M. J. The relation of parental authority to children's behavior and attitudes. *Institute for Child Welfare Monographs,* 1946, No. 22. **546**

RAY, E., *see* Walters & Ray (1960).

REDL, F., *see* Polansky et al. (1950).

RHEINGOLD, H. L. The modification of social responsiveness in institutional babies. *Monographs of the Society for Research in Child Development,* 1956, 21(2, Whole No. 63). **428, 429**

RHEINGOLD, H. L., personal communication. **421**

RIFKIN, A. H., *see* Bieber et al. (1962).

ROE, A. A psychological study of eminent psychologists and anthropologists, and a comparison with biological and physical scientists. *Psychological Monographs,* 1953, 67(2). **552**

ROE, K., *see* Feshbach & Roe (1968).

ROSENBERG, B. G., & SUTTON-SMITH, B. A revised conception of masculine-feminine differences in play activities. *Journal of Genetic Psychology,* 1960, 96, 165–70. **479**

ROSENKRANS, M. A. Imitation in children as a function of perceived similarity to a social model and vicarious reinforcement. *Journal of Personality and Social Psychology,* 1967, 7, 307–15. **467**

ROSENTHAL, M. K. The generalization of dependency behaviors from mother to stranger. Unpublished doctoral dissertation, Stanford University, 1965. **506**

ROSENTHAL, R. *Experimenter effects in behavioral research.* New York: Appleton-Century-Crofts, 1966. **515**

ROSS, D., *see* Bandura *et al.* (1961) (1963a, b).

ROSS, S. A., *see* Bandura *et al.* (1961) (1963a, b).

ROTHBART, M. K., & MACCOBY, E. E. Parents' differential reactions to sons and daughters. *Journal of Personality and Social Psychology*, 1966, 4, 237–43. **568**

RUSSELL, W. A., *see* Jenkins & Russell (1958).

SACKETT, G., PORTER, M., & HOLMES, H. Choice behavior in rhesus monkeys. *Science*, 1965, 147, 304–06. **428**

SCHACHTER, S. S. *The psychology of affiliation*. Stanford, Calif.: Stanford University Press, 1959. **507**

SCHACHTER, S. S., *see also* Nisbett & Schachter (1966).

SCHACHTER, S. S., & SINGER, J. E. Cognitive, social, and physiological determinants of emotional state. *Psychological Review*, 1962, 69, 379–99. **455**

SCHACHTER, S. S., & WHEELER, L. Epinephrine, chlorpromazine, and amusement. *Journal of Abnormal and Social Psychology*, 1962, 65, 121–28. **455**

SCHAEFER, E. S. A circumplex model for maternal behavior. *Journal of Abnormal and Social Psychology*, 1959, 59, 226–35. **560, 563**

SCHAEFER, E. S., & BAYLEY, N. Maternal behavior, child behavior, and their interactions from infancy through adolescence. *Monographs of the Society for Research in Child Development*, 1963, 28, No. 87. **564**

SEARS, P. S. Doll play aggressions in normal young children: Influence of sex, age, sibling status, father's absence. *Psychological Monographs*, 1951, 65, No. 6. **477**

SEARS, R. R., MACCOBY, E. E., & LEVIN, H. *Patterns of child rearing*. New York: Harper & Row, 1957. **449, 451, 469, 470, 478, 480, 507, 510, 565**

SHARPE, D. F., *see* Muste & Sharpe (1947).

SHIRLEY, M., & POINTZ, L. The influence of separation from the mother on children's emotional responses. *Journal of Psychology*, 1941, 12, 251–82. **508**

SINGER, J. E., *see* Schachter & Singer (1962).

SMITH, M. E. The influence of age, sex, and situation on the frequency and form and function of questions asked by preschool children. *Child Development*, 1933, 3, 201–13. **488**

SMITH, W. D., *see* Fauls & Smith (1956).

SONTAG, L. W., BAKER, C. T., & NELSON, V. L. Mental growth and personality development: A longitudinal study. *Monographs of the Society for Research in Child Development*, 1958, 23, No. 68. **528**

SPITZ, R. A., & WOLF, K. M. Anaclitic depression: An inquiry into the genesis of psychiatric conditions in early childhood. In A. Freud *et al.* (Eds.), *The psychoanalytic study of the child*, Vol. 1. New York: International Universities Press, 1946. Pp. 313–42. **507**

STEIN, R. The effects of ordinal position and identification on philosophy of life, occupational choice, and reflectiveness-impulsivity. Unpublished senior honors thesis, Harvard University, 1966. **553**

SUTTON-SMITH, B., *see* Rosenberg & Sutton-Smith (1960).

TYLER, L. E. *The psychology of human differences*. New York: Appleton-Century-Crofts, 1947. **478, 489**

VANCE, T. F., & MC CALL, L. T. Children's preference among play materials as determined by the method of paired comparisons of pictures. *Child Development*, 1934, 5, 267–77. **479**

WALTERS, J., PEARCE, D., & DAHMS, L. Affectional and aggressive behavior of preschool children. *Child Development*, 1957, 28, 15–26. **478**

WALTERS, R. H., & PARKE, R. D. Social motivation, dependency, and susceptibility to social influence. In L. Berkowitz (Ed.), *Advances in experimental social psychology*, Vol. 1. New York: Academic Press, 1964. Pp. 232–76. **500**

WALTERS, R. H., & RAY, E. Anxiety, social isolation, and reinforcer effectiveness. *Journal of Personality*, 1960, 28, 358–67. **506**

WALTERS, R. H., *see also* Bandura & Walters (1963).

WARREN, J. R. Birth order and social behavior. *Psychological Bulletin*, 1966, 65, 38–49. **552**

WATSON, S., *see* Kagan *et al.* (1961).

WEINSTEIN, J., *see* Caudill & Weinstein (1966).

WELCH, L., *see* Kagan *et al.* (1966).

WHEELER, L., *see* Schachter & Wheeler (1962).

WHITE, R. W. Motivation reconsidered: The

concept of competence. *Psychological Review*, 1959, 66, 297–333. **512**

WHITEHOUSE, E. Norms for certain aspects of the Thematic Apperception Test on a group of nine- and ten-year-old children. *Journal of Personality*, 1949, *1*, 12–15. **478**

WILBUR, C. B., *see* Bieber *et al.* (1962).

WILSON, W. C., *see* Maccoby & Wilson (1957).

WINKER, J. B. Age trends and sex differences in the wishes, identifications, activities, and fears of children. *Child Development*, 1949, 20, 191–200. **478**

WOLF, K. M., *see* Spitz & Wolf (1946).

YONDO, R., & KAGAN, J. The effect of teacher tempo on the child. *Child Development*, 1968, 39, 27–34. **535**

YOUNG, W. C., GOY, R. W., & PHOENIX, C. H. Hormones and sexual behavior. *Science*, 1964, *143*, 212–18. **410**

ZIGLER, E. F. Social deprivation and rigidity in the performance of feeble-minded children. *Journal of Abnormal and Social Psychology*, 1961, 62, 413–21. **507**

ZIMMERMAN, R. R., *see* Harlow & Zimmerman (1959).

ZUCKER, R. A., MANOSEVITZ, M., & LANYON, R. I. Birth order, anxiety, and affiliation during a crisis. *Journal of Personality and Social Psychology*, 1968, 8, 354–59. **552**

Part Four

ADCOCK, C. J. A factorial examination of Sheldon's types. *Journal of Personality*, 1948, *16*, 312–19. **650**

ADORNO, T. W., FRENKEL-BRUNSWIK, E., LEVINSON, D. J., & SANFORD, R. N. *The authoritarian personality.* New York: Harper & Row, 1950. **597**

ALLPORT, G. W. *Personality: A psychological interpretation.* New York: Holt, Rinehart and Winston, 1937. **585, 656**

ALLPORT, G. W. *The use of personal documents in psychological science.* New York: Social Science Research Council, 1942 (Bulletin 49). **778**

ALLPORT, G. W. *Pattern and growth in personality.* New York: Holt, Rinehart and Winston, 1961. **656**

ALLPORT, G. W. (Ed.) *Letters from Jenny.* New York: Harcourt, Brace & World, 1965. **623**

ALLPORT, G. W., & ALLPORT, F. H. *A-S reaction study.* Boston: Houghton Mifflin, 1928. **690**

ALLPORT, G. W., & ODBERT, H. S. Traitnames: A psycho-lexical study. *Psychological Monographs*, 1936, 47(1, Whole No. 211). **658**

ALLPORT, G. W., & VERNON, P. E. *The study of values.* Boston: Houghton Mifflin, 1931. **690, 692**

ALLPORT, G. W., VERNON, P. E., & LINDZEY, G. *The study of values.* Boston: Houghton Mifflin, 1951. **747**

ALLPORT, F. H., *see* Allport & Allport (1928).

BAILEY, D. E., *see* Sarbin, Taft, & Bailey (1960).

BARRON, F. Some personality correlates of independence of judgment. *Journal of Personality*, 1952, 21, 287–97. **750**

BARRON, F. An ego-strength scale which predicts response to psychotherapy. *Journal of Consulting Psychology*, 1953, 17, 327–33. **743**

BELLAK, L., & HOLT, R. R. Somatotypes in relation to dementia praecox. *American Journal of Psychiatry*, 1948, 104, 713–24. **651**

BIRCH, H. G., *see* Clark & Birch (1945).

BLOCK, J. *The Q-sort method in personality assessment and psychiatric research.* Springfield, Ill.: Charles C Thomas, 1961. **753, 755, 756**

BLOCK, J. *The challenge of response sets.* New York: Appleton-Century-Crofts, 1965. **645, 744**

BRUNER, J. S., & TAGIURI, R. The perception of people. In G. Lindzey (Ed.), *Handbook of social psychology*, Vol. 2. Reading, Mass.: Addison-Wesley, 1954. Pp. 634–54. **661**

BURGESS, E. W. Factors determining success or failure on parole. In A. A. Bruce (Ed.), *The workings of the indeterminate sentence law and the parole system in Illinois.* Springfield, Ill.: Illinois State Board of Parole, 1928. Pp. 205–49. **781**

BUROS, O. K. (Ed.) *The sixth mental measurements yearbook*. Highland Park, N.J.: Gryphon Press, 1965. **737**

CAMPBELL, E. H. Effects of mothers' anxiety on infants' behavior. Unpublished doctoral dissertation, Yale University, 1957. **584**

CARROLL, J. B. Ratings on traits measured by a factored personality inventory. *Journal of Abnormal and Social Psychology*, 1952, 47, 626–32. **746**

CARTWRIGHT, D. P., & FRENCH, J. R. P., JR. The reliability of life-history studies. *Character and Personality*, 1939, 8, 110–19. **600**

CATTELL, R. B. *Description and measurement of personality*. Yonkers, N.Y.: World Book Co., 1946. **659**

CATTELL, R. B. *Personality and motivation structure and measurement*. New York: Harcourt, Brace & World, 1957. **648, 658, 659**

CATTELL, R. B. Validity and reliability: A proposed more basic set of concepts. *Journal of Educational Psychology*, 1964, 55, 1–22. **634**

CHEIN, I. The logic of prediction: Some observations on Dr. Sarbin's exposition. *Psychological Review*, 1945, 52, 175–79. **797**

CLARK, G., & BIRCH, H. G. Hormonal modifications of social behavior, 1: The effect of sex-hormone administration on the social status of a male-castrate chimpanzee. *Psychosomatic Medicine*, 1945, 7, 321–29. **648**

COMREY, A. L. A factor analysis of items on the MMPI Hypochondriasis Scale. *Educational and Psychological Measurement*, 1957, 17, 568–77. **744**

COMREY, A. L. A factor analysis of items on the MMPI Psychopathic Deviate Scale. *Educational and Psychological Measurement*, 1958, 18, 91–98. **744**

COUCH, A. S., *see* Kassebaum, Couch, & Slater (1959).

COUCH, A. S., & KENISTON, K. Yeasayers and naysayers: Agreeing response set as a personality variable. *Journal of Abnormal and Social Psychology*, 1960, 60, 151–74. **645**

CRONBACH, L. J. Assessment of individual differences. In P. R. Farnsworth & Q. McNemar (Eds.), *Annual review of psychology*, Vol. 7. Palo Alto, Calif.: Annual Reviews, 1956. Pp. 173–96. **784**

CRONBACH, L. J. *Essentials of psychological testing*. (2nd ed.) New York: Harper & Row, 1960. **634**

DAHLSTROM, W. G., *see* Meehl & Dahlstrom (1960).

DAHLSTROM, W. G., & WELSH, G. S. *An MMPI handbook: A guide to use in clinical practice and research*. Minneapolis: University of Minnesota Press, 1960. **743**

DAVITZ, J. R., *et al*. *The communication of emotional meaning*. New York: McGraw-Hill, 1964. **601, 602**

DELGADO, J. M. R. Aggressive behavior evoked by radio stimulation in monkey colonies. *American Zoologist*, 1966, 6, 669–81. **648**

DEMPSEY, P. A unidimensional depression scale for the MMPI. *Journal of Consulting Psychology*, 1964, 28, 364–70. **744**

DIMITROVSKY, L. The ability to identify the emotional meaning of vocal expressions at successive age levels. In J. R. Davitz et al., *The communication of emotional meaning*. New York: McGraw-Hill, 1964. Pp. 69–86. **602**

DU BOIS, P. H. (Ed.) *The classification program*. AAF Aviation Psychology Program Research Reports, No. 2. Washington, D.C.: U.S. Government Printing Office, 1947. **783**

EBEL, R. L. Must all tests be valid? *American Psychologist*, 1961, 16, 640–47. **776, 777**

EDWARDS, A. L., & HEATHERS, L. B. The first factor of the MMPI: Social desirability or ego-strength? *Journal of Consulting Psychology*, 1962, 26, 99–100. **645**

ERIKSON, E. H. Identity and the life cycle. *Psychological Issues*, 1959, 1, Monograph No. 1. **727, 734, 768**

ERIKSON, E. H. *Childhood and society*. (2nd ed.) New York: Norton, 1963. **734, 768, 770**

ESTES, S. G. Judging personality from expressive behavior. *Journal of Abnormal and Social Psychology*, 1938, 33, 217–36. **585**

EYSENCK, H. J. The effects of psychotherapy: An evaluation. *Journal of Consulting Psychology*, 1952, 16, 319–24. **796**

EYSENCK, H. J. *The structure of human personality*. (2nd ed.) New York: Barnes & Noble, 1960. **648**

EYSENCK, H. J. *Maudsley Personality Inventory*. San Diego, Calif.: Educational and Industrial Testing Service, 1962. **746**

EYSENCK, H. J., & EYSENCK, S. B. G. *Eysenck Personality Inventory*. San Diego, Calif.: Educational and Industrial Testing Service, 1963. **746**

EYSENCK, S. B. G., *see* Eysenck & Eysenck (1963).

FELEKY, A. M. The expression of the emotions. *Psychological Review*, 1914, 21, 33–44. **601**

FISS, H. Physiognomic effects of subliminal stimulation. *Perceptual and Motor Skills*, 1966, 22, 365–66. **596**

FLANAGAN, J. C. *Factor analysis in the study of personality*. Stanford, Calif.: Stanford University Press, 1935. **638**

FRENCH, J. R. P., JR., *see* Cartwright & French (1939).

FRENKEL-BRUNSWIK, E. Intolerance of ambiguity as an emotional and perceptual personality variable. *Journal of Personality*, 1949, 18, 108–43. **597**

FRENKEL-BRUNSWIK, E., *see also* Adorno, Frenkel-Brunswik, Levinson, & Sanford (1950).

FREUD, A. Adolescence. *Psychoanalytic Study of the Child*, 1958, 13, 255–78. **735**

FREUD, S. (1887–1902) *The origins of psycho-analysis: Letters to Wilhelm Fliess, drafts and notes: 1887–1902*. London: Imago, 1954. **622**

FREUD, S. (1916) Some character-types met with in psycho-analytic work. *Standard edition*, Vol. 14. London: Hogarth Press, 1957. Pp. 309–33. **709**

FRIJDA, N. H. The understanding of facial expression of emotion. *Acta Psychologica*, 1953, 9, 294–362. **603**

GARDNER, R. W., HOLZMAN, P. S., KLEIN, G. S., LINTON, H. B., & SPENCE, D. P. Cognitive control: A study of individual consistencies in cognitive behavior. *Psychological Issues*, 1959, 1(4). **654, 757, 758, 760**

GATES, G. S. An experimental study of the growth of social perception. *Journal of Educational Psychology*, 1923, 14, 449–61. **602**

GILL, M. M., *see* Rapaport, Gill, & Schafer (1945) (1968).

GLUECK, E., *see* Glueck & Glueck (1950).

GLUECK, S., & GLUECK, E. *Unraveling juvenile delinquency*. Cambridge, Mass.: Harvard University Press, 1950. **650, 651**

GLUECK, B. C., MEEHL, P. E., SCHOFIELD, W., & CLYDE, D. J. The quantitative assessment of personality. *Comprehensive Psychiatry*, 1964, 5, 15–23. **659**

GOLDBERG, L. R. Simple models or simple processes? Some research on clinical judgments. *American Psychologist*, 1968, 23, 483–96. **742**

GOLDBERG, L. R., *see also* Hase & Goldberg (1967).

GOTTSCHALDT, K. Über den Einfluss der Erfahrung auf die Wahrnehmung von Figuren [On the influence of experience on the perception of figures], 2. *Psychologische Forschung*, 1929, 12, 1–87. **759**

GOUGH, H. G. *Manual for the California Psychological Inventory*. Palo Alto, Calif.: Consulting Psychologists' Press, 1957. **745**

GOUGH, H. G. The Adjective Check List as a personality assessment research technique. *Psychological Reports*, 1960, 6, 107–22. **750, 751**

GOUGH, H. G. Clinical versus statistical prediction in psychology. In L. Postman (Ed.), *Psychology in the making: Histories of selected research problems*. New York: Knopf, 1962. Pp. 526–84. **781, 782, 784, 785**

GOUGH, H. G. *Adjective Check List manual*. Palo Alto, Calif.: Consulting Psychologists Press, 1965. **750**

GROSS, M. *The brain watchers*. New York: Random House, 1962. **646**

GRUEN, A. A critique and re-evaluation of Witkin's perception and perception-personality work. *Journal of General Psychology*, 1957, 56, 73–93. **656**

GUILFORD, J. P. *The nature of human intelligence*. New York: McGraw-Hill, 1967. **635, 637, 760**

HARLOW, H. F. The heterosexual affectional system in monkeys. *American Psychologist*, 1962, 17, 1–9. **608, 609**

HASE, H. D., & GOLDBERG, L. R. Comparative validity of different strategies of constructing personality inventory scales. *Psychological Bulletin*, 1967, 67, 231–48. **745**

HATHAWAY, S. R., *see* Meehl & Hathaway (1946).

HATHAWAY, S. R., & MC KINLEY, J. C. *The Minnesota Multiphasic Personality Inventory*. New York: Psychological Corporation, 1943. **642, 739, 740**

HEATHERS, L. B., *see* Edwards & Heathers (1962).

HOFFMAN, P. J. The paramorphic representation of clinical judgment. *Psychological Bulletin*, 1960, 57, 116–31. **785**

HOLT, R. R. The accuracy of self-evaluations: Its measurement and some of its personological correlates. *Journal of Consulting Psychology*, 1951, 15, 95–101. **756**

HOLT, R. R. Clinical *and* statistical prediction: A reformulation and some new data. *Journal of Abnormal and Social Psychology*, 1958, 56, 1–12. **786**

HOLT, R. R. Clinical judgment as a disciplined inquiry. *Journal of Nervous and Mental Disease*, 1961, 133, 369–82. **794**

HOLT, R. R. Forcible indoctrination and personality change. In P. Worchel & D. Byrne (Eds.), *Personality change*. New York: Wiley, 1964. Pp. 289–318. **646**

HOLT, R. R. Individuality and generalization in the psychology of personality. In R. S. Lazarus & E. M. Opton, Jr. (Eds.), *Personality: Selected readings*. Baltimore: Penguin Books, 1967. Pp. 38–65. **778, 794**

HOLT, R. R., *see also* Bellak & Holt (1948).

HOLT, R. R., & LUBORSKY, L. *Personality patterns of psychiatrists*. New York: Basic Books, 1958. 2 vols. **593, 594, 613, 789**

HOLZBERG, J. D., *see* Wittenborn & Holzberg (1951).

HOLZMAN, P. S., *see* Gardner et al. (1959).

HOLZMAN, P. S., & KLEIN, G. S. Cognitive system-principles of leveling and sharpening: Individual differences in assimilation effects in visual time-errors. *Journal of Psychology*, 1954, 37, 105–22. **654, 757**

JACKSON, D. N., *see* Messick & Jackson (1961).

JACKSON, D. N., & MESSICK, S. Content and style in personality assessment. *Psychological Bulletin*, 1958, 55, 243–52. **744**

JENKINS, T. N. *How well do you know yourself?* New York: Executive Analysis Corp., 1959. **638**

JENKINS, T. N. Measurement of the primary factors of the total personality. *Journal of Psychology*, 1962, 54, 417–42. **638**

JONES, E. *The life and work of Sigmund Freud*, Vol. 1. New York: Basic Books, 1953. **622**

JUNG, C. J. (1921) *Psychological types.* New York: Harcourt, Brace & World, 1923. **638**

KALINA, W. Badania nad rozpoznawaniem wrazow mimicznych uczuc u ludzi [A study of the recognition of mimic expressions in people]. *Przeglad Psychologiczny*, 1960, 4, 177–85. **602**

KASSEBAUM, G. G., COUCH, A. S., & SLATER, P. E. The factorial dimensions of the MMPI. *Journal of Consulting Psychology*, 1959, 23, 226–36. **645**

KELLEY, H. H. The warm-cold variable in first impressions of persons. *Journal of Personality*, 1950, 18, 431–39. **592**

KENISTON, K., *see* Couch & Keniston (1960).

KLEIN, G. S. The personal world through perception. In R. R. Blake & G. V. Ramsey (Eds.), *Perception: An approach to personality*. New York: Ronald Press, 1951. Pp. 328–55. **653**

KLEIN, G. S., *see also* Gardner et al. (1959); Holzman & Klein (1954).

KLEINER, R. J. The effects of threat reduction upon interpersonal attractiveness. *Journal of Personality*, 1960, 28, 145–55. **595**

KRETSCHMER, E. (1921) *Physique and character*. New York: Harcourt, Brace & World, 1925. **649**

KUDER, G. F. *Kuder Preference Record—Vocational*. Chicago: Science Research Associates, 1948. **640**

KVALE, S., *see* Rommetveit & Kvale (1965).

LACEY, J. I. Psychophysiological approaches to the evaluation of psychotherapeutic process and outcome. In E. A. Rubinstein & M. B. Parloff (Eds.), *Research in psychotherapy*. Washington, D.C.: American Psychological Association, 1959. **653**

LEVINSON, D. J., *see* Adorno, Frenkel-Brunswik, Levinson, & Sanford (1950).

LEVITT, E. A. The relationship between abilities to express emotional meanings vocally and facially. In J. R. Davitz et al., *The communication of emotional meaning*. New York: McGraw-Hill, 1964. Pp. 87–100. **602, 603**

LEVY, I., ORR, T. B., & ROSENZWEIG, S. Judgments of emotion from facial expressions by college students, mental retardates, and mental hospital patients. *Journal of Personality*, 1960, 28, 342–49. **603**

LINDZEY, G. Thematic Apperception Test: Interpretative assumptions and related empirical evidence. *Psychological Bulletin*, 1952, 49, 1–25. **721**

LINDZEY, G. Seer versus sign. *Journal of Experimental Research in Personality*, 1965, 1, 17–26. **789**

LINDZEY, G., *see also* Allport, Vernon, & Lindzey (1951).

LINTON, H. B. Dependence on external influence: Correlates in perception, attitudes, and judgment. *Journal of Abnormal and Social Psychology*, 1955, 51, 502–07. **655**

LINTON, H. B., *see also* Gardner et al. (1959).

LORENZ, K. *King Solomon's ring*. New York: T. Y. Crowell, 1952. **607**

LORR, M., O'CONNOR, J. P., & STAFFORD, J. W. Confirmation of nine psychotic symptom patterns. *Journal of Clinical Psychology*, 1957, 13, 252–57. **617**

LOVELL, V. R. The human use of personality tests: A dissenting view. *American Psychologist*, 1967, 22, 383–93. **646**

LUBORSKY, L., *see* Holt & Luborsky (1958).

MACHOVER, K. *Personality projection in the drawing of the human figure*. Springfield, Ill.: Charles C Thomas, 1949. **610**

MASLING, J. Role-related behavior of the subject and psychologist and its effects upon psychological data. In D. Levine (Ed.), *Nebraska symposium on motivation*, Vol. 14. Lincoln: University of Nebraska Press, 1966. Pp. 67–103. **594**

MAY, H. S. A study of emotional expression among Chinese and Americans. Unpublished Master's essay, Columbia University, 1938. **602**

MC KINLEY, J. C., *see* Hathaway & McKinley (1948).

MEAD, G. H. *Mind, self, and society*. Chicago: University of Chicago Press, 1934. **610**

MEEHL, P. E. *Clinical versus statistical prediction*. Minneapolis: University of Minnesota Press, 1954. **673, 779, 784, 785, 786, 794, 797, 801**

MEEHL, P. E. Wanted—A good cookbook. *American Psychologist*, 1956, 11, 263–72. **742, 799**

MEEHL, P. E. When shall we use our heads instead of the formula? *Journal of Counseling Psychology*, 1957, 4, 268–73. **797**

MEEHL, P. E. Seer over sign: The first good example. *Journal of Experimental Research in Personality*, 1965, 1, 27–32. **784, 797**

MEEHL, P. E., *see also* Glueck, Meehl, Schofield, & Clyde (1964).

MEEHL, P. E., & DAHLSTROM, W. G. Objective configural rules for discriminating psychotic from neurotic MMPI profiles. *Journal of Consulting Psychology*, 1960, 24, 375–87. **742**

MEEHL, P. E., & HATHAWAY, S. R. The *K* factor as a suppressor variable in the MMPI. *Journal of Applied Psychology*, 1946, 30, 525–64. **643**

MEEHL, P. E., & ROSEN, A. Antecedent probability and the efficiency of psychometric signs, patterns, or cutting scores. *Psychological Bulletin*, 1955, 52, 194–216. **782, 783**

MELTZER, L., *see* Thompson & Meltzer (1964).

MERRILL, M. A., *see* Terman & Merrill (1937).

MESSICK, S. *Hidden Figures Test-cf-1*. Developed under NIMH Contract M-4186. Princeton, N.J.: Educational Testing Service, 1962. **760**

MESSICK, S., *see also* Jackson & Messick (1958).

MESSICK, S., & JACKSON, D. N. Acquiescence and the factorial interpretation of the MMPI. *Psychological Bulletin*, 1961, 58, 299–304. **645**

MILLER, R. E., MURPHY, J. V., & MIRSKY, I. A. Relevance of facial expression and posture as cues in communication of affect between monkeys. *AMA Archives of General Psychiatry*, 1959, 1, 480–88. **604**

MIRSKY, I. A., *see* Miller, Murphy, & Mirsky (1959).

MORENO, J. L. *Who shall survive?* (Rev. ed.) Beacon, N.Y.: Beacon House, 1953. **658**

MORGAN, C. D., & MURRAY, H. A. A method for investigating fantasies: The Thematic Apperception Test. *Archives of Neurology and Psychiatry*, 1935, 34, 289–306. **696**

MUNN, N. L. The effect of knowledge of the situation upon judgment of emotion from facial expressions. *Journal of Abnormal and Social Psychology*, 1940, 35, 324–38. **603**

MURPHY, G. *Personality: A biosocial approach to origins and structure*. New York: Harper & Row, 1947. **605**

MURPHY, J. V., *see* Miller, Murphy, & Mirsky (1959).

MURRAY, H. A. The effect of fear upon estimates of the maliciousness of other personalities. *Journal of Social Psychology*, 1933, *4*, 310–29. **595**

MURRAY, H. A. *Thematic Apperception Test.* Cambridge, Mass.: Harvard University Press, 1943. **696**

MURRAY, H. A., *see also* Morgan & Murray (1935).

MURRAY, H. A., *et al. Explorations in personality.* New York: Oxford University Press, 1938. **578, 644, 661, 673, 745**

MUSSEN, P. H., *see* Scodel & Mussen (1953).

NORMAN, W. T. Toward an adequate taxonomy of personality attributes: Replicated factor structure in peer nomination personality ratings. *Journal of Abnormal and Social Psychology*, 1963a, *66*, 574–83. **659, 660**

NORMAN, W. T. Personality measurement, faking, and detection: An assessment method for use iń personnel selection. *Journal of Applied Psychology*, 1963b, *47*, 225–41. **643**

O'CONNOR, J. P., *see* Lorr, O'Connor, & Stafford (1957).

ODBERT, H. S., *see* Allport & Odbert (1936).

ODEN, M. H., *see* Terman & Oden (1947).

ORR, T. B., *see* Levy, Orr, & Rosenzweig (1960).

OSS ASSESSMENT STAFF (Office of Strategic Services). *Assessment of men.* New York: Holt, Rinehart and Winston, 1948. **793**

PACKARD, V. *The naked society.* New York: McKay, 1964. **646**

PETERSON, D. R. Scope and generality of verbally defined personality factors. *Psychological Review*, 1965, *72*, 48–59. **746**

PIAGET, J. *The language and thought of the child.* New York: Harcourt, Brace & World, 1926. **610**

POLANYI, M. *Personal knowledge: Towards a post-critical philosophy.* New York: Harper & Row, 1964. **583**

POSTMAN, L. Review of H. A. Witkin *et al., Personality through perception* (1954). *Psychological Bulletin*, 1955, *52*, 79–83. **656**

RAPAPORT, D., GILL, M. M., & SCHAFER, R. *Diagnostic psychological testing,* Vol. 1. Chicago: Yearbook Publishers, 1945. **633**

RAPAPORT, D., GILL, M. M., & SCHAFER, R. *Diagnostic psychological testing.* (Rev. ed., edited by R. R. Holt.) New York: International Universities Press, 1968. **713, 749**

REDL, F. *When we deal with children.* New York: Free Press, 1966. **608**

ROMMETVEIT, R., & KVALE, S. Stages in concept formation. *Scandinavian Journal of Psychology*, 1965, *6*, 59–79. **583**

RORSCHACH, H. (1921) *Psychodiagnostics.* New York: Grune & Stratton, 1949. **711**

ROSEN, A., *see* Meehl & Rosen (1955).

ROSENZWEIG, S., *see* Levy, Orr, & Rosenzweig (1960).

SACKETT, G. P. Monkeys reared in isolation with pictures as visual input: Evidence for an innate releasing mechanism. *Science*, 1966, *154*, 1468–73. **604, 607**

SANFORD, N. (Ed.) *The American college.* New York: Wiley, 1962. **696**

SANFORD, R. N., *see* Adorno, Frenkel-Brunswik, Levinson, & Sanford (1950).

SARBIN, T. R. A contribution to the study of actuarial and individual methods of prediction. *American Journal of Sociology*, 1943, *48*, 593–602. **794**

SARBIN, T. R., TAFT, R., & BAILEY, D. E. *Clinical inference and cognitive theory.* New York: Holt, Rinehart and Winston, 1960. **794**

SAWYER, J. Measurement *and* prediction, clinical *and* statistical. *Psychological Bulletin*, 1966, *66*, 178–200. **779, 780, 784, 786, 788**

SCHAFER, R. Generative empathy in the treatment situation. *Psychoanalytic Quarterly*, 1959, *28*, 342–73. **606, 612**

SCHAFER, R., *see also* Rapaport, Gill, & Schafer (1945) (1968).

SCHOFIELD, W., *see* Glueck, Meehl, Schofield, & Clyde (1964).

SCHONBAR, R. A. Some manifest characteristics of recallers and nonrecallers of dreams. *Journal of Consulting Psychology*, 1959, *23*, 414–18. **622**

SCHWARTZ, M. S., *see* Stanton & Schwartz (1954).

SCODEL, A., & MUSSEN, P. H. Social perceptions of authoritarians and nonauthoritarians. *Journal of Abnormal and Social Psychology*, 1953, *48*, 181–84. **598**

SHELDON, W. H., *et al. The varieties of human physique.* New York: Harper & Row, 1940. **649, 693**

SHELDON, W. H., & STEVENS, S. S. *The varieties of temperament.* New York: Harper & Row, 1942. **650**

SHELDON, W. H., *et al. Varieties of delinquent youth.* New York: Harper & Row, 1949. **650**

SIEGEL, L. A biographical inventory for students. *Journal of Applied Psychology,* 1956, 40, 5–10, 122–26. **621**

SINGER, J. L. *Daydreaming.* New York: Random House, 1966. **622**

SPENCE, D. P., *see* Gardner et al. (1959).

SPRANGER, E. *Types of men: The psychology and ethics of personality.* New York: Johnson Reprint Corp., 1928. **690**

STAFFORD, J. W., *see* Lorr, O'Connor, & Stafford (1957).

STANTON, A. H., & SCHWARTZ, M. S. *The mental hospital: A study of institutional participation in psychiatric illness and treatment.* New York: Basic Books, 1954. **610**

STAR, S. A. The screening of psychoneurotics. In S. A. Stouffer, L. Guttman, E. A. Suchman, P. F. Lazarsfeld, S. A. Star, & J. A. Clausen, *Measurement and prediction.* Princeton, N.J.: Princeton University Press, 1950. Pp. 486–567. **639, 640**

STEVENS, S. S., *see* Sheldon & Stevens (1942).

STRONG, E. K., JR. *Vocational interests of men and women.* Stanford, Calif.: Stanford University Press, 1943. **641**

STRONG, E. K., JR., & TUCKER, A. C. The use of vocational interest scales in planning a medical career. *Psychological Monographs,* 1952, 66(9, Whole No. 341). **791**

SZASZ, T. S. *The myth of mental illness.* New York: Harper & Row, 1961. **586**

TAFT, R. The ability to judge people. *Psychological Bulletin,* 1955, 52, 1–23. **661**

TAFT, R., *see also* Sarbin, Taft, & Bailey (1960).

TAGIURI, R., *see* Bruner & Tagiuri (1954).

TERMAN, L. M., & MERRILL, M. A. *Measuring intelligence: A guide to the administration of the new revised Stanford-Binet tests of intelligence.* Boston: Houghton Mifflin, 1937. **692**

TERMAN, L. M., & ODEN, M. H. *Genetic studies of genius.* Vol. 4. *The gifted child grows up.* Stanford, Calif.: Stanford University Press, 1947. **693**

THOMPSON, D. F., & MELTZER, L. Communication of emotional intent by facial expression. *Journal of Abnormal and Social Psychology,* 1964, 68, 129–35. **602**

TUCKER, A. C., *see* Strong & Tucker (1952).

TYLER, F. T. A factorial analysis of fifteen MMPI scales. *Journal of Consulting Psychology,* 1951, 15, 541–46. **645**

VERNON, P. E. *Personality assessment: A critical survey.* New York: Wiley, 1964. **648, 776**

VERNON, P. E., *see also* Allport & Vernon (1931); Allport, Vernon, & Lindzey (1951).

WECHSLER, D. *Wechsler Adult Intelligence Scale.* New York: Psychological Corp., 1955. **748**

WELSH, G. S. Factor dimensions A and R. In G. S. Welsh & W. G. Dahlstrom (Eds.), *Basic readings on the MMPI in psychology and medicine.* Minneapolis: University of Minnesota Press, 1956. Pp. 264–81. **645, 744**

WELSH, G. S., *see also* Dahlstrom & Welsh (1960).

WHITE, R. W. *Lives in progress.* (2nd ed.) New York: Holt, Rinehart and Winston, 1966. **768**

WHYTE, W. H., JR. *The organization man.* New York: Simon & Schuster, 1956. **646**

WITKIN, H. A. Individual differences in ease of perception of embedded figures. *Journal of Personality,* 1950, 19, 1–15. **759**

WITKIN, H. A., *et al. Personality through perception.* New York: Harper & Row, 1954. **653, 655, 656**

WITKIN, H. A., *et al. Psychological differentiation: Studies of development.* New York: Wiley, 1962. **653**

WITTENBORN, J. R., & HOLZBERG, J. D. The generality of psychiatric syndromes. *Journal of Consulting Psychology,* 1951, 15, 372–80. **617**

WITTMAN, M. P. A scale for measuring prognosis in schizophrenic patients. *Elgin Papers,* 1941, 4, 20–33. **788**

YOUNG, K. (1940) *Personality and problems of adjustment.* (2nd ed.) New York: Appleton-Century-Crofts, 1952. **673**

Textual Material (continued)

Chapter 4   Opening quote: From Leonid Andreyev, "The Seven That Were Hanged," in *Best Russian Short Stories*, edited by Thomas Seltzer. Boni & Liveright, Inc., 1917; Random House, Inc., 1925. Courtesy of Random House, Inc.

5   Opening quote: From Thomas Mann, *Joseph in Egypt* in *Joseph and His Brothers*, translated by H. T. Lowe-Porter, Borzoi Books, Alfred A. Knopf, Inc., 1956, by permission of the publisher.

6   Opening quote: From Oscar Wilde, *De Profundis*, Philosophical Library, Inc., 1960, by permission of the publisher.

8   Opening quote: From William Faulkner, *The Town*. Copyright William Faulkner, 1957; Curtis Publishing Company, 1957. Reprinted by permission of Random House, Inc.

9   Opening quote: From pp. 49–51 of *Life on the Mississippi* by Mark Twain. Reprinted by permission of Harper & Row, Publishers, Inc.

10   Opening quote: From Dylan Thomas, "Do not go gentle into that good night" in *Collected Poems*. Copyright 1952 by Dylan Thomas. Reprinted by permission of New Directions Publishing Corporation, J. M. Dent & Sons Ltd., and the Trustees for the Copyrights of the late Dylan Thomas.

Part II opening quote: From Søren Kierkegaard, *Either/Or*, translated by D. F. and L. M. Swenson, Princeton University Press, 1944, by permission of the publisher.

11   Opening quote: From Charles Augustin Sainte-Beuve, *Sonnet to Ronsard*, translated by Jeffrey Mehlman.

Quotes from Breuer and Freud are reprinted from *Studies on Hysteria* (Standard Edition of *The Complete Psychological Works of Sigmund Freud*, Vol. 2, 1955, edited by James Strachey) by permission of the Hogarth Press Ltd., Sigmund Freud Copyrights Ltd., and the Estate of Mr. James Strachey. *Studies on Hysteria* is published in the United States by Basic Books, Inc., Publishers, New York, 1957, and the quotes are reprinted also by their permission.

12   Opening quote: Reprinted from *Narcissus and Goldmund* by Hermann Hesse, translated by Ursule Molinaro, copyright © by Farrar, Straus & Giroux 1968. Reprinted by permission of Farrar, Straus & Giroux.

Chapter 13 Opening quote: From K. F. Meyer, *Hutten's Last Days*, translated by James Strachey (Standard Edition of *The Complete Psychological Works of Sigmund Freud*, Vol. 10, 1955, edited by James Strachey), reprinted by permission of the Hogarth Press Ltd., Sigmund Freud Copyrights Ltd., and the Institute of Psycho-Analysis.

14 Quote from *Extracts from the Fliess Papers* (Standard Edition of *The Complete Psychological Works of Sigmund Freud*, Vol. 1, 1966, edited by James Strachey) reprinted by permission of the Hogarth Press Ltd., Sigmund Freud Copyrights Ltd., and the Estate of Mr. James Strachey. This material also appears in *The Origins of Psycho-Analysis: Letters to Wilhelm Fliess, Drafts and Notes, 1887–1902*, Basic Books, Inc., Publishers, New York, 1954, and is reprinted also by their permission.

Quote from Robert Waelder, "The Problem of the Genesis of Psychical Conflict in Earliest Infancy" in *International Journal of Psycho-Analysis*, 1937, 18, 406–73, by permission of *International Journal of Psycho-Analysis* and Robert Waelder.

15 Opening quote: From Denis Diderot, *Rameau's Nephew*, translated by Angela Richards (Standard Edition of *The Complete Psychological Works of Sigmund Freud*, Vol. 16, 1963, edited by James Strachey), reprinted by permission of the Hogarth Press Ltd., Sigmund Freud Copyrights Ltd., and the Institute of Psycho-Analysis.

Quotes from *Analysis of a Phobia in a Five-Year-Old Boy* (Standard Edition, Vol. 10, 1955, edited by James Strachey) reprinted by permission of the Hogarth Press Ltd., Sigmund Freud Copyrights Ltd., and the Estate of Mr. James Strachey. This material also appears in *The Collected Papers of Sigmund Freud* (5 vols., edited by Ernest Jones), Basic Books, Inc., Publishers, New York, 1959, and is reprinted also by their permission.

Quotes from Sigmund Freud, *The Interpretation of Dreams*, Basic Books, Inc., Publishers, New York, 1955, by permission of Basic Books, Inc. United Kingdom rights held by George Allen & Unwin Ltd.

16 Opening quote: Reprinted by permission of Charles Scribner's Sons and Constable & Co. Ltd. from *The Life of Reason* by George Santayana.

17 Opening quote: From D. H. Lawrence, "The Prussian Officer," in *The Complete Short Stories of D. H. Lawrence*, Vol. 1. All rights reserved. Reprinted by permission of The Viking Press, Inc., Laurence Pollinger Ltd., and the Estate of the late Mrs. Frieda Lawrence.

Quote from *Psycho-Analytic Notes on an Autobiographical Account of a Case of Paranoia* (Standard Edition of *The Complete Psychological Works of Sigmund Freud*, Vol. 12, 1958, edited by James Strachey) reprinted by permission of the Hogarth Press Ltd., Sigmund Freud Copyrights Ltd., and the Estate of Mr. James Strachey. This material also appears in *The Collected Papers of Sigmund Freud* (5 vols., edited by Ernest Jones), Basic Books, Inc., Publishers, New York, 1959, and is reprinted also by their permission.

left); Lida Moser, dpi (right); Wechsler Preschool and Primary Scale of Intelligence, Psychological Corporation (bottom). *574:* Leo Cholpin, Black Star (top); Harbrace (middle left); David Linton (middle right); George Zimbel, Monkmeyer (bottom).

Figure 2-1   Star, S. A. Psychoneurotic symptoms in the Army. In S. Stouffer et al., *The American soldier.* Vol. 2. *Combat and its aftermath.* Princeton, N.J.: Princeton University Press, 1949.

2-2   Reproduced by courtesy of Bill Mauldin.

2-3   Research Center for Mental Health, New York University. Photo by Simmons.

2-4   Archibald, H. C., & Tuddenham, R. D. Persistent stress reaction after combat. *Archives of General Psychiatry,* 1965, *12,* 475–81. Used by permission of the American Medical Association and the authors.

3-1, 3-3   Hilgard, E. R., & Atkinson, R. C. *Introduction to psychology.* (4th ed.) New York: Harcourt, Brace & World, Inc., 1967.

3-2   Campbell, D., Sanderson, R. E., & Laverty, S. G. Characteristics of a conditioned response in human subjects during extinction trials following a single traumatic conditioning trial. *Journal of Abnormal and Social Psychology,* 1964, *68,* 627–39. Copyright 1964 by the American Psychological Association, and used by permission.

5-1, 5-2   Fenz, W. D. Conflict and stress as related to physiological activation and sensory, perceptual, and cognitive functioning. *Psychological Monographs,* 1964, 78(8, Whole No. 585). Copyright 1964 by the American Psychological Association, and used by permission.

6-1   Epstein, S., & Fenz, W. D. Steepness of approach and avoidance gradients in humans as a function of experience: Theory and experiment. *Journal of Experimental Psychology,* 1965, *70,* 1–12. Copyright 1965 by the American Psychological Association, and used by permission.

6-2, 6-3   Janis, I. L. *Psychological stress.* Copyright 1958 by John Wiley & Sons, Inc., New York.

6-4   Egbert, L., Battit, G., Welch, C., & Bartlett, M. Reduction of postoperative pain by encouragement and instruction of patients. *New England Journal of Medicine,* 1964, *270,* 825–27. Used by permission of *New England Journal of Medicine.*

7-1, 7-2   Janis, I. L. Psychological effects of warnings. In G. W. Baker & D. W. Chapman (Eds.), *Man and society in disaster,* pp. 55–92, © 1962 by Basic Books, Inc., Publishers, New York.

7-3   Drawing by F. B. Modell. Copyright © 1953 The New Yorker Magazine, Inc.

8-2   Janis, I. L., & Feshbach, S. Effects of fear-arousing communications. *Journal of Abnormal and Social Psychology,* 1953, *48,* 78–92. Copyright 1953 by the American Psychological Association, and used by permission.

8-3   Janis, I. L., & Feshbach, S. Personality differences associated with responsiveness to fear-arousing communications. *Journal of Personality,* 1954, *23,* 154–66.

Figure 8-4   Zemach, M. The effects of guilt-arousing communications on acceptance of recommendations. Unpublished doctoral dissertation, Yale University, 1966.

8-5   Niles (Kafes), P. The relationship of susceptibility and anxiety to acceptance of fear-arousing communications. Unpublished doctoral dissertation, Yale University, 1964.

8-6   Janis, I. L. Effect of fear arousal on attitude change: Recent developments in theory and experimental research. In L. Berkowitz (Ed.), *Advances in experimental social psychology.* Copyright 1967 by Academic Press, New York.

8-8   Mann, L., & Janis, I. L. A follow-up study on the long-range effects of emotional role playing. *Journal of Personality and Social Psychology,* 1968, 85, 339–42. Copyright 1968 by the American Psychological Association, and used by permission.

9-1   Photo courtesy of Dr. Roger G. Barker.

9-3   Fishman, C. G. Need for approval and the expression of aggression under varying conditions of frustration. *Journal of Personality and Social Psychology,* 1965, 2, 809–16. Copyright 1965 by the American Psychological Association, and used by permission.

9-4   Milgram, S. Some conditions of obedience and disobedience to authority. *Human Relations,* 1965, 18, 57–76. Plenum Publishing Corporation.

10-1   *A Two-Year-Old Goes to Hospital,* by James Robertson. New York University Film Library.

10-2   Parkes, C. Bereavement and mental illness, Part 1: A clinical study of the grief of bereaved psychiatric patients. *British Journal of Medical Psychology,* 1965, 38, 5.

Marris, P. *Widows and their families.* London: Routledge & Kegan Paul, 1958.

10-3   Wallace, A. The Worcester tornado: An exploratory study of individual and community behavior in an extreme situation. Washington, D.C.: National Academy of Sciences–National Research Council, Committee on Disaster Studies, 1956, Publication 392. Worcester Telegram & Gazette photo.

10-4   United Press International.

11-1, 11-2   Edmund Engelman.

12-1, 12-2   Miller, N. E. Experimental studies of conflict. In J. McV. Hunt (Ed.), *Personality and the behavior disorders.* Copyright 1944 The Ronald Press Company, New York.

15-1   Courtesy of Pauline S. Sears.

15-2   Sears, P. S. Doll play aggression in normal young children. *Psychological Monographs,* 1951, 65, No. 323. Copyright 1951 by the American Psychological Association, and used by permission.

15-5   Photo courtesy of Dr. Georges Condominas.

15-6   Sigmund Freud Copyrights Ltd.

15-7   Sarnoff, I., & Corwin, S. M. Castration anxiety and the fear of death. *Journal of Personality,* 1959, 27, 374–85.

Figure 17-3   Sears, R. R. Experimental studies of projection, 1: Attribution of traits. *Journal of Social Psychology*, 1936, 7, 151–63.

19-1   Miller, N. E. Experimental studies of conflict. In J. McV. Hunt (Ed.), *Personality and the behavior disorders*. Copyright 1944 The Ronald Press Company, New York.

19-2   American Telephone and Telegraph Company.

21-2   Archives Photographiques, Paris.

21-3   Sigmund Freud Copyrights Ltd.

24-1   Lewis, M. Infant attention: Response decrement as a measure of cognitive processes, or what's new, Baby Jane? Paper presented at the meetings of the Society for Research in Child Development, symposium on The Role of Attention in Cognitive Development, New York, March 1967. Courtesy of Dr. Michael Lewis.

24-2, 24-3   Gewirtz, J. L. The course of infant smiling in four child-rearing environments in Israel. In B. M. Foss (Ed.), *Determinants of infant behavior*, Vol. 3. Copyright 1965 by John Wiley & Sons, Inc., New York. Figure 24-2 also appears in Gewirtz, J. L. Mahalach hachi-yuch aytzel teenokot be'arba sveevot geedul shonot. *Megamot*, 1966, *14*, 281–311. Photo by Dr. J. L. Gewirtz.

24-5, 24-6, 24-8   Photos courtesy of Dr. Harry F. Harlow.

24-7   Rheingold, H. L. The modification of social responsiveness in institutional babies. *Monographs of the Society for Research in Child Development*, 1956, 21(2, Whole No. 63). Copyright 1956 by the Society for Research in Child Development, Inc.

27-1   Kagan, J., & Moss, H. A. *Birth to maturity: A study in psychological development*. Copyright 1962 by John Wiley & Sons, Inc., New York.

29-1   Sontag, L. W., Baker, C. T., & Nelson, V. L. Mental growth and personality development: A longitudinal study. *Monographs of the Society for Research in Child Development*, 1958, 23, No. 68. Copyright 1958 by the Society for Research in Child Development, Inc.

29-2   By permission of Dr. Eugene S. Gollin.

29-3   Kagan, J., Pearson, L., & Welch, L. The modifiability of an impulsive tempo. *Journal of Educational Psychology*, 1966, 57, 359–65. Copyright 1966 by the American Psychological Association, and used by permission.

29-5   Stanford University, Publications Service.

30-1   Nisbett, R. E. Birth order and participation in dangerous sports. *Journal of Personality and Social Psychology*, 1968, 8, 351–53. Copyright 1968 by the American Psychological Association, and used by permission.

31-1   Schaefer, E. S., & Bayley, N. Maternal behavior, child behavior, and their interactions from infancy through adolescence. *Monographs of the Society for Research in Child Development*, 1963, 28, No. 87. Copyright 1963 by the Society for Research in Child Development, Inc.

33-1   Feleky, A. M. The expression of the emotions. *Psychological Review*, 1914, *21*, 33–44. Courtesy of the American Psychological Association.

Figure 33-2   Permission S.P.A.D.E.M. 1969 by French Reproduction Rights, Inc. Courtesy of Musée Rodin. Photo by Andrieu d'Andres.

33-4   Harlow, H. F. The heterosexual affectional system in monkeys. *American Psychologist*, 1962, 17, 1–19. Copyright 1962 by the American Psychological Association, and used by permission. Photo courtesy of Dr. Harry F. Harlow.

33-5   Machover, K. *Personality projection in the drawing of the human figure*, 1949. Courtesy of Charles C Thomas, Publisher, Springfield, Ill.

35-1   Sheldon, W. H., et al. *The varieties of human physique*. New York: Harper & Row, 1940.

35-2   Glueck, S., & Glueck, E. Unraveling juvenile delinquency. New York: Commonwealth Fund; Cambridge, Mass.: Harvard University Press, 1950.

35-3   Photo by David Linton.

35-4   Witkin, H. A., et al. *Personality through perception*, pp. 534, 545. New York: Harper & Row, 1954.

37-1   Allport, G. W., & Vernon, P. E. *The study of values*. Boston: Houghton Mifflin, 1931.

37-2a   Permission S.P.A.D.E.M. 1969 by French Reproduction Rights, Inc. Courtesy of The Cleveland Museum of Art.

39-1   Reproduced by permission. Copyright 1943, The Psychological Corporation, New York, N.Y. All rights reserved.

39-2   Allport, G. W., Vernon, P. E., & Lindzey, G. *The study of values*. Boston: Houghton Mifflin, 1951.

39-4   From Hidden Figures Test-cf-1. Copyright © 1962 by Educational Testing Service. All rights reserved. Developed under NIMH Contract M-4186. Reprinted by permission.

Table 20-1   Clark, K. B., & Clark, M. P. Racial identification and preference in Negro children. In E. E. Maccoby, T. M. Newcomb, & E. L. Hartley (Eds.), *Readings in social psychology*, 3rd ed. Copyright 1947, 1952, © 1958 by Holt, Rinehart and Winston, Inc. Used by permission of Holt, Rinehart and Winston, Inc.

27-1   Kagan, J. The child's sex role in classification of school objects. *Child Development*, 1964, 35, p. 1053, Table 1. Used by permission of the Society for Research in Child Development, Inc.

35-1   Star, S. A. The screening of psychoneurotics. In S. A. Stouffer et al., *Measurement and prediction*. Princeton, N.J.: Princeton University Press, 1950. Used by permission of the publisher.

35-2   Strong, E. K., Jr. *Vocational interests of men and women*. Palo Alto, Calif.: Stanford University Press, 1943. Used by permission of the publisher.

35-3   Bellak, L., & Holt, R. R. "Somatotypes in relation to dementia praecox," *American Journal of Psychiatry*, 1948, 104, 713–24, by permission of *American Journal of Psychiatry* and the authors.

35-4   Norman, W. T. Toward an adequate taxonomy of personality attributes: Replicated factor structure in peer nomination personality ratings. *Journal of Abnormal and Social Psychology*, 1963, 66, p.

577, Table 1. Copyright 1963 by the American Psychological Association, and reproduced by permission of the American Psychological Association and the author.

Table 39-3   Block, J. *The Q-sort method in personality assessment and psychiatric research.* Springfield, Ill.: Charles C Thomas, Publisher, 1961. Used by permission of the author.

41-1   Gough, H. G. Clinical versus statistical prediction in psychology. In L. Postman (Ed.), *Psychology in the making: Histories of selected research problems.* New York: Knopf, 1962. Used by permission of the publisher.

INDEX

Page numbers in *italics* refer to illustrations.

Avoidance learning:
  applying principles of, 59–61
  defined, 50

B

Bad news, assimilation of, 192–93
Bales, Robert F., and case study of Morris
    Brown, 667*n*
Base rate, in Burgess experience table, 782
Bashfulness, projection of, 321, *321*
Basic species identity, 607–08
Behavior:
  and motivation, 495–96
  multiple determinants of, 625–27
  structural determinants of, 578, 579
  "total," and personality assessment,
    624–25
Behavior therapy, 55–58, 338
Behavioral disturbances, examples of, 203
    (table)
Behaviorism, 585
Bender Gestalt Test, 627
Bereavement, 171, *180*, 184, 186, 197,
    293
  case studies of, 177, 178
  and research studies of widows, 181
  sexual promiscuity as reaction to, 181–83
  See also Depression; Grief; Mourning;
    Separation anxiety
Bernheim, Hippolyte, and hypnosis, 208–
    09
Bernreuter Personality Inventory, 638
Bettelheim's observation of identification
    with aggressor, 361
Binet, Alfred, and intelligence testing, 527,
    634, 635, 693, 780
Biochemistry, 652
Biographical inventory, 621–22
"Blacky Test," 280
Blanket reassurance, and reflective emotion,
    115, 120
Block, Jack, and personality assessment,
    645, 744, 755
Body image, changes in, 343–44, 345–46
Bowel training. *See* Toilet training
Bowlby, John, and separation reactions,
    172, 173, 174, 183
Brain, 578, 579
  reticular activating system in, 347
Breathing rate, as measure of emotional
    conditioning, 45–46, 47
Breuer's treatment of Anna O., 206–08
Brown, Claude, quoted, 357
Brown, Thomas, quoted, 590
Brown, Morris, case study of, 662, 664,
    667, 668, 669, 689, 738, 760, 761,
    763, 771–72, 777, 799
  adolescence of, 679–81
  adult years of, early, 683–87

Brown, Morris, case study of (*Cont.*)
  affects and impulses of, 732
  and California Q Set, 753–57, 754, 754
    (table), 756 (table)
  castration anxiety of, 705, 706, 716
  childhood of, 676–79
  clinical assessment of, 671–87, 673
    (table), 763–67
  cognitive style of, 732, 758
  criticism of assessment of, 670
  diagnostic formulation of, 734–35
  direct observation of, 669–70
  family background of, 726–29, 733–34,
    735
  formal assessment of, 689–721
  and free association, 718–20
  and Hidden Figures Test, 759
  homosexual activity of, 679, 680, 683,
    684, 730, 734, 767
  impulses and affects of, 732
  infancy of, 674–76
  informal assessment of, 662, 665–87
  I.Q. of, 693, 725, 749
  maturation of, 766, 768–70
  and MMPI, 739, 740, 741, 742, 743,
    744, 757
  motives of, 672, 685–87, 695, 732–33
  objective assessment of, comment on,
    695–96
  parental relationship with, 726, 727–29,
    733–35, 764–65, 770
  personality pattern of, 730–35
  projective assessment of, comment on,
    720–21
  and Q-sorting method, 753–57, 754, 754
    (table), 756 (table)
  results of 1966 clinical assessment of,
    763–67
  and Rorschach Test, 711–13, 715–17,
    735, 770
  sense of identity of, 708, 734, 769–70
  sexual behavior of, summary of, 729–30,
    767
  and TAT, 696, 697–702, 704–11, 715,
    717, 719, 727, 770
  values of, profile of, 691–92, 692, 733,
    747, 748
  and WAIS, 748, 749
Burgess experience table, 781–83

C

California F-Test, 661
California Psychological Inventory, 745
California Q Set, 753–57, 754, 754 (table),
    756 (table)
Cancer patient, 188
Caplan's theory of life crises, 198
Carlyle, Thomas, quoted, 663

Case studies:
altruistic surrender (Miss Eaton), 331–32
Anna O., *see* Anna O.
avoidance habits, acquisition of, 48–49
bereavement, 177, 178
body image during transition between sleep and wakefulness, 345–46
Brown, Morris, *see* Brown, Morris
castration anxiety, 277, 278, 310
chronic traumatic neurosis (Tom), 30–32, 52–53
denial, 354, 355
depression, severe, 178, 332
Don, 5–6, 7–19, 52
Dora, 293, 365
drowning man, "last thoughts" of (Don), 5–6, 7–19, 52
Duane, *see* Duane
eating conflict (Edie), 228, 229, 230, 231
Eaton, Miss, *see* Eaton, Miss
Ed, *see* Ed
Edie, *see* Edie
ego restriction, 365
female castration complex, 257–59
Freud's first, in psychoanalysis (Lucy R.), 209
generalized stimulus and response of humiliation in women, 299
grief, normal, 177–78
homosexual wishes, unconscious, and projection (Ray), 315, 318
identification with aggressor, 358, 359–60, 362–63, 364
identification with parent (Dora), 293, 365
incestuous fantasies (Ed), 310–11
interference with defenses, 337–38
isolation (Rat Man), 380
Little Hans, *see* Little Hans
love as defense against hate, 329–30
Lucy R., *see* Lucy R.
memories activated by imminent separations, 303–04
obsessional symptoms (Miss Eaton), 329–30
Oedipal complex, 263, 265, 266, 267, 268–69, 270, 275–76
over-reaction to minor loss (Miss Eaton), 332
paranoiac projections (Schreber), 320
passivity, social (S), 547–49
perceptual conflict (Duane), 223–24
personality development (Louise), 407–08
projection of unconscious homosexual wishes (Ray), 315, 318
psychoanalysis, discovery of (Anna O.), 206–08
Rat Man, *see* Rat Man

Case studies (*Cont.*)
Ray, *see* Ray
S, 547–49
Schreber, Daniel Paul, *see* Schreber, Daniel Paul
separations, memories activated by, 303–04
sex role identity, 486–87
sexual conflict (Ed), 226
social passivity (S), 547–49
standards of behavior, acquisition of (Martha), 469–70
stress tolerance in surgical patients, 98, 102
Tom, 30–32, 52–53
traumatic neurosis, chronic (Tom), 30–32, 52–53
Wolf Man, *see* Wolf Man
Women, preference of, for boy babies, 259–60
Castration anxiety, 226, 227, 239, 276–80, 278, 281, 283, 337, 352, 355, 371, 376, 384, 388, 389, 394, 396, 398
of Brown, Morris, 705, 706, 716
case studies of, 277, 278, 310
origin of, 276–79
Central nervous system, 578
Cerebrotonia, 694
Charcot, Jean-Martin, and hypnosis, 206
Chesterfield, Lord, quoted, 457, 736
Child (18 months to 3 years), 442–56 *passim*
language ability of, 443
motor abilities of, 442–43
socialization of, *see* Socialization of child
toilet training of, *see* Toilet training
Child (3 to 6 years), 458–73 *passim*
aggressive behavior of, 503
guilt feelings of, 471, 472, 473
identification of, with aggressor, 363–64
identification of, with model, 458–64
identification of, with parent, 284–85, 358, 482–83
imitative behavior of, 464, 465, 466, 467
self-concept of, 462, 473
shame felt by, 471, 472, 473
standards acquired by, 469, 470, 471, 472–73
Childhood:
and adoption, 502
aggression in, *see* Childhood aggression
amnesia for, 283
anger in, 497, 498, 500, 501
anxiety in, 504–05, 510–11, 520–22, 523, 537–38, 551
denial in, 354–55
dependency in, 505, 506, 507, 508, 509
hostility in, 263, 265, 274, 281, 497, 498, 499, 500, 501, 522, 571
language ability in, 443

Childhood (*Cont.*)
latency period of, 283–84, 286
motive-behavioral systems in, 493–516 *passim*
and parental acceptance or rejection, 561–62
and parental nurturance, anxiety over loss of, 520–22
peer group in, *see* Peer group in childhood
sexuality in, *see* Childhood sexuality
teasing in, 493
See also Father; Mother; Parents; School-age child
Childhood aggression, 247, 249, 263, 264, 272, 362–63, 498–503
and adoption, effect of, 502
changes in meaning of, 503
defined, 498–99
determinants of, 500–01
learning acts of, 501–02
mislabeling of, 500
and parental punishment, 502–03
Childhood sexuality, 246, 247, 509–11
and adult sexuality, 250–51
aggressive aspects of, 249
anal stage of, 249, 250, 252
and development of object relations, 253–60
and erotic-genital stimulation by parents, 256–57
and genitals, 510–11
Freud's investigation of, 246, 247–49
interchangeability of excitations in, 252–53
oral stage of, 249, 250, 252
phallic stage of, 249, 250
See also Sex role identity; Sex role standard
Chronic traumatic neurosis, 23, 29–30, 73
amnesia in, 19, 32, 33, 60
avoidance reaction in, 31, 49, 53
case study of (Tom), 30–32, 52–53
and psychiatric interview, 31–32
recovery from, 30–33
secondary gains in, 29
symptoms of, 30
Cigarette smoking and effects of emotional role playing, 141–44, *142, 143*
Clark, Kenneth B., on identification with aggressor, 361
Classical conditioning, 40, 41, 52
Classical conditioning model, 40, *42*
Clinical personality assessment, 586–87, 617, 631, 801
autobiographies in, 621–22
diaries in, 622
direct methods of, 618–23
free association in, 618, 619–20
indirect methods of, 623–28

Clinical personality assessment (*Cont.*)
interpretation in, 628–29
interview in, 618–20
letters in, 622–23
multiform, 629
observation in, 621
personal documents in, 621–23
prediction in, *see* Clinical prediction
projective techniques for, *see* Projective personality tests
tests in, 620, 629
Clinical prediction:
achievements of, 789–91
naive, 787 (table), 789–90
sophisticated, 788, 789–91
versus statistical prediction, 778–800, 787 (table)
Clinical Versus Statistical Prediction (Meehl), 784, 797
Clustering of symptoms, in school-age child, 523–24
Code of Ethics, of American Psychological Association, 646, 647
Codes, translation, 531–33
Cognitive-physiological theory of emotion (Schachter), 109–10
Cognitive style, objective measures of, 653–56, 718, 732, 757–61
Cognitive theories, of stress, 40, 62
Cognitive units, acquired by school-age child, 529–30
Cold, avoidance of, as biological drive, 494
Collective monologues (Piaget), 611
Communication:
and mature empathy, 611
warning, *see* Warning communication
Community mental health, 197, 198, 402
and personal disasters, 193
Compromise attitude, induced by warning communication, 115–16, 120, 125
Computers, 531, 582
Concentration, and sensory deprivation, 343
Conceptions of Modern Psychiatry (Sullivan), 296
Conditioned emotional response, 83
paradigm of, 299–300, *300*
See also Emotional conditioning
Conditioned reflex, defined, 42
Conditioned stimulus, defined, 42
Conditioned stress stimuli, 298, 307
generalized, 298, 307
Conditioning:
classical, 40, 41, *42*, 52
emotional, *see* Emotional conditioning
operant, 40, 41, 49, *50*, 53, 57, 83–84
traumatic, *see* Traumatic conditioning
Conflict(s), xxv–xxvi, 204, 205, 220, 341, 391
adaptive, 243

Conflict(s) (*Cont.*)
over aggression, 326–27, 334, 370, 397
approach-approach, 219, 220, 237
approach-avoidance, 204, 219, 221–22,
   225, 225, 227, 228, 232, 236, 237,
   237, 339, 366
appropriateness of, 240
avoidance-avoidance, 219, 223, 237, 330
case studies of, 223–24, 226, 228, 229,
   230, 231
cause of, unbearable affect as (Freud),
   210–11
conscious and unconscious, 239–41
consequences of, 240–41
dependency, 508
double approach-avoidance, 219, 222,
   222–23, 237
eating, case study of (Edie), 228, 229,
   230, 231
examples of, 223–33, 225, 227, 232
homosexual, *see* Homosexuality, projection of unconscious
individual differences in, 397, 399, 665
over-reactions to unconscious, 334
paradigm of approach-avoidance, 236–
   38, 237, 397
and past, role of, 241–42
perceptual, case study of (Duane), 223–
   24
resolution of, process of, 240, 766, 768–
   70
sexual, *see* Sexual conflict
types of, 218–23, 237
unbearable affect as cause of (Freud),
   210–11
unconscious and conscious, 239–41
See also Anxiety; Defense(s); Fear (fear
   reactions); Stress
Conformity, as sex-typed behavior, 478,
   481, 545
Conscience, 320, 334, 398, 471, 707, 709
case study of beginning of (Martha),
   469–70
fear of, 372
See also Superego
Contagion, emotional, 584, 607, 608–09,
   610
Contiguity, 53
and reinforcement, 538–39
Conversions, "deathbed" and "foxhole," 11
Correlation, statistical method of, 636
Counterphobic behavior, 378
Crime, 410
Crime and Punishment (Dostoevsky), 581
Critical score, in personality inventory, 638,
   639
Cross-family variations, within culture,
   401–02
Cuisenaire rods, 532
Cultural anthropology, 272–74, 399, 476

Cultural standards, for emotional expres-
   sion, 604–05
Cultural tradition and personality, 725–26
Cycloid personality, 725

D

Danger, 23, 65
anticipation of, 204, 238, 371
combat, and anxiety symptoms, 25, 25,
   26
denial of, 7, 96, 98, 101
and false alarms, 91–92
motor responses during, 8
and need for social reassurance, 60, 92–
   93
and panic, 8, 66
prolonged exposure to, 9–11
See also Fear (fear reactions)
Dante Alighieri, quoted, 20
Dark Ghetto (Clark), 361
Darwin's theory of evolution, 399
Daydreaming, 112, 187, 540
"Deathbed" conversions, 11
Deconditioning procedures, 54–55, 56, 57,
   58
Defense(s), xxv–xxvi, 204, 238, 240–41,
   242, 351, 389, 391, 595–96, 665,
   730–732
adaptive, 243–44
against affects, unpleasant, 372–73, 373
of avoidance, 351, 352, 353, 366, 367,
   710, 731
change of function of (Hartmann), 244
correlated, 394
of denial, *see* Denial
determinants of individual differences in,
   398–400
of displacement, *see* Displacement
against drives, motives for, 371–72
of ego restriction, 365–66, 367
of escape, 351, 352, 353, 366, 367
hierarchy of, 394–97, 395
of identification, *see* Identification
individual differences in, 397, 398–400
of inhibition, 238
interference with, 337–41, 346
of isolation, *see* Isolation
love as, 329, 384
motives for, individual differences in,
   397
of negation, 379
patterning of, 393–94
in personality assessment, 595–96, 671
of projection, *see* Projection
of reaction formation, 60, 332, 377–79,
   385, 394
of regression, *see* Regression
of repression, *see* Repression

Defense(s) (*Cont.*)
of reversal of affect, 328, 329, 370, 377, 383–85
of sublimation, *see* Sublimation
of turning around upon the self, 370, 382–83
of undoing, 329, 330, 381–82, 394
weakening of, through loss of reality contact, 346
See also Anxiety; Conflict(s); Fear (fear reactions); Stress
Defensive avoidance hypothesis:
and fear arousal, 134–35
and guilt arousal, 135–36
Delinquency, juvenile, 650, 651
Denial, 238, 353–58, 367, 379, 394, 771
case studies of, 354, 355, 732
in children, 354–55
of danger, 7, 96, 98, 101
defined, 353
experimental studies of, 355–58
Dependency, 505–09
in childhood, 505, 506, 507, 508, 509
conflict about, 508
defined, 505
determinants of, 505–07
parental influences on, 507–08
as sex-typed behavior, 478, 480, 486, 487
Depression, 15–16, 72, 171, 179, 186, 238, 333, 334, 397, 410
case studies of, 178, 332
in traumatic neurosis, 22, 23, 34
See also Bereavement; Grief; Mourning; Separation anxiety
Deprivation:
relative, 159
sensory, *see* Sensory deprivation
Depth psychology, 279
Desensitization therapy, systematic (Wolpe), 55–56, 57
Despair phase of separation reaction, 172, 174, 175, 176, 177, 179
Detachment phase of separation reaction, 172–73, 174, 175, 176, 177
Determinism, psychological, 235–36, 253
Deutsch, Helene, and case study of Miss Eaton, 327, 328, 333, 383
Development:
of object relations, 253–60
personality, *see* Personality development
Diaries, in clinical personality assessment, 622
Diderot, Denis, quoted, 261, 762
Digit-span test, 633
Disaster syndrome, 189–90
Discrimination in learning theory, defined, 42
Discriminative reassurance, and reflective emotion, 115, 122

Disorderliness, projection of, 321, *321*
Displacement, 60, 375
of affect in aggression, 165
of fear, 81–82
and isolation, 380
and Oedipal complex, 270
of target of aggression, 147, 164
Distraction effect, of frustration, 152, 153
Diven's experimental investigation of repression, 214–15
Dolls Test, 356–57
Don, case study of, 5–6, 7–19, 52
Dora, case study of, 293, 365
Dostoevsky, Fyodor, quoted, 369
Double approach-avoidance conflict, 219, 222, *222*–23, 237
Draw-a-Man Test, 628
Dreams (dreaming), 27–28, 236
castration, 279
distressing, 19, 22, 31, 67, 226
and indirect personality assessment, 623
and Oedipal complex, 266–67
and REMs, 227
in traumatic neurosis, 22, 32, 34
Drinking, 25–26, 60, 337–38, 410
Drive regression, 232
Drives, 397, 494
Drowning man, "last thoughts" of, case study of (Don), 5–6, 7–19, 52
Drug addiction, 410
Duane, case study of, 223–24
references to, 225, *225*, 232, 233, 236, 238, 241, 242, 277, 291, 327, 354, 370
Dyplastic body build (Kretschmer), 649
Dysplasia, 694

E

Eaton, Miss, case study of, 328–30, 331–33
references to, 327–28, 334, 336, 337, 365, 370, 372, 377, 378, 381, 384, 385
Ebel's critique of validity, in personality testing, 776, 777
Ectomorphy, 649, 650, 651, 651 (table), 693
Ed, case study of, 226, 310–11
references to, 227, *227*, 232, 236, 237, 238, 239, 276, 279, 281, 326, 337, 352, 370, 371, 372, 373, 375
Edie, case study of, 228–31
references to, 232, *232*, 236, 238, 239, 240, 241, 242, 251, 284, 311, 370, 385, 386
Educational guidance, 587–88
Educational selection, 588
Educational Testing Service, 759

Mesomorphy, 649, 650, 651, 651 (table), 693
Meyer, K. F., quoted, 234
Milieu, therapeutic, 193, 194–95
Miller's theory of conflict, 149–50, 237, 339–40
Minnesota Multiphasic Personality Inventory (MMPI), 642–47 *passim*, 703, 737, 738, 739, 740, 749, 750, 785
  of Brown, Morris, 739, 740, 741, 742, 743, 744, 757
  interpretation of, 742–46
Miyake, Kuzuo, on sex role identity, 490
Monkeys:
  attachment behavior in, 425–26, 426, 427, 428, 431–32, 432
  innate ability of, to recognize emotion, 604, 607
  socially deprived, 608, 609
Monologues, collective (Piaget), 611
Montaigne, Michel de, quoted, 556
Moratorium period (Erikson), 768
Moro reflex, 417
Mother:
  attachment as basis for value of, 424–27
  child's hostility toward, during severe toilet training, 448, 449
  child's interaction with, 566–67
  identification of daughter with, 459, 460, 463, 482, 483
  domination of child by, 296
  expectations of, 569, 569–70
  infant's relationship with, 423, 424–25, 429–31, 434–35, 440, 563, 565, 567, 568
  interpretations of child's attributes by, 568–69
  and Oedipal complex, 263, 274, 275, 276, 285, 385
  permissiveness of, 562, 563
  preference of, for boy baby, 259
  preoedipal attachments to, 255–56, 260
  reactions of, factors controlling, 567–70
  and rejection-acceptance continuum, 559–62, 563, 564, 564
  and restriction-autonomy continuum, 562–63, 564, 564, 565
  and separation anxiety in child, 172, 173, 174, 294, 420, 429–31
  and "sleeper" effect, 566, 567
  surrogates for, *see* Mother surrogates
  temperament of, and child's attitudes, 567
  toilet training by, 256, 430, 446–47, 449, 451
  types of behavior of, 558–65, 564
  See also Parents
Mother surrogates, 428–29
  for monkeys, 425–26, 426, 432

Motivation (motives):
  active, 494
  and aggression, *see* Aggression
  and anticipatory emotions, 109
  assessment of, 619–20, 623–28, 642–44, 665
  and behavior, relation between, 495–96
  changes in strength of, 494–95
  in child, 493–516 *passim*
  and dependency, *see* Dependency
  effectance, 511–13; *see also* Mastery
  and incentives, 494, 497
  nature of, 494–95
  potential, 494
  of school-age child for acquiring knowledge, 536–37
  sexual, *see* Adult sexuality; Child sexuality
  strength of, changes in, 494–95
  theoretical approaches to, 39–40
  See also Conflict; Frustration
Mourning, 171, 176, 179, 293
  and daydreaming, 187
  and disaster, 187–89
  incomplete, 186
  insomnia during, 26, 179
  psychoanalytic theory of, 184–87
  and resignation, 186
  work of, 100, 184, 185, 187, 189, 193, 197
  See also Bereavement; Depression; Grief; Separation anxiety
"Mourning and Melancholia" (Freud), 181
Multiple determinants of behavior, 625–27
Multiple regression, prediction by, 783–84
Murray, H. A.:
  experiment by, on fantasy activity, 309
  on personality assessment, 644, 661, 673, 699, 745
Muscle tension, as measure of emotional conditioning, 46–47

N

Narcissism, 254–55, 386
Nazism, 36, 167, 361
Near miss and remote miss, 85
Negation, 379
Negative feedback, and identification, 364
Negative therapeutic reaction, 339–41
Negroes, 154, 166, 167, 168, 355, 356, 357, 358, 361, 362, 468, 495
Nervous system:
  autonomic, 8, 45, 78, 652–53
  central, 578
Neuropsychiatric Screening Adjunct (NSA), 639, 640 (table)
Neurosis, 401
  Horney's view of, 399
  seduction theory of (Freud), 247, 248

Preschool child, *see* Child (3 to 6 years)
Primal repression, 376
Primary process functioning, shift to, 347–48
Primitivization, and frustration, 151, 152
Privacy, invasion of, and personality testing, 646–47
Problem solving, 529, 535, 538
  evaluation phases of, 534
  and sex role identity, 487, 488
Projection, 315, 376–77, 394, 398
  experimental studies of, 321, 321–24
  and homosexual wishes, unconscious, 315–16, 317, 318–19, 319
  paranoiac, of Schreber, 319–20
  in personality assessment, 596, 600
Projective identification, 332
Projective personality tests, 81, 623–27, 696–721
  clinical interpretation of, 627
  and freedom to respond, 624
  survey of, 627–28
  See also Rorschach Test; Thematic Apperception Test
Propaganda, 126, 130
Protest phase of separation reaction, 172, 175, 176, 179
Proust, Marcel, quoted, 335
Psychasthenia scale, 744
Psychoanalysis, 56, 65, 205, 215, 223, 228, 230, 236, 339, 378, 599, 705, 707, 724
  and Anna O., case study of, 206–08
  Freud's first case study in (Lucy R.), 208–10
  historical background of, 206–10
  key concepts in, from early case studies, 210–14
  See also Anxiety; Conflict; Defense(s); Mourning; Trauma
Psychodiagnosis, statistical and clinical approaches to, 797–800
Psychodynamic theories of trauma, 39, 40, 64–73
  and indiscriminate sensitization, 84–85
Psychogalvanic reaction (PGR), 45, 47, 78, 79, 214
Psychogram, of Morris Brown's Rorschach Test, 714 (table), 715
Psychological determinism, 235–36, 253
Psychological differentiation, 654–56, 655, 656, 759–60, 760
Psychometrics, 631, 632, 633, 636, 637, 775, 776, 780
Psychopathic personality, 612
Psychosexual development, in psychoanalytic theory, 249–53, 398
Psychosis, 27, 354, 401, 565, 609, 650, 651
Psychotherapy, 56, 59, 337

Puberty, 243, 286
Punishment:
  of childhood aggression, 502–03, 565
  of dependent behavior, 507, 508
  fear of, as mechanism of socialization, 444, 445, 453
  of poor school performance, 462
  of sexual curiosity, 510
Pyknic body build (Kretschmer), 649

Q

Q-sorting method, 753–57, 754, 754 (table), 756 (table), 799, 800

R

Rage, 22, 165, 333
  See also Aggression; Anger; Hatred; Hostility
Rapid eye movements (REMs), 27, 227
  experimental setup for study of, 28
Rat Man, case study of, 265, 267, 330–31, 380
  references to, 266, 269, 282, 283, 284, 290, 327, 334, 381, 382, 383
Ray, case study of, 315–16, 318
  references to, 317, 318–19, 319, 320, 324, 326, 337, 373, 377
Reaction formation, 60, 332, 377–79, 385, 394
Reality contact:
  in assessment of nonconformity, 581
  interference with, 341–48, 352
Reassurance, and reflective emotion, 115, 120, 122
Reciprocal inhibition principle, 55, 56
Reflex(es):
  conditioned, defined, 42
  Moro, 417
  in newborn period, 416–17
  psychogalvanic, 45, 47, 78, 79, 214
  sucking, 58, 416
  unconditioned, defined, 41, 42
  withdrawal, 351
Regression, 17, 238, 370, 385–86, 394
  drive, 232
Reification, fallacy of, 578
Reinforcement, 49, 50, 53
  and contiguity, 538–39
  negative, 57
  partial, 50, 57
  positive, 57
Relative deprivation, 159
Remote miss and near miss, 85
Repression, 60, 210, 211, 238, 301, 307, 374–76, 389, 391, 394, 398, 759
  after-, 376
  defined, 375
  experimental investigation of, 214–16

Repression (*Cont.*)
of guilt, 376
of hatred, 329, 384
of homosexuality, 314, 316
of Oedipal complex, 266, 274–83, 284
primal, 376
unbearable affect as cause of (Freud),
210–11
Research Center for Mental Health, 757
Response sets, in personality testing, 644–
46
Reticular activating system, in brain, 347
Reversal of affect, 328, 329, 370, 377,
383–85
Reward:
of aggression, 160, 161
in animal experiments, 51–52
of good school performance, 462
of independence, 507, 508
as mechanism of socialization, 444
occasional, in random sequence, 58
as reinforcing stimulus, 50, 53
Role playing, emotional, *see* Emotional
role playing
Rorschach Test, 348, 627, 696, 703, 710,
711–18, 759, 790, 791
of Brown, Morris, 711–13, 715–17, 735,
770
psychogram of, 714 (table), 715
scoring and interpreting, 713–17, 720
sequence analysis of, 716–17
Rousseau, Jean-Jacques, quoted, 414
Rückert's poem on mourning, 186

S

S, case study of, 547–49
Sadism, 360, 383, 384, 391, 396
Sainte-Beuve, Charles Augustin, quoted,
201
Santayana, George, quoted, 289
Sarbin, T. R., on statistical inference, 794
Scapegoat(ing), 195, 327
of minority groups, 166–67
and personality predispositions, 167–68
selection of, 165–66
Schachter's theory of emotion, 109, 110,
111, 114, 455
Schema:
as basis for affective understanding, 614–
15
relation of, to fear, 422
Schizophrenia, 254, 255, 323, 386, 394,
401, 410, 463, 609, 642, 651
(table)
Schmideberg, Melitta, on war stress, 68, 69
Scholastic Aptitude Test (SAT), 780
School-age child, 518–40 *passim*
attention in, and efficiency of learning,
539–40

School-age child (*Cont.*)
clustering of symptoms in, 523–24
cognitive units acquired by, 529–30
external versus internal symptoms in,
523–24
information decoded and interpreted by,
530–31
intelligence of, 526–29
reflective versus impulsive, 533–35, 536
in school situation, 524–26, 527, 532,
536–38
and social class differences in school
performance, 525–26
symptoms of, maladaptive, 520–24
and teacher, 514–15, 524–25, 535, 538
tempo of, 535
School phobia, 298, 352
Schreber, Daniel Paul, case study of, 254–
55, 320
references to, 319–20, 386
Scoline, 43, 45, 47
Secondary process functioning, 347
Security operations (Sullivan), 296
Selection ratio, and experience table, 782
Self-absorption, 352
Self-assessment, 582
Self-concept:
of Brown, Morris, 755
effect of identification on, 462, 473
of observer, in informal personality as-
sessment, 596–97
See also Self-definition
Self-confidence, 198
loss of, 68–72, 73
Self-definition, 462, 473, 513
Self-esteem, 296, 352, 358, 359, 367
loss of, 121, 257, 295–97, 299, 302, 365,
372, 384, 398
Self-fulfilling prophecy, 594
Self-hatred, 333
Self-love, 383, 397
Self-rating devices, in personality assessment, 750–57
Senile psychosis, 27
Sensitization to threat cues, 75–85
detection of, 76
indiscriminate, 84–85
in sports parachutists, 77–80, 83
Sensory deprivation, 341, 348, 352
and anxiety, 343–45
conflicted wishes during, 344–45
experiments in, 342, 342–45
tolerance for, 348
Sentence Completion Test, 627
Separation anxiety, 58, 172–75, 197, 293–
94, 295, 298, 299, 300, 301–08,
352, 371, 398
in adulthood, 176, 177
case study of, 303–04

Separation anxiety (*Cont.*)
  in childhood, 172–74, *174*, 420, 422,
    429–31
  despair phase of, 172, *174*, 175, 176,
    177, 179
  detachment phase of, 172–73, *174*, 175,
    176, 177
  intensity of, and memories, 305, 306
  memories activated by, 302–05
  over-reactions of, 300, *301*, 302
  protest phase of, 172, 175, 176, 179
  See also Bereavement; Depression; Grief;
    Mourning
Sex role identity, 288, 476, 481–91
  anxiety about, 523
  case study of, 486–87
  of child, 484–91
  defined, 481
  establishment of, 482–84
  and intellectual mastery, 487–91
  and social interaction, 484
  and stability, behavioral, 484–87, *485*
  and sex-typed attributes, 483–84
Sex role standard, 476–81
  content of, 477–80
  and covert attributes, 480
  defined, 477, 481
  establishment of, 480–81
  and game preferences, 479
  maintenance of, 480–81
  and overt behavior, 477–79
  and physical attributes, 477
Sex typing, 475–89 *passim*, 545
Sexual conflict, 251, 339, 366, 370, 397
  as cause of eating conflict, 229, 230,
    231, 232, 232, 233, 241, 251, 385
  examples of, 226–27, 227, 229, 230,
    231, 232
  in school-age child, 522–23
Sexual perversions, 251
Sexuality:
  adult, 250–53
  childhood, *see* Childhood sexuality
  in family relationships, 255–57
Shakespeare, William, quoted, 106, 170,
    325
Shame, 61, 64, 108, 111, 112, 113, 117,
    118, 121, 122, 140, 226
  and guilt, 471–72
  reflective, 119, 120, 122
  traumatic, 121, 122
Shaw, George Bernard, quoted, 474
Sheldon's body types, 649, 650, 651, 652,
    669–70, 693, 694
Sibling rivalry, 244, 287, 294, 328, 354,
    550–54
Siblings, 549–55
  first-born and later-born, differential
    characteristics of, 550–54, *553*

Siblings (*Cont.*)
  interacting effects of sex, birth order,
    and spacing of, 554–55
Sinus arrhythmia, 46
Skeptical Psychoanalyst, The (Colby), 215
Sleep:
  disturbances of, in traumatic neurosis,
    22, 23, 25, 26–29, 36, 61
  and wakefulness, transition between,
    345–46
Social desirability, as response set in per-
    sonality testing, 644, 645, 744
Social introversion, 741
Social perception, 585, 592, 656
Socialization of child, 443–44, 565
  first steps in, 445
  mechanisms of, 444–45
  rules for, 452
  and toilet training, *see* Toilet training
Sociometry, 658
Sociopath, 612
Sodium amytal, 43
Sodium pentothal, 6
Somatotonia, 694
Somatotyping, in personality assessment,
    649, 649–52, *650*, 651 (table), 693–
    94, 724
Spearman's method of factor analysis, 637
Species identity, basic, 607–08
Spontaneous recovery of conditioned re-
    sponse, 42, 43, 55
Sports parachutists:
  defenses used by, 81, 82, 244
  emotional adaptation in, 88–90
  fear reactions by, 77–78, 82, 88, 89, 90
  and self-ratings of fear, 89
  sensitization effects in, 77–80, 83
Spranger's personality types, 690, 691, 692
Standard(s):
  case study of acquisition of (Martha),
    469–70
  consequences of deviation from, 470–72
  establishment of, 472–73, 519
  of first-born and later-born children, 550
  importance of, 519–20
  sex role, *see* Sex role standard
Stanford-Binet Scale, 620, 692, 693, 748,
    749, 750
Staring reaction, to disaster, 190, *190*, *191*,
    191–92
Startle reaction, 25, 36, 43, 52
Statistical prediction in personality assess-
    ment:
  versus clinical, 778–800
  conditions necessary for, 792–93
  methods and achievements of, 780–84
  by multiple regression, 783–84
  and psychodiagnosis, 797–800
  See also Actuarial predictive system

Trauma (*Cont.*)
  psychodynamic theories of, *see* Psycho-
    dynamic theories of trauma
  "working through," 67–68, 72, 73
Traumatic conditioning, 41–48
  defined, 42
Traumatic neurosis, 65, 66, 72, 298
  acute, *see* Acute traumatic neurosis
  chronic, *see* Chronic traumatic neurosis
  latent, 33–37, 44
  and lost sense of invulnerability, 68–71
  prevention of, 72, 73
  therapy for, 72, 73
Trobriand Islanders, 400, 401
Turning around upon the self, as defense,
    370, 382–83
Twain, Mark, quoted, 145
Two-Year-Old Goes to Hospital, A (Rob-
    ertson), 173
Types of Men (Spranger), 690

U

Ulysses (Joyce), 5, 252, 253
Unconditioned reflex, defined, 41, 42
Unconditioned stimulus, 54, 83
  defined, 42
Unconscious fantasies, 247, 248, 251, 308,
    332, 706, 708, 728
  marital relationships influenced by, 310–
    12
Unconscious identification, as compensa-
    tory mechanism in mourning, 185,
    187
Undoing, defense mechanism of, 329, 330,
    381–82, 394

V

Values, adolescent's struggle with, 287
Values, assessment of, 665, 690–92, 716,
    733, 737, 747, 747–48
Veterans Administration Mental Hygiene
    Clinic, 743
Visceral afferent stimulation, 453, 454,
    455
Viscerotonia, 694
Vocational guidance, 587–88, 641, 690
Vocational interest tests, 640–41, 641
    (table)
Vocational selection, 588, 690
Voltaire, quoted, 349
Voyeurism, 334

W

Wakefulness and sleep, transition between,
    345–46

War neurosis, 22, 23, 34, 36
Warning communication:
  acceptance of, 126, 127, 130, 131, 140
  attention to, 126, 127
  comprehension of, 126, 127
  compromise attitude toward, 115–16,
    120, 125
  diminishing returns in, 131–36, *133,
    134*
  and discriminative vigilance, 115
  emotional arousal by, 127, 128, 129,
    131–36, *136,* 137, *138,* 138–40,
    139
  and emotional role playing, 140–44,
    142, 143
  high-threat, effectiveness of, 136–38, *138*
  and inverted U-shaped curve, 130–31
  mental efficiency affected by, 127, 128,
    129
  and optimal level of fear arousal, 138–
    41
  and reduction of emotional disturbance,
    93–95, 102–05, *104*
  resistance to, 126, 127, 135, 138, 139,
    140
Wartime bombing, near and remote misses
    in, 24
Wechsler Adult Intelligence Scale (WAIS),
    620, 692, 737, 748–50, 759
Wechsler-Bellevue Scale, 748, 790, 791
Wechsler Intelligence Scale for Children
    (WISC), 620
Whitman, Walt, quoted, 245, 392
Wilde, Oscar, quoted, 86
Withdrawal reflex, 351
Witkin's concept of field independence,
    655, 759
Wolf Man, case study of, 266, 268–69,
    277–78, 279, 394–96
  references to, 265, 267, 270, 272, 280,
    282, 283, 284, 290, 302, 375, 376,
    384, 386
Wolfe, Thomas, quoted, 541
Wolfenstein, Martha, on mourning, 176
Wolpe's systematic desensitization tech-
    niques, 55–56, 57
Woodworth, R. S., and personality inven-
    tories, 637, 638
Word Association Test, 76, 77, 78–79, 79,
    80, 627, 790
Work of mourning, 100, 184, 185, 187,
    189, 193, 197
Work of worrying, 100–05, 117, 196,
    197
  incomplete, consequences of, 101–02
  preparatory communications as prereq-
    uisite for, 102–03

B 0
C 1
D 2
E 3
F 4
G 5
H 6
I 7
J 8